The
PENGUIN
ENCYCLOPEDIA
of.
American
HISTORY

The PENGUIN ENCYCLOPEDIA of American HISTORY

Robert A. Rosenbaum

Douglas Brinkley, Advisory Editor

PENGUIN REFERENCE

PENGUIN REFERENCE
Published by the Penguin Group
Penguin Putnam Inc., 375 Hudson Street, New York, New York 10014, U.S.A.
Penguin Books Ltd, 80 Strand, London WC2R 0RL, England
Penguin Books Australia Ltd., 250 Camberwell Road, Camberwell, Victoria 3124, Australia
Penguin Books Canada Ltd, 10 Alcorn Avenue, Toronto, Ontario, Canada M4V 3B2
Penguin Books India (P) Ltd, 11 Community Centre, Panchsheel Park, New Delhi—110 017, India
Penguin Books (N.Z.) Ltd, Cnr Rosedale and Airborne Roads, Albany, Auckland, New Zealand
Penguin Books (South Africa) (Pty) Ltd, 24 Sturdee Avenue, Rosebank, Johannesburg 2196, South Africa

Penguin Books Ltd, Registered Offices:
Harmondsworth, Middlesex, England

First published in 2003 by Penguin Reference, a member of Penguin Putnam Inc.

1   3   5   7   9   10   8   6   4   2

Copyright © Robert A. Rosenbaum, 2003
All rights reserved

CIP data available

ISBN 0-670-03199-2

This book is printed on acid-free paper. ∞

Printed in the United States of America
Set in Sabon
Designed by Jaye Zimet

FOR TEDDY

PREFACE

The *Penguin Encyclopedia of American History* was conceived as a compact volume of maximum utility to readers and students of American history. Its 1,200 articles total 350,000 words. More than 300 main cross-references and hundreds of internal cross-references (indicated by asterisks) enable the reader to pursue a subject further than one might expect in a book of this modest size.

The encyclopedia focuses on political, social, economic, and military history, to the neglect—regretfully—of cultural history. Within these limits, the reader will find most of the subjects that have become conventional in historical encyclopedias. I have tried, however, to find new or neglected subjects that might interest the browser as well as the student.

For example, there are articles on all presidential elections through 2000, on all presidential administrations to George W. Bush's, and on the U.S. Supreme Court under 11 chief justices. Landmark Supreme Court decisions, from *Marbury v. Madison* (1803) to *Zelman v. Simmons-Harris* (2002), are reported. There are articles, too, on two dozen perennial public issues, including Affirmative Action, Campaign Financing, Church-State Relations, Consumer Protection, Environmentalism, Health Insurance, Poverty, and Women in the Labor Force. Seminal books, from *The Federalist* to *The Feminine Mystique*, are described.

Foreign events that have impacted American history—the French, Russian, and Mexican revolutions, the Spanish Civil War, and the Holocaust—are treated. There are articles on U.S. relations with Mexico, the Caribbean and Central America, South America, and the Middle East. Other articles cover U.S. recognition of the Latin American republics, the Soviet Union, and Israel, and describe the postwar U.S. occupations of Germany and Japan.

And of course some recent subjects make their encyclopedia debuts—Anthrax Attack, *Bush v. Gore*, Enron Bankruptcy, Globalization, New Economy, School Vouchers, Terrorism War, World Trade Center Attacks, Y2K (Year 2000) Anxiety.

Biographies as a class have been omitted, but the volume contains 12 essays on famous pairs, including Hamilton and Jefferson, Jackson and Clay, Jefferson and Madison, Lincoln and Douglas, Stanton and Anthony, Wilson and Lodge, and Truman and Acheson. In addition, there are half a dozen articles on the careers of men somehow epitomic of their ages, including John Brown, J. P. Morgan, and George C. Wallace.

Everywhere, the voices of historical actors are heard. There are excerpts from presidential inaugurals, farewells, and war messages, Supreme Court decisions, famous orations and addresses, and significant documents and manifestos. Many memorable quotations are preserved. Poets, too, are heard from, including Emerson, Longfellow, Holmes Sr., Howe, Whitman, and even Thomas Buchanan Read, who wrote ". . . and Sheridan twenty miles away."

Finally, memorable stories are retold, including Appomattox Surrender, Boston Busing, Covert Operations, ("Stonewall") Jackson's Death, Lindbergh's Flight, Montgomery Bus Boycott, *Oregon*'s Voyage, Roosevelt's Final Illness, Washington's Slaves, and Wilson's Fight for the Treaty.

I am indebted to two Viking Penguin editors—Hugh Rawson, who commissioned the encyclopedia, and Ray Roberts, who skillfully brought it to completion. I am also indebted to Douglas Brinkley for his wise counsel and to my wife, Theodora, for her invaluable editing.

R.A.R.

The PENGUIN ENCYCLOPEDIA of American HISTORY

A

ABINGTON SCHOOL DISTRICT v. SCHEMPP (1963), 8–1 decision of the *Warren Court overturning a Pennsylvania law that required morning Bible reading in the state's public schools. The Court ruled that the law breached the wall of separation between church and state that had been erected by the religion clauses—the Establishment and Free Exercise clauses—of the First Amendment.

As Justice Tom Clark explained: "[T]he Establishment Clause has been directly considered by this Court eight times in the past score of years and, with only one Justice dissenting on the point, it has consistently held that the clause withdrew all legislative power respecting religious belief or the expression thereof. The test may be stated as follows: what are the purpose and the primary effect of the enactment? If either is the advancement or inhibition of religion then the enactment exceeds the scope of legislative power as circumscribed by the Constitution. That is to say that to withstand the strictures of the Establishment Clause there must be a secular legislative purpose and a primary effect that neither advances nor inhibits religion. The Free Exercise Clause, likewise considered many times here, withdraws from legislative power, state and federal, the exertion of any restraint on the free exercise of religion. Its purpose is to secure religious liberty in the individual by prohibiting any invasions thereof by civil authority."

The one justice who dissented in this and similar cases, Potter Stewart, argued that the Court was not manifesting neutrality toward religion but hostility (see *Church-State Relations).

ABOLITIONISTS (1830–70), advocates of immediate emancipation of slaves and their integration into American society. Most antislavery people were not abolitionists. The "free-soilers" sought to prevent the extension of slavery into new regions, generally believing that slavery, confined to the states where it then existed, would eventually die out. The colonizationists (see *Colonization) coupled emancipation with deportation in the widely shared belief that the white and black races could not live together. After 1830, most Southerners were violently opposed to emancipation and most Northerners to racial equality and integration. Both abhorred abolitionists as dangerous fanatics.

Gradualist emancipation sentiment had been strong in both North and South from the American Revolution until 1830. Thereafter the South effectively suppressed such views and the North acquiesced, Northern capitalists being implicated in Southern slave-based prosperity and Northern working people being unwilling to compete with free black labor. But a wave of religious revivalism in the 1820s planted the seeds of an abolitionist movement in men—and especially women—who came to see slavery as sinful. In the early 1830s a number of able propagandists, clergymen, and philanthropists took up the cause, among them William Lloyd Garrison, Wendell Phillips, Sarah and Angelica Grimké, Theodore Dwight Weld, John Greenleaf Whittier, and Arthur and Lewis Tappan. *Free blacks were numerous in the movement—including such prominent lecturers as Frederick Douglass and Sojourner Truth—but they were denied positions of leadership. The **American Anti-Slavery Society**, founded in 1833, spawned branches throughout the North. Membership peaked in 1840 at about 200,000, the majority of them women.

The abolitionists engaged in propaganda through churches and public meetings, the press (see *Liberator, The*), and petitions to Congress (see *Gag Rules). They were met by hostility, ranging from the burning of abolitionist literature taken from the mails in the South to mob violence in the North culminating in the murder of abolitionist editor Elijah Lovejoy in 1837. In 1840 the movement split, Garrison and the American Anti-Slavery

Society continuing to pursue nonviolent but uncompromising "moral suasion." Garrison eschewed politics because he believed that the Constitution was a slaveholders' document and that voting would be a sin. Pragmatic abolitionists led by the Tappans formed (1840) the **American and Foreign Anti-Slavery Society** and entered politics through the *Liberty Party. In the 1840s Garrison, always the most extreme of the abolitionists, became a disunionist; under his influence the American Anti-Slavery Society in 1843 adopted a resolution to the effect that the U.S. Constitution was a "covenant with death and an agreement with hell."

As antislavery sentiment grew in the North in the 1850s, abolitionists were still disliked as extremists. John Brown's raid on Harpers Ferry (1859; see *Brown's Career) confirmed the South in its conviction of an abolitionist menace but horrified much of the North as well. The *Republican Party, founded in 1854, was free-soil, not abolitionist.

During the Civil War, abolitionists were impatient with Pres. Abraham Lincoln's cautious policy toward slavery and dissatisfied with the *Emancipation Proclamation. With the passage (1865) of the *13th Amendment ending slavery, Garrison considered the mission of the American Anti-Slavery Society accomplished. Others, however, led by Phillips, continued the society until 1870, when the *15th Amendment extended male suffrage to African-Americans.

ABORTION. Abortion was unregulated in the United States until the mid-19th century, when states began to prohibit it not out of moral concern but in the professional interest of physicians. During the first half of the 20th century, abortion was available to affluent women for whom sympathetic physicians found "therapeutic" reasons to justify the procedure. Poor women were compelled to undergo illegal and dangerous procedures.

By 1970, some states permitted exceptions to the outright ban on abortions, while four states and the District of Columbia had legalized them. In 1973 the U.S. Supreme Court (see *Burger Court) overturned state prohibitions when it ruled, in *Roe v. Wade, that women had a right to abortion based on their constitutional right to privacy. The Court reaffirmed its opinion that abortion was a private matter between the woman and her physician when, in *Planned Parenthood of Central Missouri v. Danforth* (1976), it struck down a state statute requiring that a married woman obtain the prior written consent of her husband and that a minor obtain the written consent of a parent. But in *Harris v. McRae* (1980), the Court upheld the constitutionality of the

"Hyde Amendment," which barred the use of Medicaid funds to pay for abortions for poor women.

Conservatives hoped that the *Rehnquist Court would overturn *Roe*, but the anti-*Roe* justices could not muster five votes. Instead, the Court upheld state restrictions on access to abortion. In *Webster v. Reproductive Health Services* (1989), the Court upheld a Missouri law that prohibited the performance of abortions in public hospitals and barred public employees from performing or assisting at such operations. In *Hogden v. Minnesota* (1990), it upheld a state law prohibiting unmarried teenage girls from obtaining abortions without notifying their parents or getting a judge's permission. In *Rust v. Sullivan* (1991), the Court upheld federal regulations adopted in the Reagan administration that cut off federal funding for family-planning clinics that discussed abortion with their patients. In *Planned Parenthood v. Casey* (1992), the Court upheld most provisions of a Pennsylvania law that required doctors to inform women of alternatives to abortion, required women to wait 24 hours before undergoing the operation, and required teenagers to get the consent of a parent or a judge. The Court rejected a requirement that a woman notify her husband of a planned abortion. The ruling set standards of "undue burden" and "substantial obstacle" by which to determine if a state's restrictions on access to abortion were constitutional.

On the other hand, in a series of decisions between 1994 and 2000, the Rehnquist Court upheld lower-court orders and local ordinances keeping antiabortion protesters at a distance from abortion clinics. And in *Stenberg v. Carhart* (2000), the Court overturned 5–4 a Nebraska law (and similar laws in 30 other states) banning late-term (so-called partial-birth) abortions.

The response of the medical profession to *Roe* was uneven. In populous states and large cities, abortion services were soon available. However, most hospitals refused to provide them: Catholic hospitals out of religious conviction; public hospitals in response to pressure from antiabortion forces; hospitals in small towns and rural areas out of deference to conservative public opinion. Many physicians, for personal reasons, also refused to perform abortions. As a result, the availability of abortion services varied widely from region to region. The great majority were performed in metropolitan areas of the West Coast and Northeast and Mid-Atlantic states and in clinics established for that purpose rather than in hospitals.

The Supreme Court's decisions divided the country into pro-life (antiabortion) and pro-choice (freedom to choose) movements, represented most prominently by the National Right to Life Committee and the National

Abortion and Reproductive Action League. Inspired by religious conviction and conservative views of family and gender roles, the pro-life people succeeded in obtaining federal and state legislation limiting access to abortion. Pro-life activists—notably members of Operation Rescue, founded in 1987 by Randall Terry—regularly picketed and harassed abortion clinics and their patrons. Extremists resorted to bombings, arson, and assassination, killing a number of physicians and clinic employees during the 1990s.

The availability of RU-486—the so-called French abortion pill—promised to alter the tactics of the abortion war. The pill could be administered by a doctor or nurse practitioner as early as the third week of pregnancy in the anonymity of a medical office rather than at an abortion clinic. Administration of the pill, however, proved more time consuming and expensive than surgical abortions, and initial acceptance was slow.

Public opinion has consistently supported the prochoice position that a woman should be free to choose whether to have an abortion. On the spectrum of public opinion, minorities at either end advocate making all abortions illegal or legal. The majority of Americans approve of abortion for "hard" or compelling reasons— rape, incest, the woman's health, deformity of the fetus— but not for "soft" reasons—the family cannot afford more children, the family has as many children as it wants, the pregnant woman is single and does not want to marry her partner.

ABRAMS v. UNITED STATES (1919), 7–2 decision of the *White Court upholding the constitutionality of the Sedition Act of 1918 (see *Espionage Act). Jacob Abrams, a Russian immigrant and anarchist, and others had been convicted under the act of publishing leaflets in English and Yiddish condemning the sending of U.S. troops to Russia (see *Russian Intervention) and calling for a general strike in protest. Justice Oliver Wendell Holmes, who had voted with a unanimous Court to uphold the Espionage Act in *Schenk v. United States, now had second thoughts and, with Justice Louis D. Brandeis, dissented.

No clear and present danger was presented by "these poor and puny anonymities," Holmes argued. The defendants were being punished "not for what the indictment alleges but for the creed that they avow."

"Persecution for the expression of opinions seems to me perfectly logical," Holmes continued. "If you have no doubt of your premises or your power and want a certain result with all your heart you naturally express your wishes in law and sweep away all opposition. . . . But

when men have realized that time has upset many fighting faiths, they may come to believe even more than they believe the very foundations of their own conduct that the ultimate good desired is better reached by free trade in ideas—that the best test of truth is the power of the thought to get itself accepted in the competition of the market, and that truth is the only ground upon which their wishes safely can be carried out. That at any rate is the theory of our Constitution. It is an experiment, as all life is an experiment. Every year if not every day we have to wager our salvation upon some prophecy based upon imperfect knowledge. While that experiment is part of our system I think that we should be eternally vigilant against attempts to check the expression of opinions that we loathe and believe to be fraught with death, unless they so imminently threaten immediate interference with the lawful and pressing purposes of the law that an immediate check is required to save the country."

ACHESON AND TRUMAN. See *Truman and Acheson.

ADAMS (JOHN) ADMINISTRATION (1797– 1801). The second president of the United States, John Adams pledged to continue the policies of his great predecessor, George Washington. Indeed, he kept Washington's cabinet intact, not realizing that three of its members looked for their instructions to Federalist leader Alexander Hamilton.

The dominant issue in the Adams administration was relations with France. The war between France and Great Britain, begun in 1793, continued, and both belligerents seized neutral ships that allegedly violated their reciprocal blockades. France was now governed by the corrupt Directory, which regarded the United States as a virtual ally of Britain as a result of *Jay's Treaty, negotiated (1794) during the *Washington administration. The Directory refused to receive the new U.S. minister, Charles C. Pinckney. When Adams sent a three-man mission, it was not only rebuffed but solicited for a bribe (see *XYZ Affair).

The incident aroused outrage in the United States, discredited the pro-French Republicans, and produced Federalist majorities in Congress. In a fever of war preparation, Congress abrogated the 1778 treaties with France. It authorized an expanded navy and established a Navy Department. An undeclared *naval war with France soon began in the West Indies. Over Adams's objections (he saw no possibility of a French invasion), Congress also authorized a 10,000-man army, which was to be commanded nominally by Washington but actually, to Adams's chagrin, by Hamilton. Military preparedness was paid for by an unprecedented federal tax on land, buildings, and slaves that led to *Fries's Rebellion. Also unsought by Adams were the *Alien and Sedition Acts (1798).

In 1799, assured that France would receive a new U.S. mission, Adams—overriding his cabinet (whose three disloyal members he dismissed the next year) and ignoring all other advisers—sent one, outraging the bellicose Federalists and ensuring his defeat in the election of 1800. This mission achieved the *Convention of 1800 with the new French government headed by Napoleon Bonaparte, although its success was not known in the United States until after the election. Adams closed his administration with his controversial *"midnight appointments." He was succeeded by Thomas Jefferson.

ADAMS (JOHN QUINCY) ADMINISTRATION
(1825–29). John Quincy Adams, sixth president of the United States, was elected over four fellow Republicans (see *Jeffersonian Republican Party) in a contest of personalities and sections rather than issues. When no candidate won a majority in the *electoral college—Adams received fewer popular and electoral votes than Andrew Jackson—the election was decided by the House of Representatives. There Henry Clay, a former rival, threw his support to Adams, assuring his election. Adams's appointment of Clay as secretary of state gave rise to the charge of a *corrupt bargain that clouded and weakened the administration.

Adams had converted from the *Federalist Party to the Republican during the *Jefferson administration. His vision for the country was an old Federalist one, now adopted by the nationalist wing of the Republican Party—a strong national government unifying the country physically by a network of highways and canals and improving it morally through national educational and scientific institutions. The program he put before Congress in his first annual address he recognized as a "perilous experiment": establishment of a department of the interior, a national naval academy, a national university, a national astronomical observatory, a uniform bankruptcy law, a uniform national militia law, a national system of weights and measures, a more effective national patent law, and, most important, a national system of federally subsidized *internal improvements. His program was ridiculed in the press and ignored by Congress, except for Southern members, who saw in the aggrandizement of the national government a threat not only to state sovereignty but to slavery as well.

Adams took a cautious approach to tariff legislation,

believing that the interests of both agriculture and industry had to be considered. Increasingly, Southerners—opposed to tariff protection for Northern manufacturers—argued that a protective tariff, as distinct from a tariff for revenue only, was unconstitutional. In 1828 Jackson forces in Congress presented Adams with a bill that raised tariffs to extraordinary heights, calculating that if he signed it he would alienate the South and that if he vetoed it he would alienate New England—in either case ensuring the election of Andrew Jackson that year. Deferring to Congress, Adams signed this *"Tariff of Abominations."

By the end of the Adams administration, the diverging wings of the Republican Party had coalesced into new parties. The states' rights, populist Republicans formed the *Democratic Party around Jackson; Adams himself was the nominal head of the *National Republican Party. Defeated in the election of 1828, he was succeeded by Andrew Jackson.

ADAMS AND JEFFERSON. John Adams and
Thomas Jefferson met and became friends in June 1775 at the Second *Continental Congress. Adams was 39, short, stout, irascible and volatile; Jefferson was 32, tall, lanky, informal but reserved. Their friendship deepened—and extended to their families—when both men served abroad, Adams as U.S. minister to Holland and Great Britain, Jefferson as U.S. minister to France.

Their devotion to the American cause hid fundamental psychological and philosophical differences between them. These first appeared when John and Abigail Adams expressed horror at the anarchy of *Shays's Rebellion, which Jefferson lightheartedly condoned. Adams, in his learned *Defense of the Constitutions of the United States* (1787), revealed his admiration of the British constitution. When copies of the newly drafted U.S. Constitution reached them, Adams regretted that the executive was not stronger while Jefferson feared that he was already a potential monarch.

Adams returned to the United States in 1788, was elected vice president, and promptly advised the U.S. Senate, as its first order of business, to create a title for President Washington comparable to those of European heads of state. His proposal: "His Highness the President of the United States and the Protector of the Rights of the Same." The Senate was satisfied with the title "President of the United States" and the address "Mr. President." In Paris, Jefferson scoffed at Adams's proposal as "the most superlatively ridiculous thing I ever heard of."

When Jefferson returned to the United States in 1790 and was appointed secretary of state, the *French Revolution was already dividing American opinion. A passionate supporter of the revolution, Jefferson feared that the American government was in the hands of antirevolutionary monarchists. He saw this not only in the economic policies of Secretary of the Treasury Alexander Hamilton (see *Hamilton and Jefferson), in the government's pro-British and anti-French foreign policy, but even in the ceremonial and almost regal estate that surrounded the president. His old friend, the vice president, was aghast at the havoc wreaked in France by illiterate and irreligious mobs. He made no secret of his preference for government by a natural aristocracy—not a hereditary one, to be sure, but far from the popular democracy celebrated by Rousseau and other French thinkers.

In 1791, Tom Paine's *Rights of Man*—a defense of the French Revolution in response to Edmund Burke's hostile *Reflections on the Revolution in France*—was published in America with an endorsement by Jefferson, who was happy that "something would at length be publicly said against the political heresies which have lately sprung up among us." Adams, not appreciating the gulf widening between him and Jefferson, denied any "heresy" on his part: "If You suppose that I have, or ever had, a design or desire of introducing a Government of kings, Lords and Commons, or in other words an hereditary Executive, or an hereditary Senate, either into the Government of the United States or that of any individual state in this country, you are wholly mistaken."

But Jefferson was convinced that the republic was endangered by "Anglomen" and "monocrats." Isolated in the cabinet, he employed the radical journalist Philip Freneau as a translator in the State Department, thereby enabling him to take on the editorship of the *National Gazette*. This was to be an organ of pro-French propaganda and opposition to the administration of which Jefferson was a member. Jefferson coolly disclaimed any responsibility for the scurrilous attacks—even touching Washington himself—that Freneau launched against the government.

Jefferson resigned as secretary of state at the end of 1793 and withdrew to his Virginia home, Monticello. Happy to be free of politics, he was nevertheless the acknowledged head of a political party, the Republican (see *Jeffersonian Republican Party). His party's candidate for president in 1796, he received fewer votes than the Federalist candidate, John Adams, and thus became vice president in an administration to which he was inveterately hostile. While the two men maintained the formalities of friendship, party politics drove them apart. Adams was deeply offended to learn what Jefferson was saying about him in private when a letter by Jefferson to an Ital-

ian friend was published in America: "It would give you a fever were I to name to you the apostates who have gone over to these heresies, men who were Samsons in the field [Washington] and Solomons in the council [Adams], but who have had their heads shorn by the harlot England."

During the presidential campaign of 1800, James Callendar, a Republican scandalmonger (he had already exposed Hamilton's affair with a married woman) and hatchet man known to be encouraged and aided by Jefferson, published a pamphlet attacking both Washington ("twice a traitor") and Adams ("successive monarchs of Braintree and Mount Vernon"). For his abuse of Adams, Callendar was imprisoned for seditious libel under the *Alien and Sedition Acts. When Jefferson became president, he promptly pardoned Callendar and other victims of the acts, only to have the ungrateful Callendar turn on him and reveal his relationship with his slave mistress, Sally Hemings.

Uncharacteristically embittered, Adams spent the last hours of his presidency appointing Federalists to judicial offices to check the tide of expected Republican anarchy (see *Midnight Appointments). Rather than participate in Jefferson's inauguration, Adams rose before dawn and was well on his way to Baltimore and home when Jefferson took the oath of office. The two men never met again.

In 1811, Benjamin Rush, the famous Philadelphia physician and signer of the Declaration of Independence, mediated a reconciliation between the two former presidents. On New Year's Day, 1812, Adams wrote a friendly letter to Jefferson conveying the published Harvard lectures of his son, John Quincy Adams; Jefferson responded promptly and warmly. A memorable correspondence ensued, formality soon dissolving into expressions of warmest affection. Their letters roamed over history, philosophy, religion, science, and politics, Adams's excitable and voluble, Jefferson's cool and composed. Over 14 years, Adams wrote 109 letters, Jefferson 49. Jefferson's last letter to Adams was written on Mar. 25, 1826, Adams's reply on Apr. 17. Both sensed that death was near.

Jefferson, aged 83, died on the morning of July 4, 1826, the 50th anniversary of the adoption of the Declaration of Independence; Adams, aged 90, died a few hours later, murmuring "Jefferson survives." The nation was profoundly struck by the triple coincidence. "Visible and palpable marks of Divine favor," John Quincy Adams mused.

ADAMSON ACT (1916). See *Railroad Regulation.

ADAMS-ONÍS TREATY (1819), diplomatic achievement of the *Monroe administration by which Spain renounced its claims to West Florida and ceded East Florida to the United States (see *Floridas, East and West) while the United States renounced its claims to Texas. The treaty, negotiated by Secretary of State John Quincy Adams and Spanish minister Luis de Onís, also defined the western limits of the *Louisiana Purchase in such a way that Spain in effect surrendered to the United States its claims to the Pacific Northwest.

ADDRESS OF THE SOUTHERN DELEGATES (Jan. 22, 1849), document written by Sen. John C. Calhoun of South Carolina at the behest of a committee of Southern members of Congress appealing for Southern unity in the face of steady Northern "aggressions and encroachments" on the slavery issue.

Calhoun reminded Southerners that the North had recognized slavery and provided for its protection in the Constitution. Indeed, the Southern states would not have joined the Union had not the North done so. But since 1819 the North had repeatedly ignored its constitutional obligations by refusing to return fugitive slaves, by enticing slaves to escape, by tolerating the abolitionist propaganda aimed at emancipation, and finally by attempting to exclude slavery from the territories, which were the common property of the states in this confederacy of sovereign states.

Calhoun hoped that Southern unity on this issue would cause the North to relent in its provocations, but unity was not to be had. Whigs and Democrats would not unite in support of Calhoun's address. Although the committee of Southern lawmakers adopted the address on Jan. 22, 1849, fewer than half the Southern members of Congress endorsed it and it had no effect.

"Moderate in manner," in Calhoun's opinion, the address is significant as the most authoritative statement of the Southern case in the growing sectional division. But it is also memorable for Calhoun's dark prediction of the consequences of emancipation:

". . . If [emancipation] ever should be effected, it will be through the agency of the Federal Government, controlled by the dominant power of the Northern States of the Confederacy, against the resistance and struggle of the Southern. It can then only be effected by the prostration of the white race; and that would necessarily engender the bitterest feelings of hostility between them and the North. But the reverse would be the case between the blacks of the South and the people of the North. Owing their emancipation to them, they would regard them as friends, guardians, and patrons, and centre, accordingly, all their sympathy in them. The people of the North would not fail to reciprocate and to favor them, instead of the whites. Under the influence of such feelings, and impelled by fanaticism and love of power, they would not stop at emancipation. Another step would be taken—to raise them to a political and social equality with their former owners, by giving them the right of voting and holding public offices under the Federal Government. . . . But when once raised to an equality, they would become the fast political associates of the North, acting and voting with them on all questions, and by this political union between them, holding the white race at the South in complete subjection. The blacks, and the profligate whites that might unite with them, would become the principal recipients of federal offices and patronage, and would, in consequence, be raised above the whites of the South in the political and social scale. We would, in a word, change positions with them—a degradation greater than has ever yet fallen to the lot of a free and enlightened people, and one from which we could not escape . . . but by fleeing the homes of ourselves and ancestors, and by abandoning our country to its former slaves, to become the permanent abode of disorder, anarchy, poverty, misery, and wretchedness."

ADKINS v. CHILDREN'S HOSPITAL (1927), 5–3 decision of the *Taft Court overturning a federal law establishing a minimum wage for women in the District of Columbia as a violation of the liberty of contract guaranteed by the Due Process Clause of the Fifth Amendment. Justice George Sutherland, for the majority, also argued that a woman's liberty of contract should not be subjected to greater restrictions than a man's. The Court reversed this decision in *West Coast Hotel Co. v. Parrish* (1937).

ADMINISTRATION OF JUSTICE ACT (1774). See *Intolerable Acts.

AFFIRMATIVE ACTION, preferential treatment of women and minorities to remedy the effects of past discrimination. Affirmative action gained currency during the *civil rights movement of the 1960s when it became apparent that the removal of discriminatory barriers was not sufficient in some areas to create a level playing field for groups that had been profoundly disadvantaged by discrimination in the past. At Howard University in 1965, Pres. Lyndon B. Johnson called for equality not just as a right and a theory but "equality as a fact and equality as a result" of affirmative action. The goal was to have women and minorities represented in desirable areas of the national life in proportion to their share of the population.

Higher Education. Under the pressure of government regulations and in the belief that a diverse student body was educationally desirable, colleges and graduate schools sought to increase the enrollment of women and minorities by instituting goals, timetables, and quotas. When a racial quota at the University of California Medical School at Davis was challenged as reverse discrimination by a rejected white applicant, the U.S. Supreme Court, in *Regents of the University of California v. Bakke* (1978), ruled that racial quotas were unconstitutional but that affirmative action in pursuit of student diversity was acceptable as long as race was only one of a number of factors weighed in the admission decision.

Controversy over race-based admissions did not end with *Bakke*. Between 1996 and 2002, in cases challenging affirmative action in admission policies of colleges and law schools in Texas, Georgia, and Michigan, federal courts reached contradictory decisions. The issue was expected to go again to the U.S. Supreme Court. (See also *School Desegregation.)

Employment. Before passage of the *Civil Rights Act of 1964, presidential executive orders had required that government contractors employ minorities and women in rough proportion to their numbers in the local labor pool. Failure to do this could result in "debarment," cancellation of federal contracts and exclusion of those firms from future bidding.

Title VII of the Civil Rights Act of 1964 made it illegal for private employers to discriminate on grounds of race, color, religion, sex, or national origin in hiring, paying, promoting, or dismissing workers. The executive agencies and courts charged with implementing the act were not content to see discriminatory practices ended; they required affirmative action to ensure that minorities and women actually moved into jobs in proportion to their numbers in the local labor force. The courts gave Title VII more force than Congress perhaps intended, viewing any employment policy that resulted in a "disparate impact" on a protected group as discriminatory. They thus prohibited as discriminatory many widespread employment practices, such as word-of-mouth recruitment of new employees (since minority workers usually had less access to such information) and partiality by employers and unions for relatives of current employees and members (since that tended to perpetuate the exclusion of minority workers).

The U.S. Supreme Court under Chief Justice Warren Burger (see *Burger Court) endorsed affirmative action in employment. In *Griggs v. Duke Power Co.* (1971), a unanimous Court ruled that all qualifications and tests for employment had to be job-related, but that they were nevertheless illegal if they had a disparate impact upon minority employees. In *Regents of the University of California v. Bakke* (1978), it found racial quotas unconstitutional but approved affirmative action that was not based exclusively on race. In *United Steelworkers of America v. Weber* (1979), it upheld the legality of a voluntary affirmative action program that gave special preference to black workers to eliminate racial imbalance among skilled-job holders. In *Fullilove v. Klutznick* (1980), it upheld a public works program that set aside 10 percent of the federal grant money for minority contractors. And in *Local 28 of Sheet Metal Workers International Association v. Equal Employment Opportunity Commission* (1986), it required a New York City union local to establish a minority membership goal of 29 percent.

The *Rehnquist Court, however, was notably hostile to affirmative action in employment. In *Richmond v. J. A. Croson Co.* (1989), it struck down a Richmond, Va., ordinance requiring prime contractors to subcontract at least 30 percent of the value of their contracts to minority contractors. And in *Ward's Cove Packing Co. v. Atonio* (1989), it rejected disparate impact as proof of discrimination, requiring plaintiffs to prove discriminatory intent. Congress reversed this requirement in the Civil Rights Act of 1991.

The Backlash. Opposition to affirmative action, unlike that to antidiscrimination legislation, was not the product of prejudice but of offended justice. Paradoxically, the pursuit of social justice inflicted individual injustice. Numerical hiring quotas for blacks, for example, penalized some white workers who themselves may never have been guilty of discrimination (although they may have profited from it) and benefited blacks who may not have been specifically discriminated against (although they may have suffered the consequences of past discrimination). In a country that had always valued individual merit, the concept of group entitlement was disquieting. Not all critics of affirmative action were white; some conservative blacks believed that affirmative action perpetuated blacks' sense of dependence and denigrated the personal achievements of successful blacks.

In 1996, California voters approved Proposition 209, which banned racial and gender preferences in college admissions, state employment, and public contracts. Later that year, the U.S. Supreme Court upheld the constitutionality of that ban. In 1998, voters in Washington State approved a similar ban on preferential treatment based on race or sex.

AFRICAN-AMERICANS. Almost all African-Americans are descendants of the 400,000 African slaves brought to America before the *slave trade ended in 1808. Since the 19th century, there has been a small *immigration of blacks from the West Indies, and since 1965 of blacks from Africa. The 2000 Census counted 34.7 million African-Americans, 12.3 percent of the U.S. population. Of these, nearly 2 million were foreign-born.

Until the great migrations to the North beginning in World War I, 90 percent of the African-American population lived in the rural South. In 2000, 54.8 percent continued to live in the South. Of those African-Americans living in the Northeast, Midwest, and West, 95 percent lived in metropolitan areas—chiefly New York, Chicago, Los Angeles, Philadelphia, and Detroit. Of those still living in the South, three-fourths lived in metropolitan areas—chiefly Washington, Atlanta, Houston, Baltimore, and Miami.

In 2000, 78.5 percent of African-Americans 25 and older (compared to 84.9 percent of whites) had completed high school, and 16.5 percent (compared to 26.1 percent of whites) had completed four years of college. In 1999, the median income for African-American families was $31,778, compared to $51,224 for white families. African-American unemployment rates have historically been twice or more those of whites. In 2000, the poverty rate for African-American individuals was 23.6 percent, compared to 9.8 percent for whites. In 1990, the National Opinion Research Center at the University of Chicago reported that, of 33 U.S. ethnic groups studied, African-Americans ranked 31st in household income and 33rd in years of schooling; they were rated 31st in "social standing."

AGRARIAN DISCONTENTS (1867–97). The last third of the 19th century was a period of distress for American farmers, especially those in the South and West who grew cotton, wheat, and corn for the national or world market. After the Civil War, farmers had moved west optimistically, bought farms and equipment on credit, and expected to prosper with the growing country. But farm production, due to expanded acreage and mechanization, grew faster than the country's population. Other food-producing countries began shipping their vast supplies to world markets. The result was that farm prices fell instead of rising. The wholesale price index for farm products fell from 133 in 1867 to 40 in 1896. Corn that sold for 66 cents a bushel in 1866 sold for 28 cents in 1889. At the same time, the price of wheat fell from $2.06 a bushel to 70 cents.

Heavily in debt, farmers found that money borrowed when farm prices were high had to be paid back when prices were low. Long periods of economic depression (1873–79, 1882–85, 1893–97) made the burden of debt especially oppressive. For many, years of hard work and privation ended in ruin.

A plausible explanation for the farmers' trouble pointed to the national currency. After the Civil War, the government stopped issuing paper money (see *Greenbacks), and in 1873 it stopped coining silver (see *Crime of '73). The country was virtually on the *gold standard, and gold was scarce. In 1865 the total amount of money in the country came to $30 per person; by 1889 it had fallen to $23. Scarce money meant low prices. The solution, according to many unorthodox thinkers, was inflation—printing paper money or coining silver to increase the money supply.

But the farmer felt victimized not only by Eastern bankers but by others upon whom he depended more directly. Credit—which he needed at the start of each planting season—was scarce and costly. The agent to whom he sold his grain or cotton was usually the only purchaser in a small rural town. With no means to store his crop until the price improved, the farmer was forced to sell at the price quoted by the agent. Then the rates charged by the railroads to ship his crop to distant cities and by grain elevators (usually owned by the railroads) to store it there seemed mysteriously resistant to the general price deflation. What the farmer produced steadily declined in price; what he needed—credit, transportation, storage—remained expensive.

Although highly individualistic and widely dispersed, farmers sought solutions to their problems in self-help and political organizations (see *Populism). The *Granger movement won the first regulation of railroad and grain elevator practices and rates. Farmers then rallied to the *Greenback Party in the belief that inflation fueled by paper money would maintain commodity prices. In the 1880s the *Farmers' Alliances sought government regulation of transportation, credit, and land ownership, new tax policies, and inflation induced by the free coinage of silver (see *Free Silver). The need for political action led the Alliances to form the *People's Party in 1892.

The political successes in which the farmers shared—such as the *Bland-Allison Act (1878), the *Interstate Commerce Act (1887), the *Sherman Antitrust Act (1890), and the *Sherman Silver Purchase Act (1890)—were more apparent than real. The farmers' problems were mitigated after 1897 when demand for farm products at last caught up with farm production. Farmland ceased to expand, relatively fewer workers were employed in agriculture, while the nation's population, increasingly urbanized, grew rapidly. At the same time, the money supply grew with the growth of gold production. With no miraculous political "fix," the period 1897–1915 became a golden age for American agriculture.

AGRICULTURAL ADJUSTMENT ACTS (1933, 1938). See *Farm Problem.

AGRICULTURAL ADJUSTMENT ADMINISTRATION (AAA). See *New Deal.

AGRICULTURAL MARKETING ACT (1929). See *Farm Problem.

AGRICULTURE. For the first 150 years of the United States, most Americans lived on or near farms. Not until 1920, when the farm population constituted 30.1 percent of the total, did the census report that the nation's urban population exceeded the rural. That same year, the number of people engaged in manufacturing exceeded the number engaged in farming for the first time.

In 1800 perhaps 85 percent of the U.S. labor force worked in agriculture. The pioneer farmer's conception of himself as independent and self-sufficient was the self-image that many Americans cherished for generations, although the percentage of the labor force engaged in agriculture fell to 52.0 in 1870, 25.2 in 1920, 4.2 in 1970, and 2.1 in 2000.

The farmers of the New England and Middle Atlantic colonies and states were self-sufficient of necessity. The difficulty of transporting bulky farm products was so great that only those farms located near towns and cities could sell their surpluses at market for cash. Farmers distant from markets consumed their own produce, providing for most of their needs from the farm or nearby woodland, and rarely saw cash.

The situation changed when Northern farmers crossed the Allegheny Mountains into the Ohio River valley. There numerous and broad rivers enabled them to transport bulky surpluses—livestock and grain—by flatboat to New Orleans, where it was sold for cash and reshipped to the East Coast or to Europe. It was cheaper to send farm products thousands of miles to market by river and sea than to haul them a few hundred miles over the mountains to Eastern cities.

With the construction of turnpikes and canals, and the development of steamboats and railroads, the Western farmer—now occupying all of the Old Northwest and moving increasingly onto the prairies and plains west of the Mississippi—became ever more market-

oriented. Specialization followed: the New England farmer specialized in dairying and vegetables, the Middle Western farmer in corn and livestock, the trans-Mississippi farmer in wheat and cattle.

Unlike Northern farmers, the large planters of the South engaged in commercial agriculture from the start. Climate, soil, topography, slave labor, and easy access to the sea permitted the South to specialize early in the large-scale cultivation of staples for sale in England—tobacco, rice, sugar, and long-staple Sea Island cotton. The invention of the *cotton gin made possible the cultivation of the short-staple upland cotton across the South, especially in the *cotton kingdom of the lower South. Here, too, numerous streams enabled the planters to ship their bales to the sea for transport to the textile mills of New England and Great Britain. Southern cotton production rose from 5 million pounds in 1793, the year the cotton gin was invented, to 2 billion pounds on the eve of the Civil War, when cotton was the nation's principal export.

Even while cotton was "king," the South grew all the other agricultural products it required for domestic consumption. In 1849, for example, when it devoted 5 million acres to cotton, the South planted 18 million acres in corn, which was the principal food for farmers, slaves, and livestock. By the end of the 20th century, cotton had been replaced as the South's principal cash crop by poultry, soybeans, corn, and peanuts. Texas was the leading cotton producer, and the country as a whole marketed 7 billion pounds of cotton annually, 15 percent of the world's total.

The mechanization of agriculture, which began in the 1830s with the introduction of the steel plow, became rapid after 1870 with the use of soil-breaking machinery like the steel harrow and the disk plow and cultivator; planting devices like the grain drill, corn and potato planters, and manure spreaders; and harvesting machinery like the mechanical reaper and thresher and the twine self-binder. This machinery was powered by horses and mules, the number of which grew rapidly. The introduction of gasoline-powered tractors and other machinery was slow because they were initially costly and unreliable. Not until 1915–25 did the number of horses and mules on farms begin to decline as animal power was replaced by the internal combustion engine.

Mechanization—together with the use of chemical fertilizers and pesticides—vastly increased the productivity of agriculture, rendered small farms uneconomical, and made much of the farm population redundant. There were 6 million farms in 1940, 3 million in 1970, and 2 million in 2000. The size of the average farm increased from 175 acres in 1940 to 434 acres in 2000, while the farm population decreased from 30.5 million (23.2 percent of the total population) in 1940 to 5.1 million (1.8 percent) in 1990.

At the end of the 20th century, with farm income low, the industry experienced rapid consolidation. The largest farms—those with sales over $250,000—accounted for 72 percent of all agricultural sales, up from 53 percent a decade before. Mergers among agribusinesses reduced the numbers of farmers' suppliers and customers. In 1999, five companies accounted for 51 percent of sow production, three companies for 88 percent of corn seed sales. Many small independent farmers became contract farmers for large agribusinesses or left the industry.

Nevertheless, with only 2.1 percent of the labor force engaged in agriculture, and agriculture contributing only 1.3 percent of the gross domestic product, the United States was the world's leading producer of meat, corn, and wheat.

(See also *Agrarian Discontents; *Farm Problem.)

AIDS (*a*cquired *i*mmune *d*eficiency *s*yndrome), an infectious viral disease that depresses the human immune system, exposing the victim to often fatal opportunistic infections. AIDS was first recognized in the United States in 1981 when physicians in California and New York reported seeing among young homosexual men an unusual number of cases of a type of pneumonia associated with immune dysfunction and a rare skin cancer usually seen in elderly men. In 1982, when 471 cases had been diagnosed and 184 people had died, the Centers for Disease Control in Atlanta termed the outbreak an epidemic.

"Gay cancer" caused panic among homosexuals and grim satisfaction in some religious circles where the disease was interpreted as divine retribution for a lifestyle condemned by the Bible as an "abomination." But AIDS was soon diagnosed in hemophiliacs, intravenous drug users, women, and infants. Discovery in 1984 of the causal virus (named HIV, or human immunodeficiency virus) was credited to U.S. and French researchers.

Communicated only by inoculation with the blood (liquid or dried) of an infected person, HIV may be active in the body for as long as ten years before the immune system becomes unable to resist other infections. The name AIDS is reserved for this last stage of the disease. Although the number of deaths from AIDS in the United States fell in the late 1990s, new HIV infections continued at about 40,000 a year. More than half of all new infections were occurring among African-Americans. By the century's end, some half million Americans had died of AIDS. Meanwhile, AIDS spread worldwide, particularly in poor and underdeveloped countries where its advance was virtually unchecked. Its ravages in sub-Saharan Africa, where it was believed to have originated, were catastrophic.

No vaccine or cure for AIDS has been discovered, although the costly drug AZT, used in a "cocktail" of other drugs, has proved effective in delaying the onset of AIDS in HIV-infected people.

AID TO FAMILIES WITH DEPENDENT CHILDREN (AFDC). See *Welfare.

AIR TRAFFIC CONTROLLERS STRIKE (1981), incident in the *Reagan administration. Having endorsed Reagan for president, the Professional Air Traffic Controllers Organization (PATCO)—which regarded its members (federal employees) as overworked, overstressed, and underpaid—called a strike on Aug. 3, 1981. Overriding his advisers, Reagan gave the strikers 48 hours to return to work or be fired. Two days later, 38 percent of the strikers had returned to work; 12,000 others were fired. Supervising personnel and military controllers took their places while new controllers were recruited and trained. PATCO was destroyed and other unions were weakened since private employers thereafter responded to strikes by hiring "replacement workers." Reagan's forcefulness enhanced his popularity.

ALABAMA CLAIMS, claims by the United States against Great Britain for damage to Northern shipping during the *Civil War inflicted by Confederate cruisers built in Britain, particularly the *Alabama, Shenandoah,* and *Florida.* By the Treaty of *Washington (1871), the two countries agreed to submit the claims to arbitration. In 1872 an international tribunal awarded the United States $15.5 million.

ALAMO SIEGE (Feb. 23–Mar. 6, 1836), incident in the Texas Revolution (see *Texas Republic). The Alamo was a fortified mission at San Antonio, Texas. Against orders from Gen. Sam Houston, a body of Texans numbering eventually 187 and led by William B. Travis and James Bowie occupied the compound and determined to defend it against the 3,000-man army of Mexican general Antonio López de Santa Anna. Having retaken San Antonio, the Mexicans besieged the Alamo on Feb. 23, 1836, and finally took it by assault on Mar. 6. All the defenders were killed; some 30 noncombatants were spared. The siege and assault cost Santa Anna 1,500 men.

ALASKA LANDS ACT (1980). See *Environmentalism.

ALASKA PIPELINE, oil pipeline carrying 1 million barrels of oil daily 789 miles from Alaska's North Slope on the Arctic Ocean to the port of Valdez on the Gulf of Alaska. Construction by a consortium of oil companies was authorized during the *oil shock of 1973 over the opposition of environmentalists who feared damage to Alaska's fragile ecosystem. It was completed in 1977.

ALASKA PURCHASE (1867), diplomatic achievement of the Andrew *Johnson administration. Russia was eager to sell Alaska (then called Russian America) because it was indefensible against the British in Canada. The U.S. secretary of state, William H. Seward, was an expansionist who dreamed of U.S. sovereignty over the entire continent. In March 1867, Seward and the Russian minister to the United States, Baron Eduard Stoeckl, negotiated the purchase of Alaska for $7.2 million. The treaty was signed on Mar. 30 and narrowly ratified by the Senate on Apr. 9. Few people were enthusiastic about "Seward's folly."

ALBANY CONGRESS (June 19–July 10, 1754), meeting of representatives from seven British North American colonies and Iroquois chiefs in Albany, New York, to unite the colonies and win the support of the Indians for the impending *French and Indian War. Its chief accomplishment was its adoption of the Albany Plan of Union, drafted by Benjamin Franklin, by which each colony would send representatives to a grand council responsible for Indian affairs and the common defense. The plan was rejected by the colonies and the British government.

ALBANY REGENCY (1820–42), political machine that governed New York State in the absence of its leader, Martin Van Buren, who, briefly governor (1828–29), served in Washington as U.S. senator (1821–28), secretary of state (1829–31), vice president (1833–37), and president (1837–41). When Van Buren supported Andrew Jackson for president in 1828, the Regency led the *Democratic Party in New York, pioneering in strict party management and the *spoils system. Its domination ended when the state party split into *Barnburner and Hunker factions.

ALDEN v. MAINE (1999), 5–4 decision of the *Rehnquist Court significantly strengthening the powers of the states in the federal system while weakening those of the federal government. It ruled that citizens of a state could not sue in state court to enforce a federally protected right, in this instance one provided in the Fair Labor Standards Act (1938). The Court had long interpreted the 11th Amendment—which bars a citizen of one state from suing another state in federal court—as also barring a citizen from suing his own state in federal court. Now the Supreme Court ruled that a state's sovereign immunity barred citizens from suing their state in state courts.

"It is unquestioned," wrote Justice Anthony M. Kennedy, "that the Federal Government retains its own immunity from suit not only in state tribunals but also in its own courts. In light of our constitutional system recognizing the essential sovereignty of the states, we are reluctant to conclude that the states are not entitled to a reciprocal privilege.

". . . Congress has vast power, but not all power. When Congress legislates in matters affecting the states, it may not treat these sovereign entities as mere prefectures or corporations. Congress must accord states the esteem due to them as joint participants in a federal system, one beginning with the premise of sovereignty in both the central Government and the separate states."

ALDRICH-VREELAND ACT (1908), legislation of the Theodore *Roosevelt administration. A response to the *Panic of 1907, it aimed to provide elasticity to the currency by permitting national banks to issue circulating notes based on commercial paper and state, county, and municipal as well as federal bonds for six years. Its most important provision established a National Monetary Commission, which, under Sen. Nelson A. Aldrich of Rhode Island, studied the banking systems of Europe. The commission's findings contributed to the *Federal Reserve Act (1913).

ALGECIRAS CONFERENCE (1906), international conference at Algeciras, Spain, that dealt with German-French rivalry over Morocco. Pres. Theodore Roosevelt persuaded France and Great Britain to attend and sent a U.S. delegation, then persuaded the kaiser to accept a settlement favorable to France that preserved Morocco's nominal independence.

ALIEN AND SEDITION ACTS (1798), legislation of the John *Adams administration passed by narrow margins by the Federalist Congress in the war fever following the *XYZ Affair. The four acts were directed against aliens—particularly the "wild Irish," who were notoriously anti-British and pro-French—and against Republican editors.

The Naturalization Act (June 18) extended from 5 to 14 years the residency requirement for new citizens and denied citizenship to anyone whose mother country was at war with the United States. It was repealed in 1802.

The Alien Act (June 25) authorized the president, in wartime or peacetime, to deport any aliens "he shall judge dangerous to the peace and safety of the United States, or shall have reasonable grounds to suspect are concerned in any treasonable or secret machinations against the government thereof." No aliens were deported under this act, which expired in 1800.

The Alien Enemies Act (July 6) authorized the president in time of war to imprison or deport alien subjects of an enemy power whom he considered dangerous. This was the only one of the four acts to become a permanent statute.

The Sedition Act (July 14) made it unlawful for persons to combine or conspire together to oppose any measure of the U.S. government or to impede the operation of any laws. More important, it forbade "any person [to] write, print, utter, or publish . . . any false, scandalous and malicious writing or writings" against the government, either house of Congress, or the president of the United States. The severity of the act was mitigated by allowing the truth of a statement to be accepted as a defense, permitting juries rather than judges to determine whether a statement was libelous, and requiring the prosecution to prove malicious intent. By the time it expired on Mar. 3, 1801 (the last day of the John Adams administration), there had been 14 prosecutions under the act.

In the *Virginia and Kentucky Resolutions, Thomas Jefferson and James Madison tried, with little success, to arouse opposition to the Alien and Sedition Acts as unconstitutional. Upon becoming president in 1801, Jefferson promptly halted all prosecutions still pending under the Sedition Act and pardoned those already convicted (see *Jefferson Administration).

ALLIANCE FOR PROGRESS, program of the *Kennedy administration calling for a ten-year, $100-billion effort by the United States and the Organization of American States to accelerate the economic and social development of Latin America. Despite initial enthusiasm, the program soon faltered due to the size of the existing Latin American debt, service of which limited new investment; the opposition of conservative circles in Latin America to necessary reforms; and the shift of Washington's attention elsewhere—especially Vietnam.

AMERICA FIRST COMMITTEE (1940–41), national organization advocating nonintervention in the European war (see *Isolationists). Led by Robert E. Wood, board chairman of Sears, Roebuck, it grew to some 450 chapters with 850,000 members, chiefly in the Middle West. Believing in hemispheric defense, it opposed aid to Britain and Russia, *Lend-Lease, convoys, and repeal of the *Neutrality Acts in 1941. Its most popular public speaker was Col. Charles A. Lindbergh, whose hint of anti-Semitism in a September 1941 speech greatly embarrassed the committee by seeming to confirm accusations that it was a transmitter of Nazi propaganda (see *Lindbergh's Career). The organization disbanded after *Pearl Harbor.

AMERICAN AND FOREIGN ANTI-SLAVERY SOCIETY. See *Abolitionists.

AMERICAN ANTI-SLAVERY SOCIETY. See *Abolitionists.

AMERICAN CIVIL LIBERTIES UNION (ACLU), organization founded in 1920 during the post–World War I *red scare to defend constitutional freedoms. Its founders included Jane Addams, Clarence Darrow, John Dewey, Felix Frankfurter, Helen Keller, and Norman Thomas. Headquartered in New York City, the organization has 250 state and local affiliates whose lawyers (salaried or volunteer) enter selected cases by filing "friend of the court" briefs or by actual litigating. The ACLU became extremely controversial for defending the First Amendment rights of communists, Nazis, and the Ku Klux Klan.

AMERICAN COLONIZATION SOCIETY. See *Colonization.

AMERICAN DREAM, a nebulous term, much abused by politicians, that seems to have evolved from the early immigrants' and pioneers' hopes for lives of political and religious liberty and personal independence in the New World to a largely materialistic expectation of upward social mobility and ever-increasing affluence.

AMERICAN EXPEDITIONARY FORCE (AEF). See *World War I.

AMERICAN FEDERATION OF LABOR–CONGRESS OF INDUSTRIAL ORGANIZATIONS (AFL–CIO), central organization of autonomous national and international labor unions. The AFL was founded in 1886 as a federation of craft unions to pursue narrow economic objectives—higher wages, shorter hours, better working conditions—within the capitalist system. Rejecting the political, reformist, utopian, and revolutionary objectives of other labor organizations, and excluding the growing masses of unskilled industrial workers, the AFL under Samuel Gompers (president 1886–94, 1895–1924) was a bastion of conservatism in the volatile labor world.

In 1935 unions led by *United Mine Workers president John L. Lewis, who wanted to organize unskilled as well as skilled workers by industry rather than by craft, seceded from the AFL, formed the Congress of Industrial Organizations (CIO), and proceeded to organize such mass-production industries as autos, steel, rubber, and electrical equipment. The bitter rivalry between the AFL and the CIO was not resolved until their merger in 1955. In 2000 the AFL–CIO claimed 1.3 million members.

AMERICAN INDEPENDENT PARTY (AIP) (1968–72), political party organized to support the presidential candidacy of Alabama governor George C. Wallace in 1968 (see *Wallace's Career). It succeeded in getting Wallace's name on the ballots in all 50 states, and ended by receiving 9 million popular votes and carrying five Southern states. In 1972 Wallace won several Democratic primaries before he was shot and paralyzed. When he declined the AIP nomination, the party nominated John Schmitz, a member of the right-wing John Birch Society. Schmitz polled 1 million popular votes and no electoral votes. By 1976 Wallace had returned to the Democratic Party while most members of the AIP joined the Republican Party.

AMERICAN INDIANS. See *Indians, American, or Native Americans.

AMERICAN PARTY. See *Know-Nothing Party or American Party.

AMERICAN PEACE SOCIETY. See *Peace Movement.

AMERICAN PLAN, name adopted in 1921 by various manufacturers' associations for the open shop (employment open to nonunion as well as union members). In their campaign to preserve the open shop, manufacturers contrasted the traditional value of rugged individualism with the foreign concept of collectivism. "Every man to work out his own salvation and not be bound by the shackles of organization to his own detriment" was their definition of the American Plan.

AMERICAN RAILWAY UNION (1893–94), labor organization founded by Eugene V. Debs to unite all railroad workers (except blacks), regardless of skills, in a single union. Despite opposition from the *Railroad Brotherhoods and the *American Federation of Labor, the union grew rapidly. A successful strike in April 1894 against James J. Hill's Great Northern Railroad was immediately followed by the *Pullman strike, in which the union collapsed.

AMERICAN REVOLUTION (1763–88), the separation of 13 North American colonies from Great Britain, a complex process—political, military, social, and cultural—extending over 25 years, during which the Americans acquired national consciousness, founded a new nation on principles of liberty and equality, declared their independence and maintained it in war (see *Revolutionary War), and finally constructed an enduring federal union.

"What do we mean by the Revolution?" John Adams asked his friend Thomas Jefferson in 1815. "The War? That was no part of the Revolution. It was only an Effect and Consequence of it. The Revolution was in the Minds of the People . . . before a drop of blood was drawn at Lexington." Nor was the revolution over, wrote Benjamin Rush, an eminent physician and signer of the Declaration of Independence, in 1786; "we have only finished the first act of the great drama. We have changed our forms of government, but it remains yet to effect a revolution in our principles, opinions, and manners so as to accommodate them to the forms of government we have adopted."

Separation began, of course, with the founding of the first American colony 3,000 miles from the mother country. As the colonies grew in population and wealth over the next century and a half, prophecies of eventual separation became frequent. Until the late 18th century, the British Empire was a loosely administered commercial empire. Britain had less interest in governing territories than in managing the commerce of its far-flung dependencies for its own advantage. Thus the *Navigation Acts, for example, required that American imports and exports be carried in British (including colonial) ships only, and that certain American exports be sold only in England whatever their ultimate market. Other acts limited American manufactures that competed with British. These restrictions on American economic activity were accepted by Americans because they protected them from the competition of foreign colonies and ensured them a favored place in the British market. Americans were mindful, moreover, that Britain protected them from the constant menace of France and Spain.

In their internal affairs, the 13 colonies were virtually

self-governing. They had been founded in the 17th century by private entrepreneurs and religious visionaries with authorization from the crown, and one school of colonial thought insisted that they were connected with Britain through the crown alone. Imperial affairs were managed by the king, his secretaries and boards, who formulated policy, and—at least in eight colonies—by royal governors, who executed it. By the mid-18th century all 13 governors—royal, proprietary, or elected—had become subordinated to their colonies' legislatures, which levied taxes and paid the cost of administration and of defense against Indians. Under Britain's policy of "salutary neglect," the colonies flourished. Total population doubled every 25 years, reaching 2.5 million (including 500,000 African slaves) in 1775, and wealth multiplied to the point that the 13 colonies were Britain's chief market for manufactured goods.

In 1763, Britain emerged victorious from the Seven Years' War with France (called the *French and Indian War in North America), possessed of extensive overseas territories—Canada and the eastern Mississippi Valley in North America—that required administration and defense. Moreover, the war had doubled Britain's national debt. Raising revenue to pay for imperial administration and to reduce the national debt was the business of Parliament, which since 1688 was constitutionally superior to the crown in the British government (although the king continued to wield great power through bribery and patronage, including the selection of the prime minister). Indeed, the term *government* now referred to the ministry, the committee of ministers who were members and leaders of Parliament (although they owed their appointments as ministers to the crown). After 1763, therefore, Parliament interjected itself into imperial administration as it had not previously.

The government's first determination was to set aside the country west of the Appalachian Mountains—country into which the colonists were steadily moving—as an Indian reserve (see *Proclamation of 1763) and to station an army in North America for which the colonists must pay. It then proceeded to tighten and enforce trade regulations, not merely, as before, to ensure Britain's commercial advantage, but to raise revenue from the colonies. The colonists, of course, pointed out that there was no need for a British army in North America now that France had been expelled from Canada. More fundamentally, the colonists regarded Parliament's intrusion into their internal affairs—in particular, Parliament's intention to raise revenue in the colonies by taxation and customs duties—as a radical and ominous violation of their liberties as Englishmen. Parliament, they insisted,

had no authority over them because they were not represented there. (Parliamentary apologists replied that the colonists were in the same position as the great majority of voteless Englishmen, who, while not directly represented in Parliament either, were *virtually* represented since members of Parliament represented the entire empire, not merely the constituents who elected them.)

In 1764, the *Sugar Act revised customs duties and tightened their enforcement, with the avowed purpose of raising revenue to pay for the army stationed in America. A currency act that same year limited the issuance of paper money by the colonies, a serious inconvenience to debtors whose specie flowed irresistibly to Britain, and in 1764 and 1765 *Quartering Acts compelled colonial legislatures to billet and supply royal troops stationed in their provinces. The *Stamp Act of 1765—the first direct tax levied by Parliament in America—aroused such massive resistance that it had to be repealed the next year, although repeal was accompanied by a Declaratory Act asserting that Parliament had the authority to legislate for America "in all cases whatsoever." The *Townshend Acts of 1767—placing import duties on a variety of useful products, the proceeds to be used to pay the cost of royal administration and military defense in the colonies—again provoked widespread resistance. Two regiments of troops were stationed in riotous Boston, a move that led to the *Boston Massacre of 1770.

These successive measures persuaded many colonists that a venal and corrupt British government had determined to reduce them to slavery before destroying the liberties of its own people. The colonies, which theretofore had been more closely linked to Britain than to each other, perceived a common threat and the necessity of a united response. Among themselves, the colonies were quarrelsome, jealous, and suspicious. There were divisions within the colonies as well—between seaboard and backcountry, between plain people and local aristocracies. Nevertheless, there were powerful unifying forces among them. The great majority of the colonists were of English descent and Protestant. They spoke the same language, shared the same historical traditions, valued personal independence and equality, and prided themselves on the possession of English liberties, carried with them when they emigrated to the New World. These liberties were expressed everywhere in representative assemblies and nonintrusive government.

Intercolonial resistance to British policy began with merchants' nonimportation pledges, first in Boston, then imitated voluntarily throughout the colonies. In 1765, the *Sons of Liberty, secret organizations established in many towns, often by leading citizens, prevented enforcement of the Stamp Act; that year, representatives of nine colonies attended the Stamp Act Congress in New York City. *Committees of correspondence, first established in Massachusetts in 1772, sprang up everywhere in the colonies, providing a network for exchanging information and coordinating activities.

A crisis in colonial relations with Britain was precipitated in 1773 by the *Boston Tea Party. In response, an outraged Parliament passed the Coercive Acts (called the *Intolerable Acts in America) to punish Massachusetts. Massachusetts's appeal for help to the other colonies was answered by the convening of the *Continental Congress.

The first Congress, which met in Philadelphia during September and October 1774, rejected a conciliatory Plan of Union proposed by Joseph Galloway of Pennsylvania (see *Galloway's Plan of Union), opting instead for economic sanctions against Britain. In the *Continental Association, the colonies agreed on a common policy of nonimportation, nonconsumption, and nonexportation and created a network of committees in every county, city, and town to monitor and enforce compliance. It also adopted a Declaration of Rights.

The second Congress assembled in Philadelphia on May 10, 1775, three weeks after the battles of *Lexington and Concord and five weeks before the battle of *Bunker Hill. Congress established a *Continental Army, appointed George Washington of Virginia its commander in chief, set about preparing for war, and began to issue paper money to pay for it. Most of the members still hoped for a redress of grievances and reconciliation with Britain. But on Aug. 23 a royal proclamation declared that the American colonies were in a state of rebellion, and on Dec. 22 a Prohibitory Act removed the colonies from the protection of the crown, prohibited trade with them, and authorized the seizure and confiscation of American ships at sea—in effect, a declaration of war.

Interest, sentiment, habit, and timidity prevented the colonists from readily embracing the idea of independence. The publication in January 1776 of Thomas Paine's pamphlet *Common Sense did much to clarify Americans' thinking and to prepare them for independence. At the same time, the news that the king was hiring 30,000 German mercenaries to use against his subjects in America and that royal officials in Georgia and South Carolina were recruiting slaves as laborers and soldiers with promises of freedom dissolved the last bonds of loyalty for many Americans, North and South.

In January 1776 Massachusetts authorized its delegates in the Continental Congress to vote for independence; South Carolina followed in March, Georgia and North Carolina in April. "Every Post and every Day," John Adams exulted on May 20, "rolls in upon us, Independence like a Torrent." In March Congress authorized the commissioning of privateers "to cruise on the enemies of these United Colonies," and in April it threw open American ports to ships of all nations except Great Britain.

Convinced that reconciliation was impossible and that Britain was determined to crush the colonial cause by force, Congress on July 2, 1776, adopted the resolution of Richard Henry Lee of Virginia "That these United Colonies are, and of right ought to be, free and independent States, that they are absolved from all allegiance to the British Crown, and that all political connection between them and the State of Great Britain is, and ought to be totally dissolved." Two days later, on July 4, Congress approved the *Declaration of Independence drafted by Thomas Jefferson.

With no change in its structure, and with no formal authorization from the states, Congress now became the sole organ of central government for the 13 independent states in its prosecution of the war. Except for brief periods of adjournment for travel, Congress remained in continuous session, its committees—foreign affairs, commerce, finance, navy, and war—performing the functions of executive departments. The need for a constitution for the United States and for a formal basis for Congress's authority was recognized by its adoption in 1777 of the *Articles of Confederation; ratification required the unanimous consent of the 13 states, which was not obtained until 1781.

The American Revolution was a conservative revolution, aiming to recover and preserve the traditional rights and liberties of English citizens. It was directed by elites whose political philosophy was republican in the classical sense rather than democratic (although they did not scruple to employ popular mobs to achieve tactical ends). Nevertheless, the Revolutionary period witnessed profound transformations in the political, social, and cultural life of the nation.

While still considering independence, Congress advised the colonies to institute governments appropriate to their new circumstances. Everywhere, royal governors had fled or been deposed. Extralegal provincial congresses and conventions proceeded to draft republican—though not notably democratic—constitutions, which in only a few cases were submitted to popular ratification. Ten states adopted new constitutions between 1776 and 1777, Massachusetts belatedly in 1780. Connecticut and Rhode Island were content to append new preambles to their colonial charters. Most of these constitutions established weak executives and strong legislatures and tried to implement the popular theory of separation of powers. All contained bills of rights. But some preserved the underrepresentation of backcountry farmers in favor of established aristocracies, and preserved property qualifications—and some religious qualifications—for voting and holding office.

Law codes were reformed to eliminate relics of feudalism in British law, such as the labor service and quitrents tenants owed proprietary landlords. Titles of nobility were forbidden. The legal devices of primogeniture and entail, which made possible the preservation of large estates in aristocratic families, were abolished. Crown lands and confiscated Loyalist estates (see *Loyalists) were broken up and sold with the intention (often frustrated) of diffusing land ownership among ordinary citizens. In Maryland, South Carolina, and North Carolina, the Anglican Church—which had been supported by taxes—was disestablished between 1776 and 1778; it was disestablished in Virginia in 1784. In three New England states, the established Congregational Church, which had played a prominent role in the Revolution, preserved its privileged status until 1817 in New Hampshire, 1818 in Connecticut, and 1833 in Massachusetts.

Between 1776 and 1786, every state but Georgia prohibited or restricted the *slave trade; Georgia abolished it in 1798. Slavery was abolished in all the Northern states between 1774 and 1804. In 1787 Congress prohibited slavery in the newly organized *Northwest Territory.

Fighting ended with the victory at *Yorktown in October 1781. Congress ratified the provisional Treaty of *Paris in April 1783, disbanded the army in October–November, and received *Washington's resignation in December. The nation then turned to the pursuits of peacetime, suffering a sharp postwar depression but then experiencing a flush of prosperity led by revived maritime commerce. But the fragile bonds of the Articles of Confederation began to unravel. An apathetic Congress, sparsely attended, was unable to halt the dissolution (although its most important work, the organization of the Northwest Territory, was accomplished in 1787). The Federal *Constitutional Convention of 1787 dramatically reversed this trend; the *ratification of the U.S. Constitution in 1788 consolidated and preserved the achievements of the Revolution and may be taken as marking the end of the Revolutionary period.

AMERICANS WITH DISABILITIES ACT (1990), legislation of the George H. W. *Bush administration intended to "mainstream" an estimated 43 million Americans with mental and physical disabilities by including

them among the groups protected from discrimination by the *Civil Rights Act of 1964. It prohibited discrimination against the disabled in employment, public services, and public accommodations. Employers were required to make "reasonable accommodations" for disabled workers. Restaurants, theaters, hotels, museums, hospitals, and retail and service establishments were required to make "readily achievable" modifications in existing facilities to accommodate the disabled. New buses and railcars were required to be accessible to them.

In 1998 the U.S. Supreme Court extended the act's protection to people infected with the HIV virus that causes *AIDS, but in 1999 it excluded people whose impairments were correctable by medication, glasses, or other devices. In 2002 the Court ruled that employers were not required to hire people whose health or safety would be put at risk on the job.

AMERICAN SYSTEM, national economic policy advocated most prominently by Henry Clay. It reflected the nationalist spirit that prevailed in the United States after the War of 1812, but it was also a considered response to changed world economic conditions. During the Napoleonic Wars, the United States had provided much of Europe's agricultural products and raw materials. The wars had also stimulated the development of new manufacturing industries in the United States. But with peace, the foreign markets disappeared, and America's infant industries were swamped by British manufactures. In these circumstances, the American System was viewed as a strategy for American economic independence.

The system entailed: a protective tariff to shield American industries from foreign competition; federally financed *internal improvements to unify the diverse sections of the country into a single home market; a national bank to facilitate economic development and ensure monetary stability (see *Bank of the United States). This system was enacted during the *Madison and *Monroe administrations and it unraveled during the *Jackson administration. The Jacksonians disliked centralized economic power, which they felt benefited privileged elites; they embraced the rising philosophy of individualism and its economic counterpart, laissez-faire; and they favored sectional and state autonomy over national planning. Jackson's reservations about internal improvements, his victory in the *Bank War, and Clay's surrender of the protective tariff in the *Compromise of 1833 mark the demise of the American System.

AMERICAN TEMPERANCE SOCIETY. See *Temperance Movement.

AMISTAD MUTINY (1839–41). In the summer of 1839 the Spanish sloop *Amistad* was transporting some 50 slaves—recently captured in Africa and sold in Havana—along the northern coast of Cuba. On July 1 the captives escaped their shackles and took over the ship, killing its captain and one crewman. Other crewmen escaped overboard, but two Spaniards were held to act as navigators and steer the vessel to Africa. Instead, they sailed *Amistad* northward until it was intercepted by a U.S. naval vessel. The Spaniards were released and the Africans imprisoned and indicted for murder. Abolitionists took up their cause, which eventually (1840) reached the U.S. Supreme Court, where former president John Quincy Adams argued on behalf of the Africans that they had been illegally enslaved and that their mutiny was therefore justified. The Court agreed (March 1841), the Africans were set free, and private funds were raised to send 35 survivors back to Africa.

AMNESTY ACT (1872). See *Reconstruction.

AMTRAK. See *Railroads; *Railroad Regulation.

ANARCHISM, political philosophy that advocates abolition of the state and voluntary cooperation among individuals in place of the state's coercion and services. The ancient tradition of philosophical anarchism, pacifist and nonviolent, is reflected in American history in various *utopian communities and in such religious sects as the Quakers and Mennonites. Its chief modern representative was the Russian novelist Leo Tolstoy. But in the Protestant Reformation, the French Revolution, and 19th-century industrial society a current of violent anarchism arose. Associated with the names of the German reformer Thomas Münzer, the French revolutionist François Babeuf, and the Russian revolutionary Mikhail Bakunin, this tradition advocated violent overthrow of the state as a prerequisite for the establishment of anarchism.

Violent anarchism was familiar in the United States in the late 19th and early 20th centuries. The *Haymarket Riot (1886) was precipitated by a bomb presumably thrown by an anarchist. The assassin of Pres. William McKinley, Leon Czolgosz, was an anarchist (see *McKinley Assassination), as was Alexander Berkman, who in 1892 attempted to assassinate the steel manufacturer Henry Clay Frick. The immigration of anarchists was barred in 1903 and 1918, and anarchists and other "reds" were deported during the post–World War 1 *red scare. In the 1920s, the principals of the *Sacco and Vanzetti case were anarchists.

ANDERSON'S CONCERT (Apr. 9, 1939). In February 1939 Howard University in Washington, D.C., asked the Daughters of the American Revolution (DAR) if it could use Constitution Hall, owned by the DAR, for a concert by the celebrated African-American contralto Marian Anderson. The DAR refused, its president declaring that no black performer would be permitted to use the hall. The incident achieved notoriety when First Lady Eleanor Roosevelt resigned from the DAR in protest. Amid widespread indignation, Anderson's manager, Sol Hurok, proposed a free, open-air concert at the Lincoln Memorial on Easter Sunday. Secretary of the Interior Harold Ickes agreed. On the afternoon of Sunday, Apr. 9, Anderson sang from the steps of the Lincoln Memorial to an audience estimated at 75,000.

ANDERSONVILLE PRISON (1864–65), Confederate prison camp for Union prisoners in southwest Georgia. Established early in 1864 as a stockade camp of 16 acres intended for 10,000 prisoners, it was enlarged to 26 acres and by August 1864 held 33,000 men. Prisoners lived in the open air with only such shelter as they themselves could create. Of 45,000 men imprisoned there, 13,000 died of disease, starvation, or exposure. After the war, a military tribunal tried and executed its commandant, Henry Wirz, for war crimes.

ANNAPOLIS CONVENTION (Sept. 11–14, 1786), meeting of state delegates at the invitation of the Virginia legislature to develop "a scheme that could be adopted by Congress to regulate the trade of the Confederated States." Delegates of only five states attended. The meeting's principal accomplishment was to call upon all the states to send delegates to a new convention, to be held in Philadelphia in May 1787, to discuss not only commercial problems but all matters necessary "to render the constitution of the Federal Government adequate to the exigencies of the Union." Congress endorsed this invitation on Feb. 21, 1787, and the Federal *Constitutional Convention convened in Philadelphia on May 25.

ANTHONY AND STANTON. See *Stanton and Anthony.

ANTHRACITE STRIKE (1902), incident in the Theodore *Roosevelt administration. In April 1902, 150,000 coal miners in eastern Pennsylvania struck for higher wages, shorter hours, and recognition of their union—the *United Mine Workers, led by John Mitchell—as their agent in collective bargaining. The mine owners refused to negotiate. Their leader, George F.

Baer, president of the Reading Railroad and an associate of J. P. Morgan, declared in July: "The rights and interests of the laboring men will be protected and cared for, not by the labor agitators, but by the Christian men to whom God in his infinite wisdom has given control of the property interests of the country." The public sided with the miners; even leading capitalists condemned the arrogance and obduracy of the owners.

As winter approached and a coal shortage loomed, the public called on Roosevelt to intervene, but he, beset by pressure from left and right, doubted his constitutional power to do so. At last he persuaded the owners to accept arbitration by a presidentially appointed Coal Strike Commission. For five weeks the commission took evidence from both sides in the dispute—the miners' case being managed by attorney Clarence Darrow. The commission awarded the strikers a 10-percent wage increase, reduced their hours to nine a day, but rejected recognition of the union and of the principle of collective bargaining. Radicals denounced both the decision and union leader Mitchell. The resolution of the strike, however, increased Roosevelt's popularity and established the principle that the federal government had a role to play in labor disputes that affected the national economy.

ANTHRAX ATTACK (2001). In September and October 2001, five envelopes containing threatening letters from a presumably Muslim source and highly virulent anthrax spores in a sophisticated aerosolized form were received by media companies in Boca Raton, Fla. (American Media, Inc., a tabloid publisher), and New York (the National Broadcasting Company and the *New York Post*), and by a U.S. senator in Washington, D.C. (a letter addressed to a second senator was intercepted before delivery). Four envelopes bore Trenton, N.J., postmarks; the fifth (the one presumably sent to Florida) was not recovered. The offices where the letters were received and nearby offices were contaminated, as were the postal facilities that had processed them; some additional postal facilities were cross-contaminated. Eighteen people were taken ill with confirmed or suspected cutaneous or inhalation anthrax; five died of the latter disease.

Nationwide anxiety, already high from the Sept. 11 attacks on the World Trade Center and the Pentagon (see *World Trade Center Attack 2), was heightened by numerous hoaxes. Investigators soon decided that the anthrax attack was an act of domestic *terrorism.

ANTICOMMUNISM. Americans' remarkable fear and hatred of Marxism—as distinct from domestic utopian or reformist socialisms—long antedates the existence of a menacing Soviet Union. It was, to begin with, a foreign ideology brought by immigrants, and thus doubly unwelcome. It attacked the institution of private property, and property owning was widespread in America. It preached class warfare, and Americans were not intensely class-conscious. It promised to exalt the proletariat, but few Americans thought of themselves as proletarians; those who in fact labored in factories and mills often considered their situation temporary, to be escaped by moving west or, like some Horatio Alger hero, by luck and pluck. Finally, Marxism was an uncompromising materialistic and atheistic philosophy, perhaps its greatest offense to zealously religious Americans.

Marxism was only one of a variety of immigrant radicalisms—including *anarchism, *socialism, and syndicalism—that Americans abhorred and generally associated with labor unions. When in 1917 Russia emerged as the aggressive champion of revolutionary Marxism and withdrew from World War 1, overwrought Americans demonized the Russians, supported the Justice Department's persecution and deportation of immigrant radicals in the *red scare of 1919–20, agreed with the State Department's attempt to contain the contagion by refusing to recognize Russia (see *Soviet Recognition), and approved of the business leaders who effectively subdued the labor movement during the 1920s.

Small and without influence in the 1920s, the American *Communist Party increased in prominence during the *Great Depression, alarming conservatives who tended to see the legislation of the *New Deal as akin to communism. In 1938 Congress established the *House Committee on Un-American Activities (HUAC) to investigate both fascist and communist subversion in the United States. The **Hatch Act** (1939) prohibited government employees from belonging to "any political party or organization which advocates the overthrow of our constitutional form of government." The **Smith Act** (1940), or Alien Registration Act, extended that prohibition to all citizens besides requiring the fingerprinting of aliens.

During America's wartime alliance with the Soviet Union, anticommunism was subdued, but it revived immediately upon the onset of the *cold war and became the dominant political force in the late 1940s and early 1950s. Revelations of Soviet espionage in Canada, Great Britain, and the United States, most notably the *Hiss case (1948–50), revitalized HUAC. Despite resolute opposition to communism in Europe through the *Marshall Plan, the *North Atlantic Treaty Organization, and the *Berlin airlift, the liberal *Truman administration was accused of being "soft on communism." To forestall his enemies, Truman, by an executive order on Mar. 21, 1947, established a Federal Employees Loyalty and Security Program to review the backgrounds of more than 4 million federal workers and dismiss those where "reasonable grounds exist for belief that the person is disloyal" (although *disloyal* was not defined). An employee accused of disloyalty could not confront his accusers, discover who they were, or even learn the nature of their charges. The order authorized the attorney general to draw up a list of subversive organizations, membership in any of which was ground for dismissal. By March 1952, 20,733 federal employees had been investigated and 384 discharged; another 2,490 had resigned. No one was indicted for any crime, and no evidence of espionage was uncovered.

Truman's pursuit of disloyal government employees (government employment, of course, was a privilege, not a right) helped him win reelection in 1948 but was soon forgotten in the rain of misfortunes that befell the administration in 1949–50: the Hiss conviction, the "loss" of China to the communists (see *China "Loss"), the explosion of a Soviet nuclear device, and the start of the *Korean War. In the minds of frantic anticommunists, such events could only be explained by the presence of communists in the highest reaches of the Roosevelt and Truman administrations. On Feb. 9, 1950, in Wheeling, W. Va., Sen. Joseph R. McCarthy, Republican of Wisconsin, claimed to possess the names of 205 (or 57) "card-carrying communists" then employed in the State Department. There followed the senator's notorious but ultimately fruitless five-year search for communists in government to justify his accusation of "20 years of treason" (see *McCarthyism).

In 1949, 11 top leaders of the Communist Party were prosecuted and convicted under the Smith Act; their conviction was upheld by the U.S. Supreme Court in *Dennis v. United States* (1951), which was followed by many other indictments and nearly a hundred convictions of other party members. In September 1950, Congress passed the **Internal Security Act**, which required the registration by the attorney general of all communist and communist-front organizations and their members, who were then denied passports and employment in defense industries and were made subject to internment during national emergencies. The act also barred the immigration of anyone who ever belonged to a totalitarian organization. Truman vetoed the act, but Congress emphatically overrode his veto.

In the spirit of the times, President Truman on Apr. 28, 1951, revised the criterion for dismissing disloyal employees enunciated in 1947. Instead of "reasonable grounds . . . for belief that the person is disloyal," the new order required only "reasonable doubt as to the loyalty of the person involved." That is, the criterion for dismissal shifted from *belief* in the subject's disloyalty to mere *doubt* of his or her loyalty.

The anticommunist crusade threatened to demoralize the Republican administration of Pres. Dwight D. Eisenhower as it had the Democratic administration of Harry Truman. Eisenhower despised McCarthy and eventually took an active part in the events that led to his downfall. But recognizing the need to placate the public's deep-seated suspicion that communists were at work even in a conservative Republican administration, Eisenhower toughened the government's personnel policies, changing the criterion for dismissal from *disloyalty* to being a *security risk* (that is, displaying "any behavior, activities, or associations which tend of show that the individual is not reliable or trustworthy"). A security officer in each federal department again reviewed personnel files, looking not only for suspect associations and wrong opinions but for alcoholism, homosexuality, and other supposed personality disorders. By October 1954, 2,611 security risks had been dismissed and 4,315 other civilian employees had resigned. Among the casualties were the "old China hands" in the State Department, who had predicted the communist victory in China, and J. Robert Oppenheimer, builder of the *atomic bomb, opponent of the *hydrogen bomb, and imprudent associate with radicals (see *Oppenheimer Affair).

In 1954 Congress passed the **Communist Control Act**, which officially defined the Communist Party as "an instrumentality of a conspiracy to overthrow the Government" and stripped it of its privileges as a political party. It also deprived communist-infiltrated (not merely communist or communist-dominated) labor unions of their rights under the National Labor Relations Act.

With McCarthy silenced, the government in the hands of a popular conservative Republican, and legislation in place that effectively disfranchised communists and their sympathizers, the anticommunist crusade began to subside. Its effects, however, lingered for another half century, allowing Republican presidents a latitude of action denied to Democrats. Thus Eisenhower accepted an armistice in Korea that Congress would never have agreed to from a Democrat, and Pres. Richard M. Nixon was able to open relations with Communist China when no Democratic president would have dared. Conversely, Democratic president Lyndon B. Johnson, in formulating U.S. policy in the *Vietnam War, had always to consider the political consequences of being perceived as "soft on communism."

ANTIETAM or **SHARPSBURG** (Sept. 17, 1862), *Civil War battle. After the second battle of *Bull Run (Aug. 29–30, 1862), Confederate general Robert E. Lee crossed (Sept. 10) the upper Potomac River into Maryland. Dispatching Gen. Thomas J. "Stonewall" Jackson with half his army to take Harpers Ferry, Lee moved toward Hagerstown with the intention of invading Pennsylvania. At South Mountain, the Union Army of the Potomac, again commanded by Gen. George B. McClellan, inflicted (Sept. 14) a sharp defeat on Lee's smaller force. Abandoning his plan to invade Pennsylvania, Lee turned back to Sharpsburg, where Jackson rejoined him.

The Confederates took up a position on the west side of nearby Antietam Creek. There McClellan, with greatly superior numbers, attacked them on Sept. 17, driving first against the Confederate left and center with little success but later pushing back the Confederate right until checked at day's end. The bloodiest single day's fighting of the war—23,000 on both sides killed or wounded—ended in a draw, although on Sept. 18–19 Lee recrossed the Potomac into Virginia. The notoriously cautious McClellan was criticized for not committing his reserves during the battle and for not pursuing the Confederates afterward.

ANTIFEDERALISTS, opponents of the Constitution in the *ratification debates of 1787–88. "Some will oppose it for pride," anticipated William Pierce, a delegate to the Federal *Constitutional Convention, "some from self-interest, some from ignorance, but the greater number will be of that class who will oppose it from a dread of its swallowing up the individuality of the States."

Whatever faults they found in the document, most Antifederalists were men for whom a national government was a remote and potentially dangerous abstraction while their states were real and familiar, the settings of their families and careers. They thought of their individual states—not the United States—as their countries, and treasured their states' unique histories, distinctive characters, even their traditional hostilities. Their great fear was of a "consolidated" national government in which the states would lose not only their sovereignty but their individuality. A national government, they feared, being distant, must inevitably be tyrannical; only government close to the people could be responsive to their needs and

protective of their liberties. Prominent Antifederalists were Patrick Henry, George Mason, James Monroe, and Richard Henry Lee of Virginia; George Clinton, John Lansing, and Robert Yates of New York; Elbridge Gerry and Samuel Adams of Massachusetts; Samuel Chase and Luther Martin of Maryland.

Better organization, leaders of greater prestige (including Washington, Franklin, and Madison), concentration in urban centers, and the promise of early amendments to the Constitution enabled the Federalists to prevail in the ratification votes. Antifederalists did not go on to organize a political party, but their sentiment reappeared frequently in U.S. history in the arguments of states' rights advocates.

ANTI-IMPERIALIST LEAGUE (1898–1901), national organization opposed to U.S. colonial expansion after the *Spanish-American War, particularly the acquisition of the Philippines. "A self-governing state cannot accept sovereignty over an unwilling people," declared its platform, adopted in Chicago in October 1899. "The United States cannot act upon the ancient heresy that might makes right." Anti-imperialists argued that political domination over alien, unassimilable peoples was contrary to American ideals, that exercising tyranny abroad would undermine democracy at home, and that distant possessions would embroil the United States in the imperialist conflicts of other powers. The reelection of Pres. William McKinley in 1900 and the suppression of the *Philippine insurrection in 1901 ended the debate, and the Anti-Imperialist League disappeared.

ANTI-MASONIC PARTY (1830–40), political party, product of a movement hostile to Freemasonry that arose after the disappearance and presumed murder in upstate New York in 1826 of one William Morgan, a Mason who had threatened to reveal the order's secrets. Resentful of the Masons for their secrecy, rituals, and upper-class membership, all of which they regarded as aristocratic, antimasons tended to be religious, principled, and democratic.

The rapid spread of the movement—from New York to New England, Pennsylvania, and the Middle West—provided a vehicle for earnest young politicians unhappy with the antiquated *National Republican Party and the proslavery *Democratic Party. A galaxy of future political leaders—including William Lloyd Garrison, William H. Seward, Thurlow Weed, and Thaddeus Stevens—joined the movement and added to its antimasonry a political program of high-minded reform.

The Anti-Masonic Party, the nation's first *third party, was also the first to hold a national nominating convention, which it did in Baltimore in 1831 when it nominated William Wirt of Virginia for president. In 1836 the party nominated William Henry Harrison, who was also running as a Whig. Thereafter the Anti-Masons merged into the *Whig Party.

ANTIQUITIES ACT (1906). See *Conservation.

ANTI-SALOON LEAGUE. See *Temperance Movement.

ANTITERRORISM ACT (2001). See *U.S.A. Patriot Act or Antiterrorism Act.

ANTIWAR MOVEMENT. See *Vietnam War.

ANZIO. See *World War 2.

APACHE WARS (1840–86), conflicts principally with the Western, Mescalero, and Chiricahua Apache Indians in Texas, Arizona, and New Mexico.

Chronic raids by Western Apaches in what is now the American Southwest intensified under the Chiricahua chief Cochise and other war leaders after 1863 when gold seekers began to enter their territory. Lt. Col. George Crook completed the pacification of the Western Apaches in 1873 and they were settled on a reservation in southern Arizona. The Mescalero Apaches were subdued at the same time and settled in New Mexico.

Nevertheless, adventurous warriors frequently escaped from the reservations and resumed raids on white settlements. In 1882 a Chiricahua leader, Geronimo, with 500 warriors, took refuge in Mexico's Sierra Madre and raided on both sides of the border. Crook (now a brigadier general) led an expedition into the mountains in 1883 and compelled Geronimo to return to the Arizona reservation. In May 1885 Geronimo returned to the Sierra Madre, where Crook pursued him and captured him on Mar. 27, 1886. Two days later Geronimo escaped and was now pursued by Brig. Gen. Nelson A. Miles, to whom Geronimo surrendered on Sept. 4.

APPEAL OF THE INDEPENDENT DEMOCRATS (Jan. 24, 1854), manifesto by six members of Congress protesting the newly introduced *Kansas-Nebraska Act. "We arraign this bill," they declared, "as a gross violation of a sacred pledge [the *Missouri Compromise prohibition of slavery in the Louisiana Purchase north of 36° 30']; as a criminal betrayal of precious rights; as part and parcel of an atrocious plot" to extend slavery. The signers, all well-known *abolitionists, were headed by Sen. Salmon P. Chase of Ohio and Sen. Charles Sumner of Massachusetts. The appeal raised an outraged protest among free-soilers and contributed significantly to the formation of the *Republican Party.

APPOMATTOX SURRENDER (Apr. 9, 1865), in the *Civil War, surrender by Confederate general Robert E. Lee of his Army of Northern Virginia to Union general Ulysses S. Grant at Appomattox Court House, a village in southern Virginia.

After the fall of *Petersburg (Apr. 2), Lee hoped to join forces with Gen. Joseph E. Johnston in North Carolina, but Grant quickly cut off his escape and surrounded the exhausted Confederates. In the afternoon of Apr. 9, Lee and Grant met in the living room of Wilmer McLean in Appomattox Court House, Lee in dress uniform, Grant in a private's uniform and muddy boots, only his shoulder straps designating his rank.

"We soon fell into a conversation about old army times," Grant recalled in his memoirs (see *Grant's Memoirs). "He remarked that he remembered me very well in the old army; and I told him that as a matter of course I remembered him perfectly, but from the difference in our rank and years (there being about sixteen years' difference in our ages), I had thought it very likely that I had not attracted his attention sufficiently to be remembered by him after such a long interval. Our conversation grew so pleasant that I almost forgot the object of our meeting. After the conversation had run on in this style for some time, General Lee called my attention to the object of our meeting, and said that he had asked for this interview for the purpose of getting from me the terms I proposed to give his army." Grant's terms were generous: parole for the Confederate soldiers; officers to retain their sidearms; officers and soldiers to retain their horses. The Union army then sent three days' rations to the starving Confederates.

On Apr. 12, in a field outside the village, the ragged Confederates marched between silent Union ranks to stack their arms and surrender their flags. "[W]hen the head of each division column comes opposite our group," recalled Gen. Joshua L. Chamberlain, "our bugle sounds the signal and instantly our whole line from right to left, regiment by regiment in succession, gives the soldier's salutation, from the 'order arms' to the old 'carry'—the marching salute. Gordon at the head of the column, riding with heavy spirit and downcast face, catches the sound of shifting arms, looks up, and, taking the meaning, wheels superbly, making himself and his horse one uplifted figure, with profound salutation as he drops the point of his sword to the boot toe; then facing to his own command, gives word for his successive brigades to pass us with the same position of the manual,—honor answering honor. On our part not a sound of trumpet more, nor roll of drum; not a cheer, nor word nor whisper of vain-glorying, nor motion of man standing again at the order, but an awed stillness rather, and breath-holding, as if it were the passing of the dead!"

ARBITRATION TREATIES (1908–13), diplomatic efforts over three administrations reflecting the concerns of the *peace movement. In the Theodore *Roosevelt administration, Secretary of State Elihu Root negotiated (1908) treaties with 24 nations providing for the referral of controversies to the Permanent Court of Arbitration at The Hague, the Netherlands. In the *Taft administration, Secretary of State Philander Knox negotiated (1910) arbitration treaties with Great Britain and France that the Senate ratified in 1911 after 18 months of opposition led by Sen. Henry Cabot Lodge. In the *Wilson administration, Secretary of State William Jennings Bryan obtained 21 treaties in which the signatories pledged to observe a "cooling-off" period of 12 months after all other means of composing a dispute had been exhausted before resorting to war.

ARMED FORCES DESEGREGATION (1948), initiative of the *Truman administration. Blacks fought in all America's wars, though usually in segregated units commanded by white officers. In World Wars 1 and 2 not only did segregation continue but the great majority of black servicemen were assigned to service rather than combat units. Responding to rising pressure from African-Americans for enforcement of their civil rights—and facing an uncertain election in November in which black votes could be crucial—Pres. Harry S. Truman bypassed a hostile Congress and by executive order on July 26, 1948, ordered the end of segregation and discrimination in the armed forces.

The services were slow to respond. The Navy and Air Force took some early steps but the Army firmly resisted. Only the desperate manpower requirements of the Korean and Vietnam wars caused the services to accept the necessity of ending segregation and opening all military specialties to blacks. The All Volunteer Force, instituted in 1973, became universally recognized as the most successfully integrated and nondiscriminating institution in American life.

At the end of the century, blacks constituted 30 percent of the Army's enlisted force and held more than 30 percent of its noncombat specialties. Almost 30 percent of the highest-ranking enlisted personnel, 11 percent of the officers, and 7 percent of the generals were black.

ARMED FORCES UNIFICATION (1947), initiative of the *Truman administration. The 1947 **National Security Act** created the National Military Establishment (reorganized in 1949 as the Department of Defense) with component departments of the Army, Navy, and Air Force, each with a secretary responsible to the secretary of defense. The Joint Chiefs of Staff (JCS), consisting of the heads of the uniformed services, was also responsible to the secretary of defense. The act also created the National Security Council (NSC) to advise the president on all aspects of security policy, the National Security Resources Board to prepare for military contingencies (abolished in 1953), and the Central Intelligence Agency (CIA) to gather foreign intelligence for the use of the president and the NSC.

ARMS CONTROL AND DISARMAMENT (1945–2002). During the *cold war, the United States and the Soviet Union built war machines of enormous overkill capacity. Peace was preserved by the informal acceptance by both superpowers of the principle of mutual assured destruction (MAD), the capacity of each power to absorb a first nuclear missile strike and still retaliate with devastating force. A series of bilateral and multilateral agreements, continuing after the dissolution of the Soviet Union, sought to reduce the danger inherent in this military standoff.

1946   The *Baruch Plan for an International Atomic Development Authority to monopolize development of atomic energy and control of atomic weapons was rejected by the Soviets.

1953   *Atoms for Peace, a proposal by Pres. Dwight D. Eisenhower, led to the establishment of the UN International Atomic Energy Agency (IAEA).

1955   *Open Skies, Eisenhower proposal made to summit meeting of the United States, Britain, France, and the Soviet Union at Geneva.

Nov. 1958–Sept. 1961 Voluntary moratorium on nuclear testing by the United States, Britain, and the Soviet Union.

1963   Limited Nuclear Test Ban Treaty, signed by the United States, Britain, and the Soviet Union, prohibited nuclear testing in the atmosphere, space, and underwater.

1967   Outer Space Treaty, signed by the United

States, Britain, the Soviet Union, and 57 other countries, banned weapons of mass destruction, weapons tests, and military bases in outer space.

1968   Nuclear Nonproliferation Treaty (NPT), signed by the United States, the Soviet Union, and 60 other countries, prohibited the transfer of nuclear weapons to nonnuclear states. Since ratified by 179 countries.

1972   Seabed Arms Treaty, signed by the United States, Britain, the Soviet Union, and 82 other countries, prohibited placement of nuclear weapons on the ocean floor outside territorial limits.

1972   Strategic Arms Limitation Treaty 1 (SALT 1), between the United States and the Soviet Union, limited the number of offensive weapons to those already under construction or deployed.

1972   Antiballistic Missile (ABM) Treaty banned space-based defensive missile systems and restricted ground-based defense systems to two (later one) fixed sites in each country.

1974   Vladivostok Accords between the United States and the Soviet Union limited each power to 2,400 strategic weapons systems (missiles, bombers, etc.) and limited the number of multiple independently targeted reentry vehicles (MIRVs) on those systems.

1974   The United States ratified the 1925 Geneva Protocol prohibiting the use of poison gas and bacteriological weapons and the 1972 Convention on the Prohibition of Bacteriological and Toxin Weapons.

1979   SALT 2 between the United States and the Soviet Union limited the number of missiles and bombers of each country. When the Soviets invaded Afghanistan in December 1979, Pres. James E. Carter withdrew the treaty from Senate consideration. The United States ratified SALT 2 in 1996; the Russian parliament did not ratify it.

1988   Intermediate-Range Nuclear Forces Treaty, signed by the United States and the Soviet Union, provided for the dismantling of all Soviet and American medium- and shorter-range land-based missiles and established a system of on-site inspection.

1990   Conventional Forces in Europe (CFE) Treaty, signed by all members of the North Atlantic Treaty Organization and the Warsaw Pact, provided for massive cuts in nonnuclear arms on both sides.

1991   Strategic Arms Reduction Treaty 1 (START 1), between the United States and the Soviet Union, reduced the number of ballistic missile warheads on both sides to 6,000 from 12,000.

1992   The United States declared a moratorium on underground nuclear tests.

1993   START 2 treaty between the United States and the Soviet Union reduced both countries' strategic arsenals to 3,000 warheads each.

1996   Pres. William J. Clinton signed the Comprehensive Test Ban Treaty prohibiting all nuclear test explosions worldwide and establishing a global network of monitoring stations to verify compliance. The treaty was signed by 164 nations and ratified by 89.

1999   The U.S. Senate rejected the Comprehensive Test Ban Treaty 51–48, a move interpreted as the most significant treaty rejection since the Versailles Treaty in 1919.

2001   The new George W. Bush administration committed itself to building a national *missile defense system, if necessary abrogating the 1972 ABM Treaty. In December President Bush formally notified Russia that the United States would withdraw from the ABM Treaty—which Bush called a "relic" of the cold war—in six months in order to develop the missile shield.

2002   The United States and Russia agreed to reduce their nuclear arsenals by two-thirds, to between 1,700 and 2,200 strategic warheads, over the next 10 years. Both countries were permitted to keep the dismantled warheads in storage. In June the United States formally abandoned the 1972 ABM Treaty; at the same time Russia announced that it was no longer bound by the 1993 START 2 accord.

ARMY-McCARTHY HEARINGS (1954). See *McCarthyism.

ARNOLD'S TREASON (1780). Hero of *Quebec and *Saratoga, Gen. Benedict Arnold was appointed military governor of Philadelphia when the Patriot army reoccupied the city in June 1778. In Philadelphia, Arnold married socially prominent Margaret Shippen, lived extravagantly, and fell into debt. Friction with Pennsylvania civilian authorities led to a military court-martial, which added to Arnold's old resentment over lack of recognition and slow promotion.

In May 1779 Arnold opened communications with Gen. Henry Clinton in New York, the British commander in North America. With the active participation of his Loyalist wife, he supplied Clinton with valuable military intelligence. When he was appointed commander of West Point, a fortress on the Hudson River, in August 1780, he arranged to turn it over to the British. On Sept. 23 British major John André, Clinton's go-between with Arnold, was captured wearing civilian clothes and carrying incriminating documents. When Arnold, who was then expecting a visit from George Washington, heard of André's capture, he fled to a British ship in the Hudson and escaped to Clinton in New York. At West Point, his wife's hysterics persuaded Washington of her innocence. André was hanged as a spy.

Clinton commissioned Arnold a brigadier general of provincial troops and sent him off to conduct marauding raids into Virginia (January 1781) and Connecticut (September 1781). In December 1781 the Arnolds moved to England, where, unable to get an army commission, Benedict Arnold engaged unhappily in business.

AROOSTOOK WAR (1839), bloodless confrontation between American and Canadian militias in disputed territory between Maine and the Canadian province of New Brunswick during the *Van Buren administration.

ARTHUR ADMINISTRATION. See *Garfield-Arthur Administration.

ARTICLES OF CONFEDERATION, first constitution of the United States (1781–88). Drafted (June 1776–November 1777) by the *Continental Congress, the Articles were ratified by the legislatures of all 13 states, Maryland finally ratifying in March 1781 after Virginia had ceded to the Confederation its claims to the territory north of the Ohio River.

The Articles in effect confirmed the informal arrangement under which the states were then conducting the *Revolutionary War. The *Confederation was defined as a firm and perpetual "league of friendship" among sovereign and independent states. The sole agency of central government was the unicameral Congress, to which each state sent delegations of two to seven persons but in which each state had only one vote. Congress was given important powers: to wage war and make peace, to conduct foreign relations, to borrow money and issue paper money, to operate a postal service, and to control trade with the Indians. But these powers were undercut by Congress's lack of authority to levy taxes, raise troops, or regulate domestic or foreign commerce. Given no powers to enforce its decisions even in the areas of its competence, Congress was dependent on the voluntary cooperation of the states.

The Articles were a major step in the evolution of a national government, earlier steps having been the *New England Confederation (1643), the *Dominion of New England, the *Albany Congress (1754), the *Stamp Act Congress (1763), the first *Continental Congress (1774), and *Galloway's Plan of Union (1774).

ASIAN-AMERICANS. The U.S. Census defines Asian-Americans as immigrants (or their descendants) from the countries of East and South Asia. In 2000, Asian-Americans numbered 10.2 million, 3.6 percent of the total U.S. population. Chinese then constituted 24 percent of the Asian-American population, Filipinos 18 percent, Asian Indians 16 percent, Vietnamese 11 percent, Koreans 11 percent, and Japanese 8 percent. Other Southeast Asians (Cambodians, Hmong, Laotians) constituted 5 percent. Other South Asians (Indonesians, Pakistanis, Bangladeshis, Sri Lankans, Burmese, Thais, and Malaysians) constituted 7 percent.

The Chinese were the first Asians to enter the United States, arriving during the California gold rush and the period of western railroad construction. Japanese began to arrive late in the 19th century to work in California agriculture. Filipinos immigrated to Hawaii after 1909 to work on sugar plantations. Chinese immigration was restricted by the Chinese Exclusion Act of 1882 (see *Chinese Exclusion). Japanese immigration was severely curtailed by the Gentlemen's Agreement of 1907 (see *Japanese Exclusion). The 1924 Immigration Act effectively banned all immigration from Asia. Since Filipinos were technically American nationals (but not citizens), Filipino immigration was not restricted until 1934, when the Tydings-McDuffie Act limited it to 50 immigrants per year (see *Immigration).

In the 1940s the ban on Asian immigrants was relaxed, Asian countries being assigned quotas of about 100 immigrants per year. In the 1950s, immigration from Asia averaged about 15,000 persons a year. The Immigration Act of 1965, which abolished national quotas, allowed Asians to enter the United States on the same terms as Europeans, and Asian immigrants soon surpassed European. After the *Vietnam War ended in 1975, there was a substantial flow of *refugees from Vietnam, Laos, and Cambodia.

In 1999 the median income of Asian-American (including Pacific Islander) families was $56,316, compared to $51,224 for white families. In 1990, the National Opinion Research Center at the University of Chicago reported that, of 33 U.S. ethnic groups studied, Chinese-Americans ranked second in household income and second in years of schooling, Japanese-Americans ranked third in household income and fourth in years of schooling, and Asian Indians ranked fifth in household income and first in years of schooling. Their "social standing" ratings were 23rd, 16th, and 28th respectively.

ATLANTA CAMPAIGN (May–September 1864), *Civil War campaign in which Union forces under Gen. William T. Sherman advanced from Chattanooga to capture Atlanta.

Sherman left Chattanooga in May with 100,000 men—the combined armies of the Ohio, Tennessee, and Cumberland—to follow a single-track railroad 100 miles to Atlanta. Opposing him was Confederate general Joseph E. Johnston, who had replaced Gen. Braxton Bragg as commander of the Army of Tennessee after the battle of Chattanooga (see *Chattanooga Campaign). Johnston, on the defensive, had the advantage of mountainous terrain, but Sherman outflanked him at Resaca (May 14–15), Cassville (May 19), and Dallas (May 25–28). On June 27 at Kennesaw Mountain, 20 miles from Atlanta, Sherman attacked entrenched Confederates and was repulsed. Resuming his flanking movements, he reached Peachtree Creek, four miles from Atlanta, on July 9.

On July 17 Confederate president Jefferson Davis replaced Johnston with the more aggressive Gen. John Bell Hood. Three times Hood attacked and was repulsed (July 20–28), suffering 15,000 casualties to Sherman's 6,000. Nevertheless, Sherman's advance was halted. From trenches outside the city, the Federals shelled Atlanta while the city's inhabitants fled.

On Aug. 26 Sherman abandoned his trenches and moved south of Atlanta to cut off the last roads and railroads connecting the city with the interior. Hood attacked again at Jonesborough, 20 miles south of Atlanta, was defeated, and on Sept. 1 evacuated the city. Sherman entered Atlanta on Sept. 2, telegraphing to Washington: "Atlanta is ours, and fairly won."

ATLANTIC, BATTLE OF THE. See *World War 2.

ATLANTIC CABLE (1866), submarine telegraph cable connecting Valentia, Ireland, with Heart's Content, Newfoundland, successfully completed on July 27, 1866. Promoted by American businessman Cyrus W. Field despite many reverses and five failures (1857–65), the cable consisted of seven strands of copper wire insulated with gutta percha (a gum from a Malayan tree), wrapped in tarred hemp and armored with steel wires. This was laid from a drum on the stern of the *Great Eastern*, the largest ship of its day, from Ireland to Newfoundland, 1,950 miles at a depth of two miles in 14 days. A few days after its completion, Queen Victoria and Pres. Andrew Johnson exchanged cabled greetings. By the end of the century there were a dozen transatlantic cables and several transpacific.

ATLANTIC CHARTER (Aug. 12, 1941), joint statement by U.S. president Franklin Roosevelt and British prime minister Winston Churchill at their Atlantic Conference (see *World War 2 Conferences) making known "certain common principles in the national policies of their respective countries on which they base their hopes for a better future for the world.

"First, their countries seek no aggrandizement, territorial or other.

"Second, they desire to see no territorial changes that do not accord with the freely expressed wishes of the peoples concerned.

"Third, they respect the right of all peoples to choose the form of government under which they will live. . . .

"Fourth, they will endeavour . . . to further the enjoyment by all States . . . of access, on equal terms, to the trade and to the raw materials of the world. . . .

"Fifth, they desire to bring about the fullest collaboration between all nations in the economic field. . . .

"Sixth, . . . they hope to see established a peace which will afford to all nations . . . freedom from fear and want.

"Seventh, such a peace should enable all men to traverse the high seas and oceans without hindrance.

"Eighth, they believe that all the nations of the world . . . must come to the abandonment of the use of force. . . ."

Having failed to get a commitment from Roosevelt that the United States would enter the war on Britain's side, Churchill took satisfaction in the "astonishing" fact that a neutral nation would join with a belligerent in making such a declaration of postwar objectives. To Churchill, the charter consisted of Wilsonian platitudes; for Roosevelt, it was a declaration of opposition to postwar territorial aggrandizement or spheres of influence, British as well as Soviet, in particular the British Commonwealth's preferential trading system.

ATLANTIC CONFERENCE (1941). See *World War 2 Conferences.

ATOMIC BOMB. On Apr. 25, 1945, Pres. Harry S. Truman was called upon by Secretary of the Army Henry L. Stimson and Gen. Leslie R. Groves, who informed him of the *Manhattan Project. (In 1943, Stimson had refused to discuss huge unexplained expenditures in the War Department's budget with Senator Truman, head of a Senate committee investigating defense contracts; see *Truman Committee.) It was Truman's 12th day in office. The war in Europe was nearing its end, and planning was under way for the invasion of Japan.

Since the Manhattan Project was close to producing an atomic bomb, Stimson appointed a civilian committee of eight members, including three scientists, to advise him on the bomb's use. This committee was joined by an advisory panel of four scientists actively engaged in the development of the bomb, including J. Robert Oppenheimer. The committee and its advisory panel reviewed and rejected various alternatives to the bomb's maximum use—a demonstration explosion, advanced warning to the target area, choice of a purely military target—and unanimously recommended that the bomb should be used against Japan as soon as possible, against war plants and associated workers' housing, and without warning. These recommendations were later adopted by all U.S. military leaders.

By now the bomb was viewed not as a means of winning the war but of ending it. Allied and Japanese leaders alike agreed that Japan had lost the war. But the Japanese government was in the hands of a military clique who felt that national honor required a final national immolation. Impressed by the suicidal defense of Iwo Jima and Okinawa, U.S. leaders did not doubt that the Japanese would fight bitterly to defend their home islands. Estimates of Allied casualties in the invasion of Japan scheduled to start in November 1945 ranged as high as half a million. Since devastating firebombing of its cities had failed to bring about Japan's surrender, the Allies believed that some tremendous shock was necessary. The bomb, then, was considered a means of ending the war and saving Allied (and Japanese) lives.

On July 16, 1945, U.S. scientists exploded a test bomb near Alamogordo, N.Mex. (see *Trinity). Official confirmation of this event reached Truman in Germany, where he was attending the Potsdam Conference, on July 21. Truman later wrote, "The final decision of where and when to use the atomic bomb was up to me." Like his predecessor, Franklin Roosevelt, Truman never expressed any reservation about using the bomb. All his most respected civilian, military, and scientific advisers recommended it. At Potsdam, British prime minister Winston Churchill urged it. Of the scientists who knew of its existence, only a minority expressed moral reservations. Use of the bomb was a political as well as a strategic imperative: to have possessed the bomb and not used it would have been incomprehensible to Allied publics.

The decision to use the bomb was confirmed (if not actually made) on July 24. That evening, Truman informed Soviet premier Joseph Stalin that the United States had a powerful new weapon. Long familiar with the bomb's development through Soviet espionage, Stalin expressed no surprise or interest. On July 26, Truman issued the Potsdam Declaration, calling upon Japan to surrender or face "prompt and utter destruction" but not mentioning the bomb. On July 31, Truman gave the final go-ahead for dropping the bomb at the earliest opportunity. Of approved target cities, Hiroshima—southern army headquarters—led the list.

On Aug. 6, a single B-29 bomber from the island of Tinian in the Marianas dropped a uranium bomb on Hiroshima. Casualties were later estimated at 80,000 killed outright, 50–60,000 dead in the next few months, many thousands more dead in succeeding years as a result of injuries sustained on Aug. 6, 1945. When no response was received from Tokyo, a second bomb was dropped on Nagasaki on Aug. 9. This was a plutonium bomb. More powerful than the Hiroshima bomb, it produced fewer casualties—35–70,000 killed outright—because the bombardier was two miles off target. That same day the Soviet army invaded Manchuria. Upon the insistence of Emperor Hirohito, the Japanese government resolved that night on surrender. At that time, the United States had only one more bomb in its arsenal.

After the war, Truman placed control of the atomic bomb in the hands of the civilian Atomic Energy Commission, firmly rebuffing a request from the military that the bomb be entrusted to the Joint Chiefs of Staff.

ATOMS FOR PEACE (1953), proposal by Pres. Dwight D. Eisenhower in a speech to the United Nations General Assembly on Dec. 8, 1953, that the United States, United Kingdom, and Soviet Union contribute fissionable atomic materials to a UN International Atomic Energy Agency (IAEA), which would study peaceful applications of atomic energy. The object was to begin the transfer of atomic energy from military to civilian control. Eisenhower's speech was well received except by the Soviets. The IAEA was not established until 1957.

ATTICA UPRISING (Sept. 9–14, 1971), inmate revolt at the Attica Correctional Facility near Buffalo, N.Y. Demanding improved prison conditions, the inmates took several guards hostage and seized control of parts of the facility. When negotiations failed, Gov. Nelson A. Rockefeller ordered state troopers to storm the prison. Using helicopters and tear gas, the troopers fired indiscriminately into a crowd of 1,281 inmates in Prison Yard D. Once in control, they brutally abused the prisoners and denied them medical care. The uprising left 11 guards and 32 prisoners dead.

In 2000, a federal court awarded $8 million in compensation to more than 500 former inmates and relatives.

AUSTRALIAN BALLOT, introduced in most states in the 1890s, replaced ballots printed by political parties that listed their candidates only. Party ballots prevented secret voting and led to intimidation and fraud. The Australian ballot was printed by the government rather than the parties, listed the candidates of all major parties rather than those of a single party, and facilitated secret voting.

AUTOMOBILES. While American inventors were tinkering with steam- and electric-powered automobiles in the 1880s, inventors in Germany and France successfully developed gasoline-powered vehicles. In 1896, Charles and Frank Duryea of Springfield, Mass., began the manufacture of gasoline-powered cars, producing 13 vehicles in their first year. Other mechanics had little difficulty entering the field—the early automobiles were essentially assembled from existing engines, carriage bodies, and wheels. By 1900 there were some 8,000 automobiles in America, most of them steam- and electric-powered; only 20 percent were gasoline-powered.

The early cars were custom-made and handcrafted by hundreds of small companies. Factory production was begun in 1901 by Ransom E. Olds and in 1903 by Henry Ford, whose Model N (1906–7) and Model T (1908–27), produced after 1914 on a moving assembly line, brought automobiles within the reach of the "great multitude." General Motors, founded in 1908, competed with Ford by offering a variety of models and colors, compelling Ford to abandon the durable black Model T for the more attractive Model A. In 1925, Chrysler joined Ford and General Motors to form the "big three" with 80 percent of the output of the American automobile industry, which had by then shrunk to 44 companies.

Auto manufacturing sparked the economic boom of the 1920s. It soon became the largest industry in the country (as railroads had been in the 19th century), bringing vast expansion to such related industries as petroleum, steel, glass, rubber, and construction. One American worker in seven worked in an auto-related job.

The automobile transformed American life as no previous invention had. Rural isolation was ended. Cities spread out into suburbs and exurbs. New roads and highways, new communities, new businesses proliferated. People's daily lives—at work, homemaking, recreation, even courtship—were forever changed. There were, of course, negative consequences: traffic congestion, air pollution, accidental injuries and deaths, dependence upon foreign oil, the decline or disruption of vital city neighborhoods. These negatives, however, barely affected Americans' preference for the individuality, independence, and mobility of the private automobile over more rational public transportation.

From the start, Americans embraced the "car culture" enthusiastically. Very early, automobiles ceased to be luxuries or playthings and became necessities. Suburban families often require two or three cars to get their members to work, school, and shopping. In 1999, there were 132.4 million automobiles registered in the United States, almost one for every two Americans.

AUTOMOBILE WORKERS UNION. See *United Automobile Workers (UAW).

B

BABY BOOM (1946–64), post–World War 2 demographic phenomenon. During the 15 years between 1931 and 1945, years of depression and war, the nation's birthrate averaged 19.8 per 1,000 population and the number of live births averaged 2.6 million per year. From 20.4 in 1945, the birthrate leaped to 24.1 in 1946, the number of live births from 2.9 million to 3.4 million. During the 19 years from 1946 to 1964 the birthrate averaged 24.2, peaking in 1957 at 25.3. From 21.0 in 1964, it fell to 19.4 in 1965 and has remained below 20.0 since then, reaching a low of 14.8 in 1975 and 1976. Live births in the same period averaged 4.0 million per year. The number fell below 4.0 million in 1965 and remained below 4.0 million until 1989. From 1945 to 1964, the population below age 15 grew from 34.6 million (25 percent of the total) to 59.0 million (31 percent of the total). As the "baby boom" cohort advanced from infancy to old age, the demographic bulge moved through the population like a pig in a python (a favorite simile of the period), taxing society's resources—from schools to Social Security—at each stage.

BACK TO AFRICA, 1920s movement among African-Americans initiated by Jamaican-born Marcus Garvey. Through his Universal Negro Improvement Association, Garvey encouraged black pride and separatism, economic independence, and eventual establishment of a black state in Africa that would earn respect and provide protection for blacks everywhere. When Garvey's Black Star Line—a steamship company intended to link non-Caucasian peoples commercially and transport American blacks to Africa—failed in 1922, Garvey was convicted of fraud, jailed, and then deported.

BACON'S REBELLION (1676), revolt in colonial Virginia led by Nathaniel Bacon, a young planter, who, contrary to the policy of Gov. William Berkeley, raised a force of volunteers and attacked friendly Indians residing in the colony in retaliation for border depredations by others. Bacon then led his volunteers against Berkeley himself, driving him out of the colonial capital, Jamestown. But Bacon died suddenly in October 1676 and Berkeley dispersed his followers.

BAILEY v. DREXEL FURNITURE CO. (1922), 8–1 decision of the *Taft Court overturning a second effort by Congress, in 1919, to eliminate *child labor by taxing its product. Chief Justice William Howard Taft found that the tax was an attempt to regulate local working conditions and thus beyond Congress's powers under the Commerce Clause.

BAKER v. CARR (1962), 6–2 decision of the *Warren Court requiring "substantial equality" among state electoral districts. The suit originated in Tennessee, where the state legislature had since 1901 ignored the state constitution's requirement that members of the state legislature be reapportioned among the state's 95 counties after every decennial census, resulting in underrepresentation of the state's urban and suburban population and overrepresentation of its rural population.

Traditionally, the Court had regarded this issue as a nonjusticiable "political question," to be resolved by voters rather than judges. Justice William Brennan, however, writing for the majority, found Tennessee's failure to reapportion equitably a violation of the Equal Protection Clause of the *14th Amendment, which was later construed to require "precise mathematical equality" among electoral districts—implementation of the "one person, one vote" principle. The decision inaugurated a wave of reapportionment throughout the country.

BAKKE. See *Regents of the University of California v. Bakke.*

BALKAN INTERVENTION (1995–   ), episode begun in the *Clinton administration. In 1991, Croatia, Slovenia, Bosnia, and Macedonia seceded from the federal republic of Yugoslavia, leaving a rump Yugoslavia consisting only of the republics of Serbia and Montenegro. The region was immediately convulsed by savage ethnic warfare designed to expel ethnic minorities from territory desired by another group.

In **Bosnia**, civil war raged among Roman Catholic Croats, Eastern Orthodox Serbs, and Muslims. European and U.S. diplomatic initiatives bore fruit in November 1995 when the leaders of Croatia, Serbia, and Bosnia met at Wright Patterson Air Force Base in Dayton, Ohio, and under U.S. pressure agreed, among other things, that Bosnia would be a multiethnic state with a collective presidency, its security assured by North Atlantic Treaty Organization (NATO) "peace enforcers." In 2002, 16,600 NATO troops, including 2,500 U.S. troops, were stationed in Bosnia.

Meanwhile, the Serbian province of **Kosovo**, populated largely by ethnic Albanians but considered by Serbs the birthplace of their nation, erupted in rebellion. In the fall of 1998, Serbian president Slobodan Milosevic ordered an invasion of Kosovo to drive out the Albanians. The campaign was marked by atrocities. Although popular sentiment in the United States did not favor U.S. military intervention, Pres. William J. Clinton decided that a limited U.S. intervention was morally and politically necessary. Under U.S. leadership, NATO on Mar. 24, 1999, launched a 78-day air campaign against Serb positions in Kosovo and against Serbia itself. The Serbs finally withdrew from Kosovo, and a NATO peacekeeping force entered the province. In 2002, 38,000 NATO troops, including 5,800 U.S. troops, were stationed in Kosovo.

BALLINGER-PINCHOT CONTROVERSY (1909–10), incident in the *Taft administration. In the summer of 1909 Louis R. Glavis, an investigator in the Interior Department, went to Gifford Pinchot, head of the Forestry Service in the Department of Agriculture and chief ally in *conservation matters to former president Theodore Roosevelt, with information suggesting that Secretary of the Interior Richard A. Ballinger was conspiring to turn over valuable Alaska coal lands to a Morgan-Guggenheim syndicate. Pinchot sent Glavis to President Taft, who sided with Ballinger and fired Glavis.

Pinchot then fed information to muckraking journals (see *Muckrakers) damaging to Ballinger, and himself publicly criticized the interior secretary. Angry at Pinchot's insubordination, Taft in January 1910 demanded his resignation. Although he replaced Pinchot with the director of the Yale School of Forestry, and later replaced Ballinger with a confirmed environmentalist, Taft appeared to Roosevelt, then on safari in Africa, to have abandoned the conservationist cause.

BANK HOLIDAY (Mar. 5–12, 1933), incident in the Franklin *Roosevelt administration. Thousands of banks had failed in the first three years of the *Great Depression. Anxiety about the safety of their savings, and the need to use them in the absence of other income, compelled millions of depositors to withdraw their money. Unsound banks—small, undercapitalized, their assets frozen in speculative loans, their managers sometimes guilty of criminal practices—faced failure. Even sound banks, however, could not survive a "run" of panicked depositors. As Roosevelt's inauguration approached, governor after governor closed or restricted access to the banks in their states.

On inauguration day, Mar. 4, 1933, all the nation's banks were closed. The next day, the president declared a national bank holiday lasting until Thursday, Mar. 9, when a special session of Congress could pass the Emergency Banking Relief Act. Congress convened on Mar. 9 and quickly passed the act, which permitted sound banks to reopen with licenses from the Treasury Department and put unsound banks under the direction of conservators. The bank holiday was extended to Sunday, Mar. 12, when Roosevelt gave his first *fireside chat, reassuring the nation of the safety of deposits in licensed banks. The panic passed. Within a month, 70 percent of the banks had reopened.

BANK OF AUGUSTA v. EARLE (1839), 8–1 decision of the *Taney Court giving corporations the freedom to operate in states in which they were not chartered. A citizen of Alabama had refused to honor bills of exchange of three corporations chartered in other states, arguing that "foreign" corporations could not do business in a "sovereign" state. Chief Justice Roger B. Taney ruled that a corporation, like a natural person, could act in states where it did not reside, although, unlike a natural person, it could be excluded from a state. Although Taney did not go so far as to accept Daniel Webster's argument that a corporation enjoyed all the protections of citizenship under the Constitution's Privileges and Immunities Clause, his decision provided a significant stimulus to economic expansion.

BANK OF THE UNITED STATES, name of the first two U.S. central banks. The First Bank of the United States (BUS; 1791–1811) was proposed by Alexander Hamilton, secretary of the Treasury in the *Washington administration, who envisioned a privately owned bank that would serve important public functions—a depository for federal revenues, a fiscal agent for the federal government, a source of loans in a national emergency, a source of credit to the business community, and regulator of a stable currency (see *Hamilton System).

The bank was opposed by Secretary of State Thomas Jefferson, who, fearing the rise of a moneyed class with close connections to the government, argued that the chartering of federal corporations was not among the powers specifically delegated to the national government by the Constitution. Hamilton responded that the bank was a necessary means for the execution of the government's enumerated economic powers: ". . . every power vested in a Government is in its nature *sovereign*, and includes . . . a right to employ all the *means* requisite, and fairly applicable to the attainment of the ends of such power; and which are not precluded by restrictions & exceptions specified in the constitution; or not immoral, or not contrary to the essential ends of political society" (see *Hamilton and Jefferson).

President Washington sided with Hamilton and on Feb. 25, 1791, signed the act establishing the bank. The bank was capitalized at $10 million, a sum obtained by selling 25,000 shares at $400 per share. The U.S. government bought 5,000 shares; private investors were limited to 100. (British investors held two-thirds of the bank's shares.) The bank proved highly successful, although its extreme conservatism curtailed the supply of money and credit. When its charter expired in 1811 during the *Madison administration, it was not renewed due to Republican hostility and continued doubts as to its constitutionality.

The proliferation of unsound state banks and the wild expansion of paper money that followed the demise of the first BUS convinced Republicans of the advisability of chartering the Second Bank of the United States (1816–36). Under the presidency (1823–33) of Nicholas Biddle, the bank was well but conservatively managed. Nevertheless, it encountered the hostility of Pres. Andrew Jackson, whose hatred of the "money power" was visceral. In 1832 Jackson vetoed a bill to recharter the bank early, and in 1833 he crippled the bank by removing govern-

ment deposits (see *Bank War). When its charter expired in 1836, the BUS became a private bank chartered in Pennsylvania.

BANK WAR (1832–36), episode in the *Jackson administration. Pres. Andrew Jackson disliked all banks—but especially the *Bank of the United States (BUS)—as bastions of a privileged "moneyed aristocracy." Under bank president Nicholas Biddle, the Second BUS had well served the government, the business community, and its stockholders. Its charter was due to expire in 1836, and Jackson's position on renewal was unknown. In 1832, Sen. Henry Clay of Kentucky, a candidate for president, brought in an early rechartering bill in the belief that, if Jackson vetoed it, the issue would benefit him in the presidential election that year.

Jackson did in fact veto the bill. In his veto message, he attacked the bank as a monopoly (it was the only bank in which the government deposited its money and therefore the largest bank in the country) whose profits came from the earnings of workers and enriched a few hundred stockholders. His veto was based on a strict construction of the Necessary and Proper Clause of the U.S. Constitution (Art. 1, sec. 8). Noting that the courts had found the bank constitutional in the past, Jackson went on to make a startling claim of presidential autonomy: ". . . the opinion of the Supreme Court . . . ought not to control the coordinate authorities of this Government. The Congress, the Executive, and the Court must each for itself be guided by its own opinion of the Constitution. . . . The opinion of the judges has no more authority over Congress than the opinion of Congress has over the judges, and on that point the President is independent of both." This assertion won Jackson the sobriquet "King Andrew."

Biddle put the bank's resources behind Clay's candidacy, but Jackson was reelected with an overwhelming electoral majority. Resolved to punish Biddle and "kill the monster" (the bank), Jackson decided to remove government funds from the bank. To do so he had to promote one uncooperative Treasury secretary and dismiss another before Roger B. Taney, promoted from attorney general to secretary of the Treasury, did the president's bidding. In September 1833 government money was removed from the BUS and deposited around the country in "pet" state banks. The Senate reacted with an unprecedented resolution of censure (see *Jackson Censure).

From Jackson's point of view, the **removal of deposits** and their distribution among state banks was a democratic measure because it made capital available to farmers and small businessmen who had no access to the BUS. The result, however, was to open the floodgates of easy credit from those banks, which financed a wave of speculation in *public lands. In July 1836 Jackson issued a **Specie Circular** directing the Treasury not to accept paper money in payment for public lands. The effect was to quickly contract the money supply and bring on the *Panic of 1837.

In 1836 the BUS was transformed into a private bank under Biddle's presidency. The bank's collapse in 1841, amid charges of fraud against Biddle (who was acquitted), was widely interpreted as vindication of Jackson's hostility.

BARBARY WARS (1801–5, 1815), naval conflicts with piratical Arab states of the Barbary Coast of North Africa—Morocco, Algiers, Tunis, and Tripoli. Nominally parts of the Ottoman Empire, these states had preyed on Mediterranean shipping since the 16th century, and the European powers paid annual tribute for protection.

The United States did likewise until the pasha of Tripoli increased his demands and declared war against the United States. Pres. Thomas Jefferson dispatched a naval force to the Mediterranean under Commodore Edward Preble, who blockaded Tripoli (1803–5). On Oct. 31, 1803, the U.S. frigate *Philadelphia* ran aground and was captured by the Tripolitans with its crew and captain, William Bainbridge. While the *Philadelphia* was anchored in Tripoli harbor, Lt. Stephen Decatur boarded and burned it (Feb. 16, 1804). The arrival of another American squadron under Commodore John Rodgers and the approach from Egypt of a small army of adventurers led by William Eaton, U.S. consul in Tunis, caused the pasha to sign a treaty (Jan. 4, 1805) by which the United States ransomed its prisoners and the pasha ended the tribute payments.

The United States continued, however, to pay tribute to the other Barbary states. During the *War of 1812, the dey of Algiers resumed attacks on American ships and the enslavement of American sailors. In May 1815 Capt. Stephen Decatur led a fleet of ten vessels to Algiers, captured several Algerine warships, and threatened to bombard the city. The dey signed a peace treaty and released all U.S. prisoners without ransom. Decatur exacted similar agreements from Tunis and Tripoli, and thereafter a U.S. squadron was stationed in the Mediterranean.

BARBED WIRE, twisted wire with frequent sharp barbs patented in 1873 by Joseph F. Glidden for fencing

cattle. No other form of fencing protected cattlemen so well from trespassing, theft, interbreeding, or dispersal of their herds by weather. By 1890 most privately owned rangeland was fenced with barbed wire, putting an end to free grazing and cattle drives but permitting improvement of breeds.

BARNBURNERS AND HUNKERS, factions of the *Democratic Party in New York State formed in the 1840s. The party split originated over state issues but had national consequences. The Barnburners, led by former president Martin Van Buren, were the radical wing of the party; their opponents accused them of putting principles above party and compared them to the farmer who burned down his barn to get rid of the rats. The Hunkers were the conservative wing of the party, "hungry" or "hankering" for political patronage. Nationally, the Barnburners opposed *Texas annexation and slavery expansion. In 1848 they bolted the Democratic national convention, and Van Buren accepted the presidential nomination of the *Free-Soil Party. The Barnburners later returned to the Democratic Party, but in the 1850s they joined the antislavery *Republican Party.

BARUCH PLAN (1946), U.S. proposal for the international control of atomic energy and weapons (see *Arms Control and Disarmament). Presented to the UN Atomic Energy Commission in June 1946 by U.S. delegate Bernard M. Baruch, it called for the establishment of an International Atomic Development Authority (IADA) that would monopolize the development of atomic energy and control of atomic weapons. Only after the IADA had proved its effectiveness would the United States dispose of its atomic weapons and turn over its scientific and technological information to the agency. The Soviet Union demanded that the United States dispose of its atomic weapons at once. The UN Atomic Energy Commission and the General Assembly accepted the Baruch Plan but Soviet opposition killed it.

BATAAN. See *World War 2.

BATTLE HYMN OF THE REPUBLIC, religio-patriotic anthem written by social reformer Julia Ward Howe in November 1861 to the tune of "John Brown's Body," which she had heard being sung by Union troops on the march. She wrote it at a single sitting, before dawn, the long lines having formed themselves in her head as she lay in bed. Published in the February 1862 issue of the *Atlantic Monthly*, the poem begins: "Mine eyes have seen the glory of the coming of the Lord: / He is trampling out the vintage where the grapes of wrath are stored; / He has loosed the fateful lightning of his terrible swift sword: / His truth is marching on."

BAY OF PIGS INVASION (1961), failed *covert operation of the *Kennedy administration.

During the *Eisenhower administration, the Central Intelligence Agency (CIA) recruited, equipped, and trained in Central America a force of fiercely anti-Castro Cuban exiles for an invasion of their homeland that the CIA confidently expected would ignite a popular rising against the new Cuban leader. Eisenhower supported the plan but put it off when the CIA could not satisfy his prerequisites—chiefly, a Cuban government-in-exile supported by the Cuban refugees in the United States.

Thus Pres. John F. Kennedy inherited an enterprise in an advanced stage of preparation, which he had the option of continuing or canceling. On the uniformly positive recommendations of his intelligence and military advisers, which reinforced his own desire to establish an image of toughness, he chose to proceed.

On Apr. 15, 1961, six repainted American B-26 bombers bombed and strafed Cuban airfields, destroying half of Castro's air force (but alerting him to the fact that an attack was at hand). On the night of Apr. 16, two U.S. destroyers guided the invasion fleet of four small chartered merchant ships and two landing craft from Nicaragua to the Bay of Pigs on the southern coast of Cuba, about 90 miles from Havana. Several miles offshore waited a U.S. aircraft carrier and task force with instructions to do nothing until the invaders had succeeded in capturing an airfield. Kennedy had rejected a plan to use the navy planes to support the landing for fear of revealing U.S. complicity in the invasion.

On Apr. 17 a landing force of some 1,400 men got ashore over unexpected reefs that prevented their supplies coming ashore until high tide. Castro's planes promptly disposed of the invaders' tiny air force and sank two of the loaded merchant ships; the others scattered. Ashore, Cuban militia confined the invaders to the swampy beachhead from which they could not escape. There was no popular uprising.

On Apr. 19, Castro's army reached the scene. Of the invaders, now out of ammunition, 114 were killed, almost 1,200 taken prisoner. (In December 1962 the prisoners were exchanged for $53 million—privately raised—worth of food and medical supplies.) The fiasco—an intelligence disaster compounded by military ineptitude—profoundly shook the confidence of the new administration and encouraged the Soviets.

BEAR FLAG REVOLT (1846), incident in the *Mexican War. American settlers in California's Sacramento Valley declared their independence from Mexico (June 1846), seized Sonoma, and established a Republic of California under a flag depicting a grizzly bear and a red star. Capt. John C. Frémont, with an armed exploration party of 60 men, lent them his support. The revolt and republic ended on July 9 when Commodore John D. Sloat proclaimed California part of the United States. Some of the Sacramento Valley settlers joined Frémont's "California Battalion" and participated in the conquest of southern California.

BELKNAP SCANDAL (1876), incident in the *Grant administration. On Mar. 2, 1876, the House of Representatives voted unanimously to impeach Secretary of War William W. Belknap for receiving annual payments from a man he had appointed to a lucrative post tradership. Belknap resigned the same day. At his trial in April and May, the Senate failed to convict him, some members arguing that the Senate had no jurisdiction over a resigned official.

BELLEAU WOOD. See *World War 1.

BEMIS HEIGHTS. See *Saratoga Campaign.

BENNINGTON (Aug. 16, 1777), *Revolutionary War battle. After a difficult march through the forested east bank of the Hudson River in the *Saratoga campaign, and with supplies running low, British general John Burgoyne on Aug. 11 dispatched a force of Germans, Loyalists, and Indians to seize an American depot at Bennington, Vt. On the afternoon of Aug. 16 a force of New Hampshire militia under Gen. John Stark intercepted them about four miles northwest of Bennington. The American victory was complete, but a second British force, sent to reinforce the first, suddenly appeared and was only repulsed by the timely arrival of Col. Seth Warner with 350 veteran Continentals. The battle of Bennington cost Burgoyne 1,000 men (700 of them captured) and substantial equipment. The widespread Loyalist uprising he had counted on did not materialize, and most of his Indians deserted.

BERING SEA FUR-SEAL CONTROVERSY (1892–98). See *Sealing Controversies.

BERLIN AIRLIFT (1948–49), episode in the *Truman administration. In response to the decision by the Western allies to institute a currency reform in their occupation zones in Germany (see *German Occupation), the Soviets on June 23, 1948, blocked rail, highway, and water traffic into and out of West Berlin, deep in the Soviet occupation zone, to force out the Western occupiers. Gen. Lucius D. Clay, the U.S. military governor, immediately ordered a limited airlift. Determined to stay in Berlin, but rejecting the idea of an armored convoy forcing its way through the Soviet blockade, Pres. Harry S. Truman on June 28 ordered a full-scale airlift to supply 2 million West Berliners. U.S. and British transports ultimately carried 2,000 tons of food and 12,000 tons of fuel and other supplies into West Berlin daily. The Soviets harassed some flights but stopped short of interfering. The blockade ended on May 12, 1949, although the airlift continued until September.

BERLIN WALL (1961–89), 113-mile stretch of fortified concrete and steel, topped with barbed wire, surrounding the Western sectors of occupied Berlin. It was built in 1961 to stop the flow of East Germans to the West after U.S. president John F. Kennedy rejected Soviet premier Nikita Khrushchev's demand for a peace treaty with East Germany, which the Western allies did not recognize. Kennedy responded to Khrushchev's belligerence by calling for additional defense spending, enlarging the draft, and calling up National Guard units. The wall became the scene of constant incidents as East Germans continued to attempt to escape over it.

On June 26, 1963, President Kennedy, standing near the wall, told cheering Berliners: "Two thousand years ago the proud boast was *Civis romanus sum* [I am a Roman citizen]. Today, in the world of freedom, the proudest boast is *Ich bin ein Berliner* [I am a Berliner]. . . . All free men, wherever they may live, are citizens of Berlin, and, therefore, as a free man, I take pride in the words *Ich bin ein Berliner*."

On June 12, 1987, Pres. Ronald Reagan, then in Berlin, addressed Soviet leader Mikhail Gorbachev with the demand, "Mr. Gorbachev, tear down this wall!"

The wall was opened on Nov. 9, 1989, when thousands of East Berliners poured into West Berlin. It was demolished over the next year.

BILLION DOLLAR CONGRESS, popular name for the 51st Congress (December 1889–March 1891), in which Republicans had majorities in both the House (173–161) and Senate (47–37). It managed to wipe out a persistent Treasury surplus by appropriating the unprecedented sum of nearly $1 billion. "This is a billion dollar country," Speaker of the House Thomas B. ("Czar") Reed observed approvingly. The electorate, however, disliked active and spendthrift government. In 1891, the next House of Representatives contained 235 Democrats, 88 Republicans, and 10 Farmers Alliance representatives. The Republicans preserved a slight majority in the Senate.

BILL OF RIGHTS (1791), the first ten amendments to the U.S. Constitution, which protect certain civil and procedural rights possessed by Americans through natural law or English common law.

The model of the Bill of Rights was the English Bill of Rights of 1689 in which Parliament codified the personal liberties formulated in English common law as far back as the 12th century. English emigrants to America believed they carried these liberties with them, and some royal charters and acts of colonial legislatures affirmed them. When the *Continental Congress, in May 1776, called upon the colonies to frame republican constitutions, the Virginia convention adopted (June 12, 1776) a Declaration of Rights, largely prepared by George Mason, whose 16 articles identified Virginians' "inherent and natural" personal rights. This declaration influenced the other states. By 1781 all except Rhode Island and Connecticut had bills of rights or other specific guarantees in their constitutions.

At the Federal *Constitutional Convention, a bill of rights was not considered until the convention's final days. The weary delegates decided that a federal bill of rights was unnecessary: the rights involved were natural and inalienable in the first place; most state constitutions already protected them; and their protection remained a state responsibility because it was not listed among the enumerated powers of the federal government. Some of the Framers, however, objected to the absence of a bill of rights in the draft constitution. George Mason, Elbridge Gerry, and Edmund Randolph refused to sign the draft in part because of this omission.

The debates in the state ratifying conventions (see *Ratification) made clear the Framers' error. The absence of a bill of rights was the chief criticism of the *Antifederalists. Several states voted to ratify only on the understanding that a bill of rights would be the first order of business of the new Congress.

A committee of the first House of Representatives, at James Madison's insistence, drafted a bill containing 17 proposed amendments to the Constitution. The Senate reduced the list to 12. These were passed by Congress on Sept. 25, 1789, and submitted to the states for ratification. In most states, the first and second proposed amendments—dealing with congressional apportionment and compensation—were defeated. Ratification of the ten remaining amendments was completed in 1791. These amendments provided:

1. "Congress shall make no law respecting an establishment of religion, or prohibiting the free exercise thereof," nor abridging freedom of speech, press, and assembly.

2. "A well-regulated militia, being necessary to the security of a free state, the right of the people to keep and bear arms shall not be infringed."

3. "No soldier shall, in time of peace, be quartered in any house without the consent of the owner, nor in time of war but in a manner to be prescribed by law."

4. "The right of the people to be secure . . . against unreasonable searches and seizures shall not be violated. . . ."

5. "No person shall be held to answer for a . . . crime" unless indicted by a grand jury; "nor shall any person be subject for the same offense to be twice put in jeopardy . . . ; nor shall be compelled . . . to be a witness against himself, nor be deprived of life, liberty, or property, without due process of law. . . ."

6. "In all criminal prosecutions, the accused shall enjoy the right to a speedy and public trial, by an impartial jury . . . and to be informed . . . of the accusation; to be confronted with the witnesses against him; to have compulsory process for obtaining witnesses in his favor, and to have the Assistance of Counsel for his defense."

7. "In suits at common law . . . the right of trial by jury shall be preserved. . . ."

8. Excessive bail and fines, and "cruel and unusual punishments," are prohibited.

9. "The enumeration in the Constitution, of certain rights, shall not be construed to deny or disparage others retained by the people."

10. "The powers not delegated to the United States by the Constitution, nor prohibited by it to the states, are reserved to the states respectively, or to the people."

The phrase "Congress shall make no law" in the First Amendment indicates that the authors of the Bill of Rights regarded it as protection against abuses by the federal government. That the Bill of Rights did not apply to state governments was affirmed by Chief Justice John Marshall in 1833. Not until the middle of the 20th century did the U.S. Supreme Court, on the basis of the Due Process and Equal Protection clauses of the *14th Amendment, rule that state governments too were forbidden to infringe on most of the rights protected by the Bill of Rights.

BIRMINGHAM CAMPAIGN (1963), episode in the *civil rights movement. Under pressure to revive its anti-segregation movement after a failure in Albany, Ga., Martin Luther King Jr.'s *Southern Christian Leadership Conference (SCLC) determined to confront segregation in Birmingham, Ala., a notorious stronghold of segregation under its iron-fisted police commissioner, Eugene "Bull" Connor. The carefully prepared plan called for a steadily escalating series of nightly mass meetings, daytime marches and *sit-ins, and a shopping boycott, all calculated to fill the city's jails, attract national attention, and compel a negotiated end to segregation.

The campaign got off to a poor start. Postponed from Mar. 6 to Apr. 3, it found the local black community hostile and the national press indifferent or critical. Mass meetings were poorly attended, and few volunteered for arrest. King himself was arrested on Apr. 12 (Good Friday) for violating an antidemonstration injunction. During nine days in jail he wrote his famous "Letter from Birmingham Jail" (see *King's Letter from Birmingham Jail).

Desperate for a tactic to energize the campaign and attract the national media, King decided to allow Birmingham's black children to march. On May 2, eager black elementary- and high-school students—children as young as six—took to the streets, from which 600 were carried off to jail in police vans and school buses. The next day, new companies of marching children were met by fire hoses and police dogs. Photographs of these encounters awakened the nation's—and the Kennedy administration's—interest in events in Birmingham, where thousands of blacks now attended the nightly mass meetings. Adults now joined the children in demonstrations, parents often accompanying their children to jail. When the jails became overcrowded, new arrests were penned in the open air on the local fairground. On May 6, black children poured into the city's highly segregated business district, paralyzing all activity there.

Finally the city's white business leaders were moved to seek negotiations—not with King but with Birmingham's black leaders. By May 10 they had worked out an agreement involving gradual desegregation of Birmingham over a period of months and the release of jailed demonstrators. This was acceptable to King and endorsed by President Kennedy. Segregationist governor George C. Wallace and Birmingham politicians remained opposed. The night following the end of the campaign was marked by bomb blasts and retaliatory black rioting. Only King's personal peacemaking and the dispatch of federal troops to the area finally brought calm.

BITBURG VISIT (May 5, 1985), incident in the *Reagan administration. In response to an invitation from West German chancellor Helmut Kohl, Pres. Ronald

Reagan agreed to combine his attendance at a seven-nation economic summit in Bonn in May with a visit to a German military cemetery as a gesture of reconciliation on the 40th anniversary of the end of World War 2 in Europe. The cemetery chosen, in the town of Bitburg, contained the graves of nearly 2,000 German soldiers, including 49 identified as members of the Waffen SS, the Nazi elite guard.

The April announcement of Reagan's plan aroused intense criticism. His remark that most of the German soldiers buried at Bitburg were as much victims of the Nazis as the inmates of concentration camps only made matters worse. Nevertheless, he refused to cancel the Bitburg visit, which had become politically important to his friend Chancellor Kohl. But he added a visit to the Bergen-Belsen concentration camp.

On May 5, Reagan spent 80 minutes at Bergen-Belsen, where he spoke, then eight minutes at the Bitburg cemetery, where he presided over the laying of a wreath but pointedly did not glance at the soldiers' graves.

BITUMINOUS COAL STRIKE (1919), strike by the *United Mine Workers for higher wages and a shorter workweek. When the federal government obtained an injunction against union officers, union president John L. Lewis called off the strike, knowing that the miners would not obey. The strike was not settled until a Bituminous Coal Commission awarded the men a 27-percent pay increase but did not reduce the workweek.

BIXBY LETTER (1864), letter of condolence by Pres. Abraham Lincoln to a Massachusetts woman who was reported to have lost five sons in the Civil War. The number was actually two. On Nov. 21, 1864, the president wrote: "Dear Madam, I have been shown in the files of the War Department a statement of the Adjutant-General of Massachusetts that you are the mother of five sons who have died gloriously on the field of battle. I feel how weak and fruitless must be any words of mine which should attempt to beguile you from the grief of a loss so overwhelming. But I cannot refrain from tendering to you the consolation that may be found in the thanks of the Republic they died to save. I pray that our heavenly Father may assuage the anguish of your bereavement, and leave you only the cherished memory of the loved and lost, and the solemn pride that must be yours to have laid so costly a sacrifice upon the altar of freedom."

BLACK BELT, 5,000-square-mile region of Alabama and Mississippi distinguished by extremely fertile black soil. Until 1880 it was the leading cotton-producing region of the South; since then it has produced diversified food crops as well as cotton.

BLACK CODES (1865–66), legislation enacted by the former Confederate states (except Tennessee) to define the status of the freed blacks as a subordinate caste.

The black codes conferred certain basic civil rights on the new freedmen—the rights to marry (but not intermarry), to own personal property, to sue in court. On the other hand, they limited the freedmen's rights to own real property, to make contracts, to testify in court, to travel, to assemble, and to keep firearms. New criminal laws aimed expressly at blacks prescribed harsh punishment for petty offenses, including "insulting" language. No Southern state gave freedmen the right to vote or allowed them to serve on juries.

In South Carolina, Mississippi, and Louisiana, where blacks outnumbered whites, the codes were particularly severe. There the codes' clear intent was to preserve and control the black agricultural workforce, which was essential to the economies of those states. Nonagricultural work was virtually prohibited. Blacks were required to work on plantations under yearlong contracts. A laborer who left his job before the expiration of his contract forfeited his pay and was subject to arrest. Unemployment was equated with vagrancy, punishable by imprisonment or forced labor. Black children were subject to unpaid agricultural "apprenticeships."

Reminiscent of the antebellum slave codes, the black codes outraged opinion in the North, which regarded them as reinstituting slavery without the name. Nothing more discredited Pres. Andrew Johnson's *reconstruction program, for these codes were defiantly enacted by the legislatures of the states Johnson himself had declared reconstructed in 1865. The *Civil Rights Act of 1866 nullified the black codes, which were repealed by the Republican state governments put in place during congressional reconstruction.

BLACK FRIDAY (Sept. 24, 1869), incident in the *Grant administration. In the summer of 1869, a group of speculators led by Jay Gould and Jim Fisk laid plans to corner the gold market. To ensure the government's neutrality, they involved a brother-in-law of President Grant and the head of the New York subtreasury. They approached Grant's private secretary and conspicuously but unsuccessfully courted the president himself. Their large purchases of gold beginning Sept. 2 amid planted rumors that the government would not intervene rapidly drove up the price, precipitating a financial panic on

"Black Friday" that was relieved by the sale of $4 million of Treasury gold. Forewarned, Gould and Fisk profited handsomely while many other speculators were ruined. Public opinion implicated the Grant administration in the affair.

BLACK HAWK WAR (1832), resistance by Sac Indians under Black Hawk to removal from ancestral lands in northern Illinois (see *Indian Removal). It was suppressed with genocidal ferocity by Illinois and Wisconsin volunteers and their Sioux allies. Engagements were small and scattered; more whites were killed by *cholera than by Indians. The war was well publicized in the national press. Taken prisoner, Black Hawk was pardoned by Pres. Andrew Jackson, then toured Eastern cities as a celebrity.

The first Indian war in the former *Northwest Territory since Tippecanoe (see *Tecumseh Confederacy), it was also the last instance of armed Indian resistance in that region.

BLACK MIGRATIONS. African-American history has been marked by dramatic migrations. First was the involuntary migration of black Africans to the American colonies, later their involuntary migration west with the cotton frontier. After the Civil War, Southern rural blacks moved in large numbers to Southern cities while smaller numbers sought better lives in the North.

In 1900, 89.7 percent of African-Americans lived in the South and the overwhelming majority were still rural. By then, however, the **Great Migration** (1890–1970) to Northern cities was under way, swelling to huge numbers during World War 1, during the 1920s when the curtailment of immigration opened industrial jobs for Southern blacks, and again during World War 2 when war industries needed labor. During the 1920s, New York City's black population grew from 152,000 to 328,000, Chicago's from 109,000 to 233,000. Between 1930 and 1970, the black population of Mississippi declined from 1,010,000 to 816,000, of Alabama from 945,000 to 903,000, of Arkansas from 478,000 to 352,000, of South Carolina from 794,000 to 789,000. The proportion of blacks in Northern cities grew even more rapidly because of "white flight" to the suburbs. In 1970, blacks constituted 43.7 percent of the population of Detroit (81.6 percent in 2000), 33.8 percent of the population of Philadelphia (43.2 percent in 2000), 32.7 percent of the population of Chicago (36.8 percent in 2000), and 21.1 percent of the population of New York (26.6 percent in 2000).

Life in the ghettos of Northern cities was not all that the migrants had hoped. Many experienced poverty, discrimination, poor schools, family breakup, drugs, and crime. Race riots were frequent where black and white populations collided—28 in as many different cities in the latter half of 1919 alone, including most notably Chicago, where 38 people were killed and 537 injured. In the late 1960s, black ghettos in dozens of Northern cities erupted in riot. After 1970, a small reverse migration to the South began to be observed. Between 1990 and 2000, the proportion of the black population living in the South rose from 52.8 percent to 54.8 percent.

BLACK MONDAY (Oct. 19, 1987), financial panic when the Dow Jones industrial average plunged a record 508 points and a record 604.3 million shares changed hands on the New York Stock Exchange. The decline in market value of 22.6 percent was the greatest since World War 1, far greater than the 12.82 percent drop on Black Thursday, Oct. 28, 1929 (see *Panic of 1929). Unlike the 1929 crash, the 1987 crash did not herald a depression. A year later the market had regained half its losses.

BLACK MUSLIMS. See *Nation of Islam or Black Muslims.

BLACK PANTHERS (1966–69), black nationalist and Marxist organization founded in Oakland, Calif., by Huey Newton and Bobby Seale. Their community service—health clinics, educational programs, breakfasts for schoolchildren—together with their militancy—black uniforms, unconcealed weapons, and confrontational tactics—won them heroic stature in black communities and on college campuses across the country, although they also engaged in criminal activities. At their peak, they may have had 5,000 members in a dozen large cities. The Federal Bureau of Investigation targeted them for infiltration and destabilization, with the result that many Black Panthers died in gun battles with the police, the FBI, other black revolutionaries, and each other.

BLACK POWER (1966), slogan popularized by black activist Stokely Carmichael of the *Student Nonviolent Coordinating Committee (SNCC) during *Meredith's "March Against Fear," signaling his break with Martin Luther King Jr.'s nonviolent and integrationist civil rights strategy. The slogan implied black self-determination, beginning with the exclusion of whites from civil rights organizations; SNCC excluded them in 1966, the *Congress of Racial Equality (CORE) in 1967. The slogan's power lay in its ambiguity: where blacks heard promises, whites heard threats. Embracing black power proved disastrous to those organizations that did so.

BLACK THURSDAY. See *Panic of 1929.

BLACK WARRIOR AFFAIR (1854), incident in the *Pierce administration. When Spanish authorities in Havana seized the U.S. steamer *Black Warrior*, Southern expansionists in Congress demanded war. The administration settled for an apology and reparations.

BLADENSBURG. See *War of 1812; *Washington Burning.

BLAND-ALLISON ACT (1878), legislation of the *Hayes administration. In response to the demand of distressed agrarian and labor groups during the depression of 1873–79 (see *Agrarian Discontents), the House of Representatives in December 1877 passed a bill sponsored by Rep. Richard P. Bland of Missouri providing for the unlimited coinage of silver at a ratio to gold of 16 to 1 (see *Free Silver). Amended by Sen. William B. Allison of Iowa, a weakened bill was passed over Pres. Rutherford B. Hayes's veto on Feb. 28, 1878. It required the government to buy $2–4 million worth of silver per month at market prices for coining into silver dollars. The purchase requirement was a victory for silver producers, but the limited coinage was a partial defeat for their "silverite" allies. Because the silver content of the new dollar was worth less than a dollar, the silver dollar and silver certificate were widely used to pay taxes but otherwise largely disappeared from circulation.

BLEEDING KANSAS (1854–58), term applied by Horace Greeley's New York *Tribune* to the strife in Kansas Territory between free-state and proslavery forces.

Passage in May 1854 of the *Kansas-Nebraska Act, which left the decision whether Kansas would be free or slave up to its inhabitants (see *Popular Sovereignty), triggered a flow of migrants to the new territory from North and South, some of them determined to affect the ultimate resolution of the question. Many Northern migrants were financed by the New England Emigrant Aid Company and similar organizations founded by *abolitionists throughout the North. Lawrence became the center of free-state settlers, Leavenworth of proslavery settlers. Most settlers in both groups, however, were more interested in obtaining clear title to land than in the slavery question.

When the first governor of the territory scheduled for Mar. 30, 1855, an election to a territorial legislature open to all "residents," proslavery men from western Missouri—the so-called border ruffians—poured across the border, voted fraudulently, and ensured the election of a proslavery legislature at Lecompton that was officially recognized by the *Pierce administration. Free-staters organized a rival (and illegal) government at Topeka. Both factions were armed and felt threatened. A series of minor clashes beginning in November 1855 culminated on May 21, 1856, with the "sack" of Lawrence, in which a party of Missourians burned and looted several buildings but killed no one (an event much exaggerated in the East) and on May 24–25 with John Brown's Pottowatomie massacre (see *Brown's Career). Guerrilla warfare ensued, with irregular forces terrorizing southeastern Kansas and inflicting some 200 casualties by the end of the year.

In September 1857 a convention called by the legal (proslavery) territorial legislature and chosen in an election boycotted by free-staters met at Lecompton to draft a state constitution. In October, however, new and fair elections to the territorial legislature in which the free-staters participated returned a free-state majority. Thus the legal territorial government was now in the hands of free-staters while the constitutional convention remained in the hands of slave-staters. That convention, as expected, drafted a proslavery constitution, which was ratified (December 1857) in an election boycotted by free-staters. Then the new territorial legislature called a second ratifying convention—this one boycotted by the proslavery faction—that rejected the Lecompton constitution.

Like his predecessor, Franklin Pierce, Pres. James Buchanan regarded the original, fraudulently elected territorial government at Lecompton as legal, and he accepted the Lecompton constitution as a valid expression of popular sovereignty (see *Buchanan Administration). On this point he clashed with Democratic senator Stephen A. Douglas of Illinois, author of the Kansas-Nebraska Act, who considered the Lecompton constitution a travesty of popular sovereignty. Buchanan submitted the Lecompton constitution to Congress, where, despite Douglas's opposition, it was accepted by the Senate but then rejected by the House. In a compromise move, Congress resubmitted the Lecompton constitution to the people of Kansas, who in August 1858 overwhelmingly rejected it. Kansas remained a territory until 1861, when it entered the Union as a free state.

BLOODY ANGLE. See *Wilderness Campaign.

BLOODY SHIRT, rhetorical device employed by Republican orators after the Civil War identifying Democrats with the Confederacy. In the congressional elections of 1866, in which the Republicans scored massive victories, Gov. Oliver P. Morton of Indiana "waved the bloody shirt" to great effect: "Every unregenerate rebel . . . calls himself a Democrat. Every bounty jumper, every deserter, every sneak who ran away from the draft calls himself a Democrat. . . . Every man who labored for the rebellion in the field, who murdered Union prisoners by cruelty and starvation, who contrived hellish schemes to introduce into Northern cities the wasting pestilence of yellow fever, calls himself a Democrat. Every wolf in sheep's clothing who pretends to preach the gospel but proclaims the righteousness of man-selling and slavery, every one who shoots down negroes in the streets, burns up negro school-houses and meeting-houses, and murders women and children by the light of their own flaming dwellings, calls himself a Democrat. . . . In short, the Democratic party may be described as a common sewer and loathsome receptacle, into which is emptied every element of treason North and South, every element of inhumanity and barbarism which has dishonored the age."

BONHOMME RICHARD AND SERAPIS. See *Jones's Cruise.

BONUS ARMY (1932), incident in the *Hoover administration. In 1924, over Pres. Calvin Coolidge's veto, Congress passed an Adjusted Compensation Act providing World War 1 servicemen bonuses of $1 per day of domestic service and $1.25 per day of overseas service. Averaging $1,000 for 3.5 million veterans, the bonus was in the form of a life insurance endowment policy payable in 1945.

Hardship brought on by the *Great Depression caused veterans to agitate for immediate payment, and in the summer of 1932 a "Bonus Expeditionary Force" of some 20,000 unemployed veterans and their families—repudiated by the American Legion and Veterans of Foreign Wars—descended on Washington, occupied abandoned buildings, and set up a makeshift camp of tents, shacks, and crates on the Anacostia Flats in Maryland, in view of the Capitol. In June, Congress rejected a bill authorizing immediate payment, but the bonus army stayed on. Disorderly demonstrations and lack of food and sanitation moved Congress to provide funds for the veterans' return home.

Charging that radicals and communists were inciting disorders, Pres. Herbert Hoover ordered the U.S. Army to disperse those who remained. On July 28, with tear gas, bayonets, cavalry, and tanks, troops drove the veterans out of downtown Washington, then pursued them to Anacostia, where they destroyed the veterans' camp. Directing this controversial operation was Army chief of staff Maj. Gen. Douglas MacArthur, accompanied by his reluctant aide, Maj. Dwight D. Eisenhower.

BORDER STATES, in the Civil War, four *slave states—Maryland, Virginia, Kentucky, and Missouri—adjacent to Northern free states. Virginia was the only one to secede, but its unionist northwestern counties promptly separated from that state and entered (1863) the Union as West Virginia. The other border states were deeply divided but were held in the Union by political and military means. Pres. Abraham Lincoln applied the first *habeas corpus suspensions against secessionist politicians in Maryland. Union armies expelled the Confederates from Kentucky. In Missouri, Lincoln in 1861 overruled an emancipation proclamation issued by Union general John C. Frémont, and in 1863 he exempted the border states from his own *Emancipation Proclamation. Border state men fought on both sides in the war.

BORK NOMINATION (1987), incident in the *Reagan administration. On July 1, 1987, Pres. Ronald Reagan nominated Robert H. Bork, then a judge on the U.S. Circuit Court of Appeals for the District of Columbia, to succeed Associate Justice Lewis F. Powell Jr., a moderate conservative, on the U.S. Supreme Court.

A strict constructionist and believer in "original intent" (that judges should be guided by the intentions of the authors of the Constitution), Bork had criticized some of the principal decisions of the *Warren and *Burger courts. Liberals believed that his conservatism was so extreme as to be out of the mainstream of American jurisprudence. They feared that his presence on the Court would tilt its balance and endanger recent decisions on abortion, school prayer, and pornography. Democrats, in particular, had not forgotten that in 1973, as U.S. solicitor general and acting attorney general, Bork had executed Pres. Richard M. Nixon's order to fire the *independent counsel investigating *Watergate after his two superiors in the Department of Justice had resigned rather than do so.

In the first of three weeks (Sept. 15–30) of hearings by the Senate Judiciary Committee, Bork was subjected to intense interrogation by Democratic senators, during which he modified many of his published conservative opinions. On Oct. 6, the committee voted 9–5 against confirmation, and on Oct. 23 the Senate rejected Bork's nomination 58–42. The next year Bork resigned from the Court of Appeals. Bork's Republican supporters accused Democrats of politicizing the confirmation process. They had their revenge in 1991 with the *Thomas nomination.

BOSNIA. See *Balkan Intervention.

BOSTON BUSING (1974–89). In June 1974, federal judge Arthur Garrity, having presided at a *school-desegregation suit brought by the *National Association for the Advancement of Colored People, concluded that the Boston public schools had been intentionally segregated by various covert administrative procedures and that *affirmative action was therefore appropriate. His initial remedy, for the 1974–75 school year, was to impose a plan that redrew the districts for 40 percent of the city's schools to end the most extreme racial concentrations. (The racial composition of the Boston public schools at that time was 52 percent white, 37 percent black, 8 percent Hispanic, and 3 percent Asian.) Two districts—black Roxbury and Irish South Boston—were to be paired, some 17,000 students being bused between them to integrate the virtually all-black schools of Roxbury and the virtually all-white schools of South Boston.

On Sept. 12, 1974, 80 of the Boston schools affected by the plan opened peacefully. But in South Boston, buses transporting black students from Roxbury to attend formerly all-white South Boston High School were stoned by angry white mobs. Over the next few months, police had to break up brawls and melees in and around the high school. When blacks in Roxbury rampaged in response, the governor called out the National Guard. Frequent demonstrations protested forced busing. Judge Garrity was burned in effigy, his suburban home targeted by demonstrators, and his mail filled with abusive letters and death threats.

For the Southies and many other white Bostonians, their ethnically and racially homogeneous neighborhoods were sources of identity and safety. Family, church, and the local public school were at the heart of their universe. Outsiders were alien and threatening. The Southies viewed busing as a scheme of social engineering imposed upon them by affluent suburban liberals.

For the 1975–76 school year, Judge Garrity's plan embraced the entire city. Boston was divided into nine districts like wedges of a pie—black neighborhoods in the center, white neighborhoods on the periphery. Integration was to be achieved by busing white students toward the center, black students toward the periphery.

Students could choose any school in the district or one of 32 citywide "magnet" schools offering special programs. But Roxbury and South Boston were again placed in the same district, and the number of students to be bused citywide increased to 25,000.

When the schools opened in September 1975, there were student boycotts and angry demonstrations. In some schools, there was violence. In all schools blacks and whites sat isolated from one another except for the exchange of taunts and insults and the occasional physical incident in the halls. As it became clear that busing would continue, white students turned to parochial and private schools. White flight, which long antedated the busing controversy, continued, the city's population falling from 641,000 (16.3 percent black) in 1970 to 563,000 (22.4 percent black) in 1980.

In 1989 court-ordered busing was replaced by a system of "controlled choice," in which the city was divided into three zones and students in each were allowed to choose among about 27 schools—so long as all the schools remained adequately integrated. Thus race was a factor in assigning students to the schools of their choice or others. In 1999—when the Boston school population was 49 percent black, 26 percent Hispanic, 15 percent white, and 9 percent Asian—the Boston School Committee voted to drop race as a factor in such assignments beginning in the year 2000.

BOSTON MASSACRE (Mar. 8, 1770), eruption of violence between British troops and a harassing crowd in Boston. A small British guard fired into a menacing crowd, killing three outright and fatally wounding two more. To prevent a general uprising, Lt. Gov. Thomas Hutchinson removed the troops from the town to an island in the harbor. The British captain of the guard and eight men were arrested for murder. Defended (October–November) by patriot leaders John Adams and Josiah Quincy, the captain and six soldiers were acquitted. Two soldiers found guilty of manslaughter were branded on the thumb.

BOSTON POLICE STRIKE (1919), strike by Boston police when they were denied the right to form a union. The night of Sept. 9, 1919, when the city had no police protection, was marked by rowdyism but no general lawlessness. The next day civilian volunteers and state police maintained order. When Samuel Gompers, president of the American Federation of Labor, asked Gov. Calvin Coolidge to remove the police commissioner and reinstate suspended union members, the governor telegraphed: "There is no right to strike against the public safety by anybody, anywhere, anytime." His response won Coolidge the Republican vice presidential nomination in 1920.

BOSTON PORT ACT (1774). See *Intolerable Acts.

BOSTON SIEGE (Apr. 19, 1775–Mar. 17, 1776), episode in the *Revolutionary War.

After the battles of *Lexington and Concord, New England militia converged upon Boston and laid siege to it. The Massachusetts provincial congress appointed Artemas Ward commander of Massachusetts troops. He established his headquarters at Cambridge, the center of the Patriot forces. Other militia leaders generally accepted Ward as commander. With little to do, the undisciplined and inexperienced soldiers, poorly equipped, supplied, and housed, were soon demoralized.

In Boston, the British commander, Gen. Thomas Gage, awaited reinforcements, which arrived in May (bringing British strength to 7,000 men) along with generals William Howe, Henry Clinton, and John Burgoyne. In June, the British decided to strengthen the defenses of Boston by occupying nearby high ground—Dorchester Heights to the south, Charlestown Peninsula to the north. The Patriots forestalled the British move by occupying Charlestown Peninsula on the night of June 16–17. At the battle of *Bunker Hill on June 17 the British drove the Americans off the peninsula at great cost to themselves.

At Philadelphia on June 15, the *Continental Congress had appointed George Washington commander in chief of a *Continental Army. Washington reached Cambridge on July 3 and took command of the army besieging Boston. He was appalled by what he found. "The People of this government have obtained a Character which they by no means deserve," he wrote to a correspondent in August: "their officers generally speaking are the most indifferent kind of People I ever saw. . . . I dare say the Men would fight very well (if properly Officered) although they are an exceeding dirty and nasty people. . . ." Washington set about organizing the army, imposing discipline, instituting training, improving supplies, and cleaning up the camp. Yet most of his troops were due to be discharged on Dec. 31.

Meanwhile, the people of Boston and the British troops there were suffering from lack of food. In September, Howe replaced Gage as the British commander in North America. Like Gage, he saw no possibility of offensive action from Boston and wanted to evacuate the city. On Mar. 4, 1776, Washington's troops occupied Dorchester Heights, where they set up the heavy artillery that had been captured at *Fort Ticonderoga and dragged to Boston. The Patriot position threatened the British fleet in Boston harbor and made the city untenable.

Having agreed with Washington that the Patriots would not interfere if Howe did not set fire to the city, Howe ordered the city's evacuation. On Mar. 7 British troops and Loyalist citizens began boarding British ships. Ten days later the ships sailed to Nantasket Roads, five miles south of Boston, and on Mar. 27 departed for Halifax, Nova Scotia. On Mar. 18, Washington led Patriot troops into Boston.

BOSTON TEA PARTY (Dec. 16, 1773), destruction of East India Company tea in Boston harbor, an early event in the *American Revolution.

To aid the straitened East India Company, which was burdened with a surplus of tea, Parliament in May 1773 passed a Tea Act exempting the company from export duties on tea shipped from England to America. This made the tea cheaper than other tea in America, legal and illegal, even with the Townshend tax on imported tea still in effect (see *Townshend Acts). But the act also permitted the company to sell its tea directly to favored agents or consignees rather than at auction, thus excluding American tea merchants from its sale. American patriots viewed the scheme as a trick to seduce Americans into buying the cheap tea and paying the Townshend tax, which their leaders considered unconstitutional.

Resistance to the landing of the tea became continent-wide. In Boston, where three tea ships arrived in late November and early December, mass meetings demanded the tea's return. Lt. Gov. Thomas Hutchinson refused to let the ships leave until they paid the Townshend duty. On the night of Dec. 16, a band of patriots disguised as Mohawk Indians boarded the three ships and threw overboard their cargoes of tea, numbering 342 chests. At Charleston, Philadelphia, New York, and Annapolis the landing of the tea was prevented.

Outraged by the defiance of Boston and the destruction of property, Parliament resolved to stamp out the fires of rebellion in that city. The result was the Coercive Acts, known in America as the *Intolerable Acts.

BOURBONS or REDEEMERS, conservative Southern Democrats who reclaimed control of their states from carpetbag Republican regimes in the 1870s (see *Reconstruction) and controlled them until the turn of the century. The name Bourbon was derogatory, a reference to the reactionary Bourbon kings restored to their thrones in Europe after the fall of Napoleon. The Bourbons called themselves Redeemers, in the sense that they had redeemed their states from black Republican rule.

The Bourbons' conservatism did not include traditional Southern values of agrarianism and states' rights. They wanted minimal government and maximum exploitation of the South's resources, which they pursued in alliance with Northern financial, industrial, and railroad interests (see *New South). Unsympathetic to the radicalism of distressed farmers (see *Agrarian Discontents), they were paternalistic toward the freedmen until the *populist challenge compelled them to adopt the tactics of Negrophobia. This did not prevent their overthrow by racist poor whites.

BOXER REBELLION (1898–1900), antiforeign uprising in China. In June 1900 the Boxers occupied Beijing and besieged the foreign legations there. From their fleets at Tientsin, Britain, France, Russia, Germany, Japan, and the United States organized an 18,000-man military force (of which 2,100 were Americans) that fought its way (Aug. 4–14) from Tientsin to Beijing, where it lifted the siege. China was compelled to pay the powers an indemnity of $333 million, to revise its commercial treaties, and to permit the stationing of foreign troops in the capital. In 1908 the United States applied part of its share of the indemnity to financing scholarships for Chinese students in America.

BOZEMAN TRAIL. See *Sioux Wars.

BRACERO PROGRAM. See *Mexican Relations.

BRADDOCK'S ROAD, military highway constructed during the *French and Indian War connecting Baltimore and Fort Pitt (Pittsburgh). Improved by Maryland during the 1780s until it was passable by wagons, it became a thoroughfare for early western migration.

BRAIN TRUST (1932–33), group of Columbia University professors—Raymond Moley, Rexford G. Tugwell, and Adolf A. Berle Jr.—who advised New York governor Franklin Roosevelt during his campaign for the presidency in 1932. When Roosevelt was elected, these three were given positions in the new administration. Other advisers soon replaced them.

BRANDYWINE (Sept. 11, 1777), *Revolutionary War battle, one of the largest (in terms of number of participants) of the war.

In planning an attack on Philadelphia, British general William Howe hoped to force Patriot general George Washington to leave his secure position in New Jersey's Watchung Mountains and fight a major engagement.

Leaving Gen. Henry Clinton in New York awaiting reinforcements with which to aid Gen. John Burgoyne in the Hudson Valley, Howe took 16,000 troops by ship to Chesapeake Bay, landing them at the head of the bay at the end of August.

Determined to protect Philadelphia, Washington moved south and took up a position on the east bank of Brandywine Creek in Maryland across Howe's line of march to Philadelphia. The river was too deep to cross except at fords. Washington placed his center at Chad's Ford under Gen. Nathanael Greene, his left and right flanks south and north. Howe divided his army, placing one wing of 7,000 men at Chad's Ford opposite Washington's center while he and Gen. Charles Cornwallis led 9,000 other troops north. This wing crossed the west and east branches of Brandywine Creek, then turned south on the east bank of the river toward Washington's unsecured right flank.

Until midafternoon, Washington was ignorant of Howe's whereabouts. When he finally learned that Howe had crossed the river and was approaching from the north, he recalled his right flank and placed it at right angles to the river to face the oncoming British. During the fierce battle that followed, the British at Chad's Ford forced a crossing, at great cost, and engaged Washington's center. The American troops gave way on all fronts. Night ended the battle. Washington's army, disorganized but still intact, retreated to Chester, still between Howe and Philadelphia.

BRETTON WOODS CONFERENCE (July 1–22, 1944), conference at Bretton Woods, N.H., attended by representatives of 44 nations to plan postwar economic cooperation. They established the International Monetary Fund (IMF) and the Bank for Reconstruction and Development (World Bank).

BRICKER AMENDMENT (1953–57), constitutional amendment proposed on Jan. 7, 1953, by Republican senator John W. Bricker of Ohio modifying Art. 6 of the U.S. Constitution to the effect that "no treaty . . . shall be the supreme law of the land unless made in pursuance of this Constitution." It continued (in a 1954 version): "A provision of a treaty or other international agreement which conflicts with this Constitution shall not be of any force or effect" and "A treaty or other international agreement shall become effective as internal law in the United States only through legislation by the Congress. . . ."

Bricker's original proposal was cosponsored by 62 other senators, including all but three Republicans. Its potential effect was unclear, but it was recognized as an effort by Congress to reduce the power of the president and an effort by isolationists to prevent internationalist presidents (like Franklin Roosevelt and Dwight Eisenhower) from making agreements that would limit American sovereignty (like Yalta or membership in the United Nations). Eisenhower opposed the amendment vigorously, but it continued as an issue until 1957. In 1954 one version came within a single vote of adoption.

BROWN'S CAREER. In October 1855, 55-year-old abolitionist John Brown (1800–1859) drove a one-horse wagon into Kansas Territory. Behind him he left a lifetime of failure as a farmer and businessman. Now he was determined to devote the remainder of his life to the mission God had assigned him—to rid the country of the monstrous evil of slavery. Five sons had preceded him to the territory and established a settlement near Osawatomie. Besides supplies for "Brown's Station," John Brown brought another son and a son-in-law (he had 20 children by two wives) and an arsenal of rifles, revolvers, ammunition, and knives for the work at hand.

Since passage of the *Kansas-Nebraska Act in 1854, settlers had been rushing into Kansas Territory to determine whether it would become a free or a slave state. Free-state settlers were still a minority, harassed and intimidated by "border ruffians" from Missouri who invaded Kansas, voted fraudulently, and established a proslavery territorial government that Washington recognized as legal. The free-state men established a rival but illegal government (see *Bleeding Kansas).

With war between free-state and proslavery forces threatening, marauding Missourians on May 21, 1856, sacked the free-state town of Lawrence. Although there were free-state military organizations in the territory, Brown was incapable of subordinating himself to anyone else's authority. Resolving to retaliate for the sack of Lawrence with an act of terrorism that would instill "a restraining fear" in the enemy, Brown recruited a war party of seven men that included four sons and a son-in-law and led them on the night of May 24–25 to a proslavery settlement along nearby Pottawatomie Creek. There they dragged five men from their cabins and hacked them to death with knives in what became known nationally as the **Pottawatomie massacre**.

The atrocity stunned the region. Free-state and proslavery men in Kansas joined in condemning the murders, although Eastern antislavery newspapers tried variously to mitigate them. But southeastern Kansas now erupted into guerrilla warfare, with free-state and proslavery bands fighting each other and looting and burning while federal troops tried to restore order. Brown's Station was destroyed, one of Brown's sons was killed and two others were taken captive. Brown himself led his small band in the war, winning a skirmish with Missourians at Black Jack in June but being driven out of Osawatomie in August. In October, Brown slipped out of Kansas with a price on his head for the Pottawatomie murders.

Back in Kansas in December 1858 to resume his private war with the Slave Power, Brown led a raid into Missouri, ransacking the homes of two planters (one planter was killed) and bringing back to Kansas horses, mules, and wagons along with 11 liberated slaves. These Brown escorted all the way to Detroit and to freedom in Canada. Although another price was put on his head, authorities did not interfere with him because of public resentment of the Fugitive Slave Act of 1850 (see *Fugitive Slave Laws).

In the summer of 1859, with funds provided by a group of distinguished Massachusetts citizens who were also militant abolitionists, Brown rented a farm in Maryland and gathered 21 armed followers—16 whites, five blacks. His plan, presumably, was to capture the federal arsenal at Harpers Ferry, Va., across the Potomac River from Maryland and 60 miles from Washington. With the arsenal's arms, he would establish a base in the mountains of western Virginia to which slaves could escape. There he would arm them, but whether for defensive or offensive purposes is unclear; Brown spoke variously of raising a slave insurrection or leading his defensively armed charges to freedom in the North—or simply of provoking a civil war.

On the night of Oct. 16, Brown led 18 of his men on the **Harpers Ferry raid**. The raiders quickly seized the arsenal and a number of prisoners. A foray into the surrounding countryside brought in several more prisoners and ten slaves. The first casualty of the raid, ironically, was a free black townsman. Gunfire aroused the sleeping town, and soon church bells tolled the alarm of a slave insurrection, summoning farmers and militia from the neighborhood. By dawn, townsmen and rapidly assembling militias besieged the arsenal. Mysteriously, Brown made no effort to escape, perhaps waiting for the arrival of escaping slaves from the neighborhood; in fact, not a single slave responded to the raid. In the morning of Oct. 18, a detachment of U.S. marines arrived commanded by Col. Robert E. Lee. When Brown refused to surrender, the marines stormed and captured the arsenal. The raid cost 17 lives, ten of them Brown's men, including two of his sons. Seven raiders, including Brown, were captured; five other participants in the plot escaped.

Brown was tried for treason against the state of Virginia and sentenced to death. His calm and dignified bearing during the trial and at his hanging on Dec. 2 evoked the grudging admiration of Southerners and the reverence of Northerners. On his way to his execution, Brown handed a note to an attendant: "I John Brown am now quite certain that the crimes of this guilty land will never be purged away but with blood. I had as I now think vainly flattered myself that without very much bloodshed it might be done."

Brown's death unleashed an outpouring of grief in the North: tolling bells, minute-gun firings, memorial meetings, sermons, editorials, the production of pictures, books, and other mementos. The South, meanwhile, was gripped with hysterical dread of slave insurrections. The spectacle of the North mourning the death of a terrorist embittered Southerners and made the sectional division irreparable.

BROWNSVILLE AFFAIR (1906), incident in the Theodore *Roosevelt administration. Around midnight, Aug. 13, 1906, a gang of perhaps 20 armed men shot up the town of Brownsville, Tex., on the Rio Grande. One person was killed, another wounded. The identity of the gang was unknown, but suspicion and circumstantial evidence pointed to members of the all-black 25th Infantry Regiment that had recently been stationed at nearby Fort Brown. After an Army investigation (not a court-martial), President Roosevelt ordered three companies—a total of 167 men, including six winners of the Medal of Honor—discharged "without honor." Roosevelt was furious at critics of his decision, and was supported in 1908 by the Senate Military Affairs Committee and again in 1909 by a military court of inquiry. Nevertheless, 14 of the discharged men were allowed to reenlist. In 1972 all the discharges were changed to honorable.

BROWN 2. See *Brown v. Board of Education of Topeka.*

BROWN v. BOARD OF EDUCATION OF TOPEKA (1954), unanimous decision of the *Warren Court on May 17, 1954, applying to four school-segregation cases that racial segregation in the public schools was unconstitutional. In discarding the "separate but equal" doctrine of *Plessy v. Ferguson* (1896), the Court doomed all other forms of legal segregation.

"In approaching this problem," wrote Chief Justice Warren for the Court, "we cannot turn the clock back to 1868 when the [14th] Amendment was adopted, or even to 1896 when *Plessy* was written. We must consider pub-

lic education in the light of its full development and its present place in American life throughout the Nation. Only in this way can it be determined if segregation in public schools deprives these plaintiffs of the equal protection of the laws. Today, education is perhaps the most important function of state and local governments. Compulsory school attendance laws and the great expenditures for education both demonstrate our recognition of the importance of education to our democratic society. It is required in the performance of our most basic public responsibilities, even service in the armed forces. It is the very foundation of good citizenship. Today it is the principal instrument in awakening the child to cultural values, in preparing him for later professional training, and in helping him to adjust normally to his environment. In these days, it is doubtful that any child may reasonably be expected to succeed in life if he is denied the opportunity of an education. Such an opportunity, where the state has undertaken to provide it, is a right which must be made available to all on equal terms.

"We come to the question presented: Does segregation of children in public schools solely on the basis of race, even though the physical facilities and other 'tangible' factors may be equal, deprive the children of the minority group of equal educational opportunities? We believe that it does. . . . To separate [schoolchildren] from others of similar age and qualifications solely because of their race generates a feeling of inferiority as to their status in the community that may affect their hearts and minds in a way unlikely ever to be undone. The effect of this separation on their educational opportunities was well stated by a finding in the Kansas case by a court which nevertheless felt compelled to rule against the Negro plaintiffs: 'Segregation of white and colored children in public schools has a detrimental effect upon the colored children. The impact is greater when it has the sanction of the law; for the policy of separating the races is usually interpreted as denoting the inferiority of the negro group. A sense of inferiority affects the motivation of a child to learn. Segregation with the sanction of law, therefore, has a tendency to retard the educational and mental development of negro children and to deprive them of some of the benefits they would receive in a [racially] integrated school system.' Whatever may have been the extent of psychological knowledge at the time of *Plessy v. Ferguson*, this finding is amply supported by modern authority. Any language in *Plessy v. Ferguson* contrary to this finding is rejected.

"We conclude that in the field of public education the doctrine of 'separate but equal' has no place. Separate educational facilities are inherently unequal. . . ."

Warren tactfully refrained from offering guidelines for the implementation of this decision. Instead, the parties to *Brown* and the other cases were asked to argue the issue of implementation the following April. On May 31, 1955, Warren issued a second unanimous ruling, called **Brown 2**, that left the implementation of *school desegregation to local federal courts, which would be best informed as to local conditions and needs. However, Warren declared, ". . . the courts will require that the defendants make a prompt and reasonable start toward full compliance with our May 17, 1954, ruling. Once such a start has been made, the courts may find that additional time is necessary to carry out the ruling in an effective manner. The burden rests upon the defendants to establish that such time is necessary in the public interest and is consistent with good faith compliance at the earliest practicable date. . . . The . . . lower courts are to take such proceedings and enter such orders and decrees consistent with this opinion as are necessary and proper to admit to public schools on a racially nondiscriminatory basis with all deliberate speed the parties to these cases."

BRYAN'S "CROSS OF GOLD" SPEECH (July 8, 1896). The Democratic Party that assembled in Chicago in July 1896 was firmly in the hands of the *free silver forces. They had no outstanding presidential candidate, but their platform contained a plank demanding the unlimited coinage of silver along with gold. "We are unalterably opposed to monometallism which has locked fast the prosperity of an industrial people in the paralysis of hard times," the platform declared. "Gold monometallism is a British policy, and its adoption has brought other nations into financial servitude to London. It is not only un-American but anti-American. . . . We demand the free and unlimited coinage of both silver and gold at the present ratio of 16 to 1. . . ." The plank was a clear repudiation of Democratic president Grover Cleveland and the *Gold Democrats.

On July 8, four delegates debated the platform before the convention—two in favor, two against. The last speaker, in support of the platform, was William Jennings Bryan, a 36-year-old two-term congressman from Nebraska. By the time Bryan ascended the rostrum his audience was tired and restless. He seized its attention in a moment. "I come to speak to you," he said, "in defense of a cause as holy as the cause of liberty—the cause of humanity."

He recounted the struggle of the silver forces to win control of the party. "[O]ur silver Democrats went forth from victory to victory until they are now assembled, not to discuss, not to debate, but to enter up the judgment already rendered by the plain people of this country. . . . We do not come as aggressors. Our war is not a war of conquest; we are fighting in the defense of our homes, our families, and posterity. We have petitioned, and our petitions have been scorned; we have entreated, and our entreaties have been disregarded; we have begged, and they have mocked when our calamity came. We beg no longer; we entreat no more; we petition no more. We defy them! . . ."

"You [Gold Democrats] come to us," he went on, "and tell us that the great cities are in favor of the gold standard; we reply that the great cities rest upon our broad and fertile prairies. Burn down your cities and leave our farms, and your cities will spring up again as if by magic; but destroy our farms and the grass will grow in the streets of every city in the country."

By now, Bryan's audience rose and cheered at the end of every sentence, then fell silent to await the next. At last his memorable peroration: "Having behind us the producing masses of this nation and the world, supported by the commercial interests, the laboring interests and the toilers everywhere, we will answer their demand for a gold standard by saying to them: You shall not press down upon the brow of labor this crown of thorns, you shall not crucify mankind upon a cross of gold."

For a moment Bryan stretched out his arms at his sides, then let them fall and stepped back. Stunned silence was followed by bedlam. "Bryan! Bryan! Bryan!" the crowd roared in a demonstration that lasted half an hour. The next day Bryan was nominated for president on the fifth ballot.

BUCHANAN ADMINISTRATION (1857–61). Democrat James Buchanan, 15th president of the United States, was immediately confronted by the Dred Scott decision (see *Scott v. Sandford*), which he accepted, and the problem of *"Bleeding Kansas," which he proposed to resolve by *popular sovereignty. A new governor of Kansas Territory held an election for a state constitutional convention that was boycotted by free-state forces; the result was the proslavery Lecompton constitution. Influenced by Southern members of his cabinet, Buchanan recommended the Lecompton constitution to Congress. Under the leadership of Sen. Stephen A. Douglas, Congress rejected it but sent it back to Kansas for reconsideration, where it was overwhelmingly rejected (August 1858). Kansas finally entered the Union as a free state in January 1861.

The *Mormon War (1857–58) established the appearance (if not the reality) of federal authority in Utah Territory. But the Lecompton issue and the *Panic of 1857 weakened the administration, and the Congress that met in 1859 was controlled by Republicans and Douglas Democrats. It frustrated Buchanan's attempts to annex Cuba and to assume a protective role in Mexico, which it believed were dictated by the South.

The Harpers Ferry raid (October 1859; see *Brown's Career) alarmed the South, and the election of Abraham Lincoln in November 1860 precipitated the *secession crisis. South Carolina seceded in December 1860, and six other states of the Deep South followed in January and February 1861. A paralyzed Congress looked for compromises (see *Crittenden Compromise). Buchanan, who believed he had no constitutional authority to compel a state to remain in the Union, blamed the situation on Northern hostility to slavery and proposed a constitutional convention. The Southern members of his cabinet soon resigned. In February 1861 the seceded states formed the *Confederate States of America and elected Jefferson Davis provisional president.

After South Carolina shore batteries drove back (Jan. 9, 1861) a ship carrying reinforcements to the isolated federal garrison at Fort Sumter in Charleston harbor, Buchanan did nothing further to relieve the fort and avoided any confrontation with the South that might precipitate war. He was succeeded by Republican Abraham Lincoln.

During the Buchanan administration, Minnesota (1858), Oregon (1859), and Kansas (1861) became the 32nd, 33rd, and 34th states.

BUCKLEY v. VALEO (1976), per curiam (unsigned) decision by the *Burger Court in which different majorities ruled on different provisions of the Federal Election Campaign Act of 1971 (see *Campaign Financing). Most important, the Court declared unconstitutional the act's limits on campaign spending, ruling that campaign spending was a form of political expression protected by the Free Speech Clause of the First Amendment. It also rejected ceilings on the amount a candidate or a candidate's family could spend on a campaign. On the other hand, the Court upheld the constitutionality of limits on contributions to a candidate's campaign from nonfamily sources (while permitting unlimited contributions to "independent" committees working on behalf of the candidate—so-called soft money), and it upheld the act's disclosure requirements as well. The Court made a significant exception to its rejection of limits on campaign spending: such limits were permissible, the Court declared, if the candidate voluntarily accepted them as a condition of receiving public campaign subsidies. The Court upheld the act's provisions for public funding of presidential campaigns.

BUENA VISTA (Feb. 22–23, 1847), *Mexican War battle. Late in 1846 Mexican general Antonio López de Santa Anna gathered an army of 20,000 men at San Luis Potosí to attack the American army of Gen. Zachary Taylor, who was moving south from Monterrey. In January 1847 Santa Anna learned that Taylor had been compelled to detach 9,000 troops for the Vera Cruz campaign. Confident of victory, Santa Anna marched his army across 300 miles of desert and mountains, losing 5,000 men along the way.

When Taylor discovered the Mexicans' approach south of Saltillo, he withdrew to the Angostura, a narrow valley six miles south of Saltillo near the Hacienda de Buena Vista. He had an excellent defensive position, but fewer than 5,000 troops (only 700 of them combat veterans) and 18 artillery pieces. Late in the afternoon of Feb. 23, Santa Anna threw his exhausted army into the attack. A cold, windy night intervened. The next day, despite the effectiveness of the American artillery, the Mexicans pushed the Americans back, drove several volunteer units into flight, and seized important high ground. By nightfall, Taylor's situation was desperate. He had suffered 673 casualties and lost 1,500 deserters. But additional men and supplies came from Saltillo, and Taylor prepared to fight a third day.

At dawn, however, the Americans discovered that Santa Anna had abandoned the field. He had suffered 2,100 casualties, and would lose several thousand more on the road back to San Luis Potosí.

BULGE, BATTLE OF THE. See *World War 2.

BULL MOOSE PARTY. See *Progressive Party or Bull Moose Party.

BULL RUN or **MANASSAS, FIRST** (July 21, 1861), first major engagement of the *Civil War. Ordered to seize Manassas, a rail junction in northern Virginia some 25 miles from Washington, Union general Irvin McDowell departed from Alexandria on July 16 with 30,000 raw troops. At a small stream called Bull Run a few miles north of Manassas he encountered a Confederate force of 20,000, commanded by generals Pierre G. T. Beauregard and Joseph E. Johnston, similarly green but entrenched on an eight-mile front on the south side of the stream. McDowell attacked at dawn, drove the Confederates back, and by afternoon appeared to be on the verge of victory. But the steady resistance of the Confederates under leaders like Gen. Thomas J. Jackson (who here won the sobriquet "Stonewall") and the timely arrival of 10,000 reinforcements turned the tide. An orderly Federal retreat dissolved into flight, the demoralized troops—who were not being pursued—pouring into Washington in a state of panic. A blow to Northern morale and a boost to Southern, the battle had no strategic consequence.

BULL RUN or **MANASSAS, SECOND** (Aug. 29–30, 1862), *Civil War battle. After the failure of the *Peninsula Campaign, the center of the war in the East shifted to the Rappahannock River between Washington and Richmond. Union general John Pope, successful in the West, was given command of a new Army of Virginia with orders to take Richmond by the direct overland route. Gen. George B. McClellan was ordered to bring his Army of the Potomac north from the Peninsula to join Pope. Lee, too, shifted his troops from the Peninsula, determined to strike at Pope before the full Union force assembled.

On Aug. 9, Confederate general Thomas J. "Stonewall" Jackson defeated two of Pope's divisions at Cedar Mountain, then outflanked Pope's main force and destroyed (Aug. 26) the Union supply depot at Manassas in Pope's rear. When Pope caught up with Jackson, entrenched near the old Bull Run battlefield, he attacked prematurely, counting on the arrival of reinforcements. These never came, in part perhaps because of the personal animosity of their commanders toward Pope. On the other hand, Jackson received timely aid from Confederate general James Longstreet. After two days of desperate and costly fighting, Pope pulled back to the defenses of Washington, warding off a Confederate attack along the way at Chantilly (Sept. 1).

BUNKER HILL (June 17, 1775), *Revolutionary War battle. To forestall a British move to occupy Dorchester Heights south of Boston, the Patriot army of New England militia besieging Boston (see *Boston Siege) occupied Charlestown Peninsula north of the city across the Charles River. The peninsula, stretching one and a quarter miles west to east between the Mystic and Charles rivers, was connected to the mainland by the narrow Charlestown Neck. Its high ground—Bunker Hill and Breed's Hill—overlooked Boston.

On the night of June 16–17, Massachusetts and Connecticut militia under Col. William Prescott built a redoubt on Breed's Hill, the more easterly of the two hills, with supporting breastworks and a reinforced rail and stone fence extending north to the Mystic River. In the morning of June 17 British warships in Boston harbor began to bombard the Patriot position. In the afternoon, 2,200 British troops under Gen. William Howe landed at the eastern end of the peninsula. Howe divided this force into two wings, one to attack the fortified fence, the other the redoubt. He himself would lead an elite force of light infantry up the beach along the Mystic River to turn the Patriot line, confident that a bayonet charge by massed regulars would rout the undisciplined Patriots.

When the assault began, Howe's force was halted by the devastating fire of Col. John Stark's New Hampshire militia at the extreme end of the Patriot line. At the same time, the two principal wings of the British force, carrying full packs over uneven ground, were met by the massed fire of the Patriots along the fence and in the redoubt, who obeyed Prescott's order: "Don't fire until you see the whites of their eyes." Twice they were driven back with heavy casualties.

By this time, however, the Americans were exhausted and out of ammunition. A third British assault swept the Patriots from the fence and breastworks and poured into the redoubt, where the British and Americans fought hand to hand. The Americans withdrew over Bunker Hill and across Charlestown Neck, the British halting on the reverse slope of the hill, unable to continue the pursuit.

British casualties exceeded 1,000 dead and wounded, a disproportionate number of them officers—a loss "greater than we can bear," the British commander in chief, Gen. Thomas Gage, reported to London. Howe, who had been in the thick of the action, was unscratched. American losses, suffered chiefly at the redoubt, were 140 dead, 271 wounded. The excited Americans considered the battle a moral victory, deriving from it an unjustified confidence in militias.

BUNTING v. OREGON (1917), 5–3 decision of the *White Court upholding an Oregon maximum-hours law in manufacturing establishments on the ground of workers' health. Harvard law professor Felix Frankfurter defended the law with a massive "Brandeis brief" documenting how long hours were detrimental to workers' health.

BURGER COURT (1969–86), the U.S. Supreme Court under Chief Justice Warren Burger. Pres. Richard Nixon's appointment of Burger as chief justice in 1969 was interpreted as marking the end of the liberal activism that had distinguished the *Warren Court. But rather than reverse direction, the Burger Court for the most part preserved and consolidated the achievements of the Warren Court.

The Court sharply checked the pretensions of Nixon's *imperial presidency when, in *New York Times Co. v. United States (1971), it rejected the administration's attempt to stop publication of the *Pentagon Papers and, in *United States v. Nixon (1974), it rejected the president's claim of executive privilege in refusing to surrender subpoenaed tapes.

In the area of *school desegregation, the Court ended the "all deliberate speed" formula of Brown 2 (see *Brown v. Board of Education of Topeka) and insisted on prompt desegregation. In *Swann v. Charlotte-Mecklenburg Board of Education (1971) it upheld the authority of federal judges to order far-reaching remedies, including massive busing, to undo school segregation, although in *Milliken v. Bradley (1974) it limited those remedies to the districts actually guilty of segregation.

The Court upheld the Free Exercise Clause (see *Church-State Relations) in *Wisconsin v. Yoder (1972) and was consistently supportive of *affirmative action.

In the area of criminal procedure, where the Warren Court had most seriously offended "law and order" conservatives by expanding the protections of criminal-law defendants, the Burger Court (with some minor restrictions) preserved rather than reversed the landmark Warren Court decisions. In Furman v. Georgia (1972), the Court declared unconstitutional *capital punishment as then conducted.

In *Buckley v. Valeo (1976) the Court ruled that campaign spending was a form of political expression protected by the First Amendment. Its most controversial decision was *Roe v. Wade (1973), finding *abortion constitutionally protected.

BURLINGAME TREATY (1868), diplomatic accord of the Andrew *Johnson administration, negotiated by Anson Burlingame, U.S. minister to China but now acting as the representative of the Chinese emperor, and Secretary of State William H. Seward. An addendum of the Treaty of *Tientsin (1858), it provided for various consular and travel arrangements and established free immigration between the two countries, in particular guaranteeing the unrestricted immigration of Chinese laborers, then in great demand by Western mine owners and railroad builders (see *Chinese Exclusion).

BURR CONSPIRACY (1805–7), plot of uncertain objective attributed to former vice president Aaron Burr. With his political career in ruins after his murder of Alexander Hamilton on July 11, 1804 (see *Burr-Hamilton Duel), restless, unstable Burr—perhaps influenced by the example of Napoleon Bonaparte—probably conceived a scheme to carve out from Spanish Mexico an independent western empire for himself. His project may have included separating some western territories from the United States.

Even before the end of his term as vice president in 1805, Burr had unsuccessfully sought British support for some western scheme from the British minister in Washington. After leaving the vice presidency, he traveled through the West as far as New Orleans, arousing speculation and rumor. He enlisted as a partner James Wilkinson, commanding general of the U.S. Army and governor of Upper Louisiana, a consummate intriguer who even then was in Spanish pay. By October 1806 Burr's plan was in motion. Armed men and supplies were moving down the Ohio and Mississippi rivers toward a rendezvous at Natchez. At this point, Wilkinson informed Pres. Thomas Jefferson of a mysterious expedition aimed at New Orleans and Veracruz, Mexico. On Nov. 27 Jefferson issued a proclamation alerting civil and military authorities to the existence of a conspiracy. In a message to Congress on Jan. 22, 1807, he named Burr as its leader, asserting that Burr's "guilt is placed beyond question." Burr surrendered to authorities in Mississippi Territory, then escaped and was captured on Feb. 19.

In Richmond, Va., in June a grand jury indicted Burr (but not Wilkinson) for treason. Trial was held in the federal circuit court in August with Chief Justice John Marshall presiding. Since Burr had been arrested before committing any overt act of treason, the prosecution based its case on the assembling of men with treasonable purposes at Blennerhassett's Island in the Ohio River in December 1806. Burr, however, had not himself been present, and Marshall ruled that the gathering did not therefore constitute proof of Burr's treason. The jury then found Burr not guilty. Jefferson was furious at the verdict, which he attributed to the political malevolence of the Federalist chief justice.

BURR-HAMILTON DUEL (July 11, 1804). The professional rivalry between Aaron Burr and Alexander Hamilton as lawyers in New York City continued into politics, Hamilton becoming leader of the *Federalist Party and Burr achieving prominence as a Republican politician in New York (see *Jeffersonian Republican Party).

Critical of Burr's public and private character, Hamilton opposed his election to the U.S. Senate in 1796 and threw his influence in the House of Representatives against him in the presidential election of 1800. Denied renomination as vice president by the Republicans in 1804, Burr ran for governor of New York with the support of Federalists who plotted to take New York and New England out of the Union. Burr lost to the official Republican candidate, who was backed by Hamilton. The campaign was bitter, and Burr blamed Hamilton for his defeat, citing in particular Hamilton's alleged statement that Burr was "a dangerous man and ought not to be trusted with the reins of government." Burr demanded an explanation, Hamilton was evasive, and Burr challenged him to a duel.

They met on the morning of July 11, 1804, at Weehawken, N.J. Hamilton fired into the air, but Burr aimed to kill. His bullet passed through Hamilton's liver and lodged in his spine. Hamilton died the next day. Indicted in both New Jersey and New York, Burr fled to Philadelphia, then traveled south, embarking upon the mysterious *Burr conspiracy.

BUSH (GEORGE H. W.) ADMINISTRATION

(1989–93). Republican George H. W. Bush, 41st president of the United States, inherited from his predecessor, Ronald Reagan, the unresolved *savings and loan crisis. An S&L bailout act provided $166 billion in federal and banking industry funds to meet the obligations— seriously underestimated—of the failed thrifts and the industry was reregulated. A significant piece of legislation was the *Americans with Disabilities Act (1990).

Budget negotiations with the Democratic-controlled Congress compelled Bush to agree to tax hikes aimed at the wealthy and middle class. This violation of his campaign pledge—"Read my lips: No new taxes"—infuriated Republican conservatives (never happy with Bush anyway), and in 1990 Bush apologized for his "mistake." Sluggish in 1989, the economy slipped into a full-fledged recession in 1990 that persisted for the remainder of the Bush administration.

Preoccupied by foreign affairs, Bush did little about the recession. His administration witnessed the collapse of communism in Europe and the dissolution of the Soviet Union. In 1989 U.S. forces invaded Panama and captured Gen. Manuel Antonio Noriega, indicted in the United States on charges of drug trafficking (see *Panama Invasion). In February 1990 a coalition of anti-Sandinista parties defeated the left-wing government of Nicaragua at the polls, ending a perceived threat to the United States in Central America. In December 1992 the United States joined a multinational military force to bring order and famine relief to Somalia (see *Somalia Intervention). When Iraq invaded Kuwait in August 1990, Bush's response was the *Gulf War.

The victory raised Bush's popularity to record heights, but the absence of a satisfactory closure to the war and his continued indifference to the ailing economy at home soon brought it down. In November 1992 Bush was defeated for reelection by a little-known former Democratic governor of Arkansas, William J. Clinton, who had correctly perceived "It's the economy, stupid."

BUSH (GEORGE W.) ADMINISTRATION

(2001–   ). Republican George W. Bush, 43rd president of the United States, campaigned as a "compassionate conservative." In office, he proved obedient to his party's right wing, rewarding it with a regressive tax cut, return of the Treasury surplus to taxpayers, and probusiness policies in domestic affairs and unilateralism in foreign affairs. The Treasury surplus was replaced by growing deficits, caused in part by a recession that began in March 2001 and from which recovery was sluggish. A wave of corporate scandals (see *Enron Bankruptcy; *Corporate Responsibility Act) touched several members of his administration, which was conspicuously filled with former corporate executives. When terrorists attacked New York and Washington on Sept. 11, 2001, Bush declared war on *terrorism (see *Terrorism War). U.S. success in Afghanistan raised his popularity to record levels. In November 2002, Republicans won control of both houses of Congress.

BUSH DOCTRINE

(2002), comprehensive state-ment of U.S. foreign policy issued by the George W. *Bush administration in September 2002. Entitled "The National Security Strategy of the United States," it dealt largely with the problems presented by international *terrorism. It rejected as obsolete the doctrines of *containment and deterrence in favor of proactive and preemptive policies aimed to "disrupt and destroy terrorist organizations."

"Our immediate focus will be those terrorist organizations of global reach and any terrorist or state sponsor of terrorism which attempts to gain or use weapons of mass destruction. . . ." The United States will defend itself by "identifying and destroying the threat before it reaches our borders. While the United States will constantly strive to enlist the support of the international community, we will not hesitate to act alone, if necessary. . . ." To that end, "The United States must and will maintain the capability to defeat an attempt by an enemy—whether a state or a nonstate actor—to impose its will on the United States, our allies, or our friends."

The document noted the division of the world between affluent and poor nations. It recognized as a "moral imperative" and top priority the need to include all the world's poor "in an expanding circle of development and opportunity." It promised U.S. aid to those countries that met "the challenge of national reform," meaning establishment of the rule of law, intolerance of corruption, and the institution of free-market economies.

BUSH v. GORE (2000), 5–4 decision of the *Rehnquist Court ending the recount of Florida votes in the 2000 presidential election, thereby awarding the election to Republican candidate George W. Bush.

Bush appealed a decision of the Florida supreme court, which, in response to a Democratic challenge to the vote count in Florida, had ordered a statewide manual recount of "undervotes," ballots that machines had read as indicating no presidential choice. The intervention of the U.S. Supreme Court surprised many observers, since the Rehnquist Court had labored for years to revive the doctrine of state sovereignty. But on Dec. 4, 2000, in response to the Bush appeal, the Supreme Court overruled the Florida court and ordered the recounting stopped.

On Dec. 12 the Court ruled that, in the absence of a statewide standard for reading the variety of ballots involved, the recount denied some voters the equal protection of the laws guaranteed by the 14th Amendment. It ordered the Florida supreme court to formulate such a standard—but then observed that it was already too late to do so since a Dec. 10 deadline for counting votes (instituted by an 1887 federal election law to permit the certification of electors on Dec. 12) had passed, although the *electoral college would not convene until Dec. 18. Confronted by a conflict between the constitutionally guaranteed right to vote and a statutory deadline for counting votes, the Court in effect ruled in favor of the technicality rather than the principle.

The decision was widely regarded as partisan, even by some of the justices. "Although we may never know with complete certainty the identity of the winner of this year's presidential election," Justice John Paul Stevens wrote in his dissent, "the identity of the loser is perfectly clear. It is the nation's confidence in the judge as an impartial guardian of the rule of law."

BUSING. See *School Desegregation; *Boston Busing.

C

CABINET, advisory body to the president consisting of the heads of executive departments together with other federal officials accorded cabinet rank. Unmentioned in the Constitution, the cabinet was initiated by Pres. George Washington. It has no authority and has been consulted by presidents to widely varying extents.

The number of executive departments grew from four in Washington's time to 15 in the George W. Bush administration: Agriculture, Commerce, Defense, Education, Energy, Health and Human Services, Homeland Security, Housing and Urban Development, Interior, Justice, Labor, State, Transportation, Treasury, and Veterans Affairs. In 1947, Congress made department heads successors to the presidency—in the absence of a president and a vice president and after the Speaker of the House and president pro tem of the Senate—in order of the creation of their departments (see *Presidential Succession).

Six other federal officials had cabinet rank in the George W. Bush administration: the vice president, the White House chief of staff, the administrator of the Environmental Protection Agency, the director of the Office of Management and Budget, the director of the Office of National Drug Control Policy, and the U.S. trade representative.

CAIRO CONFERENCES (1943). See *World War 2 Conferences.

CALHOUN AND JACKSON. See *Jackson and Calhoun.

CALIFORNIA TRAIL, overland route of migrants from Missouri to California. It was identical to the *Oregon Trail as far as Fort Hall, where migrants bound for California turned south, crossed Nevada and the Sierra Nevada, and continued to Sacramento and San Francisco (see *Donner Party).

CAMBODIA INCURSION. See *Vietnam War.

CAMDEN (Aug. 16, 1780), *Revolutionary War battle. After Patriot general Benjamin Lincoln's surrender of Charleston, S.C., Congress—without consulting Washington—appointed Gen. Horatio Gates, the hero of *Saratoga, to command the Southern Department. At Coxe's Mill, N.C., on July 25, Gates took command of 1,400 hungry and poorly equipped troops. He immediately ordered them on the road, through swampy and sandy country rife with hostile Loyalists, toward Camden, S.C., picking up reinforcements along the way. On the night of Aug. 15, Gates's army, making its way through a pine forest, encountered a British force commanded by Gen. Charles Cornwallis that was advancing from Camden to intercept it. At dawn, the experienced British troops routed the Americans, who fled north in panic toward North Carolina. Gates himself managed to reach Charlotte, 60 miles from the battlefield, by day's end. Cornwallis now controlled Georgia and South Carolina and prepared to invade North Carolina.

CAMELOT. See *Kennedy Administration.

CAMPAIGN FINANCING. The need for money to contest local, state, and national elections was recognized from the very beginning of the republic. It was natural for banks, business corporations, and wealthy individuals to support candidates sympathetic to their interests. Legislatures soon contained men who were recognized as the representatives of certain economic interests rather than those of the voters who elected them. With the introduction of the *spoils system, government employees were assessed a small percentage of their salaries to help pay for their parties' activities. The corruption inherent in private campaign financing became scandalous. Entire states were "owned" by railroads or manufacturers. Yet reform proved difficult, since the existing system always benefited incumbents. Following is a chronology of federal campaign financing reform legislation:

1883   The Pendleton Act banned the solicitation of political contributions from federal employees.

1907   The Tillman Act prohibited contributions to federal election campaigns by corporations and national banks.

1910   The Corrupt Practices Act required candidates for federal offices to disclose the sources of their campaign funds. 1911 amendments placed a ceiling of $5,000 on spending for House elections, $10,000 for Senate elections.

1921   In *Newberry v. United States* the U.S. Supreme Court ruled that spending limits imposed in 1911 did not apply to primaries, which were not essential parts of elections.

1925   The Corrupt Practices Act required that candidates and their committees file quarterly reports of receipts and expenditures.

1939   The *Hatch Act forbade political activities, including fund-raising, by federal employees. Amendments extended the act to state employees whose salaries came from federal funds. The act also limited individual contributions to $5,000 and party committee expenditures to $3 million in presidential elections.

1947   The *Taft-Hartley Act prohibited unions from contributing to national political organizations. The Congress of Industrial Organizations responded by creating the first *political action committee, the CIO–PAC, independent of the union.

1971   The Federal Election Campaign Act required candidates for federal office to disclose all campaign contributions over $100 and all campaign expenditures over $1,000. Taxpayers could indicate by checking a box on their income tax returns whether they consented to have $1 of their taxes transferred to a federal election fund to subsidize presidential election campaigns.

1974   The Campaign Finance Law required annual financial disclosure reports by all members of Congress and by candidates. Further, for each election (primary, runoff, general), it placed a ceiling of $1,000 on individual contributions to candidates and of $5,000 on contributions by PACs. It also placed ceilings on candidates' total and personal expenditures in primary and general elections. Oversight of federal elections was assigned to a bipartisan Federal Election Commission (FEC).

1976   In *Buckley v. Valeo*, the U.S. Supreme Court upheld the 1974 limits on *contributions* to federal candidates but ruled that limits on expenditures by candidates were unconstitutional, expenditures being a form of political expression protected by the First Amendment.

1976   The first presidential election campaign subsidized by public funds. Both Republican and Democratic candidates accepted public funding and expenditure limits.

1985   In *Federal Election Commission v. National Conservative Political Action Committee*, the U.S. Supreme Court ruled that Congress could not limit independent spending by PACs in presidential election campaigns as it did in the 1974 Campaign Finance Law.

1996   Both Democratic and Republican parties raised unprecedented amounts of "soft money"—contributions ostensibly to political parties but frequently diverted to the campaigns of individual candidates—from corporations, unions, and wealthy individuals, including foreigners.

1997   The McCain-Feingold Bill proposed to ban soft money, provide free or discounted television advertising and postage for candidates who adhere to voluntary spending limits, reduce ceilings on PAC contributions. Although much modified, the bill was blocked in Congress in 1997, 1998, 1999, and 2001.

2001   In *Federal Election Commission v. Colorado Republican Federal Campaign Committee*, the U.S. Supreme Court upheld 5–4 restrictions on "coordinated spending" established in 1974 under which contributors were limited in the amount of money they could give to a party to be spent on a particular candidate's campaign.

2002   The McCain-Feingold Act prohibited national political parties from accepting "soft money"—large, unlimited contributions from corporations, unions, and individuals. It raised the amount of "hard money" that individuals could contribute directly to federal candidates from $1,000 to $2,000.

CAMP DAVID ACCORDS (1978), diplomatic achievement of the *Carter administration. The historic flight of Egyptian president Anwar Sadat to Jerusalem in November 1977 revived the Middle East peace process, frozen since 1973. Meetings between Israeli and Egyptian representatives followed. From Sept. 6 to Sept. 17, 1978, Pres. James E. Carter met with Sadat and Israeli prime minister Menachem Begin at Camp David, the presidential retreat in Maryland, and hammered out frameworks for peace between Israel and Egypt and for the Middle East.

When the promised Israeli-Egyptian peace treaty missed its Dec. 17 deadline, a crisis ensued. Carter traveled to the Middle East and shuttled between Cairo and Jerusalem, promising both countries substantial foreign aid and finally announcing agreement on peace terms in Cairo on Mar. 13. An Israeli-Egyptian peace treaty was signed on Mar. 26, 1979, on the White House lawn. No other Middle East states participated, and Egypt became a pariah in the Arab world. Sadat was assassinated in 1981.

CANADIAN RECIPROCITY (1911), failed initiative of the *Taft administration. After passage of the *Payne-Aldrich Tariff, Pres. William H. Taft, with uncharacteristic energy, pursued an agreement with Canada removing tariff barriers on both sides of the border. Despite opposition from wheat farmers and industrialists, Congress approved the agreement. But statements by Taft himself, Democratic Speaker of the House Champ Clark, and newspaper publisher William Randolph Hearst suggesting that reciprocity was a step toward U.S. annexation of Canada offended Canadians, who in a national plebiscite in September 1911 rejected the treaty.

CANALS. Enthusiasm for canal building in America was stimulated by the English example and by the greater ease of transporting bulky agricultural goods over water than over existing roads. The first American canals, serving coal mines and quarries or improving existing trade routes, were privately financed. Thus the Middlesex Canal in Massachusetts, built 1793–1804, connected Boston with the Merrimac River; the Santee and Cooper Canal in South Carolina, built in the 1790s, connected these two rivers near Charleston; the Delaware and Raritan Canal connected Philadelphia and New York.

The great period of canal building was inspired by the idea of connecting the Atlantic tidewater with the western upcountry and the growing settlements across the Appalachian Mountains. The first and most successful, the *Erie Canal, was built by New York State in 1817–25 to connect the Hudson River and Lake Erie. It opened

western New York to settlement and ultimately funneled a portion of the trade of the Ohio River Valley through New York City. It had the advantages over other westward-extending canals of the most favorable terrain (keeping costs down) and the earliest start (avoiding early competition with the railroads).

To compete with the Erie Canal, Pennsylvania built (1826–34) its Mainline Canal between Philadelphia and Pittsburgh, combining a canal with 174 locks with railways to cross the Appalachians. It succumbed to competition from the railroads.

With contributions from Maryland, Virginia, and the federal government, the Chesapeake & Ohio Canal Co. began construction in 1828 along the Potomac River toward Cumberland, Md., its ultimate objective being the Ohio River. Construction was slow and costly; the canal did not reach Cumberland until 1850, at which time competition from the Baltimore & Ohio Railroad put an end to further construction.

In Virginia, the James River & Kanawha Canal extending west from Richmond never reached its goal at Buchanan across the mountains in western Virginia.

Meanwhile, the states in the Ohio Valley embarked optimistically on major canal projects. Ohio built two north–south canals to take advantage of the Erie Canal's connection with the East Coast: the Ohio & Erie Canal (completed 1833) crossed the eastern part of the state from Portsmouth on the Ohio River to Cleveland on Lake Erie; the Miami & Erie (completed 1845) connected Cincinnati and Dayton with Toledo on the lake.

In Indiana, construction of the Wabash & Erie Canal connecting Evansville, Ind., on the Ohio River with Lake Erie began in 1832 and was completed in 1853. In Illinois, the Illinois & Michigan Canal, connecting Lake Michigan at Chicago with the Illinois River, a tributary of the Mississippi, was built 1836–48.

State canal systems were financed in various ways, including land grants from the federal government and loans from foreign (mostly British) investors. The *Panic of 1837 halted or delayed most construction, while competition from steamboats and railroads soon rendered most of them obsolete.

CANNONISM (1903–10), dictatorial rule of the U.S. House of Representatives by Joseph G. Cannon, Republican of Indiana, member of the House (except for two terms) 1873–1923, Speaker 1903–11. His rule rested on his power to appoint the members of the Rules Committee, which determined what legislation would reach the floor of the House, and to recognize speakers on the floor. A coarse and reactionary politician, he used his power in the interests of the Republican Old Guard. Progressives in the House looked to President Taft for support against Cannon but Taft, always quick to avoid conflict, disappointed them. On Mar. 17, 1910, Rep. George Norris of Nebraska, a progressive Republican, slipped a resolution into House proceedings making members of the Rules Committee elective and excluding the Speaker from membership. Supported by all the Democrats and 30 Republicans, the resolution carried on Mar. 19. Stripped of his powers, Cannon was permitted to remain as Speaker.

CANTIGNY. See *World War 1.

CAPITAL PUNISHMENT. In the United States, most capital offenses have been defined and punished by the states. These offenses have varied over the years in number and kind. Capital offenses under federal law are quite different, reflecting national concerns.

The Colonial Period. The American colonies had no uniform criminal code. In 1636 the Puritans of the Massachusetts Bay Colony defined the following offenses as capital crimes: idolatry, witchcraft, blasphemy, murder, assault, sodomy, adultery, statutory rape, rape, manstealing, perjury in a capital trial, and rebellion. Each statute was sanctioned by an Old Testament text. How rigorously these laws were enforced is unknown, but during the 17th century Massachusetts executed four Quakers and 20 alleged witches, among other offenders. In Pennsylvania, by contrast, William Penn's Great Act of 1682 limited the death penalty to premeditated murder.

In the 18th century, the colonies adopted sterner criminal codes closer to the English model. By the time of the Revolution, most of the colonies treated murder, treason, piracy, arson, rape, robbery, sodomy, and sometimes counterfeiting, horse-theft, and slave rebellion as capital crimes.

Abolition and Reform. In 1845, during a period of vigorous humanitarian reform, an American Society for the Abolition of Capital Punishment was founded. Throughout the country, antigallows groups petitioned state legislatures to abolish the death penalty, as Pennsylvania had in 1794 except for first-degree murder. There were waves of abolition during the 1840s and 1850s, after the Civil War, during the Progressive Era, and again in the 1950s and 1960s, although many states that abolished capital punishment eventually restored it. All of these abolitions were achieved by legislative action. In 1972 the supreme courts of California and New Jersey ended capital punishment in those states.

Reform of the administration of capital punishment

proved easier to achieve and more permanent than abolition. In fact, the success of reform efforts probably blunted the drive for abolition. The reform movement, lasting from the start of the 19th century to the middle of the 20th, succeeded in ending public executions, transferring executions from local to state authorities, instituting more efficient and humane methods of execution, limiting the death penalty to murder in the first degree, and substituting discretionary for mandatory death sentences.

The Judicial Attack. Failing to achieve statutory abolition of capital punishment, and dissatisfied with mere reform of its administration, opponents of the death penalty turned to the courts, first to secure defendants' rights, then to launch a direct attack on the constitutionality of capital punishment. In 1932, the U.S. Supreme Court ruled that counsel had to be provided for capital defendants. In 1947 the Court prohibited racial discrimination in jury selection, and in 1957 it barred coerced confessions.

In the 1960s, the Legal Defense and Educational Fund of the National Association for the Advancement of Colored People (NAACP) undertook a systematic attack on capital punishment on the grounds of racial and economic discrimination in its application. It was well known that only about 1 percent of all homicides (10–15 percent of capital homicides) resulted in executions. Researchers found that disproportionate numbers of blacks received the death penalty. Of the 3,859 persons executed under civil authority (by the states and federal government) between 1930 and 1967, 53.5 percent were black although blacks constituted only 12 percent of the population. Blacks constituted 48.9 percent of the 3,334 persons executed for murder, 89.0 percent of the 455 executed for rape. (There were 70 other executions in 1930–67 for armed robbery, kidnapping, burglary, espionage, and aggravated assault; 44.3 percent were of blacks.) The majority of state executions—60.3 percent—occurred in the 16 Southern states and the District of Columbia. Blacks constituted 71.9 percent of all persons executed in the Southern states, 35.7 percent in the North Central states, 29.1 percent in the Northeastern states, and 16.3 percent in the Western states.

NAACP class-action suits based on the Due Process and Equal Protection clauses of the 14th Amendment succeeded in blocking executions in Florida and California in 1967. Other states thereupon suspended executions until the Supreme Court could rule on the issue. From 1968 to 1977, there were no executions in the United States.

Furman v. Georgia. On June 29, 1972, the U.S. Supreme Court handed down a decision in three capital cases—*Furman v. Georgia, Jackson v. Georgia,* and

Branch v. Texas—involving two rapists and a murderer. All three defendants had been sentenced to death under state statutes that authorized juries to impose the death penalty at their discretion. In their appeals, the NAACP lawyers had argued that these sentences were cruel and unusual because of the rare, arbitrary, and discriminatory way in which the death penalty was imposed.

The Court, split 5–4, issued a brief per curiam opinion: "The Court holds that the imposition and carrying out of the death penalty in these cases constitutes cruel and unusual punishment in violation of the Eighth and Fourteenth Amendments." All nine justices filed separate opinions. The consensus of the five concurring justices was not that capital punishment was unconstitutional in itself but that it had become unconstitutional as a result of the arbitrary way it was imposed by juries exercising discretionary authority to decide between death and imprisonment.

"These discretionary statutes," wrote Justice William O. Douglas, "are unconstitutional in their operation. They are pregnant with discrimination, and discrimination is an ingredient not compatible with the idea of equal protection of the laws that is implicit in the ban on 'cruel and unusual punishments.'" Justice Potter Stewart concurred: "The petitioners are among a capriciously selected random handful upon whom the sentence of death has in fact been imposed. . . . [T]he Eighth and Fourteenth Amendments cannot tolerate the infliction of a sentence of death under legal systems that permit this unique penalty to be so wantonly and freakishly imposed."

After *Furman*. In the years immediately following the *Furman* decision, 35 states passed new capital punishment laws to satisfy the constitutional test suggested by the Supreme Court. Death sentences—now for murder only—were rapidly meted out under the new laws, but no executions were performed until the Supreme Court could consider the issue again. In 1976 NAACP lawyers brought to the Court cases challenging death sentences imposed in murder convictions in Georgia, Florida, Texas, Louisiana, and North Carolina. The Court upheld (7–2) the Georgia, Florida, and Texas statutes and nullified (5–4) those of Louisiana and North Carolina.

The Georgia, Florida, and Texas statutes, the Court found, met the requirements of the *Furman* decision by instituting procedures that eliminated the arbitrariness and caprice that the Court had objected to in 1972. In all three states, the statutes required two trials, one to determine guilt and another to determine the sentence. For the latter trial, guidelines ensured that the jury would weigh both aggravating and mitigating circumstances. Finally, an automatic review by the state supreme court was pro-

vided for. On the other hand, the Louisiana and North Carolina statutes simply imposed mandatory death sentences for first-degree murder, allowing the jury to convict or acquit but not to choose a lesser punishment as more appropriate in view of the defendant's character and record and the particular circumstances of the crime. The Court required that state capital punishment laws provide "objective standards" to guide, regularize, and make rationally reviewable the process for imposing a sentence of death.

The Court's 1976 decision cleared the way for the resumption of executions, at least in the three states whose capital punishment laws had been specifically approved. The first execution since 1967 occurred in 1977 in Utah. By 2002, 783 executions (273 in Texas alone) had been carried out in the 38 states that had death-penalty laws; that year, there were 3,701 inmates on death rows. Meanwhile, research showed that as many as two-thirds of death-row inmates had been wrongfully convicted due to inadequate legal representation, lack of access to DNA testing, police misconduct, racial bias, and simple error. From 1973 through 2001, 98 people had been freed from death rows.

In 2002, the *Rehnquist Court banned the execution of mentally retarded offenders and required that juries, not judges, determine death penalties. But it permitted the execution of minors.

CAREY DESERT LAND ACT (1894). See *Conservation.

CARIBBEAN AND CENTRAL AMERICAN RELATIONS. Over the course of U.S. history, the Caribbean and Central American region has been by turn an area of commercial opportunity, a theater of possible expansion, and a problem of national security.

At the end of the 18th century, a third of America's foreign trade was with the Caribbean islands. American ships carried farm products to the islands to exchange for sugar, rum, and molasses. Before 1808, American slavers also brought slaves from Africa for sale in Cuba (see *Slave Trade).

U.S. acquisition of Florida from Spain in 1819 (see *Floridas, East and West) thrust the United States deep into the Caribbean. American Southerners coveted Cuba as an additional slave state (see *Ostend Manifesto), but Spain rejected two offers to buy the island. In 1871 the U.S. Senate rejected a treaty favored by Pres. Ulysses S. Grant to annex Santo Domingo (now the Dominican Republic; see *Santo Domingo Affair). When the building of an isthmian canal became a national priority, the

United States helped Panama achieve its independence from Colombia and was rewarded with a ten-mile-wide Canal Zone in perpetuity (see *Panama Canal).

From the early years of the republic, the region presented security problems. The new United States was menaced from the Caribbean by the naval power of England, France, and Spain, and by pirates of all nationalities. Bloody slave revolts in Haiti in 1791 and periodically in Cuba terrified American Southerners with the possibility of contagion. The *Monroe Doctrine barred European powers from further aggrandizement in the Caribbean as well as in South America. To enforce it, the United States later in the century assumed the role of policeman in the Caribbean, intervening where political disorder and financial mismanagement threatened to bring the intervention of European creditors (see *Roosevelt Corollary).

U.S. policy toward the Caribbean and Central American countries, while always self-interested, was also well-intentioned, although its beneficiaries tended to see the United States as domineering. Spanish misrule in Cuba brought about the *Spanish-American War, from which the United States emerged in possession of Puerto Rico and with a protectorate over Cuba (see *Platt Amendment). U.S. troops occupied Cuba in 1898–1902, 1906–9, and again in 1912 and 1917. The United States established a customs receivership in the Dominican Republic in 1905 and occupied that country militarily in 1916–24. Marines also occupied Nicaragua in 1912–33 and Haiti in 1915–34. U.S. occupiers eradicated yellow fever in Cuba and elsewhere in the region and built roads, schools, hospitals, and sanitation facilities in Haiti.

With the building of the Panama Canal, the Caribbean and Central American region was viewed as vital to the canal's defense. In the *cold war, the United States became highly sensitive to the possibility of communist penetration of the region. In Guatemala in 1954 the Central Intelligence Agency (CIA) helped overthrow the legally elected reformist government of Jacobo Arbenz Guzmán (see *Covert Operations). When Fidel Castro established a Marxist and anti-American regime in Cuba in 1959, the United States severed diplomatic relations, imposed a trade embargo, and lent its support to anti-Castro exiles (see *Bay of Pigs Invasion). Increasingly close ties between Cuba and the Soviet Union led to the *Cuban missile crisis of 1962. In 1979–84, civil war raged in El Salvador between left-wing guerrillas and a right-wing government whose "death squads" horrified the world. The United States provided military and economic assistance to the conservative government. In Nicaragua, when left-wing Sandinistas overthrew the

dictatorship of Anastasio Somoza Debayle in 1979 and established a reformist government, the United States aided the anti-Sandinista Contras (see *Iran-Contra Affair). The United States was relieved when, in 1990, a coalition of conservative democratic parties defeated the Sandinistas at the polls. In 1984 U.S. troops overthrew a Marxist government on the island of Grenada (see *Grenada Invasion). U.S. troops returned to the Dominican Republic in 1965 and to Haiti in 1994 to maintain order and support pro-American governments.

American control of the Panama Canal proved unpopular among Panamanians. Anti-American demonstrations and riots punctuated the 1950s and 1960s. In 1977, the United States signed the *Panama Canal treaties with Panama, transferring the Canal Zone to Panama in 1999 and promising not to intervene in Panama's domestic affairs. Nevertheless, in 1989 U.S. troops invaded Panama and seized strongman Manuel Antonio Noriega, once an informant for the CIA but now indicted as a drug trafficker in the United States.

Meanwhile, *immigration from the Caribbean and Central American region mounted. Large migrations of Puerto Ricans to the United States began during World War 2. In 2000, the population of Puerto Rico was estimated at 3.8 million, while 3.4 million Puerto Ricans lived in the United States. In the 1960s, half a million anti-Castro Cubans sought refuge in the United States, another 125,000 in 1980 (see *Cuban Migration). Civil wars in Nicaragua, El Salvador, and Guatemala drove millions to seek refuge in the north, while thousands of desperate Haitians reached the United States by small boats and rafts. Dominican immigration swelled after the removal of dictator Rafael Leónidas Trujillo in 1961. Between 1961 and 1998, some 800,000 Dominicans entered the United States, constituting the fourth-largest immigration stream.

CAROLINE AFFAIR (1837), incident in the *Van Buren administration. Canadian rebels established themselves on Navy Island in the Niagara River, where they were supplied by sympathetic Americans in the steamship Caroline. In December 1837 Canadian militia seized the Caroline on the American side of the river. President Van Buren protested but declared U.S. neutrality in the Canadian rebellion.

CARPETBAGGERS AND SCALAWAGS, derogatory terms for two types of white Republicans in the post–Civil War South. Carpetbaggers were Northerners who went south during or soon after the war. The name implies penniless adventurers who carried their belongings in a single carpetbag or suitcase. In fact, many were middle-class professional or business people, some motivated by idealism to help the former slaves, others seeking economic opportunities. Some who entered politics in alliance with black voters achieved short-lived prominence during congressional *reconstruction.

Scalawags were native Southerners. Some—former Unionists and Whigs—agreed with the Republican Party's nationalist and economic positions. Others hoped that they would be able, as Republicans, to mitigate the social revolution under way in the South. Still others were opportunists who sought business advantage or political patronage.

CARTER ADMINISTRATION (1977–81). Democrat James Earl Carter Jr., 39th president of the United States, having campaigned as a Washington outsider, found that he had little influence with Washington insiders in Congress. His promises of liberal reforms quickly died, and the Carter administration became known as the most conservative Democratic administration of the century. This was due not only to congressional opposition but to inflation, which rose from 6.5 percent in 1977 to 13.5 percent in 1981 fueled by rising oil prices (see *Oil Shock).

To counter inflation, Carter cut spending on social programs, provoking the criticism of liberals. Energy policy, aiming at energy independence, became a chief concern. Carter began to phase out price controls on natural gas and crude oil, but his efforts to achieve energy conservation and to prevent windfall profits through taxes were frustrated. In 1980 Congress created a Synthetic Fuels Corporation to provide incentives to companies producing coal liquids and gases, shale oil, and petroleum from tar sands. These efforts were abandoned when supplies of conventional oil increased and prices fell in the early 1980s. Hopes for *nuclear energy were dimmed by the *Three Mile Island accident in 1979. The departments of Energy (1977) and Education (1979) were established during the Carter administration.

In foreign affairs, Carter overcame conservative opposition to secure ratification of the *Panama Canal treaties transferring control of the Panama Canal to Panama in 1999. In 1979 he brokered a peace agreement between Israel and Egypt at Camp David (see *Camp David Accords). With the Soviet Union, he continued détente, in 1979 signing the SALT 2 treaty, which was never ratified (see *Arms Control and Disarmament). The Soviet invasion of Afghanistan in December 1979 shocked Carter and changed U.S. policy abruptly. A military buildup was speeded, 19- and 20-year-old men were compelled

to register for a possible draft, a wheat embargo was imposed on the Soviets (to the outrage of American farmers), and the United States withdrew from the 1980 Olympics in Moscow (to the frustration of American athletes). In Iran in November 1979 Islamic militants seized the U.S. embassy in Tehran and took 53 Americans hostage for the return of the deposed shah, who had been allowed to enter the United States for treatment of his terminal cancer (see *Iranian Hostage Crisis). Carter's inability to liberate or win the release of the hostages was the chief cause of his defeat in the November 1980 election. He was succeeded by Republican Ronald Reagan.

CASABLANCA CONFERENCE (1943). See *World War 2 Conferences.

CAUCUS, meeting of members of a legislative body sharing a common purpose. Between 1800 and 1824, caucuses of congressional members of the *Jeffersonian Republican Party regularly nominated that party's candidates for president and vice president. When the Republican caucus in 1824 nominated William H. Crawford, Crawford's rivals—Andrew Jackson, John Quincy Adams, John C. Calhoun, and Henry Clay—so effectively attacked "King Caucus" as undemocratic that no congressional caucus thereafter presumed to nominate a presidential candidate. Before the advent of party *nominating conventions, party caucuses in state legislatures also nominated—or endorsed—presidential candidates. Party caucuses for legislative purposes are of course routine, and special-interest caucuses crossing party lines— for example, the Congressional Black Caucus—are sometimes formed.

CEDAR CREEK (Oct. 19, 1864), *Civil War battle. Given command of the Army of the Shenandoah (August 1864), Union general Philip H. Sheridan defeated Confederate general Jubal A. Early at Winchester, Va. (Sept. 19) and Fishers Hill (Sept. 22), then proceeded to execute Gen. Ulysses S. Grant's order to turn "the Shenandoah Valley [into] a barren waste . . . so that crows flying over it for the balance of this season will have to carry their provender with them." On the night of Oct. 18–19, Early, with four Confederate divisions, attacked the Union army at Cedar Creek, scoring a complete surprise and apparent victory. Sheridan was then at Winchester. Hearing the distant guns ("The terrible grumble, and rumble, and roar / Telling the battle was on once more, / And Sheridan twenty miles away," sang poet Thomas

Buchanan Read in "Sheridan's Ride"), he galloped toward the battlefield, rallying stragglers along the way and turning the morning's defeat into a decisive victory.

CENTENNIAL EXPOSITION (1876), international exposition—the first in America—held at Philadelphia to celebrate the 100th anniversary of the Declaration of Independence. Thirty-seven foreign countries participated. Visitors were most impressed by the machinery and products of American industry exhibited there.

CENTER OF POPULATION. See *Westward Movement.

CENTRAL TREATY ORGANIZATION (CENTO), diplomatic achievement of the *Eisenhower administration, although the United States was not formally a member. A regional defense alliance among Turkey, Iran, Iraq, Pakistan, and Great Britain, it was promoted by the United States as part of its *cold war policy of *containment. It originated as the Baghdad Pact (1955). After Iraq withdrew in 1959, the alliance was named the Central Treaty Organization. It was dissolved in 1979.

CHALLENGER DISASTER (Jan. 28, 1986). At 11:39 a.m. on Jan. 28, 1986, the space shuttle *Challenger* lifted off from Cape Canaveral, Fla., before thousands of spectators and a national television audience. Seventy-four seconds into its flight, the craft exploded, scattering debris into the Atlantic Ocean 18 miles offshore. All seven astronauts aboard died, including Christa McAuliffe, a schoolteacher from Concord, N.H., who had been selected—for public relations purposes—to be the first ordinary citizen in space.

A four-month investigation by a presidential commission traced the immediate cause of the explosion to an O-ring seal on a booster rocket that had become brittle in the cold. The more fundamental cause was the National Aeronautics and Space Administration's slighting of safety procedures to adhere to a frequent flight schedule calculated to win increased congressional financing.

CHANCELLORSVILLE (May 2–4, 1863), *Civil War battle. After the battle of *Fredericksburg (Dec. 13, 1862), Confederate general Robert E. Lee's Army of Northern Virginia remained in a defensive position along 25 miles of the Rappahannock River. Late in April, the Union Army of the Potomac, now commanded by Gen. Joseph Hooker and numbering 120,000 men, crossed the Rappahannock. Ten thousand cavalry and 70,000 in-

fantry took up a position near Chancellorsville, west of Lee's position, while another 40,000 confronted Lee's right at Fredericksburg.

On May 2, leaving only 10,000 men at Fredericksburg, Lee sent Gen. Thomas J. "Stonewall" Jackson with the bulk of his army around Hooker's right. That evening the Confederates burst out of the woods west of the south-facing Union army; by nightfall they had pushed back the Union right two miles to the Rappahannock. The next two days, fighting raged on the Confederate right at Fredericksburg, where Union troops captured the heights behind the town before being driven back across the river by Lee.

Paralyzed by the Confederate successes, "Fighting Joe" Hooker remained uncharacteristically passive throughout the battle. On the night of May 4 he ordered the Union army to withdraw across the river. This second disaster within six months along the Rappahannock cost the Army of the Potomac 17,000 casualties. Among the Confederates' 13,000 casualties was "Stonewall" Jackson, mortally wounded by his own pickets while returning from a patrol on the night of May 2 (see *Jackson's Death). Chancellorsville is considered Lee's most brilliant victory.

CHAPLIN HILLS. See *Perryville or Chaplin Hills.

CHARLES RIVER BRIDGE v. WARREN BRIDGE (1837), decision of the *Taney Court. The Charles River Bridge had been chartered by Massachusetts in 1785 as a toll bridge and had proved highly profitable. When the nearby Warren Bridge was chartered in 1828 in the expectation that it would become a free bridge, thereby destroying the profitability of the Charles River Bridge, the latter company sued, arguing a violation of contract in that the monopoly it had enjoyed was implied in its charter.

Chief Justice Taney, for the Court, declared that corporation charters must be narrowly construed to protect the community from monopoly and vested interest; "in grants by the public," he wrote, "nothing passes by implication." "The whole community," he went on, ". . . have a right to require that the power of promoting their comfort and convenience, and of advancing the public prosperity by providing safe, convenient, and cheap ways for the transportation of produce and the purposes of travel, should not be construed to have been surrendered . . . by the State, unless it shall appear by plain words that it was intended to be done." Justice Joseph Story, longtime colleague of the late chief justice, John Marshall, dissented.

CHASE COURT or **RECONSTRUCTION COURT**
(1864–77), the U.S. Supreme Court under Chief Justice
Salmon P. Chase. The 40th Congress (1867–69), dominated by *Radical Republicans, seemed bent on transforming the U.S. government from one of checks and
balances to a parliamentary regime in which an all-
powerful Congress did as it pleased while its nominally
coequal branches, the executive and the judiciary, were
reduced to impotence. Regularly overriding presidential
vetoes, Congress reduced the power of the president and
in the end impeached him (see Andrew *Johnson Administration). Since most of the Radicals' *reconstruction
legislation was of dubious constitutionality, they necessarily regarded the Supreme Court as a potential obstacle
to their program. Their strategy was to reduce the Court
to acquiescence through simple intimidation—despite the
fact that Chief Justice Chase was a longtime friend of the
Radicals.

This, at least, is the conventional interpretation of
congressional and Court behavior after Ex parte *Milligan (1866), in which the Court ruled that martial law
was unconstitutional where the civil courts were open
and functioning. This was a direct challenge to the Radicals' program of reconstruction, which initially involved
restoring martial law in the South. When this was challenged in Ex parte *McCardle (1867), Congress hastily
stripped the Court of its authority to decide the case. The
Court submitted, acknowledging Congress's constitutional power to regulate its appellate jurisdiction (Art. 3,
sec. 2, par. 2). Thereafter the Radicals spoke menacingly
of reorganizing the Court and its procedures. To prevent
President Johnson from making new appointments to the
Court, Congress in 1866 reduced its membership from
nine to seven.

Thoroughly intimidated (it is supposed), the Court
evaded decisions involving reconstruction. In Mississippi
v. Johnson (1867) and Georgia v. Stanton (1867), in
which plaintiffs sought injunctions against enforcement
of the Reconstruction Acts, the Court disclaimed jurisdiction. In the *Test Oath Cases (1867) Congress simply
ignored the Court's ruling of unconstitutionality and
continued to require oaths of past loyalty from Southern
voters and officeholders. In *Texas v. White (1869), the
Court vigorously upheld the theory upon which Radical
reconstruction rested. A final measure of contempt was
heaped upon the Court when it reversed itself within a
single year in the *Legal Tender Cases (1870–71), the reversal having been made possible by Congress's restoring
the Court to nine members and Pres. Ulysses S. Grant's
appointing two justices favoring reversal.

The Court's revenge (if such it was) upon the Radicals
came in the *Slaughterhouse Cases (1873), when it denied the Radicals' reliance on the *14th Amendment to
protect the civil rights of the freedmen.

CHASE IMPEACHMENT (1804–5), incident in the
*Jefferson administration. Samuel Chase, a Federalist
justice of the U.S. Supreme Court, had made intemperate
attacks on the Republican administration as well as on
the new democratic constitution of his native Maryland.
He was also accused of bias in several prominent trials.
Aiming to check the power of the federal judiciary, and
particularly of the Supreme Court under Federalist chief
justice John Marshall, Jefferson directed Republicans in
the House of Representatives to bring in a bill of impeachment against Chase. Chase's trial in the Senate
(February–March 1805) was presided over by the outgoing vice president, Aaron Burr, who had killed Alexander
Hamilton in a duel the previous July. To Jefferson's chagrin, Chase was acquitted on all eight charges brought
against him.

CHÂTEAU-THIERRY. See *World War 1.

CHATTANOOGA CAMPAIGN (August–November
1863), *Civil War campaign in which Union forces expelled the Confederates from Tennessee.

While the North celebrated *Gettysburg and
*Vicksburg, Union general William S. Rosecrans, com-
manding the Army of the Cumberland, skillfully maneuvered the Confederate Army of Tennessee,
commanded by Gen. Braxton Bragg, out of middle and
eastern Tennessee. The Confederates evacuated
Knoxville on Sept. 3 and strategically important Chattanooga on Sept. 8.

Withdrawing into the Georgia mountains south of
Chattanooga, Bragg received reinforcements from the
Army of Northern Virginia—12,000 men under Gen.
James Longstreet who had been transported by rail
through the Carolinas and Georgia to the Chattanooga
front. When Rosecrans pursued Bragg into Georgia, the
Confederates hit him (Sept. 19) at **Chickamauga**
Creek, eight miles from Chattanooga. Longstreet's veter-
ans exploited a penetration in the Union right and sent a
third of the Union army in flight back to Chattanooga.
The Union left, however, commanded by Gen. George H.
Thomas—"the Rock of Chickamauga"—held its ground
during the day and withdrew to Chattanooga that night.
Bragg, who had lost 30 percent of his effectives, followed
belatedly and laid siege to Chattanooga from the high
ground to its south—Lookout Mountain and Missionary
Ridge.

Concerned over Rosecrans's position, Washington rushed reinforcements to the Chattanooga front. Under Gen. Joseph Hooker, 20,000 troops detached from the Army of the Potomac were transported by rail 1,200 miles via Indianapolis to Chattanooga. Gen. William T. Sherman was also transferred there with 17,000 troops of the Army of the Tennessee. Command of the entire Western Theater, from the Appalachians to the Mississippi, was assigned to Gen. Ulysses S. Grant, who arrived in Chattanooga on Oct. 23, having already replaced Rosecrans with Thomas as commander of the Army of the Cumberland. Meanwhile, the Confederate army was racked by dissension between its generals and its commander, Bragg.

Late in November Grant struck. On Nov. 24 Hooker drove the Confederates from **Lookout Mountain** in the "Battle Above the Clouds" but was delayed transferring his troops east to the southern end of **Missionary Ridge**. Meanwhile, Sherman had already taken his first objective at the northern end of the ridge but then stalled. On Nov. 25 Grant ordered Thomas to create a diversion at the Confederate center. Unexpectedly, the Confederate defenders there fell into confusion and Union flags soon flew on the top of Missionary Ridge. Driven from what they had believed was an impregnable position, the Confederates retreated 30 miles into Georgia. Bragg resigned his command and was succeeded by Gen. Joseph E. Johnston.

CHAUTAUQUA (c. 1875–c. 1925), adult education program popular in rural America. It originated in church camp meetings at Chautauqua, N.Y., was widely imitated across the country, and was finally converted into a commercial enterprise in which groups of preachers, politicians, lecturers, and entertainers traveled circuits of small towns, attracting thousands of rural people to one-day or weeklong programs held in circus-size tents or specially built wooden sheds much like a county fair's. A major cultural influence, particularly in the Middle West, Chautauqua declined with the advent of automobiles, motion pictures, and radio.

CHEROKEE NATION v. GEORGIA (1831), 4–2 decision of the *Marshall Court ending the independent status of the Cherokee Indians in Georgia. Theretofore the federal government had treated the Indian tribes as foreign nations. When Georgia asserted jurisdiction over Cherokee lands in the state, the tribe appealed to the Supreme Court. For the Court, Chief Justice John Marshall ruled that the Court had no jurisdiction since the tribe was not a foreign state as intended by Art. 3, sec. 2

of the Constitution but a "domestic, dependent nation" and a ward of the United States (see *Indian Policy).

CHERRY VALLEY MASSACRE (Nov. 11, 1778), incident in the *Revolutionary War. Cherry Valley was a village of some 300 inhabitants in Oswego County in New York's Mohawk Valley. On Nov. 11, 1778, a force of Loyalists, British regulars, and Seneca and Mohawk Indians totaling 700 and commanded by Capt. Walter Butler pillaged and burned the village, murdering many inhabitants and taking captives. A fort sheltering 250 Massachusetts troops was unharmed.

CHESAPEAKE AFFAIR (1807), incident in the *Jefferson administration. On June 22, 1807, the U.S. frigate *Chesapeake*, commanded by Commodore James Barron, was stopped by the British frigate *Leopard* off the Virginia coast. The British commander demanded the surrender of four alleged British deserters from the *Chesapeake*. (In fact, there were many British deserters in the crew.) When Barron refused to permit the British to board his vessel, the Leopard opened fire upon the unprepared *Chesapeake*, killing 3 crewmen and wounding 18. Barron struck his colors and the British boarded the ship, seizing the four alleged deserters. Three of them were Americans who had been impressed into the Royal Navy and later escaped. The one Englishman was later hanged at Halifax.

When the crippled *Chesapeake* returned to Norfolk, indignation in U.S. ports was intense. On July 2, Pres. Thomas Jefferson issued a proclamation ordering British warships out of U.S. territorial waters. The British responded by ordering more vigorous *impressment of British subjects from neutral ships. When war fever subsided, Jefferson—knowing that the nation was totally unprepared for war—turned to economic coercion with the Embargo (see *Embargo and Nonintercourse). In 1811 the British paid reparations for the attack on the *Chesapeake*.

In the *War of 1812 the *Chesapeake* again acquired notoriety when, now commanded by Capt. James Lawrence, it ventured (June 1, 1813) out of Boston harbor to accept a challenge from the British frigate *Shannon*. It was defeated and captured, although Lawrence, mortally wounded, had allegedly given the famous order "Don't give up the ship."

CHEYENNE-ARAPAHO WAR (1864–65), Indian war on the high plains of Colorado, Kansas, and Nebraska. Although Cheyenne and Arapaho leaders had ceded extensive lands in exchange for a small reservation in Colorado, young tribesmen continued to hunt beyond the reservation, raiding ranchers' herds and clashing with whites. Colorado militia under Col. John M. Chivington responded with attacks on Cheyenne villages. On Nov. 29, 1864, Chivington's force attacked the unsuspecting Cheyenne reservation on Sand Creek, slaughtering and mutilating hundreds of Indians in the **Sand Creek massacre**. Over the next year, other Cheyennes retaliated in bloody style. By a treaty signed Oct. 14, 1865, the Cheyennes and Arapahos were moved from their former reservation to another.

CHICAGO FIRE (Oct. 8–9, 1871), conflagration that destroyed five square miles of Chicago, then a city of 300,000 built largely of wood. Folklore blames the fire on a Mrs. O'Leary's cow, which allegedly kicked over a lamp. A hundred thousand people were made homeless, perhaps 300 killed; property loss was estimated at $200 million.

CHICAGO, MILWAUKEE & ST. PAUL RAILWAY CO. v. MINNESOTA (1890), 6–3 decision of the *Fuller Court overturning a Minnesota law that gave unappealable rate-fixing authority to a state agency. The Court ruled that judicial review of the decisions of regulatory agencies was an essential requirement of substantive due process. The Court had not asserted the requirement of judicial review in *Munn v. Illinois* (1877), which had confirmed the authority of states to regulate private businesses.

CHICAGO SEVEN (1969–70), defendants in a notorious trial arising out of the rioting outside the 1968 Democratic national convention in Chicago by *Yippies and others. Charged with conspiracy and crossing state lines to riot were *New Left activists Rennie Davis, David Dellinger, John Froines, Tom Hayden, Abbie Hoffman, Jerry Rubin, and Lee Weiner. A mistrial was declared in the case of an eighth defendant, Black Panther Bobby Seale. Judge Julius Hoffman's bias and incompetence enabled the defendants to turn the proceedings into a circus. All were acquitted of conspiracy; five were found guilty of rioting, but these convictions were reversed on appeal. All the defendants and their two lawyers were charged with criminal contempt; only three defendants and lawyer William M. Kunstler were convicted, and these were sentenced to time already served.

CHICKAMAUGA. See *Chattanooga Campaign.

CHILD LABOR. In colonial America, nonslave children of all but the wealthiest parents customarily worked on family farms or in home workshops under the supervision of their parents or were early apprenticed to craftsmen or business firms. With the coming of the Industrial Revolution (see *Industrialization), child labor was often preferred to that of adults in factories and mines. In textile mills, for example, children proved as adept as adults, were more docile, and could be paid less. In mines, their small size suited them for certain tasks, such as dragging loads of coal through narrow tunnels. The exploitation of children was accepted as the inevitable consequence of economic laws, which ordained that, in the brutal competition of laissez-faire society, wages must always be driven to the lowest subsistence level.

In the early 19th century, humanitarians realized that child labor was cruel and oppressive, that children were being denied the benefits of religion and education, and that their labor produced maimed and sickly adults. Some states passed protective legislation—in 1842, Connecticut and Massachusetts, for example, limited the labor of children in textile mills to ten hours a day. But state laws were not uniform and were rarely enforced. The 1870 census, the first to count child workers, found 765,000 children aged 10–15 employed—6 percent of the total labor force. (It did not count children working on family farms or in family enterprises.) The federal regulation of child labor became a major item on the agenda of liberal reformers.

In 1912 Congress established the Children's Bureau in the Department of Labor to collect data on the condition of working children. In 1916 the **Keating-Owen Act** barred the products of child labor from interstate commerce; the U.S. Supreme Court, however, ruled the act unconstitutional on the grounds that Congress was regulating manufacturing, where it had no constitutional authority, rather than commerce (see *Hammer v. Dagenhart). In 1919 Congress taxed products manufactured by children, but this too was ruled unconstitutional in 1922. A constitutional amendment regulating child labor was passed by Congress in 1924 but failed to win the support of the necessary three-fourths of the states. In 1938 the Fair Labor Standards Act (see *New Deal) prohibited employers engaged in interstate commerce from hiring children under 16 (under 18 in hazardous occupations). This act was unanimously upheld by a liberalized Supreme Court in 1941. A 1948 amendment barred children from farm work during school hours.

The Fair Labor Standards Act remains the principal federal statute regulating child labor, but it is often not enforced in agricultural districts where the labor of children—especially the children of migrant farm workers—is important to the local economy.

CHINA BLOC. See *China "Loss."

CHINA CLIPPER (1935–41). In October 1934, Juan Trippe, president of Pan American Airways, wrote a letter to the U.S. secretary of the Navy informing him that Pan Am planned to establish air service between the United States and China by way of Hawaii, Midway, Wake, Guam, the Philippines, and Hong Kong. Trippe requested the Navy's permission to use its facilities at Pearl Harbor and Manila and the islands of Midway, Wake (both uninhabited), and Guam, where Pan Am proposed to build marine airports for its flying boats. In the event of war, he promised, these bases would be turned over to the Navy.

The Navy Department welcomed Trippe's letter. For many years, it had watched the growing power of Japan with alarm and believed that Japan was secretly fortifying its mandated islands in the Western Pacific. The Navy wanted bases of its own there, but it was prevented by treaty from fortifying Midway, Wake, and Guam. The proposal from a civilian airline to build bases—readily convertible to military use—was very much in the national interest. The Navy gave its permission for Pan Am to use its facilities and its islands, and thereafter it provided extensive logistical and personnel support.

Pan Am was already using flying boats on Caribbean and South American routes. Trippe now ordered a new generation of flying boats from Glenn L. Martin. By the time the new flying boats arrived, Pan Am pilots had surveyed the Pacific route as far as the Philippines and the construction of bases had been completed—angering the Japanese. Each of the three new planes—the *China, Philippine,* and *Hawaiian Clipper*s—was 90 feet long, had a wingspan of 130 feet, and weighed 26 tons. Powered by four 800-horsepower Pratt & Whitney Wasp engines, it could accommodate 40 passengers (only 10 or 11 on the long Hawaii run, when additional fuel storage was needed). Fully loaded, the flying boat could cruise 3,200 miles nonstop at 156 miles per hour.

On Nov. 22, 1935, crowds watched the *China Clipper* take off from San Francisco Bay carrying mail but no passengers; six days later, after nearly 60 hours' flying time, it anchored at Manila. Weekly passenger service between San Francisco and Hong Kong, with nightly stopovers along the way, began in October 1936. After Japan invaded China in 1937, the clippers flew into a war zone. When in July 1938 the *Hawaiian Clipper* disappeared between Guam and Manila, Japanese sabotage was suspected. Clipper service ended with *Pearl Harbor.

CHINA "LOSS" (1949), episode in the *Truman administration. The civil war in China, between the Nationalists led by Chiang Kai-shek and the Communists led by Mao Tse-tung, suspended during World War 2, resumed in July 1946. U.S. general George C. Marshall, having failed in a yearlong effort to peacefully reunite the two sides in a democratic coalition government, returned to the United States in January 1947. Repressive, corrupt, incompetent, and unpopular, the Nationalist regime quickly crumbled before the Communists. At Beijing in October 1949 Mao declared the establishment of the People's Republic of China. In December, Chiang, with the remnants of his party and army, withdrew to Formosa. In February 1950 Communist China and the Soviet Union signed a formal alliance. The United States refused to recognize the new government and blocked its admission to the United Nations.

Regarding Europe and the Middle East as more important than the Far East to U.S. vital interests, the Truman administration had no choice but to accept this development, hoping to capitalize on the historic hostility between Russia and China to divide these two communist powers. In November 1949 Secretary of State Dean Acheson published a 1,000-page "China White Paper" consisting of text and documents to prove that the United States had done all in its power to support the Nationalist regime. "The unfortunate but inescapable fact," Acheson wrote, "is that the ominous result of the civil war in China was beyond the control of the government of the United States. Nothing that this country did or could have done within the reasonable limits of its capabilities could have changed that result; nothing that was left undone by this country has contributed to it."

Congressional Republicans did not accept Acheson's explanation. Led by Sen. Arthur Vandenberg of Michigan, they had supported the administration's *cold war policies in Europe. But now, frustrated by their unexpected defeat in the 1948 election, they seized upon the China issue for partisan advantage. The **China bloc**—Republican senators William Knowland of California, Styles Bridges of New Hampshire, and Kenneth Wherry of Nebraska, joined by Democratic senator Pat McCarran of Nevada—attacked the "White Paper" as a "whitewash." They would not agree that Europe was more important than Asia in the cold war, but they could suggest no alternative policy that might have averted the Nationalist collapse. Inevitably, some Republicans professed to see evidence of conspiracy and betrayal in the "loss" of China. The most extreme expression of this view was a speech by Republican senator William E. Jenner of Indiana in September 1950 in which he called General Marshall "a front man for traitors," "a living lie," "stooge" for the "communist-appeasing, communist-protecting betrayer of America, Secretary of State Dean Acheson."

The accusation that China had been "lost" had far-reaching ramifications. On a personal level, it ended the careers of an elite group of China experts in the State Department—"old China hands" John S. Service, John Paton Davies, John Carter Vincent, and O. Edmund Clubb. On a policy level, it limited the foreign policy options of subsequent administrations, none of which would pay the political price for "losing" another country to world communism.

CHINA TRADE. Cut off from the British West Indies after the Revolutionary War, American merchants found a lucrative substitute in trade with China. The *Empress of China* pioneered the trade in 1784, traveling from New York to Canton (until 1842 the only Chinese port open to Western traders) by way of the Cape of Good Hope, the Indian Ocean, and the East Indies. Other ships followed, although China had little interest in Western goods other than furs. In 1787 the *Columbia* sailed from Boston, rounded Cape Horn, and proceeded to the Pacific Northwest, where it took on a cargo of otter skins and, in 1789, continued on to Canton, where the furs proved highly salable. The *Columbia* returned to Boston in 1790 by way of the Indian and Atlantic oceans. Thereafter the China trade shifted to the Pacific, the increasingly scarce otters being replaced by sealskins and sandalwood. From Canton, the American ships brought back tea, porcelains, and silks, which became fashionable in the Northeast. The voyages were long and dangerous but highly profitable. The trade peaked in 1818–19.

CHINESE EXCLUSION. The *Burlingame Treaty (1868) encouraged the reciprocal migration of Chinese and Americans. Few Americans emigrated to China, but around 1850 Western mine owners—and later railroad builders—began importing contract coolie labor from China. These immigrants were met with intense hostility because of their low wages, low standard of living, poor health, strange costumes, language, and "heathen" religion. State laws discriminating against them were overturned by the U.S. Supreme Court, but persecution of the docile and clannish Chinese was widespread. The anti-Chinese riots that occurred in San Francisco in 1877

were not unique. Regularly, the Western states petitioned Congress for protection against the **"yellow peril."**

In 1875 Congress prohibited the importation of contract coolie labor. In 1880, when there were perhaps 200,000 Chinese in the Western states, the Burlingame Treaty was renegotiated to permit the United States to limit, suspend, and regulate but not prohibit the *immigration of Chinese laborers. Teachers, officials, students, merchants, and travelers were not affected. The Chinese Exclusion Act of 1882, a direct violation of the 1880 treaty, stopped all new immigration of Chinese laborers for ten years and barred Chinese from citizenship. The ban on Chinese laborers was extended for 20 years in 1888 and for another ten years in 1892. In 1894 it was extended indefinitely.

During World War 2, when China was a U.S. ally, Congress in 1943 repealed the exclusionary laws, established an annual quota for China of 105 immigrants, and made Chinese immigrants eligible for citizenship. The 1952 McCarran-Walter Immigration Act removed all racial barriers to immigration while retaining the Chinese quota of 105. The Immigration Act of 1965 replaced national quotas with hemisphere quotas, effectively ending discrimination against Chinese and others. In 1998, 44,000 immigrants from China and Taiwan entered the United States.

CHISHOLM v. GEORGIA (1793), early decision of the U.S. Supreme Court asserting a nationalist view of the federal union. Chisholm, a citizen of South Carolina, sued Georgia for payment for goods delivered by him. Although the Constitution (Art. 3, sec. 2) gave the federal courts jurisdiction over "controversies . . . between a state and citizens of another state," Georgia claimed immunity from the suit as a sovereign and independent state and refused to participate in the proceedings.

The Court ruled 4–1 against Georgia, Justice James Wilson categorically rejecting the concept of state sovereignty "as to the purposes of the union." This assertion of judicial nationalism profoundly shocked the new nation and led immediately to the adoption of the *11th Amendment, which denies federal courts jurisdiction over suits brought against one state by a citizen of another state or of a foreign country. Although the ruling in *Chisholm* was thereby overturned, the Court continued to deny extreme assertions of state sovereignty in cases like *Martin v. Hunter's Lessee* (1816) and *Cohens v. Virginia* (1821).

CHOLERA, a disease endemic to southern Asia that spread worldwide during six pandemics in the 19th and

20th centuries. It is caused by an intestinal bacillus and communicated by polluted water. Thus it affects countries or regions with primitive sanitary facilities. Its most prominent symptoms are dehydration resulting from vomiting and diarrhea, intense muscular cramps or seizures, and a "sinking stage" that precedes death. Despite its ravages in India and Russia, cholera was not as lethal as bubonic plague, mortality averaging about half its incidence.

The second, third, and fourth cholera pandemics (1829–75) reached North America. Cholera entered the United States from Europe in 1832, spreading westward from New York and the Eastern seaboard until it reached the West Coast in 1834. It then spread into Mexico and South America, reentering the United States from Cuba at New Orleans and eventually reaching Canada. It remained a major health threat in the United States until the end of the 19th century.

The cholera bacillus was isolated in 1883, after which mortality in treated cases fell to 10 percent. By 1945, active public health measures in much of the world had largely confined cholera to its zone of endemicity in southern Asia.

CHRISTIAN COALITION. See *Christian Right.

CHRISTIAN RIGHT, social movement of evangelical (fundamentalist) Protestants that seeks to infuse traditional values into public policy to counter the alleged moral degeneracy associated with the secularization of society and evidenced by sexual license, family breakup, and social disorder. Originating in the 1970s, it had roots in the fundamentalist crusades against "modernity" in the 1920s and communism in the 1950s.

By the 1970s, the establishment of hundreds of Christian radio and television stations enabled evangelical leaders to mobilize large constituencies in the interest of political conservatism. The best-known organization in this period was the **Moral Majority**, founded in 1979 by Baptist minister and televangelist Jerry Falwell and credited with contributing to the election of Pres. Ronald Reagan in 1980. In 1988 televangelist Pat Robertson sought the Republican presidential nomination but fared poorly, in part because of scandals among other televangelists and disunity among the evangelicals (Falwell supported George H. W. Bush). Many candidates endorsed by the Christian Right during the 1980s were defeated, and those who were elected proved unresponsive to the Christian Right's agenda. Falwell dissolved the Moral Majority in 1989, signaling a decline of Christian Right activity.

The Christian Right quickly revived, however, focusing more pragmatically on grassroots organizing and greater involvement in conventional politics. In 2000, the three largest of many Christian Right organizations were the Christian Coalition, Focus on the Family, and Concerned Women for America. Founded by Pat Robertson in 1989, the **Christian Coalition** demonstrated sophisticated organizational and communications skills, including Robertson's *700 Club* television program on the Christian Broadcasting Network and the distribution of millions of "voter guides" rating candidates on issues of conservative concern. Its avowed intention was to capture the Republican Party "one precinct at a time." In 1994 the Christian Coalition's 4 million members helped elect many right-wing Republican congressmen. Membership declined in subsequent years, and in 2001 Robertson resigned as the organization's president. **Focus on the Family**, founded in 1977, entered politics in 1987 as a lobby on behalf of family issues. **Concerned Women for America**, founded in 1979, is aggressively antifeminist and is often promoted as the conservative alternative to the National Organization for Women.

At the Republican national convention in 1992, the stridency of Christian Right speakers—calculated to please the conservative wing of the party—in fact alienated many nonideological voters. Although the party then tried to distance itself from the Christian Right, Republican politicians remained sensitive to its views. In 1999, Gary Bauer of the Christian Right Family Research Council entered the race for the Republican presidential nomination in 2000.

CHRISTMAS BOMBING. See *Vietnam War.

CHURCH COMMITTEE (1975–76), the Select Committee to Study Government Operations with Respect to Intelligence Activities, chaired by Democratic senator Frank Church of Idaho. Its 1976 report revealed that, during the 1960s and early 1970s, intelligence agencies of the federal government had spied on the American people on a scale never before approached.

This was a period of perilous international relations marked by *cold war with the Soviet Union and hot war in *Vietnam. It was also a period of domestic turmoil marked by the *civil rights and antiwar movements and by the assassinations of several national leaders. Successive presidents feared that the national security was threatened by little-understood forces, both foreign and domestic. The temptation to use federal investigative agencies to gather information about dissidents and possible subversives proved difficult to resist, although their use for such purposes was in violation of their mandates and often of the law. The presidents justified their orders by a claim of "inherent powers" to override the law in the interests of national security.

The principal agency used in domestic intelligence was the Federal Bureau of Investigation (FBI). From Franklin Roosevelt on, presidents regarded the FBI as the intelligence arm of the government and used it frequently to gather information about Americans. Some of this information was for purely political purposes, as when Attorney General Robert F. Kennedy, during the Kennedy administration, used the FBI to investigate the sugar lobby in Washington and when Pres. Lyndon Johnson sent FBI agents into the Democratic national convention in 1964 to gather behind-the-scenes information. Most was sought for purposes of national security. As World War 2 approached, President Roosevelt assigned the FBI to monitor the possibly subversive activities of Nazis and communists in the United States. In the cold war that followed World War 2, the FBI intensified its efforts against communists and other Marxist groups.

With the rise of the civil rights and antiwar movements, the FBI turned its attention to every manifestation of dissent, of the right as well as the left. During the 1960s and early 1970s, FBI targets included such right-wing organizations as the Ku Klux Klan, the John Birch Society, the Christian Nationalist Crusade, the American Nazi Party, and the National States' Rights Party; such African-American organizations as the National Association for the Advancement of Colored People, the Southern Christian Leadership Conference, the Congress of Racial Equality, the Student Nonviolent Coordinating Committee, the Black Panther Party, and the Nation of Islam; and such antiwar organizations as the Institute for Policy Studies, the American Friends Service Committee, Students for a Democratic Society, the Weathermen, and Women Strike for Peace.

The FBI gathered information through agents and informers within the target organizations, extensive interviews, and physical surveillance; and through warrantless wiretaps and buggings, illegal mail openings, and hundreds of burglaries in search of incriminating documents. Passing beyond mere information-gathering, the FBI undertook to disrupt and neutralize certain organizations by sowing suspicion among their leaders and provoking conflicts among their factions. FBI director J. Edgar Hoover's personal animus toward civil rights leader Martin Luther King Jr. caused the FBI to attempt to destroy his reputation and replace him with another black leader more acceptable to the agency.

The Central Intelligence Agency (CIA), vainly seeking foreign connections to the U.S. antiwar movement, opened overseas mail from organizations and individuals on its "watch lists" and spied on antiwar and civil rights activists traveling abroad. The National Security Agency (NSA) intercepted cables and other electronic messages sent overseas. Because of the Army's role in dealing with civil disturbances, military intelligence agents infiltrated and spied upon civil rights and other groups. The Internal Revenue Service (IRS), which has the legal authority to audit the tax returns of any American, was used by successive administrations to harass dissidents and opponents.

Congress disregarded most of the Church Committee's recommendations to prevent the recurrence of these abuses, but it did establish oversight committees in both houses to monitor domestic intelligence activities.

CHURCHILL'S ADDRESS TO CONGRESS (Dec. 26, 1941). While conferring with Pres. Franklin Roosevelt in Washington two weeks after *Pearl Harbor, British prime minister Winston Churchill was invited to address a joint session of Congress. He was aware that, until Pearl Harbor, many in his audience had opposed Roosevelt's efforts to aid Britain in its war against Germany.

"I cannot help reflecting," he began, "that if my father had been an American and my mother British, instead of the other way round, I might have got here on my own." Cheers and laughter filled the Senate chamber.

Churchill went on soberly to outline the difficulties lying ahead for the allies. "We have . . . a time of tribulation before us. In this time some ground will be lost which it will be hard and costly to regain. Many disappointments and unpleasant surprises await us. Many of them will afflict us before the full marshaling of our latent and total power can be accomplished."

Of the enemies confronting the two allies he demanded: "What kind of a people do they think we are? Is it possible they do not realize that we shall never cease to persevere against them until they have been taught a lesson which they and the world will never forget?"

"It is not given to us to peer into the mysteries of the future," he concluded. "Still, I avow my hope and faith, sure and inviolate, that in the days to come the British and American peoples will for their own safety and for the good of all walk together side by side in majesty, in justice, and in peace."

CHURCH-STATE RELATIONS. The First Amendment to the U.S. Constitution—the first article of the *Bill of Rights—begins: "Congress shall make no law affecting the establishment of religion [the Establishment Clause] or prohibiting the free exercise thereof [the Free Exercise Clause]. . . ." In 1802, Pres. Thomas Jefferson famously interpreted these clauses as "building a wall of separation between church and state."

The Establishment Clause. During the 19th century, Protestant Christianity was virtually the established religion in the United States. School prayer and Bible reading (from the King James Version) were universal. Public events were solemnized by prayer and religious symbolism. Protestant theology and morality were reflected in laws enforcing Sabbath observance, banning alcohol, and prohibiting the teaching of evolution.

The courts had few occasions to examine the Establishment Clause until the 20th century, by which time American society had become notably diverse and secular. Two views of the "wall of separation" emerged, the separationist and the accommodationist. The classic statement of the separationist view was written by Justice Hugo Black in *Everson v. Board of Education of Ewing Township* (1947): "The 'establishment of religion' clause of the First Amendment means at least this: Neither a state nor the Federal Government can set up a church. Neither can pass laws which aid one religion, aid all religions, or prefer one religion over another. Neither can force or influence a person to go or remain away from church against his will or force him to profess a belief or disbelief in any religion. No person can be punished for entertaining or professing religious beliefs or disbeliefs, for church attendance or nonattendance. No tax in any amount, large or small, can be levied to support any religious activities or institutions, whatever they may be called, or whatever form they may adopt to teach or practice religion. Neither a state nor the Federal Government can, openly or secretly, participate in the affairs of any religious organizations or groups and vice versa. In the words of Jefferson, the clause against establishment of religion by law was intended to erect a 'wall of separation between Church and State.' . . . That law must be kept high and impregnable."

For the accommodationists, Justice William O. Douglas in *Zorach v. Clauson* (1952) wrote: "We find no constitutional requirement which makes it necessary for government to be hostile to religion and to throw its weight against efforts to widen the effective scope of religious influence. . . . [The First Amendment] does not say that in every and all respects there shall be separation of Church and State."

The meaning of the Establishment Clause has occupied the Court in areas involving public aid to religious schools, religious instruction in public schools, school prayer, and public displays of religious symbols.

PUBLIC AID TO RELIGIOUS SCHOOLS

Pierce v. Society of the Sisters of the Holy Names of Jesus and Mary (1925) ruled unconstitutional a Ku Klux Klan–sponsored anti-Catholic Oregon law that required all parents to send their children to public schools.

*Everson v. Board of Education of Ewing Township (1947) upheld the constitutionality of state funding for bus transportation for children attending parochial as well as public schools in New Jersey on the grounds that the aid was a general welfare benefit to children, not to religious schools.

Board of Education v. Allen (1968) approved the loan of secular textbooks to children in sectarian schools in New York as a direct benefit to students rather than to the schools.

Lemon v. Kurtzman (1971) struck down a Pennsylvania law authorizing the state to pay parochial schools for teaching certain secular subjects, the instructional material to have been approved by the state. The Court formulated a three-part test for determining if a law or program violated the Establishment Clause: (1) whether the law or program had a secular purpose; (2) whether the primary effect of the law or program was to advance or inhibit religion; and (3) whether the law or program promoted excessive entanglement of government and religion.

Committee for Public Education and Religious Liberty (PEARL) v. Nyquist (1973) struck down a New York law providing (1) direct grants to nonpublic schools serving children from low-income families, (2) tuition reimbursements for low-income families that sent their children to nonpublic schools, and (3) a tax deduction for low-income families that sent their children to nonpublic schools on the grounds that the primary effect of the law was to fund the mission of religious schools.

Meek v. Pittenger (1975) struck down a Pennsylvania law that provided for loans of equipment (such as projectors) and materials (such as maps) to religious schools and that authorized the state to furnish "auxiliary services" (remedial reading, psychological and therapeutic services, guidance counseling and testing) as advancing the schools' sectarian mission and promoting excessive entanglement of government and religion. The Court continued to uphold the loan of secular textbooks.

Wolman v. Walter (1977) approved certain forms of public aid to religious schools in Ohio: loans of secular textbooks; state-financed standardized tests; state-subsidized speech, hearing, and psychological diagnostic services administered by public school employees; state-subsidized therapeutic services such as guidance counseling and remedial speech and reading provided away from the parochial school.

Mueller v. Allen (1983) upheld a Minnesota law that allowed state income tax deductions for tuition, textbooks, and transportation for parents of children attending any school. The Court found that the law's secular purpose was to provide a well-educated citizenry, that it did not have the primary effect of advancing religion because the aid went to parents no matter what schools their children attended, and that it did not create excessive entanglement of government and religion.

Aguilar v. Felton (1985) struck down a program in which public school teachers were sent to religious schools to teach academic subjects as promoting excessive entanglement of government and religion.

Zobrest v. Catalina Foothills School District (1993) upheld the use of government money under the Individuals with Disabilities Education Act (1975) to provide a sign language interpreter for a deaf student at a religious high school on the grounds that the money was provided to the student, not to the school.

*Mitchell v. Helms (2000) upheld a federal program that placed computers and other instructional equipment in parochial as well as public schools.

*Zelman v. Simmons-Harris (2002) upheld a Cleveland, Ohio, *school voucher program as religiously neutral, public money going to parents who decided whether to send their children to public or private (including religious) schools.

RELIGIOUS INSTRUCTION IN PUBLIC SCHOOLS

McCollum v. Board of Education (1948) struck down a "released time" program in which unpaid instructors came into public schools during the regular school day to offer religious instruction to those children whose parents consented.

Zorach v. Clauson (1952) approved a "released time" program in which children attended religious instruction or services during the regular school day but away from school premises.

Epperson v. Arkansas (1968) struck down a law forbidding the teaching of evolution in public schools because its purpose was to advance fundamentalist religion.

Stone v. Graham (1980) struck down a Kentucky law that required that the Ten Commandments be posted on the wall in every public school classroom. The posters were to be bought with private funds and carry a disclaimer of any religious intent.

Edwards v. Aguillard (1987) struck down a Louisiana law that required the teaching of "creation science" whenever evolution was taught.

Board of Education of the Westside Community Schools v. Mergens (1990) upheld the 1984 Equal Access Act, which requires that public secondary schools that receive federal financial assistance allow student religious groups to meet at school on the same student-initiated voluntary basis as other noncurriculum-related clubs.

Lamb's Chapel v. Center Moriches Union Free School District (1993) prohibited a public school from banning a church from showing a film on family issues on the school premises after school hours when the school allowed other films on family issues to be shown by outside groups. The Court ruled that the school's "limited public forum" must be "viewpoint neutral."

*Good News Club v. Milford Central School (2001) opened public elementary schools to after-school religious activity on the same basis as other after-school activities.

PRAYER IN PUBLIC SCHOOLS

*Engel v. Vitale (1962) prohibited the reading of a prayer composed by school officials at the beginning of each school day.

*Abington Township School District v. Schempp (1965) banned the state-sponsored recitation of any prayer or devotional reading from the Bible, although it approved teaching about religion in a nondevotional manner and as part of the school's secular curriculum.

Wallace v. Jaffree (1981) struck down an Alabama law requiring a moment of silence at the beginning of the school day for "meditation or voluntary prayer" as promoting prayer. The decision suggested that a moment of silence for a secular purpose would be constitutional.

Lee v. Weisman (1992) prohibited a clergyman's recitation of a nondenominational prayer at a high school graduation both as coercive to the students and as giving the appearance of the school's endorsement of religion.

*Santa Fe Independent School District v. Doe (2000) found unconstitutional the practice of student-initiated and student-led prayer at public high school football games.

PUBLIC DISPLAY OF RELIGIOUS SYMBOLS

Lynch v. Donnelly (1984) upheld the display of a crèche, erected by the city of Pawtucket, R.I., in the heart of the shopping district, as having a secular purpose. In a concurring opinion, Justice Sandra Day O'Connor argued that the crèche was part of the "overall holiday setting" and was not "intended to endorse nor had the effect of endorsing Christianity."

Allegheny County v. ACLU (1989) held that a crèche displayed in the county courthouse, unaccompanied by secular symbols of the Christmas season, violated the Establishment Clause, whereas a Christmas tree and a Jewish Hanukkah menorah, displayed on the front steps of the city hall, were not a government endorsement of religion but rather a recognition that "both Christmas and Hanukkah are part of the same winter-holiday season, which has attained a secular status in our society."

Capitol Square Review and Advisory Board v. Pinette (1995) upheld the erection by the Ku Klux Klan (a private organization) of a cross in a state park.

The Free Exercise Clause. The "free exercise" of religion, as Justice Owen J. Roberts explained in *Cantwell v. Connecticut* (1940), involves both the freedom to believe and the freedom to act. "The first is absolute but, in the nature of things, the second cannot be. Conduct remains subject to regulation for the protection of society."

Reynolds v. United States (1878) upheld Congress's power to impose criminal sanctions against the Mormon practice of polygamy.

Minersville School District v. Gobitis (1940) upheld a school board's expelling two children who refused to salute the flag because of their religious beliefs as Jehovah's Witnesses.

West Virginia State Board of Education v. Barnette (1943) reversed *Gobitis* and protected Jehovah's Witnesses' refusal to salute the flag.

Sherbert v. Verner (1963) ruled that government could not burden religious practice without a "compelling interest," and then it must use the "least restrictive alternative" to achieve its end.

Wisconsin v. Yoder (1972) found that the state's "compelling interest" in compulsory education to age 16 did not override the free-exercise rights of Amish parents, who refused on religious grounds to send their children to school beyond the eighth grade.

TWA v. Hardison (1977) ruled that an employer does not have to accommodate an employee's religious observance if that results in more than a *de minimis* cost.

Frazee v. Illinois Department of Employment Security (1990) ruled that unemployment benefits could not be withheld from a worker who refused to work on his Sabbath.

Employment Division, Department of Human Resources v. Smith (1990) abandoned the "compelling interest" requirement of *Sherbert v. Verner* and ruled that any law of general application was sufficient to override a religious observer's free-exercise right.

Church of the Lukumi Babalu Aye, Inc. v. City of Hialeah (1993) struck down Hialeah's ban on ritual animal sacrifice practiced by adherents of Santeria, a religion derived from West Africa and practiced by Caribbean immigrants in the United States.

City of Boerne v. Flores (1997) struck down the Religious Freedom Restoration Act (RFRA) passed by Congress in 1993—unanimously in the House, 97–3 in the Senate—in reaction to the Court's decision in *Smith* abandoning the "compelling interest" requirement in burdening religious practice. For the Court, Justice Anthony M. Kennedy wrote: "[T]he provisions of the federal statute here involved are beyond congressional authority; it is this court's precedent, not RFRA, which must control."

CINCINNATI, SOCIETY OF THE, fraternal order of former *Continental Army officers, formed in 1783 and named for the Roman general Cincinnatus, who, like George Washington, had been called from his farm to lead the army and then returned to it after the victory rather than seek power for himself. Membership was to be hereditary through the eldest son. Its formation aroused a storm of protest, some Americans seeing in it the beginning of a military nobility and a menace to republican institutions. The society continues to the present day.

CITIES. See *Urbanization.

CIVIL DISOBEDIENCE (1849), essay by transcendentalist author Henry David Thoreau, written after the *Mexican War. "How does it become a man to behave toward this American government to-day?" Thoreau asked. "I answer, that he cannot without disgrace be associated with it. . . . [W]hen a sixth of the population of a nation which has undertaken to be the refuge of liberty are slaves, and a whole country is unjustly overrun and conquered by a foreign army, and subjected to military law, I think that it is not too soon for honest men to rebel and revolutionize."

Thoreau symbolized his dissociation from the U.S. government by refusing to pay his Massachusetts poll tax. For this he spent a night in jail, before friends paid his fine. He recommended the experience to others:

"Under a government which imprisons any unjustly, the true place for a just man is also a prison. . . . It is there that the fugitive slave, and the Mexican prisoner on parole, and the Indian come to plead the wrongs of his race should find them; on that separate, but more free and honorable ground, where the State places those who are not *with* her, but *against* her,—the only house in a slave State in which a free man can abide with honor. If any think that their influence would be lost there, and their voices no longer afflict the ear of the State, that they would not be as an enemy within its walls, they do not know by how much truth is stronger than error, nor how much more eloquently and effectively he can combat injustice who has experienced a little in his own person. Cast your whole vote, not a strip of paper merely, but your whole influence. A minority is powerless while it conforms to the majority; it is not even a minority then; but it is irresistible when it clogs by its whole weight. If the alternative is to keep all just men in prison, or give up war and slavery, the State will not hesitate which to choose."

Thoreau's doctrine of nonviolent resistance to government authority had wide influence, notably on Indian nationalist Mohandas K. Gandhi and American civil rights leader Martin Luther King Jr.

CIVILIAN CONSERVATION CORPS (CCC). See *New Deal.

CIVIL RIGHTS ACT (1866), legislation of the Andrew *Johnson administration. The first civil rights act, passed to nullify the discriminatory Southern *black codes, it conferred civil equality on the former slaves and extended unprecedented federal protection to them.

"[A]ll persons born in the United States," the act began, ". . . excluding Indians not taxed, are hereby declared to be citizens of the United States," thereby reversing the Supreme Court's 1857 ruling in the Dred Scott case (see *Scott v. Sandford) that blacks were not citizens. It went on to declare that "such citizens, of every race and color, without regard to any previous condition of slavery . . . , shall have the same right, in every State and Territory . . . , to make and enforce contracts, to sue, to be parties, and give evidence, to inherit, purchase, lease, sell, hold, and convey real and personal property, and to [enjoy] full and equal benefit of all laws and proceedings for the security of person and property, as is enjoyed by white citizens, and shall be subject to like punishment, pains, and penalties, and to none other, any law, statute, ordinance, regulation, or custom, to the contrary notwithstanding." Where persons were denied these equal rights, the act authorized federal courts and officers, including the president and the armed forces, to enforce them. The act did not give freedmen the right to vote, which the Constitution left to the states to determine.

President Johnson vetoed the bill as infringing on states' rights. "In all our history," he wrote, "in all our experience as a people living under Federal and State law, no such system as that contemplated by the details of this bill has ever before been proposed or adopted. . . . It is another step, or rather stride, toward centralization and the concentration of all legislative powers in the National Government." First passed on Mar. 13, 1866, the act was repassed over the president's veto on Apr. 9.

CIVIL RIGHTS ACT (1875), legislation of the *Grant administration seeking to ensure the social as well as the political equality of freedmen. Since "it is essential to just government [that] we recognize the equality of all men before the law," the act declared "That all persons within the jurisdiction of the United States shall be entitled to the full and equal enjoyment of the accommodations, advantages, facilities, and privileges of inns, public conveyances on land or water, theaters, and other places of public amusement. . . ." And further: "That no citizen possessing all other qualifications which are or may be prescribed by law shall be disqualified for service as grand or petit juror in any court of the United States, or of any State, on account of race, color, or previous condition of servitude. . . ."

The act was passed in honor of Sen. Charles Sumner of Massachusetts, its author, who had died the previous year. Sumner's original bill had prohibited racial discrimination in all "common schools and public institutions of learning or benevolence supported in whole or in part by general taxation." Passed by the Senate, this provision was rejected by the House, which was not ready for integrated schools.

To secure their rights under the act, it was necessary for blacks who had been denied equal accommodations or jury service to sue, which few did. When five *Civil Rights Cases reached the Supreme Court in 1883, the act was declared unconstitutional.

CIVIL RIGHTS ACT (1957), legislation of the *Eisenhower administration. The first civil rights act since 1875, it established a two-year Civil Rights Commission to investigate the denial of voting rights and a permanent Civil Rights Division within the Justice Department. It also authorized the attorney general to institute civil suits in federal district courts on behalf of blacks whose voting rights had been denied rather than leaving the burden on them to seek redress. The act's effectiveness was nullified, however, by its provision of jury trials for state officials accused of violating court orders on voting rights, although everyone knew that Southern juries would not convict where black voting rights had been denied. In the Senate, Democratic majority leader Lyndon Johnson persuaded enough moderates that it was this bill or nothing to get the bill passed. Many civil rights leaders were outraged, as was President Eisenhower, for whom voting rights was the one black issue toward which he was sympathetic.

CIVIL RIGHTS ACT (1964), legislation of the Lyndon *Johnson administration. It prohibited the application of different standards in the same political subdivision in determining qualification for voting in federal elections and made a sixth-grade education a presumption of literacy. It forbade discrimination or segregation on grounds of race, color, religion, or national origin in any place of public accommodation and authorized the attorney general to bring suit to eliminate discrimination in any public place, including schools, hospitals, libraries, and museums. It outlawed discrimination in employment not only on the basis of race, color, religion, and national origin but also on the basis of sex, and created the Equal Employment Opportunity Commission to investigate and remedy complaints. It cut off funding to any state or local government that discriminated in the administration of federally funded programs.

Passed only after a three-month filibuster by Southern senators, the most far-reaching civil rights bill since *Reconstruction was vigorously enforced by the Johnson administration.

CIVIL RIGHTS CASES (1883), 8–1 decisions of the *Waite Court in five cases testing the *Civil Rights Act of 1875, which prohibited discrimination in public accommodations on account of race. That law was intended to implement the *13th and *14th Amendments, from which it claimed to derive its authority.

For the majority, Justice Joseph P. Bradley rejected the appeal to either amendment. As for the 14th Amendment, he wrote: "It is state action of a particular character that is prohibited. Individual invasion of individual rights is not the subject-matter of the Amendment. . . . Positive rights and privileges are undoubtedly secured by the Fourteenth Amendment, but they are secured by way of prohibition against state laws and state proceedings affecting those rights and privileges." For Congress to pass legislation covering "the whole domain of rights appertaining to life, liberty and property . . . would be to establish a code of municipal law regulative of all private rights between man and man in society. It would be to make Congress take the place of the state legislatures and to supersede them."

As for the 13th Amendment, Bradley denied that "mere discriminations on account of race or color" were "badges of slavery." "When a man has emerged from slavery, and by the aid of beneficent legislation has shaken off the inseparable concomitants of that state, there must be some stage in the progress of his elevation when he takes the rank of a mere citizen, and ceases to be the special favorite of the law, and when his rights as a citizen, or a man, are to be protected in the ordinary mode by which other men's rights are protected. . . ."

In dissent, Justice John Marshall Harlan, a Southerner and former slave owner, wrote: "I agree that government has nothing to do with social, as distinguished from technically legal, rights of individuals. No government ever has brought, or ever can bring, its people into social intercourse against their wishes. . . . The rights which Congress, by the Act of 1875, endeavored to secure and protect are legal, not social rights. The right, for instance, of a colored citizen to use the accommodations of a public highway, upon the same terms as are permitted to white citizens, is no more a social right than his right, under the law, to use the public streets of a city or a town, or a turnpike road, or a public market, or a post office, or his right to sit in a public building with others, of whatever race, for the purpose of hearing the political questions of the day discussed."

As a result of the Court's decision in the *Civil Rights Cases*, the federal government withdrew from the enforcement of civil rights until after World War 2.

CIVIL RIGHTS MOVEMENT (1954–68), movement by African-Americans, supported by white sympathizers, to end segregation and racial discrimination in the United States.

Background. When slavery was ended after the Civil War, the Southern states passed *black codes, laws designed to preserve the subordination of the black race to the white. Congress, however, made the federal government the protector of the former slaves. In the *13th, *14th, and *15th Amendments to the Constitution, and in the *Civil Rights Acts of 1866, 1870, 1871, and 1875, Congress sought to erase all the "badges" and "incidents" of slavery, all racial distinctions that had any support in law or custom. Slavery was abolished; all persons born or naturalized in the United States were citizens; and all (male) citizens, without regard to race, were to enjoy the rights to vote, to serve on juries, to sue and be sued, to give evidence in courts of law, to inherit, buy, sell, or lease property, to make and enforce contracts, to obtain accommodations in places of public resort, and to be subject to like punishments and penalties—in all respects to enjoy the full and equal protection of the laws.

With the end of *Reconstruction in 1877, the federal government withdrew from active protection of blacks' civil rights. The civil rights legislation of the Reconstruction period was soon a dead letter. By law in the South, by custom in much of the rest of the country, segregation became the accepted solution to the problem of race relations. In 1883 the Supreme Court found the public-accommodations sections of the Civil Rights Act of 1875 unconstitutional: the 14th Amendment, on which the act was based, prohibited discriminatory *state* action, not discriminatory *private* action. Furthermore, the Court did not consider racial discrimination in hotels, theaters, or railroads a "badge" of slavery. In 1896 the Court ruled that the provision of separate but equal facilities for blacks satisfied the constitutional requirement of equal protection of the laws. For more than 50 years, the Court legitimized segregation by upholding the "separate but equal" doctrine—despite the fact that public facilities provided for blacks were conspicuously unequal and sometimes nonexistent, despite the growing awareness that separate facilities were inherently unequal.

In those 50 years, the country's black population experienced a profound transformation. During World War 1 and again during World War 2 and the postwar years, blacks in great numbers migrated from the rural South to the industrial cities of the Northeast and Midwest. The black migration made civil rights a national rather than a Southern concern. Nevertheless, conservative presidents, legislators, and judges made sure that patterns of segregation and discrimination yielded only slowly. Starting in the 1930s, the *National Association for the Advancement of Colored People (NAACP), through its Legal Defense and Educational Fund, cautiously challenged the constitutional foundations of segregation: in 1948 the Supreme Court ruled that racially restrictive covenants were not enforceable in the courts; in several cases between 1938 and 1950 it compelled state professional and graduate schools in the South to admit black students. Yet, at the beginning of the 1950s, segregation was still legally established in the South, and racial discrimination was customary in much of the rest of the country.

The consequences of the blacks' stigmatized social status—first as slaves, then as a segregated social caste—were discernible in every index of life quality when whites and blacks were compared, including life expectancy, infant mortality, death rates, educational attainment, illiteracy, unemployment, labor force participation, poverty, family income, family composition, and crime. The gulf between whites and blacks belied the American ideals of nationhood and equality.

The Movement. The great victory of the NAACP Legal Defense and Educational Fund was the unanimous decision of the U.S. Supreme Court in *Brown v. Board of Education of Topeka* outlawing racial segregation in public schools. The Court's ruling that separation was inherently unequal put an end to the "separate but equal" doctrine in schools and doomed all other forms of legalized segregation. *School desegregation in the South initially met massive resistance, which had to be overcome in notable instances by federal troops and marshals (see *Little Rock Crisis).

While the nation's courts continued for many years to carry out the *Brown* decision, black civil rights organizations—the *Southern Christian Leadership Council (SCLC), the *Student Nonviolent Coordinating Committee (SNCC), the *Congress of Racial Equality (CORE), the *National Urban League, and the NAACP—determined to confront other forms of segregation physically, by nonviolent direct action, in order to provoke a resistance that would arouse the conscience of the country and bring the federal government to their aid. This was the story of the *Montgomery bus boycott, the *Birmingham campaign, the *sit-ins and *freedom rides, *Freedom Summer, and the *Selma-to-Montgomery march. Blacks and white sympathizers were killed and brutalized by Southern police and racist mobs while television news cameras recorded the violence. The high point of the movement was the dignified 1963 March on Washington when Martin Luther King Jr. inspired a large crowd with his "I Have a Dream" speech that concluded with the moving verse from an old spiritual, "Free at last! Free at last! Thank God almighty, we are free at last!" The black civil rights movement contributed significantly to passage of the *Civil Rights Acts in 1957, 1960, 1964, and 1968 and the *Voting Rights Act of 1965.

Its immediate political goals won, the movement turned to the intractable economic and social problems of blacks in Northern inner cities. Now its unity began to fray. Youthful activists lost patience with the nonviolent strategy of the older leaders and turned to *black power, racial separation, radical social policies, and criticism of the war in Vietnam. The eruption of riots in urban ghettos, North and South, in the summers of 1963–68 signaled the movement's loss of leadership, which was dramatized on Apr. 4, 1968, by the assassination of Martin Luther King Jr. King's *Poor People's Campaign, carried out with misgivings by his followers as a tribute to their fallen leader, marked the end of the movement.

Its Achievements. During the administrations of presidents John F. Kennedy and Lyndon B. Johnson, the executive branch vigorously enforced the new civil rights acts. The cooperation of the judicial, legislative, and executive branches, however, did not last beyond the 1960s. When the civil rights movement began to affect communities outside the South and to arouse widespread opposition there, the politically sensitive branches of the government—Congress and the president—deserted the cause, leaving civil rights policy largely to the courts.

It was soon discovered that civil rights fell into two groups. In the first—comprising principally voting rights, public accommodations, and criminal justice—racial justice seemed to require only the removal of discriminatory barriers that prevented blacks from exercising their equal rights. In a second group—education, employment, and housing—the mere prohibition of racial discrimination did not alter old patterns of deprivation. Here the federal government and the courts ordered *affirmative action— positive measures to ensure that blacks actually received the material benefits of rights long denied.

Voting. After the withdrawal of federal troops in 1877, the Southern states moved promptly to disfranchise blacks. The means employed included poll taxes, tests of literacy or of knowledge of the Constitution, required character references, and physical and economic coercion. In 1959, the U.S. Civil Rights Commission reported that whereas 62 percent of the white population of voting age in ten Southern states were registered as voters, only 25 percent of blacks were registered. Disfranchisement was most common in rural counties where blacks constituted a majority of the population. In 16 of the 158 Southern counties where blacks were a majority, there was not one black voter; in 49 others, fewer than 5 percent of eligible blacks were registered. (Once registered, of course, blacks were often prevented from voting by physical and economic intimidation.)

The Civil Rights Acts of 1957, 1960, and 1964, along with the *24th Amendment to the Constitution (barring poll taxes) ratified in 1964, proved ineffective. Southern election officials were resourceful in circumventing each successive act and raising new legal challenges. Ultimately, the Voting Rights Act of 1965 swept aside all tests for voter registration and ensured the registration of eligible blacks, by federal examiners if need be. Black voting power has made public officials increasingly responsive to black interests. This is most dramatically evident in the South, where the overt racial demagogues of former years have largely vanished from political life. The most impressive evidence of black voting power, however, is the number of black elected officials. In 1964, there were only 103 black elected officials nationwide; in 1999 there were 8,896.

In many Southern cities and counties where blacks constitute substantial minorities, their political impact has been nullified to a significant extent by such devices as the creation of electoral districts that dilute or divide black voting strength; the requirement of election by a majority rather than a plurality, with the result that runoff elections often pit a minority black candidate against a white; and the preservation of the at-large system of voting in which public officials are elected not by districts but by the total electorate of a jurisdiction.

Public Accommodations. In 1946 the U.S. Supreme Court declared racial segregation on interstate buses unconstitutional, in 1952 it banned segregation on interstate railroads, and in 1960 it banned segregation at interstate terminals. Segregation on buses running within a state—13 Southern and Border states required such segregation—was declared unconstitutional in 1956. In 1955 the Court abolished segregation in such public recreational facilities as parks, playgrounds, golf courses, and beaches.

All these prohibitions were largely ignored by local communities, as was revealed by sit-ins and freedom rides in 1960–61 that subjected civil rights demonstrators to beatings, shootings, bombings, and riots. On occasion, federal law-enforcement agents had to be sent into the South to protect civil rights workers when local officials proved unwilling or unable to maintain order. Eventually sick of violence, the South gradually acquiesced in the end of legally enforced segregation, although subtle segregation is still widespread.

Criminal Justice. By law and custom, black criminals in the post-Reconstruction South were subjected to severer punishments than whites for committing the same offenses. This was most conspicuous in the punishment of blacks who violated the South's sexual code. The systematic exclusion of blacks from Southern juries ensured the absence of any restraint in a judicial system dedicated to upholding white supremacy.

In 1959, the U.S. Supreme Court upheld an appeals court ruling reversing the murder conviction of a black on the ground that blacks were excluded from juries in the Mississippi county where the trial had taken place. (Although more than half the county's population was black, no blacks were included on the list of registered voters from which juries were chosen.) In 1967, an all-white federal jury in Meridian, Miss., convicted seven white defendants of the murder of three civil rights workers, one of whom was black. This was the first time a Mississippi jury had convicted white defendants in the murder of a black.

Nationally, racial discrimination is still a factor in the disproportionate numbers of blacks sentenced to state and federal prisons, and particularly among persons sentenced to death. In 1997 blacks constituted 44.1 percent of all state prison inmates. Of 4,542 persons executed for all causes between 1930 and 2000, 51.0 percent were blacks. Blacks often receive significantly longer sentences than whites for the same crimes, particularly crimes of violence.

CIVIL SERVICE REFORM (1850–83). A small, respected federal civil service was thrown into disorder in 1829 when Pres. Andrew Jackson instituted the *spoils system, replacing existing officeholders, whom he considered a privileged elite, with his own partisans. Jackson rationalized the change as a democratic rotation of offices, but its true purpose was to reward faithful party workers with federal jobs. This enhanced party discipline, but it contributed to incompetence and corruption in the civil service. The spoilsmen often had no qualifications for the offices they filled, were subject to exactions from their salaries to meet party needs, and could expect to be turned out with the election of the opposition party with its own workers to reward.

In the 1850s, demand grew for a permanent, tenured civil service built on the merit system. During the *Grant administration, reform-minded Republicans like E. L. Godkin, Carl Schurz, Charles Sumner, and Lyman Trumbull took up the cause. In 1871 Congress established a Civil Service Commission authorized to make recommendations for reform. Grant soon lost interest in the issue, and the commission's chairman, George William Curtis, resigned. Civil service reform became a major objective of the *Liberal Republican Party in the election of 1872.

The assassination in 1881 of Pres. James A. Garfield by a disappointed office seeker renewed the demand for reform. The **Pendleton Act** (1883) authorized the appointment of a three-member, bipartisan commission to administer competitive examinations on the basis of which future appointments would be made. Government jobs were organized in a hierarchy of classifications, and appointees were assured of tenure and freedom from enforced political contributions. Only a small fraction of federal employees were covered initially, but the number was gradually extended in subsequent administrations and the system itself extensively revised to make it a professional career service.

During the *New Deal and World War 2, the federal civil service was rapidly enlarged and the merit system for a time abandoned. In 1949 the service was critically reviewed by the Commission on Organization of the Executive Branch (the Hoover Commission). Its most comprehensive reform was effected by the **Civil Service Reform Act** of 1978. This act abolished the old Civil Service Commission, dividing its functions between an Office of Personnel Management to supervise personnel policies like those used in the private sector—for example, executive development and regular performance appraisals—and a Merit System Protection Board to adjudicate alleged violations of established procedures. The latter board was also charged to protect "whistleblowers" who report on waste, fraud, or corruption in their agencies.

CIVIL SERVICE REFORM ACT (1978). See *Civil Service Reform.

CIVIL WAR (1861–65), conflict between 11 Southern states, constituting the *Confederate States of America and fighting for independence, and 23 Northern and Border states, still the United States of America, fighting to preserve the federal Union.

Causes. The South went to war in 1861 to win independence, the North to suppress an "insurrection." The controversies over slavery—its existence, its extension, its limitation, its influence—that had convulsed the country for the preceding ten years were suddenly replaced by the uncomplicated issue of *secession. Northerners who disliked blacks and were indifferent to slavery united in support of a Republican president who denied that there was a constitutional right to secede and who was resolved to preserve the Union. Not until the *Emancipation Proclamation in 1863 did the abolition of slavery become a Union war aim, to the discomfiture of many Northerners and Border staters. But contemporaries knew—although some later historians denied—that slavery was the cause of the war. "[S]laves constituted a peculiar and powerful interest [in 1861]," Pres. Abraham Lincoln recalled in 1865. "All knew that this interest was, somehow, the cause of the war."

Until 1860, the ties holding Americans together were stronger than the issues that divided them. Most Americans shared a common language and religion, a common history and vision of a glorious future. Most were farmers who worked their own land, believed in personal independence, social egalitarianism, and the virtues of hard work and honest acquisition. The three great sections of the country—Northeast, Northwest, and South (see *Sectionalism)—were economically complementary and interdependent. They were fast becoming even more so with the development of new means of communication such as the steamboat, the railroad, and the telegraph.

But the South possessed one institution that the other sections did not—slavery. To protect its "peculiar institution," the South developed a distinctive civilization and constitutional theory. Born into a slave society, Southerners accepted its ethos with little question. Those who owned slaves—a quarter of the white population—were dependent upon them for their prosperity. Those who did not own slaves derived social status from the presence of a stigmatized caste. Most white Americans of all classes, North as well as South, believed that Africans were an inferior race naturally fitted for slavery and could not conceive of any social order in which whites and free blacks could live together. In 1820 Thomas Jefferson said of slavery: "[W]e have the wolf by the ears, and we can neither hold him nor safely let him go." Abraham Lincoln in 1854 said: "I surely will not blame them [Southerners] for not doing what I should not know how to do myself."

The rising criticism of slavery, especially after 1850, seemed to Southerners uninformed, hypocritical, intrusive, and ultimately insulting. They keenly resented the lack of respect manifested by the North for the Southern way of life, which they regarded as superior to the Northern. As the population of the Northeast and Northwest grew, the South saw itself reduced to a permanent minority in which its unique civilization was threatened. Feeling forced to choose between preserving the Southern way of life and accepting domination by "Yankees" in a hostile federal Union, Southerners increasingly inclined toward independence. With the election in 1860 of a "black Republican" as president, that choice suddenly became an urgent one.

The Adversaries. The Union and the Confederacy went to war in a mood of wild enthusiasm, although at first glance the two sides seemed distinctly uneven. In its 23 states, the Union had a population of 22 million; in its 11 states, the Confederacy had only 9 million, of whom 3.5 million were slaves. During the course of the war, the Union was able to put more than 1.5 million men (186,000 of them black) into military service, the Confederacy 900,000. The Confederate army reached its largest size in 1863; in the last year of the war, the Union had 800,000 men under arms, the Confederacy 200,000.

The Northern states had 110,000 manufacturing plants and 1.3 million industrial workers compared to the South's 18,000 plants and 110,000 industrial workers. At the start of the war, the North manufactured 97 percent of the nation's firearms and 96 percent of its railroad equipment. It contained 70 percent of the country's 31,300 miles of railroads.

The apparent advantages of the North were balanced to some degree by less apparent advantages possessed by the South. The South intended to fight a defensive war, in which it would have the advantage of internal lines of communication and would require fewer troops than the North, which had the task of invading the South on several fronts, protecting ever longer lines of communication, and occupying hostile territory in addition to actually defeating Confederate forces in battle. In this last particular, the Confederates had the advantage of a martial tradition and, at least in the first years of the war, superior generalship.

The strategies of the two sides reflected their particular advantages. Confederate president Jefferson Davis eschewed a war of conquest: the Confederacy, he said, "seeks no conquest, no aggrandizement, no concession of any kind from the States with which we were lately confederated; all we ask is to be let alone." Although the Confederacy precipitated the war by its attack on Fort Sumter, its strategy thereafter was largely defensive. It did not have to defeat the North to secure its war aims; a stalemate, in which the North wearied of the struggle, would be sufficient. This was the same strategy pursued by George Washington in the Revolutionary War.

The North had to subdue the Confederacy, a task it at first hoped to accomplish in a short war. Initially there was some thought that a blockade of the Atlantic and Gulf coasts and the Mississippi River would bring the Confederacy to its knees. Public opinion, however, demanded aggressive action. When the North lost its first great battle, it realized that the war would not be short. President Lincoln perceived the necessary Union strategy: "I state my general idea of this war to be that we have the *greater* numbers, and the enemy has the *greater* facility at concentrating forces upon points of collision; that we must fail, unless we can find some way of making *our* advantage an overmatch for his; and that this can only be done by menacing him with superior forces at *different* points at the same time. . . ."

The war was fought in two principal theaters, divided by the Appalachian Mountains, which run from Pennsylvania to Alabama: the Western, extending from the mountains to the Mississippi River, and the Eastern, extending from the mountains to the Atlantic Ocean. In both theaters, the North carried the war into the South. While Union and Confederate armies grappled on a narrow Eastern Front, the war was won in the West.

The War Starts. The six Southern states that seceded December 1860–February 1861 quickly seized federal property—forts, arsenals, customs houses—in their territories. South Carolina's demands for the surrender of Fort Sumter in Charleston harbor was refused. When President Lincoln attempted to reprovision the fort, Confederate authorities ordered its seizure by force. A bombardment (Apr. 12–13) ended in the fort's surrender (see *Fort Sumter Bombardment).

The next day Lincoln summoned 75,000 militiamen into federal service for 90 days to put down an insurrection "too powerful to be suppressed by the ordinary course of judicial proceedings." Seeing in Lincoln's call a measure of coercion against the South, four more Southern states quickly seceded.

Public pressure for action, and a belief that a quick military success might deflate Southern enthusiasm, caused Lincoln to direct Gen. Irvin McDowell to lead the army that was quickly massing in the Washington area into Virginia and seize Manassas, a railroad junction 30 miles away. When McDowell protested that his troops were untrained, Lincoln observed, "You are green, it is true, but they [the Confederates] are green, also; you are all green alike." At the first battle of *Bull Run (July 21, 1861), McDowell's 30,000 troops were routed by the Confederates. Victory filled the South with optimism; defeat sobered the North.

The War in the East, 1861–63. For three years, Union and Confederate armies in the East fought in Virginia for possession of the Confederate capital, Richmond, only 100 miles from Washington.

After Bull Run, Lincoln called to Washington Gen. George B. McClellan, who had recently driven the Confederates out of the western counties of Virginia (which later entered the Union as West Virginia). From July 1861 to March 1862 McClellan organized, equipped, and drilled the 150,000-man Army of the Potomac. Impatiently, the nation demanded action, but McClellan procrastinated. "He has the slows," Lincoln complained. When he finally chose to move, McClellan rejected the direct overland route to Richmond preferred by Lincoln for a movement from the east along the peninsula between the James and York rivers. The result was the failed *Peninsula Campaign (March–July 1862).

Command of the Army of the Potomac was then entrusted to Gen. John Pope, who took the overland route to Richmond. He got only as far as Manassas, where he suffered a disastrous defeat in the second battle of *Bull Run (Aug. 29–30).

Confederate general Robert E. Lee then took the offensive with his Army of Northern Virginia, moving north into Maryland with the idea of cutting off Washington from the rest of the North. Returned to command of the Army of the Potomac, McClellan stopped Lee at *Antietam (Sept. 17, 1862). When McClellan failed to pursue the withdrawing Confederates, Lincoln again replaced him, this time with Gen. Ambrose E. Burnside. Burnside pursued Lee as far as the Rappahannock River, where he met defeat at the battle of *Fredericksburg

(Dec. 13). Burnside's replacement, Gen. Joseph Hooker, shortly led the army to another disaster at *Chancellorsville (May 2–4, 1863).

Lee now moved north again, this time through the Shenandoah Valley into Pennsylvania, again with the idea of cutting off Washington and encouraging defeatism in the North. The Army of the Potomac, now commanded by Gen. George G. Meade, followed him. The two armies met at *Gettysburg (July 1–3, 1863) in the greatest battle of the war. Lee's advance was checked, and he withdrew into Virginia, his army still intact.

The War in the West, 1861–63. In the Western Theater, the Union forces had three successive objectives: first, to keep the Confederates out of neutral Kentucky and to clear them out of strategically important Tennessee; second, to win control of the Mississippi River; and third, to bring the Western armies east to support Union efforts in Virginia.

Union forces entered Kentucky in September 1861. Despite a victory (Jan. 19, 1861) at Mill Springs in eastern Kentucky, they were not able to enter Tennessee to support the unionist population in the eastern portion of that state. In western Kentucky, Gen. Ulysses S. Grant captured (Feb. 6 and 16, 1862) *forts Henry and Donelson on the Tennessee and Cumberland rivers, opening the way to Nashville. The Confederates evacuated Nashville on Feb. 25. On Apr. 6–7, Grant inflicted a costly but decisive defeat on the Confederates at *Shiloh, and on May 25 Union troops entered Corinth, Miss. In August, Confederate general Braxton Bragg launched an offensive from eastern Tennessee into Kentucky; he was stopped at *Perryville (Oct. 8, 1862), and at *Murfreesboro, Tenn. (Dec. 31, 1862–Jan. 3, 1863), was compelled to fall back upon Chattanooga.

Meanwhile, Union forces extended their control over the Mississippi River. On Apr. 7, 1862, Gen. John Pope captured the Confederate river base at Island No. 10, while Commodore David G. Farragut entered the Mississippi from the Gulf of Mexico and seized (Apr. 29) New Orleans (see *New Orleans Capture). On June 6, Union riverboats took Memphis. The last Confederate stronghold on the Mississippi fell to General Grant on July 4, 1863 (see *Vicksburg Campaign).

In eastern Tennessee, Union general William S. Rosecrans maneuvered Bragg out of Knoxville and Chattanooga, but Bragg then inflicted (Sept. 19–20) a sharp defeat on Rosecrans at Chickamauga. Appointed commander of the entire Western Theater, Grant went to Chattanooga and in the battle of Chattanooga (Nov. 24–25) drove the Confederates south into Georgia (see

*Chattanooga Campaign). The way was now open for Union armies in the West to enter Georgia and lend support to the Union army fighting in Virginia.

The Naval War. Of 46 ships in commission at the start of the war, the Union had fewer than a dozen available for immediate service in home waters when President Lincoln declared (Apr. 19, 1861) a blockade of the 3,500-mile Confederate coast. The blockade became increasingly effective as the North rapidly built new ships. The Confederates built small, swift blockade runners that at first penetrated the blockade almost at will although they were capable of carrying only a small fraction of the South's prewar trade. As the blockade became tighter, chances of capture rose from one in ten in 1861 to one in three in 1864. The Confederate ironclad *Virginia* was intended to destroy blockading vessels, but it was scuttled after only a single engagement (see *Monitor* and *Merrimack*).

Lacking the resources to build a seagoing fleet, the Confederates concentrated on building gunboats and torpedo boats for harbor and coastal defense. In Britain, it commissioned or bought 12 commerce raiders, of which the *Florida, Shenandoah,* and *Alabama* became the most famous. Under Capt. Raphael Semmes, the *Alabama,* on a 22-month cruise, captured or destroyed 64 Union merchantmen before it was destroyed in combat with the USS *Kearsarge* in the English Channel on June 19, 1864.

In support of the blockade, Union amphibious operations during the first year of the war seized the coastal islands off North Carolina and South Carolina and key points on the coast itself. By April 1862 Union forces held or had closed every important Atlantic coast harbor except Charleston and Wilmington, N.C. Wilmington was captured by an army-navy task force in January 1865. In September 1861 the Union navy occupied Ship Island off the Gulf coast of Mississippi; from there, in April 1862, Farragut captured *New Orleans and in August 1864 closed *Mobile Bay to blockade runners.

Union riverboats played a crucial role in the Western Theater, supporting Grant at forts Henry and Donelson and winning control of the Mississippi at Island No. 10, Memphis, and Vicksburg.

War Diplomacy. The object of Confederate diplomacy during the war was to win foreign recognition of its independence, for with recognition could come military and financial aid. The object of Union diplomacy was to prevent recognition of the Confederacy and foreign intervention in the war.

The Confederacy was initially optimistic that British dependence on Southern cotton would bring British recognition. But in 1861 the British had a two-year supply of cotton and felt no pressure to accede to Confederate desires. Britain did, however, declare its neutrality early in the war, which in effect recognized at least Confederate belligerency—that is, that the war was not merely an internal rebellion. The United States protested vigorously, but President Lincoln's own establishment of a blockade and treatment of Confederate captives as prisoners of war rather than as rebels had already established the Confederacy as a belligerent.

The Union blockade of Southern ports and seizure of neutral ships strained U.S. relations with Britain. The two powers came close to war in the *Trent* Affair (1861). British sale of munitions and the building of cruisers and rams for the Confederacy were continuing causes of complaint by U.S. representatives in Britain (see *Alabama* Claims). The British upper classes—unlike the middle and lower classes—were sympathetic to the South, and in the fall of 1862 the government came close to intervening in the war in the role of mediator. But the possibility of British intervention rapidly faded after the Union success at Antietam and especially the issuance of the Emancipation Proclamation.

Napoleon III of France, his offer to mediate having been rebuffed, took advantage of the American war to install an Austrian archduke, Maximilian, as his puppet emperor of Mexico in defiance of the Monroe Doctrine. The Confederacy was willing to recognize the new regime in Mexico in exchange for recognition of its independence, but Napoleon would not act independently of Great Britain. After the war, U.S. pressure—combined with European developments—compelled Napoleon to withdraw French troops from Mexico and abandon Maximilian to his fate.

Final Year of the War, May 1864–April 1865. After repeated disappointments, Lincoln finally found in Grant a general who shared his strategic views and was not reluctant to fight. In March 1864 Grant was called to Washington and promoted to lieutenant general and general in chief of all Union armies. He designated Gen. William T. Sherman his successor as commander in the Western Theater. Grant now planned a combined offensive to end the war. Making his headquarters with the Army of the Potomac, which was commanded by General Meade, he would drive against Richmond while Sherman, with the combined armies of the Ohio, Tennessee, and Cumberland, would advance against Atlanta.

The offensives began in May 1864. Meeting the usual initial reverse in the battle of the Wilderness on May 5–6, the Army of the Potomac did not retreat but continued south, repeatedly outflanking General Lee and bloodying the Confederates at Spotsylvania Court House (May 8–12) and Cold Harbor (June 1–3) at enormous cost in Union casualties (see *Wilderness Campaign). On June 12, Grant broke off his deadly duel with Lee, slipped away from Cold Harbor, and reappeared on June 15 at Petersburg, a railroad junction 20 miles south of Richmond through which Lee's army and the Confederate capital were supplied. The siege of *Petersburg lasted until Apr. 2, 1865, when Lee's starving army escaped to the west.

Meanwhile, Sherman had taken Atlanta on Sept. 2, 1864 (see *Atlanta Campaign). In his rear, Confederate general John Bell Hood conceived the idea of fighting his way through Tennessee to join Lee in Virginia; this plan was frustrated at the battle of *Nashville (Dec. 15–16). At the same time, Sherman, having left Atlanta on Nov. 14, was marching to the sea, devastating the countryside in his path (see *Sherman's March Through Georgia). At Savannah he turned north into South Carolina and North Carolina against the feeble opposition of Confederate general Joseph E. Johnston.

In Virginia, Lee was quickly surrounded after leaving Petersburg. On Apr. 9 he surrendered to Grant at Appomattox Court House (see *Appomattox Surrender). On Apr. 26 Johnston surrendered to Sherman near Durham Station, N.C. The remaining Confederate troops east of the Mississippi surrendered at Citronelle, Ala., on May 4. Troops in the trans-Mississippi West surrendered at New Orleans on May 26.

Consequences. The greatest war of the 19th century, for the United States the Civil War was more costly than all its other wars combined. The Union suffered 360,000 dead (killed in battle or died of wounds), the Confederates 258,000. The cost in treasure was incalculable. It left the South devastated and embittered—and struggling with a far-reaching social revolution—for generations.

But the war put an end to the doctrine of secession. The constitutional theory that the United States was a confederation of sovereign states received its deathblow. In place of a confederation of states there now stood a single nation under a central government of unprecedented powers. The war also put an end to slavery, transforming 4 million ill-prepared African-Americans from chattel to citizenship and from economic dependence to independence. Finally, it launched the nation— particularly the Northern states—onto the course of rapid industrialization, large-scale business enterprise, and urbanization.

CIVIL WORKS ADMINISTRATION (CWA). See *New Deal.

CLAYTON ANTITRUST ACT (1914), legislation of the *Wilson administration. Aimed to close loopholes in the *Sherman Antitrust Act (1890), it prohibited price discrimination where it tended to lessen competition, purchase contracts that prevented the purchaser from buying the products of a competitor, and interlocking directorates in industrial organizations capitalized at $1 million or more. Corporation officials were made personally responsible for their corporation's violations. Businessmen had little difficulty circumventing the act's restrictions, and legislators realized that it was impossible to specify all possible unfair competitive practices. A remedy for this problem was sought in the *Federal Trade Commission Act (1914).

For labor, the act declared that "the labor of a human being is not a commodity or article of commerce." It reaffirmed labor's right to organize, exempted unions from antitrust laws (as combinations in restraint of trade), legalized strikes, peaceful picketing, and boycotts, and outlawed the use of the injunction in most labor disputes. Samuel Gompers, president of the American Federation of Labor, hailed the Clayton Act as labor's "Magna Carta," but the deliberately ambiguous language of its labor provisions enabled the courts to largely nullify them. The weaknesses of the Clayton Act's labor provisions were corrected only by the *National Labor Relations Act (1935).

CLAYTON-BULWER TREATY (1850). See *Panama Canal.

CLEAN AIR ACT (1970). See *Environmentalism.

CLEAN WATER ACT (1972). See *Environmentalism.

CLEVELAND ADMINISTRATION, FIRST (1885–89). Gruff, frugal, and honest, Grover Cleveland became the 22nd president of the United States—the first Democrat since James Buchanan—with a reputation as a reformer, although his reformist impulse derived from conservative Jacksonian principles (see *Jacksonian Democracy): strict construction of the Constitution, limited government honestly and economically administered, and hostility to government favoritism.

His most notable achievement was his assertion of presidential independence against an aggressive Senate.

During *Reconstruction, Congress, dominated by *Radical Republicans, had significantly reduced the powers of the presidency. Now a Republican Senate, stretching the terms of the revised Tenure of Office Act (1867), demanded to see all the documents pertaining to presidential dismissals and appointments. Cleveland resisted successfully and in the end obtained (1887) repeal of the act.

Although he supported *civil service reform in principle and eventually extended the number of protected federal employees from 16,000 to 27,000, he believed in the necessity of patronage as a means of controlling his party and influencing Congress. Finding the federal bureaucracy almost 100 percent Republican when he took office, he had no qualms about replacing 75 percent of the unprotected officeholders with deserving Democrats.

In his appointments to federal jobs, Cleveland showed no preference for unqualified Civil War veterans. Moreover, he regarded many of the private pension bills that came before him as fraudulent appeals for government favor. He vetoed 228 of them (approving 1,871) and also vetoed a Dependent Pension Bill (passed in the next administration) that would have given pensions to disabled veterans with only 90 days' service and to their dependents. His disregard of the veterans lobby—and especially his willingness to return *Confederate battle flags to the Southern states—solidified the alliance between the *Grand Army of the Republic and the Republican Party.

Cleveland's egalitarianism was troubled by the unequal conflict between labor and capital, and he proposed the establishment of a permanent board for the voluntary arbitration of labor disputes. His hostility to government favoritism led him to halt the fraudulent land claims of Western land-grant railroads, timber and cattle interests, and speculators. He perceived the high protective tariff maintained by the Republican Party since the Civil War as a prime example of government favoritism to business interests, a form of inequitable taxation that raised the cost of living for workers while enriching monopolists (see *Tariffs). In December 1887 he devoted his entire third annual message to Congress to an argument for tariff reform.

Important legislation of the first Cleveland administration included the Interstate Commerce Act of 1887 (see *Railroad Regulation), the Dawes General Allotment Act of 1887 (see *Indian Policy), and the *Hatch Act (1887).

Seeking reelection in 1888, Cleveland made tariff reform his central issue and lost. He was succeeded by Republican Benjamin Harrison.

CLEVELAND ADMINISTRATION, SECOND

(1893–97). Returned to office as the 24th president of the United States, Democrat Grover Cleveland seemed inflexibly conservative. His cabinet contained no representative of the agrarian wing of his party, no sympathizer with labor; all were champions of "sound money."

The new administration was confronted at once by the *Panic of 1893, which was followed by a four-year economic depression. Cleveland attributed the panic to the decline of U.S. gold reserves, caused, he believed, by the *Sherman Silver Purchase Act (1890). He demanded and obtained repeal of the Sherman Act, splitting his party between silver and gold Democrats. When gold reserves continued to decline below $100 million (the minimum necessary to support the currency, as was commonly believed), Cleveland resorted to several public bond issues to finance gold purchases, then to a private bond issue through Wall Street bankers headed by J. P. Morgan, an alliance that mortally offended the silver Democrats and sealed Cleveland's reputation as a conservative.

Cleveland's hope for tariff reform was disappointed in the *Wilson-Gorman Tariff (1894). He pleased advocates of *civil service reform by doubling the number of covered civil servants (to 87,000 out of a total of 200,000). Although deeply concerned about the condition of labor, he felt compelled to adopt a law-and-order stance against popular manifestations of economic distress such as *Coxey's Army (1894) and the *Pullman strike (1894).

In foreign affairs, Cleveland condemned U.S. involvement in the revolution in Hawaii and withdrew a treaty of annexation that Pres. Benjamin Harrison had laid before the Senate (see *Hawaii Annexation). By dangerous bluster, he forced Great Britain to submit the *Venezuelan boundary dispute to arbitration.

During Cleveland's second administration, Utah became (1896) the 45th state. Cleveland was succeeded by Republican William McKinley.

CLINTON ADMINISTRATION   (1993–2001).

Democrat William J. Clinton, 42nd president of the United States, defined himself as a "New Democrat," resolved to bring his party from the left of the ideological spectrum to the broad middle—where presidential elections are won. At the start of his presidency, he had four major objectives, only one of which (the third) was popular with party liberals: deficit reduction, free trade, universal *health insurance, and *welfare reform.

In 1993 Congress narrowly passed Clinton's package of tax increases and spending cuts intended to reduce the budget deficit. No Republican in either house supported it. But the policy of deficit reduction contributed to the country's recovery from the recession of 1990–91 and to the economic expansion that continued throughout Clinton's presidency (see *New Economy). Committed to global economic engagement rather than economic nationalism, Clinton overcame the opposition of congressional liberals to win approval in 1993 of the *North American Free Trade Agreement, to lead the country into the World Trade Organization in 1994, and, in 2000, to normalize trade with China (ending annual congressional reviews of China's human rights record). An overelaborate plan for universal health insurance was rejected by Congress in 1995, but in 1996 Congress passed the Personal Responsibility and Work Opportunity Act, fulfilling Clinton's promise to "end welfare as we know it."

At the start of his presidency, Clinton had Democratic majorities in both houses of Congress, but in 1994 Republicans won control. Conservative Republicans in the House launched a *Republican Revolution, which self-destructed in 1996 when they forced the government to shut down in a budget controversy with the president. Clinton was reelected in 1996—the first Democrat to be elected president twice since Franklin Roosevelt. Congress, again in Republican hands, was mired in partisanship. Forced to abandon large schemes of the sort that had characterized his first term, Clinton now concentrated on undramatic but constructive initiatives in welfare, education, crime, gun control, health insurance, the environment, foreign trade, and telecommunications. Two major legislative achievements of his second term were the *Freedom to Farm Act (1996), which sought to end *New Deal production controls on major crops and income-support payments to farmers, and the *Financial Services Modernization Act (1999), which partially repealed the Glass-Steagall Act of 1932 and permitted banks to enter the brokerage and insurance businesses.

In foreign affairs, Clinton directed U.S. intervention in Somalia and the Balkans (see *Somalia Intervention; *Balkan Intervention), futilely bombed Iraq in 1998 for not cooperating with weapons inspectors, and took a prominent role in the Arab-Israeli peace process. His support of Russian president Boris Yeltsin helped preserve Russia's democratic government, while his intervention in Mexican and Asian financial crises averted international economic disasters. During his administration, the United States experienced several acts of *terrorism, both domestic (see *Oklahoma City Bombing) and international (see *World Trade Center Attack 1; *Embassy Bombings).

A master politician, Clinton was gifted, well informed, articulate, and empathic. His political enemies pursued him relentlessly but fruitlessly in the *Whitewater scandal.

His self-destructive character flaws included persistent womanizing, most notoriously a relationship with a young White House intern. His lying about this under oath brought about his impeachment (see *Clinton Impeachment), which he narrowly survived. (On his last day in office, he signed an agreement with Independent Counsel Robert W. Ray in which he avoided criminal liability by admitting that he had given false testimony and by surrendering his law license for five years.) Clinton departed the White House in a cloud of marital discord, outrage over some unsavory last-minute pardons, and disgust over his solicitation of expensive gifts from friends and supporters. He was succeeded by Republican George W. Bush.

CLINTON IMPEACHMENT (1998–99), the second impeachment of a president in U.S. history. Both were unsuccessful. (See *Johnson Impeachment.)

In 1994 an *independent prosecutor, Kenneth W. Starr, began investigating a number of scandals in which Pres. William J. Clinton was allegedly involved. One was an Arkansas land deal, when Clinton was governor of that state, called "Whitewater"; another, involving the White House travel office, was called "Travelgate"; the third, involving White House use of Federal Bureau of Investigation files, was called "Filegate." He also investigated the suicide in 1994 of White House aide Vincent Foster. After four years and the expenditure of some $35 million, Starr failed to produce any evidence of Clinton wrongdoing.

In January 1998 it was revealed that Clinton—who had a reputation as a womanizer and was even then being sued for sexual harassment by one Paula Jones in Arkansas (that case was dismissed in April 1998, but a year later Clinton was cited for contempt of court for having given "false, misleading and evasive answers" in a deposition)—had for two years conducted an affair with a young White House intern. On Jan. 26, 1998, on national television, Clinton flatly (and untruthfully) denied the story. From the U.S. attorney general, the independent prosecutor had already sought and obtained permission to enlarge his investigation of the president to include this latest scandal.

For the next eight months, Starr's prosecutors examined witnesses before a Washington grand jury. Clinton's own testimony—a videotaped deposition broadcast nationwide—was evasive and hairsplitting. On Sept. 9, Starr presented his "findings"—a report of 445 pages containing excerpts of the grand jury testimony—to the House Judiciary Committee. He advised the committee that the material contained in his report supported 11 possible grounds for impeachment.

On Dec. 11–12, 1998, the House Judiciary Committee approved four articles of impeachment. A week later, on Dec. 19, the House of Representatives (a "lame duck" House, 7 of whose members had failed of reelection in November and 23 who would retire in January) approved two articles—one charging perjury, the other obstruction of justice. Both in the committee and then on the House floor, the president's defenders conceded that his conduct had been reprehensible but that it did not meet the constitutional test of impeachable offenses, namely, "treason, bribery, or other high crimes and misdemeanors." The partisan nature of the proceedings is evidenced by the votes. The House Judiciary Committee divided on party lines. In the House itself, the first article of impeachment was approved 228 (all Republicans) to 206 (all Democrats), the second 221 (all Republicans) to 212 (all Democrats plus six Republicans).

The trial of the president was held in the U.S. Senate from Jan. 7 to Feb. 12, 1999, the chief justice of the United States presiding. The case against the president was made by 13 "House managers," the defense conducted by the president's attorneys. No witnesses were called; as was the case in the House, the Senate had access to the 445-page record of sworn grand jury testimony. To convict the president on either article of impeachment, a two-thirds vote of the Senate (67 senators) was necessary. On Feb. 12 the Senate rejected the first article 55–45 (all 45 Democrats and 10 Republicans opposed) and the second 50–50 (all 45 Democrats and 5 Republicans opposed, 50 Republicans in favor). Clinton was declared acquitted on both articles.

CLIPPERS, merchant sailing ships built for speed rather than cargo capacity. Long and narrow, they carried three or more masts crowded with sails—including lofty skysails and moonrakers. They were employed on the transatlantic run but especially on long voyages to California, China, and Australia. The great American designer and builder was Donald McKay, whose *Flying Cloud* in 1851 sailed from New York to San Francisco in a record 89 days. By 1870 the clippers had succumbed to competition from steamships.

COERCIVE ACTS (1774). See *Intolerable Acts.

COHENS v. VIRGINIA (1821), 6–0 decision of the *Marshall Court asserting the position of the U.S. Supreme Court as the final interpreter of the Constitution. The plaintiffs appealed a decision of the Virginia supreme court, which argued that the appellate power of the U.S. Supreme Court "cannot . . . be exercised against the judgment of a state court."

Chief Justice Marshall rejected that argument and took the opportunity to expound his philosophy of judicial nationalism: "America has chosen to be, in many respects, and to many purposes, a nation; and for all these purposes, her government is complete; to all these objects, it is competent. The people have declared, that in the exercise of all powers given for these objects it is supreme. It can, then, in effecting these objects, legitimately control all individuals or governments within the American territory. The constitution and laws of a state, so far as they are repugnant to the constitution and laws of the United States, are absolutely void. These states are constituent parts of the United States. They are members of one great empire—for some purposes sovereign, for some purposes subordinate."

COINAGE ACT (1873). See *Crime of '73.

COLD HARBOR. See *Wilderness Campaign.

COLD WAR (1945–91), limited conflict between the United States and the Soviet Union. Although "hot wars" were fought between clients of the two superpowers (e.g., Cuba in Angola) and between one superpower and a client of the other (e.g., the United States and North Korea, the Soviet Union and Afghanistan), the "balance of terror" restrained the two superpowers from direct military confrontation.

At its root, the hostility between the United States and the Soviet Union was the inherent conflict between an open society and a closed one and between economic systems that both sides considered incompatible. Soviet leaders and many American politicians believed that war between the two systems was inevitable. The World War 2 alliance between the United States and its allies and the Soviet Union was not prompted by shared principles but by a common enemy. When the war was over, that tenuous alliance ended abruptly.

In the Western view, the immediate cause of the cold war was the establishment by the Soviet Union of a security zone in Eastern Europe consisting of countries whose communist governments were imposed and maintained by the Red Army. In the case of Poland, the Soviet Union's imposition of a communist government violated a pledge made at Yalta to hold free elections there. The Western Allies, who had quickly demobilized after the war, became convinced that the massively armed Soviet Union was bent upon expansion, determined to exploit weakness and instability in countries on its periphery either by military threat (e.g., Iran, Greece, Turkey) or by subversion through national communist parties (e.g.,

France, Italy). The communist takeover of Czechoslovakia in 1948 confirmed this view. The Soviets, moreover, sought to obstruct efforts to reconstruct Western Europe on capitalist lines and were particularly incensed by the resurrection in 1949 of an independent West Germany (the Federal Republic of Germany), to which they responded by transforming their occupation zone into an independent communist East Germany (the German Democratic Republic).

In "fighting" the cold war, the United States made several crucial assumptions: (l) that the world's communist countries formed a monolithic bloc led by the Soviet Union; (2) that the Soviet Union in particular and communism in general was inherently expansionist; and (3) that if any noncommunist country was permitted to fall to communism, its neighbors would soon also succumb like "falling dominoes." The strategy adopted by the United States was *containment—resistance to communist expansion wherever it threatened by appropriate political, economic, or military means.

The cold war was experienced in the United States as a time of mortal danger, with nuclear holocaust always at hand. While Soviet espionage was real enough (see *Hiss Case; *Rosenberg Case), the exaggerated fear of communist infiltration and subversion poisoned public life (see *Anticommunism; *McCarthyism). In international affairs, the United States lost moral standing because of its covert destabilization of legitimate governments suspected of Marxism and its support of repressive and corrupt—though professedly anti-Marxist—regimes in many parts of the world (see *Covert Operations).

The cold war ended with the dissolution of the Soviet bloc in Europe in 1989–90 and of the Soviet Union itself in 1991. U.S. politicians declared victory, but it is debatable whether the Soviet collapse was due to external pressures (e.g., the burden of an arms race with the *Reagan administration) or internal ones (e.g., the inefficiency and corruption inherent in a command economy). For all its dangers, the cold war was a period of basic stability, the two superpowers being careful to avoid rash or irreversible provocations and restraining regional and ethnic tensions that erupted when the cold war was over. To many observers, the world after the cold war seemed more complicated and only slightly less dangerous.

COLONIZATION (1815–60), movement to settle emancipated slaves in Africa, the West Indies, or Central America. The founders of the **American Colonization Society** (1816–1912) had varied motives. Some were sincerely antislavery but believed that emancipation had to be accompanied by emigration to be acceptable. Others were concerned only to deport *free blacks, whom they considered a dangerous influence on the slave population. Many *abolitionists abandoned the colonization movement when they discovered the hostility to blacks inherent in its program.

With prominent supporters—including James Madison and Henry Clay—the American Colonization Society enjoyed early success. The federal government appropriated $100,000 for its use; this and state and private donations enabled it to buy land on the west coast of Africa and begin to settle free blacks there in colonies that eventually coalesced as Liberia. By 1860 the society had transported some 5,000 people there. After Liberia was declared independent in 1846, the society continued to interest itself in Liberian affairs.

Before the Civil War, the majority of free blacks opposed colonization, regarding the United States as their native country and recognizing that colonization strengthened slavery. Some, however, endorsed it, notably Martin R. Delany. In the 1920s, Marcus Garvey attempted unsuccessfully to revive the colonization idea in his *"Back to Africa" movement.

COMMAND OF THE ARMY ACT (1867). See *Reconstruction.

COMMISSION ON INDUSTRIAL RELATIONS (1912–14), commission authorized by Congress to investigate the causes and remedies of the warfare between capital and labor. Of its nine members, three represented employers, three labor, and three the public. The most influential members were its chairman, Frank Walsh, a liberal Missouri attorney, and John Rogers Commons, professor of political science at the University of Wisconsin. The commission held hearings in cities across the country at which more than 700 persons of all walks of life and political persuasions testified. The records of the hearings were published in 1914 in 11 volumes. The commission's findings included:

"1. The control of manufacturing, mining, and transportation industries is to an increasing degree passing into the hands of great corporations through stock ownership, and control of credit is centralized in a comparatively small number of enormously powerful financial institutions. These financial institutions are in turn dominated by a very small number of powerful financiers. . . .

"5. In such corporations, in spite of the large number of stockholders, the control through actual stock ownership rests with a very small number of persons. . . .

"6. Almost without exception the employees of the

large corporations are unorganized as a result of the active and aggressive 'nonunion' policy of the corporation management. . . .

"9. These industrial dictators for the most part are totally ignorant of every aspect of the industries which they control except the finances, and are totally unconcerned with regard to the working and living conditions of the employees in those industries. . . .

"10. . . . the labor conditions of these corporation-controlled industries are subject to great criticism and are a menace to the welfare of the Nation. . . .

"12. The domination of the men in whose hands the final control of a large part of American industry rests is not limited to their employees, but is being rapidly extended to control the education and 'social service' of the Nation [through philanthropic foundations and membership on university boards of trustees]. . . ."

COMMITTEE ON THE CONDUCT OF THE WAR
(1861–65), during the *Civil War, a joint committee of Congress established Dec. 10, 1861, after a Union defeat at Ball's Bluff, Va., "to inquire into the conduct of the present war." It was chaired by Sen. Benjamin F. Wade of Ohio and generally reflected the views of *Radical Republicans in its advocacy of more vigorous prosecution of the war and its criticism of politically conservative and unsuccessful generals.

COMMITTEES OF CORRESPONDENCE (1772–76), town, county, and provincial committees that provided the early communications infrastructure of the *American Revolution. The first committee was established by the Boston town meeting in November 1772 at the urging of patriot leaders Samuel Adams, Joseph Warren, and James Otis to communicate with other Massachusetts towns and coordinate resistance to British measures. Committees were quickly established in towns and counties throughout New England. In March 1773 the Virginia House of Burgesses established a provincial committee of correspondence.

The committees of correspondence usually enlisted the intellectuals of the revolutionary movement. Acquaintanceships begun with distant correspondents often ripened into personal friendships at meetings of provincial congresses or the *Continental Congress. In time, the committees of correspondence—later called committees of safety—assumed many governmental functions in their localities, giving force to the decisions of provincial and national revolutionary authorities. The committees disappeared with the establishment of effective state governments.

COMMON SENSE (1776), pamphlet by English-born Thomas Paine. Self-educated and impecunious, Paine arrived in Philadelphia in November 1774 at age 34, found work as a journalist, and quickly absorbed American sentiments. His pamphlet, calling for American independence from Great Britain, was published in January 1776. Welcomed by Patriot leaders, it became an enormous popular success and played a major part in preparing the popular mind in America for total separation from Britain.

"The sun never shined on a cause of greater worth," Paine wrote. " 'Tis not the affair of a city, a colony, a province, or a kingdom; but of a continent—of at least one eighth part of the habitable globe. 'Tis not the concern of a day, a year, or an age; posterity are virtually involved in the contest, and will be more or less affected, even to the end of time, by the proceedings now. Now is the seed time of continental union, faith, and honor."

COMMUNIST CONTROL ACT (1954). See *Anticommunism.

COMMUNIST PARTY. The *Russian Revolution splintered the socialist movement in the United States (see *Socialism). Radicals dissatisfied with the gradualism of the existing socialist parties and eager to identify with the revolutionaries in Russia formed two communist parties in 1919. These combined in 1921 on orders from Moscow. Thereafter the American Communist Party—variously named the Workers Party, the Workers (Communist) Party, and the Communist Party U.S.A.—took its orders from Moscow and obediently served the interests of the Soviet Union.

During the 1920s, the Stalinist dictatorship in the USSR, through the Communist International or Comintern, established its control over the American and other national communist parties. In 1929 the U.S. party had some 7,000 members, mostly in and around New York City. With the coming of the *Great Depression, it attracted many new members and "fellow travelers" who believed that capitalism had failed. The party's presidential candidate in 1932 received a record 103,000 votes—less than one-eighth of the votes for the Socialist Party candidate. During the 1930s the party's high profile on cynically selected issues like the *Scottsboro Case and unwinnable coal-mining and textile strikes made it appear a progressive ally of the *New Deal. But its dizzying reversals of position at Moscow's dictation cost it all credibility with most Americans.

From 1935 to 1939, the party adhered to the

Moscow-dictated policy of the "popular front," cooperating with noncommunists (as it never had before) against the growing threat of Nazi Germany. But when Hitler and Stalin signed a nonaggression pact in August 1939, days before the start of World War 2, the party abandoned the popular front and urged American neutrality in a war that it now attributed to British imperialism. When Germany attacked the Soviet Union in June 1941, the war suddenly became a peoples' war and the Communist Party urged U.S. involvement. In the *cold war that followed World War 2, the party continued to serve Soviet interests by peace propaganda and espionage (see *Hiss Case; *Rosenberg Case). In 1948 it controlled the *Progressive Party of presidential candidate Henry A. Wallace.

Thereafter, the party organization suffered devastating blows. Congress investigated alleged communist penetration of the government (see *Anticommunism; *House Committee on Un-American Activities; *McCarthyism). In 1949, 11 top communist leaders were convicted under the Smith Act (1940) of conspiring to overthrow the U.S. government; when the U.S. Supreme Court upheld the Smith Act in *Dennis v. United States (1951), nearly a hundred more convictions followed. In 1949–50, the Congress of Industrial Organizations expelled communist-dominated unions. The Internal Security Act (1950) required the registration of members of communist and communist-front organizations and their members, while the Communist Control Act (1954) stripped the party of its privileges as a political party. The party was shaken, too, by events abroad—the communist seizure of power in Czechoslovakia in 1948, Soviet suppression of the Hungarian Revolution in 1956, the revelation that same year by Soviet premier Nikita Khrushchev of Stalin's "crimes," and the suppression by the Warsaw Pact of the "Prague Spring" in 1968.

In the 1960s a *New Left arose in the United States that claimed a Marxist ideology but was—in its spontaneity, youth, disorganization, and self-indulgence—the antithesis of the disciplined Old Left epitomized by the Communist Party. The final blow to the party was the dissolution of the Soviet Union in 1991. At the end of the century, the Communist Party was virtually invisible on the American scene.

COMPARABLE WORTH. See *Women in the Labor Force.

COMPROMISE OF 1820. See *Missouri Compromise or Compromise of 1820.

COMPROMISE OF 1833, second of three Union-saving compromises attributed in significant part to Henry Clay (see also *Missouri Compromise; *Compromise of 1850). That of 1833 was a tariff act that lowered duties over a nine-year period to an average ad valorem of 20 percent—at which point it would no longer be a protective tariff but one for revenue only. This satisfied the complaints of South Carolina over the tariffs of 1828 and 1832, which had led to the *nullification crisis.

The bill was prepared by Clay and John C. Calhoun and rushed through Congress in time to be signed simultaneously with a Force Bill authorizing the president to use the armed forces to compel South Carolina's compliance with federal law. Both Clay and Calhoun hoped to become president, and both sacrificed principle in pursuit of electoral gain. Calhoun, the theorist of nullification, accepted the principle of a protective tariff for nine years; Clay surrendered that principle—one of the foundations of the *American System—at the end of nine years. But he won the sobriquet "The Great Compromiser."

COMPROMISE OF 1850, legislation of the *Taylor-Fillmore administration. "The United States will conquer Mexico," wrote Ralph Waldo Emerson during the *Mexican War, "but . . . Mexico will poison us." Indeed, the territory acquired from Mexico proved to be a source of domestic conflict for the United States. Although twice rejected by Congress, the *Wilmot Proviso—which would have excluded slavery from the entire *Mexican Cession—was still supported in the North. Southern extremists demanded that all the new territories be open to slavery; Southern moderates would accept an extension of the *Missouri Compromise line to the Pacific Ocean. Behind the South's demands was its awareness that with the admission of California as a free state, which seemed inevitable, the balance between North and South at 15 states each would be ended and the South would be reduced to the status of a permanent minority in a Union increasingly hostile to slavery.

The slavery issue had prevented Pres. James K. Polk from obtaining territorial organization for California and New Mexico. Pres. Zachary Taylor encouraged both regions to apply directly for statehood, with or without slavery, thereby avoiding the territorial stage when Congress would have to confront the divisive Wilmot Proviso again. California organized a state government in November 1849 and in March 1850 applied to Congress for admission to the Union as a free state.

Henry Clay, author of the compromises of 1820 and

1833 and newly returned to the Senate, saw the problem of the new territories more comprehensively than Taylor did. He recognized that the South would not accept permanent minority status in the Union without compensation, that a broad sectional adjustment was therefore necessary. Hoping to complete his career with a third Union-saving compromise, on Jan. 26, 1850, Clay presented to the Senate a series of proposals dealing with a number of long-festering issues: admission of California as a free state; organization of the remainder of the Mexican Cession (New Mexico and Utah) without restriction as to slavery; resolution of the *Texas boundary dispute; noninterference with slavery in the District of Columbia but prohibition of the slave trade there; disavowal by Congress of authority to interfere with the internal slave trade; and a more effective *fugitive slave act.

The debate that followed was memorable for bringing together for the last time the great triumvirate of Clay, John C. Calhoun, and Daniel Webster. On Feb. 5–6, Clay developed his proposals and appealed to both sides for mutual concessions. On Mar. 4, the ailing Calhoun, in a speech read for him by a colleague, demanded equality and safety for the South (he died on Mar. 31). On Mar. 7, Webster exalted the Union over slavery concerns (see *Webster's Seventh of March Speech). After the giants had spoken, the debate continued. William H. Seward, a "conscience" Whig from New York, in his maiden Senate speech denounced compromise and slaveholders alike and invoked "a higher law than the Constitution" as the basis for freedom in the territories. The phrase became famous.

Clay combined his proposals into a single Omnibus Bill, to be voted up or down together, on the theory that the whole would attract more supporters than would the measures taken singly. The bill was assigned to a committee chaired by Clay that reported on May 8. Debate dragged on into the summer. On July 9, President Taylor, who had resented Clay's usurpation of leadership and opposed the compromise, died and was succeeded by Vice Pres. Millard Fillmore, who supported the bill.

In the end, the Omnibus Bill had to be given up in favor of five separate bills. These were shepherded through the Senate for the exhausted Clay by Stephen A. Douglas of Illinois, who found varied majorities for each, passed Sept. 9–20, and promptly signed by President Fillmore: (1) an act admitting California to the Union as a free state; (2) an act organizing New Mexico as a territory without restriction as to slavery (leaving the matter to be decided by *popular sovereignty) and resolving the boundary dispute with Texas; (3) an act organizing Utah as a territory, also with no restriction as to slavery; (4) a stiff new fugitive slave act; and (5) an act abolishing the slave trade in the District of Columbia.

In Congress and across the country, the Compromise of 1850 was hailed as the final settlement of the slavery question.

COMPROMISE OF 1877, informal understanding between Southerners and representatives of President-elect Rutherford B. Hayes that ended *Reconstruction.

The election of 1876 had resulted in 184 uncontested electoral votes for Democrat Samuel J. Tilden (185 being necessary for election) and 166 for Republican Hayes. South Carolina, Florida, and Louisiana, the last of the "unredeemed" states, where virtual civil war reigned between native Democrats and carpetbag Republicans, returned two sets of 19 electoral votes. To resolve the issue, Congress in January 1877 appointed a 15-member electoral commission consisting of five senators, five representatives, and five justices of the Supreme Court—eight Republicans, seven Democrats. On strict party lines, the commission voted to validate the Republican votes in all three contested states, giving the election to Hayes by a margin of one vote.

Democrats in Congress threatened to filibuster when the counting of electoral votes resumed, but a number of influential Southerners saw advantage in negotiation. They and friends of Hayes agreed that they would accept Hayes's election if the new president would withdraw federal troops from the South, appoint a Southerner to his cabinet, and support Southern interest in federally subsidized internal improvements, particularly a projected Texas & Pacific Railroad. Hayes agreed and was duly declared elected and inaugurated.

On Apr. 10, federal troops in Columbia, S.C., were withdrawn from the statehouse, permitting Democrats to take control of the state, as they soon did also in Florida and Louisiana. Hayes appointed a Southerner postmaster general and hoped to establish a native white Republican party in the South by appointing Democrats and former Whigs to federal offices there. This hope was disappointed, as was the South's hope for federally financed internal improvements.

The eventual withdrawal of all federal troops from the South ended federal protection of the former slaves, whose formal civil rights were quickly nullified.

COMPUTERS, electronic devices for storing, processing, and presenting data. The first electronic

computer—ENIAC—was built during World War 2 by
John Mauchly and J. Presper Eckert of the University of
Pennsylvania under a contract with the U.S. Army. It
filled a large room, contained 18,000 vacuum tubes, and
consumed 174 kilowatts of energy. The invention of the
transistor made possible the construction of smaller,
solid-state computers. Rapid technological progress affecting every element of computer design and programming resulted in the 1980s in desktop computers with
many times the power, capacity, speed, and versatility of
ENIAC, making the computer indispensable to business
and science. In the 1990s, the linking of personal computers by telephone to a worldwide network created a
communications, marketing, and entertainment Internet
of incalculable potential.

COMSTOCK LODE, silver deposit in western Nevada
near Virginia City, discovered in 1859. In the next 20
years it produced $500 million in silver and gold, enrich-
ing half a dozen "silver kings" who made their homes in
San Francisco.

CONCERNED WOMEN FOR AMERICA. See
*Christian Right.

CONCURRENT MAJORITY, doctrine developed by
John C. Calhoun to protect slavery and expounded in his
posthumous *Disquisition on Government*. Calhoun conceived of society as comprising not only individuals but
interests. Government by a *numerical* majority of individuals inevitably becomes absolute; truly constitutional
(limited) government must be by a *concurrent* majority
of interests: "[T]here are two different modes in which
the sense of the community may be taken. . . . [O]ne regards numbers only, and considers the whole community
as a unit, having but one common interest throughout;
and collects the sense of the greater number of the whole,
as that of the community. The other, on the contrary, regards interests as well as numbers;—considering the
community as made up of different and conflicting interests, as far as the action of the government is concerned;
and takes the sense of each, through its majority or appropriate organ, and the united sense of all, as the sense
of the entire community."

In Calhoun's conception, each interest (acting through
its "appropriate organ") would have a self-protecting
veto over government action; in fact, no government action would be possible without the concurrence of all the
interests. Since for Calhoun the nation's varied interests
were represented by the states, his doctrine was less a

foreshadowing of the Fascist corporate state than a rationale for *nullification and *secession.

CONFEDERATE BATTLE FLAGS RETURN
(1889), incident in the first *Cleveland administration.
Cleveland's approval of a routine War Department
order—initiated by a general who was both a Republican
and a member of the *Grand Army of the Republic—to
return captured Civil War battle flags to the Southern
states aroused such protest from Republican and veterans
groups that he had quickly to revoke the order. The flags
were finally returned in 1905 during the Theodore *Roosevelt administration.

CONFEDERATE STATES OF AMERICA (1861–
65), short-lived republic comprising 11 seceded states.

Establishing the Confederacy. As soon as the
election of Abraham Lincoln as president of the United
States was certain, the South Carolina legislature called a
*secession convention, which, on Dec. 20, 1860, re-
solved unanimously on secession. Between Dec. 20,
1860, and Feb. 1, 1861, six other Southern states followed South Carolina out of the Union.

On Feb. 4, 1861, 50 delegates from the seven seceded
states met at Montgomery, Ala. In quick order they
formed the Confederate States of America, adopted a
provisional constitution, elected a provisional president
and vice president—Jefferson Davis of Mississippi and
Alexander H. Stephens of Georgia—then resolved themselves into a congress to write a permanent constitution.

When the *Civil War began in April, Virginia and
three more states seceded and joined the Confederacy.
The Confederate congress thereupon voted to move the
republic's capital to Richmond, Va., where it arrived on
May 29. In a general election held in November 1861,
Davis and Stephens were elected permanent president
and vice president without opposition, and on Feb. 22,
1862, they were inaugurated in Richmond. Meanwhile,
secessionist factions expelled from Missouri and Kentucky had formed governments-in-exile whose representatives were seated in the Confederate congress.

The Confederate Constitution. The Montgomery convention was dominated by moderates—men
not inclined to experiment with the radical ideas of the
*fire-eaters but concerned to modify existing political
arrangements as little as possible. Thus the constitution
of the Confederacy was modeled not on the *Articles of
Confederation but on the U.S. Constitution, departing
from that familiar document only on points of special
concern to the South.

"We, the people of the Confederate States," its preamble read, "each State acting in its sovereign and independent character, in order to form a permanent government, establish justice, insure domestic tranquillity, and secure the blessings of liberty to ourselves and our posterity—invoking the favor and guidance of Almighty God—do ordain and establish this Constitution for the Confederate States of America."

The phrase "We, the people," promptly modified by "each State acting in its sovereign and independent character," indicated that the constitution was a compact among sovereign states, not the work of the Southern "nation" so much talked about before secession. In listing the objectives to be achieved by their constitution, the Confederates omitted some in the U.S. Constitution—"to form a more perfect union," "promote the general welfare"—that had been interpreted to justify the centralizing powers of the U.S. government. The parenthetical phrase "invoking the favor and guidance of Almighty God" was a touch of 19th-century religiosity altogether absent from the 18th-century document.

The president of the Confederacy was to be elected for a single term of six years. Slavery was explicitly recognized and protected, although the foreign slave trade was prohibited—a point that outraged radicals, since it implied a negative judgment on slavery. Congress was prohibited from enacting a protective tariff, giving "bounties" (subsidies), or appropriating money for internal improvements. In fact, Congress was not permitted to appropriate money for any purpose not recommended by the president except by a two-thirds majority. These obstacles to spending money were intended to prevent the Confederate government from growing powerful as the U.S. government had.

Mobilizing for War. When it became clear that the war would be long and costly, the South had to learn to organize its limited resources for maximum effectiveness. Ironically, the prewar Southern ideology of small government, states' rights, and unconstrained individualism succumbed quickly to the need for regimentation and discipline.

Manpower. With a white population of only 5.5 million, the Confederacy mobilized every white male of military age into service. A conscription act in March 1862 made all white males aged 18 to 35 (soon extended to 50) eligible for three years of military service. There were numerous exemptions for essential civilian occupations. Administration of the draft fell to the national government, which assumed the responsibility for recruiting and organizing military units that had formerly been the

states'. Some 70–80 percent of Southern men of military age served in the Confederate army at some time.

This high percentage was possible only because many farms and factories continued to be worked by slaves. Slaves were also impressed—to the outrage of their owners—into military service as construction workers, teamsters, cooks, and hospital orderlies. In the last, desperate weeks of the war, the War Department permitted blacks to become soldiers in the Confederate army—if they volunteered and were emancipated by their masters.

Industry. With only one-tenth of the North's industrial capacity, the Confederacy was at first compelled to buy its military supplies abroad. But it soon ran out of cash and credit, and the ever-tightening Union blockade prevented the export of cotton and the import of war matériel. To an extraordinary degree, the Confederacy succeeded in producing its own supplies. It accomplished this with a combination of state-controlled and state-owned industries, the latter created and managed by officials of the War and Navy Departments in the absence of a Southern entrepreneurial class. By 1863 the Confederacy could claim self-sufficiency in military production, although this condition declined as Union armies increasingly occupied Southern territory where mines and industrial plants were located. Nevertheless, at the very end of the war, the Confederate army, while lacking food and clothing, was well supplied with munitions.

Food. Anticipating the war, the South had been confident that it could always feed itself while using its valuable cotton to acquire war supplies abroad. During the war, much cotton land was converted to food production, but production suffered when the male farmer or planter was absent. Devastation of farmlands by passing armies, occupation by the Union army, the breakdown of railroads, and raging inflation compounded the problems of food production and distribution. In 1863 there were food riots in Richmond, Atlanta, Mobile, and other cities. At the end of the war, Confederate general Robert E. Lee's army was starving.

Finances. To finance the war, the Confederacy resorted to taxes, loans, and the printing press. Only about 5 percent of war costs were met by taxation. Having no machinery to collect taxes, the Confederate government apportioned them among the states, which often met their obligations by borrowing or printing money.

Borrowing was also a major expedient of the Confederate government, which negotiated one costly foreign loan but depended largely on the sale of government bonds to its citizens. There was, however, little liquid capital in the South, and the interest rate on the bonds was soon exceeded by the rate of inflation. Inevitably, the printing press became the government's chief recourse. The government promised to redeem its notes at face value in specie two years after the war, but the notes depreciated rapidly.

Dissension and Division. Jefferson Davis's qualifications for the presidency of a nation at war seemed superior to those of Abraham Lincoln. A graduate of West Point who had served with distinction in the Mexican War, Davis had been a U.S. senator and secretary of war in the Pierce administration. He would have preferred to command the Confederacy's armies, and he accepted the presidency reluctantly as an onerous duty. Unfortunately for him, he lacked the human qualities necessary for successful political leadership. Aloof, arbitrary, inflexible, and rigidly self-controlled, he was also sensitive to criticism and tormented by ill health. The necessities of war compelled him to conduct a government repugnant to ideological Confederates, a centralizing administration very similar to the one from which they sought to escape. No one foresaw the suspension of habeas corpus and imposition of martial law, the impressment (expropriation) of private property for use of the army, heavy and ubiquitous taxes, state-controlled industry, and—most offensive—military conscription. Like Lincoln, Davis was accused of despotism.

The South was beset by dissension and division, although probably not more so than the North. Strong unionist sentiment persisted in the Appalachian region and elsewhere. Inflation, taxes, food shortages, but especially exemption of slave overseers from the draft exacerbated class tensions and gave rise to the complaint of "a rich man's war and a poor man's fight." As the war progressed, peace movements arose in Georgia, North Carolina, Arkansas, Alabama, and Tennessee. In the backcountry, outlaw bands of draft evaders and deserters evidenced the erosion of Southern patriotism.

Political ideology underlay some of the dissension. States' righters could not accept the necessity for the regimentation of civilian as well as military life. Governors Joseph E. Brown of Georgia and Zebulon A. Vance of North Carolina obstructed the draft in their states and hoarded food and supplies. Vice President Stephens became an enemy of the administration's "despotic" policies. "Away with the idea of getting independence first, and looking for liberty afterwards," he argued. "Our liberties, once lost, may be lost forever."

Some of the opposition was personal, born of military reverses, dislike of Davis, and loss of faith in the administration's competence. Members of congress and even generals blamed Davis for Confederate military failures.

Newspapers like the Charlotte *Mercury* (owned by fire-eater Robert B. Rhett) and the Richmond *Examiner* were merciless in their criticism.

The End of the Confederacy. On Apr. 2, 1865, Lee withdrew his disintegrating Army of Northern Virginia from Petersburg and Richmond and marched west in the hope of breaking through the encircling Federals and joining forces with Gen. Joseph E. Johnston in North Carolina. That night, Jefferson Davis, his cabinet, government officials, and military personnel boarded trains loaded with government records and property and traveled to Danville, leaving Richmond to looting and arson. Federal troops arrived the next morning to restore order. On Apr. 4, Abraham Lincoln, with a small escort of sailors, walked the streets of the fallen Confederate capital.

Davis passed an anxious week in Danville, desperately hoping to hear that Lee was in the clear, confident that Lee and Johnston together could defeat Union generals Ulysses S. Grant and William T. Sherman separately and restore Confederate fortunes. But on Apr. 10 he learned that Lee had surrendered. That night the government moved by train to Greensboro, N.C. At cabinet meetings, Davis was deaf to counsel that the war was lost and he should escape to Mexico.

From Greensboro Davis's party proceeded by wagon and horseback to Charlotte. There Davis learned of Lincoln's assassination and of Johnston's unconditional surrender to Sherman. Davis pushed on through South Carolina and into Georgia, his cabinet members now departing, his escort steadily shrinking. At Washington, Ga., on May 4, he "temporarily" dissolved the Confederate government until it could reassemble across the Mississippi. He had the notion that if he could make his way to Louisiana he could assemble 100,000 Confederate troops to carry on the fight.

At Irwinville, Ga., on May 10, Union cavalry came upon Davis's party and took the fugitive prisoner. Davis was held at Fort Monroe in Virginia for two years while the authorities—who regretted that he had not escaped abroad—tried to formulate charges against him and argued whether he should be tried by a military or a civilian court. Meanwhile, all other Confederate leaders, military and civilian, were amnestied or pardoned. Finally, in May 1867, Davis was remanded from military to civil custody, then released on bond. He was never brought to trial.

CONFEDERATION (1781–88), period between the ratification of the *Articles of Confederation and the ratification of the U.S. Constitution, called by 19th-century historian John Fiske "the critical period of American history." The Articles provided for a unicameral legislature (the *Continental Congress) but no executive or judiciary. Congress was given large powers but little means to exercise them—the states continued to control taxation and to regulate trade. Amendment of the Articles proved impossible since it required the unanimous agreement of all 13 states.

This weak central government reflected the colonies' unhappy experience under a powerful British government, but it left the country too feeble to protect its national interests. Heavily in debt, the government had no means of raising money except the sale of western lands. Its currency was worthless. Lacking an army and navy, it had no credibility in diplomatic relations and had to submit to continued British occupation of frontier posts in violation of the Treaty of *Paris, to Spanish control of the mouth of the Mississippi, and to the depredations of the Barbary pirates. Lacking the power to regulate foreign trade, the government could not retaliate against the mercantilist policies of European governments that disadvantaged U.S. commerce—for example, the British exclusion of American vessels from Canada and the West Indies. Meanwhile, the states competed commercially against each other and in some cases enacted debtor-relief legislation, including the issuing of paper money, that horrified conservatives as demagogic, unjust, and unsound.

The one great success of the Confederation was the nationalization of western lands (see *Public Lands) and, through its organization of the *Northwest Territory, the establishment of a process by which new states could be formed and admitted to the Union on a basis of equality with the original states, thereby avoiding the kind of colonialism from which the colonies had suffered.

During the last years of the Confederation, Congress was poorly attended and largely inactive. A sense of dissolution and impending anarchy pervaded the country (see *Shays's Rebellion). The impulse for constitutional reform arose outside of Congress among statesmen who feared for the survival and security of the country and among businessmen concerned for the security of their property. "Let us have [a government] by which our lives, liberties, and properties will be secured," George Washington wrote in 1786. "To be more exposed in the eyes of the world, and more contemptible than we already are, is hardly possible." Only grudgingly did Congress ratify the summons to the *constitutional convention that met in Philadelphia in 1787.

CONFISCATION ACTS (1861, 1862), legislation of the *Lincoln administration. The first (August 1861) clarified the status of the growing numbers of slaves who had escaped into Union lines. It permitted those who had been employed by the Confederate armed forces to remain within Union lines as contraband of war, although it did not go so far as to declare them free. Constitutionally unable to legislate emancipation, Congress was free to legislate punishment for treason by confiscation of property.

The second Confiscation Act (July 1862) punished treason, rebellion, or insurrection by fine, imprisonment, or confiscation of property as well as by death, thereby forestalling mass executions after the war. It now provided that confiscated slaves should thereafter be free. At Lincoln's insistence, it provided that confiscated estates should be returned to the heirs of the guilty parties after their deaths, thereby preventing the wholesale destruction of the Southern planter aristocracy.

Never enforced, the second Confiscation Act was superseded by Lincoln's Proclamation of Amnesty and Reconstruction (Dec. 8, 1863), which permitted most Confederates to escape punishment for participation in the rebellion simply by taking an oath of allegiance to the United States. Confederate leaders could avoid penalties by appealing for individual pardons, which Lincoln's successor, Pres. Andrew Johnson, granted liberally (see *Reconstruction).

CONGRESSIONAL RECONSTRUCTION. See *Reconstruction.

CONGRESS OF INDUSTRIAL ORGANIZATIONS (CIO). See *American Federation of Labor–Congress of Industrial Organizations (AFL–CIO).

CONGRESS OF RACIAL EQUALITY (CORE), civil rights organization, originally interracial and pacifist, founded in 1942. It played a prominent role in the *freedom rides (1961) and *Freedom Summer (1964). In the late 1960s, CORE embraced *black power and expelled white members. Its commitment to racial separation, black self-determination, and black capitalism led it to adopt conservative political positions.

CONRAIL. See *Railroads; *Railroad Regulation.

CONSCRIPTION or **DRAFT.** In colonial America, males were required to train in militias, and selective drafts brought men to arms in emergencies such as Indian attacks and colonial wars. The *Revolutionary War was fought by a volunteer *Continental Army aided by voluntary state militias. The states occasionally attempted to draft men for local defense or for duty with the Continental Army, but numerous exemptions nullified these efforts.

At the start of the *Civil War, the Union relied on volunteer state forces to supplement Regular Army units; the Confederate army consisted entirely of volunteer state forces. The Confederacy instituted conscription of white males aged 18–35 (later 17–50) in April 1862. The Union followed in March 1863 with conscription of men aged 20–45. In the North, the draft was directly administered by the army. Those drafted could avoid service by employing substitutes or buying exemptions. The inequity of this system provoked intense opposition (see *Draft Riots). In the South, numerous exemptions, including those for slave overseers, also made the draft inequitable. In both North and South, draftees complained that it was "a rich man's war and a poor man's fight." However, relatively few combatants in the Civil War were draftees.

The **Selective Service System**, established upon U.S. entry into *World War 1, avoided the inequities of the Civil War draft. The World War 1 draft was administered by local civilian boards, which called registrants to service in order of numbers drawn in a national lottery. The draft boards also determined who met the law's conditions for exemption. There were no substitutions or purchased exemptions. Despite dire predictions of bloody resistance, the World War 1 draft was perceived as equitable and worked smoothly. Some 2.8 million men were drafted into the "National Army" before the war and the draft ended. The Regular Army, National Guard, Navy, Marines, and Coast Guard were manned entirely by volunteers.

The United States resorted to a military draft again in September 1940, 15 months before the country entered *World War 2. Up until the attack on *Pearl Harbor, the necessity of the draft was seriously challenged; in August 1941 the original one-year term of service was extended by 18 months by a one-vote margin in Congress. When war came, the term of service was extended to the duration of the war plus six months. The fairness of the system, modeled on that of World War 1, was broadly accepted. During World War 2 more than 10 million men—almost two-thirds of the nation's military forces—were drafted.

The World War 2 draft expired in March 1947. A new draft, in response to the *cold war, was instituted in March 1948. It made all men aged 18.5–26 liable for eight years of military service divided between two years of active duty and six in the reserves. But active duty could be avoided by enlistment in the National Guard or federal reserve forces. Deferments were permitted on ed-

ucational, occupational, and family grounds. Many middle-class youths were able to avoid active service, with the result that working-class youths were disproportionately represented among those drafted. Poor and minority youths were underrepresented because many failed to meet induction standards.

As long as the military had absorbed nearly all the available manpower to maintain massive forces and as long as exemptions had been few and reasonable, the draft had encountered little opposition. But after 1948 the military needed only a fraction of those eligible for conscription. At this point, the system began to be perceived as unfair. When draftees were sent into combat in Korea and Vietnam (see *Korean War; *Vietnam War), it began to be perceived as intolerable.

The inequity of the draft was a major element in civilian opposition to the Vietnam War and in the demoralization of the armed forces in the early 1970s. The armed forces were already composed largely of volunteers when the decision to return to an all-volunteer military force was made by Pres. Richard M. Nixon. No one was drafted after January 1973. The Selective Service System, reduced to a skeleton staff, was placed on "deep standby."

In January 1980, in response to the Soviet Union's invasion of Afghanistan, Pres. James E. Carter called for the registration of 19- and 20-year-old men and women as a step toward expediting any future mobilization. Congress quickly rejected the president's proposal to register women, but it voted funds to revive the Selective Service System and to begin registration of men 19 and 20 and then of all men as they turned 18. In 1981 the U.S. Supreme Court ruled that Congress could constitutionally restrict the draft to men.

CONSERVATION, national effort begun in the 19th century to preserve America's publicly owned natural resources—land, minerals, forests, grasslands, water, wildlife—that were being heedlessly despoiled. Its foundations were laid with the establishment of the Department of the Interior in 1849 and its Geological Survey in 1879 and Division of Forestry in 1887. Its beginnings may be dated from the creation of Yellowstone National Park in 1872 and Yosemite National Park in 1891.

The **Forest Reserve Act** (1891) authorized the president to set aside select forest lands from commercial exploitation. Pres. Benjamin Harrison set aside 13 million acres, Pres. Grover Cleveland 25 million acres, Pres. William McKinley 7 million acres, and Pres. Theodore Roosevelt 235 million acres before the act was repealed in 1907 at the behest of lumber and grazing interests.

The **Carey Desert Land Act** (1894) encouraged the states to undertake land reclamation by authorizing the president to give Western states up to 1 million acres of public lands for irrigation, reclamation, and cultivation by private developers. The problem proved too large for individual developers or states.

Theodore Roosevelt, an outdoorsman, made conservation a major concern of his administration, aided by Gifford Pinchot, chief of the U.S. Forest Service, now in the Department of Agriculture. It was Pinchot who gave the name conservation to the movement. The **Newlands Reclamation Act** (1902) replaced the Carey Act and returned the problem of land reclamation to the federal government. It assigned the proceeds from all public land sales in Western states to be used for federal irrigation projects. Under this act, a dozen great dams were built, including the Hoover Dam on the Colorado River and the Grand Coulee Dam on the Columbia River. The **Antiquities Act** (1906) authorized the president to withdraw from the public domain lands of great natural or historic interest for preservation as national monuments. Two such sites designated by Roosevelt were the Grand Canyon and Niagara Falls. To dramatize the subject in the public mind, Roosevelt in 1908 convened a **White House Conference on Conservation** in which most governors and hundreds of other public officials and experts participated. That conference led to the appointment (1908) of a **National Conservation Commission**, chaired by Pinchot, which inventoried the nation's mineral, water, forest, and soil resources.

The efforts of government conservationists were increasingly supported by private conservation organizations, including the Sierra Club (founded 1892), the National Audubon Society (1905), the Izaak Walton League (1922), and the Wilderness Society (1935).

Despite its successes in protecting the nation's mineral resources, the *Taft administration was made to appear indifferent to conservation by the *Ballinger-Pinchot Controversy. The *Wilson administration saw the creation (1916) of the **National Park Service** (which in 2000 managed 365 national parks, monuments, preserves, trails, seashores, and other units) and the signing (1918) of a Migratory Bird Treaty with Canada.

Conservation was a major concern as well of the Franklin *Roosevelt administration, which combined human and land reclamation in such programs as the *Tennessee Valley Authority, the *Civilian Conservation Corps, and the *Works Projects Administration. Conservation was an essential component of agricultural and power projects as well.

The conservation imperative expressed itself again in a second White House conference called by Pres. John F. Kennedy in 1962. By then, however, the conservation current was broadening into the new *environmentalism.

CONSTITUTION, USS, 44-gun frigate, launched in 1797, that saw service in the undeclared *naval war with France, the Tripolitan War (see *Barbary Wars), and the *War of 1812. Condemned (1830) as unseaworthy, she was saved from destruction by public opinion aroused by Oliver Wendell Holmes Sr.'s poem "Old Ironsides" ("Ay, tear her tattered ensign down! / Long has it waved on high, / And many an eye has danced to see / That banner in the sky . . ."). Since 1925 the *Constitution* has been preserved and exhibited at the Boston navy yard.

CONSTITUTIONAL CONVENTION, FEDERAL (May 25–Sept. 17, 1787), meeting of state delegates in Philadelphia that produced the U.S. Constitution.

In the years following the Revolutionary War, national-minded Americans grew increasingly dissatisfied with the feeble central government established by the *Articles of Confederation. An abortive meeting in Annapolis, Md., in 1786, called to develop uniform commercial regulations among the states, ended by inviting the states to send delegates to a meeting in Philadelphia in May 1787 that would recommend to Congress revisions of the Articles intended to make the central government more effective (see *Annapolis Convention).

The convention met in the Pennsylvania State House (now Independence Hall), in the same room where the *Continental Congress had met and the *Declaration of Independence had been signed. States sent delegations of various sizes, but each state had only one vote in the convention's deliberations. A total of 55 delegates representing 12 states (Rhode Island did not participate) attended at one time or another, although there were rarely more than 30 present at any one time.

Among the delegates, nationalists—men who wanted a strong and "energetic" central government rather than a mere federation of states—were in the majority. Prominent nationalists included George Washington and James Madison of Virginia, James Wilson and Gouverneur Morris of Pennsylvania, Alexander Hamilton of New York, Rufus King of Massachusetts, and Charles Pinckney of South Carolina. Prominent defenders of states' rights against a strong national government were William Paterson of New Jersey, John Dickinson of Delaware, Luther Martin of Maryland, and John Lansing and Robert Yates of New York.

Absent in Paris, Thomas Jefferson commented on the

convention, "It is really an assembly of demigods." A Georgia delegate, William Pierce, recorded his impressions of the delegates, among them:

"Colo. Hamilton is deservedly celebrated for his talents. He is a practitioner of the Law, and reputed to be a finished Scholar. To a clear and strong judgment he unites the ornaments of fancy, and whilst he is able, convincing, and engaging in his eloquence the Heart and Head sympathize in approving him. Yet there is something too feeble in his voice to be equal to the strains of oratory;—it is my opinion that he is rather a convincing Speaker, [than] a blazing Orator. Colo. Hamilton requires time to think,—he enquires into every part of his subject with the searchings of phylosophy, and when he comes forward he comes highly charged with interesting matter, there is no skimming over the surface of a subject with him, he must sink to the bottom to see what foundation it rests upon.—His language is not always equal, sometimes didactic like Bolingbroke's at others light and tripping like Stern's. His eloquence is not so defusive as to trifle with the senses, but he rambles just enough to strike and keep up the attention. He is about 33 years old, of small stature, and lean. His manners are tinctured with stiffness, and sometimes with a degree of vanity that is highly disagreeable. . . .

"Mr. Maddison is a character who has long been in public life; and what is remarkable every Person seems to acknowledge his greatness. He blends together the profound politician, with the Scholar. In the management of every great question he evidently took the lead in the Convention, and tho' he cannot be called an Orator, he is a most agreeable, eloquent, and convincing Speaker. From a spirit of industry and application which he possesses in a most eminent degree, he always comes forward the best informed Man of any point in debate. The affairs of the United States, he perhaps, has the most correct knowledge of, of any Man in the Union. He has been twice a Member of Congress, and was always thought one of the ablest Members that ever sat in that Council. Mr. Maddison is about 37 years of age, a Gentleman of great modesty,—with a remarkable sweet temper. He is easy and unreserved among his acquaintance, and has a most agreeable style of conversation. . . .

"Mr. Wilson ranks among the foremost in legal and political knowledge. He has joined to a fine genius all that can set him off and show him to advantage. He is well acquainted with Man, and understands all the passions that influence him. Government seems to have been his peculiar Study, all the political institutions of the World he knows in detail, and can trace the causes and effects of every revolution from the earliest stages of the Grecian commonwealth down to the present time. No man is more clear, copious, and comprehensive than Mr. Wilson, yet he is no great Orator. He draws the attention not by the charm of his eloquence, but by the force of his reasoning. He is about 45 years old."

The delegates began by electing Washington their presiding officer, deciding to deliberate in secret, and scrapping the instructions from their state legislatures merely to propose amendments to the Articles of Confederation. Instead, they determined to draw up a completely new national constitution. They did so with a confidence characteristic of men of the Enlightenment. "The science of politics," Hamilton wrote later in The *Federalist (No. 9), ". . . like most other sciences has received great improvement. The efficacy of various principles is now well understood, which were either not known at all, or imperfectly known to the ancients. The regular distribution of power into distinct departments—the introduction of legislative ballances and checks—the institution of courts composed of judges, holding their offices during good behaviour—the representation of the people in the legislature by deputies of their own election—these are either wholly new discoveries or have made their principal progress towards perfection in modern times. They are means, and powerful means, by which the excellencies of republican government may be retained and its imperfections lessened or avoided."

In The Federalist (No. 37), Madison identified four great tasks that the convention faced: (1) "combining the requisite stability and energy in government, with the inviolable attention due to liberty and to the republican form"; (2) "marking the proper line of partition between the authority of the general and that of the State governments"; (3) reconciling the "pretensions of the larger and smaller States"; and (4) reconciling the "contending interests and local jealousies" of "the different parts of the United States [which] are distinguished from each other by a variety of circumstances."

The document that emerged from the convention was necessarily a product of compromises large and small. The dispute between large and small states over whether states should be represented in the national legislature equally or in proportion to their populations, for example, was resolved in the "great compromise": states would be represented equally in the Senate, proportionately in the House of Representatives. Other important compromises were effected between nationalists and advocates of states' rights, between democrats and conservatives, and between North and South.

The great achievement of the convention was its conception of federalism, the combining of preexisting sovereign states with a newly created sovereign nation. The federal government was to be more than the agent of confederated states yet less than the all-powerful master of those states. Its powers were limited to specifically enumerated areas, but in those areas they were supreme. All other powers remained with the states, and in these areas the states were supreme. The Framers were careful by their language ("We the people . . .") and by their recommended method of ratification (not by existing state legislatures but by special popular conventions elected for the purpose) to make clear that the legitimacy of the federal government emanated from the sovereignty of the whole people, whereas the legitimacy of the state governments emanated from the sovereignty of their particular portions of the whole people. This combination of sovereignties was entirely novel and was not in fact understood or accepted by many Americans until the Civil War.

The Constitution was completed and ready for signing on Sept. 17. Few delegates were entirely satisfied. Three of those present refused to sign, but most saw the choice as between the proposed constitution and anarchy. Venerable Benjamin Franklin, too weak to address the delegates personally, distributed printed remarks to them before the signing: ". . . I agree to this constitution, with all its faults—if they are such; because I think a general government necessary for us, and there is no *form* of government but may be a blessing to the people, if well administered; and I believe, further, that this is likely to be well administered for a course of years, and can only end in despotism, as other forms have done before it, when the people shall become so corrupted as to need despotic government, being incapable of any other. I doubt, too, whether any other convention we can obtain may be able to make a better constitution; for, when you assemble a number of men, to have the advantage of their joint wisdom, you inevitably assemble with those men all their prejudices, their passions, their errors of opinion, their local interests, and their selfish views. From such an assembly can a *perfect* production be expected? It therefore astonishes me, Sir, to find this system approaching so near to perfection as it does; and I think it will astonish our enemies, who are waiting with confidence to hear that our councils are confounded like those of the builders of Babel, and that our states are on the point of separation, only to meet hereafter for the purpose of cutting one another's throats. Thus I consent, Sir, to this constitution, because I expect no better, and because I am not sure that this is not the best."

On Sept. 17, 1787, 39 delegates signed the Constitution, which was then forwarded to the Confederation Congress in New York with the recommendation that it be submitted to specially elected state conventions for *ratification. "The business being thus closed," wrote Washington in his diary, "the Members adjourned to the City Tavern, dined together and took a cordial leave of each other,—after which I returned to my lodgings—did some business with, and received the papers from the secretary of the Convention, and retired to meditate on the momentous wk. which had been executed. . . ."

CONSTITUTIONAL UNION PARTY (1860), short-lived political party composed of conservative former Whigs and Know-Nothings. Its platform recognized "no political principle other than THE CONSTITUTION OF THE COUNTRY, THE Union OF THE STATES, AND THE ENFORCEMENT OF THE LAWS . . . believing that thereby peace may once more be restored to the country. . . ." Nominating John Bell of Tennessee for president and Edward Everett of Massachusetts for vice president, the party hoped to deny the Republican candidate an electoral majority and thus throw the election into the House of Representatives, which might then elect a pro-Southern president. In the November 1860 election, the Constitutional Union Party carried Tennessee, Kentucky, and Virginia but won less than 3 percent of the Northern vote.

CONSUMER PRODUCT SAFETY ACT (1972). See *Consumer Protection.

CONSUMER PROTECTION. Before the 20th century, Americans were regularly victimized by adulterated foods, quack medicines, and unethical business practices. In the 20th century, however, the federal government began to intervene in what had become a national marketplace to redress the disparity between the feeble power of the individual consumer and the great power of manufacturers and marketers.

The 20th century experienced three waves of consumer concern, all climaxing during activist administrations. The first wave, during the Theodore *Roosevelt administration—the era of the *muckrakers—saw the passage of the **Pure Food and Drug Act** (1906) and the **Meat Inspection Act** (1906). The former prohibited adulterated or fraudulently labeled foods and drugs; the latter—in part a response to Upton Sinclair's novel *The Jungle*, which exposed horrendous conditions in meatpacking plants—introduced federal inspectors into the plants to enforce new sanitary regulations.

The second wave, during the Franklin *Roosevelt administration, saw the strengthening of the Federal Trade Commission (FTC), which had been established in 1914, and the passage of a new **Pure Food, Drug, and Cosmetics Act** (1938), which required manufacturers of foods, drugs, and cosmetics to list the ingredients of their products on the labels.

The third wave of consumer concern began in the administration of Pres. John F. Kennedy, swelled to unprecedented proportions during the Lyndon *Johnson administration, and diminished only in the 1970s. Areas of significant consumer protection legislation in this period included medicine, automobile safety, packaging, meat and poultry, product safety, and consumer credit and debt collection.

A Senate investigation of drug prices, begun in 1959, soon extended to misleading advertising by pharmaceutical houses and finally to the safety and effectiveness of both prescription and nonprescription drugs. The revelation that the sedative thalidomide, which had caused gross birth defects when given to pregnant women in Europe, had only narrowly been kept off the U.S. market by the Food and Drug Administration (FDA) resulted in the **Drug Amendments Act** (1962), which required that new drugs be approved by the FDA for effectiveness as well as safety.

A highway death toll approaching 50,000 a year in the 1950s prompted congressional interest in automobile safety. It became apparent that automobile manufacturers considered safety unmarketable; their investment went almost entirely into yearly style changes and other popular features at the expense of durability, economy, and safety. Publication of Ralph Nader's *Unsafe at Any Speed* (1965) aroused public support for the **National Traffic and Motor Vehicle Safety Act** (1966), which directed the secretary of commerce to prescribe safety standards for all new motor vehicles and required manufacturers to notify purchasers of any safety-related defects within a reasonable time after their discovery.

In a "packaged goods economy," manufacturers use packaging not only to attract consumers but sometimes to deceive them. The **Fair Packaging and Labeling Act** (1966) required the FDA and the FTC to set standards for the disclosure of net quantity on every package. The size and form of these quantity declarations were to be prescribed by the government, and qualifying adjectives were prohibited.

The Meat Inspection Act of 1906 regulated slaughterers and packers engaged in interstate commerce. But as much as a quarter of the nation's meat supply, prepared in small plants serving local markets, remained subject only to often ineffectual state regulation. The **Wholesome Meat Act** (1967) and **Wholesome Poultry Products Act** (1968) brought intrastate meat and poultry processors under federal regulation when state regulation fell short of federal standards.

In the late 1960s and early 1970s, Congress passed acts to protect consumers, especially children, from injury and illness caused by hazardous products. These included the **Flammable Fabrics Act** (1967), the **Child Protection and Toy Safety Act** (1969), and the **Poison Prevention Packaging Act** (1970). The piecemeal approach to product safety was abandoned with passage of the **Consumer Product Safety Act** (1972). This act established an independent Consumer Product Safety Commission empowered to set safety standards for consumer products, to conduct safety studies and tests, and to ban hazardous products.

Varied and deceptive means of calculating the cost of consumer credit—the finance charges on installment purchases, the interest on borrowed money, the mortgage rates on home purchases—often misled consumers and prevented them from shopping for credit as they would for products. The **Truth-in-Lending Act** (1968) required lenders and mortgagors to disclose in writing and in advance the cost of credit both in dollars and as an annual percentage.

Because creditors pooled their information about borrowers in credit bureaus, these had the power, through adverse credit reports, to deny credit for reasons unknown to the consumer. They also routinely sold their information to lenders, employers, government agencies, and other inquirers. The **Fair Credit Reporting Act** (1970) remedied many of these abuses. The **Fair Debt Collection Practices Act** (1977) curbed some of the intrusive, embarrassing, and intimidating tactics of debt-collection agencies.

CONTAINMENT, *cold war policy toward the Soviet Union and later Communist China adopted by the *Truman and successive administrations. The policy was proposed in an article, "The Sources of Soviet Conduct," in the prestigious quarterly *Foreign Affairs* in July 1947 by a "Mr. X," in reality George F. Kennan, a State Department official. Describing the Soviet Union as expansionist wherever its supposed security interests dictated or the weakness of a neighbor invited, Kennan argued that the United States should adopt a "policy of firm containment designed to confront the Russians with unalterable counterforce at every point where they show signs of encroaching upon the interests of a peaceful and stable world," the object being "the gradual mellowing of Soviet power." Kennan was not clear whether U.S. counterforce should be primarily political, economic, or military or whether containment was equally desirable in all geographical areas. The influential columnist Walter Lippmann criticized the proposal as leading to "unending intervention" by the United States in all countries on the Soviet periphery.

Lippmann proved correct. To contain Soviet and then Chinese communism, the United States provided military aid to Greece and Turkey in 1947 (see *Truman Doctrine), financed the postwar recovery of 17 European nations in 1948–51 (see *Marshall Plan), and continued to provide *foreign aid to endangered anticommunist governments around the world. It organized military alliances in Western Europe (the *North Atlantic Treaty Organization [NATO], 1949), Southeast Asia (the *Southeast Asia Treaty Organization [SEATO], 1954), and the Middle East (the *Central Treaty Organization [CENTO], 1955). It fought wars in Korea (see *Korean War) and Vietnam (see *Vietnam War), shielded Taiwan from Chinese threat (see *Formosa Straits Crisis), and supported the mujahideen in their resistance to the Soviet invasion of Afghanistan (1979–88). It also intervened in many local conflicts, sometimes covertly (see *Covert Operations).

The theory—but not the practice—of containment came into disfavor in the *Eisenhower administration. An exponent of that policy as U.S. Army chief of staff and military commander of NATO, Gen. Dwight D. Eisenhower, as a presidential candidate in 1952, had to placate conservative Republicans by criticizing the very policies he had been closely associated with in the Truman administration. Like other conservative Republicans, Secretary of State John Foster Dulles thought it was immoral to abandon the captive peoples of Eastern Europe to Soviet rule; he advocated their "liberation" by whatever means necessary. Eisenhower restrained his belligerent secretary by insisting that liberation be achieved by peaceful means only. Eisenhower himself practiced containment by accepting an armistice in Korea that did nothing more than contain communist aggression, checking Chinese threats to Taiwan, and creating SEATO and CENTO. When anticommunist revolutions broke out in Poland and Hungary in 1956, the administration did nothing to aid them.

Eisenhower did, however, give a new twist to containment, promising "massive retaliation," with nuclear weapons if necessary, in response to any communist aggression. He saw massive retaliation as more cost-effective than maintaining large conventional forces (it would provide "more bang for the buck"). But massive retaliation had its own difficulties—how large must an aggression be to trigger it?—and soon proved as empty as liberation.

With its rejection of massive retaliation in favor of "flexible response," the *Kennedy administration returned to the original concept of containment, which called for resistance to communist expansion by all appropriate means.

CONTINENTAL ARMY (1775–84), army of the United States during the *Revolutionary War. The *Continental Congress created the army on June 15, 1775, adopting into it the 17,000 militiamen then besieging Boston (see *Boston Siege). George Washington was named commander in chief, and four major generals and eight brigadier generals were appointed. During 1776, Congress filled the army by adopting into it existing state militia units.

Thoroughly dissatisfied with short-term militias, Washington in 1775 instituted one-year enlistments directly into the Continental Army. After 1776 Congress set the term of enlistment at three years or the duration of the war and offered a bounty of $20 and 100 acres of land to each volunteer. Congress aimed at an army of 75,000 men but never obtained half that number. At its greatest strength, in November 1778, the Continental Army numbered 35,000 men. During campaigns, it was always necessary to supplement the Continentals with local militias.

The long-term Continentals proved the equal of British regulars, especially after their training in European combat drill at *Valley Forge in 1777–78. Their junior officers were considered excellent; their senior officers were a mixed bag, which time and experience sorted out. Service was hard, supplies and equipment were often lacking, and pay was often late and in the form of paper money of dubious value. Desertion was frequent, but significant mutinies did not occur until after the end of hostilities (see *Newburgh Conspiracy; *Philadelphia Mutiny).

Congress officially declared the Revolutionary War over on Apr. 11, 1783, and on Nov. 3 discharged the last enlistees. Washington formally resigned his commission on Dec. 23. On June 2, 1784, Congress abolished the Continental Army but then created a new Regular Army of 700 men.

CONTINENTAL ASSOCIATION (Oct. 18, 1774), agreement among the delegates at the *Continental Congress to boycott trade with Great Britain in retaliation for the *Intolerable Acts. The delegates agreed not to import British goods or slaves after Dec. 1; not to consume British or foreign luxury products after Mar. 1, 1775; and not to export colonial products to Britain, Ireland, or the West Indies after Sept. 1, 1775. Local committees were to ensure compliance, punishing violators by publicity and boycott. By April 1775, when war began, the Association was in operation in all the states except Georgia.

CONTINENTAL CONGRESS (1774–88), sole organ of central government of the 13 colonies (later states) during the *American Revolution. It was convened initially to formulate a united response to the *Intolerable Acts. When the *Revolutionary War began, it assumed direction of the country's military and diplomatic affairs, although its authority rested entirely on the acquiescence of the states. The *Articles of Confederation (1781) regularized its status—but scarcely increased its authority— as a de facto national government. Thereafter it is informally known as the Confederation Congress.

"It is to be a School of Political Prophets . . . a Nursery of American Statesmen," wrote Massachusetts delegate John Adams in anticipation of the Congress's first meeting. The first Congress met in Carpenters Hall in Philadelphia Sept. 5–Oct. 26, 1774, the second in the Pennsylvania State House (now Independence Hall) in Philadelphia May 10–Aug. 2, 1775. Congress reconvened on Sept. 13 and thereafter remained in more or less continuous session. The approach of British troops in December 1776 caused it to remove to Baltimore, Md., where it remained until February 1777. While the British occupied Philadelphia, Congress met in York, Pa. (September 1777–June 1778). A mutiny of Pennsylvania troops prompted it to move to Princeton, N.J. (June–November 1783). It then moved to Annapolis, Md. (November 1783–June 1784), to Trenton, N.J. (November–December 1784), and finally to New York City (January 1785).

At Philadelphia in June 1775 Congress recognized the war that had begun in Massachusetts as a continental cause, adopting the militia forces around Boston as a *Continental Army and appointing George Washington its commander in chief. A year later, on July 2, 1776, Congress passed Richard Henry Lee's resolution that the "United Colonies are, and of right ought to be, free and independent states," and on July 4 it approved Thomas Jefferson's draft of the *Declaration of Independence. From July 1776 to November 1777 Congress drafted a written constitution for the United States, the Articles of Confederation, which was not adopted until 1781. At York, Pa., on May 4, 1778, Congress ratified treaties of commerce and alliance with France. At Annapolis, Md., on Dec. 23, 1783, it received *Washington's resignation and on Jan. 14, 1784, it formally ratified the treaty that ended the Revolutionary War (see *Paris Treaty [1783]).

The Articles of Confederation established a quorum of at least two representatives from seven states that was mustered with increasing infrequency after the war. The great achievement of Congress's waning years was its organization of the *Northwest Territory. On Feb. 22, 1787, the Congress formally called for the meeting of the Federal *Constitutional Convention. The new Constitution having been ratified, Congress, on Sept. 13, 1788, ordered that the states should appoint their presidential electors on the first Wednesday in January 1789, that those electors should meet and vote on the first Wednesday in February, and that the new Congress should meet and count the presidential ballots in New York City on the first Wednesday in March. The old Congress mustered a quorum for the last time on Oct. 10, 1788.

CONTINENTAL NAVY (1775–84), the U.S. navy during the *Revolutionary War, established by the *Continental Congress on Nov. 25, 1775. In 1776 its first commander, Esek Hopkins, sailed a small fleet of converted merchantmen to the Bahamas, where it raided Nassau, took several prizes, then returned to Providence, R.I., where it was bottled up by the British blockade. Operating from France in the *Ranger* and the *Bonhomme Richard*, Capt. John Paul Jones carried the war into British home waters. American privateers—not naval vessels—captured some 600 British ships. Congress dismantled the Continental Navy after the war.

CONTRACT WITH AMERICA. See *Republican Revolution.

CONVENTION OF 1800 or **TREATY OF MOR-FONTAINE,** diplomatic achievement of the John *Adams administration ending the undeclared *naval war with France. The chief objective of the three negotiators sent by President Adams in 1799 was indemnification for the depredations of French privateers on American commerce. The French refused to pay indemnities, wanted the 1778 treaties of commerce, amity, and alliance between the United States and France reaffirmed (Congress had abrogated them in 1798), and would not accept commercial privileges in the United States inferior to what the British had obtained in *Jay's Treaty. The two positions were irreconcilable.

After six months, the negotiators—in a treaty signed (Sept. 30, 1800) at Morfontaine—agreed on minimal terms, including peace, abrogation of the 1778 treaties, and commercial privileges for France on a most-favored-nation basis.

Back in the United States, Republicans and Federalists alike disliked the treaty—Republicans because it was less than a treaty of friendship, Federalists because it seemed like one more humiliation at the hands of France. But gradually they perceived some clear gains: an end to the depredations of French privateers, a chance to resume profitable trade with France, and release from the 1778 treaties, America's only "entangling alliance." Having rejected the treaty on Jan. 27, 1801, the Senate reconsidered and ratified it on Feb. 3 after fixing its duration at eight years.

CONVENTION OF 1818, diplomatic achievement of the *Monroe administration. This Anglo-American convention fixed the northern boundary of the United States from Lake of the Woods to the crest of the Rocky Mountains along the 49th parallel. West of the mountains lay Oregon country, which the signatories agreed would be jointly occupied (that is, open to citizens of both countries) for ten years (extended indefinitely in 1827). The convention also confirmed American fishing rights off the Labrador and Newfoundland coasts.

CONWAY CABAL (1777–78), intrigue among some generals and members of Congress during the *Valley Forge winter of the *Revolutionary War to replace George Washington as army commander with Gen. Horatio Gates, then celebrated as the victor of *Saratoga. Instigators included Gen. Thomas Mifflin, the incompetent army quartermaster general, and Gen. Thomas Conway, an Irish-born French soldier contemptuous of American amateurs. When Washington confronted Conway with evidence of the intrigue, those involved backed away from the affair. A congressional committee investigated the army at Valley Forge, blamed its problems on Mifflin and Congress itself, and supported Washington's defensive policy.

COOLEY v. BOARD OF WARDENS (1851), 6–2 decision of the *Taney Court defining a line between federal supremacy and concurrent state powers in the federal system. Cooley refused to pay a fee required by a Pennsylvania law regulating the employment of pilots at Philadelphia. For the Court, Justice Benjamin Curtis ruled: "The grant of commercial power to Congress does not contain any terms which expressly exclude the States from exercising an authority over its subject matter. If they are excluded it must be because the nature of the power, thus granted to Congress, requires that a similar

authority should not exist in the States. . . . Now, the power to regulate commerce embraces a vast field, containing not only many, but exceedingly various subjects, quite unlike in their nature; some imperatively demanding a single uniform rule, operating equally on the commerce of the United States in every port; and some, like the subject now in question, as imperatively demanding that diversity which alone can meet the local necessities of navigation."

COOLIDGE ADMINISTRATION (1923–29). Republican Calvin Coolidge, 30th president of the United States, succeeded to the presidency on the death of Warren G. Harding. A prototypical New Englander—unpretentious, dour, frugal, taciturn—he was a thorough conservative perfectly content with the status quo. "The business of America is business," Coolidge boasted, accurately voicing the ethos of the 1920s. He became immensely popular in a country whose extravagant hedonism contrasted with his own cautious virtues. Editor William Allen White called his biography of Coolidge *A Puritan in Babylon.*

Except for the shift from corruption to respectability, there was no break in policy between the Harding and Coolidge administrations. "Coolidge prosperity" had begun under Harding but was stimulated by the revenue bills of 1924 and 1926 pushed by millionaire secretary of the Treasury Andrew Mellon that drastically slashed personal income, corporate, and inheritance taxes. The two revenue bills increased the already extreme maldistribution of income and wealth and fed the frenzy of private investment and stock speculation that led to the *Panic of 1929 and the *Great Depression. Antitrust laws were forgotten.

Other important legislation of the Coolidge administration was the Immigration Act of 1924, which drastically reduced the size and changed the character of the annual *immigration; the Veterans Bonus Act of 1924 (passed over Coolidge's veto), which led to the *Bonus Army of 1932; and the Air Commerce Act of 1926, which placed civil aviation under the Department of Commerce. In 1928 Coolidge vetoed the persistent McNary-Haugen Bill (see *Farm Problem).

In foreign affairs, Secretary of State Frank B. Kellogg negotiated the visionary *Kellogg-Briand Treaty of 1928, in which 62 countries renounced war as an instrument of national policy except for self-defense.

In 1928, in response to reporters' badgering about his reelection plans, Coolidge issued his famous statement, typically laconic: "I do not choose to run for president in 1928." A decision he later regretted (he disliked Herbert

Hoover, who succeeded him), it was nevertheless one of his luckiest. In the depth of the Great Depression, when some people remembered Coolidge prosperity and considered nominating him for president again, Coolidge, only a few months before he died, issued a poignant statement: "We are in a new era to which I do not belong, and it would not be possible for me to adjust myself to it."

COOPER v. AARON (1958), unanimous decision of the *Warren Court rejecting an appeal of the Little Rock, Ark., School Board for a two-and-a-half-year delay in implementing a court-approved *school-desegregation plan because of public disorders (see *Little Rock Crisis) and pending state efforts to nullify the Court's ruling in *Brown v. Board of Education of Topeka*. "The constitutional rights of respondents [the black students]," wrote Chief Justice Earl Warren, "are not to be sacrificed or yielded to the violence and disorder which have followed upon the actions of the Governor and the Legislature." Moreover, under the Constitution's Supremacy Clause (Art. 6), "the interpretation of the Fourteenth Amendment enunciated by this Court in the *Brown* case is the supreme law of the land. . . . Every state legislator and executive and judicial officer is solemnly committed by oath . . . 'to support this Constitution.' "

COPPERHEADS, in the *Civil War, Northern "Peace Democrats" who opposed the war effort and the policies of the *Lincoln administration. They were particularly numerous in Illinois, Indiana, and Ohio. The most prominent was Clement L. Vallandigham, an Ohio congressman (1858–63) who supported states' rights and opposed the war. He was arrested by military authorities (see *Habeas Corpus Suspensions), but President Lincoln commuted his sentence to banishment to the Confederacy. From there he went to Canada, returning to the United States in 1864. His demand for immediate cessation of hostilities was included in the Democratic Party platform that year. The Copperheads were largely responsible for the stigma of disloyalty that the Republicans attached to the Democrats for many years.

CORAL SEA. See *World War 2.

CORINTH (Oct. 3–4, 1862), *Civil War battle. To support Confederate general Braxton Bragg's invasion of Kentucky from Tennessee (August–October 1862), Confederate troops in Mississippi under Gen. Sterling Price pushed north, driving the Federals from Iuka on Sept. 14 and hitting Corinth on Oct. 3. Union defenders under Gen. William S. Rosecrans fell back but counterattacked the next day, putting the Confederates to flight and ending the last Confederate offensive in Mississippi.

CORPORATE RESPONSIBILITY ACT or **SAR-BANES-OXLEY ACT** (2002), legislation of the George W. *Bush administration in response to a wave of corporate scandals involving aggressive accountants, complicit auditors, lax regulators, and huge bankruptcies from which insiders walked away with millions (see *Enron Bankruptcy). These events contributed to a plummeting stock market, which reached five-year lows in July 2002.

Influenced by conservative advisers, President Bush reacted by assuring the country that the economy was sound and by exhorting corporate executives to be honest. But Congress—members of both parties, in an election year—heeded the public's demand for corporate accountability and passed the Corporate Responsibility Act (sponsored by Democratic senator Paul S. Sarbanes of Maryland and Republican representative Michael G. Oxley of Ohio) by near-unanimous votes in both houses. Although he had opposed central provisions of the act only weeks before, President Bush signed it approvingly, describing it as "the most far-reaching reforms of American business practices since the time of Franklin Delano Roosevelt."

The act required chief executives and chief financial officers of publicly traded companies to personally certify their financial statements and fixed stiff prison terms for "knowingly and willfully" publishing misleading information. It required companies to disclose "material" changes in their financial condition promptly. It also prohibited company loans to executives. The act barred accounting firms from providing consulting services to the companies they audit, and it established a regulatory board with investigative and enforcement powers to oversee the accounting industry.

The New York Stock Exchange also initiated reforms affecting corporate governance.

CORRUPT BARGAIN (1825), charge leveled against the incoming John Quincy *Adams administration after Adams appointed Henry Clay secretary of state. Clay, a rival candidate for president in the election of 1824, which was decided by the House of Representatives, had thrown his support to Adams, assuring his election over Andrew Jackson, although Jackson had led in the popular and electoral votes. Historians doubt that there was any explicit bargain. Clay preferred Adams to Jackson for many reasons, and Adams respected Clay's qualifications for the cabinet post. Although Clay and Adams denied the charge, it hung over the administration for four years. Jackson felt that an injustice had been done and was determined to oust Adams in 1828.

COTTON GIN, machine for separating cotton fibers from the seed, patented by Eli Whitney in 1794. Whitney's gin—from "engine"—used spiked teeth set in a revolving wooden cylinder to pull the cotton fibers through slots too narrow to admit the seed. Brushes attached to a second cylinder then freed the fiber from the teeth. Whitney claimed his machine could do the work of 50 men, and indeed it made possible the rapid expansion of so-called green-seed cotton across the South and the increase of annual cotton production from 3,000 bales in 1790 to more than 2 million in 1850.

COTTON KINGDOM, before the Civil War, five states of the lower South—South Carolina, Georgia, Alabama, Mississippi, and Louisiana. These states accounted for over three-fourths of U.S. cotton production.

COUNTERCULTURE (1960s), rebellion of alienated youths against the values and conventions of their parents, often affluent members of the middle class. The disaffected *baby boomers, known as **hippies**, were generally high-school or college students, though they were joined by numbers of immature adults. Wearing raffish dress, sandals, long hair, and beads, they affected a smattering of Eastern religion. Their mantras were "Love" and "Peace." Following the advice of Harvard psychologist Timothy Leary, an advocate of drug experimentation, many of them "tuned in, turned on, and dropped out." Those who left home congregated in city neighborhoods where they supported themselves by panhandling when they were not indulging in the counterculture's alleged chief activities—sex, drugs, and rock and roll (folk music was preferred by some).

The epitome of the counterculture was the **Woodstock Music Fair** (Aug. 15–17, 1969), a three-day rock festival held on a farm in New York's Sullivan County where 300,000 well-behaved young people (more thousands were prevented by massive traffic jams from reaching the site) camped in rain and mud to hear a succession of rock bands.

COURT-PACKING PLAN (1937), incident in the Franklin *Roosevelt administration. In February 1937, shortly after his landslide reelection, President Roosevelt sent to Congress a bill proposing a number of reforms of the federal judiciary, most notably the appointment of one new federal judge for every sitting judge over age 70 up to a maximum of 50—including a maximum of six to the U.S. Supreme Court. The plan was recognized as a device to circumvent the hostility of a largely conservative Republican judiciary to the administration's broad view of federal regulatory powers. In 1935 and 1936 the Supreme Court (see *Hughes Court) had overturned two cornerstones of the *New Deal—the National Industrial Recovery Act (see *Schechter Poultry Corp. v. United States) and the Agricultural Adjustment Act of 1933 (see *United States v. Butler).

Roosevelt pushed his scheme against bitter opposition even in his own party. In March, however, a shift within the Supreme Court created a 5–4 majority in support of a state minimum wage law, signaling the Court's tactical retreat from its obstructionist stance (see *West Coast Hotel Co. v. Parrish). In April, the same 5–4 majority validated the National Labor Relations Act, considered the administration's most radical legislation (see *National Labor Relations Board v. Jones & Laughlin Steel Corp.), and in May the Social Security Act was upheld in 5–4 and 7–2 decisions (see *Steward Machine Co. v. Davis). In May, also, conservative justice Willis Van Devanter announced his retirement, enabling Roosevelt to make his first appointment to the Court. Between 1937 and 1943, he would appoint eight justices to the Supreme Court and elevate a chief justice.

In August 1937 Congress passed a Judicial Procedures Reform Act incorporating some of Roosevelt's recommendations but leaving unchanged the number of federal judges.

COVERT OPERATIONS (1945–90), during the *cold war, secret interventions—both political and military—into foreign countries by the United States. Typically, these were carried out by the Central Intelligence Agency (CIA), sometimes with the collaboration of civilian and military departments. Their objectives, according to a 1955 National Security Council directive, included: "Create and exploit troublesome problems for International Communism . . . [;] Discredit the prestige and ideology of International Communism . . . [;] Counter any threat of a party or individuals . . . responsive to Communist control to achieve dominant power in a free world country . . . [;] Reduce International Communist control over any areas of the world . . . [;] Strengthen the orientation toward the United States of the peoples and nations of the free world. . . ." A desired characteristic of such operations was "plausible deniability."

There were literally thousands of covert operations,

major and minor, during the cold war. A few of the now better known were these:

In 1953, the CIA engineered the overthrow of Iranian premier Muhammad Mussadegh, who had nationalized the British-owned Anglo-Iranian Oil Co. and who, in the American view, was tilting toward Moscow. Shah Mohammed Reza Pahlevi was restored to absolute power and ruled as an American client for 26 years.

In 1954, the CIA sponsored an invasion of Guatemala, whose popular president, Jacobo Arbenz Guzmán, had expropriated (with compensation) 400,000 acres of land owned by the United Fruit Co. for distribution to peasants. The invasion proved farcical but it was sufficient to cause the ouster of Arbenz.

In 1958 the CIA supplied a short-lived colonels' revolt against dictatorial Indonesian president Sukarno, who, although an anticommunist, had offended Washington by choosing (with India, Burma, and Egypt) "nonalignment" in the cold war. The U.S. role was discovered and exposed, strengthening Sukarno's position.

From 1956, the CIA flew high-altitude photo reconnaissance planes over the Soviet Union. These secret flights were known to the governments that provided bases for the planes, and they were of course known to the Soviets, who were chagrined at their inability to bring the planes down. In 1960, however, they succeeded in downing a plane and captured its pilot. The flights were exposed and halted (see *U-2 Affair).

During 1960–61, the CIA recruited, equipped, trained, and transported a force of Cuban exiles intending to overthrow Cuban dictator Fidel Castro, who, though not yet known to be a communist or aligned with the Soviet Union, had expropriated (without compensation) American property in Cuba. The *Bay of Pigs fiasco resulted.

In the fragmenting Republic of the Congo (formerly the Belgian Congo, later Zaire) in 1961, the CIA backed army strongman Joseph Mobutu against the nationalist premier Patrice Lumumba. Lumumba was captured by Mobutu's troops and murdered. Seizing power with CIA help in 1965, Mobutu ruled Zaire despotically until 1997, vastly enriching himself while reducing the country to economic disaster.

From 1954, the CIA covertly violated the sovereignty of Laos, first to subvert the country's cold war neutralism, then to employ a secret army of Meo (Hmong) tribesmen to fight Laotian and North Vietnamese communists. The U.S. air force secretly bombed the Ho Chi Minh Trail and North Vietnamese positions within Laos.

When Marxist Salvador Allende Gossens was elected president of Chile in 1970—despite large U.S. govern-

ment and corporate contributions to his opponent—Washington added to rising popular unrest in Chile by cutting off economic assistance and blocking American and international loans, while the CIA spent large sums to subsidize opposition newspapers and encouraged an army revolt. In 1973 Allende was overthrown and died in an army coup that brought to power Gen. Augusto Pinochet. In 16 years of authoritarian rule, Pinochet bloodily repressed left-wing opposition while encouraging capitalist development.

As Angola neared independence, scheduled for 1975, three political movements—the MPLA, FNLA, and UNITA—fought for power. All were tribally based and leftist. Since the MPLA received support from the Soviet Union and later from Cuba, Washington automatically rushed to the support of the FNLA, the CIA shipping arms and other equipment and recruiting mercenaries. In so doing, it found itself allied with Zaire, South Africa, and Communist China, which also supported the FNLA. Learning about the operation, Congress was shocked at the CIA's unsavory allies and in December 1975 cut off funds for Angola.

In the 1980s, the CIA shipped weapons through Pakistan to Afghan mujahideen resisting the Soviet invasion of their country. The Afghan war proved a training ground for later Muslim terrorists hostile to the United States.

Also in the 1980s, the CIA financed and trained Contra opponents of Nicaragua's leftist Sandinista government, going so far as to mine Nicaraguan ports in 1983 to isolate the country. When Congress cut off government funds for the Contras, the CIA tried to raise money from other countries, a tactic that led to the *Iran-Contra Affair.

COWPENS (Jan. 17, 1781), *Revolutionary War battle. While Gen. Nathanael Greene, newly appointed to replace Gen. Horatio Gates as commander of the Southern Department, remained in North Carolina facing British general Charles Cornwallis, Gen. Daniel Morgan led a force of 1,000 Patriots into South Carolina, where he threatened Cornwallis's rear. Cornwallis detached Col. Banastre Tarleton to deal with Morgan.

With 1,100 men, Tarleton tracked Morgan relentlessly, coming upon his hastily deserted camp on Jan. 16. Morgan prepared for battle at a wooded pasture, or cowpen, nearby. When Tarleton approached the American line in the morning of Jan. 17, he ordered a frontal attack. Patriot militia in the first two lines fired and withdrew; the line of Continentals behind them held firm for a while and then withdrew to a nearby crest.

Thinking they had the Patriots in retreat, the British broke ranks and pursued them. At this point the Continentals turned, fired, and launched a bayonet attack upon the disorganized British, driving them in headlong retreat.

The British suffered 110 dead, 200 wounded, 500 captured, a major loss; the Patriots counted 12 dead, 60 wounded. *King's Mountain and Cowpens significantly weakened Cornwallis in his confrontation with Greene in North Carolina.

COXEY'S ARMY (1894), march on Washington of unemployed workingmen during the severe economic depression that followed the *Panic of 1893. It was organized by a Massillon, Ohio, businessman, Jacob Sechler Coxey, who conceived of it as a "petition with boots on" seeking federal public works to alleviate unemployment.

Coxey envisioned an "army" of 100,000 men, but only 100 departed from Massillon on Easter Sunday, Mar. 24, and only 500 camped outside Washington on Apr. 29. Sympathetic crowds along the way and especially in Washington gave the demonstration greater impact on public opinion than its numbers might have warranted. On May Day, police barred the marchers from the Capitol grounds, then assaulted them. Coxey and other leaders were arrested and the army was dispersed.

At the same time, other and larger "industrial armies" originated on the West Coast and came east in boxcars, on captured trains, and on foot. Some 1,200 remnants of such armies reached Washington during the spring of 1894.

CRATER, THE. See *Petersburg Siege.

CRÉDIT MOBILIER SCANDAL (1876), incident in the *Grant administration. Crédit Mobilier was a company formed by leading shareholders of the Union Pacific Railroad to act as general contractor during building of the railroad (see *Transcontinental Railroad) while diverting construction profits to themselves. Its owners profited hugely. Since the railroad securities used to finance the company were backed by government loans and land grants, the public considered those profits illegitimate.

When it appeared in 1867 that Congress might investigate the company, its managers distributed shares to influential senators and representatives to forestall such an event. In September 1872, during the presidential election campaign, a list of share recipients came into the possession of the New York *Sun*, which published it. A subsequent congressional investigation of the affair resulted in the formal censure of two congressmen and sullied the reputations of Vice Pres. Schuyler Colfax and Rep. James A. Garfield.

CREEK WAR (1811–14), Indian war on the Southern frontier fought during the *War of 1812. In 1811, a portion of the Creek Indians, the so-called Red Sticks, led by Chief William Weatherford, were aroused by the Shawnee chief Tecumseh to war against the whites (see *Tecumseh Confederacy). Raids on frontier settlements were climaxed by a massacre at Fort Mims, Ala., on Aug. 30, 1813. In response, Gen. Andrew Jackson led an army of Tennessee militia south into Creek territory, cutting a road as he went, facing down mutinous troops, and inflicting heavy casualties on the Creeks in a series of battles culminating at **Horseshoe Bend** (Mar. 27, 1814). In the Treaty of Fort Jackson (Aug. 9, 1814), Jackson imposed a punitive peace on the Creeks, friendly and hostile alike, stripping them of almost all their territory in Alabama and Georgia.

CREOLE AFFAIR (1842), incident in the *Tyler administration. A U.S. vessel, the *Creole*, was carrying a cargo of 135 slaves from Virginia to New Orleans when 19 of the slaves forcibly seized the ship and compelled the captain to take them to Nassau in the Bahamas. There British authorities held the 19 mutineers on criminal charges but released the other slaves. Secretary of State Daniel Webster demanded the return of the ship and cargo or indemnification, to the satisfaction of Southerners and the distress of abolitionists. The issue was resolved in 1855 with a British payment of $110,530.

CRIME AGAINST KANSAS, THE. See *Sumner Assault.

CRIME OF '73, the demonetization of silver, accomplished by omitting the silver dollar from the list of coins authorized by the **Coinage Act** of 1873. The omission may have been inadvertent, since the silver dollar (whose silver content was worth more than a dollar) had not circulated for many years. But it's possible that the authors of the act knew that new silver discoveries in the West would soon cause the price of silver to fall and bring a flood of silver bullion to the mints for coinage into dollars. Because the silver content of these dollars would be worth less than a dollar, they would soon drive gold out of circulation. The effect of the Coinage Act was to place the United States de facto on the gold standard, imposing on the country a relatively static money supply during a period of economic expansion.

The result, according to silverites, was a decades-long price deflation, causing hardship to debtors generally and to farmers in particular (see *Agrarian Discontents). Silver producers and bimetallists seeking to enlarge the money supply (see *Free Silver) attributed the 1873 Coinage Act to a conspiracy among British and American financial interests to establish the gold standard in the United States. Belief in this conspiracy persisted among silverites for many years.

CRITTENDEN COMPROMISE (January 1861), attempt to resolve the *secession crisis. The compromise consisted of a number of proposals drawn up by Sen. John J. Crittenden of Kentucky, a Democrat, as a member of the Senate Committee of Thirteen appointed to review compromise plans. These were to be enacted as constitutional amendments that were never to be overridden. The principal proposals were: no interference by the national government with slavery in the states; no interference with the interstate slave trade; slavery prohibited in the territories north of 36°30' but protected south of that line in all present and future territories; slaveholders to be compensated for unrecovered fugitives.

From Springfield, Ill., President-elect Abraham Lincoln advised Republican senators: "Entertain no proposition for a compromise in regard to the *extension* of slavery." Republican opposition in the committee and on the Senate floor killed the compromise.

CROWN POINT, promontory on the west shore of Lake Champlain in New York, ten miles north of *Fort Ticonderoga. It was fortified by France in 1731 and by the British in 1759. On the invasion route between the United States and Canada, it was captured (May 12, 1775) by the *Green Mountain Boys at the start of the *Revolutionary War but changed hands several times in the course of that war.

CUBAN MIGRATION. During the 19th century, Cuban political exiles sought refuge in the United States, and a moderate immigration continued during the 20th. After Fidel Castro took power in 1959, middle-class, educated Cubans began coming to the United States under normal immigration procedures. When diplomatic relations between the United States and Cuba were severed in 1961 and Cubans could no longer obtain visas, Cuban refugees began to be paroled into the United States by the U.S. attorney general. Commercial flights from Cuba to the United States were terminated in Oc-

tober 1962, and the number of refugees dropped sharply.

These first Cuban migrants were intensely anticommunist and expected to return to Cuba and overthrow Castro. But the failure of the *Bay of Pigs invasion in 1961 and the settlement of the *Cuban Missile Crisis in 1962, by which the United States pledged not to invade Cuba, persuaded them that their stay would be more permanent.

Between December 1965 and April 1973 an airlift brought further large numbers of Cuban refugees to the United States. During 1959–79, 665,000 Cuban refugees entered the United States, 420,000 of them as parolees. In 1966 Congress permitted the Cuban refugees to adjust their status as permanent residents after two years.

Between April and June 1980 some 125,000 new Cuban refugees reached Florida in the so-called **Mariel boatlift**. The first came in their own small boats, but soon a flotilla of U.S. fishing and pleasure boats began to shuttle between Florida and Cuba bringing in refugees, sometimes at steep prices, until the Castro government put a stop to the traffic. The refugees professed anti-Castro sentiments, but it was clear that their migration was motivated by economic troubles at home and a desire to be united with relatives in the United States. Many were criminals and mental patients deported by Castro. Half of these refugees were released to sponsors in Miami, while the other half were detained in army camps.

The Cuban migrants concentrated in Florida, New Jersey, and New York City. In the 1970s they became a conservative political force in Florida and nationally. The rising generation of Cuban-Americans were more moderate in their political views than their parents. The 2000 Census counted 1.2 million Cuban immigrants or their descendants in the United States, 54 percent of them in Florida.

CUBAN MISSILE CRISIS (1962), incident in the *Kennedy administration. During the summer of 1962 a Soviet military buildup was observed in Cuba. On Oct. 15 U-2 reconnaissance photographs revealed the construction of launching sites for intermediate-range missiles. Since these were clearly offensive weapons, their emplacement in Cuba could not be tolerated.

How to respond was the issue that engrossed Pres. John F. Kennedy and his advisers. An invasion of Cuba and an air attack on the missile sites were ruled out as reminiscent of Pearl Harbor. (U.S. intelligence was unaware that the Soviets had 42,000 troops in Cuba and may have had tactical nuclear weapons as well.) It was finally decided to impose a naval "quarantine" (a blockade would have been an act of war) around Cuba, stopping Soviet ships carrying military equipment there.

Soviet premier Nikita Khrushchev was informed of the quarantine on Oct. 22. That evening Kennedy described the situation to the American people on television. The quarantine went into effect on Oct. 24. Kennedy and his advisers held their breath while the world balanced on the edge of nuclear war. To their vast relief, the next day Soviet ships approaching Cuba turned back. As Secretary of State Dean Rusk remarked, "We're eyeball to eyeball, and the other fellow just blinked."

However, construction continued at the missile sites, and the uncrating and assembly of Russian bombers on Cuban airfields was observed. Kennedy insisted to Khrushchev that the missiles had to be removed and the sites inspected; Khrushchev agreed on condition that the quarantine end and the United States promise not to invade Cuba. In secret negotiations, the United States agreed also to remove its intermediate-range missiles stationed in Turkey and Italy (now rendered obsolete by the development of the missile-firing Polaris submarine).

Kennedy has been both criticized and praised for his management of the missile crisis. Khrushchev's management at his end contributed to his removal from power in 1964. Fidel Castro was furious at the Soviets' desertion. He refused to accept inspection of the missile sites, and the 42,000 Soviet troops remained on the island.

CULTURE WARS, conflict of worldviews in late-20th-century America. Opposing worldviews have always coexisted, but the sharpness of their conflicts in this period seemed to portend the fragmenting of American society. The fault lines may be suggested by such dichotomies as religion/secularism, nation/ethnicity, family/self, authority/self-determination, sacrifice/hedonism. The battlefields of the culture wars were politics, law, education, religion, and media and the arts. Some notable battles concerned abortion, affirmative action, child care, feminism, homosexuality, pornography, school prayer, and school vouchers.

A more arcane culture war was fought in the universities between the conservative establishment and some former student radicals of the 1960s who, a decade later, had become tenured professors, critically challenging the status quo in the humanities and social sciences. The philosophical differences between conservative and radical academics may be suggested by the dichotomies tradition/innovation, objectivism/perspectivism, universalism/multiculturalism.

CUMBERLAND ROAD. See *National Road or Cumberland Road.

CUSHING'S TREATY (1844). See *Wanghia Treaty or Cushing's Treaty.

CUSTER'S LAST STAND. See *Little Bighorn.

D

DANBURY HATTERS' CASE. See *Loewe v. Lawlor* or *Danbury Hatters' Case.*

DARK HORSE, an unexpected presidential nominee selected by a convention unable to nominate a more prominent candidate. At the Democratic national convention in 1844, when neither Martin Van Buren nor Lewis Cass could get the two-thirds majority necessary for nomination, the delegates turned to little-known James K. Polk. In 1852, the Democratic convention, deadlocked between James Buchanan and Stephen A. Douglas, finally chose Franklin Pierce. In the 1876 Republican convention, his managers thrust forward Rutherford B. Hayes to prevent the nomination of James G. Blaine when the other leading candidates began to fail. In 1920, Republican party managers meeting in the famous *"smoke-filled room" produced Warren G. Harding to break a deadlock between Leonard Wood and Frank Lowden.

DARTMOUTH COLLEGE v. WOODWARD (1819), 5–1 decision of the *Marshall Court that protected private corporations from state regulation. In 1816, the Republican governor and legislature of New Hampshire attempted to convert Federalist-controlled Dartmouth College from a private to a public institution by revising the college's 1769 charter. Chief Justice Marshall agreed with the college's lawyers that the charter was a contract protected by the Contract Clause of the U.S. Constitution ("No state shall . . . pass any . . . law impairing the obligation of contracts . . ."). This was the first time that the protection of the Contract Clause was extended to a corporate charter, and the precedent later served to exempt business corporations from state regulation— although Justice Joseph Story, in a concurring opinion, suggested that legislatures could include "reservation" clauses in corporate charters preserving certain state powers.

DAWES GENERAL ALLOTMENT ACT (1887). See *Indian Policy.

DAWES PLAN (1924). See *War Debts.

D-DAY. See *World War 2.

DEBS, IN RE (1895), unanimous decision of the U.S. Supreme Court denying to Eugene V. Debs, president of the *American Railway Union, a writ of habeas corpus that would have released him from six months' imprisonment for contempt of court for his role in the *Pullman strike (1894). At the request of U.S. attorney general Richard Olney, the federal circuit court in Chicago had issued an injunction forbidding anyone to hinder the railroads in their tasks of carrying the mail and engaging in interstate commerce. The injunction, based on the *Sherman Antitrust Act (1890), in effect found the union a "combination in restraint of trade."

"The national government," wrote Justice David Brewer in denying Debs's appeal, "given by the Constitution power to regulate interstate commerce, has by express statute assumed jurisdiction over such commerce when carried upon railroads. It is charged, therefore, with the duty of keeping those highways of interstate commerce free from obstruction, for it has always been recognized as one of the powers and duties of a government to remove obstructions from the highway under its control. . . ."

The use of injunctions in labor disputes was ended by the *Norris–La Guardia Act (1932).

DECLARATION OF INDEPENDENCE, document adopted July 4, 1776, by the *Continental Congress to explain and justify "to a candid world" the resolution of independence already adopted by the 12 colonies (New York had abstained) on July 2. That resolution, offered by Richard Henry Lee of Virginia on June 7, read: "Resolved, That these United Colonies are, and of right ought to be, free and independent States, that they are absolved from all allegiance to the British Crown, and that all political connection between them and the State of Great Britain is, and ought to be totally dissolved" (see *American Revolution).

After Lee's resolution was introduced (its adoption a foregone conclusion), Congress on June 10 appointed a committee consisting of John Adams, Benjamin Franklin, Roger Sherman, Robert R. Livingston, and Thomas Jefferson to compose the supplemental document. Jefferson was asked to prepare a draft; Adams and Franklin emended it; and the emended draft was submitted to Congress on June 28.

The colonists had long tried to base their claims to governmental autonomy on the British constitution. Finally persuaded that this was impossible, they took their stand on the more radical ground of natural law, which they believed antedated and underlay the British constitution itself. Their argument came principally from the English philosopher John Locke, whose theory of the social contract seemed "the common sense of the subject," as Jefferson recalled in 1825. "[Not] aiming at originality of principle or sentiment, . . . it [the Declaration] was intended to be an expression of the American mind. . . ." In this theory, rights were inherent and therefore natural, society and government were constructed and therefore artificial. (Conservative political philosophers, of course, argued the exact opposite.) Humans established governments to protect their rights, the consent of the governed legitimizing whatever form of government they adopted. When government abused their rights, the people could withdraw their consent, abolish the government, and establish a new one to better meet their needs.

If Jefferson's principles were not new, his concise and masterful statement of them in the Declaration became the official democratic creed of the new republic: "We hold these truths to be self-evident, that all men are created equal, that they are endowed by their Creator with certain unalienable Rights, that among these are Life, Liberty and the pursuit of Happiness. That to secure these rights, Governments are instituted among Men, deriving their just powers from the consent of the governed, That whenever any Form of Government becomes destructive of these ends, it is the Right of the People to alter or to abolish it, and to institute new Government, laying its foundation on such principles and organizing its powers in such form, as to them shall seem most likely to effect their Safety and Happiness."

There followed a long list of charges leveled against George III, since the colonists, having rejected subordination to Parliament, believed they were connected to Britain only through the crown. "The history of the present King of Great Britain is a history of repeated injuries and usurpations, all having in direct object the establishment of an absolute Tyranny over these States," Jefferson declared. These offenses against the natural rights of his American subjects justified them in ending their fealty to him.

Jefferson concluded: "We, therefore, the Representatives of the united States of America, in General Congress, Assembled, appealing to the Supreme Judge of the world for the rectitude of our intentions, do, in the Name, and by Authority of the good People of these Colonies, solemnly publish and declare, That these United Colonies are, and of Right ought to be Free and Independent States. . . . And for the support of this Declaration, with a firm reliance on the Protection of Divine Providence, we mutually pledge to each other our Lives, our Fortunes and our sacred Honor."

Congress considered Jefferson's draft as a committee of the whole July 2–4, making a number of changes—significantly, deleting his accusation that George III had allowed the "cruel" slave trade to continue, to which the Southern colonies objected. On July 4, the Declaration was formally adopted and copies were distributed to the army and throughout the states. Five days later the New York provincial congress voted for independence, and on July 15 the word "Unanimous" was inserted in the declaration's title: "The Unanimous Declaration of the Thirteen United States of America." On Aug. 2 a copy of the Declaration, engrossed on parchment, was signed by the members of Congress.

DECLARATORY ACT (1766). See *Stamp Act.

DE LÔME LETTER (1898), private letter written by Enrique Depuy de Lôme, Spanish minister to the United States, stolen from the mails in Havana by Cuban insurgents, and published (Feb. 9, 1898) with great sensation in William Randolph Hearst's New York *Journal* (see *Yellow Press). De Lôme called Pres. William McKinley "weak and a bidder for the admiration of the crowd, besides being a would-be politician who tries to leave a door open behind himself while keeping on good terms with the jingoes of his party." De Lôme promptly resigned.

DEMOCRACY. Democracy did not come to America on the *Mayflower*. While England was governed by a landed aristocracy, colonial New England was governed by a clerical oligarchy and the Middle and Southern colonies by landowning elites. Religious and property qualifications for voting and holding office were widespread. Everywhere it was taken for granted, as in England, that the "better sort" should rule and that ordinary folks should defer to them in opinion as well as in manners.

But the absence in the New World of feudal institutions and hereditary social classes, together with the leveling influence of the frontier, gave rise to an American ideology subversive of an established aristocracy. "We hold these truths to be self-evident," proclaimed the *Declaration of Independence, "that all men are created equal, that they are endowed by their Creator with certain unalienable rights. . . ." The ideology of equality and natural rights contained the seeds of democracy that were destined to flower and expand irresistibly in succeeding generations.

The Framers of the Constitution were fearful of special interests of all kinds, not least the "popular" interest. To some of them democracy meant mob rule. To others, who had witnessed the abuses of popular parties in control of state governments during the *Confederation period, democracy meant fiscal irresponsibility and social injustice. In designing the new government, the Framers entrusted the selection of the president not to the ill-informed people but to a sagacious *electoral college. They devised an ingenious mechanism of checks and balances to prevent any one of the three branches of government—the executive, the legislative, and the judicial—from exercising excessive power. They specifically prohibited the states from behaving unjustly toward the propertied classes: "No state shall . . . coin money; emit bills of credit; make anything but gold and silver coin a tender in payment of debts; pass any . . . law impairing the obligation of contracts. . . ."

More than two centuries since the adoption of the Constitution have witnessed the steady democratization of American life (see, for example, *Jacksonian Democracy; *Women's Rights; *Civil Rights Movement), including that of its political institutions. Most important has been the extension of the franchise, beginning with the removal of religious and property qualifications for

voting and officeholding, then the enfranchisement of former (male) slaves (see *15th Amendment) and women (see *19th Amendment), and finally the lowering of the voting age to 18 (see *26th Amendment). At the same time, the electoral college became a mere formality; state senates and the U.S. Senate were made popularly elected (see *17th Amendment); the method of nominating candidates for state and national offices evolved from narrow party *caucuses to state and national *nominating conventions and finally to *primary elections. Reforms such as the secret ballot (see *Australian Ballot) and the *initiative, referendum, and recall were instituted.

Like any other system of government, democracy is vulnerable to abuse and corruption. The Framers never expected their handiwork to last two centuries. At times, the survival of the American democracy has seemed almost providential. Some of this good fortune must be attributed to certain remarkable individuals, more perhaps to the existence of various informal elites—professional, business, scientific, scholarly, journalistic—whose members shape public opinion, advise government leaders, and often themselves serve in the government in elected or appointive positions.

DEMOCRACY IN AMERICA (1835), classic analysis of American society by French observer Alexis de Tocqueville. A young civil servant (later statesman and historian), Tocqueville spent (1831–32) ten months in the United States during the *Jackson administration, officially to study prison conditions but actually to study American society, which he believed to be in the forefront of a great democratic revolution that was making its way in Europe as well as in America. To cope with the consequences of that revolution, "a new science of politics is needed for a new world." America was to be Tocqueville's laboratory.

"Nothing [in America] struck me more forcibly," Tocqueville observed at the start of his book, "than the general equality of condition among the people. . . . This equality of condition is the fundamental fact from which all others seem to be derived." He went on to examine the influence of equality in all areas of American society and culture. In politics, equality meant that "the very essence of democratic government consists in the absolute sovereignty of the majority." No institution, group, or class could withstand the tyranny of the majority (see *Jacksonian Democracy).

"In my opinion," Tocqueville concluded, "the main evil of the present democratic institutions in the United States does not arise . . . from their weakness, but from their irresistible strength. I am not so much alarmed at the excessive liberty which reigns in that country as at the inadequate securities which one finds there against tyranny."

DEMOCRATIC PARTY, one of two major contemporary political parties. It traces its origins to the *Jeffersonian Republican Party, which formed in the 1790s to oppose the *Federalist Party. From Jefferson it received its character as a small government, states' rights party devoted to the agrarian interest, especially in the South. It opposed *tariffs and *internal improvements favored by the Federalists and later the Whigs (see *Whig Party), who were sympathetic to industrial and commercial interests. Andrew Jackson's populism reinforced the Jeffersonian democratic heritage (see *Jacksonian Democracy).

By the time of the Civil War, the Democratic Party was largely associated with the Southern interest. Northern Democrats' support for the Union was ambivalent. As a consequence, the *Republican Party controlled the presidency from Lincoln to Wilson, except for the two separate terms of Democrat Grover Cleveland, who was every bit as conservative as his Republican opponents. The Democratic Party dominated only the *Solid South, sunk in racism and reaction.

Jacksonian populism reemerged in the Democratic Party with the populist (see *Populism) and *free silver movements late in the 19th century, and these contributed to the current of *progressivism represented by Theodore Roosevelt in the Republican Party and by Woodrow Wilson in the Democratic. In the 1920s the party reverted to its traditional conservatism and minority status until Franklin Roosevelt revived the Wilsonian reform impulse and permanently transformed the party (except in the South) into an agent of centralizing liberal reform. The Roosevelt revolution rested upon a coalition of the urban working class, labor unions, the rising middle class, ethnic and religious minorities, and Southern Democrats (on selected issues).

Against growing conservative opposition, subsequent liberal Democratic presidents—Harry S. Truman, John F. Kennedy, Lyndon B. Johnson—preserved the Roosevelt coalition, causing the party to be perceived as overly partial to minorities and the poor. Republican Ronald Reagan, supported by many "Reagan Democrats," led the conservative backlash. The South ceased to be solidly Democratic and became increasingly Republican. Democratic president William J. Clinton steered the party back toward the political center, coopting some traditional Republican positions. Even the moderate liberalism of the *Clinton administration contrasted sharply with the fierce conservatism of a Republican-dominated Congress

after 1995. Personal scandals surrounding Clinton contributed to the party's defeat in the 2000 presidential election.

DEMOCRATIC-REPUBLICAN PARTY. See *Jeffersonian Republican Party or Democratic-Republican Party.

DEMOCRATIC SOCIETIES (1793–95), political clubs inspired by the *French Revolution with the purpose of protecting republican principles by means of vigilant attention to the activities of the U.S. government. They had no formal connection with the Jeffersonian opposition. Some 35 appeared nationwide in 1793–94. Two in western Pennsylvania were implicated in the *Whiskey Rebellion. They disappeared rapidly after Pres. George Washington condemned them as "certain self-created [and therefore illegitimate if not illegal] societies" that "disseminated . . . suspicions, jealousies, and accusations of the whole Government."

DENMARK VESEY PLOT (1822). See *Slave Revolts.

DENNIS v. UNITED STATES (1951), 6–2 decision of the U.S. Supreme Court upholding the Smith Act (1940), which made it a crime to teach, advocate, or organize the violent overthrow of any government of the United States (see *Anticommunism). Responding to political criticism of being "soft on communism," the *Truman administration, in July 1948, belatedly indicted 11 leaders of the American *Communist Party. They were convicted in a controversial trial in 1949 and their conviction was upheld on appeal. The Supreme Court determined that the Smith Act was constitutional, Chief Justice Fred Vinson rejecting the "clear and present danger" test of impermissible speech enunciated by Justice Oliver Wendell Holmes in *Schenck v. United States (1919) in favor of the "grave and probable danger" rule developed by appeals court judge Learned Hand. With the Court's sanction in *Dennis*, the U.S. Justice Department indicted 141 other communists throughout the country, of whom 29 served jail terms.

DEPENDENT PENSION ACT (1890), legislation of the Benjamin *Harrison administration. A tribute to the electoral clout of the *Grand Army of the Republic, this act provided a monthly pension of $6–12 for Civil War veterans of 90 days' service who could not support themselves by manual labor because of some disability, war-connected or not. Widows, children, and dependent parents were also provided for. The act doubled the number of Civil War pensioners and increased expenditures for pensions from $81 million in 1890 to $135 million at the end of Harrison's term in 1883.

DEPOSIT, RIGHT OF, the right to store goods in New Orleans before duty-free reshipment by sea. Granted to the United States by Spain in *Pinckney's Treaty, the right of deposit was important for Western farmers who shipped their produce down the Mississippi River to New Orleans, from where they had access to Eastern and world markets.

DESERET, state name proposed by a constitutional convention that met (March 1849) in Salt Lake City to seek statehood for the Mormon settlement in Utah. The convention proposed state boundaries that would have included all present-day Utah and Arizona, most of Nevada, and parts of Idaho, Wyoming, Colorado, and southern California. In the face of congressional opposition, the convention changed its request to one for territorial organization. As part of the *Compromise of 1850, Congress organized Utah Territory to include all present-day Utah, most of Nevada, and parts of Colorado and Wyoming. Pres. Millard Fillmore appointed Mormon leader Brigham Young the territorial governor. Despite the presence of non-Mormon appointed officials, the territory was efficiently governed by the Church of Jesus Christ of Latter-Day Saints.

DESERT LAND ACT (1877). See *Public Lands.

DESTROYERS-FOR-BASES DEAL (1940), wartime incident in the Franklin *Roosevelt administration. After the fall of France in June 1940, and while Britain faced an imminent German invasion with her destroyer fleet greatly reduced at Dunkirk and in the Atlantic, British prime minister Winston Churchill asked Roosevelt to transfer to Britain 50 overaged U.S. destroyers that had only recently been saved from consignment to the scrap heap.

Such a transfer required the approval of Congress, where Republicans were certain to block it. When it was suggested that the transfer be made in exchange for British bases in the Western Hemisphere, it seemed legitimate to argue that the president—as commander in chief and head of state—had the authority to make such an exchange without congressional approval so long as the net result was an increase in America's national security. Roosevelt announced the exchange of the 50 destroyers for 99-year leases on nine British bases on Sept. 3, 1940.

Congressmen protested the president's arbitrary action, but public opinion approved the deal as advantageous to the United States.

DINGLEY TARIFF (1897), legislation of the *McKinley administration. Pointing out that the object of tariff legislation was protection, not exclusion, Pres. William McKinley opposed any significant increase in the *Wilson-Gorman Tariff (1894). The bill drafted by Rep. Nelson Dingley satisfied the president, but then Senate protectionists raised tariff rates to the highest level in U.S. history, higher even than the unpopular *McKinley Tariff (1890). McKinley took what satisfaction he could from an expanded provision for reciprocity agreements that the president could negotiate. The Dingley Tariff remained in effect until 1909.

DISASTERS. Of the hundreds of disasters that have punctuated American history—earthquakes, floods, hurricanes, fires, explosions, wrecks—perhaps two dozen have acquired folkloric status in the national memory.

1865	(Apr. 27) Mississippi steamboat *Sultana*, repatriating 2,400 Union prisoners, blew up near Memphis; 1,500 died
1871	(Oct. 8–9) *Chicago fire; 300 died
1888	(Mar. 11–13) New York City blizzard; 200 died
1889	(May 31) *Johnstown flood; 2,500 died
1900	(Apr. 30) Wreck of the *Cannon Ball Express* near Vaughan, Miss., in which engineer Casey Jones was killed
1900	(Sept. 8) Galveston, Tex., hurricane; 5,000 died
1903	(Dec. 30) Iroquois Theater fire in Chicago; 639 died
1904	(June 15) Excursion streamer *General Slocum* burned in New York's East River; 1,021 died
1906	(Apr. 18) *San Francisco earthquake; 700 died
1911	(Mar. 25) *Triangle fire in New York; 146 died
1912	(Apr. 15) *Titanic* sinking; 1,500 died
1918–19	*Influenza pandemic; 500,000 died in the United States
1933–39	*Dust Bowl
1934	(Sept. 8) Cruise ship *Morro Castle* burned; 134 died
1937	(May 6) *Hindenburg* crash; 36 died
1938	(Sept. 21) New England hurricane; 680 died
1941	(Dec. 7) *Pearl Harbor; 2,400 died
1942	(Nov. 28) Coconut Grove nightclub fire in Boston; 493 died
1944	Circus fire at Hartford, Conn.; 168 died

1979	(Mar. 28) *Three Mile Island nuclear accident
1986	(Jan. 28) *Challenger space shuttle explosion; 7 died
1989	(Mar. 24) *Exxon Valdez oil spill
1989	(Sept. 16–22) Hurricane Hugo; 504 died
1992	(Aug. 22–26) Hurricane Andrew; 38 died
1995	(Apr. 19) *Oklahoma City bombing; 168 died
2001	(Sept. 11) *World Trade Center attack, 3,000 died

DISPLACED PERSONS ACT (1948). See *Refugees.

DIXIE, name of uncertain origin for the Southern states. The song "Dixie" was composed by Daniel D. Emmett for Bryant's Minstrel Troupe of New York in 1859. Emmett's tune was fitted with many lyrics, including some by Confederate general Albert Pike, who thereby made it a Confederate marching song and anthem. Emmett's original lyrics began: "I wish I was in de land ob cotton, / Old times dar am not forgotten; / Look away, look away, look away, Dixie land!" Pike's version began: "Southrons, hear your country call you! / Up, lest worse than death befall you! / To arms! To arms! To arms, in Dixie!"

DIXIECRATS. See *States' Rights Party or Dixiecrats.

DIXON-YATES SCANDAL (1955), incident in the *Eisenhower administration. Because of Pres. Dwight D. Eisenhower's hostility toward the Tennessee Valley Authority (TVA), the Atomic Energy Commission in 1954 contracted with a private firm, Dixon-Yates, to build an electricity-generating plant in Tennessee. In 1955 it became known that a government consultant who had recommended the contract had a financial interest in Dixon-Yates. The contract was canceled. TVA's generating capacity continued to expand throughout the Eisenhower administration.

DOLLAR DIPLOMACY, effort of the *Taft administration to achieve diplomatic objectives in Latin America and China by use of economic rather than military power. The administration intervened to protect Honduras, Nicaragua, and Haiti from European creditors, and it encouraged American bankers to participate in international enterprises in China to preserve U.S. influence there. Taft's successor, Woodrow Wilson, repudiated "dollar diplomacy," rejecting U.S. participation in an international loan to China because its conditions were "obnoxious to the principles upon which the government of our people rests."

DOMINION OF NEW ENGLAND (1686–89), consolidation of the New England colonies into a single unit for more efficient administration. New York and New Jersey were added in 1688 to strengthen the defenses against France. The dominion was governed from Boston by a governor-general, Sir Edmund Andros, and a council, both appointed by the crown. There was no dominion representative assembly, and all popularly elected legislatures in the colonies were abolished. Andros's determination to enforce the *Navigation Acts made his regime unpopular. Upon receiving news of the Glorious Revolution in England, the Massachusetts Puritans overthrew Andros and the dominion expired.

DONIPHAN'S MARCH (June 1846–May 1847), episode in the *Mexican War. During their one-year enlistment, the men of the First Missouri Mounted Infantry, under Col. Alexander W. Doniphan, marched 3,500 miles over barren wasteland from Fort Leavenworth to Santa Fe, El Paso, Chihuahua, Parras, Monterrey, and Matamoros. Along the way they pacified hostile Navajos, defeated Mexicans in two battles (Brazito, Dec. 25, 1846, and Sacramento, Feb. 28, 1843), and took the city of Chihuahua. They were discharged at New Orleans.

DONNER PARTY (1846–47), emigrant party that suffered disaster on the *California Trail. The original party of 32 people comprised the three extended families of the brothers George and Jacob Donner and James Reed and their hired teamsters. This group left Springfield, Ill., on April 15, 1846, with nine wagons and additional oxen, cows, horses, and dogs. Arriving at Independence, Mo., on May 11, it attached itself to a large wagon train and was joined by other groups until the party numbered 89 persons.

The emigrants proceeded west along the California Trail by way of forts Kearney and Laramie. Arriving late at Fort Bridger, the Donner party turned off the main route, which circled Great Salt Lake to the north via Fort Hall, and chose the untested Hastings Cutoff to the south, thought to be 400 miles shorter. At this time it elected George Donner its captain. Leading through the Wasatch Mountains and the Great Salt Lake Desert, the Hastings Cutoff proved disastrous. By the time the weak and disorganized party rejoined the main California Trail at the Humboldt River, it had lost valuable time as well as people, wagons, and animals.

The Donner party began the ascent of the Sierra Nevada in California in October. On November 3, when it was three miles from the summit, a heavy snowfall blocked its path. The party's 81 members retreated to Truckee (now Donner) Lake, where they built a crude camp and sent a group ahead to Sutter's Fort for help. In the months that followed, the party endured cold, disease, and starvation. In their extremity, some resorted to murder and cannibalism. Rescuers from Sutter's Fort arrived in February and over the next two months led the survivors to safety. Forty-seven members of the Donner party survived the ordeal. The Donner brothers were not among them.

DOOLITTLE RAID. See *World War 2.

DORR'S REBELLION (1842), incident in the *Tyler administration. In the 1840s, Rhode Island, still governed under a modified version of its 1663 royal charter, had the most restricted suffrage of all the states. A popular reform movement led by Thomas Dorr, a Jacksonian Democrat, held a convention in October 1841 and framed a new "People's Constitution" providing white manhood suffrage. A rival "Landowners' Constitution" sponsored by the state legislature preserved suffrage restrictions.

Both constitutions were ratified by their supporters, and the factions behind each proceeded to elect rival state governments. The reformers elected Dorr governor; the conservatives reelected the sitting governor, who declared Dorr in insurrection. The Dorr party crumbled in the face of federal and state military force. Dorr was tried and sentenced to life imprisonment but soon amnestied. A new state constitution extending the franchise was adopted in 1843.

DOUGHFACES, Northern politicians who voted with the South on slavery issues. The term was applied contemptuously in 1819 by John Randolph of Virginia to 18 Northern members of the House of Representatives who voted against an amendment to the bill admitting Missouri to the Union that would have prohibited the further introduction of slaves into the state (see *Missouri Compromise). Presidents Franklin Pierce and James Buchanan were prominent doughfaces.

DOUGLAS AND LINCOLN. See *Lincoln and Douglas.

DRAFT. See *Conscription or Draft.

DRAFT RIOTS (July 13–16, 1863), mob resistance to the implementation in New York City of the new *Civil War draft law (see *Conscription). Believing the draft to be both inequitable and unconstitutional, mobs of workingmen, mostly Irish-Americans, seized arms from a state armory and proceeded to loot and burn the city. Blacks and abolitionists were attacked, a black orphanage was burned, and business was brought to a standstill. Casualties numbered as high as 1,000. The riots were finally suppressed by federal troops (rushed to the city from the Gettysburg front), militia, police, and West Point cadets. The draft was resumed in August without incident.

DRAGO DOCTRINE (1902), opinion by Argentine foreign minister Luis María Drago, communicated to the United States on Dec. 19, 1902, in response to the *Venezuelan Boundary Dispute, that a creditor nation did not have the right to use force to collect a debt from another sovereign state.

DRED SCOTT CASE (1857). See *Scott v. Sandford or Dred Scott Case.

DRUG AMENDMENTS ACT (1962). See *Consumer Protection.

DRUG WAR, much-publicized effort by the federal government to suppress traffic in and use of illegal drugs, principally heroin, cocaine, and marijuana.

Federal drug regulation began in 1914, but a "war on drugs" was proclaimed only in the *Nixon administration, when drug use was conspicuous in the *counterculture. Pres. Lyndon B. Johnson had already taken drug enforcement duties from the Treasury Department and drug regulation from the Food and Drug Administration and assigned them to a Bureau of Narcotics and Dangerous Drugs in the Justice Department. In 1973 this became the Drug Enforcement Administration. At the same time, a Senate-confirmed "drug czar" was established in the White House to devise drug war strategy. The appearance in the mid-1980s of crack, an inexpensive and immediately addictive form of cocaine, imparted new urgency to the drug war. In 1988, the Office of National Drug Control Policy, directed by the drug czar, was established in the Office of the President to coordinate federal, state, and local efforts to control illegal drugs.

The war on drugs focused largely on suppressing the supply of drugs, most of which originated abroad. The U.S. government helped Asian and Latin American governments to eradicate crops of poppy and coca (sources of heroin and cocaine respectively) and marijuana (much of which is grown in the United States) and to persuade growers to switch to other crops. In 2000, it committed $2 billion in mostly military aid to Colombia to fight Marxist guerrillas allied with coca growers and drug traffickers. The U.S. Customs Service, Border Patrol, and armed forces worked to interdict the flow of drugs into the United States.

Finally, federal, state, and local law-enforcement authorities pursued drug distributors within the United States. Draconian laws mandating long prison terms for the possession or sale of even small quantities of drugs filled the prisons to overflowing but hardly dented the traffic. The profit was so great, at every stage of the traffic from grower to street "pusher," that new participants in the drug trade quickly replaced those who were arrested. The profit in drugs was a function of their illegal status and the intensity of the demand, which education, advertising, and treatment barely affected. The parallel to *Prohibition was clear, but it proved politically costly to advocate decriminalization (if not deregulation) of drugs.

The drug market in the United States has been estimated at $150 billion a year. Forty million Americans are believed to use drugs although only 6 million are considered steady users.

DUMBARTON OAKS CONFERENCE (Aug. 21–Oct. 7, 1944), conference held at an estate in Washington, D.C., at which representatives of the United States, Great Britain, the Soviet Union, and China laid preliminary plans for the United Nations Organization.

DUPLEX PRINTING CO. v. DEERING (1921), 6–3 decision of the *Taft Court upholding an injunction against a labor union engaged in an illegal secondary boycott despite the *Clayton Antitrust Act's exemption of unions from antitrust legislation. An effectual ban on the use of injunctions in labor disputes was achieved only by the *Norris–La Guardia Act in 1932.

DUST BOWL, 150,000-square-mile area of the Great Plains region encompassing parts of Oklahoma, Texas, Kansas, Colorado, and New Mexico stricken by drought in 1934–37. Once grazing land, it was plowed and planted in wheat during *World War 1 to take advantage of high wartime prices. In the drought of the 1930s, the light topsoil, unanchored by grass, was blown off in dense dust clouds. Many destitute residents, like the Joad family in John Steinbeck's novel *The Grapes of Wrath* (1939), abandoned their homes and fled west.

The *New Deal's Soil Conservation Service, established in 1935, taught farmers to plant trees and grass to hold down the soil and to plow in contour patterns to retain rainwater. The government also bought and took out of production 11.3 million acres of submarginal land. In World War 2, farmers again plowed up the plains to plant wheat, and the danger of drought and devastation was renewed.

E

EARTH DAY. See *Environmentalism.

EAST FLORIDA. See *Floridas, East and West.

EATON AFFAIR (1829–31), incident in the *Jackson administration. In January 1829, incoming secretary of war Thomas Eaton, a Tennessee crony of President-elect Andrew Jackson, married the notorious Margaret (Peggy) O'Neale Timberlake, daughter of a Washington tavern keeper and recently widowed. The wives of Jackson's cabinet members, led by Floride Calhoun, wife of Vice Pres. John C. Calhoun, refused to receive her socially. Jackson was outraged, recalling the slanders directed at his own wife that had contributed to her death, and defended Mrs. Eaton gallantly.

Secretary of State Martin Van Buren, wifeless and daughterless, befriended the Eatons. Having thereby earned the president's gratitude, he adroitly encouraged Jackson's growing estrangement from Calhoun, who aspired to succeed Jackson as president. The problem was resolved in 1831 when Van Buren and Eaton resigned from the cabinet, permitting Jackson to ask for the resignations of the other members, including three Calhoun supporters. Jackson then appointed Van Buren U.S. minister to Great Britain. When the Senate rejected his nomination, Jackson picked him for vice president (and eventual successor) in 1832.

ECONOMIC OPPORTUNITY ACT (1964), legislation of the Lyndon *Johnson administration, the centerpiece of its "war on poverty." It established an Office of Economic Opportunity (terminated 1974) to administer a wide-ranging program of job training and education. For the most disadvantaged youths aged 16–21, it established a Job Corps to provide education, counseling, vocational training, and useful work experience for up to two years at residential centers. It also established a domestic Peace Corps called Volunteers for Service to America (VISTA) and a Neighborhood Youth Corps to engage in antipoverty projects in inner cities. For unemployed adults, it provided work-training programs, and for college students from low-income families opportunities for part-time employment on campus. It established basic education programs to make illiterate adults employable. It authorized loans of up to $2,000 to farmers and small businessmen where there was a reasonable possibility of effecting a permanent increase in the incomes of those families.

Most significantly, the act sought to empower the poor to help themselves by authorizing the formation of "community action programs" to develop employment opportunities in local communities. These programs were to be "developed, conducted, and administered with the maximum feasible participation of residents of the areas and members of the groups served."

ECONOMIC ROYALISTS (1936), term applied by Pres. Franklin Roosevelt to opponents of the *New Deal in accepting the Democratic Party's presidential nomination in Philadelphia on June 27, 1936.

"For too many of us," Roosevelt declared, "the political equality [won against political royalists in the American Revolution] was meaningless in the face of economic inequality. A small group had concentrated into their hands an almost complete control over other people's property, other people's money, other people's labor—other people's lives. . . . [T]he collapse of 1929 showed up the despotism for what it was. The election of 1932 was the people's mandate to end it. . . .

"These economic royalists complain that we seek to overthrow the institutions of America. What they really complain of is that we seek to take away their power. . . . [H]ere in America we are waging a great and successful war. It is not alone a war against want and destitution and economic demoralization.... [I]t is a war for the survival of democracy."

Roosevelt's speech marked the end of the administration's attempts to conciliate business and a decisive turn to the left toward the groups that constituted the Roosevelt coalition.

EDUCATION REFORM ACT (2002), legislation of the George W. *Bush administration enlarging the federal role in education. The act mandated annual testing nationwide of children in grades 3–8 in reading and math on a single standardized test starting in the 2005–6 school year. Students in poorly performing schools would be eligible for tutoring and other supplemental services and for transfer to more successful public schools. The act set a 12-year timetable for closing the chronic gaps among students of different racial and socioeconomic backgrounds and provided increased funding for schools in poverty areas.

EIGHTEENTH AMENDMENT (1919), the *Prohibition amendment, constitutional amendment barring "the manufacture, sale, or transportation of intoxicating liquors within, the importation thereof into, or the exportation thereof from the United States." It was repealed by the *21st Amendment in 1933.

EIGHTH AMENDMENT. See *Bill of Rights.

EISENHOWER ADMINISTRATION (1953–61). Dwight D. Eisenhower, 34th president of the United States, was the first Republican to occupy the White House in 20 years. A staunch conservative on fiscal matters, he believed that a sound economy was the foundation of national security, and he set about balancing the budget not only by downsizing the federal government but by making large cuts in what he considered excessive defense spending.

An advocate of limited government, he gave the oil-rich tidelands to the coastal states for private development (see *Submerged Lands Act), tried to halt the growth of the Tennessee Valley Authority (see *Dixon-Yates Scandal), and ensured the private development of atomic and hydroelectric energy. On the other hand, his administration created the U.S. Department of Health, Education and Welfare, expanded *Social Security coverage and benefits, enlarged the supply of private and public *housing, increased federal regulation of labor unions (see *Landrum-Griffin Act), and undertook major public works (see *St. Lawrence Seaway; *Interstate Highway System). On three occasions he dramatically enlarged

presidential powers—in the *Formosa Straits crisis, with the *Eisenhower Doctrine, and by claiming an unprecedented executive privilege in dealing with Congress (see below).

His most stubborn opponents were the Old Guard of his own party, who resisted his domestic program, argued for the centrality of Asia over Europe in the *cold war, tried to reduce presidential power through the *Bricker Amendment, and urged limitless defense spending. Led until his death in 1953 by Sen. Robert A. Taft of Ohio, they did not consider Eisenhower a true Republican.

Although he effectively advanced desegregation in the armed forces (see *Armed Forces Desegregation) and desegregated the public buildings in Washington, D.C., Eisenhower failed to provide leadership in the *school-desegregation crisis precipitated by the Supreme Court's decision in *Brown v. Board of Education of Topeka (1954). He never endorsed the decision, never saw desegregation as a moral imperative; in his public comments, he was always sympathetic to the Southern viewpoint. He studiously avoided the disorders in the South attendant on implementing desegregation until he was compelled to send federal troops to restore order in Little Rock, Ark. (see *Little Rock Crisis). But he felt strongly about black voting rights and supported the (ineffective) *Civil Rights Act of 1957.

In both foreign and domestic affairs, the Eisenhower administration was dominated by the cold war. Eisenhower's first challenge was to end the hot war in Korea (see *Korean War). He visited Korea for five days in November–December 1952 and concluded that the stalemate in the peace talks was intolerable. As president, he let the Chinese know that if negotiations did not progress he was prepared to resume the war and would not be inhibited in his choice of weapons. Negotiations resumed, and on July 26, 1953, a truce, not a peace, was signed, ending the war along the same line where it began. Only Eisenhower's military prestige persuaded Congress to accept this result.

During the 1952 presidential election campaign, Eisenhower had criticized the *Truman administration's doctrine of *containment, but except for some bombastic talk about "massive retaliation" and "liberating the enslaved peoples," Eisenhower adhered to the established doctrine. He regarded the *North Atlantic Treaty Organization (NATO) as the centerpiece of America's defense, and he dispatched Secretary of State John Foster Dulles to the Middle East and to Southeast Asia to create similar alliances—the *Central Treaty Organization (CENTO) and the *Southeast Asia Treaty Organization (SEATO)—on the Soviet and Chinese periphery. He also worked for the entry of West Germany into NATO and its rearmament (see *German Occupation).

In the spirit of the cold war, Eisenhower was zealous in rooting out subversives in the federal government. He changed the criterion for discharge from disloyalty to security risk, a much broader category (see *Anticommunism). One notable casualty of the new rules was J. Robert Oppenheimer, builder of the first atomic bomb (see *Oppenheimer Affair). Eisenhower sternly refused to commute the death sentences of convicted spies Ethel and Julius Rosenberg (see *Rosenberg Case).

Eisenhower's concern for security did not immunize his administration from the attacks of Sen. Joseph R. McCarthy, who now sought subversion in the Republican administration as he had in the Democratic (see *McCarthyism). Dulles proved an eager appeaser, purging the State Department, the Voice of America, and government libraries overseas to meet McCarthy's criticisms. Eisenhower loathed McCarthy but refused to denounce him in the belief that McCarthy would only thrive on the publicity. In the end, Eisenhower took the one step that brought McCarthy down, refusing to allow any employee of the executive branch to be subpoenaed by McCarthy's investigative committee. Eisenhower's assertion of executive privilege in this instance was an unprecedented enlargement of presidential powers.

Finally, because of the cold war, Eisenhower found it expedient to sell some of his major initiatives to Congress and the public on the grounds of their contribution to national defense. Among these were the St. Lawrence Seaway, the Interstate Highway System, the *National Defense Education Act of 1957 (a result of the *Sputnik alarm), and creation of a civilian space agency, the National Aeronautics and Space Agency (NASA).

Eisenhower was appalled at the cost of the arms race with the Soviet Union, which he believed would eventually lead to war. He tried to check American expenditures on excessive armaments and sought an understanding with the Soviets banning the testing of atomic weapons. Twice he made interesting (if propagandistic) proposals for a start on disarmament: *Atoms for Peace and *Open Skies. Most important, repeatedly he stood alone against a chorus of advisers urging him to take belligerent steps—in Korea, Indochina, the Formosa Straits, and Berlin—that might have led to war. In 1956 he stopped a war in the Middle East (see *Suez War) and in 1958 demonstrated his ability to deploy American force to keep peace in that dangerous region (see *Lebanon Interventions).

Although he avoided a hot war, Eisenhower was not averse to employing *covert operations—in Iran, Guatemala, Indonesia, North Vietnam, the Congo, and even in the skies above the Soviet Union (see *U-2 Affair)—in what he saw as a worldwide struggle against communism.

By the end of his administration, Eisenhower was no longer sure that communism was the only danger facing the United States. In a farewell address to the American people he warned of the threat of the new "military-industrial complex" to democratic government (see *Eisenhower's Farewell Address). He was succeeded by Democrat John F. Kennedy.

During the Eisenhower administration, Alaska (1959) and Hawaii (1959) became the 49th and 50th states.

EISENHOWER DOCTRINE (1957), statement of U.S. policy in the Middle East made by Pres. Dwight D. Eisenhower in an address to Congress on Jan. 5, 1957, after the *Suez War and embodied in a congressional resolution signed by him on Mar. 9.

To reassure U.S. friends in the region, and to warn enemies against miscalculation, the Eisenhower Doctrine declared that "the United States regards as vital to the national interest and world peace the preservation of the independence and integrity of the nations of the Middle East." Congress authorized the president in advance to extend economic assistance to any nation or group of nations in the Middle East desiring it and "to use armed force to assist any such nation or group of nations requesting assistance against armed aggression from any country controlled by international communism."

EISENHOWER'S FAREWELL ADDRESS (Jan. 17, 1961), delivered by Pres. Dwight D. Eisenhower on national radio and television in the last days of his administration to advise the American people of some of the problems involved in long-term commitment to the *cold war. Chief among these was the existence of a large military establishment and a new armaments industry.

"This conjunction of an immense military establishment and a large arms industry," the president said, "is new in the American experience. The total influence—economic, political, even spiritual—is felt in every city, every statehouse, every office of the federal government. We recognize the imperative need for this development. Yet we must not fail to comprehend its grave implications. Our toil, resources, and livelihood are all involved; so is the very structure of our society.

"In the councils of government, we must guard against the acquisition of unwarranted influence, whether sought or unsought, by the military-industrial complex. The potential for the disastrous rise of misplaced power exists and will persist.

"We must never let the weight of this combination endanger our liberties or democratic processes. We should take nothing for granted. Only an alert and knowledgeable citizenry can compel the proper meshing of the huge industrial and military machinery of defense with our peaceful methods and goals, so that security and liberty may prosper together."

ELECTORAL COLLEGE, device invented by the Framers of the U.S. Constitution for the indirect election of the president and vice president. It was entirely the product of theory, having no basis in colonial experience. Nevertheless, it was hardly criticized in the *ratification debates.

Disinclined to trust the people at large to elect magistrates as important as the president and vice president, the Framers decided that these officials would be selected by a body of presidential electors, informed and judicious men who would survey the entire continent and identify the most eminent and qualified candidates. The Constitution provided no other nominating process, nor did it make provision for political parties.

States were assigned as many electors as they had members of Congress (senators and representatives). Assembled in the state capital, each elector would vote for two people, at least one of whom was not an inhabitant of that state. A sealed report of their votes would then be sent to the nation's capital and the votes counted in the presence of both houses of Congress. The individual receiving the most votes would be declared president, the runner-up, vice president. (In 1804 the *12th Amendment required electors to vote separately for president and vice president.) If no candidate received a majority of the electoral vote, the election would go to the House of Representatives, where each state delegation would cast a single vote for one of the electoral college's candidates.

How electors were chosen was left up to the states. In the first presidential election, in 1789, electors were chosen by the legislatures in six states, by popular election in three, and by a combination of the two methods in two. (Two states had not yet ratified the Constitution.) As the country became more democratic, states increasingly switched to the popular election of electors. From 1832 until the Civil War, South Carolina was the only state where presidential electors were still chosen by the state legislature.

The ideal of a panel of wise, informed, and dispassionate statesmen selecting the best men in the country for president and vice president soon succumbed to the realities of party politics. With the rise of political parties, party leaders in *caucus, then *nominating conventions, nominated party candidates. Electors, being party members, were pledged to vote for their parties' choices. The popular election of electors assured that the candidate who "carried" a state in fact carried his party's slate of electors and thus won all that state's electoral votes (the winner-take-all rule). Today citizens still technically vote for electors rather than directly for a presidential candidate, although the names of the electors rarely appear on the ballot. The electoral vote merely (and unnecessarily) ratifies the popular vote.

The electoral college system has consistently produced presidents accepted by the American people, even when on 13 occasions it produced presidents with less than half of the popular vote. There have, however, been a few mishaps. In 1796 the electoral college produced a president of one party and a vice president of the opposition party. In 1800 it produced a tie between one party's presidential and vice presidential candidates that the House of Representatives had to resolve. In 1824 the House was again called upon to elect a president when the electoral college failed to do so. In 1876 contested vote counts had to be resolved by a special electoral commission. In general, however, the electoral college has been so successful as to be barely noticed by the American people.

ELEMENTARY AND SECONDARY EDUCATION ACT (1965), legislation of the Lyndon *Johnson administration intended to improve the achievement of poor children by funding preschool enrichment and compensatory-education programs for them. Project **Head Start** enrolled 3- and 4-year-olds in special enrichment programs so they would enter kindergarten at the same level of school readiness as middle-class children. For poor elementary-school children, federal money made possible a variety of compensatory-education programs intended to close the gap between them and high-achieving middle-class children. The effects of these efforts on IQ proved small and temporary, but they seemed to produce significant gains in motivation and achievement among the children who participated.

ELEVENTH AMENDMENT (1795), constitutional amendment denying federal courts jurisdiction in suits brought against a state by a citizen of another state or of a foreign country. It explicitly reversed the Court's decision in *Chisholm v. Georgia* (1793), which offended believers in state sovereignty.

ELKINS ACT (1905). See *Railroad Regulation.

EMANCIPATION PROCLAMATION (Jan. 1, 1863), executive order of Pres. Abraham Lincoln liberating the slaves in those parts of the Confederacy still in rebellion against the United States.

Except for *abolitionists, emancipation was not a war aim of the Union at the start of the *Civil War. Most Northerners, anticipating a short war, expected the Union to be restored without so fundamental a social revolution in the Southern states. Although morally opposed to *slavery, Lincoln was a moderate on the issue, aware that many Northerners were strongly antiblack in sentiment and concerned not to jeopardize the loyalty of the slaveholding Border states. He himself favored gradual, compensated emancipation, paid for out of the national Treasury since North and South alike were responsible for slavery. In September 1861 he revoked as unconstitutional and inexpedient an emancipation order issued by Gen. John C. Frémont in Missouri, and in May 1862 he overruled an order of emancipation by Gen. David Hunter in the South Carolina sea islands.

"My paramount object in this struggle," Lincoln wrote to New York *Tribune* editor Horace Greeley on Aug. 22, 1862, "*is* to save the Union, and is *not* either to save or to destroy slavery. If I could save the Union without freeing *any* slave I would do it, and if I could save it by freeing *all* the slaves I would do it, and if I could save it by freeing some and leaving others alone I would also do that."

During the war, abolitionist sentiment grew and emancipation became a fact of life. Southern blacks in large numbers entered Union lines, where they were put to work in all capacities except as soldiers. The *Confiscation Acts of 1861 and 1862 prohibited their return to slavery. Increasingly, Northern leaders perceived that there would be a military advantage in denying the South the use of its reserve army of slave labor. Moreover, by the summer of 1862 Lincoln had become persuaded that the president's war powers permitted him to emancipate slaves by executive order when that appeared to be a military necessity. On the advice of his cabinet, however, he deferred any move until the Union had achieved a significant military victory lest emancipation be viewed as a sign of weakness. The Union success at *Antietam (Sept. 17, 1862) provided the desired opportunity, and on Sept.

22 Lincoln issued a preliminary proclamation announcing that emancipation would be declared on Jan. 1, 1863, in those areas still in rebellion.

On Dec. 1, 1862, in his second annual message to Congress, Lincoln justified his decision. "[W]e cannot escape history," he said. ". . . The fiery trial through which we pass will light us down in honor or dishonor to the last generation. We say we are for the Union. . . . We know how to save the Union. . . . In giving freedom to the slave, we assure freedom to the free—honorable alike in what we give and what we preserve. We shall nobly save or meanly lose the last, best hope of earth." On Jan. 1, after a New Year's reception in the White House, Lincoln signed the Emancipation Proclamation.

The proclamation was issued "by virtue of the power in me vested as Commander-in-Chief of the Army and Navy of the United States in time of actual armed rebellion against the authority and government of the United States, and as a fit and necessary war measure for suppressing said rebellion." Lincoln ordered and declared "that all persons held as slaves within said designated States and parts of States [still in rebellion] are, and henceforward shall be, free. . . ." He went on to "enjoin upon the people so declared to be free to abstain from all violence, unless in necessary self-defense; and I recommend to them that, in all cases when allowed, they labor faithfully for reasonable wages." He announced further "that such persons of suitable condition will be received into the armed service of the United States to garrison forts, positions, stations, and other places, and to man vessels of all sorts in said service."

The Emancipation Proclamation was criticized by abolitionists for being based on military necessity rather than on antislavery principles and, since it applied only to areas not yet occupied by Union troops, for actually emancipating no one. Conservatives and Southerners criticized it as an act of constitutional usurpation, inviting a servile insurrection and precipitating a social revolution in the South of unforeseeable consequences. The proclamation, however, made emancipation an official war aim of the Union and decisively affected the sympathies of foreign observers. Its promise of total emancipation for all slaves was fulfilled with the adoption in 1865 of the *13th Amendment to the U.S. Constitution.

EMBARGO ACT (1807). See *Embargo and Nonintercourse.

EMBARGO AND NONINTERCOURSE (1807–12), U.S. responses to British and French depredations against American shipping during the Napoleonic Wars (1803–15). During the 1790s, the threat of war with Britain over her seizure of American ships and *impressment of American seamen was superseded by an actual but undeclared *naval war with France (1798–1800). A new phase of the European war, beginning in 1803, again exposed U.S. shipping to the depredations of Britain and France as both countries enforced their reciprocal blockades.

The *Chesapeake affair (1807) compelled Pres. Thomas Jefferson to act (see *Jefferson Administration). Frugal and pacific, Jefferson put his faith in economic coercion, believing that the European powers could be brought to terms if they were deprived of U.S. trade. Congress had already enacted a nonimportation measure directed against selected British goods. Jefferson now put an end to all foreign trade. The **Embargo Act** (December 1807) forbade U.S. ships to sail to foreign ports. Foreign ships could not carry cargoes from American ports. Coastal trade was permitted but was highly regulated. The embargo produced economic stagnation and hardship in the port cities of New England and the Middle Atlantic states despite widespread evasion. An Enforcement (or "Force") Act (January 1809) gave the federal government unprecedented (and perhaps unconstitutional) powers over citizens' economic activities. The president himself became obsessively preoccupied with the minutiae of enforcement, inspired both by conviction of the correctness of his policy and by dislike of the commercial states.

Economic distress brought the Federalists back to power in New England, where protests and petitions multiplied and enforcement of the Embargo Act was obstructed. Conscious of the failure of the embargo, Jefferson in the last months of his administration uncharacteristically refused to provide any leadership in resolving the national dilemma—embargo, war, or submission—so as not to tie the hands of his successor.

In Congress, Federalists and dissident Republicans passed, and Jefferson signed (March 1809), a **Nonintercourse Act** repealing the embargo and reopening trade with all nations except Britain and France until they ended their restrictions on American shipping. Like the embargo, nonintercourse was felt chiefly—and negatively—in the United States.

For the failed Nonintercourse Act, Congress in 1810 substituted **Macon's Bill No. 2**, which opened American trade unconditionally but with the proviso that if either belligerent lifted its restrictions on American commerce the United States would renew nonintercourse with the other. Napoleon was quick to exploit the opportunity. He announced that French restrictions would be lifted on condition that the United States "shall cause their rights to be respected by the English." Pres. James Madison (see *Madison Administration) accepted this dubious declaration in the hope of putting pressure on Britain. On Nov. 2, 1810, he announced that nonintercourse would be reimposed on Britain if she failed to revoke her restrictive measures within three months. To the renewal of nonintercourse Britain responded with more seizures of American ships and impressments of American sailors. At the same time, French duplicity was revealed by continued confiscations of American ships in French ports.

Although both belligerents were guilty of acts of war against the United States, British actions were far more injurious to American interests than were the French. As British depredations brought war inexorably closer, the assembling of the *"war hawk" Congress in November 1811 promised an end to indecision. On June 1, 1812, President Madison sent his war message to Congress; Congress voted a declaration of war on June 18—two days after Britain suspended her restrictions on American commerce (see *War of 1812).

EMBASSY BOMBINGS (Aug. 7, 1998), simultaneous terrorist attacks on the U.S. embassies in Nairobi, Kenya, and Dar es Salaam, Tanzania. The Nairobi blast killed 224 people, including 12 Americans; the explosion in Dar es Salaam killed 11 Africans. The United States retaliated by sending cruise missiles against terrorist training camps in Afghanistan and a suspected chemical-weapons factory in Sudan. Four low-level followers of Afghanistan-based Islamic militant Osama bin Laden—a Lebanese, a Saudi, a Jordanian, and a Tanzanian—were apprehended in Africa and extradited to the United States. In 2001 all four were convicted in a federal court in New York for their parts in the bombings and sentenced to life imprisonment. (See *Terrorism.)

EMERGENCY RAILROAD TRANSPORTATION ACT (1933). See *Railroad Regulation.

EMPLOYMENT ACT (1946), legislation of the *Truman administration. Although Congress failed to specify full employment as the act's goal as Pres. Harry S. Truman wished—this would have required government spending to create jobs in a recession—the act declared that it was the "responsibility of the Federal Government . . . to promote maximum employment, production, and purchasing power." It created the Council of Economic Advisers to assist the president and required him to report to Congress annually on the state of the economy.

EMPLOYMENT DIVISION, DEPARTMENT OF HUMAN RESOURCES v. SMITH (1990), 5–4 decision of the *Rehnquist Court upholding the denial of unemployment benefits to two Oregon state employees discharged for ingesting peyote, a hallucinogenic drug, in a Native American Church ceremony on the basis of a "neutral law of general applicability" against drug use. Although the law burdened a religious practice, the Court abandoned its previous requirement that the government demonstrate a "compelling state interest" for doing so as long as the law did not single out the religious practice for discriminatory treatment.

In his decision, Justice Antonin Scalia narrowly interpreted the First Amendment's Free Exercise Clause as prohibiting only laws "specifically directed at . . . religious practice," not laws of general applicability that incidentally burdened religion. If courts exempted religious practices from "neutral, generally applicable laws," he wrote, "they would destroy the power of government to make any rules at all"; they would be "courting anarchy." "Precisely because we value and protect [America's religious diversity], we cannot afford the luxury of deeming presumptively invalid, as applied to religious objectors, every regulation of conduct that does not protect an interest of the highest order." Scalia advised religious minorities penalized by neutral laws to seek relief from state legislatures or Congress, not from the courts. He conceded that they would be at a disadvantage in the political process, "but that unavoidable consequence of democratic government must be preferred to a system in which each conscience is a law unto itself. . . ."

In dissent, Justice Harry Blackmun wrote: "I do not believe the Founders thought their dearly bought freedom from religious persecution a 'luxury,' but an essential element of liberty—and they could not have thought religious intolerance 'unavoidable,' for they drafted the Religion Clauses precisely in order to avoid that intolerance."

Congress quickly passed the Religious Freedom Restoration Act restoring the compelling-government-interest requirement for burdening religious practice, but in *City of Boerne v. Flores* (1997) the Supreme Court ruled that act unconstitutional. (See *Church-State Relations.)

ENDANGERED SPECIES ACT (1973). See *Environmentalism.

ENGEL v. VITALE (1962), 7–1 decision of the *Warren Court prohibiting the use in public schools of a government-mandated prayer. The New York State Board of Regents, as part of its interest in "moral and spiritual training in the schools," had composed a nondenominational prayer for voluntary morning recital in schools that it believed would be "be subscribed to by all men and women of good will. . . ." The prayer read: "Almighty God, we acknowledge our dependence upon Thee, and we beg Thy blessings upon us, our parents, our teachers and our Country."

For the Court, Justice Hugo Black ruled that government authorship of the prayer violated the First Amendment's Establishment Clause: "It is neither sacrilegious nor antireligious to say that each separate government in this country should stay out of the business of writing or sanctioning official prayers and leave that purely religious function to the people themselves and to those the people choose to look to for religious guidance" (see *Church-State Relations).

ENLARGED HOMESTEAD ACT (1909). See *Public Lands.

ENRON BANKRUPTCY (2001), largest (at the time) corporate bankruptcy in the nation's history, with wide-reaching political and regulatory consequences. (Involving assets of $63 billion, the Enron bankruptcy was surpassed seven months later by the bankruptcy of the telecommunications giant WorldCom, with claimed assets of $107 billion.)

Houston-based Enron Corporation evolved during the 1980s and 1990s from a small natural-gas distributor to a multibillion-dollar energy broker. Its arcane business and technological innovations and dazzling earnings reports awed the business community. Enron executives ceaselessly touted the company's limitless future. The corporation made large contributions to both national political parties but was particularly close to the new Republican administration of George W. Bush, where it influenced the formulation and administration of energy policy.

Appearances were deceiving. The business was not as profitable as represented; large losses were hidden in numerous off-the-books partnerships; financial statements were incomplete and misleading. As suspicions grew, Enron stock prices declined through 2001, collapsing the corporation's intricate financial scaffolding and wiping out its employees' retirement funds (largely invested in Enron stock). Corporate executives, however, made fortunes by selling out in time. In December 2001 Enron filed for bankruptcy protection.

Enron's debacle destroyed its auditors, the accounting firm Arthur Andersen (which was convicted of obstructing justice in a Securities and Exchange Commission investigation of its client). It provided the necessary impetus for passage of the long-pending McCain-Feingold *campaign financing bill. It also inspired investigations into criminal conduct, political influence, financial reporting, and accounting procedures that led to passage of the *Corporate Responsibility Act of 2002.

ENVIRONMENTALISM. Rising concern over the quality of the nation's—and the world's—environment manifested itself in the late 1960s in a powerful environmental movement. Unlike the *civil rights and antiwar (see *Vietnam War) movements that immediately preceded it, the environmental movement at first encountered little opposition. Indeed, politicians embraced it, and business interests acquiesced in it, as an innocuous cause around which a national consensus had formed. Resistance developed quickly, however, when affected interests realized the costs of pollution controls.

Pres. Richard M. Nixon called in 1970 for a "new American revolution" in the cause of environmentalism. On Jan. 1 of that year, he signed the **National Environmental Policy Act (NEPA)**, which declared protection of the environment to be a major goal of national policy and required all federal agencies to prepare environmental impact statements before undertaking major activities. On Apr. 22, the first annual **Earth Day** was celebrated with teach-ins and cleanup projects across the nation. In October, the president established the Environmental Protection Agency (EPA) to control pollution in the areas of air, water, solid waste, and toxic substances.

The **Clean Air Act** of 1970 (which had been preceded by clean air acts in 1963, 1965, and 1967) authorized the EPA to set "national ambient air quality standards" for seven major pollutants: carbon monoxide, hydrocarbons, lead, nitrogen dioxide, ozone, particulates, and sulfur dioxide. The act established emission standards for motor vehicles and authorized the EPA to set emission standards for factories. The Clean Air Act Amendments (1990) imposed stricter federal standards on urban smog, automobile exhausts, toxic air pollution, and acid rain.

The **Clean Water Act** of 1972 (which had been preceded by water-quality acts in 1948, 1965, and 1966, largely concerned with sewage treatment, and in 1970,

concerned with oil spills) set water-quality standards for all U.S. navigable waters and limited discharges by polluters. The goals of the act were to achieve a water quality safe for fish, shellfish, wildlife, and recreation by 1983 and to eliminate all pollutant discharges by 1985. Industries were required to use the "best practicable" technology for treatment of discharges by 1977 and the "best available" technology by 1983. No discharges were allowed without a discharge permit issued by a state authority or by the EPA if state permit programs failed to meet EPA standards. The act was passed over President Nixon's veto. A 1987 act authorizing additional funds for clean water programs was passed over a veto by Pres. Ronald Reagan.

The 1976 **Resource Conservation and Recovery Act** provided federal funds to encourage state and local governments to develop and implement solid waste disposal programs. To obtain funding, these programs were required to provide for the closing or upgrading of existing open dumps and to recycle or safely dispose of all solid wastes. The act required the EPA to develop regulations for "cradle to grave" handling of hazardous wastes. The EPA regulations, published in 1980, required most generators of hazardous waste to register with the EPA, keep records of waste transportation and disposal, and monitor their disposal sites for up to thirty years. Also in 1980, Congress created a $1.6 billion toxic waste **Superfund**—80 percent of it raised by excise taxes on the chemical industry—to enable the federal government to clean up thousands of toxic waste sites abandoned by industry. Over the years, Congress proved reluctant to fund the increasingly costly program.

The **Pesticide Control Act** (1972), inspired by Rachel Carson's *Silent Spring (1962), gave the EPA authority to control the manufacture, distribution, and use of all pesticides. That year the EPA banned use of the pesticide DDT.

Other priorities of the environmental movement were wilderness and wildlife preservation. In the **Wilderness Act** of 1964, Congress established the principle that the permanent preservation of certain wilderness areas in their pristine condition was in the national interest. As a result, Congress has been able to protect portions of the public domain from development by including them in either the wilderness system or the national park system. A major environmental victory was the 1980 **Alaska Lands Act**, which removed most of the public domain in Alaska from possible development by designating more than 104 million acres as national parks, wildlife refuges, and wilderness areas. In 2001, outgoing president William J. Clinton placed nearly 30 percent of the national forests (58.5 million acres) off-limits to road-building, logging, and oil and gas development.

Beginning in 1966, a series of progressively more comprehensive statutes extended federal protection over endangered and threatened plant and animal species. The acts gave the Fish and Wildlife Service responsibility for maintaining lists of endangered and threatened species and for managing the listed species (for example, by acquiring their habitats). The **Endangered Species Act** (1973) prohibited federal agencies from taking any actions that would jeopardize a listed species or its habitat. In 1978 the U.S. Supreme Court upheld the act against a challenge by the Tennessee Valley Authority, which was compelled to abandon a dam on the Little Tennessee River whose construction threatened to destroy the habitat of a small fish, the snail darter.

EPIC (END POVERTY IN CALIFORNIA) (1934),

program of radical writer Upton Sinclair, whose grass-roots campaign won him the Democratic nomination for governor of California in 1934. In a pamphlet, *I, Governor of California*, Sinclair outlined a reform program that included turning over idle farmlands and factories to cooperatives of the unemployed. Republican and business interests attacked Sinclair's radicalism, and Pres. Franklin Roosevelt failed to support him. In November 1934 Sinclair lost to the incumbent Republican governor.

EQUAL EMPLOYMENT OPPORTUNITY COMMISSION (EEOC). See *Fair Employment Practices Committee (FEPC).

EQUAL PAY ACT (1963). See *Women in the Labor Force; *Women's Rights.

EQUAL RIGHTS AMENDMENT (ERA) (1971–

82), proposed amendment to the U.S. Constitution guaranteeing equal rights for women (see *Women's Rights). Equal rights amendments were introduced into every Congress from 1923 to 1971. The 1971 ERA ("Equality of rights under the law shall not be denied or abridged by the United States or by any State on account of sex") was passed by the requisite two-thirds vote of the House of Representatives in October 1971 and of the Senate in March 1972. The resolution submitting the amendment to the states required ratification within seven years—that is, by March 1979.

Twenty-two states ratified ERA in 1972, eight in

1973, three in 1974, and one each in 1975 and 1977—a total of 35, three short of the constitutionally required three-fourths of the states, or 38. Five states rescinded their ratifications, although constitutional authorities doubted that they could do so. As the 1979 deadline approached, ERA advocates prevailed upon Congress to extend the ratification period. In October 1978 Congress, by means of a resolution passed by simple majorities in both houses, extended the ratification period to June 30, 1982. This action was controversial for several reasons: the constitutionality of such an extension, particularly by simple majorities, was uncertain; and the choice of extension rather than of resubmission of the amendment, while permitting nonratifying states to reconsider the issue, prevented states that had already ratified from reconsidering.

In the end, ERA failed to win ratification by the requisite 38 states. However, many states adopted equal rights amendments to their own constitutions, and Congress, the courts, and federal agencies steadily applied the principle of equal rights—under the Equal Protection Clause of the *14th Amendment and the *Civil Rights Act of 1964—in such important areas as employment, education, jury service, Social Security benefits, pension rights, and credit.

ERA OF GOOD FEELINGS, name applied by a

Boston newspaper to the James *Monroe administration (1817–25) celebrating the end of party strife (the *Federalist Party had disappeared as a national party, its principles largely coopted by the *Jeffersonian Republican Party) and the enthusiastic reception of the new president on his tour of Northern states in 1817.

ERIE CANAL, artificial waterway through New York

State connecting the Hudson River above Albany with Lake Erie at Buffalo. Built (1817–25) by the state under the leadership of DeWitt Clinton (governor 1817–23, 1825–28), it was 40 feet wide, four feet deep, and used 84 locks to raise or lower boats 650 feet between the Hudson and the lake. It was profitable from the start, carrying immigrants west, bringing Western farm products east, spurring the growth of Buffalo, Rochester, and Syracuse, and making New York City the country's principal seaport. Despite competition from railroads starting in the 1850s, the canal remained profitable. It was modernized (1905–18) as the New York State Barge Canal. (See *Canals.)

ESCH-CUMMINS TRANSPORTATION ACT

(1920). See *Railroad Regulation.

ESPIONAGE ACT (1917), legislation of the *Wilson administration during *World War I. It prohibited acts of espionage, defined to include obstructing the operations of the government and the military or naval forces. Penalties of $10,000 and 20 years' imprisonment were provided for anyone who might "willfully cause or attempt to cause insubordination, mutiny, or refusal of duty . . . or shall willfully obstruct the recruiting or enlistment service." It barred from the mails any "letter, writing, circular, postal card, . . . newspaper, pamphlet, book . . . advocating or urging treason, insurrection, or forcible resistance to any law of the United States," leaving it to the postmaster general to determine which items met this description.

Amending the Espionage Act, the **Sedition Act** of 1918 made it illegal to "willfully utter, print, write, or publish any disloyal, profane, scurrilous, or abusive language about the form of government of the United States, or the Constitution of the United States, or the military or naval forces of the United States, or the flag . . . or the uniform of the Army or Navy of the United States, or any language intended to bring the form of government . . . or the Constitution . . . or the military or naval forces . . . or the flag . . . of the United States into contempt, scorn, contumely, or disrepute" or to "willfully advocate, teach, defend, or suggest the doing of any of the acts or things in this section enumerated" or "by word or act support or favor the cause of any country with which the United States is at war or by word or act oppose the cause of the United States therein. . . ."

The acts were zealously enforced by the postmaster general and the attorney general. The former banned from the mails periodicals, however small and obscure, that he deemed radical or subversive. The latter, with the help of an enlarged Federal Bureau of Investigation and of the American Protective League, a volunteer secret service, reported arresting 6,700 spies and conspirators and catching 220,747 draft dodgers. The acts reflected—if they did not cause—the patriotic hysteria that gripped the country once it was at war. Socialists, anarchists, pacifists, conscientious objectors, union members were harassed, beaten, and arrested. Distinguished professors were fired (and others resigned in protest). Immigrants deemed undesirable by virtue of their nationality, supposed opinions, or alleged immorality were deported. Americans with German names were persecuted, the German language ceased to be taught in high schools, and the music of Beethoven and Wagner was boycotted.

The U.S. Supreme Court upheld the constitutionality of the Espionage Act in *Schenk v. United States and of the Sedition Act in *Abrams v. United States.

ESSEX JUNTO, a group of "high" Federalists related by educational and professional background, marriage, and residence in Essex County, Mass. They included Fisher Ames, George Cabot, John Lowell, Theophilus Parsons, and Timothy Pickering. Both John Adams and Thomas Jefferson suspected them of conspiratorial proclivities.

EUROPEAN RECOVERY PROGRAM (1948). See *Marshall Plan.

EUTAW SPRINGS (Sept. 8, 1781), *Revolutionary War battle. With insufficient numbers to capture Charleston in late summer 1781, Patriot general Nathanael Greene attacked a British force at Eutaw Springs, S.C., on Sept. 8. After a hard fight between veteran forces, the British broke and fell back. The Patriots entered the British camp, found food and rum, and celebrated their victory, only to be counterattacked by the reformed British and driven from the field. Casualty rates on both sides were high, but the British rate—mostly prisoners—was the highest suffered by any force in the war. The British retired to Charleston, leaving Greene in control of the rest of the state.

EVERSON v. BOARD OF EDUCATION OF EWING TOWNSHIP (1947), 5–4 decision of the U.S. Supreme Court upholding a New Jersey statute reimbursing parents for the cost of transporting their children to and from school, whether public or parochial.

Justice Hugo Black, for the Court, began his ruling with a classic exposition of the First Amendment's Establishment Clause (see *Church-State Relations) but then concluded: "The [First] Amendment requires the state to be neutral in its relations with groups of religious believers and non-believers; it does not require the state to be their adversary. State power is no more to be used so as to handicap religions than it is to favor them.

"This Court has said that parents may, in the discharge of their duty under state compulsory education laws, send their children to a religious rather than a public school if the school meets the secular educational requirements which the state has power to impose. . . . It appears that these parochial schools meet New Jersey's requirements. The State contributes no money to the schools. It does not support them. Its legislation, as applied, does no more than provide a general program to help parents get their children, regardless of their religion, safely and expeditiously to and from accredited schools."

EXCEPTIONALISM, the idea that the United States has been singled out by Providence to play a redemptive role in human affairs. According to this idea, the United States may act as an exemplary nation that other, degenerate nations can emulate or as a regenerative nation, actively intervening in world affairs as a force for good.

Consciousness of exemplary nationhood preceded the founding of the nation. The New England Puritans, who saw their migration to the New World as a reenactment of the biblical Exodus, anticipated that their godly community in this Promised Land would be the object of intense, universal interest. "We must consider," wrote John Winthrop in 1630, "that we shall be as a city upon a hill; the eyes of all people are upon us."

The Revolutionary generation considered the American Revolution an event of world-historical significance. " 'Tis not the concern of a day, a year, or an age," Thomas Paine wrote in *Common Sense*; "posterity are virtually involved in the contest, and will be more or less affected, even to the end of time, by the proceedings now." "Our cause is noble, it is the cause of Mankind!" George Washington wrote during the Revolutionary War. The Confederation Congress commissioned a seal for the new republic that proclaimed: "A new order for the ages."

As the Civil War approached, Americans felt that the rest of the world watched with concern. In "The Building of the Ship" (1849), Henry Wadsworth Longfellow wrote: ". . . sail on, O Ship of State! / Sail on, O Union, strong and great! / Humanity with all its fears, / With all the hopes of future years, / Is hanging breathless on thy fate." Longfellow's poem was a favorite of Abraham Lincoln, for whom, too, America was an exemplary nation, "the last best hope of earth." The dead at Gettysburg, he said, gave their lives so that "government of the people, by the people, and for the people shall not perish from the earth."

In the 20th century, Americans came to think of themselves less as an exemplary nation than as a regenerative one. On Apr. 2, 1917, in asking Congress for a declaration of war against Germany, Pres. Woodrow Wilson declared: "We are glad . . . to fight thus for the ultimate peace of the world and for the liberation of its peoples, the German people included: for the rights of nations great and small and the privilege of men everywhere to choose their way of life and of obedience. The world must be made safe for democracy. Its peace must be planted upon the tested foundations of political liberty. We have no selfish ends to serve. We desire no conquest, no dominion. We seek no indemnities for ourselves, no material compensation for the sacrifices we shall freely make. We are but one of the champions of the rights of mankind."

And a quarter century later, when the United States entered World War 2, Pres. Franklin Roosevelt told Congress on Jan. 6, 1942: "Our own objectives are clear: the objective of smashing the militarism imposed by war lords upon their enslaved peoples—the objective of liberating the subjugated nations—the objective of establishing and securing freedom of speech, freedom of religion, freedom from want, and freedom from fear everywhere in the world."

EXCLUSIONARY RULE. See *Mapp v. Ohio*.

EXXON VALDEZ OIL SPILL (1989). At 9 p.m. on Mar. 23, 1989, the 987-foot tanker *Exxon Valdez* departed from the Alyeska Marine Terminal (southern terminus of the *Alaska pipeline), across the harbor from the town of Valdez on Alaska's Prince William Sound, carrying 1.26 million barrels of Prudhoe Bay crude oil. Shortly after midnight, the tanker grounded on a reef, rupturing eight of its 13 cargo tanks. In two days, 260,000 barrels of crude oil leaked into the sound; the remaining 1 million barrels were successfully transferred to other tankers.

The worst in U.S. history at that time, the spill eventually covered more than 1,000 square miles with devastating effect on fish, birds, and mammals and on people dependent on fishing for their livelihoods. Cleanup continued for three years, but the spill's long-term environmental impact would not be known for decades. After a 2001 survey, federal scientists estimated that 10,000 gallons of oil remained under the Prince Edward Sound shoreline.

F

FAIR CREDIT REPORTING ACT (1970). See *Consumer Protection.

FAIR DEAL, Pres. Harry S. Truman's label for his domestic program, suggesting continuity with Franklin Roosevelt's *New Deal (see *Truman Administration).

The liberal impulse behind the New Deal had expired by 1938 in the face of an increasingly conservative Congress and Roosevelt's preoccupation with foreign affairs. In his first postwar message to Congress, on Sept. 6, 1945, Truman surprised many people by presenting for congressional consideration a 21-point domestic program emphatically in the Roosevelt tradition. Truman adhered to this program—indeed, broadened it—throughout his administration, naming it the Fair Deal only in his State of the Union message on Jan. 5, 1949, when he proposed repeal of the *Taft-Hartley Act, a more progressive tax system, a 75-cent minimum wage (it was then 40 cents), agricultural reform, resource and public-power development, broadening of Social Security, national medical insurance, federal aid to education, civil rights, and expansion of federal housing programs. Congress enacted very little of it.

FAIR DEBT COLLECTION PRACTICES ACT (1977). See *Consumer Protection.

FAIR EMPLOYMENT PRACTICES COMMITTEE (FEPC) (1941–46), wartime federal agency established by executive order of Pres. Franklin Roosevelt in response to a threatened march on Washington by African-Americans led by A. Philip Randolph, head of the Brotherhood of Sleeping Car Porters, to demand an end to discrimination in defense employment and to segregation in the armed forces. By his executive order of June 25, 1941, Roosevelt ordered the end of discrimination by government agencies and defense contractors (but not military segregation) and created the FEPC to investigate violations. Largely powerless and unpopular among Southerners in Congress, the FEPC was terminated in 1946 although Pres. Harry S. Truman unsuccessfully advocated a permanent FEPC.

In the Lyndon *Johnson administration, the *Civil Rights Act of 1964 established the **Equal Employment Opportunity Commission (EEOC)** charged with eliminating discrimination in government and private employment based on race, color, religion, sex, and national origin, and later on disability and age.

FAIR LABOR STANDARDS ACT (1938). See *New Deal.

FAIR OAKS. See *Peninsula Campaign.

FAIR PACKAGING AND LABELING ACT (1966). See *Consumer Protection.

FALAISE GAP. See *World War 2.

FALLEN TIMBERS (Aug. 20, 1794), battle between 2,000 U.S. troops under Gen. Anthony Wayne and a like number of Miami, Shawnee, and other Indians on the Maumee River in northwest Ohio. Wayne brought his well-trained and disciplined force from present-day Greenville, Ohio, to the Maumee near present-day Toledo. When the Indians refused to negotiate, Wayne advanced (Aug. 20) against their position behind a natural breastworks of fallen trees. Mounted dragoons leaped the barricades, infantry fired and charged with bayonets. The Indians fled, and Wayne destroyed their villages and cornfields. The battle led to the Treaty of Greenville

(Aug. 3, 1795), which brought peace to the *Northwest Territory and opened it to rapid settlement.

FAMILY. The nuclear family—a married man and woman with children, autonomous and private—has been the American norm since its colonial beginnings. For much of the time, it was self-sufficient, dependent on its own resources. Often it was an economic unit, all its members working, inside the home and out, to maintain its independence. With little outside assistance, it reared its young and cared for its aged.

But gradually the family changed. Except for rural families, it ceased to be an economic unit: typically, the father went out to work, leaving wife and dependent children at home. It grew smaller: since the 17th century, the average number of children per family has decreased from perhaps eight to fewer than two. Many of the family's former functions have been taken over by society: for example, only infrequently do parents now care for their aged, since social insurance enables the elderly to maintain separate households, and nursing homes accommodate them when they become disabled.

The diminished nuclear family was subjected to ideological attacks from almost every quarter. Marxists condemned it as a bourgeois invention, founded on property relations and male supremacy. Racial minorities rejected it as the norm of the white middle class. Feminists rebelled against it for condemning women to sex-defined roles as homemakers and mothers. Ecologists feared its contribution to overpopulation. But perhaps most influential were the attacks of some radical psychologists, who condemned the nuclear family as tyrannical and oppressive, destructive of children's free human potential and unfulfilling of the personal needs of adults. Virtually all the neuroses and psychoses of the modern age, according to these critics, were generated in the nuclear family. Few defenders of the traditional family could withstand such concentrated attacks.

Since 1960, all the indicators of family health have been negative: family size has decreased; young people are postponing marriage; fertility rates have fallen; divorce rates have risen and remain high; growing numbers of children are being raised by mothers alone; wives and mothers in record numbers are leaving home to go to work. The 2000 Census found that nuclear families constituted only 23.5 percent of all households, down from 45 percent in 1960. Experts debate whether the traditional nuclear family is mortally ill or simply adapting to the enormous social and cultural changes that are transforming other institutions as well.

FARM BLOC. See *Farm Problem.

FARMERS' ALLIANCES, two organizations founded in the 1880s by distressed farmers in the West and South (see *Agrarian Discontents). Like many other farmers' organizations of the time (see *Granger Movement), the National Farmers' Alliance, or the Northern Alliance, and the National Farmers' Alliance and Industrial Union, or Southern Alliance, were originally self-help organizations that sought to improve the farmers' condition by means of buying and selling cooperatives. Although sectional and racial issues prevented their uniting, both eventually recognized the need for political action to combat railroads, trusts, and banks. In 1892 they helped form the *People's Party.

FARM PROBLEM (1919–40). The years immediately preceding World War 1 were a golden age for American agriculture. After decades of agricultural depression in the 19th century, farmers at last enjoyed decent incomes. The years 1909–14 would later be selected as the basis for the parity index—the ratio of the prices farmers received to those they paid. The index 1909–14 = 100 meant that farmers in those years shared proportionately in the general prosperity.

During World War 1 farm prosperity increased even more as American farmers were called upon to feed U.S. allies and later devastated areas of Europe. High prices and government encouragement induced farmers to bring marginal land under cultivation, buy new land, replace horses and mules with modern machinery, and thereby greatly increase production. Farm income doubled during the war—but so did farm debt, which rose from $4.7 billion in 1914 to $8.4 billion in 1920, then to $10.8 billion in 1923.

After the war, farm prices fell precipitately. European farmers resumed production, and the crops of great food-producing areas like Russia, Canada, Australia, and Argentina glutted world markets. At the same time, the domestic market for agricultural products proved inelastic. Despite the nation's unprecedented prosperity, people did not greatly increase their demand for food. The situation became worse with the beginning of the *Great Depression. American investments and loans that had financed European imports of American farm products ceased. The prohibitive *Hawley-Smoot Tariff of 1932 provoked retaliatory measures abroad. As a result of all these factors, the 25 percent of U.S. farm income traditionally dependent on exports disappeared. Between 1920 and 1932, American farm income declined from $15.5 billion to $5.5 billion.

Farmers understood that they were caught in a crisis of overproduction, but no one dared cut production because of the need to preserve as much income as possible. This was the farm problem that occupied government policy makers through the 1920s and 1930s. In Congress, a bipartisan group of farm state senators and representatives known as the **farm bloc** pushed for legislation to relieve farmers' distress.

The government's response was high tariffs on agricultural imports, then financial support for cooperative marketing enterprises. The **McNary-Haugen Farm Relief Bill** proposed to deal with the source of the problem, overproduction, by establishing a Federal Farm Board that would set a price for each commodity, buy the annual surpluses for either storage or sale abroad, then charge producers for any losses incurred. Defeated in 1924 and 1926, the bill passed in 1927 and 1928, only to be vetoed both times by Pres. Calvin Coolidge as "special interest" legislation.

In the *Hoover administration, an **Agricultural Marketing Act** (1929) established a Federal Farm Board that subsidized marketing cooperatives and bought up large quantities of surplus commodities without stabilizing their prices. The *Reconstruction Finance Corporation supported land and livestock banks and loaned money to farmers on the value of their crops.

The chief strategy of the *New Deal was to raise farm prices by drastically reducing the production of such basic farm commodities as corn, wheat, cotton, tobacco, and hogs. (The list of enumerated commodities was later extended several times.) Under the **Agricultural Adjustment Act** of 1933, farmers who agreed to reduce future acreages planted in enumerated crops were paid a subsidy derived from a tax on the processors of those commodities. As for current plantings, farmers were paid to destroy a portion of existing crops. Millions of pigs were slaughtered and given to relief agencies for distribution to the hungry. By 1936, the New Deal's farm program had raised commodity prices 66 percent and gross farm income 50 percent.

When the Agricultural Adjustment Act of 1933 was declared unconstitutional in 1936, it was quickly replaced by the **Soil Conservation and Domestic Allotment Act**, which sought to reduce production by paying farmers to substitute soil-conserving crops like soybeans and alfalfa for such soil-depleting crops as corn, cotton, tobacco, wheat, and oats and for other conservation practices. This act was superseded by the **Agricultural Adjustment Act** of 1938, under which production continued to be controlled by voluntary acreage allotments and subsidies for acreage not planted. If a surplus in an export crop threatened to lower its price, the Agricultural Adjustment Administration (AAA) was authorized to establish marketable quotas; production in excess of these could be stored and the farmer given a loan on the value of the stored crop. When a shortage developed and the price of the stored crop reached or exceeded "parity"—the equivalent in purchasing power of the 1909–14 price—the stored commodity could be sold. The desired result was the "ever normal granary," a steady supply of commodities in times of plenty and shortage at a steady price. The 1938 act was the basis of U.S. farm policy until 1996, when the *Freedom to Farm Act proposed to phase out controls and subsidies over seven years.

Other New Deal measures provided credit to farmers to refinance mortgages, prevent foreclosures, and recover property already lost by foreclosure; to finance crop production, harvesting, and storage; to enlarge farms to make them economically viable; to resettle marginal farmers and enable tenant farmers to buy farms and tools; and to facilitate electrification of remote farms.

During the course of the New Deal, farm prices and farm incomes rose significantly. Some of this improvement was due to the general rise of national income. A special factor was the severe droughts that affected portions of the country and resulted in unplanned reductions of farm output (see *Dust Bowl). On the other hand, New Deal farm programs tended to benefit large farmers rather than small, and did little for Southern tenant farmers and sharecroppers, mostly black, many of whom were evicted rather than given a share of government subsidies and forced to migrate to Northern cities.

FARM WORKERS UNION. See *United Farm Workers (UFW).

FAVORITE SON, a candidate for the presidency put forward by his native state. Before the institutionalization of the national party *nominating convention, state legislative caucuses (that is, the members of one party in a state legislature) often nominated a favorite son for the consideration of the national party. At a national convention (before the day of *primary elections), a state delegation might nominate a favorite son not as a serious candidate but as a device to withhold its votes from one of the leading candidates for bargaining purposes.

FEDERAL EMERGENCY RELIEF ADMINISTRATION (FERA). See *New Deal.

FEDERALISM REVOLUTION. See *Rehnquist Court.

FEDERALIST, THE (1788), a collection of 85 essays advocating ratification of the proposed federal constitution by the state of New York. The essays were published in New York City newspapers and in papers in other states between Oct. 27, 1787, and Apr. 2, 1788. In the spring of 1788 they were collected in two volumes entitled *The Federalist: A collection of Essays, written in favour of the new constitution, as agreed upon by the federal convention, September 17, 1787.*

All the essays were signed "Publius." (It was then customary for writers on public affairs to use pseudonyms, often classical.) In fact, their three authors were Alexander Hamilton and John Jay of New York and James Madison, a Virginian then in New York as a member of the *Continental Congress. Hamilton and Madison had been delegates to the Federal *Constitutional Convention.

Because opposition to the proposed constitution was particularly strong in New York, Hamilton conceived and planned a massive propaganda campaign on its behalf and recruited Madison and Jay to help him. The trio—largely Hamilton and Madison, since Jay was injured in a street riot and could not do his share—wrote three or four essays a week for more than five months. Hamilton wrote 50, Madison 29, Jay 6.

"Publius" argued that a strong central government was necessary to protect national interests; that although the government would be strong, its powers would be strictly limited and so divided among the three branches of government in a system of checks and balances as to prevent their abuse; and that the nation's diverse economic and political interests would be reconciled in the national legislature.

The New York State convention ratified the constitution on July 26, 1788, by a vote of 30–27. Passage was probably due less to the influence of *The Federalist* than to the facts that New Hampshire, the ninth state to ratify, had done so on June 21, thereby bringing the constitution into effect in nine states, and that Virginia had ratified on June 26. Thus New York had a choice between ratification and exclusion from the already existing new republic.

FEDERALIST PARTY, one of the nation's first two political parties, the other being the *Jeffersonian Republican Party.

The name Federalist was adopted by nationalists at the Federal *Constitutional Convention who succeeded in writing a centralizing constitution and then, by effective propaganda, narrowly winning its ratification. All the members of the new government were Federalists. The economic policies of Secretary of the Treasury Alexander Hamilton attached the nation's financial and commercial elements to the government and to the "Federalist interest," while driving into opposition not only *Antifederalists but farmers, workingmen, and others of democratic inclination. Foreign affairs further divided the two groups, Federalists favoring close commercial ties with monarchical England while their opponents supported revolutionary France, England's enemy. Anti-administration forces rallied behind Thomas Jefferson, who left his post as secretary of state in 1793 to lead the opposition "Republican interest," which eventually became the Republican Party.

Fisher Ames, a prominent Massachusetts Federalist, described his as the party of "the good and the wise, the lovers of liberty and owners of property" and castigated the Republicans as "violent Jacobins." Jefferson, in turn, referred to the Federalists as an "Anglican monarchical and aristocratical party." In fact, both parties were led by elites—the Federalists by a Northeastern financial and commercial elite, the Republicans by a Southern agrarian elite.

Enjoying control of the government and the enormous prestige of George Washington (president 1789–97), the Federalists, under Hamilton's leadership, failed to organize as effectively as the Republicans. They only narrowly elected John Adams (president 1797–1801), then lost the election of 1800. Thereafter Federalist influence in national affairs declined. Their work of nation-building was done. As the country moved rapidly toward new concerns and greater democracy, the Republicans increasingly appropriated nationalist positions while the Federalists shrank to the party of a single section (New England). The Federalists nominated a presidential candidate for the last time in 1816, but a Federalist chief justice, John Marshall, continued to implement the party's original principles until 1835.

FEDERAL RESERVE ACT (1913), legislation of the *Wilson administration that established the Federal Reserve System. Its purpose was to end Wall Street's domination of the nation's banking system (see *Pujo Committee), to manage the credit supply in the national interest, and to assure all businesses access to credit on equal terms.

In large part, the design of the Federal Reserve System followed the plan developed by the National Monetary Commission (1908–12), appointed after the *Panic of

1907 and headed by Sen. Nelson W. Aldrich of Rhode Island, except that the control of the system was vested in the government, not in private hands. The act created a central Federal Reserve Board, whose six members were appointed by the president, and 12 regional Federal Reserve Banks, of whose nine-member boards three members were also presidential appointees. The regional banks acted as "bankers' banks," all national banks being required to join the system and other banks permitted to join if qualified. Member banks were required to keep a portion of their reserves on deposit with the regional Federal Reserve Bank. On the basis of member banks' discounted commercial paper, rediscounted by the regional Federal Reserve Bank, the latter could issue Federal Reserve notes that became part of the circulating money supply. By its power to set interest rates charged by member banks, the Federal Reserve Board could expand or contract the nation's credit supply as conditions required.

FEDERAL TRADE COMMISSION ACT (1914),
legislation of the *Wilson administration intended to compensate for the weakness of the *Clayton Antitrust Act arising from the impossibility of specifying in advance all possible unfair competitive practices. It established a five-member bipartisan Federal Trade Commission (FTC) with broad investigative authority and the power to order companies to stop unfair practices, enforcing its orders through the courts if necessary. Its interpretations of the antitrust laws were expected to build a body of precedents arising from actual conditions that could be applied flexibly to new cases. The FTC's powers have been steadily enlarged, notably in the area of *consumer protection.

FEMININE MYSTIQUE, THE (1963), book by Betty
Friedan that revived the feminist movement in America (see *Women's Rights). Friedan reported widespread, acute discontent—"the problem that has no name"—among middle-class, educated, suburban housewives, which she traced to their efforts to conform to the "feminine mystique," society's notion that women should find identity and fulfillment in marriage, motherhood, and homemaking. "The only way for a woman, as for a man, to find herself, to know herself as a person," Friedan prescribed, "is by creative work of her own. There is no other way. But a job, any job, is not the answer. . . . [T]he only kind of work which permits an able woman to realize her abilities fully, to achieve identity in society in a life plan that can encompass marriage and motherhood, is the kind that was forbidden by the feminine

mystique: the lifelong commitment to an art or science, to politics or profession."

The book was hailed as liberating by the women to whom it was addressed; others attacked it as elitist, denigrating the lives that most women led.

FENIAN UPRISING (1866), incident in the Andrew
*Johnson administration. The Fenian Brotherhood was an Irish revolutionary society aiming for independence from Great Britain. American Fenians supported it with arms and money. On June 1, 1866, some 600 American Fenians crossed the Niagara River at Buffalo, occupied the Canadian village of Fort Erie, and the next day had a brush with Canadian militia. Returning across the river, the raiders were arrested by U.S. authorities but soon released. Later Fenian attempts to invade Canada from St. Albans, Vt., and Malone, N.Y., were frustrated by U.S. troops.

FETTERMAN MASSACRE (1866). See *Sioux Wars.

FIFTEENTH AMENDMENT (1870), constitutional
amendment that enfranchised blacks, North as well as South. After long temporizing, the Republican Congress approved the measure for both principled and practical reasons. The latter was the Republicans' need for black voters to enable the party to compete with the resurgent Democratic Party. In 1868, Republican Ulysses S. Grant had won the presidency with a small popular margin provided by Southern blacks. Black suffrage was unpopular in the North, where blacks voted in only five New England and four Midwestern states. Under congressional *reconstruction, Southern states had been required to write black suffrage into their constitutions, but Republicans recognized the necessity of a federal guarantee of that right.

The amendment's first section declared: "The right of citizens of the United States to vote shall not be denied or abridged by the United States or by any State on account of race, color, or previous condition of servitude."

The 15th Amendment had little immediate effect in the South. Illegal intimidation increasingly kept blacks from the polls, and the amendment did not prohibit such seemingly racially neutral devices as literacy tests, *poll taxes, property requirements, *grandfather clauses, and *white primaries. For a time the federal courts found these devices constitutionally permissible, and after 1877 the federal government ceased to protect black voters. Not until the *Voting Rights Act of 1965 did the federal government effectively assure the right of Southern blacks to vote.

FIFTH AMENDMENT. See *Bill of Rights.

FILIBUSTERING, in the 1850s, the invasions of Latin American countries by private American military expeditions for politics or profit. The most notable filibuster was William Walker, who led an abortive invasion of Lower California (1853–54), joined a revolution in Nicaragua, where he made himself president (1856–57), and died before a firing squad in Honduras (1860).

FILLMORE ADMINISTRATION. See *Taylor-Fillmore Administration.

FINANCIAL SERVICES MODERNIZATION ACT (1999), legislation of the *Clinton administration repealing the depression-era Glass-Steagall Act and later legislation aimed to prevent another 1929-style speculative collapse by restricting the banking, securities, and insurance industries from expanding into one another's businesses. In anticipation of the emergence of new financial conglomerations, the new act provided for shared supervision by the Treasury, the Federal Reserve, and the Securities and Exchange Commission. A significant provision required that banks must have satisfactory records of lending to the disadvantaged before being permitted to expand into new businesses.

FIRE-EATERS, Southern nationalists, defenders of slavery, and advocates of *secession as early as the 1840s. Prominent among them were Edmund Ruffin of Virginia, Robert B. Rhett of South Carolina, and William L. Yancey of Alabama. Opposed by moderates (including John C. Calhoun), they played minor roles in the Confederacy (see *Ruffin's Career).

FIRESIDE CHATS (1933–44), feature of the Franklin *Roosevelt administration. Roosevelt took advantage of the new medium of radio to circumvent a hostile press and speak directly and informally to the American people. Chats were scheduled irregularly as events warranted. In character they were explanatory rather than argumentative. There were 27 in all, beginning with an explanation of the banking crisis on Mar. 12, 1933 (see *Bank Holiday) and ending with an account of the Normandy invasion on June 12, 1944. Roosevelt spoke from the White House for about 30 minutes, usually on Sunday evenings, to huge audiences. The fireside chats contributed immeasurably to his popularity.

FIRST AMENDMENT. See *Bill of Rights.

FIVE CIVILIZED TRIBES, the Choctaws, Chickasaws, Creeks, Cherokees, and Seminoles, who in the early 19th century inhabited what is now the southeastern United States. By that time they had abandoned earlier modes of life and become agriculturalists and village dwellers. Marriage with whites and blacks was frequent; some kept black slaves. The Cherokees by 1820 had acquired a written language, invented by Sequoya. Between 1827 and 1842 the five tribes were removed to Indian Territory in present-day Oklahoma (see *Indian Removal), where they maintained autonomous states until 1907.

FLAG BURNING. During the *Vietnam War, no action of antiwar protesters offended veterans and other conventional patriots more than burning the American flag. Many states passed laws forbidding flag desecration, but in *Texas v. Johnson* (1989) the *Rehnquist Court ruled 5–4 that flag burning was a form of political speech protected by the First Amendment. In the next 11 years four constitutional amendments intended to reverse the Court's ruling passed the U.S. House of Representatives but narrowly failed to win the necessary two-thirds vote of the Senate.

FLETCHER v. PECK (1810), 4–1 decision of the *Marshall Court upholding the law of property and contracts from legislative interference. In 1794 a corrupt Georgia legislature authorized the sale of 35 million acres in the region of the Yazoo River (present-day Alabama and Mississippi) to four land companies at 1.5 cents an acre (see *Yazoo Land Fraud). A new legislature in 1796 rescinded the grant and invalidated all property rights resulting from it. Fletcher, a purchaser of Yazoo land, sued his seller, Peck, for breach of warranty of title with the object of having the rescission invalidated.

Chief Justice Marshall confined himself to the issue of title, arguing that political corruption was a matter for the political, not the judicial, process. On the matter of title, Marshall held the rescission of the grant unconstitutional under the Contract Clause, since the sale of the land to indirect purchasers had been legally valid.

FLORIDAS, EAST AND WEST. Spain held all of Florida from the 16th century until 1763, when it was ceded to Great Britain, which divided it into two provinces, East and West Florida, at the Apalachicola River. Both Floridas returned to Spain in 1783.

The United States claimed West Florida as far east as

the Perdido River as part of the *Louisiana Purchase, but it acquiesced in the temporary continuance of Spanish administration. Spain, however, was impotent, and the Madison administration feared that France or Great Britain would occupy the area. Some 15,000 people, most of them Americans, lived in the portion of West Florida between the Mississippi and Pearl Rivers. Secretly encouraged by Washington, these Americans revolted against Spanish authority in 1810, captured Spanish-held Baton Rouge, declared their independence, and sought annexation by the United States. On Oct. 27, 1810, President Madison obliged.

The portion of West Florida between the Pearl and Perdido rivers was seized by the United States during the War of 1812. West Florida from the Perdido to the Apalachicola, with its capital at Pensacola, remained in Spanish hands until 1819.

Meanwhile, East Florida remained a refuge for hostile Seminole Indians, escaped slaves, and smugglers and privateers. In 1818 Gen. Andrew Jackson entered Florida to pacify the Seminoles (see *Seminole Wars) but also seized the Spanish posts of St. Marks and Pensacola and declared an American occupation. Although the posts were returned to Spain, Spain relieved itself of the troublesome colony by ceding it to the United States in the *Adams-Onís Treaty (1819), in which it also relinquished its claims to West Florida.

FOCUS ON THE FAMILY. See *Christian Right.

FOOD STAMPS. See *Welfare.

FORAKER ACT (1900), legislation of the *McKinley administration providing temporary civil government for Puerto Rico. It was named for Sen. Joseph B. Foraker of Ohio, chairman of the special Senate committee on dependencies. The government was to consist of a governor and an 11-member executive council (at least five members being Puerto Ricans) appointed by the president. This council would also serve as the upper house of the legislature, the lower house being popularly elected. A resident commissioner was to represent Puerto Rico in the U.S. House of Representatives but could not vote except in committees. Puerto Ricans were to be citizens of Puerto Rico, not of the United States. They were exempted from U.S. internal revenue taxes but not from customs laws. Pres. William McKinley had promised them free trade with the United States, but protectionists objected and a compromise imposed a two-year tariff of 15 percent of *Dingley Tariff rates on Puerto Rican

goods entering the United States and on U.S. goods entering Puerto Rico, all proceeds being returned to the Puerto Rican treasury.

FORBES'S ROAD, military highway constructed during the *French and Indian War connecting Philadelphia and Fort Pitt (Pittsburgh). Improved by Pennsylvania during the 1780s until it was passable by wagons, it became a thoroughfare for early western migration.

FORCE BILL (1833). See *Nullification.

FORD ADMINISTRATION (1974–77). Republican Gerald Ford, appointed vice president in 1973 after the resignation of Spiro Agnew, became the 38th president of the United States on the resignation of Pres. Richard M. Nixon (Aug. 9, 1974). To fill the office of vice president, Ford nominated—and Congress approved—Gov. Nelson A. Rockefeller of New York. For the first time, the nation's two highest offices were occupied by men who had not been elected to them.

Ford's decency and candor, as well as his popularity with his former colleagues in the House of Representatives, where he had served as Speaker, promised to heal the wounds of *Watergate. But a month after assuming the presidency Ford ignited a firestorm of criticism by granting a full pardon to former president Nixon. Many people had looked forward to Nixon's indictment and trial for his role in Watergate as necessary to establish the truth about that complex event. But Ford thought that the legal process would distract and divide the nation for years, and since a posttrial pardon was universally accepted as desirable to prevent a past president from going to prison, Ford reasoned "If eventually, why not now?" Suspicion of a secret deal between Nixon and Ford was widespread, and the pardon proved a significant factor in Ford's failure to be reelected in 1976.

Most of Ford's energies were devoted to fighting inflation and recession at home. When South Vietnam collapsed in April 1975 (U.S. troops had been removed in 1972; see *Vietnam War), Ford ordered the evacuation of Americans remaining in Saigon. A thousand Americans and some 5,500 Vietnamese were taken by helicopter to U.S. naval vessels offshore. In foreign affairs, Secretary of State Henry Kissinger brokered a truce between Israel and Egypt following their 1973 war.

Narrowly renominated by the Republican national convention in 1976 over challenger Ronald Reagan, Ford lost the election to Democrat James E. Carter of Georgia.

FORDNEY-McCUMBER TARIFF (1922), legislation of the *Harding administration. A high tariff being the only answer the Republican Party had for economic problems, the Fordney-McCumber Tariff was another record-breaker designed to achieve American economic as well as political isolation after World War 1. It raised average rates on imports to 33 percent.

FORD PEACE SHIP (1915), quixotic attempt by auto manufacturer Henry Ford to end *World War 1. A life-long pacifist, Ford was prevailed upon in November 1915 to lead a party of well-known pacifists to Europe in the hope of ending the war through the mediation of a conference of neutrals. He chartered a Scandinavian liner, *Oscar II*, which departed from Hoboken, N.J., on Dec. 2, 1915, Ford telling reporters, "We're going to try to get the boys out of the trenches before Christmas." Shortly after the ship reached Oslo on Dec. 18, Ford left the party and returned home. The pacifists remaining in Europe were ridiculed and rebuffed at every turn and riven by dissension. Eventually they drifted back to the United States empty-handed.

FOREIGN AID, the transfer of economic and military resources from the U.S. government to other governments, was virtually unknown—except in emergencies—before World War 2. *Lend-Lease, begun in 1941, marked the beginning of large-scale government-to-government transfers between the United States and friendly governments engaged in World War 2.

During the war, multinational institutions were created in anticipation of the postwar needs of devastated countries for relief and reconstruction—the United Nations Relief and Rehabilitation Agency, the International Bank for Reconstruction and Development, and the International Monetary Fund. When urgent needs proved beyond the capacities of these institutions, the United States began providing unilateral aid, first through military assistance to Greece and Turkey, then through the *Marshall Plan. The latter aid was offered to the Soviet Union and its satellites but was rejected by them.

With the outbreak of the Korean War and the intensification of the *cold war, U.S. foreign aid, chiefly military equipment, was sent to countries on the Soviet and Chinese peripheries to forestall communist attack or subversion. Developmental aid went to poor countries in the Middle East, Asia, Africa, and Latin America. Eventually, its determination to aid any anticommunist regime led the United States to support corrupt and repressive governments around the world. In reaction, Congress in the 1970s made a country's human rights record one criterion for receiving U.S. foreign aid (see *Human Rights).

After the cold war, foreign aid became increasingly unpopular. In 2000 Congress approved only $13.3 billion in foreign aid, slightly more than 0.5 percent of federal spending. The leading recipients of U.S. foreign aid have been Israel and Egypt.

FOREST RESERVE ACT (1891). See *Conservation.

FORMOSA STRAITS CRISIS (1953–56), incident in the *Eisenhower administration. To appease congressional advocates of Chinese Nationalist leader Chiang Kai-shek, who had withdrawn from the mainland to Formosa in 1949, Pres. Dwight Eisenhower in February 1953 removed the U.S. Seventh Fleet from the straits between Formosa and Communist China (where it had been put by Pres. Harry Truman in 1950), thereby "unleashing" Chiang to invade the mainland. Chiang, as Eisenhower well knew, had no such capacity, but he did manage to send bombers to the mainland, for which the Communists retaliated (September 1954) by shelling Quemoy and Matsu, small islands two miles off the Chinese coast (although 150 miles apart) garrisoned by Nationalist troops. Hawks in the administration urged that the United States now bomb China, but Eisenhower refused and in December signed a mutual defense treaty with Chiang in which the generalissimo agreed to stop harassing the mainland and the United States agreed to protect Formosa (but not the coastal islands).

When the Communists in January 1955 occupied one of the Tachen Islands 200 miles north of Formosa and increased their attacks on Quemoy and Matsu, Eisenhower requested a resolution from Congress authorizing him in advance to use U.S. armed forces in the defense of Formosa and the Pescadores and "such related positions and territories . . . as he judges to be required or appropriate" for that defense, deliberately not mentioning Quemoy and Matsu. When the Communists stepped up their shelling of Quemoy and Matsu in March 1956, Eisenhower responded with a matter-of-fact statement in a press conference that tactical atomic weapons were no different from other weapons in a strictly military situation. The Communist shelling decreased and stopped in May. No war resulted, and Eisenhower's resoluteness and deliberate ambiguity were widely credited with quieting his congressional critics, restraining Chiang, and deterring the Chinese Communists.

FORT BRIDGER, Wyoming trading post built by *mountain man Jim Bridger in 1843. It was an important stop on the *Oregon, *California, and *Mormon trails. An army post after 1858, it was abandoned in 1890.

FORT PILLOW MASSACRE (Apr. 12, 1864), incident in the *Civil War. Union-held Fort Pillow, on the Mississippi River north of Memphis, was captured by Confederate raider Gen. Nathan B. Forrest. Many of its defenders were black soldiers; several dozen of these and some whites, including their commander, were shot after surrendering. President Lincoln decided against retaliation.

FORTS HENRY AND DONELSON (February 1862), *Civil War battles. The Confederate forts, on the Tennessee and Cumberland rivers respectively, barred the river approaches to Nashville. Union general Ulysses S. Grant, with a fleet of gunboats commanded by Commodore Andrew H. Foote, took Fort Henry on Feb. 6, 1862.

Grant then invested Fort Donelson, 12 miles away, on Feb. 14. But Foote's gunboats were driven off, and on Feb. 15, in Grant's absence, the garrison fought its way out of the besieged position. Grant directed a successful counterattack. When the Confederate commander, Simon Bolivar Buckner, an old army friend, asked for terms, Grant replied, "No terms except unconditional surrender can be accepted. I propose to move immediately upon your works." Buckner accepted Grant's "ungenerous and unchivalrous terms" on Feb. 16.

The capture of the two forts was the first important Union victory of the war. The North celebrated. Grant became nationally known, was promoted to major general, and was given the sobriquet "Unconditional Surrender" (for his initials "U.S."). On Feb. 23, the Confederates abandoned Nashville, the first Southern state capital to fall.

FORT SUMTER BOMBARDMENT (Apr. 12–13, 1861), opening event of the *Civil War. Fort Sumter was built 1829–60 on an island at the entrance to Charleston harbor. When South Carolina seceded on Dec. 20, 1860, Fort Sumter and nearby Fort Moultrie remained in federal possession. On Dec. 26, Maj. Robert Anderson moved his 80-man garrison from Fort Moultrie to the more defensible Fort Sumter. South Carolina requested transfer of the fort. Pres. James Buchanan refused, but after a merchant ship sent to reinforce the garrison was turned back by South Carolina batteries on Jan. 9, 1861, he took no further action to save the fort.

Pres. Abraham Lincoln, inaugurated on Mar. 4, agonized for weeks over what to do. Finally, overriding the advice of most of his cabinet to evacuate the fort, he informed South Carolina governor Francis W. Pickens on Apr. 6 that a naval expedition was being sent to reprovision the garrison. The decision to resist or not now lay with the Confederate government in Montgomery, Ala., which had placed Gen. Pierre G. T. Beauregard in command of Charleston. It ordered him to reduce the fort before aid arrived. On Apr. 11 Beauregard demanded the fort's surrender. When Anderson refused, Beauregard, at 4:30 a.m. on Apr. 12, began a 34-hour bombardment of the fort. Anderson surrendered on Apr. 13. Given the choice between war and peace, the Confederate government had decided for war.

FORT TICONDEROGA, stone fort on the southwest side of Lake Champlain in New York, commanding the entrance to it from Lake George. It was built by the French in 1755 and captured by the British in 1759. Fifty British soldiers manned the fort when it was captured (May 10, 1775) by some 200 *Green Mountain Boys led by Ethan Allen and accompanied by Col. Benedict Arnold at the start of the *Revolutionary War. When asked by what authority he acted, Allen allegedly replied, "In the name of the Great Jehovah and the Continental Congress!"

Cannon stored at Ticonderoga were later hauled to Boston and mounted on Dorchester Heights, compelling the British to evacuate the city (see *Boston Siege). Early in the *Saratoga campaign, the Americans abandoned (July 6, 1777) the fort when the British positioned artillery atop nearby Mount Defiance. They reclaimed it later that year.

FORT WAGNER ASSAULT (July 18, 1863), incident in the *Civil War. Preliminary to a major assault on Charleston, S.C., Union commanders decided it was necessary to capture Morris Island at the mouth of Charleston harbor, from which Union artillery could destroy Fort Sumter. Fort Wagner was a sand redoubt on the island, approachable only across a 200-yard-wide neck of sand.

On July 11, a Union assault was repulsed with heavy casualties. A second assault on July 18 was preceded by a seven-hour bombardment from naval and land guns. At twilight, 6,000 Union troops moved forward, led by the black 54th Massachusetts Infantry commanded by Boston blue blood Col. Robert Gould Shaw. Again the attackers were repelled with heavy casualties, the 54th losing half its effectives, including Shaw. The Confederates buried Shaw in a common grave with his black troops as a form of insult. The incident, however, demonstrated that black troops would fight (one black sergeant received the Medal of Honor) and speeded their recruitment.

FORTY ACRES AND A MULE, disappointed expectation of emancipated slaves immediately after the Civil War. In January 1865 Gen. William T. Sherman designated a portion of the Georgia and South Carolina coast extending 30 miles inland for settlement by freedmen, each family to receive 40 acres and the use of army mules. The expectation that the government would distribute confiscated and abandoned land swept across the South, and indeed officials of the *Freedmen's Bureau began to implement such a policy. They were stopped by Pres. Andrew Johnson, who determined to restore the land to its former owners. Even *Radical Republicans shrank from violating the prevailing laissez-faire ideology, fearing that such substantial aid would weaken the freedmen's character. The "Sherman reservation" was terminated in the fall of 1865, and early in 1866 blacks were evicted from other settlements in Virginia and Louisiana.

FOUR FREEDOMS (1941), aspirations for a better world voiced by Pres. Franklin Roosevelt in a message to Congress on Jan. 6, 1941. The four freedoms, to be enjoyed universally, were freedom of speech and expression, freedom of worship, freedom from want, and freedom from fear. These were later incorporated in the *Atlantic Charter.

FOURTEEN POINTS (Jan. 8, 1918), Pres. Woodrow Wilson's "only possible program" for world peace following *World War 1, drafted after the failure of an Interallied Conference at Paris to agree upon a statement of Allied war aims. Contained in an address to Congress, the 14 Points were:

(1) "[o]pen covenants of peace, openly arrived at";
(2) "[a]bsolute freedom of navigation upon the seas";
(3) "removal . . . of all economic barriers and the establishment of equality of trade conditions" among all nations;
(4) national armaments to be "reduced to the lowest level consistent with domestic safety";
(5) "impartial adjustment of all colonial claims," with "the interests of the populations concerned given equal weight with the equitable claims of the government whose title is to be determined";
(6) "evacuation of all Russian territory," "independent determination of her own political develop-

ment," and "a sincere welcome into the society of free nations";
(7) Belgium to be "evacuated and restored";
(8) "[a]ll French territory . . . freed and the invaded portions restored," and Alsace-Lorraine returned;
(9) "readjustment of the frontiers of Italy . . . along clearly recognized lines of nationality";
(10) "[t]he peoples of Austria-Hungary" to be "accorded the freest opportunity of autonomous development";
(11) Romania, Serbia, and Montenegro to be evacuated, occupied territories to be restored, and Serbia accorded free and secure access to the sea;
(12) the Turkish portion of the Ottoman Empire to be assured a secure sovereignty, other nationalities under Turkish rule to be assured "unmolested opportunity of autonomous development," and the Dardanelles permanently opened to the commerce of all nations;
(13) an independent Polish state with secure access to the sea;
(14) "[a] general association of nations. . . ."

"An evident principle runs through the whole program I have outlined," Wilson explained. "It is the principle of justice to all peoples and nationalities, and their right to live on equal terms of liberty and safety with one another."

In October 1918 Germany sought an armistice on the basis of the 14 Points. Britain and France objected, since they had never agreed to Wilson's program, but they were compelled to grant the armistice with reservations concerning free navigation and war reparations that Germany accepted.

FOURTEENTH AMENDMENT (1868), constitutional amendment intended to preserve the results of the Civil War. In particular, it protected the *Civil Rights Act of 1866 against possible rejection by the U.S. Supreme Court.

The amendment's first section declared: "All persons born or naturalized in the United States, and subject to the jurisdiction thereof, are citizens of the United States and of the State wherein they reside. No State shall make or enforce any law which shall abridge the privileges and immunities of citizens of the United States; nor shall any State deprive any person of life, liberty, or property, without due process of law; nor deny to any person within its jurisdiction the equal protection of the laws."

Its second section abrogated the Constitution's

*Three-fifths Clause, by which the Southern states had been permitted to count three-fifths of their slaves in calculating their congressional representation, but it reduced a state's representation proportionately to the number of male inhabitants denied the right to vote. (This provision was never enforced.)

Section 3 barred from national and state office all men who had taken an oath to uphold the U.S. Constitution and then engaged in "insurrection or rebellion," thereby excluding from public life the South's prewar political leadership. (The Amnesty Act of 1872 removed this disability from all but a few hundred Confederate leaders.)

The fourth section asserted the validity of the Union war debt and required the repudiation of the Confederate debt.

The amendment was passed by Congress on June 13, 1866, against the opposition of Pres. Andrew Johnson. Ten Southern states rejected it, but it was declared ratified on July 28, 1868.

The impact of the 14th Amendment on racial discrimination was severely limited by the Supreme Court's narrow readings in the *Slaughterhouse Cases* (1873), the *Civil Rights Cases* (1883), and *Plessy v. Ferguson* (1896). Not until the middle of the 20th century was the amendment's Equal Protection Clause effectively used against racial discrimination, notably in *Brown v. Board of Education* (1954). At the same time, the Court interpreted the amendment broadly in defense of corporate interests, finding that a business corporation was a "person" and thus protected against state regulation by the Due Process Clause.

FOURTH AMENDMENT. See *Bill of Rights.

FRANK LYNCHING (1915). On Apr. 27, 1913, Mary Phagan, a 14-year-old employee of the National Pencil Co. in Atlanta, was found murdered in the factory basement. The factory's manager, Leo Frank, was arrested and charged with the crime. Despite lack of evidence and the dubious testimony of prosecution witnesses, the jury—intimidated by anti-Semitic crowds in and out of the courtroom—brought in a verdict of guilty. The verdict was appealed unsuccessfully up to the U.S. Supreme Court. Shortly before Frank's scheduled execution, the governor of Georgia commuted his sentence to life imprisonment. But on Aug. 16, 1915, a mob—incited in part by an anti-Semitic campaign conducted by racist politician Tom Watson, 1904 presidential candidate of the People's (Populist) Party and later a U.S. senator—dragged Frank from the jail and lynched him.

FREDERICKSBURG (Dec. 13, 1862), *Civil War battle. After the battle of *Antietam (Sept. 17, 1862), the Union Army of the Potomac, now numbering 110,000 men, did not resume its drive on Richmond until Oct. 26. Exasperated by the procrastination of its commander, Gen. George B. McClellan, President Lincoln replaced him on Nov. 7 with Gen. Ambrose Burnside.

By Nov. 17 Burnside had brought the army to the Rappahannock River in Virginia opposite Fredericksburg. Rather than contest the crossing, Confederate general Robert E. Lee entrenched his 75,000 troops on Marye's Heights behind the town. Crossing the river on Dec. 11–12, the Federals looted Fredericksburg. At dawn on Dec. 13 they left the protection of the town to cross half a mile of open field before the Confederate position. All day they threw themselves futilely against devastating Confederate fire, never getting beyond a stone wall at the foot of the heights. On Dec. 15 the disheartened Federal survivors recrossed the Rappahannock.

FREE BLACKS, before the Civil War, former slaves (and their descendants) who had obtained their freedom by emancipation (in the North), flight, self-purchase, or manumission. There were half a million free African-Americans on the eve of the Civil War. Half of these lived in the North, where legal or customary segregation was universal. Some states forbade their immigration, curtailed their civil rights, and barred them from public schools. In 1860 blacks could vote only in Maine, Vermont, New Hampshire, Massachusetts, and Rhode Island. In 1855 Massachusetts became the only state to accept them as jurors. Five Western states prohibited the testimony of blacks in cases involving white people. Although poor, Northern free blacks had a vigorous communal life, including newspapers, churches, and social, cultural, and economic organizations.

Free blacks in the South had no comparable communal life and no more civil rights than slaves, although they could make contracts and own property. Often better educated and more skilled than their Northern brothers, they typically worked as barbers, waiters, and artisans in Southern towns. In Charleston, Mobile, and New Orleans, a small cultivated class of mulattoes worked at skilled crafts and trades. Some entered the planter class and owned slaves.

Hostility to free blacks in the South was intense, since they contradicted the prevalent view that blacks' natural status was slavery and were imagined to incite slaves to aspire to freedom. Many Southerners wanted free blacks expelled from their states or reenslaved. Some states required manumitted blacks to leave or refused to readmit them if they left. Any person of color was presumed to be a slave unless he or she had documents to prove otherwise.

FREEDMEN'S BUREAU (1865–72), agency of the U.S. War Department established by Congress on Mar. 3, 1865, as the Bureau of Refugees, Freedmen, and Abandoned Lands to provide emergency relief to people displaced and made destitute by the Civil War and to facilitate the transition of the former slaves to economic independence. Its work was to end one year after the close of the war.

The bureau provided food, shelter, and medical care to people of both races, built schools and hospitals, settled freedmen on abandoned lands, supervised the labor contracts between other freedmen and white planters, and guarded the freedmen's interests in Southern courts. Directed by Gen. Oliver O. Howard, it employed some 900 agents throughout the South, often army officers. These inevitably aroused the hostility of Southerners, who accused them of incompetence, corruption, stirring up the blacks, and working on behalf of the Republican Party. Some of these accusations were valid, but on the whole the Freedmen's Bureau operated conscientiously despite insufficient resources.

In July 1866, Congress passed over Pres. Andrew Johnson's veto a New Freedmen's Bureau Act extending the life of the bureau indefinitely and enlarging its powers. Johnson's veto marked the beginning of his open conflict with Congress over *reconstruction. When Congress replaced the Johnson state governments in the South with Republican governments, most of the activities of the Freedmen's Bureau were discontinued (July 1, 1869). Its educational work continued until 1872.

FREEDOM OF INFORMATION ACT (1966), legislation of the Lyndon *Johnson administration empowering citizens to obtain documents held by agencies of the executive branch of the federal government. Nine classes of documents were exempted from the act, but citizens may appeal refusals in the federal courts. The act has been invaluable to journalists and scholars.

FREEDOM RIDES (1961), episode of the *civil rights movement. To test compliance with a U.S. Supreme Court decision (*Boynton v. Virginia*, 1960) that segregated waiting rooms, rest rooms, and restaurants in interstate bus terminals were unconstitutional, the *Congress of Racial Equality (CORE) determined to send nonviolent "freedom riders" by bus across the South from Washington, D.C., to New Orleans.

On May 4, 1961, 13 riders (joined by others at Atlanta), in two interracial groups, boarded two regularly scheduled commercial buses in Washington. At Anniston, Ala., the first bus was firebombed and the freedom riders were beaten by a mob. Photos of the burning bus were published around the world. When the second bus reached Anniston, it was boarded by whites who beat the freedom riders aboard. The bus continued to Birmingham, where gangs of Klansmen beat the riders again. Nevertheless, 18 freedom riders regrouped at Birmingham and on May 15 attempted to go on to Montgomery. When bus drivers refused to drive them down a highway reportedly lined by angry whites, the unnerved riders, surrounded by a hostile crowd though now protected by police, gave up and eventually escaped by air to New Orleans.

In Nashville, Tenn., student veterans of the *sit-ins resolved to continue the freedom ride. Upon their arrival in Montgomery on May 20, they were attacked and beaten by a mob. On May 24, 12 freedom riders appeared at the Montgomery bus terminal for a bus to Jackson, Miss. Together with a crowd of reporters, they were put aboard a bus and transported nonstop in a police convoy to Jackson, where they were immediately jailed.

The sensational media coverage of the freedom rides produced an outpouring of funds for CORE and announcements of many other freedom rides. But the movement quickly faded. Media coverage ceased when prompt jailings forestalled mob violence. (By June, Mississippi jails held nearly 200 freedom riders.) National editorial comment was hostile, condemning the riders as provocative. U.S. attorney general Robert F. Kennedy, who had demanded that Alabama authorities protect the freedom riders and had sent federal marshals to Birmingham, considered the publicity harmful to America's image abroad. Having obtained from the Interstate Commerce Commission an order prohibiting segregated facilities in interstate travel, Kennedy persuaded the civil rights organizations to turn their attention from freedom rides to voter registration (see *Freedom Summer).

FREEDOM SUMMER (1964), episode of the *civil rights movement. In 1962, three civil rights organizations—the *Congress of Racial Equality (CORE), the *Student Nonviolence Coordinating Committee (SNCC), and the *National Association for the Advancement of Colored People (NAACP)—formed a Council of Federated Organizations (COFO) headed by a young SNCC activist, Robert Moses, to undertake a voting rights campaign in Mississippi. Moses tried to organize local voting rights organizations in rural areas and to encourage blacks to register, but his efforts were frustrated by intimidation and violence and by registration requirements designed to disfranchise blacks.

The assassination on June 12, 1963, of NAACP official Medgar Evers led to COFO's declaring the summer of 1964 Freedom Summer and inviting Northern college students to come to Mississippi to help register blacks to vote. Some 900 male and female volunteers—mostly white—received a brief orientation at Oxford, Ohio, then traveled to Mississippi where, directed by SNCC staff, they canvassed potential black registrants, conducted literacy and voter education classes for adults, and taught children in "freedom schools." Moses believed that the exposure of the white volunteers to racist violence would focus national attention on the disfranchisement of Mississippi blacks. Two early arrivals—Michael Schwerner and Andrew Goodman, both from New York, together with James Chaney, a local black youth—were murdered near Philadelphia, Miss., on June 15, 1964. Hundreds of other volunteers endured shootings, bombings, beatings, and jailings.

Freedom Summer ended with burnout and strife among the volunteers. Although they had registered only 1,200 blacks, the publicity generated by their effort contributed to passage of the *Civil Rights Act of 1964 and the *Voting Rights Act of 1965. It also led to the creation of the *Mississippi Freedom Democratic Party (MFDP).

FREEDOM TO FARM ACT (1996), legislation of the *Clinton administration intended to reform the system of federal farm subsidies created during the *New Deal. These had grown ever more complicated and inequitable, rewarding chiefly wealthy farming corporations in a handful of states. The act failed to achieve its purpose, yearly emergency appropriations essentially preserving the subsidy system. In 2002—an election year—a new farm act abandoned the reform effort altogether, providing $180 billion in subsidies over the next ten years, including a $40-billion increase in subsidies for large grain and cotton farmers. It also provided increased spending for food stamp and nutrition programs and for environmental and conservation efforts.

FREEMAN'S FARM. See *Saratoga Campaign.

FREEMEN. See *Radical Right.

FREEPORT DOCTRINE. See *Lincoln-Douglas Debates.

FREE SILVER, the unlimited coinage of silver as well as gold at a ratio of 16 to 1, the prescription of silver producers and inflationists for curing the price deflation that followed the Civil War and persisted to the end of the 19th century.

When the demonetization of silver in 1873 (see *Crime of '73) and the *Specie Resumption Act (1875) promised to contract rather than expand the money supply, silver producers joined with greenbackers (see *Greenback Party) and other inflationists to demand resumption of the free coinage of silver. They won partial victories with the *Bland-Allison Act (1878) and the *Sherman Silver Purchase Act (1890), but these created monetary confusion and caused a drain on U.S. gold reserves that contributed to the *Panic of 1893. The defeat of William Jennings Bryan, the great advocate of free silver (see *Bryan's "Cross of Gold" Speech), in the 1896 presidential election ended the agitation.

FREE-SOIL PARTY (1848–54), political party formed (August 1848) by antislavery ("conscience") Whigs (see *Whig Party) at a convention in Buffalo, N.Y. Joined by members of the *Liberty Party and by antislavery Democrats (see *Barnburners and Hunkers), the convention nominated former president Martin Van Buren and adopted a platform endorsing the *Wilmot Proviso and free homesteads for settlers in the West. Its slogan was "Free Soil, Free Speech, Free Labor, Free Men."

Although the Free-Soil Party carried no state, it deprived the Democratic candidate, Lewis Cass, of New York State and thus ensured the election of the Whig candidate, Zachary Taylor. The party's 1852 candidate, John P. Hale, received only half the votes that Van Buren had received. In 1854 most of its members joined the *Republican Party.

FREE SPEECH MOVEMENT. See *New Left.

FRENCH AND INDIAN WARS (1689–1763), the North American phases of wars between England and France fought worldwide.

King William's War (1689–97), in Europe the War of the Grand Alliance, began with French and Indian attacks on English frontier settlements. Massachusetts troops seized and briefly held Port Royal on Cape Breton Island. Fleets sent from France and England accomplished nothing. The war ended with the Treaty of Ryswick (1697).

Queen Anne's War (1702–13), in Europe the War of the Spanish Succession, saw bloody frontier warfare, most notably the destruction of Deerfield, Massachusetts, in 1704 by Abenaki Indians. The British failed to take Quebec but New Englanders took Port Royal on Cape Breton Island. The Peace of Utrecht (1713) transferred Newfoundland and Hudson Bay to Great Britain.

King George's War (1744–48), in Europe the War of the Austrian Succession, began with a French failure to capture Port Royal in 1744, and New Englanders captured Louisbourg in 1745. English plans to capture Montreal and Quebec were abandoned, and French fleets failed in their mission to attack colonial targets. The Treaty of Aix-la-Chapelle (1748) restored Louisbourg to France.

The French and Indian War (1754–63), in Europe the Seven Years' War, began in the Ohio Valley when George Washington, in command of a body of Virginia militia, was compelled to abandon Fort Necessity near the French Fort Duquesne on the site of present-day Pittsburgh. In 1755, the British sent Gen. Edward Braddock, guided by Washington, to take Fort Duquesne. He was surprised, defeated, and killed by an inferior French and Indian force near the fort. Three years later, Gen. John Forbes, also accompanied by Washington, reached Fort Duquesne and found it abandoned. In 1758 Gen. Jeffrey Amherst captured Louisbourg; in 1759 Gen. James Wolfe captured Quebec; and in 1760 Amherst took Montreal, ending French control of Canada. By the Treaty of *Paris (1763), France was expelled from North America.

FRENCH REVOLUTION (1789–99). The French Revolution was greeted in America with universal enthusiasm. No one doubted that it had been inspired by the American Revolution, that the French Declaration of the Rights of Man and the Citizen imitated the American Declaration of Independence, and that the constitution being prepared by the National Assembly would be modeled on that of the United States. When the French repelled invading Austrian and Prussian armies in September 1792 and then declared a republic, American enthusiasm reached its peak. Americans believed that France would now champion human liberty in the heart of monarchical Europe. When Edmund Genêt, the minister of the new French republic, reached America in April 1793, he was received everywhere with celebrations (see Genêt Affair). *Democratic Societies, in imitation of the Jacobin clubs in France, sprang up in Philadelphia and other places.

By 1793, however, conservative Americans—including those in the *Washington administration—were beginning to have second thoughts about the French Revolution. French constitutional experiments had unwisely—in their view—rejected British and American examples. Mob vio-

lence, the flight abroad of the heroic La Fayette in June 1972, the execution of King Louis XVI in January 1793, and the French declaration of war against England in February 1793 disturbed the administration. Diverging opinions on the revolution in France fed growing partisan divisions in the United States.

Washington's cabinet was led by Secretary of the Treasury Alexander Hamilton, whose policies Secretary of State Thomas Jefferson abhorred (see *Hamilton and Jefferson). Hamilton's admiration for the British constitution—like Vice Pres. John Adams's—was well known. Jefferson, who hated England, was convinced that these "anglomen" were conspiring to restore monarchy in America. He believed that the success of republicanism in France was vital for the security of republicanism in the United States. Jefferson and his followers were therefore ardently pro-French, blandly excusing revolutionary excesses in France as a small price to pay for liberty. Thus in addition to hostility to the *Hamilton system, pro-French and anti-British sentiments distinguished the emerging *Jeffersonian Republican Party from the emerging *Federalist Party.

The Republicans interpreted Washington's 1793 proclamation of neutrality in the Anglo-French war as pro-British, and they opposed *Jay's Treaty in 1794 for the same reason. Their partiality for France—and their incomprehension of events there—continued into the John *Adams administration. They were indifferent to French depredations on American commerce in retaliation for Jay's Treaty; they were embarrassed by the *XYZ affair, when the French Directory showed its contempt for the United States; they opposed preparations for war against France (see *Naval War with France); and they vehemently resisted the *Alien and Sedition Acts, which were directed as much against them as against French subversion.

The French Revolution ended in the dictatorship of Napoleon Bonaparte. In 1803, President Jefferson was happy to end French control of New Orleans—a source of potential conflict—by the *Louisiana Purchase.

FRIES'S REBELLION (1799), incident in the John *Adams administration. John Fries aroused resistance among Pennsylvania Germans to the direct property tax passed (1798) by Congress to finance preparations for war with France. The rebellion was roughly suppressed by the Philadelphia militia. Fries was convicted of treason, sentenced to death, but pardoned by President Adams.

FRONTIER. See *Westward Movement.

FUGITIVE SLAVE LAWS, laws requiring the return of fugitive slaves to their owners. In the colonial period, most of the colonies restricted the movements of white indentured servants and black slaves; authorized the recapture, punishment, and even death of runaways; and severely punished anyone who aided or harbored a fugitive. Similar laws were written into the slave codes of the Southern states (see *Slavery).

The ending of slavery in the Northeast and its prohibition in the *Northwest Territory created "free" areas where the status of an escaped slave was problematic. The Ordinance of 1787, which organized the Northwest Territory, recognized an owner's right to reclaim a fugitive slave in the territory. The U.S. Constitution (Art. 4, sec. 2) recognized the right of owners to reclaim their property across state lines.

The Fugitive Slave Act of 1793 provided the means of enforcing the Constitution's provision. It permitted slave owners or their agents to cross state lines to recapture an escaped slave and, upon proving ownership to a state or federal magistrate, to return the captive to slavery. The fugitive had no legal defense. To protect fugitives and *free blacks from professional slave catchers and kidnappers, some Northern states enacted *personal liberty laws assuring the fugitives such rights as habeas corpus and jury trial and punishing kidnappers. In *Prigg v. Pennsylvania (1842) the U.S. Supreme Court ruled that state personal liberty laws were unconstitutional, a slave owner's constitutional right to his property taking precedence over any state legislation. At the same time, the Court held that enforcement of the fugitive slave law was entirely a federal responsibility and that state officers had no obligation to help.

The Fugitive Slave Act of 1850, part of the *Compromise of 1850, was intended to correct defects in the 1793 law. It created a class of U.S. commissioners who were authorized to return an alleged fugitive to slavery on the basis merely of the claimant's affidavit of ownership and the testimony of white witnesses. Ostensibly to cover the cost of additional paperwork, the commissioner received a $10 fee for accepting the claim and only $5 for refusing it. U.S. marshals, their deputies, and ordinary citizens were required to assist the commissioners in the performance of their duty and were heavily penalized for refusing or obstructing them. Criminal penalties were also levied on citizens concealing or rescuing a fugitive.

In New England, northern New York State, and portions of the Middle West settled by New Englanders condemnation of the act was intense. It was a law "which no man can obey or abet the obeying, without loss of self-respect and forfeiture of the name of a gentleman," declared Ralph Waldo Emerson. Press, pulpit, and public meetings denounced the act and pledged defiance. The South was outraged by this vocal denial of its constitutional rights, which it saw as a new form of *nullification.

During the first year after passage of the act, the number of fugitive slaves seized in the North increased sharply. Many fugitives and free blacks fled to Canada. A handful of well-publicized instances of violent resistance to seizures inflamed sentiment on both sides, although the great majority were effected without incident.

FULLER COURT (1888–1910), the U.S. Supreme Court under Chief Justice Melville W. Fuller. To a remarkable degree, the Fuller Court mirrored the popular sentiment of the period. In economic matters, it reflected the dominant laissez-faire philosophy. The economic laws propounded by Adam Smith and Herbert Spencer appeared to most contemporaries as natural laws to which the Constitution itself must conform. These laws postulated the absolute freedom of the individual in the marketplace.

To ensure that freedom, the Court consistently struck down state regulatory statutes, using an enlarged interpretation of the *14th Amendment's Due Process Clause. Whereas that clause had originally merely guaranteed a person (individual or corporate) fair procedure in the juridical system, it was now expanded to guarantee the person's natural liberties, of which the epitome was liberty of contract. State regulatory laws that arbitrarily deprived a person of his property or infringed his liberty violated **substantive due process**.

Further, the Court limited the regulatory power of the federal government by restricting the reach of the Constitution's Commerce Clause. Separating manufacturing from commerce, the Court prevented Congress from using its powers under the Commerce Clause to regulate conditions within manufacturing plants (even when their products were destined for interstate commerce) and confined its jurisdiction to the interstate traffic itself. By relieving entrepreneurs of regulatory burdens, the Court greatly encouraged the nation's rapid industrialization—at whatever cost to those persons (individual or corporate) who found their property taken and their liberty infringed not by the state but by more powerful persons.

In *Chicago, Milwaukee & St. Paul Railway Co. v. Minnesota (1890), the Court made judicial review of the decisions of regulatory agencies an integral component of substantive due process—thereby restricting the power of regulators. In *United States v. E. C. Knight Co.* (1895), it made the distinction between manufacturing and commerce that limited Congress's ability to regulate businesses until the 1930s. That same year, in *Pollock v. Farmers' Loan & Trust Co.* (1895), it ruled a national income tax unconstitutional. In *Northern Securities Co. v. United States* (1904), the Court revived the moribund *Sherman Antitrust Act to give Pres. Theodore Roosevelt a narrow victory over a major *trust that was restraining free competition. But the next year, in *Lochner v. New York* (1905), it overturned a ten-hour law as a violation of the workers' liberty of contract. In *Loewe v. Lawler* (1908), it used the Sherman Act to destroy a small union. In *Muller v. Oregon* (1908), it seemed to reverse its stance in *Lochner* by upholding an Oregon ten-hour law for women, but this was in conformity with the popular view that women workers required special protection.

On racial matters, the Court accurately reflected the prevailing racism. In *Plessy v. Ferguson* (1896), it upheld legal segregation in the South but with the proviso—which became significant only 50 years later—that the segregated accommodations be "equal" as well as "separate." In *Williams v. Mississippi* (1896), it found no discrimination in laws that prevented blacks from voting and serving on juries. Finally, in the *Insular Cases* (1901–4), by distinguishing between incorporated and unincorporated territories, the Court prevented nonwhite inhabitants of the nation's new insular possessions from becoming American citizens.

FURMAN v. GEORGIA (1972). See *Capital Punishment.

FUR TRADE, generally the first economic activity on each successive American frontier, since furs could always be readily and profitably sold. The fur trade went hand in hand with exploration; it played a central role in relations with the Indian tribes and in the rivalry among English, French, Spanish, and Americans for control of North America.

In the eastern half of the continent, popular furs were raccoon, otter, mink, muskrat, and fox; in the western half, the beaver predominated until overtrapping and changing European fashions caused profits to plummet. Furs were usually acquired from the Indians in exchange for weapons, tools, clothing, ornaments, tobacco, and alcohol. But white trappers also roamed far afield, most notably the *mountain men of the Rocky Mountains. For several decades in the first half of the 19th century, the North American fur trade was dominated by two great rivals, John Jacob Astor's American Fur Company in the United States and the Hudson's Bay Company in Canada.

As the area of settlement expanded, the area of fur trapping diminished. The great days of the fur trade ended around 1850.

G

GABRIEL PROSSER PLOT (1800). See *Slave Revolts.

GADSDEN PURCHASE (1854), last addition to the contiguous United States, acquired from Mexico for $10 million. Some 29,670 square miles in the southern parts of present-day Arizona and New Mexico south of the Gila River, the area was thought necessary for a southern transcontinental railroad route. The purchase treaty was negotiated by James Gadsden, U.S. minister to Mexico, but was much modified by the U.S. Senate before ratification on Apr. 29, 1854.

GAG RULES (1836–44), rules adopted by both the Senate and the House of Representatives to prevent debate on antislavery petitions. In the 1830s, Northern antislavery groups began to flood Congress with petitions for the abolition of slavery, at least in the District of Columbia, where Congress had legislative authority. (It was arguable if Congress could regulate slavery in the states.) The petitions enraged Southern congressmen as agitating a question that the Constitution had closed. Moreover, they professed to be insulted by the petitions: many were from women, whose involvement in politics they considered immoral; all offended by branding slave-owning congressmen as sinners.

In 1836 the Senate decided to receive the petitions but instantly reject them. The House voted to receive them but to automatically table them, thus preventing any consideration. In 1840 the House voted not to receive them at all.

Former president and from 1831 U.S. representative John Quincy Adams shrewdly challenged the gag rules as violations of First Amendment rights of free speech and petition. Almost daily he protested the gag rules on the floor of the House, taking special delight in mocking the apoplectic Southerners. On one occasion he asked to present a petition from 22 slaves who—when the petition was finally examined over Southern protests—requested to remain enslaved.

Adams's efforts made Northerners realize that the defense of slavery, which was already restricting the liberties of white Southerners, must inevitably restrict Northern liberties as well. In 1844 Northern Democrats joined with Northern Whigs to end the gag rules.

GALLOWAY'S PLAN OF UNION (Sept. 28, 1774), proposal by Joseph Galloway of Pennsylvania at the first *Continental Congress to establish an American legislature that would administer intercolonial affairs jointly with the British Parliament. Congress narrowly rejected the plan (see *American Revolution).

GARFIELD-ARTHUR ADMINISTRATION (1881–85). The brief administration of Republican James A. Garfield, 20th president of the United States, was occupied with problems of patronage. A "Half-Breed" (see *Stalwarts and Half-Breeds), Garfield appointed a collector of customs for the Port of New York (a prime patronage post) who was not acceptable to the "Stalwart" Republican boss of the state, Sen. Roscoe Conkling. He also appointed Conkling's enemy, James G. Blaine, secretary of state. In protest, Conkling resigned his Senate seat, mistakenly expecting to be immediately reelected; instead, his political career was ended. On July 2, 1881, Garfield was shot by a disappointed office seeker; he died on Sept. 19 (see *Garfield Assassination).

His successor, Vice Pres. Chester A. Arthur, had been a Stalwart follower of Conkling in New York who had been given the vice-presidential nomination to mollify Conkling and balance the ticket. In office, the 21st president of the United States proved an efficient if lethargic executive. Public opinion, aroused by the Garfield assassination and the *Star Route Frauds, compelled him to support *civil service reform; the Pendleton Act (1883) was the major legislative achievement of his administration. Arthur appointed an expert tariff commission that recommended cuts of 25 percent in tariff rates. Congress objected, and Arthur reluctantly signed the *Mongrel Tariff (1883), which reduced rates less than 1.5 percent. He vainly vetoed a pork-filled Rivers and Harbor Act in 1882 and signed a *Chinese Exclusion Act (1882) that prohibited the immigration of Chinese laborers for ten years.

Arthur was succeeded by Democrat Grover Cleveland.

GARFIELD ASSASSINATION (July 2, 1881). Having stalked Pres. James A. Garfield for several weeks, Charles J. Guiteau, a disappointed and deranged office seeker, found him on July 2 strolling with Secretary of State James G. Blaine in the waiting room of the Baltimore and Potomac Railroad station in Washington. Guiteau shot twice, exclaiming, "I am a Stalwart; Arthur is now president of the United States!" (See *Stalwarts and Half-Breeds.)

Garfield suffered a minor wound in his right arm and a serious wound in his abdomen, where the bullet lodged near his pancreas. Three operations followed to drain abscesses and remove bone fragments. Meanwhile, physicians probed the wound with bare fingers and unsterilized instruments in vain attempts to remove the bullet. Blood poisoning set in, and the president died on Sept. 19.

At his trial, Guiteau pleaded not guilty by reason of insanity. He was hanged on June 30, 1882.

GAULT, IN RE (1967), 8–1 decision of the *Warren Court mandating procedural safeguards for juvenile defendants.

Adjudicated a "delinquent child" for making an obscene phone call while on probation for another offense, 15-year-old Gerald Gault was sentenced to a state training school until his majority (six years), whereas an adult would have been subject to a $50 fine or two months in jail for the same offense. This anomaly was a consequence of the separate juvenile justice system, created to protect juveniles, where judges, probation officers, and social workers adjudicated cases in consultative (not adversarial) proceedings in which the defendants had no procedural safeguards.

"There may be grounds for concern," Justice Abe Fortas had written in Kent v. United States (1966), "that the child receives the worst of both worlds: that he receives neither the protections accorded to adults nor the solicitous care and regenerative treatment postulated for children." In Kent, Gault, and In re Winship (1970), the Court mandated for juveniles such adult procedural safeguards as written notification of charges against them, the right to counsel, the right to cross-examine witnesses, protection against self-incrimination, and conviction only on proof beyond a reasonable doubt.

GENERATION X, children of the *baby boom generation, allegedly distinguished from their self-absorbed, striving parents by cynicism and ironic detachment. They are reputed to have left their impress on popular music, television, and film. Comedian Jerry Seinfeld (technically a boomer) exemplified the ethos of the Gen-Xers.

GENÊT AFFAIR (1793), incident in the *Washington administration. Edmond Charles Genêt, age 30, was the first minister to the United States from the new French Republic, which was already at war with half of Europe. His arrival (Apr. 8, 1793) at Charleston, S.C., was hailed by enthusiastic crowds sympathetic to the *French Revolution. He began at once to arm and commission privateers to attack British ships in U.S. waters and to set in motion a grandiose scheme to arouse the peoples of Florida, Louisiana, and Canada to revolt against their Spanish and British masters.

Genêt's journey from Charleston to Philadelphia was a virtual triumphal progress. Pres. George Washington received him on May 18, and he was soon embarked on negotiations, by letter and in person, with an initially very sympathetic secretary of state, Thomas Jefferson. Jefferson let him know that he and Washington were not in agreement about U.S. policy toward France. Nevertheless, it became Jefferson's duty to reject Genêt's proposal for a new commercial treaty and for advance payment of America's *Revolutionary War debt to France. Finally, Jefferson had to tell Genêt that Washington had decided that Genêt's commissioning of privateers on American soil violated U.S. sovereignty and must cease.

Enraged at the unfraternal behavior of the U.S. government, Genêt dispatched another privateer from Philadelphia and threatened to appeal over Washington's head to the American people. The government thereupon requested his recall. By then, however, control of the French Republic had passed from the moderate Girondins to the radical Jacobins. Prudently, Genêt decided to remain in the United States. He married the daughter of Gov. George Clinton of New York and passed the remaining 40 years of his life as a farmer in Dutchess County.

GENTLEMEN'S AGREEMENT (1907). See *Japanese Exclusion.

GERMAN OCCUPATION (1945–55). At the end of *World War 2, a truncated Germany (its territory east of the Oder and Neisse rivers was transferred to Poland) was divided into four occupation zones. The Soviets occupied the eastern zone, the British a zone in the northwest, the French a zone in the southwest, and the Americans a zone in the south comprising the *Länder* of Bavaria, Hesse, and Württemberg-Baden plus the North Sea port of Bremen. Berlin, in the Soviet zone, was similarly divided into four sectors. An Allied Control Council in Berlin was to set policy, but when it failed to work, the military commanders of the four occupation zones had free hands.

At the Potsdam Conference in July 1945 (see *World War 2 Conferences), the Allied leaders asserted their purpose "to assure that Germany never again [would] threaten her neighbors or the peace of the world." Thus the occupation policies of the Allies were initially punitive. The military government in the American zone prohibited fraternization between Americans and Germans, prosecuted war criminals and former Nazis (see *War Crimes Trials), and reduced the Germans' standard of living. Agricultural reconstruction was pursued, industrial reconstruction was ignored; indeed, German factories were dismantled and sent to the Soviet Union as reparations.

In 1947 occupation policy became less harsh in the western zones when the Western Allies realized that German economic recovery was essential to the recovery of Europe. The American and British zones were combined into a single economic unit, to which the French later adhered, and economic development was emphasized. American policy was to set Germany onto the path to free enterprise. When several *Länder* attempted to nationalize the coal and steel industries, the American military governor, Gen. Lucius D. Clay, overrode them, with the concurrence of the British, whose Labour government actually favored nationalization but was economically dependent upon the United States. In June 1948 the Western Allies instituted a currency reform in their zones that caused the Soviets to retaliate with the Berlin Blockade (see *Berlin Airlift).

The inability of the four powers to resolve their fundamental differences convinced the Western Allies that there would be no general peace treaty in the foreseeable future, and they now encouraged the organization of a west German federal government that would be economically integrated with Western Europe. In 1948, a Parliamentary Council elected by the parliaments of the 11 western *Länder* drew up a "basic law" (a provisional constitution for a provisional federal republic), and on May 23, 1949, the Federal Republic of Germany (FRG, or West Germany), with its capital at Bonn, came into existence. In August, the Germans elected a federal parliament, or Bundestag. Theodor Heuss became the first federal president, Konrad Adenauer the first federal chancellor. The FRG was subject to an Occupation Statute drawn up by the United States, Great Britain, and France, but the occupation now changed from military to civilian, the military governors giving way to civilian high commissioners.

Under Adenauer, the FRG pursued a policy of political and economic integration with the West. In October 1949 it joined the Organization for European Economic Cooperation, which managed the distribution of *Marshall Plan funds. In April 1951 it joined the European Coal and Steel Community and the next month it became a member of the Council of Europe. With each step, the Occupation Statute was relaxed to give the FRG ever larger measures of independence. In July 1951, the United States, Britain, and France ended their state of war with West Germany.

Although the Occupation Statute prohibited the existence of any military force in Germany, the intensification of the *cold war persuaded the Allies of the necessity of German participation in the defense of Western Europe. By a treaty between the FRG and the occupying powers signed at Paris in the fall of 1954, the FRG became a member of the Western European Union and the *North Atlantic Treaty Organization (NATO) and was permitted to raise an army of 500,000 that would be entirely subordinated to NATO. The treaty imposed certain other military restrictions on the FRG, but when it went into effect in May 1955 the Occupation Statute lapsed and the FRG assumed full sovereignty. Foreign troops remained on its soil, but these were NATO, not occupying, forces.

GERMANTOWN (Oct. 4, 1777), *Revolutionary War battle. When the British occupied Philadelphia in September 1777, Gen. William Howe stationed 3,000 troops in the city while he remained at Germantown, six miles northwest of Philadelphia, with 9,000 more. Confident that the Americans were too weak to attack after their losses at *Brandywine and *Paoli, Howe did not bother to fortify his camp.

At this extremity of his fortunes, Patriot general George Washington reacted as he had a year earlier at *Trenton: he attacked. His plan was bold but complicated. Four columns of troops, totaling 11,000 men and marching by night on separate roads across a seven-mile front, would converge in a pincers movement on Germantown at dawn on Oct. 4. Despite delays in all the columns and a heavy ground fog, the initial attack succeeded. For three hours the British were driven back, except for a force trapped in a stone mansion in the American rear. But the exhausted Patriots ran low on ammunition, became confused by the firing in their rear, and apparently fired on each other in the fog. They began to fall back even as the British re-formed and pushed forward. By 10 a.m. the retreat was general, but the British limited their pursuit.

Their initial success buoyed the morale of Patriots overly familiar with defeat. Washington's aggressiveness favorably impressed French observers.

GETTYSBURG (July 1–3, 1863), largest and most important battle of the *Civil War, turning point of the war in the East.

After the battle of *Chancellorsville (May 2–4, 1863), Confederate general Robert E. Lee led his Army of Northern Virginia, now numbering 75,000, up the Shenandoah Valley through Maryland and into Pennsylvania. The Union Army of the Potomac, numbering 90,000 and after June 28 commanded by Gen. George G. Meade, followed. On June 30, units of the two armies collided at Gettysburg, Pa. Recognizing that a major battle loomed, both commanders hurriedly concentrated their armies at the small town.

In the developing battle, Union generalship proved uncharacteristically competent. Lee, however, was beguiled by belief in his army's invincibility, although it now lacked the aggressive drive of Gen. Thomas J. "Stonewall" Jackson (killed at Chancellorsville) and the intelligence-gathering of Gen. J. E. B. Stuart (absent on a raid).

On July 1, outnumbered Federals were driven out of Gettysburg to defensive positions south of the town. The Confederates did not push their attack, and during the night three Union corps arrived and took up positions on a three-mile-long Union front, curved like a fishhook from Culp's and Cemetery hills in the north (the bend of the hook), along Cemetery Ridge (the shank), and ending at Little Round Top (the eye). The Confederates occupied Seminary Ridge, about a mile west of and parallel to Cemetery Ridge.

On July 2, Lee ordered two frontal attacks—Gen. James Longstreet's corps against the Union left and Gen. Richard S. Ewell's against the right. The attacks were uncoordinated. Longstreet did not move until 4 p.m.; his late-starting attack on the Union left drove back a for-

ward salient and briefly penetrated the Union line but failed to capture Little Round Top, from which the Confederates could have enfiladed the entire Union position. On the Union right, Ewell's evening attack took Culp's Hill, but the Confederates were dislodged the next morning.

Believing that Meade had weakened his center to defend his flanks on July 2, Lee on July 3 ordered a frontal attack on the Union center. Shortly after 1 p.m. the Confederates launched an unprecedented two-hour artillery barrage against Cemetery Ridge. At 3 p.m. three Confederate divisions moved out to cross three-quarters of a mile of open ground under Federal guns (see *Pickett's Charge). The attack was repulsed with heavy losses, and Lee's army was probably saved only by Meade's failure to counterattack.

The next day, July 4, Lee abandoned the field in a heavy rain and turned his once-invincible army south. On the night of July 13–14, with Meade in reluctant pursuit, Lee recrossed the Potomac into Virginia. The three-day battle had cost 23,000 Union casualties, 28,000 Confederate.

GETTYSBURG ADDRESS. See *Lincoln's Gettysburg Address.

GHENT TREATY (1814), treaty between the United States and Great Britain ending the *War of 1812.

Efforts to end the war began soon after it started. In August 1814 a U.S. delegation consisting of Henry Clay, Jonathan Russell, James Bayard, Albert Gallatin, and John Quincy Adams met their British counterparts in the Flemish city of Ghent, then in the Netherlands. The great fear of the Americans was the possible loss of American territory; their primary demand was for an end to *impressment. The British refused to discuss that subject, but the end of the war in Europe in April rendered it moot. British demands—an Indian buffer state between the United States and Canada, boundary revisions that would give them access to the Mississippi River, an end to American rights to the Newfoundland fisheries—were rejected by the Americans.

When the negotiators learned that a British army had captured and burned Washington, the British proposed a peace in which both parties would retain their present territorial holdings (the British held territory in eastern Maine). News of Commodore Thomas Macdonough's victory on Lake Champlain restored the balance between the parties. In November, the Duke of Wellington, declining a command in North America, advised the British government that victory was impossible without control of the Great Lakes and that Britain had no military grounds for demanding any cession of territory.

The parties thereupon agreed on a return to the status quo ante bellum (prewar conditions). Mixed commissions would settle the U.S.-Canadian boundary. Other matters were postponed. The Newfoundland fisheries and navigation of the Mississippi were not mentioned. In fact, none of the issues that caused the war figured in the peace treaty. The treaty was signed on Dec. 24, 1814 (two weeks before the battle of *New Orleans) and ratified unanimously by the U.S. Senate on Jan. 15, 1815. "We have obtained nothing but peace," observed John Quincy Adams.

GHETTO RIOTS (1963–68). Summer nights in the 1960s were illuminated by the flames of burning black ghettos in the inner cities of both North and South. Beginning in 1963 with disorders in Birmingham, Savannah, and Cambridge, Md., provoked by civil rights demonstrations, they spread in 1964 to New York, Philadelphia, Cleveland, and Chicago. The riot in the Watts district of Los Angeles in 1965 absorbed the nation for five days. The next summer, 43 disorders and riots were counted nationwide. In 1967, 164 disorders included major riots in Tampa, Cincinnati, Atlanta, Newark, and Detroit. The assassination of civil rights leader Martin Luther King Jr. on Apr. 4, 1968, was answered by 130 riots, including three days of looting and arson in Washington, D.C.

In 1967, Pres. Lyndon Johnson appointed a National Advisory Commission on Civil Disorders chaired by Otto Kerner, governor of Illinois. In its report issued in March 1968, the **Kerner Commission** found no evidence of organized provocation. Rather, the riots were spontaneous eruptions of black anger at the racial discrimination that blighted black lives at every turn, compounded by the disappointment of expectations heightened by the rhetoric of the *civil rights movement and the War on Poverty (see Lyndon *Johnson Administration). When black anger was exacerbated by the stresses of poverty, congestion, and idleness pervasive in the black ghettos, the mere addition of summer heat created a combustible mixture that minor confrontations with the police were often sufficient to ignite.

The riots revealed no revolutionary strategy—they did not aim to capture some symbolic bastille or seat of government. Their simple anarchy, their rage and jubilation, was captured in the exclamation "Burn, baby, burn!" Their primary effect was to destroy large portions of the blacks' own communities, driving essential stores (some of them black-owned) out of business and inhibiting new investment while at the same time strengthening the conservative "law and order" reaction that followed the disorderly 1960s.

The Kerner Commission's many recommendations were largely ignored, but its sad conclusion was remembered: "This is our basic conclusion," its report read: "Our Nation is moving toward two societies, one black, one white—separate and unequal. . . .

"What white Americans have never fully understood—but what the Negro can never forget—is that white society is deeply implicated in the ghetto. White institutions created it, white institutions maintain it, and white society condones it."

GHOST DANCE. See *Sioux Wars.

GIBBONS v. OGDEN (1824), decision of the *Marshall Court broadly construing the Commerce Clause of the U.S. Constitution. New York State had granted a monopoly of steam navigation on the state's waterways to Robert Fulton and Robert Livingston, who in turn licensed Aaron Ogden. Ogden sued to restrain Thomas Gibbons, who (with a federal license) operated boats between New York and New Jersey.

Chief Justice Marshall, for a unanimous Court, interpreted the Commerce Clause ("To regulate commerce with foreign nations, and among the several states, and with the Indian tribes") to give the federal government power to regulate all foreign and interstate commerce ("commercial intercourse . . . in all its branches," including navigation) without regard to state boundaries. The only power reserved to the states was the power to regulate intrastate commerce—that is, commerce confined within the borders of a single state. Marshall ruled that Gibbons's federal license nullified the New York State grant of monopoly, which infringed on an area where the national government was supreme.

The decision freed transportation from state restraints and thereby gave great impetus to its development. In the 20th century, the broad construction of the Commerce Clause served to validate much federal regulatory legislation.

G.I. BILL OF RIGHTS or **SERVICEMEN'S READJUSTMENT ACT** (1944), legislation of the Franklin *Roosevelt administration. For veterans of *World War 2—often called G.I.s (from "*government* *issue*"), slang for army enlisted men—it provided tuition grants and monthly allowances for vocational training or college; loan guarantees for the purchase of houses, farms, or businesses; and unemployment compensation of $20 per week for 52 weeks ("the 52–20 club"). The act was later extended to other veterans, and the benefits were progressively increased.

GIDEON v. WAINWRIGHT (1963), unanimous decision by the *Warren Court that the Sixth Amendment's guarantee of right to counsel was made applicable through the Due Process Clause of the *14th Amendment to all the courts in the land. Gideon, a Florida indigent, was tried for breaking into a poolroom to commit a felony. Denied a court-appointed lawyer, he defended himself and was convicted.

"[R]eason and reflection," wrote Justice Hugo Black for the Court, "require us to recognize that in our adversary system of criminal justice any person haled into court, who is too poor to hire a lawyer, cannot be assured a fair trial unless counsel is provided for him. This seems to us to be an obvious truth. Governments, both state and federal, quite properly spend vast sums of money to establish machinery to try defendants accused of crime. Lawyers to prosecute are everywhere deemed essential to protect the public's interest in an orderly society. Similarly, there are few defendants charged with crime, few indeed, who fail to hire the best lawyers they can get to prepare and present their defenses. That government hires lawyers to prosecute and defendants who have the money hire lawyers to defend are the strongest indications of the widespread belief that lawyers in criminal cases are necessities, not luxuries.

"The right of one charged with crime to counsel may not be deemed fundamental and essential to fair trials in some countries, but it is in ours. From the very beginning, our state and national constitutions and laws have laid great emphasis on procedural and substantive safeguards designed to assure fair trials before impartial tribunals in which every defendant stands equal before the law. This noble ideal cannot be realized if the poor man charged with crime has to face his accusers without a lawyer to assist him."

This ruling was originally thought to pertain to defendants charged with felonies, but in 1972 it was extended to defendants charged with lesser crimes who faced a single day in jail and in 2002 to defendants who received suspended sentences where there was even a remote possibility of imprisonment.

GILDED AGE, title of an 1873 novel by Mark Twain and Charles Dudley Warner satirizing the greed, materialism, vulgarity, and corruption of the post–Civil War period. Much used by historians, the term is usually applied to the 1870s and 1880s, although sometimes to the entire period from the end of the Civil War to the McKinley administration.

GITLOW v. NEW YORK (1925), 7–2 decision of the *Taft Court upholding the New York conviction of Benjamin Gitlow, a communist, for writing a pamphlet urging the establishment of socialism by strikes and "class action." While acknowledging that freedom of speech and of the press were among the fundamental liberties protected by the Due Process Clause of the *14th Amendment, Justice Edward T. Sanford, for the majority, ruled that "a state may punish utterances endangering the foundations of organized government and threatening its overthrow by unlawful means."

In dissent, Justice Oliver Wendell Holmes appealed to the test of "clear and present danger" that he had formulated in *Schenk v. United States* (1919). "If what I think the correct test is applied, it is manifest that there was no present danger of an attempt to overthrow the government by force on the part of the admittedly small minority who shared the defendant's views. It is said that this Manifesto was more than a theory, that it was an incitement. Every idea is an incitement. . . . Eloquence may set fire to reason. But whatever may be thought of the redundant discourse before us, it had no chance of starting a present conflagration."

Despite Justice Sutherland's appreciation of First Amendment freedoms, the federal *Bill of Rights was not then considered binding on the states. Not until 1931 did the Supreme Court rule a state law unconstitutional on First Amendment grounds.

GLOBALIZATION, worldwide economic transformation, accelerating since the end of the cold war, driven by technology, and marked by an unprecedented flow of capital, goods, people, and information among nations. Some people equate globalization with Americanization, believing that the major international institutions charged with economic development and trade facilitation—the World Bank, the International Monetary Fund, and the World Trade Organization—are dominated by the United States and that the United States is the chief beneficiary of globalization. In recent years, protesters have tried to disrupt meetings of the international financial organizations in the United States and abroad, charging that those institutions served a capitalist elite, were not benefiting the world's poorest people, and were pursuing development projects harmful to the environment.

GOLD DEMOCRATS (1896), faction of the *Democratic Party that rejected the party's presidential nominee, William Jennings Bryan, formed the National Democratic Party, and nominated former Union general John M. Palmer of Illinois for president and former Confederate general Simon Bolivar Buckner of Kentucky for vice president. By cutting into Bryan's Democratic vote, they were responsible for Republican William McKinley's carrying Michigan, Indiana, Kentucky, and West Virginia.

GOLD RUSHES. The discovery of gold near Sutter's Fort in California's Sacramento Valley in January 1848 precipitated the greatest gold rush of the 19th century (see *Sutter's Gold). News of the discovery spread rapidly on the West Coast, reached the East Coast in August, and was confirmed by Pres. James K. Polk in his annual message to Congress in December.

By then Californians had long since deserted homes and jobs for the goldfields. Gold seekers from other parts of the country were slower to arrive. Some came over the *California Trail, some across the isthmus of Panama, some by sailing ship around the Horn. Other gold seekers came from Europe, Australia, Mexico, and China. Relatively few "struck it rich." But in a few months San Francisco was transformed from a village to a city of 25,000. California's non-Indian population grew from 14,000 in 1848 to 224,000 in 1852. As part of the *Compromise of 1850, California entered the Union as the 31st state in September 1850.

Other gold rushes of the 19th century brought prospectors to Colorado (1858–59, 1892), Nevada (1859–60), Idaho (1860–63, 1882), Montana (1862–64), South Dakota (1876), and Alaska (1899).

GOLD STANDARD, the valuation of a unit of currency in terms of a fixed quantity of gold. The object is a stable currency—that is, one neither inflationary nor deflationary. (Although gold fluctuates in value according to supply and demand, it is relatively more stable than alternative standards.)

In the late 19th century, the major nations of the world adopted the gold standard. The United States had been on a bimetallic (gold and silver) standard until the Civil War, when it went onto a paper standard. After the war, business interests (and working people) equated a gold standard with "sound money," putting them at odds with farmers and small merchants, whose universal indebtedness made them partisans of inflationary *greenbacks and *free silver. Sound money prevailed. The Coinage Act of 1873 (see *Crime of '73) ended the minting of silver dollars, and the *Specie Resumption Act of 1875 put the country effectively on a gold standard. Sil-

verite agitation, however, resulted in the *Sherman Silver Purchase Act of 1890, which alarmed foreign and domestic holders of paper dollars and set off a run on the nation's gold reserves. The Sherman Act was repealed in 1893, and the *Gold Standard Act of 1900 put the United States (like its chief trading partners) unequivocally on a gold standard.

World War 1 caused many nations to temporarily abandon the gold standard; the Great Depression of the 1930s caused them to abandon it permanently in favor of managed economies. In the United States, the Gold Reserve Act of 1934 took the country largely off the gold standard: gold could no longer be used as a medium of domestic exchange and the ownership of gold bullion was made illegal.

The dollar was completely separated from gold in 1971 when the United States ran a large trade deficit and foreigners demanded the conversion of their dollars to gold. With its gold reserves under attack, the United States announced that it would no longer redeem foreign-held dollars in gold. All U.S. currency, paper as well as coins, is now fiat money—intrinsically valueless but made legal tender by law.

GOLD STANDARD ACT (1900), legislation of the *McKinley administration. It moved the country closer to a true gold standard by fixing the content of the gold dollar, declaring it the standard unit of value, and requiring that all forms of money issued or coined by the United States should be maintained at a parity with the gold dollar (although the silver dollar remained legal tender). A gold reserve of $150 million, to be maintained by the sale of bonds when necessary, was established for the redemption of all paper money. For rural areas, the act authorized the establishment of national banks with a capital of not less than $25,000.

GOLIAD MASSACRE (Mar. 27, 1836), incident in the Texas Revolution (see *Texas Republic). On Mar. 19, 1836, Col. James W. Fannin with 420 American volunteers evacuated Goliad, Texas, before an approaching Mexican army. They were overtaken by the Mexicans and, after a short fight, surrendered as prisoners of war. They were returned to Goliad, where, by order of Mexican general Antonio López de Santa Anna, 371 were executed because, as foreigners, they were regarded under Mexican law as pirates.

GOOD NEIGHBOR POLICY (1933–45), policy of the Franklin *Roosevelt administration toward Latin America. Announced in Roosevelt's first inaugural as

U.S. policy toward all countries, it came to be associated particularly with U.S. relations with Latin America, where for economic, strategic, and idealistic reasons the administration was eager to end decades of U.S. hegemonic oversight. At a Pan-American Conference in Montevideo, Uruguay, in 1933, the United States subscribed to a Convention on the Rights and Duties of States, which included the declaration: "No State has the right to intervene in the internal affairs of another"—thereby repudiating the Theodore *Roosevelt Corollary to the *Monroe Doctrine. The success of the administration's Latin America policy was demonstrated when every Latin American country—including Argentina at the last minute—declared war on the Axis powers in World War 2.

GOOD NEWS CLUB v. MILFORD CENTRAL SCHOOL (2001), 6–3 decision of the *Rehnquist Court opening public elementary schools to after-school religious activities on the same basis as other after-hours activities. The Good News Club, an evangelistic Christian youth group, proposed to move its daily after-school children's religious program from a church to a public school classroom. Justice Clarence Thomas, writing for the majority, ruled that to deny the use of the schoolroom to the Good News Club would violate the club's free-speech rights while to grant it "would ensure neutrality, not threaten it."

The decision abandoned the Court's previous position that young children—unlike college students—were especially impressionable to religious indoctrination and likely to mistake equal access for official endorsement. In dissent, Justice David H. Souter wrote: "It is beyond question that Good News intends to use the public school premises not for the mere discussion of a subject from a particular, Christian point of view, but for an evangelical service of worship calling children to commit themselves in an act of Christian conversion" (see *Church-State Relations).

GRADUATION ACT (1854). See *Public Lands.

GRAND ARMY OF THE REPUBLIC (GAR) (1866–1956), organization of Union veterans of the Civil War, founded in Illinois in 1866. Its membership peaked in 1890 at 409,000. Its last national encampment, attended by six members, was held in 1949. Its last member died in 1956, when the organization was considered dissolved.

From the start, the GAR was virtually a department of the Republican Party, which had been the party of the Union in the Civil War and which proved most generous in providing veterans' benefits—although the Democrats were also obedient to the veterans' lobby. The connection between the GAR and the Republican Party was solidified in the first *Cleveland administration, when Democratic president Grover Cleveland alienated veterans by vetoing many private pension bills as well as the *Dependent Pension Bill (passed in the Benjamin *Harrison administration) and by proposing to return *Confederate battle flags to the Southern states.

GRANDFATHER CLAUSE, a legislative device exempting a citizen from a legal requirement if he or an ancestor had been exempt in the past. In the late 19th century, when some Southern states imposed literacy or property requirements on voters in order to disfranchise blacks, unqualified whites were allowed to vote if they had been eligible in 1867 (before the *15th Amendment was ratified) or were the legal descendants of such voters. In *Quinn v. United States (1915) the U.S. Supreme Court found the grandfather clause unconstitutional.

GRANGER CASES (1877), group of cases decided by the *Waite Court in March 1877 arising out of attempts by some Midwestern states to fix maximum prices charged by railroads and grain elevators. The issue in all was whether a state could regulate a private corporation whose business affected the public interest. The railroads and elevators argued that regulation was a deprivation of property in violation of the Due Process Clause of the *14th Amendment. The Court found such regulation a constitutionally permissible exercise of state police power as long as the effect on interstate commerce was incidental. The case most often cited is *Munn v. Illinois.

GRANGER MOVEMENT (1867–76), agrarian protest movement that grew out of the National Grange of the Patrons of Husbandry, a fraternal and educational organization of farmers founded by Oliver H. Kelley in 1867. From slow beginnings the network of local granges grew rapidly after 1873 in the Middle West as a vehicle for farmers' protests against the monopolistic practices of railroads and grain elevators (see *Agrarian Discontents).

Unsuccessful in the organization of cooperatives, the Grangers succeeded in politics, capturing state legislatures in Illinois, Wisconsin, Minnesota, and Iowa, where they passed so-called Granger laws regulating the rates and practices of railroads and elevators. In *Munn v. Illinois (1877), the *Waite Court upheld the principle of state regulation of businesses affected with a "public interest." But in *Wabash, St. Louis & Pacific Railway Co. v. Illinois* (1886), it restricted state regulation to intrastate commerce, necessitating federal legislation like the Interstate Commerce Act of 1887 (see *Railroad Regulation).

GRANT ADMINISTRATION (1869–77). "Let us have peace," wrote Ulysses S. Grant in accepting the Republican Party's presidential nomination in 1868. The sentiment was welcomed by millions of Americans who idolized the victorious general but who did not see an end to the nation's strife (see *Reconstruction). Unfortunately, the 18th president of the United States came to office with little political experience or comprehension of the problems that confronted him. His cabinet consisted largely of army cronies and millionaire contributors to his election campaign; the few men of ability and integrity were soon disposed of and the administration was naïvely delivered to the spoilsmen and corruptionists. The chief exception was Hamilton Fish, who served as secretary of state throughout Grant's two terms.

During the Andrew *Johnson administration, Grant, general of the Army, had been courted by *Radical Republicans as an unbeatable presidential candidate. As president, Grant conscientiously furthered the Radical program of reconstruction, presiding over a Union restored by the Radicals, supporting with federal troops carpetbag administrations in the Southern states (see *Carpetbaggers and Scalawags), and vigorously enforcing the laws against the *Ku Klux Klan. The *15th Amendment was ratified in 1870. But Grant (like many other Americans) wearied of the turmoil in the South and was relieved to sign the Amnesty Act (1872), which restored political rights to all but a few hundred former Confederates.

In economic matters, Grant was guided by the conservative, hard-money interests in the Republican Party. He endorsed the continuation of high wartime tariffs (see *Morrill Tariffs), the redemption of war bonds (bought with depreciated *greenbacks) with gold, and the redemption of the greenbacks themselves with specie (see *Specie Resumption Act). Neither Grant nor his advisers had any solution to the prolonged depression that followed the *Panic of 1873.

From the start, the administration was rocked by scandals—most notably *Black Friday, the *Crédit Mobilier Scandal, the *Salary Grab, the *Whiskey Ring Scandal, and the *Belknap Scandal. Grant reneged on a promise to pursue *civil service reform, alienating reform-minded Republicans, who in 1872 formed the

*Liberal Republican Party and unsuccessfully campaigned against his reelection. At the end of his administration, Grant felt impelled to make an unprecedented apology to Congress for his sorry record (see *Grant's Apology).

Only in foreign affairs was the administration's record respectable. Secretary of State Fish saved Grant from premature recognition of Cuban rebels and from annexation of Santo Domingo (see *Santo Domingo Affair). These issues, plus the *Virginius affair, threatened to involve the United States in war with Spain. Fish's great achievement was the Treaty of *Washington (1871), by which the United States and Great Britain agreed to submit to arbitration the principal controversies disturbing their relations—the *Alabama claims, the *San Juan boundary dispute, and a dispute over Canadian fisheries.

In 1876 the Republican bosses wanted to run the inadequate but unbeatable and willing Grant for a third term, but the party adhered to the two-term precedent and nominated Rutherford B. Hayes, who was narrowly elected.

During the Grant administration, Colorado (1876) became the 38th state.

GRANT AND LEE. Out of the carnage of the Civil War emerged a new America—rootless, striving, acquisitive, coarse. Consigned to history was the Old South, a land of stratified social classes ruled by aristocratic families, with codes of noblesse oblige for the gentry, courtesy to the common folks, and slavery for the unfortunate blacks. The two generals who met at Appomattox in April 1865 personified the new and the old orders—slouching Ulysses S. Grant in his muddy private's uniform, erect Robert E. Lee in dress uniform and gilded sword. Two men could not have been more dissimilar, although they shared a secret passion for war and a gnawing fear of disgrace.

The Lees, descended from English earls, had been planters in Virginia since 1642. They were related by marriage to many other leading Virginia families—Carters, Randolphs, Fitzhughs, Custises, Harrisons. Two Lees had signed the Declaration of Independence. Robert E. Lee seemed to carry the weight of his ancestry lightly. Five feet ten inches tall, he was handsome, charming, and universally liked. Yet he maintained an impenetrable reserve. "Can anyone say they know Robert E. Lee?" asked one admirer. Having learned from his mother the meaning of Honor and Duty, he resolved even as a child to excel at every undertaking. Perhaps this was from pride in his origins. Or perhaps it was from fear of disgrace that had already stained his family. His father, the

Revolutionary War's dashing Light-Horse Harry Lee, had gone through the fortunes of two wives and died a bankrupt, leaving Robert's mother in genteel poverty; a half brother had been ostracized from society for having made his wife's sister pregnant.

In four years at West Point, Robert E. Lee did not earn a single demerit. He graduated second in his class in 1829 and was selected for the elite corps of engineers. He emerged from the Mexican War a hero, indispensable to the victory, according to Gen. Winfield Scott, the American commander. Scott believed that Lee was the finest officer in the U.S. army and in 1861, as the Civil War approached, offered him its field command. After 35 years of national service, Lee decided that his first loyalty was to Virginia. Although he considered slavery "a moral and political evil" and opposed secession, he believed that the South had a right to independence if it chose. He would never fight against the South—the Old South of home and kinsmen—but he would fight to defend it if it was attacked by "those people," the boorish Yankees.

If Lee had known genteel poverty, Grant's early poverty was of the hardscrabble sort. His ancestors had drifted west with the frontier from Connecticut to Ohio. Even in Ohio his father had moved restlessly from town to town, finally prospering as a tanner. There was nothing promising about Ulysses, small and withdrawn, whose only desire was to get away from the foul-smelling tannery. His tightfisted father got him an appointment to West Point and thus a free education. Cadet Grant graduated in 1843, 21st in a class of 39, having accumulated 290 demerits. He was assigned to the infantry, and endured the tedium and loneliness of remote army posts. The Mexican War was a bright interlude, after which he returned to the monotony of peacetime army life. In 1854 Captain Grant was compelled to resign because of drunkenness. Joining his wife and children in St. Louis, he tried his hand at farming, woodcutting, and real estate—all jobs provided by his contemptuous father-in-law. By 1860, at 38, he was destitute, galled by the disgrace of failure and poverty. Five feet eight inches tall, shoulders stooped in despair, hands shaking from recurrent malaria, dressed in a slouched hat and shabby army coat, he was an object of condescension among the people of the town. In his darkest hour, his implacable father relented and made him a clerk in a leather goods store he owned in Galena, Ill., that was managed by two younger sons.

The coming of the Civil War brought both men to life—escape from military routine for Lee, escape from failure and obscurity for Grant. Lee's emergence as the preeminent general of the Confederacy surprised no one. By every measure, he was destined for success. Although he believed that the Confederacy was doomed, he dutifully accepted a losing hand and played it brilliantly, prolonging the war for years—with the help, of course, of Union generals who had no stomach for war. Lee loved war. "It is well that war is so terrible," he said at Fredericksburg, "else men would learn to love it too much."

No one ever accused Grant of brilliance—or of lacking a stomach for war. From depths no one had perceived, perhaps least of all himself, the great captain emerged. People who had known him in civilian life marveled: was the shabby down-and-out Sam Grant they had known in St. Louis and Galena the same Grant who had demanded the unconditional surrender of forts Henry and Donelson? (His given name was Hiram Ulysses, but at West Point he had been erroneously enrolled as Ulysses Simpson—his mother's maiden name—Grant. From his initials, U.S., the cadets called him Uncle Sam, then simply Sam.)

At West Point, Grant, like Lee, had studied the battles of the great Napoleon, but with little interest. Perhaps Lee felt at home in the 18th century, his father's century. But Grant was 15 years younger, a product of the 19th century and unburdened by distinguished ancestry. Intuitively, he understood that war in the age of industry, railroads, steamships, and the telegraph would be total war in which all of society's resources would be engaged. He grasped that the purpose of an army was not to capture real estate but to destroy the enemy's capacity to wage war—in particular, to destroy the enemy's army. To do this with certainty required bringing superior resources and manpower to bear on that army, forcing it to fight without remission, bleeding it to death.

This is what Grant did when, in 1864, as lieutenant general commanding all the armies of the United States, he at last confronted Lee in the bloody corridor between Washington and Richmond while, far to the south, Gen. William T. Sherman drove on Atlanta. He was not a cruel or insensitive man. On the second night in the Wilderness, in the solitude of his tent, he wept. But he had told Lincoln, "Whatever happens, there will be no turning back," and the next morning, instead of withdrawing to the north as his predecessors had routinely done after a mauling, he led the Army of the Potomac south.

Doggedly, Grant pushed the Confederates back through horrific battles at Spotsylvania and Cold Harbor, costly standoffs from which he disengaged only to push farther south around Lee's flank. The North groaned as casualties mounted. Once hailed as the savior of the

Union, Grant was now execrated as a butcher. But new troops replaced the fallen and Grant pushed on. "I propose to fight it out on this line if it takes all summer," he said. The Army of Northern Virginia fell back in good order, but always smaller and hungrier. By July 1864 it was bottled up in Petersburg. In the spring of 1865 the remnants of Lee's army fought their way westward out of Petersburg. Grant pursued them relentlessly until, starving and exhausted, they could fight no more.

At Appomattox, Grant's terms were generous and Lee appreciated them. But the old man (he was 58) was heartbroken, able to console himself only with a maxim he had once written: "There is a true glory and a true honor—the glory of duty done, the honor of integrity of purpose." Grant, 43, went back to Washington to receive the cheers of multitudes; three years later he was elected president of the United States. Lee became president of a small college with 4 professors and 40 students.

GRANT'S APOLOGY (Dec. 5, 1876). Conscious that his two terms in office had been sullied by scandals (see *Grant Administration), due in part to his political naïveté and to betrayal by trusted friends, Pres. Ulysses S. Grant appended to his last annual report to Congress an unprecedented apology: "It was my fortune, or misfortune, to be called to the office of Chief Executive without any previous political training. . . . Mistakes have been made, as all can see and I admit, but it seems to me oftener in the selections made of the assistants appointed to aid in carrying out the various duties of administering the Government—in nearly every case selected without a personal acquaintance with the appointee, but upon recommendations of the representatives chosen directly by the people. . . . History shows that no Administration from the time of Washington to the present has been free from these mistakes. But I leave comparisons to history, claiming only that I have acted in every instance from a conscientious desire to do what was right, constitutional, within the law, and for the very best interests of the whole people. Failures have been errors of judgment, not of intent. . . ."

GRANT'S MEMOIRS, autobiography of former general and president Ulysses S. Grant through the Civil War. Considered a classic of military narrative, the *Personal Memoirs* was composed by Grant in the last year of his life when, bankrupt and dying of throat cancer at his home near Saratoga, N.Y., he labored to provide for his family. He completed the two volumes shortly before his death on July 23, 1885. They were published by Mark Twain and ultimately brought the Grant family $450,000 in royalties.

GREAT AWAKENING (1739–44), wave of religious revivalism initiated by English Methodist preacher George Whitefield. It was welcomed for a time by American clergymen as an antidote to the religious complacency of their parishioners, but eventually many perceived that the religious enthusiasm it inspired was divisive within existing denominations ("new lights" vs. "old lights") and subversive of ministerial authority. Lesser waves of revivalism—in which the Calvinist doctrines of human sinfulness and divine judgment shook multitudes—preceded and followed the Great Awakening and became a feature of frontier life.

GREAT DEPRESSION (1929–41), longest, deepest, and most transforming economic recession in American history, precipitated by the *Panic of 1929. Its complex causes, both domestic and foreign, are still debated by economists and historians. Domestically, they are to be found in fundamental imbalances in the American economy during the 1920s that produced a crisis of underconsumption—the inability of a large portion of the American people to buy the goods produced by a rapidly expanded and efficient industrial plant.

After a steep but transitory depression following World War 1, the United States entered upon an industrial boom based on the automobile and related industries—steel, rubber, glass, and petroleum. This led to a bull market on Wall Street. In the heady optimism induced by the new prosperity, much consumer spending and stock speculation was financed by credit. By 1929, public and private debt totaled as much as $150 billion, a third of the national wealth.

The prosperity, however, was not shared by all sectors of the economy. Agriculture never emerged from the postwar depression. Coal mining, textiles, and railroads were also stagnant.

Nor was the prosperity shared by all segments of the population. The richest fifth of the population in 1929 received 54.4 percent of the nation's money income—more, that is, than the other four-fifths combined. That year, 71 percent of American families had incomes below $2,500; only 2.3 percent had incomes above $10,000. The aggregate income of the top 0.1 percent (24,000 families with incomes over $100,000) was equal to that of the bottom 42 percent. Between 1920 and 1929, while the disposable income of all Americans increased 9 percent, that of the top 1 percent increased 75 percent.

The income of the top 20 percent of the population

derived in part from investments (the other 80 percent had no savings). An extremely high rate of savings in the 1920s resulted in an expanded industrial plant and greatly increased worker productivity. Over the decade, worker productivity in manufacturing increased 43 percent, but most of the benefits of this increase went into profits and thus to shareholders.

For manufacturing workers themselves—who, with their families, constituted more than a third of the nation's population in 1920—employment and wages stagnated. Although manufacturing employment fluctuated during the decade, the number of manufacturing jobs was the same in 1929 as in 1920. The average hourly wage in all manufacturing in 1920 was 55 cents; in 1929 it was 56 cents. Average *weekly* wages actually declined as average weekly hours of work fell from 47.4 to 44.2. Largely unorganized, subject to frequent unemployment, and increasingly displaced by laborsaving machinery, manufacturing workers were excluded from the national prosperity.

Farmers, too, were excluded. Farmers and their families constituted 30 percent of the total population in 1920. During the decade, farm prices steadily declined and farm debt rose. Farm families, who received 15 percent of the national income in 1920, received only 9 percent in 1929. In that year, when the average per capita income for all Americans was $750, that for farm families was $273 (see *Farm Problem).

For several years, the maldistribution of income—the lack of purchasing power in a large portion of the population—was masked by a feverish prosperity based on credit buying and financial speculation. When the stock market crash of 1929 put an end to the optimism that fed both, depression quickly followed.

Between 1929 and the depth of the depression in 1933, the gross national product (the sum of all goods and services produced in the country) declined 29 percent, national income 55 percent, industrial production 47 percent, construction 78 percent, investment 98 percent. Unemployment rose from 4 million to 12–15 million; it hovered around 10 million as late as 1939. Consumer prices fell 18 percent; farm prices fell 50 percent from already depressed 1929 levels; wages fell 40 percent. The value of the stock on the New York Stock Exchange fell 80 percent—a loss of $74 billion (the prices of 50 leading industrial stocks declined from an average of $252 to $61). Some 124,000 businesses and 9,000 banks failed.

For 15 million unemployed and their families (more than a third of the population) the depression was a period of unprecedented suffering, often unrecognized by the wealthy. On vacant lots and city dumps across the country, homeless families lived in shantytowns ironically called "Hoovervilles." Downcast and silent, jobless men stood in long breadlines, barely sustained by local relief agencies and private charities. On street corners, men in suits and ties sold apples. ("Many persons," former president Herbert Hoover recalled 30 years later, "left their jobs for the more profitable one of selling apples.")

Dispossessed farm families—tenants displaced by machinery, marginal farmers whose mortgages had been foreclosed—took to the highways in old jalopies, many headed west hoping to sell their labor in the green valleys of California, as portrayed by John Steinbeck in *The Grapes of Wrath*. Millions of men and boys—and women too—crossed the country in freight cars looking for work, living in hobo "jungles," asking for handouts at back doors. (Henry Ford is reported to have remarked that the young men and boys crossing the country in search of work were getting a good education.)

While millions went hungry, farmers burned their crops or left them to rot in the fields rather than sell them at prices below the cost of production.

The rich were fearful of revolution. But the unemployed were too frightened and dispirited to revolt. Having believed in the American dream that any man who worked hard would succeed, they now blamed themselves for their incomprehensible calamity. It was not unusual for beggars to apologize for their condition.

No one had a cure for the depression. Conservatives advised waiting it out; in the past, depressions had proved self-correcting over time. Pres. Herbert Hoover believed that the cure lay in restoring business confidence, which he attempted to do by balancing the budget, consulting numerous committees of businessmen, and finding grounds for optimism in the most transient events. (The cheerful prediction "Prosperity is just around the corner," frequently attributed to Hoover, was in fact made by Vice Pres. Charles Curtis.) He also believed that extending federal aid to the unemployed would destroy their spirit of self-reliance—although aid to banks and railroads was acceptable.

Hoover's rival for the presidency in 1932, Democrat Franklin Roosevelt, announced no specific plans during the campaign. Once he was in office, however, his *New Deal set off in energetic pursuit of relief, recovery, and reform. Unfortunately, a balanced budget was a philosophical and political necessity for Roosevelt as it was for Hoover. Thus the New Deal, for all its experimentation, employed deficit spending—the cure for the depression—timidly, with little result. In 1939 the unemployment rate was still 17.2 percent. Only the military buildup of 1940–41 made a dent in the depression. Politicians would tolerate deficit spending for national defense sooner than for social programs. As the military budget—and the deficits—mounted, the nation's economic engine restarted. In 1940 the unemployment rate was 14.6 percent, in 1941 it was 9.9 percent. By then, industrial production was 30 percent ahead of 1929 levels.

GREATEST GENERATION, name given in a book by television commentator Tom Brokaw to the generation of Americans that lived through the *Great Depression and *World War 2. Schematically, they were the parents of the *baby boom generation and the grandparents of *Generation X.

GREAT MIGRATION. See *Black Migrations.

GREAT SOCIETY. See Lyndon *Johnson Administration.

GREAT WHITE FLEET (1907–9), incident in the Theodore *Roosevelt administration. To test the navy's capability and impress the Japanese, Pres. Theodore Roosevelt dispatched 16 white-painted warships on a global voyage. The fleet sailed from Hampton Roads, Va., on Dec. 16, 1907, proceeded around South America through the Strait of Magellan, then from San Francisco crossed the Pacific to Japan, Australia, and New Zealand, and returned home through the Suez Canal, arriving at Hampton Roads on Feb. 22, 1909. The voyage of 46,000 miles was accomplished without a serious breakdown. At the time, the U.S. navy was ranked second in the world, the Japanese fifth.

GREENBACK LABOR PARTY. See *Greenback Party or Greenback Labor Party.

GREENBACK PARTY or **GREENBACK LABOR PARTY** (1876–84), political party organized during the hard times following the *Panic of 1873 (see *Agrarian Discontents) to repeal the *Specie Resumption Act (1875) and to increase the money supply, first by expanding the use of paper money (*greenbacks) and later by coining silver (see *Free Silver).

In 1876 the party's presidential nominee, New York industrialist and philanthropist Peter Cooper, won only 80,000 votes, in part because Republican and Democratic candidates in depressed agricultural areas endorsed the inflationary greenbacks. After the *railroad strikes of 1877, industrial workers joined the party, which in 1878 sent 14 greenbackers to Congress and many more to state legislatures. The party now adopted a broad range

of issues: limitation of hours of labor; Chinese exclusion; regulation of interstate commerce; and woman suffrage. But the temporary return of prosperity after 1879 caused the party to decline. James B. Weaver, its presidential candidate in 1880, won 300,000 votes; Benjamin F. Butler won only 175,000 in 1884, the last year the party fielded a presidential candidate.

GREENBACKS, paper money authorized by the *Legal Tender Act (1862) to help pay for the Civil War. Before that, there had been no federal paper money. The constitutional provision empowering Congress "to coin money" (Art. 1, sec. 8) was understood (correctly) to mean metallic money only, the Framers having for good reason abhorred paper money. The paper money that did circulate before the Civil War was banknotes, backed by the assets of the issuing banks. Greenbacks, however, were pure fiat money, required to be accepted as legal tender although unredeemable in specie (gold or silver). The printing of $450 million in greenbacks contributed to the inflation that doubled prices during the Civil War.

When the government undertook in 1866 to retire the greenbacks, strong public pressure developed to retain and expand them, since inflation was beneficial to farmers and debtors generally. A compromise was reached to keep $356 million of greenbacks in circulation. In 1871, the U.S. Supreme Court declared the Legal Tender Act constitutional, partially satisfying the demands of inflationists.

In the hard times that followed the *Panic of 1873, farmers demanded the issuance of more greenbacks as a means of sustaining commodity prices (see *Agrarian Discontents). The *Greenback Party, founded in 1876, took up the cause of expanding the money supply on behalf of farmers, small businessmen, and industrial workers. But the hard-money men triumphed in the *Specie Resumption Act (1875), which authorized the redemption of greenbacks in gold starting in 1879. Confidence in the government was so great that few greenbacks were redeemed. They remained in circulation, their value assured, but their number was not increased.

GREEN MOUNTAIN BOYS, irregular military companies formed around 1770 in the New Hampshire Grants (Vermont) to prevent the absorption of the region by New York. At stake were the land titles of settlers and speculators issued by New Hampshire and declared invalid by New York. Under the leadership of Ethan Allen, the Green Mountain Boys succeeded, by intimidation and violence, in keeping Vermont independent of New York.

At the start of the *Revolutionary War, Allen led a party of Green Mountain Boys in the capture of *Fort

Ticonderoga. A few months later, Congress incorporated a regiment of Green Mountain Boys into the Continental Army. Under Col. Seth Warner, the regiment participated in the *Quebec and *Saratoga campaigns, most notably at the battle of *Bennington.

GREEN v. COUNTY SCHOOL BOARD OF NEW KENT COUNTY (1968), unanimous decision of the *Warren Court rejecting a plausible freedom-of-choice response to the Court's school-desegregation order in *Brown v. Board of Education of Topeka (1954). New Kent County in Virginia, a rural, residentially integrated area, allowed students to attend either a formerly all-white or a formerly all-black school. No whites chose to attend the formerly all-black school, and only 15 percent of the black students chose to attend the formerly all-white school.

Justice William J. Brennan did not find freedom of choice unconstitutional except where its result, as in this instance, was to perpetuate a dual school system. *Brown*, Brennan declared, required a plan that "promise[d] realistically to convert promptly to a system without a 'white' school and a 'Negro' school, but just schools."

GRENADA INVASION (1983), incident in the *Reagan administration. On Oct. 19, 1983, a left-wing faction within the Grenadian government (which had come to power in a 1979 coup) overthrew its opponents and executed several of them. The nations of the Organization of Eastern Caribbean States (OECS) appealed to the United States to intervene.

Expressing concern for the safety of U.S. students on the island, Pres. Ronald Reagan ordered an invasion of Grenada on Oct. 25 by 6,000 American and 1,000 OECS troops supported by a U.S. carrier battle group. They were opposed by 750 Grenadian troops and 600 Cuban construction workers. Nineteen Americans died before resistance ended on Oct. 28. The United States vetoed a UN Security Council resolution condemning the invasion.

GRISWOLD v. CONNECTICUT (1965), 7–2 decision of the *Warren Court nullifying a Connecticut law prohibiting the use of contraceptives on the ground that it violated a right to privacy that, although not mentioned in the Constitution, was created by various guarantees in the *Bill of Rights.

Justice William O. Douglas, for the Court, pointed out other rights unmentioned in the Constitution that had been derived from those that were mentioned. For example: "The right of freedom of speech and press includes not only the right to utter or to print, but the right to dis-

tribute, the right to receive, the right to read and freedom of inquiry, freedom of thought, and freedom to teach—indeed the freedom of the entire university community."

"The foregoing cases," Douglas continued, "suggest that specific guarantees in the Bill of Rights have penumbras, formed by emanations from those guarantees that help give them life and substance. Various guarantees create zones of privacy. The right of association contained in the penumbra of the First Amendment is one, as we have seen. The Third Amendment in its prohibition against the quartering of soldiers 'in any house' in time of peace without the consent of the owner is another facet of that privacy. The Fourth Amendment explicitly affirms the 'right of the people to be secure in their persons, houses, papers, and effects, against unreasonable searches and seizures.' The Fifth Amendment in its Self-Incrimination Clause enables the citizen to create a zone of privacy which government may not force him to surrender to his detriment. The Ninth Amendment provides: 'The enumeration in the Constitution, of certain rights, shall not be construed to deny or disparage others retained by the people.' "

GUADALCANAL. See *World War 2.

GUADALUPE HIDALGO TREATY (1848), treaty between the United States and Mexico ending the *Mexican War. Signed Feb. 2, 1848, by the insubordinate Nicholas P. Trist, the American commissioner who had been recalled to Washington, it achieved all of Pres. James K. Polk's original objectives.

Mexico relinquished all claims to Texas above the Rio Grande and ceded to the United States California and New Mexico (territory comprising all present-day Texas, California, Nevada, and Utah, most of Arizona, New Mexico, and Colorado, and parts of Wyoming, Nebraska, and Oklahoma, a total of more than 900,000 square miles). For this territory the United States agreed to pay $15 million and to assume the claims of U.S. citizens against Mexico (worth $3 million). The U.S.-Mexican boundary was fixed at the Rio Grande to New Mexico, then along the Gila and Colorado rivers, and west between Upper and Lower California to the Pacific. (The present southern boundaries of Arizona and New Mexico were fixed by the *Gadsden Purchase in 1853.)

The treaty was ratified by the U.S. Senate on Feb. 27, by the Mexican congress on May 25, and proclaimed in effect by President Polk on July 4.

GUILFORD COURTHOUSE (Mar. 15, 1781), *Revolutionary War battle. Having withdrawn from North

Carolina after the battle of *Cowpens, Patriot general Nathanael Greene returned in March with 4,400 troops (mostly militia and volunteers) and established a sound defensive position at Guilford Courthouse. British general Charles Cornwallis, with 2,000 battle-tested veterans, was eager to give battle. "The Americans fought like Demons," Cornwallis testified. As on other occasions, Greene chose to preserve his army rather than risk a decisive defeat. He withdrew from the field in good order; the British, with casualties of nearly 25 percent, were unable to pursue. Cornwallis sought shelter for his exhausted army in Wilmington, N.C. Greene pushed on into South Carolina.

GULF OF TONKIN RESOLUTION (1964). See *Vietnam War.

GULF WAR (1991), episode in the George H. W. *Bush administration. Throughout the Iran-Iraq War (1980–88), the United States had befriended the brutal Iraqi dictator Saddam Hussein as a strategic check to Iranian fundamentalism and anti-Americanism. After the war it tolerated Saddam Hussein's human rights abuses and military buildup. When on Aug. 2, 1990, Iraq seized its small neighbor Kuwait and menaced oil-rich Saudi Arabia, a surprised Pres. George Bush vowed, "This will not stand."

At the behest of the United States, the United Nations imposed economic sanctions on Iraq to enforce its demand that Iraq withdraw from Kuwait. Bush, meanwhile, had determined upon a military response. While organizing a coalition of 43 nations, Bush sent 200,000 U.S. troops to defend Saudi Arabia (Operation Desert Shield), then (after the November elections) another 300,000. Other nations provided 150,000 more. The coalition forces were commanded by U.S. general Norman H. Schwarzkopf.

A UN Security Council resolution on Nov. 29, 1990, authorized the use of "all means necessary" if Iraq did not withdraw from Kuwait by Jan. 15, 1991. On Jan. 12, 1991, Congress approved Bush's request to use military force under UN auspices. When Iraq failed to comply with the UN ultimatum, the coalition launched a military offensive against Iraq and Kuwait (Operation Desert Storm) beginning with a five-week aerial assault. On Feb. 24, 1991, a massive ground attack drove forward to encircle Kuwait. Saddam Hussein had threatened the "mother of all battles," but the Iraqis were quickly routed. Having already ignited the Kuwaiti oil fields and befouled the Persian Gulf by spilling oil from offshore facilities, the Iraqis streamed north out of Kuwait under continuous air attack. Abruptly, after 100 hours, President Bush declared Kuwait liberated and called off the assault. On Feb. 27 Iraq accepted 12 UN Security Council resolutions as the basis for an end to the hostilities.

The coalition had suffered 240 battle casualties (148 American), the Iraqis more than 25,000. Saddam Hussein remained in power in Baghdad with sufficient military strength to crush a rebellion of Kurds in his north and another of Shiite Arabs in his south. The UN retained its economic sanctions against Iraq while investigators entered the country to dismantle its capacity to manufacture nuclear, chemical, and biological weapons of mass destruction.

GUN CONTROL. One of the profound effects of the frontier on American society is the widespread prevalence of gun ownership. In 1995, the U.S. Bureau of Alcohol, Tobacco, and Firearms reported that Americans owned 62 million shotguns, 66 million handguns, and 73 million rifles.

Classical political philosophy banned private justice and gave the state a monopoly of armed force. In England, however, standing armies and professional police forces were considered dangerous to individual liberty, which was thought best protected by an armed yeomanry (landowners). This tradition was carried to America and expressed in the Second Amendment to the U.S. Constitution, which confirms Americans' right "to keep and bear arms," although it justifies that right by the need to maintain a "well-regulated militia"—indeed, in the 18th century, "to bear arms" meant to serve in a military organization. That important qualification would seem to make the right "to keep and bear arms" less than absolute.

Guns are so much a part of American culture, however, that the U.S. Supreme Court has been reluctant to interfere. In the 19th century it ruled that the Second Amendment applied only to the federal government; the states were free to regulate gun ownership if they wished. The first federal regulation of gun ownership was the National Firearms Act of 1934, a product of *Prohibition, which restricted interstate traffic in sawed-off shotguns. This act was unanimously upheld by the Supreme Court in *United States v. Miller* (1935), the Court ruling that the Second Amendment protected the citizen's right to own only ordinary militia weapons. The only other Supreme Court action on gun control was a 1983 decision not to review a lower court's upholding of a village ordinance banning the possession of handguns.

The demand for more effective gun control usually rises in response to a sensational assassination or mass killing. The Omnibus Crime Control and Safe Streets Act (1968) followed the assassinations of Robert F. Kennedy and Martin Luther King Jr. that year. The Brady Gun Control Act (1993), named for presidential press secretary James S. Brady, who was permanently disabled in the attempt to assassinate Pres. Ronald Reagan in 1981, imposed a five-day waiting period for possession of a pistol or revolver bought from a licensed dealer during which the background of the purchaser could be checked for disqualifying information. (In 1997, the *Rehnquist Court struck down the provision of the Brady Act that required state officials to check the backgrounds of gun purchasers.) A 1994 anticrime act banning 19 types of semiautomatic assault weapons was easily circumvented by making minor alterations in the guns' designs. The great obstacle to meaningful gun control remained the National Rifle Association, a powerful lobby that few legislators dared oppose.

H

HABEAS CORPUS SUSPENSIONS (1861–65), incidents in the *Lincoln administration. A writ of habeas corpus is issued by a judge to bring a prisoner before him so he can decide if that prisoner is being legally detained. The U.S. Constitution prescribes (Art. 1, sec. 9), "The privilege of the writ of habeas corpus shall not be suspended, unless when in cases of rebellion or invasion the public safety may require it."

On Apr. 27, 1861, a week after a Baltimore mob attacked Union troops moving through that city, Pres. Abraham Lincoln suspended habeas corpus in the Washington area, thereby permitting the arrest by military authorities of persons thought to be disloyal and likely to interfere with the prosecution of the *Civil War. Those arrested at that time included the mayor and police chief of Baltimore; in September, nine members of the Maryland legislature were arrested to prevent that state from joining the Confederacy.

The arrest of John Merryman, a Southern sympathizer in Baltimore, led to a decision by Chief Justice Roger B. Taney in *Ex parte *Merryman* (1861) that Lincoln had acted unconstitutionally. Lincoln ignored the decision. On Sept. 24, 1862, and again on Sept. 15, 1863, Lincoln suspended habeas corpus "throughout the United States."

During the Civil War more than 15,000 people were arbitrarily arrested—spies and saboteurs in some cases, disloyal or defeatist citizens in others. They were usually held for several weeks, then released without trial. Because of these arrests, the Democratic opposition accused Lincoln of tyranny.

HALF-BREEDS. See *Stalwarts and Half-Breeds.

HAMILTON AND JEFFERSON. When Thomas Jefferson joined Washington's cabinet in March 1790 as secretary of state, the program of Secretary of the Treasury Alexander Hamilton was already far advanced. The relationship between the two men was at first amicable, but as Jefferson came to understand Hamilton's program he became intensely hostile to it. Toward Hamilton he came to feel profound suspicion and eventually hatred.

At its heart, the conflict between Hamilton and Jefferson was one between radically different visions of the kind of country the United States should be. Jefferson envisioned an idealized version of his native Virginia—a country inhabited by sturdy independent farmers deriving their modest wealth from the soil, prizing their natural liberties, deferentially selecting their governors from among their superior (and richer) neighbors. For Jefferson, this agrarian society had a moral object: it instilled such virtues as simplicity, frugality, honesty, republicanism, and patriotism. "The mobs of great cities," he wrote, "add just as much to the support of pure government, as sores do to the strength of the human body."

If Jefferson's vision was rural and agrarian, Hamilton's was urban and commercial, modeled very much on English lines. He was notorious for his belief that the British constitution was the best in the world. He even admired the corruption—the distribution by king and ministry of places, honors, and pensions in order to control Parliament—that made the British government effective. He recognized that the new financial institutions of burgeoning British capitalism vastly enlarged the government's resources. To create a similarly powerful government in the United States he proposed to transplant those British institutions to America: a funded national debt, held by a narrow class of bondholders; a national bank; excises and other federal taxes; active government encouragement of industrial development.

Jefferson viewed the *Hamilton system with horror. To him, nothing better illustrated its moral effects than the orgy of speculation that preceded Hamilton's consolidation and funding of the national debt. Believing that land alone was the source of wealth, Jefferson detested the people who made money by manipulating paper, who—he believed—stole wealth from its honest creators. These vulgar new "money men"—speculators, stock-jobbers, gamblers—were nothing like the cultivated and public-spirited Virginia gentry whom Jefferson knew. Their influence would lead to extremes of wealth and poverty, love of luxury, subservience to Britain, corruption, and ultimately monarchy.

Hamilton's success, made possible by Federalist majorities in Congress (see *Federalist Party) and the support of President Washington himself, drove Jefferson and his followers to unanticipated expedients. They succeeded in removing the new national capital to the banks of the Potomac, far from the money men of New York and Philadelphia. They developed a strict-constructionist reading of the Constitution that in time led them to the doctrine of *nullification. They initiated a newspaper war of remarkable ferocity against the government. They encouraged the formation of a political party (something hitherto foreign to republican ideology) in opposition to the government of which Jefferson himself was a member (see *Jeffersonian Republican Party). They made hatred of Britain and uncritical attachment to France the foundations of domestic as well as foreign policy.

The political differences and personal animosity between Jefferson and Hamilton dominated Washington's cabinet during the four years they were together. "Hamilton and myself were daily pitted in the cabinet like two cocks," Jefferson related. The situation was extremely unpleasant for him, and he longed to be permitted to retire. But Washington wanted both men to stay, perhaps to demonstrate that his government was above faction.

"How unfortunate," Washington wrote feelingly to Jefferson on Aug. 23, 1792, "and how much is it to be regretted then, that whilst we are encompassed on all sides with avowed enemies and insidious friends, that internal dissensions should be harrowing and tearing our vitals. . . . My earnest wish, and my fondest hope therefore is, that instead of wounding suspicions, and irritable charges, there may be liberal allowances, mutual forbearances, and temporizing yieldings on *all sides*."

A similar letter went to Hamilton. Both men promised to reconcile their differences, and both urged Washington to accept a second term since he was the only man who could hold the country together. Jefferson resigned from the cabinet on Dec. 31, 1793, Hamilton on Jan. 31, 1795.

HAMILTON-BURR DUEL. See *Burr-Hamilton Duel.

HAMILTON SYSTEM, fiscal program implemented in the *Washington administration. Alexander Hamilton, appointed secretary of the Treasury on Sept. 11, 1789, brought to the office a vision of economic development, of a dynamic America made strong by flourishing agriculture, commerce, and industry. It was a very different vision from that of the static agrarian society cherished by his colleague and rival, Secretary of State Thomas Jefferson (see *Hamilton and Jefferson).

Of the three prerequisites for realizing that vision—a strong national government, a sound public credit, and financial institutions supportive of development—the first was in place. To provide the other two, Hamilton proposed: (1) assumption by the national government of the states' war debts; (2) consolidation of these with the foreign and domestic debts inherited from the *Confederation; (3) funding of the consolidated debt—that is, exchanging new, interest-bearing debt certificates (bonds) for the old certificates at their face value; (4) establishment of a federal revenue, in specie, through tariffs, excises, and other taxes committed to payment of the interest on the debt; (5) establishment of a national bank to serve as the government's fiscal agent, to manage a stable currency, and to provide credit to entrepreneurs; (6) encouragement of the growth of a concentrated class of bondholders who would identify their interests with that of the national government and whose collective capital would form a pool of capital available for investment in new enterprises; and (7) systematic encouragement of industry by the federal government.

Hamilton's system—all but the last item—was in place by the end of 1791. In December 1791 Hamilton submitted to Congress his Report on Manufactures in which he proposed a combination of protective tariffs, subsidies, and premiums to expedite the development of particular manufactures. A financial panic in 1792, which only confirmed Jefferson and his followers in their conviction of the nefarious consequences of Hamilton's policies, prevented its acceptance.

HAMMER v. DAGENHART (1918), 5–4 decision of the *White Court overturning the Keating-Owen Child Labor Act of 1916 (see *Child Labor), which prohibited the transportation in interstate commerce of goods made by child labor. For the majority, Justice William Rufus Day argued: "The necessary effect of this act is . . . to regulate the hours of labor of children in factories and mines within the States, a purely state authority. Thus the act in a twofold sense is repugnant to the Court. It not only transcends the authority delegated to Congress over commerce, but also exerts a power as to a purely local matter to which the federal authority does not extend."

"[I]f an act is within the powers specifically conferred upon Congress," wrote Justice Oliver Wendell Holmes in dissent, "it seems to me that it is not made any less constitutional because of the indirect effects that it may have. . . . I should have thought that the most conspicuous decisions of this court had made it clear that the power to regulate commerce . . . could not be cut down or qualified by the fact that it might interfere with the carrying out of the domestic policy of any state. . . .

"[I]f there is any matter upon which civilized countries have agreed . . . it is the evil of premature and excessive child labor. I should have thought that if we were to introduce our own moral conceptions where, in my opinion, they do not belong, this was preeminently a cause for upholding the exercise of all its powers by the United States."

HAMPTON ROADS PEACE CONFERENCE (Feb. 3, 1865), secret meeting of Union and Confederate officials to end the *Civil War. Pres. Abraham Lincoln and Secretary of State William H. Seward represented the Union; Confederate vice president Alexander H. Stephens, Sen. Richard M. T. Hunter, and Assistant Secretary of War John A. Campbell represented the Confederacy. The meeting had been proposed by Francis P. Blair with the idea of restoring peace by common action against the French in Mexico. Confederate president Jefferson Davis went along with the proposal to discredit Confederate advocates of negotiation.

At the meeting, Lincoln proved inflexible, demanding national reunion, disbanding of Confederate armed forces, and Southern acceptance of emancipation. After four hours, the conference ended. Davis exploited the meeting by publicizing Lincoln's "humiliating" demand for unconditional surrender.

HANNA AND MCKINLEY. See *McKinley and Hanna.

HARDING ADMINISTRATION (1921–23). Republican Warren G. Harding, 29th president of the United States, alleged product of the *smoke-filled room, had been a small-town Ohio newspaper publisher and an undistinguished senator. A thoroughly commonplace person, he was ill at ease as president (although everyone commented that he looked the part), grateful for the distinction lent to his administration by Charles E. Hughes,

secretary of state, Andrew Mellon, secretary of the Treasury, and Herbert Hoover, secretary of commerce, but unable to control the corruption of the "Ohio gang" he brought to Washington with him.

Indeed, his brief administration is remembered chiefly for its corruption. Secretary of the Interior Albert B. Fall went to prison for his part in the *Teapot Dome Scandal; his coconspirator, Secretary of the Navy Edwin Denby, was forced to resign. Attorney General Harry M. Daugherty avoided jail but was dismissed for his illegal sale of liquor permits and pardons. The director of the Veterans Bureau, Charles R. Forbes, went to prison for the corrupt sale of government property. And the alien property custodian, Thomas W. Miller, went to jail for defrauding the government by selling German chemical patents.

On the other hand, it is to Harding's credit that he appointed the able Charles G. Dawes first director of the Bureau of the Budget and pardoned socialist Eugene V. Debs, who had served three years of a ten-year sentence in the Atlanta penitentiary for his opposition to U.S. participation in *World War I.

In foreign affairs, Harding made final U.S. refusal to enter the League of Nations (although he favored U.S. participation in the World Court), signed (July 2, 1921) without ceremony a separate peace treaty with Germany, and approved the *Fordney-McCumber Tariff (1922), which matched U.S. political isolation with economic isolation. The significant foreign policy achievement of his administration was the *Washington Naval Conference (1921–22), the work of Secretary of State Hughes, which committed the great powers to substantial naval disarmament while creating a variety of peacekeeping arrangements.

Inadequate to the demands of his office, and probably increasingly aware of the betrayal of his friends, Harding broke down under the strain. He died on Aug. 3, 1923, on a trip to Alaska and was succeeded by Vice Pres. Calvin Coolidge.

HARPERS FERRY RAID (1859). See *Brown's Career.

HARRISON (BENJAMIN) ADMINISTRATION (1889–93). Republican Benjamin Harrison, 23rd president of the United States, received fewer popular votes than his opponent, Democrat Grover Cleveland. But he was given a Congress (the 51st, 1889–91) with Republican majorities in both houses. With the House led by the dictatorial Thomas B. ("Czar") Reed (see *Cannonism), and encouraged by a persistent Treasury surplus, this Congress proceeded to legislate almost the entire 1888

Republican platform, earning the dubious title of the *Billion Dollar Congress.

Cold and aloof, Harrison believed in legislative supremacy and did not initiate legislation beyond recommendations contained in his speeches. Nevertheless, the 51st Congress, during the first two years of the Harrison administration, was one of the most productive of major legislation in history. The *McKinley Tariff (1890) raised tariff rates to new highs. The *Sherman Antitrust Act (1890) gratified but ultimately disappointed the growing numbers of people who demanded control of the burgeoning *trusts. The *Sherman Silver Purchase Act (1890) pleased Republican mining interests in the West without satisfying the demands of inflationists for *free silver. The *Dependent Pension Act (1890) doubled the number of Civil War pensioners. The Forest Reserve Act (1890) permitted the president to set aside timber areas as national parks; Harrison reserved 13 million acres (see *Conservation). The 51st Congress continued rapid construction of a modern *steel navy. A Federal Elections Bill, sponsored by Rep. Henry Cabot Lodge of Massachusetts to protect the voting rights of Southern blacks, provided for federal supervision of all congressional elections, with federal district courts settling disputed election procedures. This bill narrowly passed the House but failed to pass the Senate despite Harrison's support.

Harrison declared himself a friend of *civil service reform, and pleased reformers by appointing the energetic Theodore Roosevelt to the Civil Service Commission. But he replaced unprotected Democratic civil servants in almost the same high proportions as Grover Cleveland had replaced Republicans.

In foreign affairs, the United States in 1889 joined (with Germany and Great Britain) in a three-power protectorate over Samoa. That same year saw the convening in Washington of the first Inter-American Conference, long sought by Secretary of State James G. Blaine. In 1893 an international arbitration panel resolved the Bering Sea Fur-Seal Controversy (see *Sealing Controversies) with Great Britain against the United States. At the end of his term, Harrison submitted to the Senate a treaty annexing Hawaii (see *Hawaii Annexation). Renominated for president in 1888, Harrison was defeated by Grover Cleveland.

During the Harrison administration, North Dakota (1889), South Dakota (1889), Montana (1889), Washington (1889), Idaho (1890), and Wyoming (1890) became the 39th through 44th states.

HARTFORD CONVENTION (Dec. 15, 1814–Jan. 5, 1815), meeting of New England Federalists (see *Fed-

eralist Party) in Hartford, Conn., on the initiative of the Massachusetts legislature, to promote a "radical reform of the national compact" intended to restore New England's waning influence in the Union.

At the time of the Massachusetts summons, the *War of 1812 was dragging ignominiously on, New England commerce was at a standstill, the British navy was blockading the New England coast, and British troops occupied part of Maine. But Federalist grievances ran deeper than the conduct of the war. The Federalists were unhappy with successive Republican (see *Jeffersonian Republican Party) administrations (and consequent Republican patronage), with Republican policies hostile to commercial interests, with the Republicans' pro-French and anti-British foreign policy, with the disproportionate influence of slave states in the national government, with the admission of new states that altered the original balance of the Union, with the prominence of naturalized foreigners. Disaffection was so intense that talk of *nullification was common, and it was feared that the Hartford meeting would even call for secession.

The meeting, however, was dominated by moderates and contented itself with publishing a list of Federalist grievances and proposing seven constitutional amendments, including: representation and taxes to be apportioned according to the number of free persons in the states (abolishing the *Three-Fifths Clause that gave the slave states their disproportionate influence); a two-thirds vote of both houses of Congress required to admit a new state; naturalized persons to be ineligible for any office in the federal government; no second term for presidents, and no successive presidents from the same state.

The commissioners who carried the convention's resolutions to Washington arrived in the midst of celebrations occasioned by news of the battle of *New Orleans and the Treaty of *Ghent. They soon abandoned their mission, but the Federalist Party was now stigmatized as unpatriotic and its national influence was irretrievably lost.

HATCH ACT (1887), legislation of the first *Cleveland administration. It provided federal funds for the creation of state agricultural experiment stations.

HATCH ACT (1939), legislation of the Franklin *Roosevelt administration prohibiting partisan political activity by federal employees except those in policy-making positions. A 1940 amendment extended the act to state and local government employees paid in whole or in part with federal funds. The act originated in criticism of political activity by Works Progress Administration workers (see also *Anticommunism).

HAWAII ANNEXATION (1898). In January 1893 American sugar planters in Hawaii led by Sanford B. Dole, with the assistance of the U.S. minister and of marines from an offshore cruiser, overthrew the government of Queen Liliuokalani and established a provisional government with Dole as president. The U.S. minister recognized the new government and declared Hawaii a U.S. protectorate. Commissioners from the provisional government drafted a treaty of annexation that outgoing U.S. president Benjamin Harrison submitted to the Senate.

The new president, Grover Cleveland, withdrew the treaty and launched an investigation of recent events in the islands, discovering that the planters' revolution had not been supported by the Hawaiian people. A new minister was sent to Hawaii with instructions to restore Liliuokalani. Dole, however, would not step aside, and on July 4, 1894, he proclaimed the independent Republic of Hawaii. Not willing to use force, President Cleveland reluctantly recognized the republic on Aug. 7.

Cleveland's successor, William McKinley, was favorable to annexation and in 1897 submitted a new treaty, which was opposed for more than a year by anti-imperialists in the Senate (see *Anti-Imperialist League). Opinion changed during the *Spanish-American War, when the strategic value of the islands became apparent. To avoid defeat over the treaty, President McKinley sought annexation by a joint congressional resolution, which required only simple majorities in both houses of Congress rather than the two-thirds Senate vote required to ratify a treaty. Congress passed the resolutions on July 7, 1898. Hawaii became a territory of the United States with Dole as its governor.

HAWLEY-SMOOT TARIFF (1930), legislation of the *Hoover administration. The highest in American history, it was Congress's reflexive response to the deepening *Great Depression. A thousand economists petitioned Pres. Herbert Hoover not to sign the bill, pointing out that foreign countries could not pay their debts to the United States if they could not sell their products here. Hoover's orthodoxy, however, was unyielding. The tariff, which raised average rates on imports to 40 percent, provoked retaliatory measures abroad that brought U.S. foreign trade to a virtual halt.

HAY-BUNAU-VARILLA TREATY (1903). See *Panama Canal.

HAYES ADMINISTRATION (1877–81). Republican Rutherford B. Hayes, 19th president of the United States, was a distinguished soldier and three-term governor of Ohio, but he was widely perceived as having achieved the presidency by fraud (see *Compromise of 1877). He further weakened himself by announcing at the start that he would not seek a second term. With the House of Representatives in Democratic hands, there was little Hayes could accomplish.

The two important issues facing his administration were *reconstruction and *civil service reform. Hayes honored the Compromise of 1877, withdrawing federal troops from the South and bringing an end to the period of Reconstruction. Eager to conciliate the South, he promised white Southerners that there would be no further federal coercion if they would treat the black freedmen fairly. Southerners ignored this condition but Hayes nevertheless abandoned the Republican commitment to defending the freedmen. His policy divided the Republican Party into *Stalwarts and Half-Breeds, the former faction opposed to conciliating the South, the latter favoring conciliation.

Hayes proclaimed himself a supporter of civil service reform and conscientiously sought to place able men in major positions, but he disappointed reformers by rewarding the politicians who had been responsible for his election. He replaced the top managers of the New York customshouse, a federal office rich in patronage and corruption, with men independent of the state's Republican boss, Sen. Roscoe Conkling, thereby reclaiming a measure of presidential authority that had been significantly diminished by a Congress dominated first by *Radical Republicans and then by party bosses like Conkling.

Hayes had little comprehension of the social and economic forces that were rapidly changing the country. He had no cure for the depression that followed the *Panic of 1873 except to cling to the gold standard. Hostile to silver coinage, he vainly vetoed the *Bland-Allison Act (1878) and welcomed in 1879 the redemption of *greenbacks with gold in conformity with the *Specie Resumption Act (1875). Although not unsympathetic to laboring people, he used federal troops to suppress the *railroad strikes of 1877.

In foreign affairs, Hayes vetoed a congressional measure that would have unilaterally abrogated the *Burlingame Treaty (1868), which permitted Chinese laborers to immigrate, and directed Secretary of State William M. Evarts to negotiate the U.S.-China Treaty of 1881 that restricted but did not bar Chinese immigration (see *Chinese Exclusion). In 1880, when a French company was attempting to build a canal across the Isthmus of Panama (see *Panama Canal), Hayes told Congress: "The policy of this country is a canal under American control. The United States cannot consent to the surrender of this control to any European power or to any combination of powers."

Hayes was succeeded by Republican James A. Garfield.

HAY-HERRÁN TREATY (1903). See *Panama Canal.

HAYMARKET RIOT (May 4, 1886), incident during an *anarchist rally in Chicago's Haymarket Square to protest the police shooting the previous day of strikers at the McCormick Harvesting Machine Co. Some 1,300 people attended, listened to speeches, then started to leave when rain began. Three hundred remained when 180 police arrived and demanded that they disperse. At that moment a bomb exploded among the police, who then opened fire on the crowd. Seven policemen and four civilians were killed and many wounded.

In the following days, hundreds of known radicals were arrested. Eight anarchists (seven of them German immigrants) were tried for conspiracy; seven were sentenced to hang, the eighth to a long prison term. One of the condemned men committed suicide in prison, two had their sentences commuted to life imprisonment. On Nov. 11 the remaining four were executed. In 1893 Illinois governor John Peter Altgeld pardoned the three survivors.

HAY-PAUNCEFOTE TREATY (1901). See *Panama Canal.

HAYWOOD TRIAL (1907), trial of William D. "Big Bill" Haywood for the murder of Frank R. Steunenberg, former governor of Idaho. Steunenberg died in a bomb blast on Dec. 30, 1905, presumably in retaliation for having ordered the National Guard to put down a strike of the *Western Federation of Miners (WFM) in the Coeur d'Alene district in 1899. Harry Orchard, a professional terrorist employed by the union, was arrested and confessed that he had planted the bomb at the instigation of Haywood and two other WFM officers. These three were kidnapped in Denver and taken to Boise for trial. Haywood was tried first. William E. Borah, newly elected U.S. senator, was appointed special prosecutor; Haywood's defense was conducted by Chicago lawyer Clarence Darrow. The trial, which attracted national attention, ended on July 28, 1907, with Haywood's acquittal.

HEAD START. See *Elementary and Secondary Education Act (1965).

HEALTH INSURANCE. Before World War 1, American social reformers, having studied the comprehensive social insurance programs instituted in Germany and Great Britain, developed plans for compulsory, government-sponsored health insurance for industrial workers to be paid for by the states, employers, and the workers themselves. The debates inspired by this proposal foreshadowed the debates over all future health insurance proposals: Should health insurance be universal, compulsory, and provided by the government or partial, voluntary, and private? How should universal health insurance—or the cost of caring for the uninsured—be paid for? Following are some milestones—chiefly failed legislative initiatives—in the evolution of health care financing policy:

1921   The Shephard-Towner Act provided federal funds to state health departments for maternal and child-care programs.

1930s   Rise of Blue Cross and Blue Shield, private, voluntary, nonprofit insurance plans whereby all members of the same community paid at the same rate rather than at rates proportionate to their medical risk. Benefits were paid directly to hospitals and physicians.

1935   The Social Security Act included maternal, child-care, and crippled children programs, authorized grants to states for public health research, and financed continuing study of medical care. Health insurance was excluded from the act because of the opposition of organized medicine.

1935–45 Rise of prepaid cooperative group medical practices (health maintenance organizations, or HMOs), most prominently the Kaiser-Permanente Medical Care Program in California and the Health Insurance Plan of New York. These were opposed by medical societies because they limited the autonomy of physicians.

1939   The Wagner Bill and the Wagner-Murray-Dingle Bill (1943) proposed universal government-sponsored health insurance.

1946   The Hill-Burton Act provided low-cost, government-insured loans to build hospitals.

1947   The Wagner Bill proposed state programs of medical care for the needy, compulsory health insurance for workers and their dependents, and free choice of physicians and hospitals.

1960   The Kerr-Mills Act made federal funds available to the states to enable them to provide medical care to low-income aged persons who were ineligible for old-age assistance.

1961 The King-Anderson-Javits Bill anticipated Medicare by proposing nonmeans-tested medical benefits for the elderly.

1965 Medicare, hospital insurance for the aged, and Medicaid, medical insurance for the poor, were established (see *Social Security; *Welfare).

1971 The Kennedy-Griffiths Bill proposed compulsory universal medical coverage financed by payroll and income taxes.

1973 A Comprehensive Health Insurance Program was proposed by the Nixon administration for voluntary health insurance for working people, the poor, the unemployed, and the elderly.

1974 The Long-Ribicoff Bill proposed federal insurance for medical catastrophes.

1974 The Kennedy-Mills Bill was a more conservative version of the Kennedy-Griffiths Bill.

1980s Crisis of escalating medical care costs, accompanied by growing numbers of uninsured or inadequately insured people. People who lost jobs in corporate "downsizing" lost their group medical insurance as well and rarely could afford the cost of an individual policy. If they had a "preexisting condition," they could not buy insurance at any price. In the expanding service sector, where low-paying jobs were the norm, health insurance was a rarity.

1994 The Clinton plan, developed by a commission headed by Hillary Rodham Clinton, was based on universal, mandated coverage. While compelling participation, it tried to take advantage of free-market mechanisms rather than government control by requiring the formation of large regional groups or "alliances" of employers and consumers that could choose from a variety of plans offered by providers, using their size and economic power to negotiate optimum terms. The regulations required by compulsory universal coverage made the plan seem incomprehensible and unworkable. Its rejection was a major setback for the new Clinton administration.

1999 Medicaid and Medicare were expanded to enable people with disabilities to return to work without losing their health insurance benefits.

1999 In response to protests against abuses of "managed care," wherein insurance companies rejected physicians' recommendations and referrals to control costs, the House of Representatives passed a sweeping bill to control the managed-care industry and to protect patients' rights—most significantly, opening up managed-care companies to lawsuits.

2001 The Senate passed the Kennedy-Edwards-McCain "patient's bill of rights," which provided patients who had private health insurance or Medicare guaranteed access to specialty care, emergency care, and necessary drugs as well as independent medical reviews of decisions denying claims. It also created a right to sue the insurer for injuries.

2001 The United States remained the only industrialized country that did not provide some form of universal health coverage for its citizens. Some 41.2 million people—including 10 million children—were without private or government medical insurance.

HEART OF ATLANTA MOTEL v. UNITED STATES (1964), unanimous decision of the *Warren Court upholding the public-accommodations sections of the *Civil Rights Act of 1964. In the *Civil Rights Cases* (1883), the Court had overturned the very similar *Civil Rights Act of 1875, which had been based on the *14th Amendment. That amendment, the Court had ruled, prohibited state, not private, discrimination.

The Civil Rights Act of 1964, however, was based on the Commerce Clause. When the Heart of Atlanta Motel—which drew 75 percent of its guests from out of state—challenged the act on the grounds that Congress had exceeded its power under the Commerce Clause, Justice Tom Clark replied, "The commerce power invoked here by the Congress is a specific and plenary one authorized by the Constitution itself." "[T]he power of Congress to promote interstate commerce," he explained, "also includes the power to regulate the local incidents thereof, including local activities in both the States of origin and destination, which might have a substantial and harmful effect upon that commerce. . . . [Thus] Congress may—as it has—prohibit racial discrimination by motels serving travelers, however 'local' their operations may appear."

HENRY'S "LIBERTY OR DEATH" SPEECH (Mar. 23, 1775), speech by patriot Patrick Henry, the "forest Demosthenes," to the Virginia revolutionary convention at Richmond in support of resolutions calling for the colony's military readiness.

Its peroration has a permanent place in anthologies of

American patriotic literature: "Gentlemen may cry, peace, peace—but there is no peace. The war is actually begun! The next gale that sweeps down from the north will bring to our ears the clash of resounding arms! Our brethren are already in the field! Why stand we here idle? What is it that gentlemen wish? What would they have? Is life so dear, or peace so sweet, as to be purchased at the price of chains and slavery? Forbid it, Almighty God! I know not what course others may take; but as for me, . . . give me liberty or give me death!"

There is no manuscript copy, stenographic report, or contemporary version of the speech. It was reconstructed by William Wirt in his biography of Henry published 40 years later.

HEPBURN ACT (1906). See *Railroad Regulation.

HINDENBURG CRASH (May 6, 1937). During 1936, the 830-foot dirigible *Hindenburg*, the pride of Nazi Germany, made ten round trips carrying passengers between Germany and the United States and promised to make transatlantic passenger service routine. On its first crossing in 1937, however, the hydrogen-filled *Hindenburg* caught fire and crashed as it approached its mooring tower at the Lakehurst, N.J., Naval Air Station on May 6. Thirty-six passengers and crew died. The event put an end to dirigible development.

HIPPIES. See *Counterculture.

HISPANIC-AMERICANS, U.S. residents of any race whose origins are the Spanish-speaking countries of Latin America and Europe. The 2000 Census counted 35.3 million Hispanics, 12.5 percent of the total population and the country's largest minority.

Of the 2000 Hispanic population, Hispanics of Mexican origin constituted 58.4 percent, of Central and South American origin 28.3 percent, of Puerto Rican origin 9.6 percent (the population of Puerto Rico itself is not counted in the U.S. Hispanic population), of Cuban origin 3.4 percent. Two-thirds of all Hispanic-Americans were immigrants or the children of immigrants. A third were not citizens. Thirty-five percent of Hispanic-Americans were under 18, compared to 26 percent of the total U.S. population.

Mexicans resident in Texas and the present U.S. Southwest became U.S. citizens when those areas were absorbed by the United States in 1845 and 1848. By 1920 only about 750,000 immigrants from Mexico, the Caribbean, and other parts of Latin America had entered the United States. The United States imposed no restrictions on *immigration from Western Hemisphere countries until 1965, when the immigration act of that year established a ceiling of 120,000 immigrants for the Western Hemisphere and set quotas for individual countries.

Immigration from Latin America increased rapidly. In the 1980s, 3.5 million Latin Americans entered the United States, 47 percent of the total immigration. In 1998, more than 131,000 immigrants were admitted from Mexico alone, constituting the largest immigrant stream. There are, moreover, an estimated 2.7 million undocumented Mexican aliens living in the United States. Mexicans have concentrated in California, Texas, and Illinois, Puerto Ricans and Dominicans in New York, Cubans in Florida.

In 1999, the median income of Hispanic families was $31,663, compared to $51,224 for white families. The poverty rate for Hispanic individuals was 22.8, compared to 9.8 for whites. In 2000, 57 percent of Hispanics 25 and older had completed high school and 10.6 percent had completed college. In 1990, the National Opinion Research Center at the University of Chicago reported that, of 33 U.S. ethnic groups studied, Mexicans and Puerto Ricans (the only Hispanic groups studied) ranked 32nd and 33rd respectively in household income and 31st and 32nd in years of schooling; they were rated 32nd and 33rd in "social standing."

HISS CASE (1948–50), perjury trials of Alger Hiss, a former State Department official accused of membership in the Communist Party and of espionage on behalf of the Soviet Union. His accuser was Whitaker Chambers, an editor of *Time* magazine and a confessed former communist spy. Whereas Hiss was tall, affable, and self-assured, Chambers was short and plump, dressed in rumpled clothes, his hesitant speech suggesting an introverted and conflicted personality. In the country at large, the case pitted the liberal middle class, for whom Hiss was the paragon of the well-born, Ivy League–educated New Dealer, against conservatives of both parties who were increasingly fearful of communist subversion and distrustful of the nation's liberal leadership.

The case began on Aug. 3, 1948, when Chambers, testifying before the *House Committee on Un-American Activities, mentioned Hiss as one of several members of an underground communist cell to which he had belonged in the 1930s. Hiss, then president of the Carnegie Endowment for International Peace in New York, demanded an opportunity to refute the accusation. Before the committee—whose questioning was led by freshman representative Richard M. Nixon of California—Hiss denied knowing Chambers, despite Chambers's intimate knowledge of the Hiss household at that time. Finally, at a dramatic confrontation in a New York hotel room arranged by Nixon, Hiss recognized Chambers as George Crosley, an unemployed journalist he had befriended. Hiss thereupon challenged Chambers to repeat his accusations in a forum where he would not be protected against a suit for libel. Chambers obliged on the Aug. 30 broadcast of the national radio program *Meet the Press*, and Hiss promptly sued.

Chambers had not yet accused Hiss of espionage, but at pretrial hearings in November he produced State Department documents that he said Hiss had given him in 1937 and 1938 for transmission to the Soviet Union. From a hollowed-out pumpkin in the garden behind his Maryland farmhouse, he also produced three rolls of microfilm containing additional documents copied on an old Woodstock typewriter once owned by Hiss. In December, a New York grand jury indicted Hiss on two counts of perjury, the statute of limitations on espionage having run out.

Hiss went on trial in the U.S. district court in New York on May 31, 1949 In six weeks of testimony, Hiss and Chambers repeated their contradictory stories, Hiss denying that he had ever passed State Department documents to Chambers and explaining the documents typed on his Woodstock typewriter as "typewriter forgery." Two Supreme Court justices and other jurists, a former and a future Democratic presidential candidate, and a number of State Department officials testified to Hiss's good character. On July 8, the trial ended in a hung jury that had voted 8–4 for conviction.

A second trial, from Nov. 7, 1949, to Jan. 21, 1950, ended in Hiss's conviction. Sentenced to five years' imprisonment and fined $10,000, Hiss served 44 months in the federal prison at Lewisburg, Pa. For the remainder of his life (he died in 1996 at 92) he continued to insist on his innocence, but careful examination of an ever-growing body of evidence has caused historians to vindicate Chambers. Meanwhile, having established a reputation as a dogged anticommunist, Richard M. Nixon went on to become vice president and president of the United States. Chambers wrote an anguished and profoundly antiliberal autobiography, *Witness* (1952).

HOBKIRK'S HILL (Apr. 25, 1781), *Revolutionary War battle. From *Guilford Courthouse, Patriot general Nathanael Greene, with a much diminished force, proceeded into South Carolina and encamped at Hobkirk's Hill, near Camden. There he was attacked by 900 British regulars and Loyalists commanded by Francis Rawdon. The Patriots performed poorly, and Greene was forced to retreat. Nevertheless, the British soon gave up Camden. "We fight, get beat, rise, and fight again," Greene wrote after Hobkirk's Hill.

HO CHI MINH TRAIL. See *Vietnam War.

HOLLYWOOD TEN (1947), ten motion picture writers, producers, and directors who in 1947 refused to tell the *House Committee on Un-American Activities whether they were or had been communists. All served short prison terms and then were blacklisted by the industry for many years. They were: Ring Lardner Jr., John Howard Lawson, Alvah Bessie, Dalton Trumbo, Samuel Ornitz, Lester Cole, Albert Maltz, Herbert Biberman, Adrian Scott, and Edward Dmytryk.

HOLOCAUST RESPONSE. The Holocaust (1942–45), the extermination by Nazi Germany and its collaborators of 6 million Jews during World War 2, was preceded by eight years of official anti-Semitism in Germany beginning with the accession of Adolf Hitler to the chancellorship in January 1933. Between 1933 and 1941, Nazi policy aimed at the pauperization and emigration of Germany's thousand-year-old Jewish community. Jews were stripped of their citizenship and civil rights, expelled from government service and the professions, denied opportunities for education and employment, and had their businesses and property confiscated.

When Germany invaded the Soviet Union in June 1941, *Einzatsgruppen*—special killing squads following in the wake of the army—murdered Jews in the captured territories. The "final solution to the Jewish problem," in Nazi terminology, was launched at a meeting of high-ranking Nazis in the Berlin suburb of Wannsee in January 1942. Finding that shooting was too slow, the Nazis secretly built death camps in Poland such as Auschwitz and Treblinka to which Jews were transported from all parts of Nazi-occupied Europe. At the camps, they were moved with assembly-line efficiency from freight cars to gas chambers and thence to crematoria. So determined were the Nazis on completing the extermination of the Jews that until the very end of the war—long after they had recognized that the war was lost—they continued to devote scarce military and transportation resources to the task.

Throughout the years of persecution and extermination, Americans resolutely closed their doors to the victims. Racked during the 1930s by the Great Depression, they opposed all immigration as threatening to deprive Americans of jobs. But it is also true that the country was pervasively anti-Semitic. The national origins quota system adopted in 1924 (see *Immigration) to stem the flow of immigrants from Southern and Eastern Europe—many of whom were Jewish—was one reflection of this attitude. German Jews seeking to emigrate during the period of persecution found few countries willing to accept them. The U.S. State Department so effectively obstructed the issuing of visas to refugees that only small fractions of the German quota—26,000 per year—were filled between 1933 and 1937 and only a third of these immigrants were Jews. The greatest concession that the United States would make at the unsuccessful Evian conference—called by the United States to deal with the problem of "political refugees"—that met in France in July 1938 was to admit refugees from Germany and Austria up to the quota limits for those countries. In the 11 years from 1933 to 1943, when worldwide immigration quotas totaled 1.6 million, barely half a million immigrants entered the United States; of these, 138,000 were Jewish refugees.

When the first reports of the Holocaust reached the United States in 1942, the State Department suppressed them pending verification. But even when verified, the news received little media attention. Americans were understandably skeptical of stories of war atrocities. In any case, winning the war was the first priority; no resources could be spared to rescue potential victims, halt or interrupt the killing, or relieve Jews living in refugee camps. The **War Refugee Board**, established by executive order in January 1944 but funded in large part by American Jewish organizations, is credited with saving the lives of several hundred thousand Jews and other refugees, chiefly in Eastern Europe. One small project was the transportation in 1944 of 984 refugees—most of them Jews—from Italian detention camps to internment in an abandoned army camp at Oswego, N.Y., with the understanding that they would be repatriated after the war. Technically, these refugees were never in the United States but in a "free port."

The horrors of the Holocaust were at last revealed and publicized when Allied armies liberated concentration camps and death camps in Central and Eastern Europe in the spring of 1945. On Apr. 15, 1945, radio correspondent Edward R. Murrow reported on his visit to newly liberated Buchenwald, a slave-labor camp in southern Germany that housed prisoners of many nationalities, including Jews. Its horrors beggared description. "I pray you to believe what I have said about Buchenwald," Murrow implored his American listeners. "If I've offended you by this rather mild account . . . I'm not in the least sorry."

Still there was little response. Preoccupied by the problems and prospects of the coming peace, Americans could not comprehend the meaning of an event that so fundamentally challenged the principles of Western civilization. Little concern was expressed for Holocaust survivors, who could not return to their homelands, were barred from Palestine, and were unwelcome everywhere else. Sheltered in camps maintained by American Jewish relief organizations, many continued to die of disease and malnutrition.

In 1946 Pres. Harry S. Truman expedited the immigration to the United States of 40,000 "displaced persons" (a minority of them Jewish) under existing quotas. The Stratton Displaced Persons Act of 1948 gave immigration priority not to Holocaust survivors but to refugees from communist regimes (regardless of their wartime sympathies). Of the 220,000 displaced persons admitted to the United States under the first two years of the Stratton Act, only 2,500 were Holocaust survivors. Altogether, an estimated 250,000 Jewish refugees from Nazism eventually reached safety in the United States.

Fifty years later, the Holocaust was being studied in dozens of American colleges and universities. American churches, banks, industrial corporations, and even art museums were beginning to confront their roles in it. Their complicity ranged from the silence of the churches, to banks' trading in looted Nazi gold, to industrial corporations' profiting from the slave labor used by German subsidiaries, to museums' acquisition of artworks stolen from Holocaust victims. In 1993 a U.S. Holocaust Memorial Museum opened in Washington, D.C.

HOMESTEAD ACT (1862). See *Public Lands.

HOMESTEAD STRIKE (1892), strike of the Amalgamated Association of Iron and Steel Workers against the Carnegie Steel Co. in Homestead, Pa. Determined to break the union, plant manager Henry Clay Frick on July 2 locked out the skilled union men, whereupon the entire workforce struck. Frick summoned 300 *Pinkerton guards, who arrived by barge on July 6 and were met by 10,000 strikers. In the ensuing battle, nine strikers and seven Pinkertons were killed. A week later the arrival of 8,000 state militia enabled Frick to reopen the plant with strikebreakers. Public sympathy was with the strikers until an anarchist, Alexander Berkman, attempted on July 23 to assassinate Frick. The strike ended on Nov. 20 with the union destroyed and the men working longer hours at reduced wages.

HOOVER ADMINISTRATION (1929–33). Republican Herbert Hoover, 31st president of the United States, was a self-made millionaire who, as secretary of commerce in two previous administrations, had been recognized as the ablest member of the cabinet. Nevertheless, the "great engineer" was suspected by his own party of having been infected by *progressivism. And indeed he began his administration with a flurry of activity affecting the civil service, prison reform, conservation, child welfare, civil liberties, and racial justice. In a progressive mode, he appointed commissions to study law enforcement (see *Prohibition), education, and the administration of the public domain.

The *Panic of 1929 may not have surprised Hoover (he had warned against the dangers of speculation), but the onset of the *Great Depression certainly did, and here his true commitment to orthodox laissez-faire, individualism, and voluntarism was revealed. He believed that periodic economic slumps were natural and self-correcting. Not understanding the underlying causes or the depth of this one, he thought the cure lay simply in restoring business confidence, and this he attempted to do both by optimistic pronouncements and by appointing numerous (and ultimately futile) committees of business leaders to restart the economic engine.

Believing that business confidence required a high tariff and a balanced budget, he accepted the *Hawley-Smoot Tariff of 1930, which brought U.S. foreign trade to a virtual halt, and abandoned an early interest in job-creating public works. Fearing that it would destroy the self-reliance of the unemployed, he refused to provide federal relief, wrongly supposing that state agencies and private charities were adequate to the task. But moral scruples did not prevent him from providing federal aid to banks and other financial institutions through the *Reconstruction Finance Corporation.

Other legislation of the Hoover administration included the Agricultural Marketing Act of 1929, under which a Federal Farm Board bought up agricultural surpluses in a futile attempt to stabilize prices (see *Farm Problem) and the *Norris–La Guardia Act of 1932, which finally banned the use of injunctions in labor disputes. The *20th ("lame duck") Amendment was passed in 1932 and ratified in 1933.

In foreign affairs, the Hoover Moratorium of 1931 on intergovernmental payments temporarily eased the international economic crisis (see *War Debts). The United States participated in the 1930 London Naval Conference, which revised a treaty negotiated at the *Washington Naval Conference to permit Japan to enlarge its fleet. In 1932 the *Stimson Doctrine denied recognition to Japanese territorial gains in the Far East.

Hoover's unpopularity grew with the deepening of the depression. He contributed to it not only by his doctrinaire inaction but by his failure to empathize with the suffering of the depression's victims. This was particularly evident in his hostility toward the *Bonus Army. The Republicans had no choice but to renominate Hoover in 1932, but the contrast in the presidential campaign between the Democratic candidate, the ebullient Franklin Roosevelt, and the glum, despairing, and even angry Hoover only ensured his defeat.

HOOVER COMMISSION (1947–48), initiative of the *Truman administration. Responding to Pres. Harry S. Truman's desire to reorganize the executive branch for efficiency and economy, Congress in 1947 established a bipartisan Commission on Organization of the Executive Branch of the Government, and Truman invited former president Herbert Hoover to be its chairman. Some 70 percent of the commission's recommendations were adopted. Hoover chaired a similar commission in the Eisenhower administration, but its recommendations were not so well received.

HOOVER MORATORIUM (1931). See *War Debts.

HORSESHOE BEND. See *Creek War.

HOUSE COMMITTEE ON UN-AMERICAN ACTIVITIES (HUAC) (1938–75), special committee of the House of Representatives authorized on May 26, 1938, to investigate fascist and communist subversion in the United States (see *Anticommunism). Under its first chairman, conservative Democrat Martin Dies of Texas, the committee concentrated instead on *New Deal liberals, whom it often accused of being communists or communist dupes. It compiled lists of 640 organizations (including the *American Civil Liberties Union and the Boy Scouts of America), 438 newspapers, and 280 labor groups as possible communist fronts. The committee achieved its greatest notoriety when it investigated alleged communist infiltration into the motion picture industry in 1947 (see *Hollywood Ten) and the *Hiss case in 1948.

In 1953–54 HUAC was overshadowed by the activities of the Permanent Subcommittee on Investigations of the Senate Committee on Government Operations, headed by Republican senator Joseph R. McCarthy of Wisconsin (see *McCarthyism). HUAC was made a standing committee of the House in 1945, renamed the House Internal Security Committee in 1969, and abolished in 1975.

HOUSING. In 1937, Pres. Franklin Roosevelt observed "one-third of a nation ill-housed, ill-clad, ill-fed." Sixty-five years later, the perennial "housing problem" looked quite different. More than 80 percent of the nation's 99.5 million year-round housing units had been built since 1940. One result was that the large proportion of substandard housing in the 1930s—units without plumbing or kitchens, overcrowded, or in serious disrepair—had shrunk to very low numbers. Indeed, the quality of housing was now measured by neighborhood conditions rather than the condition of the unit itself. On the other hand, increasing numbers of Americans were experiencing an unfamiliar form of housing deprivation— excessively costly housing that consumed a disproportionately large share of their incomes.

Housing the Affluent. In the last 65 years, the majority of Americans ceased to be renters and became home owners. In 1940, fewer than half (43.6 percent) of the nation's occupied housing units were owner-occupied; in 2000, 67.7 percent were. This change reflected the value Americans placed on home ownership for its privacy, independence, and social status. Their ideal was the single-family house on its own plot of ground—the most costly and inefficient of all types of housing. Of all year-round occupied units in 2000, nearly two-thirds were single-family detached houses.

A major cause of this phenomenon was government encouragement not only of home ownership but of ownership of single-family houses. Committed to the idea that widespread home ownership was socially desirable, the federal government encouraged it through mortgage guarantees, credit, tax incentives, highway building, and other policies. Its bias in favor of building new houses rather than rehabilitating old contributed to the creation of burgeoning suburbs and the neglect of older housing in central cities.

Because of rising demand from the *baby boom generation, and reduced government funding for low- and moderate-income housing, the cost of housing in the 1980s began to surpass the increase in median family income. Rents rose faster than the cost of living. In 2002, a congressionally appointed Millennial Housing Commission reported that the housing shortage was as severe as in the immediate postwar years.

Housing the Poor. Traditionally, the housing needs of middle- and upper-income families, both owners and renters, were adequately met by the housing market. The market also met the needs of the poor, although less adequately: low-income families often occupied older dwellings relinquished by upper-income families. By 2000, the situation had changed dramatically. Housing costs taxed the resources of middle-income families, and the cost of new housing rapidly passed beyond the reach

of all but a fraction of American families. Meanwhile, the scarcity of standard-quality units had caused good older housing to appreciate rather than decline in value and so remain beyond the reach of low-income families. Without government subsidies, private developers had no incentive to build housing for the poor.

With the Housing Act of 1937, the federal government began sharing with local agencies the cost of **public housing** for low-income families. The favored model was "projects" of high-rise buildings in parklike settings to be occupied by the working poor as well as the welfare poor. Limited financing resulted in poor construction and early disrepair. Over time, preference was given to the welfare poor over the working poor, with the result that the projects concentrated and segregated the very poorest people and were soon made uninhabitable by crime, drugs, and vandalism. A number of major projects, considered beyond salvage, had to be destroyed.

As enthusiasm for public housing declined, alternative models were tried—low-rise, less isolated buildings, mixed projects where the market rents of some tenants subsidized the rents of low-income tenants. For a time, vouchers enabled clients to seek their own housing, paying the landlord 30 percent of their incomes while the housing agency paid the balance. Congress ceased funding for vouchers in 1995. In 2000, only 28 percent of the poor lived in public housing or received rent subsidies.

Meanwhile, the rental housing stock available to poor people shrank rapidly. On any given night, perhaps 300,000 Americans were homeless in 2000.

Housing Discrimination. Discrimination in housing was first made illegal by the *Civil Rights Act of 1866, which declared that all citizens, regardless of race or color, should have the same right to inherit, purchase, lease, sell, hold, or convey real and personal property. But this act was not enforced, and in 1883 the U.S. Supreme Court excluded these and other rights from constitutional protection when it ruled that the *14th Amendment prohibited only discriminatory state action, not discriminatory private action.

Consistent with the view of the constitutionality of private discrimination, the Court in 1948 held that private restrictive covenants (by which property owners in a community agreed not to sell to persons of a particular race or religion) were constitutionally permissible though not enforceable in the courts, since that would cloak them with state protection. Not until 1968 did the Supreme Court reverse its 1883 decision when it ruled that an owner's refusal to sell a publicly advertised house to an African-American was a violation of the Civil Rights Act of 1866.

States began to pass fair-housing laws in the 1950s. The *Civil Rights Act of 1964 forbade discrimination under any program receiving federal assistance, including housing subsidies, urban-renewal and community-development funds, and mortgage insurance. The Fair Housing Act of 1968 barred discrimination in the sale or rental of housing based on race, color, religion, sex, or national origin, exempting units bought directly from the owner or rented in an owner-occupied house. The enforcement provisions of the act were weak, and landlords and real-estate agents evaded them with impunity. The Fair Housing Act of 1988 significantly increased the government's enforcement powers while adding the handicapped and families with young children to the protected groups.

Although the law prohibited racial discrimination, it did not prohibit economic discrimination. By zoning residential areas for large lots and single-family houses, suburban communities effectively excluded the poor (and black). In 1976 the Supreme Court ruled that federal courts could require the introduction of public housing only in communities that had violated antidiscrimination statutes. But in 1977 it found that a Chicago suburb had not violated the Constitution when it refused to rezone to permit the building of low-income housing because its intention—to preserve the community's low-density character—had not been discriminatory.

HUGHES COURT (1930–41), the U.S. Supreme Court under Chief Justice Charles Evans Hughes. Despite the *Great Depression, Chief Justice Hughes and Associate Justice Owen Roberts, both appointed by Pres. Herbert Hoover in 1930, joined four conservative sitting justices—Willis Van Devanter, James C. McReynolds, George Sutherland, and Pierce Butler—to form a majority committed to preserving the laissez-faire jurisprudence of the *Taft Court. This meant adhering to a restrictive interpretation of the Commerce Clause, the constitutional basis for congressional regulation of business. In this interpretation, manufacturing, mining, and agriculture were not considered commerce and were thus beyond the reach of Congress. There were only three liberals on the Court—Oliver Wendell Holmes Jr. (who would be replaced in 1932 by Benjamin Cardozo), Louis D. Brandeis, and Harlan Fiske Stone.

Between 1934 and 1936, the Court overturned *New Deal legislation in nine of 16 cases that came before it, including the cornerstone National Industrial Recovery Act (see *Schechter Poultry Corp. v. United States, 1935) and the Agricultural Adjustment Act of 1933 (see *United States v. Butler, 1936). Furious at the Court,

and made overconfident by his landslide reelection in 1936, Pres. Franklin Roosevelt proposed to appoint additional justices to the Court (see *Court-Packing Plan). His plan was defeated in Congress, but even before it had been announced Hughes and Roberts, responding to new intellectual currents in the legal community, had abandoned their commitment to laissez-faire ideology. In *West Coast Hotel Co. v. Parrish (1937), they joined the three liberal justices to a create a 5–4 majority upholding a Washington State minimum wage law. The same majority upheld the radical Wagner Act in *National Labor Relations Board v. Jones & Laughlin Steel Corp (1937). And in *Steward Machine Co. v. Davis (1937) and a related case the Court upheld the Social Security Act.

The historic switch from opposition to support of New Deal legislation divided the Hughes Court into two periods, as did the changes in its personnel. Between 1936 and Hughes's retirement in 1941, all four of the conservative justices retired. Cardozo died in 1938, and Brandeis retired in 1939. Thus Roosevelt was able to appoint six new justices to the Hughes Court—Hugo Black, Stanley Reed, Felix Frankfurter, William O. Douglas, Frank Murphy, and James F. Byrnes.

A famous decision of the "second" Hughes Court, made as the nation prepared for war, upheld the expulsion from school of two Jehovah's Witnesses children for refusing to salute the flag (see *Minersville School District v. Gobitis, 1940). Justice Frankfurter, for the 8–1 majority, argued that patriotic ceremonies were necessary to strengthen national unity. Three years later (after Hughes's departure), the Court reversed itself 6–3, Justice Robert Jackson writing a classic defense of First Amendment freedoms (see *West Virginia State Board of Education v. Barnette, 1943).

HÜLSEMANN LETTER (1850), incident in the *Taylor-Fillmore administration. In September 1850, the Austrian chargé in Washington, J. G. Hülsemann, formally protested U.S. sympathy for Hungary during the recent Hungarian revolution. Secretary of State Daniel Webster resolved not only to justify U.S. conduct but to use the occasion to strike a nationalistic note calculated to revive American patriotism after the divisive debates surrounding the *Compromise of 1850.

With deliberate arrogance, Webster wrote in part in his letter to Hülsemann of Dec. 21, 1850: "The power of this republic, at the present moment, is spread over a region one of the richest and most fertile on the globe, and of an extent in comparison with which the possessions of the house of Hapsburg are but a patch on the earth's surface. Its population, already twenty-five millions, will [soon] exceed that of the Austrian empire. . . . Its navigation and commerce are hardly exceeded by the oldest and most commercial nations. . . . Life, liberty, property, and all personal rights, are amply secured to all citizens, and protected by just and stable laws. . . . [T]he country . . . partakes most largely in all the improvements and progress which distinguish the age."

A few months later, Louis Kossuth, the leader of the failed revolt, was enthusiastically received in America.

HUMAN RIGHTS. Human rights were not a concern of international law until after World War 2. In 1945–46, the victorious Allies prosecuted war criminals on the novel charge of crimes against humanity. At the founding conference of the United Nations in San Francisco in 1945, the American delegation inserted a commitment to human rights into the preamble of the organization's charter. Three years later, the UN General Assembly unanimously adopted the Universal Declaration of Human Rights, in the formulation of which Eleanor Roosevelt had played a prominent role. This resolution was not given the legal force of a treaty until 1966, when two International Human Rights Covenants—one concerned with civil and political rights, the other with economic, social, and cultural rights—were presented for signing. By then, however, U.S. enthusiasm for human rights had given way to *cold war concerns.

During the cold war, the United States equated anti-communism with support for freedom and readily embraced repressive regimes around the world—in Bolivia, Chile, Guatemala, Haiti, Iran, Liberia, Pakistan, Paraguay, Somalia, South Africa, South Korea, South Vietnam, Sudan, Zaire, and elsewhere. In time, public opinion—informed by private organizations like Amnesty International that monitored and publicized human rights abuses—protested and Congress responded. During the 1970s, Congress made a country's human rights record one criterion in the decision to extend *foreign aid to it. In 1976, Congress established the Bureau of Human Rights and Humanitarian Affairs (now the Bureau of Democracy, Human Rights, and Labor) in the State Department. In 1977, incoming president James E. Carter promised to make human rights the cornerstone of U.S. foreign policy. His successors, Ronald Reagan and George H. W. Bush, took a dimmer view of human rights as the basis for American foreign policy, but in 1993 Pres. William J. Clinton again asserted their primacy.

Rhetoric aside, through all four administrations the pursuit of human rights was distinctly subordinated to other foreign policy objectives. This was most notable in Clinton's trade negotiations with China, conducted despite constant criticism of China's human rights abuses. Nevertheless, in 1992 the Senate ratified the International Covenant on Civil and Political Rights (but not the International Covenant on Economic, Social, and Cultural Rights) presented in 1966. In 1994 it ratified conventions on women's rights (drafted in 1979) and torture (drafted in 1984). As of 2002, it had not ratified conventions on genocide (drafted in 1948) and children's rights (1989).

In 2002, the George W. Bush administration renounced a treaty (signed but not ratified in the Clinton administration) setting up a permanent international criminal court to try individuals accused of genocide, crimes against humanity, and war crimes. (Disputes between states are tried before the International Court of Justice, or World Court.)

HUNDRED DAYS (Mar. 9–June 16, 1933), episode in the Franklin *Roosevelt administration. The day after his inauguration, Roosevelt called the 73rd Congress—the one elected with him in November 1932 but not scheduled to meet until December 1933 (see *20th Amendment)—into special session, starting Mar. 9, to deal with the emergencies presented by the *Great Depression. The special session did not adjourn until June 16. During those 100 days, it enacted an unprecedented amount of major legislation, instituting much of the *New Deal.

In European history, the term "Hundred Days" refers to the critical period between the escape of Napoleon I from exile on the island of Elba on Mar. 1, 1815, and his final defeat at Waterloo on June 18.

HYDROGEN BOMB, nuclear weapon that derives its energy from the fusion of atomic nuclei rather than from their fission as in the *atomic bomb. Indeed, detonation of a fission device is necessary to generate the extreme temperatures necessary to achieve a thermonuclear or fusion reaction.

The theoretical feasibility of a hydrogen bomb was demonstrated by physicist Edward Teller while he was employed on the *Manhattan Project during World War 2. After the Soviets exploded an atomic device in August 1949, the Atomic Energy Commission began to discuss the development of the much more powerful hydrogen bomb. It finally voted 3–2 against its development; its General Advisory Committee of scientists headed by Robert Oppenheimer opposed it unanimously for both moral and technical reasons. Scientists, administration officials, members of Congress, and the press took sides on the issue. The Joint Chiefs of Staff urged its development, although the JCS chairman, Gen. Omar Bradley, regarded it as militarily useless.

In November 1949 Pres. Harry S. Truman appointed a committee consisting of Secretary of State Dean Acheson, Secretary of Defense Louis Johnson, and AEC chairman David Lilienthal to review the matter. On Jan. 31, 1950, the committee reported to the president its unanimous recommendation to develop the bomb, Lilienthal having reversed his previous position. In a seven-minute meeting, Truman asked: "Can the Russians do it?" Assured that they could, he responded: "In that case we have no choice. We'll go ahead."

The United States detonated a thermonuclear device at Eniwetok Atoll in the Pacific Ocean on Oct. 31, 1952; the Soviets followed suit in April 1953.

HYPHENATED AMERICANS, term apparently coined during World War 1 to designate those Americans who were overly conscious of their ethnic origins. For former president Theodore Roosevelt and Pres. Woodrow Wilson, a hyphenated American was no patriot. In 1915, Roosevelt wrote: ". . . among the very many lessons taught by the last year has been the lesson that the effort to combine fealty to the flag of an immigrant's natal land with fealty to the flag of his adopted land, in practice means not merely disregard of, but hostility to, the flag of the United States. When two flags are hoisted on the same pole, one is always hoisted undermost. The hyphenated American always hoists the American flag undermost."

Wilson was no less emphatic: "For my part," he declared in 1919, "I think the most un-American thing in the world is a hyphen. I don't care what it is that comes before the word 'American.' It may be a German-American, or it may be an Italian-American, or a Swedish-American, or an Anglo-American, or an Irish-American. It don't make any difference what comes before the 'American,' it ought not to be there, and every man that comes to take counsel with me with a hyphen in his conversation, I take no interest in whatever."

From a term of opprobrium, "hyphenated American" evolved in the 1960s—when patriotism was suspect and multiculturalism the fashion—into a term of respect if not honor. No longer "one nation . . . indivisible," America was seen by some opinion makers as a multiethnic society in which hyphens were the norm.

I

IMMIGRATION. For nearly a century, the United States made no effort to limit immigration. Indeed, many groups actively encouraged immigration: states seeking larger populations, industries seeking cheap labor, railroads seeking settlers along their routes, shipping companies seeking passengers. On the other hand, a nativist movement—antiforeign and anti-Catholic—arose in response to the influx of Irish and German immigrants (see *Nativism). The anti-Catholic and anti-immigrant *Know-Nothing Party flourished briefly in the 1850s.

"Old" and "New" Immigrations. Between 1820 (when immigration records began to be kept) and 1890, the United States received 15.4 million immigrants. Slow at first, the immigrant flow mounted rapidly after 1840. Until 1890, the immigrants came overwhelmingly from the countries of Western and Northern Europe—chiefly England, Ireland, Germany, and the Scandinavian countries—to which most Americans at that time traced their ancestry. This immigration is called the old immigration.

After 1890, the size and character of the immigration flow shifted dramatically. In the 30 years between 1891 and 1920, 18.2 million immigrants reached the United States; 8.8 million came in the single decade 1901–10. The majority of these came from the countries of Southern and Eastern Europe, chiefly Italy, Austria-Hungary, Greece, Romania, and Russia. Historians call this the new immigration.

During the 19th century, the U.S. Supreme Court struck down state laws regulating the admission of aliens and restricting immigration, upholding the exclusive power of Congress in this area. Not until 1875, however, did Congress pass its first act establishing controls on the admission of aliens and excluding certain classes of immigrants. Convicts were excluded in 1875, and the list of excluded persons was steadily extended in subsequent acts to include paupers, criminals, the insane, the dis-

eased, prostitutes, polygamists, sexual deviants, anarchists, communists, alcoholics, and illiterates—33 classes in all. An act of 1882 prohibited the entry of Chinese laborers (see *Chinese Exclusion); in 1907, a "Gentlemen's Agreement" with Japan virtually ended the immigration of Japanese laborers as well (see *Japanese Exclusion).

The National-Origins Quota System. The "new immigration" after 1890 gave rise to intense opposition to the continuation of unlimited immigration. Pseudoscientific racial theories provided a veneer of respectability to arguments that at heart were based on prejudice and privilege. Americans were warned that the newcomers from Southern and Eastern Europe were racially inferior to the "Nordic" immigrants from Western and Northern Europe, that their great numbers could not be absorbed, and that they therefore posed a threat to American ideals, institutions, and living standards. The result was the introduction in 1921 of the national-origins quota system that governed U.S. immigration policy until 1965.

The Immigration Act of 1921 limited the number of immigrants from any one country in a single year to 3 percent of the number of persons born in that country who were living in the United States in 1910. This quota system had the effect of placing a ceiling of 358,000 on the total number of immigrants admissible in one year and ensuring that more than half of them would come from Western and Northern Europe.

But advocates of immigration restriction were not satisfied. The Immigration Act of 1924, therefore, reduced national quotas to 2 percent and used 1890 rather than 1910 as the base year. One effect of the reduced quotas was to lower the immigration ceiling to 165,000 per year. In 1929, the ceiling was further reduced to 150,000, and national quotas were set at the percentage of that figure that each national group had constituted of the total population in 1920. The Immigration and Nationality (McCarran-Walter) Act of 1952 set the quota for each national group at one-sixth of 1 percent of its number in 1920, causing the overall ceiling on immigration to rise slightly to 155,000 persons per year. The national-origins quota system had the effect of restoring, at least formally, the character of the "old immigration."

The Immigration and Nationality Act of 1965 and After. The discriminatory national-origins quota system was already repugnant to many Americans when Congress passed the Immigration Act of 1952 over Pres. Harry S. Truman's veto. Not until 1965, however, during the liberal tide of Pres. Lyndon B. Johnson's "Great Society," did Congress finally abolish it.

The Immigration and Nationality Act of 1965 discarded national origin as the criterion for admission; instead, it stressed the reuniting of families and the admission of needed workers. The act fixed a limit of 290,000 immigrants a year, although immediate relatives of U.S. citizens (minor children and spouses of citizens, and parents of citizens over 21) were exempt from this limit. For the Western Hemisphere, the act set a ceiling (for the first time) of 120,000 immigrants a year. For the Eastern Hemisphere (all countries outside North and South America and the Caribbean area) the act set a ceiling of 170,000 immigrants a year, with no more than 20,000 from any one country. Whereas Western Hemisphere immigrants were to be admitted on a first-come-first-served basis, Eastern Hemisphere immigrants had to apply for visas under one of seven "preference categories" favoring family unification and needed workers.

It was almost as an afterthought that Congress placed the ceiling of 120,000 on Western Hemisphere immigrants. Previous immigration acts had placed no limits on Western Hemisphere immigrants, and the national-origins quota system had not been applied there. Few people foresaw the steep rise in immigration from Western Hemisphere countries that developed after 1965. In 1976 a new immigration act extended to the Western Hemisphere the limit of 20,000 immigrants per country and the preference system that the 1965 act had applied only to the Eastern Hemisphere. In 1978 another act ended hemispheric quotas and established a single worldwide ceiling of 290,000 immigrants a year. The Refugee Act of 1980 raised the ceiling for immigrants and refugees to 320,000 persons per year.

The Immigration and Nationality Act of 1965 and its revisions had a striking effect on both the size and the composition of the stream of immigration. Southern and Eastern Europeans again replaced Northern and Western Europeans as the predominant European group. Meanwhile, Asians, competing with Europeans on an equal basis for the first time, quickly outnumbered them. But immigration from the Western Hemisphere exceeded immigration from both Europe and Asia.

The problem of illegal immigration was addressed by the Immigration Reform and Control Act of 1986, which provided for sanctions against employers who knowingly hired illegal immigrants, for increased border enforcement, and for legalizing the status of illegal aliens who could prove they had lived in the United States for five years.

In 1990 a new immigration act raised the annual number of legal immigrants from 500,000 to 700,000 for three years, thereafter to 675,000. Again, preference was given to family members of U.S. citizens and to skilled workers. The act also eliminated the barring of foreigners because of their political beliefs and sexual orientation.

Concern about the growing numbers of immigrants—916,000 legal immigrants in 1996, perhaps 300,000 illegals—prompted Congress to pass new legislation in 1996 increasing preventive measures against illegal entrants, authorizing the deportation or detention of aliens without judicial review (a provision overturned by the U.S. Supreme Court in 2001), denying public assistance to illegal aliens, and restricting some welfare benefits to most legal aliens. Nevertheless, the number of illegal immigrants in the United States rose from 5 million in 1996 to 6.5–7 million in 2001.

An immigration act in 2000 increased the number of visas for highly skilled foreign workers from 115,000 to 195,000 for three years.

Between 1991 and 2000, 11.3 million legal immigrants entered the United States. The foreign-born population in 2000 numbered 31.1 million—11.1 percent of the total—up 57 percent over 1990. Of the foreign born, more than half—52 percent—came from Latin America.

IMPERIAL PRESIDENCY, label for a presidential administration in which the executive branch dominates the others to an arguably unconstitutional degree. Historian Arthur M. Schlesinger Jr., in his *The Imperial Presidency* (1973), pointed out that the authors of the Constitution placed the executive, legislative, and judicial functions of government into separate branches and, by a system of checks and balances, tried to ensure that no one branch would be able to exercise excessive power. Recognizing that the system of checks and balances was a recipe for inertia, they gave the president sufficient powers so that an "energetic" executive could move the government toward desired ends. The line between presidential primacy and presidential supremacy, however, was always a blurred one. Andrew Jackson and Franklin Roosevelt were accused of usurping unconstitutional powers. There is little question that Lyndon Johnson, Richard Nixon, and Ronald Reagan, by well-documented secrecy, deception, and extralegal expedients, exercised unconstitutional power. Periods of executive supremacy tend to be followed by periods of congressional supremacy.

IMPRESSMENT, forcible recruitment into military or naval service. England, like other countries, long relied on "press gangs" to fill vacancies in army units or ship crews preparing for active service. During the Napoleonic Wars, Britain insisted on its right to reclaim British citizens—often deserters from the Royal Navy—serving on American ships, frequently stopping and searching American ships, including warships, on the high seas and kidnapping alleged deserters (see *Chesapeake Affair). In his war message of June 1, 1812, Pres. James Madison listed British impressment of American seamen as the first cause of the *War of 1812.

INCHON LANDING. See *Korean War.

INCOME TAX CASES. See *Pollock v. Farmers' Loan & Trust Co.

INDENTURED SERVITUDE (1620–1800), contract labor system in the English colonies in which a migrant paid the cost of his transportation to America by committing himself to a period of labor for an American employer who bought his contract. Most indentured servants were single young men. Although they retained some legal rights, they had no control over the conditions of their employment. Upon the completion of their period of servitude—generally four to seven years—they were free to find employment on their own or establish farms on the frontier. African laborers were first treated as indentured servants, but in time racial prejudice debased their condition to chattel slavery.

INDEPENDENT COUNSEL or **SPECIAL PROSECUTOR,** federal official created in 1978 to investigate wrongdoing in the executive branch of the U.S. government. The Independent Counsel Act was a response to Pres. Richard M. Nixon's firing in 1973 of special prosecutor Archibald Cox, who had been appointed by the attorney general to investigate *Watergate. The act provided for a prosecutor, appointed by a three-judge panel, who would have unlimited scope, tenure, and budget and be removable only by the attorney general. An independent counsel pursued the *Iran-Contra Affair during the *Reagan administration; another's pursuit of alleged wrongdoing by Pres. William J. Clinton led to the *Clinton impeachment. Reauthorized in 1994, the act expired on June 30, 1999.

INDEPENDENT TREASURY SYSTEM or **SUB-TREASURY SYSTEM** (1840–41, 1846–1920), federal fiscal system, separate from the banking system, initiated by the *Van Buren administration. Rejecting reestablishment of a national bank but recognizing the stimulus to speculative credit expansion of federal deposits in state banks, Pres. Martin Van Buren proposed in the Independent Treasury Act (1840) establishment of a federal independent Treasury in Washington and subtreasuries or depositories in major cities to receive public revenues and pay Treasury obligations independently of banks and exclusively in specie. The Whigs, favoring a national bank, repealed the act in 1841, but Pres. John Tyler objected to a national bank on constitutional grounds. The Democratic administration of Pres. James K. Polk reinstituted the Independent Treasury System in 1846. The system restrained speculation, but the hoarding of specie in federal depositories restricted credit in good times and aggravated economic difficulties in bad times. The system survived, with modifications, until replaced (1913) by the *Federal Reserve System.

INDIAN POLICY. The newly independent United States formulated a policy toward the native inhabitants (see *Indians, American) of its national territory at once respectful of their independent sovereignty and sensitive to their vulnerability before the more numerous and more civilized white population. "The utmost good faith shall always be observed toward the Indians," the Confederation Congress determined in the Ordinance of 1787; "their lands and property shall never be taken from them without their consent; and, in their property, rights, and liberty, they never shall be invaded or disturbed, unless in just and lawful wars authorized by Congress; but laws founded in justice and humanity shall, from time to time, be made, for preventing wrongs being done to them and for preserving peace and friendship with them."

The resolve to deal with Native Americans justly and humanely was soon forgotten in the expansion of the ever-growing white population into Indian country. By purchase and military force, the United States took possession of Indian lands on the trans-Appalachian frontier and relocated many tribes beyond the Mississippi (see *Indian Removal). When the tide of settlement crossed the Mississippi, the Indians were again relocated, this time to isolated reservations on the least desirable Western lands. To be sure, these successive land cessions and resettlements were accomplished with the nominal consent of the Indians. Bowing to necessity, the Indians signed treaties accepting compensation for their lands in the form of money, livestock, clothing, blankets, guns, and ammunition. In their long retreat, however, their numbers were decimated and their societies demoralized.

For a hundred years the United States dealt with the Indian tribes as with foreign nations. Treaties negotiated by agents of the executive branch were formally ratified by the U.S. Senate. As early as 1831, however, Chief Justice John Marshall dispelled this solemn fiction. "It may well be doubted," he wrote in *Cherokee Nation v. Georgia, "whether those tribes which reside within the acknowledged boundaries of the United States can, with strict accuracy, be denominated foreign nations. They may, more correctly, perhaps be denominated domestic dependent nations. . . . [T]hey are in a state of pupilage. Their relation to the United States resembles that of a ward to his guardian." In 1871 Congress finally determined that future relations between the United States and the Indian tribes would be conducted by executive agreement rather than formal treaty.

By then, however, hundreds of treaties, as well as statutes and court decisions, had clearly established the unique legal status of the Indians. Like no other group in the population, the Indians in their tribal organizations possessed permanent homelands (reservations) on which they lived as sovereign (though dependent) self-governing nations. At the same time, they were wards of the federal government, for in the treaties establishing the reservations the United States had pledged permanently to protect the Indians' lands and rights—a commitment known as the "trust responsibility." The federal agency most responsible for the Indians' welfare is the Bureau of Indian Affairs (BIA), established in 1836 in the Department of the Interior. Created to manage U.S. relations with the Indians, the BIA came in time to manage the Indians themselves. It long exercised a benign but stifling paternalism that stripped the Indians of all responsibility for their own welfare.

The BIA, however, did not make Indian policy. That was made by the U.S. Congress, usually in response to initiatives of the executive branch. Since the 1870s, that policy has swung between two extremes: at some peri-

ods, the policy has aimed at the dissolution of the Indian tribes and the assimilation of the Indians as individuals into the general population; at other periods, the policy has aimed at the preservation and strengthening of the Indian tribes and of individual Indian identity.

The most important assimilationist measure was the **Dawes General Allotment Act** (1887). By this act Congress, in violation of U.S. guarantees to the tribes, undertook to dissolve the reservations, allotting tribal lands to individual Indians on the assumption that they would thereby become independent and self-sufficient farmers. Each family head was to receive 160 acres, each single person over 18 years of age 80 acres. These allotments were to remain under trust protection—untaxed and unsalable—for 25 years. "Surplus" tribal lands left over after the distribution of allotments were to be sold to non-Indians.

Under the Dawes Act, 118 reservations were allotted. For the Indians affected, the consequences were disastrous. The small sizes of the allotments, the poor quality of the land, their lack of training, capital, and credit, and their preference for traditional communal ownership rather than private ownership assured the Indians' failure as farmers. Between 1887 and 1934, two-thirds of all Indian lands were lost. The number of landless Indians rose from 5,000 in 1887 to 100,000 in 1934.

In 1934, the **Indian Reorganization Act** reversed the policy of assimilation. It ended the allotment program, extended indefinitely the federal trusteeship over lands already allotted, restored unsold "surplus" lands to tribal ownership, and provided for the purchase of additional lands to consolidate and make economically viable existing Indian landholdings. To stimulate economic development of the reservations, the act established loan funds to finance Indian business ventures and to pay Indians' tuition in vocational and trade schools. It recognized the right of the Indian people to be self-governing, permitting the tribes to adopt written constitutions and bylaws (subject to approval by the secretary of the interior) and giving the new governments enlarged powers to manage reservation affairs.

In the 1950s, Congress reverted to the assimilation policy. Determined "to make the Indians within the territorial limits of the United States subject to the same laws and entitled to the same privileges and responsibilities as are applicable to other citizens," Congress in 1953 declared its intention that "at the earliest possible time, all of the Indian tribes and individual members thereof . . . should be freed from Federal supervision and control." Between 1954 and 1962, a series of termination acts dissolved a dozen tribes, removing their members and lands from federal protection. Vehement Indian protests caused this policy to be abandoned.

Meanwhile, tribal governments had acquired new vigor as a result of their designation as eligible recipients of federal grants in the War on Poverty initiated by the Lyndon *Johnson administration. Presidents Johnson and Richard M. Nixon promised a new policy of Indian self-determination. This was finally embodied in the **Indian Self-Determination and Education Assistance Act** (1975), in which Congress reaffirmed its commitment to maintaining the federal government's "unique and continuing relationship with and responsibility to the Indian people." Indian self-determination meant that the Indian tribes could assume greater responsibility for their own governance by contracting with the BIA to conduct educational and other programs that formerly would have been administered for them. At the same time, an impressive series of court decisions confirmed the powers of reservation governments, giving increased reality to their claims to the status of local governments like municipalities and counties.

At the start of the 21st century, with declining federal support for health and education programs, some tribes were deriving revenue from gambling casinos on their reservations. Despite the well-publicized success of a few of these, Native Americans living on reservations remained the poorest segment of the U.S. population, blighted by high unemployment, low educational achievement, and poor health.

INDIAN REMOVAL (1825–50), policy of resettling Eastern Indians west of the Mississippi River. Reversing the previous policy of assimilation, it was formulated by Secretary of War John C. Calhoun in the *Monroe administration and involved the idea of a permanent Indian frontier west of the 95th meridian. Removal treaties—superseding earlier treaties that had guaranteed the tribes their ancestral lands—were obtained by persuasion, bribery, and misrepresentation. The Indian Removal Act (1830) provided for compensation for old lands, perpetual title to new, government payment of the cost of removal, and a year's subsistence in the tribe's new home; most significant, it authorized the president to use force when necessary to effect removal. To protect the tribes in their new homes, the Indian Intercourse Act (1834) prohibited all white men except licensed traders from entering the reservations. That same year the Bureau of Indian Affairs was established.

By the early 1830s, most of the tribes of the Old Northwest—Shawnee, Delaware, Chippewa, Miami, and others—had been resettled in the eastern part of present-day Kansas or western Iowa. The fate of the Sac and Fox in the *Black Hawk War (1832) persuaded the northern tribes of the futility of resistance.

In the South, the *Five Civilized Tribes were more resistant. The Choctaws, Chickasaws, and Creeks moved from Arkansas, Mississippi, Alabama, and Georgia in the early 1830s to *Indian Territory in the eastern part of present-day Oklahoma. The Cherokees in Georgia protested a fraudulent treaty but, denied the protection of their treaty rights by the federal government (see *Cherokee Nation v. Georgia, *Worcester v. Georgia), they were finally and forcibly removed to Indian Territory in the tragic *Trail of Tears. In Florida, the Seminoles resisted removal until 1842 (see *Seminole Wars).

INDIAN REORGANIZATION ACT (1934). See *Indian Policy.

INDIANS, AMERICAN, or **NATIVE AMERICANS.** When Europeans reached North America in the 16th century, the territory that is now the United States was inhabited by about 1 million Indians, descendants of peoples from northeastern Asia who had migrated across the Bering Strait over a long period of time, beginning perhaps 25,000 years ago. They differed in physical type, spoke several hundred languages, and inhabited eight "culture areas" defined by the natural environment—Eastern Woodland, Southeastern, Southwestern, Plains, Basin, Plateau, Northwest Coast, and California. Their societies differed markedly in level of civilization, political organization, and economies—some Indians were primitive food gatherers, others nomadic hunters, still others settled agriculturalists. The Indian peoples dealt with each other as sovereign nations, and the European newcomers did likewise. Although Europeans laid claim to great portions of North America on the basis of discovery, exploration, settlement, or Christian mission, they acknowledged the Indians' right of occupancy of the territories they customarily inhabited. These rights could be extinguished only by purchase or treaty.

Indian rights were increasingly disregarded as the British colonies and then the United States expanded westward. The Indians were decimated by war, disease, dislocation, starvation, and poverty. U.S. policy toward them varied between protection, destruction, assimilation, and preservation (see *Indian Policy).

The Indian population reached its lowest point in the 1920s and has since increased. In 2000 the U.S. Census counted 2.5 million Indians (including Alaska natives), 0.9 percent of the population. Somewhat less than half lived on reservations or trust lands. For all Indian individuals, the poverty rate was 31.2 percent.

INDIAN SELF-DETERMINATION AND EDUCATION ASSISTANCE ACT (1975). See *Indian Policy.

INDIAN TERRITORY, eastern portion of present-day Oklahoma, never formally organized as a territory, to which the *Five Civilized Tribes were relocated in 1830–40 (see *Indian Removal). The western part of Oklahoma was opened to white settlement in 1889 and organized as a territory in 1890. In 1906 tribal lands were converted to individual holdings (which could be bought by whites), and the next year Indian Territory was combined with Oklahoma Territory to form the state of Oklahoma.

INDIAN WARS. See *Apache Wars; *Black Hawk War; *Cheyenne-Arapaho War; *Creek War; *Fallen Timbers; *King Philip's War; *Nez Percé War; *Pequot War; *Pontiac's Rebellion; *Seminole Wars; *Sioux Wars; *Tecumseh Confederacy.

INDUSTRIALIZATION. The Industrial Revolution—the movement of manufacturing from homes and workshops to factories where a numerous workforce tended powered machines—spread to the United States from Great Britain in the late 18th century. A factory established at Pawtucket, R.I., in 1790 produced yarn by water-powered machines copied from British models. Another, established at Waltham, Mass., in 1813 wove cotton cloth on power-driven looms, also copied from British machines. Cotton manufacturing, concentrated in New England where energy could be harnessed from numerous swift streams, became the first major industry to develop in America.

The Napoleonic Wars, which interrupted the flow of manufactured goods from Europe, provided the original window of opportunity for American entrepreneurs. The federal government encouraged them with *tariff protection, state governments with *internal improvements—roads and canals, then railroads—that facilitated the movement of raw material to factories and the distribution of finished goods to regional markets.

By 1840 the substitution of steam for water power was well under way. Manufacturers could now build their factories in cities and towns where labor was readily available rather than at remote streamsides. Wood, bituminous coal, and finally anthracite coal fueled regularly improved steam engines. In 1860, manufacturing was heavily concentrated in the Northeast, particularly in New York, Pennsylvania, and Massachusetts. Leading industries were cotton goods, lumber, boots and shoes, iron, clothing, flour and meal, machinery, leather, and woolen goods.

The Civil War provided a great impetus to industrial expansion. In the postwar years, conditions were ripe for unprecedented industrialization: a continental market, knit together by a vast railroad network; a growing urban workforce, enlarged each year by migrants from farms and immigrants from abroad; vast natural resources, especially coal, iron, oil, and timber; technological virtuosity, for which Americans became famous, measured by the rise in the number of new patents from 12,000 in 1860 to 40,000 in 1914; high tariffs, instituted in the Civil War to raise revenue but retained into the 20th century to protect and enrich manufacturers; and the ready availability of American and European capital.

Between 1860 and 1914, manufacturing in the United States expanded 12.5 times, making the United States the world's leading industrial nation. By 1884 the value of manufactures had exceeded those of agriculture, and farmers constituted less than half of the nation's labor force. Exploitation of the rich iron deposits around Lake Superior extended the nation's industrial belt from the Northeast to the Great Lakes region. By 1910, the Middle West—the region north of the Ohio River and east of the Mississippi—employed 70 percent of U.S. industrial workers. Manufacturing businesses were becoming increasingly large publicly held corporations. In 1900 the five most important industries were: iron and steel; slaughtering and meatpacking; foundry and machine-shop products; lumber and timber products; and flour and gristmill products.

After World War 1, the manufacture of consumer durable goods—automobiles, home appliances, telephones—flourished. World War 2 made the United States a major producer of military equipment of all kinds, and the role of the federal government in financing research and purchasing heavy goods became important. In the 1950s, automated machinery began to replace the moving assembly line in many places. Data processing, aerospace, and biotechnology represented industries of the future. At the end of the century, America's principal manufacturing industries were: chemical and allied products; transportation equipment; food and kindred products; industrial machinery and equipment; electronics and other electrical equipment; and printing and publishing. The manufacturing region had extended from the Northeast and Middle West to include the Southern piedmont and the Gulf Coast. The leading manufacturing states were California, New York, Ohio, Texas, Illinois, Michigan, Pennsylvania, North Carolina, Indiana, New Jersey, and Georgia.

INDUSTRIAL WORKERS OF THE WORLD (IWW) (1905–20), labor organization founded by left-wing critics of the *American Federation of Labor (AFL) to unite all workers, skilled and unskilled, into "one big union." Openly revolutionary, the IWW eschewed political action in favor of economic action, which was to culminate in a general strike overthrowing the capitalist system and establishing a workers' government. Samuel Gompers, president of the AFL, condemned it as "fallacious, injurious, reactionary." Nevertheless, the **"Wobblies"** successfully organized miners, lumberjacks, and migrant farmworkers in the West and immigrant textile workers in the East, where their greatest success was the *Lawrence, Mass., textile strike (1912). IWW membership was unstable and transitory, never exceeding 70,000. Its aggressive radicalism and opposition to U.S. entry into World War 1 caused it to be widely abhorred as unpatriotic and it declined rapidly after 1917.

INFLUENZA PANDEMIC (1918–19), worldwide course of virulent "Spanish flu" in the wake of *World War 1. Its origin was uncertain and its cause unknown; there was no cure. Fatalities worldwide have been estimated at 20–100 million; in the United States they numbered 500,000.

INITIATIVE, REFERENDUM, AND RECALL, political devices popular in the Progressive Era (see *Progressivism) as promising to increase citizen participation in local and state government (the U.S. Constitution precludes their use at the federal level).

The **initiative** permits citizens to initiate legislation by getting a specified number of signatures on a petition supporting it. In a direct initiative, the proposal goes directly onto the ballot in a regular election; in an indirect initiative, it goes first to the legislature for action, failing which it may then go onto the ballot.

A **referendum** is the vote by citizens on an issue placed on the ballot either by initiative or by the legislature itself seeking an advisory vote.

Recall is the procedure by which citizens, by getting a specified number of signatures on a petition, may call a special election to remove an elected official from office.

All three devices have been criticized as examples of direct democracy, inconsistent with the representative democracy characteristic of the United States. Fewer than half the states have adopted the initiative; smaller numbers, the referendum and recall.

INQUIRY, THE. See *World War 1.

INSULAR CASES (1901–4), 14 decisions in which the *Fuller Court attempted to define the constitutional status of newly acquired island possessions—Puerto Rico, Hawaii, and the Philippines—as concerned tariff laws and the Bill of Rights. The Court's problem—in keeping with public sentiment—was to deny these islands territorial status, which meant that they might eventually become states and their nonwhite inhabitants citizens.

The Court ultimately concluded that the islands were not foreign and therefore not subject to the tariff laws but, since Congress had not expressly incorporated them into the United States, neither were they territories in which the Bill of Rights applied.

"As near as I can make out," puzzled Secretary of War Elihu Root, "the Constitution follows the flag—but doesn't quite catch up with it." More perceptively, *Mr. Dooley observed: "No matter whether th' Constitution follows th' flag or not, th' Supreme Court follows th' illiction returns."

INTERNAL IMPROVEMENTS, a term used before the Civil War for state or federally subsidized improvement or building of rivers, harbors, roads, canals, and other transportation infrastructure.

The early republic was so deficient in means of communication as to prompt fears of political disintegration. In 1806 Congress authorized construction of the *National Road, to be paid for with revenue from the sale of *public lands. Albert Gallatin, secretary of the Treasury in the cabinet of Pres. Thomas Jefferson, prepared (1808) a report advocating construction by the national government of a network of unifying roads and canals. Jefferson doubted the constitutionality of such a federal project, and the War of 1812 intervened. Under the General Survey Act (1824) some 90 projects were begun, most notably the Chesapeake and Ohio Canal.

The question of constitutionality persisted for strict-constructionist presidents James Madison and James Monroe. Pres. Andrew Jackson favored a constitutional amendment that would clarify the role of the federal government in such projects; lacking that, he opposed local but supported national projects. His Democratic successors continued to oppose internal improvements, the Whig opposition—especially Henry Clay—to favor them. They were popular in the West but became unpopular in the South, where an active federal government was perceived as a potential threat to slavery.

States and private businesses seized the opportunities neglected by the federal government (as Jackson anticipated they would). New York's *Erie Canal (built 1817–25) was enormously successful, with the result that other states rushed into debt to launch similar projects. Many of these had to be abandoned after the *Panic of 1837 or in the face of competition from the rapidly developing railroad network. Increasingly, private capital replaced state and federal money in the development of the nation's transportation infrastructure.

INTERNAL SECURITY ACT (1950). See *Anticommunism.

INTERNATIONAL BROTHERHOOD OF TEAMSTERS (IBT), labor union formed in 1899 among drivers of horse-drawn wagons that grew into the country's second-largest union with iron control over the trucking industry and considerable political power. Long plagued by corruption, the union experienced the jailing of successive presidents and ouster (1957–87) from the *American Federation of Labor–Congress of Industrial Organizations. In 1989, the union settled a racketeering lawsuit against it by agreeing to close federal oversight of its affairs and elections. To end government oversight, the union amended its constitution in 2000 to permit the direct election of officers by the membership instead of by the union's board. The IBT then claimed 1.6 million workers.

INTERNATIONAL LADIES' GARMENT WORKERS' UNION (ILGWU), labor union formed in 1900 to fight exploitative conditions in the garment industry. Under David Dubinsky (president 1932–66), the ILGWU expelled communists and pioneered social welfare benefits for its members. Over the years, its membership shifted from Italian and Jewish to Hispanic and African-American, while many jobs shifted overseas. In 1995 the ILGWU merged with the Amalgamated Clothing and Textile Workers' Union to form the Union of Needletrades, Industrial and Texile Employees with 355,000 members.

INTERSTATE COMMERCE ACT (1887). See *Railroad Regulation.

INTERSTATE HIGHWAY ACT (1956), legislation of the *Eisenhower administration authorizing the construction over ten years of the 42,500-mile National System of Interstate and Defense Highways at a cost of $82 billion, shared by federal and state governments on a 90–10 matching basis. The administration supported the act on the grounds of increasing automobile congestion (auto registrations had risen from 25 million in 1945 to 51 million in 1955), the need to evacuate cities quickly in case of an atomic attack, and its value as a countercyclical measure (more could be spent when unemployment was high, less when unemployment was low). Construction took longer than anticipated, cost more, and had a negative impact upon many urban neighborhoods. But it greatly stimulated the petroleum, automobile, and construction industries.

INTOLERABLE ACTS or **COERCIVE ACTS** (March–May 1774), four acts of Parliament—called Coercive Acts in Britain—intended to punish Boston and Massachusetts for the rebelliousness manifested most recently in the *Boston Tea Party.

The **Boston Port Act** (March 1774) closed the port of Boston to all shipping until the East India Company and the customs had been compensated for their losses.

The **Massachusetts Government Act** (May 1774) fundamentally revised the Massachusetts charter of 1691. Members of the Provincial Council were henceforward to be appointed by the crown instead of elected by the House of Representatives. The chief justice and judges of the superior court were also to be appointed by the crown. Lesser judges and judicial officers were to be appointed and removed by the governor. Juries were to be selected by the sheriff instead of elected locally. No more than one town meeting could be held yearly without prior consent of the governor.

The **Administration of Justice Act** (May 1774) permitted the governor, with the assent of the Provincial Council, to transfer to Britain the trial of any royal official accused of a capital offense.

The **Quartering Act** (May 1774) accompanied the appointment of Gen. Thomas Gage, commander of the British army in North America, to the post of governor of Massachusetts. Gage anticipated that four regiments of troops would be sufficient to restore order in Boston, and this act provided for their accommodation—in private dwellings if need be.

The **Quebec Act** (May 1774) was not regarded by Parliament as one of the Coercive Acts, but the colonists found it intolerable nonetheless. It organized the government of Quebec on centralized, authoritarian French lines. The governor and legislative council were to be appointed by the crown, and legislation was subject to a royal veto. Civil trials would be held without juries. Catholics were granted complete civil rights, and existing privileges of the Catholic Church were confirmed. Most alarming to the 13 colonies, the border of Quebec was extended to the Ohio and Mississippi Rivers, bringing into question the western land claims of several seaboard colonies.

Rather than pacifying Massachusetts and Boston, the Intolerable Acts led directly to the convening of the *Continental Congress.

IRAN-CONTRA AFFAIR (1985–92), episode of the *Reagan administration. Zealously anticommunist, the Reagan administration supported rebel forces (the Contras) fighting the legal but left-wing Sandinista government of Nicaragua until Congress, in 1984, prohibited further aid. Members of the National Security Council staff then sought other sources of money. One secret expedient was to sell American arms to Iran, then engaged in a costly war with Iraq, and divert the profits from these sales to the Nicaraguan Contras. A secondary objective was to persuade Iran to order its terrorist clients in Lebanon to release seven American hostages (see *Lebanon Hostages). This enterprise violated the congressional prohibition of further aid to the Contras; a U.S. arms embargo against Iran (the United States officially supported Iraq in the Iran-Iraq War); and U.S. policy against exchanging arms for hostages.

Revealed in November 1986, the Iran-Contra scheme was investigated by a presidential commission (the Tower Commission), a joint committee of Congress, and an *independent counsel. Pres. Ronald Reagan was criticized for lax management (he may, in fact, have been a party to the scheme), and criminal indictments were returned against a number of participants. The convictions of National Security Adviser John M. Poindexter and his aide, Lt. Col. Oliver L. North, were overturned. In 1992 Pres. George H. W. Bush pardoned six others indicted or convicted in the affair.

IRANIAN HOSTAGE CRISIS (1989–91), episode in the *Carter administration. Deposed in the fundamentalist Iranian revolution in 1978, Shah Muhammad Reza Pahlavi, a former U.S. client, was permitted to come to the United States for treatment for terminal cancer. In retaliation, militant Iranian students on Nov. 4, 1979, seized the U.S. embassy in Tehran, taking its 53 occupants hostage for the shah's return.

All of Pres. James E. Carter's efforts to secure the release of the hostages—including an air rescue mission in April 1980 that met disaster in the desert 250 miles southeast of Tehran—proved futile, and his failure was a major factor in his defeat for reelection in November. Finally, Algeria intervened and negotiated a settlement whereby the United States released $8 billion in Iranian assets in exchange for the hostages. The hostages were released on Jan. 20, 1981, hours after Ronald Reagan was inaugurated president.

IRONCLAD OATHS. See *Test Oath Cases.

IRRECONCILABLES (1919–20), during the *Wilson administration, 16 U.S. senators unalterably opposed to the Treaty of Versailles (which included the covenant of the League of Nations) although for different reasons. Some were isolationists—notably William E. Borah of Idaho and Hiram W. Johnson of California. Others were conservative internationalists—notably Philander C. Knox of Pennsylvania, Joseph Medill McCormick of Illinois, and Miles Poindexter of Washington. Still others were "peace progressives," sympathetic to the early Wilsonian goal of "peace without victory"; these included Robert M. La Follette of Wisconsin and George W. Norris of Nebraska.

ISOLATIONISTS (1933–41), during the Franklin *Roosevelt administration, members of Congress concerned to preserve U.S. sovereignty (freedom of action) by avoiding membership in international organizations and "entangling alliances" with other countries that might involve the United States in foreign wars. They were not pacifists—they believed in active defense of the Western Hemisphere and were prepared to pursue U.S. interests aggressively. Nor were they necessarily conservatives, although most were Republicans—some were progressives in domestic affairs who believed that the United States could best lead the world by setting an isolated example rather than by risky participation in world affairs. By and large, their views reflected an American past when foreign events had little impact on American consciousness and when Americans believed that they were uniquely protected by geography in the working-out of their national destiny. It was a view bound to be made obsolete by the integration of world markets and by the development of modern means of communication that reduced the effectiveness of America's ocean ramparts.

Some of the isolationists responsible for U.S. rejection of membership in the League of Nations (see *Irreconcilables) were still in Congress during the Roosevelt administration. These included Republican senators William E. Borah of Idaho, Hiram Johnson of California, and George W. Norris of Nebraska, and Rep. Hamilton Fish of New York. These were joined in the 1920s and 1930s by Republican senators Arthur Capper of Kansas, Robert La Follette Jr. of Wisconsin, Gerald P. Nye of North Dakota, Henrik Shipstead of Minnesota, Robert A. Taft of Ohio, and Arthur Vandenburg of Michigan, and by Democratic senators Bennett Champ Clark of Missouri and Burton K. Wheeler of Montana. Besides reflecting the sentiments of their (mostly) Middle Western and Great Plains states, they probably reflected at first the view of 80 percent of the American public. The public's view—if not that of the isolationists—gradually changed during the 1930s under the force of events and Roosevelt's skilled leadership.

Beginning in July 1940 (after the fall of France and the beginning of Roosevelt's active intervention in *World War 2), isolationist sentiment outside Congress was mobilized by the *America First Committee. In the presidential election of 1940, both major parties were led by interventionists. *Pearl Harbor put an end to the debate and united Americans for war.

ISRAEL RECOGNITION (May 14, 1948), diplomatic move of the *Truman administration. In 1947, Great Britain announced that it would resign its mandate in Palestine and return it to the United Nations on May 14, 1948. On Nov. 29, 1947, the UN voted (with U.S. support) to partition Palestine into two independent states, Arab and Jewish. The Jews accepted partition, the Arabs promised war.

In the aftermath of the Holocaust (see *Holocaust Response), Pres. Harry S. Truman regarded the establishment of a Jewish state in Palestine as an act of justice and humanity. He was, of course, not unmindful of the political consequences of his support: Jewish voters in New York, Pennsylvania, and Illinois could very well determine the electoral votes of those states in the 1948 presidential election. The State Department, which had a reputation of anti-Semitism and pro-Arabism, opposed the establishment of a Jewish state. Along with the Defense Department and the Central Intelligence Agency, it argued that the U.S. national interest depended upon access to Arab oil. Secretary of State George C. Marshall believed that support for a Jewish state could only be politically motivated.

Despite his sympathy for the Jewish cause, Truman was irritated and exhausted by Zionist pressure to adhere to partition and statehood. At one point he wavered and supported as a temporary expedient a State Department position favoring a UN trusteeship for Palestine. But two meetings with Chaim Weizmann, the 74-year-old world Zionist leader and future first president of Israel—the second meeting arranged, over Truman's resistance, by Eddie Jacobson, the president's onetime business partner—had deeply impressed him, and he had given Weizmann his personal promise to support statehood.

A day after Truman's second meeting with Weizmann, Warren Austin, the U.S. ambassador to the UN, voicing Marshall's understanding of the situation, told the General Assembly that the United States was abandoning its support for partition and now favored a UN trusteeship. The Zionists cried betrayal and the press accused the administration of vacillation and ineptitude. Truman in turn accused the State Department of reversing U.S. policy and reaffirmed his support for partition.

On May 12, two days before the expiration of the British mandate, high administration officials met in the president's office to discuss recognition of the Jewish state. Marshall's vehement opposition stunned Truman, who feared his secretary of state might resign. On the afternoon of May 14, however, Marshall informed the president that he would not oppose him publicly. That evening, at 6 p.m. Washington time—midnight in Jerusalem—the State of Israel was proclaimed in Jerusalem. Eleven minutes later, the White House announced de facto recognition. The next day, five Arab armies attacked the fledgling state.

IWO JIMA. See *World War 2.

J

JACKSON ADMINISTRATION (1829–37). Seventh president of the United States, Andrew Jackson was swept into office on a tide of democratic reform (see *Jacksonian Democracy). He believed he had replaced a regime of corrupt elitists, and he was resolved to continue the struggle against privilege wherever he found it. The democratic tone of his administration was epitomized by the postinaugural reception, when a mob of very ordinary citizens stormed the White House.

Jackson immediately found himself beset by domestic problems in his political family. The *Eaton affair divided the cabinet. Vice Pres. John C. Calhoun and Secretary of State Martin Van Buren already competed to be Jackson's successor, a problem solved by the unraveling of Jackson's alliance with Calhoun (see *Jackson and Calhoun). Unhappy with his official cabinet, Jackson preferred to consult his *"kitchen cabinet" until 1831, when he was able to replace his official cabinet with a more congenial one.

Jackson's assault on antidemocratic forces in the country began with his instituting the *spoils system, which he considered a method of dispossessing a class of elite officeholders and rotating public offices among ordinary people. The great bastion of privilege, in his view, was the *Bank of the United States; in the *Bank War, Jackson prevented the renewal of the bank's charter and then dealt the bank a severe blow by removing federal deposits from it. His autocratic behavior in this incident—of the sort that earned him the sobriquet "King Andrew"—led to an unprecedented censure of the president by the Senate (see *Jackson Censure). His distribution of federal deposits to "pet" state banks caused a vast expansion of credit and speculation in *public lands that his Specie Circular (1836) was designed to check. The result was the *Panic of 1837, which blighted the administration of his successor.

A believer in small and frugal government, Jackson opposed federal subsidization of local *internal improvements (see *Maysville Road Veto) but supported national projects, particularly if they related to national defense.

A Southerner sympathetic to states' rights, Jackson was nonetheless a nationalist devoted to the Union. He handled South Carolina's experiment with *nullification with tact (see *Compromise of 1833) backed by determination to use force if necessary. At the same time he deferred to Georgia on Indian questions, preferring to remove the Indians to the trans-Mississippi west rather than use federal troops to enforce their treaty rights against Georgia (see *Indian Removal). When the U.S. Supreme Court ruled against Georgia in *Worcester v. Georgia* (1832), Jackson did nothing to enforce its decision. During his two terms, Jackson appointed a chief justice (Taney) and six associate justices to the Court.

Much to the displeasure of Southerners and Westerners in the Democratic Party, Jackson dictated the party's choice of his successor, Martin Van Buren. Anti-Jackson Democrats and National Republicans united (1836) in the *Whig Party.

During Jackson's administration, Arkansas (1836) and Michigan (1837) became the 25th and 26th states.

JACKSON AND CALHOUN. Vice president in the John Quincy *Adams administration, John C. Calhoun defected to the Andrew Jackson camp and was again elected vice president when Jackson was elected president in 1828. A number of cabinet posts were filled with Calhoun supporters, and Calhoun expected to succeed Jackson as president—although here he had a wily rival in Secretary of State Martin Van Buren (see *Jackson Administration).

The estrangement between Jackson and Calhoun derived inevitably from the conflict between Jackson's frontier egalitarianism and Calhoun's patrician elitism.

Insofar as events played a role, it began with the *Eaton affair, in which Calhoun's wife played a leading role. At some point, Jackson learned that Calhoun was the author of the *South Carolina Exposition and Protest, the fundamental document in the developing *nullification controversy. The differences between the two men on this issue were revealed in the famous Jefferson birthday toasts on Apr. 13, 1830. Jackson offered: "Our Federal Union—it must be preserved!" To which Calhoun responded: "The Union—next to our liberty, the most dear!"

Jackson then learned from William H. Crawford, who had been secretary of the Treasury in the cabinet of Pres. James Monroe, that, contrary to what Calhoun had led Jackson to believe, then secretary of war Calhoun had voted to censure Jackson for his conduct in Florida in 1818 (see *Seminole Wars), a censure prevented only by then secretary of state John Quincy Adams. Confronted with this information, Calhoun could not defend himself. When Jackson reorganized his cabinet in 1831, Calhoun's supporters were dismissed and Calhoun was isolated in the administration. His alienation from Jackson was completed when, in his role as presiding officer of the Senate, he cast the deciding vote in the Senate's rejection of Martin Van Buren's nomination as U.S. minister to Great Britain.

Calhoun resigned as vice president in December 1832 after being elected senator from South Carolina.

JACKSON AND CLAY. The enmity between Andrew Jackson and Henry Clay dated from 1819, when Congress considered censuring the insubordinate general for waging an undeclared war against Spain in his Florida campaign against the Seminoles (see *Seminole Wars). For Clay, Jackson represented a potential rival for the votes of Westerners. Both men were Westerners by adoption—Clay a Kentuckian, Jackson a Tennessean—but of markedly different types: Jackson was the illiterate frontier brawler and iron-fisted soldier; Clay was the "gamester," as John Quincy Adams described him, "with a vigorous intellect, an ardent spirit, a handsome elocution, though with a mind very defective in elementary knowledge, and a very undigested system of ethics. . . ."

Clay seized the opportunity of the congressional debate to try to destroy Jackson's political future. He warned the House, of which he was Speaker, against the danger of military usurpation: "Greece had her Alexander, Rome her Caesar, England her Cromwell, France her Bonaparte." Congress refused to censure Jackson, but the general was mortally offended. When Clay later proffered his friendship, Jackson rebuffed him. "The

hypocrisy & baseness of Clay," Jackson told a friend, "in pretending friendship to me, . . . make me despise the Villain."

In 1824, Clay, having finished fourth in a field of four Republican presidential candidates, threw his influence in the House of Representatives to John Quincy Adams, who was elected although he had won fewer popular votes than Jackson. "[T]he voice of the people of the west have been disregarded," Jackson raged, "and demagogues barter them as sheep in the shambles, for their own views, and personal aggrandisement." When Adams then appointed Clay secretary of state, Jackson was convinced that there had been a *corrupt bargain. "[T]he *Judas* of the West has closed the contract and will receive the thirty pieces of silver. His end will be the same. Was there ever witnessed such a bare faced corruption in any country before?"

In 1832, when Jackson sought a second term as president, Clay ran against him as the candidate of the *National Republican Party. Before the election, Jackson had vetoed a bill to recharter the *Bank of the United States, and Clay believed he could use this issue to defeat the enormously popular Jackson. He failed. But when Jackson, reelected, continued his feud with the bank by removing federal deposits and placing them in state banks, Clay—together with other Jackson opponents, including John C. Calhoun and Daniel Webster—moved to censure the president (see *Jackson Censure). If the veto had been "a perversion of the veto power" (as Clay called it), the removal of deposits was an executive usurpation of the first order.

"The land is filled with spies and informers, and detraction and denunciation are the orders of the day," Clay told the Senate. "People, especially official incumbents in this place, no longer dare speak in the fearless tones of manly freemen, but in the cautious whispers of trembling slaves. The premonitory symptoms of despotism are upon us; and if Congress do not apply an instantaneous and effective remedy, the fatal collapse will soon come on, and we shall die—ignobly die—base, mean, and abject slaves; the scorn and contempt of mankind; unpitied, unwept, unmourned."

"Oh, if I live to get these robes of office off me," Jackson raged, "I will bring the rascal to a dear account."

The censure was passed, but two years later, in 1836, it was expunged from the record. Jackson passed off the Washington stage in 1837, but Clay continued to attribute the country's ills to Jackson's "usurpations."

JACKSON CENSURE (1834–36), incident in the *Jackson administration. Beginning in September 1833,

Pres. Andrew Jackson began removing government money from the *Bank of the United States and depositing it in selected state banks (see *Bank War). Outraged by this high-handed action and the way it was accomplished, Sen. Henry Clay of Kentucky offered a resolution of censure that read in part: "That the President . . . has assumed upon himself authority and power not conferred by the Constitution and laws, but in derogation of both." Clay expected this resolution, passed by the Senate on Mar. 28, 1834, to "destroy" Jackson. Jackson, furious at this unprecedented censure, responded on Apr. 15 with a long justification of his actions and an extreme statement of executive power. (See *Jackson and Clay.)

Two years later, Sen. Thomas Hart Benton of Missouri moved to have the vote of censure expunged from the record. The giants of the Senate—Henry Clay, John C. Calhoun, and Daniel Webster, united in hostility to Jackson—orated against the motion, but it passed, a measure of Jackson's dominance. For Jackson, the expunging was the "crowning mercy" of his political life, as the battle of New Orleans had been of his military life.

JACKSONIAN DEMOCRACY, controversial term
sometimes applied broadly to the political and social currents of the 1830s and sometimes applied narrowly to the policies of Pres. Andrew Jackson and the *Democratic Party.

The period experienced an expansion of *democracy in which Jackson himself played no part. Significant developments included: extension of white male suffrage; greater participation in the political process; emergence of the modern two-party system; appearance of the national party *nominating convention in place of the elite *caucus; popular election of presidential electors; and a great number and variety of humanitarian reform movements.

For many Americans, Jackson—if he was not responsible for these developments—nevertheless embodied the expanding democratic spirit. Although aristocratic in lifestyle and autocratic in political style, he was an authentic democrat, having absorbed the egalitarian ethos of the southwestern frontier. Like Jefferson, he believed in the natural goodness of the common people, by which he meant white farmers, mechanics, and laborers. Unlike Jefferson, he distrusted elites. He believed in majority rule and that, as president, he personified the will of the majority (see *Jackson Administration).

His consistent object was to destroy privilege, to rid the country of the influence of the corrupt "moneyed aristocracy" represented most notably in the *Bank of the United States (see *Bank War). By instituting the *spoils system, he believed he was abolishing an elite of-

ficeholding class. Because privileged elitists always managed to use government institutions for their own profit, he was necessarily a "small government" man and a strict constructionist. He advocated direct election of the president, popular election of senators and judges, term limits, and the right of voters to instruct their representatives. No agency of government, he believed, not even the courts, should be able to obstruct the majority's exercise of its will.

Jacksonian democracy did not extend to slaves. A slave owner himself, Jackson considered opposition to slavery "unconstitutional and wicked" because property was inviolable. *Abolitionists he classified among antidemocratic elites, and he proposed prohibiting the circulation by mail of abolitionist literature in the South.

JACKSON'S DEATH (May 10, 1863). His devoted
troops called him "Old Jack" although he was only 39 when he died. A zealous Presbyterian, exacting commander, and stern disciplinarian, Confederate general Thomas Jonathan Jackson was also so eccentric that some of his associates thought he was insane. He won his sobriquet "Stonewall" at First *Bull Run. His campaign in the Shenandoah Valley in 1862 prevented the Federals from reenforcing their army before Richmond (see *Jackson's Valley Campaign). He served Gen. Robert E. Lee brilliantly at Second *Bull Run, *Antietam, *Fredericksburg, and *Chancellorsville.

Shortly after nine o'clock on the first night of Chancellorsville (May 2, 1863), while Jackson and his staff were returning from a reconnaissance in the dense Wilderness, they were fired upon by rattled Confederate infantry. One ball struck Jackson in his left arm just below the shoulder, severing an artery and smashing the bone; another passed through his left forearm and a third hit his right hand. In the firing, his horse bolted and Jackson's head crashed into a tree branch.

The surviving members of his party placed Jackson, bleeding profusely and in great pain, upon the ground under a pine tree. Eventually a litter was brought and Jackson was carried through the burning woods under Federal artillery fire out to a road where he was placed in a crowded ambulance and carried to a field hospital. There surgeons amputated his left arm. The next day he was carried beyond the battle some 24 miles to a plantation at Guiney's Station.

In a small house, attended by army physicians, Jackson began to recover. But by the time his wife, Anna, arrived on May 7 pneumonia had set in. Heavily sedated, slipping in and out of consciousness, in his delirium he was again with his troops. He weakened rapidly. On

Sunday, May 10, he was told he would die that day. "It is the Lord's day," he replied. "I have always desired to die on Sunday." Sinking into unconsciousness, at 3:30 p.m. he said distinctly "Let us cross over the river and rest under the shade of the trees" and died.

JACKSON'S VALLEY CAMPAIGN (March–June 1862), in the *Civil War, a series of battles in Virginia's Shenandoah Valley by which fast-moving Confederate general Thomas J. "Stonewall" Jackson, with 16,000 troops—the famed "foot cavalry"—kept nearly three times that number of Union troops engaged and thus unable to reenforce Union general George B. McClellan in the *Peninsula Campaign. In June, Jackson and his troops joined Confederate general Robert E. Lee for the Seven Days' Battles that closed the Peninsula Campaign.

JAMESTOWN (1607–99), first settlement of English colonizers in Virginia, on a marshy island in the James River. Of about 100 original settlers, 60 died during the first year. The survivors, helped by friendly Indians, were augmented by 120 new arrivals in December 1608. During 1609 Capt. John Smith's firm governance—he required all men, including gentlemen, to work—averted disaster, but Smith's return to England late in 1609 was followed by a "starving time" during the winter of 1609-10 when 90 percent of the settlers died.

Prosperity began with the cultivation of tobacco, the arrival of African laborers in 1619, and the establishment at Jamestown of the Virginia legislative assembly in 1622. But the colony's population settled on tobacco plantations along the many navigable rivers in the neighborhood rather than in the town. By 1629 Jamestown had only 124 inhabitants. Jamestown was burned in 1678 and again in 1698, after which the colonial government was moved to Williamsburg and the old town left to decay.

JAPANESE-AMERICAN RELOCATION (1942–46), removal from West Coast "military zones" of over 110,000 Americans of Japanese descent, two-thirds of them American citizens, and confinement in relocation centers during World War 2. They were compelled to dispose of their property, then transported to ten relocation centers in California, Arizona, Utah, Wyoming, and Arkansas where they lived in tar-paper barracks guarded by armed troops. A quarter were paroled before the end of the war on condition that they not return to their former homes. The last were not released until 1946.

The episode was a product of wartime hysteria—in December 1941 residents of the West Coast lived in fear of Japanese air raids and even a Japanese invasion—and of the racial prejudice endemic in the region, which now saw Japanese-Americans as members of the "enemy race." There had been espionage by Japanese living in Hawaii, and Japanese-Americans on the West Coast suspected of disloyalty were promptly rounded up by the Federal Bureau of Investigation after *Pearl Harbor. Of the great majority, no evidence of disloyalty was ever produced. More than 1,000 Japanese-Americans enlisted in the army from the relocation centers and fought with distinction in Italy in the segregated 442nd Combat Team.

In three cases arising out of the relocation, the U.S. Supreme Court avoided the constitutional issue by deferring to unproved "military necessity." In April 1988, Congress voted a formal apology and a grant of $20,000 to each survivor of the relocation.

JAPANESE EXCLUSION. Japanese immigrants began to arrive on the West Coast in the 1890s; by 1910 they numbered nearly 130,000, mostly laborers. Like the Chinese, they encountered hostility and ostracism, besides arousing renewed fear of the "yellow peril." In 1900 the Japanese government voluntarily agreed to limit the emigration of laborers to the United States, but Japanese laborers continued to reach the United States through Mexico and Hawaii. When in 1906 the San Francisco school board proposed to establish segregated schools for Oriental children, Pres. Theodore Roosevelt persuaded it to desist while he, under an act of Congress passed in February 1907, personally negotiated with Japan a **Gentlemen's Agreement** by which Japan agreed to stop the emigration of laborers to the United States and Roosevelt agreed to block exclusionary legislation, to which Japan was extremely sensitive.

Congress never passed a Japanese exclusion law as it had (in 1882) a Chinese exclusion law, but neither did it revise the law governing naturalization, which prescribed (in 1790) that only a "free white person" and (in 1870) "persons of African descent" could be admitted to citizenship. On the basis of this language, the U.S. Supreme Court in 1922 ruled that Japanese were not eligible for naturalization—although many Japanese and Chinese had in fact been naturalized and the United States had, by annexing Hawaii, extended its citizenship to Japanese, Chinese, and others who were neither white nor black. The Immigration Act of 1924 (see *Immigration) then prohibited the immigration of "aliens ineligible for citizenship." Anti-American demonstrations erupted in Japan, and in Tokyo on July 1, 1924, the Japanese observed "Humiliation Day."

The McCarran-Walter Immigration Act of 1952 eliminated race as a bar to immigration and naturalization and set a quota for Japan of 185 immigrants per year. The Immigration Act of 1965 replaced national quotas with hemisphere quotas, effectively ending discrimination against Japanese and others. From 1991 through 1998, 50,000 immigrants from Japan entered the United States.

JAPANESE OCCUPATION (1945–52). Stunned by the sudden and calamitous end of *World War 2, the Japanese passively accepted Allied occupation. In theory, it was an international occupation, supervised by a 13-nation Far Eastern Commission in Washington and a four-power Allied Council for Japan in Tokyo. In fact, the occupation was directed by U.S. general Douglas MacArthur with American and some British troops. Its object was to transform Japan from a militaristic to a democratic society.

The Japanese empire was dissolved, Japanese troops and civilians overseas were brought home, the Japanese armed forces were demobilized, and the Japanese armaments industry was dismantled. Twenty-five wartime leaders were tried for war crimes (see *War Crimes Trials); seven were hanged. Two hundred thousand former politicians, officers, and businessmen were barred from public office. Ultranationalist organizations were banned, the Shinto religion was disestablished, and political prisoners were released.

Land was redistributed from large landowners to tenants in ten-acre lots. Eighty-three large *zaibatsu*—banking and industrial holding companies—were dissolved and the formation of labor unions was encouraged.

A new constitution, drafted by occupation authorities, went into effect in 1947. The emperor was retained as a symbol of national unity but was stripped of political power; his position derived from the people's rather than divine will. Both houses of the Diet (parliament) were made elective, all men and women aged 20 and above given the vote. Governors of prefectures and mayors of municipalities were also made elective. The judiciary was made independent, the supreme court empowered to pass on the constitutionality of the Diet's legislation. A list of civil and human rights—more extensive than those recognized in the West—were given constitutional sanction. In Article 9 of the constitution, "the Japanese people forever renounce[d] war as a sovereign right of the nation" and rejected the maintenance of armed forces.

On Sept. 9, 1951, the United States and 47 other countries—but not the Soviet Union or Communist China—signed a peace treaty with Japan. The same day, the United States and Japan signed a mutual security treaty in which Japan granted the United States the right to maintain military bases in Japan and agreed to establish a small National Security Force while the United States guaranteed Japan's security.

The occupation ended on Apr. 28, 1952, an independent Japan taking its place in the *cold war defense perimeter of the United States opposite the Soviet Union and China.

JAPAN OPENING (1853–58). Except for a Dutch trading post at Nagasaki, Japan had been hermetically sealed to foreigners for 250 years when, on July 8, 1853, Commodore Matthew C. Perry appeared in Yedo (Tokyo) Bay with two steam and two sail warships bearing a letter from U.S. president Millard Fillmore to the emperor of Japan. Fillmore requested protection for shipwrecked American sailors (theretofore routinely executed), the right of reprovisioning for American ships, and trading privileges at one or more Japanese ports.

Rejecting a command to go to Nagasaki, Perry presented Fillmore's letter to Japanese officials at an elaborate ceremony at Yedo on July 14, then took his fleet to the Chinese coast while the Japanese considered their reply. He returned in February 1854 with seven ships. Near present-day Yokohama he signed (Mar. 31) the Treaty of Kanagawa, by which the Japanese acceded to the American requests, opening two ports for trade. Perry returned to the United States in 1855.

In 1855 New York merchant Townsend Harris was appointed American consul in Japan, where in 1858 he negotiated additional treaties opening other ports, granting Americans rights of residence, and establishing diplomatic relations between the two countries. The arrival of a Japanese delegation in the summer of 1860 created a sensation in New York.

JAY'S TREATY (1794), diplomatic achievement of the *Washington administration settling troublesome issues between the United States and Great Britain arising out of the Treaty of *Paris (1783) and later events.

Issues arising from the peace treaty included: continued British occupation of posts in the U.S. Northwest; failure of U.S. courts to enforce payment of prewar private debts owed to British creditors; confiscation of the estates of returning *Loyalists; and claims of U.S. slave owners for slaves taken by the British during the *Revolutionary War.

Issues arising after 1783 included: British intrigue with Indians in the Northwest; British refusal to admit U.S. ships in West Indies ports; and, most urgently, British seizure of U.S. ships and *impressment of American seamen incidental to the ongoing Anglo-French war. By early 1794, this last issue threatened to involve the two countries in war.

For Pres. George Washington, peace was essential. U.S. revenues were largely derived from tariffs, and nine-tenths of tariff income came from British imports. War, or even a temporary suspension of commerce, would destroy U.S. credit. In April 1794 Washington dispatched John Jay, chief justice of the United States, as special envoy to Britain to negotiate a comprehensive settlement of all outstanding differences.

The treaty that Jay signed on Nov. 19, 1794, provided for (among other things): British evacuation of the Northwest posts by June 1796; referral to mixed commissions of private debts, compensation for British seizure of U.S. ships, and settlement of northern boundary questions; placing of British trade with the United States on a most-favored-nation basis (no discriminatory tariffs or tonnage duties); opening of the West Indies to U.S. vessels under 70 tons, but prohibiting them from carrying molasses, sugar, coffee, cocoa, and cotton. Britain did not acknowledge the illegality of its interference with neutral shipping, and the treaty was silent on impressment, Indians, captured slaves, and Loyalists' claims.

When the terms of the treaty became known in the United States (March 1795), Republicans condemned it as a betrayal of American interests by a pro-British and monarchically inclined Federalist administration. It was "an infamous act," fumed Thomas Jefferson, ". . . a treaty of alliance between England and the Anglomen of this country against the legislature and people of the United States." A furious controversy ensued, but the treaty averted war and Washington, after long hesitation, sent it to the Senate, where it was ratified (June 24, 1795) except for the article on the West Indies trade.

JEFFERSON ADMINISTRATION (1801–9). Thomas Jefferson, third president of the United States, established a tone of simplicity and frugality at the start of his administration. On Mar. 4, 1801, eschewing the ceremonial trappings enjoyed by his predecessors, he walked in a plain brown suit from his boardinghouse in Washington, D.C., to the Capitol for his inauguration. In his address his tone was conciliatory and reasonable: "[E]very difference of opinion," he said, "is not a difference of principle. We have called by different names brethren of the same principle. We are all Republicans, we are all Federalists. If there be any among us who wish to dissolve this Union or to change its republican form, let them stand undisturbed as monuments to the safety with which error of opinion may be tolerated where reason is left free to combat it."

Jefferson's political philosophy—strict construction of the Constitution, deference to the coequal branches of the federal government, respect for states' rights—promised a government of harmony and collegiality. But Jefferson was strong-willed, determined to control the legislative branch no less than the executive, and prepared to contest the independence of the Federalist-dominated judiciary.

At his behest, a willing Congress revised the Naturalization Act of 1798 (see *Alien and Sedition Acts) and repealed the *Judiciary Act of 1801, abolished all internal taxes ("what farmer, what mechanic, what laborer, ever sees a tax gatherer of the United States?" he asked in his second inaugural), reduced the army and navy to skeletons, "downsized" the federal establishment, and shrank the national debt. But strongly held principles bent before political exigencies. Frugal and pacific, Jefferson nevertheless employed the fleet built in the John *Adams administration to wage (1801–5) a successful war against Tripoli (see *Barbary Wars). He had to override constitutional scruples to consummate the *Louisiana Purchase and to dispatch the *Lewis and Clark Expedition. After *Marbury v. Madison, the removal of one Federalist judge (John Pickering in New Hampshire), and the failed impeachment of a justice of the U.S. Supreme Court (see *Chase Impeachment), he abandoned his war against the judiciary.

Jefferson was reelected in a landslide in 1804, but his second term was marked by frustration and failure. In 1807 he was outraged at the acquittal of Aaron Burr on treason charges when he had already pronounced Burr guilty (see *Burr Conspiracy). But foreign affairs were his chief concern. Britain and France, again at war after 1803, enforced their blockades of each other at the expense of neutral shipping. After the *Chesapeake affair, the country demanded war with Britain, but Jefferson responded with his favored policy of economic coercion by embargoing all American overseas commerce (see *Embargo and Nonintercourse). To enforce the embargo, Jefferson wielded unprecedented federal powers heavy-handedly and intrusively but succeeded only in causing hardship and disaffection in the commercial states. Frustrated and eager to return to private life, he abandoned the problem to his successor, James Madison.

During the Jefferson administration, Ohio (1803) became the 17th state.

JEFFERSON AND ADAMS. See *Adams and Jefferson.

JEFFERSON AND HAMILTON. See *Hamilton and Jefferson.

JEFFERSON AND MADISON. Thomas Jefferson and James Madison met in 1776 in the Virginia House of Delegates. Jefferson, 33 years old and already the author of the Declaration of Independence, was eight years Madison's senior, and Madison willingly accepted junior status in what was to prove a 40-year collaboration in Virginia and national politics. But though younger, Madison was the wiser of the two, a deeper student of history and politics, and the greater realist. The brilliant Jefferson, a man of the Enlightenment, was interested in everything, fascinated by ideas although sometimes indifferent to their consequences.

Both men were republicans (see *Republic), committed to the sovereignty of the people. But Jefferson—in theory, at least—was a radical democrat, trusting ultimately in a wise and virtuous people, whereas Madison saw the people as passionate and motivated by self-interest. Thus Jefferson's casual response to *Shays's Rebellion (which horrified Madison): "I like a little rebellion now and then. It is like a storm in the Atmosphere" and "The tree of liberty must be refreshed from time to time with the blood of patriots and tyrants."

He shocked Madison again when he took up the notion that "the earth belongs to the living." "[B]y the law of nature," Jefferson deduced from this principle, "one generation is to another as one independent nation to another. . . . [N]o society can make a perpetual constitution, or even a perpetual law. . . . Every constitution then, and every law, naturally expires at the end of 19 years [his calculation of the length of a generation]."

In 1793 Jefferson hotly defended the Jacobin Terror in revolutionary France (see *French Revolution). "In the struggle which was necessary, many guilty persons fell without the forms of trial, and with them some innocent. . . . The liberty of the whole earth was depending on the issue of the contest, and was ever such a prize won with so little innocent blood? . . . [R]ather than it should have failed, I would have seen half the earth desolated. Were there but an Adam & an Eve left in every country, & left free, it would be better than as it now is."

Jefferson's favored solution to any constitutional question was to consult the whole people, reassembled in their primal conventions. Of course, the "people" to whom Jefferson would appeal existed only in his fantasy of an agrarian Arcadia. "Those who labour in the earth are the chosen people of God," he wrote in *Notes on the State of Virginia*, "if ever he had a chosen people, whose breasts he has made his peculiar deposit for substantial and genuine virtue. . . . Corruption of morals in the mass of cultivators is a phaenomenon of which no age nor nation has furnished an example. . . . The mobs of great cities add just so much to the support of pure government, as sores do to the strength of the human body."

Madison had no romantic illusions about the nature of the "people," whose governments of various states during the *Confederation had been characterized by faction, injustice, and instability. "Liberty," observed Madison in *Federalist* No. 10, "is to faction, what air is to fire."

"So strong is this propensity of mankind to fall into mutual animosities," he continued, "that where no substantial occasion presents itself, the most frivolous and fanciful distinctions have been sufficient to kindle their unfriendly passions, and excite their most violent conflicts. But the most common and durable source of factions, has been the various and unequal distribution of property. Those who hold, and those who are without property, have ever formed distinct interests in society. Those who are creditors, and those who are debtors, fall under a like discrimination. A landed interest, a manufacturing interest, a mercantile interest, a monied interest, with many lesser interests, grow up of necessity in civilized nations, and divide them into different classes, actuated by different sentiments and views."

For Madison, the great political problem was to contain the passions of a faction-riven people within a just and stable government. He believed that the Constitution's separation of powers and system of checks and balances, but especially the great geographic extent of the new republic, would diminish the undesirable effects of faction and permit governors to pursue the public good. Where Jefferson saw in the Constitution the seeds of tyranny, Madison saw a mechanism creating order and continuity. Where Jefferson saw periodic revolutions and frequent recourse to popular conventions as beneficial, Madison saw them as only generating passion, disorder, and injustice.

Despite their fundamental philosophical differences (always tactfully muted by the deferential Madison), Jefferson and Madison collaborated effectively in opposing the nationalist policies of the Federalist *Washington and John *Adams administrations on the grounds of strict constructionism (see *Jeffersonian Republican Party).

But when they succeeded to the presidency in turn, they proved no less nationalist. Jefferson was a strong-willed president who dominated Congress and expanded federal powers (see *Jefferson Administration; *Louisiana Purchase; *Embargo and Nonintercourse). Madison, an ineffective war president (see *Madison Administration), nevertheless closed his administration advocating a program that broke with the Old Republicans of small government and states' rights and inaugurated the *National Republican Party.

JEFFERSONIAN REPUBLICAN PARTY or DEMOCRATIC-REPUBLICAN PARTY, one of the nation's first two political parties, the other being the *Federalist Party.

The Republican Party arose in opposition to the economic policies of the *Washington administration effected by Secretary of the Treasury Alexander Hamilton, which, while establishing the public credit and resources of the federal government, seemed to benefit unduly Northeast financial, commercial, and manufacturing groups. Its leaders, Secretary of State Thomas Jefferson in the cabinet and James Madison in the House of Representatives, challenged the "loose construction" of the Constitution by which Hamilton aggrandized the power of the federal government at the expense of states' rights and Southern agrarians. Federalist and Republican "interests" divided further over the *French Revolution, the Republicans being ardently pro-French, the Federalists strongly pro-British. The controversy over *Jay's Treaty (1794) saw the two "interests" transformed into political parties with their own newspapers and national organizations.

The Jacobin revolution that the Federalists feared would follow the election of Jefferson (president 1801–9) failed to materialize, and Jefferson himself proved to be a strong-willed loose constructionist. Indeed, the Republicans pragmatically embraced Federalist principles of strong government. A minority of Old Republicans preserved the original commitment to small government and states' rights, a position now increasingly adopted by the Federalists, who were compelled to oppose the reigning Republicans on any grounds.

Under James Madison (president 1809–17) and James Monroe (president 1817–25, the so-called *Era of Good Feelings), the Republicans faced no viable national opposition. (The Federalists nominated a presidential candidate for the last time in 1816.) Fragmenting into sectional and personal factions, and facing new issues like *tariffs and *internal improvements, the party gradually formed "national" and "democratic" wings, the former represented by John Quincy Adams (president 1825–29), the latter by Andrew Jackson (president 1829–37). From these evolved the *National Republican Party and the *Democratic Party.

JEWS. The first Jews in America arrived in *New Amsterdam from Brazil in 1654. Twenty-three men, women, and children, they were descendants of the Jews—Sephardim—who had been expelled from Spain in 1492, some of whom had found refuge in Holland. When the Dutch occupied a portion of Portuguese Brazil, some of these Jews migrated there. With the return of the Portuguese (and the Inquisition), they fled to tolerant Dutch New Amsterdam. By 1750 there were Sephardic congregations in New York, Newport, Savannah, Philadelphia, and Charleston. In 1790, the U.S. Jewish population was about 2,000.

By then, Jews from Central and Eastern Europe—Ashkenazim—were beginning to arrive. Their numbers increased after 1815 as a result of the political reaction and economic distress in Europe following the Napoleonic Wars. German Jews predominated. Frequently they became peddlers in the South and West before achieving the status of merchants. They rapidly acculturated and entered the middle class. Cincinnati and San Francisco were flourishing Jewish centers. By 1880 there were 250,000 Jews in the United States, predominantly of German origin.

Beginning in 1882, Jewish migrants from Eastern Europe—Russia (including Poland) and the Austro-Hungarian Empire—began coming in great numbers, driven from their homelands by oppression and economic hardship. Generally young and often skilled workers, they crowded into the tenements of great cities like New York, Philadelphia, and Chicago, working under sweatshop conditions in the clothing and tobacco industries. With the assistance of the more affluent German Jews (whose social acceptance was endangered by the arrival of the impoverished East European Jewish masses), the newcomers zealously pursued education, economic advancement, and Americanization. In 1927 (three years after mass immigration had been cut off; see *Immigration), there were 4.2 million Jews in the United States, 80 percent of them of East European origin.

Due in part to restrictive national immigration quotas, Jewish immigration was slight during the Great Depression and World War 2 (which were also the years of Hitler and the Holocaust in Europe; see *Holocaust Response). Some Jewish *refugees were admitted after the war, but there was no other major Jewish immigration until the 1980s, when several hundred thousand Soviet Jews arrived.

At the end of the 20th century, the Jewish population of the United States was estimated at 6 million, 2.2 percent of the total U.S. population. (Because of low fertility and intermarriage, it was in fact declining.) Foreign-born constituted 9 percent (for the population as a whole, the rate of foreign-born was 10 percent). Forty percent of American Jews lived in the Northeast, most of them in the New York–New Jersey–Long Island metropolitan area. Outside New York, the largest Jewish concentrations were in the Los Angeles and Miami metropolitan areas. According to a 1998 American Jewish Committee survey, American Jews were more likely (39 to 23 percent) to describe themselves as "liberal" than "conservative"; 52 percent identified themselves as Democrats, 30 percent as independents, and 16 percent as Republicans. In 1990, the National Opinion Center at the University of Chicago reported that, of 33 U.S. ethnic groups studied, Jews ranked first in household income and third in years of schooling, but were rated only 17th in "social standing."

JIM CROW LAWS(1890–1910), laws passed by Southern states and localities at the end of the 19th century legally segregating the black and white races.

Before the Civil War, segregation had been almost universal in the North (see *Free Blacks) but unusual in the rural South where slavery brought the races into close contact. For a generation after the war, through *Reconstruction and the *New South, Southern segregation was largely confined to schools, hospitals, and other institutions. In Southern cities, blacks patronized railroads, streetcars, theaters, restaurants, bars, and parks without incident. In the rural South, where the great majority of blacks lived, they were subjected to the terror of white supremacists (see *Ku Klux Klan; *Lynching). Nevertheless, throughout the South in this period, blacks—patronized first by *Radical Republicans and then by upper-class conservative Democrats (see *Bourbons)—voted in large numbers, served on juries, held many minor political offices, and sat in state legislatures and even in the U.S. Congress.

Late in the century, the country experienced a wave of Negrophobia. In the North, liberals had tired of the "Negro question" and sought reconciliation with the South by accepting Southern views—which were not very different from their own—on racial matters. In a series of notable decisions, the U.S. Supreme Court nullified the promises of protection extended to the freedmen by the *14th Amendment and the *Civil Rights Acts (see *Slaughterhouse Cases, *Civil Rights Cases). In the South, agricultural distress (see *Agrarian Discontents)

loosened the influence of the traditional conservative white leadership, permitting an upwelling of extreme racism among poor whites that quickly reversed the South's 25-year accommodation with the freedmen. This was the climate in which Jim Crow flourished.

The first assault, beginning in Mississippi in 1890, was the disfranchisement of blacks by means of poll taxes, property requirements, literacy tests, and white primaries that received the sanction of the Supreme Court in *Williams v. Mississippi (1898). In rapid succession, segregation was required in railroad cars (sanctioned by the Court in *Plessy v. Ferguson, 1896), waiting rooms, and at ticket windows; on streetcars, in workplaces, and in state institutions; in theaters, bars, restaurants, parks, and even drinking fountains. Segregation so complete had never been known in the South before, but it was immediately represented as the traditional Southern way of life, the legal enactment of ancient custom.

Legal segregation in the South (there was little *legal* segregation in the North) was not overturned until after World War 2 (see *Civil Rights Movement; *Brown v. Board of Education of Topeka).

JOHN BIRCH SOCIETY. See *Radical Right.

JOHNSON (ANDREW) ADMINISTRATION (1865–69). Andrew Johnson, 17th president of the United States, succeeded to the presidency on the death of Abraham Lincoln. A Democratic senator from Tennessee, he was the only Southern senator to remain loyal to the Union in the *secession crisis. In 1862 Lincoln appointed him military governor of occupied Tennessee, and in 1864 he was nominated for the vice presidency by the National Union Party, a wartime coalition of Republicans and War Democrats.

As president, Johnson was disowned by the Democrats and had little in common with the Republicans. He was, in fact, an old-fashioned Jacksonian Democrat who shared with his hero—in addition to a passionate Unionism—belief in strict construction of the Constitution, limited federal government and states' rights, faith in the small independent farmer as the backbone of the nation, and dislike of social privilege and economic power. By 1864, these views were antithetical to those of the Republicans. Having risen from very humble origins, Johnson nourished a profound hostility to the planter aristocrats who had governed the South and led it into war—causing the *Radical Republicans briefly to believe he was sympathetic to their desire for a vengeful peace.

But he had also been a slave owner, and he shared the Southern poor white's contempt for the black man.

Johnson preserved Lincoln's cabinet and proceeded to carry out a conciliatory policy of *reconstruction. During his first eight months in office, while Congress was in recess, Johnson oversaw the reconstruction of eight Confederate states (three had been reconstructed by Lincoln), but his hopes for an egalitarian South led by white yeoman farmers were dashed when Southern voters returned to office many traditional Southern leaders, to whom Johnson now gave wholesale pardons. Convinced that Johnson had given away the fruits of victory, the Republican Congress determined to repudiate his reconstruction program and institute one of its own founded on the enfranchisement of the freedmen. Johnson's opposition to black suffrage—indeed, to any special treatment for the vulnerable freedmen—prevented any accommodation with Congress.

Stubborn, pugnacious, intemperate (see *Swing Around the Circle), Johnson drove conservative and moderate Republicans into the Radical camp. All the notable legislation of his administration—the New Freedmen's Bureau Act (see *Freedmen's Bureau), the *Civil Rights Act of 1866, the Reconstruction Acts, and the *14th and *15th Amendments—were passed over Johnson's vetoes or opposition. His reconstruction program was overturned, the Johnson state governments being replaced first by military governments, then by Republican regimes led by *carpetbaggers and scalawags supported by black votes. By the Command of the Army Act (1867) and the Tenure of Office Act (1867), his powers as president were diminished, and he himself escaped impeachment by only a single vote (see *Johnson Impeachment).

In foreign affairs, the firm line taken by Secretary of State William H. Seward toward the French intervention in Mexico contributed to Napoleon III's decision to abandon (1867) the puppet emperor Maximilian. Seward also negotiated (1867) the purchase of Alaska from Russia (see *Alaska Purchase) and (1868) the *Burlingame Treaty with China.

During the Johnson administration, Nebraska (1867) became the 37th state. Johnson was succeeded by Republican Ulysses S. Grant.

JOHNSON (LYNDON) ADMINISTRATION

(1963–69). Democratic vice president Lyndon B. Johnson became the 36th president of the United States upon the assassination of Pres. John F. Kennedy.

Not a popular or greatly respected public figure, but ambitious to become a great president, Johnson found it expedient initially to depict himself as Kennedy's heir and efficiently accomplished some unfinished business of the Kennedy administration: an economic stimulus tax cut; the *Civil Rights Act of 1964; and the *Economic Opportunity Act, the centerpiece of the multifaceted **War on Poverty**. In 1964, the Social Security Administration defined a poverty line or threshold according to which more than 20 percent of the population was living in poverty—that is, at or below a subsistence level (see *Poverty). The approach of the War on Poverty was to enlarge opportunities for the disadvantaged through education and job training. The Civil Rights Act of 1964 was an important element in the war, since it enlarged opportunity by prohibiting discrimination in employment on the basis of race and sex.

After the presidential election of 1964, which he won in a landslide and which produced large Democratic majorities in Congress (294–140 in the House, 68–32 in the Senate), Johnson believed he had a mandate to implement the **Great Society**. A torrent of legislation followed, comparable in volume and significance to that of the *New Deal:

Civil Rights. The *Voting Rights Act of 1965; an Open Housing Act (1968) prohibited discrimination in the sale or renting of much housing.

Minimum Wage. Raised the minimum wage and extended coverage to new classes of workers.

Education. The *Elementary and Secondary School Act (1965); the Higher Education Act (1965) provided the first federal college scholarships.

Social Insurance. Medicare, hospital insurance for the aged (1965; see *Social Security).

Welfare. Medicaid, hospital insurance for the poor (1965); the food stamp program (1964; see *Welfare).

Criminal Justice. The Omnibus Crime Control and Safe Streets Act (1968) created the Law Enforcement Assistance Administration in the Justice Department to administer grants to the states for upgrading police training and equipment.

Housing and Urban Affairs. The Urban Mass Transportation Act (1964) subsidized mass transit; the Omnibus Housing Act (1965) provided rent supplements to low-income families; the Department of Housing and Urban Affairs was established in 1965; the Demonstration Cities and Metropolitan Area Redevelopment Act (1966) financed slum rehabilitation; the Area Planning and Housing Act (1968) subsidized the building or rehabilitation of low-income housing (see *Housing).

Immigration. The Immigration Act (1965) ended the national quota system (see *Immigration).

Consumer Protection. The National Traffic and Motor Vehicle Safety Act (1966) required safety standards for all vehicles; the Department of Transportation was established in 1966; the Truth-in-Lending Act (1968) required full disclosure of lending terms (see *Consumer Protection).

Conservation. The Wilderness Preservation Act (1964) preserved certain wilderness areas in their pristine condition; the Scenic Rivers Act (1968); the Redwood and North Cascades National Parks were established in 1968 (see *Conservation).

Environment. Water Quality Act (1965); Air Quality Act (1968); Clear Water Restoration Act (1966; see *Environmentalism).

Cultural Affairs. The National Foundation of the Arts and Humanities was established in 1965; the Public Broadcasting Corporation was established in 1967.

The *24th and *25th Amendments were ratified during the Lyndon Johnson administration.

Johnson, who—unlike Kennedy—was primarily interested in domestic affairs, had hoped that foreign affairs would be quiescent during his administration. The tragedy of Lyndon Johnson was that he became drawn ever deeper into the *Vietnam War, in which all his dreams for the Great Society foundered. In March 1968, he announced that he would not be a candidate for reelection that year. He was succeeded by Republican Richard M. Nixon.

JOHNSON AND McNAMARA. When Lyndon Johnson became president after the assassination of John F. Kennedy in November 1963 (see *Kennedy Assassinations), he inherited a cabinet whose outstanding member was 47-year-old Robert S. McNamara. Briefly president of the Ford Motor Co. when Kennedy appointed him secretary of defense, McNamara with his team of "defense intellectuals" had, in three years, imposed strict budgetary controls on the sprawling defense establishment, reshaped the armed forces, and presided over a massive military buildup. The business community hailed McNamara as a managerial genius. Not so the Pentagon brass, many of whose favorite programs McNamara had challenged and overridden.

A masterful politician, energetic, coarse, and domineering, Johnson burst upon the Oval Office like a hurricane. His ambition was to be a great president in the image of Franklin Roosevelt, and indeed his Great Society program (see Lyndon *Johnson Administration) was comparable in some respects to the *New Deal. But from the start Johnson felt ensnared by the war in Vietnam (see *Vietnam War), where the United States already had 16,000 military

advisers supporting a feeble South Vietnam government. He had "the terrible feeling that something has grabbed me around the ankles and won't let go."

The new president agonized about Vietnam. To be perceived as "soft" on communism—to "lose" Vietnam as Harry Truman had "lost" China (see *China "Loss")—would be political suicide. But the unpredicable duration and potential cost of involvement in Vietnam could destroy the Great Society. Johnson, like most of his advisers, truly believed that an independent South Vietnam was essential to the *containment of communism. The war in Vietnam was another front in the constant expansion of a monolithic communist bloc directed by Moscow. If South Vietnam fell to the communists, other Southeast Asian countries would topple like dominoes. The resolution and credibility of the United States—leader of the free world—were challenged in Vietnam.

Unable to find an acceptable alternative, Johnson finally committed himself to winning that war. "We will not be defeated," he declared in 1965. "We will never grow tired. We will not withdraw, either openly or under the cloak of a meaningless agreement." Nevertheless, to protect the Great Society, he determined to hide the human and economic costs from the American people by secrecy and deception, by half-measures and half-truths.

Johnson was relieved to have the management of the war in McNamara's hands. McNamara had known Johnson only slightly as vice president, but he was quickly impressed by the new president's mastery of his office and by his ambitious domestic program. He became Johnson's loyal lieutenant, willing to follow wherever Johnson led. In turn, Johnson admired and trusted McNamara.

Since 1961, McNamara had managed the U.S. involvement in Vietnam as he had managed Ford—objectively, rationally, quantitatively. Everything countable in Vietnam was counted, and the statistics were analyzed for evidence of progress. At the end of 1963, all McNamara's "measurable indices" predicted success in Vietnam, encouraging him to plan the withdrawal of American advisers by the end of 1965. He was, in fact, misinformed.

The guerrilla war in South Vietnam was then in its fifth year. In the countryside, the communist Vietcong, directed by North Vietnam, moved invisibly among the peasants, alternately courting and terrorizing them, and constantly recruiting new members. They regularly assassinated provincial officials and ambushed government troops; periodically, they inflicted embarrassing defeats on elite army units staffed with American advisers. Areas controlled by the Vietcong expanded steadily. Beginning in the spring of 1964, the Vietcong were joined by North Vietnamese regular troops, infiltrated down the Ho Chi Minh Trail. In Saigon, the South Vietnamese government was unstable, corrupt, and unpopular; generals jockeyed for power, seemingly heedless of their country's moral peril.

A trip to Vietnam in December 1963 alarmed McNamara. He found the Saigon government near collapse and the Vietcong ranging unchecked. U.S. officials, whose careers depended on the perception of success, had discouraged negative assessments; their reports to Washington were false and self-serving, describing nonexistent progress on both the political and military fronts.

McNamara returned to Washington gloomy and apprehensive, but firmly committed to Johnson's decision to stand in Vietnam. The war he now had to manage was strictly limited. There could be no invasion of North Vietnam for fear of provoking China's intervention. Nuclear weapons were ruled out. Nevertheless, it was inconceivable to McNamara that the vast military power of the United States could not prevail in a small agrarian country. Sufficient inputs, he believed, would produce desired results. Subjected to enough pain through prudently calibrated escalations (intended to minimize the risk of Chinese or Soviet intervention), a rational enemy would quit. Missing from this calculus, because unquantifiable, was the enemy's morale.

During 1964, the number of military advisers in South Vietnam was increased to 26,000. Covert penetrations of the north by South Vietnamese were organized and facilitated. One of these—a coastal raid—provoked the North Vietnamese response that Johnson seized upon to obtain passage of the Tonkin Gulf Resolution, which gave him a free hand to wage war in South Vietnam.

By 1965, Johnson—on the strong advice of McNamara and other advisers—had decided that direct U.S. intervention in the war was necessary to prevent a complete South Vietnamese collapse. In March, sustained but limited air attacks on the north were begun from offshore carriers. At the same time, 3,500 marines were deployed to Vietnam to defend the U.S. base at Danang. By the end of 1965, there were 210,000 U.S. troops in Vietnam. In June, huge B-52 bombers based on Guam began attacking "suspected enemy concentrations" in South Vietnam, dropping heavy explosives and napalm on invisible targets. Other planes sprayed herbicides and defoliants to deny the enemy cover. In 1966, another 200,000 troops were sent to Vietnam, and bombing raids on the north increased from 6,000 sorties a month to 12,000.

Despite the escalation, the infiltration of men and matériel from the north increased. Suffering heavy casu-

alties themselves, the communists inflicted significant losses on U.S. troops. In 1967, U.S. battle deaths averaged 1,000 a month. U.S. overtures for negotiation were met with silence. The enemy's resolve showed no sign of weakening.

The carnage wreaked on South Vietnam was televised into American living rooms. Antiwar protests, beginning in churches and on college campuses, began to spill into the streets. McNamara was heckled in public appearances, where he continued to promise victory. In November 1965 McNamara was horrified to observe an antiwar protester immolate himself under his Pentagon window.

The war took a toll on Johnson and McNamara. Frustrated by military stalemate, trapped in endless deceptions, buffeted by criticism he considered irresponsible, Johnson became increasingly volatile and paranoid, attributing opposition to personal enmity and communist influence. McNamara too, exhausted and haggard, was increasingly conflicted by his private despair and public optimism. In late 1965, he urged a simultaneous bombing pause and diplomatic offensive to bring the North Vietnamese to the negotiating table. The 37-day bombing halt produced no result except to irritate Johnson and the Joint Chiefs of Staff. In May 1966 McNamara delivered a public address in which he advocated economic development—not military assistance—as the solution to third-world turmoil. In May 1967 he opposed a request from Gen. William C. Westmoreland, the U.S. commander in Vietnam, for an additional 200,000 troops. In August, before a congressional committee, he opposed his generals' demand for an expanded air war. Implicit in these arguments was McNamara's conviction that the war was unwinnable—a view he made explicit in a memo to Johnson on Nov. 1.

The Joint Chiefs had been furious at McNamara's congressional testimony and had considered a mass resignation. Johnson, too, was angry, concluding that McNamara had finally broken under the pressure. Johnson also suspected that McNamara had become close to his enemy, Robert Kennedy, brother of the former president and now an antiwar senator from New York. McNamara had to go.

On Nov. 27, 1967, McNamara learned from the London *Financial Times* that Johnson had nominated him to become president of the World Bank. His last day at the Pentagon was Feb. 29, 1968—an election year. A month before McNamara's departure, during the Tet national holiday, the Vietcong had simultaneously attacked 36 South Vietnamese provincial capitals and five large cities, penetrating Saigon to the gates of the U.S. embassy. Although the offensive was repulsed, its surprise and magnitude exposed the hollowness of official optimism about the war. A month after McNamara's departure, at the close of a televised address about the war on Mar. 31, Johnson unexpectedly announced: "I shall not seek, and I will not accept, the nomination of my party for another term as your president."

JOHNSON IMPEACHMENT (1868). In the acrimonious congressional elections of 1866, Republicans opposed for personal as well as political reasons to Pres. Andrew Johnson—conservatives, moderates, and Radicals (see *Radical Republicans)—won large majorities in both houses of Congress. Masters of their party, the Radicals would no longer suffer Johnson's obstruction of their *reconstruction program (see Andrew *Johnson Administration). They now had the votes not only to override presidential vetoes but to impeach the president himself.

Twice the House Judiciary Committee tried and failed to find "high crimes and misdemeanors" for which the president could be indicted. When, on Feb. 21, 1868, Johnson dismissed Secretary of War Edwin M. Stanton in apparent violation of the Tenure of Office Act, the Radicals seized their opportunity. The House quickly resolved (Feb. 24) to impeach Johnson and appointed a committee to draw up articles of impeachment. Eight of the 11 articles dealt with some aspect of Stanton's dismissal, although the Tenure of Office Act was of dubious constitutionality and, in any case, did not technically apply in this instance since Lincoln, not Johnson, had appointed Stanton to his position. The tenth article revealed the temper of the Congress; it declared that President Johnson "did attempt to bring into disgrace, ridicule, hatred, contempt, and reproach the Congress of the United States . . . ; and, in pursuance of his said design and intent, openly and publicly, and before divers assemblages . . . did . . . make and deliver with a loud voice certain intemperate, inflammatory, and scandalous harangues, and did therein utter loud threats and bitter menaces . . . amid the cries, jeers, and laughter of the multitudes. . . ."

The trial began in the Senate on Mar. 30, 1868, when Johnson had only 11 months of his term remaining. Chief Justice Salmon P. Chase presided. The prosecution was conducted by a committee of House members led by Radicals Thaddeus Stevens, George S. Boutwell, and Benjamin F. Butler. Johnson was defended by four prominent attorneys, chief among them William M. Evarts, a distinguished corporation lawyer, and Benjamin R. Curtis, a former justice of the U.S. Supreme Court, both Republicans. Johnson did not attend.

It quickly became apparent that the prosecutors had no legal or constitutional case. They came ultimately to the argument that Johnson was not "fit" to be president, transforming the case from a criminal into a political one. In the end, seven Republicans decided that impeaching the president on political grounds would disgrace the country and permanently weaken the presidency. Joining with the Senate's 12 Democrats (who had supported Johnson's reconstruction policy), they denied the Radicals the two-thirds Senate majority necessary to convict. On May 16, the Senate voted 35 to 19 (ten Southern states were not then represented) to approve the 11th and broadest article of impeachment, one vote short of a two-thirds majority. On May 23 the votes were the same on the second and third articles. With that, the Radicals gave up and the trial was adjourned.

JOHNSTOWN FLOOD (May 31, 1889), disaster at Johnstown, Pa., caused by the collapse of an earthen dam across the Conemaugh River above the town. Over 2,500 people died; property losses totaled more than $10 million.

JOINT COMMITTEE ON RECONSTRUCTION. See *Reconstruction.

JONES'S CRUISE (Aug. 14–Oct. 3, 1779), naval episode in the *Revolutionary War. In 1779, Commodore John Paul Jones was famous in America and France—and notorious in Britain—for his cruise in the Irish Sea the year before. During 28 days in April and May 1778, Jones, sailing from Brest, France, in command of the 18-gun sloop *Ranger*, had captured a British naval sloop, *Drake*, taken seven prizes and 200 prisoners, spiked the guns of the forts at Whitehaven, and raided the estate of the earl of Selkirk on the Scottish coast.

On Aug. 14, 1779, Jones put to sea again, now in command of a squadron of American and French ships, for another cruise in British waters. His flagship was a converted French East Indiaman, refitted with 34 guns and renamed *Bonhomme Richard* (the French title of Benjamin Franklin's *Poor Richard's Almanack*) in honor of Franklin, the American minister to France, who had been instrumental in obtaining the ship. Although most of its officers were Americans, its crew was largely foreign and it carried 140 French marines. Accompanying the *Bonhomme Richard* was the U.S. frigate *Alliance*, with a French captain and an Anglo-American crew, the French frigate *Pallas*, and the French brig *Vengeance*. The four-ship squadron sailed up the west coast of Ireland, around Scotland, and down the east coast of England, taking 17 ships.

On Sept. 23, off Flamborough Head on the Yorkshire

coast, Jones's squadron encountered a fleet of merchantmen being convoyed by the 44-gun British frigate *Serapis* and the 20-gun sloop *Countess of Scarborough*. The *Bonhomme Richard* closed with the *Serapis*, whose broadsides wreaked havoc in the outclassed American vessel. Desperately, Jones grappled his ship to the *Serapis*, stem to stern, and the fight continued into the night under a full moon— the cannon firing muzzle to muzzle, marines and crews shooting from the tops. When the captain of the *Serapis* demanded that Jones surrender, Jones replied (in a much later account), "I have not yet begun to fight." By now both vessels were burning wrecks. At 10:30 p.m. an explosion in the *Serapis* forced its captain to strike his colors.

While British warships searched for them, Jones's squadron made for the Continent against contrary winds. On Sept. 25 the *Bonhomme Richard* sank. The survivors reached Texel in Holland on Oct. 3. The battle of the **Bonhomme Richard and Serapis** made the indomitable John Paul Jones one of America's great naval heroes.

JONESTOWN, site in Guyana, South America, settled in 1977 by members of the Peoples Temple, a San Francisco–based religious cult led by Rev. Jim Jones. Jones founded the temple—an integrated and socially active congregation—in Indianapolis during the 1950s, then moved it to California in 1965. Apocalyptic, drug-addicted, and increasingly deranged, Jones subjected his largely black followers to mind-numbing discipline and abuse, sustained by faked "miracles." After exposure of the temple's bizarre practices, Jones compelled his submissive congregation to follow him to Guyana, where he established a primitive and harshly disciplined "paradise." Relatives of temple members complained to the U.S. State Department, and California congressman Leo Ryan led a party of relatives and journalists to Guyana in November 1978 to investigate. Returning from Port Kaituma with a number of defectors on Nov. 18, Ryan's party was attacked by temple gunmen; Ryan and four others were killed. That night, Jones ordered his followers to commit mass suicide; 913 people drank cyanide-laced Kool-Aid and died. Jones shot himself.

JUDICIAL REVIEW, the power of the courts to nullify a legislative act as unconstitutional, first asserted nationally by Chief Justice John Marshall in *Marbury v. Madison* (1803). Federal and state courts have generally exercised this power sparingly out of deference to legislatures and a philosophy of judicial self-restraint. The *Rehnquist Court overturned acts of Congress with unusual frequency.

JUDICIARY ACTS (1789, 1801), legislation of the *Washington and John *Adams administrations. The first Judiciary Act fleshed out the Constitution's terse provision for a "Supreme Court" and "inferior courts." It provided that the Supreme Court should consist of five justices and the chief justice, and it created two lower levels of federal courts: district courts and circuit courts. It established 13 judicial districts, one for each state except Massachusetts and Virginia, which received two (North Carolina and Rhode Island had not yet ratified the Constitution), and three circuit courts, which were to meet twice a year under two itinerant Supreme Court justices and one district judge. The act permitted appeals from state courts to federal courts under certain circumstances; it also provided for *judicial review of state legislation. More a constitutive than a legislative act, it established the basic framework of the federal judicial system that survives today. It was a victory for the nationalists in Congress, who wanted federal rather than state courts to try cases involving federal-state relations.

The Judiciary Act of 1801, conceived as a reform measure, reduced the Supreme Court from six justices to five, raised the number of circuits from three to six, and established five new judicial districts. The incoming *Jefferson administration viewed the act as a partisan measure, designed to entrench Federalists even more strongly in the federal judiciary, and repealed it in 1802 (see *Midnight Appointments).

K

KANSAS-NEBRASKA ACT (1854), legislation of the *Pierce administration. On Jan. 4, 1854, Democratic senator Stephen A. Douglas of Illinois introduced a bill to organize Nebraska Territory, a vast region lying west of Missouri, Iowa, and Minnesota Territory and entirely north of the *Missouri Compromise line of 36°30'. Using the same language as the acts that had organized Utah and New Mexico territories as part of the *Compromise of 1850, Douglas's bill provided that "when admitted as a State or States, the said territory, or any portion of the same, shall be received into the Union, with or without slavery, as their constitution may prescribe at the time of their admission." Douglas reasoned that the Compromise of 1850, by providing for *popular sovereignty in Utah and New Mexico, which extended north of the Missouri Compromise line (but were not in the Louisiana Purchase), had implicitly repealed that portion of the Missouri Compromise and established a precedent for the application of popular sovereignty in the remaining unorganized portions of the Louisiana Purchase.

Southern senators were dissatisfied with Douglas's bill, which in fact prohibited slavery in the territory until a state constitution was drafted—when, since no slavery interest would then be represented, a free state constitution was assured. To win their support, Douglas revised his bill to include an explicit repeal of the Missouri Compromise, thereby permitting slavery in the new territory at once. At the same time, the revised bill established two territories in the region—Kansas Territory, west of Missouri, and Nebraska Territory, extending north to the Canadian border. Whatever the motive here, this provision was universally interpreted as meaning that Kansas would likely become a slave state and Nebraska a free state. The issue would be decided by whether the two territories were settled by proslavery or antislavery immigrants.

Despite a groundswell of Northern opposition aroused by the *Appeal of the Independent Democrats, the highly controversial bill, brilliantly managed by Douglas, became law on May 30.

Douglas's motives in championing a bill tailored to Southern demands and offensive to antislavery sentiment in the North have long been debated. The organization of Nebraska Territory was essential to Douglas's plan for a northern *transcontinental railroad with its eastern terminus in Chicago in which he had a large personal as well as political interest. Southern senators, who favored a central or southern route, would not support Douglas's measure without special inducements. Douglas proved peculiarly insensitive to the consequences of repealing the Missouri Compromise, which for 30 years had been regarded by many—himself included—not merely as an act of Congress but as an inviolable "solemn compact." He was aware that Congress's power to exclude slavery from a territory was being challenged as unconstitutional (the Supreme Court would declare the Missouri Compromise unconstitutional in 1857), and he sincerely considered popular sovereignty as a more democratic method of achieving the same end—for, in his view, geography assured that Kansas-Nebraska would not become slave states. He did not appreciate that, for most Americans, the Missouri Compromise prohibition of slavery north of 36°30' represented a moral condemnation of slavery. He himself was not proslavery, but he believed that slavery had already reached its natural limits and that issues of nation-building, such as a transcontinental railroad, were of more pressing importance.

The consequences of the Kansas-Nebraska Act were far-reaching. A race promptly ensued between Southerners (mostly Missourians) and Northerners to settle and control Kansas. The result was a local civil war (see *Bleeding Kansas) that foreshadowed a national civil war. The Democratic Party, which had dominated the country since Andrew Jackson, now became a distinctly Southern rather than a national party. Its Northern wing was decimated by its support of the Kansas-Nebraska Act. Of 91 seats in the House of Representatives won by Northern Democrats in 1852, they retained only 25 in 1854–55. In the political turmoil caused by the act, the *Whig Party disintegrated, the nativist *Know-Nothing Party quickly rose and briefly flourished, and the *Republican Party was founded as a purely Northern party committed to the containment of slavery.

One consequence of the act was to bring Abraham Lincoln, a leader of the Whig Party in Illinois, back into active politics. Lincoln was "thunderstruck" by the moral indifference of the act. This ignoble law, he believed, declared "that we have no longer a choice between freedom and slavery—that both are equal to us—that we yield our territories as readily to one as the other."

KASSERINE PASS. See *World War 2.

KEATING-OWEN ACT (1916). See *Child Labor.

KELLOGG-BRIAND PEACE PACT or **PACT OF PARIS** (1928), diplomatic agreement of the *Coolidge administration, negotiated by U.S. secretary of state Frank B. Kellogg and French foreign minister Aristide Briand and signed on Aug. 27, 1928, by 15 powers; ultimately, 62 countries adhered to the agreement. The signatories "renounce[d war] as an instrument of national policy" and "agree[d] that the settlement or solution of all disputes or conflicts . . . which may arise among them, shall never be sought except by pacific means."

KENNEDY ADMINISTRATION (1961–63). Democrat John F. Kennedy, 35th president of the United States, was elected with 49.7 percent of the popular vote—a plurality of only 120,000 votes. While Democrats constituted majorities in both houses of Congress, Congress was in fact controlled by a coalition of Republicans and conservative Southern Democrats. Kennedy could not, therefore, claim a mandate for the *New Frontier, a liberal legislative program in the tradition of Franklin Roosevelt and Harry Truman.

Not surprisingly, Kennedy's domestic record was marked by major legislative failures: federal aid to the states for public schools; hospital insurance for the aged; high price supports for farmers in exchange for mandatory production and marketing controls; a Depressed Areas Act authorizing redevelopment grants for areas with high unemployment, passed in 1961 but denied funding in 1963.

Modest legislative successes included a Housing Act (1961) that extended existing programs and authorized low-interest loans for the construction of middle-income housing; a Trade Expansion Act (1962); a Manpower Development and Training Act (1962); an Equal Pay Act (1963), guaranteeing equal pay for women doing the same work as men; a Higher Education Facilities Act (1963), aiding the construction of college and university buildings; an increased minimum wage; and acts affecting consumer protection, mental health, and the environment. The *23rd Amendment was ratified in 1961.

Important legislative initiatives left incomplete at Kennedy's death were: an economic stimulus tax cut; a comprehensive civil rights bill; and an attack on *poverty.

Notable executive initiatives during the Kennedy administration included: compelling steel companies to rescind price increases made in violation of a wage settlement (1962); appointment of the President's Committee on Juvenile Delinquency (1961) and the President's Commission on the Status of Women (1962); a war against organized crime waged by Attorney General Robert F. Kennedy; and the president's recommendation (1961) of a national commitment to put a man on the moon by 1970 (see *Moon Landing).

Kennedy did not mention his domestic program in his inaugural address (see *Kennedy's Inaugural), which was concerned solely with the *cold war. In that conflict, he declared, "we shall pay any price, bear any burden, meet any hardship, support any friend, oppose any foe to assure the survival and the success of liberty." He reversed Pres. Dwight D. Eisenhower's policy of military sufficiency with one of military superiority. Cold war crises regularly distracted Kennedy from domestic concerns, particularly in Cuba (see *Bay of Pigs Invasion; *Cuban Missile Crisis), in Berlin (see *Berlin Wall), and in Vietnam (see *Vietnam War). Initiatives for peace included the *Alliance for Progress, the *Peace Corps, and a nuclear test ban treaty with the Soviets and Great Britain (1963; see *Arms Control and Disarmament).

The Kennedy administration is remembered for the aura of glamour that the handsome and stylish first family created in the White House, where the nation's artistic and intellectual elite were frequently entertained. After Kennedy's death, his widow, recalling a Broadway musical they had enjoyed, compared the Kennedy White House to **Camelot**, the court of the mythical British king Arthur.

Kennedy was assassinated in Dallas, Tex., on Nov. 22, 1963 (see *Kennedy Assassinations) and was succeeded by Vice Pres. Lyndon B. Johnson.

KENNEDY ASSASSINATIONS (1963, 1968). On a political fence-mending trip to Texas, Pres. John F. Kennedy was assassinated at about 12:30 p.m. on Friday, Nov. 22, 1963, while riding in a motorcade in Dallas. The president and his wife, who had just arrived at Love Field, were in an open car with Texas governor John Connally and the governor's wife. As the motorcade passed the Texas School Book Depository Building on Elm Street on its way downtown, three shots were fired from the sixth floor of the depository. One wounded Governor Connally, two struck the president—one in his lower neck, another in his head, killing him. The motorcade sped to Parkland Hospital, where the president was pronounced dead at 1 p.m.

Shortly thereafter, Lee Harvey Oswald, an employee of the book depository, was arrested in a movie theater and charged with the murder of a Dallas policeman who had tried to detain him on the street. The assassination weapon found in the depository—a mail-order Mannlicher-Carcano 6.5mm carbine—proved to belong to Oswald. Charged with the assassination as well as the policeman's murder, Oswald denied knowledge of either event. On Sunday morning, while Oswald was being transferred from police headquarters at City Hall to the county jail, in police custody and in full view of television cameras, he was approached by one Jack Ruby, a strip-joint operator well known to the police, who shot Oswald dead.

The new president, Lyndon B. Johnson, promptly appointed a commission chaired by Chief Justice Earl Warren to investigate the assassination. The **Warren Commission**'s lengthy report, presented on Sept. 24, 1964, concluded that Oswald alone had killed the president and that Ruby too had acted alone. The report debunked many conspiracy theories that had sprung up immediately after the assassination—often involving a second shooter on the grassy knoll in Dealey Plaza—on the basis of witness testimony, photographs, and a film of the assassination itself.

In the 1970s, new information unknown to the Warren Commission came to light that inspired a new crop of conspiracy theories. It was learned that the Central Intelligence Agency (CIA) had tried to use organized crime (Mafia) figures to assassinate Cuban dictator Fidel Castro and that Castro was aware of the plot; that the Mafia hated President Kennedy for not getting rid of Castro (who had closed their Havana casinos) and the president's younger brother, Attorney General Robert F. Kennedy, for prosecuting Mafia leaders; that the FBI had been negligent in its surveillance of Oswald, a onetime resident of the Soviet Union and a Castro partisan; that both Oswald and Ruby had had tenuous Mafia connec-

tions. Some theories implicated the Soviets, the CIA, and even President Johnson in the assassination.

In 1979 a select committee of the House of Representatives, after a two-year investigation of the assassination, confirmed the conclusions of the Warren Commission. Both investigative bodies, however, sealed sensitive evidence, thereby failing to definitively end the proliferation of conspiracy theories.

On June 5, 1968, Robert Kennedy was shot and killed in the Ambassador Hotel in Los Angeles. A U.S. senator from New York, Kennedy had entered in March the race for the Democratic presidential nomination as an opponent of the *Vietnam War. He had just celebrated his victory in the California primary when he was shot at 12:16 a.m. by a 24-year-old Palestinian immigrant, Sirhan B. Sirhan. Sirhan was seized on the spot, convicted of murder, and sentenced to death. In 1972 the sentence was commuted to life imprisonment.

KENNEDY'S INAUGURAL (Jan. 20, 1961). On a snowy winter day in Washington, D.C., newly inaugurated Pres. John F. Kennedy said in part:

"The world is very different now. For man holds in his mortal hands the power to abolish all forms of human poverty and all forms of human life. And yet the same revolutionary beliefs for which our forefathers fought are still at issue around the globe. . . .

"We dare not forget today that we are the heirs of that first revolution. Let the word go forth from this time and place, to friend and foe alike, that the torch has been passed to a new generation of Americans—born in this century, tempered by war, disciplined by a hard and bitter peace, proud of our ancient heritage—and unwilling to witness or permit the slow undoing of those human rights to which this nation has always been committed, and to which we are committed today at home and around the world.

"Let every nation know, whether it wishes us well or ill, that we shall pay any price, bear any burden, meet any hardship, support any friend, oppose any foe to assure the survival and the success of liberty. . . .

"Now the trumpet summons us again—not as a call to bear arms, though arms we need—not as a call to battle, though embattled we are—but a call to bear the burden of a long twilight struggle, year in and year out, 'rejoicing in hope, patient in tribulation'—a struggle against the common enemies of man: tyranny, poverty, disease, and war itself. . . .

"In the long history of the world, only a few generations have been granted the role of defending freedom in its hour of maximum danger. I do not shrink from this responsibility—I welcome it. I do not believe that any of us would exchange places with any other people or any other generation. . . .

"And so, my fellow Americans: ask not what your country can do for you—ask what you can do for your country. . . .

". . . With a good conscience our only sure reward, with history the final judge of our deeds, let us go forth to lead the land we love, asking His blessing and His help, but knowing that here on earth God's work must truly be our own."

KENT STATE SHOOTINGS (1969). See *Vietnam War.

KERNER COMMISSION. See *Ghetto Riots.

KING ASSASSINATION (Apr. 4, 1968). Angered by the diversion of national resources from the promised War on Poverty to the war in Vietnam, civil rights leader Martin Luther King Jr. became an outspoken opponent of that war—thereby alienating Pres. Lyndon Johnson and distancing himself from more prudent civil rights leaders—and a champion of economically distressed urban blacks.

On Mar. 28, 1968, King led a march on the Memphis, Tenn., city hall in support of striking black sanitation workers that ended in violence precipitated by black marchers. Profoundly depressed by this violation of his principle of nonviolence, he addressed a Memphis rally on Apr. 3 in somber mood, concluding: "We've got some difficult days ahead. But it doesn't matter with me now. Because I've been to the mountaintop. And I don't mind. Like anybody, I would like to live a long life. Longevity has its place. But I'm not concerned about that now. I just want to do God's will. And He's allowed me to go up to the mountain. And I've looked over. And I've seen the promised land. I may not get there with you. But I want you to know tonight that we, as a people, will get to the promised land. And I'm happy, tonight. I'm not worried about anything. I'm not fearing any man. Mine eyes have seen the glory of the coming of the Lord."

King spent the next day at the Lorraine Motel working with his aides on plans for another march scheduled for Apr. 5. At 6 p.m., while he stood on the second-floor balcony of the motel, a bullet from a high-powered .30-06 rifle fired from a building across the motel parking lot shattered his jaw. He died at St. Joseph's Hospital at 7:05 p.m.

That night riots erupted in 130 cities across the country. Forty-six people (all but five of them black) died,

thousands were injured, property valued at $100 million was destroyed.

On June 8, escaped convict James Earl Ray was arrested at London's Heathrow Airport. Extradited to the United States, he pleaded guilty to King's murder on Mar. 10, 1969, and was sentenced to 99 years in prison. Ray later recanted and claimed that he had been set up to take the blame for the killing. The King family pressed for a new trial for Ray, but Ray died in prison on Apr. 23, 1998.

Convinced that the assassination had been the work of a conspiracy, the Kings in 1999 brought a civil wrongful-death suit against a retired Memphis café owner, Loyd Jowers, and other "unknown coconspirators" alleging that they had been part of a vast conspiracy that included government agencies. The Memphis jury quickly found Jowers—who claimed to have arranged the murder—guilty. The Kings professed to be satisfied that the truth had been established.

KING GEORGE'S WAR. See *French and Indian Wars.

KING PHILIP'S WAR (1675–76), war between Massachusetts settlers and the Wampanoag Indians under Philip, son of Massasoit, longtime friend of *Plymouth Colony. The war consisted originally of Indian raids and ineffectual white counterattacks, which provoked the hostility of other tribes. In 1675 white settlements in Massachusetts, Maine, and New Hampshire were devastated and two colonial forces were ambushed and destroyed. The tide turned in 1676, and Philip's capture and execution in August ended the war.

KING'S LETTER FROM BIRMINGHAM JAIL (Apr. 16, 1963), letter by civil rights leader Martin Luther King Jr., jailed for his participation in antisegregation demonstrations in Birmingham, Ala. (see *Birmingham Campaign), to eight white Alabama clergymen who had criticized his campaign as "unwise and untimely." An angry rebuttal of the white clergymen—whose need for respectability, in King's view, deadened them to the moral imperative of the black protest—the letter was written in the margins of newspapers and smuggled out of the jail for recopying.

"You deplore the demonstrations that are presently taking place in Birmingham," King wrote. ". . . You are exactly right in your call for negotiation. Indeed, this is the purpose of direct action. Nonviolent direct action seeks to create such a crisis and establish such creative tension that a community that has constantly refused to negotiate is forced to confront the issue. It seeks so to dramatize the issue that it can no longer be ignored. . . .

"[You state] that our acts are untimely. . . . [But] freedom is never voluntarily given by the oppressor; it must be demanded by the oppressed. Frankly, I have never yet engaged in a direct action movement that was 'well timed,' according to the timetable of those who have not suffered unduly from the disease of segregation. For years now I have heard the word 'Wait!' It rings in the ear of every Negro with a piercing familiarity. This 'wait' has almost always meant 'never.' . . .

"You express a great deal of anxiety over our willingness to break laws. . . . There are *just* laws and there are *unjust* laws. I would be the first to advocate obeying just laws. One has not only a legal but moral responsibility to obey just laws. Conversely, one has a moral responsibility to disobey unjust laws. . . . Any law that uplifts human personality is just. Any law that degrades human personality is unjust. All segregation statutes are unjust because segregation distorts the soul and damages the personality. It gives the segregator a false sense of superiority and the segregated a false sense of inferiority. . . . Isn't segregation an existential expression of man's tragic separation, an expression of his awful estrangement, his terrible sinfulness? . . .

"You spoke of our activity in Birmingham as extreme. . . . I stand in the middle of two opposing forces in the Negro community. One is a force of complacency made up of Negroes who, as a result of long years of oppression, have been so completely drained of self-respect and a sense of 'somebodiness' that they have adjusted to segregation, and of a few Negroes in the middle class who, because of a degree of academic and economic security, and because at points they profit by segregation, have unconsciously become insensitive to the problems of the masses. The other force is one of bitterness and hatred and comes perilously close to advocating violence. It is expressed in the various black nationalist groups that are springing up over the nation. . . .

"I have tried to stand between these two forces saying that we need not follow the 'do-nothingism' of the complacent or the hatred and despair of the black nationalist. There is the more excellent way of love and nonviolent protest. I'm grateful to God that, through the Negro church, the dimension of nonviolence entered our struggle. If this philosophy had not emerged I am convinced that by now many streets of the South would be flowing with floods of blood. And I am further convinced that if our white brothers dismiss us as 'rabble rousers' and 'outside agitators'—those of us who are working through the channels of nonviolent direct action—and refuse to support our nonviolent efforts, millions of Negroes, out of frustration and despair, will seek solace and security in black nationalist ideologies, a development that will lead inevitably to a frightening racial nightmare.'"

KING'S MOUNTAIN (Oct. 7, 1780), *Revolutionary War battle. After his victory at Camden, S.C. (Aug. 16, 1780), British general Charles Cornwallis moved into North Carolina and occupied Charlotte. Protecting his left flank was Maj. Patrick Ferguson and a force of Loyalists operating in the mountains of western North Carolina and South Carolina.

In September, an army of frontier militias—Tennesseans, Virginians, and North Carolinians led by John Sevier, Isaac Shelby, and William Campbell and totaling 1,300 men—crossed the mountains and went in pursuit of Ferguson. On Oct. 7 they found him with 1,100 Loyalists positioned on the grassy top of King's Mountain in North Carolina, a mile from the border between the Carolinas. The backcountry horsemen dismounted and fought their way on foot in small groups up the heavily wooded sides of the mountain, using their long rifles to good effect.

In the battle on the mountaintop Ferguson was killed. When the Loyalists sought to surrender, many were slaughtered by frontiersmen shouting "Tarleton's quarter!" in revenge for atrocities associated with British colonel Banastre Tarleton. The entire Loyalist force was killed, wounded, or captured. The defeat at King's Mountain brought Cornwallis back to South Carolina.

KING WILLIAM'S WAR. See *French and Indian Wars.

KITCHEN CABINET (1829–31), group of unofficial presidential advisers in the early years of the *Jackson administration. Because his official cabinet was divided by factionalism—there was personal rivalry between Vice Pres. John C. Calhoun and Secretary of State Martin Van Buren, complicated by the *Eaton affair in which the two rivals took opposite sides—Pres. Andrew Jackson stopped holding cabinet meetings and sought advice instead from his "kitchen cabinet" of trusted friends. Its members included Amos Kendall and Francis Blair, newspaper editors; Andrew J. Donelson, Jackson's secretary; and William B. Lewis, a friend from his army days. Van Buren and Secretary of War John H. Eaton were the only members of the official cabinet to participate. Duff Green, another editor, was a partisan of Calhoun's and left the kitchen cabinet in 1830.

In 1831 Van Buren's resignation from the cabinet gave

Jackson the opportunity to request the resignations of its other members, most of whom were Calhoun supporters. By then Jackson and Calhoun were no longer allies (see *Jackson and Calhoun). Jackson was more comfortable with his new cabinet, and the kitchen cabinet receded in importance.

KNIGHTS OF LABOR (1869–95), national labor organization that sought to unite all wage earners, whatever their trades or levels of skill. Founded as a secret society by Philadelphia tailors in 1869, it expanded rapidly under the leadership (1879–93) of Terence V. Powderly, a visionary less interested in direct economic action (he opposed strikes as an outmoded industrial weapon) than in education, political action, and especially producers' and consumers' cooperatives.

Yet it was a wave of spontaneous strikes in 1883–85, culminating in a successful strike against the western railroads of Jay Gould, that raised the Knights to a peak membership of 700,000. The next year, the failure of new strikes—ineptly opposed by Powderly—precipitated the organization's rapid dissolution. Disappointed strikers deserted, the skilled workers gravitating to the craft unions affiliated with the *American Federation of Labor.

KNOW-NOTHING PARTY or **AMERICAN PARTY** (1849–56), political party that originated in New York City as the Order of the Star-Spangled Banner, an anti-immigrant and anti-Catholic secret society. By 1854 it had become a national organization with lodges in most states. The party's popular name derived from its members' response to questions about it: "I know nothing."

The rapid rise of the Know-Nothings was a result of long-standing anti-Catholic sentiment in the country heightened by an influx of Irish and German Catholic immigrants in the late 1840s. Widespread electoral successes in 1854 and 1855 raised the possibility that the Know-Nothings might elect a president in 1856. "Americans must rule America," proclaimed the Know-Nothing platform that year; "and to this end, native-born citizens should be selected for all state, federal, or municipal offices. . . ." Moreover (addressing the Catholic menace), "No person should be selected for political station . . . who recognizes any alliance or obligation of any description to any foreign prince, potentate or power. . . ." But when the convention (which nominated former president Millard Fillmore) endorsed the *Kansas-Nebraska Act, Northern members bolted. Fillmore (who was also the candidate of the *Whig Party) carried only Maryland, and the party soon dissolved.

Many Northern Know-Nothings joined the *Republican Party, which drew its supporters from the same social group as the Know-Nothings—rural Protestants who were antislavery, antiforeigner, and protemperance. The accession of the Know-Nothings probably gave the Republican Party its margin of victory in 1860. Although he recognized the importance of their numbers, Abraham Lincoln rejected the Know-Nothings' principles. "How can anyone who abhors the oppression of negroes," he wrote to a friend, "be in favor of degrading classes of white people?"

KOREAN WAR (1950–53). A Japanese colony since 1910, Korea was promised independence at the Cairo Conference during World War 2 (see *World War 2 Conferences). When Japan surrendered, Soviet troops entered Korea from the north, U.S. troops from the south; the 38th parallel, which bisects the peninsula, was accepted as a temporary dividing line between the two occupation zones.

The Soviets, however, severed communications across the 38th parallel and proceeded to erect a communist regime in the north while blocking a United Nations proposal to hold free elections for the entire country. An election in the south in 1948 resulted in the establishment of a Republic of Korea (ROK), after which U.S. troops were withdrawn except for an advisory group to train an ROK military force denied offensive weapons such as tanks and aircraft. The Soviets withdrew from the north, leaving in place, however, a heavily armed Democratic People's Republic of Korea. Both governments claimed to rule all of Korea, and clashes along the 38th parallel became frequent.

On June 25, 1950, North Korea, having sought and received permission from Soviet dictator Joseph Stalin, launched a full-scale invasion of South Korea across the 38th parallel. In Washington, the *Truman administration assumed that the invasion had been ordered by Moscow. Although U.S. military authorities had excluded any part of the Asian mainland from the American defense perimeter in the Far East, Pres. Harry S. Truman determined that the supposed Soviet-sponsored aggression in Korea had to be resisted if American *cold war commitments were to have any credibility.

At the request of the United States, the UN Security Council on June 25 passed a resolution (in the fortuitous absence of the Soviet delegate) calling for the withdrawal of North Korean troops and an immediate end to hostilities. Two days later a second resolution called on UN members to assist the ROK. President Truman had already ordered U.S. air and naval forces in Japan to support the South Koreans. On July 7 the Security Council authorized a unified UN command in Korea under U.S. leadership. Truman appointed Gen. Douglas MacArthur, at that time head of the Allied occupation of Japan, its commander.

Meanwhile, the North Korean invaders were routing the outnumbered and poorly trained and equipped South Koreans. Seoul was captured on June 28. When U.S. air and naval intervention proved insufficient to halt the rout, ill-prepared American occupation troops from Japan were rushed into combat. In the next few weeks, three army divisions, a marine brigade, and other units entered the battle as the U.S. Eighth Army, to which 20 other UN members eventually provided small contingents. By the beginning of August, U.S. and South Korean troops had been driven back to within 50 miles of the southeast Korean port of Pusan. There they formed a defensive perimeter that they held in furious fighting. By the end of August the North Korean offensive drive was spent, while within the Pusan perimeter the Eighth Army was being steadily reinforced.

On Sept. 13, the Eighth Army launched a counteroffensive northward from the Pusan perimeter. Two days later, MacArthur directed a brilliant but very risky amphibious landing of marine and army divisions at **Inchon** on the west coast of the peninsula. By Sept. 26, this force had taken Seoul. Fleeing north to avoid entrapment, the North Koreans recrossed the 38th parallel.

MacArthur's decision to pursue and destroy the defeated North Koreans—conventional military strategy—was supported by Washington despite warnings from China. At a meeting on Wake Island on Oct. 15, MacArthur assured Truman that there was no danger of Chinese or Soviet intervention and that the fighting would be over by Christmas. MacArthur sent the Eighth Army up the west coast of the peninsula and the separate Tenth Corps up the east coast, intending a pincers movement to prevent the North Koreans from escaping into Manchuria.

On Nov. 21, the first UN troops reached the Yalu River, the border between Korea and Manchuria (Communist China). On Nov. 24 MacArthur launched a major offensive intended to close the trap on the North Koreans. Two days later 200,000 Chinese troops unexpectedly struck UN forces and drove them back in disarray. Sustaining heavy losses and suffering intensely in the Korean winter, the Eighth Army was driven back across the 38th parallel, while the remnants of Tenth Corps were evacuated by sea from the port of Hungnan. The Chinese captured Seoul on Jan. 5. Not until the end of January 1951 did the UN forces halt their retreat and hold a defensive line 75 miles below the 38th parallel.

In December, Lt. Gen. Matthew B. Ridgway assumed command of the Eighth Army. Reorganizing and restoring the morale of his exhausted troops, Ridgway launched an offensive on Jan. 25, recapturing Seoul on Mar. 15 and reaching the 38th parallel by the end of the month. Washington had by now concluded that victory was impossible in Korea except at the risk of starting World War 3. Its aim was to hold the 38th parallel, thereby denying the communists any reward for their aggression, while seeking a negotiated settlement. For repeatedly differing publicly with U.S. policy, in particular for advocating widening the war to China, MacArthur on Apr. 11 was relieved of his command (see *MacArthur Firing) and replaced by Ridgway.

Now commanded by Lt. Gen. James A. Van Fleet, the Eighth Army fell back before a final Chinese offensive in April and May but counterattacked on May 22 and regained positions north of the 38th parallel in June. Here the battle lines hardened despite bitter fighting for limited tactical advantages.

Armistice talks between communist and UN forces began on July 10, 1951, at Kaesong but later moved to Panmunjom. Negotiations proved difficult and were broken off on Oct. 8, 1952, over UN refusal to repatriate North Korean and Chinese prisoners against their will. They were resumed only on Apr. 26, 1953, following the death of Stalin and a discreet warning from U.S. president Dwight D. Eisenhower implying the use of nuclear weapons.

The truce agreement, signed July 27, 1953, provided for a demilitarized buffer zone 2.5 miles wide extending across the peninsula between the two Koreas. The war—which cost 54,000 American dead (both killed in battle and dead of injuries or disease) and much greater numbers of North and South Koreans and Chinese—produced no other result.

KOSOVO. See *Balkan Intervention.

KU KLUX KLAN, during *Reconstruction, secret organization formed (May 1866) at Pulaski, Tenn., to preserve white supremacy in the post–Civil War South by punishing independent or assertive freedmen and later subverting Republican local and state governments. These it did by murder, arson, and beatings, or by silent intimidation by its white-sheeted and masked night riders. Klan terror was directed against white *carpetbaggers and scalawags as well as blacks.

The Klan spread rapidly through the mountains and piedmont of the South, absorbing many smaller vigilante groups. Its organization in local, county, and state "dens," "provinces," "dominions," and "realms" culminated in an "empire" whose "grand wizard" for a time was former Confederate general Nathan B. Forrest. Former Confederates of all social classes were active in the Klan, which played an important part in "redeeming" Southern states from Republican control. The Klan nominally dissolved in 1869, but violence continued throughout the South.

The federal government responded in 1870–71 with three force or enforcement acts directed against the Klan. Whereas the *Civil Rights Act of 1866 prohibited the denial of civil rights by states, these later acts prohibited individuals from preventing other citizens from exercising their civil rights. The activities of the Klan thus became federal offenses, to be prosecuted by federal district attorneys backed where necessary by military force. Thousands of Klansmen were prosecuted; many fled their states. In October 1871 federal troops occupied nine western counties in South Carolina and put an end to Klan depredations there. By 1872 Klan violence had been significantly reduced throughout the South.

After World War I the Klan name was taken by a patriotic, Protestant-fundamentalist fraternal order with an antiblack, anti-Catholic, anti-Semitic, and anti-immigrant agenda. The organization achieved considerable political power in the Midwest and South but, having acquired a reputation for violence and corruption, virtually disappeared by the 1930s. A third Klan appeared during the civil rights disturbances of the 1960s (see *Radical Right).

L

LABOR. Colonial America dealt with a shortage of agricultural labor with *indentured servitude and *slavery. In the towns, wage-earning artisans and laborers often had to be recruited in England. Although relations between master and worker in the small shops of the period were close, the perennial conflict between capital and labor soon manifested itself. The hours of labor for townsmen were by custom the same as for agricultural labor—from dawn to dark. Town governments or associations of employers could set wages, but a combination of workers for that purpose was considered an illegal conspiracy. Nevertheless, workers in various crafts—shoemakers, printers, tailors, carpenters—organized secretly. But as quickly as these early unions took shape, they were dispersed by the blasts of panic and depression.

With the coming of *industrialization—the assembling of workers in factories—the condition of the workers deteriorated. Employers lengthened hours and depressed wages. The flow of *immigration ensured a large labor supply, while differences between native and foreign-born workers made united action difficult. Enticed by the many reform movements of the period, workers often failed to perceive their own economic interests. Some were drawn to utopian socialism, others to producers' and consumers' cooperatives, still others to agitation for the free distribution of *public lands to settlers.

*Workingmen's parties pursued workers' interests as well as broad social reform programs through political action. During the 1840s and 1850s, the ten-hour day was won for certain federal employees and legislated in seven states—although it was easily avoided. Belatedly, in the prosperity of the 1850s, the union movement revived, with skilled craftsmen (generally native-born Protestants) separating themselves from unskilled Catholic immigrants to pursue their special interests.

Burgeoning industrialization after the Civil War vastly increased the scale and character of the conflict between capital and labor until contemporaries spoke of "industrial warfare." Corporate organization interposed managers between owners and workers long before there was any "science" of management. Large industrial enterprises brought great numbers of workers of varied ethnic backgrounds together under a single roof. Technological advances diminished the importance of skilled mechanics, often reducing them to the ranks of the unskilled immigrants who performed single monotonous tasks at their stations.

In an age of ferocious competition, owners and managers callously exploited their human resources as they did all others. In this they were sustained by the prevailing laissez-faire ideology, popular belief in the sanctity of private property, the sympathy of the courts and the ready accessibility of the police power, and widespread fear of immigrants, disorder, and "radical" ideas.

On the other side, the law considered each worker individually responsible for negotiating the terms of his or her employment—this was "liberty of contract." Unions were few, inexperienced, and of uncertain legality. There were no government mechanisms to mitigate the severity of the conflict, and society provided no "safety net" for losers beyond private charity. A strike, when possible at all, was the last resort of men and women driven to desperation by inhuman working conditions and below-subsistence wages. Strikes, which in the past had rarely been violent, now became increasingly so (see *Molly Maguires; *Railroad Strikes of 1877; *Haymarket Riot; *Homestead Strike; *Pullman Strike; *Ludlow Massacre; *Steel Strikes).

The new industrial landscape was as perplexing to labor strategists as to everyone else. How should industrial workers be organized? In combination with distressed farmers? By craft, excluding the growing masses of unskilled laborers? By all-inclusive unions of both skilled and unskilled workers? What objective should they pursue and by what means? The transformation of society by education, political action, utopian experimentation, revolutionary violence? Or the immediate economic interests of the workers—wages, hours, job security, and conditions of employment—by means of collective bargaining, strikes, and boycotts?

Out of the varied experiences of the *Greenback Party, the *People's Party, the *Railroad Brotherhoods, the *National Labor Union, the *Knights of Labor, the *American Railway Union, and the *Western Federation of Miners emerged the "new unionism" represented by the American Federation of Labor (AFL; see *American Federation of Labor–Congress of Industrial Organizations)—a national federation of trade (craft) unions that pursued the economic interests of its members within the framework of the existing capitalist system.

Except for a few industrial unions like the *United Mine Workers and the *International Ladies Garment Workers Union, the AFL excluded the bulk of immigrant mass-production workers, and its conservative policies failed to reflect the increasingly radical temper of unorganized labor. The *Industrial Workers of the World (IWW), founded in 1905, sought to organize these workers in "one big union" and lead them aggressively toward the ultimate goal of a general strike that would overthrow the capitalist system. During World War 1, the IWW's radicalism was considered unpatriotic and the union disintegrated, while the AFL's support of the war effort earned it a measure of respectability.

The flagrant inequality of the two sides in the conflict between capital and labor began to be addressed during the progressive period (see *Progressivism). In 1902, Pres. Theodore Roosevelt compelled mine owners to submit to mediation in the *Anthracite Strike. The *Commission on Industrial Relations (1912–14) exposed (among many other things) the remoteness of capital from the concerns of labor. The U.S. Department of Labor was established in 1913. The *Clayton Antitrust Act (1914) assured labor of the right to strike and forbade the use of the injunction in labor disputes (a prohibition made effectual only with the *Norris–La Guardia Act of 1932). The Adamson Act (1916; see *Railroad Regulation) established the eight-hour day for railroad workers. Meanwhile, state laws limited *child labor, regulated the wages and hours of women workers, and improved health and safety conditions in factories.

World War 1 was followed by a wave of strikes—4 million workers took part in 3,600 strikes in 1919—that turned public opinion against labor. Unions declined during the 1920s while the prestige of businessmen rose. Employing the physical force of courts, police, and strikebreakers, the propaganda of antiradicalism and pro-Americanism (see *American Plan), and sometimes the seduction of *"welfare capitalism," management significantly reduced the power of labor.

In the 1930s, however, with the encouragement and protection of the *New Deal, labor revived. The National Labor Relations Act (1935) assured workers of the right to organize and bargain collectively; the Social Security Act (1935; see *Social Security) provided a "safety net" for workers, including unemployment and old age and survivors' insurance; and the Fair Labor Standards Act (1938) established minimum wages and maximum hours for firms engaged in interstate commerce and regulated child labor.

In such a climate, union membership grew rapidly. The old trade unions recruited millions of new members. The Congress of Industrial Organizations, which split from the AFL in 1935 over the issue of industrial vs. craft organization (they were reunited in 1955), successfully organized the auto, steel, rubber, and electrical industries (see *Sit-Down Strikes; *United Automobile Workers). Its efforts to organize Southern textile workers, however, were defeated.

During World War 2, labor—with the notable exception of the United Mine Workers—generally adhered to a "no strike" pledge. But in the inflationary spiral that followed the end of wartime price and wage controls an explosion of strikes made the unions unpopular. Moreover, some unions were discovered to be corrupt (see *International Brotherhood of Teamsters) and others penetrated by communists. In an antilabor mood, Congress passed the *Taft-Hartley Act (1947) and the *Landrum-Griffin Act (1959) to shift the balance between capital and labor somewhat more in capital's favor. Union membership, which had sunk to 11.6 percent of wage and salary workers in 1930, then reached a postwar peak of 34.7 percent in 1954, declined steadily thereafter to 13.5 percent in 2000.

LA FOLLETTE'S COLLAPSE (Feb. 3, 1912). While former president Theodore Roosevelt insisted that he would not be a candidate for president in 1912 and kept a foot in both the progressive and regular Republican camps, Sen. Robert M. La Follette of Wisconsin, leader of western progressives, in June 1911 announced his candidacy for the Republican presidential nomination. The nation's leading progressives—many of whom would have preferred Roosevelt—rallied to La Follette.

On Feb. 3, 1912, La Follette spoke in Philadelphia at a banquet of the Periodical Publishers' Association. Exhausted by campaigning, distracted by a daughter's serious illness, and fortified by a shot of whiskey on an empty stomach, he began to speak (following a notable address by New Jersey governor Woodrow Wilson) after 11 p.m., reading from a manuscript. When his weary audience heckled him, he responded abusively, abandoned his text, returned to it, and finally rambled incoherently for two hours as his audience deserted.

The next day hostile newspapers headlined that La Follette had suffered a "nervous breakdown." Friends took it upon themselves to announce that he was withdrawing his candidacy. Neither report was true, but progressive leaders were stunned, convinced that La Follette was too nervously unstable to be trusted. When, on Feb. 21, Roosevelt announced that his "hat was in the ring," many deserted La Follette for Roosevelt.

LA FOLLETTE SEAMEN'S ACT (1915), legislation of the *Wilson administration, championed by Sen. Robert M. La Follette of Wisconsin. It regulated the working conditions for seamen aboard U.S. ships.

LAKE ERIE (Sept. 10, 1813), naval battle in the *War of 1812 that preserved American control of the lake. Capt. Oliver Hazard Perry, commanding a makeshift fleet of boats built over the preceding months, confronted a similar British fleet off Put-in-Bay near the western end of the lake. Perry's flagship, the *Lawrence*, displayed a flag bearing the dying words of Capt. James Lawrence in the battle between the *Chesapeake* and the *Shannon* (June 1, 1813): "Don't give up the ship." Perry, however, was forced to abandon the seriously damaged *Lawrence* in the midst of the battle, but from the *Niagara* he bombarded the two strongest British ships, which had fouled with each other, and compelled their surrender. To Gen. William Henry Harrison he sent the famous message, "We have met the enemy, and they are ours."

LANDRUM-GRIFFIN ACT (1959), legislation of the *Eisenhower administration intended to protect union members from wrongdoing by union officers, including misuse of union funds and collusion with employers. It contained a bill of rights for union members that included freedom of speech and periodic free elections.

LANSING-ISHII AGREEMENT (1917), diplomatic accord of the *Wilson administration, negotiated by Secretary of State Robert Lansing and Japanese diplomat Kikujiro Ishii to harmonize U.S.-Japanese relations during World War 1. In an exchange of notes, both parties reaffirmed the *Open Door Policy and the territorial integrity of China but acknowledged Japan's "special interests in China." The United States and Japan canceled the agreement in 1923.

LaROUCHITES. See *Radical Right.

LATIN AMERICAN RECOGNITION (1822–26), issue confronting the *Monroe administration. The French invasion of Spain in 1808 precipitated independence movements in Spain's American colonies. In 1819 Spain refused to ratify the *Adams-Onís Treaty until the United States agreed not to recognize the Latin American revolutionary governments.

After the treaty's ratification, Rep. Henry Clay of Kentucky renewed his advocacy of Latin American recognition, begun in 1815, on the grounds that the Latin American revolutions were continuations of the American Revolution. He envisaged the United States at the head of a Western Hemisphere independent of reactionary European politics. "We should become the center of a system which would constitute the rallying point of human freedom against the despotism of the Old World," he argued. Monroe's secretary of state, John Quincy Adams, was notably skeptical, believing that the leaders of the Latin American revolutions were mere desperadoes and that their countries were incapable of self-government.

In March 1822—by which time Clay was no longer in the House—Pres. James Monroe proposed to Congress that the United States recognize the Latin American republics. The United States recognized Colombia and Mexico in 1822, Chile and Argentina in 1823, Brazil and the Federation of Central American States in 1824, and Peru in 1826. In 1823 the *Monroe Doctrine extended U.S. protection to those "Governments who have declared their independence and maintained it, and whose independence we have, on great consideration and on just principles, acknowledged. . . ."

LATIN AMERICAN RELATIONS. See *Caribbean and Central American Relations; *Mexican Relations; *South American Relations.

LAWRENCE TEXTILE STRIKE (1912), strike (Jan. 12–Mar. 12, 1912) of 20,000 textile workers in Lawrence, Mass., directed by the *Industrial Workers of the World (IWW). The strikers, immigrants earning less than $9 a week, were protesting a wage cut on top of a speedup on the production line. The IWW preserved discipline in the face of police violence and provided relief for the strikers' families. The companies finally granted the workers' demands, but later discharged union militants and shifted production to nonunion mills.

LEBANON HOSTAGES (1982–91), incident in the *Reagan administration. Lebanon in 1982 was racked by civil war between Christians and Muslims, occupied by Palestinians and Syrians, invaded by Israelis, and home to a variety of terrorist groups, some controlled by Iran. For obscure reasons, these last groups began to seize Western hostages. Because of U.S. support for Israel, a number of Americans were taken hostage between 1982 and 1985. Three were released in connection with the *Iran-Contra affair but immediately replaced by three others. In 1991 seven American hostages and the bodies of two others who had been slain by their captors were released, along with three Britons. Two Germans remained in captivity.

LEBANON INTERVENTIONS (1958, 1982–84), incidents in the *Eisenhower and *Reagan administrations.

Fearful of radical Arab nationalism in the Middle East and of Soviet influence in Egypt and Syria (recently united as the United Arab Republic), Pres. Dwight D. Eisenhower welcomed a request from the president of Lebanon for U.S. intervention in a domestic political crisis as an opportunity to implement the *Eisenhower Doctrine and to demonstrate U.S. ability to deploy force in the region. The U.S. Sixth Fleet landed marines in Lebanon on July 15, 1958; army troops transported from Germany by air and sea brought the total of U.S. personnel to 8,500. A new Lebanese president took office on Sept. 23, and the last U.S. troops were withdrawn by Oct. 25. There were no casualties.

In August 1982, with Lebanon convulsed by civil war, occupied by Syria and the Palestine Liberation Organization, and invaded by Israel, U.S. marines returned as part of a multinational peacekeeping force. On Apr. 18, 1983, terrorists destroyed the U.S. embassy in Beirut (63 killed, including 17 Americans). On Oct. 23, 1983, a terrorist truck bomb destroyed the marine headquarters at the Beirut Airport (241 marines killed). In February 1984, the marines were redeployed to U.S. ships offshore (see *Terrorism).

LEE AND GRANT. See *Grant and Lee.

LEE'S DECISION (April 1861). In February 1861, Lt. Col. Robert E. Lee, age 54, was summoned to Washing-

ton from Texas, promoted to full colonel, and given command of the First Cavalry Regiment. This was the work of General in Chief Winfield Scott, who considered Lee the finest officer in the U.S. Army—scion of one of the first families of Virginia, second in his class at West Point, possessor of a brilliant record in the Mexican War and in a succession of choice military assignments since then. At a time when Southern officers were choosing between the Union and the new Confederacy, Scott hoped to persuade Lee to remain with the Union.

Lee's views on the growing crisis were well known. He considered slavery "a moral and political evil." He opposed secession: "I can anticipate no greater calamity for the country than a dissolution of the Union." But he could never fight against his native state.

On Scott's recommendation, Lee was offered field command of the federal army. He rejected the offer: "Though opposed to secession and deprecating war, I would take no part in an invasion of the Southern states." "Lee," Scott told him, "you have made the greatest mistake of your life, though I feared it would be so." On Apr. 20, Lee submitted his resignation from the army, telling Scott: "Save in defense of my native State, I never desire again to draw my sword."

On Apr. 23, Lee accepted appointment as commander of Virginia's military forces, and a week later he was commissioned a brigadier general in the Confederate army.

LEGAL TENDER ACT (1862), legislation of the *Lincoln administration creating paper money (*greenbacks) unredeemable in specie (gold and silver) to help pay for the Civil War. Greenbacks were declared full legal tender for all private and most public debts: the government accepted them in payment of all taxes except customs duties and did not use them to pay interest on the federal debt. First issued in the spring of 1862 in the amount of $150 million, they eventually totaled $450 million.

LEGAL TENDER CASES (1870–71), two contradictory decisions of the *Chase Court on the constitutionality of the *Legal Tender Act of 1862, which had authorized the issuance of fiat paper money (*greenbacks) during the Civil War.

Hepburn v. Griswold (1870) asked if a debt contracted in gold before 1862 could be repaid in paper. For a 4–3 majority, Chief Justice Salmon P. Chase (who as secretary of the Treasury had agreed to the necessity of issuing paper money) now found the Legal Tender Act unconstitutional as impairing the obligation of contracts made before its passage.

The following year, the Court, now increased to nine members, reversed itself 5–4. *Knox v. Lee* (1871) and *Parker v. Davis* (1871) concerned debts contracted after 1862. If the unconstitutionality of the Legal Tender Act was sustained, debtors who had borrowed paper money would be required to repay in specie. The two new justices and the three dissenters in *Hepburn* accommodated them by overturning *Hepburn* and declaring the Legal Tender Act constitutional.

LEND-LEASE (1941–45), wartime program of the Franklin *Roosevelt administration designed to furnish military assistance to any country whose defense the president deemed vital to the United States.

The act establishing it was conceived in response to the confession of British prime minister Winston Churchill in December 1940 that Britain would not be able to pay cash for American war matériel after June 1941 as required by the cash-and-carry provision of the 1939 Neutrality Act (see *Neutrality Acts). Roosevelt ingeniously proposed to lend or lease rather than sell the matériel, thereby avoiding the issue of *war debts that had so embittered international relations after World War 1 since the recipients' war efforts would be considered in the final settlement of accounts.

Roosevelt won over dubious public opinion by his homely analogy—at a press conference on Dec. 17, 1940—of a man lending his garden hose to a neighbor whose house was on fire, thereby protecting his own house, and by a stirring *fireside chat on Dec. 29 in which he defined the U.S. role in the war as serving as the "arsenal of democracy."

The Lend-Lease Bill (H.R. 1776) was attacked by isolationists including the aviator Charles Lindbergh, the historian Charles A. Beard, and Republican senator Robert A. Taft. But Wendell Willkie, the 1940 Republican candidate for president, supported the bill, telling the House Foreign Affairs Committee: "If the Republican Party . . . allows itself to be presented to the American people as the isolationist party, it will never again gain control of the American government."

The bill passed both houses with substantial majorities, and Roosevelt signed it on Mar. 11, 1941. By the end of World War 2, the United States had furnished war matériel and other goods worth $48 billion to 38 countries, chiefly Great Britain and the Soviet Union, in what Churchill called "the most unsordid act in the history of any nation." Lend-Lease was terminated at the end of the war and most outstanding debts were canceled. A Soviet debt estimated at $10 billion was reduced in 1972 to $722 million.

LEVITTOWN, a community on Long Island, N.Y., 30 miles east of New York City, a harbinger of the vast expansion of American suburbs after World War 2.

Built 1948–51 by developers Levitt and Sons, all the mass-produced Levittown houses had the same floor plan, but exterior colors varied and they were placed at different angles on their 60×100-foot lots. The first floor contained a living room, kitchen, bath, and two bedrooms; above was an unfinished attic. A refrigerator, electric strove, and washing machine were provided. The original Cape Cod style houses sold for $6,990 to $7,990.

When completed in November 1951, the community contained 17,447 houses as well as schools, stores, parks, and a community center. Young couples with children stood in line to buy them, then proceeded to individualize them with improvements and landscaping.

The developers built two other Levittowns in Pennsylvania and New Jersey.

LEWIS AND CLARK EXPEDITION (1804–6), expedition that explored the northern reaches of the *Louisiana Purchase, recently acquired from France, en route to the junction of the Columbia River with the Pacific Ocean.

Pres. Thomas Jefferson had an avid interest in the geography of Louisiana before it became part of the United States. In a secret message to Congress in January 1803 (when Louisiana was still believed to belong to Spain), he proposed an exploratory expedition to extend "the external commerce of the United States." This, in Jefferson's view, was an object that Congress was constitutionally permitted to pursue (unlike "the advancement of geography"). Moreover, the phrase covered certain urgent specifics: to find a commercially practicable water route to the Pacific (the old dream of a Northwest Passage); to divert the Canadian *fur trade to the Missouri River; to establish an overland connection with the maritime trade of the Northwest (from where sea otter skins were carried to Canton for exchange for Chinese products); and to strengthen U.S. claims to Oregon, first established by Robert Gray in 1792. Congress approved the venture and appropriated $2,500 for it (its ultimate cost was some $40,000).

A few months later, Louisiana, which had secretly passed from Spanish to French possession, was acquired by the United States. The expedition would traverse American soil after all.

Leadership of the expedition was entrusted to 29-year-old Meriwether Lewis, Jefferson's private secretary and a captain in the U.S. army. Lewis chose a former army acquaintance, William Clark, as coleader. Five years older than Lewis, Clark was only a lieutenant but was represented to the expedition as a captain. The main party consisted of 14 soldiers plus 9 civilians and various watermen, interpreters, and hunters who were enlisted as army privates. Clark was accompanied by a slave. A small party of soldiers and watermen accompanied the expedition as far as the country of the Mandan Indians in present-day North Dakota to help with portage and defense.

The expedition left its base on the Mississippi River near St. Louis on May 14, 1804, and moved laboriously up the Missouri River to the site of present-day Bismarck, N.D., where they spent the winter. Here they were joined by a French interpreter and his wife, Sacajawea, a captive Shoshone Indian who later proved helpful as a translator when the expedition reached her people.

In April 1805 the expedition resumed its ascent of the Missouri River through country teeming with wildlife. On Apr. 25, at the confluence of the Yellowstone and Missouri rivers, Lewis recorded: "I ascended the hills from whence I had a most pleasing view of the country, particularly of the wide and fertile vallies formed by the missouri and the yellowstone rivers, which occasionally unmasked by the wood on their borders disclose their meanderings for many miles in their passage through these delightful tracts of country. . . . the whol face of the country was covered with herds of Buffaloe, Elk & Antelopes; deer are also abundant, but keep themselves more concealed in the woodland. The buffaloe Elk and Antelope are so gentle that we pass near them while feeding, without appearing to excite any alarm among them; and when we attract their attention, they frequently approach us more nearly to discover what we are. . . ."

In June, the expedition spent two weeks carrying their boats and equipment around the Great Falls of the Missouri in present-day Montana. They crossed the Continental Divide and the Bitterroot Range, then descended the Clearwater, Snake, and Columbia rivers to the sea, which they reached on Nov. 18, 1805. The "men appear much Satisfied with their trip," Clark wrote, "beholding with estonishment the high waves dashing against the rocks & this emence Ocean."

The expedition began its homeward journey in April 1806, generally retracing the route by which they had come. Descent of the Missouri was swift, and they reached St. Louis on Sept. 23, 1806.

The expedition's rich collection of flora and fauna was never seriously studied. Lewis and Clark's journals of the expedition were not published until 1904–5. Nevertheless, the expedition proved the nonexistence of a practicable water route to the Pacific in the last area of North America where it might have existed; discovered the populousness of beavers, thus opening the fur trade in the Far West; strengthened U.S. claims to Oregon; pioneered one of the main courses of western migration; and provided the first reliable account of western Indian tribes.

LEXINGTON AND CONCORD (Apr. 19, 1775), first battles of the *Revolutionary War. On the night of Apr. 18, 1775, Gen. Thomas Gage, commander of the British army in North America and governor of Massachusetts, dispatched 700 troops from Boston to seize military stores accumulated by the Patriots at Concord, 20 miles away. Patriots Paul Revere, William Dawes, and Samuel Prescott rode ahead to warn the countryside of their coming (see *Revere's Ride).

At dawn on Apr. 19 the British advance guard reached Lexington, where some 70 *minutemen under Capt. John Parker met them on the town green. Parker and his men had already agreed not to resist the British—"Don't fire unless fired upon," Parker is reputed to have told his men, "but if they mean to have a war let it begin here." When the Americans did not disperse immediately upon the order of British major John Pitcairn, a shot of unknown origin precipitated an exchange of fire and a British charge. The Americans fled but fired as they went; Parker, who held his ground, and seven other Patriots were killed.

The British troops proceeded to Concord, seven miles farther, where they found and destroyed a small quantity of Patriot stores. But now 300–400 militiamen were firing on the redcoats, and hundreds more were streaming to the scene. An exchange at the North Bridge in Concord was commemorated by Ralph Waldo Emerson in "Concord Hymn": "By the rude bridge that arched the flood, / Their flag to April's breeze unfurled, / Here once the embattled farmers stood / And fired the shot heard round the world."

The British returned to Lexington, harassed along the way by militiamen firing from houses and from behind fences and trees. A relief column sent by Gage met the withdrawing troops at Lexington, and the combined force marched under continual fire back to Boston. There a motley army of New England militias, swelling to 15,000 in the next few days, laid siege to the city (see *Boston Siege).

Lexington and Concord cost the British 73 dead, 174 wounded, 26 missing; the Patriots, 49 dead, 41 wounded, 5 missing.

LEYTE GULF. See *World War 2.

LIBERAL REPUBLICAN PARTY (1872), political party formed by reform-minded Republicans disaffected from the *Grant administration and determined to rid the party of corruption and vindictiveness toward the South. At their convention in Cincinnati in May, they failed to nominate the distinguished but unpopular Charles Francis Adams, settling instead on the eccentric editor of the New York *Tribune*, Horace Greeley. The Democrats also nominated him, although Greeley had opposed them in the *Tribune* for 30 years. The reformers campaigned for *civil service reform and an end to the military occupation of the South (see *Reconstruction). Grant was reelected by a wide margin, and the reformers returned to the Republican Party.

LIBERATOR, THE, weekly periodical edited and published by abolitionist William Lloyd Garrison from 1831 to 1865 (see *Abolitionists). The first issue, dated Jan. 1, 1831, carried the motto "Our country is the world—Our countrymen are mankind." An editorial by Garrison demanded immediate and complete emancipation of the slaves. He closed with: "I am in earnest—I will not equivocate—I will not excuse—I will not retreat a single inch—and *I will be heard.*"

Although subscriptions at $2 per year—bought largely by *free blacks in the North—never exceeded 3,000, the *Liberator* infuriated Southerners, who blamed it for the Nat Turner revolt in 1831 (see *Slave Revolts). With ratification of the *13th Amendment, Garrison decided his work was done; the last issue of the *Liberator* was dated Dec. 29, 1865.

LIBERTY LEAGUE (1934–40), anti-*New Deal organization in which wealthy leaders of big business were especially prominent. Well financed by corporate funds (the du Ponts provided 30 percent of its resources) and enlisting conservative Democrats as well as Republicans, it bitterly attacked the New Deal as unconstitutional and compared Roosevelt to the European dictators. Its aim was to return to unfettered free enterprise. The league had no popular base. In 1936, Republican presidential candidate Alfred Landon called its endorsement of him "the kiss of death."

LIBERTY PARTY (1840–48), antislavery political party founded by *abolitionists James G. Birney and Gerritt Smith. Birney, its presidential candidate in 1840 and 1844, received few votes but enough to deprive Whig candidate Henry Clay of New York State in 1844 and thus ensure the election of Democrat James K. Polk.

In 1848, the party's nominee, John P. Hale, withdrew and the party merged with the *Free-Soil Party.

LINCOLN ADMINISTRATION (1861–65). The election of Abraham Lincoln, a Republican, as 16th president of the United States led to the *secession of seven Southern states. In his first inaugural address (see *Lincoln's First Inaugural) Lincoln assured the South that he would take no offensive action against it but that he was determined to uphold his oath to maintain the Constitution. When the Confederates fired on *Fort Sumter, Lincoln called 75,000 militia into federal service to put down an "insurrection," whereupon four more Southern states seceded and the *Civil War began.

Lincoln proved a masterful war president. He presided firmly but tactfully over a cabinet that contained the most eminent politicians of his party, including his principal rivals for the presidential nomination. He took an increasingly broad view of the president's war powers. The war having begun while Congress was in recess, Lincoln, on his own authority, called militia into federal service, ordered a naval blockade of the Southern coast, and issued the first of several suspensions of habeas corpus, permitting the arbitrary arrest by military authorities of persons suspected of disloyalty (see *Habeas Corpus Suspensions). In 1862 he instituted *conscription six months before Congress passed a Conscription Act. Believing that Congress did not have the power to abolish slavery (that required a constitutional amendment), he issued the *Emancipation Proclamation on the basis of "military necessity." At the same time, he ordered the enlistment of black soldiers in the Union army. Without congressional assent he instituted *reconstruction measures in seceded states occupied by Union forces. He prudently avoided war with Great Britain in the *Trent affair, and with the Emancipation Proclamation he ensured continued British and French neutrality.

As commander in chief, Lincoln appointed and removed generals and sometimes directed military operations. He understood the priority of destroying the Confederate army over capturing territory, but not until the appointment of Gen. Ulysses S. Grant as general in chief of all Union armies did he find a general who shared his strategic views and did not shrink from the cost.

Above all, on many occasions and in imperishable language, Lincoln articulated the war's meaning for a suffering and faltering people (see, for example, *Lincoln's Gettysburg Address; *Lincoln's Second Inaugural; *Bixby Letter).

Because of the withdrawal of Southern members of Congress, Republicans controlled both the House and the Senate throughout the war. They quickly passed legislation desired by Northern agricultural and business interests that had long been blocked by the South, most notably the Homestead and Morrill Acts (both 1862; see *Public Lands), the *Morrill Tariffs (1861–64), the Pacific Railroad Act (1862) authorizing construction of a *transcontinental railroad, and the *National Banking Act (1863). The *Legal Tender Act (1862) authorized the issuance of paper money (*greenbacks) to help pay for the war.

Within the Republican Party, the dominant faction was the *Radical Republicans, *abolitionists who were determined to impose severe terms upon the defeated South (see *Confiscation Acts). They formed the *Committee on the Conduct of the War to press the fight, and later they challenged Lincoln's moderate approach to reconstruction, announced in his Proclamation of Amnesty and Reconstruction, in the Wade-Davis Bill and Manifesto. In January 1865 all the Republicans (and a handful of Democrats) passed the *13th Amendment abolishing slavery.

In the summer of 1864 enormous casualties incurred by Grant's *Wilderness Campaign exacerbated war weariness in the Union. The Democrats adopted a peace platform and nominated the failed general George B. McClellan for president. Lincoln was convinced he would not be reelected, but Union successes at *Mobile Bay and *Atlanta raised Northern spirits and changed the political picture. On Nov. 8, 1864, Lincoln was reelected. In his second inaugural address, Lincoln prayed for national reconciliation "with malice toward none, with charity for all."

On Apr. 9, 1865, Confederate general Robert E. Lee surrendered to Grant at Appomattox Court House (see *Appomattox Surrender), effectively ending the war. On Apr. 14 the Lincolns attended a performance at Ford's Theater in Washington where the president was assassinated (see *Lincoln Assassination). He was succeeded by Vice Pres. Andrew Johnson.

During the Lincoln administration, Kansas (1861), West Virginia (1863), and Nevada (1864) became the 34th, 35th, and 36th states.

LINCOLN AND DOUGLAS.

In the small world of frontier Illinois politics, Abraham Lincoln and Stephen A. Douglas were professional and political rivals from young manhood. They were distinctly unalike. Douglas was short (five feet three inches), stocky, energetic, pragmatic. Lincoln was tall (six feet four inches), rawboned, slow, melancholic.

The younger Douglas rose rapidly in the *Democratic Party, early earning the sobriquet "the Little Giant." He was elected a U.S. representative in 1843 and a U.S. senator in 1847. A leading proponent of *popular sovereignty, he was prominently associated with the *Compromise of 1850, the *Kansas-Nebraska Act, and the controversy over the Lecompton constitution (see *Bleeding Kansas). He sought the Democratic presidential nomination in 1852 and 1856.

At the time of the 1858 debates with Lincoln (see *Lincoln-Douglas Debates), Douglas was the most famous politician in the country. He was then fighting for his political life. Ambitious to be president, he was distrusted in the North for his authorship of the Kansas-Nebraska Act and hated in the South for his opposition to the proslavery Lecompton constitution in Kansas. In the Illinois senatorial election, he was opposed by administration Democrats (see *Buchanan Administration) as well as by Republicans. But victory would make him leader of Northern Democrats and a leading candidate for the Democratic presidential nomination in 1860.

In 1858, Lincoln, a former Whig and a prosperous lawyer, was a leader of the new *Republican Party in Illinois. He had served (1845–47) one term in Congress, where he had opposed the *Mexican War—an unpopular position in Illinois. He was largely unknown outside Illinois until the debates with Douglas made him a national figure.

In the political philosophy of both men, the Union was paramount. Both had been influenced by the romantic nationalism of Daniel Webster and Henry Clay. For Douglas, the Union seemed to mean progress, development, expansion, and wealth. For Lincoln, the Union had transcendent meaning as the carrier of the regenerative ideals contained in the *Declaration of Independence (see *Exceptionalism).

Both men were antislavery. But Douglas regarded slavery merely as an anachronism. He believed that it had already reached its fullest extent and that popular sovereignty would prevent its further spread; he was indifferent to its continuance in the states where it existed. Indeed, he considered slavery a local issue, not important enough to be allowed to obstruct national development. He regarded blacks as an inferior species for whom subordination to whites was the only practical means of coexistence. "This government," he declared, ". . . was made by white men, for the benefit of white men and their posterity forever. . . ." In the debates, he baited Lincoln for Lincoln's alleged desire for social equality for blacks.

Lincoln had no such desire. He shared the prevailing view of black inferiority and never advocated social and political equality for blacks. Since he would allow no exceptions to the Declaration of Independence's assertion that *all* men were created equal, he opposed slavery on moral grounds and rejected popular sovereignty for its moral indifference. Out of concern for the Union, he was no *abolitionist; he wanted only to prevent the further extension of slavery. He had no plan for emancipation, which he deferred to a remote future. Nor did he know how to organize a society in which blacks and whites could live together except on the basis of black subordination. But he believed that blacks possessed all the natural rights enumerated in the Declaration of Independence. "In the right to eat the bread, without leave of anybody else, which his own hand earns," Lincoln said, "he is my equal . . . and the equal of every living man."

Douglas won the senatorial election in 1858. In 1860, the Democratic Party split, Northern Democrats nominating Douglas for president. When he realized that Lincoln, the Republican candidate, would win the presidential election, Douglas campaigned in the South urging support for the Union. In the last months of his life, he strongly supported the new president. In a famous gesture, he held Lincoln's hat while the president read his inaugural address. Douglas died of typhoid fever on June 21, 1861.

LINCOLN ASSASSINATION (Apr. 14, 1865), first assassination of an American president (although there had been an attempt on the life of Pres. Andrew Jackson).

As early as August or September 1864, the actor John Wilkes Booth, a passionate Southern sympathizer, recruited accomplices to kidnap Pres. Abraham Lincoln. Not until Apr. 14, 1865, did he decide instead to assassinate the president together with Vice Pres. Andrew Johnson and Secretary of State William H. Seward.

That night—while his accomplices failed to kill Johnson and Seward—Booth entered the president's box at Ford's Theater in Washington during a performance of *Our American Cousin* and at 10:15 p.m. shot the president in the back of the head with a single-shot derringer. He then leaped 12 feet to the stage, breaking his left leg, shouted "Sic semper tyrannis" ("Thus ever to tyrants," the state motto of Virginia), and escaped on a horse being held for him behind the theater. Lincoln was carried to a boardinghouse across the street where, without regaining consciousness, he died at 7:22 the next morning. "Now he belongs to the ages," pronounced Secretary of War Edwin M. Stanton at the president's bedside.

Booth and a coconspirator, David E. Herold, rode out of Washington and at 4 a.m. stopped at the Maryland home of Dr. Samuel A. Mudd, who splinted Booth's simple fracture. Booth and Herold then went on to the home of Samuel Cox, a Confederate sympathizer, who hid them for six days. Eventually they crossed the Potomac River into Virginia and were hidden in a tobacco barn on the farm of Richard A. Garrett near Port Royal. There before dawn on Apr. 26 they were surrounded by Union cavalry. Herold surrendered. The troopers set fire to the barn to smoke Booth out, but a shot—allegedly fired by Sgt. Boston Corbett—mortally wounded the assassin.

The government, making no distinction between the kidnap and the murder plots, charged nine persons in the assassination. Eight were tried (May 9–June 30) by a military court without a jury and found guilty. Four were hanged, three were sentenced to life imprisonment, and one was sentenced to six years. The trial in 1867 of the ninth person ended in a hung jury. In 1869, Pres. Andrew Johnson pardoned the three surviving imprisoned men.

LINCOLN-DOUGLAS DEBATES (August–October 1858), series of debates between Abraham Lincoln and Stephen A. Douglas in the Illinois senatorial election campaign of 1858. Douglas, a nationally prominent Democrat, was seeking a third term as U.S. senator; the little-known Lincoln represented the rising *Republican Party. Because senators were then chosen by state legislatures, the campaign was in fact for the election of members of the state legislature.

There were seven debates—at Ottawa (Aug. 21), Freeport (Aug. 27), Jonesboro (Sept. 15), Charleston (Sept. 18), Galesburg (Oct. 7), Quincy (Oct. 13), and Alton (Oct. 15)—each three hours long and attended by large crowds. Their subject—the extension of slavery in the territories—was of vital interest due to the controversies surrounding the *Kansas-Nebraska Act, *Bleeding Kansas, and the Dred Scott decision (see *Scott v. Sandford). The debates attracted national attention.

By his opposition to the admission of Kansas under the proslavery Lecompton constitution, Douglas had antagonized the South and won the admiration of some Republicans. It was essential for Lincoln, therefore, to make clear the difference between the Democratic and Republican positions on slavery. The difference was that Republicans regarded slavery as a moral evil, inconsistent with the principles enunciated in the Declaration of Independence. Failure to check slavery now, Lincoln argued, and put it "in the course of ultimate extinction," would lead to its "perpetuity and nationalization."

Douglas, on the other hand, was indifferent to the morality of slavery. The author of the Kansas-Nebraska Act continued to advocate *popular sovereignty as the democratic way of determining whether or how far slavery would be extended beyond the states where it already existed. He personally did not care if it was "voted up or down" (though he anticipated that it would be voted down in the new territories for geographical reasons); more important to him than the fate of slavery was the principle of democratic, local self-government.

The fact that the Supreme Court in the Dred Scott case had ruled that nothing, including popular sovereignty, could prevent slave owners from taking their property into a new territory did not faze Douglas. In the famous **Freeport doctrine**, he argued that slavery could always be excluded from any territory whose inhabitants refused to pass the laws and ordinances that actually protected slave property. Popular sovereignty, he believed, would enable free and slave states to coexist indefinitely, whereas congressional prohibition of the extension of slavery would mean war.

In the November election, the Illinois Republicans slightly outpolled the Democrats, but the holdover of incumbent Democratic legislators assured Douglas's reelection as senator. Nevertheless, the debates made Lincoln known beyond Illinois. Invitations to speak came from Eastern states, and Lincoln began to be spoken of as a Republican presidential candidate in 1860.

LINCOLN'S FIRST INAUGURAL (Mar. 4, 1861).

By the time Abraham Lincoln was inaugurated as president of the United States, seven Southern states had seceded and were seizing federal property—forts, arsenals, customshouses—within their borders. In his inaugural address, the new president struck notes of moderation and firmness. He reassured the South that the new government had no right or desire to interfere with slavery where it then existed. He disclaimed any aggressive intentions toward the South. But, he insisted, "the Union of these States is perpetual. . . . [N]o State, upon its own mere motion, can lawfully get out of the Union. . . . [T]o the extent of my ability, I shall take care . . . that the laws of the Union be faithfully executed in all the States. . . . I trust this will not be regarded as a menace, but only as the declared purpose of the Union that it *will* constitutionally defend and maintain itself."

"In *your* hands, my dissatisfied fellow countrymen," Lincoln concluded, "and not in *mine*, is the momentous issue of civil war. The government will not assail *you*. You can have no conflict, without being yourselves the aggressors. *You* have no oath registered in Heaven to destroy the government, while *I* shall have the most solemn one to 'preserve, protect and defend' it.

"I am loth to close. We are not enemies, but friends. We must not be enemies. Though passion may have strained, it must not break our bonds of affection. The mystic chords of memory, stretching from every battlefield, and patriot grave, to every living heart and hearthstone, all over this broad land, will yet swell the chorus of the Union, when again touched, as surely they will be, by the better angels of our nature."

LINCOLN'S FUNERAL (Apr. 18–May 4, 1865).

Abraham Lincoln's body lay in state Apr. 18–20 in the White House and then in the Capitol. On Apr. 21 it was placed aboard a funeral train that for 16 days moved slowly across the country through grieving crowds, pausing for ceremonies at Baltimore, Harrisburg, Philadelphia, New York, Albany, Buffalo, Cleveland, Columbus, Indianapolis, and Chicago.

The poet Walt Whitman described the journey in his elegy "When Lilacs Last in the Dooryard Bloom'd": ". . . Through day and night with the great cloud darkening the land, / With the pomp of inloop'd flags, with the cities draped in black, / . . . With the countless torches lit, with the silent sea of faces, and the unbared heads. . . ."

On May 3 the train brought Lincoln home to Springfield, Ill., where his body was temporarily interred the next day in Oak Ridge Cemetery. In 1871 it was moved to a newly constructed tomb nearby.

LINCOLN'S GETTYSBURG ADDRESS (Nov. 19,

1863), short address by Pres. Abraham Lincoln at the dedication of the military cemetery on the *Gettysburg battlefield. It is the definitive statement of Lincoln's deeply held belief that the survival of the United States was a matter of world-historical significance, since the United States, alone among the nations of the world, embodied the precious ideals of liberty and equality (see *Exceptionalism). The complete address (271 words):

"Four score and seven years ago our fathers brought forth on this continent, a new nation, conceived in Liberty, and dedicated to the proposition that all men are created equal.

"Now we are engaged in a great civil war, testing whether that nation, or any nation so conceived and so dedicated, can long endure. We are met on a great battlefield of that war. We have come to dedicate a portion of that field, as a final resting place for those who here gave their lives that that nation might live. It is altogether fitting and proper that we should do this.

"But, in a larger sense, we can not dedicate—we can not consecrate—we can not hallow—this ground. The brave men, living and dead, who struggled here, have consecrated it, far above our poor power to add or detract. The world will little note, nor long remember what we say here, but it can never forget what they did here. It is for us the living, rather, to be dedicated here to the unfinished work which they who fought here have thus far so nobly advanced. It is rather for us to be here dedicated to the great task remaining before us—that from these honored dead we take increased devotion to that cause for which they gave the last full measure of devotion— that we here highly resolve that these dead shall not have died in vain—that this nation, under God, shall have a new birth of freedom—and that government of the people, by the people, for the people, shall not perish from the earth."

LINCOLN'S "HOUSE DIVIDED" SPEECH (June 18, 1858), delivered at the closing session of the Illinois Republican state convention at Springfield that nominated Abraham Lincoln for the U.S. Senate seat held by Stephen A. Douglas. Douglas was the great advocate of *popular sovereignty as a solution to the controversy over the extension of slavery. Lincoln condemned the doctrine as morally neutral—indeed, indifferent—toward slavery. Indifference, he felt, must lead to slavery's perpetuation. Thus the necessity to make clear the Republicans' moral condemnation of slavery. His use of the biblical phrase (Mark 3:25) gave authority to what at that time was a radical position for a politician. Lincoln knew his audience would accept the metaphor as both biblically and self-evidently true.

In the most memorable passage of his speech, Lincoln declared: " 'A house divided against itself cannot stand.' I believe this government cannot endure, permanently half *slave* and half *free*. I do not expect the Union to be *dissolved*—I do not expect the house to *fall*—but I *do* expect it will cease to be divided. It will become *all* one thing, or *all* the other. Either the *opponents* of slavery, will arrest the further spread of it, and place it where the public mind shall rest in the belief that it is in the course of ultimate extinction; or its *advocates* will push it forward, till it shall become alike lawful in all the States, *old* as well as *new*—North as well as *South*."

LINCOLN'S SECOND INAUGURAL (Mar. 4, 1865). The *Civil War was in its final weeks, and the *13th

Amendment, ending slavery in the United States, had been passed by Congress, when Pres. Abraham Lincoln delivered his brief, meditative second inaugural address.

There was no triumphalism in it. Instead, Lincoln saw in the war the unfolding of divine purpose, an exaction of expiation for national sin. "Fondly do we hope— fervently do we pray—that this mighty scourge of war may speedily pass away," Lincoln said. "Yet, if God wills that it continue, until all the wealth piled by the bondman's two hundred and fifty years of unrequited toil shall be sunk, and until every drop of blood drawn with the lash, shall be paid by another drawn with the sword, as was said three thousand years ago, so still it must be said, 'the judgments of the Lord, are true and righteous altogether."

His conclusion, a virtual benediction, called upon the newly forgiven to forgive in turn: "With malice toward none; with charity for all; with firmness in the right, as God gives us to see the right, let us strive on to finish the work we are in; to bind up the nation's wounds; to care for him who shall have borne the battle, and for his widow, and his orphan—to do all which may achieve and cherish a just, and a lasting peace, among ourselves, and with all nations."

LINDBERGH'S CAREER. In the years following his celebrated Paris flight (see *Lindbergh's Flight), Charles A. Lindbergh (1902–1974) and his wife, Anne Morrow Lindbergh, surveyed air routes to the Orient, Europe, Africa, and South America for Pan American Airways. In February 1932 their infant son was kidnapped and murdered; a Bronx, N.Y., carpenter, Bruno Richard Hauptmann, was eventually convicted of "the crime of the century" and electrocuted in April 1936. Harassment by the press and threats to a second infant son caused the Lindberghs to leave the United States in December 1935 and settle first in England and then in France.

Invited to inspect the air forces of the European powers, Lindbergh was particularly impressed by the German air buildup. In Berlin in October 1938 (after the dismemberment of Czechoslovakia) he accepted a medal from Luftwaffe chief Herman Göring.

After war began in Europe in September 1939, Lindbergh, back in the United States, became active on behalf of the isolationist *America First Committee, speaking against U.S. involvement in the war. At Des Moines, Iowa, on Sept. 11, 1941, he said: "The three most important groups who have been pressing this country toward war are the British, the Jewish, and the Roosevelt administration." When Pres. Franklin Roosevelt likened him to disloyal Civil War *Copperheads, Lindbergh resigned his reserve commission as a colonel in the Army Air Corps.

His attempt to reenlist after the Japanese attack on *Pearl Harbor was rebuffed. He then worked as a civilian consultant and test pilot for several aircraft manufacturers. In May 1944 the United Aircraft Corp. sent him to the South Pacific to observe the performance of its Corsair fighter-bomber. With the complicity of local commanders, Lindbergh flew 50 combat missions, shooting down at least one Japanese plane.

After the war, Lindbergh became active in conservationist causes. His autobiography, *The Spirit of St. Louis* (1953), received a Pulitzer Prize.

LINDBERGH'S FLIGHT (May 20–21, 1927). In 1926 a French hotel owner offered a prize of $25,000 for the first nonstop flight in either direction between France and the United States. Within a year, six men died preparing for or attempting the flight.

In May 1927, at Roosevelt Field on Long Island, N.Y., Navy commander Richard E. Byrd with a crew of four was readying a trimotor Fokker for the flight. He was joined there by Charles A. Lindbergh, a 25-year-old Army-trained airmail pilot from St. Louis. With financing from St. Louis businessmen, Lindbergh had ordered a single-engine, high-wing monoplane from Ryan Airlines in San Diego and had flown the plane, the *Spirit of St. Louis*, from California to New York in record time. Press interest in the competition to be first across the Atlantic was intense, and the boyish Lindbergh became the center of attention while the fliers waited for rainy weather to pass.

Learning that the weather over the Atlantic was clearing, Lindbergh, early on Friday, May 20, with only a few minutes' sleep, determined to take off. At 7:42 a.m., the small, stripped-down Spirit of St. Louis, overloaded with 450 gallons of gasoline, lumbered down the sodden runway at Roosevelt Field and struggled into the air. Lindbergh headed north, traveling 100 miles per hour on the 3,600-mile great circle route to Paris.

An anxious nation cheered when he was sighted over New England, Nova Scotia, and Newfoundland. Then he disappeared into the night over the North Atlantic. All night he struggled to stay awake. Morning found him over Ireland. On he flew, over southern England and the English Channel. A second night was approaching as he crossed the French coast. At 10:24 p.m. on Saturday, May 21, after 33.5 hours in the air, he landed at Le Bourget airport outside Paris and was immediately engulfed in a mass of cheering humanity.

Lindbergh's celebrity was totally unprecedented. Pres.

Calvin Coolidge sent the cruiser *Memphis* to bring the hero home. In Washington he was awarded the Medal of Honor and promoted to colonel in the Army reserve. There was a ticker-tape parade in New York, then a national tour. Everywhere he was greeted with hysterical adulation. It was the high point in "Lucky Lindy's" life (see *Lindbergh's Career).

LINE-ITEM VETO, executive power to veto individual items in an appropriation measure without rejecting the entire bill. In the 1980s, 43 state governors had a form of line-item veto. The power has been sought by many presidents as a defense against special interest and pork-barrel spending as well as against objectionable riders (amendments) frequently attached to appropriation bills.

In 1996, a Republican Congress passed a bill giving Democratic president William J. Clinton the functional equivalent of a line-item veto (a true line-item veto would require a constitutional amendment). But in 1998 the U.S. Supreme Court ruled in *Clinton v. City of New York* that Congress could not change the procedure for enacting legislation spelled out in the Constitution.

LITTLE BIGHORN (June 25, 1876), battle in the *Sioux Wars. Headstrong and aggressive, Lt. Col. George Armstrong Custer (he had been brevetted a brigadier general in the Civil War at 23 and his troops called him general) commanded the Seventh Cavalry Regiment in Brig. Gen. Alfred H. Terry's 1876 campaign in present-day Montana to drive the Sioux under Sitting Bull back to their reservation. On June 22, Terry ordered Custer ahead to locate the elusive Indians.

With more than 600 men and a pack train of 175 mules, Custer pushed along Rosebud Creek to Davis Creek, then after noon on June 25 west along Medicine Dance Creek toward its confluence with the Little Bighorn River. The Sioux encampment, some 15 miles ahead, was still invisible, but Custer's scouts warned him that the Sioux and their Cheyenne allies were extremely numerous. Custer, however, believed that the Indians were in flight. To prevent their escaping to the south, he sent Capt. Frederick Benteen with one battalion on a reconnaissance sweep to the south. Maj. Marcus Reno with another battalion proceeded west along the south bank of the creek while Custer held to the north bank with 220 men.

Around 3 p.m. Reno made contact with fleeing Indians and Custer ordered him to attack. He himself turned north along the Little Bighorn, perhaps intending to cross the stream and trap the Indians on Reno's front. To Reno's surprise, the Indians in front of him did not flee but attacked in overwhelming numbers. Reno's panicked battalion was driven with heavy casualties across the creek to high ground on the north side. There Benteen joined them.

From bluffs above the Little Bighorn, Custer saw Reno engaged and also saw for the first time the huge Indian encampment on the opposite shore. He sent orders to Benteen to join him, then, ever aggressive, looked for a way to cross the river to attack. But unknown to Custer, the Indians had already crossed the river to his side and hidden themselves in ravines to the north and west of the ridge where he, with 220 men, was advancing.

Indian agent James McLaughlin described the battle as it was told him by Gall, Crow King, Bear Cap, No Neck, and other Indian leaders: "Custer swung his troops to the left of the ridge and turned down to the river. As the men rode down into the bottom, the Indians saw that they were apprehensive, but they did not falter and were well down to the river before the Sioux showed themselves on that shore. . . .

"With the first shot that was fired the truth undoubtedly dawned upon Custer and his people that they had met a formidable force. The Indians rose up in front of them and in a very considerable number, and went directly to the attack. The soldiers retreated instantly to the ridge behind and to their right. . . .

"While a considerable body of Indians followed and harassed the men in this movement, another even larger body was sent around the ravine to the rear of the position aimed at by Custer. . . . The elevation was surrounded to the west and north, while a considerable mass of the Sioux were advancing on what might be called the front of Custer's position. . . .

"While the troops were getting into this position, they were fighting continuously, but the onslaught of the Indians did not take on its deathly and irresistible form until Gall, in carrying his men around the ravine to the north and east of the position, struck the cavalry horses. . . . The shouting and shooting incident to the stampeding of the horses was the signal for the attack on the troops from three sides of the ridge.

". . . When Gall gave the signal, the Indians rose up out of the ravines, the Cheyennes led by Crazy Horse. . . . They came straight at the ridge, riding fiercely and swiftly, stayed by nothing, a red tide of death; and almost without pause they rode over the field, and the desperate shooting of the white men did not halt them for a moment. When the tide had passed, Custer and his men were reckoned with the dead."

The entire battle had lasted barely half an hour.

A few miles away, the men of Reno's and Benteen's battalions heard the firing at the Little Bighorn. When at last the guns fell silent the Indians turned back to deal with the surviving troopers. That night and all day on June 26 the troopers held off the Indians. Late in the afternoon of the 26th the Indians disappeared. The next day troops under Col. John Gibbon arrived from the north. The combined forces proceeded to the battlefield above the Little Bighorn, where they found the mutilated corpses of Custer and his command.

News of the massacre stunned a nation proudly celebrating its centennial year.

LITTLE ROCK CRISIS (1957), incident in the *Eisenhower administration. In the summer of 1957, Little Rock, Ark., officials resolved to comply with the U.S. Supreme Court's *school-desegregation decisions by enrolling a token nine black students in the city's Central High School. To prevent that, segregationist governor Orval Faubus ordered the National Guard to surround the school, ostensibly to maintain law and order. When the black students, escorted by white and black ministers, appeared on the second day of school, the Guard turned them away through a hostile crowd.

On Sept. 20 a federal court cited Faubus for contempt. He responded by removing the National Guard from Central High on Sept. 23. When the black children returned to the school on Sept. 25, they were driven out by an angry mob, whereupon the mayor of Little Rock called upon the White House for federal troops. Reluctantly, Eisenhower sent 1,100 paratroopers to Little Rock that same day and federalized the Arkansas National Guard (removing it from Faubus's control)—the first time since *Reconstruction that federal troops had been used to protect Southern blacks.

The paratroopers left at the end of November, the Guard at the end of the school year. Eight of the nine black students completed the year despite the hostility of their classmates. An appeal by the Little Rock School Board for a two-and-a-half-year delay in implementing the city's desegregation plan was rejected by the U.S. Supreme Court in *Cooper v. Aaron. Reelected in a landslide, Faubus in 1958 closed all four Little Rock high schools for the 1958–59 academic year. They reopened integrated in 1959.

LITTLE STEEL. See *Steel Strikes.

LOCHNER v. NEW YORK (1905), 5–4 decision of the *Fuller Court overturning a New York law limiting the hours of labor in bakeries to ten per day or 60 per week. Lochner, a "boss baker," claimed that the law deprived him of a liberty—freedom of contract—in violation of the *14th Amendment's guarantee of "due process."

Justice Rufus Peckham, for the Court, agreed. While recognizing that so fundamental a freedom as freedom of contract was subject to the police powers of a state—powers that "relate to the safety, health, morals and general welfare of the public"—Peckham insisted that the ostensible purpose of the New York law—to protect the health of bakery workers—was a "mere pretext." He denied that the act was, "within any fair meaning of the term, a health law." Rather, it was "an illegal interference with the rights of individuals, both employers and employees, to make contracts regarding labor upon such terms as they may think best. . . ."

Justice John Marshall Harlan, in dissent, argued that an act of a legislature should be accepted at face value and enforced unless it was demonstrably in violation of the Constitution. Justice Oliver Wendell Holmes, another dissenter, wrote: "The Fourteenth Amendment does not enact Mr. Herbert Spencer's Social Statics. . . . [A] constitution is not intended to embody a particular economic theory. . . ."

LOCOFOCOS (1834–43), a radical, working-class wing of the Jacksonian *Democratic Party in New York. Calling themselves Equal Rights Democrats, they were hostile to privilege, government, business, even labor-saving machinery; they embraced every reform scheme. Their popular name derived from a party nominating meeting in 1835. The *Tammany regulars declared their ticket carried, adjourned the meeting, and extinguished the lights; whereupon the Equal Righters produced the new sulfur friction matches (called locofocos), lit candles, and nominated their own ticket. By 1843 most Locofocos had been absorbed into Tammany.

LODGE AND WILSON. See *Wilson and Lodge.

LODGE COROLLARY (1912), Senate resolution introduced by Henry Cabot Lodge of Massachusetts prompted by reports that a Japanese syndicate was negotiating to buy a large site near Magdalena Bay in Lower California, Mexico. The resolution declared that the United States viewed with "grave concern" any purchase of a strategically important area by a foreign corporation whose government would be able to exercise practical control over it. The Lodge Corollary thus applied the *Monroe Doctrine to non-European powers and to foreign companies as well as countries.

LODGE RESERVATIONS (1919), 14 reservations to the Treaty of Versailles (which included the covenant of the League of Nations) negotiated by pro-League Republican senators with Republican members of the Senate Foreign Relations Committee headed by Henry Cabot Lodge of Massachusetts and introduced on Nov. 6, 1919. Stronger reservations, issued by the committee in September, had been rejected by Republican senators who supported the League. The negotiations leading to the revised "mild" reservations were boycotted by Democrats on the instruction of Pres. Woodrow Wilson.

The most important reservation dealt with Art. 10 of the covenant, which obliged members of the League to "preserve as against external aggression the territorial integrity and existing political independence" of all members of the League as the League's Council "shall advise." The reservationists declared that the United States would not enforce sanctions against aggressors without the explicit consent of Congress in each case. Wilson commented that this "cuts the very heart out of the Treaty."

Other reservations declared that the United States would not accept a League mandate without congressional approval, that no arms-limitation agreement would be binding on the United States without congressional consent, that Congress would be the sole judge of what constituted a "domestic" issue, and that no issue arising out of the Monroe Doctrine would be submitted to the League.

The fact that Lodge supported these reservations may indicate that he accepted the treaty and the League in deference to the advice of former secretary of state Elihu Root, who formulated Republican Party policy on the issue. Or he may have been confident that Wilson would reject even these mild reservations and in consequence suffer a humiliating—if self-inflicted—political defeat (see *Wilson and Lodge). If the latter, he was correct. Wilson instructed Senate Democrats to vote against the reservations, with the result that the treaty was rejected by the Senate on Nov. 19, 1919.

LOEWE v. LAWLOR or **DANBURY HATTERS' CASE** (1908), unanimous decision by the *Fuller Court finding the United Hatters of North America a "combination in restraint of trade" under the *Sherman Antitrust Act for its use of a national boycott to support a strike against a Danbury, Conn., hat manufacturer. The 191 local members of the union were ultimately held individually responsible for $250,000 in damages, with disastrous consequences to them.

LONDON ECONOMIC CONFERENCE (June 12–July 28, 1933), international conference called to deal with the worldwide depression. U.S. president Franklin Roosevelt instructed the American delegates to seek tariff reductions and removal of artificial trade restrictions. But France and other gold bloc countries proposed a plan of currency stabilization based on the gold standard, which the United States had already abandoned. Roosevelt feared that currency stabilization would be disadvantageous to the United States and hinder his efforts to raise U.S. commodity prices. Roosevelt's decision to put national interest above international agreement on this issue caused the conference to fail.

LONG ASSASSINATION (Sept. 7, 1835). Mobilizing small farmers against the conservative oligarchy that had ruled backward Louisiana since Reconstruction, coarse, flamboyant, and intimidating Huey P. Long was elected governor in 1928 on the slogan "Every Man a King." Unlike other Southern demagogues, Long kept his campaign promises, building new schools, hospitals, and highways, a new state capitol and governor's mansion, and a new airport for New Orleans, while pouring funds into the state university. By patronage, corruption, electoral fraud, and violence, but with undeniable popular support, Long created a political machine through which he governed Louisiana as a virtual dictator.

Long was elected to the U.S. Senate in 1930, remaining as governor until he took his Senate seat in December 1931. From Washington, he continued to exercise absolute control over Louisiana. Proposing the redistribution of the nation's wealth as the cure for the *Great Depression, Long briefly supported Pres. Franklin Roosevelt, but by the end of 1933 had separated himself from the administration and had alienated most other senators by his contemptuous behavior toward them. It was clear that he had his eye on the presidency in 1936 or 1940. His vehicle would not be one of the conventional political parties but the *Share Our Wealth Society, which he founded in February 1934 and which quickly attracted millions of members.

Facing a presidential election in 1936, the administration worried about the damage Long was doing to its prospects. Roosevelt considered Long one of the two most dangerous men in the country (the other was Gen. Douglas MacArthur) and debated sending federal troops into Louisiana to restore republican government. His "turn to the left" in the *Second New Deal in 1935 was partly intended to weaken Long.

In September 1935 Long returned to Louisiana and summoned a meeting of the state legislature. Among other legislation, Long proposed a measure (clearly unconstitutional) that would have empowered state officials to arrest agents of the Roosevelt administration. Another proposed to gerrymander the district of state judge Benjamin Pavy, a longtime personal enemy. At 9 p.m. on Sept. 7, Long was confronted in a capitol corridor by a single gunman who shot him twice. The gunman, Carl A. Weiss, a son-in-law of Judge Pavy, was immediately shot to death by Long's bodyguards. Long was rushed to a nearby hospital, where surgeons, repairing his wounds, failed to notice a damaged kidney. Long died on Sept. 10.

Without its leader, the Share Our Wealth Society collapsed. The Long political machine, however, continued to control Louisiana.

LONG ISLAND (Aug. 27, 1776), *Revolutionary War battle. Anticipating a British move against New York City, strategic center of the United States, Patriot general George Washington moved his army there from Boston and began fortifying the city at the tip of Manhattan Island and Brooklyn Heights across the East River on the western end of Long Island.

In August, British fleets from Nova Scotia and Great Britain converged on New York, bringing a British army totaling 35,000 men to Staten Island in New York harbor. During Aug. 22–25, 20,000 British troops were carried across the harbor, landing unopposed near Gravesend on Long Island and advancing four miles inland to the village of Flatbush. Three miles away a Patriot army of 9,000—half of Washington's total army—formed a line extending from the East River to Jamaica Pass, anchored by fortified Brooklyn Heights.

On Aug. 27 a British attack at Jamaica Pass rolled up the Patriot left flank while frontal attacks routed the Patriot center and right. The Patriots streamed into Brooklyn Heights, where they awaited the next British move. But British general William Howe, overcautious, prepared for a siege. Adverse winds kept the British fleet out of the East River, where it could have cut off the Patriot army on Long Island. On the night of Aug. 29–30, under cover of fog, Washington withdrew his troops from Brooklyn Heights to Manhattan by small boats.

The Americans had lost some 500 dead and wounded and more than 1,000 captured, including two generals; British casualties totaled fewer than 400.

LOOKOUT MOUNTAIN. See *Chattanooga Campaign.

LOUISIANA PURCHASE (1803), acquisition by the United States of the western half of the Mississippi River watershed, a diplomatic achievement of the *Jefferson administration.

As early as May 1801 rumors that Spain was about to return Louisiana to France (Spain had acquired it in 1762 and had already returned it to France by secret treaty in 1800) alarmed Pres. Thomas Jefferson. Louisiana was a vast area of uncertain boundaries. Its most important point was the city of New Orleans at the mouth of the Mississippi; the possessor of New Orleans could deny western American farmers—who floated their wheat and pork down the Mississippi for transportation by sea—access to eastern and foreign markets. Jefferson preferred that New Orleans remain in feeble Spanish hands rather than be transferred to militarily powerful France. "There is on the globe one single spot, the possessor of which is our natural and habitual enemy," he wrote in 1802. "It is New Orleans. . . . France placing herself in that door assumes to us the attitude of defiance."

In January 1803 Jefferson sent James Monroe as a special envoy to France and Spain with authorization to buy New Orleans and West and East Florida for $9 million, thereby securing U.S. control of the mouth of the Mississippi. (The Federalist opposition, led by Alexander Hamilton, clamored for a U.S. attack on New Orleans and the *Floridas.) Before Monroe reached Paris, First Consul Napoleon Bonaparte, having abandoned his plan for an American empire, had decided to offer the entire region (exclusive of the Floridas, which remained in Spanish hands) to the United States for $15 million. Monroe and Robert R. Livingston, U.S. minister to France, signed the purchase treaty on May 2, 1803.

Jefferson the strict constructionist saw only one obstacle to Senate ratification of the treaty: the acquisition of foreign territory (like the establishment of a national bank, which Jefferson had once opposed) was not one of the enumerated powers of the federal government. Unwilling to miss the extraordinary opportunity to double "the empire of liberty," Jefferson rejected as too slow the idea of seeking a constitutional amendment and permitted himself to be persuaded that the president's treaty-making powers (loosely constructed) were sufficient for the purchase. On Oct. 20, 1803, the Senate ratified the treaty 24–7; the negative votes were cast by Federalists, who feared that doubling U.S. territory would decrease the influence of New England in national affairs.

LOYALISTS or **TORIES,** American adherents of Great Britain in the *Revolutionary War. The name Tories, which is often applied to them, is certainly a misnomer for many who in England would have been recognized as Whigs—upholders of the Parliamentary system of king, lords, and commons.

Loyalists may have constituted 15–30 percent of the colonial population. They were found in all localities, in all social classes, and at all economic levels, but were probably proportionately most numerous in New York, New Jersey, Massachusetts, North and South Carolina, and Georgia. Compared to the general population, they were probably more often urban dwellers, public officials, business and professional people, and Anglicans.

The motives for their loyalism were varied. Some were inherently conservative, preferring traditional allegiances and institutions and fearing mob rule and anarchy. Officeholders and wealthy merchants had strong career and economic incentives. Others had political, social, religious, and even personal motives.

Sometimes prewar attitudes carried over into the Revolution. Thus in New England poor farmers and small businessmen who resented the control of provincial governments by wealthy merchants became Patriots opposed to Loyalist aristocrats. In some Southern states, backcountry farmers who resented the dominance of tidewater plantation owners, many of whom were Patriots, took up the Loyalist cause. Many people who became Loyalists were active in the revolutionary movement until the *Declaration of Independence forced them to choose sides.

Thousands of Loyalists fought on the British side during the war, usually in Loyalist battalions and regiments that served as auxiliaries to the British army. In the South, Loyalist militias and armed bands waged a savage civil war with their similarly organized Patriot neighbors.

The war uprooted those Loyalists who did not choose or were not able to hide their sympathies. Revolutionary authorities persecuted, imprisoned, and exiled Loyalists and confiscated their property (the Treaty of *Paris provided for compensation to Loyalists for these confiscations). Thousands of Loyalists fled from their homes to take refuge in cities controlled by the British army—Boston, Philadelphia, New York, Charleston. When the British evacuated these cities, the Royal Navy carried many Loyalists into exile. Some 80–100,000 Loyalists left the United States to settle in Canada, the West Indies, or Great Britain.

LUDLOW MASSACRE (Apr. 20, 1914), incident during a *United Mine Workers strike (November 1913–August 1914) against Rockefeller-owned coal mines at Ludlow, Colo. Evicted from company-owned houses, the miners and their families set up tent colonies on the plain. On Apr. 20, 1914, fighting between strikers and company guards was followed by the machine-gunning and burning of 200 miners' tents, in which 12 children and two women died. Two weeks of fighting and 40 more deaths followed before federal troops restored order. The strike failed.

The episode received wide publicity through the interrogation of John D. Rockefeller Jr. before the *Commission on Industrial Relations, a panel created by Congress to study labor-management relations.

LUDLOW RESOLUTION (1935–38), proposal by Republican representative Louis Ludlow of Indiana for a constitutional amendment that would have required—except in cases of actual invasion—a national referendum before a declaration of war by Congress became effective. First initiated in 1935 as a result of the *Nye Munitions Investigation, it was rejected several times but seemed likely to pass in 1938 until Pres. Franklin Roosevelt strongly opposed it.

LUSITANIA SINKING (May 7, 1915), incident in the *Wilson administration. Despite warnings published in the U.S. press by the German embassy that Americans traveling in the German-declared war zone around the British Isles did so at their own risk, many Americans took passage on the British liner *Lusitania*, which was sunk without warning by a German submarine off the Irish coast. Among the 1,198 casualties were 128 Americans.

Pres. Woodrow Wilson composed a restrained, even conciliatory note in which he professed to believe that the sinking was contrary to German policy. Nevertheless, he pointed out "the practical impossibility of employing submarines in the destruction of commerce without disregarding" the rules of warfare, and he declared that the U.S. government "confidently expects . . . that the Imperial German Government will disavow the acts of which the Government of the United States complains, that they will make reparation so far as reparation is possible for injuries which are without measure, and that they will take immediate steps to prevent the recurrence of anything so obviously subversive of the principles of warfare. . . ."

The note was signed reluctantly by Secretary of State William Jennings Bryan, a pacifist, who recognized that

Wilson had determined to uphold neutral rights against Germany even at the risk of war. Rather than sign a second note, Bryan resigned.

While negotiations over the *Lusitania* continued, a German submarine on Aug. 19 sank the British liner *Arabic* with the loss of two Americans. The United States demanded that the German government repudiate the attack. Deciding that the advantages of unrestricted submarine warfare were outweighed by the risk of involving the United States in the war, Berlin agreed not to sink passenger liners or unarmed merchant ships without warning. Germany did not resume unrestricted submarine warfare until 1917.

LYNCHING. The execution—by hanging, shooting, burning, or other means—of suspected lawbreakers by vigilantes occurred frequently in the American past. It was most common where law enforcement was weak or undeveloped, as on the frontier or in isolated rural communities. But lynch mobs were not unknown in cities and towns.

In the post–Civil War South, lynching became a primary means of enforcing white supremacy, particularly the idealized position of Southern white womanhood. Especially in backward areas, blacks were lynched for alleged crimes serious and trivial, from murder to "disrespect." Lynching could be secret or public. In the latter case, large crowds might gather to witness the torture, mutilation, and burning alive of the victim, then scrounge for souvenirs.

Between 1882 and 1968 some 4,742 lynchings were recorded nationwide. In 72 percent of these, the victim was black. Over the years, lynching was increasingly confined to the Southern states and its victims were increasingly black. In the 1920s, 95 percent of all lynchings occurred in the South and blacks constituted 90 percent of all victims.

The lynching of blacks in the South peaked in the late 19th century. Thereafter other forms of racial control—segregation, disfranchisement, and tenant farming—reduced the "need" for exemplary lynchings. The number of lynchings in the South declined gradually in the first decades of the 20th century, rapidly after 1930. But sporadic lynchings occurred as late as the 1950s.

M

MacARTHUR FIRING (Apr. 10, 1951). After World War 2, at his headquarters in Tokyo as head of the Allied occupation, Gen. Douglas MacArthur, the imperious and theatrical conqueror of Japan, assumed the role of American proconsul in Asia, virtually independent of his nominal civilian and military superiors. When the *Korean War broke out, he took command of the United Nations forces in Korea and in the Inchon landing (Sept. 15, 1950) brilliantly transformed military disaster into victory, confirming the popular view of him as the greatest American soldier who had ever lived.

MacArthur's task then was to pursue the routed North Korean army across the 38th parallel, destroy it, and reunite the peninsula. At a meeting on Wake Island (Oct. 15), MacArthur assured Pres. Harry S. Truman that neither the Chinese nor the Soviets would intervene and that the war would be over by Christmas. But when UN troops approached the Yalu River border between North Korea and China, the Chinese intervened in overwhelming numbers, sending UN forces reeling 300 miles back below the 38th parallel.

Subject now to unaccustomed criticism in the American press, MacArthur in late November gave his version of events to friendly journalists. He denied that his strategy had provoked Chinese intervention and blamed his inability to repel the Chinese offensive on restrictions placed upon him by Washington. Truman's response (Dec. 6) was to order all military officers and diplomatic officials to "refrain from direct communication on military or foreign policy with newspapers, magazines, or other publicity media."

At the end of December, facing the destruction of his army, MacArthur called for a naval blockade of China, the bombing of Chinese cities to destroy the country's industrial capacity, use in Korea of Chinese Nationalist troops from Formosa, and allowing the Nationalists to in-vade southern China as a diversion. Truman and his advisers opposed enlargement of the war. Recognizing that victory in Korea was now impossible—as Secretary of State Dean Acheson explained, "They can put in more than we can"—Truman decided to fight a limited war with the objective of regaining the 38th parallel and then seeking an armistice, having at least successfully stopped communist aggression. In the age of the atomic bomb, Truman believed that limited war was the only feasible war.

In January 1951, a new commander of UN ground forces, Gen. Matthew B. Ridgway, halted the UN retreat south of Seoul and counterattacked, reaching the 38th parallel in March. Late that month, Truman sent MacArthur a copy of a cease-fire proposal he intended to communicate to the Chinese. MacArthur promptly issued a bombastic ultimatum of his own, threatening the Chinese with destruction and offering to meet with their commander to negotiate a settlement. Truman's proposal was never sent; the Chinese rebuffed MacArthur with contempt. Then on Apr. 5 Republican Joe Martin of Massachusetts read to the House of Representatives a letter he had received from MacArthur agreeing with Martin's call for the use of Chinese Nationalist troops in Korea. In contradiction to U.S. policy, MacArthur declared that the war against communism had to be won in Asia, not Europe. He concluded with a phrase that was soon famous: "There is no substitute for victory."

Truman's civilian and military advisers agreed unanimously that MacArthur's insubordination was intolerable. On Apr. 10, Truman relieved MacArthur of all his commands in the Far East. A storm of abuse from Congress, the public, and much of the press immediately broke around the president's head. Talk of impeachment was in the air.

Returning to the United States for the first time in 16 years, MacArthur was greeted in San Francisco on Apr.

17 by delirious throngs. Two days later he delivered a dramatic address to a joint session of Congress, followed by triumphal parades in Washington and New York. On May 3, the Senate Foreign Relations and Armed Services committees began joint hearings on MacArthur's dismissal. MacArthur's self-justifying testimony over three days—particularly his indifference to the global consequences of his policies as a theater commander—forced once-worshipful senators to confront the fact that they had no intention of adopting his recommendations. Moreover, Secretary of Defense George C. Marshall and the Joint Chiefs of Staff flatly denied MacArthur's claim that they agreed with him and supported his dismissal. By the time the disgruntled senators completed their seven-week investigation, the MacArthur hysteria, like the old soldier himself, had faded away.

MACON BILL NO. 2 (1810). See *Embargo and Nonintercourse.

MADISON ADMINISTRATION (1809–17). From Thomas Jefferson, James Madison, fourth president of the United States, inherited the intractable problem of British and French depredations against American shipping. Madison's response, like Jefferson's—economic coercion—was ineffectual and led inexorably to war (see *Embargo and Nonintercourse). As war approached, Madison urged military preparedness on Congress, but his Treasury secretary, Albert Gallatin, insisted on a balanced budget. Old Republicans, frugal and pacific, and Federalists heeded Gallatin. To make up a shortfall in tariff revenues due to nonimportation, Congress in 1810 slashed army and navy appropriations rather than raise taxes.

In 1811 Congress refused to renew the charter of the *Bank of the United States—now supported by Madison, who had led the opposition to its charter in 1791—thereby depriving the government of a valuable fiscal agent in the approaching crisis. At last the "war hawk" Congress (see *War Hawks) that convened in November 1811 agreed to enlarge the army; the House voted to increase the army by 10,000 men, the Senate by an impractical 25,000. Both houses rejected Madison's recommended increase in the navy. Grudgingly, Congress approved a war loan and tax increases—to take effect in case of war, which Congress voted on June 18, 1812.

Lacking a commanding personality, and constrained by his Republican principles, Madison failed to exert dynamic leadership as a war president (see *War of 1812). His military directives were vigorous and intelligent, but he was frustrated at every turn by meager resources, in-

competent civilian and military authorities, congressional foot-dragging, and Federalist obstruction. His popularity reached its nadir in August 1814 when the British burned Washington (see *Washington Burning); six months later—after the battle of *New Orleans and receipt of a favorable peace treaty (see *Ghent Treaty)—it reached its zenith.

In his annual message to Congress in December 1815, Madison outlined a program remote from the small-government Republican philosophy of 1800: national defense, protective *tariffs, retention of some wartime taxes, *internal improvements, a national bank, and a national university. The national bank was rechartered in 1816. But when Congress presented Madison with an internal improvements bill at the close of his administration in 1817, he vetoed it in the conviction that federally subsidized internal improvements required a constitutional amendment. Madison was succeeded by his secretary of state, James Monroe.

During Madison's administration, Louisiana (1812) and Indiana (1816) became the 18th and 19th states.

MADISON AND JEFFERSON. See *Jefferson and Madison.

MAINE SINKING (Feb. 15, 1898), incident that precipitated the *Spanish-American War. Sent to Cuba in January 1898 to protect American lives and property during the Cuban war of independence, the 6,682-ton battleship *Maine*, anchored in Havana harbor, was rocked at 9:40 p.m. on Feb. 15 by two explosions, the second in its forward magazine. The ship sank with the loss of 266 of its 354-man crew. "Remember the *Maine*!" became the battle cry of U.S. troops in the war that followed.

A U.S. investigation soon after the sinking blamed it on the explosion of a submarine mine that in turn detonated a powder magazine. A Spanish investigation at the same time concluded that the explosions had been entirely of internal origin. In 1976 the U.S. Navy Department published a report by Adm. Hyman J. Rickover that attributed the explosions to spontaneous combustion in a coal bunker (a common occurrence on coal-burning ships) adjacent to powder magazines.

MALARIA, worldwide disease caused by one or more of four plasmodium parasites carried from host to host by the female *Anopheles* mosquito. It is endemic in tropical and subtropical coastal areas and river valleys. Its classic symptoms are alternating chills and fevers, then a period of exhaustion before the cycle starts again. These symptoms may continue for six to ten weeks, then disappear for as long as 28 weeks before recurring. If the victim leaves the malarial area, the infection wears out in two to four years. Only one type of parasite causes death; in other cases, death results from other infections invading the already weakened body.

Because of its debilitating effects on whole populations, malaria has been implicated in the decline of powerful states and the depopulation of large areas. It was also a major barrier to European penetration of Africa, India, China, and South and Central America. In the 17th century, quinine—contained in cinchona bark—was recognized as the major specific for preventing and controlling malaria in individuals. In 1898 the role of the *Anopheles* mosquito as its vector was established. Thereafter antimalaria programs were aimed at halting the breeding of mosquitoes in standing water.

Spanish colonizers and their African slaves probably introduced malaria into the Western Hemisphere. In the 17th and 18th centuries, malaria became endemic in North America, affecting New England, the southern Atlantic and Gulf coasts, and the Mississippi Valley. Early in the 19th century, Illinois was notoriously unhealthful. Malaria persisted in the upper Middle West until the 1880s. It remained a problem in the Southern states until after World War 2, when DDT spraying checked mosquito breeding. By 1960, the disease had disappeared from the United States. Elsewhere in the world, however, the cost and effort involved in continuing mosquito control have proved too great for underdeveloped countries, and these have experienced a recrudescence of the disease.

MALMÉDY. See *World War 2.

MANASSAS. See *Bull Run, First; *Bull Run, Second.

MANHATTAN PROJECT (1942–46), secret Army project during *World War 2 for the development of an *atomic bomb. In 1939, Pres. Franklin Roosevelt was informed by a letter from physicist Albert Einstein of the possible military implications of the discovery of nuclear fission in Germany the year before. Roosevelt obtained funding for new theoretical and experimental research. The project eventually consumed $2 billion, provided by Congress for secret purposes to which it was not privy.

Because development of a bomb required a significant industrial infrastructure, the project was turned over to the Army, and Gen. Leslie R. Groves, builder of the Pentagon, was put in charge. Groves built plants at Oak Ridge, Tenn., for the separation of fissionable uranium-235 from U-238 and reactors at Hanford, Wash., for the production of plutonium.

After physicist Enrico Fermi produced the first controlled nuclear chain reaction at the University of Chicago in December 1942, Groves put theoretical physicist J. Robert Oppenheimer in charge of a weapons laboratory at Los Alamos, N.Mex., with the task of building a bomb. Oppenheimer's team succeeded in building bombs of two types—first a uranium bomb in which two hemispheres of U-235, fired at each other, created a critical mass and exploded; second, a plutonium bomb in which ingots of plutonium were compressed by surrounding explosives to the point of criticality. This was the type of device tested near Alamogordo, N.Mex., on July 16, 1945 (see *Trinity).

Control of the atomic bomb passed in 1946 from the Manhattan Project to the U.S. Atomic Energy Commission.

MANIFEST DESTINY, phrase used by editor John O'Sullivan in the July 1845 issue of *United States Magazine and Democratic Review* to justify the expansionist program of the *Polk administration. "Away, away with all these cobweb tissues of rights of discovery, exploration, settlement, contiguity, etc. . . . ," wrote O'Sullivan in an editorial supporting *Texas annexation. "The American claim is by right of our manifest destiny to overspread and to possess the whole of the continent which Providence has given us for the development of the great experiment of liberty and federative self-government entrusted to us. . . . It is in our future far more than in our past . . . that our True Title is to be found."

MANILA BAY. See *Spanish-American War.

MANN-ELKINS ACT (1910). See *Railroad Regulation.

MAPP v. OHIO (1961), 5–3–1 decision of the *Warren Court applying to the states, through the Due Process Clause of the *14th Amendment, the Fourth Amendment's prohibition of unreasonable searches and seizures—including its logical corollary, the **exclusionary rule** (that illegally seized evidence may not be used in a criminal trial) then binding on federal but not state officers. The police had entered Dolly Mapp's home without a warrant in search of gambling paraphernalia and a fugitive but had instead found obscene literature, for possession of which Mapp was imprisoned.

For the Court, Justice Tom Clark closed "the only

courtroom door remaining open to evidence secured by official lawlessness in flagrant abuse of that basic right [of privacy]. . . ." Clark continued: "There are those who say, as did Justice (then Judge) Cardozo, that under our constitutional exclusionary doctrine '[t]he criminal is to go free because the constable has blundered.' . . . The criminal goes free, if he must, but it is the law that sets him free. Nothing can destroy a government more quickly than its failure to observe its own laws, or worse, its disregard of the charter of its own existence. As Mr. Justice Brandeis . . . said . . . : 'Our Government is the potent, the omnipresent teacher. For good or for ill, it teaches the whole people by its example. . . . If the government becomes a lawbreaker, it breeds contempt for law; it invites every man to become a law unto himself; it invites anarchy.' "

MARBURY v. MADISON (1803), unanimous decision of the *Marshall Court claiming the power of *judicial review, the power of the judicial branch of the government to nullify acts of the legislative or executive branch that it found in violation of the Constitution.

Pres. John Adams had appointed Federalist William Marbury a justice of the peace in the District of Columbia—one of Adams's *midnight appointments. Secretary of State John Marshall (newly appointed chief justice but still acting as secretary of state) neglected to deliver the signed and sealed commission to Marbury. The new Republican president, Thomas Jefferson, ordered his secretary of state, James Madison, not to deliver the commission. Marbury appealed to the Supreme Court under the *Judiciary Act of 1789 for a writ of mandamus compelling Madison to deliver his commission.

Chief Justice Marshall ruled that the commission was valid and wrongfully withheld. But he dismissed Marbury's suit on the grounds that the Judiciary Act of 1789 had unconstitutionally enlarged the Supreme Court's original jurisdiction when it gave it the power to issue writs of mandamus. "It is emphatically the province and duty of the judicial department to say what the law is," declared Marshall. Since "the constitution is superior to any ordinary act of the legislature," it followed that "an act of the legislature, repugnant to the constitution, is void."

By denying Marbury his commission, Marshall adroitly avoided exacerbating the conflict between the Republican administration and the Federalist judiciary. Contemporaries were slow to appreciate that the Court, while renouncing a minor power (to issue writs of mandamus), had claimed a potentially great one (judicial review).

MARIEL BOATLIFT (1980). See *Cuban Migration; *Refugees.

MARRIED WOMEN'S PROPERTY ACTS. See *Women's Rights.

MARSHALL COURT (1801–35), the U.S. Supreme Court under Chief Justice John Marshall. Federalist John Marshall was appointed chief justice of the United States by Pres. John Adams at the very dawn of Thomas Jefferson's "Revolution of 1800," which ended Federalist control of the national government and heralded a new era of strict construction, small government, and states' rights. For the next 35 years, Marshall was the principal champion of nationalism against often contrary political currents.

Marshall had three conscious objectives as chief justice: to make the federal judiciary a coequal branch—with the legislative and executive—of the federal government; to establish the supremacy of the federal government over the states and to make the Constitution the supreme law of the land; and to ensure that the national government had the power to govern effectively.

To make the judiciary a coequal branch of the federal government, Marshall early asserted the Supreme Court's power of *judicial review—that is, the power to nullify an act of Congress or of the executive that it determined to be in violation of the Constitution. This power is not mentioned in the Constitution, although the very existence of a written constitution implies it. Alexander Hamilton argued for it in *Federalist* No. 78, and Marshall made use of his argument. His first (and only) assertion of the power of judicial review involving other branches of the federal government occurred in *Marbury v. Madison* (1803), in which he found both Congress and the executive in error. (This power was not asserted again until *Scott v. Sandford*, 1857.)

To establish the supremacy of the national government and of the Constitution as the law of the land, it was necessary to assert the power of judicial review over state legislatures and state courts. In *Fletcher v. Peck* (1810) and *Dartmouth College v. Woodward* (1819) the Marshall Court found actions of state legislatures unconstitutional; in *Martin v. Hunter's Lessee* (1816) and *Cohens v. Virginia* (1821), Marshall asserted the appellate powers of the Supreme Court over state court decisions. In *McCulloch v. Maryland* (1819), Marshall declared explicitly: "The government of the Union, though limited in its powers, is supreme within its sphere of action."

To ensure that the national government had the powers necessary to govern effectively, Marshall relied on an expansive reading of the Constitution, adopting Hamilton's argument in favor of "implied powers" that was based on the last of the Constitution's enumerated powers in Art. 1, sec. 8: "To make all laws which shall be necessary and proper for carrying into execution the foregoing powers." To accomplish important national purposes like chartering a national bank (*McCulloch*) or extending congressional authority over broadly defined "commerce" (*Gibbons v. Ogden*, 1824), Marshall refused to be constrained by the absence of specific empowering language in the Constitution.

The Marshall Court is often credited with laying the foundations for modern American capitalism by the protection it afforded to property interests. Thus *Dartmouth College* established the immunity of private corporations from state regulation, and *Fletcher* protected the law of property and contracts from even well-intentioned legislative interference. At the same time, *Gibbons*, which endorsed the competitive rather than the monopoly model of economic development, provided the basis for future federal regulation of economic activity by its very broad construal of the Commerce Clause.

MARSHALL PLAN or **EUROPEAN RECOVERY PROGRAM** (1948–51), diplomatic achievement of the *Truman administration. Alarmed at the destitution of postwar Europe, U.S. secretary of state George C. Marshall, in a commencement address at Harvard University on June 5, 1947, offered substantial U.S. financial aid if the European countries—including, by inference, the Soviet Union—would unite on a comprehensive plan for the industrial, agricultural, and commercial recovery of the continent.

A few weeks later the foreign ministers of Great Britain, France, and the Soviet Union met in Paris to consider the proposal. The Soviet delegation soon withdrew, denouncing the proposal as an imperialist plot and preventing their satellites from participating. In July, 16 European nations (later joined by West Germany) met in Paris, created the Organization for European Economic Cooperation (OEEC), and drafted a recovery program requiring $16–22 billion over four years. The absence of the Soviet Union and its satellites assured bipartisan approval of the program by Congress, which in April 1948 created the Economic Cooperation Administration (ECA), through which grants and loans totaling $14 billion were eventually made to Europe.

The program proved highly successful. Often hailed as an example of American altruism, the program was advantageous to the United States since almost all the money loaned to Europe was spent here.

MARTIN v. HUNTER'S LESSEE (1816), unanimous decision of the *Marshall Court asserting the appellate jurisdiction of the U.S. Supreme Court over state courts where federal statutes or treaties were involved. During the Revolutionary War, Virginia had confiscated the estate of Loyalist Thomas Lord Fairfax. The Fairfax interests challenged the confiscation as violating Virginia's obligations under both the Treaty of *Paris (1783) and *Jay's Treaty (1794), which protected Loyalist property.

In 1813, Justice Joseph Story upheld the Fairfax interests, but the Virginia court of appeals refused to obey. The case returned to the Supreme Court in 1816 under the title *Martin v. Hunter's Lessee,* and again Justice Story, for a 6–0 Court, rejected Virginia's claim to equal sovereignty with the United States based on a states' rights theory of the Constitution as a compact among the states.

MASON-DIXON LINE, the southern border of Pennsylvania, partially surveyed in 1763–67 by Charles Mason and Jeremiah Dixon to resolve disputes over the Pennsylvania-Maryland boundary and extended 1782–84 to settle the Pennsylvania-Virginia boundary. It has been regarded as the border between North and South.

MASSACHUSETTS BAY COLONY (1630–91), English colony on Massachusetts Bay founded by a "Great Migration" of English Puritans—members of the Anglican Church, unlike the Puritan Separatists at nearby *Plymouth Colony—as a "Bible commonwealth." "We shall be as a city upon a hill," admonished John Winthrop, leader of the first migration. "The eyes of all peoples are upon us."

The migration consisted of entire families, well prepared for life in the wilderness; thus they escaped the privations of the Plymouth settlers. Winthrop led 900 settlers in 11 ships in 1630; by 1642 the colony had 21,000 inhabitants. Large families assured rapid population growth. Boston was the principal settlement, but smaller communities were established around the bay and in its hinterland. Each family was given 150 acres to farm; many settlers, however, turned to the *fur trade, fishing, and commerce.

The original settlers brought with them their royal charter for a trading company and transformed the company into a civil society with a government including a governor, magistrates, and a legislature (the General Court). Although Congregationalism soon replaced Anglicanism as the established religion, Massachusetts Bay was a Puritan theocracy rather than a democracy. The vote was restricted to male church members—a steadily diminishing minority—and clergymen proved the strongest political force in the colony, although they could not hold civil offices.

Massachusetts Bay became noted for its intolerance of religious dissenters. Roger Willliams was expelled in 1635, Anne Hutchinson in 1638; Baptists and Quakers were persecuted; in 1692 witches were discovered at Salem and executed (see *Salem Witchcraft Trials). Nevertheless, a highly educated clergy—originally trained at Cambridge University in England but later increasingly trained locally at Harvard College (founded 1636)—left a permanent impress of intellectualism and idealism on New England life.

Massachusetts Bay fought genocidal wars with local Indians (see *Pequot War; *King Philip's War). During the Anglo-Dutch War (1664–67) it extended its jurisdiction south into the Connecticut River valley and north over Maine and New Hampshire. After the Restoration in England (1660), the Massachusetts charter was revoked (1684) and the colony was combined (1686) with other colonies in the *Dominion of New England. Upon news of the Glorious Revolution (1688), Puritan leaders overthrew the dominion's governor, Sir Edmund Andros, and in 1691 Massachusetts (together with Plymouth and Maine) became a royal colony. The abolition of church membership as a requisite for voting ended the Puritan theocracy.

MASSACHUSETTS GOVERNMENT ACT (1774).
See *Intolerable Acts.

MAYFLOWER COMPACT (Nov. 21, 1620), organic
document drawn up by the *Pilgrims aboard the *Mayflower* shortly after they sighted the Massachusetts coast. The problem of a government was acute since they were outside the territory of the Virginia Company, from which they had received a patent, and the "Strangers" among them were rebellious of their authority.

The document read: "Having undertaken for the Glory of God, and Advancement of the Christian Faith, and the Honour of our King and Country, a Voyage to plant the first colony in the northern Parts of Virginia; [We] Do by these Presents, solemnly and mutually in the Presence of God and one another, covenant and combine ourselves together into a civil Body Politik, for our better Ordering and Preservation, and Furtherance of the Ends aforesaid; And by Virtue hereof do enact, constitute, and frame, such just and equal Laws, Ordinances, Acts, Constitutions, and

Offices, from time to time, as shall be thought most meet and convenient for the general Good of the Colony; unto which we promise all due Submission and Obedience."

Forty-one adult males, both "Saints" and "Strangers," signed the compact, which remained the only constitution *Plymouth Colony ever had.

MAYSVILLE ROAD VETO (1830), veto by Pres. Andrew Jackson of a bill authorizing federal participation in the construction of a 60-mile extension of the *National Road from Maysville (on the Ohio River opposite Cincinnati) to Lexington, Ky. In addition to constitutional scruples, he believed that federal expenditures on such local *internal improvements—what a later generation would call "pork"—had a corrupting influence on elections. He was particularly irate that this bill was passed at a time when the government was in debt. To emphasize his point, he simultaneously vetoed several other projects in the interest of "reform, retrenchment, and economy."

McCARDLE, EX PARTE (1869), case in which Congress reduced the appellate jurisdiction of the *Chase Court to prevent the Court from passing upon the constitutionality of the Reconstruction Acts (see *Reconstruction). McCardle, a Mississippi editor, was arrested by the military authorities governing the state under congressional reconstruction. Challenging the constitutionality of the Reconstruction Acts on the basis of the Court's decision in *Ex parte *Milligan* (1866), which held that martial law was unconstitutional where the civil courts continued to function, McCardle appealed to the Supreme Court under a provision of the Habeas Corpus Act of 1867.

After arguments in the case had been heard, Congress, fearing that the Court might indeed find the Reconstruction Acts unconstitutional, repealed the provision of the Habeas Corpus Act under which McCardle had appealed. Acknowledging Congress's constitutional power to reduce its appellate jurisdiction (Art. 3, sec. 2), the Court dismissed the case for lack of jurisdiction.

McCARTHYISM, term derived from Sen. Joseph R. McCarthy, Republican of Wisconsin, who during 1950–54 achieved national prominence and intimidating political power by unsubstantiated accusations of communism accompanied by bullying investigative methods.

An obscure and unpopular conservative senator—he continually defied Senate rules of courtesy—McCarthy stumbled into notoriety on Feb. 9, 1950, when he made a speech at Wheeling, W.Va., on a then-popular subject—communists in government (see *Anticommunism). In that speech, McCarthy claimed to possess the names of 205 (or 57—no record of the speech was preserved) "card-carrying" members of the Communist Party, known to the secretary of state, then employed in the State Department.

Before a Senate committee appointed to investigate his charges, McCarthy was unable to produce a single name that fitted his description. Nevertheless, supplied with information from friendly sources in the government and from professional anticommunists, he went on to make extravagant new allegations against individuals in and out of government, including Owen Lattimore, a Far East scholar at Johns Hopkins University ("the top Russian agent" in the United States, "boss" of Alger Hiss), and Secretary of Defense George C. Marshall (the central figure in "a conspiracy so immense and an infamy so black as to dwarf any previous venture in the history of man") without ever proving his cases.

With public opinion polls showing 50 percent of the country favorable to McCarthy, Republican senators encouraged or tolerated his attacks because of their damage to the *Truman administration.

In 1953, McCarthy became chairman of the unimportant Senate Committee on Government Operations and turned its Permanent Subcommittee on Investigations into a virtual inquisition in pursuit of alleged communists, now in the newly elected Republican *Eisenhower administration. Investigations of the International Information Agency and the Army Signal Corps at Fort Monmouth, N.J., forced the administration at last to take a stand against McCarthy.

In March 1954 the Army charged that McCarthy had sought preferential treatment for a staff member who had been drafted; McCarthy countercharged that the Army was holding the private hostage to prevent further investigations at Fort Monmouth. The result was the **Army-McCarthy hearings** (Apr. 22–June 17, 1954) before McCarthy's own subcommittee (from which he removed himself). Televised nationally, the disorderly 36-day hearings revealed McCarthy to the public as a crude and reckless bully. The subcommittee produced four reports that failed to resolve the issues, but on Dec. 2, 1954, the Senate voted 67–22 to censure McCarthy for "act[ing] contrary to senatorial ethics and tend[ing] to bring the Senate into dishonor and disrepute. . . ." His influence abruptly ended, McCarthy descended into alcoholism, from which he died in 1957.

McCULLOCH v. MARYLAND (1819), unanimous decision of the *Marshall Court asserting a nationalist interpretation of the Constitution. Although a Republican administration in 1816 rechartered the *Bank of the United States (BUS), many states' rights Republicans continued to oppose it as unconstitutional, using the same strict-construction arguments that Thomas Jefferson had used 25 years before. In 1818, Maryland imposed a tax on the notes of banks operating in the state not chartered by the state legislature. James McCulloch, cashier of the Baltimore branch of the BUS, refused to pay. Chief Justice Marshall ruled that the Maryland tax was unconstitutional and void.

Marshall first dealt with the constitutionality of the bank in much the same terms that Alexander Hamilton had used in 1791. The method of the Constitution's ratification, he declared, made clear that the Constitution was not a compact among the states but "proceeds directly from the people." Although the powers of the federal government are limited to those specifically enumerated, the Constitution empowers it "to make all laws which shall be necessary and proper for carrying into execution the foregoing powers. . . ."

"Let the end be legitimate," Marshall expounded, "let it be within the scope of the constitution, and all means which are appropriate, which are plainly adapted to that end, which are not prohibited, but consist with the letter and spirit of the constitution, are constitutional." Thus the chartering of a national bank was justified as a legitimate means of executing the government's specifically enumerated powers.

Under the Supremacy Clause ("the laws of the United States . . . shall be the supreme law of the land"), Marshall continued, "the constitution and the laws made in pursuance thereof are supreme; . . . they control the constitution and laws of the respective states, and cannot be controlled by them." Since "the power to tax involves the power to destroy," "if the right of the states to tax the means employed by the general government be conceded, the declaration that the constitution, and the laws made in pursuance thereof, shall be the supreme law of the land, is empty and unmeaning declamation. . . ."

McKINLEY ADMINISTRATION (1897–1901). Having triumphed over the forces of monetary heresy in the presidential election of 1896, William McKinley, 25th president of the United States, presided over an administration of sound Republican orthodoxy. The *Dingley Tariff (1897) established the highest tariff rates in U.S. history. The *Gold Standard Act (1900) ended "ambiguity and doubt" about the U.S. financial system.

In foreign affairs, Cuba and the *Spanish-American War were the central concerns of the administration.

During the war, Hawaii was annexed (see *Hawaii Annexation). After the war, the administration set about suppressing the *Philippine Insurrection and organizing the country's new empire (see *Foraker Act; *Platt Amendment) and clearing the way for an isthmian canal (see *Panama Canal). It also began to play an enlarged role in world affairs, formulating the *Open Door Policy toward China and participating in the international expedition that relieved the siege of Beijing during the *Boxer Rebellion.

McKinley's renomination and reelection in 1900 seemed assured. The problem for Republican leaders was to prevent the nomination for vice president from going to the hyperactive governor of New York, Theodore Roosevelt. McKinley did not want Roosevelt, but publicly he took a neutral stance and Roosevelt won the nomination unanimously, to Mark Hanna's frustration and rage (see *McKinley and Hanna). McKinley's second term was short. On Sept. 5, 1901, he was shot by an anarchist; he died on Sept. 14 (see *McKinley Assassination). At his funeral, Hanna growled to a companion, "Now look, that damned cowboy is president of the United States."

McKINLEY AND HANNA. The most expensive sport in America, it has been said, is the sport of president-making. That sport appealed to Marcus Alonzo Hanna, a Cleveland industrialist who was appalled by the corruption and inefficiency of politics. He believed that much could be accomplished by the introduction of business management into politics. His objective was not the spoils of office but a prosperous country rationally run by people of wealth. Central to the country's prosperity, he believed, was the protective tariff, which, since the Civil War, had spread its blessings generously, if not equally, on all classes. What Hanna needed was a politician who shared his vision.

Hanna found his partner in William McKinley, a member of the House of Representatives from Ohio who early adopted the tariff as his legislative specialty and who climaxed his legislative career in 1890 by authoring the *McKinley Tariff, which raised rates higher than they had ever been before. Like Hanna, McKinley, "the Napoleon of the tariff," believed that the tariff was necessary not only to protect new, infant, and prospering industries but to ensure the job security and high wages (at least relative to those in other industrializing countries) of American workingmen.

The partnership of Hanna and McKinley has often been misrepresented. Although six years older, Hanna was in fact the junior partner. An amateur in politics, he

respected McKinley's national eminence and superior political skills. Hanna was willing to provide the money and organization to make McKinley president for the good of the country.

Although he had established a national reputation in Congress, McKinley in 1891 was gerrymandered out of his seat in the House. With Hanna's funding and organizing, McKinley was elected governor of Ohio in 1891 and again in 1893. In 1895, when McKinley was caught in the failure of a friend's business and found himself liable for more than $100,000 in cosigned notes, Hanna mobilized friends and farsighted corporations across the country to come to McKinley's rescue. He then retired from business to devote himself full-time to making McKinley the Republican presidential nominee in 1896.

With superb management skill and great sums of money, Hanna sewed up the convention for McKinley, that "Advance Agent of Prosperity," before Eastern party bosses became aware of his efforts. As Republican national chairman in the ensuing campaign, he mobilized the nation's business interests to finance a vast organizational and informational campaign on behalf of McKinley and "sound money" against William Jennings Bryan's dangerous call for *free silver.

The relationship between Hanna and McKinley was one of mutual regard and affection. President McKinley offered Hanna a cabinet office, but Hanna's great ambition was to sit in the U.S. Senate. The only political office he ever held was senator from Ohio, 1897–1904.

McKINLEY ASSASSINATION (Sept. 6, 1901). While greeting visitors in the Temple of Music at the Pan American Exposition in Buffalo, N.Y., Pres. William McKinley was approached by Leon F. Czolgosz, an anarchist, who concealed a revolver in his bandaged right hand. Czolgosz fired twice, wounding the president in the abdomen. The president was rushed to a hospital, where two operations were performed. He seemed to be recovering, but on Sept. 12 suffered a relapse and died two days later. Czolgosz was electrocuted on Oct. 29, 1901.

McKINLEY TARIFF (1890), legislation of the Benjamin *Harrison administration. Largely written by Rep. William McKinley of Ohio, chairman of the House Ways and Means Committee, the act raised average tariff rates to the highest levels ever, 49.5 percent. It contained, however, a reciprocity element—advocated by Secretary of State James G. Blaine—that permitted bilateral reductions. The act was highly unpopular, being widely blamed for price rises.

McNAMARA AND JOHNSON. See *Johnson and McNamara.

McNAMARA CASE (1910). On Oct. 1, 1910, the building of the antiunion *Los Angeles Times* was dynamited and 20 (nonunion) workers were killed. The *Times*'s owner, Harrison Gray Otis, saw in the event a labor conspiracy; labor and its sympathizers saw a capitalist conspiracy to discredit labor. When two brothers, J.B. and J.J. McNamara, were kidnapped in Indiana, brought to Los Angeles, and accused of the dynamiting, labor rallied to their cause and employed Chicago attorney Clarence Darrow to defend them. In the face of persuasive evidence of their guilt, the McNamaras confessed in order to escape execution. The shock to the labor movement was profound.

McNARY-HAUGEN FARM RELIEF BILL (1924–28). See *Farm Problem.

MEAT INSPECTION ACT (1906). See *Consumer Protection.

MEDICAID. See *Welfare.

MEDICARE. See *Social Security.

MEMORIAL DAY MASSACRE (1937). See *Steel Strikes.

MEREDITH'S "MARCH AGAINST FEAR" (1966). James Meredith, who had been protected by U.S. marshals and troops during his senior year (1962–63) at the University of Mississippi, announced in the summer of 1966 that he would undertake a 220-mile walk alone from Memphis, Tenn., to Jackson, Miss., to encourage Mississippi's blacks to register to vote. He left Memphis on June 5 but was felled on the highway the next day by shotgun blasts.

Leaders of the nation's civil rights organizations— Martin Luther King Jr. of the *Southern Christian Leadership Conference, Roy Wilkins of the *National Association for the Advancement of Colored People, Whitney Young of the National Urban League, Stokely Carmichael of the *Student Nonviolent Coordinating Committee, and Floyd McKissick of the *Congress of Racial Equality—rallied at Meredith's hospital bedside and resolved to continue the march. The march resumed on June 9, the number of marchers growing from a few dozen to several thousand. Large crowds met them at towns along the way.

But the marchers were riven by controversy. The rejection by young militants of King's nonviolent philosophy was only reinforced by the gassing and beatings the marchers suffered at Philadelphia and Canton, Miss. At Greenwood, Carmichael's call for *black power was enthusiastically received by his black audience. In protest, Wilkins and Young abandoned the march; King remained to preserve a semblance of unity. This he accomplished through a rally at the state capital in Jackson on June 26 attended by 15,000. Thereafter, the fragmentation of the *civil rights movement could not be denied.

MERRYMAN, EX PARTE (1861), case in the Baltimore federal court. Among persons suspected of disloyalty and arrested by military authorities in April 1861 (see *Habeas Corpus Suspensions) was John Merryman, an active Baltimore secessionist. While Merryman was held in Fort McHenry, his lawyers petitioned the circuit court, then presided over by Chief Justice Roger B. Taney, for a writ of habeas corpus.

Taney issued the writ, the military authorities refused to honor it, and Taney filed an opinion that only Congress, and not the president, had the constitutional authority to suspend habeas corpus. Lincoln ignored the opinion (and Taney as well, who expected to be arrested), only asking rhetorically in his address to the special session of Congress in July 1861: "Are all laws, *but one* [the right of habeas corpus], to go unexecuted, and the government itself go to pieces lest that one be violated?"

MEUSE-ARGONNE OFFENSIVE. See *World War I.

MEXICAN CESSION (1848), territory acquired from Mexico by the Treaty of *Guadalupe Hidalgo. Totaling 529,189 square miles, it comprised all present-day California, Nevada, and Utah, and parts of present-day Arizona, New Mexico, Colorado, and Wyoming. Texas was not part of the Mexican Cession.

MEXICAN RELATIONS. Differences in geography, culture, social systems, and political traditions have produced as neighbors a postindustrial superpower in the United States and a country perilously close to third-world status in Mexico. Their relationship has been characterized by domineering attitudes on the U.S. side and resentment on the Mexican.

The United States recognized Mexican independence from Spain in 1821 and extended to Mexico the protection of the *Monroe Doctrine in 1823. But American expansionism resulted in the annexation of Texas in 1845 (see *Texas Annexation) and of half a million square miles of northern Mexican territory after the *Mexican War in 1848. In the *Gadsden Purchase (1853) the United States acquired 54,000 more square miles of Mexican territory.

During the long dictatorship of Porfirio Díaz (1876–1911), U.S. capital flowed into Mexico, feeding national resentment that burst forth in the *Mexican Revolution (1910–17), during which the United States twice intervened militarily. A new Mexican constitution in 1917 gave the government the power to expropriate foreign property. The fears of U.S. oil corporations were realized in 1938 when Mexican president Lázaro Cárdenas nationalized Mexican oil. Rather than intervene, U.S. president Franklin D. Roosevelt accepted compensation (although the United States then boycotted Mexican oil for 30 years). An ally during World War 2, Mexico asserted an independent foreign policy during the *cold war.

Initiated during World War 2, the **bracero program** (1942–64) brought 5 million Mexican farm laborers temporarily to the United States, touching off a massive flow of permanent *immigration. From ranking fourth among sources of legal immigration in 1940, Mexico has ranked first since 1960. Moreover, there are an estimated 2.7 million illegal Mexican aliens in the United States. The *North American Free Trade Agreement (NAFTA, 1993), abolishing trade barriers among Canada, the United States, and Mexico, was believed to be especially favorable to Mexico. NAFTA proponents argued that it would slow illegal immigration into the United States by creating new jobs in Mexico. The new George W. Bush administration promised a major reform of Mexican immigration.

Mexico and the United States maintain a partnership in the *drug war troubled by the corruption endemic in the Mexican government. The explosive growth of the Mexican population, the depth of Mexican poverty, and the increasing inability of its government to cope augurs an uncertain future.

MEXICAN REVOLUTION (1910–17). The overthrow of Mexican dictator Porfirio Díaz in 1911 by democrat Francisco I. Madero jeopardized U.S. investments in Mexico. In February 1913 Madero was murdered in a military coup that brought reactionary Gen. Victoriano Huerta to power. Because of Madero's murder, newly inaugurated U.S. president Woodrow Wilson refused to recognize Huerta, proposing instead an election in which Huerta would not be a candidate. When Huerta rejected this proposal, Wilson imposed an arms blockade on Mexico, stationing naval units off Veracruz to prevent European arms from reaching Huerta, and adopted a policy of "watchful waiting."

On Apr. 9, 1914, unarmed U.S. sailors who had gone ashore at Tampico to obtain supplies were arrested but then promptly released with apologies. The U.S. naval commander, however, demanded a formal apology and a 21-gun salute to the American flag. Huerta refused, and Wilson ordered the bombardment and occupation of Veracruz. The result was an explosion of anti-American protests across Mexico that took Wilson by surprise and threatened war. Mediation by the ABC Powers (Argentina, Brazil, and Chile) at a conference at Niagara Falls, Ont. (May 18–July 2, 1914) failed because of Wilson's insistence on the elimination of Huerta, but in July Huerta fled to Spain. U.S. forces evacuated Veracruz in November.

After a year of civil war, Venustiano Carranza, leader of the Constitutionalist Party, secured control of the country, and in October 1915 Wilson extended de facto recognition to his regime. In March 1916, however, the Mexican revolutionary and bandit Pancho Villa, seeking to embarrass his opponent Carranza, raided the town of Columbus, N.Mex., killing 18 Americans. Wilson mobilized U.S. forces on the Mexican border and sent 10,000 troops under Gen. John J. Pershing into Mexico in fruitless pursuit of Villa. A clash between American and Mexican forces at Carrizal on June 21 resulted in 9 American dead and 30 Mexican. Pershing's column was not withdrawn until February 1917.

Meanwhile, a new Mexican constitution raised the prospect (not realized until 1925) of nationalization of the country's mineral resources. U.S. oil interests agitated for renewed intervention, but Wilson, whose clumsy interventions in Mexico had always been idealistically motivated, rejected their demands and granted full de jure recognition to the Carranza government. The issue of Mexican expropriation of U.S. holdings was not resolved until 1927.

MEXICAN WAR (1846–48), war between the United States and Mexico resulting from U.S. annexation of Texas (see *Texas Republic; *Texas Annexation), over which Mexico claimed sovereignty. The annexation of Texas, in turn, was caused by two factors: the desire of the Southern states to expand the area of slavery and thereby increase their influence in national affairs, and the operation of *manifest destiny, the self-fulfilling prophecy that the United States must inevitably extend its sway west to the Pacific Ocean and south to the Tropics.

Background. James K. Polk was elected president in 1844 on a platform of expansion in Texas and Oregon (see *Polk Administration). His predecessor, John Tyler, had completed the annexation of Texas (pending only Texas approval) in his last days in office. Polk was determined to acquire all or part of California and New Mexico from Mexico as well, by purchase if possible, by war if necessary. Soon after Polk became president, Mexico formally protested U.S. annexation of Texas and broke off diplomatic relations with the United States. In November 1845, Polk sent an emissary to Mexico charged with resolving the Texas issue, purchasing other Mexican territories, and settling the claims of American citizens against Mexico. Mexico rejected Polk's proposals, and both countries recognized that war was likely.

The Republic of Texas had claimed the Rio Grande as its western boundary, and when the United States annexed Texas Polk accepted that border. Mexico, however, regarded the Nueces River, 150 miles east of the Rio Grande, as the Texas border, and indeed Texas had never exercised any authority between the two rivers. On Jan. 13, 1846, Polk ordered Gen. Zachary Taylor to take up a position on the east side of the Rio Grande opposite Matamoros. The Mexicans considered Taylor to be on Mexican territory, and on Apr. 25 Mexican and U.S. troops clashed on the east side of the Rio Grande. This event provided Polk with a moral justification for war. "After reiterated menaces," he declared in his war message to Congress on May 11, "Mexico has passed the boundary of the United States, has invaded our territory and shed American blood upon the American soil." Congress passed a declaration of war on May 12.

Neither side was prepared for war, but both were confident of victory. Mexico was a feudal society of 7 million mostly poor Indian peons exploited by a white and mestizo (mixed) upper class. In the turmoil of its endless revolution, its two stable institutions were the church and the army. Mexico's premodern army of some 35,000 men was overofficered and underequipped, enmeshed in politics, and addicted to pageantry and display. Its proud officers were eager to humble the North Americans.

The United States, with a population of 20 million, had a regular army of 7,500, expandable with short-term militia (three months) and untrained volunteers (one year). The country had no military tradition (in fact, it was notably hostile to the military) and a reputation (won in the War of 1812) for military incompetence. But it had modern organizational skills and, in the army, a leaven of professional engineering and artillery officers trained at West Point.

The War in Northern Mexico. By the time Congress passed a declaration of war, General Taylor with some 2,000 regulars had won two victories. A Mexican force had crossed the Rio Grande and attempted to cut off Taylor from his base of supplies. Taylor bloodied it at Palo Alto (May 8) and routed it at Resaca de la Palma (May 9). On May 18 Taylor crossed the Rio Grande and entered undefended Matamoros. After building up his army over the summer with volunteer regiments, he captured Monterrey (Sept. 24) and pushed south to Saltillo. In January 1847 he was ordered to detach 9,000 of his best troops for the Veracruz campaign. With fewer than 5,000 men, almost all of them untested volunteers, he fought his most famous battle at *Buena Vista (Feb. 22–23), where he held off Mexican general Antonio López de Santa Anna's 15,000.

The War in the Far West. With the outbreak of war, plans made far in advance were executed in California and New Mexico. Commodore John D. Sloat, commander of the Pacific Squadron, seized Monterey, Sonoma, and San Francisco and proclaimed California part of the United States. When American settlers in the Sacramento Valley declared (June 1846) their independence of Mexico as the Republic of California (see *Bear Flag Revolt), Capt. John C. Frémont was on hand with his armed exploratory expedition to support them. With naval personnel and Frémont's "California Battalion," Commodore Robert F. Stockton, who had replaced the ill Sloat, took possession of southern California, occupying (Aug. 17) Los Angeles (which was retaken by the Californios—descendants of the original Spanish settlers—a month later).

Meanwhile, Gen. Stephen W. Kearny, commander of the Army of the West, led his 1,600-man army from Fort Leavenworth to Santa Fe, which he occupied on Aug. 18. In September, with only 100 men, he proceeded to California, joining forces with Stockton at San Diego. Their combined army of 600 men recaptured (Jan. 10, 1847) Los Angeles. Three days later the last Californios surrendered to Frémont.

The War in Central Mexico. When the occupation of its northern provinces failed to bring Mexico to the negotiating table, President Polk decided to strike directly at Mexico City. On Mar. 9, 1847, Gen. Winfield Scott landed 12,000 men on a beach south of Veracruz, the largest amphibious operation in history at that time. After a three-day bombardment, Veracruz surrendered (Mar. 27). Eager to get away from the unhealthy lowlands, Scott left Veracruz early in April for Mexico City, taking the same route that Cortés had followed in 1519. At mountainous Cerro Gordo the Americans routed

(Apr. 18) a larger Mexican army under Santa Anna (recently returned from Buena Vista), then pushed on to Puebla on the high Mexican Plateau. There the army remained three months, weakened by disease and the departure of seven regiments of volunteers whose one-year enlistments had expired. These were replaced by an equal number of new arrivals.

Lacking manpower to maintain his supply line to the coast, Scott abandoned all his stations between Veracruz and Puebla. On Aug. 7 he resumed his march inland with 11,000 effectives. A few days later the Americans emerged from the mountains into the Valley of Mexico. In its center, amid lakes and marshes, stood walled Mexico City, approachable only along elevated causeways. On Aug. 20 the outnumbered Americans won battles at Contreras and Churubusco, seven miles apart. Two strongpoints now stood in their path guarding causeways into the city. In a fierce fight the Americans took Molino del Rey (Sept. 8), then scaled the walls and captured the castle of Chapultepec (Sept. 13). From Chapultepec the troops rushed down the causeways to the gates of Mexico City. In triumph on Sept. 14 Scott entered the Mexican capital, from which Santa Anna had fled.

Peace and After. After the fall of Veracruz, Polk sent Nicholas P. Trist, chief clerk at the State Department, to negotiate peace with Mexico. Early in September the Mexicans rejected the American terms and Trist was recalled. After the fall of Mexico City and the flight of Santa Anna, a new Mexican government was willing to reconsider the American terms. Ignoring his order to return to Washington, Trist remained in Mexico and negotiated the Treaty of *Guadalupe Hidalgo (signed Feb. 2, 1848), by which the United States achieved all of Polk's original objectives.

The treaty reached Washington on Feb. 19. Despite his anger at Trist's insubordination and his displeasure with the treaty (Polk now wanted to annex more of Mexico), the president submitted the treaty to the Senate, where it was ratified (Feb. 23) by a vote of 38–14. U.S. troops evacuated Mexico City on June 12 and Veracruz on Aug. 2.

The war cost the United States 1,721 dead in combat, 11,155 dead of disease, 4,102 wounded. Mexican casualties were many times greater. The United States acquired more than 900,000 square miles of territory (including Texas), making it a Pacific power but exacerbating the national debate over the extension of slavery and thereby hastening the coming of the Civil War (see *Wilmot Proviso). Many junior officers in the Mexican War became senior commanders in the Civil War, including Union generals Ulysses S. Grant, Joseph Hooker, George B. McClellan, George G. Meade, John Pope, William T. Sherman, and George H. Thomas, and Confederate generals Pierre G.T. Beauregard, Braxton Bragg, Richard S. Ewell, Daniel H. Hill, Thomas J. Jackson, Albert Sidney Johnston, Joseph E. Johnston, Robert E. Lee, and James Longstreet.

MIDDLE EAST RELATIONS. Until World War 2, the Middle East was of little interest to Americans other than archaeologists and missionaries. When, after World War 2, Britain and France withdrew from the Arab world, the United States replaced them in order to block Soviet expansion southward toward the Indian Ocean, to prevent communist subversion of conservative pro-Western governments, and to ensure the continued flow of Middle East oil to itself, other Western powers, and Japan.

The United States quickly discovered that the Islamic world was inherently hostile to modernity in any form—the atheistic, communist Soviet model no less than the secular, capitalist American model. U.S. recognition of Israel in 1948 (see *Israel Recognition) and support for Israel in subsequent Arab-Israeli wars fed the flames of preexisting nationalism and fundamentalism in the region. Israel—the only democratic country in the region—proved an invaluable ally as the United States navigated through dangerous currents often unrelated to Israel.

To contain the Soviet Union, the United States brought Greece and Turkey into the *North Atlantic Treaty Organization in 1952 and organized a *Central Treaty Organization in 1955 consisting of Iraq, Iran, Turkey, Pakistan, and Great Britain (see *Containment). But it was not communists but nationalists who overthrew the pro-Western governments in the region: led by Muhammad Mussadegh, nationalists took power in Iran in 1952; led by Gamal Abdel Nasser, they deposed King Farouk and took power in Egypt, also in 1952; led by the socialist Baath Party, they took control of Iraq in 1968; led by Muammar Qaddafi, they took power in Libya in 1969; led by Hafez al-Assad, they took power in Syria in 1970. Jordan's King Hussein narrowly survived a revolt of nationalist Palestinians in "Black September" in 1970.

Since Arab and Iranian nationalisms were anti-American as well as anti-Israel and anti-Western, the United States was confronted with complex new problems. In Iran, the Central Intelligence Agency engineered the overthrow of Mussadegh and the restoration of the pro-Western shah—who, in 1979, was himself overthrown by an Islamic fundamentalist revolution (see *Covert Operations). In Egypt, when the United States tried to punish Nasser for buying weapons from communist countries, the Egyptian leader responded by nationalizing the Suez Canal, provoking an attack by Britain, France, and Israel. Only the intervention of U.S. president Dwight D. Eisenhower saved Egypt (see *Suez War).

When the United States supported Israel in the 1973 Arab-Israeli war, the Arab oil states tripled the price of their oil (which was increased again by the Iranian revolutionaries in 1979; see *Oil Shock). But the Iranian and Arab producers had nowhere else to sell their oil, so when high prices brought new sources of oil into the market their prices fell. During the 1970s, Iran, Syria, and Libya turned to *terrorism and hostage-taking against the Western powers (see *Iranian Hostage Crisis; *Lebanon Hostages). When Lebanon dissolved in civil war—due in part to the basing of terrorists there—the United States intervened disastrously (see *Lebanon Interventions).

In 1980, Iraq, ruled by the brutal despot Saddam Hussein, attacked its neighbor Iran, then in the throes of revolution. To Saddam's surprise, Iran resisted successfully and the war dragged on for eight years at enormous cost to both countries. The United States officially supported Iraq as less dangerous to the West than Iranian fundamentalism, but individuals in the *Reagan administration sold arms to Iran to raise money for the illegal support of Nicaraguan Contras and to gain the release of American hostages (see *Iran-Contra Affair). Consistent U.S. placating of Saddam encouraged him to invade and annex Kuwait in 1990. Again to Saddam's surprise, U.S. president George H. W. Bush determined to reverse the move. The *Gulf War followed, in which Bush assembled a coalition that included many Arab countries—who would not permit Israel to participate nor Saddam to be deposed. Thus the war ended with Saddam still in power and a threat to the region despite United Nations surveillance—as indeed was Iran, which was rapidly developing missiles and chemical and biological weapons without any international constraints.

Meanwhile, the United States continued to play a unique role as facilitator of the Israeli-Palestinian peace process. In 1978 Pres. James E. Carter brokered the *Camp David accords between Israeli prime minister Menachem Begin and Egyptian president Anwar Sadat that led to an Israeli-Egyptian peace treaty in 1979, Egypt thus becoming the first Arab country to recognize and make peace with Israel. When Israeli prime minister Yitzhak Rabin and Palestine Liberation Organization chairman Yasser Arafat, under great American pressure, agreed to officially recognize each other, Pres. William J. Clinton brought the two old enemies together on the White House lawn on Sept. 13, 1993, for a famous if gingerly handshake. In subsequent years Clinton regularly acted as a mediator between Israeli and Palestinian

leaders. When the peace process broke down, the new George W. Bush administration rejected Clinton's policy of engagement and determined to remain aloof from the renewed Israeli-Palestinian conflict.

After Arab terrorists attacked the World Trade Center in New York City and the Pentagon near Washington, D.C., on Sept. 11, 2001 (see *World Trade Center Attack 2), President Bush launched a military campaign in Afghanistan against the Al Qaeda terrorist organization responsible for the attacks and the fundamentalist Taliban government that sheltered it (see *Terrorism War). Discovering that the continuing Israeli-Palestinian conflict hindered its recruitment of Arab allies in the terrorism war, the Bush administration reversed course and became deeply engaged in mediation, committing itself to the eventual establishment of a Palestinian state. In 2002, it prepared for a preemptive attack (see *Bush Doctrine) against Iraq, where Saddam Hussein was believed to be developing weapons of mass destruction.

MIDDLE PASSAGE. See *Slave Trade.

MIDDLETOWN (1929), pioneering sociological study of a typical American town by Robert S. and Helen M. Lynd. Attempting to objectify sociology with the observational techniques of anthropologists, the Lynds and their researchers in 1924–25 examined work, homemaking, education, leisure, religion, and community activities in Muncie, Ind., a town of 30,000. They found a society sharply divided between business and working classes and, compared to 1890, undergoing rapid change in work and leisure, little change in education and religion. The Lynds revisited Muncie in 1935, and in 1937 they published *Middletown in Transition*.

MIDNIGHT APPOINTMENTS (1801), episode in the final weeks of the John *Adams administration. Adams's defeat in the presidential election of 1800 was known before the electoral votes were formally counted on Feb. 11, 1801. On Jan. 20, the lame-duck president appointed his secretary of state, John Marshall, chief justice of the United States. On Feb. 27, the outgoing Federalist-controlled Congress passed a new *Judiciary Act, repealing the act of 1789. The new act reduced from six to five the number of Supreme Court justices, delaying the next president's opportunity to appoint a Republican to the Court (two sitting justices would have to die or retire before one could be appointed). It also created 16 circuit courts, providing an opportunity for Adams to appoint Federalist judges, marshals, clerks, and other judicial officers. This he continued to do even on his last night in office. These "midnight appointments" deeply offended his successor and onetime friend, Thomas Jefferson, who contested the appointments in *Marbury v. Madison*.

MIDWAY. See *World War 2.

MILITIAS. See *Radical Right.

MILLENNIUM ANXIETY. See *Y2K (Year 2000) Anxiety or Millennium Anxiety.

MILLIGAN, EX PARTE (1866), unanimous decision of the *Chase Court overturning a conviction by a military court in Indiana during the Civil War. Milligan, a Southern sympathizer, was arrested in 1864 by military authorities in Indiana, tried for conspiracy by a military court without a jury although the civil courts were open, and sentenced to be hanged.

Martial law was legitimate, ruled Justice David Davis for the Court, only where civil authority had been overthrown. "No doctrine, involving more pernicious consequences," Davis wrote, "was ever invented by the wit of man than that any of [the Constitution's] provisions can be suspended during any of the great exigencies of government."

Coming a year after the war, the decision could not undo all the military arrests and trials, but it restated the primacy of civilian over military authority and threatened the *Radical Republicans' plan of *reconstruction.

MILLIKEN v. BRADLEY (1974), 5–4 decision of the *Burger Court limiting the power of federal courts to effect *school desegregation over metropolitan areas. The student population of the Detroit school district was 65 percent black, that of the Detroit metropolitan area (city plus suburbs) 19 percent black. A district court, having found that the Detroit school district had maintained a dual school system, ruled that a unitary, integrated system was possible only if the city and its suburbs were combined in a single busing area. The Supreme Court reversed, ruling that since the largely white suburbs had not engaged in segregation practices, they could not be compelled to participate in the solution to Detroit's problem. As white flight from central cities continued, creating de facto segregated suburbs, meaningful school desegregation confined to central cities became increasingly difficult.

MINERSVILLE SCHOOL DISTRICT v. GOBITIS (1940), 8–1 decision of the *Hughes Court upholding a school board for expelling two children who refused to participate in the daily salute to the flag and Pledge of Allegiance because the ceremony violated their religious beliefs as Jehovah's Witnesses.

At a time when war in Europe and Asia already threatened to engulf the United States, Justice Felix Frankfurter wrote for the Court: "The religious liberty which the Constitution protects has never excluded legislation of general scope not directed against doctrinal loyalties of particular sects. . . . National unity is the basis of national security. . . . The ultimate foundation of a free society is the binding tie of cohesive sentiment. Such a sentiment is fostered by all those agencies of the mind and spirit which may serve to gather up the traditions of a people, transmit them from generation to generation, and thereby create that continuity of a treasured common life which constitutes a civilization. 'We live by symbols.' The flag is the symbol of our national unity, transcending all internal differences, however large, within the framework of the Constitution" (see *Church-State Relations).

MINE WORKERS UNION. See *United Mine Workers (UMW).

MINNESOTA UPRISING (1862). See *Sioux Wars.

MINUTEMEN, in colonial Massachusetts, selected members of the militia prepared at all times to assemble on short notice. In October 1774, the Massachusetts provincial congress directed that each militia regiment assign 25 percent of its members to 50-man companies ready to respond at a moment's notice to orders from the committee of safety. On Apr. 19, 1775, the minutemen won immortality at the battles of *Lexington and Concord.

MIRANDA v. ARIZONA (1966), 5–4 decision of the *Warren Court extending the Fifth Amendment's right against self-incrimination to criminal suspects in "custodial interrogation" as well as in a criminal trial. Twenty-three-year-old Ernesto Miranda had confessed to kidnapping and rape after two hours of police interrogation during which he had not been advised of his right to consult an attorney or have an attorney present.

"[W]ithout proper safeguards," wrote Chief Justice Earl Warren for the Court, "the process of in-custody interrogation of persons suspected or accused of crime contains inherently compelling pressures which work to undermine the individual's will to resist and to compel him to speak where he would not otherwise do so freely."

"Prior to any questioning," Warren ruled, "the person must be warned that he has a right to remain silent, that any statement he does make may be used as evidence against him, and that he has a right to the presence of an attorney, either retained or appointed. The defendant may waive effectuation of these rights, provided the waiver is made voluntarily, knowingly and intelligently. If, however, he indicates in any manner and at any stage of the process that he wishes to consult with an attorney before speaking there can be no questioning. Likewise, if the individual is alone and indicates in any manner that he does not wish to be interrogated, the police may not question him. The mere fact that he may have answered some questions or volunteered some statements on his own does not deprive him of the right to refrain from answering any further inquiries until he has consulted with an attorney and thereafter consents to be questioned."

Miranda was long opposed by law-enforcement conservatives, although it was never demonstrated to have reduced police effectiveness. In *Dickerson v. U.S.* (2000), the *Rehnquist Court confirmed *Miranda* when it overturned an obscure 1968 federal law that had been intended to reverse it. "[B]eing a constitutional decision of this Court," Chief Justice Rehnquist ruled, *Miranda* "may not in effect be overruled by an act of Congress." *Miranda*, he observed, "has become embedded in routine police practice to the point where the warnings have become part of our national culture."

MISSILE DEFENSE. In the Antiballistic Missile (ABM) Treaty of 1972, the United States and the Soviet Union undertook "not to develop, test or deploy ABM systems or components which are sea-based, air-based, space-based or mobile land-based." Because the Soviets had already deployed fixed, land-based point defenses and the United States planned to do so, the treaty permitted the deployment of point defenses around each national capital and a single intercontinental ballistic missile (ICBM) site.

Both superpowers recognized that the development of an effective missile shield would neutralize the other's missile arsenal. The treaty had the effect of freezing the status quo—the so-called balance of terror, by which the threat of retaliation deterred aggression. Throughout the *cold war, deterrence seemed to prove a beneficial strategy for both.

In 1983 Pres. Ronald Reagan called for a defense against ballistic missiles that would render them "impotent and obsolete," and in 1985 he put forward a research-and-development program called the **Strate-**

gic Defense Initiative (SDI). He envisioned a system of artificial satellites capable of detecting hostile missiles from space and destroying them with laser beams. The Soviets were alarmed at the threat to strategic stability. At home, critics ridiculed SDI as "**Star Wars**" after a popular science-fiction film. They argued that it violated the 1972 ABM Treaty, that the technology for it did not exist, and that the cost would be prohibitive. Nevertheless, Reagan adhered to the plan unshakably. The idea of missile defense proved popular, and Congress began appropriating $3–4 billion a year to support the program although it consistently failed to meet its technical goals and disappeared from public awareness.

Despite the end of the cold war and scandalous misrepresentations of SDI's achievements, the George H. W. *Bush administration preserved it in deference to Republican conservatives, now rationalizing it as a defense against missile attacks from "rogue states" like North Korea and Iran or against accidental launchings from Russia or China. The *Clinton administration abandoned the idea of a space-based missile shield in favor of a limited system of land-based interceptors, but it did not pursue this plan when the Russians refused to amend the ABM Treaty.

Early in his administration, Pres. George W. *Bush declared that the ABM Treaty was obsolete and announced that a missile shield—to protect the country from rogue states and terrorists—would be central to his defense policy. In June 2002 he formally withdrew from the ABM Treaty.

MISSIONARY RIDGE. See *Chattanooga Campaign.

MISSISSIPPI FREEDOM DEMOCRATIC PARTY (MFDP) (1964), political party founded by newly registered black voters in Mississippi (see *Freedom Summer) to supplant the state Democratic Party, which denied blacks any meaningful participation in party affairs, demanded repeal of the *Civil Rights Act of 1964, and went on to urge Mississippi whites to vote for the Republican candidate, Barry Goldwater, in the 1964 presidential election.

At the Democratic national convention in Atlantic City in July 1964, a MFDP delegation contested the seating of the state party's delegation. Pres. Lyndon Johnson opposed their claim, and Sen. Hubert Humphrey proposed a compromise by which the MFDP would be given two at-large seats in the convention—not in the Mississippi delegation. Although Martin Luther King Jr. and other civil rights leaders supported the compromise in their anxiety for a Democratic victory in the fall, the

MFDP delegation rejected it and left the convention feeling betrayed by Northern liberals.

At the 1968 Democratic convention, the credentials committee barred the regular Mississippi delegation and seated a biracial delegation in its place.

MISSOURI COMPROMISE or COMPROMISE OF 1820 (1820–21), resolution of the first national crisis over the extension of slavery into the trans-Mississippi territories. In 1819, slave and free states were evenly balanced at 11 each. The statehood application of Missouri Territory—which had been settled by Southerners, including slave owners—threatened to disrupt that balance. The fortuitous statehood application of Maine, theretofore a district of Massachusetts, presented an obvious solution. But antislavery forces in Congress resisted any extension of slavery beyond the states where it was already established. In the end, Congress approved Maine's admission as a free state, Missouri's admission as a slave state, and the exclusion of slavery from the remainder of the *Louisiana Purchase north of latitude 36°30', Missouri's southern boundary.

A second crisis arose when the newly drafted Missouri constitution excluded "free negroes and mullatos" from the state, in violation of Art. 4, sec. 2 of the U.S. Constitution ("The citizens of each state shall be entitled to all the privileges and immunities of the citizens of the several states"). The North protested and, in a further compromise, Missouri was finally admitted (1821) to the Union on a pledge by its legislators not to ban *free blacks from the state. This pledge was later violated. Credit for the second of the two compromises is traditionally given to Rep. Henry Clay of Kentucky.

Although the settlement was generally considered favorable to the South, neither side was satisfied. The crisis quickly passed, but it was universally recognized that it had exposed deepening sectional differences in the country. "This momentous question, like a fire bell in the night, awakened and filled me with terror," wrote ex-president Thomas Jefferson at Monticello. "It is hushed, indeed, for the moment. But this is a reprieve only, not a final sentence." "I have favored this Missouri compromise," Secretary of State John Quincy Adams recorded in his diary, but "If the Union must be dissolved, slavery is precisely the question upon which it ought to break."

The Missouri Compromise was superseded by the *Kansas-Nebraska Act (1854), then declared unconstitutional by the U.S. Supreme Court in *Scott v. Sandford (1857).

MITCHELL COURT-MARTIAL (1925). Two setbacks to naval aeronautics within a few days—the failure of three flying boats to reach Hawaii from California and the wreck of the dirigible Shenandoah in a thunderstorm over Ohio—made headlines in September 1925. Both the planes and the dirigible were on publicity-seeking missions ordered by authorities ignorant of their hazards.

At San Antonio, Tex., Col. William "Billy" Mitchell—formerly brigadier general in command of AEF aviation in World War 1, then zealous prophet of the air age and advocate of an independent air force—issued a public statement calculated to bring about his court-martial: "These accidents are the result of the incompetency, criminal negligence, and almost treasonable administration of the national defense by the War and Navy Departments." Charged with insubordination and conduct prejudicial to military discipline, Mitchell welcomed the court-martial that soon followed. He considered it an opportunity to educate the American people about aviation and the state of the national defense.

The trial, held at Washington before 12 (soon reduced to nine) generals from Oct. 28 to Dec. 17, was a national sensation. Defense witnesses—among them World War 1 aces Reed Chamber and Eddie Rickenbacker and future *World War 2 generals Maj. Henry Arnold, Maj. Carl Spaatz, and Capt. Ira Eaker—testified to the truth of Mitchell's allegations about the neglect of aviation by hidebound generals and admirals fighting over meager military appropriations. The nation learned that the Army had only 59 modern planes fit for duty, that the Army had refused to pay $1 a year to rent a field for gunnery practice, and that it had prohibited long-distance telephone calls to ascertain weather conditions at planned flight destinations. Prosecution witnesses—chiefly brass from the War and Navy departments—derided Mitchell, belittled the military role of aviation, and insisted that the United States was invulnerable to foreign air attack.

On Dec. 17, the court found Mitchell guilty on all counts (only Maj. Gen. Douglas MacArthur, as he later wrote, cast a dissenting vote). Suspended from duty and pay for five years, Mitchell resigned from the Army in February 1926.

MITCHELL v. HELMS (2000), 6–3 decision of the *Rehnquist Court upholding a federal program that placed computers and other instructional equipment in school classrooms, including those in parochial schools.

For the Court, Justice Clarence Thomas wrote: "[T]he question whether governmental aid to religious schools results in governmental indoctrination [i.e., governmental support of parochial schools' religious teaching] is ultimately a question whether any religious indoctrination that occurs in those schools could reasonably be attributed to governmental action. . . .

"In distinguishing between indoctrination that is attributable to the state and indoctrination that is not, we have consistently turned to the principle of neutrality, upholding aid that is offered to a broad range of groups or persons without regard to their religion. If the religious, irreligious, and areligious are all alike eligible for governmental aid, no one would conclude that any indoctrination that any particular recipient conducts has been done at the behest of the government" (see *Church-State Relations).

MOBILE BAY (Aug. 5, 1864), *Civil War naval battle. Suppressing blockade-running in the Gulf of Mexico, Union admiral David G. Farragut, with a fleet of 14 wooden warships and five ironclads, fought his way past Confederate forts on Aug. 5, 1864, and entered Mobile Bay. Losing one ironclad to mines in the channel, Farragut—lashed to the mainmast of his flagship—declared, "Damn the torpedoes [mines]! Full speed ahead!" and led the way through the mines. His force attacked and defeated a Confederate fleet and later captured the forts. The city of Mobile, 30 miles away at the head of the bay, remained in Confederate hands until April 1865 but was no longer a center of blockade-running.

MOLLY MAGUIRES (1865–75), a secret organization among Irish-American coal miners in the anthracite fields of eastern Pennsylvania. During prolonged labor strife, the Molly Maguires allegedly resorted to intimidation, arson, and murder against strikebreakers and mine owners. A *Pinkerton detective infiltrated and exposed the organization. On dubious evidence, 20 of its members were hanged and the organization was destroyed.

MONGREL TARIFF (1883), legislation of the *Garfield-Arthur administration. Embarrassed by a Treasury surplus, Pres. Chester Arthur favored tariff reform (federal revenues came largely from customs duties) and proposed to the Democratic Congress that a commission be appointed to study the matter scientifically and make recommendations to Congress. A commission was duly appointed, took evidence around the country, and proposed several reforms: reduced tariff rates, a court of customs, and simplification of revenue collection. Furious debate ensued in Congress, which finally passed a bill slightly reducing the existing average tariff

rate but so full of contradictions that it soon became known as the Mongrel Tariff.

MONITOR AND MERRIMACK (Mar. 9, 1862), *Civil War naval battle, the first between ironclads.

To combat the Union blockade of Southern ports, the Confederates at Norfolk salvaged the hull of the frigate *Merrimack*, attached iron plates to it extending three feet below the waterline, built a barnlike armored superstructure on top of it that housed ten guns, and powered the affair with a feeble engine capable of only four or five knots. The ship was named the *Virginia*, but the Federals insisted on calling it the *Merrimack*.

The Federals responded to the threat to their wooden navy by building the *Monitor*, an ironclad designed by John Ericsson—a low iron-plated hull 172 feet long, a flat deck, and a revolving armored turret nine feet high and 21 feet in diameter housing two 11-inch guns. The vessel was dubbed the "cheese box on a raft." With a draft of only ten feet compared to the *Merrimack*'s 22 feet, the *Monitor* was capable of eight knots.

On Mar. 8, 1862, the *Merrimack* steamed down the James River from Norfolk, meeting five wooden Union ships—three sail, two steam—at Hampton Roads. She promptly destroyed two of them and drove one aground. Shells from the Union ships bounced off her armor. The *Monitor*, however, was already on its way from Brooklyn to Hampton Roads and was waiting for the *Merrimack* the next day. The two-hour duel on Mar. 9 ended in a draw, the guns of neither ship being able to penetrate the other's armor.

The two did not fight again. When the Confederates evacuated Norfolk during the *Peninsula Campaign, the *Merrimack*—incapable of going up the river or out to sea—had to be destroyed. On Dec. 31, 1862, the *Monitor* sank in a storm off Cape Hatteras while being towed to a position in the blockade. The wreck was located in 1973 at 230 feet, and recovery began in 1977. The 120-ton turret was raised in 2002.

MONMOUTH (June 28, 1778), *Revolutionary War battle. Ordered to evacuate Philadelphia and concentrate his forces in New York City, British general Henry Clinton sent his sick and 3,000 Philadelphia Loyalists to New York by ship and on June 17, 1778, started his army on an overland march through New Jersey to Sandy Hook, from where British ships would carry it to New York.

The extended British line of march, including a baggage train 12 miles long, presented a tempting target for

Patriot general George Washington, whose army, newly trained at *Valley Forge in European-style combat drill, marched north parallel to the British. Washington decided against a general engagement but sent 4,000 men under Gen. Charles Lee (who had only recently returned from a long captivity) to see if the British rearguard could be cut off while the main Patriot army lay ready to exploit whatever opportunity this presented.

At noon on June 28, in very hot weather, Lee's force attacked Clinton's rearguard near Freehold in Monmouth County. Expecting an attack by Washington, Clinton ordered Gen. Charles Cornwallis with 8,000 men to turn back and deal with the Americans. For reasons that remain controversial, Lee lost control of the quickly developing battle. By 1:30 p.m., Lee was in retreat and his command in confusion. When Washington encountered retreating Americans between 2 and 3 p.m., he rushed to the front and took command. The American line firmed up and with its newly acquired discipline withstood repeated attacks by the British regulars.

At day's end, Clinton left the field in the possession of the Americans—technically signaling an American victory. But he had stopped the American pursuit and eventually brought his army and baggage to New York—a victory in his eyes.

For his conduct at Monmouth, Lee was court-martialed and suspended from command for one year.

MONROE ADMINISTRATION (1817–25). Republican James Monroe, fifth president of the United States and last of the *Virginia dynasty, believed with his predecessors Thomas Jefferson and James Madison in the nonparty—or one-party—state. In his inaugural address he adopted Federalist principles on national defense and promotion of manufacturing. He favored *internal improvements as well, although he believed that a constitutional amendment was necessary to enable the federal government to subsidize them. (In 1822, he vetoed a bill to repair the *National Road as unconstitutional.)

A diffident man, Monroe assembled a talented cabinet that included John Quincy Adams of Massachusetts as secretary of state, William H. Crawford of Georgia as secretary of the Treasury, and John C. Calhoun of South Carolina as secretary of war (Henry Clay of Kentucky had declined the appointment). Three months after his inauguration the new president traveled to Federalist New England, where he was enthusiastically received. A Boston newspaper hailed the start of an *Era of Good Feelings free of party strife. The calm of this new era was sharply but briefly roiled by the *Panic of 1819 and by the crisis leading to the *Missouri Compromise, in which Monroe played little part.

The Monroe administration was distinguished by its accomplishments in foreign affairs. Some matters deferred by the Treaty of *Ghent were resolved in the *Rush-Bagot Agreement (1817) and the Anglo-American *Convention of 1818. The *Seminole War (1818), in which Gen. Andrew Jackson established U.S. military control over Spanish East Florida, led to the *Adams-Onís Treaty (1819), in which Spain renounced claims to West Florida (seized by the United States in 1812) and ceded East Florida (see *Floridas, East and West). The administration then defied Spain by recognizing the newly independent Latin American states (see *Latin American Recognition). The revolutions in Latin America and Russian claims on the Pacific coast of North America led to the *Monroe Doctrine (1823), by which the United States unilaterally declared the American continents closed to future colonization by European powers.

Monroe's administration saw the breakup of the dominant *Jeffersonian Republican Party into sectional and personal factions, four of whose leaders contested the presidency in 1824. Monroe was succeeded by John Quincy Adams.

During the Monroe administration, Mississippi (1817), Illinois (1818), Alabama (1819), Maine (1820), and Missouri (1821) became the 20th, 21st, 22nd, 23rd, and 24th states.

MONROE DOCTRINE (1823), declaration by Pres. James Monroe in his annual message to Congress, Dec. 2, 1823, that the United States considered the Western Hemisphere no longer subject to European colonization. Immediately dubbed the Monroe Doctrine, the declaration reflected U.S. concerns over Russian expansionism on the northwest coast of North America and the possibility that the reactionary powers of the Holy Alliance would attempt to restore to Spain her former American colonies, now recognized by the United States as independent republics.

Great Britain had proposed a joint British-U.S. declaration against interference in the Americas by the Holy Alliance, but U.S. secretary of state John Quincy Adams thought it would be more dignified—and would give the United States more freedom of action—if the United States issued such a declaration unilaterally. Adams was largely responsible for drafting the declaration, which warned the European powers against intervening in the Americas while disclaiming U.S. intent to interfere in European affairs.

The United States asserts, said Monroe in his message

to Congress, "as a principle in which the rights and interests of the United States are involved, that the American continents, by the free and independent condition which they have assumed and maintain, are henceforth not to be considered as subjects for future colonization by any European powers. . . .

"We owe it . . . to candor and to the amicable relations existing between the United States and those powers to declare that we should consider any attempt on their part to extend their system to any portion of this hemisphere as dangerous to our peace and safety. With the existing colonies or dependencies of any European power we have not interfered and shall not interfere. But with the Governments who have declared their independence and maintained it, . . . we could not view any interposition for the purpose of oppressing them, or controlling in any other manner their destiny, by any European power in any other light than as the manifestation of an unfriendly disposition toward the United States."

Her hostility to the Holy Alliance, her interest in trade with North and South America, and her command of the Atlantic sea lanes made Britain a silent underwriter of the Monroe Doctrine and a defender of U.S. hegemony in the Western Hemisphere. "With [Great Britain] on our side we need not fear the whole world," wrote former president Thomas Jefferson (whose career had been predicated on hostility to Britain) to President Monroe in October 1823. Britain's acceptance of the Monroe Doctrine marked the beginning of an informal alliance between the two English-speaking powers against aggressive European reaction.

MONTGOMERY BUS BOYCOTT (1955–56). On Dec. 1, 1955, Rosa Parks, a 45-year-old black seamstress, refused to give up her seat on a Montgomery, Ala., bus to a white person. She was arrested and jailed. Activists in the black community—an officer of the Brotherhood of Sleeping Car Porters, a committee of churchwomen—resolved to boycott the city buses. For that purpose they organized a Montgomery Improvement Association (MIA), and drafted a little-known newcomer to Montgomery, 26-year-old Baptist minister Martin Luther King Jr., as its president.

Eloquent and courageous, King inspired Montgomery's black community to persevere for an entire year, walking and carpooling rather than riding the buses, enduring police harassment, verbal abuse, and economic retaliation. At the same time, the MIA brought suit in federal court, and on Nov. 13, 1956, the U.S. Supreme Court affirmed the decision of a lower court

that Montgomery's bus-segregation ordinances were unconstitutional. On Dec. 21 the boycott ended with the desegregation of the buses. Everywhere else in Montgomery, however, segregation remained unchanged. The boycott brought King to national prominence as a leader of the *civil rights movement.

MOONEY CASE (1916–39). On July 22, 1916, a bomb was thrown into a *preparedness parade in San Francisco, killing nine people and wounding many. Four labor leaders, including Thomas Mooney, were arrested. Charged with murder, convicted on perjured testimony, and sentenced to death in February 1917, Mooney was hailed internationally as a labor martyr. In 1918 the governor of California commuted Mooney's sentence to life imprisonment. Mooney was pardoned and released in 1939.

MOON LANDING (July 20, 1969). In 1957, the Soviet Union shocked Americans with the launching of *Sputnik* (see *Sputnik* Alarm). In 1959, Soviet *Luna* spacecraft flew by the moon, crash-landed on its surface, and studied its far side. Responding to the Soviet challenge to U.S. preeminence in space, Pres. John F. Kennedy on May 25, 1961, recommended to Congress that the United States commit itself to "landing a man on the moon and returning him safely to earth" before the end of the decade.

There followed a decade of intense scientific and technological competition between the two superpowers. The United States mobilized an immense industrial complex to produce rockets and spacecraft. In 1964, *Ranger* spacecraft took photographs of the lunar surface while crash-landing. In 1966–67, *Surveyor* spacecraft soft-landed on the moon, took photographs and analyzed lunar soil, and executed the first takeoff from the lunar surface. At the same time, *Lunar Orbiters* were orbiting the moon and taking photographs from which maps of the lunar surface were made. Meanwhile, Soviet *Luna* spacecraft soft-landed on the moon and transmitted photographs back to Earth.

On July 16, 1969, half a million people at Cape Canaveral, Fla., and millions more by television watched the launch of *Apollo 11*, borne on a Saturn 5 rocket and carrying astronauts Neil A. Armstrong, Edwin E. Aldrin Jr., and Michael Collins. After two Earth orbits, *Apollo 11* headed for the moon, entering lunar orbit on July 19, 76 hours after launching. On July 20, the lunar landing module, *Eagle*, carrying Armstrong and Aldrin, separated from the orbiting command module, *Columbia*, carrying Collins, and descended to the moon's surface in a basin called the Sea of Tranquillity.

At 4:17 p.m. (EDT) Armstrong radioed to National Aeronautics and Space Administration headquarters in Houston, Tex.: "Houston. Tranquillity Base here. The *Eagle* has landed." Six and a half hours later, Armstrong, wearing a protective space suit, descended the ladder from *Eagle* to the moon's surface. "That's one small step for man, one giant leap for mankind," he announced. Aldrin soon followed. During a two-hour "moon walk," the two astronauts raised the American flag, set up scientific instruments, and collected rocks and soil samples. Back in the landing module, they rested for eight hours, then took off and successfully rendezvoused with *Columbia*.

Discarding the landing module, the astronauts accelerated *Columbia* out of the moon's gravitational field and toward Earth. On July 24, *Columbia* splashed down in the Pacific Ocean 950 miles southwest of Hawaii.

Six more *Apollo* missions (*Apollos 12–17*) placed ten more astronauts on the moon before the moon-landing program was abandoned in 1972 (*Apollo 13* had to turn back after a mechanical failure in space). Abandoning the effort to put a man on the moon, the Soviets in 1972 sent a *Luna* spacecraft to the moon that returned lunar samples to Earth and in 1973 placed an automated rover on the moon.

MORAL MAJORITY. See *Christian Right.

MORFONTAINE TREATY (1800). See *Convention of 1800 or Treaty of Morfontaine.

MORGAN'S CAREER. When J. Pierpont Morgan (1837–1913) died at 75, he was vilified by millions as the rapacious and autocratic master of the American economy. Others admired him as a financial statesman who had served his country in ways that no other man could have. In the last 50 years, Morgan's reputation has changed along with those of some of the *"robber barons" with whom his name has sometimes been coupled. Historians now tend to view their "crimes" as characteristic of the age while increasingly appreciating their constructive achievements in transforming the United States from an agrarian, debtor nation into the world's greatest industrial and financial power.

Morgan was born to great wealth. His father, Junius Morgan, having made a fortune as a Boston merchant, moved to London and in 1854 became a partner of the American-born banker George Peabody. John Pierpont, his only son, served his business apprenticeship in New York during the *Panic of 1857 and the Civil War, opening a New York affiliate of his father's bank—J. Pierpont Morgan & Co. in 1862, Drexel, Morgan & Co. in 1871,

J. P. Morgan & Co. in 1895. From 1873, the firm occupied a building at 73 Broad Street on the corner of Wall Street, opposite the New York Stock Exchange and near the U.S. Subtreasury Building.

For many years, Junius Morgan supervised the affairs of the New York branch, early reprimanding his son for recklessness and greed for a wartime speculation in gold. Thereafter, by hard work, prudence, rectitude—"a man I do not trust could not get money from me on all the bonds in Christendom," he said late in life—and not least by a brusque and domineering personality, Pierpont Morgan established himself as a leading financier. The name Morgan on an issue of stocks or bonds was taken as a guarantee of its soundness.

In the mid-19th century, the Morgans and other international bankers funneled European—chiefly British—capital to the capital-starved United States to be invested in state and federal bonds and to finance the building of canals, railroads, and industrial plants. The period was one of rampant speculation and cutthroat competition, rife with fraud, corruption, and bankruptcies. Busts followed booms with predictable regularity. To Morgan, the turbulence of the American economy meant waste and lost opportunities. Order—especially an end to ruinous competition—was necessary if European capital was going to be attracted to America. The country's growth and prosperity depended upon it.

For many years, Morgan was deeply involved in the financing of *railroads. Then the nation's largest business, the railroads epitomized the prevailing economic anarchy. Rails were laid with no overall planning. Tracks were often shoddy and redundant. There was no standard gauge, necessitating the transfer of freight and passengers from one train to another at the end of a stretch of track. Investment prospectuses were sometimes fraudulent, stock was often "watered" (that is, issued in excess of the value of the company), managers were known to loot their own firms (typically by forming a separate construction company, then hiring it at exorbitant rates), and bankruptcies were welcomed because they freed the roads from debt.

When a troubled railroad came to Morgan for help, he—empowered by his control of capital—took charge of it, restructured its finances, appointed new managers, and placed himself or a partner on the board of directors. The process, usually successful, came to be called Morganization. In the 1880s, Morgan was acclaimed for ending the warfare between the New York Central and the Pennsylvania railroads, in the 1890s for creating the profitable Southern Railroad out of a collection of bankrupt or mismanaged smaller lines.

Only in 1892, after he had resolved the conflict between two Northwestern railroads, did Morgan encounter a formidable critic. The Northern Pacific and the Great Northern ran in parallel lines 200 miles apart from the Great Lakes to the Pacific. Both coveted the Chicago, Burlington, & Quincy for its access to Chicago and connections to the East Coast. Morgan brought these railroads, nominally independent, into a holding company called Northern Securities, ending the competition among them and providing an efficient coast-to-coast rail network of enormous benefit to U.S. industry. Astounded when Pres. Theodore Roosevelt announced that he would prosecute the Northern Securities Co. for violation of the *Sherman Antitrust Act, Morgan hurried to Washington, where to the president he famously proposed, "If we have done anything wrong, send your man to my man and they can fix it up." But Roosevelt was in a *trust-busting mood, and in 1906 the U.S. Supreme Court narrowly supported him (see *Northern Securities Co. v. United States).

At the turn of the century, American industry experienced a wave of consolidations. Rival companies in the same industry sought to escape competition by combining to form large "consolidated" companies, popularly called *trusts. They generally found consolidation beneficial. Besides ending costly competition with one another, they now benefited from professional management, economies of scale, and market positions that enabled them to dominate rivals outside the trust. Andrew Carnegie and John D. Rockefeller had shown the way. Carnegie dominated the steel industry because the efficiency of his operation enabled him to undersell his rivals, and Rockefeller dominated the oil industry by brutally destroying his rivals.

Morgan's way was negotiation, but his financial power generally ensured that he got what he wanted. Having played a leading role in the formation of General Electric and International Harvester, in 1901—the same year he organized the Northern Securities Co.—Morgan formed the United States Steel Corp., a vertically integrated colossus that owned iron and coal mines, coke ovens, railroads and steamships, blast furnaces and rolling mills. The climax of this consolidation was Morgan's purchase of Carnegie Steel at Carnegie's own valuation—$480 million—to get rid of a potential competitor. U.S. Steel was capitalized at $1.4 billion, the world's first billion-dollar corporation. Morgan appointed all the top managers, and he and three partners took seats on the board of directors. (In 1913, Morgan and his ten partners sat on the boards of 72 corporations.)

The creation of U.S. Steel was the financial wonder of the age. Bankers celebrated Morgan as the Napoleon of Wall Street, but some people wondered if so much power in the hands of one man was good for the country. One result was the investigation by the *Pujo Committee in 1913 of the "money trust."

Morgan, of course, believed that all his accomplishments served the interests of the country. A sentimental patriot, he took special satisfaction when afforded an opportunity to serve the government directly. In 1875 he took a share in a government loan to refinance the Civil War debt, playing junior partner to the Rothschilds, but in 1879 he secured the right to sell abroad an entire new issue of government bonds. In 1895, when U.S. gold reserves were shrinking dangerously because foreign creditors were exchanging their dollars for gold and Congress refused to authorize a public bond issue to finance the purchase of more gold, Morgan organized a syndicate whose successful private bond issue enabled Morgan to buy $65 million worth of gold abroad and sell it to the U.S. Treasury. In all these transactions, Morgan was bitterly reviled for enriching himself in the service of his country.

Despite his suit against the Northern Securities Co., Pres. Theodore Roosevelt appealed to Morgan for help during the *anthracite strike of 1902. The coal mines were owned by railroads controlled by Morgan. When their obstinate presidents refused to negotiate with labor, Morgan persuaded them to accept arbitration by a specially appointed commission that gave the miners most of their demands. It is revealing that labor leaders regarded Morgan as a fair-minded referee.

In October 1907 a severe financial panic struck Wall Street (see *Panic of 1907). Depositors flocked to withdraw their money from all kinds of financial institutions. Bankers blamed the panic on the government's attacks on big business; Roosevelt blamed it on "malefactors of great wealth." The basic cause was an inadequate money supply and an antiquated banking system's inability to remedy the problem.

As the crisis deepened, Morgan assembled a committee of bankers, identified the financial institutions that could be saved, and dictated to the other banks their contributions to a fund to support the selected firms. He also summoned gold from Europe and received a substantial supply of cash from the U.S. Treasury. Morgan had assumed the role of central banker, a functionary missing from the United States since Andrew Jackson abolished the *Bank of the United States in 1836 (see *Bank War) but destined to be re-created in 1913 with the establishment of the Federal Reserve System (see *Federal Reserve Act).

When the panic appeared to be over, the collapse of

an independent steel manufacturer in Birmingham, Ala., the Tennessee Coal and Iron Co., threatened to renew it. Morgan's solution was to have U.S. Steel buy the Birmingham company. This would be a violation of the Sherman Act, and Morgan sought and obtained Roosevelt's approval before U.S. Steel (reluctantly, it claimed) made the purchase. The panic soon passed.

Throughout the Panic of 1907, Roosevelt played almost no part. Its resolution was entirely Morgan's work, for which he was highly praised by European and American bankers. Roosevelt himself congratulated "those conservative and substantial business men who in this crisis have acted with such wisdom and public spirit." But again Morgan was publicly assailed, accused of having engineered the panic to enrich himself and particularly to acquire the Tennessee Coal & Iron Co. for U.S. Steel.

After his death, the executors of Morgan's estate estimated it at $80 million. "And to think," marveled John D. Rockefeller, who was then worth nearly a billion, "he wasn't even a rich man."

MORGENTHAU PLAN (1944), proposal by U.S. secretary of the Treasury Henry Morgenthau Jr. at the Quebec Conference in September 1944 (see *World War 2 Conferences) that postwar Germany be transformed into a country "primarily agricultural and pastoral in character." This was to be accomplished by internationalizing the highly industrialized Ruhr and Kiel Canal areas, transferring the Saar and adjacent areas to France, and partitioning the remainder of the country into northern and southern states.

Both U.S. president Franklin Roosevelt and British prime minister Winston Churchill initially accepted the plan, but later changed their minds in recognition of the facts that much eastern German agricultural land was going to be transferred to Poland and that an agricultural Germany would not be a market for British or American manufactures.

MORMON TRAIL, overland migration route followed by Mormons joining the main body of their church in Utah's Salt Lake Valley. Pioneered in 1847 by 148 persons led by Brigham Young, the trail coincided with the *Oregon Trail as far as Fort Bridger, where it diverged to the southwest toward Utah. Thousands of Mormons traversed the trail every year by wagon, handcart, and foot until the construction of the transcontinental railroad.

MORMON WAR (1857–58), incident in the *Buchanan administration. Popular antipathy to the Mormons and outrage over reports that Mormon authorities in Utah Territory were ignoring federal law prompted Pres. James Buchanan to appoint a non-Mormon governor to replace Gov. Brigham Young and sent him to Utah in the company of 1,500 troops from Fort Leavenworth. Believing that the federal government intended to destroy his church, Young organized guerrilla warfare against the troops, compelling them to winter at Fort Bridger without entering Utah. Meanwhile, in September 1857, a group of Mormons, at a place in southwest Utah called **Mountain Meadows**, massacred 120 members of an emigrant train that was passing through Utah on its way to California.

During the winter, a federal mediator was sent to Salt Lake City to assure Young that the troops would not interfere with the Mormon establishment. Young thereupon accepted the new governor, who arrived without military protection and occupied the governor's office. He soon found, however, that he had no role to play in the government of Utah Territory.

MORRILL ACT (1862). See *Public Lands.

MORRILL TARIFFS (1861–64), legislation of the *Lincoln administration, made possible by the absence of Southern members of Congress. Three acts of 1861, written by Rep. Justin S. Morrill of Vermont, were originally intended to increase federal revenues, first to recover shortfalls due to the *Panic of 1857 and then to pay for the *Civil War. As the war continued, new acts in 1862 and 1864 raised tariff rates to unprecedented heights, not only for revenue but—under pressure from iron, cotton, and woolen manufacturers—for protection against foreign competition. Since 1832, the South had blocked the efforts of Northern manufacturers to pass tariffs other than for revenue. During the war, tariff rates were raised from an average of 20 percent of the value of imports to between 40 and 50 percent. After the war, most wartime internal taxes were repealed, but high wartime tariff rates were retained despite budget surpluses.

MOTION PICTURES. Americans' chief entertainment medium during the 20th century, the "movies" were also a cultural influence of immeasurable power as well as an authentic new art form.

Motion pictures emerged in America during the 1890s with Thomas Edison's Kinetoscope (1894), in which a single viewer, peering into a peep-show contrivance, saw a brief film sequence—perhaps a galloping horse or an oncoming locomotive. Edison's Vitascope (1896) projected the moving image onto a screen observable by a large audience. Successful when displayed as part of vaudeville programs, in 1905 films began to be shown in "nickelodeons," storefront theaters where for a nickel the customer might see several short, silent films accompanied by piano music. In 1914, the first "picture palace," capable of seating 3,300 people, opened on Broadway in New York City. Within a few years there were 20,000 similar motion picture theaters in American downtowns, many of sumptuous and exotic design suggesting royal opera houses or palaces of ancient Egypt or Moorish Spain.

For perhaps 40 years, a weekly night at the movies was an American family custom. A host of film magazines made celebrities of glamorous actors and actresses whose often scandalous lives helped transform the nation's morals. Only television eventually challenged the primacy of the movies in shaping the American imagination.

The "show" itself early evolved from a mere curiosity to telling a simple story. The replacement of the single static camera by several cameras and the invention of the art of film editing greatly enlarged the film's narrative capacity. The first full-length (three-reel) motion picture, a French import, was shown in 1912. Sound arrived in 1927, color in 1935. These and countless other technical developments were utilized by innovative directors, cinematographers, and editors to enrich the narrative power of film. Great films, however, comparable to the best novels in character and story, were never the product of technology but of the vision of writers, directors, and actors.

MOUNTAIN MEADOWS MASSACRE (1857). See *Mormon War.

MOUNTAIN MEN (1824–40), fur-trappers of the Rocky Mountains who hunted beaver in solitude, then brought their pelts to an annual rendezvous conducted by the fur companies (see *Fur Trade). There hundreds of trappers and Indians sold their pelts and indulged in a general debauch before dispersing again into the mountains. Competition, overtrapping, Indian hostility, changing fashions, and dwindling profits put an end to the era of the mountain men. The last, thinly attended rendezvous was held in 1840. Mountain men celebrated in folklore included Jedediah Smith, Thomas Fitzpatrick, Christopher ("Kit") Carson, Jim Bridger, and William Sublette.

MOYNIHAN REPORT (1965), document prepared by sociologist Daniel Patrick Moynihan, then assistant secretary of labor in the Lyndon *Johnson administration, examining the problem of translating equality of opportunity (promised in civil rights legislation) into equality of socioeconomic results for African-Americans.

Moynihan located the problem in the "tangle of pathologies" besetting the black family—unemployment, illegitimacy, educational failure, delinquency, welfare dependency, matriarchy. He concluded: "[T]o bring the Negro American to full and equal sharing in the responsibilities and rewards of citizenship . . . the programs of the Federal government . . . shall be designed to have the effect, directly or indirectly, of enhancing the stability and resources of the Negro American family."

The report served as the basis for a speech (cowritten by Moynihan) delivered by President Johnson at Howard University on June 4, 1965. "[I]t is not enough just to open the gates of opportunity," the president declared. "All our citizens must have the ability to walk through those gates. This is the next and most profound stage of the battle for civil rights. We seek . . . not just equality as a right and a theory but equality as a fact and as a result."

The Moynihan Report, published as *The Negro Family: The Case for National Action*, aroused a storm of controversy, many black activists faulting Moynihan for indicting the black family rather than the racist society that created it.

MR. DOOLEY, literary invention of journalist Finley Peter Dunne, in the Chicago *Post* and *Journal* (1893–1900), then in *Collier*'s magazine until 1919. Martin Dooley's observations on the passing scene were delivered from behind the bar of his Archer Avenue saloon in Chicago in a rich Irish brogue, often to his friend Malachi Hennessy. His famous "review" of Theodore Roosevelt's *The Rough Riders* appeared in November 1899:

" 'I haven't time f'r to tell ye the wurruck Tiddy did in ar-hmin' an' equippin' himself, how he fed himself, how he steadied himself in battles an' encouraged himself with a few well-chosen worruds whin th' sky was darkest. Ye'll have to take a squint into the book ye'erself to l'arn thim things.'

" 'I won't do it,' said Mr. Hennessy. 'I think Tiddy Rosenfelt is all r-right an' if he wants to blow his horn lave him do it.'

" 'True f'r ye,' said Mr. Dooley. . . . 'But if I was him I'd call th' book "Alone in Cubia." ' "

MUCKRAKERS (1890–1912), a group of authors and journalists whose exposures of corporate and political wrongdoing aroused public opinion in behalf of *progressivism. Jacob Riis's *How the Other Half Lives* (1890) revealed the appalling conditions of New York's slums. Henry Demarest Lloyd's *Wealth Against Commonwealth* (1894) attacked monopolies. Gustavus Myers's *History of the Great American Fortunes* (1910) portrayed American businessmen in unflattering light.

Beginning in 1903 with *McClure's Magazine*, low-priced popular magazines discovered that exposure was a great circulation builder. In *McClure's*, Lincoln Steffens wrote his exposures of the corrupt links between business and politics in American cities and states, later published as *The Shame of the Cities* (1904), and Ida Tarbell wrote her account of the ruthless machinations of Standard Oil, later published as *The History of the Standard Oil Co.* (1904). Ray Stannard Baker, Samuel Hopkins Adams, Thomas Lawson, and Burton J. Hendrick also muckraked for *McClure's*. David Graham Phillips's *The Treason of the Senate* (1906), documenting the connections between leading senators and corporate interests, appeared first as articles in *Cosmopolitan*, which, with *Everybody's*, *Collier's*, and the *American Magazine* followed *McClure's* with frequent articles on food adulteration, patent medicines, insurance, child labor, prostitution, electoral fraud, railroad accidents, and great fortunes.

The literature of exposure extended to fiction, most notably Upton Sinclair's novel *The Jungle* (1906), whose incidental exposure of unsanitary conditions in the meat-packing industry ensured passage of the Meat Inspection Act of 1906.

The name muckrakers was given this group of writers by Pres. Theodore Roosevelt. Originally a fan of the genre, Roosevelt began to fear that its excesses would contribute to radicalism. In speeches in 1906, Roosevelt compared these writers to the man with the muckrake in John Bunyan's 17th-century work *Pilgrim's Progress* who was too intent on the filth on the floor about him to look up. Muckraking passed from fashion after 1912.

MUGWUMPS, derisive name for a small group of high-minded Republicans who in 1884 deserted their party's candidate for president, the morally sullied James G. Blaine, to support the Democratic candidate, honest Grover Cleveland. Leading Mugwumps were E. L. Godkin, editor of the *Nation*, George W. Curtis, editor of *Harper's Weekly*, and former senator and cabinet officer Carl Schurz. The word was alleged to be an Indian term meaning "great chiefs."

MULLER v. OREGON (1908), unanimous decision of the *Fuller Court upholding an Oregon statute limiting the work of women in factories and laundries to ten hours a day. In *Lochner v. New York* (1905), the Court had overturned a similar New York statute by denying that long hours were detrimental to the health of bakery workers. In *Muller*, Boston attorney Louis D. Brandeis demonstrated the legitimacy of the Oregon statute by assembling a mass of medical and sociological evidence of the detrimental effect of long hours of labor on women's health. The "Brandeis brief" was used thereafter to defend reform legislation or challenge existing social evils. From the later point of view of the *women's rights movement, the decision confirmed women's protected but confining "special place."

MULLIGAN LETTERS (1876, 1884), letters written in 1876 by Speaker of the House James G. Blaine to one Warren Fisher Jr. and made public by an employee of Fisher, James Mulligan, who claimed that they implicated Blaine in a corrupt business deal. Blaine obtained possession of the letters and read selectively from them on the floor of the House to show their innocence, but the incident probably cost him the Republican presidential nomination in 1876. In 1884, when Blaine was the Republican presidential candidate, the letters were published—including the cryptic postscript "Burn this letter"—and contributed to his defeat.

MULTICULTURALISM, view of U.S. society that emphasizes its racial, religious, and cultural diversity and the contributions of each ethnic group. It is often advocated for therapeutic reasons in the belief that an appreciation of their cultural backgrounds will enhance the self-esteem of minority students. Its proponents sometimes distort history by magnifying minor figures and events while undervaluing the national enterprise. In fact, some proponents use multiculturalism as a critique of the dominant national culture, which they see as the work of white European males.

It is undeniable that the values and institutions that distinguish the United States—for example, republican government, the rule of law, legal equality, and individual liberty—derive almost entirely from British historical experience as modified by British colonists in the New World. Paradoxically, these values and institutions—unlike those of other cultures—have proved uniquely accommodating to an increasingly diverse society.

MUNN v. ILLINOIS (1877), 7–2 decision of the *Waite Court, one of the *Granger Cases*. The decision validated an Illinois law regulating the rates charged by Chicago grain elevators. "Property," wrote Chief Justice Morrison R. Waite, "... become[s] clothed with a public interest when used in a manner to make it of public consequence, and affect the community at large. When, therefore, one devotes his property to a use in which the public has an interest, he, in effect, grants to the public an interest in that use, and must submit to be controlled by the public for the common good, to the extent of the interest he has thus created."

MURCHISON LETTER (1888), letter purportedly written by Charles F. Murchison, who described himself as a naturalized Englishman, asking the British minister in Washington, Sir Lionel Sackville-West, how he (Murchison) should vote in that fall's presidential election. Sackville-West foolishly advised the unknown Murchison to vote for Grover Cleveland. Republicans charged that Sackville-West's advice proved that Cleveland's program of tariff revision served British interests and was perhaps even paid for by British gold.

MURFREESBORO or **STONES RIVER** (Dec. 31, 1862–Jan. 3, 1863), *Civil War battle. After the battle of *Perryville (Oct. 8, 1862), Union troops under Gen. William S. Rosecrans followed the Confederate army of Gen. Braxton Bragg back to central Tennessee. In a furious battle at Murfreesboro, the Federals were driven back but finally held their ground. Each side lost about a third of its effectives. On Jan. 3, 1863, Bragg had no choice but to withdraw toward Chattanooga; Rosecrans was too weak to follow.

MUSLIMS. Estimates of the Muslim population of the United States vary greatly, are seldom based on credible scientific methodology, and seem to have undergone inflation in recent years. Crude estimates from Census and Immigration and Naturalization Service figures suggest a Muslim population between 1.5 and 3.4 million, or 0.5–1.2 percent of the total population. In 2001, the General Social Survey of the National Opinion Research Center at the University of Chicago estimated the Muslim population at 1.9 million.

That year, some 1,200 mosques stretched from Florida to Alaska. About 25 percent of American Muslims were immigrants (or their descendants) from South Asia, 12 percent from Arab countries, and smaller proportions from Afghanistan, Iran, and Turkey. Most had immigrated to the United States after the national quota system was ended in 1965 (see *Immigration).

More than half of American Muslims were native converts, the great majority (42 percent of all American Muslims) African-Americans. Some African slaves had been Muslims, but the modern affinity of African-Americans for Islam was largely inspired by black separatist Elijah Muhammad, whose *Nation of Islam was distinctly unorthodox. After Elijah Muhammad's death, his son, Wallace D. Muhammad, dissolved the Nation of Islam and led his followers into orthodox Islam. The Nation of Islam was revived, however, by Louis Farrakhan, who preached Elijah Muhammad's doctrines of black separation, to which he added a virulent anti-Semitism.

Islamic fundamentalism, rampant in the Middle East, was reported to have a significant presence in the United States, funded by the governments of Iran, Saudi Arabia, and Libya. Anti-Semitic and anti-American, Islamic fundamentalists (both foreign and domestic) were responsible for terrorist acts against American interests abroad and targets within the United States (see *Terrorism). After the attacks on the World Trade Center and Pentagon by Arab terrorists on Sept. 11, 2001 (see *World Trade Center Attack 2), American Muslims of Middle Eastern origin were subjected to heightened government scrutiny and some public harassment.

MY LAI MASSACRE (1968). See *Vietnam War.

N

NASHVILLE (Dec. 15–16, 1864), *Civil War battle. While Union general William T. Sherman marched from Atlanta to the sea (see *Sherman's March through Georgia), hard-driving Confederate general John Bell Hood led his dispirited Army of Tennessee, 40,000 strong, from Alabama into Tennessee with the intention of smashing Union general George H. Thomas's Army of the Tennessee and then joining Gen. Robert E. Lee in Virginia.

On Nov. 30 Hood hurled his army against entrenched Federals at Franklin, 15 miles south of Nashville, eventually dislodging them but at a cost of 7,000 casualties. Pushing his shattered army on toward Nashville, he established a defensive line four miles south of the city and waited for Thomas to attack. After careful preparation, Thomas did so on Dec. 15, throwing 50,000 troops against Hood's 25,000. Hood fell back that night and was hit again the next day. Under Thomas's pounding, the Confederate army dissolved. Thousands surrendered, more thousands fled south. Their flight ended at Tupelo, Miss., where fewer than half of Hood's original force assembled. Hood resigned his command on Jan. 13, 1865.

NASHVILLE CONVENTION (1850), meeting of slave-state delegates called by a Mississippi convention to establish Southern unity in the face of expected antislavery legislation by Congress. The first session (June), attended by more than a hundred delegates selected by the legislatures of 9 (out of 15) slave states, was controlled by moderates. Held while Congress was debating the *Compromise of 1850, it passed resolutions defending slavery and accepting an extension of the *Missouri Compromise line to the Pacific Ocean.

A second session (November), boycotted by Unionists, was attended by 59 irregularly selected delegates from only seven states. More radical than the first session, the second rejected the Compromise of 1850 and asserted the right of *secession. The Nashville Convention revealed the disunity and general moderation of the South on the issue of secession at that time.

NATIONAL ASSOCIATION FOR THE ADVANCEMENT OF COLORED PEOPLE (NAACP), civil rights organization, interracial and integrative, founded in 1909 to promote the equal citizenship of black Americans. It opposed the strategy of black educator Booker T. Washington, who advocated black accommodation to segregation. Chapters spread rapidly across the country, eventually numbering nearly 2,000. During the 1930s blacks assumed complete leadership of the organization.

The NAACP's early campaign, by publicity and education, to obtain federal antilynching legislation failed. The organization was more successful when it turned to legal action, overturning death penalties (see *Capital Punishment) and winning Supreme Court decisions outlawing the *grandfather clause, the *white primary, and residential segregation (see *Housing). Beginning in 1940, through the NAACP Legal Defense and Educational Fund (which became independent of the NAACP in 1961), it undermined the legal foundations of segregation in a series of successful challenges to the "separate but equal" doctrine of *Plessy v. Ferguson (1896) that culminated in the Court's decision in *Brown v. Board of Education of Topeka (1954) outlawing segregation in public schools.

In the *civil rights movement that grew up after Brown, new organizations, impatient with the NAACP's legal strategy, criticized the organization as middle class and conservative and advocated direct action against segregation and in support of voting rights. But in the 1970s, with the movement in disarray, the NAACP Legal

Defense and Educational Fund returned to the courts to sue for implementation of the long-deferred promise of *Brown*.

NATIONAL BANKING ACT (1863), legislation of the *Lincoln administration made possible by the absence of Southern members of Congress. Intended to stabilize state banks, create a uniform national currency, and enlarge the market for war bonds, the act authorized the granting of federal charters to banks that invested a third of their capital in U.S. securities. These banks could then issue notes up to 90 percent of the value of such bonds. (In 1865, Congress levied a 10-percent tax on other banknotes, driving them out of circulation.)

Repairing the Jacksonian separation of government from banking (see *Bank War), this measure reflected the centralizing pressures of the Civil War. "The policy of this country," declared John Sherman, chairman of the Senate Finance Committee, "ought to be to make everything national as far as possible."

NATIONAL CONSERVATION COMMISSION. See *Conservation.

NATIONAL DEFENSE EDUCATION ACT (1958), legislation of the *Eisenhower administration inspired by the *Sputnik* alarm. Intended to advance education in science, mathematics, and foreign languages, the act—among other things—authorized the use of federal money to improve facilities and instruction in elementary and (nonvocational) high schools. The act was controversial because of the fear of federal control of the nation's schools.

NATIONAL ENVIRONMENTAL POLICY ACT (1970). See *Environmentalism.

NATIONAL INDUSTRIAL RECOVERY ACT (1933). See *New Deal; *Schechter Poultry Corp. v. United States*.

NATIONAL LABOR REFORM PARTY. See *National Labor Union (NLU).

NATIONAL LABOR RELATIONS ACT or WAGNER ACT (1935). See *New Deal.

NATIONAL LABOR RELATIONS BOARD v. JONES & LAUGHLIN STEEL CORP. (1937), 5–4 decision of the *Hughes Court upholding the *National Labor Relations Act (1935). The act guaranteed labor the right to organize, bargain collectively, and strike and protected workers from discrimination by their employer because of union membership.

In the past, the Court had interpreted the liberty of contract protected by the Due Process Clause of the Fifth Amendment as insulating labor-management relations from government interference. It had also considered manufacturing as only indirectly related to interstate commerce and thus beyond the power of Congress to regulate. But now, only weeks after Pres. Franklin Roosevelt had proposed his *court-packing plan to circumvent judicial obstruction of New Deal measures, Chief Justice Charles E. Hughes and Justice Owen Roberts abandoned their earlier views and adopted the view that the government possessed broad powers to regulate the economy.

NATIONAL LABOR UNION (NLU) (1866–72), federation of trade unions founded at Baltimore in 1866. Its pursuit of reformist objectives through producers' cooperatives and political action caused many unions interested in immediate economic gains to withdraw. In 1872 the NLU became the **National Labor Reform Party**. When its nominee for president, David Davis of Illinois, failed to get the Democratic nomination as well, he withdrew from the race and the party collapsed. The NLU was partially responsible for Congress's establishing in 1868 the eight-hour day for laborers and mechanics employed by the federal government.

NATIONAL ORGANIZATION FOR WOMEN (NOW). See *Women's Rights.

NATIONAL-ORIGINS QUOTA SYSTEM. See *Immigration.

NATIONAL PARK SERVICE. See *Conservation.

NATIONAL RECOVERY ADMINISTRATION (NRA). See *New Deal.

NATIONAL REPUBLICAN PARTY (1824–34), political party formed by the division of the *Jeffersonian Republican Party into two groups, the National Republicans following Pres. John Quincy Adams and the Democratic Republicans (see *Democratic Party) following Andrew Jackson. The National Republicans preserved the Federalist tradition of a government that actively enhanced national unity and prosperity in contrast to the Jeffersonian states' rights and laissez-faire tradition preserved by the Democrats. The party unsuccessfully nominated Adams for president in 1828 and Henry Clay (author of the *American System) in 1832. In 1834 the National Republicans merged with other anti-Jackson groups to form the *Whig Party.

NATIONAL ROAD or **CUMBERLAND ROAD,** federally built road intended to facilitate communication with the West. Authorized by Congress in 1806, the road was not begun until 1815. Starting at Cumberland, Md., it reached Wheeling on the Ohio River in western Virginia in 1818, Columbus, Ohio, in 1833, and Vandalia, Ill., in 1850. Pres. Andrew Jackson, opposed to federal *internal improvements, turned over control of the road to the states through which it passed for maintenance and repair. In the 20th century, it became part of U.S. Route 40.

NATIONAL SECURITY ACT (1947). See *Armed Forces Unification.

NATIONAL TRAFFIC AND MOTOR VEHICLE SAFETY ACT (1966). See *Consumer Protection.

NATIONAL UNION FOR SOCIAL JUSTICE (NUSJ) (1934–36), national "people's lobby" created by Father Charles E. Coughlin, the Royal Oak, Mich., Catholic priest whose weekly radio sermons, begun in 1926, were listened to by an estimated 40 million Americans in the early 1930s.

From pastoral topics, Coughlin turned to political issues during the *Great Depression, which he blamed on "predatory capitalists" and international bankers. He offered a variety of inflationary panaceas, including abandonment of the gold standard, remonetization of silver, and nationalization of the banks. For a time he supported the Franklin *Roosevelt administration, but when the administration rebuffed his pretensions to be an "insider" he turned against it.

In November 1934 Coughlin announced over the air the creation of the NUSJ, which could be joined simply by writing to him. Its great numbers, used at his direction to support selected candidates and issues, would, he expected, give him the influence in national affairs that he desired. And in fact the perfervid response of Coughlin's followers to his denunciation in January 1935 of an administration proposal to join the World Court may have been decisive in defeating that plan.

In 1936 Coughlin formed the *Union Party out of the NUSJ, supporters of the *Townsend Plan, and the remnants of Huey Long's *Share Our Wealth Society to contest Roosevelt's reelection. Compelled to choose between Coughlin and Roosevelt, Coughlin's followers deserted him en masse. After the election, Coughlin officially dissolved the organization.

NATIONAL YOUTH ADMINISTRATION (NYA). See *New Deal.

NATION OF ISLAM or **BLACK MUSLIMS,** black nationalist organization that practices an unorthodox version of Islam. Founded in Detroit in 1930 by one Wali Farrad Muhammad (Wallace Fard), it was directed for 40 years (1934–75) from Chicago by Elijah Muhammad (Robert Poole), who taught blacks the necessity of economic self-reliance, a puritanical lifestyle, and separation from whites, the source of evil.

In 1964, Elijah Muhammad's chief lieutenant, Malcolm X (Malcolm Little), left the Nation of Islam, converted to orthodox (nonracist) Sunni Islam, and founded the Organization of Afro-American Unity. Malcolm X became a popular advocate of nonracist but still militant black nationalism and an opponent of the mainstream integrationist *civil rights movement until his assassination by Black Muslims in New York City on Feb. 21, 1965.

Elijah Muhammad was succeeded (1975) as head of the Nation of Islam by his son, Wallace D. Muhammad, who, moving toward orthodox Sunni Islam, abandoned the organization's racist tenets, renaming it the American Muslim Mission (1980–85). His changes precipitated a schism in 1978 when the leading Black Muslim minister, Louis Farrakhan (Louis Walcott), restored the Nation of Islam, adding to its black-nationalist and separationist doctrines a virulent anti-Semitism.

NATIVE AMERICANS. See *Indians, American, or Native Americans.

NATIVISM. Hostility to immigrants on racial, religious, political, and economic grounds has been a recurrent theme in American history (see *Immigration). Eagerly welcomed in colonial America, immigrants fell under suspicion in the 1790s as possible carriers of the virus of the *French Revolution. The *Alien and Sedition Acts, passed by a Federalist Congress in 1798, were aimed primarily at certain foreign-born editors prominent in the *Jeffersonian Republican Party, which endorsed the revolution in France and proclaimed its intention of planting its egalitarian principles in the United States.

When at last the revolutionary fever passed, immigrants discovered that they were unpopular as economic competitors, willing to accept lower wages and more menial work than native-born workers would accept (see *Labor). The fact that many immigrants were Catholics added the fuel of bigotry to the basic dislike of foreigners. Repeated waves of Protestant revivalism, accompanied by books and pamphlets that "exposed" the unspeakable vices of priests and nuns, fanned into flame the embers of anti-Catholicism that the first settlers had brought from England and that had never died out. This sentiment was exacerbated in the 1840s when masses of Catholic immigrants began to arrive from famine-stricken Ireland and from Germany after the failed revolutions of 1848. Many Americans believed that their republican institutions, derived from English Protestantism, were threatened with subversion.

Anti-Catholicism moved from the pulpit to politics in the 1840s. In New York City, the Catholic demand for public funds for parochial schools and protest over the use of the (Protestant) King James Bible in the public schools led to the formation of an anti-Catholic American Republican Party that won local elections in New York, Boston, and Philadelphia. Ten years later, the anti-immigrant and anti-Catholic *Know-Nothing Party experienced a meteoric rise as a national party, threatening to win the presidential election of 1856. Its decline, caused by the growing crisis over slavery, was almost as precipitous as its rise.

Hostility to immigrants in the latter half of the 19th century was reflected in successive restrictions on their admission—first convicts, then paupers, criminals, the insane, the diseased, and numerous other categories. Chinese and Japanese immigrants were entirely barred (see *Chinese Exclusion; *Japanese Exclusion). Animosity toward immigrants was heightened in World War 1, when again they were suspected of un-American radicalism. Many foreign-born radicals were deported in the *red scare of 1919–20. Anti-immigrant sentiment was reflected in the 1920s in the revival of the *Ku Klux Klan, the popularity of pseudoscientific race theories, and the consequent adoption of a national-origin immigration policy intended to check the flow of the "new immigration" from Southern and Eastern Europe—often Catholic and Jewish—and restore the "old immigration" of Protestants from Northern Europe.

Anti-Catholic sentiment contributed to the defeat of presidential candidate Alfred E. Smith in 1928. Anti-Jewish sentiment contributed to obstructions to the immigration of refugees from Nazi Germany (see *Holocaust Response).

A remarkable change in public sentiment was indicated by the election of Catholic John F. Kennedy as president in 1960 and by the rejection in 1965 of the national-origin immigration policy in favor of a new policy indifferent to race. Since then, the perennial debate on immigration has dwelt not on racial, religious, or political issues but on whether immigrants are economic assets or liabilities to American society—productive new citizens or competitors to native-born workers and a drain on public services. Nevertheless, racism, xenophobia, and religious bigotry remain strong in the *Radical Right.

NAT TURNER REVOLT (1831). See *Slave Revolts.

NAVAL WAR WITH FRANCE (1798–1800), undeclared war between the United States and France growing out of French resentment of *Jay's Treaty. The French Directory unleashed a horde of privateers against U.S. merchant shipping with catastrophic results, particularly in the West Indies, a region that accounted for a third of U.S. foreign commerce. The West Indies privateers were effectively suppressed by the new U.S. navy, authorized by Congress in the war fever following the *XYZ Affair and created and directed by Secretary of the Navy Benjamin Stoddert. The most notable engagement involving U.S. and French vessels was the victory of the U.S. frigate *Constellation*, commanded by Capt. Thomas Truxtun, over the French frigate *Insurgente* off the island of Nevis on Feb. 9, 1799. The war was ended by the *Convention of 1800.

NAVIGATION ACTS (1649, 1651, 1660, 1696), acts of Parliament to protect English shipping from foreign competition and to maximize revenues from the colonial trade. No goods could be imported into or exported from any English colony except in English or colonial ships. Certain enumerated colonial products—originally tobacco, sugar, indigo, cotton wood, ginger, and dyewoods—could be exported only to other colonies or to England itself. If they were intended for Europe, they had to be reshipped from England. Similarly, European and Asian products destined for the English colonies had to go first to England and be reshipped.

NEOCONSERVATIVES (1960s–90s), group of intellectuals who abandoned Marxist and liberal views in favor of a moderate conservatism based on historical American values and moral standards (in reaction to the *counterculture) and concern about the threat of Soviet aggression (rather than internal communist subversion). A leading member of the group once defined a neoconservative as a liberal who had been mugged by reality.

NEO-NAZIS. See *Radical Right.

NEUTRALITY ACTS (1935–41), legislation of the Franklin *Roosevelt administration to prevent U.S. involvement in foreign wars. Characteristic of these acts was voluntary American curtailment of its neutral rights (assertion of which had led to U.S. involvement in World War 1) and refusal to differentiate between aggressor and victim, both of whom were simply labeled "belligerents."

The Neutrality Act of 1935 authorized the president, upon finding that a state of war existed, to declare an embargo on arms shipments to belligerents and to withhold protection of U.S. citizens traveling on belligerents' ships. Passed after the Italian invasion of Ethiopia, the act did not prohibit trade in strategic materials, and U.S. oil shipments to Italy increased.

The Neutrality Act of 1936 extended the 1935 act and prohibited loans or credits to belligerents.

The Neutrality Act of 1937, passed during the *Spanish Civil War, covered civil as well as international wars, prohibited travel by American citizens on belligerents' ships, and forbade the arming of American merchant ships. It empowered the president to embargo strategic materials as well as weapons and to place the sale of non-embargoed goods on a "cash-and-carry" basis. When Japan attacked China in July 1937, Roosevelt refused to declare that a state of war existed, thereby permitting the sale of war materials to China (as well as to Japan).

The Neutrality Act of 1939 repealed the arms embargo, permitting belligerents to buy war materials in the United States if they paid in cash and transported the materials in their own ships. It also permitted the president in time of war to designate "war zones" through which U.S. citizens and ships were forbidden to travel.

A 1941 act repealed portions of the 1939 act, authorizing the arming of American merchant vessels and permitting them to sail to belligerents' ports.

NEW AMSTERDAM. See *New Netherland.

NEWBURGH CONSPIRACY (1783). The *Continental Army's last cantonment was at New Windsor, N.Y., 60 miles north of New York City, from the summer of 1782 to the summer of 1783. Gen. George Washington made his headquarters at nearby Newburgh.

Disgruntled by lack of back pay and pensions, the army's officers complained to Congress in December 1782 without satisfaction. In March 1783 an anonymous printed "address" called for a meeting of officers in tones implying a threat to the civilian government. On Mar. 15 Washington appeared at the meeting and

pleaded with his officers "to rely on the plighted faith of your Country" and repudiate anyone "who wickedly attempts to open the flood Gates of Civil discord." To demonstrate Congress's good intention, he proposed to read a letter from a Virginia congressman, putting on a pair of spectacles to do so and apologizing: "Gentlemen, you must pardon me. I have grown gray in your service and now find myself growing blind as well."

The incident moved Washington's officers in a way that his speech had not. After Washington left the meeting, the officers adopted a resolution rejecting the "infamous propositions . . . in a late anonymous address." Congress soon adopted a pension plan agreeable to the officers.

NEW DEAL (1933–38), domestic program of the Franklin *Roosevelt administration to combat the *Great Depression. New Deal measures are conventionally categorized as relief, recovery, or reform. These aspects of the New Deal were not distinct stages but were pursued simultaneously. Sometimes a major piece of legislation contained components reflecting several aspects of the New Deal.

Relief. The administration was immediately confronted with the need to funnel federal money to the relief of victims of the depression. The depression was now at its greatest depth, and most state and local relief agencies had exhausted their resources. The **Federal Emergency Relief Administration (FERA)**, created in May 1933, distributed federal funds for the first time to states and localities—half as outright grants, half to be matched by the recipient governments—for emergency relief to the destitute.

The dole, however, was as unpalatable to Roosevelt as it had been to Hoover. "Our greatest primary task," Roosevelt had declared in his inaugural address, "is to put people to work." Pending the revival of the economy, the launching of job-creating public works projects was indispensable.

The first of these was the **Civilian Conservation Corps (CCC)** (1933–43), established in the administration's first month. The CCC employed single young men 17–25 on conservation projects like reforestation, fire fighting, land reclamation, and erosion control. The men lived in camps run by the Army and were paid $30 per month, of which $25 was sent directly to their families. Three million young men—never more than 500,000 at any one time—passed through the CCC during its nine years. The CCC was the most popular and least controversial of New Deal programs.

The **Public Works Administration (PWA)**

(1933–43) was authorized by the National Industrial Recovery Act of June 1933. Headed by Secretary of the Interior Harold L. Ickes, the PWA was intended to act as an economic "pump primer" by undertaking major construction projects that would employ large numbers of jobless. Ickes's meticulous management of the program to prevent waste and corruption caused the PWA to move slowly; furthermore, much of its funds were spent on building materials rather than wages. Between 1933 and 1939, the PWA spent $6 billion constructing public buildings, schools, hospitals, bridges, tunnels, and sewer systems.

In November 1933, as a winter of unparalleled destitution approached, the administration created the **Civil Works Administration (CWA)** (1933–34), directed by Harry Hopkins, which put 4 million unemployed to work on federal, state, and local make-work projects. The CWA was terminated in March 1934.

For his success with the CWA, Hopkins was appointed director of the **Works Progress Administration (WPA)** (1935–43; from 1939, the **Work Projects Administration**), the administration's principal work-relief program. Excluded from large-scale construction projects of the sort undertaken by the PWA, the WPA undertook thousands of small-scale, labor-intensive projects that made it vulnerable to criticism for waste and inefficiency. Over its eight-year life, the WPA employed 8.5 million people (never more than 3.2 million at one time) in building libraries, schools, stadiums, airports, rural roads, bridges, dams, parks, tennis courts, and golf courses. To preserve the skills of white-collar and professional workers, it created of the Federal Theater Project, the Federal Arts Project, and the Federal Writers Project. The WPA, however, was never able to provide jobs for more than a third of those who needed them. Wages were not allowed to compete with those in private industry, the average wage per recipient being $55 per month. The WPA was terminated in 1943 as war production absorbed the unemployed.

The **National Youth Administration (NYA)** (1935–43) sought to provide work for youths, whose unemployment rate was estimated at 30 percent. High schools and colleges were given money to pay students, mainly from families on relief, for part-time work on campus. More than 2 million students had been aided in this way by 1943. For out-of-school youth, the NYA provided vocational training, especially for defense work after 1939.

Recovery. The revival of industry was the object of the **National Recovery Administration (NRA)**, established by the National Industrial Recovery Act of June 1933. It sought to do this by eliminating destructive competition. All the firms in a particular industry were encouraged to negotiate a code of fair competition, to be approved by the government, that fixed production levels, prices, wages, and hours for that industry. Participating firms were exempted from antitrust prosecution. In its famous Section 7a, the act also guaranteed workers the right to organize and bargain collectively.

Although some 550 codes were negotiated, amid great initial enthusiasm, the NRA did not work. The codes, often dictated by the largest firms in the industry, set production levels, prices, and wages agreeable to the large firms but often disadvantageous to the small. The codes did little to increase employment, and by fixing wages at low levels did nothing to stimulate mass purchasing power. Moreover, they were administered in the interests of large firms by business executives temporarily employed in Washington. Small-business people, farmers, unions, and consumers soon protested. Businesses, many involved in multiple codes, complained about bureaucratic interference. The NRA was widely unpopular and perceived as unsuccessful when the U.S. Supreme Court declared it unconstitutional in *Schechter Poultry Corp. v. United States* (1935). It was abolished on Jan. 1, 1936.

Agricultural recovery was the task of the **Agricultural Adjustment Administration (AAA)** (1933–35), created in May 1933. Its diagnosis of the *farm problem was overproduction, and its solution was voluntary reduction of acreage devoted to certain key commodities, which was rewarded by government subsidies. Found unconstitutional in *United States v. Butler* (1935), the original Agricultural Adjustment Act was replaced in 1938 by a new one similar in its emphasis on reducing production through acreage allotments and government subsidies.

A major recovery project was the **Tennessee Valley Authority (TVA)**, created in May 1933 as an experiment in regional development. By providing hydroelectric power, flood control, river navigation, land reclamation, and scientific farming, the TVA revitalized the economies of the seven Southern states that shared the valley of the Tennessee River. Private power companies blocked the creation of other regional development projects.

The results of the New Deal's recovery efforts were mixed. Its agricultural policy enjoyed a measure of success. Farm prices and farm income rose significantly during the 1930s. Most of the benefits, however, went to farm owners, particularly owners of large farms, despite many administration efforts to aid marginal farmers, tenants, sharecroppers, and migratory workers. While its industrial policy was considered a failure, gross national product (GNP) increased from $55.6 billion in 1933 to $90.4 billion in 1937, when it stood at 88 percent of the 1929 level—although 7.7 million Americans (14.3 percent of the labor force) remained unemployed.

Reform. Reform of the institutions that had made the depression possible was a high priority of the New Deal. The Federal Securities Act of May 1933 reformed the securities business, requiring full disclosure of relevant information to purchasers of securities and the registration of new securities with the Federal Trade Commission (later the Securities and Exchange Commission). The Banking Act of June 1933 separated commercial from investment banking to end speculation with depositors' money and established federal insurance of bank deposits (originally under $5,000). The Securities Exchange Act of June 1934 established federal regulation of securities exchanges by the Securities and Exchange Commission. The Banking Act of 1935 increased the powers of the Federal Reserve Board over the reserve requirements, discount operations, interest rates, and open market operations of member banks, making the Federal Reserve a true central bank. The Public Utility Holding Company Act of August 1935 set in motion the dissolution of monopolistic public utility holding companies.

Labor benefited from important New Deal reforms. Section 7a of the National Industrial Recovery Act guaranteed workers the right to organize and bargain collectively through unions of their own choice. The **National Labor Relations Act (Wagner Act)** of July 1935 again guaranteed (the NIRA having been declared unconstitutional) workers the right to organize, bargain collectively, and strike. It outlawed company unions and discrimination against workers because of union membership, and it permitted the "closed shop"— the requirement that only union members could be hired. To supervise the workers' choice of a union and to certify that union as the workers' representative in collective bargaining, the act established the National Labor Relations Board, which was also authorized to monitor employers' unfair labor practices and to issue cease-and-desist orders enforceable by the courts. The **Fair Labor Standards Act** of June 1938, applying to many occupations involved in interstate commerce, established a national minimum wage and a maximum of workweek hours. In deference to the South, the minimum wage—originally 40 cents an hour—was to be phased in over eight years, starting at 25 cents an hour. The maximum hours standard—40 per week—was to be phased in over three years, starting at 44 hours. The act also outlawed the labor of

children under 16 and limited youths under 18 to nonhazardous occupations.

The **Social Security Act** of August 1935 established a system of federal-state unemployment insurance, a federal program of old-age and survivors' insurance, and federal-state cooperation for aid to children and the disabled (see *Social Security; *Welfare).

Two other important reform measures were the National Housing Act of September 1937, under which the U.S. Housing Authority provided, to local housing authorities that furnished 10 percent of the cost, low-interest loans for slum clearance and low-rent public housing (see *Housing), and the Food, Drug, and Cosmetic Act of June 1938, which required informative and accurate labeling and prohibited false and misleading advertising of these products (see *Consumer Protection).

Results. By 1940, war production was beginning to absorb the unemployed, although work relief programs continued until 1943. Roosevelt's attention was now focused on foreign affairs, and in his annual message to Congress in January 1939 for the first time he recommended no new domestic reforms.

For all its efforts, the New Deal did not cure the depression. That the underlying problem was underconsumption and not overproduction, "wasteful" competition, or monopoly power, and that the solution was deficit spending on a truly wartime scale, became clear only after a decade of stagnation. Nevertheless, the New Deal defused a national crisis of ominous potential and preserved the American political and economic systems—an achievement unappreciated by its conservative critics and condemned by its radical critics. It legitimized an active role for government in managing the economy. Its permanent institutional reforms gave Americans a greater sense of economic security and social justice.

NEW ECONOMY (1991–2001), popular term for the longest economic expansion in U.S. history, which began in March 1991 and ended in 2001 (see *Clinton Administration).

Similar expansions had followed the introduction of such technologies as steam, steel, railroads, petroleum, home appliances, and automobiles. The "new economy" of the 1990s was driven by the development of information and communication technologies, principally computers, software, and the Internet. This resulted in increased productivity, large capital investments by business, extraordinary affluence among people in high-tech industries, and government budget surpluses. The gross domestic product grew from $5.7 trillion in 1990 to $10.0 trillion in 2000; the number of civilian jobs grew from 118.8 million to 135.2 million; median family income climbed 9.5 percent; unemployment declined from 5.6 percent to 3.9 percent; and the poverty rate for individuals fell from 13.5 percent to 11.8 percent. A long bull market, which started from a low of 777 in 1982, accelerated in the 1990s, the Dow Jones industrial average doubling between 1995 and 2000 (peaking on Jan. 14, 2000, at 11,773).

Enthusiasts for the new economy believed that the "information revolution" had fundamentally altered the economy, promising permanent high productivity, low unemployment and inflation, and steady economic expansion. Their "irrational exuberance" (a cautionary phrase of Federal Reserve chairman Alan Greenspan) was epitomized by the high-flying "dot-com" companies, which sold goods and services over the Internet. The dot-com bubble burst in 2000, exposing a sluggish economy. A recession that began in March 2001 was pushed deeper by the terrorist attack of Sept. 11, 2001 (see *World Trade Center Attack 2).

NEW ENGLAND CONFEDERATION (1643–84), military alliance among Massachusetts Bay, Hartford, New Haven, and Plymouth directed against the Dutch, French, and Indians. Two commissioners from each colony formed an executive committee with authority in all military affairs. The confederation was disbanded when the Massachusetts charter was abrogated.

NEW FRANCE (1608–1763), French colony in North America, founded at Quebec in 1608, that eventually stretched through the Great Lakes region and the entire Mississippi Valley. First left to private companies, the colony was taken under royal control by Louis XIV in 1661 and actively developed and extended.

During the *French and Indian Wars, which paralleled a series of European wars between England and France, English troops and colonists fought against the French and their Indian allies in North America. The capture of Quebec in 1759 sealed the doom of New France. By the Treaty of *Paris (1763), Canada and all French territory east of the Mississippi were ceded to England; French territory west of the Mississippi (Louisiana) passed to Spain.

NEW FREEDOM (1912), slogan adopted by Democratic presidential candidate Woodrow Wilson to contrast his policy toward big business with that of former president and *Progressive Party candidate Theodore Roosevelt.

Roosevelt believed that trusts and monopolies were natural developments; in his doctrine of the *New Nationalism, he proposed regulating them in the national interest. Wilson, on the other hand, believed that trusts developed from lack of competition, compounded by the advantages offered to large-scale capitalists by the banking system and protective tariff. Instead of regulating the trusts, which he foresaw leading to massive and pervasive government controls, Wilson proposed dismantling them and reforming the banking system and the protective tariff. In free competition among smaller economic units, he believed, talented individuals would be able to rise to their full potential unimpeded by monopoly and privilege.

Wilson's speeches of 1911 and 1912 developing this theme were published as *The New Freedom* (1912).

NEW FRONTIER, term selected by John F. Kennedy to describe his presidential campaign and legislative program. He first used it in accepting the Democratic presidential nomination in Los Angeles on July 15, 1960, when he said: "[T]he problems are not all solved and the battles are not all won—and we stand today on the edge of a new frontier—the frontier of the 1960s—a frontier of unknown opportunities and perils—a frontier of unfulfilled hopes and threats."

NEW GUINEA CAMPAIGN. See *World War 2.

NEWLANDS ACT (1913). See *Railroad Regulation.

NEWLANDS RECLAMATION ACT (1902). See *Conservation.

NEW LEFT (1960s), radical college and university students, distinguished from the **Old Left** (communist and socialist parties, labor unions) by indifference to doctrine, lack of bureaucratic organization, and a moralistic rather than an instrumental politics.

As the *baby boom generation approached maturity, unprecedented numbers of students entered the nation's colleges. A minority of them were awakened to societal problems and radicalized by the *civil rights movement, the war on poverty (see Lyndon *Johnson Administration), and the *Vietnam War.

The first manifestation of student radicalism was the **Free Speech Movement** on the Berkeley campus of the University of California in 1964, precipitated by the university's prohibiting the distribution of political literature on the campus. Student rebellions spread rapidly. The colleges and universities were perceived as large, impersonal, authoritarian, and controlling, preparing students not for freedom but for places in the corporate economy. Moreover, they were found to be complicit in the Vietnam War through government-contracted research and investments in military suppliers. Revolts against the universities culminated in May 1968 in a violent strike at Columbia University in New York City.

Student opposition to the Vietnam War began in March 1963 with the first Vietnam "teach-in" at the University of Michigan. Students were prominent in antiwar marches and demonstrations. They also picketed employee recruitment on campus by firms like Dow Chemical, occupied or tried to destroy campus ROTC buildings, and publicly burned draft cards and flags. Antiwar protests reached their height after the U.S. invasion of Cambodia in 1970. In May that year, four students at Kent State University in Ohio were killed by National Guardsmen and two at Jackson State College in Mississippi by police.

Of the many groups that constituted the New Left, the largest and most representative was **Students for a Democratic Society (SDS)**. Its moderate manifesto, the Port Huron Statement, drafted in 1962 by Tom Hayden and heavily influenced by the writings of sociologist C. Wright Mills and critic Paul Goodman, identified the social problems as perceived by middle-class youths: racial injustice, the cold war, personal alienation and helplessness, and the failure of mainstream politics. Pledging SDS to nonviolence and morality in politics, it especially emphasized the organization's commitment to "participatory democracy," by which it meant, on the small or organizational scale, group decision-making and, on the larger or national scale, the view that "politics have the function of bringing people out of isolation and into community."

SDS began with antipoverty and civil rights work in inner cities. Radicalized by the Vietnam War, it turned its energies against the universities, which it saw as pillars of the immoral society. As the war escalated, SDS became ever larger and more radical, refusing to exclude communists from its leadership, then abandoning peaceful protests for confrontation and civil disobedience. In 1969 the organization fragmented, an extreme element—the **Weathermen**—committing itself to revolutionary violence. In support of the *Chicago Seven, 300 Weathermen and other radicals rampaged through Chicago's streets in October 1969 in "Days of Rage."

For several months in 1969–70, Weathermen participated in a wave of bombings of corporate headquarters, university buildings, and federal offices. In March 1970, three Weathermen died in an explosion in a Greenwich Village townhouse where they were making bombs. Other Weathermen quickly disappeared underground. SDS lingered on until 1974.

NEW NATIONALISM, concept of the national government as active promoter of social justice, borrowed by former president Theodore Roosevelt from Herbert Croly's The *Promise of American Life* (1909) and used by him in his presidential campaign of 1912.

"The New Nationalism," Roosevelt explained at Osawatomie, Kans., on Aug. 31, 1910, "puts the national need before sectional or personal advantage. It is impatient of the utter confusion that results from local legislatures attempting to treat national issues as local issues. It is still more impatient of the impotence which springs from overdivision of governmental powers, the impotence which makes it possible for local selfishness or for legal cunning, hired by wealthy special interests, to bring national activities to a deadlock. This New Nationalism regards the executive power as the steward of the public welfare. It demands of the judiciary that it shall be interested primarily in human welfare rather than in property, just as it demands that the representative body shall represent all the people rather than any one class or section of the people."

NEW NETHERLAND (1624–64), Dutch colony in the Hudson River Valley. Some of the first 30 families settled in 1624 at Fort Orange (now Albany), a smaller number at the mouth of the Hudson on what is now Governors Island. In 1625 the latter group moved to Manhattan Island, which Gov. Peter Minuit bought from the Indians for $24 in trinkets and named **New Amsterdam**.

The government of the colony was entirely in the hands of the governor and the Dutch West India Co., which, to encourage colonization, provided in 1629 for the establishment of large feudal estates called patroonships (see *Patroons). Only one of these, Rensselaerswyck, proved successful. Small farmers were given as much free land as they could cultivate. The governorship of Peter Stuyvesant (1647–64) saw the beginning of self-government in the colony, constant warfare with Indians, and friction with the New England colonies, which encroached on territory claimed by the Dutch. In 1664, Stuyvesant surrendered New Netherland to an English fleet. The English renamed the colony New York.

NEW ORLEANS (Jan. 8, 1815), last battle of the *War of 1812, fought two weeks after the signing of the Treaty of *Ghent.

On Dec. 15, 1814, a large British fleet entered Lake Borgne, east of defenseless New Orleans, and began to disembark an army of veteran troops commanded by Gen. Edward Pakenham. Gen. Andrew Jackson, commander of the U.S. army in the southwest, declared martial law in New Orleans and conscripted the city's male population, forming a motley army of regulars, Creoles, sailors, pirates, blacks, and Tennessee and Kentucky volunteers.

On Dec. 23, Jackson attacked a British advance party at the Villere plantation, eight miles south of New Orleans. The fight was inconclusive, and Jackson withdrew two miles north and established a mile-long defensive line in a dry irrigation canal that ran from the Mississippi River to a cypress swamp. Here he placed the main body of his force—some 5,000 men and 12 batteries of artillery—to await the British attack. The British gathered their force slowly. A British attack on Dec. 26 was turned back by American artillery, and an artillery duel on Jan.1, 1815, ended in an American success.

Pakenham launched his major attack on Jan. 8. His army of 5,300 elite troops advanced in two columns through early-morning fog. When the fog lifted, the British were exposed to the view of the Americans waiting behind earthworks raised along the edge of the canal. Concentrated American fire from artillery, rifles, and muskets halted the British advance and inflicted horrendous casualties. Twice the British re-formed and attacked against devastating fire. Pakenham was killed. His next in command broke off the fight and withdrew. On Jan. 25 the British fleet sailed from Lake Borgne.

In two hours' combat on Jan. 8, the British had suffered 291 killed, 1,262 wounded, and 484 captured or missing; American losses were 13 killed, 39 wounded, 19 missing. "Such a disproportion in loss," Jackson reported to Washington, ". . . must, I know, excite astonishment, and may not, every where, be fully credited. . . ." The battle had no effect on the peace, but it closed a dreary and ignominious war with a burst of glory for Americans and made a military hero and future president of Jackson.

NEW ORLEANS CAPTURE (April 29, 1862), incident in the *Civil War. Campaigns in Tennessee during the early part of 1862 stripped Louisiana of Confederate troops. The city of New Orleans was protected only by a pair of forts on either side of the Mississippi River 75 miles below the city, some river batteries just below the city, a small fleet of gunboats, and 3,000 short-term militia in the city itself.

In February, Union commodore David G. Farragut took command of a task force in the Gulf of Mexico consisting of 8 shallow-draft steam sloops, 1 sailing sloop, 14 gunboats, 19 schooners, and transports carrying 15,000 troops under Gen. Benjamin Butler. In early April, his flotilla entered the Mississippi and anchored below the forts. When six days (Apr. 18–23) of concentrated mortar fire failed to reduce the forts, Farragut, in the early hours of Apr. 24, sent two gunboats under the forts to cut a chain holding a boom of hulks across the river. They succeeded in opening a space wide enough for the Union flotilla to proceed in single file.

Seventeen of Farragut's warships then steamed upriver past the forts, receiving and returning heavy fire from the forts and from Confederate gunboats. Four ships were lost and 137 men killed in the hour-and-a-half battle. (Four days later the forts surrendered.) The next morning Farragut's fleet silenced the river batteries below New Orleans and arrived before the hostile but defenseless city. Marines entered the city on Apr. 29; on May 1 Butler's troops began a strict occupation.

NEW SOUTH, term popularized by Henry Grady, editor of the Atlanta *Constitution*, in speeches to Northern audiences, particularly a famous address in New York in December 1886, to describe a rapidly industrializing post-Reconstruction South. After the Civil War, and especially after the depression of 1873–79, Northern and European capital poured into the South. Railroad construction, lumbering, and the manufacture of textiles, tobacco products, and iron and steel increased dramatically. The rest of the country, however, grew even more rapidly, and in 1900 the South remained predominantly rural and relatively poor.

NEW SWEDEN (1638–55), Swedish colony on the Delaware River. Its vigorous but autocratic governor, Johan Printz (1643–53), developed and expanded the colony, expelling English and Dutch fur traders. In 1655, the Dutch at New Netherland under Peter Stuyvesant seized New Sweden.

NEW YORK TIMES CO. v. SULLIVAN (1964), unanimous decision by the *Warren Court that criticism of the conduct of public officials, even if inaccurate, was protected by the First and *14th Amendments unless "actual malice" could be proved.

On Mar. 29, 1960, during the civil rights struggle in

Montgomery, Ala., the *New York Times* published an advertisement protesting the brutality of the Montgomery police. Because the ad's description of incidents of brutality contained several factual errors, the Montgomery police commissioner considered himself libeled and sued four signers of the ad and the New York Times Co. The Alabama circuit court and the Alabama supreme court upheld his claim, but the U.S. Supreme Court reversed them.

"[W]e consider this case," wrote Justice William J. Brennan for the Court, "against the background of a profound national commitment to the principle that debate on public issues should be uninhibited, robust, and wide-open, and that it may well include vehement, caustic, and sometimes unpleasantly sharp attacks on government and public officials. The present advertisement, as an expression of grievance and protest on one of the major public issues of our time, would seem clearly to qualify for the constitutional protection. The question is whether it forfeits that protection by the falsity of some of its factual statements and by its alleged defamation of respondent. . . .

"A rule compelling the critic of official conduct to guarantee the truth of all his factual assertions—and to do so on pain of libel judgments virtually unlimited in amount—leads to . . . 'self-censorship.' Allowance of the defense of truth, with the burden of proving it on the defendant, does not mean that only false speech will be deterred. Even courts accepting this defense as an adequate safeguard have recognized the difficulties of adducing legal proofs that the alleged libel was true in all its factual particulars. Under such a rule, would-be critics of official conduct may be deterred from voicing their criticism, even though it is believed to be true and even though it is in fact true, because of doubt whether it can be proved in court or fear of the expense of having to do so. . . . The rule thus dampens the vigor and limits the variety of public debate. It is inconsistent with the First and Fourteenth Amendments.

"The constitutional guarantees require, we think, a federal rule that prohibits a public official from recovering damages for a defamatory falsehood relating to his official conduct unless he proves that the statement was made with 'actual malice'—that is, with knowledge that it was false or with reckless disregard of whether it was false or not."

NEW YORK TIMES CO. v. UNITED STATES

(1971), 6–3 decision of the *Burger Court overturning an injunction against publication of the *Pentagon Papers in the *New York Times* and the *Washington Post*.

To prevent their publication, the *Nixon administration had sought and failed to get injunctions from district courts in New York City and the District of Columbia. The Court of Appeals for the Second Circuit, however, granted the injunction, which the *Times* appealed to the U.S. Supreme Court. In a per curiam (unsigned) opinion, the Court agreed with the district courts that the government had not met the burden of proof necessary to impose prior restraint on publication.

All nine justices wrote separate opinions in the case. "In the First Amendment," wrote Justice Hugo Black, "the Founding Fathers gave the free press the protection it must have to fulfill its essential role in our democracy. The press was to serve the governed, not the governors. The Government's power to censor the press was abolished so that the press would remain free to censure the Government. The press was protected so that it could bare the secrets of government and inform the people. Only a free and unrestrained press can effectively expose deception in government. And paramount among the responsibilities of a free press is the duty to prevent any part of the government from deceiving the people and sending them off to distant lands to die of foreign fevers and foreign shot and shell. . . . In revealing the workings of government that led to the Vietnam war, the newspapers nobly did precisely that which the Founders hoped and trusted they would do."

NEZ PERCÉ WAR

NEZ PERCÉ WAR (1877), Indian war precipitated by U.S. pressure to move "nontreaty" Nez Percés from Oregon to a tribal reservation in Idaho. Negotiations broke down when conflict erupted between Nez Percés and neighboring whites. Confronted by overwhelming military force, the Nez Percé chief, Joseph, determined to escape to Canada. From June to October, he led his band of 145 fighting men and 500 women and children 1,200 miles through Idaho, Montana, and Wyoming, fighting off their pursuers three times. In northern Montana, only 30 miles from the Canadian border, they were compelled to surrender to Col. Nelson A. Miles on Oct. 5, 1877. To his people, Chief Joseph declared: "I am tired; my heart is sick and sad. From where the sun now stands, I will fight no more forever."

NINETEENTH AMENDMENT

NINETEENTH AMENDMENT (1920), the woman suffrage amendment (see *Women's Rights), constitutional amendment declaring: "The right of citizens of the United States to vote shall not be denied or abridged by the United States or by any State on account of sex."

NINTH AMENDMENT.

NINTH AMENDMENT. See *Bill of Rights.

NIXON ADMINISTRATION

NIXON ADMINISTRATION (1969–74). Republican Richard M. Nixon, 37th president of the United States, was elected with 43.2 percent of the popular vote. A shrewd politician, Nixon as president abandoned a lifetime of ideological baggage and proved himself flexible and pragmatic. Largely indifferent to domestic affairs, he was often content to follow the lead of his Democrat-controlled Congress—except where his strategy for reelection was affected. As a result, the Nixon administration was the most liberal Republican administration since that of Theodore Roosevelt.

Welfare. Despite Nixon's inveighing against the "welfare mess," his administration saw increased spending for food stamps, Medicaid, and a greatly enlarged Aid to Families with Dependent Children (AFDC; see *Welfare). Supplemental Security Income (SSI) for the indigent aged, blind, and disabled was established in 1972. SSI and the newly federalized food stamp program were indexed to the cost of living. For a time, Nixon supported a Family Assistance Program (FAP), proposed by adviser Daniel Patrick Moynihan, a Democrat, that would have substituted a guaranteed annual income for all poor families in place of the complex and bureaucratic AFDC program, but he lost interest when the plan was opposed from both left and right.

Social Insurance. Congress raised *Social Security benefits and indexed them to the cost of living.

Civil Rights. Nixon approved extension of the *Voting Rights Act of 1965 and a measure banning sex discrimination in higher education. His administration pushed the concept of *affirmative action to the point of requiring government agencies and contractors to establish quotas and timetables for the hiring of minorities. On the other hand, it tried to delay *school desegregation—especially by means of court-ordered busing—to gain political advantage in the South and in Northern suburbs.

Environmentalism. Nixon saw no advantage in opposing the rising tide of environmental concern (see *Environmentalism). His administration saw passage of the National Environmental Policy Act (1969), the Water Improvement Act (1970), the Occupational Safety and Health Act (1970), the Clean Air Act (1970), the Federal Water Pollution Act (1972), and the Endangered Species Act (1973). Earth Day was celebrated for the first time on Apr. 22, 1970.

A professedly "law-and-order" administration, the Nixon administration initiated a number of anticrime acts in 1970, including the Organized Crime Control Act and the Drug Abuse Prevention and Control Act. It also ended the military draft, creating in its place the All Volunteer Force (see *Conscription). The *26th Amendment was ratified in 1971.

Nixon's primary interest was foreign affairs, where he saw an opportunity to exploit the hostility between the Soviet Union and the People's Republic of China. In pursuing this policy, he was aided by Henry Kissinger, national security adviser (1969–73) and secretary of state (1973–77). In 1970 and 1971, Nixon and Soviet premier Leonid Brezhnev secretly resolved Cuban and Berlin issues. Publicly in 1972, the two leaders signed a Strategic Arms Limitation Treaty (SALT 1) limiting the number and deployment of intercontinental ballistic missiles and another treaty restricting the deployment of defensive antiballistic missile systems (see *Arms Control and Disarmament). The new spirit of détente was welcomed on both sides. Also in 1972, Nixon paid a carefully prepared visit to China, where he was well received.

In Vietnam, Nixon pursued a policy of Vietnamization—removing American troops while increasing support for the South Vietnamese army—while raising pressure on North Vietnam through bombing for terms on which the United States could "honorably" withdraw from the war. In the end, he accepted terms that abandoned South Vietnam to inevitable defeat (see *Vietnam War). The last American troops were withdrawn from Vietnam in March 1973. In November, overriding a presidential veto, Congress passed the *War Powers Act limiting the president's power to take the country into war.

In 1973, Kissinger brokered a peace between Israel and Egypt in the Yom Kippur War.

The Nixon administration was the high point of the *imperial presidency, a product of the *cold war. Much of Nixon's foreign and military policy was conceived and executed in secrecy, outside normal administrative channels and without consultation with Congress. The power thus wielded by the president—magnified by his ability to control news and to command television time—was totally unprecedented. At the same time, Nixon's concern about opponents and enemies led him to employ federal intelligence and law-enforcement agencies in illegal surveillance and harassment of individuals and organizations on alleged grounds of national security. The civil liberties of the American people were violated by these domestic intelligence programs on a scale never before known (see *Church Committee; *Pentagon Papers; *Covert Operations; *Watergate).

No sooner had Nixon been reelected in 1972 by a huge margin than his "law-and-order" administration began to be revealed as a place of pervasive lawlessness. In January 1973 the seven "plumbers" caught breaking into the offices of the Democratic National Committee in the Watergate apartment complex the previous June went on trial. In October, Vice Pres. Spiro Agnew resigned and pleaded no contest to charges of evading federal income taxes on payoffs from construction companies while he was governor of Maryland and also vice president (Agnew was replaced as vice president by Speaker of the House Gerald Ford of Michigan). In May 1974, after nine months of investigation, the House Judiciary Committee began closed hearings on five impeachment resolutions against President Nixon passed by the House; in July, the committee voted three articles of impeachment. Advised that the Senate would certainly vote to convict, Nixon resigned on Aug. 9 and was succeeded by Vice Pres. Gerald Ford.

NIXON DOCTRINE (1969), casual statement by Pres. Richard M. Nixon during a stopover at Guam on a return trip from Vietnam that in the future the United States would expect Asian nations to assume responsibility for their own defense—"except for the threat of a major power involving nuclear weapons." The statement was basically an elaboration of the policy of Vietnamization then being implemented in the *Vietnam War, but the press treated it as a significant policy departure.

NOMINATING CONVENTIONS, periodic meetings of local, state, and national political parties to transact party business and, most important, to nominate candidates for public office. *Primary elections have generally replaced the nominating function of local and state conventions, but national party conventions every four years still nominate party candidates for president and vice president.

The national nominating convention was instituted as a democratic reform, replacing the congressional party *caucus as the source of party nominations. "King Caucus" was officially dethroned after the 1824 election. The first national conventions were held in 1831 by the *Anti-Masonic and the *National Republican parties. The Democratic-Republican Party (later the *Democratic Party) met for the first time in 1832. Convention procedures were formalized during the 1840s.

Delegates to national conventions were generally elected by state conventions until the 20th century, when the institution of primary elections permitted party members in some states to directly elect some or all of their state delegation to the national convention (some delegation slots are reserved for party leaders and office-

holders). In some states, party conventions continue to select delegates to the national convention.

NONINTERCOURSE ACT (1809). See *Embargo and Nonintercourse.

NONPARTISAN LEAGUE (1915–24), organization of North Dakota wheat farmers to protest monopolistic control of wheat marketing. Demanding state-owned grain elevators and mills, hail insurance, rural credits, and tax reform, the league in 1916 captured the state Republican Party, elected its ticket, and enacted its program. It quickly spread to other Western states, where it was less successful. The league's radical program made it suspect during World War 1 and it faded during the postwar depression.

NORMANDY INVASION. See *World War 2.

NORRIS–LA GUARDIA ACT (1932), legislation of the *Hoover administration. It effectively prohibited the use of court injunctions against strikes, boycotts, and picketing by labor unions after the anti-injunction provisions of the *Clayton Antitrust Act had been circumvented by the courts.

NORTH AMERICAN FREE TRADE AGREEMENT (NAFTA), *Clinton administration measure, approved by Congress in 1993, establishing an eventual free trade area consisting of Canada, the United States, and Mexico. An initiative of the George H. W. *Bush administration, it was taken up by Pres. William J. Clinton, a strong advocate of free trade. It was supported by business and Republicans, opposed by labor unions and some environmentalists (and thus by a majority of House Democrats) who feared that high-paying American manufacturing jobs would be moved to Mexico to take advantage of the low labor costs and the absence of environmental regulations there. To address these fears, the administration negotiated side agreements with Mexico on labor and environmental standards.

NORTH ATLANTIC TREATY ORGANIZATION (NATO), diplomatic achievement of the *Truman administration. A regional defense alliance among the United States, Canada, and ten European countries— Belgium, Denmark, France, Iceland, Italy, Luxembourg, the Netherlands, Norway, Portugal, and the United Kingdom—it was established in 1949 as part of the U.S. *cold war policy of *containment. Germany, Spain,

Greece, and Turkey joined later. It was the first peacetime military alliance in American history. With the end of the cold war, rather than disband, NATO expanded with the addition in 1999 of the Czech Republic, Poland, and Hungary. In 2002, Estonia, Latvia, Lithuania, Slovakia, Slovenia, Bulgaria, and Romania joined; Russia became an associate member.

NORTHERN SECURITIES CO. v. UNITED STATES (1904), 5–4 decision of the *Fuller Court dissolving a holding company formed by James J. Hill, Edward H. Harriman, and J.P. Morgan—three titans of Wall Street—to control the stock of the Great Northern and Northern Pacific railroads in violation of the *Sherman Antitrust Act. "What the Government particularly complains of," wrote Justice John Marshall Harlan for the Court, "indeed, all that it complains of here, is the existence of a combination among the stockholders of competing railroad companies which in violation of the act of Congress restrains interstate and international commerce through the agency of a common corporate trustee designated to act for both companies in repressing free competition between them."

To the vast annoyance of Pres. Theodore Roosevelt, who had appointed him in 1902, Justice Oliver Wendell Holmes dissented. Holmes found no restraint of trade in "an arrangement by which competition is ended through community of interest," a common occurrence in business. Although any railroad may be said to be a monopoly in the area it serves, Holmes went on, in the present case "there is no attempt to monopolize . . . until something is done with the intent to exclude strangers to the combination from competing with it in some part of the business which it carries on."

The suit was initiated by Roosevelt to demonstrate his opposition to the *trusts. His success revitalized the Sherman Act and greatly enhanced his own popularity.

NORTHWEST TERRITORY, created in 1787 by the Congress under the *Articles of Confederation. The territory embraced the "Old Northwest," the region northwest of the Ohio River. Between 1781 and 1784, New York, Massachusetts, Connecticut, and Virginia ceded to the *Confederation government territorial claims in this region deriving from their colonial charters, thus creating a public domain that the Congress regarded as a potential source of revenue from land sales as well as a place where veterans of the Revolutionary War could redeem the land warrants given them in payment for their service.

In the **Ordinance of 1785,** the Confederation Congress ordered the region surveyed and divided into six-mile-square townships, each subdivided into 36 one-mile-square (640 acres) sections, the smallest unit to be sold to settlers at a price of $1 per acre. The plan ensured the orderly settlement of the region (unlike the Southern frontier) but, since few settlers could afford or wanted an entire section, also ensured that speculators would buy up large areas at discount prices and resell them profitably in small parcels to settlers.

The **Ordinance of 1787**—the most important act of the Confederation Congress—was written in New York at the same time that the new federal constitution was being drafted in Philadelphia. It organized the Old Northwest politically, establishing a congressionally appointed governor, secretary, and judges, and providing for an elected territorial legislature. A humane and liberal document, it forbade primogeniture, thus preventing the preservation of large hereditary estates; it provided a bill of rights for inhabitants of the territory that included freedom of religion, habeas corpus, jury trial, and bail for all but capital offenses; and it prohibited slavery. "Religion, morality, and knowledge, being necessary to good government and the happiness of mankind," the Ordinance observed, "schools and the means of education shall forever be encouraged." And: "The utmost good faith shall always be observed toward the Indians. . . ."

Most important, the Ordinance established the steps by which portions of the territory, as their populations grew, could form states that would be admitted to the Union on a basis of equality with existing states. This method of territorial organization and state formation, which served the country thereafter, prevented the development of a U.S. colonialism such as the American colonies had themselves escaped from.

Migration into the Northwest Territory was slow until 1794. In that year Great Britain evacuated military posts it had retained south of the Great Lakes in violation of the Treaty of *Paris that ended the Revolutionary War, and Gen. Anthony Wayne broke the power of hostile Indians in the battle of *Fallen Timbers (Aug. 20) near present-day Toledo, Ohio. Thereafter, swelling streams of settlers entered the territory from the Great Lakes in the north and the Ohio River in the south. In 1800 the Northwest Territory was divided into Ohio and Indiana territories and thereafter into smaller territories. Eventually five states were created out of the Northwest Territory: Ohio (1803), Indiana (1816), Illinois (1818), Michigan (1837), and Wisconsin (1848).

NUCLEAR ENERGY. During the *oil shock of the 1970s, policy makers viewed nuclear energy as most likely to replace oil and gas in the generation of electricity. They confidently envisioned 1,000 large nuclear reactors satisfying 40 percent of the nation's total energy requirements by the year 2000.

Disenchantment followed fast as the nuclear power industry encountered construction delays, steeply rising construction and operating costs, low operating efficiency, declining growth in electricity consumption, and growing concern over reactor safety fueled by the *Three Mile Island accident in 1979 and the Chernobyl disaster in the Soviet Union in 1986. Moreover, planners had underestimated the costs of dismantling obsolete nuclear plants and the environmental impact of disposing of nuclear wastes.

At the start of the 21st century, 104 reactors were providing 20 percent of the nation's electricity. No new plants had been ordered since 1978, and all orders placed between 1973 and 1978—for 108 plants—had been canceled. The George W. Bush administration, committed to enlarging energy supplies by increased extraction of coal and oil, took a positive view toward accelerating the production of nuclear energy.

NULLIFICATION, doctrine that each state had a right to suspend within its borders the operation of a federal law that it deemed unconstitutional. The doctrine reflected uncertainty about the nature of the federal union that prevailed until the *Civil War.

The Framers understood the Constitution as an act of the whole people, not a compact among states (see Federal *Constitutional Convention). That the meaning of federalism was not understood or accepted by many Americans is evidenced by the survival of the *Antifederalist tradition, at first in the *Jeffersonian Republican Party but later in the *Federalist Party itself. The Framers' expectation that the federal courts would in time define the nature of the federal union was frustrated by the Republican challenge to the federal courts, which they regarded as part of the problem rather than the solution.

The theory of nullification was first developed in the *Virginia and Kentucky Resolutions (1798), written by Thomas Jefferson and James Madison to protest the *Alien and Sedition Acts. They received no support from the other states, to which they appealed for *collective* resistance to unconstitutional acts of the federal government. Connecticut and Massachusetts appealed to a form of nullification when they violated President Jefferson's Embargo Act of 1807 (see *Embargo and Nonintercourse). Georgia successfully defied a U.S. treaty with the Creek Indians and later a decision of the U.S. Supreme

Court. But the defining act of nullification was South Carolina's resistance to the tariffs of 1828 and 1832.

Outraged by the *Tariff of Abominations, the South Carolina legislature asked John C. Calhoun to prepare a rationale for resistance. This he did in the *South Carolina Exposition and Protest, in which he argued, anonymously, that a state could nullify federal legislation within its own borders, subject only to a constitutional amendment specifically giving the federal government the disputed power. When Congress passed a new and still unacceptable tariff in 1832, the South Carolina legislature, controlled by nullifiers, assembled a convention at Columbia in November 1832 and adopted an ordinance declaring the tariffs of 1828 and 1832 "null, void, and no law," forbade state and federal officers to collect duties in the state, forbade appeals from state to federal courts, and warned that if the federal government attempted to enforce the tariffs the state would secede.

Pres. Andrew Jackson responded vigorously. On Dec. 10, 1832, he issued a **Proclamation to the People of South Carolina** refuting the doctrine of nullification. "I consider," he declared, ". . . the power to annul a law of the United States, assumed by one State, incompatible with the existence of the Union, contradicted expressly by the letter of the Constitution, unauthorized by its spirit, inconsistent with every principle on which it was founded, and destructive of the just object for which it was formed." He sought and received from Congress a **Force Bill** authorizing him to use the armed forces to compel South Carolina's compliance with the law.

At the same time, Jackson asked Congress to revise downward the 1832 tariff schedules to mollify South Carolina. Senators Henry Clay and Calhoun prepared and rushed through Congress a new tariff bill that reduced rates over a nine-year period (see *Compromise of 1833). Jackson signed both the revised tariff and the Force Act on Mar. 2, 1833. The South Carolina convention reassembled, nullified the Force Act, but repealed its ordinance nullifying the tariffs of 1828 and 1832. The nullifiers were a minority in South Carolina and no other Southern state supported them. Both sides claimed victory in the confrontation, but it is clear that Jackson preserved the Union in a particularly dangerous crisis.

Twenty years later, the spirit of nullification reappeared in the North in response to the Fugitive Slave Act of 1850 (see *Fugitive Slave Laws) and the Dred Scott case (see *Scott v. Sandford) in 1857. In the 20th century it revived after the Supreme Court's decision in 1954 declaring segregation in public schools unconstitutional.

NYE MUNITIONS INVESTIGATION (1934–36), episode of the Franklin *Roosevelt administration. In response to pressure from peace organizations, a special Senate committee was appointed in 1934 to investigate the armaments industry—"merchants of death," as the title of a best-selling 1934 book called it. The committee chairman was Sen. Gerald P. Nye of North Dakota, a progressive Republican and staunch isolationist.

On the basis of the huge profits made by firms like du Pont and Bethlehem Shipbuilding during World War 1 and the exposed machinations of the armament industry's executives, some witnesses alleged that the industry actually fomented and prolonged wars. To "take the profit out of war," the committee recommended that the government be empowered to fix prices in wartime and tax away excess profits and inflated salaries. It only narrowly failed to endorse nationalization of the armaments industry. Its recommendations were unpalatable not only to business but to the administration as well.

O

OIL SHOCK (1973). In 1973, nearly half of America's energy needs were supplied by oil, and more than a third of that oil was imported. When Arab oil producers that year embargoed shipments to the United States and the Organization of Oil Exporting Countries (OPEC) quadrupled the price of its oil (world oil prices tripled again in 1974–80), the result in the United States was an acute gasoline shortage, double-digit inflation, and in 1975 a sharp recession.

The federal government responded with measures encouraging energy conservation, use of coal in place of oil, and increased production of coal and domestic oil. It approved an *Alaska pipeline, licensed new *nuclear energy plants, and launched programs to develop synthetic fuels. Of all these initiatives aimed at energy independence, conservation proved the most successful: between 1973 and 1980, energy consumption in the United States grew only 2.3 percent compared to 51.5 percent in the 1960s and 11.7 percent between 1970 and 1973.

The crisis was relieved in the 1980s by a glut of oil on the world market.

OKINAWA. See *World War 2.

OKLAHOMA CITY BOMBING (Apr. 19, 1995), act of domestic *terrorism in which a rented truck loaded with ammonium nitrate fertilizer and diesel fuel was detonated outside the Alfred P. Murrah Federal Office Building in Oklahoma City, Okla., destroying the building, killing 169 people (including children in a day care center), and damaging many nearby buildings.

The bombing occurred on the second anniversary of the assault by federal agents on the Branch Davidian compound near Waco, Tex. (see *Waco Siege), an event that deeply angered members of the *Radical Right. Suspects were quickly identified and apprehended. Timothy McVeigh, a recent army veteran, gun enthusiast, drifter, reader of white-supremacist literature, and hater of the federal government, was convicted in June 1997 of conspiracy and murder and sentenced to death. A friend, Terry L. Nichols, was convicted in a separate trial later that year of conspiracy and involuntary manslaughter and sentenced to life imprisonment.

The remnants of the Murrah Building were razed, and the site was turned into a memorial park.

OLD LEFT. See *New Left.

OPEN DOOR POLICY (1899–1900), diplomatic initiative of the *McKinley administration. The United States had not participated in the seizure of treaty ports and the carving-out of spheres of influence in China by the major European powers and Japan. However, it saw in the progressive partition of China and the weakening of the imperial authority threats to its own growing economic interest in China.

To ensure equality of treatment of all foreign trade throughout China, Secretary of State John Hay on Sept. 6, 1899, sent a circular letter to the powers asking each to subscribe to three principles: (1) noninterference with any treaty port or vested interest within its sphere of influence; (2) continued collection by the Chinese of existing tariffs within its sphere of influence; (3) nondiscrimination in harbor dues and railroad rates within its sphere of influence in favor of its own nationals. All the powers accepted on condition that all the others did so. On Mar. 20, 1900, Hay informed the powers that all had agreed and that "this Government will therefore consider the assent given to [this policy—i.e., the Open Door] as final and definitive."

A few weeks later, during the *Boxer Rebellion, Hay, on July 3, again circularized the powers to make clear that "the policy of the government of the United States is to . . . preserve Chinese territorial and administrative entity, protect all rights guaranteed to friendly powers by treaty and international law, and safeguard for the world the principle of equal and impartial trade with all parts of the Chinese Empire."

OPEN SKIES (1955), proposal by Pres. Dwight D. Eisenhower on July 22, 1955, at a Geneva summit conference that the United States and the Soviet Union open their skies to each other's aircraft, providing bases from which they could operate, to permit effective mutual inspection as a first step toward disarmament. The Soviets rejected the proposal out of hand.

OPPENHEIMER AFFAIR (1953–54), incident in the *Eisenhower administration. In November 1953, the Federal Bureau of Investigation sent to Pres. Dwight D. Eisenhower a report suggesting the disloyalty of J. Robert Oppenheimer, the brilliant theoretical physicist who had directed the Los Alamos laboratory during World War 2 when the *atomic bomb was built. Concerned that the information would reach red-baiting Sen. Joseph R. McCarthy and be exploited by him to the embarrassment of the administration (see *McCarthyism), Eisenhower ordered the Atomic Energy Commission (AEC) to investigate the matter and meanwhile to place a "blank wall" between Oppenheimer, who held consultant contracts with the AEC and the Department of Defense, and secret data.

From Apr. 12 to May 6, 1954, a three-man AEC Personnel Security Board held hearings on the Oppenheimer allegations. As Oppenheimer himself willingly admitted, as a young man he had been entirely absorbed in physics and literature and had no interest in economics or politics. He had not voted, did not read newspapers or magazines, did not own a radio or telephone. In 1936, however, events in Germany, the Spanish Civil War, and the effects of the Great Depression on his students awoke him to public issues. Like many intellectuals of the period, he found himself in agreement with some positions held by the Communist Party, although he rejected the party's dogma and never became a member. His wife, however, and his brother and sister-in-law, had been party members for a time, as were many of his academic friends. Oppenheimer joined organizations and supported causes that were later identified by the *House Committee on Un-American Activities as communist fronts.

All this had been known before his appointment to Los Alamos but took on new significance in light of current criteria for determining loyalty (see *Anticommunism). Moreover, his testimony before the board raised issues of arguable lack of candor and especially questions about his opposition to the development of the *hydrogen bomb. (Lewis Strauss, then chairman of the AEC, had been a strong proponent of the bomb, and Eisenhower was critical of Oppenheimer for not taking part in the program once the decision to build the bomb had been made.)

On May 27, the Security Board voted 2–1 to end Oppenheimer's security clearance, the majority feeling that under current guidelines "any doubts whatsoever must be resolved in favor of the national security." The AEC accepted the board's recommendation 4–1, finding, in Strauss's words, "fundamental defects in [Oppenheimer's] 'character'" and "persistent and continuing association with Communists."

In 1963, Pres. Lyndon B. Johnson presented to Oppenheimer the AEC's highest honor, the Fermi Award.

ORDINANCES OF 1785 AND 1787. See *Northwest Territory.

OREGON DISPUTE (1818–46). Oregon country lay west of the Rocky Mountains between the 42nd parallel and 54° 40'. Spanish and Russian claims in the area having been relinquished, the United States and Great Britain remained the only claimants. By the Anglo-American *Convention of 1818, the two countries agreed on joint occupancy of Oregon for ten years; in 1827 this arrangement was extended indefinitely. Pres. John Quincy Adams proposed dividing the country at the 49th parallel—that is, extending the U.S.-Canadian border established by the Convention of 1818 to the Pacific. The British rejected this proposal, wanting to retain the Columbia River.

Oregon did not become a serious issue for the two countries until American settlers began to migrate there in organized fashion in 1841 (see *Oregon Trail). In his first annual message to Congress in December 1845, Pres. James K. Polk claimed all of Oregon for the United States, and in May 1846, with congressional approval, he gave the British the required one-year notice that he was terminating the joint-occupancy agreement. Bellicose expansionists had already taken up the cry "Fifty-four forty or fight!"

Rankled at first, the British proved conciliatory. The British foreign secretary, Lord Aberdeen, submitted a draft treaty accepting a division at the 49th parallel with the island of Vancouver remaining British. At the same time, he also made clear that Britain would not interfere between the United States and Mexico (see *Mexican War). Polk submitted this treaty to the Senate, which ratified it on June 15, 1846. Oregon Territory, extending from the 42nd to the 49th parallels, was organized in 1848.

OREGON'S VOYAGE (Mar. 19–May 24, 1898), incident in the *Spanish-American War. In preparation for war with Spain in the Caribbean, the U.S. Navy Department ordered the 10,288-ton battleship *Oregon* to leave San Francisco and join Commodore Winfield S. Schley's squadron at Key West, Fla. The ship accomplished the 14,000-mile voyage around South America by way of the Strait of Magellan in 68 days, arriving in time to participate in the destruction of the Spanish fleet outside Santiago, Cuba, on July 3. The voyage dramatized the necessity of an isthmian canal.

OREGON TRAIL, overland route of emigrants from Missouri to Oregon. Pioneered by fur trappers and traders, the trail was traversed by small parties of migrants beginning in 1839. From 1843, the year of the "Great Emigration," annual migrations exceeded 1,000 people.

The journey usually began at Independence on the Missouri River in western Missouri. The trail proceeded to Fort Kearney on the Platte River in present-day Nebraska, followed the Platte and North Platte to Fort Laramie in present-day Wyoming, then followed the Sweetwater River. It crossed the Continental Divide through South Pass to reach Fort Bridger in the southwest corner of Wyoming. From there it led overland to Fort Hall on the Snake River in present-day Idaho; migrants to California here turned south to Nevada (see *California Trail). The Oregon Trail then continued along the Snake River to the Blue Mountains, which it crossed before descending the Columbia River to Fort Vancouver in Oregon. From there the migrants dispersed into the fertile Willamette Valley.

Most migrants traveled in families with their household goods in covered wagons generally pulled by six oxen. Additional oxen, cows, and horses accompanied the wagons. The 2,000-mile journey had to be accomplished between the appearance of spring grass (necessary for the cattle) on the plains and winter snow in the mountain passes.

With the completion of the *transcontinental railroad in 1869, travel on the trail declined and finally ceased in the 1870s.

ORGANIZATION OF AMERICAN STATES (OAS), international organization founded at Bogotá, Colombia, in 1948 for the defense and the "economic, social, and cultural development of the peoples of the [Western] Hemisphere." Headquartered in Washington, D.C., where the **Pan-American Union** serves as its secretariat, it comprises the 35 independent states of North, Central, and South America and the Caribbean. Cuba was excluded in 1962 because of its Marxist-Leninist ideology. Resentment of U.S. dominance and criticism of U.S. policy toward Cuba, the Falkland Islands, Grenada, Nicaragua, Panama, and Haiti have been persistent in the organization.

ORISKANY (Aug. 6, 1777), *Revolutionary War battle. Coming to the relief of Fort Stanwix, which was besieged by Col. Barry St. Leger's force of Loyalists and Indians (see *Saratoga Campaign), Patriot general Nicholas Herkimer led a mile-long column of 800 militia and oxcarts into a marshy-bottomed ravine two miles from the village of Oriskany, N.Y., and six miles from the fort. There they were ambushed by 400 of St. Leger's men. Bloody hand-to-hand fighting raged for hours. Eventually the Loyalists and Indians withdrew and the Patriot survivors retreated to their base without relieving the fort. Mortally wounded, Herkimer died ten days later.

ORPHAN TRAINS (1854–1929), social experiment conducted by the New York Children's Aid Society, the New York Foundling Hospital, and other humanitarian agencies by which some 200,000 orphaned, abandoned, neglected, or poor children, often immigrants, were sent in groups from East Coast cities to small towns in the West where they were taken in by rural families. The agencies believed that the children would be better off in wholesome rural environments, away from the cities' squalor. Many children were indeed well provided for, but many others were abused and treated as slave laborers. The program ended with the onset of the Great Depression.

OSTEND MANIFESTO (1854), policy recommendation toward Cuba drafted by James Buchanan, John Mason, and Pierre Soulé—U.S. ministers to Great Britain, France, and Spain respectively—at Ostend, Belgium, at the request of Secretary of State William L. Marcy.

"It must be clear to every reflecting mind," the ministers (all proslavery Democrats) wrote, "that, from the peculiarity of its geographical position, . . . Cuba is as necessary to the North American republic as any of its present members, and that it belongs naturally to that great family of States of which the Union is the providential nursery." If Spain, "dead to the voice of her own interest, and actuated by stubborn pride and a false sense of honor, should refuse to sell Cuba to the United States . . . then, by every law, human and divine, we shall be justified in wresting it from Spain. . . ."

Marcy repudiated the doctrine; Soulé resigned; and Buchanan was elected (1856) president of the United States.

OTHER AMERICA, THE (1962), book by Michael Harrington that called the attention of the "affluent society" to the existence of 40–50 million "invisible" poor in their midst (see *Poverty). Some were invisible because they lived in depressed rural areas, others because they were segregated in inner cities. These were "new" poor who had been left behind when the rest of the country moved out of the *Great Depression. Minorities, the mentally and physically ill, the incompetent, uneducated, and unskilled—all were mired in a "culture of poverty" marked by apathy, hopelessness, and helplessness.

"To be impoverished," Harrington wrote, "is to be an internal alien, to grow up in a culture that is radically different from the one that dominates the society." The problem could be addressed only by the federal government, which must do so in a comprehensive and magnanimous way. Harrington's book inspired the War on Poverty undertaken by the Lyndon *Johnson administration.

P

PANAMA CANAL. The acquisition of California in 1848 and the discovery of gold there the same year excited interest in the United States in a canal across Central America that would connect the Atlantic and Pacific Oceans. The **Clayton-Bulwer Treaty** (1850) with Great Britain envisioned a joint Anglo-American enterprise, but this was never popular in the United States. The *Spanish-American War dramatized the need for a canal entirely in American hands. By the **Hay-Pauncefote Treaty** (1901), Britain acquiesced in an entirely American project, which Pres. Theodore Roosevelt was determined to accomplish.

During the 1880s, a French company had tried and failed to build a canal across the Isthmus of Panama, then part of Colombia. By the **Hay-Herrán Treaty** (1903) with Colombia, the United States, which proposed to buy French rights in Panama for $40 million, secured the right to build its canal for $10 million. When the Colombian congress rejected the treaty in expectation of a larger payment, Roosevelt arranged with Philippe Bunau-Varilla, a representative of the French interests, to support a revolution arranged by him that would result in the independence of Panama.

The revolution came off on Nov. 3, with U.S. naval vessels standing offshore to prevent a Colombian response. On Nov. 6 the U.S. recognized the independent republic of Panama. And on Nov. 18, 1903, by the **Hay–Bunau-Varilla Treaty**, Panama granted to the United States in perpetuity a ten-mile-wide strip of land across the isthmus for construction of a canal.

Roosevelt's chicanery in this series of events was castigated by some moralists but heartily approved by a chauvinistic public. He himself wrote in extenuation: "To talk of Colombia as a responsible Power to be dealt with as we would deal with Holland or Belgium or Switzerland or Denmark is a mere absurdity. The analogy is with a group of Sicilian or Calabrian bandits. . . . You could no more make an agreement with the Colombian rulers than you could nail currant jelly to a wall."

In 1922 the United States paid Colombia $25 million "to remove all misunderstandings growing out of the political events in Panama in November 1903."

Authorized by Congress in 1902, construction of the canal was delayed by indecision between a sea-level and a lock canal as well as by high mortality caused by disease. The sanitation work of Col. William C. Gorgas led to the eradication of *malaria and *yellow fever in the Canal Zone. In 1906 Roosevelt decided on a lock canal, and in 1907 he appointed Col. George W. Goethals of the U.S. Army Corps of Engineers chief engineer of the project. The canal, 40.3 miles long between Cristobal on the Caribbean and Balboa on the Pacific, was opened to traffic on Aug. 15, 1914, although not completed and formally dedicated until July 12, 1920.

The *Panama Canal Treaties signed in 1977 by the United States and Panama returned the Canal Zone to Panamanian jurisdiction with full control of the canal to revert to Panama on Dec. 31, 1999. In the interim, the United States retained responsibility for the operation, maintenance, and defense of the canal. Both signatories agreed to maintain the neutrality of the canal.

PANAMA CANAL TREATIES (1977), diplomatic achievement of the *Carter administration. Although the 1903 Hay–Bunau-Varilla Treaty (see *Panama Canal) gave the United States sovereignty in perpetuity over a ten-mile-wide Canal Zone in Panama, anti-American rioting in Panama in January 1964 caused Pres. Lyndon Johnson to promise to renegotiate control of the canal. Subsequent administrations agreed on the principles of a new treaty, and on Sept. 7, 1977, Pres. James E. Carter and Panamanian "Supreme Leader" Omar Torrijos Herrera signed two treaties.

The first, the Panama Canal Treaty, transferred control of the canal to Panama on Dec. 31, 1999, Panama assuming an increasing role in the canal's operation and an increasing share in its revenues in the interim. The second, the Neutrality Treaty, obligated Panama to keep the canal neutral and open to all nations. Amendments added by the U.S. Senate gave both countries the right, should the canal be closed, to use force to reopen it but prohibited U.S. intervention in Panama's internal affairs.

PANAMA CONGRESS (1826), meeting of delegates of Latin American republics called by Simón Bolívar to which the United States was invited. Pres. John Quincy Adams and Secretary of State Henry Clay favored U.S. attendance, and although the invitation was controversial the Senate approved and the House appropriated funds. President Adams appointed two delegates, but one died en route and the other had got only as far as Mexico City when the congress adjourned. The delegates signed a treaty of confederation, but their governments did not ratify it and no subsequent congress was held.

PANAMA INVASION (1989), incident in the George H. W. *Bush administration. Gen. Manuel Antonio Noriega, commander of the Panama Defense Forces (PDF), had been useful to the United States in its support of the Contras in Nicaragua before he discovered more lucrative opportunities in the service of the Medellín drug cartel in Colombia. In 1988 a federal grand jury in Miami indicted Noriega on a variety of drug charges but had no way of bringing him to trial. Economic sanctions against Panama and a coup by the PDF failed to dislodge him. Moreover, in May 1989 Noriega refused to let a newly elected president of Panama take office and thereafter ruled Panama dictatorially.

On Dec. 20, 1989, in Operation Just Cause, 22,000 U.S. troops invaded Panama from the Canal Zone and fought their way to Noriega's headquarters in Panama City. Noriega took refuge in the Vatican embassy but surrendered on Jan. 3, 1990. He was taken to Miami, tried and convicted of cocaine trafficking, and imprisoned.

Operation Just Cause cost 23 American lives and the lives of more than 500 Panamanians. Originally welcomed by the Panamanians, it aroused a nationalist reaction as a violation of the U.S.-Panamanian Neutrality Treaty of 1977 (see *Panama Canal Treaties) and by the death and destruction it wreaked on Panama.

PANAMA TOLLS REPEAL (1914), incident in the *Wilson administration. In the Panama Tolls Act (1913), Congress exempted U.S. coastal shipping from payment of *Panama Canal tolls. This violated the Hay-Pauncefote Treaty (1902), in which the United States had pledged that the canal would be open on equal terms to all nations. Great Britain protested, and President Wilson obtained repeal of the act in June 1914.

PAN-AMERICAN UNION. See *Organization of American States (OAS).

PAN AM FLIGHT 103 BOMBING (Dec. 21, 1988), terrorist act allegedly committed by a Libyan-sponsored Palestinian group that put a suitcase containing as much as 30 pounds of plastic explosive aboard a Pan American Boeing 747 jetliner at Frankfurt, West Germany. The plane stopped at London and was en route to New York when the suitcase bomb in the forward cargo hold exploded at 31,000 feet over Lockerbie, Scotland. All 259 people aboard the plane, including 189 Americans, were killed, as were 11 people on the ground when the plane's wreckage plowed through two rows of houses.

In 1991, the United States indicted two Libyan intelligence officers in the bombing, in effect accusing the government of Muammar Qaddafi of complicity. After considerable negotiation involving concerned governments and the United Nations, Qaddafi, on Apr. 5, 1999, turned over the two suspects to be tried in the Netherlands before a Scottish court. In return, the United Nations lifted economic sanctions against Libya. In January 2001, one Libyan was convicted for his part in the bombing while the second was acquitted (see *Terrorism).

PANIC OF 1837, financial panic followed by a severe depression lasting until 1843, the worst the country had yet experienced.

The removal of federal funds from the Bank of the United States and their deposit in state banks (see *Bank War) fueled speculation in *public lands and borrowing by states to finance ambitious *internal improvements. On June 23, 1836, Congress passed a Surplus Revenue Act directing that the surplus in the federal Treasury be distributed as loans to the states rather than deposited in state banks. On July 11, 1836, Pres. Andrew Jackson issued his Specie Circular requiring that the Treasury accept only specie (gold and silver) in payment for public land. At the same time, a financial crisis in England caused British creditors to call in American loans.

The resulting contraction of credit brought on a financial panic. Bank closings, unemployment, hunger, and rioting followed. The depression was most heavily felt in the West and South.

PANIC OF 1857, financial panic following upon a decade of prosperity fueled by California gold, speculation in railroads, and expansion of manufacturing. The depression that followed intensified sectional differences as the Civil War approached: the South, prospering with cotton, blocked the tariff protection and free public lands wanted by Eastern manufacturers and Middle Western farmers.

PANIC OF 1873, business collapse initiated by the failure of the great banking house of Jay Cooke and Co., financiers of the Civil War, that was followed by a severe economic depression lasting until 1879. Its complex causes included overexpansion of railroad construction, excessive speculation, business corruption and fraud, an inadequate banking system, and a distrusted paper currency (see *Greenbacks).

The depression that followed was marked by the bankruptcies of many railroads, thousands of other business failures, and the destitution of many working people. Nascent labor unions were destroyed; spontaneous strikes like the *railroad strikes of 1877 were disorganized, violent, and futile. Hard-pressed farmers turned to the *Granger movement, inflationists to the *Greenback Party. The *Grant and *Hayes administrations had no nostrum other than to wait for the return of "business confidence." This was supposed to be inspired by the *Specie Resumption Act (1875), which reaffirmed the country's commitment to the *gold standard, but was more likely occasioned by the return of bumper farm crops in the United States and scarcity abroad.

PANIC OF 1893, financial crisis that led to a severe economic depression lasting until 1897. Its complex causes included overexpansion of railroad construction, industrial manufacturing, and agricultural production; draining U.S. gold reserves (exacerbated by the *Sherman Silver Purchase Act [1890]) and consequent contraction of the money supply and of credit; and the withdrawal of foreign capital.

A prolonged agricultural depression preceded the panic (see *Agrarian Discontents). Then, ten days before the end of the Benjamin *Harrison administration and without warning, the Philadelphia and Reading Railroad went bankrupt. Other businesses and banks quickly followed. By the end of 1893, 500 banks and 16,000 businesses had closed. Unemployment in 1894 was estimated

at 2.5 million (although reliable statistics are lacking). Highways and railways were populated by wandering tramps; city streets sheltered unnumbered homeless. The year 1894 witnessed 1,394 strikes (including the *Pullman strike) as well as popular protests like *Coxey's Army. In August 1896 stock prices stood at 68 percent of their August 1892 level.

The second *Cleveland administration obtained the hasty repeal of the Sherman Silver Purchase Act, but that had no effect on the crisis; thereafter Cleveland grimly, even courageously, defended the *gold standard, but business confidence failed to revive. Increasingly, large portions of the country—particularly the West and South—attributed the problem to an inadequate money supply. The stage was set for the battle between *free silver and sound money in the presidential election of 1896. But by then recovery was already under way.

PANIC OF 1907, incident in the Theodore *Roosevelt administration. Called "the bankers' panic," it resulted from excess speculation and a shortage of credit. Several unexpected business failures led to runs on banks and a stock market panic in October. To relieve the crisis, the government made large deposits in several banks, and a group of bankers headed by J. P. Morgan spent $40 million rescuing others (see *Morgan's Career).

To save one brokerage house, Morgan obtained from President Roosevelt permission for U.S. Steel to buy stock in a competitor, the Tennessee Coal and Iron Co., owned by the broker. Pres. William Howard Taft's prosecution of U.S. Steel under the *Sherman Antitrust Act for this acquisition contributed to the *Roosevelt-Taft split.

Europeans criticized the United States for lacking a central bank, a condition remedied by the *Aldrich-Vreeland Act (1908) and the *Federal Reserve Act (1913).

PANIC OF 1929, stock market crash that precipitated the *Great Depression. In reality, the "crash" was a two-month decline punctuated by a number of steep sell-offs.

An industrial boom in the first half of the 1920s led into a bull market on Wall Street. Speculative fever affected not only individuals but banks and other financial institutions as well. Contemporaries imagined that they had entered a new era of permanent prosperity. Much of the decade's consumer buying and stock speculation, however, was financed by credit.

In the spring and summer of 1929 economic indicators pointed to a business downturn, but warning voices went unheeded. The bull market peaked on Sept. 3, 1929, when the Dow Jones industrial average closed at 381 (up from 191 only 18 months before), then drifted down for several weeks. On Monday, Oct. 21, and again on Wednesday, Oct. 23, there were steep sell-offs. On Thursday, Oct. 24 (**Black Thursday**), stocks plummeted. A group of bankers bought heavily to support prices and the market stabilized briefly, but on Monday, Oct. 28, the Dow fell 38 points and on Tuesday, Oct. 29 (Black Tuesday), it fell another 30, closing at 230. A brief recovery was followed by further collapses in November. At the end of the year, the Dow—having closed as low as 199 on Nov. 13—closed at 248, down 35 percent from its Sept. 3 high.

The **stock market crash** did not cause the depression. Only 4 million Americans (out of a population of 120 million) owned stocks and most of them only a few shares (74 percent of all dividends in 1929 went to only 600,000 shareholders). But it put an abrupt end to the optimism that had supported market speculation and credit-based consumption, exposing fundamental weaknesses in the economy. The loss of $30 billion in assets set in motion widening circles of personal ruin, business and bank failures, factory closings, and rising unemployment that the economy could not sustain.

PAOLI MASSACRE (Sept. 21, 1777), incident in the *Revolutionary War. Ten days after the battle of *Brandywine, British troops staged a night attack on a small Patriot force under Gen. Anthony Wayne encamped near Paoli, Pa. In a confused retreat, the Patriots suffered heavy casualties. The fact that the British had removed the charges from their muskets to prevent premature firing gave rise to the legend that they had surprised the unguarded camp and silently bayoneted the Americans while they slept.

PARIS PACT (1928). See *Kellogg-Briand Peace Pact or Pact of Paris.

PARIS PEACE CONFERENCE (1919–20), meeting of World War 1 victors that drew up the peace treaties with their former enemies, the principal one being the **Treaty of Versailles** with Germany.

Determined to exert to the maximum America's power and prestige to achieve a just peace, Pres. Woodrow Wilson personally led the American delegation to the conference. French, English, and Italian masses, stirred by his idealism, received him rapturously. But at Paris he quickly discovered that his partners in peacemaking—French premier Georges Clemenceau, British prime minister David Lloyd George, and Italian prime minister Vittorio Orlando—were vengeful and opportunistic.

One by one, Wilson surrendered principles enunciated in his speeches and *14 Points. The secret sessions of the negotiators violated his pledge of "open covenants, openly arrived at." Instead of a "peace without victory" negotiated among equals, Germany was excluded from the conference, which in the end assigned to Germany sole responsibility for the war and attempted to extract from her the war's total costs. Germany's colonies were awarded to the Great Powers (except the United States), nominally as League of Nations mandates, without consulting the populations concerned. Eastern Europe's new boundary lines frequently violated Wilson's principles of nationality and self-determination. But Wilson did succeed in drafting the covenant of the League of Nations and getting it incorporated into the final treaty. The League, he persuaded himself, would in time right the wrongs of the peace settlement.

The Treaty of Versailles was presented to a German delegation on May 9, 1919; resentful Germans signed it on June 28. Wilson promptly returned to the United States, where he found the people and Congress deeply divided over whether to accept the international obligations that membership in the League would entail or retreat into America's traditional isolationism (see *Wilson's Fight for the Treaty).

On Nov. 19, the U.S. Senate rejected the Treaty of Versailles. The United States was not a party to the peace treaties with Austria, Hungary, Bulgaria, and Turkey that were also drafted at the Paris Conference, but in 1920 it negotiated separate bilateral peace treaties with Germany, Austria, and Hungary.

PARIS TREATY (1763), treaty between Great Britain, France, and Spain ending the Seven Years' War in Europe and the *French and Indian War in North America. In North America, France ceded to Britain all of Canada and all territory east of the Mississippi River, together with the right of navigation on the Mississippi. (France had already ceded to Spain its territory west of the Mississippi, including the city of New Orleans.) In exchange for Cuba, Spain ceded East Florida and West Florida to Great Britain (see *Floridas, East and West).

PARIS TREATY (1783), treaty between the United States and Great Britain ending the *Revolutionary War. This and simultaneous treaties between Britain and the other belligerents—France, Spain, and the Netherlands—constituted the Peace of Paris.

The Anglo-American treaty was negotiated by John Adams, Benjamin Franklin, and John Jay for the Americans and by Richard Oswald for the British. Considered a diplomatic triumph for the Americans, the treaty recognized American independence; established U.S. boundaries at the St. Croix River and the Great Lakes in the north, the Mississippi River in the west, and Spanish Florida in the south; provided for the evacuation of British troops "with all convenient speed"; and guaranteed U.S. rights to the Newfoundland fisheries and the navigation of the Mississippi.

PATERSON SILK STRIKE (1913), five-month strike of silk mill workers in Paterson, N.J., led by the *Industrial Workers of the World and marked by the brutality of the police, who were determined to crush the revolutionary menace represented by the union. Passionately supported by the advanced spirits of New York City's Greenwich Village, including journalist John Reed, the strike was a failure.

PATROONS, Dutch colonizers authorized in 1629 to establish large estates in *New Netherland which they would rule with full feudal jurisdiction limited only by their oath of fealty to the Dutch West India Co. The patroons were required to purchase Indian rights to their land and then settle at least 50 colonists on it within five years. Five patroonships were reported in 1630—two on the Hudson River, two on the Delaware, and one on the Connecticut. Only one, Rensselaerwyck, founded by Killiaen van Rensselaer on the west bank of the Hudson around Fort Orange (Albany), succeeded.

PAYNE-ALDRICH TARIFF (1909), legislation of the *Taft administration. To honor a Republican Party platform pledge, Pres. William H. Taft in 1909 summoned a special session of Congress to reform the tariff. A House bill by Rep. Sereno Payne of New York placed important commodities on the free list and lowered duties on others. But the version that was passed in the protectionist Senate, led by Nelson A. Aldrich of Rhode Island, reversed direction. Although the resulting Payne-Aldrich bill lowered average rates to 38 percent from the record 57 percent of the *Dingley Tariff (1897), it was still a highly protective measure. For four months, Senate progressives led by Robert M. La Follette of Wisconsin fought the bill item by item, documenting the connection between the tariff and the trusts. Nevertheless, the bill passed and Taft signed it. Later, he unwisely characterized it as "the best tariff bill the Republican Party ever passed," outraging Republican progressives, including former president Theodore Roosevelt.

PEACE CORPS, volunteer international service organization, established by the *Kennedy administration in 1961 and made an independent agency in 1981. Volunteers train for 9–14 weeks, then spend two years on community projects in some 90 countries in the areas of education, agriculture, health, small business development, urban development, and the environment.

PEACE MOVEMENT, one of many humanitarian and reformist movements that arose in the early 19th century. The **American Peace Society**, founded in 1828 by William Ladd, propagandized against war and for arbitration of international disputes. The **Universal Peace Union**, founded in 1866 by Alfred Love, advocated arbitration of domestic as well as international disputes. American peace organizations sent representatives to Universal Peace Congresses that began in 1889.

Early in the 20th century, with the convening of the Hague Conferences (1899, 1907), the establishment of the Permanent Court of Arbitration at The Hague (1899), the award of the first Nobel Peace Prize in 1901, the signing of *arbitration treaties by the United States with some 40 other countries (1908–13), and the creation by steel magnate Andrew Carnegie of the Carnegie Endowment for International Peace (1910), it appeared that most of the objectives of the peace movement had been achieved. World War 1 stunned the movement, but the creation of the League of Nations after the war seemed to cap the peace edifice.

In the interwar period, American peace societies advocating membership in the League of Nations and the World Court proliferated. Their great achievement was the *Kellogg-Briand Peace Pact (1928). After World War 2, with the United States a member of the United Nations, the old peace organizations disappeared, replaced by movements for such ad hoc causes as nuclear disarmament and peace in Vietnam (see *Vietnam War).

PEARL HARBOR. On Dec. 7, 1941, some 350 Japanese planes attacked the U.S. naval base at Pearl Harbor on Oahu in the Hawaiian Islands where almost the entire Pacific Fleet was anchored, many ships side by side. (The fleet's three aircraft carriers and their escorts were at sea.) Army planes were parked closely together at nearby Hickam and Wheeler fields. The Japanese came in two waves, at 7:50 a.m. and an hour later. Initial surprise was complete, as evidenced by the alarm: "Air raid! This is no drill!" Eight battleships, three light cruisers, three destroyers, and four auxiliary vessels were sunk, capsized, or damaged. Nearly 200 planes were destroyed. Casualties totaled 2,403 dead and 1,178 wounded.

Washington officials who had been negotiating with Japan expected that Japan would go to war rather than accept U.S. conditions for peace. From an intercepted coded diplomatic message, they knew in November that a Japanese attack was near and alerted U.S. army and naval forces throughout the Pacific. But no one in authority expected an attack on Pearl Harbor. This was the idea of Japanese admiral Isoroku Yamamoto, who hoped that by crippling the U.S. fleet at Pearl Harbor Japan would gain six months to consolidate its intended conquests in the Western Pacific and be able to defend them against a U.S. counterattack.

An assault force of 30 vessels, including six aircraft carriers, commanded by Adm. Chuichi Nagumo left the Kurile Islands on Nov. 26, steamed undetected 3,400 miles through the North Pacific, and at dawn on Dec. 7 reached a position 220 miles north of Oahu from which the attack was launched. Japanese losses were 29 planes destroyed and 74 damaged, plus one large and five midget submarines sunk. Otherwise undamaged, the fleet returned to Hiroshima on Dec. 23.

The first of numerous investigations of the Pearl Harbor disaster, in December 1941, placed the blame on the army and navy commanders there. Lt. Gen. Walter C. Short and Rear Adm. Husband E. Kimmel were relieved of their commands and reprimanded. Republicans later blamed the Roosevelt administration for multiple failures, and some historians accused Roosevelt himself of withholding information about the impending attack from authorities at Pearl Harbor in order to bring the United States into World War 2. The ultimate explanation perhaps lies in the failure of the American military imagination to anticipate so dramatic a Japanese maneuver, compounded by the laxness and inexperience of a peacetime and still developing army and navy.

PENDLETON ACT (1883). See *Civil Service Reform.

PENINSULA CAMPAIGN (March–July 1862), *Civil War campaign in which the Union Army of the Potomac failed to take Richmond from the east.

In March and April 1862, Union general George B. McClellan transported the 100,000-man Army of the Potomac down the Potomac River and Chesapeake Bay to Union-held Fort Monroe at the tip of the peninsula between the James and York Rivers in Virginia, 70 miles from Richmond. Advancing with excessive caution against less numerous Confederates, McClellan occupied

Yorktown (May 4) and Williamsburg (May 5). On May 10 the Confederates evacuated Norfolk, opening the James River as far as Drewrys Bluff, nine miles from Richmond.

Establishing a base at White House on the Pamunkey River, McClellan placed his army on both sides of the narrow Chickahominy River, then—erroneously convinced that he was greatly outnumbered—waited for reinforcements from Fredericksburg. These, however, had to be diverted to the Shenandoah Valley to face Confederate general Thomas J. "Stonewall" Jackson's threat to Washington (see *Jackson's Valley Campaign).

Late in May heavy rains swelled the Chickahominy and flooded the surrounding countryside. Choosing this moment to attack, Confederate general Joseph E. Johnston threw his Confederates against the southern wing of the Union army in the battle of **Fair Oaks** (May 31–June 1). The Confederate attack, across flooded terrain, was poorly coordinated and was repulsed with heavy casualties. Johnston himself was seriously wounded and was succeeded in command by Gen. Robert E. Lee.

Lee fell back on Richmond, regrouped his forces (now called the Army of Northern Virginia), and prepared a major counteroffensive against McClellan. On June 12 he dispatched cavalry general J.E.B. Stuart with 1,200 horsemen on a reconnaissance mission behind Union lines. During June 12–15, **Stuart's ride** completely circled McClellan's army, gathering information, destroying Union supplies, and capturing 165 Federals while losing only a single trooper.

Lee launched his attack on June 26, hitting McClellan's right flank on the north side of the Chickahominy. At Mechanicsville, the first of the so-called **Seven Days' Battles** (June 26–July 2), the Federals repelled the attack, but then withdrew to Gaines's Mill. There superior Confederate forces drove them (June 27) across the Chickahominy, where they joined the main body of the Union army.

By then McClellan had abandoned the attempt to take Richmond and had decided to move his base from White House to Harrison's Landing on the James River, where he would be covered by the guns of Union warships. As the Union army withdrew, through swampy and wooded terrain, Lee attacked furiously but futilely at Savage's Station (June 29) and Frayser's Farm (June 30). Reaching the safety of the north bank of the James, McClellan took up a position on Malvern Hill, where he fought off (July 1) repeated Confederate attacks in some of the hardest fighting of the war. On July 2 the Confederates withdrew.

Malvern Hill marked the end of the Peninsula Campaign. Having failed to take Richmond, McClellan at least brought his army to safety in good order. During August, the Army of the Potomac was withdrawn from the Peninsula. Lee had saved Richmond, but he had failed to destroy the Union army and had suffered heavy casualties.

PENTAGON ATTACK (2001). See *World Trade Center Attack 2.

PENTAGON PAPERS (1971), a 47-volume, 7,000-page collection of documents and analyses tracing U.S. involvement in the *Vietnam War from 1945 to 1968. It was commissioned by Secretary of Defense Robert S. McNamara. Twenty copies were published in 1969 under the title *History of U.S. Decision-Making on Viet Nam Policy*.

One of the 36 military and civilian researchers who compiled the work was Daniel Ellsberg, a former marine, Defense Department employee, and Vietnam hawk, at that time an employee of the Rand Corporation in Los Angeles on loan to the Defense Department. Ellsberg had become an opponent of the war while on assignment in Vietnam for the Defense Department, and his work on the papers had convinced him that they should be made public.

With the help of a colleague at Rand, Anthony J. Russo Jr., Ellsberg copied a large part of the papers and in 1971 gave them to the *New York Times* and the Washington *Post*, which began publishing excerpts on June 13, 1971. After three installments had appeared, the government obtained an injunction preventing further publication. The *Times* appealed directly to the U.S. Supreme Court, which decided in its favor on June 30 (see *New York Times Co. v. United States*).

Meanwhile, Ellsberg and Russo had been indicted in Los Angeles on a variety of criminal charges, including conspiracy, theft, and violation of the *Espionage Act. Because of procedural delays, Judge Matthew Byrne Jr. declared a mistrial in December 1972. A second trial began on Jan. 18, 1973, but at its conclusion on May 11 Judge Byrne dismissed all charges against the defendants because of government misconduct, including illegal wiretapping, a break-in at the office of Ellsberg's former psychiatrist, and a strong intimation to Judge Byrne himself that he might be appointed director of the Federal Bureau of Investigation.

PEOPLE'S PARTY (1892–1908), political party of the populist movement (see *Populism). It held its first con-

vention in July 1892 at Omaha, where it adopted a platform whose preamble was written by Ignatius Donnelly of Minnesota.

"We meet," Donnelly wrote, "in the midst of a nation brought to the verge of moral, political, and material ruin. Corruption dominates the ballot-box, the Legislatures, the Congress, and touches even the ermine of the bench. . . . The newspapers are largely subsidized or muzzled, public opinion silenced, business prostrated, homes covered with mortgages, labor impoverished, and the land concentrating in the hands of capitalists. The urban workmen are denied the right to organize for self-protection, imported pauperized labor beats down their wages, a hireling standing army, unrecognized by our laws, is established to shoot them down. . . . The fruits of the toil of millions are boldly stolen to build up colossal fortunes for a few. . . . From the same prolific womb of governmental injustice we breed two great classes—tramps and millionaires. . . .

"Silver," he went on, ". . . has been demonetized to add to the purchasing power of gold by decreasing the value of all forms of property as well as human labor, and the supply of currency is purposely abridged to fatten usurers, bankrupt enterprise, and enslave industry." Then that curious mark of the otherwise liberal early populist mind: "A vast conspiracy against mankind has been organized on two continents, and it is rapidly taking possession of the world. . . ."

Finally, in language that anticipated that of the *New Nationalism and *New Deal of the next century, he declared: "We believe that the power of government—in other words, of the people—should be expanded . . . as rapidly and as far as the good sense of an intelligent people and the teachings of experience shall justify, to the end that oppression, injustice, and poverty shall eventually cease in the land."

The platform itself advocated free and unlimited coinage of silver, a graduated income tax, and government ownership of the railroads, telegraph, and telephone.

The party nominated for president James B. Weaver of Iowa, who 20 years before had been the candidate of the *Greenback Party. Weaver received 1 million votes and carried five states. But soon Western politicians of both the Democratic and Republican parties began to talk like populists and took votes from the People's Party. In the South, conservative Democrats stifled the People's Party with their familiar appeal for white supremacy.

When the Democratic Party was taken over by silver men and nominated William Jennings Bryan for president in 1896, many in the People's Party urged a fusion with the Democrats to enhance the possibility of electing a silverite. The People's Party therefore nominated Bryan too, although, in a feeble effort to maintain its identity, it named a vice presidential candidate of its own. Bryan made *free silver the sole issue of his campaign and he lost. The focus on silver had cost the party the labor vote, since workingmen, unlike farmers, were not generally debtors and wanted their wages paid in "sound money."

Thereafter an agrarian party, the People's Party succumbed to electoral defeat and rising farm prices. It nominated its last presidential candidate in 1908.

PEQUOT WAR (1637), war between the settlers of Massachusetts and the Pequot Indians in the Connecticut River valley. It began with a preemptive massacre of 400 Indians near the Mystic River and continued until most of the tribe had been exterminated.

PERRYVILLE or **CHAPLIN HILLS** (Oct. 8, 1862), *Civil War battle. In August 1862 Confederate general Braxton Bragg led his Army of Tennessee from east Tennessee into Kentucky, confident that the invasion would bring Kentucky into the Confederacy. The Confederates occupied Richmond, Lexington, and Frankfort, but Kentuckians remained passive. On Oct. 8 Union general Don Carlos Buell's Army of the Ohio attacked a portion of the Confederate force at Perryville. The battle was inconclusive, but that night Bragg abandoned his campaign and withdrew.

PERSONAL LIBERTY LAWS, laws passed by many Northern states before the Civil War to hinder the constitutionally permitted recapture of fugitive salves (see *Fugitive Slave Laws). Search warrants, jury trials, and other requirements made the task of the slave owner or his agent difficult. In *Prigg v. Pennsylvania* (1842), the U.S. Supreme Court ruled these personal liberty laws unconstitutional, although it acknowledged that enforcement of the fugitive slave law was entirely a federal responsibility. Massachusetts promptly passed a new personal liberty law prohibiting state officials from cooperating in the recapture of fugitives. The Fugitive Slave Act of 1850 authorized federal commissioners to compel state officials and private citizens to assist in recapturing fugitives on pain of severe penalties.

PERSONAL RESPONSIBILITY AND WORK OPPORTUNITY ACT (1996). See *Welfare.

PESTICIDE CONTROL ACT (1972). See *Environmentalism.

PETERSBURG SIEGE (June 15, 1864–Apr. 2, 1865), episode in the *Civil War. After the battle of Cold Harbor (June 1–3, 1864; see *Wilderness Campaign), Union general Ulysses S. Grant and the Army of the Potomac slipped away (June 12–13) from Confederate general Robert E. Lee, crossed the James River (June 14), and appeared before Petersburg on June 15. A railroad junction 20 miles south of Richmond through which supplies for Lee's army and the Confederate capital passed, Petersburg was heavily fortified but then held by Confederate general Pierre G. T. Beauregard with only 2,500 troops. Due to caution engendered by recent costly battles, Grant missed the opportunity to seize the city at once.

By June 18 Lee had arrived with 55,000 troops. For five days Grant battered the city at great cost, then settled down to a siege in which the most dramatic event was the explosion (July 30) of four tons of gunpowder in a 511-foot shaft dug under Confederate lines. This blasted a pit 170 feet long, 60 feet wide, and 30 feet deep. Instead of passing around the **Crater** and penetrating Confederate defenses, unprepared Union troops rushed into it and were slaughtered by Confederate artillery and mortars.

By the spring of 1865 Grant had 120,000 men before Petersburg. Steadily he pushed his lines west to cut off Petersburg's road and rail connections with the south. Lee's costly efforts to break out of the encircling Union army were frustrated at Fort Stedman (Mar. 25) and Five Forks (Apr. 1). On Apr. 2 the Federals broke into the city. That night Lee evacuated Petersburg, pulling his troops from Richmond as well, and moved west, hoping to get around the Union army and join Gen. Joseph E. Johnston in North Carolina. His starving and rapidly diminishing army, now fewer than 35,000, was soon surrounded by Federals, and on Apr. 9 Lee offered to surrender (see *Appomattox Surrender).

PHILADELPHIA MUTINY (June 1783), incident in the *Revolutionary War. Disgruntled by lack of pay, a small number of troops of the Pennsylvania line left their camp at Lancaster and marched on Philadelphia to present their grievances to Congress. In Philadelphia they were joined by some local troops, raising their total number to several hundred. Armed with weapons from the state arsenal, they menaced the Congress and the Pennsylvania executive council, both sitting in the Pennsylvania State House. When Pennsylvania authorities proved unable or unwilling to protect the Congress, that body moved to Princeton, N.J.

Meanwhile, Gen. George Washington, informed of

the mutiny, had sent 1,500 troops from Newburgh, N.Y., taking the opportunity to distinguish between the legitimate discontents of his veteran regiments and those of the mutineers, who were "recruits and soldiers of a day" and had not "borne the heat and burdens of the war." With the belated mustering of the Pennsylvania militia and the approach of Washington's troops, the mutiny collapsed. Several leaders were arrested and sentenced to death but later pardoned by Congress.

PHILIPPINE INSURRECTION (1899–1902). A Filipino revolt against Spain began in 1895. When Commodore George Dewey sailed to Manila at the outbreak of the *Spanish-American War, he carried with him the Filipino leader Emilio Aguinaldo from exile in Hong Kong. After destroying the Spanish fleet in Manila Bay, Dewey remained offshore awaiting American land troops. Aguinaldo, however, went ashore, established a provisional government, and proceeded to occupy all of Luzon except Manila. When Gen. Wesley Merritt arrived with 14,000 American troops, these and the Filipinos together took Manila on Aug. 13, 1898, one day after an armistice had ended the war.

The Filipinos regarded the Americans as liberators, but they became restive when there was no word from Pres. William McKinley confirming their independence. In January 1899 they learned that, at the Paris peace conference, the United States had demanded all of the Philippine Islands from Spain. To McKinley, who professed reluctance at this step, it seemed the best of the possible alternatives. The Filipinos, he reasoned, were not ready for self-government. To return the islands to Spain would be dishonorable. To allow another power to take them would be dangerous. American possession of the islands became a moral obligation. "There was nothing left for us to do," McKinley explained, "but to take them all, and to educate the Filipinos, and uplift and civilize and Christianize them." (Most Filipinos were already Roman Catholics.)

Feeling betrayed, Aguinaldo on Jan. 5, 1899, proclaimed an independent Philippine Republic. Fighting between Americans and Filipinos broke out in February. The American commander, Gen. Elwell S. Otis, conducted a cautious, conventional campaign while calling for reinforcements. A sweep through Luzon in October 1899 ended organized Filipino resistance. Aguinaldo fled to the mountains, from where he directed guerrilla warfare against Otis and his successor, Gen. Arthur MacArthur, who now had 70,000 troops. As the army expanded the area of pacification, it organized local governments, conducted public health programs, and established public schools to win the allegiance of Filipino civilians.

McKinley was determined that the Filipinos must recognize American sovereignty before he would make any promises of ultimate independence. Knowing almost nothing about the islands, in 1899 he sent a civilian fact-finding commission headed by Jacob G. Schurman, president of Cornell University. Schurman agreed that the Filipinos were not ready for self-government and urged the establishment of an American government. The next year another commission, this one headed by Judge William Howard Taft, went to the Philippines with instructions to establish a civil government to replace military rule. This was accomplished in July 1901 with Taft as governor-general.

The reelection of McKinley in November 1900 and the capture of Aguinaldo in March 1901 took the heart out of the insurgency. In 1902 the last Filipino commanders surrendered, and Secretary of War Elihu Root declared the insurrection over. The Philippine Government (or Organic) Act, passed on July 1, 1902, constituted the Philippines an unorganized territory of the United States, confirmed the reforms of the Taft Commission, and provided for the establishment of a bicameral legislature, the lower house to be popularly elected, the upper house to consist of the members of the Taft Commission (to which three Filipinos had now been added).

PHILIPPINE SEA. See *World War 2.

PHYSICAL VALUATION ACT (1913). See *Railroad Regulation.

PICKETT'S CHARGE (July 3, 1863), climactic episode in the three-day battle of *Gettysburg.

On the third day of the battle, Confederate general Robert E. Lee ordered a frontal attack on the Union center, which he believed had been weakened by attacks on the Union flanks the day before. From the protection of Seminary Ridge, the attackers would have to advance across three-quarters of a mile of gently rolling valley floor, under Federal guns, to reach the Federal position on 100-foot-high Cemetery Ridge, where the Federals were entrenched behind stone walls and breastworks. Veterans on both sides were reminded of *Fredericksburg.

Shortly after 1 p.m. on a clear, hot day, 160 Confederate guns began a two-hour barrage intended to disable the Union artillery and demoralize the troops on Cemetery Ridge. Union artillery responded, but after an hour its firing slackened and stopped, persuading the Confederates that they had put the Union artillery out of action. In fact, their aim had been high, the Union position had not been seriously damaged, and the Union artillerymen were conserving their ammunition for the expected attack.

At 3 p.m., three Confederate divisions—38-year-old Gen. George E. Pickett's fresh all-Virginia division on the right—formed a mile-long line of 14,000 men and started across the valley. Their objective was a 1,000-yard segment of the Union center, then held by three depleted divisions numbering only 5,700 men under Gen. Winfield S. Hancock. The Union artillery revived at once. Swept by artillery from the front and flanks, then by massed musket fire from the front, the Confederates struggled up to the first Union line, momentarily broke through (the "high tide of the Confederacy"), and then fell back. In the half-hour assault they had suffered 7,500 killed, wounded, or captured; Union losses were 1,500.

As his beaten troops streamed back across the valley, Lee rode out to meet them, acknowledging "It is all my fault, it is all my fault." When he directed Pickett to place his division in position to repel a Union counterattack, Pickett—who had lost all his brigade and regimental commanders—exclaimed tearfully, "General Lee, I have no division now."

PIERCE ADMINISTRATION (1853–57). Democrat Franklin Pierce, 14th president of the United States, regarded the *Compromise of 1850 as a final resolution of the slavery issue and hoped to avoid further contention by pursuing an expansionist foreign policy. In this desire he was frustrated by the bitter controversy over the *Kansas-Nebraska Act, which he did not initiate but actively supported, and by the ensuing civil war in Kansas (see *Bleeding Kansas).

An expansionist in the spirit of *Young America, Pierce obtained (1853) the *Gadsden Purchase from Mexico (providing territory for a southern transcontinental railroad), although he had sought much more. He quickly recognized (1856) the short-lived Nicaragua regime of filibuster William Walker (see *Filibustering), who opened that Central American country to slavery. Eager to acquire Cuba (a slaveholding colony of Spain), Pierce for a time supported a projected large-scale filibustering expedition against that island. He resisted (1854) demands for war with Spain aroused by the *Black Warrior affair but then attempted to buy Cuba. When Spain refused to sell, Secretary of State William L. Marcy authorized a meeting of the three principal U.S. ministers in Europe to recommend a Cuba strategy. They produced (1854) the embarrassing *Ostend Manifesto, which portrayed the United States as an aggressor. Pierce's expansionism, which appeared to serve Southern

interests, ended the appeal of *Manifest Destiny in the North.

Pierce hoped to be renominated by the Democrats in 1856, but the party rejected the now unpopular president and turned to James Buchanan, whose absence as U.S. minister to Great Britain had left him untouched by the controversies of the Pierce administration. Buchanan was elected.

PILGRIMS, Puritan Separatists (see *Puritanism) who founded *Plymouth Colony in 1620, although the name Pilgrims was not applied to them until 1799.

In the summer of 1620, 46 of the 500-member Separatist community at Leyden, Holland, sailed for America, in whose isolation they hoped to build a godly society. Their passage was paid by a group of London merchants in exchange for seven years' service (see *Indentured Servitude). At Southampton, the emigrants were joined by 67 others, including several more "Saints" and a larger number of "Strangers" employed by the sponsors. One of their ships proving unseaworthy, 102 migrants (and 48 crew members) crowded aboard the small *Mayflower*, which departed from Plymouth, England, on Sept. 16.

Their destination was the mouth of the Hudson River in territory owned by the Virginia Company (see *Virginia and Plymouth Companies), but on Nov. 19 they made landfall in Massachusetts in territory of the Council for New England. After five weeks spent exploring the coast of Cape Cod, they went ashore on Dec. 26 at the site of present-day Plymouth, Mass., having earlier organized a temporary government in the *Mayflower Compact.

During their first winter, some of the colonists remained aboard the *Mayflower* while others built shelters on the shore. Their principal diet was shellfish and groundnuts. By spring—when the *Mayflower* sailed for England—half the company had died. Expected hostility from Indians did not materialize since the local tribes had recently been decimated by an epidemic. Indeed, friendly Indians taught the surviving colonists how to plant crops in abandoned Indian fields. A successful harvest in 1621 and the arrival of a ship carrying new settlers, provisions, and a patent from the Council for New England—the occasion for the first Thanksgiving—ensured the colony's survival.

PINCKNEY'S TREATY or **TREATY OF SAN LORENZO** (1795), treaty between the United States and Spain negotiated by U.S. minister to Great Britain Thomas Pinckney. In it, Spain recognized the western and southern boundaries of the United States established by the Treaty of *Paris (1783) as the Mississippi River and the 31st parallel. Spain, which at that time possessed all of Louisiana, also granted Americans free navigation of the Mississippi and the right of *deposit (the right to store goods pending reshipment) at New Orleans.

PINKERTONS, detectives employed by the Pinkerton National Detective Agency, founded by Allen Pinkerton in 1850. Hired to provide security for railroads, they supplied intelligence to the Union army during the Civil War, then won notoriety for their pursuit of railroad and stagecoach bandits. Late in the century they were often employed in labor disputes (see *Molly Maguires; *Homestead Strike).

PITTSBURG LANDING. See *Shiloh or Pittsburg Landing.

PLATT AMENDMENT (1901), legislation of the *McKinley administration governing U.S. relations with independent Cuba. Drafted by Secretary of War Elihu Root and named for Sen. Orville H. Platt of Connecticut, chairman of the Senate special committee on Cuba, the amendment (to an Army appropriations bill) contained eight articles, the most important providing that: (1) Cuba would make no treaty with any foreign power that would "tend to impair" its independence; (2) Cuba would not contract any public debt beyond its ability to pay; (3) Cuba would permit the United States "to intervene for the preservation of Cuban independence [and] the maintenance of a government adequate for the protection of life, property, and individual liberty"; (4) Cuba would lease or sell to the United States "lands necessary for coaling or naval stations."

The United States required that these articles be included in the new Cuban constitution as a condition of U.S. withdrawal from the island. Resenting the articles as an infringement on Cuban sovereignty, the members of the Cuban constitutional convention narrowly agreed. The Platt Amendment was later embodied in a 1903 treaty between the United States and Cuba.

The United States withdrew from Cuba on May 20, 1902. The Platt Amendment was used to justify intervention in Cuba in 1906–9 and 1917–23. It was finally abrogated in 1934.

PLEDGE OF ALLEGIANCE, patriotic declaration customarily recited as part of the salute to the flag. It was composed by Francis Bellamy, an editor of the *Youth's Companion*, and published in that magazine in 1892. In 1942 Congress adopted it as part of the U.S. flag code. The pledge originally read: "I pledge allegiance to my flag and to the republic for which it stands, one nation indivisible, with liberty and justice for all." In 1923, "the flag of the United States" was substituted for "my flag." In 1954, Congress added the phrase "under God" after "indivisible."

In 2002, a three-judge panel of the Ninth Circuit Court of Appeals in California ruled 2–1 that the phrase "under God" violated the Establishment Clause of the First Amendment and was therefore unconstitutional (see *Church-State Relations). The decision was widely denounced.

PLESSY v. FERGUSON (1896), 7–1 decision of the *Fuller Court that established the constitutionality of racial segregation by means of the "separate but equal" doctrine.

In 1890, the state of Louisiana adopted a *Jim Crow law providing "equal but separate accommodation for the white and colored races" on railroads within that state. Homer Plessy, a black man, refused to sit in a segregated car on the grounds that segregation imposed a badge of servitude in violation of the *13th Amendment and denied him the equal protection of the laws guaranteed by the *14th Amendment.

For the Court, Justice Henry Billings Brown ruled that such a mere "legal distinction" as the Louisiana statute made had to be viewed "with reference to the established usages, customs, and traditions of the people, and with a view to the promotion of their comfort, and the preservation of the public peace and good order. Gauged by this standard, we cannot say that a law which authorizes or even requires the separation of the two races in public conveyances is unreasonable or more obnoxious to the 14th Amendment than the acts of Congress requiring separate schools for colored children in the District of Columbia, the constitutionality of which does not seem to have been questioned. . . ."

Brown went on: "We consider the underlying fallacy of the plaintiff's argument to consist in the assumption that the enforced separation of the two races stamps the colored race with a badge of inferiority. If this be so, it is not by reason of anything found in the act, but solely because the colored race chooses to put that construction upon it. . . . The argument also assumes that social prejudices may be overcome by legislation, and that equal rights cannot be secured to the negro except by an enforced commingling of the two races. We cannot accept this proposition. If the two races are to meet on terms of social equality, it must be the result of natural affinities, a mutual appreciation of each other's merits and a voluntary consent of individuals."

In sole dissent, Justice John Marshall Harlan, a Kentuckian and former slave owner, wrote: "The white race deems itself to be the dominant race in this country. And so it is, in prestige, in achievements, in education, in wealth, and in power. So, I doubt not that it will continue to be for all time, if it remains true to its great heritage and holds fast to the principles of constitutional liberty. But in the view of the Constitution, in the eye of the law, there is in this country no superior, dominant, ruling class of citizens. There is no caste here. Our Constitution is color-blind, and neither knows nor tolerates classes among citizens. In respect of civil rights, all citizens are equal before the law. The humblest is the peer of the most powerful. The law regards man as man, and takes no account of his surroundings or of his color when his civil rights as guaranteed by the supreme law of the land are involved. It is therefore to be regretted that this high tribunal, the final expositor of the fundamental law of the land, has reached the conclusion that it is competent for a state to regulate the enjoyment by citizens of their civil rights solely upon the basis of race.

"In my opinion, the judgment this day rendered will, in time, prove to be quite as pernicious as the decision made by this tribunal in the *Dred Scott Case*. . . ."

The "separate but equal" doctrine justifying racial segregation was overturned only in 1954 in *Brown v. Board of Education of Topeka*.

PLYMOUTH COLONY (1620–91), founded by the *Pilgrims. After initial hardships, it prospered modestly through farming, fishing, and fur trading. In 1627, the colonists settled their debt with their London sponsors and abandoned communal for private property. Attendance at church—the first Congregational church in America—was compulsory for all residents, "Saints" and "Strangers" alike, although only Saints could become members. Because laymen controlled the church, Plymouth escaped the clerical domination that characterized their Puritan neighbor, *Massachusetts Bay Colony. All freemen who paid taxes were permitted to vote. In 1691 Plymouth was combined with Massachusetts Bay to form the royal province of Massachusetts.

PLYMOUTH COMPANY. See *Virginia and Plymouth Companies.

POINT FOUR (1949), initiative of the *Truman administration to make the benefits of American science and technology available to underdeveloped nations. The last of four foreign policy undertakings listed by President Truman in his 1949 inaugural address, technical assistance continued as a part of U.S. *cold war policy long after the program's original name and origin were forgotten.

POLIOMYELITIS, an intestinal infection caused by one of three types of virus. Humans are the only reservoir of the poliovirus, which is found worldwide. Infection is common, but the great majority of infections pass unnoticed or as short-lived flu symptoms. Infection confers immunity. Clinical symptoms appear only when the virus passes into the bloodstream and is carried to the central nervous system. Then paralysis, of varying degree and permanence, occurs. Because polio was once common in children, the disease was called infantile paralysis. But as hygiene and public health measures improved, children increasingly escaped infection (and immunity), and polio began to appear more frequently in adults.

An increase in the number of cases of paralytic polio (the only cases clinically observable) in the late 19th century caused alarm. Early in the 20th century, polio epidemics struck a number of U.S. cities. In 1916, New York City reported 9,000 polio cases—185.2 per 100,000 population. Nationwide, the incidence rate reached 18.5 per 100,000 population. In the 1950s, the United States had more than 50,000 cases annually, half of them adults. Franklin D. Roosevelt contracted paralytic polio in 1921; his celebrity in the 1930s focused unusual attention and resources on the polio problem.

One strain of poliovirus was identified in 1908, two others were identified in 1931. In 1937, polio was recognized as an intestinal infection. Intensified search for an effective vaccine was rewarded in 1955 with the announcement of the successful testing of a killed-virus vaccine developed by Jonas Salk at the University of Pittsburgh. Although the Salk vaccine was safe, it required a series of shots and a booster to achieve immunity. In 1960 the successful testing of a live-virus oral vaccine developed by Albert Sabin at the University of Cincinnati was announced. The ease with which the Sabin vaccine could be administered made it preferred to the Salk vaccine, particularly in underdeveloped countries. But in rare instances the Sabin vaccine caused polio—about eight cases a year in the United States, one for every 2.4 million oral doses given. For this reason the American Academy of Pediatrics in 1999 recommended a return to the Salk killed-virus vaccine.

POLITICAL ACTION COMMITTEES (PACS), organizations established by business corporations, labor unions, and other economic and ideological interest groups to collect and disburse funds on behalf of political candidates, chiefly candidates for Congress.

The first PAC was formed by the Congress of Industrial Organizations (CIO) in 1947 after the *Taft-Hartley Act barred unions from contributing to political campaigns; the CIO–PAC was technically independent of the union. PACs multiplied after the Federal Election Campaign Act of 1971, which placed a ceiling on contributions to candidates but allowed unlimited contributions—soft money— to political parties or independent committees helping the candidates (see *Campaign Financing).

In 1974, approximately 600 PACs contributed $12.5 million to congressional candidates; in 1999–2000, some 3,700 PACs contributed $259.8 million to House and Senate candidates.

POLK ADMINISTRATION (1845–49). Democrat James K. Polk, 11th president of the United States, defined four objectives for his administration: (1) settlement of the *Oregon dispute with Great Britain; (2) acquisition of California; (3) tariff reduction (see *Tariffs); and (4) reestablishment of the *Independent Treasury System. He accomplished all four.

The settlement of the Oregon dispute was made possible by Polk's acceptance of the 49th parallel as the northern boundary of Oregon instead of 54°40.' which he had originally demanded. Many expansionist Northern Democrats felt betrayed by his compromise, since they had coupled the acquisition of a large free Oregon with that of a large slave Texas and felt that Southern interests had dictated the abandonment of the maximum claims.

In any case, Polk was now free to deal with Mexico. His original intention was to acquire California, but when Mexico refused to receive his emissary, Polk determined to go to war. As a result of the *Mexican War, the United States not only confirmed the annexation of Texas but acquired the Mexican provinces of California and New Mexico (see *Mexican Cession).

The Walker Tariff (1846) gratified the South by lowering import duties to the level of revenue only, and the Independent Treasury System—originally created by the *Van Buren administration and repealed by the *Tyler administration—was reinstituted the same year.

Polk had promised to serve only one term. He was succeeded by Whig Zachary Taylor and died a few months later.

During the Polk administration, Texas (1845), Iowa (1846), and Wisconsin (1848) became the 28th, 29th, and 30th states.

POLLOCK v. FARMERS' LOAN & TRUST CO. (1895), one of three **income tax cases** appealed to the *Fuller Court by financial interests fearful of the effects of the income tax provision of the *Wilson-Gorman Tariff of 1894. This act placed a flat 2 percent tax on personal and corporate incomes over $4,000. A Civil War tax on incomes, first over $800 and then over $600, that lasted from 1861 to 1872 had been upheld by the Supreme Court in 1881 on the ground that an income tax was not a direct tax, which the Constitution required to be apportioned among the states (Art. 1, sec. 2). Indeed, the Supreme Court in 1796 had ruled that only *poll taxes and taxes on land were direct taxes.

Passions in this case ran high. One attorney argued that the tax would lead to "communism, anarchy, and . . . despotism." Another bewailed "this army of 60,000,000—this triumphant and tyrannical majority— who want to punish men who are rich and confiscate their property." By 5–4 the Court decided that a tax on the income from real or personal property was a direct tax and that the income tax as a whole was unconstitutional. The *16th Amendment (1913) reversed this decision.

POLL TAX, a head tax levied upon every adult citizen by a state or local government. They were common in colonial and early America but were rejected as undemocratic as the country moved toward universal white manhood suffrage. In the late 19th century, Southern states used poll taxes to keep blacks from voting. The *24th Amendment (1964) outlawed poll taxes in federal elections, and in 1966 the U.S. Supreme Court declared poll taxes as a requirement for voting in state elections unconstitutional.

PONTIAC'S REBELLION (1763–66), Indian uprising against the British, named after one of its leaders, the Ottawa chief Pontiac. After the *French and Indian War, the tribes north of the Ohio River, finding the British victors less generous than the French and unprotective of Indian lands, resolved upon war. Detroit and Fort Pitt withstood sieges in 1763, but the Indians captured many other British posts and spread terror along the Pennsylvania, Virginia, and Maryland frontiers. In 1764 the British subdued the Shawnees and Delawares in Pennsylvania. Lacking allies, Pontiac submitted in 1766 and was pardoned.

PONY EXPRESS (1860–62), short-lived mail service between Independence, Mo., and Sacramento, Calif. Departing twice weekly, relays of horsemen made the 2,000-mile trip in eight days, changing mounts every ten or 15 miles. As a business, the pony express was unprofitable. It was made obsolete by the extension of the telegraph to San Francisco in 1861.

POOR PEOPLE'S CAMPAIGN (1968), episode in the *civil rights movement. Several summers of *ghetto riots persuaded civil rights leader Martin Luther King Jr. that the movement had to turn its attention—after passage of the *Civil Rights Act of 1964 and the *Voting Rights Act of 1965—to the condition of the impoverished black masses in Northern inner cities. How intractable these conditions were he learned in Chicago in 1966, where his Southern Christian Leadership Conference had gone to campaign for jobs, housing, and better schools. Leading black marches into white ethnic neighborhoods to protest housing segregation, King had been greeted by rage and hatred that surpassed anything he had encountered in Alabama and Mississippi.

Nevertheless, against the advice of his colleagues, King pursued his plan for a national multiethnic coalition of poor people to gather in Washington, D.C., and by their nonviolent demonstrations bring the government to a halt to dramatize their need for jobs and training. After King's assassination on Apr. 4, 1968, his followers, despite profound misgivings, felt they had to continue the project as a tribute to King.

Poorly planned and managed, the Poor People's Campaign quickly degenerated into a public relations disaster. The first participants arrived in Washington while the city was recovering from three days of looting and arson in response to King's assassination. They took shelter in unfinished Resurrection City, a collection of plywood and plastic shanties in West Potomac Park, but heavy rains soon reduced their encampment to a quagmire. Tensions among ethnic groups—blacks, whites, Mexican-Americans, Puerto Ricans, Native Americans—escalated into disorders and violence. Several hundred street gang members enlisted as marshals to keep the peace had to be sent home for their lawlessness. Meanwhile, nightly revival meetings were poorly attended, and bedraggled daytime demonstrations at government offices were simply ignored.

On June 19, some 50,000 people celebrated Solidarity Day before the Lincoln Memorial, but a few days later, when the campaign's permit had expired, the police who closed Resurrection City found only a few hundred stragglers. The organizers accepted the police action with relief for extricating them from a frightening debacle. The Poor People's Campaign had accomplished nothing.

POPULAR SOVEREIGNTY or **SQUATTER SOVEREIGNTY** (1847–60), doctrine that the decision

whether a territory should be slave or free should be left to its inhabitants. It was first advocated by Sen. Lewis Cass in 1847, applied by Henry Clay to Utah and New Mexico territories in the *Compromise of 1850, and applied again to Kansas and Nebraska territories by Stephen A. Douglas in the *Kansas-Nebraska Act (1854).

The doctrine was superficially attractive because it was based on local and democratic self-government, but especially because it promised to remove from Congress the contentious debate over the extension of slavery. Southerners were willing to accept popular sovereignty, whereas they regarded congressional prohibition of slavery as both unconstitutional and insulting to their "peculiar institution." On the other hand, it was never clear at what point in a territory's development toward statehood popular sovereignty would come into play. Southerners argued that slavery could not be excluded from a new territory under any circumstances. But once established in a territory, it was unlikely to be expelled at a later period—for example, when that territory drafted a state constitution. Abraham Lincoln abhorred the doctrine because it—unlike the Ordinance of 1787 and the *Missouri Compromise, which excluded slavery from large areas of the country—adopted a stance of moral neutrality (or indifference) toward the evil of slavery.

In *Scott v. Sandford* (1857), the U.S. Supreme Court, in ruling that neither Congress nor a territorial legislature could exclude slavery from a territory, seemed to end popular sovereignty as an option. Douglas, however, continued to argue that even if slavery could not be excluded, it could not survive in a territory whose inhabitants failed to pass the police regulations necessary for its protection.

POPULATION. In 1790 the first U.S. Census counted 3.9 million Americans. Thereafter, population growth was explosive. Between 1790 and 1860, the population grew at an average annual rate of 3.5 percent, doubling every 24 years. From 1870 to 1910, the average annual growth rate was 2.4 percent; from 1920 to 2000, 1.3 percent. The U.S. population reached 25 million in 1853, 50 million in 1880, 100 million in 1915, 200 million in 1968. The 2000 Census counted 281.4 million Americans, an increase of 32.7 million (13.2 percent) over 1990. Hispanics, now the largest minority group, constituted 12.5 percent of the total; African-Americans, 12.3 percent.

Most of the population increase was natural, resulting from the excess of births over deaths. From an astonishing 55.2 births per 1,000 population in 1820, birthrates generally declined to 32.3 in 1900 and to 19.4 in 1940. During the post–World War 2 *baby boom, the birthrate peaked in 1957 at 25.3, then declined irregularly to 15.5 in 1993.

*Immigration has contributed a significant proportion of the decennial population increase. At the peak of immigration in 1901–10, when immigrants arrived at an annual rate of 10.4 per 1,000 population, the new arrivals accounted for 55.1 percent of the decade's population increase. Between 1991 and 2000, when immigrants arrived at an annual rate of 3.5 per 1,000 population, immigrants accounted for 34.6 percent of the population increase. In 2000, 11.1 percent of the U.S. population—31.1 million people—was foreign-born.

The population has grown older with the country. Except for a slight dip between 1950 and 1980 reflecting the arrival of the baby boomers, the median age of the population has steadily increased from about 16.0 years in 1800 to 35.3 years in 2000. Life expectancy at birth increased from 47.3 years (47.6 for whites, 33.0 for blacks and others) in 1900 to 77.0 years (77.5 for whites, 72.2 for blacks) in 2000. Americans 65 and over, who constituted 9.8 percent of the population in 1970, constituted 12.4 percent in 2000 and were projected to constitute 20.0 percent in 2050.

POPULATION, CENTER OF. See *Westward Movement.

POPULISM, agrarian protest and reform movement growing out of the *Farmers' Alliances that swept the South and West in the late 1880s (see *Agrarian Discontents).

The movement, which originally sought to unite farmers (white and black) and industrial workers, attracted all the disparate reformers of the period—Greenbackers, Knights of Labor, free silverites, single taxers, and utopians of the Edward Bellamy stamp. Its leaders included Ben Tillman in South Carolina, Tom Watson in Georgia, David Waite in Colorado, Ignatius Donnelly in Minnesota, James B. Weaver in Iowa, Mary Lease in Kansas, and William Jennings Bryan in Nebraska. It produced a bumper crop of egalitarian and democratic heterodoxies to alarm the conservative political parties—the free coinage of silver, government ownership of railroads and telegraph, the eight-hour day, the direct election of senators, and many more. Populists were portrayed unflatteringly by Kansas newspaper publisher William Allen White in his famous 1896 *Emporia Gazette* editorial *"What's the Matter with Kansas?"

Without political organization, the movement in 1890 elected four U.S. senators and more than 50 members of the U.S. House of Representatives, besides winning control of legislatures in a dozen states. In 1892 the populists organized the *People's Party, which thereafter embodied the movement.

PORT CHICAGO MUTINY (1944). On July 17, 1944, during World War 2, an explosion at Port Chicago, Calif., just north of San Francisco, killed 320 sailors, including 202 members of black work crews who had been loading ammunition onto Navy ships. When the black work crews were ordered to resume the dangerous loading, 50 men refused, were court-martialed, found guilty of mutiny by all-white panels, and sentenced to long prison terms (later reduced). Most of the convicted men rejoined the Navy after serving their sentences and were eventually discharged "under honorable conditions." The episode focused attention on segregation in the armed services.

PORTSMOUTH TREATY (1905), treaty ending the Russo-Japanese War (1904–5), mediated by Pres. Theodore Roosevelt at a conference held in the navy yard at Portsmouth, N.H. Japan's control of Korea was recognized and its position in Manchuria was strengthened by acquisition of Russia's Liaotung leasehold and of the South Manchuria Railroad. Roosevelt prevented Japan from obtaining all of Sakhalin Island (it got only the southern half) and an indemnity. For his mediation, Roosevelt received the Nobel Peace Prize in 1906.

POTSDAM CONFERENCE (1945). See *World War 2 Conferences.

POTTAWATOMIE MASSACRE (1856). See *Brown's Career.

POVERTY. Although America was spared the horrendous mass poverty of premodern Europe, its experience with poverty was close and hard enough. Defining poverty as existence at or below the subsistence level, one expert has calculated that 67 percent of American families lived in poverty in 1896, 63 percent in 1918, 51 percent in 1935–36, 30 percent in 1950, and 20 percent in 1960.

Students of poverty have long distinguished between people who are poor through no fault of their own (the aged, disabled, chronically ill, women with dependent children) and others, once thought to be morally deficient but now more kindly considered structurally poor—victims of an economy unable to provide jobs for all who want them and a social order that distributes wealth inequitably. The poverty of the former, it was realized in the 1930s, could be permanently alleviated by government social welfare programs (see *Social Security; *Welfare), the poverty of the latter by government policies that encouraged economic growth. Indeed, the declining proportion of American families living in poverty between 1896 and 1960 testifies primarily to the growth of the American economy, gross national product having grown from $18.7 billion in 1900 to $503.7 billion in 1960.

Not until the 1960s did the federal government adopt an official definition of poverty by formulating the poverty index or threshold. Developed by the Social Security Administration (SSA) in 1964, the poverty threshold was based on the Economy Food Plan devised by the Department of Agriculture to provide a minimally adequate diet at lowest cost. Having found that low-income families spent approximately one-third of their income on food, the SSA analysts in 1964 set the poverty threshold—that is, the subsistence standard of living—at three times the cost of the Economy Food Plan at that time. Updated every year to reflect changes in the consumer price index, the poverty threshold also varies with household size. In 2000, the poverty threshold for a household of four was $17,603, about 30 percent of the median income nationally for all four-person households. ("Households" includes families as well as unmarried people living alone or with friends.)

It should be noted that the official poverty index is controversial. The method by which it was constructed, either by error or by political calculation, tends to underestimate the number of the poor. On the other hand, its focus on money income—to the exclusion of other resources—tends to overestimate their number. Plans now under way to update the poverty index on the basis of the current spending habits of poor people would raise it to at least $20,000 for a four-person household.

In the rapid economic growth that followed World War 2, Americans lost sight of poverty and had to be reminded of its existence in their midst by Michael Harrington, whose The *Other America (1962) described an invisible poverty in depressed rural and urban areas. The problem was taken up by Pres. John F. Kennedy and inherited by Pres. Lyndon Johnson, who in 1964 launched a multifaceted **War on Poverty** (see Lyndon *Johnson Administration). First were measures to stimulate the economy and create new jobs: a massive tax cut in 1964 and the *Vietnam War after 1965 had this effect. Second were employment, job-training, compensatory education, and community development programs, launched under the *Economic Opportunity Act of 1964, intended to improve the skills, productivity, and economic self-sufficiency of the poor. Third was the removal of obstacles to the employment of the minority poor: the *Civil Rights Act of 1964 banned discrimination in employment on the basis of race and sex and led shortly to vigorous *affirmative action efforts. Finally, expansion of the welfare system (food stamps in 1964, Medicaid in 1965, Supplemental Security Income in 1974) channeled enlarged cash and in-kind benefits to the poor, who took advantage of this largesse in ever-increasing numbers.

The 1960s saw a striking reduction in the number of the poor. Their number declined from 39.9 million in 1960 to 25.4 million in 1970, the poverty rate from 22.2 percent in 1960 to 12.6 percent in 1970. It would appear, therefore, that the War on Poverty was highly successful. In fact, however, the rate of *pretransfer* poverty—that is, the percentage of the population that was poor before the receipt of social insurance and welfare benefits—was the same in 1976 as in 1965. The decline in the poverty rate during the 1960s was not due to poor people finding productive employment but entirely to the expansion of welfare programs and the increased rate of participation among eligible persons. As Pres. Ronald Reagan remarked, "We fought a war on poverty, and poverty won."

The experience of the War on Poverty inhibited further large-scale efforts to solve the poverty problem. Government policy continued to emphasize education and job-training as means of preventing individuals from falling into poverty. The government continued to offer loan guarantees and tax incentives to entrepreneurs who invested in certain depressed rural and urban areas designated enterprise zones. An economic boom in the 1990s (see *New Economy) brought the poverty rate for individuals down from 15.1 percent in 1993 to 11.3 percent in 2000 (the lowest level since 1979). In 2000, with a national unemployment rate of 4.0 percent, 31.8 million Americans lived at or below the poverty level.

PREEMPTION ACT (1841). See *Public Lands.

PREPAREDNESS (1915–16), episode in the *Wilson administration. Pres. Woodrow Wilson's policy of neutrality in the European war gave rise to numerous private organizations, such as the National Security League, the American Defense Society, the League to Enforce Peace, and the American Rights Committee that were avowedly pro-Ally. Wilson's most vociferous critic was former president Theodore Roosevelt, who in speeches, articles, and books inveighed against the president's pusillanimity and urged entrance into the war on the Allied side. He was seconded by Gen. Leonard Wood, senior officer in the U.S. Army, who in the face of presidential disapproval organized an officer-training program for volunteer business and professional men at Plattsburgh, N.Y., in the summers of 1915 and 1916.

Wilson opposed preparation for war as likely to involve the country in war, as inconsistent with American neutrality, and as detracting from America's moral standing as an eventual peacemaker. But the *Lusitania* sinking and subsequent sinkings altered his view. In the summer of 1915 he laid plans for the expansion of the Army and Navy. In October he led a preparedness parade up New York City's Fifth Avenue, and in December he proposed to Congress a comprehensive plan for national defense. In January 1916 his speaking tour urging preparedness through antiwar Midwestern states was well received. The National Defense Act of June 1916 provided for an enlarged Regular Army and National Guard and established a reserve officers corps. In August, a Naval Appropriations Bill authorized construction of many new ships. In September, the U.S. Shipping Board Act provided funds for an enlarged merchant marine. And in October, the Council of National Defense, consisting of six cabinet officers and an advisory board drawn from industry and labor, was organized to coordinate industry and resources for national defense.

Wilson was reelected in November 1916 on the slogan "He Kept Us Out of War," but Germany was already moving toward its decision to resume unrestricted submarine warfare.

PRESIDENTIAL ELECTIONS. The U.S. Constitution limits the terms of president and vice president to four years and thus requires quadrennial presidential elections. The Framers devised a fanciful method—the *electoral college—for the nomination and election of these officers, but this quickly succumbed to political realities. When political parties first formed, party leaders selected their party's candidates. Sometimes a party *caucus in Congress or in one or more state legislatures nominated candidates. Not until the 1830s did the national party *nominating convention become the means for nominating candidates for president and vice president. In recent years, presidential *primary elections have diminished the role of the party convention, which often only ratifies the decision of the primaries.

For many years, presidential candidates took little part in election campaigns, affecting a classical republican dignity that did not permit them to solicit public favor. They generally remained on their farms, writing occasional letters, receiving delegations, speaking—if

necessary—only in platitudes to local audiences. Party activists, however, campaigned vigorously on the candidates' behalf, writing laudatory campaign biographies, blackening opponents' reputations in the press, whipping up a carnival atmosphere, and generally distracting the public from the real issues to artificial ones.

Not until the 20th century did presidential candidates routinely "stump" the country, traveling by train, airplane, and bus caravan to show themselves to the people. Radio and television made candidates even more familiar to voters, but these media were rarely employed to realize the educative possibilities of the campaign. Increasingly, presidential campaigns have been managed by marketing experts, more concerned with image than substance and with winning above all else.

Perhaps for this reason (although analysts disagree), voter participation rates—the percentage of eligible voters who actually vote in presidential elections—have irregularly declined in recent years, reaching a low of 44.9 percent in 1988.

Elections of 1789 and 1792. When they created a single, powerful executive, the Framers of the Constitution knew they were creating the office for George Washington. In the state ratifying conventions, despite the vigorous arguments for and against the Constitution, the knowledge that Washington supported it and would certainly be the first president helped ensure the Constitution's ratification.

Reluctant but unable to resist a call to duty, Washington acquiesced in the urgings of his friends that he accept the presidency in 1789. Classical republican ideology, of course, prevented him from declaring his willingness (or unwillingness) to accept the presidency. Like an old Roman, he remained silent and aloof on his farm until his countrymen called him.

Washington's popularity was so great that no *Antifederalist dared oppose him. Instead, the politicians focused their attention on the choice of a vice president. The Constitution prescribed that each elector cast two votes; the person receiving the most votes would become president, the runner-up vice president. Under Alexander Hamilton's leadership, the Federalists agreed to support John Adams of Massachusetts, a man of great distinction but little popularity. The Antifederalists inclined toward Gov. George Clinton of New York, who had led the fight against the Constitution in the New York ratifying convention.

On Jan. 5, 1789, ten states chose presidential electors—three by popular vote, five by state legislatures, and two by a combination of popular nomination and legislative selection. North Carolina and Rhode Island had not yet ratified the Constitution, and New York, where the state legislature was to choose the electors, failed to select any when the two houses of the legislature, one Federalist and the other Antifederalist, could not agree on a slate. A total of 69 electors were chosen, the majority of them Federalists. Hamilton's concern now was to prevent Adams from getting as many votes as Washington—or even, by some fluke, more. This he did by persuading some Federalist electors to cast their second votes for minor candidates.

The electors met in their respective state capitals on Feb. 4, voted, and sent their sealed ballots to New York. Congress was supposed to convene there on Mar. 4, but a quorum did not assemble until Apr. 1. On Apr. 6 the electoral ballots were opened in the presence of Congress and counted. All 69 electors had voted for Washington. Adams, to his great chagrin, received only 34 votes, fewer than half, although he had no major rival, but enough to elect him vice president. Clinton received only three votes, and 32 other second votes were scattered among other Federalists and Antifederalists.

Washington did not want to serve more than one term as president, and as the end of that term approached he longed more than ever to retire to private life. But government affairs caused increasing anxiety. The strife between Secretary of the Treasury Hamilton and Secretary of State Thomas Jefferson grew in intensity. The Hamiltonian or Federalist "interest" and the Jeffersonian or Republican "interest" were fast hardening into rival political parties (see *Federalist Party; *Jeffersonian Republican Party). Both men implored Washington to stay on, arguing that he alone was capable of holding the country together.

As in 1789, John Adams was the Federalist choice for vice president and George Clinton the choice of the Republicans. But the accomplishments of Washington's first administration had put the Federalists in an even stronger position than in 1789. Washington was unanimously reelected with all 132 electoral votes of the 15 states. Adams received 77 to Clinton's 50.

Election of 1796. Washington's decision not to accept a third term—withheld until Sept. 17, 1796, when his farewell address was published (see *Washington's Farewell Address)—meant that 1796 would see the presidency pass from the godlike Washington to a fallible mortal, indeed a mere politician, since by then the Federalist and Republican parties had become clearly demarcated. Fear that party strife would destroy the fragile Union was widespread.

John Adams, vice president during Washington's two terms, seemed the natural successor and as such was nominally the leader of the Federalist Party. Although he professed otherwise, he aspired to be president—but he refused to seek the office as representative of a party. Thomas Jefferson, leader of the Republican Party, also refused to actively seek the office. Politics, he wrote to Adams, was "a subject I never loved and now hate." Both men, adhering to classical decorum, awaited the call of the people. To attract Southern votes from Jefferson, the Federalists chose Thomas Pinckney of South Carolina as their candidate for vice president; to attract Northern votes from Adams, the Republicans chose Aaron Burr of New York as theirs.

The choice of presidential electors in November 1796 promised a Federalist victory. Alexander Hamilton, the real leader of the Federalists, was sufficiently optimistic to try to rig the election in favor of Pinckney over Adams, whom he disliked. Hamilton arranged for South Carolina electors to refrain from voting for Adams while voting for Pinckney, in the expectation that Pinckney would emerge with more votes than Adams and thus become president. Hamilton's scheme became known, however, and New England electors refrained from voting for Pinckney, with the result that, while Adams was elected president with a bare majority of 71 votes, Jefferson, leader of the opposition, was elected vice president with 68. Pinckney received 59 votes, Burr 30.

Elections of 1800 and 1804. In May 1800 a Federalist congressional caucus—that is, a meeting of Federalist members of Congress—nominated John Adams for president and Charles Cotesworth Pinckney of South Carolina for vice president. The Federalists, however, were distinctly cool toward President Adams—he was too eccentric, too independent for their taste. Some of them secretly calculated that Pinckney, their choice for vice president, might actually poll more electoral votes than Adams and thus become president. Certainly that was the desire of Alexander Hamilton, Federalist Party leader, who in October astonished the country by publishing a letter in which he declared that Adams was temperamentally unfit to be president.

Among Republicans, there was no question that Vice Pres. Thomas Jefferson would be their candidate for president as he had been in 1796. For vice president, a Republican congressional caucus in May selected Aaron Burr of New York, who had just managed the election of a Republican majority to the New York legislature, thereby assuring that the Republican candidates would get all of New York's electoral votes.

The Republicans campaigned for strict construction of the Constitution and for simple and frugal government—no standing army or large navy, little or no diplomatic establishment, discharge of the national debt. They portrayed Jefferson as the farmers' friend and the author of the *Declaration of Independence. The Federalists were compelled to run on the record of President Adams, which they tried to link to that of the great George Washington. Moreover, they attacked Jefferson personally as an atheist and a Jacobin.

When the electoral votes were counted on Feb. 11, 1801, the results were: Jefferson and Burr, 73 each; Adams 65 and Pinckney 64; and John Jay, a New York Federalist, one. No Republican elector had thrown away his vice presidential vote to ensure that Jefferson would get more votes than Burr. The unexpected tie between the two Republican candidates (Burr refused to withdraw in favor of his party leader) threw the election into the House of Representatives.

This was not the newly elected House in which the Republicans had a majority but the still-sitting House elected in 1798 with a Federalist majority. Although they constituted a majority of House members, the Federalists actually controlled only six state delegations and the election in the House would be by state—that is, each state delegation would cast one vote. Republicans controlled eight delegations and two were evenly divided. Hamilton urged Federalist representatives to vote for Jefferson as the lesser of two evils, but for 35 ballots they ignored his advice and voted for Burr. Finally, convinced that Burr could not be elected, on the 36th ballot several Federalists in the two divided delegations cast blank ballots, permitting those states to go for Jefferson. The Federalist representatives in two Federalist states abstained or cast blank ballots rather than vote for Jefferson. Thus Jefferson was elected president with the votes of ten states. Burr, with the votes of only four New England states, became vice president.

In 1804 Jefferson's popularity was at its zenith. On Feb. 25, a Republican congressional caucus nominated him for president and, ignoring Aaron Burr, selected George Clinton of New York for vice president. The party was well organized: there was a national Republican campaign committee and state, county, and town committees wherever there was Federalist opposition. By contrast, the Federalists were in disarray. There was no nominating caucus, merely a private consensus among Federalist leaders to support Charles Cotesworth Pinckney of South Carolina for president and Rufus King of New York for vice president.

The 1804 election was the first held under the *12th Amendment, requiring separate votes for president and vice president. Jefferson and Clinton carried 14 states with 162 electoral votes; Pinckney and King received

only the 12 electoral votes of Connecticut and Delaware plus two in Maryland. "The two parties which prevailed with so much violence when you were here," Jefferson wrote with satisfaction to a French friend after the election, "are almost wholly melted into one."

Elections of 1808 and 1812. Weighed down by the disaster of the embargo (see *Embargo and Nonintercourse) and eager to retire to private life, Jefferson happily fulfilled his earlier resolution to follow Washington's precedent and not seek a third term. His heir apparent was Secretary of State James Madison, and in January 1804 a Republican congressional caucus nominated Madison for president and George Clinton of New York for vice president. Deep in despair and lethargy, the Federalists in September renominated—how remains unclear—their 1804 ticket: Charles Cotesworth Pinckney for president, Rufus King for vice president.

But factionalism now roiled Republican calm. Sen. James Monroe also wanted to be president, as did the party's vice presidential candidate, George Clinton. Since the candidates themselves perforce remained silent, a vicious press war raged as Clintonites, Monroeites, and Federalists collaborated to discredit Madison. The chief accusation against Madison was that, as secretary of state, he had been biased against England and subservient to France. But this accusation was refuted when President Jefferson released diplomatic correspondence of 1804–8 that revealed Madison forthrightly defending U.S. interests against both powers. On Jan. 4, 1809, the count of electoral ballots gave Madison 122, Pinckney 47, and Clinton 6.

The election of 1812 was a referendum on the war that Congress had declared in January of that year (see *War of 1812). In May, the Republican congressional caucus renominated Madison for president and nominated Elbridge Gerry of Massachusetts for vice president. But ten days later Republicans in the New York State legislature nominated DeWitt Clinton, nephew of Vice Pres. George Clinton. New York's opposition to Madison was sectional rather than personal—New Yorkers were jealous of the fact that for 20 of the nation's 24 years Virginians had held the presidency.

In September, Federalists held a national "peace" convention in New York City at which they agreed to support Clinton rather than nominate a ticket of their own. Clinton repaid them by straddling the war issue: in sections of the country opposed to the war his spokesmen promised an early and honorable peace; in sections where the war was popular, they promised vigorous prosecution of the war. President Madison properly took no part in the campaign beyond letters to several state conventions justifying the war and suggesting that Clinton's opposition was hampering the president's conduct of it.

The result was far closer than Madison's victory in 1808—128 electoral votes for Madison, 89 for Clinton. Madison carried all the Southern and Western states except Maryland and Delaware; Clinton carried all the New England and Middle Atlantic states except Pennsylvania and Vermont.

Elections of 1816 and 1820. As secretary of state in Madison's cabinet, James Monroe was widely recognized as heir apparent. But there was dissatisfaction in the Republican Party with the colorless and old-fashioned Monroe, who would be the fourth Virginian to occupy the presidency. The dissidents turned to the able and popular William H. Crawford, the secretary of war. But Crawford declined to oppose the older Monroe, and on Mar. 16, 1816, the Republican congressional caucus nominated Monroe for president and Daniel Tompkins of New York for vice president.

The Federalists, virtually destroyed by the *Hartford Convention, did not bother to nominate anyone. In the end, 34 Federalist electors from Massachusetts, Connecticut, and Delaware voted hopelessly for Rufus King of New York, the last Federalist candidate for president. Monroe and Tompkins received 183 Republican electoral votes. "Monroe," King observed, "had the zealous support of nobody, and he was exempt from the hostility of everybody."

The demise of the Federalists as a national party ushered in a strange period when party conflicts were stilled. The Republicans had gradually adopted the Federalist program and had become the party of nationalism and centralism, while the surviving Federalists now spoke the language of strict construction and sectionalism. A Boston newspaper described the Monroe administration as the *"Era of Good Feelings." But foreign and domestic troubles were brewing beneath the placid surface; most alarming was the crisis in 1820 over the admission of Missouri as a slave state.

Monroe's acceptance of the *Missouri Compromise, which prohibited *slavery in the northern *Louisiana Purchase, might have cost him the South in the election of 1820. It did not. Monroe's reelection in 1820 was so taken for granted that no one even bothered to nominate him. Even Federalist electors voted for him. Of 231 votes cast in the electoral college, Monroe received 230; one dissident Republican cast his vote for John Quincy Adams. The unanimity with which the country returned Monroe to office in 1820, explained the Virginia Republican senator John Randolph, was "the unanimity of indifference, and not of approbation."

Election of 1824. Early in Monroe's second administration speculation began about his successor. The contest would be confined entirely to the Republican Party, which produced five contenders: William H. Crawford of Georgia, John C. Calhoun of South Carolina, Andrew Jackson of Tennessee, Henry Clay of Kentucky, and John Quincy Adams of Massachusetts. Crawford, secretary of the Treasury and a favorite of the "old" states' rights Republicans, was considered the favorite, and indeed was nominated by the Republican congressional caucus in February 1824 despite the fact that he had suffered a paralytic stroke the previous September. So effectively did the supporters of his rivals attack "King Caucus" as undemocratic that a congressional caucus never again nominated a presidential candidate.

Three of Crawford's rivals were "new" Republicans, advocates of *internal improvements, protective *tariffs, banking regulations, and a strong national defense. Jackson's political views were unknown, but he and Clay were identified with the rising tide of *democracy in opposition to government by elites.

Jackson was nominated—technically, endorsed—by the Tennessee legislature, Calhoun by the South Carolina legislature, Clay by legislative caucuses in Kentucky and other Western states, and Adams by a legislative caucus in Massachusetts. Jackson's candidacy proved unexpectedly popular. When he captured the state Republican convention in Pennsylvania, Calhoun withdrew from the race, content to seek the vice presidency, in which role he was welcomed by both the Adams and Jackson camps. When the electoral votes were counted in January 1825, Jackson had 99, Adams 84, Crawford 41, and Clay 37. Calhoun was elected vice president with two-thirds of the votes cast, but none of the presidential candidates had a majority.

Under the 12th Amendment, the House of Representatives was now required to select a president from among the three leading candidates. Clay was thus out of the race, but in a position to throw his influence to one of the others. There was long-standing animosity between Jackson and Clay, not least because they were rivals for the political leadership of the West. There was no personal liking between Adams and Clay either, but their political views were similar and Adams presented less of an obstacle to Clay's ambition than Jackson did. When it became known that Clay was urging his supporters in the House to vote for Adams, a Jackson man accused Adams of having bought Clay's support. The charge was never proved (although there was probably an understanding of some sort), but when Adams was elected with the votes of 13 states to Jackson's 7 and Crawford's 4, and soon thereafter appointed Clay secretary of state, Jackson became convinced that the election had been stolen from him, and the suspicion of a *"corrupt bargain" lived on to haunt the new administration.

The election of 1824 was the first in which a candidate who lost the popular and electoral votes nevertheless became president. It was also the last to be decided by the House of Representatives.

Elections of 1828 and 1832. Having been cheated of the presidency—as he thought—by the "corrupt bargain" of 1824, Andrew Jackson would not be denied in 1828. By then the Republican Party had divided into two factions. The Democratic-Republicans (soon to become the *Democratic Party) comprised the advocates of small government, states' rights, and the interests of farmers and workingmen; they backed Jackson with great enthusiasm. The *National Republicans (soon to become the *Whig Party) comprised advocates of energetic federal government and of institutions and policies—a national bank, protective tariff, internal improvements—intended to overcome sectional differences and unite the country; they backed their nominal leader, Pres. John Quincy Adams (their real leader was Secretary of State Henry Clay), but with less enthusiasm and little of the organizational skill of the Jackson men.

Jackson was nominated as early as 1825 by the Tennessee legislature (the old congressional caucus, discredited as antidemocratic, was abandoned after 1824). His campaign was ably organized by politicians like Martin Van Buren of New York with committees at state, county, and local levels. Jackson supporters joined Hickory Clubs (in honor of "Old Hickory") and carried hickory sticks. Rallies, parades, and barbecues substituted for discussion of the issues. Jackson newspapers accused Adams of aristocratic proclivities: a billiard table he had installed in the White House at his own expense was described as "gambling furniture" and a "royal extravagance." Henry Clay was denounced for using English stationery. National Republicans retaliated by depicting Jackson as crude and uneducated, a frontier brawler, and a bigamist and adulterer (nearly 40 years before, Jackson had married in good faith before his wife's divorce from her previous husband had been finalized).

But nothing could stem the democratic tide of which Jackson had become the symbol and leader. Both sides regarded the election as a revolution. All but 2 of the 24 states chose electors by popular vote; in those states the number of voters tripled over that of 1824. Jackson received 56 percent of the popular vote and 178 electoral votes to Adams's 83. Adams carried New England, Delaware, and New Jersey, and received electoral votes in New York and Maryland; but Jackson carried the entire West and South plus Pennsylvania. John C. Calhoun, who had been vice president under Adams but had deserted to the Jackson camp, was reelected vice president.

The election of 1832 was the first in which the political parties held national nominating conventions. The new *Anti-Masonic Party held the first such convention in September 1831 in Baltimore, selecting William Wirt, who had been attorney general under presidents Monroe and John Quincy Adams, as its candidate for president. The National Republicans met in Baltimore in December and chose Henry Clay, now a U.S. senator, as their standard-bearer. The Democratic-Republicans also met in Baltimore in May 1832, renominating Jackson and nominating Van Buren for vice president.

Jackson's popularity was now greater than ever. His recent veto of a bill to recharter the Second *Bank of the United States had seemed to draw the line between the party of the "moneyed aristocracy" (the National Republicans) and the party of the common man (the Democratic-Republicans). Jackson and Van Buren won 55 percent of the popular vote, amassing 219 electoral votes to Clay's 49 and Wirt's nine.

Election of 1836. Andrew Jackson selected as his successor his vice president and loyal political adviser, Martin Van Buren. For vice president he picked Rep. Richard M. Johnson of Kentucky. Despite dissension within the party—Southerners distrusted Van Buren, the "little magician" from New York, hated Johnson for keeping a black mistress, and resented Jackson's suppression of the *nullification movement—the convention that met in Baltimore in May 1835 ratified "King Andrew's" choices.

The Whig Party was still too new and disunited to hold a convention and select a single candidate to oppose Van Buren. Instead, it encouraged the nomination by state legislatures and conventions of *"favorite sons" in the hope that these might collectively take enough votes from Van Buren to force the election into the House of Representatives. Thus Sen. Daniel Webster of Massachusetts, Sen. Hugh L. White of Tennessee, and Gen. William Henry Harrison of Ohio ran for president as Whigs. "The remarkable character of this election," John Quincy Adams grumbled in his diary, "is that all the candidates are at most third-rate men whose pretensions rest not on high attainments or upon eminent services, but upon intrigue and political speculation."

Despite dissension in their ranks and three Whig opponents, the Democrats had the advantages of national prosperity (which would soon end) and superior organization. Van Buren received 51 percent of the popular vote and 170 electoral votes; the three Whig candidates together received 124.

Election of 1840. The election of 1840 was held in the midst of a severe economic depression triggered by the *Panic of 1837. Sensing a national desire for a change of administration, the Whigs passed over the celebrated but controversial giants of their party—Henry Clay and Daniel Webster—and at their convention in Harrisburg, Pa., in December 1839 nominated Gen. William Henry Harrison of Ohio for president and former governor and senator John Tyler of Virginia for vice president. In May 1840 the Democrats, meeting in Baltimore, nominated Pres. Martin Van Buren for a second term.

Determined to employ against the Democrats the populist strategy that the Democrats had used so effectively against John Quincy Adams in 1828, the Whigs conducted a campaign carnival intended to sway the masses rather than appeal to their reason. The aged Harrison had been a dubious hero in wars against Indians and British and an undistinguished governor and senator. Unlike Andrew Jackson, he was wellborn and college-educated. Nevertheless, the Whigs transformed him into a frontiersman of humble origin. Log cabins and hard cider were the themes, "Tippecanoe and Tyler Too" was the slogan, at countless rallies, revivals, barbecues, and parades. On the issues, Harrison was silent. "Let him say nothing, promise nothing," counseled banker Nicholas Biddle, and "General Mum" obeyed. Meanwhile, Whig propagandists depicted Van Buren as an "effete sybarite" who maintained a "royal establishment" in the "presidential palace."

The disgraceful campaign, which John Quincy Adams likened to a hurricane, ended with an electoral landslide for Harrison—234 electoral votes to 60—although he received only 52 percent of the popular vote.

Election of 1844. The overriding issue in 1844 was the annexation of Texas (see *Texas Annexation), which was certain to cause war with Mexico and would add a large slave area to the United States. At their convention in Baltimore in May 1844, the Whigs nominated Henry Clay, who opposed annexation. The Democratic convention, which also met in Baltimore later that same month, deadlocked between former president Martin Van Buren (antiannexation) and former governor Lewis Cass of Michigan (proannexation), neither of whom could get the two-thirds majority required for nomination. On the ninth ballot, the convention turned to little-known former congressman and governor James K. Polk of Tennessee (the first *"dark horse" in American history), a forthright advocate of annexing both Texas and Oregon (see *Oregon Dispute).

Although Clay was one of the great statesmen of the era, he was confronted by a dilemma: how to keep the support of Southern Whigs, who favored annexation, without losing the support of Northern Whigs, whose antislavery element had formed a *Liberty Party and nominated *abolitionist James G. Birney. His decision to straddle the issues of both annexation and slavery proved fatal. Once opposed to annexation, he now declared that he would not object if it could be had "without dishonor, without war." The presence of slavery in Texas was not a problem because slavery was a "temporary institution." Clay's equivocation failed to satisfy Southerners and alienated antislavery Northerners.

While Clay mired himself ever more deeply in contradiction, Polk remained quietly at home. His Democratic followers, however, cheered for "Texas and Democracy" and "Fifty-four Forty or Fight," a reference to U.S. claims to all of Oregon as far as Alaska. They also attacked Clay's moral fitness to be president, since he had a reputation as a gambler, duelist, and debauchee.

Polk edged Clay in the popular vote but won 170 electoral votes to Clay's 105. Birney's small antislavery vote cost Clay New York, Pennsylvania, and Ohio and thus the election.

Election of 1848. In 1848 the major issue facing the country was the extension of slavery in territory won in the *Mexican War. But the two major parties, Democrats and Whigs, ignored it, since they were national parties dependent on supporters in all sections of the country. But antislavery men increasingly looked for a new party that would represent their principles.

Since President Polk refused to run for a second term, the Democrats at their convention in Baltimore in May 1848 nominated Sen. Lewis Cass of Michigan. Cass opposed the *Wilmot Proviso, which would have prohibited slavery in all the new territories, preferring instead what he called "squatter sovereignty" (see *Popular Sovereignty), the right of the settlers in a territory to decide whether to admit or bar slavery. Antislavery delegates—particularly New York "Barnburners" (see *Barnburners and Hunkers), led by former president Martin Van Buren—walked out of the convention and in the following months joined with other antislavery groups, including James G. Birney's Liberty Party, to form the *Free-Soil Party. The Free-Soilers nominated Van Buren for president and Charles Francis Adams (son of the president whose defeat Van Buren had engineered in 1828) for vice president.

The Whigs, meeting in Baltimore in June, still smarted from their defeat in 1844 with Clay. Remembering their success in 1840 with an alleged military hero, they now passed over Clay and nominated Gen. Zachary Taylor, a genuine hero of the Mexican War, for president and former congressman Millard Fillmore of New York for vice president. A lifelong professional soldier, Taylor was totally apolitical. He had never voted, never belonged to a political party, and his views on national issues were unknown. For Southerners, it was enough that he was a large Louisiana planter and slave owner and father-in-law of Sen. Jefferson Davis of Mississippi.

For the first time, voters in all 30 states (except Massachusetts) went to the polls on the same day, Nov. 7. They gave a slight majority of the popular vote to Taylor, who received 163 electoral votes to Cass's 127. Van Buren received 10 percent of the popular vote. Although he did not carry a single state, he took enough votes from Cass—particularly in New York—to cost Cass the election.

Election of 1852. Both Democrats and Whigs in 1852 endorsed the *Compromise of 1850, which most Americans wanted to believe had permanently settled the slavery issue. At the Democratic convention in Baltimore that June, the leading contenders were Sen. Lewis Cass of Michigan, former secretary of state James Buchanan of Pennsylvania, and Sen. Stephen A. Douglas of Illinois, but none could get the two-thirds majority required for nomination. On the 49th ballot, the party turned to dark horse Franklin Pierce of New Hampshire, a former governor and senator who had served as a brigadier general in the Mexican War.

The Whigs met later that month, also in Baltimore. Millard Fillmore, who had succeeded to the presidency on the death of Zachary Taylor, believed that he deserved the party's nomination. But the Whigs—having elected Harrison in 1840 and Taylor in 1848—were enamored of military heroes. On the 53rd ballot they chose Winfield Scott, general in chief of the U.S. Army and a hero of the Mexican War, as their candidate. Antislavery Whigs thereupon abandoned their party and, as Free-Soil Whigs, nominated Sen. John Parker Hale of New Hampshire for president.

Since slavery was, by mutual agreement, not an issue between Democrats and Whigs, the contest was one of personalities, which Scott, now aged, fat, vain, and foolish, lost. Pierce received 51 percent of the popular vote, Scott 44 percent; but Pierce amassed 254 electoral votes to Scott's 42. The Free-Soil Whigs polled only half the votes that the Free-Soil Party had in 1848.

Election of 1856. The truce between the major parties on the slavery issue was ended by the passage of the *Kansas-Nebraska Act, which repealed the Missouri Compromise and established the principle of popular sovereignty in the territories. Devastated by its overwhelming defeat in 1852, the Whig Party dissolved in the new crisis. Its antislavery members joined with others to form (1854) the new *Republican Party, which preserved Whig political and economic principles but committed itself to preventing the extension of slavery into the territories. At their convention in Philadelphia in June 1856, the Republicans nominated the popular young explorer John C. Frémont.

The Democrats, meeting in Cincinnati in June, passed over Pres. Franklin Pierce and Sen. Stephen A. Douglas of Illinois and nominated James Buchanan of Pennsylvania. Absent from the country as U.S. minister to Great Britain when the Kansas-Nebraska Act was passed, Buchanan was untouched by the controversies that had surrounded it. He had never, according to one Southern newspaper, "uttered a word which would pain the most sensitive Southern heart." The Democratic platform endorsed the Kansas-Nebraska Act and popular sovereignty and condemned continued agitation over the slavery question.

Another new party, the American Party—formerly the *Know-Nothing Party—split over the Kansas-Nebraska Act. Its Northern members joined the Republicans; its Southern rump nominated former president Millard Fillmore.

Republicans campaigned for "Free Soil, Free Speech, Free Men, Frémont." They made clear they were not abolitionists but were determined to prevent the spread of slavery beyond the states where it then existed. The Democrats labeled the "Black Republicans" disunionists, and indeed some Southern states threatened to secede (see *Secession) if Frémont was elected. In November, Buchanan won 45 percent of the popular vote and 174 electoral votes, carrying every Southern state except Maryland plus Pennsylvania, New Jersey, Indiana, Illinois, and California. Frémont won 30 percent of the popular vote and 114 electoral votes, all of them in the North. Fillmore carried only Maryland with 8 electoral votes.

Elections of 1860 and 1864. The election of 1860 was held in a mood of national crisis. A Republican victory seemed certain, and that would mean dissolution of the Union with all its imponderable consequences.

The Democrats met in Charleston, S.C., in April 1860 and promptly split apart. When Northern delegates refused to agree to a proslavery platform, the delegates of eight Southern states walked out. The rump convention, unable to provide the necessary two-thirds majority for any candidate, adjourned and reassembled in June in Baltimore, where it was joined by new delegates. There the convention split again. Northern Democrats nominated Sen. Stephen A. Douglas of Illinois; Southern Democrats nominated Vice Pres. John C. Breckinridge of Kentucky.

The Republicans met in Chicago in May. Writing off the South, they adopted a platform not only opposing the extension of slavery but advocating Northern policies that Southerners had stymied in the past—protective tariffs, internal improvements, and free land for Western settlers. The leading candidate for the Republican nomination was Sen. William H. Seward of New York. But Seward was widely perceived as too radical on slavery for Northern tastes and too friendly toward immigrants to please the Know-Nothings who had joined the party. On the third ballot, the convention nominated Abraham Lincoln of Illinois, a moderate on the slavery issue, a staunch supporter of the Union—and the only candidate capable of carrying the key Western states of Indiana and Illinois.

One other party entered the race. The *Constitutional Union Party, made up of former Whigs who simply ignored the slavery issue and committed themselves single-mindedly to the preservation of the Union, nominated former senator John Bell of Tennessee.

The Republicans did not campaign in the South, where Lincoln's name was not even on the ballots. Although Douglas had been repudiated by the South, he campaigned there extensively, speaking on behalf of the Constitution and the Union—becoming, incidentally, the first presidential candidate to "stump" the entire country. Bell and Breckinridge confined their efforts to the South.

Lincoln received 40 percent of the popular vote, but these votes were concentrated in the populous Northern states, winning him 180 electoral votes—more than those of all his rivals combined. Douglas received 29 percent of the popular vote but carried only Missouri and New Jersey with 12 electoral votes. Breckinridge, with 18 percent of the popular vote, carried every state of the Deep South plus North Carolina, Delaware, and Maryland with 72 electoral votes. Bell, with 13 percent of the popular vote, carried Tennessee, Virginia, and Kentucky with 39 electoral votes.

Since Breckinridge was the only candidate favoring disunion, it can be said that the American people in 1860 voted overwhelmingly for the Union. Since Lincoln was the only candidate proposing to limit the spread of slavery, it can also be said that most American voters did not oppose slavery.

Four years later, with the North weary of the *Civil War and its enormous casualties, Lincoln despaired of re-election. But Gen. William T. Sherman's capture of Atlanta in September 1864 raised Northern spirits and altered the political picture. The Democrats nominated the discredited Gen. George B. McClellan, who ignored his party's peace platform and strongly endorsed the war. Lincoln received 55 percent of the popular vote and 212 electoral votes, McClellan 45 percent of the popular vote and 21 electoral votes.

The remarkable fact about this election—in which 25 states participated—was that it was held at all. Speaking a few days later to a group of visitors, Lincoln said: "We can not have free government without elections; and if the rebellion could force us to forgo, or postpone a national election, it might fairly claim to have already conquered and ruined us. . . . But the election . . . has demonstrated that a people's government can sustain a national election, in the midst of a great civil war. Until now it has not been known to the world that this was a possibility."

Elections of 1868 and 1872. The great issue in 1868 was *Reconstruction: would Republicans, under a president of their own party, complete the Radical program (see *Radical Republicans) on which they had embarked in defiance of Pres. Andrew Johnson, or would a Democratic president pursue Johnson's course of quick and easy reconciliation? The latter seemed improbable, for the Republicans had long since hit upon and cultivated an unbeatable presidential candidate, Gen. Ulysses S. Grant, who would prove a docile tool of the Radicals and a patriotic cover for the impatient spoilsmen. At their convention in Chicago, the Republicans nominated Grant for president on their first ballot; for vice president they selected Radical representative and Speaker of the House Schuyler Colfax.

The Democrats in New York City required 22 ballots to nominate former governor Horatio Seymour of New York, a onetime Peace Democrat who had declared the *Emancipation Proclamation unconstitutional and had opposed *conscription. Their vice presidential nominee was Francis P. Blair of Missouri, a former congressman and Union general.

In the campaign that followed, the Democrats attacked Radical reconstruction and Republicans waved the *bloody shirt. Grant won, but by a surprisingly small margin—3 million popular votes to Seymour's 2.7 million. (Grant's plurality of 300,000 votes was more than accounted for by 500,000 Republican votes cast by freedmen in six Southern states controlled by Radicals.) Grant received 214 electoral votes, Seymour 80.

By 1872, numbers of Republicans had become disaffected from Grant's corrupt administration. They were also becoming weary of Radical coercion of the South and wanted to turn to new issues like *civil service reform. At Cincinnati in May they founded the *Liberal Republican Party and nominated for president Horace Greeley, eccentric reformer and publisher of the New York *Tribune,* and for vice president Gov. Benjamin Gratz Brown of Missouri. Astonishingly, the Democratic national convention adopted the Liberal Republican ticket, although Greeley had been a lifelong foe of their party. The Republicans renominated Grant for president and Radical senator Henry Wilson of Massachusetts for vice president.

Grant received 3.6 million popular votes, 286 electoral votes. Greeley received 2.8 million popular votes; because he died shortly after the election, his electoral votes were distributed among four other men.

Election of 1876. The Republican Old Guard or "Stalwarts" (see *Stalwarts and Half-Breeds) were eager to renominate Grant for a third term, and Grant was willing to serve, but the party refused to break the two-term precedent. Passing over the party favorite, Rep. James G. Blaine of Maine, who was then embarrassed by the *Mulligan letters, it nominated for president Civil War general and three-term Ohio governor Rutherford B. Hayes, a man of irreproachable character. For vice president the party nominated Rep. William W. Wheeler of New York.

The Democrats nominated reform governor Samuel J. Tilden of New York, destroyer of the *Tweed Ring, for president and Gov. Thomas A. Hendricks of Indiana for vice president.

Tilden received 4.3 million popular votes to Hayes's 4.0 million. But three Southern states—Florida, South Carolina, and Louisiana—turned in two slates of electoral votes. Without one vote from those states, Tilden fell one electoral vote short of election. To resolve the disputed electoral-vote returns, Congress created an electoral commission of 15 members that, voting strictly along party lines, awarded all the disputed electoral votes to Hayes, who on Mar. 2 was declared elected with 185 electoral votes. Tilden chose not to contest the decision, but a group of Southern politicians seized the opportunity presented by Hayes's vulnerability to negotiate the *Compromise of 1877. Hayes was inaugurated without incident on Mar. 5.

Election of 1880. Again in 1880 Republican Stalwarts advanced the candidacy of former president Ulysses S. Grant. The Half-Breed candidate, James G. Blaine, appeared to be the favorite. Grant led on the first ballot, but on the 36th ballot Blaine and Sen. John Sherman of Ohio threw their support to a dark horse, Civil War general and Ohio representative James A. Garfield. To appease the Stalwarts, the vice presidential nomina-

tion went to Chester A. Arthur, a follower of New York boss Roscoe Conkling though himself an honest and able executive. The party platform advocated civil service reform, a protective tariff, and veterans' benefits.

The Democrats nominated for president Gen. William Scott Hancock, hero of Gettysburg, and for vice president former congressman William H. English of Indiana.

Garfield received 4.5 million popular votes, 214 electoral votes; Hancock, 4.4 million popular votes, 155 electoral votes.

Election of 1884. The Republicans at last nominated for president the popular former senator and secretary of state James G. Blaine of Maine, with Sen. John A. Logan of Illinois for vice president. The Democrats nominated corpulent Gov. Grover Cleveland of New York for president and former governor Thomas A. Hendricks of Indiana for vice president. Cleveland's reputation for honesty was such that *Tammany Hall, the Democratic machine in New York, opposed him, while liberal Republicans—*"mugwumps"—deserted the corrupt Blaine for the Democratic candidate.

No issue was involved in this election other than possession of the government. Both candidates were attacked on personal grounds. Republicans hooted at Cleveland, who acknowledged that he had fathered an illegitimate child, "Ma, Ma, where's my pa? / Gone to the White House, ha, ha, ha!" And Democrats replied, "Blaine, Blaine, James G. Blaine, / Continental liar from the state of Maine!" Blaine was plagued as usual by the compromising Mulligan letters.

With New York ripe to be stolen by the Republicans because of Tammany's inactivity, Blaine may have lost it by his failure to promptly disavow the characterization of the Democratic Party by a Protestant clerical supporter, the Rev. Samuel D. Burchard, as the party of *"rum, Romanism, and rebellion." He lost New York by only 1,149 votes out of 1.125 million cast there, many by Irish Catholics, and with it the election.

Cleveland received 4.9 million popular votes, 219 electoral votes; Blaine got 4.8 million popular votes, 182 electoral.

Election of 1888. Pres. Grover Cleveland again led the Democrats, this time with Allen G. Thurman of Ohio for vice president. The Republicans selected little-known Gov. Benjamin Harrison of Indiana for president and former U.S. senator and minister to France Levi P. Morton of New York for vice president.

Cleveland refused to campaign, believing it undignified for the president of the United States to solicit votes. In any case, his position favoring tariff revision—for him, the central issue of the campaign—was well known.

But his stern integrity during his first term had won him few friends. His conscientious management of the civil service pleased neither office seekers nor reformers. Veterans were furious with him for resisting increased pensions and for proposing to return captured *Confederate battle flags to the Southern states. The *Murchison letter cost the Democrats dearly among Irish-Americans. Meanwhile, powerful manufacturing interests supported the Republicans' promise of upward tariff revision.

In November, Cleveland received 5.5 million popular votes to Harrison's 5.4 million, a plurality of 100,000; but the electoral college gave Harrison 233 votes, Cleveland 168.

Election of 1892. Unenthusiastically, the Republicans renominated the unpopular Pres. Benjamin Harrison (this time with newspaper publisher Whitelaw Reid of New York for vice president) while the Democrats renominated (for an unprecedented third time) former president Grover Cleveland (now with former congressman Adlai E. Stevenson of Illinois for vice president). For the first time the contest was between two presidents, one former, one sitting.

Cold and remote, Harrison was unpopular with both liberal and conservative wings of his party. The public, moreover, regarded his administration as having been an unconscionable raid on the Treasury. The *McKinley Tariff was particularly disliked, although the administration made high tariffs the centerpiece of its campaign. The suppression by state and federal troops of the *Homestead Strike and other labor disorders also disturbed public opinion.

Even more ominous were the forces gathering in the West over the *free silver issue. The *People's Party had nominated for president Gen. James B. Weaver of Iowa, former candidate of the *Greenback Party, and for vice president James G. Field. To the alarm of the older parties, the People's Party carried five states (Kansas, North Dakota, Colorado, Idaho, and Nebraska), electing five senators, ten representatives, and three governors (Kentucky, North Dakota, and Colorado).

On Nov. 8, Cleveland received 5.6 million popular votes and 277 electoral votes, Harrison 5.2 million popular votes and 145 electoral votes, Weaver 1 million popular votes and 22 electoral votes.

Elections of 1896 and 1900. A severe depression and a split in the Democratic Party between Eastern *Gold Democrats and Western Silver Democrats promised to make 1896 a Republican year. The leading candidate for the Republican nomination was the able and genial governor of Ohio, William McKinley. As early as 1895, president-maker Marcus Alonzo Hanna had devoted himself full-time to applying his money and organizational skills to ensure McKinley's nomination (see *McKinley and Hanna). McKinley and Hanna shared a belief in the protective tariff as the centerpiece of national prosperity. Indeed, Hanna billed McKinley as the "Advance Agent of Prosperity." By the time the Republican convention convened in Philadelphia, Hanna had sewed up the majority of the delegates for McKinley. When the Eastern bosses came belatedly to negotiate for patronage in exchange for their support, Hanna and McKinley were able to turn them away. McKinley was nominated on the first ballot. For vice president, the convention chose Garret A. Hobart of New Jersey. The party platform advocated a high tariff and "sound money." When the party adopted its gold plank, a small number of Western *Silver Republicans bolted.

The Democratic Party, now in the possession of the silverites, met in Chicago. No candidate stood out above the others. But when 34-year-old William Jennings Bryan, former congressman and delegate from Nebraska, gave his stirring "Cross of Gold" speech (see *Bryan's "Cross of Gold" Speech) during debate on the platform, the crowded auditorium was roused to frenzy. The next day, crying "Bryan, Bryan, Bryan, Bryan!" it nominated the young Nebraskan on the third ballot. Arthur Sewall of Maine was the party's choice for vice president. The People's Party also nominated Bryan for president, but chose Thomas E. Watson of Georgia as its candidate for vice president.

Bryan's nomination alarmed the conservative forces in the Republican Party. They had expected to win the election on the issue of the protective tariff, but Bryan insisted on fighting the campaign on the radical issue of free silver. While McKinley remained at home in Canton, Ohio, receiving on his front porch several delegations daily (a total of 750,000 persons between June and November), Bryan, campaigning virtually alone, traveled 13,000 miles across the country, speaking 600 times on behalf of silver and the common man. Republican national chairman Mark Hanna mobilized corporate money in the Republican Party for vigorous electioneering and for an antisilver educational campaign in which hundreds of millions of pamphlets were distributed across the country to refute Bryan's seductive fallacies.

On Nov. 3, McKinley received 7 million popular votes and 271 electoral votes; Bryan, 6.5 million popular votes and 176 electoral votes.

1900 was a reprise of 1896, except that now the country was prosperous and the issue of free silver had lost much of its appeal. McKinley again headed the Republican ticket; war hero Theodore Roosevelt, governor of New York, was the Republican candidate for vice president. They ran on the slogan "The Full Dinner Pail." Bryan again headed the Democratic ticket, together with Adlai E. Stevenson of Illinois for vice president. Again Bryan argued for free silver, but now he also condemned U.S. imperialism in the Philippines.

McKinley received 7.2 million popular votes, 292 electoral votes; Bryan received 6.4 million popular votes, 155 electoral votes.

Election of 1904. Theodore Roosevelt desperately wanted to be elected president in his own right. Betraying an uncharacteristic loss of confidence, he feared the conservative Republican Party would seek another candidate, but the party—whatever its misgivings—could not reject a popular president. At its Chicago convention in June, it nominated Roosevelt for president and conservative Charles W. Fairbanks of Indiana for vice president.

At St. Louis in July, the Democrats, now controlled by the Eastern Gold Democrats, rebuffed William Jennings Bryan and nominated a conservative New York judge, Alton B. Parker, for president and an obscure 82-year-old West Virginia millionaire, Henry G. Davis, for vice president.

Neither candidate campaigned. Parker had no hope of winning, although his cause was heavily financed by Wall Street tycoons Thomas Ryan and August Belmont. Roosevelt's advisers persuaded him he had more to lose than to gain by speaking in public. Nevertheless, Roosevelt suffered another bout of anxiety in October when he feared he might not carry New York State. He appealed to E. H. Harriman, president of the Union Pacific Railroad, and Henry Clay Frick, head of U.S. Steel, for emergency funds. They came through handsomely, but when Roosevelt, safely reelected, resumed his denunciations of "malefactors of great wealth," Frick reportedly grumbled, "We bought the son of a bitch and then he didn't stay bought!"

In November, Roosevelt received 7.6 million popular votes and 336 electoral votes, Parker 5.1 million popular votes and 140 electoral votes. Roosevelt exclaimed happily: "I am no longer a political accident!"

Election of 1908. Theodore Roosevelt had declared in 1904 that he would not seek a third term (a pledge he later regretted), but he did not hesitate to pick his own successor. He chose Secretary of War William Howard Taft, a personal friend who he assumed shared his progressive enthusiasms (see *Progressivism). Taft, who would have preferred appointment to the Supreme Court, accepted the honor dutifully—although he and his wife feared a possible betrayal at the last minute. Their fears seemed justified when the Republican convention,

which Roosevelt had stacked in Taft's favor, erupted at the mention of Roosevelt's name into a 49-minute demonstration that might have led to Roosevelt's renomination by acclamation. But discipline prevailed, and the convention, with diminished enthusiasm, nominated Taft on the first ballot. For vice president it chose Rep. James S. Sherman, a New York conservative. Taft accepted the nomination with a promise to preserve and extend Roosevelt's "practical reforms"—a hint that he was no progressive zealot.

In Denver in July, the Democratic Party returned with affection to William Jennings Bryan, whom it had nominated in 1896 and 1900 but passed over in 1904. For vice president it nominated John W. Kern of Indiana. The progressive spirit pervaded the platforms of both parties, although the Democratic platform was more adamantly antimonopolistic.

As usual, Bryan campaigned strenuously, speaking several times a day on the theme "Shall the People Rule?" Taft played golf. In November, Taft received 7.7 million popular votes and 312 electoral votes (close to Roosevelt's showing in 1904), Bryan 6.4 million popular votes and 162 electoral votes. The Republicans retained control of both houses of Congress.

Elections of 1912 and 1916. In 1912, both major parties experienced a struggle between conservatives and progressives for possession of the parties' souls. In the Republican Party, the progressives lost. At the party's Chicago convention, the Old Guard rolled over the progressive minority and renominated William Howard Taft for president and James S. Sherman for vice president. (Sherman died in October and was replaced on the ticket by Nicholas Murray Butler, president of Columbia University in New York.) The progressives bolted, formed a new *Progressive Party, and in August nominated their hero, Theodore Roosevelt, for president and Gov. Hiram Johnson of California for vice president. At its Baltimore convention, the Democratic Party was saved from inconsequence when William Jennings Bryan, that much-belittled relic of lost causes, threw his influence behind progressive New Jersey governor Woodrow Wilson, who was nominated on the 46th ballot. Thomas R. Marshall of Indiana was nominated for vice president.

For Taft and Roosevelt, the campaign that followed was a bitter contest between former friends bent on punishing one another. Buoyed by the division in the Republican Party, Wilson campaigned serenely and eloquently, preaching a *New Freedom that was actually backward-looking compared to Roosevelt's *New Nationalism in its hostility to large aggregations of capital. For better or worse, that's where the future lay.

When the votes were counted, Taft and Roosevelt had accomplished their ends: each had prevented the election of the other. Wilson, with 6.3 million popular votes (41.9 percent of the total), won 435 electoral votes; Roosevelt, with 4.1 million popular votes, won 88 electoral votes; Taft, with 3.5 million popular votes, had only eight electoral votes. The Democrats gained control of both houses of Congress.

In June 1916, with war raging in Europe, a confident Republican Party, reunited and again the majority party, convened in Chicago. There it rebuffed the chastened Theodore Roosevelt and nominated for president Charles Evans Hughes, a justice of the U.S. Supreme Court, who resigned from the bench to accept the nomination. As a gesture to Roosevelt, the convention nominated for vice president Charles W. Fairbanks of Indiana, who had been vice president in Roosevelt's second term. The Democrats, meeting in St. Louis the same month, renominated Pres. Woodrow Wilson and Vice Pres. Thomas R. Marshall.

The Democratic convention was electrified by the slogan "He Kept Us Out of War." Wilson embraced the claim only gradually as its vote-getting power became evident; the vast majority of Americans opposed involvement in the European war. Hughes, however, was in a dilemma. If he criticized Wilson's diplomacy, he would seem to be prowar. His situation was made especially difficult by Roosevelt's clamoring for America to enter the war against Germany.

On election night, Hughes appeared to have swept most Eastern and some Midwestern states. When he went to bed he was only 12 electoral votes short of victory and he expected California, whose votes were not then counted, to provide those. By midnight, New York newspapers were headlining his election. But during a campaign visit to California Hughes had snubbed former governor Hiram Johnson, the 1912 Progressive Party candidate for vice president and now Republican candidate for the U.S. Senate. Many California progressives, therefore, split their tickets, voting for Johnson for senator and Wilson for president. By a small margin—3,800 out of 1 million votes cast—Wilson carried California along with the Western states and the Solid South and was elected.

One story has it that a newspaper reporter tried to telephone Hughes at his New York hotel in the early morning hours and was told, "The president has retired." To which the reporter replied, "When he wakes up, tell him he is no longer president."

Wilson received 9.1 million popular votes (49.4 percent of the total) and 277 electoral votes, Hughes 8.5 million popular votes and 254 electoral votes. The Democrats retained control of both houses of Congress.

Election of 1920. By the summer of 1920, in the aftermath of World War 1, most Americans were heartily sick of wartime ideals and duties, of postwar high prices, unemployment, and labor strife. More than anything else they longed to forget the world's troubles and return to the halcyon life of prewar small-town America—fast becoming a golden age in the popular imagination.

At the Republican national convention in Chicago that June, the leading candidates for the party's presidential nomination were Gen. Leonard Wood, onetime Army chief of staff, and Gov. Frank Lowden of Illinois. When these two champions deadlocked, the convention turned, on the tenth ballot, to handsome, genial Warren G. Harding, U.S. senator from Ohio, where he published a small-town newspaper, the *Marion Star*. Legend has it that Harding was picked by party bosses in a *smoke-filled hotel room. The reality is that Harding was everyone's second or third choice, a man devoid of convictions and therefore without enemies, "the best of the second raters," as another senator declared in his praise. Republican progressives were appalled, then doubly depressed by the nomination for vice president of another nullity, Gov. Calvin Coolidge of Massachusetts, who had won a moment of fame for breaking the *Boston police strike of 1919.

At San Francisco in July, the leading candidate for the Democratic presidential nomination was William G. McAdoo, who had been an effective wartime secretary of the Treasury and railroad administrator. But he was also President Wilson's son-in-law, now a fatal connection. Instead of the "crown prince," the party, on the 44th ballot, chose James M. Cox, three-term reform governor of Ohio and, like Harding, the publisher of small-town Ohio newspapers. For vice president it chose the attractive Franklin D. Roosevelt of New York, assistant secretary of the Navy, now universally recognized as a political "comer."

The stricken president had asked that the election of 1920 be "a great and solemn referendum" on the League of Nations. Cox and Roosevelt dutifully visited Wilson in the White House, then campaigned earnestly for the League while Harding generally remained on his front porch in Marion, issuing impenetrable statements about a "return to normalcy" and "agreement among nations."

On election day, Harding received 16 million popular votes (60.2 percent of the total) and 404 electoral votes to Cox's 9 million popular votes and 127 electoral votes. Harding carried every state outside the Solid South plus Tennessee.

Election of 1924. President Harding died on Aug. 2, 1923, and was succeeded by Vice President Calvin Coolidge. Something about that dour, laconic, frugal little man appealed to the country. Untouched by the scandals of his predecessor, he was down-to-earth, unpretentious, and given to commonplace utterances that could be taken as insightful—for example, "The business of America is business." Not one to rock the boat, he was borne along on the national tide of prosperity to his party's presidential nomination at its national convention in Cleveland in June 1924. Budget Director Charles G. Dawes was chosen as the Republican vice presidential candidate.

The Democrats, meeting in New York City in late June, were profoundly divided over *Prohibition and the *Ku Klux Klan, neither of which they dared to condemn. The anti-Klan, anti-Prohibition delegates, representing Eastern and urban Democrats, backed New York governor Alfred E. Smith, called "the Happy Warrior" by Franklin Roosevelt in his nominating speech, his first public appearance after having been stricken with polio. The Southern and Western delegates supported William G. McAdoo. Neither candidate could get the two-thirds majority necessary for nomination. After nine hot days and 103 ballots, the convention turned to John W. Davis, a conservative New York banker, then sought to balance the ticket by nominating William Jennings Bryan's brother, Nebraska governor Charles Bryan, for vice president.

Confronted by two conservative major party candidates, the remnants of progressivism assembled in Cleveland in July and nominated Republic insurgent Sen. Robert M. La Follette of Wisconsin for president and Democratic senator Burton K. Wheeler of Montana for vice president.

The result was predictable. Coolidge received 15.7 million popular votes (54.1 percent of the total) and 382 electoral votes; Davis received 8.4 million popular votes (28.8 percent) and 136 electoral votes. La Follette won only 4.8 million popular votes (16.6 percent) and the 13 electoral votes of his native Wisconsin. Both houses of Congress remained in Republican control.

Election of 1928. After Pres. Calvin Coolidge withdrew as a candidate for reelection, the front-runner for the 1928 Republican presidential nomination was Secretary of Commerce Herbert Hoover. The outstanding member of the Harding and Coolidge cabinets, Hoover was universally admired as the "great engineer," the nation's ablest executive. At the Republican national convention in Kansas City, Mo., June 12–15, Hoover was nominated on the first ballot; for vice president the Republicans chose Sen. Charles Curtis of Kansas.

The front-runner for the Democratic nomination was Alfred E. Smith, whose four terms as governor of New York had been marked by liberal social legislation. The sources of Smith's popularity among urban Democrats— his big-city origin, immigrant associations, and liberalism—were liabilities among rural and small-town Democrats. Worse, Smith was a Catholic and a "wet," an avowed opponent of Prohibition. Nevertheless, at the Democratic convention in Houston, June 26–29, the delegates fell into line and nominated Smith for president on the first ballot and Sen. Joseph Robinson of Arkansas for vice president.

Hoover campaigned on Republican prosperity, which he promised to extend until—in the words of a Republican campaign slogan—there was "a chicken in every pot and a car in every garage." The underdog from the start, Smith had to face a firestorm of religious bigotry, fanned by the Ku Klux Klan in the South and Midwest but pervading even liberal circles in the East.

On Nov. 4, 1928, Hoover received 21.4 million popular votes (58.2 percent of the total) and 444 electoral votes. Smith received 15.0 million popular votes (40.8 percent), carrying only six states of the once-solid South plus Massachusetts and Rhode Island with 87 electoral votes.

Elections of 1932, 1936, 1940, and 1944. Gloom, desperation, even talk of revolution pervaded the depression-racked country (see *Great Depression) as the 1932 election approached. Constrained by his ideology of laissez-faire, individualism, and voluntarism, Pres. Herbert Hoover refused to extend government aid to the growing numbers of unemployed (although he extended it to banks and railroads). By contrast, the leading candidate for the Democratic nomination, two-term New York governor Franklin D. Roosevelt, had declared: "The country needs and . . . demands bold, persistent experimentation." Neither man had a cure for the depression, but voters understood that the choice would be between action and inaction.

The Republican convention in Chicago in mid-June renominated Hoover and Curtis for president and vice president. The party's platform favored reduced government spending, a balanced budget, a high tariff, and maintenance of Prohibition.

At the Democratic convention, also in Chicago later that month, Roosevelt was opposed by party conservatives led by the now rancorous Al Smith. His name introduced to the strains of "Happy Days Are Here Again," Roosevelt fell short of the necessary two-thirds majority on the first three ballots. His support threatened to dissolve, but rather than see a conservative nominated,

William G. McAdoo, who had hoped for the nomination himself, delivered the California and Texas delegations to Roosevelt, who was nominated on the fourth ballot. Texas congressman John Nance Garner was nominated for vice president.

From Albany, N.Y., Roosevelt flew to Chicago in a Ford trimotor airplane—a nine-hour flight in bad weather with two refueling stops—to accept the nomination in person. "I pledge you, I pledge myself," he told the convention, "to a new deal for the American people." The Democratic platform, like the Republican, called for reduced government spending and a balanced budget, but it proposed lower tariffs and repeal of Prohibition.

In the campaign that followed, Hoover predicted that "grass [would] grow in the streets of a hundred cities, a thousand towns" if Roosevelt was elected. Roosevelt spoke (as he had the previous April) of economic reconstruction "from the bottom up and not from the top down, that puts the faith once more in the forgotten man at the bottom of the economic pyramid."

On Nov. 8, when 52.5 percent of the electorate voted for president, Roosevelt received 22.8 million popular votes (57.4 percent of the total) and 427 electoral votes; Hoover received 15.8 million popular votes (39.7 percent) and 59 electoral votes. The Democrats won control of both houses of Congress.

In June 1936, the Republican national convention in Cleveland nominated Alfred E. Landon, a progressive governor of Kansas and onetime follower of Theodore Roosevelt, for president and conservative Chicago newspaper publisher Frank Knox for vice president. Later that month, in Philadelphia, the Democrats renominated Roosevelt and Garner.

Landon attacked the New Deal for stifling American freedoms. Eighty percent of the press supported Landon; some Republican papers charged that the Democratic administration was in the hands of communists. Roosevelt denounced opponents of the New Deal as *economic royalists. The Literary Digest, which had correctly predicted the outcome of every presidential election since 1920, again polled millions of voters—owners of automobiles and/or telephones—and on Oct. 31 confidently reported that Landon would be elected with 370 electoral votes.

On Nov. 3, when 56.9 percent of the electorate voted for president, Roosevelt carried every state but Maine and Vermont, winning 27.8 million popular votes (61.1 percent of the total) and 523 electoral votes. Landon won 16.7 million popular votes (36.7 percent of the total) and eight electoral votes. Democrats retained control of both houses of Congress.

Roosevelt did not intend to run for a third term in 1940, but the fall of France that summer (see *World War 2) convinced him that he must (see *Roosevelt's Third-Term Decision). Nevertheless, he refused to declare his candidacy, informing the Democratic convention in Chicago that he had "no wish to be a candidate again" and that the delegates were "free to vote for any candidate." The announcement threw the delegates into confusion, but a cry over the loudspeakers of "We want Roosevelt!," originating in the basement of the convention hall at the instigation of Chicago mayor Edward Kelly, stampeded the convention. Roosevelt was renominated on the first ballot, but not by acclamation as he had wished. To preserve the liberal character of the party, Roosevelt demanded the nomination for vice president of Henry A. Wallace, secretary of agriculture. The choice was unpopular with the conservative-dominated convention, but Roosevelt was determined to reject his own nomination if the convention rejected Wallace. Eleanor Roosevelt flew to Chicago and in a memorable address calmed the incipient rebellion and secured Wallace's nomination on the first ballot.

In Philadelphia a few weeks earlier, the Republicans had nominated Wendell Willkie, a newcomer not only to politics but to the Republican Party. Willkie had been a distant third choice after Sen. Robert A. Taft of Ohio and gang-busting New York City district attorney Thomas E. Dewey. But a shrewdly managed publicity campaign supported by Time magazine and other Republican powers, culminating in packed convention galleries chanting "We want Willkie!," brought him the nomination on the sixth ballot. His running mate was conservative Oregon senator Charles McNary.

Willkie identified himself as the peace candidate against an administration that was leading the country to war. Roosevelt felt compelled to respond. At a speech in Boston on Oct. 30, he promised the mothers and fathers of America: "I have said this before, but I shall say it again, and again, and again. Your boys are not going to be sent into any foreign war."

On Nov. 5, when 58.9 percent of the electorate voted for president, Roosevelt carried 38 states, winning 27.3 million popular votes (54.7 percent of the total) and 449 electoral votes to Willkie's 22.3 million popular votes (44.8 percent) and 82 electoral votes. The Democrats retained control of both houses of Congress.

At their Chicago convention in June 1944, the Republicans had only one viable candidate. A short-lived boomlet for Gen. Douglas MacArthur had been ended by the general himself. Wendell Willkie's hopes for a second nomination had been dashed by defeat in the Wisconsin primary. That left Thomas E. Dewey, now governor of New York, who was selected almost unanimously on the first ballot (only one delegate voted gainst him). His running mate was conservative governor John A. Bricker of Ohio.

With American troops now fighting in France, Roosevelt felt he had an obligation to run yet again if the people commanded him. The Democratic convention in Chicago in July nominated him on the first ballot, although people close to him were shocked by the state of his health (see *Roosevelt's Final Illness). Roosevelt again preferred Wallace as his running mate but wearily bowed to the opinion of party leaders and accepted Sen. Harry S. Truman of Missouri instead.

With the war at its climax, Americans were not inclined to exchange their tested war leader for a young man with no experience in foreign affairs. Roosevelt roused himself from his enormous fatigue to prove himself an unbeatable campaigner one last time. The climax of his campaign was a four-hour tour of New York City in an open car during a chill October rain, followed that night by a major foreign policy address.

On Nov. 7, when 56.0 percent of the electorate voted for president, Roosevelt carried 36 states, winning 25.6 million popular votes (53.4 percent of the total) and 432 electoral votes to Dewey's 22.0 million popular votes (45.9 percent) and 99 electoral votes. The Democrats retained control of both houses of Congress.

Election of 1948. A Republican victory was certain in 1948, but the Eastern Republicans in control of the party were taking no chances. Passing over "Mr. Republican" himself, the estimable but unappealing Sen. Robert A. Taft of Ohio, at the party convention in Philadelphia in July, the Easterners won the nomination of Gov. Thomas E. Dewey of New York for president on the third ballot and of Gov. Earl Warren of California for vice president. A ticket that paired the youthful, popular governors of the nation's two most populous states was surely unbeatable.

The Democrats, on the other hand, were sunk in gloom. The old New Dealers were contemptuous of blundering, colorless Pres. Harry S. Truman and hoped only that Gen. Dwight D. Eisenhower—a man who had never voted or betrayed any political leaning—would reveal himself a Democrat and accept their nomination. Eisenhower disappointed them, and at the party convention in July, also in Philadelphia, they had no alternative but to nominate Truman for president and the aged Sen. Alben Barkley of Kentucky for vice president.

Even as they did so, the party was falling apart around them. Henry Wallace had already carried off its

left wing to his new *Progressive Party, and when the convention passed a strong civil rights plank the party's right wing—Southern conservatives—bolted to form a segregationist *States' Rights Party. But at 2 a.m. on July 14 the moribund rump of the party was roused from its despair by its feisty nominee. "Senator Barkley and I will win this election and make those Republicans like it," Truman told them, "—and don't you forget it!"

Truman promptly recalled the 80th Congress into special session, presented it with an agenda of the nation's pressing business—from civil rights to housing and education—and watched it depart two weeks later having done nothing. Thereafter Truman would campaign not against Dewey but against that "do-nothing" 80th Congress.

In Dewey's view, victory was certain if only he made no mistakes. The press and the pollsters assured him he was right. Thus he moved cautiously, avoided controversy, and spoke in banalities. "America's future is still ahead of us," he said.

Between Labor Day and Election Day, Truman whistle-stopped across the country, traveling 22,000 miles, speaking 275 times, often from the rear platform of his train at ten-minute stops to ever-growing crowds, attacking the "special interests" and that "do-nothing" 80th Congress, pleading for a Democratic Congress, and promising what he would later call his *Fair Deal. "Give 'em hell, Harry!" the crowds responded.

On Nov. 2, when 51.1 percent of the electorate voted for president, Truman received 24.2 million popular votes (49.6 percent of the total) to Dewey's 22.0 million (45.1 percent), carried 28 states to Dewey's 16, and won 303 electoral votes to Dewey's 189. The Democrats won control of both houses of Congress.

J. Strom Thurmond, candidate of the States' Rights Party, received 1.2 million popular votes and carried four Southern states with 39 electoral votes. Wallace also received 1.2 million popular votes but no electoral votes.

Elections of 1952 and 1956. In January 1952, Gen. Dwight D. Eisenhower revealed that he was, in fact, a Republican. In June, he resigned his position as military commander of the North Atlantic Treaty Organization and returned to the United States to seek the Republican nomination for president. Recognizing a sure winner, the Republicans again deserted "Mr. Republican," Sen. Robert A. Taft of Ohio, who exemplified the dominant conservative and isolationist element in the party, and at their convention in Chicago in July nominated Eisenhower on the first ballot. For vice president they chose Sen. Richard M. Nixon of California, a leader in the fight against communist subversion.

Pres. Harry S. Truman had decided not to run for re-election, although he was exempted from the *22nd Amendment's third-term prohibition. He selected Gov. Adlai E. Stevenson of Illinois as his candidate and was annoyed by Stevenson's unwillingness to sacrifice himself in an unwinnable contest against Eisenhower. It was Stevenson's misfortune to deliver such an eloquent address welcoming the delegates to the Democratic convention in Chicago in July that they drafted him as the party's nominee on the third ballot. For vice president the Democrats chose Sen. John Sparkman of Alabama.

Stevenson was witty, intellectual, and eloquent, but he could not touch Eisenhower, whose emphasis on the "mess in Washington" and the communist menace reflected the nation's discontent with the tired Democratic administration. Eisenhower found himself condemning Democratic foreign policies that he had helped formulate and had supported; he had to endure the embraces of reactionary and isolationist politicians he loathed; and he shamed himself by dropping a tribute to his friend and mentor, Gen. George C. Marshall, from a speech in Wisconsin in which he had to support Sen. Joseph R. McCarthy for reelection (see *McCarthyism).

The only setback for the Republicans was the revelation in September that a group of wealthy Californians had provided a secret fund to cover Nixon's expenses as senator. The fund was not illegal or uncommon, but it suggested corruption and Eisenhower was prepared to drop Nixon from the ticket. Nixon, however, went on national television, recounted the story of his humble origins, his struggle to get ahead, and his limited financial resources (his wife wore a "respectable Republican cloth coat"). Defiantly, he refused to give back their dog, Checkers, which his daughters had received as a gift "all the way from Texas." The speech was tasteless and maudlin, but millions of Americans wrote and wired their forgiveness for his transgressions and Eisenhower welcomed him back on the team.

In the last week of the campaign, Eisenhower promised to go to Korea (where the *Korean War had stalemated). This alone would have won him the election but was probably not necessary. On Nov. 4, when 61.6 percent of the electorate voted for president, Eisenhower received 33.9 million popular votes (55.1 percent of the total) and 442 electoral votes to Stevenson's 27.3 million popular votes (44.4 percent) and 89 electoral votes. Stevenson carried only nine Southern and Border states. The Republicans won slim majorities in both houses of Congress.

In 1956, the Republican convention in San Francisco renominated Eisenhower and Nixon. This time, Adlai Stevenson dutifully sought the Democratic nomination, and received it on the first ballot at the party's convention in Chicago. The Democrats chose Sen. Estes Kefauver of Tennessee as their vice presidential candidate.

Eisenhower was more popular than ever, and a tense international situation—revolution in Hungary, war in the Middle East—worked to his advantage. On Nov. 6, when 59.3 percent of the electorate voted for president, Eisenhower received 35.6 million popular votes (57.4 percent of the total) and 457 electoral votes, Stevenson 26.0 million popular votes (42.0 percent) and 74 electoral votes, now from only seven Southern states. But the Democrats won majorities in both houses of Congress.

Election of 1960. At Los Angeles in July 1960, the Democratic national convention nominated on its first ballot the attractive but undistinguished senator from Massachusetts, John F. Kennedy. The youngest presidential candidate of a major party in U.S. history, Kennedy, at 43, was handsome, sophisticated, stylish, and witty. He surrounded himself with intellectuals and shrewd political operatives. His young, fashionable wife and large, active family were other assets. Behind them stood his father, multimillionaire Joseph P. Kennedy, who was prepared to spend anything to see his son elected president of the United States.

To strengthen the Democratic ticket in the South, Kennedy chose for the vice presidential nomination the Senate majority leader, Lyndon B. Johnson, generally considered a conservative, a wheeler-dealer, and less than honest. Johnson had sought the presidential nomination; his reason for accepting the nomination for the vice presidency, where he would have less power than he enjoyed in the Senate, remains a matter of speculation.

The Republicans met at Chicago later the same month and, also on the first ballot, nominated Vice Pres. Richard M. Nixon for president. At 47, Nixon was awkward and ill at ease in public. Pres. Dwight D. Eisenhower wondered that his vice president seemed to have no friends. Eisenhower's secretary wrote that Nixon seemed "like a man who is acting like a nice man rather than being one." Having tirelessly—even ruthlessly—struggled upward from modest origins, befriended by few, humiliated even by Eisenhower, Nixon entered the presidential race with a load of resentment difficult to mask. For the vice presidential nomination, Nixon chose Henry Cabot Lodge, former senator from Massachusetts and U.S. representative to the United Nations.

The principal issues in the election were the economy and the *cold war. Since both men were centrists in their parties, they differed little in the substance of their campaigns. Both talked about "moving forward." Nixon (falsely) claimed some credit for Eisenhower's conduct of the cold war; Kennedy (falsely) alleged the existence of a "missile gap" between the United States and the Soviet Union.

A more important issue, unspoken, was Kennedy's religion. A Catholic, Kennedy confronted the problem directly before a meeting of Protestant clergy at Houston. Reaffirming his commitment to the separation of church and state, he declared: "I am not the Catholic candidate for president. . . . I do not speak for my church on public matters—and the church does not speak for me." Still, many Americans cast their votes along religious lines.

In the end, the greatest single issue was the personalities of the two candidates, particularly when they appeared together in a series of four television debates. The cameras were kinder to Kennedy, and that probably proved decisive.

On Nov. 8, when 62.8 percent of the electorate voted for president, Kennedy received 34.2 million popular votes (49.7 percent of the total) and 303 electoral votes to Nixon's 34.1 million popular votes (49.5 percent) and 219 electoral votes. Kennedy's plurality of only 120,000 votes was the smallest since 1888. Democratic voting irregularities were alleged in Illinois and Texas, and Nixon was urged to contest the counts but he refused. "No one steals the presidency of the United States," he said. Democrats retained control of both houses of Congress.

Election of 1964. Demoralized by the popularity of the martyred John F. Kennedy and by the success of Lyndon Johnson posing as Kennedy's heir, the Republican Party was captured between 1961 and 1964 by its extreme right wing, whose hero was Arizona senator Barry M. Goldwater. At the Republican national convention in San Francisco in July 1964 the conservative zealots hooted down moderates like Gov. Nelson A. Rockefeller of New York and nominated Goldwater on the first ballot; for vice president, Goldwater chose William Miller, an obscure but like-minded congressman from upstate New York. In his acceptance speech, Goldwater declared: ". . . extremism in the defense of liberty is no vice . . . moderation in the pursuit of justice is no virtue."

The Democrats met at Atlantic City in August and nominated Lyndon Johnson for president and Minnesota senator Hubert H. Humphrey for vice president.

The campaign that followed was a disaster for the Republicans. Goldwater, "shooting from the lip," virtually proposed to repeal the New Deal—he opposed Social Security, the Tennessee Valley Authority, price supports for farmers. He was against the *Civil Rights Act of 1964 and the War on Poverty. In foreign affairs, he wanted to break off relations with the Soviet Union, withdraw

from the United Nations, and fight communism everywhere with nuclear weapons. The Republican slogan "In your heart you know he's right" was answered by the Democrats with "In your guts you know he's nuts." By the time Goldwater tried to moderate his views, it was too late.

Not content to win the election, Johnson's enormous ego required a landslide. In the last six weeks of the campaign he traveled across the country, promising to pass the legislation that Kennedy would have wanted and assuring voters that American boys would not fight in Vietnam (while already planning to escalate the war there in the spring of 1965).

On Nov. 4, when 61.9 percent of the electorate voted for president, Johnson received 43.1 million popular votes (61.1 percent of the total) and 486 electoral votes. Goldwater received 27.2 million popular votes (38.5 percent) and 52 electoral votes from Arizona and five Southern states. Democrats strengthened their control of both houses of Congress.

Elections of 1968 and 1972. 1968 began with the Tet offensive in January (see *Vietnam War); Pres. Lyndon Johnson withdrew as a candidate for reelection in March; Martin Luther King Jr. was assassinated in April and the ghettos erupted; Robert Kennedy was assassinated in June. As the major party conventions approached, the country seemed to be fragmenting ever more deeply.

For years, Richard Nixon, defeated for president in 1960 and for governor of California in 1962, had toiled for other Republican candidates. He was now perceived as the centrist who could reunite the Republican Party after the Goldwater debacle of 1964. At the Republican national convention in Miami Beach, Fla., in early August, Nixon was nominated on the first ballot. He chose Gov. Spiro T. Agnew of Maryland as the Republican vice presidential candidate. The Republican platform called for de-Americanizing the war in Vietnam and for law and order at home.

Even before the Democratic national convention met in Chicago in late August, protesters of every stripe descended upon the city. Mayor Richard Daley mobilized the police and National Guard to keep the rebellious youths under control. In the convention amphitheater, the forces of Vice Pres. Hubert Humphrey, at the behest of Pres. Lyndon Johnson, pushed through a proadministration platform plank on Vietnam: no unilateral withdrawal, no bombing halt. That night Humphrey was nominated on the first ballot while Daley's police clubbed and gassed antiwar demonstrators infuriated by the fact that both major parties had nominated prowar candidates. "The whole world is watching!" the demonstrators chanted, and indeed the country watched horrified as the violence was broadcast over the television networks and threw the convention itself into turmoil. The next day, Humphrey chose Sen. Edmund Muskie of Maine for the vice presidential spot.

Meanwhile, in February, Alabama governor George Wallace had entered the race as the candidate of the *American Independent Party. Wallace's opposition to desegregation made him a powerful threat to both major parties in the South; his contempt for "liberals, intellectuals, and long-hairs" protesting the war and his promise of law and order threatened to win support among Northern blue-collar workers as well.

The events in Chicago left the Democratic Party shattered. Nixon led in the polls, enjoying the advantages of a united party, an efficient staff, the support of most newspapers, and plenty of money. He assumed a statesmanlike posture, hinted at a secret plan for ending the war in Vietnam, and promised an administration of law and order.

Humphrey, perceived as the administration candidate, was beset by hecklers wherever he went. In late September he began to separate himself from the administration, proposing a bombing halt in Vietnam. His modest departure from administration orthodoxy made him the peace candidate. Democratic liberals and organized labor belatedly rallied to him and he began to climb in the polls. On Oct. 31, President Johnson halted the bombing, allegedly in response to progress at the Paris peace talks but perhaps also to boost Humphrey's cause.

On Nov. 5, when 60.9 percent of the electorate voted for president, Nixon received 31.8 million popular votes (43.4 percent of the total) and 301 electoral votes to Humphrey's 31.3 million popular votes (42.7 percent) and 191 electoral votes. Wallace received 9.9 million popular votes (13.5 percent), carrying five Southern states with 45 electoral votes (a 46th came from a maverick North Carolina elector). The Democrats retained control of both houses of Congress.

Four years—and 25,000 more deaths in Vietnam—did not make Nixon a popular candidate for reelection in 1972. But the Democratic Party obliged him by self-destructing. Its leading figures—senators Edward Kennedy of Massachusetts, Edmund Muskie of Maine, and Hubert Humphrey of Minnesota—declined to run or faded in the primaries. New party rules multiplied the number of primaries and favored the election of nonprofessionals as convention delegates. Little-known South Dakota senator George McGovern—liberal, antiwar, and neoisolationist (his battle cry was "Come home, America")—swept the primaries. The Democratic convention at Miami Beach in July—in which youthful radicals of every persuasion were conspicuous—nominated him on the first ballot and endorsed Sen. Thomas Eagleton of Missouri for vice president. (Eagleton was soon replaced by R. Sargent Shriver when it became known that he had been hospitalized for depression.)

The Republican convention met in Miami Beach in August and renominated Nixon and Agnew. With his sole conservative rival, Alabama governor George Wallace, eliminated in May—a would-be assassin's bullet had left him paralyzed from the waist down—Nixon had only to claim the wide American center to be assured of a landslide victory.

On Nov. 7, when 55.2 percent of the electorate voted for president, Nixon received 47.2 million popular votes (60.7 percent of the total) and 520 electoral votes to McGovern's 29.2 million popular votes (37.5 percent) and 17 electoral votes. But the Democrats retained control of both houses of Congress.

Election of 1976. As 1976 approached, an unknown former one-term governor of Georgia, James E. Carter Jr., saw an opportunity to capitalize on his status as a Washington outsider and a born-again Southern Baptist to win the presidency against establishment politicians besmirched—at least in the public mind—by *Watergate and other scandals. Carter toured the country assiduously, entered 30 Democratic primaries, and won more than half of them against nationally known Democrats. "I'll never lie to you," he promised. Nominated on the first ballot at the Democratic national convention in New York in July, Carter selected Minnesota senator Walter F. Mondale as his running mate.

The incumbent Republican president, Gerald Ford, who as vice president had succeeded to the presidency on the resignation of Pres. Richard M. Nixon, was subjected to the indignity of having to compete for his party's nomination in the primaries against former California governor Ronald Reagan, leader of the party's conservative wing. Ford had dissipated his early popularity by pardoning Nixon, and he had alienated Republican conservatives by appointing liberal Nelson Rockefeller as vice president. Nevertheless, at the Republican national convention in Kansas City in August, Ford won the nomination—narrowly—on the first ballot and chose Kansas senator Robert Dole for the vice presidential spot.

No profound issues divided the candidates. The moralist Carter made a laughingstock of himself by confessing, in a *Playboy* interview, to "lusting in my heart." Ford, himself decent and popular, committed an inexplicable gaffe in a television debate by denying that the

Soviet Union dominated Eastern Europe. These blunders only briefly diverted an apathetic public.

On Nov. 2, when 53.5 percent of the electorate voted for president, Carter received 40.8 million popular votes (50.1 percent of the total) and 297 electoral votes to Ford's 39.1 million popular votes (48.0 percent) and 240 electoral votes. The Democrats won majorities in both houses of Congress.

Elections of 1980 and 1984. Pres. James E. Carter approached the 1980 election mired in stagflation (the unprecedented combination of high unemployment and inflation) and the *Iranian hostage crisis. Americans were offended when he complained on television that they suffered from a "national malaise," a loss of confidence. At the Democratic national convention in New York in August, he and Vice Pres. Walter Mondale were renominated without enthusiasm.

In Detroit in July, the Republicans had nominated former California governor Ronald Reagan, whose reputation as an archconservative was moderated by his amiability and grace. Reagan had swept most of the Republican primaries with the theme that government was the problem, not the solution. He offered lower taxes, less regulation, increased defense spending, and a balanced budget and promised to make America "stand tall" again. For vice president, Reagan chose George H.W. Bush, a moderate Republican who had served as party chairman, United Nations ambassador, and head of the Central Intelligence Agency.

A third-party candidate, former representative John Anderson of Illinois, ran on a National Unity ticket. Although he appeared on the ballot in all 50 states and received prominent liberal endorsements, he lacked the means to compete with the major party candidates.

Both major candidates committed embarrassing gaffes, but Reagan had the advantage of better organization and skilled handlers, while Carter often seemed querulous and spiteful. In what appeared to be a close race, Reagan's summation at the end of the candidates' single television debate was credited with giving him the lead. "Are you better off than you were four years ago?" he asked.

On Nov. 4, when 52.8 percent of the electorate voted for president, Reagan received 43.9 million popular votes (50.7 percent of the total) and 489 electoral votes to Carter's 35.5 million popular votes (41.0 percent) and 49 electoral votes. Anderson received 5.7 million popular votes (6.6 percent).

By 1984 the economy was recovering vigorously from the recession of 1981–83 and Reagan was at the peak of his popularity. Criticism did not stick on the "Teflon president." Inequitable taxes, slashed social programs,

ballooning deficits were dismissed by many who claimed that Reagan had restored their pride and optimism. At Dallas in August, the Republicans enthusiastically renominated Reagan and Bush.

The Democratic national convention in San Francisco in July nominated former vice president Walter Mondale, who selected New York congresswoman Geraldine Ferraro as the party's vice presidential candidate—the first woman ever nominated for national office by a major party. But the Democrats could not dent Reagan's shining armor.

On Nov. 6, when 53.3 percent of the electorate voted for president, Reagan received 54.5 million popular votes (58.8 percent of the total) and 525 electoral votes to Mondale's 37.6 million popular votes (40.6 percent) and 13 electoral votes. Republicans retained control of the Senate and gained seats in the House.

Election of 1988. With the endorsement of retiring Pres. Ronald Reagan to reassure conservatives, Vice Pres. George H.W. Bush emerged victorious in Republican party primaries and was nominated for president in New Orleans in August. He chose Indiana senator Dan Quayle for vice president. At Atlanta in July, the Democrats nominated Massachusetts governor Michael Dukakis for president and Sen. Lloyd Bentsen of Texas for vice president.

The campaign was notable for its negativity. Major issues were ignored and trivialities exploited. The hapless and inept Dukakis was on the defensive from the start, accused of being soft on crime because a convicted murderer, Willie Horton, had raped a woman while on a weekend furlough from a Massachusetts prison while Dukakis was governor. Dukakis was also accused of lack of patriotism for vetoing an unconstitutional Massachusetts bill requiring schoolchildren to recite the Pledge of Allegiance. Bush made a point of campaigning in a flag factory and incautiously promised, "Read my lips: No new taxes."

On Nov. 4, when 50.3 percent of the electorate voted for president, Bush received 48.9 million popular votes (53.4 percent of the total) and 426 electoral votes to Dukakis's 41.8 million popular votes (45.6 percent) and 111 electoral votes. Democrats won control of both houses of Congress.

Elections of 1992 and 1996. As a result of the 1991 *Gulf War, Pres. George H.W. Bush's popularity reached record heights and his reelection in 1992 seemed a certainty. Most prominent Democrats withdrew from the race. But a recession, begun in 1990, continued into 1992, and Bush's do-nothing response—a result of his conservative economic philosophy and preoccupation with foreign affairs—presented an opportunity that little-known Arkansas governor William J. Clinton seized.

Posting a reminder in his Little Rock headquarters that "It's the economy, stupid," Clinton entered the Democratic primaries with a program of economic revitalization directed at the middle class: higher taxes on the rich, national health insurance, support for education, welfare reform, rebuilding the country's infrastructure. Clinton had been a leader in moving the Democratic Party toward the political center in order to win back the Reagan Democrats, middle- and working-class voters who were unsympathetic to the party's long partiality for the poor and minorities. Young, well-informed, and articulate, this "New Democrat," preaching equal opportunity for all rather than spending on the poor, outdistanced other Democratic contenders despite wounding allegations of marital infidelity and evasion of military service in the Vietnam War. In New York in July, the Democratic national convention nominated Bill Clinton for president on the first ballot and chose Tennessee senator Albert Gore for vice president.

At Houston in August, the Republican national convention celebrated family values to placate the restive conservative wing of the party. Bush and Quayle were renominated, Bush defining the issue as "Who do you trust?"

A third major candidate—self-nominated and self-financed—was Texas billionaire Ross Perot, who organized United We Stand America to support his candidacy. Perot's chief issue was the budget deficits and ballooning national debt. He projected a folksy, commonsense, but simplistic approach to all problems, but his personal peculiarities and erratic behavior—he entered the race in January, dropped out in July, and reentered it in October—cost him millions of followers.

On Nov. 3, when 55.1 percent of the electorate voted for president, Clinton received 44.9 million popular votes (43.0 percent of the total) and 370 electoral votes to Bush's 39.1 million popular votes (37.4 percent) and 168 electoral votes. Perot received 19.7 million popular votes (18.9 percent) but no electoral votes. Democrats won control of both houses of Congress.

The Clinton administration was stunned in 1994 when the *"Republican Revolution," led by House Speaker Newt Gingrich, captured both houses of Congress. But the new Republicans—zealous conservatives—overplayed their hand by proposing large tax cuts that threatened Medicare, then shutting down the government when Clinton vetoed their bill. Clinton's popularity rose, and, riding a growing economic boom, he and Vice President Gore were renominated at the Democratic national convention in Chicago in August 1996.

At San Diego in August, the Republicans nominated Kansas senator Bob Dole for president and former housing secretary Jack Kemp for vice president. Aging and inarticulate, Dole could offer nothing more inspiring than the usual Republican tax cut.

Ross Perot again entered the race, now nominated—by mail and telephone vote—by the new *Reform Party, which he had created.

On Nov. 5, when 49.0 percent of the electorate voted for president, Clinton received 47.4 million popular votes (49.2 percent of the total) and 379 electoral votes to Dole's 39.2 million popular votes (40.7 percent) and 159 electoral votes. Perot received 8.1 million popular votes (8.4 percent) but no electoral votes. Republicans retained their control of both houses of Congress.

Election of 2000. Because of the Clinton scandals, character was the chief issue in the 2000 election. The Democratic candidate, Vice Pres. Al Gore, selected as his running mate Connecticut senator Joseph Lieberman, an outspoken critic of Clinton's behavior (and the first Jew on a major party national ticket), and during the campaign distanced himself from Clinton despite the president's undoubted popularity.

The Republican candidate, Texas governor George W. Bush, compounded his image of inexperience by a reputation as a onetime hard-drinking playboy (including a 1976 conviction for drunk driving). He selected as his running mate Richard Cheney, president of a Texas oil services company who had been a conservative Republican congressman and secretary of defense in the George H. W. Bush administration.

Bush campaigned as a "compassionate conservative," Gore as the champion of the working family. Gore came across as stiff and pedantic, Bush as amiably incoherent ("More and more of our imports come from overseas," he said). On election day, Nov. 7, Gore carried the West Coast, the Upper Midwest, and the Northeast, Bush the small-state "heartland." That night, with Florida still in doubt, Gore had 267 electoral votes, Bush 246; 270 were needed to win, and Florida's 25 would decide the election.

Voting in the United States is managed by counties. Irregularities are frequent and widespread due to the variety of ballots that may be used in a single state, the availability and condition of voting machines, and the competence of county election officials. All states provide for manual recounting of votes in contested elections.

In November 2000 irregularities were most glaring in Florida. Many Hispanic and African-American voters complained that they had been erroneously denied opportunities to vote. The validity of large numbers of absentee ballots was challenged. Most important were problems arising from the use in some counties of unfamiliar "butterfly" ballots. These ballots listed candidates in an order confusing to some voters, who often voted for a candidate other than the one they intended. Moreover, the voter had to indicate his choice by punching a stylus through the paper ballot. If the hole made by the stylus was incomplete or imperfect, the machine that read the ballot might reject it as "unmarked"—although in many cases the intention of the voter would be apparent to a manual counter. Because of the butterfly ballot, 19,000 "unmarked" ballots were discarded in heavily Democratic Palm Beach County alone.

Bush's extremely narrow lead in Florida was challenged by Democrats, and a manual recount began in four counties. The Republican Florida secretary of state set a deadline of Nov. 14 for the recounting, but she was overruled by the Florida supreme court, which extended the deadline to Nov. 26. Although the recounts were not completed by then, the secretary of state certified Bush as the winner by a 537-vote margin. Gore appealed to the Florida supreme court, which ordered the manual recount to resume in all Florida counties and be completed by Dec. 10. This was a deadline established by an 1887 federal election law to permit electors to be certified on Dec. 12 in time for the convening of the electoral college on Dec. 18.

Bush appealed the Florida court's ruling to the U.S. Supreme Court, which ordered the recounting stopped and on Dec. 12 ruled 5–4 that, without uniform statewide standards for counting the ballots, the recount was unconstitutional but that the deadline for certifying electors left no time to remedy the situation (see *Bush v. Gore). The effect was to award Florida's electoral votes to Bush. In the final official count, with a voter participation rate of 50.7 percent, Bush had 50.5 million popular votes (47.9 percent of the total) and 271 electoral votes, while Gore had 51.0 million popular votes (48.4 percent) and 266 electoral votes.

A year later, a consortium of eight news organizations that had recounted all the Florida ballots found that either candidate might have won by a very slight margin depending upon the system of recounting adopted. Significantly, 113,000 of the controversial butterfly ballots on which confused voters had voted for two or more presidential candidates were not counted because there was no clear indication of the voters' intentions. On these, 75,000 voters had voted for Gore and a minor candidate, 29,000 for Bush and a minor candidate.

PRESIDENTIAL RECONSTRUCTION. See *Reconstruction.

PRESIDENTIAL SUCCESSION. The U.S. Constitution made no provision for succession to the office of president in the event of the death, removal, resignation, or disability of both the president and the vice president. This omission was remedied in 1792 when Congress decided that, in the absence of both a president and a vice president, the president pro tempore of the Senate (an officer elected by the Senate to preside over it in the absence of the vice president, who normally presides) should succeed. If the Senate should have no president pro tempore, the Speaker of the House would succeed.

In 1886, Congress made the members of the president's *cabinet, in order of their rank (that is, the order in which their departments were created), successors to the president in the absence of a vice president. The order was then the secretaries of state, war, and Treasury, the postmaster general, the attorney general, then the secretaries of the Navy and the interior.

The *20th Amendment, ratified in 1933, provides that if a president-elect has not been chosen, or dies, or does not qualify at the beginning of his term, the vice president-elect should become president. If the vice president-elect does not qualify, then Congress decides who would become president. An act of Congress in 1947 made the Speaker of the House, then the president pro tempore of the Senate, followed by cabinet members in order of their rank successors to the presidency in the absence of both a president and a vice president.

The *25th Amendment in 1975 authorizes a president to fill the vacant office of vice president by appointment, subject to confirmation by majorities of both houses of Congress.

PRIGG v. PENNSYLVANIA (1842), 8–1 decision of the *Taney Court that state *personal liberty laws were unconstitutional as obstructing a slave owner's constitutional right to recapture his property (see *Fugitive Slave Laws). At the same time, the Court made clear that enforcement of the Fugitive Slave Act of 1793 was entirely a federal responsibility, in which state authorities need take no part. The result was new personal liberty laws in Massachusetts and other states prohibiting state officials from assisting in the return of escaped slaves. The Fugitive Slave Act of 1850 authorized federal commissioners to compel state officials and even private citizens to assist in the recapture of fugitives.

PRIMARY ELECTIONS, method by which members of a political party choose their party's nominees for public office—city, county, state, or national. It became a popular reform during the Progressive Era (see *Progressivism) as a means of limiting the influence of party bosses and special interests in party *nominating conventions. Today, almost all states have some form of primary election; others use the party caucus or convention.

Primary elections are instituted by the states (not by the parties) and regulated by them. Most states have primary elections for city, county, and state offices; 22 have presidential primaries.

Presidential primaries are of various kinds. In an open primary, a citizen of any party or no party may vote in the party primary of his choice; in a closed primary, only registered party members may vote. In a preference primary, voters register their preference for their party's nominee, which may or may not be binding on the state party's delegation to the national nominating convention. In other primaries, voters elect some or all of the members of the state party's delegation, who may or may not be pledged to a particular candidate. (Some places in a state party's delegation may be reserved for party "notables"—officeholders or party leaders.)

Contesting state presidential primaries—beginning with New Hampshire's in February of a presidential election year—is a long, arduous, and costly process that eliminates minor candidates but does not necessarily assure any candidate of enough delegate support to secure the nomination. In that case, the convention is free to nominate whomever it chooses, a decision in which party leaders usually play a major role.

PRINCETON (Jan. 3, 1777), *Revolutionary War battle. After his victory at *Trenton, Patriot general George Washington briefly rested his ragged and freezing troops in Pennsylvania, inducing some short-term veterans to serve another six weeks for a bounty of $10. On Dec. 30, 1776, he reoccupied Trenton, and there received militia reinforcements bringing his strength to 5,000 men.

British general Charles Cornwallis, however, was approaching with 8,000 regulars. Washington withdrew across Assunpink Creek, and took up a position with the Delaware River at his back. Believing that he had his fox "bagged," Cornwallis delayed his attack overnight (Jan. 2–3, 1777), only to find in the morning that Washington had slipped away to the east behind a screen of deceptive campfires, had circled around Cornwallis's army, and was marching toward Princeton, where Cornwallis had stationed his rearguard of some 1,200 men.

At Princeton, the Americans drove the British from the field, Washington himself leading the decisive charge fully exposed to enemy fire. The frustrated Cornwallis arrived only after the Americans had withdrawn toward Morristown, where they went into winter quarters.

PRINCETON EXPLOSION (Feb. 28, 1844), incident in the *Tyler administration. On Feb. 28, 1844, Pres. John Tyler and guests cruised the Potomac River aboard the USS *Princeton*, a new 1,000-ton steam warship—the first driven by a screw propeller—designed by Swedish engineer John Ericsson and commanded by Capt. Robert F. Stockton. The ship's principal armament was a pair of 12-inch iron guns. On a third test firing, one of these guns exploded, killing six people, including Secretary of State Abel P. Upshur and Secretary of the Navy Thomas W. Gilmer. Tyler was uninjured.

PROCLAMATION OF AMNESTY AND RECONSTRUCTION (1863). See *Reconstruction.

PROCLAMATION OF 1763, royal proclamation setting aside the region between the Appalachian Mountains and the Mississippi River as an Indian reserve where American colonists were forbidden to settle. The ostensible purpose of the proclamation (issued Oct. 7, 1763) was to protect the Indians from the encroachments of whites and to prevent costly conflicts like *Pontiac's Rebellion. Another purpose was to confine the American colonies to the Atlantic seaboard, where they would remain economically dependent on Great Britain. Westward-moving colonists and land speculators ignored the proclamation.

PROCLAMATION TO THE PEOPLE OF SOUTH CAROLINA (1832). See *Nullification.

PROGRESS AND POVERTY (1880), influential book by Henry George, a self-taught economist. George observed that the more advanced a civilization was, the greater its material progress and affluence, the more numerous and miserable were its poor. "This association . . . of progress with poverty is the great enigma of our time."

The explanation lay in the private ownership of land, since, of the three factors of production—land, capital, and labor—land increased in value with the growth of population and productive power, and the landowner was able to appropriate through rent the wealth created by labor and capital, invariably depressing wages to the subsistence level. "Rent swallows up the whole gain and pauperism accompanies progress." George's solution was to tax economic rent—the value of land created by society. This one tax, he believed, would yield enough to cover all the costs of government and would result in a more productive and equitable economic order in which labor earned the full value of its production.

Progress and Poverty sold millions of copies around the world and inspired a vigorous single-tax movement in the United States.

PROGRESSIVE PARTY or BULL MOOSE PARTY

(1912), political party formed by supporters of former president Theodore Roosevelt who bolted the Republican national convention in Chicago after it nominated Pres. William Howard Taft for a second term. On Aug. 5 the party held its national convention in Chicago, where it became known as the Bull Moose Party from Roosevelt's ebullient declaration upon arriving, "I feel as strong as a bull moose."

"If the Progressives were a party of protest, they were not in the least proletarian," recalled national committeeman William Allen White 30 years later. "[T]he movement which Theodore Roosevelt led in 1912 was . . . in its heart of hearts *petit bourgeois*; little businessmen, professional men, well-to-do farmers, skilled artisans from the upper brackets of organized labor."

The party nominated Roosevelt for president and Gov. Hiram Johnson of California for vice president. "Behind the ostensible government sits enthroned an invisible government," its platform declared, "owing no allegiance and acknowledging no responsibility to the people. To destroy this invisible government, to dissolve the unholy alliance between corrupt business and corrupt politics is the first task of the statesmanship of the day."

Reflecting Roosevelt's *New Nationalism and anticipating Franklin Roosevelt's *New Deal, the platform favored: direct primaries for nomination to state and national offices; nationwide preferential primaries for the presidency; direct election of U.S. senators; the initiative, referendum, and recall; woman suffrage; limits on campaign contributions and expenditures; registration of lobbyists; reversal of state court decisions by popular vote; prohibition of the injunction in labor disputes; health and safety standards in the workplace; the prohibition of child labor; wage and hour regulation; workmen's compensation; unemployment, health, and old age insurance; national regulation of interstate corporations; strengthening of the Sherman Act; tariff revision; inheritance and income taxes; supervision of the stock market; and public ownership of natural resources.

By dividing the Republican vote, the Progressive Party assured the election of Democrat Woodrow Wilson. In defeat, the Progressives scattered. Some, including Roosevelt and Johnson, returned to the Republican Party, others became Wilson Democrats. In 1916 a remnant of the party met in Chicago and again nominated Theodore Roosevelt for president. Roosevelt promptly declined, declaring: "There is no place for a third party in our politics." The party thereupon dissolved.

PROGRESSIVE PARTY (1924), political party

formed by progressive, socialist, and labor organizations in response to the nomination by the major parties in 1924 of two conservative candidates—Republican Calvin Coolidge and Democrat John W. Davis.

A convention at Cleveland, Ohio, in July nominated Sen. Robert M. La Follette of Wisconsin for president and Sen. Burton K. Wheeler of Montana for vice president. The party's platform reflected the issues La Follette had advocated for years, including public ownership of water power, reduction of tariff and railroad rates, farm relief, abolition of the injunction in labor disputes, a child labor amendment, and election of federal judges. The party polled 5 million votes—17 percent of the total—chiefly in the Middle and Far West but carried only one state, Wisconsin.

PROGRESSIVE PARTY (1948), political party or-

ganized to support the presidential candidacy of Henry A. Wallace. Secretary of agriculture in Franklin Roosevelt's first two terms, vice president in Roosevelt's third term, and secretary of commerce in his fourth, Wallace was forced to resign from Pres. Harry S. Truman's cabinet because of his opposition to the administration's *cold war policy (see *Truman Administration). Viewing himself as an advocate of peace and bearer of the liberal New Deal tradition, Wallace declared his presidential candidacy in December 1947, rallied other disaffected liberals to his cause, and at Philadelphia in July 1948 was nominated by acclamation by the Progressive Party. Democratic senator Glen Taylor of Idaho, "the Singing Cowboy," was nominated for vice president.

Wallace's defection threatened to cost the Democrats the most populous states and thus the election, but his early strength eroded when he refused to repudiate the endorsement of the *Communist Party, tolerated the presence of communists in influential positions in the party, denounced the *Marshall Plan, the draft, and U.S. nuclear weapons, and blamed the United States for the cold war. The communist coup in Czechoslovakia and the Berlin blockade (see *Berlin Airlift) that year contradicted his position. In November, Wallace received 1.2 million popular votes, mostly in New York and California (denying

New York to Truman), but no electoral votes. He resigned from the Progressive Party in 1950 when it opposed U.S. intervention in Korea (see *Korean War).

The party ran a presidential ticket in 1952 that received only 140,000 popular votes.

PROGRESSIVISM (1890–1917), broadly based reform impulse responding to the antidemocratic and corrupting consequences of industrialism by seeking greater political, economic, and social democracy. Editor William Allen White, a prominent progressive, described it as "the middle class protest (perhaps 'revolt' is a truer word) that had begun with the demand for free labor in abolition times—that had bloomed modestly in the agrarian protest of the Grangers and the Greenbackers—that had flowered in Populism and almost fruited under Bryanism in the Democratic party, and was ripening under the [Theodore] Roosevelt policies and the *Progressive party into a responsible middle-class rebellion at the slow-moving economic progress made by our government."

In politics, progressives sought woman suffrage (see *Women's Rights); *primary elections; the direct election of U.S. senators; and the *initiative, referendum, and recall. In economics they supported antitrust legislation; public ownership or regulation of utilities; banking and currency reform; *consumer protection; and the income tax. Their social objectives included *prohibition; wage, hour, and safety regulation in the workplace; abolition of *child labor; workmen's compensation; improved *housing; and immigrant education.

Progressivism is chiefly associated with presidents Theodore Roosevelt and Woodrow Wilson, but there were many senators and representatives, governors and mayors in both major parties who were counted as progressives or insurgents. Moreover, the reform impulse manifested itself in other fields besides politics—in religion (see *Social Gospel), journalism (see *Muckrakers), social work (see *Settlement Houses), law, social sciences, education, and literature. Some of its most important objectives were achieved during the *Wilson administration. World War 1 effectively put an end to the movement, although many progressives reappeared in the Franklin *Roosevelt administration. Progressive parties entered presidential elections in 1912, 1924, and 1948.

PROHIBITION (1920–33). Ratification of the *18th Amendment, which prohibited the "manufacture, sale or transportation of intoxicating liquors within . . . the United States," climaxed a century-long effort to limit the consumption of hard liquor in America (see *Temperance Movement). Congress passed the amendment in December 1917 in the heightened moral climate of World War 1. Ratified in 1919, it was implemented that year (over Pres. Woodrow Wilson's veto) by the **Volstead Act**, which defined intoxicating liquor as any beverage containing at least 0.5 percent alcohol. The act also authorized measures for the enforcement of prohibition and penalties for its violation. It permitted the retention of private stocks of liquor bought previously and allowed brewers to make beer weaker than 0.5 percent. Proponents of prohibition celebrated the imminent demise of crime, vice, and poverty.

The wartime moral climate of idealism and sacrifice ended as abruptly as the war and was replaced by a climate of greed and hedonism. Urban Americans, at least, repented of the national folly. Liquor, conspicuous in their new lifestyle, was now served in clubs and speakeasies instead of saloons, purchased from bootleggers and gangsters instead of licensed merchants, or made at home ("bathtub gin") with sometimes unfortunate consequences.

Enforcement of prohibition proved costly and ineffectual. Corruption of local officials and police was widespread. Out of the criminal gangs that fought for control of local liquor markets developed the organized crime "families" of later ill repute. On the other hand, consumption of liquor noticeably decreased—although the fivefold increase over the preprohibition price may have contributed to that.

In the presidential election of 1928, native-born, Protestant, rural and small-town "drys" united to reject the candidacy of Al Smith, a "wet" who uniquely personified immigrant, urban, and non-Protestant America. Instead they elected Republican Herbert Hoover, who had endorsed the "noble experiment" but then appointed the **Wickersham Commission**—the National Commission on Law Observance and Enforcement, chaired by former attorney general George W. Wickersham—in part to study the prohibition issue. The commission dealt with prohibition in the first of 14 lengthy reports issued in 1931, concluding that prohibition was unenforceable but that it should be retained.

In 1932 the Republican platform endorsed prohibition, the Democratic platform called for repeal. The election of Democrat Franklin Roosevelt signaled the end of prohibition. In February 1933 Congress passed the *21st Amendment repealing prohibition; it was promptly ratified, and the states again assumed responsibility for the issue.

PROHIBITION PARTY, political party founded in 1869 to advocate the nationwide banning of the manu-

facture and sale of intoxicating liquors, an issue then ignored by the major parties. It has nominated a candidate
for president in every election since 1872 but has never
won any electoral votes. In 1892 its candidate received a
record 271,000 votes. (See *Temperance Movement;
*Prohibition.)

PROMISE OF AMERICAN LIFE, THE (1909), influential book by Herbert Croly that was hailed by people
like Theodore Roosevelt, Walter Lippmann, and Felix
Frankfurter for providing a philosophical basis for *progressivism. By the promise of American life, Croly meant
the advance of democracy and of social and economic
equality. In the 20th century, marked by great industrial
corporations and growing disparities of wealth, the old
Jeffersonian ideals of individualism and small government
were proving inimical to the fulfillment of that promise.
What was needed in modern circumstances, Croly argued, was an enlarged and activist federal government
that would employ "Hamiltonian means" to effect "Jeffersonian ends" (see *Hamilton and Jefferson). In 1914
Croly became founding editor of the *New Republic*.

PUBLIC ASSISTANCE. See *Welfare.

PUBLIC HOUSING. See *Housing.

PUBLIC LANDS. Between 1781 and 1802, the seven
original states that claimed lands west of the Appalachian Mountains surrendered them to the federal
government. Thereafter, all the territory belonging to the
United States outside the original states was owned by
the federal government on behalf of the people as public
land. Contemplating this vast territory, which stretched
to the Great Lakes and the Mississippi River, Pres.
Thomas Jefferson observed in 1801 that there was
"room enough for our descendants to the hundredth and
thousandth generation."

Yet this original territory was rapidly augmented by
the *Louisiana Purchase (1803), the purchase of Florida
(1819), the annexation of *Texas (1846), the settlement
of the *Oregon Dispute (1846), the *Mexican Cession
(1848), the *Gadsden Purchase (1853), the *Alaska Purchase (1868), and the annexation of *Hawaii (1898).

From the start, Congress viewed these lands as a
source of revenue far into the future as it was bought and
settled by independent small farmers, the backbone of
the republic. By the **Ordinance of 1785**, Congress
began to survey the *Northwest Territory, dividing it
into six-mile-square townships and 36 one-mile-square
sections (640 acres). Congress designated the section as

the smallest unit of land a settler could buy, and it was
priced at $1 an acre. Few westward-moving pioneers,
however, could afford to buy or were able to farm 640
acres; as a result, the land was bought by speculators, divided into smaller tracts, and sold profitably to settlers.

Initially land sales were slow, since all the states still
possessed unoccupied lands of their own. Congress
therefore reduced the minimum area of Western land a
settler could buy and lowered prices. Western land was
also given to war veterans, to new states to endow education, and to Indian tribes.

As the West filled up, Westerners demanded cheaper
and even free land. They were opposed by Eastern manufacturers who feared that free land would entice away
their workers and increase wages. Southerners too opposed free land, anticipating that it would be taken up by
small farmers who would form free states, disrupting the
balance between slave and free states. Western Democrats led by Sen. Thomas Hart Benton of Missouri scored
a significant victory with the **Preemption Act**
(1841), which expressed Westerners' preference for actual settlers over distant speculators by legitimizing the
hitherto illegal position of squatters on surveyed public
land and allowing them first right to buy up to 160 acres
on which they had made improvements for $1.25 an
acre. A second victory was the **Graduation Act**
(1854), which progressively lowered the price of public
land the longer it remained unsold.

Beginning in the 1850s, Congress abandoned the
policy of treating public lands as a source of revenue
and undertook to use them to accomplish important national purposes. By giving free land to the *railroads,
Congress subsidized the construction of strategically
important railroads, first between the Great Lakes and
the Gulf of Mexico, then linking the Mississippi Valley
with the Pacific Ocean (see *Railroad Land Grants). Altogether, the railroads received 223 million acres of federal and state land, the sale of which helped pay the
costs of construction. The land grants enriched the railroads, but they achieved the national objective of developing a continental rail system (see *Transcontinental
Railroad).

During the Civil War, while Southern representatives
were absent, Congress passed the **Homestead Act**
(1862) to speed settlement of the West. The act provided
that any adult citizen who headed a family could receive
a grant of 160 acres of public land by paying a small fee
and living on and improving the land continuously for
five years. Alternatively, the settler could buy the land at
$1.25 an acre after six months' residence.

The act was less successful in achieving its aim than

its advocates had hoped. Much public land had already been given to railroads, states, and Indian tribes and was therefore not available for homesteading—although it could be purchased from railroads and states. Much that was available lay west of the 99th meridian in the arid and semiarid High Plains where 160 acres was not a viable economic unit. Congress therefore enlarged the amount of land homesteaders could acquire. The **Timber Culture Act** (1873) permitted homesteaders who kept 40 acres in timber to acquire 160 additional timbered acres. The **Desert Land Act** (1877) authorized homesteaders to acquire 640 additional arid acres at 25 cents an acre if they irrigated the land within three years. The **Timber Cutting Act** (1878) allowed homesteaders to cut timber on the public domain free of charge for their own use—in effect enlarging their farms through the use of nearby woodland. The **Enlarged Homestead Act** (1909) raised the acreage available to homesteaders from 160 to 320, and the **Stock-Raising Homestead Act** (1916) raised it again to 640 acres of land not suitable for irrigation. As a consequence of these supplementary acts, more land was taken up under the Homestead Act after 1904 than before.

Also during the Civil War, the **Morrill Act** (1862) gave to each state that had remained in the Union 30,000 acres of public land for each member of its congressional delegation. Proceeds from the sale of this land were to be used to establish colleges that would offer courses in agriculture, engineering, and home economics in addition to academic subjects. Seventy land-grant colleges were established under the act.

Late in the 19th century the remaining public lands began to be thought of as a national heritage of surpassing beauty, rich in mineral and water resources, unspoiled forests, and irreplaceable wildlife. Public rather than private ownership, and preservation rather than exploitation, became the new concerns (see *Conservation).

In 2000, the federal government owned 630 million acres of public lands, including lands devoted to forest and wildlife, to grazing, and to parks and historic sites.

PUBLIC WORKS ADMINISTRATION (PWA).
See *New Deal.

PUJO COMMITTEE
(1912), subcommittee of the House Committee on Banking and Currency created to determine if there was a concentration of financial and banking power in the United States that constituted a "money trust." Chaired by Rep. Arsène Pujo of Louisiana, with Samuel Untermyer of New York as counsel, the committee examined a mine of evidence and in-

terrogated J.P. Morgan and other financiers. Its conclusion that a money trust in the hands of "comparatively few men" did in fact exist contributed to the passage in 1913 of the *Federal Reserve Act.

PULLMAN STRIKE
(1894), labor dispute in the severe economic depression that followed the *Panic of 1893. In 1894 the Pullman Palace Car Co., manufacturer of railroad dining, parlor, and sleeping cars, laid off large numbers of workers and slashed wages (but not workers' rents in the company town of Pullman). Its economies enabled the company to earn $9.6 million in 1894 (compared to $11.4 million in 1893) while actually increasing dividends to stockholders.

In the spring of 1894, 4,000 desperate Pullman workers joined the *American Railway Union. When the company dismissed members of a grievance committee, the workers, against the advice of union president Eugene V. Debs, struck. In short order, the company rejected compromise, the union boycotted Pullman cars, the railroads fired trainmen who refused to handle Pullmans, and the union struck 24 Chicago-based railroads.

On the grounds that the strike threatened the movement of the U.S. mail, federal authorities on July 2 secured an injunction against the union. This provoked a riot in the Rock Island yards. To suppress the "reign of terror," Pres. Grover Cleveland ordered 2,000 federal troops to Chicago despite the protest of Illinois governor John Peter Altgeld that they were not needed. The arrival of the troops precipitated mob violence that resulted in extensive destruction of property and 12 deaths.

Debs and other union leaders were arrested, tried for contempt of court for ignoring the antistrike injunction, and sentenced to three to six months in jail. By July 20 the strike had been broken and federal troops withdrawn. In January 1895 the U.S. Supreme Court upheld the use of the injunction in labor disputes (see *In re Debs*).

PURE FOOD AND DRUG ACT
(1906). See *Consumer Protection.

PURE FOOD, DRUG, AND COSMETICS ACT
(1938). See *Consumer Protection.

PURITANISM,
a reform movement in the Church of England that arose in the 16th century to "purify" that church of Catholic liturgy and ritual and to impose on it the Calvinist doctrines of biblical fundamentalism and human depravity. A corollary of this last view was that God had arbitrarily preselected a minority of the human

race—the "Saints" or "elect"—for salvation; it was impossible to deserve or earn election, but those elected might know it through the authenticity of their conversion experience and through lives of sober, pious, and prosperous work.

Some Puritans—"Separatists"—despairing of the Church of England, separated from it altogether and formed autonomous "Congregational" churches. Persecuted in England, hundreds of Separatists early in the 17th century sought refuge in Holland, from where a few dozen *Pilgrims emigrated to North America in 1620 and founded *Plymouth Colony. Ten years later, thousands of English Puritans, still nominally members of the Church of England, emigrated to America in the "Great Migration" and founded *Massachusetts Bay Colony.

Puritanism's radical individualism contained the seeds of its own dissolution, for in time Puritanism gave rise to numerous competing sects. Nevertheless, it indelibly stamped the New England character and profoundly influenced the rest of the country by its emphasis on self-reliance and moral and intellectual vigor.

Q

QUARTERING ACTS (1765, 1766, 1774), parliamentary measures requiring the American colonies to provide shelter and supplies to British troops stationed there. The first required barracks, the second billeting in inns and unoccupied dwellings. The 1774 act (one of the *Intolerable Acts, the only one that applied to all the colonies) legalized the billeting of troops in occupied dwellings. The Third Amendment to the U.S. Constitution (see *Bill of Rights) prohibited the U.S. government from quartering troops "in any house" without the consent of the owner in peacetime and except by law in wartime.

QUEBEC ACT (1774). See *Intolerable Acts.

QUEBEC CAMPAIGN (1775–76), unsuccessful Patriot invasion of Canada in the *Revolutionary War.

The failure of Canadians to respond to the invitation of the first *Continental Congress to join the 13 southern colonies in their resistance to British policy did not disabuse Americans of the notion that the Canadians might still be won to the cause—perhaps by an invasion, which, if successful, would deny the British an operational base in the north. The capture of *Fort Ticonderoga and *Crown Point in May 1775 seemed to invite such an enterprise, which the second Congress promptly authorized (June 27, 1775).

At the end of August 1775, Patriot general Richard Montgomery led 1,200 New York and Connecticut militia up Lake Champlain and the Richelieu River. They captured Chambly (Oct. 18) and Saint Johns (Nov. 2). On Nov. 13 undefended Montreal surrendered to the Americans. British general Sir Guy Carleton, governor of Quebec, who had tried to halt the American advance, escaped from Montreal with a handful of troops and made for the fortress at Quebec City.

Meanwhile, Col. Benedict Arnold with some 1,100 men on Sept. 25 started up the Kennebec River in Maine toward Quebec. During the arduous seven-week journey through uncharted wilderness, Arnold lost most of his boats and equipment; a third of his men died or turned back. Only 600 exhausted and starving men descended the Chaudière River and reached the St. Lawrence River opposite Quebec on Nov. 3. On Dec. 2 Montgomery joined them with 300 men.

With insufficient men and equipment for a siege, Montgomery decided to attack the fortress through the supposedly unfortified "lower town." But Carleton had anticipated the move, and when the Americans entered the lower town in a blinding snowstorm on Dec. 31 they were met by devastating fire from strong points and barricades. Sixty Americans were killed or wounded, 426 captured. Montgomery was killed, Arnold seriously wounded.

A few hundred American survivors clung to their position outside Quebec through the winter. Spring brought reinforcements and a new commander, Gen. John Thomas (Arnold had by then gone to Montreal). But it also brought a British fleet of 15 ships carrying Gen. John Burgoyne and 13,000 British and German troops.

The Americans, starving and now decimated by smallpox, retreated toward Montreal, pursued by the British. Thomas died of smallpox and was succeeded by Gen. John Sullivan. After an attack on Three Rivers was repelled (June 8, 1776), the Americans evacuated Montreal (June 15). In July the dejected remnants of the invasion army returned to Fort Ticonderoga.

Congress now appointed Gen. Horatio Gates to command the Canadian front. Gates energetically prepared to defend Ticonderoga against the oncoming British. During July and August, Benedict Arnold assembled a fleet of small boats on Lake Champlain to bar the British advance. Carleton assembled a superior fleet, manned by experienced sailors, and on Oct. 11, near Valcour Island,

and again on Oct. 13, near Crown Point, defeated Arnold's fleet. But the season was now too far advanced to lay siege to Ticonderoga. Carleton withdrew into Canada, postponing until 1777 a British invasion of the United States from the north.

The Quebec campaign cost the Americans 5,000 dead, mostly from disease.

QUEBEC CONFERENCES (1943, 1944). See *World War 2 Conferences.

QUEEN ANNE'S WAR. See *French and Indian Wars.

QUINN v. UNITED STATES (1915), decision of the *White Court finding the *grandfather clause in the constitutions of some Southern states unconstitutional. The decision had no effect, since in some states time limits for registering to vote under the grandfather clause had expired and in other states African-Americans continued to be denied the vote on other grounds.

R

RADICAL REPUBLICANS, extreme faction of the Republican congressional delegation during the *Civil War and *Reconstruction. Their leaders in the Senate were Charles Sumner and Henry Wilson of Massachusetts, Benjamin F. Wade of Ohio, and Zachariah Chandler of Michigan. In the House, they were led by Thaddeus Stevens of Pennsylvania, George S. Boutwell of Massachusetts, George W. Julian of Indiana, and James F. Wilson of Iowa.

Varying widely on economic and social issues, the Radicals were united on the principle of racial equality. Former *abolitionists, they were zealous in the prosecution of the war, controlling the *Committee on the Conduct of the War; insistent on early emancipation (and impatient with President Lincoln on this score); determined, through their control of the Joint Committee on Reconstruction, to inflict a punitive peace upon the South, which they regarded as a conquered province; and committed to black suffrage and civil rights, North as well as South.

The Radicals were a minority in the *Republican Party, although their strong sense of purpose gave them considerable influence. From 1867 to 1869, after Pres. Andrew Johnson had alienated conservative and moderate Republicans, the Radicals dominated Congress. They were able to institute their own reconstruction program, employing the powerful national government—a new phenomenon, produced by the war—to impose Republican regimes and black suffrage on recalcitrant Southern states. Injudiciously, they impeached President Johnson (see *Johnson Impeachment); their failure to convict him marked a turning point in their fortunes. With the election of Ulysses S. Grant as president in 1868, their influence quickly faded along with wartime idealism.

Radical reconstruction failed because the Radicals were constrained by their laissez-faire economic philosophy from providing sustained assistance—especially land—to the freedmen, which might have assured their economic independence. Political rights, unprotected by military force after 1877, proved ephemeral in the hostile Southern environment. The permanent heritage of Radical reconstruction are the *13th, *14th, and *15th Amendments to the U.S. Constitution.

RADICAL RIGHT, a collection of fringe groups outside the mainstream of U.S. politics distinguished by racist and paranoid ideologies.

White supremacists believe in the superiority of the white race and are hostile to African-Americans, Jews, and other minorities to the point of committing vicious hate crimes and random murders. Many profess to believe in a coming race war that will "purify" a white, Christian America. The *Ku Klux Klan, founded in 1866, was the original white-supremacist organization; its name has been used repeatedly by a variety of organizations claiming ideological descent from the original Klan. White-supremacist organizations multiplied in opposition to the *civil rights movement of the 1960s. Among the better known in a large and ever-changing field are the Aryan Nations and The Order. White-supremacist ideology is often shared by other radical-right movements.

Neo-Nazis appeared in America with the founding of the National Socialist White People's Party by George Lincoln Rockwell in 1959. Anti-Semitic, antiblack, and preaching violence, the group wore Nazi-style uniforms with swastika armbands and conducted provocative public demonstrations. The publicity these generated masked the party's small size. Rockwell was murdered by a rival in 1967, after which Nazi parties and organizations proliferated, all of them small and ineffectual.

The **John Birch Society**, an ultraconservative

organization founded in 1958 by Robert H. W. Welch and named for a U.S. intelligence officer killed by the Chinese communists in 1945, won notoriety by its discovery of ubiquitous communist conspiracies. It accused Pres. Dwight D. Eisenhower and other prominent individuals of being "dedicated agents" of an international communist conspiracy. In 2000 it claimed 50,000 members and described itself as an educational organization advocating abolition of most federal regulatory agencies, termination of foreign aid, and U.S. withdrawal from the United Nations.

LaRouchites, followers of Lyndon LaRouche, founder of a cultlike movement masked by multiple and ever-changing front organizations. The movement is characterized by rampant paranoia—LaRouche himself has accused the British royal family of drug trafficking. Its objectives are unclear.

Militias, armed bodies that arose throughout the country in the 1990s preparing for war—defensive or offensive is unclear—against the U.S. government. Members believe that the government is conspiring with the United Nations to create a one-government New World Order. Militias sometimes intimidate or harass courts and local government officials. In 2001 the Southern Poverty Law Center reported that the number of militias peaked at 858 in 1996, then fell to 194 by 2000.

Skinheads, young, shaven-headed street toughs, alienated and violent, who first appeared in the United States in the 1980s in imitation of British models. Loosely organized in local federations, they often ape Nazi regalia and conduct, and parrot Nazi ideology.

Freemen, an anarchistic movement that denies the legitimacy of all American governments and thus justifies such criminal activity as filing fraudulent liens, passing bad checks, robbing banks, kidnapping, and murder.

Survivalists, individuals who, for religious or ideological reasons, expect a coming Armageddon and are preparing by arming themselves and stockpiling food and other supplies in isolated retreats.

RADIO AND TELEVISION. Radios dominated American living rooms for about 25 years, beginning in the early 1920s. Far from the mere "music box" its creators had foreseen, radio provided a complete menu of entertainment—all of it purely audio, thus leaving much of its enjoyment to the imagination.

Afternoons were devoted to "soap operas," 15-minute chapters in the lives of long-suffering women, typically sponsored by manufacturers of laundry and beauty products. Late afternoon offered children a succession of 15-minute episodes in a number of adventure

series. The evening's adult programming began with the phenomenally popular daily 15-minute episode of *Amos and Andy*, followed by weekly half-hour or hour comedy, drama, and variety shows. Almost all radio in this "golden age" was live.

As World War 2 approached, radio networks expanded their news departments. Correspondents in European capitals brought the growing international crisis directly into Americans' living rooms. When the Japanese attacked Pearl Harbor, Americans rushed to their radios for news. By then, radio had replaced print media as Americans' principal source of news.

After the war, television quickly displaced radio as the primary entertainment and news medium, leaving radio stations to find local "niche" markets, often by specializing in ever narrower (recorded) music genres or provocative talk shows. Television even threatened to displace motion pictures until the two industries were absorbed into entertainment conglomerates.

The need to fill so many hours of airtime with entertainment for mass audiences guaranteed that the quality of most commercial television programming would sink to the lowest common denominator of viewer taste. Television was partially redeemed, however, by a number of superior comedy and drama series, by its coverage of news, sports, and special events, and by talk shows that provided forums for the discussion of public issues in which Americans could participate if only as observers. The Public Broadcasting System, created in 1967, in particular provided a rich fare of educational and cultural programming.

Perhaps television's greatest redeeming feature was its power to weld—however briefly—a diverse and fragmented country into a national community at times of extraordinary celebration, shock, or grief. Such a time was the assassination of Pres. John F. Kennedy, when the nation sat before its television sets for days, transfixed by a succession of sensational and poignant images. The same was true after the terrorist attacks on the World Trade Center and the Pentagon in 2001.

At the start of the new century, television's future was already clouded by the multiplication of channels and development of the Internet that threatened to fragment the mass audiences television required for advertising revenue.

RAIL PASSENGER SERVICE ACT (1970). See *Railroad Regulation.

RAIL REORGANIZATION ACT (1974). See *Railroad Regulation.

RAILROAD ADMINISTRATION, U.S. See *Railroad Regulation.

RAILROAD BROTHERHOODS, five unions of railroad-operating employees—locomotive engineers (organized 1863), conductors (1868), firemen and enginemen (1873), trainmen (1883), and switchmen (1894). Originally organized for fraternal and insurance purposes, the brotherhoods became highly militant in railroad labor conflicts. As railroad employment declined after World War 2, the conductors, firemen, trainmen, and switchmen merged in 1969 to form the United Transportation Union.

RAILROAD LABOR ACT (1934). See *Railroad Regulation.

RAILROAD LAND GRANTS (1850–72). Having earlier subsidized the building of wagon roads and canals with grants of *public land, Congress in 1850 embarked on a major program of subsidizing the development of strategically important railroads. Gifts of several million acres to Illinois, Alabama, and Mississippi were intended to encourage the development of a railroad connecting Lake Michigan and the Gulf of Mexico. By 1860 Chicago and New Orleans were linked by rail.

During and after the *Civil War, Congress provided grants to subsidize construction of a *transcontinental railroad. The Union Pacific and Central (later Southern) Pacific—and later the Santa Fe and Northern Pacific—were given alternate mile-square sections (640 acres) of public land extending six miles on both sides of the projected routes. The Union Pacific received 20 million acres, the Central and Southern Pacific 24 million, the Santa Fe 17 million, and the Northern Pacific 44 million—areas totaling almost the size of Texas.

The land was to be sold at prices above those charged for public land because of the enhanced value created by the presence of the railroad, and revenues from the sales were to be applied to the costs of construction. (The railroads kept for themselves sections containing valuable timber and mineral resources.) Settlers were recruited from as far away as Europe to buy the railroads' land and eventually become the railroads' customers.

Since the alternate sections retained by the government increased in value with the sections owned by the railroads, it was anticipated that the land grants would actually cost the government nothing. In fact, the government was not able to sell its sections at the expected premium prices and suffered a loss on that part of the transaction.

The government also loaned money to the railroad companies, in exchange for which it was permitted to transport troops, supplies, and mail by rail at discounted rates. The loans were all repaid, and by the time the discounted rates were discontinued in 1946 they were calculated to have been worth more than $1 billion.

RAILROAD REGULATION. The nation's largest business in the 19th century, the railroads long wielded their power with impunity. Their freight rates, based upon inflated construction costs and watered stock, were exorbitant and extended to grain elevators and other storage facilities they owned. They discriminated among commodities and locations and granted secret rebates to major shippers. They controlled the politics of many states by their party contributions and free passes to influential people, including legislators. Their monopolistic practices eventually aroused the protests of the *Granger movement and the *Farmers' Alliances (see also *Agrarian Discontents).

After the U.S. Supreme Court, in *Wabash, St. Louis & Pacific Railroad v. Illinois (1886), limited state regulatory authority to intrastate commerce, Congress responded with passage of the **Interstate Commerce Act** (1887), making the railroads the first industry to experience federal regulation. The act prohibited railroad pooling (combining), rebates, and discrimination among persons, places, and commodities; required the railroads to post their rates; and established the first federal regulatory agency, the Interstate Commerce Commission (ICC), to ensure that these rates were "reasonable and just." The courts, however, quickly took upon themselves the right to review ICC decisions, reversing 15 of the first 16 to be appealed to the Supreme Court and virtually nullifying the powers of the ICC.

The **Elkins Act** (1905) prohibited the railroads from deviating from published rates, provided that shippers as well as railroad officials were liable for receiving rebates, and substituted civil for criminal penalties.

The **Hepburn Act** (1906) extended the ICC's authority from interstate railroads to storage, refrigeration, and terminal facilities; to sleeping car, express, and pipeline companies; and in 1910 to telephone and telegraph companies. It authorized the ICC to set maximum rates for the railroads—although the power to set *minimum* rates would have ended the railroads' practice of giving rebates to favored shippers. The ICC was empowered to settle disputes between railroads and shippers and to impose a standardized accounting system on the railroads. Railroads were prohibited from carrying without charge commodities produced by them or by companies in which they held interests. Free passes were prohibited except for railroad employees.

The **Mann-Elkins Act** (1910) empowered the ICC to suspend any rate increases pending its review and created a Commerce Court to hear appeals from the ICC.

The **Physical Valuation Act** (1913) authorized the ICC to establish the value of railroad property as a basis for rate-making. The same year, the **Newlands Act** established a four-member Board of Mediation and Conciliation to deal with labor problems on the railroads.

The **Adamson Act** (1916) reduced from ten hours to eight the workday on interstate railroads and provided for time and a half for overtime. Alternatively, a run of 100 miles counted as a workday.

During World War 1, the railroads—2,905 companies—were nationalized and placed under the direction of the **U.S. Railroad Administration**, headed by Secretary of the Treasury William G. McAdoo.

Under the **Esch-Cummins Transportation Act** (1920) the railroads were returned to private operation. However, the powers of the ICC were further enlarged, now to set minimum as well as maximum rates and to establish fair returns to stockholders. Railroads were required to turn over to the ICC half of all earnings over 6 percent, to be used to subsidize railroads with low earnings. The act also created a Railroad Labor Board to adjudicate wage disputes.

During the *New Deal, the **Emergency Railroad Transportation Act** (1933) sought to avoid unnecessary duplication of services and facilities and to promote financial reorganization of the railroads. The **Railroad Labor Act** (1934) recognized the right of railroad employees to organize and bargain collectively and established a National Railroad Adjustment Board to deal with labor issues where collective bargaining had failed. The **Railroad Retirement Act** (1937) established government pensions for retired railroad workers.

The decline of the nation's railroads, dramatized in 1970 by the bankruptcy of the Penn Central, the nation's largest, resulted in the **Rail Passenger Service Act** (1970), which established a nationwide passenger system, **Amtrak**, to which railroads could transfer their unprofitable passenger services. The **Rail Reorganization Act** (1974) provided for the reorganization of the Penn Central and six other bankrupt Northeastern and Midwestern railroads, established a federal agency to unite the bankrupt lines in a new profit-making rail system, and created the Consolidated Railroad Corporation (**Conrail**) to run it.

The railroads were partially deregulated by the **Staggers Rail Act** (1980), which gave them greater flexi-

bility in rate-setting, made it easier to abandon unprofitable lines, and encouraged mergers (see also *Railroads).

RAILROAD RETIREMENT ACT (1937). See *Railroad Regulation.

RAILROADS. During 1830–35, the first railroads designed to carry freight and passengers pulled by steam-powered locomotives ventured from Charleston, Albany, Baltimore, Philadelphia, Petersburg, Boston, and New Orleans into transportation-starved hinterlands. They were built with both private and public capital in a climate of growing enthusiasm only temporarily dampened by the *Panic of 1837. All were local enterprises of limited objectives. No one thought of coordination or of uniformity of track gauges and rolling stock.

Mileage multiplied by the decade. From 3,328 miles in 1840 (nearly twice as many as in all of Europe), U.S. railroad lines totaled 9,000 miles in 1850, 31,000 miles in 1860. The tangled web of local lines eventually meshed into a national system. Most lines ran generally east and west, uniting the Northeastern and Middle Western states. By 1855, it was possible to travel from New York to Chicago by rail—with many changes and stopovers. In 1860, Chicago was joined by rail to New Orleans.

The American Civil War was the first "railroad war," railroads transporting matériel and equipment and moving whole armies between theaters. During the war, Congress authorized construction of a *transcontinental railroad uniting the Mississippi Valley with the West Coast, subsidizing the enterprise with grants of land from the public domain (see *Railroad Land Grants). When completed in 1869, the united Union Pacific and Central Pacific connected Omaha, Nebr., to Sacramento, Calif. Four other lines soon pushed across the trans-Mississippi West. By 1882, the Southern Pacific connected New Orleans with San Diego; in 1883, the Northern Pacific connected Duluth, Minn., to Portland, Ore., and the Atchison, Topeka & Santa Fe connected Kansas City, Kans., to Los Angeles; in 1893, the Great Northern connected St. Paul, Minn., to Seattle, Wash.

Consolidation of numerous railroad lines began before the war and continued after. In 1849–55 four Illinois railroads were united to form the Chicago, Burlington & Quincy. In 1853, three New York State railroads connecting New York to Buffalo formed the New York Central, which by 1885 connected New York to Chicago and St. Louis. The Pennsylvania Railroad soon also extended from New York, Baltimore, and

Washington to Chicago and St. Louis. By 1904, six major railroad systems—controlled by J. P. Morgan (see *Morgan's Career), August Belmont, Edward H. Harriman, James J. Hill—controlled three-fourths of the country's railroad mileage.

Consolidation brought (1883) replacement of hundreds of different local times by four broad time zones and (1886) conversion of diverse track gauges to a standard four feet, eight and a half inches. Crucial inventions like car couplers and air brakes were developed and standardized, making it possible for cars to be shunted from system to system. By 1890, welded steel rails had replaced iron rails. Mileage continued to expand, peaking finally in 1916 at 254,000.

Relative to other transportation modes, the railroads declined after World War 1. Between 1916 and 1999, the railroads' share of intercity passenger traffic fell from 98.0 percent to 0.6 percent, of intercity freight traffic from 77.2 percent to 40.3 percent. Track mileage declined from 254,000 in 1916 to 122,000 in 2000.

The principal cause of this decline was competition from other transportation modes—automobiles, trucks, buses, airplanes, pipelines. Significant improvement in operating efficiency during the 1930s and 1940s made possible by electronic communications, centralized traffic control, diesel engines, and improved passenger cars slowed but did not halt the decline. Government regulation contributed to the railroads' difficulties. The Interstate Commerce Commission (ICC) blocked abandonment of unprofitable lines, limited rate flexibility, and discouraged diversification and mergers. Finally, the railroads were affected by the changing economic fortunes of the regions they served.

Annual deficits after 1929 (except during World War 2) caused railroads to steadily curtail passenger service. In 1920, there were 20,000 passenger train departures daily, in 1970 fewer than 300. Meager profits from freight service starved the railroads of the capital necessary to maintain roadbeds and replace deteriorating equipment and facilities. After 1950, the decay of much of the railroad network outdistanced efforts at maintenance and rehabilitation.

The bankruptcy in 1970 of the nation's largest railroad, the Penn Central (formed in 1968 by a merger of the New York Central and the Pennsylvania railroads), brought a shift in federal policy. Since the optimum role of the railroads in the nation's transportation system was to carry bulk freight—coal, grain, ore, steel—over long distances and passengers over short distances in densely populated urban corridors, Congress in 1970 created the National Railroad Passenger Corporation (**Amtrak**), a quasi-public, government-sponsored corporation to operate about 90 percent of the nation's passenger service. Despite subsidies, Amtrak was forced steadily to eliminate routes and reduce service.

In 1976, Congress provided the financial assistance to make possible the organization of the Consolidated Railroad Corporation (**Conrail**), a private corporation uniting six bankrupt Northeastern and Midwestern railroads, including the Penn Central. Expectations were again disappointed; in 1981 Congress separated Conrail's freight operations from its money-losing commuter operations, which were turned over to the states, and in 1987 transferred Conrail to the private sector through a stock offering.

In 1980, 39 Class I railroads (those earning more than $50 million a year) continued to carry a substantial proportion of the nation's intercity freight and a small number of passengers aided by government subsidies in the form of grants, loans, and loan guarantees. In 1980 the **Staggers Rail Act** partially deregulated the railroads, allowing them to raise freight rates within certain limits without ICC approval, to abandon unprofitable routes more easily, and to merge more readily. The result was lower freight rates and increased revenues, but not to the point of attracting the capital necessary for long-term service improvements. In 2000, nine Class I railroads (earning over $92 million a year) continued to operate. Analysts considered the condition of the railroads stabilized but not fundamentally cured (see also *Railroad Regulation).

RAILROAD STRIKES OF 1877, wave of spontaneous strikes against the railroads that spread across the country in July 1877. During the economic depression that followed the *Panic of 1873, the railroads, like other businesses, sought to reduce labor costs. When major lines slashed wages in 1877, a Trainmen's Union, which united low-paid brakemen, conductors, and switchmen, struck the Baltimore & Ohio Railroad in Baltimore on July 16. Strikers then seized B&O yards at Martinsburg, W. Va., where they battled state militia and federal troops.

Spreading quickly to other rail centers—Buffalo, Pittsburgh, Indianapolis, Chicago, St. Louis—the strikes were marked by mob violence and widespread property destruction, testifying to the desperation of the railroad workers and their sympathizers. Rail service was disrupted throughout much of the country, and the country itself seemed on the verge of revolution.

Pres. Rutherford B. Hayes dispatched federal troops to strike centers to protect property and restore order.

Lacking national leadership and resources, the strikes had collapsed by the beginning of August.

RATIFICATION OF THE U.S. CONSTITUTION

(1787–88). The Federal *Constitutional Convention adjourned on Sept. 17, 1787, forwarding its draft constitution to the Confederation Congress (see *Continental Congress) in New York City. It recommended that the draft be submitted for ratification to specially elected state conventions rather than to existing state legislatures—a violation of the *Articles of Confederation but a device the Framers felt essential to found the new government on the sovereignty of the whole people. On Sept. 28, Congress grudgingly transmitted the document to the legislatures of the states for submission to ratifying conventions.

There ensued a national debate carried on in newspapers and pamphlets—most notably the articles written by Alexander Hamilton, James Madison, and John Jay and published as The *Federalist—as well as in public meetings and on the floors of state conventions. Supporters of the Constitution took the name Federalists, implying that the Constitution would create a federal union of more or less sovereign states and avoiding the word "nationalists," which implied a unitary or "consolidated" government in which the separate states would disappear. Opponents of the Constitution had little choice but to call themselves *Antifederalists.

In each state, the decision to ratify or not was influenced by varied factors: local political conditions, the prestige of leaders on both sides (the knowledge that George Washington and Benjamin Franklin favored the Constitution weighed heavily in the Federalists' favor), even the timing of the state conventions. The convention debates themselves, for all their richness of argument, probably changed few minds. In the end, the Constitution was ratified by a very small margin. The change of a few votes in a number of states would have reversed the result. Thus the Federalists carried the key states of Massachusetts, Virginia, and New York by a total of only 32 votes out of 580 votes cast.

The debates centered first on the absence of a *bill of rights, which the Federalists readily promised to make the first business of the new Congress. Beyond that, the Antifederalists found fault with virtually every clause of the proposed Constitution. All their objections, and the Federalists' rebuttals, can be viewed as a dialogue between those voicing fear of government and those voicing need of government.

The Antifederalists were suspicious of government—any government—and passionately devoted to their "liberties," which they associated with their states. A national government, they feared, would override and suppress not only the sovereignty but the distinctive characters of the states. Confident of the ability of free and virtuous men to govern themselves in small communities, they believed that the least government was the best. Much in the Constitution seemed to promise tyranny and oppression—a strong executive; an aristocratic Senate; a House of Representatives elected biannually rather than annually; a federal judiciary; a standing army and navy; federal excises and taxes; even salaries for members of Congress. They found little fault with the Articles of Confederation.

To the Federalists, the Articles promised early dissolution of the union. Only in union, they believed, was national security, domestic order, and economic prosperity possible. Under the Articles, the states were mutually jealous and hostile. Arenas of factional strife, they often legislated irresponsibly in the interests of the dominant faction. Only under a central government capable of defending the national interest could the people preserve their independence and liberties and win the respect of other nations.

By and large, the small states, satisfied by the "great compromise" that gave them equal representation with large states in the Senate, recognized the value of federal union. Delaware and New Jersey ratified in December 1787, Georgia and Connecticut in January 1788. Pennsylvania, a large state, ratified in December after the Federalists rushed through elections to a convention before the Antifederalists could mobilize.

The great debates on the Constitution took place in the other large states, beginning in February 1788 with Massachusetts, where the trauma of *Shays's Rebellion was still fresh. Despite an initial Antifederalist majority in the convention, Massachusetts ratified by a vote of 187 to 168. Three more small states—Maryland, South Carolina, and New Hampshire—ratified between April and June 1788. New Hampshire was the ninth state to ratify, bringing the Constitution into effect in those nine states. But with Virginia and New York still to be heard from (as well as North Carolina and Rhode Island), the viability of the new union was highly uncertain.

The realization that the Constitution was already ratified by the requisite nine states probably tipped the balance in those two large states. Virginia ratified 89–79 on June 26, New York 30–27 on July 26. North Carolina did not finally ratify until Nov. 21, 1789, and Rhode Island until May 29, 1790.

On July 2, 1788, the Confederation Congress recognized the ratification of the Constitution by the required nine states. On Sept. 13, it declared New York City the site of the new government and set the first Wednesday in January 1789 for the states to choose their presidential electors (see *Electoral College), the first Wednesday in February for the electors to meet and cast their ballots, and the first Wednesday in March for the new Congress to convene and count the electoral ballots.

REAGAN ADMINISTRATION (1981–89). Ronald Reagan, 40th president of the United States, was the leader of Republican conservatives who had long struggled with Eastern "establishment" Republicans for control of their party.

Unabashedly patriotic, serenely optimistic, a passive and detached manager, and poorly informed, he nevertheless had certain convictions that powerfully affected U.S. and world history. In domestic affairs, he believed that lower taxes and business deregulation would spur economic growth and actually increase revenues (what George H. W. Bush, his rival for the presidential nomination, then his vice president, called "voodoo economics" and which became known as "Reaganomics"). In foreign affairs he believed that the Soviet Union was an "evil empire" destined to collapse. Abhorring the prospect of nuclear war, he was prepared to negotiate nuclear disarmament with the Soviets, but only from a position of strength. For this reason a massive military buildup was central to his program.

In the Reagan administration's first year, the Omnibus Budget Reconciliation Act slashed social welfare programs and the budgets of regulatory agencies while increasing defense spending 7 percent a year (on top of Pres. James E. Carter's 5 percent increase). At the same time, the Economic Recovery Tax Act cut individual income tax rates 25 percent over three years, reduced the rates on investment income and capital gains, and speeded the depreciation of new plants and equipment. The tax act, which conspicuously favored the wealthy, reflected Reagan's conversion to **supply-side economics**, the doctrine that the tax system should favor investors and businesses rather than consumers. Some of the inequities of the 1981 tax act were corrected in the Tax Equity and Fiscal Responsibility Act of 1982 and the Tax Reform Act of 1986.

Reagan's attempt to stimulate the economy, mired in rising unemployment but double-digit inflation (an unprecedented situation called "stagflation"), came at the same time that the Federal Reserve had resolved to induce a recession to sweat inflation out of the economy. With interest rates at 20 percent, the country slipped into a severe recession in 1981–82. Recovery began in mid-1983, but the combination of recession, reduced taxes,

and increased military spending (plus increased spending on *welfare programs, which continued to grow despite Reagan's efforts to curtail them) produced enormous budget deficits. Conservatives were aghast, but Reagan believed—correctly—that voters would not feel the deficits and would credit Reaganomics for the recovery (which, though fueled by budget deficits, was no stronger than other recent postrecession recoveries had been). The national debt increased from $1 trillion in 1980 to $4 trillion a decade later, transforming the United States from a creditor to a debtor nation, making debt service a major component of the budget, and preventing the launching of any new social programs for years to come.

Reagan's military buildup alarmed the Soviets, but not as much as his decision in 1983 to pursue his Strategic Defense Initiative (SDI), a costly antiballistic missile defense system that threatened to end the existing "balance of terror" (see *Missile Defense). This brought Soviet premier Mikhail Gorbachev to the negotiating table. At a summit meeting at Reykjavík, Iceland, in October 1986, the two leaders agreed in principle to destroy all ballistic missiles and nuclear weapons over a ten-year period, but Reagan broke up the meeting by refusing to compromise on SDI.

The shock to Gorbachev proved salutary, for the Soviets now concluded that they had to abandon the arms race. Over the objections of hard-liners on both sides, Reagan and Gorbachev signed the Intermediate Nuclear Forces (INF) Treaty in Washington in December 1987. Eliminating certain classes of nuclear weapons and missiles, this treaty marked the end of the U.S.-Soviet arms race (see *Arms Control and Disarmament). For Gorbachev, however, it was too late; the Soviet Union was already spiraling toward dissolution.

In other foreign affairs, the Reagan administration supported anticommunist forces in Poland and Afghanistan. In Central America, with right-wing allies, it combated what it perceived as communist threats in El Salvador and Nicaragua. It suffered a disaster when it intervened in Lebanon (see *Lebanon Interventions) but scored an easy success in Grenada (see *Grenada Invasion). Reagan's concern for American hostages in Lebanon (see *Lebanon Hostages) led to his participation in the *Iran-Contra Affair, which clouded the last years of his administration.

Nevertheless, he left office at a peak of personal popularity, anointing his vice president, George H. W. Bush, as his successor.

REAGAN ASSASSINATION ATTEMPT (Mar. 30, 1981). On the 69th day of his presidency, as he and his

entourage emerged from a side entrance of the Washington Hilton Hotel at 2:25 p.m., Pres. Ronald Reagan was fired upon by John W. Hinckley Jr., a 25-year-old Coloradan. Hinckley fired six shots from a .22-caliber pistol, wounding presidential press secretary James Brady, a Secret Service agent, and a Washington, D.C., policeman. Reagan was struck by a ricochet that penetrated his left side, collapsed a lung, and lodged a quarter of an inch from his heart. Rushed to George Washington University Hospital, the 70-year-old president was bleeding internally and near death. In a two-hour operation the bullet was removed, the bleeding stopped, and his condition stabilized.

In a dangerous *cold war world, reports of the assassination attempt, often misleading, caused consternation across the country and especially in the White House. In the absence of Vice Pres. George H. W. Bush (who returned that night), Secretary of State Alexander Haig—to the vast irritation of his cabinet colleagues—asserted his authority as senior cabinet officer, although by law the Speaker of the House of Representatives followed the vice president in the line of *presidential succession. When asked at a press conference who was "in charge," Haig replied, "I am in control here." Meanwhile, at the hospital, presidential aides James A. Baker, White House chief of staff, Michael Deaver, deputy chief of staff, and Edwin Meese, presidential counselor, maintained the impression that the president was not incapacitated. No one invoked the *25th Amendment, under which an incapacitated president could temporarily transfer his powers and duties to the vice president.

Reagan was discharged from the hospital after 12 days. His recovery was slow, and observers later commented on a permanent diminution of his energies.

Hinckley, son of an affluent Republican family and a former psychiatric patient, had been expelled from the American Nazi Party for excessive militancy. His motivation for the assassination was to impress a film actress with whom he was infatuated although they had never met. In June 1982 a Washington jury found him not guilty by reason of insanity. The judge committed him to a mental hospital for an indefinite period.

RECALL. See *Initiative, Referendum, and Recall.

RECESSION OF 1937–38, incident in the Franklin *Roosevelt administration. After four years of steady economic improvement, the Federal Reserve in 1937 tightened the money supply to prevent inflation and the administration cut spending to balance the budget. The result was a sharp recession lasting from September 1937 to June 1938, during which GNP fell from $90.4 billion to $84.7 billion while unemployment rose from 14.3 percent to 19.0 percent. The administration shifted gears in March 1938, pouring money back into programs that had recently been cut or terminated. The experience convinced government economists of the effectiveness of deficit spending and monetary expansion in overcoming the *Great Depression.

RECONSTRUCTION (1865–77), post–*Civil War period during which relations between the former Confederate states (see *Confederate States of America) and the federal government were normalized.

Presidential Reconstruction. Pres. Abraham Lincoln believed that *secession had been illegal, that the Confederate states were therefore never out of the Union, and that they could be restored to their normal relations with the federal government as soon as loyal governments could be established. He also believed that reconstruction was the responsibility of the president, deriving from his constitutional power "to grant reprieves and pardons for offenses against the United States."

Lincoln's **Proclamation of Amnesty and Reconstruction** (Dec. 8, 1863) offered full pardons to all Confederates (except certain classes of leaders) who would swear allegiance to the United States and accept the wartime legislation affecting slavery. When the number of such persons in any state equaled 10 percent of the number of votes cast in that state in the 1860 presidential election, they could form a state government that would be recognized by the president as the "true government of the State." The decision to seat congressional delegations from such states, however, would remain with the two houses of Congress.

While Lincoln was still alive, reconstruction governments were instituted in Tennessee, Virginia, Louisiana, and Arkansas on the basis of his "10-percent plan." Lincoln hoped that former Southern Whigs, many of whom had opposed secession, would rally to a conservative Republican Party.

Lincoln's policy was challenged by the *Radical Republicans, who declared that reconstruction was a congressional prerogative because of Congress's responsibility to ensure every state a republican form of government. In the **Wade-Davis Bill** (February 1864), Sen. Benjamin F. Wade of Ohio and Rep. Henry Winter Davis of Maryland asserted the congressional claim to direct reconstruction. Their bill provided for the appointment by the president of provisional governors to administer former Confederate states until 50 percent of their populations had subscribed to an oath to support the Constitution and wartime laws respecting slavery. Then those who swore additionally that they had not supported the Confederacy or voluntarily borne arms against the Union would elect conventions to write new state constitutions that would abolish slavery and repudiate the Confederate debt. Lincoln killed this measure with a pocket veto, to which Wade and Davis responded (Aug. 5) with a manifesto attacking the president ("A more studied outrage of the legislative authority of the people has never been perpetrated. . . . [T]he authority of Congress is paramount. . . . [The president] must confine himself to his executive duties—to obey and execute, not make the laws . . .").

Lincoln's successor, Andrew Johnson, shared Lincoln's views on the status of the former Confederate states and on the president's responsibility for reconstruction. But he had a reconstruction plan of his own. A Tennessee Democrat who had risen from humble origins, he was determined to end the influence of the planter aristocracy in the government of the Southern states in favor of the independent small farmers. Thus his amnesty proclamation (May 29, 1865) exempted, along with 13 other categories, all persons who had participated in the rebellion whose taxable property was valued at over $20,000.

The Radicals believed that Johnson shared their desire for a harsh peace, for he had declared, "Treason must be made odious, and traitors must be punished and impoverished." But not only did Johnson disagree with the Radicals on presidential responsibility for reconstruction, he had no sympathy for the Radicals' interest in enfranchising and elevating the new freedmen. A former slave owner, he believed the Radicals' policy toward the freedmen would "Africanize" the South (see Andrew *Johnson Administration).

During Congress's long recess in the summer and fall of 1865, Johnson appointed provisional governors of the Southern states who convoked constitutional conventions (from which blacks were excluded) that nullified secession, repudiated Confederate debts, and ratified the *13th Amendment abolishing slavery. He left the question of suffrage up to the states, none, of which gave freedmen the vote.

When Southerners thereafter voted for government officials, Johnson was disheartened to discover that many members of the old ruling elite—planters and Confederate leaders—had been elected. Constrained by his respect for states' rights, Johnson would not interfere with what Southern voters had done. To prevent further social revolution in the South, he issued wholesale pardons to the former Confederates, legitimizing their elections. When

Congress assembled in December 1865, Johnson declared reconstruction completed.

Republicans constituted large majorities in both houses of the new Congress. They were angered to discover former Confederates—Democrats all, and still rebellious—in public office throughout the South. They were outraged by the *black codes quickly passed by the reconstructed governments to ensure continued subordination of the freedmen to their former oppressors. Moreover, they realized with dismay that, since blacks were now counted as whole persons rather than as three-fifths of persons when they were slaves, Southern membership in the House of Representatives would be increased by some 15 members. To the Republicans, especially the minority Radical faction, it appeared that Johnson had given away the fruits of victory.

Refusing to seat the delegates from the Southern states (and thereafter indicted by Johnson as a Congress of only part of the country), Congress in December 1865 appointed a **Joint Committee on Reconstruction** consisting of six senators and nine representatives. Although chaired by Sen. William P. Fessenden of Maine, it was dominated by its eight Radical members led by Rep. Thaddeus Stevens of Pennsylvania. All resolutions and bills pertaining to reconstruction had to be referred to this committee. Having investigated conditions in the former Confederate states, the committee reported on June 20, 1866, that disloyalty was still rife in the South.

Johnson's vetoes of a bill extending the life of the *Freedmen's Bureau and of the *Civil Rights Act of 1866 were quickly overridden. Vainly Johnson opposed the *14th Amendment, which Congress passed in June and which was rejected by the legislatures of ten Southern (Johnson) state governments. Race riots in Memphis and New Orleans were attributed to Johnson's leniency to the former Confederates.

The conflict between Congress and the president came to a head in the congressional elections of 1866. Johnson's pugnacious and intemperate campaigning in his *Swing Around the Circle drove moderate Republicans into the Radical camp. Anti-Johnson Republicans won every Northern state and more than two-thirds majorities in both houses of Congress. They were now in position to overturn Johnson's reconstruction program and institute a new one designed to punish treason and establish the Republican Party—still entirely a Northern party—in the South on a foundation of blacks and white Unionists.

Congressional Reconstruction. On Mar. 2, 1867, the Radical-dominated Congress passed the first of four **Reconstruction Acts** (three supplemental acts followed on Mar. 23 and July 19, 1867, and Mar. 11, 1868). Together they repudiated the Democratic state governments recognized by Johnson. They divided ten of the 11 former Confederate states (Tennessee, having ratified the 14th Amendment, was exempted) into five military districts, each commanded by a major general with extraordinary power over civilian affairs.

The generals were instructed to register loyal voters (including blacks) in each state to elect delegates to constitutional conventions, which in turn would draft new state constitutions providing for black suffrage. These constitutions had then to be ratified by the people of those states (that is, by majorities of the small numbers permitted to vote) and approved by Congress. When the state legislature under a new constitution ratified the 14th Amendment, that state would be entitled to representation in Congress. By 1870, Republican governments in all the Southern states had fulfilled the acts' requirements and their delegations had been seated in Congress. That year, ratification of the *15th Amendment put black male suffrage into the U.S. Constitution.

To the scandal of white Southerners, the constitutional conventions and new state governments were dominated by white Republican *carpetbaggers and scalawags. Although numerous in the constitutional conventions, blacks at first deferred to these whites and received few offices in the new state governments. Before the end of Reconstruction, however, one became a state governor (in Louisiana); 14 were elected to the U.S. House of Representatives and two (both from Mississippi) to the U.S. Senate. In state legislatures, blacks constituted a majority only in South Carolina.

The new state constitutions and state governments were moderately progressive in extending democratic government, reforming legal codes, improving public education, and enlarging public services. White Southerners, however, despised the "black and tan" governments and unfairly condemned their extravagance and corruption. The states, it is true, went deeply into debt to repair war damage, to pay for enlarged state services, and to float costly loans in the North—all at a time of diminished land values, crop failures, and depression. Corruption, which was characteristic of many states in this period, often resulted from the enthusiasm for economic development, especially railroad construction, and the jostling of Northern business interests for advantage.

Never reconciled to Republican government, white Southerners resisted by violence and intimidation (see *Ku Klux Klan). Gradually, they "redeemed" their states, installing conservative white Democratic governments in Tennessee in 1869; in Virginia and North Carolina in 1870; in Georgia in 1871; in Alabama, Arkansas, and Texas in 1874; in Mississippi in 1875; and in South Carolina, Florida, and Louisiana in 1877. The resultant Democratic *Solid South persisted for 80 years.

For a time, the Radical-dominated Congress altered the constitutional balance among the executive, legislative, and judicial branches of the federal government. In 1868 Congress limited the jurisdiction of the U.S. Supreme Court in a case (*Ex parte *McCardle*) challenging the constitutionality of the Reconstruction Acts. But the Radicals' chief target was the president. The 14th Amendment transferred from the president to Congress the power to restore political rights to Confederate leaders through pardons. Over presidential vetoes, Congress asserted the right to call itself into special session and moved the first meeting of the next Congress from December (more than a year after its election) to the preceding March, thereby preventing eight months of presidential government. By the **Command of the Army Act** (1867) Congress required that the president and secretary of war issue military orders only through the commanding general of the Army, who could not be removed without Senate approval. By the **Tenure of Office Act** (1867) it forbade the president to remove any official who had been appointed with Senate approval. Finally, provoked by Johnson's persistent resistance to Congress's reconstruction program, the House of Representatives impeached the president for "high crimes and misdemeanors," the Senate failing to convict him (and thus removing him from office) by only one vote (see *Johnson Impeachment).

End of Reconstruction. The election of Ulysses S. Grant as president in 1868 signaled a change in the Republican Party from an ideological to a patronage party, one that existed solely for the spoils of electoral victory and that therefore allied itself to those large business interests capable of financing the party's campaigns and willing to reward the politicians who served them. Big-business orthodoxy and blatant political corruption became the hallmarks of the new *Gilded Age. Radicals declined in number and zeal, the North wearied of reconstruction turmoil, and antiblack sentiment grew.

In 1872, Congress passed an **Amnesty Act** restoring the right to hold office to the great majority of former Confederates who had been disqualified by the 14th Amendment. Among perhaps 500 exempted men were those who before the Civil War had served in the U.S. government as senators and representatives, judges, cabinet officers, foreign ministers, and Army and Navy officers. As Democrats recaptured the Southern states, the

Republicans consoled themselves with the realization that their newly won control of Midwestern states assured them of majorities in Congress and the electoral college. In 1876 the outcome of the presidential elections hinged on disputed vote counts in South Carolina, Florida, and Louisiana. By a straight party vote, a special electoral commission awarded the electoral votes of these states to the Republican candidate, Rutherford B. Hayes, while the states themselves went Democratic. In return, Hayes, in the *Compromise of 1877, withdrew federal troops from those states, signaling the end of Reconstruction and, with it, federal concern for the freedmen.

Reconstruction left a mixed heritage. The Radicals' pursuit of political equality for the freedmen embittered race relations in the South and resulted in generations of reactionary, racist state governments, while their failure to provide long-term assistance—especially land—to the freedmen ensured their continued dependence and servitude. On the other hand, the 14th and 15th Amendments provided the tools by which later black generations would reclaim for themselves the equal citizenship that the Radical Republicans once thought was in their gift.

RECONSTRUCTION ACTS (1867, 1868). See *Reconstruction.

RECONSTRUCTION COURT. See *Chase Court or Reconstruction Court.

RECONSTRUCTION FINANCE CORPORATION (RFC) (1932–53), government agency established during the *Hoover administration to lend money to banks, other financial institutions, and railroads in the depths of the *Great Depression.

Under Hoover, RFC loans totaled $3 billion. In the Franklin *Roosevelt administration, the RFC became a pillar of the *New Deal and it was empowered to lend to states and local governments and to public agencies. Its "pump-priming" loans—$50 billion over 22 years—saved many firms from failure and financed important public works, but the underlying problem of the depression was lack of consumption, not of credit.

To Hoover's critics, the RFC epitomized his willingness to provide government aid to banks but not to people. Surveying the Republican electoral defeat in 1932, Republican senator Hiram Johnson of California observed: "I am afraid we began fertilizing the tree at the top and forgot its roots."

The RFC was terminated by Pres. Dwight D. Eisenhower.

REDEEMERS. See *Bourbons or Redeemers.

RED SCARE (1919–20), episode of the *Wilson administration. The perennial American fear of radicals, exaggerated by wartime superpatriotism and legitimized by the *Espionage and Sedition acts, was exacerbated to the point of hysteria by the *Russian Revolution and then by postwar waves of industrial strikes and terrorist bombings.

A. Mitchell Palmer, appointed U.S. attorney general in March 1919, turned the energies of the Justice Department against labor unions and alien radicals. Federal agents raided the headquarters of radical organizations, often without search warrants. Thousands were arrested, hundreds deported—among them the famous anarchists Emma Goldman and Alexander Berkman. Twenty-eight states passed peacetime sedition acts and pursued suspicious teachers. State legislatures sometimes expelled or refused to seat members who held unorthodox views. In 1919 Socialist Victor Berger was expelled from the U.S. House of Representatives and sentenced to prison for 20 years for sedition (a conviction overturned by the U.S. Supreme Court).

Pres. Woodrow Wilson did nothing to stop the wartime and postwar persecution of radicals.

REFERENDUM. See *Initiative, Referendum, and Recall.

REFORM PARTY, national political party organized and financed entirely by Texas billionaire Ross Perot to support his candidacy for president in 1992. Perot won 19 percent of the popular vote that year and 8 percent in 1996, when the party again dutifully nominated him. (Party "conventions" were then held by mail and telephone.) That year, a handful of Reform Party members won election to municipal offices around the country, and in 1998 a former professional wrestler, Jesse Ventura, was elected governor of Minnesota.

In 2000, a fractured party gave its presidential nomination to former Republican conservative columnist Patrick J. Buchanan, who polled only 0.8 percent of the vote. Thereafter, the small remnant of the party remained firmly in the hands of right-wing Buchanan supporters, although Buchanan himself took little part in its affairs.

REFUGEE ACT (1980). See *Refugees.

REFUGEE FAIR SHARE ACT (1960). See *Refugees.

REFUGEE INTELLECTUALS (1930–40). During the 1930s, a galaxy of European intellectuals—authors, artists, scholars, scientists—fled European totalitarianism and found refuge, permanent or temporary, in the United States. Their contributions to the nation's cultural life—and later to its war effort—were incalculable. The hundreds of refugee intellectuals included:

George Balanchine, Russian dancer and choreographer, to U.S. 1933

Hans Bethe, German physicist, to U.S. 1935

Bertolt Brecht, German playwright and poet, in U.S. 1941–49

Marcel Breuer, Hungarian architect, to U.S. 1937

Rudolf Carnap, German philosopher, to U.S. 1936

Albert Einstein, German physicist, to U.S. 1933

Erik Erikson, German psychoanalyst, to U.S. 1933

Max Ernst, German painter, in U.S. 1939–49

Enrico Fermi, Italian physicist, to U.S. 1938

Erich Fromm, German psychoanalyst, to U.S. 1934

Walter Gropius, German architect, to U.S. 1937

George Grosz, German painter, to U.S. 1933

Paul Hindemith, German composer, in U.S. 1940–52

Hans Hofmann, German painter, to U.S. 1930

Karen Horney, German psychoanalyst, to U.S. 1932

Wolfgang Kohler, German psychologist, to U.S. 1934

Fritz Lang, German film director, to U.S. 1934

Thomas Mann, German author, in U.S. 1938–53

Herbert Marcuse, German political philosopher, to U.S. 1934

Ludwig Mies van der Rohe, German architect, to U.S. 1937

László Moholy-Nagy, Hungarian painter, to U.S. 1937

Hans Morgenthau, German political scientist, to U.S. 1937

Erwin Panofsky, German art historian, to U.S. 1935

Erwin Piscator, German theatrical director, in U.S. 1939–51

Arnold Schoenberg, Austrian composer, to U.S. 1931

Joseph Schumpeter, Austrian economist, to U.S. 1932

Isaac Bashevis Singer, Polish-Yiddish novelist, to U.S. 1935

Igor Stravinsky, Russian composer, to U.S. 1937

George Szell, Hungarian conductor, to U.S. 1939

Leo Szilard, Hungarian physicist, to U.S. 1938

Edward Teller, Hungarian physicist, to U.S. 1935

Paul Tillich, German theologian, to U.S. 1933

Arturo Toscanini, Italian conductor, to U.S. 1930

John Von Neumann, Hungarian mathematician, to U.S. 1930

Bruno Walter, German conductor, to U.S. 1938

Kurt Weill, German composer, to U.S. 1935

Max Wertheimer, German psychologist, to U.S. 1933

Eugene Wigner, Hungarian physicist, to U.S. 1930

REFUGEE RELIEF ACT (1953). See *Refugees.

REFUGEES. The United States has traditionally regarded itself as a place of asylum for persons fleeing religious or political persecution. Until World War 2, such persons entered the country like other immigrants, subject to the various restrictions and quotas of the prevailing immigration laws (see *Immigration).

After World War 2, special legislation was passed to facilitate the entry of persons uprooted by the war and the political upheavals that followed. The **Displaced Persons Act** of 1948 provided for the admission through 1951 of over 415,000 displaced persons (see *Holocaust Response). The **Refugee Relief Act** of 1953 authorized the admission through 1956 of 214,000 refugees, primarily persons who had fled from the communist countries of Eastern Europe. In 1960, the **Refugee Fair Share Act** permitted the admission of up to 25 percent of the refugees in the charge of the United Nations commissioner for refugees.

The Immigration and Nationality Act of 1965 provided a separate preference category for refugees, allotting 6 percent of each hemisphere's yearly quota of visas to refugees. The act defined a refugee very narrowly as someone who had fled a communist or communist-dominated country, or any country in the Middle East, because of persecution or fear of persecution on account of race, religion, or political opinion. In the years after 1968, the Eastern Hemisphere refugee quota was always oversubscribed, the Western Hemisphere quota undersubscribed.

In 1978, all hemispheric immigration quotas, including those for refugees, were combined, establishing a worldwide total of 17,400 refugee visas. Refugees were granted conditional entry, not immigrant status, but they could acquire immigrant status after two years' residence.

The 1965 act provided a second means by which refugees could be admitted to the United States. This was the discretionary authority of the U.S. attorney general to "parole" into the United States individuals or groups of aliens in special emergency circumstances. Congress had intended the parole authority to be used on an individual, case-by-case basis, but circumstances dictated that the attorney general use his authority to admit large groups of refugees—Hungarians in 1956–58, Cubans from 1959, Chinese in 1962, Ugandan Asians in 1972–73, Indochinese after 1975, Chileans in 1975–78, Lebanese in 1978, Soviets in 1977–79.

The **Refugee Act** of 1980 aimed to establish "a

permanent and systematic procedure" for admitting and resettling refugees that would eliminate the need for special legislation and the frequent use of the attorney general's parole authority. It ended the restrictive definition of "refugee," defining a refugee now as anyone from any part of the world—not just communist countries or the Middle East—who had been persecuted or who had a well-founded fear of persecution if he returned to his homeland. It raised the annual number of refugees regularly allowed into the United States from 17,400 to 50,000, a number that Congress considered to represent the "normal flow" of refugees.

No sooner had the Refugee Act been signed—in March 1980—than two new refugee problems arose that required special handling. Between April and June 1980, some 125,000 new Cuban refugees reached Florida in the **Mariel boatlift**. These were admitted as political refugees. At the same time, a flood of Haitian "boat people" (in 1982 the number of Haitians illegally in the United States was estimated at 50–60,000) were denied asylum on the grounds that they were economic rather than political refugees. In the 1990s, new waves of Cuban and Haitian boat people overwhelmed U.S. asylum procedures. This time the Haitians were treated on the same terms as the Cubans. However, the United States reduced the number of refugees it would accept and made asylum-granting procedures more stringent.

Between 1991 and 1998, more than 915,000 refugees were admitted to the United States as permanent residents. The principal sources of these refugees were the former Soviet Union (308,000), Vietnam (197,000), and Cuba (122,000).

REGENTS OF THE UNIVERSITY OF CALIFORNIA v. BAKKE (1978), 5–4 decision of the *Burger Court approving *affirmative action. Rejected by the University of California Medical School at Davis although his test scores were superior to those of 16 applicants who were accepted under a minority quota, Bakke sued, charging racial discrimination in violation of the *14th Amendment's Equal Protection Clause and the *Civil Rights Act of 1964. The university argued that its discrimination was "benign," providing opportunities to minorities and diversity to the student body.

Justice Lewis Powell's adroitly crafted opinion combined the opposing views of an otherwise divided Court: the racial quota at Davis was unconstitutional on equal protection grounds, and Bakke was ordered admitted; but race could legitimately be considered along with other factors in making admission decisions.

In a constitutionally acceptable admissions program,

Justice Powell wrote, "race or ethnic background may be deemed a 'plus' in a particular applicant's file, yet it does not insulate the individual from comparison with all other candidates for the available seats. The file of a particular black applicant may be examined for his potential contribution to diversity without the factor of race being decisive when compared, for example, with that of an applicant identified as an Italian-American if the latter is thought to exhibit qualities more likely to promote beneficial educational pluralism. Such qualities could include exceptional personal talents, unique work or service experience, leadership potential, maturity, demonstrated compassion, a history of overcoming disadvantage, ability to communicate with the poor, or other qualifications deemed important. In short, an admissions program operated in this way is flexible enough to consider all pertinent elements of diversity in light of the particular qualifications of each applicant, and to place them on the same footing for consideration, although not necessarily according them the same weight. . . ."

REGULATORS, backcountry protesters against provincial governments in pre-Revolutionary South Carolina and North Carolina. Neglected by the provincial assembly, settlers in western South Carolina established their own courts to suppress lawlessness and settle disputes. In 1769, the province established six court districts in the backcountry. In North Carolina, backcountry farmers organized as Regulators to rid themselves of extortionate officials. Violence led to their suppression by the provincial militia at the battle of Alamance Creek (May 16, 1771). Leaders of the movement were executed.

REHNQUIST COURT (1986–), the U.S. Supreme Court under Chief Justice William H. Rehnquist. The Rehnquist Court was notable for the deep division between its conservative and liberal justices, which resulted in 5–4 decisions in many of its most important cases. Three consistently conservative justices (including the chief justice) were often joined by two moderate conservatives to form a majority. Less frequently, one of the moderate conservatives would join with the four liberal justices. In its 2000–01 term, the Court decided 26 of its 79 cases (33 percent) by 5–4 votes. In its 2001–02 term, 21 of its 75 cases (28 percent) were decided 5–4. On the other hand, nearly half its decisions were generally unanimous.

The Court's conservative bent was reflected in its efforts to curb the alleged "overreaching" of the legislative and executive branches and to transfer power from

Washington to the states—the so-called **federalism revolution**.

Congress overreached, in the Court's view, by basing regulatory legislation on the Commerce Clause—as it had famously done since the 1930s—when that legislation bore little relation to interstate commerce. Thus, in *U.S. v. Lopez* (1995), the Court threw out 5–4 a law banning guns within 1,000 feet of a school. And in *U.S. v. Morrison* (2000), it overturned 5–4 a law making violence against women a federal crime. (Said Chief Justice Rehnquist: "The Constitution requires a distinction between what is truly national and what is truly local.")

In *Printz v. U.S.* (1997), the Court disallowed 5–4 a crucial provision of the Brady Gun Control Act on the ground that Congress could not compel state officials to enforce a federal program—in this case, doing background checks on gun purchasers. And in *Clinton v. City of New York* (1998), it overturned 6–3 an act granting the president a *line-item veto on the ground that the Constitution prescribed the procedure for enacting legislation. Between 1995 and 2001, the Court overturned 28 acts of Congress for a variety of reasons.

The Court was no more deferential to the executive branch. In *Department of Commerce v. U.S. House of Representatives* (1999), the Court rejected 5–4 Clinton administration plans to conduct the 2000 Census with the help of statistical sampling, insisting on the Constitution's specific requirement for a literal head count for the purpose of apportioning membership in the House of Representatives. And in *Food and Drug Administration (FDA) v. Brown & Williamson* (2000), it rejected 5–4 a claim by the FDA to regulate the marketing of cigarettes to young people because nicotine had recently been determined to be an addictive drug. The Court ruled that Congress had not specifically given the FDA authority to regulate tobacco products.

While the Court continued to uphold the Constitution's federal supremacy clauses, it formulated a doctrine of states' "sovereign immunity" on the basis of which it rejected federal "incursions" into traditional states' rights areas. Thus in *Alden v. Maine* (1999), it ruled 5–4 that states were immune from lawsuits by their employees under the federal Fair Labor Standards Act. In *Kimel v. Florida* (2000), it protected 5–4 states from employees' lawsuits under the federal Age Discrimination in Employment Act. In *Board of Trustees of the University of Alabama v. Garrett* (2001), it held 5–4 that states could not be sued by their employees under the federal *Americans with Disabilities Act. And in *Federal Maritime Commission v. South Carolina State Ports Authority* (2002), it ruled that a person whose rights under a

federal law had been violated by a state could not appeal to the federal agency charged with enforcing that law. These and similar decisions raised concern over Congress's power to make national policy binding on the states.

The Court's sensitivity to state sovereignty, however, did not prevent it in *Bush v. Gore* (2000) from overruling 5–4 the Florida supreme court and in effect deciding the 2000 presidential election in favor of Republican George W. Bush, creating the appearance, at least, of partisanship.

Many conservatives had hoped that the Court would overturn *Roe v. Wade, the 1973 ruling of the *Warren Court that a woman's right to an *abortion was protected by a constitutional right to privacy, but the four justices known to favor overturning *Roe* failed to attract a fifth. On the one hand, the Court endorsed state restrictions on access to abortion so long as those restrictions did not create an "undue burden" on women seeking abortions. On the other hand, the Court sustained lower-court orders and local ordinances keeping antiabortion protesters at a distance from abortion clinics. In 2000, the Court overturned 5–4 laws in 31 states banning late-term (so-called partial-birth) abortions.

Hostile to *affirmative action, the Court allowed white males to sue on the basis of "reverse discrimination," threw out "set-aside" quotas favoring minority-owned businesses, and made it more difficult for minorities and women to prove employment discrimination—they were required to prove intent to discriminate, not merely discriminatory outcomes.

On *church-state relations, the Court upheld prohibitions on organized school prayer and government-sponsored displays of religious symbols. But it allowed religious groups to meet in public elementary schools, allowed public school teachers to teach in parochial schools in federally funded remedial programs, and upheld a federal program that placed computers and other instructional equipment in parochial schools. In 2002, it upheld a Cleveland, Ohio, *school voucher program in which 96 percent of the participating students attended parochial schools.

Generally lenient on police conduct and tough on criminal defendants, the Court in *Dickerson v. U.S.* (2000) nevertheless confirmed 7–2 the Warren Court's decision in *Miranda v. Arizona* (1966) requiring that criminal suspects be advised of their constitutional rights before police interrogation. Two landmark decisions in 2002 dealt with *capital punishment. In *Atkins v. Virginia*, the Court ruled 6–3 that the execution of mentally retarded offenders was unconstitutional under the Eighth

Amendment. In *Ring v. Arizona*, it ruled 7–2 that a jury, not a judge, must make the factual determination whether "aggravating factors" warranted a death sentence in a murder conviction. The decision invalidated death-penalty laws in five states and called into question the laws in four others as well as the federal death-penalty law.

RELIGIOUS RIGHT, envisioned political alliance of traditionalists of all religious groups, including conservative Protestants, traditionalist Catholics, Orthodox Jews, and others. Such an alliance never materialized, although conservative Protestants and Catholics cooperate in the *abortion controversy. The *Christian Right is a movement among evangelical Protestants.

REMOVAL OF DEPOSITS. See *Bank War.

REPUBLIC, state in which the people govern themselves, either directly (in popular assemblies) or indirectly (by elected representatives), rather than being governed by a hereditary monarch or aristocracy.

The doctrine of republicanism was given its classic form by Roman writers like Tacitus and Plutarch, who contrasted an idealized Roman Republic with the later Empire. The Republic, in their view, was characterized by simplicity, egalitarianism, virtue, and patriotism, the Empire by luxury, inequality, corruption, and tyranny. The classical republican tradition was revived in the European Renaissance; reformulated by English writers like John Milton, James Harrington, and Algernon Sidney during the English Civil War in the 17th century; and adopted by the American colonists in their confrontation with what they viewed as a corrupt and oppressive British monarch.

Republicanism was both a political and a moral system. It depended upon the citizens' public spirit and private virtues, and in turn it inculcated that spirit and those virtues. A principal republican virtue, in the eyes of many American republicans, was deference to those superior citizens—the natural aristocracy—who had the capacity and leisure to actually govern.

In establishing a republic in America, the Founding Fathers were not unduly optimistic. The geographical extent of the United States was unprecedented for a republic, which had succeeded elsewhere only in city-states and small countries. Moreover, the inevitable corruption of the people was taken for granted. An ingenious constitution might delay that corruption for a time, but eventually the people would become so self-interested and fractious as to require a monarchy to maintain order.

Some of the Founders lived long enough to mourn the death of republican ideals due to economic prosperity and the growth of *democracy.

REPUBLICAN PARTY, one of two major contemporary political parties. It was founded in 1854 as an antislavery, prounion party. Former Whigs (see *Whig Party) who flocked to it gave it a bias toward business interests, and during the absence of Southerners from Congress during the Civil War the party implemented policies favorable to business and Northern farmers—high *tariffs, a *transcontinental railroad, and Western homesteads (see *Public Lands). Union victory in the war, under a Republican administration, ensured Republican control of the presidency until 1913—with the exception of the two separate terms of Democrat Grover Cleveland.

The 20th century exposed two major divides within the Republican Party. First, Pres. Theodore Roosevelt assumed the leadership of reform-minded progressives (see *Progressivism) and in 1912 led them temporarily out of the party. World War 1 exposed a second divide, between Eastern internationalists and Western *isolationists. The two divides were not congruent—a Republican could be a liberal isolationist like Sen. William Borah or a conservative internationalist like Herbert Hoover. When the party regained the presidency in 1920, it was clearly in the hands of conservatives, who with blind hubris drove the country into the *Great Depression of the 1930s. The repeated electoral victories of Democratic president Franklin Roosevelt first frustrated and then embittered Republicans, causing them to obstinately oppose constructive *New Deal measures and to exploit isolationism and *anticommunism as electoral tactics.

After World War 2, the struggle between the conservative-isolationist and the moderate-internationalist elements of the party was exemplified by the contest between Sen. Robert A. Taft and Gen. Dwight D. Eisenhower for the party's 1952 presidential nomination. Conservatives captured the party in 1980 with the nomination and election of Ronald Reagan. Like his moderate predecessors, Eisenhower and Nixon, Reagan found it expedient to retain New Deal and Great Society institutions while preaching a conservative doctrine of small government and low taxes—to be achieved by transferring powers from the federal government to state and local governments. The election in 1992 of Democrat William J. Clinton, who had coopted some Republican positions, angered Republicans. In control of both houses of Congress after 1995, they fought Clinton with a bitterness more personal than ideological (see *Republican Revolution; *Clinton Impeachment).

The party regained the White House in 2000 under Texas governor George W. Bush, who lost the popular vote but won the electoral vote by carrying Florida in a hotly contested count.

REPUBLICAN PARTY, JEFFERSONIAN. See *Jeffersonian Republican Party or Democratic-Republican Party.

REPUBLICAN REVOLUTION (1994–96), episode in the *Clinton administration. In November 1994 the administration was stunned by the loss of its majorities in both houses of Congress. Whereas the 103rd Congress, elected with Pres. William J. Clinton in 1992, had large Democratic majorities—258–176 in the House, 57–43 in the Senate—the newly elected 104th Congress was solidly in Republican hands—230–204 in the House, 52–48 in the Senate. Of 73 Republican freshmen in the House, many had been personally recruited, trained, and helped by Rep. Newt Gingrich of Georgia, soon to be Speaker of the House. These freshmen tended to be zealous conservative ideologues, confrontational and uncompromising, and intensely loyal to Gingrich.

For many years, Gingrich had planned a Republican "revolution" that would dismantle the Democratic welfare state. Its agenda was contained in his **Contract with America**, to which all the new Republican representatives subscribed and which pledged, among other things, a balanced-budget amendment, a line-item veto, welfare reform, a middle-class tax cut, increased defense spending, reduced regulation, and congressional term limits. Gingrich vowed to enact the Contract with America during the first 100 days of the new Congress.

On Jan. 4, 1995, in an unprecedented 14-hour opening day, the House under Gingrich's leadership revised its rules and procedures to restore to the Speaker powers that over the years had passed to committee chairmen. Three committees and 25 subcommittees were abolished, committee staffs were cut by a third, the seniority system that produced committee chairmen was scrapped, and term limits were established for committee chairmen. Moreover, Gingrich packed crucial committees with his followers.

The Contract with America fared less well. By the end of the year, senate opposition or presidential vetoes had blocked the balanced-budget amendment, the line-item veto, congressional term limits, and welfare and regulatory reform.

The revolution died of self-inflicted wounds. When their balanced-budget amendment failed, the Republicans proposed a budget calling for spending and tax cuts that they believed would result in a balanced budget in seven years. Clinton responded with a plan of less severe cuts, preserving Medicare and other social programs, that he asserted would result in a balanced budget in ten years. Unwilling to compromise, the House Republicans threatened to shut down the government.

This happened on Nov. 13, when Clinton vetoed a stopgap funding measure. A week later he accepted the Republicans' seven-year schedule for a balanced budget, but only on condition that the Republican plan provide adequate funding for social programs. This the Republicans refused to do, and when the stopgap measure expired on Dec. 21 the government was forced to shut down partially again, this time for 21 days.

The Republicans then discovered that public opinion blamed them for the shutdown. A compromise was finally reached in April 1996, but Clinton was credited with having stood fast in defense of popular social programs against Republican blackmail.

In November, Clinton was elected to a second term, although the Republicans increased their majorities in Congress. In November 1998 Gingrich announced his resignation from Congress.

RESOURCE CONSERVATION AND RECOVERY ACT (1976). See *Environmentalism.

REVERE'S RIDE (Apr. 18–19, 1775), incident at the start of the *Revolutionary War. When Joseph Warren, a member of the Boston committee of safety (see *Committees of Correspondence), learned that British general Thomas Gage intended to send troops to seize Patriot military supplies stored at Concord, he dispatched William Dawes, a tradesman, and Paul Revere, a silversmith, to warn Patriot leaders Samuel Adams and John Hancock at Lexington and to alert the countryside.

Dawes left Boston across the Neck to the south; Revere rowed across the Charles River to Charlestown, where he borrowed a horse. At Lexington, he awoke Adams and Hancock. There he was joined by Dawes and by Samuel Prescott, a Concord physician, and the three rode off toward Concord. Revere was captured by British soldiers almost immediately and brought back to Lexington. Dawes and Prescott escaped and reached Concord, having roused the *minutemen for the battles of *Lexington and Concord.

The story is told inaccurately but irresistibly in the galloping rhythm of Henry Wadsworth Longfellow's "Ride of Paul Revere" (1861), which begins: "Listen, my children, and you shall hear / Of the midnight ride of Paul Revere, / On the eighteenth of April, in Seventy-five;

/ Hardly a man is now alive / Who remembers that famous day and year."

REVOLUTIONARY WAR (1775–83), military side of the *American Revolution.

The Adversaries. Great Britain emerged from the worldwide Seven Years' War (called the *French and Indian War in North America) in 1763 rich and powerful. In 1775 Britain (England, Wales, and Scotland), with a population of 8 million, was a center of banking, commerce, and increasingly—with the advent of the Industrial Revolution—manufacturing. As a result of her wartime conquests, she was also Europe's leading colonial power. But her very eminence assured her of enemies. When Britain went to war with her American colonies, France, Spain, and the Netherlands soon entered the war against her.

The 13 North American colonies in 1775 had a population of 2.5 million, including half a million African slaves. Typical of colonial areas, the colonies exchanged the products of farms, forests, and fisheries for the manufactured goods and luxury items of the mother country. Thus in war the Americans could feed and clothe themselves but they could not make or buy war matériel—muskets, cannon, gunpowder, and other equipment—in necessary quantities. Some of this matériel was captured from the enemy; much was supplied, on credit, by France and Spain beginning in 1777.

To suppress the rebellion in America, Britain had to wage war across 3,000 miles of ocean. Communication was slow; three months might elapse before a message sent from London received its answer. Her navy enabled Britain to undertake such a war. But that navy, which was without peer in 1763, had been allowed to decay, and in 1775 it was probably only the equal—not the superior—of the combined navies of France and Spain.

The British army was experienced and well disciplined, but it was small and scattered in garrisons from Gibraltar to Detroit. To wage war in America, Britain had to hire German mercenaries, who were less reliable than British regulars and peculiarly offensive to Americans. In America, the British army had to fight in a large (1,500 miles north to south, an average 150 miles east to west), unfamiliar country, among a hostile population, where there were no large cities or strategic points whose possession would assure victory.

At the start of the war, the Americans had no army at all, only provincial and local militias—citizen soldiers who were untrained, undisciplined, sometimes dangerous marksmen, but prone to panic in the face of concentrated fire or bayonet charges. They were highly individualistic, showing up to fight at their convenience, then returning home when other duties called. In time, these militias became experienced and reliable adjuncts to the professional soldiers of the *Continental Army. The *Continental Congress created the army in 1775, appointed George Washington of Virginia its commander in chief, and authorized the enlistment of men for one year. In 1777, enlistment was extended to three years or the duration of the war. The Continentals suffered the most extreme privations of the war, but with experience and training they became a match for the British regulars.

The British officers were veterans of combat in Europe. In America, they tended to be arrogant, overconfident, indolent, and cautious, aware that losses could be replaced only with difficulty and that defeat could mean disgrace. Some American officers were veterans of the French and Indian War; most were amateurs, and they blundered egregiously at the start. But as time passed they acquired professional expertise, and the best of them rose to positions of command.

The fundamental difference between the military postures of the two adversaries was that, in order to win, the British had to destroy the force opposing them whereas the Americans had only to survive. The Americans fought a defensive war, avoiding combat on unfavorable terms, determined to keep an army in the field until such time as the British wearied of the effort or were called away to face other challenges.

The War in the North. The theater of the Revolutionary War was vast. Fighting ranged from Canada to Florida, from the Atlantic Ocean to the Mississippi River. Regulars and irregulars—British, German, and American soldiers, Patriot and Loyalist militias and guerrilla bands, Canadian volunteers and American frontiersmen, and Indian allies of both sides—were involved in innumerable engagements, large and small.

Fighting began in Massachusetts when British troops were sent from Boston to seize Patriot military stores at Concord (see *Lexington and Concord). New England militias followed the British back to Boston and laid siege to that city (see *Boston Siege). The British won a costly victory at *Bunker Hill, but in March 1776, under Washington's threatening guns on Dorchester Heights, they evacuated Boston and withdrew to Halifax, Nova Scotia. In the meantime, a Patriot invasion of Canada ended in a rout (see *Quebec Campaign).

From Boston in the spring of 1776 Washington moved his army to New York City, dividing it between Manhattan Island and the western end of Long Island. In July and August, British troops—from Halifax under Gen. William Howe and from Britain in a fleet commanded by Howe's brother, Adm. Richard Howe—collected on Staten Island in New York harbor. During Aug. 22–25, Admiral Howe transferred this army to Long Island. There, on Aug. 27, General Howe drove the Patriots from their lines extending from the East River to Jamaica Pass and back to their fortified position on Brooklyn Heights. Spared an immediate attack, Washington evacuated his troops to Manhattan on the night of Aug. 29–30 (see *Long Island).

Unaccountably dilatory, General Howe did not put troops on Manhattan Island until Sept. 15, when he landed north of the city. Washington, who had by then abandoned the city, retreated north to Harlem Heights, where his troops drove off (Sept. 16) a British advance column. Outflanked on Manhattan, he withdrew north to White Plains, where he suffered another defeat (Oct. 28). Howe then marched off to the west. Unsure of Howe's destination, Washington left a portion of his army under Gen. Charles Lee and took the remainder across the Hudson River into New Jersey. Howe's destination proved to be Fort Washington, on the northeast tip of Manhattan Island, which he captured on Nov. 16; on Nov. 18, Gen. Charles Cornwallis seized Fort Lee on the opposite side of the Hudson.

These stunning losses left Washington adrift in New Jersey. Joining at Hackensack with Patriot forces under Gen. Nathanael Greene, he began a grim retreat through New Jersey toward the Patriot capital at Philadelphia. He summoned Lee to join him; Lee was captured by the British, but his troops, commanded by Gen. John Sullivan, followed Washington south. Gripped by despair, and suffering from cold and hunger, the army melted away. On Dec. 8, Washington, with the remnants of his army, crossed the Delaware River and found safety in Pennsylvania. Sullivan crossed on Dec. 20.

This was the nadir of the Patriot cause. Washington had suffered a succession of defeats, from which he had in large part been saved only by the excessive caution of the enemy. His army was in a pitiable state and many of his troops were due to be discharged on Dec. 31. Cornwallis was in pursuit, and Howe threatened Philadelphia, which Congress had abandoned for Baltimore. In this extremity, Washington turned and inflicted sharp blows on the enemy at *Trenton (Dec. 26) and *Princeton (Jan. 3, 1777), then withdrew into winter quarters at Morristown.

For 1777 the British had a comprehensive plan to separate New England from the other colonies and crush the rebellion where it had started. This was the ultimate objective of the *Saratoga Campaign, in which British armies coming from the north, west, and south would converge at Albany, establishing British control of the entire Hudson Valley and opening New England to invasion.

The failure of this plan was assured when General Howe, instead of advancing up the Hudson, took a large British force from New York City for an attack on Philadelphia. Landing on Chesapeake Bay in August, he defeated Washington at *Brandywine (Sept. 11), entered Philadelphia (Sept. 26), and withstood Washington's counterattack at *Germantown (Oct. 4). Howe spent the winter in comfort in Philadelphia while the Patriots suffered at *Valley Forge.

News of treaties of alliance between the United States and France (February 1778) compelled the British to adopt a new strategy. Gen. Henry Clinton, who had succeeded Howe during the winter as British commander in America, decided to concentrate his forces in New York City in preparation for a French attack. Evacuating Philadelphia (May 1778), the British marched north through New Jersey, drove off a Patriot attack at *Monmouth (June 28), and reached New York in July. Washington established his headquarters north of the city at White Plains. The war in the North had reached a stalemate.

The War in the South. Frustrated in the North, General Clinton saw promising opportunities in the South, where Loyalists were numerous and active. A British army sent by Clinton from New York and another moving up from Florida took Savannah on Dec. 29, 1778, and Augusta on Jan. 29, 1779. Patriot general Benjamin Lincoln failed to retake Augusta in April 1779 and, even with the support of a French fleet under Adm. the Comte d'Estaing, failed to recover Savannah in October.

In January 1780 Clinton led 8,000 British troops from New York to South Carolina and besieged Charleston, which Lincoln surrendered on May 12. Clinton returned to New York, leaving Gen. Charles Cornwallis to expand British control in the South. British control of Georgia and South Carolina was contested only by guerrilla bands led by Andrew Pickens, Francis Marion, and Thomas Sumter.

In June 1780 Congress appointed Gen. Horatio Gates commander in the South. On Aug. 16, Cornwallis crushed Gates at *Camden, S.C., then invaded North Carolina, but a victory by Patriot frontiersmen under John Sevier and Isaac Shelby over a Loyalist force at *King's Mountain, N.C., on Oct. 7, exposed his flank and forced him to return to South Carolina.

Gen. Nathanael Greene now replaced Gates. A portion of his small army under Gen. Daniel Morgan smashed British colonel Banastre Tarleton at *Cowpens on Jan. 17, 1781. When Greene and Cornwallis met at

*Guilford Courthouse on Mar. 15, Cornwallis drove the Americans from the field, but at such a cost that he had to retire to his base at Wilmington on the North Carolina coast. Greene entered South Carolina, and though he continued to meet reverses—at *Hobkirk's Hill, Ninety-six, and *Eutaw Springs—he inflicted such losses on the British that they were compelled to abandon most of the state except Charleston.

From Wilmington, Cornwallis moved north into Virginia, convinced that that state held the key to victory. There he conducted destructive raids against Patriot property but could not engage the small Patriot force in the state commanded by Gen. the Marquis de Lafayette. In August 1781 he established a base at *Yorktown on Chesapeake Bay. There a French fleet under Adm. the Comte de Grasse bottled him up while Patriot and French armies under Washington and Gen. the Comte de Rochambeau hurried south from New York. The allies laid siege to Yorktown on Sept. 28. On Oct. 19 Cornwallis surrendered with his army of 8,000 men, a politically irreparable loss that meant the end of the war for the British.

Washington returned to his headquarters near New York City, which was still in British possession. The French fleet and troops were gone from America by the end of 1782.

The War in the West. The trans-Appalachian Indians were the natural allies of the British, since it was the Americans who were steadily encroaching on their hunting grounds and the British king who promised to preserve them. British agents incited the Indians to fight and provided them with weapons and other inducements. The Cherokees ravaged the Southern frontier until subdued by border leaders like John Sevier. In the North, the Iroquois fought alongside British regulars in the Saratoga campaign. With Loyalist units, they committed such atrocities as the massacres at *Wyoming Valley, Pa. (July 3, 1778), and *Cherry Valley, N.Y. (Nov. 11, 1778). In 1779, Patriot general John Sullivan laid waste the heart of Iroquois country in central New York, but the Indians were not finally subdued until 1782.

Far to the west in the Ohio Valley, Kentucky settlers were attacked by Shawnees and other tribes from north of the Ohio River supplied by the British at Detroit. In 1778, George Rogers Clark led a small army of frontiersmen into Illinois country, captured British-held settlements, but was unable to proceed to Detroit. In 1782 Clark administered a severe defeat to the Shawnees at Chillicothe. His exploits provided the basis for U.S.

claims to the Old Northwest (see *Northwest Territory), which were recognized in the peace treaty.

The War at Sea. During the early years of the war, the British navy commanded the seas. Subject only to the vicissitudes of the weather, it was able to transport troops and supplies from Britain to America and from point to point on the long American coastline. In December 1775 the Continental Congress created an American navy of eight converted fishing and merchant vessels. The states also created navies, and both Congress and the states commissioned privateers. Some 2,000 American privateering vessels inflicted heavy damage on British shipping along the coast and in the West Indies. An American naval captain, John Paul Jones, operated in British waters, preying on coastal shipping, raiding the English coast itself, and, on Sept. 23, 1779, winning a famous victory over the British frigate *Serapis* in the North Sea (see *Jones's Cruise).

With the entry of France, Spain, and the Netherlands into the war, the British navy had to be widely dispersed. British and French fleets fought frequently in the West Indies. From the West Indies in September 1781, Admiral de Grasse brought a French fleet to Chesapeake Bay, trapped Cornwallis at Yorktown, drove away a British fleet sent to relieve him, and transported the armies of Washington and Rochambeau from the head of the bay to Yorktown, thereby ensuring a decisive allied victory.

War Diplomacy. The Continental Congress early recognized the need for foreign allies. In September 1776 it appointed three commissioners—Silas Deane, Benjamin Franklin, and Arthur Lee—to seek a French alliance. Commissioners were also appointed to Austria, Prussia, Spain, and Tuscany to seek recognition of American independence, treaties of alliance and commerce, and loans. They also sought to recruit professional army officers for service in America.

As early as December 1775 a French agent had assured Congress that France was well disposed to the American cause. French military supplies began to arrive secretly in the United States in March 1777. Before recognizing American independence, France required evidence that the Patriots could be relied upon to fight. Saratoga and Germantown provided that evidence, and in February 1778 the U.S. commissioners to France signed treaties of amity and commerce and of military alliance with France that Congress ratified on May 4. France sent a minister to the United States, and Congress appointed Benjamin Franklin U.S. minister to France.

By June 1778 France and Britain were at war. When

Britain refused to cede Gibraltar to Spain as the price of Spanish neutrality, Spain entered the war as an ally of France—but without recognizing American independence for fear of the effect on her own colonies in the Western Hemisphere. In 1780 Britain declared war on the Netherlands, which had been openly aiding the Americans.

In June 1781 Congress appointed a commission to conduct peace negotiations with Britain, giving it freedom to negotiate all issues except U.S. independence and sovereignty. It also instructed the commissioners to consult with French foreign minister the Comte de Vergennes and to be guided by his advice. Suspicious of French intentions, commissioners John Adams, Benjamin Franklin, and John Jay ignored these instructions and negotiated a separate peace with Britain. On the basis of the provisional treaty, Congress, on Apr. 11, 1783, declared the war ended. The final treaty was signed at Paris on Sept. 3, 1783, and ratified by Congress on Jan. 14, 1784 (see *Paris Treaty [1783]).

REYNOLDS v. SIMS

REYNOLDS v. SIMS (1964), 8–1 decision of the *Warren Court that the *14th Amendment's Equal Protection Clause required electoral districts for state legislatures as well as for Congress of approximately equal populations.

Reynolds originated in Alabama, where the populations of electoral districts for state senators varied as much as 41 to 1, those for state representatives 16 to 1. Upholding the concept of one person, one vote, Chief Justice Earl Warren wrote, "Legislators represent people, not trees or acres. Legislators are elected by voters, not farms or cities or economic interests." Insofar as possible, all electoral districts were required to have approximately equal populations; any divergence from strict population equality must be based on a "rational state policy."

The Court specifically rejected the analogy of the federal government, in which political divisions (states) were represented equally in the Senate, populations proportionately in the House of Representatives. Historically, the Court observed, most state constitutions based both houses of state legislatures on population.

ROBBER BARONS

ROBBER BARONS, some leading industrialists and financiers of the *Gilded Age, notorious for their greed, ruthlessness, and corruption. Although the term was used contemporaneously, it entered the historian's lexicon with the publication of Matthew Josephson's *The Robber Barons: The Great American Capitalists, 1861–1901* (1934) during the Great Depression, when businessmen were generally held in low repute. Josephson's barons included Daniel Drew, Jay Gould, James Fisk, Cornelius Vanderbilt, Jay Cooke, James J. Hill, Edward H. Harriman, Andrew Carnegie, Henry Clay Frick, J. Pierpont Morgan, and John D. Rockefeller. In recent years, historians have begun to appreciate the constructive achievements of some of the robber barons (see *Morgan's Career).

ROE v. WADE

ROE v. WADE (1973), 7–2 decision of the *Burger Court legalizing *abortion within certain limits on the basis of a woman's right to privacy. Justice Harry Blackmun ruled that a woman's decision to have an abortion should be unhindered in the first trimester of pregnancy but subject to state regulation in the second and state prohibition in the third.

Some people, Blackmun wrote, "argue that the woman's right is absolute and that she is entitled to terminate her pregnancy at whatever time, in whatever way, and for whatever reason she alone chooses. With this we do not agree. . . . The Court's decisions recognizing a right of privacy also acknowledge that some state regulation in areas protected by that right is appropriate. . . . [A] State may properly assert important interests in safeguarding health, in maintaining medical standards, and in protecting potential life. At some point in pregnancy, these respective interests become sufficiently compelling to sustain regulation of the factors that govern the abortion decision. The privacy right involved, therefore, cannot be said to be absolute. . . .

"With respect to the State's important and legitimate interest in the health of the mother, the 'compelling' point, in the light of present medical knowledge, is at approximately the end of the first trimester. This is so because of the now-established medical fact that until the end of the first trimester mortality in abortion may be less than mortality in normal childbirth. It follows that, from and after this point, a State may regulate the abortion procedure to the extent that the regulation reasonably relates to the preservation and protection of maternal health. . . .

"With respect to the State's important and legitimate interest in potential life, the 'compelling' point is at viability. This is so because the fetus then presumably has the capability of meaningful life outside the mother's womb. State regulation protective of fetal life after viability thus has both logical and biological justifications. If the State is interested in protecting fetal life after viability, it may go so far as to proscribe abortion during that period, except when it is necessary to preserve the life or health of the mother."

ROOSEVELT (FRANKLIN) ADMINISTRATION

ROOSEVELT (FRANKLIN) ADMINISTRATION (1933–45). Democrat Franklin Delano Roosevelt, 32nd president of the United States, assumed office in the depths of the *Great Depression. The nation's banks were closed. Roosevelt declared a *bank holiday, after which approved banks would be allowed to reopen. On Mar. 12, he gave his first *fireside chat to assure Americans that the reopened banks would be safe. Resolution of the banking crisis (followed by significant banking reforms) and devaluation of the dollar in relation to gold enlarged the money supply and encouraged spending and investment.

During its first *100 days, the administration proposed and Congress passed an unprecedented quantity of major legislation putting in place Roosevelt's program for combating the depression—the *New Deal. Its relief programs sustained millions of destitute Americans. Its institutional reforms gave Americans greater economic security. But the results of its recovery efforts were mixed. The Agricultural Adjustment Administration raised farm prices and farm income. But the National Recovery Administration, intended to restart industry and expand employment, failed. Nevertheless, recovery—buoyed in part by the optimism generated by the administration's activity—began and continued uninterrupted for four years, the gross national product rising an average 12 percent a year and unemployment falling from 24.9 percent in 1933 to 14.3 percent in 1937.

Facing an uncertain election in 1936, Roosevelt in 1935 recognized enemies on his right and on his left. On his right were the *economic royalists—business leaders represented by the *Liberty League, the National Association of Manufacturers, and the U.S. Chamber of Commerce. Also on his right was the U.S. Supreme Court (see *Hughes Court), led by a group of elderly conservatives who overturned the most important New Deal legislation. On the left, Roosevelt was criticized by progressives, socialists, and communists for failing to take advantage of the crisis to make more fundamental social and economic reforms. More dangerous—in his estimation—were the hugely popular movements spawned by demagogues Huey Long (see *Share Our Wealth Society), Charles E. Coughlin (see *National Union for Social Justice), and Francis E. Townsend (see *Townsend Plan).

Exasperated by the shortsighted hostility of business and responding to pressure from the left, Roosevelt abandoned efforts to conciliate business leaders. He now turned to the groups that came to form the Roosevelt coalition—labor, big cities, minorities, the poor—and declared a *Second New Deal, more radical than the first. The principal achievements of this period were the Works Progress Administration, the Social Security Act, and the National Labor Relations Act.

Roosevelt won reelection in 1936 in a landslide. Overconfident, he determined to curb the obstructive power of the Supreme Court (see *Court-Packing Plan). Here he suffered his greatest defeat, although a shift within the Court began to produce majorities that supported New Deal legislation. The next year he took an active part in Democratic Party primaries in an attempt to defeat conservative Democrats hostile to the New Deal (see *Roosevelt's Purge). Here, too, he failed. At the same time, his reduction in government spending to balance the budget precipitated the sharp *recession of 1937–38. Despite these reverses, and with his party increasingly dominated by conservatives, Roosevelt was still able to win a national housing act, the Agricultural Adjustment Act of 1938, and the Fair Labor Standards Act. By the end of 1938, however, the liberal momentum of the New Deal was finally checked.

From 1939, Roosevelt's attention was chiefly devoted to foreign affairs. Early in his administration, he had sought a unilateral solution to the nation's economic problems, putting U.S. interests ahead of international cooperation. Thus he refused to cooperate with the *London Economic Conference of 1933. The need for foreign trade, however, contributed to his decision to recognize the Soviet Union in 1933 (see *Soviet Recognition) and to establish the Export-Import Bank in 1934 to finance foreign purchases of American goods. Secretary of State Cordell Hull successfully pursued reciprocal trade agreements to circumvent tariff barriers. The *Good Neighbor policy toward Latin America indicated the primacy of hemispheric affairs in the administration's early thinking.

But as war clouds gathered in Europe and Asia, and as Roosevelt began to perceive that the security of France and Britain was essential to the security and interests of the United States, he gradually parted company with the *isolationists in Congress, who were anxious to prevent U.S. involvement in a foreign war. Milestones in the isolationists' campaign were: the *Nye Munitions Investigation (1934–36), which seemed to demonstrate that "merchants of death" worked to involve the United States in wars; the Johnson Debt Default Act (1934), which barred loans to foreign countries that had defaulted on their World War I debts to the United States (see *War Debts); the Senate's rejection (1935) of Roosevelt's recommendation that the United States join the World Court; the *Ludlow Resolution (1935–38), a failed proposal for a constitutional amendment that would have required a national referendum before a congressional declaration of war became effective; the *Neutrality Acts (1935–41), passed to reduce the risk of involvement in the Italo-

Ethiopian War (1935–36), the *Spanish Civil War (1936–39), and the Sino-Japanese War (from 1937) through commerce with the belligerents.

When war began in Europe in September 1939, Roosevelt proclaimed U.S. neutrality. "This nation will remain a neutral nation," he said in a fireside chat on Sept. 3, "but I cannot ask that every American remain neutral in thought as well." Roosevelt was of course not neutral. When France fell in June 1940, he resolved to seek a third term (see *Roosevelt's Third-Term Decision). Meanwhile, he began to supply surplus or obsolete stocks of weapons and munitions to Britain, negotiated the *destroyers-for-bases deal, organized the executive branch for preparedness, and, in a fireside chat on Dec. 29, 1940, roused the country at last by his appeal that it become the "arsenal of democracy."

In January 1941, he initiated secret U.S.-British staff talks, met with British prime minister Winston Churchill at Placentia Bay, Newfoundland, in August (see *World War 2 Conferences), and brought the United States more deeply into the battle of the Atlantic. Over isolationist opposition, he obtained from Congress progressively larger appropriations for a defense buildup, passage of a Selective Service Act (see *Conscription) in September 1940 (extended a year later by a single vote), and passage of *Lend-Lease in March 1941. When Japan occupied French Indochina in July 1941, Roosevelt froze Japanese assets in the United States, preventing Japan from further purchases of steel and oil here. Japan then had the choice of abandoning its imperial ambitions or going to war with the United States. It announced its decision at *Pearl Harbor on Dec. 7.

With the United States now involved in *World War 2, Roosevelt, together with Churchill and Soviet premier Joseph Stalin, actively planned war strategy and peace aims. As the vast American production capacity came on line, putting an end at last to the depression, Allied victory became increasingly inevitable. The war, however, took its toll on the president. In 1944 he was diagnosed with hypertensive heart disease (see *Roosevelt's Final Illness). Critically ill, he campaigned for a fourth term, conferred with other war leaders at Yalta, then died suddenly at Warm Springs, Ga., with victory in Europe less than a month away. He was succeeded by Vice Pres. Harry S. Truman.

ROOSEVELT (THEODORE) ADMINISTRATION

(1901–9). Republican Theodore Roosevelt, 26th president of the United States, succeeded to the office upon the assassination of Pres. William McKinley. The popularity he enjoyed in the country at large because of his youth, attractive family, conspicuous energy, and war record did not extend to his own party, which, except for a small band of insurgent or progressive congressmen (see *Progressivism), was deeply conservative and suspicious of the new president.

Roosevelt dutifully promised to continue McKinley's policies, and indeed he had little other choice. But as his popularity grew through friendly publicity, he was able to convert the presidency into a "bully pulpit" from which, with the enthusiastic support of the *muckrakers, he vigorously advocated the *Square Deal—which included labor justice (see *Anthracite Strike), *trust-busting (see *Northern Securities Co. v. United States), *railroad regulation,*consumer protection, and *conservation. A dark spot on his administration was the *Brownsville affair.

Roosevelt had more freedom of action in foreign affairs, where he did not hesitate to practice "big stick diplomacy" (after the old maxim "Speak softly but carry a big stick"). The *Roosevelt Corollary (1904) asserted a policeman's role for the United States in the affairs of Latin America. The Hay-Pauncefote (1901), Hay-Herrán (1903), and Hay–Bunau-Varilla (1903) treaties, plus Roosevelt's personal chicanery, cleared the way for the building of the *Panama Canal. Roosevelt interjected the United States into European affairs at the *Algeciras Conference (1906).

His most persistent foreign policy concern was Japan. He successfully mediated the Russo-Japanese War, bringing the parties together in New Hampshire to sign the Treaty of *Portsmouth (1905). Japanese immigration presented a delicate problem, which he handled adroitly with the Gentlemen's Agreement of 1907 (see *Japanese Exclusion). The *Taft-Katsura Memorandum (1905) and the *Root-Takahira Agreement (1908) seemed to resolve U.S.-Japanese issues in the western Pacific. Nevertheless, Roosevelt thought it prudent to impress Japan with U.S. naval power, so he sent the *Great White Fleet around the world (1907–9).

Having declared (to his later regret) that he would not seek a third (second elected) term, Roosevelt chose as his successor his old friend William Howard Taft, not realizing that he was thereby returning the Republican Party to the grip of its Old Guard.

In the Theodore Roosevelt administration, Oklahoma (1907) became the 46th state.

ROOSEVELT COROLLARY (1904), an expansion of

the *Monroe Doctrine contained in Pres. Theodore Roosevelt's annual message to Congress on Dec. 6, 1904. It was occasioned by the United States' taking over the Dominican customs to ensure payment of that chaotic country's foreign debts, thereby preventing intervention by European powers.

"Chronic wrongdoing," Roosevelt wrote, "or an impotence which results in a general loosening of the ties of civilized society, may . . . ultimately require intervention by some civilized nation, and in the Western Hemisphere the adherence of the United States to the Monroe Doctrine may force the United States, however reluctantly, . . . to the exercise of an international police power."

The Monroe Doctrine was thus transformed from a prohibition of European intervention in the Western Hemisphere to a justification of U.S. intervention.

ROOSEVELT'S "ARMAGEDDON" SPEECH (Aug.
7, 1912), speech by Theodore Roosevelt at the *Progressive Party convention in Chicago accepting its presidential nomination. Before some 15,000 wildly cheering supporters, Roosevelt elaborated a program of reform largely identical to that contained in the party's platform. "Our cause is based on the eternal principles of righteousness," he concluded, "and even though we who now lead may for the time fail, in the end the cause itself shall triumph. We stand at Armageddon, and we battle for the Lord!"

Afterward, Sen. William E. Borah and editor William Allen White, both leading progressives, walked along Michigan Avenue discussing the speech. Borah "was tremendously impressed with it," White recalled; "but he was a little frightened, as I was. We had no idea of the hidden forces beneath our feet, the volcanic social substance that was burning deep in the heart of humanity."

ROOSEVELT'S "EYES AND EARS." As governor
of New York and then president of the United States, Franklin Roosevelt, a paraplegic since an attack of polio in 1921, valued information provided by his wife, Eleanor. Although she had no official position in the presidential administration, circumstances encouraged her to become its unofficial ombudsman. Besides investigative missions on behalf of the president, she traveled widely as a public lecturer and invariably used these trips to inspect government programs and institutions and to meet people from every walk of life. Her unexpected appearances in unlikely places—coal mines, prisons, migrant-labor camps—was grist for the mills of cartoonists and humorists.

As a popular radio speaker and (nonpolitical) newspaper columnist—her column "My Day" appeared in 62 newspapers with 4 million readers in 1937—she received vast quantities of mail, some of it critical of the administration of government programs. These she shared with the responsible officials, who felt obligated to respond to the first lady. Special cases she took directly to the president. She had her own causes as well—women in the party and in government, rural poverty, race relations, youth—which she pressed upon her sometimes-resistant husband, often assembling for his benefit groups of knowledgeable people to discuss these issues at White House luncheons, teas, and dinners.

In 1940 she calmed a rebellious Democratic national convention and won its support for Henry A. Wallace, the president's unpopular choice for the vice presidential nomination. During World War 2 she served briefly with the Office of Civilian Defense, then later toured American bases in England, the South Pacific, and the Caribbean, spending long days visiting the sick and wounded and reporting back to Washington on matters great and small affecting the troops' condition.

Republican men often coarsely criticized her, only to find that Republican women admired her no less than Democratic women. Her poise, unaffected dignity, good sense, and evident caring won over the most critical audiences. At one lecture, a hostile questioner asked if the president's illness had affected his mind. "I'm glad that question was asked," she replied evenly. "The answer is yes. Anyone who has gone through great suffering is bound to have a greater sympathy and understanding of the problems of mankind."

"He might have been happier with a wife who was completely uncritical," Eleanor wrote after her husband's death. "That I was never able to be, and he had to find it in some other people. Nevertheless, I think I sometimes acted as a spur, even though the spurring was not always wanted or welcome. I was one of those who served his purposes."

ROOSEVELT'S FINAL ILLNESS (1944–45). During
his first 11 years as president, Franklin Roosevelt radiated an impression of buoyant good health. His large handsome head, often tilted at a jaunty angle, topped a powerful upper body. He was tireless at work and at play, hugely enjoying the company of large groups.

His personal physician was Ross T. McIntire, a career Navy doctor who had been recommended to the president because he was an ear, nose, and throat specialist and Roosevelt had a chronic sinus condition that made him susceptible to colds. McIntire routinely checked up on the president twice daily. In the mornings he watched the president eat breakfast. At the end of the day he made sure the president swam or rested. Apparently out of deference to presidential privacy, he rarely took Roosevelt's blood pressure and conducted few physical exams. As presidential physician, he rose from lieutenant commander to vice admiral and surgeon general of the Navy.

Roosevelt's confinement to a wheelchair may have prevented early observation of heart disease. But the question of the president's health could not be avoided after his return from the Tehran Conference in December 1943. The 18,000-mile trip would have been exhausting for any 62-year-old man. Roosevelt came down with what appeared to be influenza, but he failed to bounce back as he had after bouts with the flu in 1937 and 1941. For weeks he was overcome with fatigue, coughing, headaches, and nightly fevers.

Becoming alarmed, his daughter, Anna, demanded a thorough physical examination. This was conducted at the Bethesda Naval Hospital on Mar. 28, 1944. Lt. Comdr. Howard G. Bruenn, a cardiologist at Columbia-Presbyterian Hospital in New York City before his wartime Navy service, was appalled to discover that the president suffered from hypertension, hypertensive heart disease, and cardiac failure, as well as the acute bronchitis that McIntire had diagnosed.

There was then no medication for hypertension, but digitalis for his heart produced excellent results. The president was put on a diet and every effort was made to shield him from stress. But prolonged bed rest was impossible.

From then on, the president's decline was irregular but continuous. People who saw him infrequently were struck by the change in his appearance—falling weight, gray skin, haggard face, dark circles around his eyes, shaking hands. There were memory losses as well, and errors of judgment. During the last year of his life, Roosevelt was able to work only a few hours a day. In this condition important decisions were made in weariness or simply deferred. Yet he was capable of rousing himself to vigorous action, as in the presidential campaign of 1944 when his Republican opponent, Thomas E. Dewey, described the administration as composed of "tired old men."

Roosevelt's illness was considered by officials as a national security secret. When it was learned that doctors at Bethesda and the Mayo Clinic were gossiping about the president, J. Edgar Hoover, director of the Federal Bureau of Investigation, sent agents to intimidate them into silence. McIntire assured the press that the president was in fine health for a man his age. The doctors, in fact, never told Roosevelt everything they knew, and he did not press them. He recognized that his new attending physician was a cardiologist, but he did not understand that his condition was critical.

Roosevelt accepted his party's renomination in 1944 as a duty and expected to live out his term. Nothing else would explain his weary indifference to the party leaders' choice of Harry S. Truman as his running mate. Roosevelt barely knew Truman and made little effort to know him after the nomination. After his reelection, Roosevelt did absolutely nothing to initiate Truman into presidential concerns. Yet the politicians who selected Truman realized that they were probably choosing the next president of the United States.

Roosevelt returned from the Yalta Conference in February 1945 thoroughly spent. On Mar. 1 he delivered a rambling report on the conference to Congress while seated. At the end of the month, still exhausted, with no strength or appetite, he traveled to the "Little White House" at Warm Springs, Ga. There, at noon on Apr. 12, he suffered a cerebral hemorrhage and fell into a coma. He died at 3:30 that afternoon.

ROOSEVELT'S FIRST INAUGURAL (Mar. 4, 1933). On a cold, gloomy day in late winter, with the country's economic life paralyzed, a fourth to a third of its workforce unemployed, and fear gnawing at the nation's heart, the new president, Franklin Delano Roosevelt, addressed the people. Like a biblical prophet, he comforted and reassured them, identified transgressors among them, recalled the nation to former values, and promised swift and forceful action.

"This great nation will endure as it has endured," he promised, "will revive and will prosper.

"So first of all let me assert my firm belief that the only thing we have to fear is fear itself—nameless, unreasoning, unjustified terror which paralyzes needed efforts to convert retreat into advance. . . .

"Yet our distress comes from no failure of substance. . . . Nature still offers her bounty and human efforts have multiplied it. Plenty is at our doorstep, but a generous use of it languishes in the very sight of the supply.

"Primarily, this is because the rulers of the exchange of mankind's goods have failed through their own stubbornness and their own incompetence, have admitted their failure and abdicated. . . .

"The money changers have fled from their high seats in the temple of our civilization. We may now restore that temple to the ancient truths.

"The measure of the restoration lies in the extent to which we apply social values more noble than mere monetary profit. . . .

"Restoration calls, however, not for changes in ethics alone. This nation asks for action, and action now. . . .

"I am prepared under my constitutional duty to recommend the measures that a stricken nation in the midst of a stricken world may require.

"[Should Congress not respond,] I shall ask the Congress for the one remaining instrument to meet the crisis—broad executive power to wage a war against the emergency as great as the power that would be given me if we were in fact invaded by a foreign foe."

ROOSEVELT'S PURGE (1938),

incident in the Franklin *Roosevelt administration. Despite his landslide reelection in 1936 and Democrat majorities in both houses of Congress, Roosevelt found his liberal agenda for 1937 blocked by a coalition of Republicans and conservative Democrats. In 1938, therefore, he announced that he would support the opponents of selected conservative Democrats in that year's party primaries.

Despite Roosevelt's efforts, Sen. Guy Gillette of Iowa, Sen. Walter George of Georgia, Sen. "Cotton Ed" Smith of South Carolina, Sen. Millard Tydings of Maryland, and Rep. Howard Smith of Virginia won renomination and reelection. That year the Republicans gained eight seats in the Senate and 81 in the House, and Congress continued to block New Deal legislation.

ROOSEVELT'S SECOND INAUGURAL (Jan. 20, 1937).

In his second inaugural address, Pres. Franklin Roosevelt stated the modern liberal view of government. Government, he declared, is "the instrument of our united purpose to solve for the individual the ever-rising problems of a complex civilization. . . . [A]s intricacies of human relationships increase, so power to govern them also must increase—power to stop evil, power to do good. The essential democracy of our Nation and the safety of our people depend not upon the absence of power, but upon lodging it with those whom the people can change or continue at stated intervals through an honest and free system of elections. . . ."

"[I]n these last four years," he continued, "we have made the exercise of all power more democratic; for we have begun to bring private autocratic powers into their proper subordination to the public's government."

Although "we have set our feet upon the road of enduring progress," much remains to be done.

"I see a great nation, upon a great continent, blessed with a great wealth of natural resources. . . .

"But here is the challenge to our democracy: In this nation I see tens of millions of its citizens—a substantial part of its whole population—who at this very moment are denied the greater part of what the very lowest standards of today call the necessities of life.

"I see millions of families trying to live on incomes so meager that the pall of family disaster hangs over them day by day.

"I see millions whose daily lives in city and on farm continue under conditions labeled indecent by a so-called polite society half a century ago.

"I see millions denied education, recreation, and the opportunity to better their lot and the lot of their children.

"I see millions lacking the means to buy the products of farm and factory and by their poverty denying work and productiveness to many other millions.

"I see one-third of a nation ill-housed, ill-clad, ill-nourished.

". . . The test of our progress is not whether we add more to the abundance of those who have much; it is whether we provide enough for those who have too little."

ROOSEVELT'S THIRD-TERM DECISION (1940).

As 1940 opened, Pres. Franklin Roosevelt could not make up his mind about a third term. He was physically tired and longed to retire to Hyde Park, where he was already building a Roosevelt Library. In January 1940, he signed a contract to write for *Collier's* magazine. On the other hand, he enjoyed the powers of the presidency, feared for the survival of the New Deal without strong liberal leadership in the Democratic Party, and was apprehensive about events in Europe once the "phony war" ended.

Publicly, he said nothing about a third term, thereby retaining powers that would have fled from a lame duck. Still, he encouraged other Democratic aspirants to organize—Vice Pres. John N. Garner, Secretary of State Cordell Hull, and Postmaster General James A. Farley.

Quick Nazi victories in Scandinavia and Western Europe between April and June settled the issue. Roosevelt saw no other Democrat equal to the tasks ahead. In public opinion polls, only he scored ahead of the attractive Republican candidate, Wendell Willkie, nominated in June. Still, he insisted on being drafted.

At the Democratic national convention in Chicago in July, the chairman read a message from the White House: ". . . the President has never had, and has not today, any desire . . . to continue in the office of President . . . all delegates are free to vote for any candidate." The message confused the delegates, and the expected "Draft Roosevelt" demonstration stalled until the loudspeakers began to blare "Illinois wants Roosevelt, New York wants Roosevelt, America wants Roosevelt, the world wants Roosevelt!"—the work of Chicago mayor Ed Kelly. Roosevelt was nominated on the first ballot with 946 votes to 72 for Farley, 61 for Garner, nine for Sen. Millard Tydings of Maryland, and five for Hull.

To complete his victory over party conservatives,

Roosevelt then demanded the nomination for vice president of Secretary of Agriculture Henry A. Wallace, whose liberal credentials were beyond dispute. Consternation swept the hall, where Wallace was intensely unpopular; some delegates rebelled. But in the end Roosevelt had his way.

ROOSEVELT'S WAR MESSAGE (Dec. 8, 1941). At noon on Monday, Dec. 8, 1941, Pres. Franklin Roosevelt addressed a joint session of Congress in the House chamber. Solemn and angry, he spoke for only six minutes.

"Yesterday, December 7, 1941—a date which will live in infamy—the United States of America was suddenly and deliberately attacked by naval and air forces of the Empire of Japan.

"The United States was at peace with that nation and, at the solicitation of Japan, was still in conversation with its government and its Emperor looking toward the maintenance of peace in the Pacific. Indeed, one hour after Japanese air squadrons had commenced bombing in Oahu, the Japanese ambassador to the United States and his colleague delivered to the Secretary of State a formal reply to a recent American message. . . . [I]t contained no threat or hint of armed attack. . . .

"The attack yesterday on the Hawaiian Islands has caused severe damage to American naval and military forces. . . .

"Yesterday the Japanese government also launched an attack against Malaya.

"Last night Japanese forces attacked Hong Kong.

"Last night Japanese forces attacked Guam.

"Last night Japanese forces attacked the Philippine Islands.

"Last night the Japanese attacked Wake Island.

"This morning the Japanese attacked Midway Island.

"Japan has, therefore, undertaken a surprise offensive extending throughout the Pacific area. . . .

"As Commander-in-Chief of the Army and Navy, I have directed that all measures be taken for our defense. . . .

"No matter how long it may take us to overcome this premeditated invasion, the American people in their righteous might will win through to absolute victory. . . .

"With confidence in our armed forces—with the unbounding determination of our people—we will gain the inevitable triumph—so help us God.

"I ask that the Congress declare that since the unprovoked and dastardly attack by Japan on Sunday, December 7th, a state of war has existed between the United States and the Japanese Empire."

Congress gave Roosevelt the greatest ovation of his presidency. Two and a half hours later, the declaration of war was on his desk. It had passed both houses of Congress with only a single negative vote. Pacifist representative Jeannette Rankin of Montana voted against war in 1941 as she had in 1917.

On Dec. 11, Germany and Italy declared war on the United States. Congress thereupon recognized a state of war with those countries as well (see *World War 2).

ROOSEVELT-TAFT SPLIT. Concerned to preserve the progressive movement in the Republican Party (see *Progressivism), Pres. Theodore Roosevelt in 1908 chose Secretary of War William Howard Taft as his successor and ensured his nomination by the Republican national convention. The amiable Taft, a friend since 1890, had been a supportive cabinet member, and Roosevelt assumed that he was a progressive. Taft was, in fact, profoundly conservative, legalistic, indolent, and averse to politics (he had risen through appointive offices only). A reluctant president, he nourished a desire to be chief justice.

Strains had already begun to appear in the relations between the new and former presidents before Roosevelt went off on safari in Africa. Although Taft professed to want to continue Roosevelt's program, his fall from progressive grace and into the embrace of the Old Guard was swift: appointment of a cabinet containing no Roosevelt loyalists; the *Payne-Aldrich Tariff; the *Ballinger-Pinchot controversy; an attempt to purge progressive Republicans in the 1910 primaries; an antitrust suit against U.S. Steel for an acquisition that Roosevelt had personally approved (see *Taft Administration).

Back in the United States from his African and European travels, Roosevelt felt increasingly constrained by his pledge not to seek a third term. He recognized that the Republican Party was firmly controlled by the Old Guard and that a third-party movement would be doomed to failure. He expected that Taft would be defeated by a conservative Democrat in 1912 and that a reformed Republican Party under his leadership would return to power in 1916.

Roosevelt's frustration and fears for the future of progressivism were reflected in speeches that became increasingly and uncharacteristically radical. The list of necessary and urgent reforms that constituted the *New Nationalism grew long. His attack on the courts as obstacles to social justice outraged Taft and scandalized even his friends. Taft's prosecution of U.S. Steel was a personal affront and perhaps the last straw. Reluctantly, Roosevelt acceded to the pressure of his friends, especially the argument that he himself was responsible for Taft's presidency and that he owed it to the progressive cause to challenge Taft at whatever cost.

One obstacle was the candidacy, announced in June 1911, of Sen. Robert M. La Follette of Wisconsin. The two progressives had a visceral dislike of each other. To Roosevelt, La Follette was a raw, dogmatic radical; to La Follette, Roosevelt was a shallow reformer, given to compromise, and beholden to "the interests." The hostility between the leaders of Eastern and Western progressivism threatened to tear the movement apart. For most progressives, who preferred Roosevelt, the problem was resolved by *La Follette's "collapse" on Feb. 3, 1912, although Roosevelt's decision to run had been made previously. Professing to believe that La Follette's candidacy was doomed, the progressives flocked to Roosevelt's banner when on Feb. 21 he announced that his "hat was in the ring."

There followed a fight for convention delegates marked by ungentlemanly name-calling by both Taft and Roosevelt. Of 12 state primaries, Roosevelt won nine, La Follette two, and Taft one. But the Old Guard controlled the convention that met in June 1912 and Taft was renominated on the first ballot. Roosevelt and his followers bolted and formed the *Progressive Party with Roosevelt as its nominee.

But Roosevelt now faced a progressive Democrat, Woodrow Wilson, as well as the conservative Taft. Knowing that he could not win, he was determined to punish Taft and preserve the forces of Republican progressivism. Indeed, he outpolled Taft and made Wilson a minority president.

In May 1918 Roosevelt and Taft met accidentally in a Chicago hotel dining room and embraced affectionately.

ROOT-TAKAHIRA AGREEMENT (Nov. 30, 1908), accord between Secretary of State Elihu Root and Japanese ambassador Kogoro Takahira that the United States and Japan would respect each other's territorial possessions in the Pacific, uphold the *Open Door Policy in China, and support by peaceful means the independence and integrity of China. The agreement relieved Americans' fears of eventual war with Japan.

ROSENBERG CASE (1950–53). An electrical engineer employed by the Army Signal Corps, Julius Rosenberg, together with his wife, Ethel, had once been an active member of the Communist Party in New York. On June 15, 1950, Ethel's brother, David Greenglass, a machinist on the *Manhattan Project at Los Alamos, N.Mex., told the Federal Bureau of Investigation (FBI)—

which was investigating Karl Fuchs, a German-born British physicist who had spied for the Russians at Los Alamos—that he had passed information about the atomic bomb not only to one Harry Gold, who had already confessed to conspiring with Fuchs, but also to Julius and Ethel Rosenberg.

The Rosenbergs denied Greenglass's story but refused to cooperate with the FBI. Then another source involved in defense work told the FBI that the Rosenbergs had sought classified military information from him. Moreover, one Morton Sobell was named as an accomplice of the Rosenbergs. These accusations were supported by no hard evidence but by some damning circumstantial evidence: upon the news of Fuchs's arrest in London in February 1950, Sobell had fled to Mexico and Julius Rosenberg had applied for a passport. In August 1950 a federal grand jury indicted the Rosenbergs for conspiracy to commit espionage.

The Rosenbergs and Sobell went on trial in New York City on Mar. 6, 1951. The Rosenbergs insisted on their innocence and refused on Fifth Amendment grounds to answer questions about their membership in the Communist Party. The jury found all three defendants guilty. Intemperately calling their crime "worse than murder" as already having caused the *Korean War, Judge Irving Kaufman, on Apr. 5, 1951, sentenced Sobell to 30 years in prison and the Rosenbergs to death in the electric chair. They died at Sing Sing prison on June 18, 1953.

The trial was widely denounced as unfair and the severity of the sentence as unprecedented—both, of course, reflected the climate of the *cold war. Later evidence suggests that Julius Rosenberg—but not his wife—had in fact committed nonatomic espionage.

ROUGH RIDERS, in the *Spanish-American War, popular name for the First U.S. Cavalry, a much-publicized volunteer regiment composed of cowboys and Ivy Leaguers, organized and led by Col. Leonard Wood and Lt. Col. Theodore Roosevelt. The regiment fought in Cuba without horses, most notably at San Juan Hill. Roosevelt emerged a war hero and wrote *The Rough Riders* (1899).

RUFFIN'S CAREER. A member of one of Virginia's oldest and wealthiest planter families, Edmund Ruffin (1794–1865) early won recognition as a scientific farmer for his discovery that the application of marl would restore the fertility of Virginia soil exhausted by excessive tobacco culture. His *Essay on Calcareous Manures* went through four editions.

Although he was both a planter and a publisher of agricultural journals, Ruffin's true and obsessive passion was Southern nationalism. With other *fire-eaters like Robert B. Rhett and William L. Yancey, he defended slavery and advocated Southern independence. Restless and volatile, he had a need to be where the action was.

On Dec. 2, 1859, the white-haired 65-year-old veteran of the War of 1812 was in Charlestown, Va., dressed in an ill-fitting uniform and parading with the teenage cadets of the Virginia Military Institute. Afterward they stood at attention before the gallows where abolitionist John Brown was hanged. (Ruffin may have seen John Wilkes Booth, who was present in the uniform of a Virginia regiment.)

In the spring of 1860, although he was not a delegate, Ruffin attended both the Richmond and the Baltimore rump sessions of the Democratic national convention at which the party irremediably split, then in December 1860 managed to be present at the South Carolina convention that voted for secession.

On Apr. 12, 1861, on Morris Island in Charleston Bay, Ruffin, now dressed in the borrowed uniform of a Palmetto Guard, was given the honor of firing the first shell at Fort Sumter. Three days later he was present when the surrendered federal troops filed out of the ruined fort.

In July 1861 Ruffin left his plantation, Beechwood, on the James River, and hurried north to Manassas Junction, where he rejoined the Palmetto Guards and was present at the first battle of *Bull Run. He fired the shell that destroyed a bridge on Cub Run over which a panicked mob of Federal soldiers and civilian sightseers was trying to flee.

During the Civil War, two Ruffin plantations were sacked by Union soldiers. Ruffin lost one son and a grandson (another son deserted). On June 17, 1865, the unreconstructed fire-eater wrote a final entry in his diary ("... I hereby ... proclaim my unmitigated hatred to Yankee rule—to all political, social, & business connection with Yankees, & to the perfidious, malignant, & vile Yankee race"), then put a bullet through his head.

RULE OF REASON. See *Standard Oil Co. of New Jersey v. United States*; *White Court.

RUM, ROMANISM, AND REBELLION (1884). In October 1884, Republican presidential candidate James G. Blaine visited New York City. There, at the Fifth Avenue Hotel on Oct. 29, he received a large delegation of Protestant clergymen. Addressing the candidate, the delegation's leader, Rev. Samuel D. Burchard, described the Democratic Party as the party of "rum, Romanism, and rebellion." Blaine believed that his failure to disavow the description cost him the Irish Catholic vote, New York State, and the election. He lost New York by 1,149 votes.

RUSH-BAGOT AGREEMENT (1817), diplomatic achievement of the *Monroe administration limiting naval forces on Lake Champlain and the Great Lakes, in fulfillment of a provision of the Treaty of *Ghent. The agreement was effected by an exchange of notes between British minister Charles Bagot and Acting Secretary of State Richard Rush, but was given the force of a treaty by being unanimously ratified by the U.S. Senate on Apr. 16, 1818.

RUSSIAN INTERVENTION (1918–20), episode of the *Wilson administration. Russia's withdrawal from World War 1 in March 1918 enabled the Germans to transfer 40 divisions from the Eastern Front to participate in their final offensive in the west. In response, Britain and France conceived a plan to land troops at Murmansk in northern Russia, ostensibly to protect Allied munitions stored there but also to rally anti-Bolshevik forces and reopen an Eastern Front against Germany.

At the same time, 70,000 Czech troops—Russian prisoners of war and deserters from the Austro-Hungarian army—who had been fighting the Germans in Russia were now stranded there and asking to be evacuated via the Trans-Siberian Railroad and Vladivostok and transported around the world to the Western Front. To facilitate their evacuation, Japan agreed to land troops at Vladivostok.

Britain and France urged U.S. president Woodrow Wilson to join them in their scheme. Cool to the idea of a northern expedition, Wilson was sympathetic to the plight of the Czech Legion and suspicious of Japanese intentions in Siberia. Reluctantly, in August 1918 he dispatched 5,000 U.S. troops to Murmansk and 10,000 to Vladivostok. These moves, largely clothed in secrecy, were seen as intervention in the Russian civil war and were highly unpopular.

No Eastern Front was reopened in north Russia. In Siberia, U.S. troops patrolled the eastern end of the Trans-Siberian Railroad, over which the Czechs were evacuated in 1919. Allied troops left Murmansk in 1919. U.S. troops left Vladivostok in 1920. The Japanese did not leave until 1922.

RUSSIAN REVOLUTION (1917–20). The abdication of Czar Nicholas II in March 1917 and the apparent assumption of power by a liberal provisional government astonished and thrilled Americans. Pres. Woodrow Wilson, who was even then preparing to ask Congress for a declaration of war to make the world safe for democracy, was spared the embarrassment of having the world's oldest autocracy as an ally. "The autocracy that crowned the summit of [Russia's] political structure," he told Congress on Apr. 2, "... has been shaken off and the great, generous Russian people have been added in all their naive majesty and might to the forces that are fighting for freedom in the world, for justice, and for peace" (see *Wilson's War Message).

The seizure of power by the Bolsheviks in November 1917 changed this picture. Western statesmen feared not only the contagion of Marxist revolution but also the demoralizing effect on their war-weary peoples of the Bolshevik demand for a peace without annexations or indemnities with self-determination for subject peoples.

To demonstrate his own enlightened war aims, President Wilson hastened to publish his *14 Points. Point 6, addressed to the Bolsheviks, masked Wilson's personal hostility to the new regime. "The evacuation of all Russian territory," it proposed, "and such a settlement of all questions affecting Russia as will secure the best and freest cooperation of the other nations of the world in obtaining for her an unhampered and unembarrassed opportunity for the independent determination of her own political development and national policy and assure her of a sincere welcome into the society of free nations under institutions of her own choosing. . . ."

But when the Bolsheviks signed a separate peace with Germany at Brest-Litovsk in March 1918 and left the war, the Allies were outraged at Russia's bad faith. The United States joined them in small-scale and ineffectual interventions in support of anti-Bolshevik forces in the Russian civil war (see *Russian Intervention). Adamant hostility now characterized official Western attitudes—including that of the U.S. government—toward communist Russia.

Ordinary Americans cheered the fall of the czar as the beginning of the end of the European monarchies. (Of 20 principal European countries in 1914, only three—France, Switzerland, and Portugal—were republics.) Although profoundly ignorant of events in Russia, they understood that the Bolshevik revolution was another matter entirely.

The Bolsheviks' attacks on religion, their distribution of land to the peasants, and their turning the management of factories over to the workers were alarming and thoroughly un-American. After Russia left the war, they accepted their government's view of Russia as outside the family of civilized nations and deserving of ostracism. The United States did not recognize communist Russia—then the USSR—until 1933 (see *Soviet Recognition).

For American radicals of all stripes, however, the Bolshevik revolution heralded the dawn of a new age. With one stroke, the Bolsheviks had solved the problem of establishing socialism—not by long historical evolution, as Marx had predicted, but by revolution led by a small disciplined vanguard. Demoralized by wartime persecution (see *Espionage Act; *Red Scare), American radicals took heart and excitedly sought news from Russia.

Several well-known American radicals had actually witnessed the stirring events in Russia. The dashing war correspondent John Reed had been present at the Bolshevik coup in Petrograd, which he vividly described in his international best-seller *Ten Days That Shook the World* (1919). Reed became a passionate communist. When he died in Russia in 1920, he was buried in the Kremlin wall. The onetime muckraking journalist Lincoln Steffens visited Russia in April 1917 and again in April 1919. Already pessimistic about the prospects of democracy, he too became a propagandist for the Bolshevik regime. "I have seen the future, and it works," he said famously in 1919.

Excitement was particularly high in U.S. immigrant communities. Many Russian immigrants returned to Russia, some voluntarily, others at the behest of the U.S. Department of Justice. Among the latter were the well-known anarchists Emma Goldman and Alexander Berkman, who were deported to Russia in December 1919 and went enthusiastically. They soon discovered that the Bolshevik state was a naked dictatorship and bureaucratic nightmare. Disillusioned, Goldman left in 1921, Berkman in 1922.

The Russian Revolution inspired decades of intellectual warfare on the American left. It led directly to the founding in 1921 by left-wing socialists and labor radicals of the American *Communist Party.

S

SACCO-VANZETTI CASE (1920–27). On Apr. 15, 1920—in the midst of the post–World War 1 *red scare—the paymaster of a shoe factory and his guard were held up and killed in South Braintree, Mass., by two men who were driven off in a waiting car. Three weeks later, Nicola Sacco, a shoe operative, and Bartolomo Vanzetti, a fish peddler, were arrested and charged with the murders. Both of the accused were Italian immigrants who had evaded the wartime draft, were committed anarchists, and carried revolvers, although neither had a criminal record. When arrested, fearing (they claimed) that they were going to be deported as radicals, they betrayed "consciousness of guilt" by lying and behaving ambiguously.

At their trial before Judge Webster Thayer in Dedham, Mass., from May 31 to July 14, 1921, "consciousness of guilt" was a major argument of the prosecution. Other prosecution arguments were improbable identifications by eyewitnesses (contradicted by other eyewitnesses) and the fact that, of six bullets taken from the two dead men, one bore markings "consistent with" having been fired from Sacco's revolver. For the defense (ineptly conducted by an out-of-state lawyer), witnesses testified that both men had been elsewhere at the time of the crime and none of the holdup money was found in their possession. The police, moreover, believed that the robbery had been committed by a gang of professional criminals.

That either or both defendants were guilty "beyond a reasonable doubt" was certainly never proved. But the courtroom was pervaded by antiradical passion. When it was suggested to the foreman of the jury that the defendants might be innocent, he reportedly replied, "Damn them, they ought to hang them anyway." Judge Thayer's charge to the jury was a crude appeal to their patriotism. (Later he was reported to have said to a friend, "Did you see what I did with those anarchist bastards the other day? I guess that will hold them a while.") On July 14, Sacco and Vanzetti were found guilty.

The case soon became an international cause célèbre. The prisoners' quiet dignity, and especially Vanzetti's eloquence despite his imperfect English, elevated them to the role of martyrs in the eyes of their sympathizers. In Massachusetts, motions for a new trial—based on judicial error and on the discovery of new evidence pointing to other perpetrators—were denied by Judge Thayer and by the Massachusetts Supreme Judicial Court.

In the spring of 1927, Judge Thayer finally pronounced the sentence of death. Responding to worldwide demonstrations, Massachusetts governor Alvin T. Fuller appointed an advisory committee consisting of the presidents of Harvard University and the Massachusetts Institute of Technology and a retired jurist. The committee reported that the trial had been fair and the evidence persuasive. Last-minute appeals were rejected by the Massachusetts Supreme Judicial Court, a federal district court, and three justices of the U.S. Supreme Court—Holmes, Brandeis, and Stone. While thousands of sympathizers kept vigil in the streets, Sacco and Vanzetti were electrocuted in Charlestown prison on Aug. 23, 1927.

For many American liberals and intellectuals, the Sacco-Vanzetti case proved a watershed. Moved by a perceived miscarriage of justice at the hands of a narrow-minded establishment, some were radicalized, others driven to despair and apathy. Numerous plays, novels, and poems were inspired by the case, and scholars have not ceased debating the convicted men's guilt or innocence.

In May 1927, after they had been sentenced to death, Sacco and Vanzetti were visited in Dedham jail by Philip D. Strong, a reporter for the North American Newspaper Alliance. In the first of three syndicated articles about the prisoners, Strong quoted—with what degree of accuracy cannot be known—remarks by Vanzetti intended to cheer the disconsolate visitor. The quotation has survived as a literary gem:

"If it had not been for these thing, I might have live out my life talking at street corners to scorning men. I might have die, unmarked, unknown, a failure. Now we are not a failure. This is our career and our triumph. Never in our full life could we hope to do such work for tolerance, for joostice, for man's understanding of man as now we do by accident. Our words—our lives—our pains—nothing! The taking of our lives—lives of a good shoemaker and a poor fish-peddler—all! That last moment belongs to us—that agony is our triumph!"

SALARY GRAB (1873), incident in the *Grant administration. A bill passed in the closing hours of the 42nd Congress in March 1873 provided for substantial salary increases for the president, vice president, cabinet members, Supreme Court justices, and members of Congress (for whom the increase was retroactive for the preceding two years). A public already soured by scandals in the administration protested, and the next Congress, in January 1874, repealed the act except for provisions affecting the president and justices.

SALEM WITCHCRAFT TRIALS (1692–93). Belief in witchcraft pervaded Europe and America in the 16th and 17th centuries. In Puritan Massachusetts, where Satan was ever a malevolent neighbor, several accusations of and executions for witchcraft occurred before the outbreak of witchcraft mania in Salem (now Danvers).

In February 1692 two adolescent girls, frightened by the tales of a slave woman, became hysterical and began accusing respectable people of bewitching them. Panic ensued as accusations multiplied on all sides, motivated by revenge, malice, or spite. The clergy and civil authorities had no choice but to give credence to them, and between May and September hundreds of people were arrested and 19 hanged. The eminent divine Cotton Mather, who had written a learned treatise on witchcraft, lent his authority to the proceedings.

In October, the provincial governor halted the Salem trials and ordered the accused brought before the Superior Court, which acquitted 49 of 52 defendants. The governor then pardoned all others under suspicion. After the frenzy had subsided, Mather (in the privacy of his diary) expressed contrition for his role. Judge Samuel Sewall apologized publicly before his congregation.

SAND CREEK MASSACRE (1864). See *Cheyenne-Arapaho War.

SAN FRANCISCO EARTHQUAKE (Apr. 18, 1906), unprecedented shocks followed by fire that over three days destroyed a third of the city, killing 700 people and driving 250,000 homeless into the streets and parks. Reconstruction, under stringent new building codes, was rapid.

SANITARY COMMISSION (1861–65), volunteer war-relief organization during the *Civil War. Bringing about reform of the Army Medical Board, it sent its agents into army camps to investigate hygiene conditions, organized and staffed field hospitals, recruited and trained female nurses, and pioneered the use of hospital ships and trains. Members of 7,000 local affiliates, mostly women, sent medical supplies, food, and clothing to army camps and provided meals and lodging for soldiers traveling on furlough. A Sanitary Commission nurse, Clara Barton, later founded the American Red Cross.

SAN JACINTO (Apr. 21, 1836), decisive battle in the Texas Revolution (see *Texas Republic). In command of the last Texas armed force, Gen. Sam Houston led his 900 men in a monthlong retreat before the army of Mexican general and president Antonio López de Santa Anna. Santa Anna divided his army, the better to destroy Texas farms and ranches, from which their owners had fled. Thus he had only some 1,200 men when he cornered Houston at the San Jacinto River at a spot in the present-day city of Houston.

The Mexicans were overconfident and careless. The Texans turned and attacked, inspired by Houston's admonition, "Remember the Alamo!" The battle, which lasted only 20 minutes, was a complete Texan victory. It was followed by a massacre of Mexicans in revenge for Mexican atrocities at the Alamo and Goliad. Mexican casualties were estimated at 800; the Texans suffered 16 dead, 24 wounded.

Santa Anna was captured and compelled to sign a treaty recognizing Texas independence, which the Mexican congress repudiated. Mexico did not again seriously attempt to repossess Texas.

SAN JUAN BOUNDARY DISPUTE, controversy between the United States and Great Britain arising out of the 1846 treaty that established the boundary between Oregon and British Columbia (see *Oregon Dispute) but left unclear the status of the San Juan Islands in the Strait of Juan de Fuca. U.S. troops occupied the islands in 1859 and were soon joined by British troops in joint occupation. By the Treaty of *Washington (1871), the two powers agreed to submit the issue to arbitration. In 1872 German emperor William I decided in favor of the United States.

SAN JUAN HILL. See *Spanish-American War.

SAN LORENZO TREATY (1795). See *Pinckney's Treaty or Treaty of San Lorenzo.

SANTA CLARA COUNTY v. SOUTHERN PACIFIC RAILROAD CO. (1886), unanimous decision of the *Waite Court upholding a California court judgment preventing Santa Clara County from taxing railroad property. The case is famous for a prefatory announcement by Chief Justice Morrison R. Waite that the Court accepted the doctrine that the term *person* in the *14th Amendment applied to corporations as well as to individuals. The Court thereby explicitly extended the protection of the amendment's Due Process and Equal Protection clauses to corporations.

SANTA FE INDEPENDENT SCHOOL DISTRICT v. DOE (2000), 6–3 decision of the *Rehnquist Court declaring the practice of student-initiated and student-led prayer at public high school football games unconstitutional.

"Regardless of whether one considers a sporting event an appropriate occasion for solemnity," wrote Justice John Paul Stevens for the Court, "the use of an invocation to foster such solemnity is impermissible when, in actuality, it constitutes prayer sponsored by the school."

In dissent, Chief Justice William H. Rehnquist declared that the Court's opinion "bristles with hostility to all things religious in public life" (see *Church-State Relations).

SANTA FE TRAIL, overland route from Missouri to New Mexico pioneered in 1821 by William Becknell, a Missouri trader. A wagon train made the 780-mile trip between Independence, Mo., and Santa Fe and back once a year until supplanted by a monthly stage (1850) and the Santa Fe Railroad (1880).

SANTO DOMINGO AFFAIR (1870–71), incident in the *Grant administration. Pres. Ulysses S. Grant was eager to annex Santo Domingo (the Dominican Republic), a scheme proposed by the country's president, Buenaventura Báez, and seconded by Grant's private secretary, Gen. Orville Babcock, who saw opportunities for personal gain in the acquisition. Grant advocated annexation on the grounds that Santo Domingo was a rich country that would provide a market for American goods and a haven for discontented American blacks. Its existence as a free and stable territory, moreover, would cause Puerto Rico, Cuba, and Brazil to abolish slavery to prevent the flight of their workforces.

The project was opposed by Charles Sumner, chairman of the Senate Foreign Relations Committee, who argued that annexation would embark the United States on the course of imperialism at the expense of one of the world's two black republics. The Senate rejected a treaty of annexation, but for his opposition Sumner was forced to resign his committee chairmanship.

SARATOGA CAMPAIGN (June–October 1777), unsuccessful British attempt to seize control of the Hudson River valley during the *Revolutionary War.

The British strategy in 1777 was to cut off New England from the Middle and Southern states by taking control of the Hudson River valley in a three-pronged offensive: Gen. John Burgoyne would lead one British army from Canada down Lake Champlain and the Hudson River; Col. Barry St. Leger would lead a smaller force from Canada by way of Lake Ontario and through the Mohawk Valley; and Gen. William Howe in New York City would advance up the Hudson. All three forces would converge at Albany.

Burgoyne, with some 8,000 British regulars, German mercenaries, Indians, Canadians, and American Loyalists, moved south from Saint Johns, descended Lake Champlain by boat, and on July 6 occupied *Crown Point and *Fort Ticonderoga. Winning minor engagements at Hubbardton and Fort Ann, the British pursued the Americans southward along the east bank of the Hudson. From Skenesboro, the army, obstructed and harassed by the Americans, advanced through densely forested country at a rate of only a mile a day. On July 30 the British occupied Fort Edward. With supplies running low, Burgoyne dispatched (Aug. 11) two bodies of troops to seize an American depot at *Bennington, Vt. These were turned back with heavy casualties by local militia.

Meanwhile, St. Leger had moved from Montreal to Oswego on Lake Ontario. On July 26, with 2,000 Loyalists and Indians, he left Oswego and on Aug. 3 laid siege to Fort Stanwix at the head of the Mohawk Valley. When a relief force of New York militia under Gen. Nicholas Herkimer came to the relief of the fort, it was trapped and driven back near *Oriskany. News of the approach of another American force caused St. Leger's Indians to desert. On Aug. 22 he abandoned the siege of Fort Stanwix and retreated to Oswego.

To complete Burgoyne's predicament, General Howe on July 23 had taken a large part of the British army in New York City by ship to Chesapeake Bay for an attack on Philadelphia. Gen. Henry Clinton, left in command in New York, awaited reinforcements. Not until Oct. 3 did Clinton, seeking only to relieve pressure on Burgoyne, venture up the Hudson. He quickly captured forts Clinton and Montgomery, then returned to New York City. Burgoyne was isolated in the New York wilderness with no prospect of relief.

On Sept. 13 Burgoyne crossed to the west side of the Hudson with 6,000 men. His road south was barred by an American army entrenched on **Bemis Heights**, 24 miles north of Albany, under the command of Gen. Horatio Gates. Steadily enlarged by the arrival of Continental units and streams of militia, Gates's army had grown from 4,000 men in August to 11,000 in October. Although outnumbered and short of supplies, Burgoyne determined to fight his way south in the belief that he would find Clinton at Albany.

On Sept. 19, three British columns advanced over wooded and hilly terrain toward the American position on Bemis Heights. Gates, aware that most of his troops were raw militia, held his hand, then cautiously committed Patriot units piecemeal to the battle. A major engagement, uncontrolled by Gates, developed around **Freeman's Farm**, a 15-acre clearing one mile north of the American lines. American superiority in numbers failed to prevail against the superior training of the British regulars. At the end of the day the British had suffered heavy casualties but possessed the field. Yet the Americans remained securely entrenched on Bemis Heights.

The British dug in on the ground they had won, building a line of entrenchments and several log redoubts. There Burgoyne waited for news of Clinton's advance up the Hudson. Meanwhile his supplies were shrinking and his Loyalists, Canadians, and Indians were deserting. Burgoyne realized he must either attack or retreat. On Oct. 7, with fewer than 5,000 troops, Burgoyne sent a reconnaissance-in-force forward toward Bemis Heights. The Americans drove the British back into their fortified lines, portions of which they overran. In this action, Gen. Benedict Arnold, denied a command of his own, displayed reckless bravery in the thick of the fight.

On the night of Oct. 8, in heavy rain, Burgoyne retreated toward Saratoga. Exhausted and starving, his army was now surrounded by steadily increasing American forces. On Oct. 17 he formally surrendered to Gates. According to the terms of the "convention" (not "capitu-lation"), his army was to be allowed to march to Boston and from there be transported to England on the understanding that it would not serve in North America again. Gates accepted these terms because he feared Clinton's approach from the south. Congress, however, rejected them, and Burgoyne's army spent the remainder of the war as prisoners in Virginia.

SARBANES-OXLEY ACT (2002). See *Corporate Responsibility Act or Sarbanes-Oxley Act.

SAVINGS AND LOAN CRISIS (1989), incident in the George H. W. *Bush administration. Savings and loan institutions (S&Ls or thrifts) are traditionally conservative, modestly profitable banks that pay low interest on depositors' accounts and provide mortgages to home buyers at a slightly higher rate. In the 1980s, interest rates rose, and the S&Ls had to pay ever higher rates to attract depositors while their capital remained frozen in long-term, low-interest mortgages. The pressure for profits caused many to look for better-paying (though riskier) investments. Lax regulation and the fact that depositor accounts were insured by the federal government up to $100,000 encouraged reckless speculation in so-called junk bonds and in Southwestern real estate, where a boom fueled by high oil prices was under way. When oil prices fell in the mid-1980s, the real-estate boom ended, leaving hundreds of S&Ls insolvent and taxpayers obligated to pay depositors $180 billion.

In 1989, the Financial Institutions Reform, Recovery, and Enforcement Act created the Resolution Trust Corporation to take over hundreds of failed S&Ls and sell them, debt-free, to new owners. It also imposed stricter regulations and required larger cash reserves, thereby restoring stability to the shaken industry.

SCALAWAGS. See *Carpetbaggers and Scalawags.

SCHECHTER POULTRY CORP. v. UNITED STATES (1935), unanimous decision of the *Hughes Court ruling the **National Industrial Recovery Act (NIRA)** of 1933 unconstitutional. The NIRA was the major emergency initiative of the Franklin *Roosevelt administration (see *New Deal) to counter the depression. It called for industry groups to draw up codes of fair competition in the expectation that these would relax antitrust restraints and encourage business revival. In two years some 750 codes were drawn up. Schechter, a local slaughterhouse, had been found guilty of violating its industry's code.

For the Court, Chief Justice Charles Evans Hughes

ruled, first, that the national economic emergency did not justify the legislation: "extraordinary conditions do not create or enlarge constitutional powers." Second, he found that the act had unconstitutionally delegated legislative powers to the president (who approved and signed the individual codes). Finally, he found that Schechter was a local processor with no direct effect on interstate commerce and thus beyond the reach of congressional legislation. Roosevelt criticized the Court's "horse and buggy" interpretation of the Constitution.

SCHENCK v. UNITED STATES (1919), unanimous decision of the *White Court that speech creating a "clear and present danger" was not protected by the First Amendment. Charles Schenck, general secretary of the Socialist Party, was convicted under the *Espionage Act (1917) for distributing 15,000 antidraft leaflets to Philadelphia men being conscripted into the U.S. army for service in World War 1. Schenck and his fellow socialists argued that their leaflet was protected by the free speech and free press provisions of the First Amendment.

"We admit," wrote Justice Oliver Wendell Holmes for the Court, "that in many places and in ordinary times the defendants, in saying all that was said in the circular, would have been within their constitutional rights. But the character of every act depends upon the circumstances in which it is done. The most stringent protection of free speech would not protect a man in falsely shouting fire in a theater, and causing a panic. . . . The question in every case is whether the words used are used in such circumstances and are of such a nature as to create a clear and present danger that they will bring about the substantive evils that Congress has a right to prevent. It is a question of proximity and degree. When a nation is at war many things that might be said in time of peace are such a hindrance to its effort that their utterance will not be endured so long as men fight, and that no court could regard them as protected by any constitutional right."

SCHOOL DESEGREGATION. In *Brown v. Board of Education of Topeka (1954), the U.S. Supreme Court ruled unanimously that "in the field of public education the doctrine of 'separate but equal' has no place. Separate educational facilities are inherently unequal." It declared that "all provisions of federal, state, or local law requiring or permitting" racial discrimination in public education were unconstitutional. A year later, in Brown 2, it assigned the implementation of school desegregation to local federal courts, with the injunction that they proceed "with all deliberate speed."

"All deliberate speed" proved very slow indeed. Resis-

tance, evasion, and delay were universal in the South. During the 1950s, no significant desegregation occurred in the South except as a result of a lawsuit and a court order, always appealed. In *Cooper v. Aaron (1958), the Supreme Court refused to tolerate desegregation delays out of fear of public disorder. By 1964, ten years after Brown, only 8 percent of black schoolchildren in the South went to school with white children.

The *Civil Rights Act of 1964 put an end to the South's obstructive tactics. It authorized the U.S. Department of Justice to bring suits against school districts maintaining segregation. More important, it cut off federal funds from segregated districts. Southern school districts that wanted federal funds had to conform to desegregation guidelines drawn up by the Office of Civil Rights in the U.S. Department of Health, Education and Welfare (HEW, since 1980 the Department of Health and Human Services).

At first, HEW accepted a Southern formula of freedom of choice. Southern districts retained their dual school systems—separate white schools and black schools—but pupils were free to attend the schools of their choice. No white pupils, however, enrolled in black schools and few black pupils dared to enroll in white schools.

In 1966 HEW began to require *affirmative action to ensure that desegregation actually took place. To qualify for federal funds, school districts had to provide statistical evidence of increased black attendance at white schools every year. In *Green v. County School Board of New Kent County (1968), the Supreme Court rejected dual school systems altogether, requiring a unitary school system "without a white school and a Negro school, but just schools."

A school district could accomplish desegregation in various ways. Where blacks and whites lived in close proximity, school-attendance zones could be redrawn or schools paired to achieve a racial mix. Where the races were widely separated, as in many big-city districts, busing was the necessary solution. In *Swann v. Charlotte-Mecklenburg Board of Education (1970), the Supreme Court unanimously upheld the authority of federal judges to mandate busing until such time as racial integration had been achieved.

"Forced busing"—that is, court-ordered busing to achieve school desegregation—generated intense hostility. Whites experienced it as an exercise of remote and arbitrary authority that destroyed neighborhood schools, ended local control of education, and subjected children to physical danger for no educational purpose. In opinion polls, whites opposed busing for desegregation by large margins; blacks divided almost evenly. In 1977, of nearly 42 million children in public elementary and secondary schools, more than half (21.8 million) rode buses to school, but only 7 percent (1.5 million) were bused for reasons of desegregation. Most of the latter were black.

Close cooperation between executive agencies—the Justice Department and HEW—and the federal courts in enforcing the Civil Rights Act of 1964 produced rapid school desegregation in the South. But schools in the North and West did not escape federal scrutiny. Dual school systems did not exist in the North and West as they did in the South, but it required little investigation to discover deliberate segregation in those regions as well.

Thus mandatory desegregation—including busing—came in the 1970s to the cities of the North and West, and those regions, which had been indifferent to the South's complaints, protested vociferously (see *Boston Busing). Their representatives in Congress responded. Congress limited HEW's authority to mandate busing (almost all forced busing was court-ordered) and forbade HEW to cut off federal funds from school districts that failed to meet its desegregation standards. Pres. Richard M. Nixon curtailed the activities of the Justice Department and HEW in desegregation matters. Pres. Ronald Reagan was opposed to busing, and his administration determined no longer to seek the desegregation of entire school districts but only of specific schools where there was evidence of official segregation. Almost alone, the federal courts continued to bear responsibility for desegregation policy. In 1982, Congress considered legislation that would have restricted the courts' power in this area by prohibiting federal courts from ordering, for purposes of racial integration, the busing of children more than five miles from home or ordering children to travel by bus more than 15 minutes.

Even the courts, in the view of civil rights advocates, began after 1974 to restrict the application of their own desegregation rulings. The courts had always maintained that segregation was unconstitutional if it resulted from deliberate action of state or local governments. Thus the drawing of attendance zones, the assignment of teachers and pupils, and the construction of new schools could be evidence of discrimination if these acts perpetuated patterns of segregation.

While intentional (de jure) segregation was unconstitutional, accidental (de facto) segregation—the result, for example, of residential patterns unaffected by discriminatory statutes or policies—was constitutional. In the late 1970s the Supreme Court sharpened the distinction between de jure and de facto segregation by requiring

that the discriminatory intent of a particular act be proved rather than simply inferred from the act's effects as in the past. When in 1979 the Court found that the school systems of Dayton and Columbus had been intentionally segregated, it upheld court-ordered busing plans for those two Ohio cities.

However, in *Milliken v. Bradley* (1974), the Court also ruled that where segregative intent had been proved, the remedy could not extend beyond the jurisdiction guilty of the violation. Thus the courts could not impose desegregation on Detroit and its independent suburbs unless it could be shown that the city and its suburbs had acted together in drawing jurisdictional lines deliberately to exclude blacks from suburban schools. In 1978, the Court found that to have been the case in Wilmington, Del., and upheld a lower-court order merging two predominantly black Wilmington school districts with nine predominantly white suburban districts. But in 1980 the Court rejected the argument that patterns of residential segregation in Atlanta and its suburbs had been encouraged by government policies and refused to order the busing of students between black Atlanta school districts and white suburban districts. By requiring proof of segregative intent before ordering desegregation across jurisdictional lines, the Supreme Court effectively prevented metropolitan-area desegregation, without which significant desegregation in many central cities was virtually impossible.

Finally, once a school district had been desegregated, according to the Supreme Court, no further action need be taken if its schools became resegregated as a result of changing residential patterns. Resegregation in such circumstances would represent accidental or de facto segregation, which is constitutionally permissible, not intentional or de jure segregation, which is not.

Mandatory school busing ended in the mid-1990s. Thereafter school districts devised a variety of race-conscious pupil-assignment plans to achieve integration, but these were uniformly rejected by the courts, which insisted that school choice be entirely voluntary. Districts then experimented with magnet schools, subsidized transportation, and other devices to encourage voluntary integration, but with limited success. In the few cities where they were tried, *school vouchers tended to produce integrated classrooms.

But the trend nationally was toward resegregation. A Harvard University study released in July 2000 reported that 70 percent of black children attended predominantly minority schools in the 1998–99 academic year, up from 66 percent in 1991–92 and 63 percent in 1980–81. In 2000, more than a third of all black students attended schools in which 90 percent of the students were non-white. The trend was attributed to court decisions limiting and revising desegregation orders, declining federal support for desegregation, demographic changes, and residential segregation.

SCHOOL PRAYER. See *Church-State Relations.

SCHOOL VOUCHERS, device by which public school students could take their share of state public school expenditures and apply it toward tuition in a private school. The idea was advanced in 1955 by conservative Nobel Prize–winning economist Milton Friedman as a free-market way to improve education by stimulating competition among schools for students. It also proved attractive as a means of permitting inner-city students to escape their failing public schools.

The value of a school voucher never approached the tuition of elite private schools, but many church-subsidized private schools arose to take advantage of the voucher system. Because programs were small, there was little evidence that students in those private schools achieved more than those who remained in the public schools or that "competition" was improving the public schools. And critics argued that vouchers siphoned off resources as well as the better students from the already underfunded public schools.

In 2002, voucher programs were operating in Cleveland, Milwaukee, and Florida. More than 30 states had rejected them. The constitutionality of voucher programs had been challenged under both federal and state constitutions. The question of their constitutionality under the U.S. Constitution was resolved by the *Rehnquist Court in *Zelman v. Simmons-Harris* (2002), which upheld the Cleveland program against an Establishment Clause challenge although 96 percent of the participating students attended religious schools (see *Church-State Relations).

SCOPES TRIAL (July 10–21, 1925), trial of high-school teacher John Thomas Scopes for teaching evolution in violation of Tennessee law. The notorious "monkey trial," held in a circus atmosphere at Dayton, Tenn., attracted national attention. Chicago attorney Clarence Darrow led the defense team, while statesman William Jennings Bryan, a fundamentalist Presbyterian who had been influential in the drafting of the statute, advised the prosecution. The highlight of the trial was Darrow's examination of Bryan as an expert witness on the Bible, which revealed the naïveté of Bryan's faith and his ignorance of science. Expert scientific testimony having been ruled irrelevant, the jury found Scopes guilty

and the court fined him $100. The state supreme court set aside the verdict on a technicality.

SCOTTSBORO CASE (1931–37). In March 1931, nine black youths, aged 13–20, were taken off a freight train at Scottsboro, Ala., and charged with the rape of two young white women who had shared the same boxcar. In an Alabama court, the unsupported accusations of the white women (both of whom were prostitutes, and one of whom later recanted) outweighed substantial evidence and testimony favoring the defendants. Eight were quickly convicted and condemned to death; the youngest was temporarily saved by a hung jury unable to decide between death and a prison term. Eager to exploit the case for propaganda purposes, the Communist Party, through its legal arm, the International Labor Defense, took charge and appealed the convictions. In 1932, the U.S. Supreme Court ruled that the defendants had not received adequate counsel and remanded the cases for new trials (*Powell v. Alabama*, 1932).

Haywood Patterson, the first of the "Scottsboro boys" to be retried, was again convicted and sentenced to death. But this judge set aside the verdict as unsupported by the evidence and granted a third trial. (The judge was removed from the case and defeated in his next bid for reelection.) In his third trial, Patterson was again convicted and sentenced to death, as was Clarence Norris in his second trial. Upon appeal, the U.S. Supreme Court again overturned the Alabama verdicts on the grounds that the systematic exclusion of blacks from Alabama juries had denied the youths a fair trial (*Norris v. Alabama*, 1935).

Patterson was tried for a fourth time in 1936, found guilty, and sentenced not to death but to 75 years in prison. Clarence Norris, however, was found guilty in his third trial and sentenced to death (later commuted to life imprisonment). Two other defendants were convicted of rape and sentenced to 99 and 75 years' imprisonment respectively. A fifth was convicted of assault and sentenced to 20 years. The four remaining men, after six and a half years in jail, were released (although the case against them was the same as that against the convicted men).

Patterson escaped in 1948. The other imprisoned men were paroled in 1943, 1946, and 1950.

SCOTT v. SANDFORD or **DRED SCOTT CASE** (1857), 7–2 decision of the *Taney Court. Dred Scott was a slave who had been taken (1834–38) by his owner from Missouri (a slave state) to Illinois (where slavery was prohibited by the state constitution) and then to that part of Wisconsin Territory that is now Minnesota (where slavery had been excluded by the *Missouri Compromise) before returning to Missouri. In 1846 Scott sued for his liberty on the grounds of his temporary residence in a free state and a free territory. (Until 1852, when the Missouri supreme court ruled against Scott, the established legal principle in Missouri had been "once free, always free" as a matter of interstate comity, which the Missouri court felt free to reject in those increasingly rancorous times.)

When the case came to the U.S. Supreme Court, the justices were at first inclined simply to confirm the judgment of the Missouri courts that Scott, as a resident of Missouri, was subject to the laws of that state and was therefore still a slave. Such a narrow decision would have been relatively uncontroversial. But eventually the justices decided to take advantage of the opportunity presented by this case to settle the whole issue of the extension of slavery into the territories, a complex and explosive issue that Congress had failed to resolve. Thus Chief Justice Roger B. Taney undertook to write a broad rather than a narrow decision.

In the third and briefest part of his long decision, read in the Supreme Court on Mar. 6, 1857, Taney ruled that, once Scott had returned to Missouri, his status was determined by the laws of that state. Thus Scott was still a slave, he was not entitled to sue, and the Court had no jurisdiction in the matter.

But Taney reached this point only after a long discourse on Scott's citizenship. First, he argued that Scott—and, indeed, any black person, slave or free—could not be a citizen because the Framers had excluded them from the classes of "the people" and "citizens." At the time the Constitution was written, Taney wrote, blacks "had for more than a century been regarded as beings of an inferior order . . . so far inferior that they had no rights which white men were bound to respect."

Second, Taney argued that Scott was not a citizen because he was not free, and he was not free—notwithstanding his residence in a free territory—because the Missouri Compromise, which had excluded slavery from the *Louisiana Purchase north of 36°30', had been unconstitutional: its blanket prohibition of one kind of property (slaves) violated the Due Process Clause of the Fifth Amendment. Neither Congress nor a territorial legislature could exclude slavery from a territory.

Taney's decision was accompanied by five generally concurring decisions, one partially concurring decision, and two dissents.

The Dred Scott decision unleashed a storm of controversy and ended all possibility of political compromise on the extension of slavery into the territories. Both

proslavery and antislavery factions had, in fact, desired a judicial resolution of this intractable issue and both had pledged to respect such a resolution as final. But the decision that Congress could not regulate slavery in the territories—put forward by six justices, five of whom were Southerners—threw the antislavery people into confusion. It completely undercut the *Republican Party, whose principal objective was congressional prohibition of slavery in the territories. It demolished *popular sovereignty, since a territorial legislature would also violate the Constitution if it prohibited slavery. It even raised the question whether states could exclude slavery.

The solution to the dilemma of antislavery people was suggested in the dissent of Justice Benjamin R. Curtis: once the Court had disclaimed jurisdiction in the case, Curtis argued, everything else in its decision was mere obiter dicta, collateral but nonbinding discussion. Abraham Lincoln (who saw in the decision evidence of a deliberate conspiracy to nationalize slavery) could thus assert that the decision was not "settled doctrine."

SEALING CONTROVERSIES (1892, 1911), diplomatic incidents of the Benjamin *Harrison and *Taft administrations. Having acquired the Pribilof Islands—valuable for their fur seals—with the *Alaska purchase, the United States asserted the old Russian claim to the entire **Bering Sea**. It forbade pelagic (ocean) sealing as a means of protecting the Pribilof herd, and enforced its order by seizing Canadian sealing ships. Great Britain rejected the doctrine of a closed sea, and the controversy was submitted to international arbitration in 1893. U.S. claims were rejected and compensation to Canadian sealers was ordered, although pelagic sealing was prohibited for a portion of each year within a 60-mile zone around the Pribilof Islands.

The restriction on sealing expired in 1908, whereupon unrestricted hunting soon threatened the extinction of the seal herd. In 1911, the United States, Great Britain, Russia, and Japan signed a treaty prohibiting pelagic sealing north of the 30th parallel for 15 years. The United States received a monopoly of sealing but agreed to share its profits with Great Britain and Japan.

SEATTLE GENERAL STRIKE (1919), strike called by the city's Central Labor Committee when the demand of shipyard workers for higher wages was rejected. It paralyzed the city for five days. When local unions, unsure of their objective, withdrew, the strike collapsed.

SECESSION, withdrawal of one or more states from the federal Union. Secession is not mentioned in the Constitution. The nationalists at the Federal *Constitutional Convention sought to base a powerful national government on the sovereignty of the whole people, the nation. They conceived the Union as perpetual and secession as impossible. For the descendants of the *Antifederalists, however, the nation was an abstraction compared to the living reality of their states. Despite the constitutional expositions of John Marshall, Andrew Jackson, and Daniel Webster, they continued to view the Constitution as a compact among sovereign states and the federal government as merely the agent of the states. Any state could withdraw from the compact when its interests dictated.

The ultimate right of secession was perhaps implied in the *Virginia and Kentucky Resolutions of 1798, written by James Madison and Thomas Jefferson, and certainly implied in the doctrine of *nullification formulated by John C. Calhoun, who hoped that nullification would obviate the need for secession. Secession was openly advocated in New England at the time of the *Hartford Convention. Beginning with the controversies over the extension of slavery, first in the *Missouri Compromise but especially after the Mexican War, the appeal to secession became ever more frequent and strident in the Southern states. In the North there were many people prepared to accept Southern secession as a solution to the intractable problem of slavery.

Shortly after the election of Abraham Lincoln, a South Carolina convention voted (Dec. 20, 1860) to secede. Six other states of the Deep South quickly followed—Mississippi (Jan. 9, 1861), Florida (Jan. 10), Alabama (Jan. 11), Georgia (Jan. 19), Louisiana (Jan. 26), and Texas (Feb. 1)—sometimes, in the great excitement, overriding substantial unionist sentiment. At Montgomery, Ala., in February 1861 delegates from these states founded the *Confederate States of America. After the firing on *Fort Sumter and Lincoln's call for volunteers (which the South interpreted as coercion), four more states seceded and adhered to the Confederacy—Virginia (Apr. 17), Arkansas (May 6), Tennessee (May 7), and North Carolina (May 20).

In his first inaugural address (see *Lincoln's First Inaugural), delivered at a time (Mar. 4, 1861) when seven states had already seceded, Lincoln firmly rejected the constitutionality of secession: "[T]he Union of these States is perpetual. . . . [N]o State upon its own mere motion can lawfully get out of the Union; . . . resolves and ordinances to that effect are legally void; and . . . acts of violence, within any State, against the authority of the United States, are insurrectionary or revolutionary. . . ."

"If a minority," he reasoned, prophetically for the Confederacy, ". . . will secede rather than acquiesce [in the will of the majority], they make a precedent which in turn will divide and ruin them. . . . Plainly, the central idea of secession is the essence of anarchy."

Union victory in the Civil War put an end to secession as an issue in American constitutional thought.

SECOND AMENDMENT. See *Bill of Rights.

SECOND NEW DEAL, the reform stage of the *New Deal, announced by Pres. Franklin Roosevelt in his annual message to Congress on Jan. 4, 1935. Exasperated by the unreasoning hostility of business to the New Deal, and concerned by disaffection on the left among progressives and the followers of demagogues Charles Coughlin, Huey Long, and Charles Townsend, Roosevelt proposed a radical "turn to the left." Major achievements of the Second New Deal were the establishment of the Works Progress Administration, the Resettlement Administration, the Rural Electrification Administration, the National Youth Administration, and the passage of the National Labor Relations Act, the Social Security Act, and the Revenue Act of 1935, which steeply raised taxes on wealthy individuals and large corporations.

SECTIONALISM. Climate, physiography, soil, and ecology demarcate distinct regions of the United States. While these regions are complementary and interdependent, their separate economic interests have always determined their politics. The history of the United States before the Civil War is largely that of the struggle among its three major regions—Northeast, Northwest, and South—for economic advantage over such issues as *tariffs, *internal improvements, and the disposition of *public lands. On several occasions these struggles were so severe as to threaten the dissolution of the Union, which finally happened in 1861. After the Civil War, when a national identity submerged regional identities, sectional economic interests continued to affect national politics and require carefully adjusted compromises.

Another sectional determinant may be said to be distance from the East and West coasts, with their varied connections with Europe and Asia respectively. The isolationist strain in American politics tends to be strongest in the central states.

SEDITION ACT (1918). See *Espionage Act.

SELECTIVE SERVICE. See *Conscription or Draft.

SELMA-TO-MONTGOMERY MARCH (1965), incident in the *civil rights movement. Selma, Ala., had been the target of a faltering voter-registration drive conducted by the *Student Nonviolent Coordinating Committee (SNCC) when civil rights leader Martin Luther King Jr. selected it for his 1965 campaign. To arouse national support for federal voting rights legislation, he intended to provoke two notoriously violent lawmen, county sheriff Jim Clark and state police commander Al Lingo, into typically brutal responses to his nonviolent demonstrations. Beginning on Monday, Jan. 18, 1965, daily marches to the county courthouse by would-be registrants were blocked by Clark's deputies and the marchers beaten, tortured with cattle prods, and jailed in full view of television news cameras.

King then determined upon a 54-mile march by blacks from Selma to the state capital, Montgomery, to petition Gov. George C. Wallace for protection for black registrants. On Sunday, Mar. 7 (while King was in Atlanta), King's associate Hosea Williams and SNCC chairman John Lewis led 600 marchers out of Selma to Highway 80. At the Edmund Pettus Bridge they were attacked by state troopers, who clubbed and gassed them and drove them back into Selma. There Sheriff Clark's deputies rioted in black neighborhoods, sending dozens more to the hospital. "Bloody Sunday," recorded by television news cameras, outraged the nation.

On Mar. 15—a day when demonstrators in Selma held a memorial service for James J. Reed, a white Unitarian minister from Boston who had been clubbed to death by white citizens of Selma—Pres. Lyndon Johnson, before a joint session of Congress, solemnly committed himself to a far-reaching Voting Rights Act. Two days later in Alabama, federal judge Frank Johnson rejected Governor Wallace's request for an injunction against the Selma–Montgomery march and forbade state and local officials to interfere with it. When Wallace protested that the state could not afford to protect the marchers, President Johnson happily federalized the Alabama National Guard.

On Sunday, Mar. 21, several thousand marchers, black and white, led by King, left Selma for Montgomery along Highway 80, accompanied by an assistant U.S. attorney general and protected by federal marshals and National Guard troops. The marchers entered Montgomery on Thursday, Mar. 25, their numbers now swollen to 25,000—including the nation's civil rights leaders and a bevy of celebrity entertainers—and rallied before the state capitol. King prophesied more suffering ahead, "but it will not be long," he promised. "Not long, because the arc of the moral universe . . . bends toward justice. Not long, 'cause mine eyes have seen the glory of the coming of the Lord."

That night, as the marchers dispersed and made their way home, a Detroit housewife named Viola Liuzzo, who was ferrying marchers back to Selma along Highway 80, was murdered by Klansmen.

SEMINOLE WARS, two wars (1818, 1835–42) between the United States and the Seminole Indians of Florida and a third (1855–58) in which Florida attempted to expel the surviving Seminoles from the state.

The first Seminole war (1818) resulted from the inability of Spain to keep peace on the Florida-Georgia border. Seminole Indians crossed the border to raid settlements in Georgia, Georgia slaves escaped across it, and smugglers and privateers made St. Amelia Island, off the Atlantic coast, their headquarters. When, in November 1817, Americans and Seminoles committed reciprocal atrocities on the border, Pres. James Monroe ordered Gen. Andrew Jackson to pacify the area—well knowing and sharing Jackson's desire to expel Spain from North America.

In March 1818, Jackson—with 3,000 regulars and Tennessee volunteers and 2,000 Creek Indian allies, but no declaration of war—invaded Florida along the Apalachicola River and drove the panicked Seminoles before him for 150 miles to the Suwanee River, destroying their villages and seizing their cattle and food stores. At St. Marks, a Spanish post, he executed two British citizens who had befriended the Indians. Then, reversing direction, he marched to Pensacola, another Spanish post, captured the city, expelled the Spanish authorities, and proclaimed an American occupation until such time as Spain put a military force in Florida capable of maintaining order.

In Washington, President Monroe and his cabinet faced the possibility of war with Spain and Great Britain because of Jackson's high-handed actions. Secretary of War John C. Calhoun and two other cabinet members urged censure of Jackson; the general's only defender was Secretary of State John Quincy Adams, who realized that Jackson's campaign would induce Spain to cede Florida to the United States. A report of the House Committee on Military Affairs in January 1819 recommended a censure, but the House rejected it. A similar report by a Senate committee was not acted upon due to the successful conclusion of the *Adams-Onís Treaty.

The second Seminole war (1835–42) resulted from an 1832 removal treaty (see *Indian Removal) that a majority of the tribe, under the leadership of Osceola, rejected as fraudulent. The Seminoles waged inconclusive guerrilla warfare against the U.S. army for six years, although Osceola was seized at a parley and died soon after in imprisonment. Captured and surrendered Seminoles were carried west to *Indian Territory, but a number remained in Florida in the inaccessible Everglades.

In the third Seminole war (1855–58), Florida attempted to expel the few hundred Seminoles still in the state. In 1858 about half of the surviving Seminoles were sent west.

SENECA FALLS CONVENTION (July 19–20, 1848), first public meeting of the *women's rights movement. On July 13, 1848, five women gathered around a tea table in Waterloo, N.Y. All were married and mothers, and all were indignant at what they perceived as the subjugation and degradation of women by men. Prompted by the passion of one of their number, Elizabeth Cady Stanton, the five resolved to call a "convention to discuss the social, civil, and religious condition and rights of women." Arrangements were quickly made, and on July 19 and 20 some 300 women and men assembled in the Wesleyan Methodist Chapel in Seneca Falls, N.Y.

Stanton had prepared a Declaration of Sentiments that the convention adopted. Modeled on the Declaration of Independence, it substituted *man* for *George III* and matched Jefferson's list of colonial grievances with a list of women's grievances. "We hold these truths to be self-evident," Stanton wrote, "that all men and women are created equal. . . . The history of mankind is a history of repeated injuries and usurpations on the part of man toward woman, having in direct object the establishment of an absolute tyranny over her." The last of the list of grievances began: "He has never permitted her to exercise her inalienable right to the elective franchise." The Declaration of Sentiments was followed by ten Resolves, including: "*Resolved*, that it is the duty of the women of this country to secure to themselves their sacred right to the elective franchise," which Stanton carried over the opposition of some of her own supporters. More than 100 men and women signed the Declaration of Sentiments and Resolves.

The first women's rights convention was reported by newspapers in New York, Philadelphia, and elsewhere with ridicule and condemnation. But conventions soon followed, in Rochester, N.Y., and then in other states. In 1850 national women's rights conventions began to meet annually in different cities (see *Stanton and Anthony).

SERVICEMEN'S READJUSTMENT ACT (1944). See *G.I. Bill of Rights or Servicemen's Readjustment Act.

SETTLEMENT HOUSES. Originally educational facilities to acquaint social workers with the lives of the poor, they quickly became providers of social services and advocates of social reform. Of some 400 settlement houses established by 1910, the most famous were Chicago's Hull House headed by Jane Addams, New York's Henry Street Settlement headed by Lillian Wald, and Boston's South End House headed by Robert A. Woods. They contributed significantly to the Americanization of immigrants. By lobbying in state legislatures, they helped obtain laws improving housing, health, and safety for slum dwellers.

SEVEN DAYS' BATTLES. See *Peninsula Campaign.

SEVENTEENTH AMENDMENT (1913), constitutional amendment providing for the popular election of U.S. senators rather than their election by state legislatures.

SEVENTH AMENDMENT. See *Bill of Rights.

SEXUAL HARASSMENT. Title VII of the *Civil Rights Act of 1964 prohibits discrimination in employment on the basis of gender as well as race, color, religion, and national origin. In 1976 a U.S. circuit court found that sexual harassment in the workplace—the demand for sexual favors as a condition of employment or promotion—"created an artificial barrier to employment which was placed before one gender and not another." The Equal Employment Opportunity Commission, which enforces Title VII, thereupon defined two types of sexual harassment: quid pro quo harassment, in which the victim's cooperation in unwanted sex is a factor in employment decisions, and "hostile environment" harassment, in which unwanted sexual advances create an intimidating or abusive workplace environment.

Sexual harassment cases reached the U.S. Supreme Court in 1986 and 1993. The number of complaints grew rapidly after the 1991 televised Senate hearings on the nomination of Clarence Thomas to the Supreme Court, during which Thomas was accused of having sexually harassed a former female colleague (see *Thomas Nomination). In 1998 the Court decided four sexual harassment cases.

SHARE OUR WEALTH SOCIETY (1934–35), national organization created by Louisiana senator Huey P. Long, presumably as the vehicle to carry him to the presidency in 1936 or 1940. The society consisted of autonomous local clubs promoting Long's Share Our Wealth Plan, which would end the *Great Depression by redistributing the nation's wealth. The plan called for a sharply graduated income tax that would effectively limit personal fortunes to a few million dollars and a confiscatory inheritance tax. The revenues from these taxes would be used to provide every American family with a grant of $5,000 toward a "homestead" (a house, furnishings, car) and a guaranteed annual income of at least $2,500.

The growth of the Share Our Wealth Society during 1934–35—to 27,000 clubs claiming 8 million members—greatly alarmed the Franklin *Roosevelt administration, which faced an uncertain election in 1936. Long's society, however, had no national structure, and when Long was assassinated in September 1935 (see *Long Assassination) the society collapsed and disappeared.

SHARPSBURG. See *Antietam or Sharpsburg.

SHAYS'S REBELLION (1786–87), protest movement of western Massachusetts farmers burdened by debt and taxes and facing imprisonment and forfeiture of their property. Many of the farmers were veterans of the *Revolutionary War; one of their leaders was Daniel Shays, formerly a captain in the *Continental Army. Their petitions for relief having been ignored, and in many cases unable to vote, the farmers forcibly prevented the convening of the courts that would foreclose their property. Gov. James Bowdoin dispatched a military force under Gen. Benjamin Lincoln that dispersed the farmers. Shays and other leaders were sentenced to death but eventually pardoned.

The rebellion caused panic and outrage among conservatives in Boston, some of whom had been firebrands in the Revolution. One of the judges prevented from holding court was Artemas Ward, who had commanded Massachusetts troops at the siege of Boston. General Lincoln was a hero of Saratoga and Yorktown. The violently antifarmer president of the state senate was Samuel Adams, onetime radical patriot.

In London, Abigail Adams wrote excitedly to the Adamses' friend Thomas Jefferson in Paris: "Ignorant, wrestless desperadoes, without conscience or principals, have led a deluded multitude to follow their standard, under pretence of grievances which have no existence but in their imaginations." Jefferson was unperturbed. To another correspondent he wrote: "What signify a few lives lost . . . ? The tree of liberty must be refreshed from time to time with the blood of patriots and tyrants. It is it's natural manure."

Shays's Rebellion persuaded many national-minded politicians that a central government more effective than that provided by the *Articles of Confederation was necessary to halt the country's descent into anarchy.

SHERMAN ANTITRUST ACT (1890), legislation of the Benjamin *Harrison administration. Many states had attempted to regulate monopolistic business practices within their borders, and the Interstate Commerce Act (1887) had sought to prevent monopolistic abuses in interstate transportation, but the Sherman Act (named for Sen. John Sherman of Ohio) was the first attempt at national regulation of *trusts, combinations, and monopolies. It was passed by large bipartisan majorities in both houses of Congress.

The act's first section read: "Every contract, combination in the form of a trust or otherwise, or conspiracy, in restraint of trade or commerce among the several states, or with foreign nations, is hereby declared illegal." Its second section outlawed monopolies and conspiracies to monopolize. Later, critics found in its vague and ambiguous language—for example, the act failed to define such terms as *trust, combination,* and *restraint*—evidence that Congress had no serious intention of curbing the trusts, but the act's language was consistent with the language of the common law and would be interpreted by the courts. Contemporaries believed that Congress had acted in good faith.

Understaffed and underfunded, the U.S. Department of Justice initiated only seven antitrust cases during the Harrison administration, eight during the second *Cleveland administration, and three during the *McKinley administration. (Four of these 18 were against labor unions.) In *United States v. E. C. Knight Co. (1895), the U.S. Supreme Court distinguished between manufacturing and commerce, limiting the act's reach to the latter.

More vigorous prosecutions during the Theodore *Roosevelt and *Taft administrations succeeded in dissolving some trusts only to have them reappear in new form. In 1911 the Supreme Court further weakened the act by adopting the "rule of reason," finding that only "unreasonable" restraint of trade was forbidden.

The *Clayton Antitrust Act and the *Federal Trade Commission Act, both in 1914, supplemented the Sherman Act, which was frequently employed during the Franklin *Roosevelt administration (see *Trust-Busting).

SHERMAN SILVER PURCHASE ACT (1890), legislation of the Benjamin *Harrison administration, obtained by "silverite" lawmakers in exchange for their support of the *McKinley Tariff. Repealing the *Bland-Allison Act (1878), the act required the government to purchase 4.5 million ounces of silver (now valued at 20 to 1 of gold) per month, at market prices, using new Treasury certificates. Legal tender, these certificates were redeemable in either gold or silver as the Treasury preferred. Anxiety about U.S. monetary policy caused foreigners and Americans alike to convert paper and silver money to gold. The drain on U.S. gold reserves contributed to the *Panic of 1893, which repeal of the Sherman Silver Purchase Act failed to check.

SHERMAN'S MARCH THROUGH GEORGIA

(November–December 1864), episode in the *Civil War. Occupying Atlanta on Sept. 2, 1864 (see *Atlanta Campaign), Union general William T. Sherman found himself at the end of a line of supply stretching back to Chattanooga and from there all the way to Louisville. Licking his wounds in Alabama was Confederate general John Bell Hood, certain to exploit Sherman's vulnerability.

To accept a defensive posture at this point, Sherman reasoned, would be costly, unprofitable, and destructive of his army's high morale. Instead, he proposed to his chief, Gen. Ulysses S. Grant, that he resume the offensive, taking his army through Georgia to the sea and then north through South Carolina and North Carolina into Virginia. "If we can march a well-appointed army right through [Jefferson Davis's] territory, it is a demonstration to the world, foreign and domestic, that we have a power which Davis cannot resist. . . . I can make the march, and make Georgia howl!" Hesitantly, Grant and President Lincoln approved.

After placing Gen. George H. Thomas in Tennessee with 60,000 men to deal with the Confederates in his rear (which Thomas did decisively at the battle of *Nashville on Dec. 15–16), Sherman left burning Atlanta on Nov. 15 with an army of 62,000 high-spirited veterans. Severing all connections to its rear and with no communication with the outside world, the army disappeared into the Georgia countryside. Four infantry corps, forming a front from 25 to 60 miles wide, cut a swath of destruction through the heart of the state, meeting little resistance. Sherman had determined to live off the country as Grant had done in Mississippi during the *Vicksburg Campaign, and now his "bummers" foraged like locusts in the well-stocked countryside, burning what the troops could not consume or carry. "My aim then," Sherman wrote later, "was to whip the rebels, to humble their pride, to follow them to their utmost recesses, and make them fear and dread us."

On Dec. 10, 285 miles from Atlanta, Sherman's army reappeared at Savannah, which was soon abandoned by its defenders. To Lincoln on Dec. 22 Sherman telegraphed: "I beg to present you, as a Christmas gift, the city of Savannah, with 150 heavy guns and . . . about 25,000 bales of cotton."

SHILOH or **PITTSBURG LANDING** (Apr. 6–7, 1862), *Civil War battle, the largest and most costly fought in the Western Theater.

Having been driven from forts Henry and Donelson and from Nashville, Confederate general Albert Sidney Johnston concentrated his forces at Corinth, Miss. Union general Ulysses S. Grant based his Army of the Tennessee around Pittsburg Landing, 12 miles north of Corinth in Tennessee, where he waited to be joined by Gen. Don Carlos Buell's Army of the Ohio before attacking the Confederates.

But Johnston struck first (Apr. 6), driving the unentrenched Federals (always offensive-minded, Grant had not prepared for defense) back to the Tennessee River. Johnston, mortally wounded, was succeeded by Gen. Pierre G. T. Beauregard, who retired that night believing the Confederates had won a great victory. But during the stormy night units of Buell's army arrived, and at daybreak on Apr. 7 Grant, now with superior numbers and fresh troops, counterattacked, driving the Confederates back to Corinth in disorder. Grant was unable to pursue.

The battle cost North and South a total of 20,000 dead and wounded, casualties far greater than any suffered previously. Since most of the Union casualties were Midwesterners, newspapers in that region demanded Grant's dismissal. To one of Grant's detractors President Lincoln said: "I cannot spare this man—he fights." The battle persuaded Grant that the rebellion would not be put down by a single decisive victory but would require "complete conquest."

SILENT SPRING (1962), book by Rachel Carson, called one of the most influential books of the 20th century and credited with the launching of the environmental movement (see *Environmentalism). Carson described the poisoning by indiscriminately used chemical pesticides of water, soil, wildlife, and man himself, with potentially catastrophic effect on the infinitely complex balance of nature.

"Along with the possibility of the extinction of mankind by nuclear war," she warned, "the central problem of our age has therefore become the contamination of man's total environment with such substances of incredible potential for harm—substances that accumulate in the tissues of plants and animals and even penetrate the germ cells to shatter or alter the very material of heredity upon which the shape of the future depends."

SILICON VALLEY, popular name for a 1,500-square-mile region southeast of San Francisco, Calif., embracing all of Santa Clara County and parts of three adjoining counties that became the research and development center for the U.S. electronics industry after *World War 2. Intel, IBM, Fairchild, Apple, and Xerox are among the many companies with facilities in the Valley. Stanford University is located there.

SILVER REPUBLICANS (1896), Western "silverite" delegates who, led by Sen. Henry M. Teller of Colorado, bolted the Republican convention when it adopted a gold plank in its platform and later supported William Jennings Bryan, the presidential candidate of the Democratic and People's parties.

SIMPSON CASE (1994–97). On June 12, 1994, Nicole Brown Simpson and a friend, Ronald Goldman, were found brutally stabbed to death in the affluent Brentwood section of Los Angeles. Ms. Simpson was the ex-wife of O.J. Simpson, an African-American former football player and film actor. The circumstances of the murders and copious evidence pointed to Simpson.

The ensuing trial lasted from Jan. 24 to Sept. 29, 1995. Despite a strong case, the prosecution was stymied by a defense that successfully painted the Los Angeles Police Department as racist and incompetent. On Oct. 2, a jury of nine African-Americans, one Hispanic, and two whites found Simpson not guilty. The long trial had been followed intensely throughout the country. The verdict stunned white viewers but was cheered by blacks, who saw it as revenge for many years of police abuse of minorities.

On Feb. 4, 1997, in a civil suit filed by the victims' families, a Santa Monica, Calif., jury found Simpson liable for the two deaths and awarded the families $33.5 million.

SIOUX WARS (1860–90), conflicts with the Sioux Indians in Minnesota and on the Northern Plains.

The Eastern or Santee Sioux, village farmers, had by 1860 ceded their land in southern Minnesota in exchange for reservations in the north. There they were victimized by corrupt government agents and suffered the encroachments of white settlers. In 1862, a band of Santee Sioux, led by Little Crow, devastated 200 miles of frontier and massacred over 700 whites in the **Minnesota uprising**. White militia retaliated in kind, and on Sept. 23, 1862, state troops under Col. H.H. Sibley defeated Little Crow at Wood Lake. Treaties signed in 1867 expelled the Santees from Minnesota and settled them on reservations in Nebraska and the Dakotas.

Also in the 1860s, the Teton Sioux under the Oglala chief Red Cloud, with Cheyenne and Arapaho allies, went on the warpath along the **Bozeman Trail** on the Northern Plains of Colorado, Wyoming, and Montana. This trail—mapped out by John M. Bozeman in 1862–63 and protected by forts Reno, Phil Kearny, and C.F. Smith—connected Colorado with the goldfields around Virginia City, Mont., but it passed through Indian hunting grounds reserved by treaty. The **Fetterman massacre** at Fort Kearny on Dec. 21, 1866, when the Sioux ambushed and annihilated an 80-man detachment commanded by Capt. William J. Fetterman, a novice at Indian warfare, put an end to civilian and military traffic on the trail. In a peace treaty signed with the Sioux in 1868, the Bozeman Trail and the forts protecting it were abandoned, while the Sioux were confined to a reservation in South Dakota with hunting privileges in the Powder River country in Montana.

The ground was laid for renewed conflict when the army failed to prevent gold seekers from trespassing on the South Dakota Sioux reservation after the discovery of gold in the Black Hills in 1875. Fighting was precipitated when the army arbitrarily tried to drive the Sioux under Sitting Bull, Crazy Horse, and Gall from the Powder River country back to their reservation in South Dakota. The fighting was marked by the battle of the *Little Bighorn, in which the Sioux and their allies under Crazy Horse wiped out the 220-man command of Lt. Col. George A. Custer. By the spring of 1877 Crazy Horse was forced to surrender while Sitting Bull escaped to Canada. By an agreement in 1876, the Teton Sioux ceded the Black Hills.

Sunk in destitution and despair, the Sioux were reinspirited in 1890 by the **Ghost Dance**, a messianic religious cult originated in Nevada by a Paiute named Wovoka that promised the return of the dead and the buffalo herds and the demise of the whites. Excitement generated by the cult—together with the recent killing of Sitting Bull—created tension between the Indians and the troops guarding them on the Pine Ridge Reservation in South Dakota. On Dec. 29, 1890, when troops of the Seventh Cavalry attempted to disarm a band of Sioux on Wounded Knee Creek, fighting broke out and quickly intensified. The **Wounded Knee massacre** resulted in 146 Indian dead (including women and children) and 51 wounded; the army suffered 25 dead and 39 wounded. It was the final event in the centuries-long Indian wars.

SIT-DOWN STRIKES (1936–37), labor tactic in which strikers remained in their factories. It was successfully employed (Dec. 30, 1936–Feb. 11, 1937) at a Chevrolet plant in Flint, Mich., by autoworkers seeking recognition of their union, the *United Automobile Workers, by General Motors. Sit-down strikes were then used against the Chrysler Corporation and in the rubber, glass, and textile industries. The tactic was eventually ruled illegal as a trespass on private property.

SIT-INS (1960), episode of the *civil rights movement. On Feb. 1, 1960, four freshmen from black North Carolina A&T College in Greensboro sat down at the whites-only lunch counter in the otherwise unsegregated local F. W. Woolworth store and politely waited to be served. They returned to their campus that night unserved but hailed as heroes. The next day 20 more A&T students joined them at the Woolworth lunch counter.

There had been short-lived lunch-counter sit-ins in Southern towns before, but none had precipitated a regional movement the way the Greensboro sit-in did. Within days, black students were sitting at whites-only lunch counters in drugstores, department stores, shopping malls, theaters, and drive-ins throughout North Carolina, then in Virginia and South Carolina, and soon throughout the South, the Border states, and beyond. In Northern states, sympathetic whites picketed branch stores of the chains resisting the sit-ins in the South.

Committed to nonviolence, the students—both black and white—absorbed verbal abuse and physical harassment, were often arrested while their tormentors went free, and were sometimes expelled from colleges dependent on public funding.

The sit-ins succeeded in some cities—the Greensboro Woolworth's began serving blacks in July 1960—and were brutally suppressed in others. They became, however, a major tactic in the repertory of the nonviolent antisegregation effort. And they introduced into the civil rights movement a youthful element not always deferential to their elders.

SIXTEENTH AMENDMENT (1913), constitutional amendment reversing the U.S. Supreme Court's ruling in *Pollock v. Farmers' Loan & Trust Co.* (1895) that a national income tax was unconstitutional. It authorized Congress "to lay and collect taxes on income, from whatever source derived, without apportionment among the several States, and without regard to any census or enumeration."

SIXTH AMENDMENT. See *Bill of Rights.

SKINHEADS. See *Radical Right.

SLAUGHTERHOUSE CASES (1873), 5–4 decisions of the *Chase Court virtually nullifying the federal pro-tection of the freedmen's civil rights promised by the *14th Amendment.

To protect the community's health, and using its police power in a conventional way, the state of Louisiana in 1869 granted a monopoly to a New Orleans slaughterhouse company. Other butchers sued, making the novel claim that the grant violated the Privileges and Immunities Clause (among others) of the 14th Amendment by denying their freedom to work.

Justice Samuel F. Miller rejected this claim. He distinguished between U.S. citizenship and state citizenship, and narrowly read the 14th Amendment to apply only to the privileges and immunities—that is, the civil rights—enjoyed by Americans as citizens of the United States. These included the "protection of the Federal government . . . when on the high seas or within the jurisdiction of a foreign government," the "right to peaceably assemble and petition for redress of grievances, the privilege of the writ of habeas corpus . . . [and the] right to use the navigable waters of the states. . . ."

All other privileges and immunities Americans enjoyed as citizens of states. "[B]eyond the very few express limitations which the Federal Constitution impose[s] upon the states—such, for instance, as the prohibition against *ex post facto* laws, bills of attainder, and laws impairing the obligation of contracts . . . , the entire domain of the privileges and immunities of citizens of the states . . . [lies] within the constitutional and legislative power of the states, and without that of the Federal government." The 14th Amendment, he asserted, was never "intended to bring within the power of Congress the entire domain of civil rights, heretofore belonging exclusively to the states."

SLAVE CODES. See *Slavery.

SLAVE POWER CONSPIRACY, alleged Southern plot to establish slavery nationwide through its control of the presidency, Congress, and the Supreme Court. Proof of the conspiracy, believed in by *abolitionists, lay in a succession of events favorable to slavery: the annexation of Texas (see *Texas Annexation); the *Mexican War; the Fugitive Slave Act of 1850 (see *Fugitive Slave Laws); the *Kansas-Nebraska Act; and the Dred Scott decision (see *Scott v. Sandford).

The mirror image of the slave power conspiracy was the South's conviction that abolitionists intended to raise a slave insurrection or even invade the South. Some Southerners connected the Nat Turner insurrection (see

*Slave Revolts) with the publication of the first issue of William Lloyd Garrison's *Liberator*. John Brown's raid on Harpers Ferry (see *Brown's Career) was widely taken as proof of abolitionists' intentions.

SLAVE REVOLTS. After the sanguinary slave revolt in Haiti in the 1790s, the dread of slave insurrections never ceased to haunt the South. Although slave codes restricted the freedom of blacks so severely as to make concerted action almost impossible, one historian counted some 200 insurrectionary incidents—North and South, actual or abortive—from colonial days to the Civil War. In the 19th century, three were significant enough to be attached to the names of their perpetrators.

In 1800 **Gabriel Prosser**, a Richmond blacksmith, and his brother Martin, a preacher, assembled slaves in the Richmond neighborhood for an attack on the city, in which they planned to kill all the whites except Quakers and Methodists. A storm prevented the attack and dispersed the rebels.

In 1822 **Denmark Vesey**, a free black carpenter, organized Charleston servants and rural slaves for an attack on that city. The plot was betrayed and Vesey and 34 followers were hanged.

In 1831 **Nat Turner**, a slave preacher, with as many as 80 followers, moved for 12 hours from farm to farm in Southampton County, Va., murdering 55 whites, chiefly women and children because the men were attending a religious revival. The insurrection was suppressed by militia, but in a reign of terror vigilantes continued to kill blacks indiscriminately. The most serious uprising in the history of American slavery, it led to stricter slave codes and put an end to abolitionist sentiment in the South.

News of the Harpers Ferry raid (see *Brown's Career) in October 1859 alarmed and frightened the South, but no slaves rose to follow John Brown.

SLAVERY. Introduced into the American colonies at Jamestown, Va., in 1619, African laborers were at first treated little differently from white *indentured servants. By the end of the 18th century, however, African servants had been legally defined as personal property (chattel), their servitude fixed for life, and their color made a badge of degradation—the hallmarks of the American slavery system. During the *American Revolution, slavery was ended in all the Northern states (where it was not economically important). Nevertheless, fortunes continued to be made by Massachusetts and Rhode Island merchants in the *slave trade.

In the Southern *slave states, where climate, soil, and topography favored the large-scale production of staple export crops (cotton, tobacco, sugar, rice, hemp, and indigo), slavery was considered indispensable. Although its profitability declined in the older colonies with the exhaustion of the soil, slavery received a new lease on life with the invention of the *cotton gin, the opening of western lands ideally suited for cotton growing, and a rising world demand for cotton. Cotton was king, Southerners said. Cotton production increased from 335,000 bales in 1820 to 3.8 million bales in 1860, when it constituted two-thirds of all U.S. exports. Slavery was highly profitable, as evidenced by the steady rise in the price of slaves. Northern bankers, merchants, manufacturers, and shipowners participated in Southern prosperity, largely indifferent to the fact that it rested on slave labor.

From the Revolution to the eve of the Civil War, the slave population grew from 500,000 to 4 million. Most of this growth was natural increase, the older states of the Upper South exporting their surplus slaves to the Gulf Coast states in a vigorous domestic slave trade. In 1860, blacks constituted more than 50 percent of the populations of South Carolina and Mississippi and more than 40 percent of the populations of Alabama, Florida, Georgia, Louisiana, and Virginia (exclusive of West Virginia).

The great majority of slaves were employed in agriculture, chiefly cotton growing. On large plantations (half of all slaves belonged to planters who owned 50 or more), field slaves, both men and women, labored in gangs from dawn to dusk five and a half or six days a week. Strict discipline was enforced by white or black overseers. On smaller farms, owners and slaves worked side by side but separated at night. Sundays were free, and there were holidays at Christmas, Good Friday, Independence Day, and after the harvest. The slaves' monotonous diet consisted chiefly of corn meal and pork. Housing was usually primitive, health conditions deplorable, infant mortality high, and life expectancy short.

A small number of slaves were employed in their masters' houses as domestics. To some extent these shared the masters' lifestyle, and ties of intimacy and affection sometimes developed between blacks and whites.

Perhaps 10 percent of slaves were hired out as factory workers or artisans in urban areas; these lived like *free blacks, except that their wages belonged to their owners.

Despite ceaseless propaganda (and some genuine testimony) about benevolent masters and contented slaves, black resistance to slavery was universal. During the Revolutionary War many slaves escaped to the British. Afterward, a relatively small number of slaves escaped to freedom in the North or Canada, some assisted by the *underground railroad. Others, incapable of armed uprising, resisted subtly by malingering, pretended incompetence, self-mutilation, and sabotage. A distinctive black culture, combining African traditions and American experience, was radically subversive of the Southern system. In the Civil War, thousands of slaves fled to Union lines. Those who remained on plantations and farms often became ungovernable in the absence of white masters.

Although only a quarter of Southern families owned slaves, all classes joined in defending slavery even in defiance of their own economic interests. Slavery was defended as being ordained by both nature and Scripture and as beneficial to the blacks. Most Southerners could conceive of no other way the two races could coexist.

Believing that blacks were an inferior race, phobic about sexual contact between black men and white women, and dreading *slave revolts, Southern legislatures enacted **slave codes** that enforced the subordination of blacks. These variously prohibited the education of blacks, forbade their marriages, restricted their movements, and denied them weapons. Slave status was inherited from the mother; no amount of white blood could affect it, nor could conversion to Christianity. Infractions of the slave codes were punished severely by imprisonment, flogging, or "selling south"—the last involving separation from family and community and consignment to harsher conditions in the Deep South. Crueler punishments such as brandings, mutilations, and death were prohibited or constrained by consideration of the slave's monetary value. The unremitting need to control the black population resulted in a virtual reign of terror over blacks and a culture of stultifying orthodoxy for whites.

By threatening to stay outside the Union, the slave states won important concessions in the Federal *Constitutional Convention: slaves were to be counted in the apportionment of representation in the House of Representatives, a slave counting as three-fifths of a white person; the importation of slaves was allowed to continue for another 20 years (until 1808); and a fugitive slave clause recognized the obligation of the free states to return escaped slaves to their masters.

In 1787, the Confederation Congress prohibited slavery in the *Northwest Territory, but under the Constitution the Southern states prevented any further restrictions on the preservation and spread of slavery. The admission of each new free state was balanced by the admission of a slave state (see *Missouri Compromise; *Compromise of 1850); *fugitive slave laws forcefully asserted the property rights of slave owners; the annexations of Texas and California opened the possibility of unlimited extension of slavery west and south.

After 1850 the slave states constituted a minority within the Union. Their defensiveness, perceived in the North as the arrogance of the "slave power," provoked increasing hostility to slavery (see *Abolitionists). That hostility was solidified by the stringent Fugitive Slave Act of 1850, publication of Harriet Beecher Stowe's *Uncle Tom's Cabin in 1853, passage of the *Kansas-Nebraska Act in 1854, and the Dred Scott decision (see *Scott v. Sandford) in 1857 (see *Slave Power Conspiracy). After 1854, the new *Republican Party, committed to preventing the further spread of slavery into western territories, quickly became the dominant party in the North. The election of Republican Abraham Lincoln in 1860—following upon John Brown's attempted slave insurrection at Harpers Ferry, Va., in 1859 (see *Brown's Career)—precipitated the *secession of a number of slave states and led quickly to the Civil War. During the war, many slaves liberated themselves by fleeing to Union lines. The *Emancipation Proclamation (1863) theoretically freed the slaves in states still in rebellion and made emancipation a war aim of the Union. Slavery was formally ended with ratification of the *13th Amendment.

SLAVE STATES. At the start of the *American Revolution, slavery was legal in all 13 colonies. Between 1774 and 1804, its immediate or gradual abolition was accomplished in seven Northeastern states—Rhode Island (1774), Pennsylvania (1780), Massachusetts (1781), New Hampshire (1781), Connecticut (1784), New York (1799), and New Jersey (1804)—where it was not economically important. It persisted in six of the original states—Delaware, Georgia, Maryland, North Carolina, South Carolina, and Virginia. By the Ordinance of 1787, the Confederation Congress prohibited slavery in the *Northwest Territory; there was no comparable prohibition in the Southwest.

By 1796, the admission of Vermont (1791) as a free state and of Kentucky (1792) and Tennessee (1796) as slave states had achieved a balance of eight slave and eight free states, assuring the equal representation of these blocs in the U.S. Senate although not in the U.S. House of Representatives. This balance was roughly preserved for 50 years, the admission of a free state being soon followed by that of a slave state. In 1848, the two blocs were balanced at 15 each; the admission of California (1850), Minnesota (1858), and Oregon (1859) raised the total of free states on the eve of the Civil War to 18.

In 1860–61, 11 slave states—South Carolina, Mississippi, Florida, Alabama, Georgia, Louisiana, Texas,

Arkansas, North Carolina, Virginia, and Tennessee—seceded from the Union and formed the *Confederate States of America. Four slave states—Delaware, Maryland, Kentucky, and Missouri—remained in the Union.

SLAVE TRADE. The Atlantic slave trade was inaugurated in the 15th century by Portuguese explorers who carried African captives back to Portugal and Spain. In the 16th century, Portuguese, French, Dutch, Danish, Swedish, Prussian, and English ships began carrying Africans to the West Indies, Brazil, and the Spanish possessions in America. A Dutch ship brought the first Africans to Virginia in 1619 (see *Slavery). In the 18th century, British and colonial American ships dominated the slave trade. By the time the trade was legally prohibited in the 19th century, as many as 15 million Africans had been uprooted, about half a million carried to North America.

American slavers—chiefly based in Rhode Island and Massachusetts—customarily imported molasses from the West Indies, converted it into rum, exchanged the rum and other trading goods for slaves on the West African coast, and brought the slaves to the West Indies or to South Carolina. This was the famous **triangular trade**, each leg of which was profitable. The westward voyage across the Atlantic was the notorious **middle passage**, during which—despite the slavers' interest in preserving the lives of their cargoes—as many as 50 percent of the captives died.

As a concession to the Southern states, the U.S. Constitution, adopted in 1788, permitted the African slave trade to continue for another 20 years. Great Britain prohibited the slave trade for its nationals in 1807, the United States in 1808. By then slavery had been abolished in the Northern states, and the importation of slaves was prohibited in most of the Southern states. Nevertheless, thousands of slaves continued to be imported illegally every year. Joint Anglo-American naval patrols off the African coast proved ineffective, as did a U.S. act in 1820 that made the slave trade piracy punishable by death—Southern juries refused to convict captured slavers.

The legal end of the African slave trade coincided with the opening of extensive new cotton lands in the U.S. Southwest. The existing slave population of about 1 million was inadequate to meet the growing demand for labor in this region. As a result, the price of slaves rose steadily and a brisk domestic slave trade began. Natural increase of the slave populations in the Atlantic and *Border states, together with declining agriculture there, enabled those states to export their surplus slaves, first to Alabama, Mississippi, and Louisiana, then, in the 1850s, to Arkansas and Texas. Virginia, South Carolina, North Carolina, Maryland, and Kentucky were the principal exporters.

Bought on speculation by despised traders (genteel planters in the old states were embarrassed by the trade), the slaves were transported by coastal vessel, by flatboat and steamer on inland rivers, but chiefly by foot in long, shackled coffles along dusty roads. In the Deep South, the trader sold them by whatever means he could. Traders were not scrupulous to preserve families or to admit that some slaves were troublemakers or diseased. The federal government made little effort to regulate this interstate commerce, although in 1850 it ended the slave trade in the District of Columbia.

In the late 1850s, a continued labor shortage in the South and high prices for slaves prompted some Southerners to advocate reopening the African slave trade, which in any case was flagrantly conducted despite the prohibitions against it. Most responsible Southern leaders rejected the proposal, and the constitution of the Confederate States of America retained the prohibition on the foreign slave trade.

SMALLPOX, highly infectious viral disease, considered eradicated since 1975. Communicated in droplets discharged from the nose or mouth in face-to-face exposure, the disease, after an incubation period, produced a high fever, then a rash whose papules erupted with pus and ended in scabs deeply scarring the face and in some cases causing blindness. Infection, common in populous areas, conferred immunity. When infection occurred in a population without immunity, mortality as high as 90 percent resulted.

Such was the case with the native populations of South America, which were decimated by the smallpox, measles, influenza, and typhus carried by Spanish colonizers in the 16th century. In North America in the 17th and 18th centuries, smallpox exterminated entire Indian villages and tribes.

During a smallpox epidemic in Boston in 1721, clergyman and scientist Cotton Mather, informed of the technique of inoculation then practiced in Constantinople, persuaded Dr. Zabdiel Boylston to employ it in Boston. Boylston inoculated members of his family and some 200 other Bostonians by placing infected matter from a smallpox pustule into an open cut in the patient's skin. Although dangerous, the experiment was successful. Boylston and Mather, however, suffered popular abuse for their impiety.

At the same time, the wife of the British ambassador to the Ottoman Empire brought the technique of inoculation to London. In 1796 the English country physician Edward Jenner discovered that inoculation with matter from a lesion of the relatively benign cowpox conferred immunity to smallpox.

By the 1940s, vaccination had eliminated smallpox in the United States and other advanced countries. A campaign by the World Health Organization to eliminate it worldwide was launched in the 1960s. The world's last known case of smallpox was reported in 1975. After *World Trade Center Attack 2, concern grew over the possible weaponizing of smallpox by "rogue states" and terrorists (see *Anthrax Attack).

SMITH ACT (1940). See *Anticommunism.

SMITH-LEVER ACT (1914), legislation of the *Wilson administration intended to bring the benefits of science and business management to farmers. It provided federal subsidies for farm demonstration projects conducted by county agricultural agents under the supervision of state agricultural colleges. Although the act contributed to increased farm production, it tended to benefit most the largest and most prosperous farmers. Many small, tradition-bound farmers resisted instruction from county agents, and the poorest farmers—tenant farmers and sharecroppers—were unaffected.

SMOKE-FILLED ROOM, in political folklore, site of the selection of presidential candidates. The term was given currency in February 1920 when Harry M. Daugherty, campaign manager for Sen. Warren G. Harding of Ohio, predicted in a *New York Times* interview how his candidate would be nominated at the Republican national convention in Chicago that June. When the convention had deadlocked, he predicted, some 15 or 20 men, worn out and bleary-eyed from lack of sleep, would meet in a smoke-filled hotel room and select Harding as their nominee. Daugherty facetiously timed the event for 2:11 a.m.

His prediction was remarkably accurate. The two leading candidates for the Republican nomination, Gen. Leonard Wood and Illinois governor Frank Lowden, were deadlocked when the convention adjourned on June 11. That night, in suite 404–6 on the 13th floor of the Blackstone Hotel, which was shared by magazine publisher George Harvey and Republican National Committee chairman Will H. Hays, senators and other party leaders came and went, debating the alternatives. As names were considered and rejected, Harding's name always remained. Although recognized as a mediocrity, Harding was personally popular. The delegates realized, moreover, that no Republican had ever been elected without Ohio's electoral votes and that the Democrats seemed likely to nominate Ohio governor James M. Cox.

By 1 a.m. a consensus had formed in favor of Harding as "the most available candidate." About 2 a.m. Harvey sent for Harding and told him he would probably be nominated that day. On June 12, Harding was nominated on the tenth ballot.

SMOOT-HAWLEY TARIFF (1930). See *Hawley-Smoot Tariff.

SOCIAL DARWINISM, application to social philosophy of English naturalist Charles Darwin's theory of evolution by means of natural selection as misinterpreted by English philosopher Herbert Spencer. Spencer's epitome of Darwinism, "survival of the fittest," appeared to many Americans—including some social scientists and probably most businessmen—to provide scientific validation of the rapacious individualism of the *Gilded Age. Its leading academic exponent was William Graham Sumner, professor of political and social science at Yale. Among Sumner's many works was *What Social Classes Owe to Each Other* (1883). His answer: Nothing.

SOCIAL GOSPEL, late-19th-century movement in the Protestant churches to apply the teachings of the Bible to the social problems of the industrial age. Its leading exponent was Walter Rauschenbusch of the Rochester Theological Seminary, author of *Christianity and the Social Crisis* (1907). In 1908 the Federal Council of the Churches of Christ in America adopted a "social creed" advocating improved wages and conditions for workers, a six-day workweek, and abolition of child labor.

SOCIAL INSURANCE. See *Social Security.

SOCIALISM. Many varieties of socialism have bloomed and faded on the American scene. In the 18th and early 19th centuries, Mennonites, Shakers, Rappites, and other religious sects founded egalitarian communities in which goods were communally owned. Secular communities inspired by European socialists like Charles Fourier, Etienne Cabet, and Robert Owen flourished briefly, as did Brook Farm, founded by transcendentalists, and the Oneida Community, founded by free-love advocate John Humphrey Noyes. All of these communities were "utopian" in their withdrawal from the main society and their trust in human cooperativeness (see *Utopian Communities).

Other varieties of socialism, native to America, were the "single tax" movement inspired by Henry George's

Progress and Poverty (1879), the Nationalist movement inspired by Edward Bellamy's *Looking Backward* (1887), and the Christian Socialist movement that arose in the 1880s (see *Social Gospel). The **Socialist Party**, founded in 1901 by Eugene V. Debs, had roots in these and other native sources—including *populism—as well as European sources.

Late-19th-century European socialism was more theoretically rigorous than American socialism. In midcentury, German immigrants fleeing the failed revolutions of 1848 brought Marxism to the United States, and in 1869 they founded the American section of Marx's International Workingmen's Association, the so-called First International. Marxism professed to be "scientific," based upon laws of historical evolution. This evolution, driven by class conflict, would end eventually in the triumph of the working class, which would replace bourgeois capitalism with proletarian socialism.

Other German immigrants were followers of Ferdinand Lasalle, founder of German social democracy. Unlike Marx, who believed that the revolution of the working class must await objectively favorable conditions, Lasalle believed in political action to improve workers' condition in the present. The success of the German Social Democratic Party in obtaining social legislation favorable to labor—a success Marxists could not claim—inspired the founding of the American **Socialist Labor Party** in 1877.

Two other ideologies on the American scene may be considered here because of their anticapitalist stance and their utopian vision of a communitarian future. *Anarchism, propounded by the Russian revolutionist Mikhail Bakunin and taught in America by his German disciple, Johann Most, aimed to destroy capitalism by violence, after which human benevolence could be counted upon to create a society of liberty and equality. The anarchists founded a Revolutionary Socialist Party in 1881, but the movement never recovered from the popular revulsion inspired by the *Haymarket riot in 1886.

Syndicalism, arising in America out of the brutal labor conditions in the Far West, was represented by the *Industrial Workers of the World (IWW), founded by socialists and labor radicals in 1905. The IWW was an industrial union, aiming to organize all workers, unskilled as well as skilled, in single industries, unlike the trade unions represented by the *American Federation of Labor (AFL), which organized only skilled craftsmen across industries. But the IWW was only marginally interested in traditional union objectives such as higher wages and shorter hours. Its ultimate objective was revolution, to be achieved by strikes and violence leading to a final general strike, after which industries would be owned and run by their workers. IWW radicalism offended patriotic Americans during World War 1, and the organization faded from view.

At the start of the 20th century, many labor leaders were socialists. The socialists, aiming to reconstruct society, despised the AFL not only for its elitism but for its conservative concentration on short-term "bread-and-butter" issues. Increasingly, the labor movement left political action to the socialists. In time, the AFL accepted the necessity of industrial unions, but without the revolutionary purpose such unions had for socialist theorists. The socialist and labor movements diverged, although in the 1930s the communists began systematically to penetrate and control labor unions for political, not labor, purposes.

In 1920 socialism in the United States was represented by two political parties, the Socialist and the Socialist Labor. Both were by then Marxist, the doctrinaire Daniel De Leon having converted the latter from its original Lasallean orientation, and the democratic Debs having been gradually influenced by Marxist literature. The Socialist Labor Party remained small and militant. Although it nominated candidates for president in every election from 1872 to 1968, it never received more than 55,000 votes. The Socialist Party, on the other hand, a basically reformist party in the progressive mode, reached its high point in 1912 when Debs, its candidate for president, received nearly 1 million votes, and 1,200 Socialists were elected to public offices across the country. During the *Great Depression, its perennial candidate, Norman Thomas, received 882,000 votes in 1932. The party nominated a candidate for president for the last time in 1972.

The *Russian Revolution precipitated a realignment of the socialist movement in America. Radicals impatient with the existing socialist parties and eager to emulate the Bolsheviks with a truly revolutionary party, established two communist parties in 1919; these combined in 1921 on orders from Moscow, and the American *Communist Party remained thereafter an instrument of Soviet foreign policy. Always a small party, it was virtually suppressed in the 1950s by the prosecution of its leaders and the forging of legal constraints on its activities (see *Anticommunism).

With the demonstration of the American economy's capacity to reform itself in the *New Deal and the Great Society, and with the disappointing performance of socialist governments in many parts of the world and the success of free-market economies, the socialist movement in America diminished to insignificance.

SOCIALIST LABOR PARTY. See *Socialism.

SOCIALIST PARTY. See *Socialism.

SOCIAL SECURITY, social insurance system—in fact, an income-transfer system by which revenues derived from the better-off portions of the population are used to maintain incomes for the needy portions—established by the **Social Security Act** of 1935, a major legislative achievement of the Franklin *Roosevelt administration.

The act contained both a social insurance and a public assistance (see *Welfare) component. The **social insurance** component consisted of federal programs of old-age insurance (OAI) and a federal-state system of unemployment insurance (UI). Under both these programs, payroll taxes paid by workers and their employers were used to provide incomes for workers who had lost their jobs or retired. Benefits were based on previous contributions. Contributions to Social Security—that is, payroll taxes—began in 1937; the first benefits were paid in 1940. Beginning in 1972, Social Security benefits were increased annually in relation to the cost of living.

The authors of the Social Security Act believed that as social insurance became more fully operative, the need for welfare would disappear. And indeed the comprehensive system of social insurance that they envisioned was largely realized. Over the years, the system expanded to cover ever wider categories of risk: the original OAI became old age and survivors insurance (OASI) in 1939, old age, survivors, and disability insurance (OASDI) in 1957, and old age, survivors, disability, and hospital insurance—**Medicare**—(OASDHI) in 1965.

At the same time, coverage was extended to additional categories of persons: to the employees of industrial and commercial firms covered in 1935 were later added farm and domestic workers, self-employed businesspeople, and state and local government employees (1951), farmers and professional people, except physicians (1955–56), members of the armed forces (1957), physicians (1965), and newly hired federal employees, judges, congressmen, and other federal officeholders (1984).

Social Security is not managed like an insurance fund, with benefits paid from the interest on invested capital. Instead, benefits are paid immediately out of revenues and the surplus invested in Treasury securities—that is, loaned to the government for spending elsewhere. In the 1970s a crisis appeared on the horizon when expenditures began to exceed revenues. In 1983 the recommendations of a Social Security commission were put in

place: the Social Security payroll tax was increased, Social Security benefits were made taxable, and the age of retirement was raised to 66 for people born after 1938 and to 67 for people born after 1954.

Concern for the viability of Social Security arose again in the 1990s as the *baby boom generation approached retirement age. A commission appointed by the George W. Bush administration called in 2001 for sweeping reform of the system—including the institution of private investment accounts—to prevent eventual benefit cuts, tax increases, or massive borrowing to meet projected obligation.

SOCIAL SECURITY ACT (1935). See *New Deal; *Social Security; *Welfare.

SOIL CONSERVATION AND DOMESTIC ALLOTMENT ACT (1936). See *Farm Problem.

SOLID SOUTH, term reflecting the fact that the 11 former Confederate states voted consistently Democratic from the end of *Reconstruction until well into the 20th century. On the eve of the Civil War, Southern Whigs (see *Whig Party) moved into the proslavery *Democratic Party, although the new *Republican Party better reflected their political and economic views. Pres. Abraham Lincoln hoped that former Whigs would establish the Republican Party in the South after the war, but the *Radical Republicans' enfranchisement of the former slaves confirmed Southern Whigs in their Democratic allegiance.

The South voted solidly Democratic in presidential elections until 1928, when five Southern states went Republican rather than vote for the Catholic Democratic candidate. In the 1950s, the civil rights policies of the Democratic Party drove conservative Southern Democrats increasingly into the Republican camp. Between 1952 and 1968, Republican presidential candidates carried from three to five Southern states; in 1972, Pres. Richard M. Nixon carried them all.

SOMALIA INTERVENTION (1992–95), episode of the George W. *Bush and *Clinton administrations. In December 1992 the United States contributed 22,000 troops to a United Nations force to restore order and alleviate famine in civil war–torn Somalia. This humanitarian purpose having been accomplished, the United States withdrew some of its troops in May 1993, leaving 17,500 to participate in a UN program of political and economic reconstruction (a 1,600-man rapid response force remained under U.S. command).

UN efforts were forcibly resisted by Somali clan leaders or warlords, principally Gen. Mohammed Farah Aidid, who accused the UN of trying to recolonize the country. While UN leaders argued over policy, the U.S. rapid response force tried to disarm the Somalis and capture Aidid. In October 1993, Aidid's troops trapped a body of U.S. soldiers in Mogadishu, killed 18 of them, and dragged their bodies through the streets.

All U.S. troops were withdrawn from Somalia in March 1994 and the U.S. embassy in Mogadishu was closed in September. The remaining UN troops were evacuated in March 1995 under the protection of U.S. marines, leaving Somalia in anarchy.

SONS OF LIBERTY, intercolonial organization formed in 1763 to prevent enforcement of the *Stamp Act. Although local organizations opposing the Stamp Act sprang up spontaneously in many places, a New York City committee undertook by correspondence to create an intercolonial opposition.

Existing social, civic, and religious groups, whose members were drawn from the middle and upper levels of society, often served as nuclei for local branches of the Sons of Liberty. Seeking a mass base, these organizations recruited members from the lower classes. The respectable members of the Sons of Liberty conceived of themselves as a loyal and responsible opposition to a misguided British government. Their preferred tactics were petitions, mass meetings, parades, and electioneering. Often they were compelled to restrain the lower-class members' proneness to burning effigies, intimidating or assaulting stamp officials and Tories, tarring and feathering, and rioting.

When the Stamp Act was repealed in 1766, the Sons of Liberty disbanded, but they reappeared in many locations in 1768–70 to enforce the nonimportation agreements with which the colonists resisted the duties levied by the *Townshend Acts. By then the name Sons of Liberty was applied to all patriots who engaged in extralegal direct action.

SOUTH AMERICAN RELATIONS. U.S. sympathy for the independence movement in South America (see *Latin American Recognition) turned to disillusionment when the revolutionaries failed to establish stable and democratic republics. Thereafter U.S. attitudes toward South America varied between indifference and condescension.

Trade between the United States and South America was insignificant; that continent's commercial and cultural ties were with Europe. U.S. policy—as manifest in the *Monroe Doctrine—was chiefly aimed to prevent

European intervention in Western Hemisphere affairs, while the policy of the South American countries aimed increasingly to prevent U.S. intervention, which they deplored in the Caribbean and Central America (see *Caribbean and Central American Relations).

A series of inter-American conferences did little to enlarge commerce between the United States and South America and failed to satisfy the demand of the South American countries for guarantees of their sovereignty (see *Drago Doctrine). Growing South American hostility toward the United States was not mollified by the creation at a Buenos Aires conference in 1910 of the Pan-American Union, whose headquarters were in Washington and whose chairman was the U.S. secretary of state.

After World War 1, the United States replaced the European powers as the chief investor in South America. Pres. Franklin D. Roosevelt's *Good Neighbor Policy, which repudiated intervention in the affairs of the Western Hemisphere, greatly improved inter-American relations. All the South American states except Argentina and Chile supported the Allied cause in World War 2.

After the war, mutual interest in strengthening the inter-American system led to the Inter-American Treaty of Reciprocal Assistance, signed at Rio de Janeiro in 1947, and the creation at Bogotá in 1948 of the *Organization of American States, a regional organization under the United Nations—again based in Washington and largely funded by the United States.

The advent of the *cold war renewed U.S. security concerns in South America as in the Caribbean and Central America. U.S. preoccupation with affairs in Europe and Asia—the *Alliance for Progress was one casualty—and support for anticommunist dictatorships and military regimes in the Western Hemisphere renewed South American fears of U.S. interventionism and hegemony. In the 1990s, political and economic alliances among the South American states reflected their growing self-determination.

SOUTH CAROLINA EXPOSITION AND PROTEST (1828), document prepared anonymously by Vice Pres. John C. Calhoun at the invitation of the South Carolina legislature to justify South Carolina's revival of the doctrine of *nullification to protest the *Tariff of Abominations.

Calhoun was concerned to find a constitutional way to protect the liberty of a minority (here South Carolina or the South) against the tyranny of the majority (the federal government, dominated by an ever more populous North). The Constitution, he argued, was a compact among sovereign states. The federal government was merely the states' agent, and when it acted in violation of the Constitution any state had a right to nullify that act for itself. However, three-fourths of the states could override a nullification by amending the Constitution to specifically give the federal government the disputed power.

Calhoun believed his plan would preserve the Union from sectional differences, currently reflected in disputes over tariff legislation. Former president James Madison, both a Framer of the Constitution and an author of the *Virginia and Kentucky Resolutions, called the South Carolina Exposition a "preposterous and anarchical pretension."

SOUTH CAROLINA v. KATZENBACH (1966),

unanimous decision of the *Warren Court (one justice dissented on a minor point) upholding the *Voting Rights Act of 1965, passed to enforce the *15th Amendment's prohibition of racial discrimination in voting. The act provided novel and effective correctives to the practices of certain states that, while not necessarily unconstitutional, had the effect of denying the vote to black citizens. South Carolina challenged the act on the grounds that those provisions "exceed the powers of Congress and encroach on the area reserved to the States by the Constitution," in Chief Justice Warren's words.

"The basic test to be applied," Warren ruled, ". . . is the same as in all cases concerning the express powers of Congress with relation to the reserved powers of the States. Chief Justice Marshall [in *McCulloch v. Maryland, 1819] laid down the classic formulation, 50 years before the Fifteenth Amendment was ratified. 'Let the end be legitimate, let it be within the scope of the constitution, and all means which are appropriate, which are plainly adapted to that end, which are not prohibited, but consist with the letter and spirit of the constitution, are constitutional.' . . .

"We therefore reject South Carolina's argument that Congress may appropriately do no more than to forbid violations of the Fifteenth Amendment in general terms—that the task of fashioning specific remedies or of applying them to particular localities must necessarily be left entirely to the courts. Congress is not circumscribed by any such artificial rules. . . . In the oft-repeated words of Chief Justice Marshall, referring to another specific legislative authorization in the Constitution, 'This power, like all others vested in Congress, is complete in itself, may be exercised to its utmost extent, and acknowledges no limitations, other than are prescribed in the constitution.' "

SOUTHEAST ASIA TREATY ORGANIZATION (SEATO),

diplomatic achievement of the *Eisenhower administration. A regional defense alliance among the Philippines, Thailand, Pakistan, Australia, New Zealand, Great Britain, France, and the United States, it was established in 1954 as part of the U.S. *cold war policy of *containment (see *North Atlantic Treaty Organization; *Central Treaty Organization). The omission of India, Indonesia, Burma, and Malaysia and the organization's ineffectiveness in the *Vietnam War led to its dissolution in 1977.

SOUTHERN CHRISTIAN LEADERSHIP CONFERENCE (SCLC),

civil rights organization of Southern black ministers founded in 1957 by Martin Luther King Jr. after the *Montgomery bus boycott as the institutional vehicle for further nonviolent confrontations with segregation. SCLC conducted notable campaigns in Albany, Ga. (1961), Birmingham, Ala. (1963; see *Birmingham Campaign), and Selma, Ala. (1965; see *Selma-to-Montgomery March). In the late 1960s, King led it in campaigns for economic change in Chicago (1966) and Cleveland (1967) that culminated in his *Poor People's Campaign in 1968. After King's death, the organization faded due to the absence of strong leadership and the alienation of young activists increasingly impatient with nonviolence.

SOUTHERN MANIFESTO ON INTEGRATION

(1956), protest against the U.S. Supreme Court decision in *Brown v. Board of Education of Topeka (1954) declaring public school segregation unconstitutional. It was signed by 101 members of Congress, including all but three senators of the former Confederate states, and published in the *New York Times* on Mar. 12, 1956. It read in part:

"We regard the decision of the Supreme Court in the school cases as clear abuse of judicial power. It climaxes a trend in the Federal judiciary undertaking to legislate, in derogation of the authority of Congress, and to encroach upon the reserved rights of the states and the people.

"The original Constitution does not mention education. Neither does the Fourteenth Amendment nor any other amendment. The debates preceding the submission of the Fourteenth Amendment clearly show that there was no intent that it should affect the systems of education maintained by the states.

"The very Congress which proposed the amendment subsequently provided for segregated schools in the District of Columbia.

"When the amendment was adopted in 1868, there were thirty-seven states of the Union. Every one of the twenty-six states that had any substantial racial differences among its people either approved the operation of segregated schools already in existence or subsequently established such schools by action of the same lawmaking body which considered the Fourteenth Amendment.

"As admitted by the Supreme Court in the public school case (*Brown v. Board of Education*), the doctrine of separate but equal schools 'apparently originated in *Roberts v. City of Boston* (1849), upholding school segregation against attack as being violative of a state constitutional guarantee of equality.' This constitutional doctrine began in the North—not in the South—and it was followed not only in Massachusetts but in Connecticut, New York, Illinois, Indiana, Michigan, Minnesota, New Jersey, Ohio, Pennsylvania and other northern states until they, exercising their rights as states through the constitutional processes of local self-government, changed their school systems.

"In the case of *Plessy v. Ferguson* in 1896 the Supreme Court expressly declared that under the Fourteenth Amendment no person was denied any of his rights if the states provided separate but equal public facilities. This decision has been followed in many other cases. It is notable that the Supreme Court, speaking through Chief Justice Taft, a former President of the United States, unanimously declared in 1927 in *Lum v. Rice* that the 'separate but equal' principle is ' . . . within the discretion of the state in regulating its public schools and does not conflict with the Fourteenth Amendment.'

"This interpretation, restated time and again, became a part of the life of the people of many of the states and confirmed their habits, customs, traditions and way of life. It is founded on elemental humanity and common sense, for parents should not be deprived by Government of the right to direct the lives and education of their own children

"Though there has been no constitutional amendment or act of Congress changing this established legal principle almost a century old, the Supreme Court of the United States, with no legal basis for such action, undertook to exercise their naked judicial power and substituted their personal political and social ideas for the established law of the land. . . ."

SOUTHWEST TERRITORY (1790–96), territory created out of western land ceded to the United States by North Carolina and comprising present-day Tennessee.

SOVIET RECOGNITION (Nov. 16, 1933), diplomatic move of the Franklin "Roosevelt administration. Three Republican administrations had refused to establish diplomatic relations with the Soviet Union "so long as the present rulers of Russia persist in aims and practices in the field of international relations that are inconsistent with international friendship," as the acting secretary of state wrote on the last day of the Hoover administration. Those "aims and practices" included the repudiation of wartime debts incurred by the czarist and provisional governments of Russia, the confiscation of American property, and the conduct of revolutionary propaganda and actual subversion against capitalist states.

The new president, Franklin Roosevelt, was indifferent to Soviet debts. For him it simply defied common sense that two of the world's great powers should not have diplomatic relations. Recognition, moreover, promised to increase trade between the two countries at a time of economic depression and to send a cautionary message to Japan, which in 1932 had solidified its conquest of Manchuria from China by establishing the puppet state of Manchukuo. Fear of Japanese aggression in the Far East was the chief factor in Soviet dictator Joseph Stalin's desire for U.S. recognition.

Circumventing his own State Department, which opposed recognition, Roosevelt on Oct. 10, 1933, invited Soviet president Mikhail Kalinin to send an envoy to Washington to work out the terms of recognition directly with him. Soviet foreign minister Maxim Litvinov arrived in Washington on Nov. 7. On Nov. 16, the two announced a number of agreements, including religious freedom for Americans resident in the Soviet Union and Soviet promises "to refrain from interfering in any manner in the internal affairs of the United States" and "not to permit the formation or residence on its territory of any organization . . . which has as its aim the overthrow . . . of the political or social order . . . of the United States."

In one agreement, not then made public, Roosevelt canceled all Soviet debts owed to the United States except a sum of "not less than $75 million," which the Soviet Union agreed to pay in the form of a surcharge on the interest of any loan made by the United States to the Soviet Union. No loan was made before World War 2 and no part of the $75 million was ever paid.

SPANISH-AMERICAN WAR (1898), war between the United States and Spain for the independence of Cuba.

Background. The brutality of Spanish efforts to suppress a Cuban insurrection that began in 1895

brought both official and public opinion in America onto the side of the rebels—despite the fact that the rebels regularly destroyed American-owned sugar plantations on the island. The *yellow press—notably William Randolph Hearst's New York *Journal* and Joseph Pulitzer's New York *World*—inflamed American opinion with tales of Spanish atrocities and insults to the United States (see *De Lôme Letter).

Both Pres. Grover Cleveland and Pres. William McKinley tried to avoid war over Cuba, but the sinking of the battleship *Maine* in Havana harbor on Feb. 15, 1898 (see *Maine* Sinking) made the public's demand for war irresistible. Despite Spain's last-minute acceptance of a U.S. demand for an armistice in Cuba, President McKinley on Apr. 11 asked Congress to authorize "forcible intervention" to pacify Cuba. The recognition of Cuban independence, he said, was "impracticable and indefensible," and "forcible annexation . . . by our code of morality, would be criminal aggression." His concern was "the very serious injury to the commerce, trade, and business of our people . . . and the wanton destruction of property and devastation of the island."

Congress, however, responded on Apr. 20 with four resolutions, the first recognizing Cuban independence, the second demanding the withdrawal of Spanish armed forces, the third authorizing the president "to use the entire land and naval forces of the United States . . . to carry these resolutions into effect," and the fourth disclaiming any intention to take possession of Cuba (see *Teller Amendment). An ultimatum was sent to Spain that same day, and on Apr. 22 the United States blockaded Cuban ports. Spain declared war on Apr. 24, the United States on Apr. 25 (retroactive to Apr. 21).

Operations. The newly built U.S. *steel navy far outclassed the decrepit Spanish fleet. The Asiatic squadron, based at Hong Kong and commanded by Commodore George Dewey, had been alerted for war as early as Feb. 25 by Assistant Secretary of the Navy Theodore Roosevelt. On Apr. 30 it sailed into **Manila Bay** and the next day destroyed a Spanish fleet so weak that it had remained at anchor under the protection of shore batteries. In the Caribbean, U.S. squadrons commanded by Rear Adm. William T. Sampson and Commodore Winfield S. Schley blockaded Cuba, bottling up a Spanish force under Adm. Pascual Cervera that had slipped into Santiago harbor on May 19.

To face 150,000 Spanish troops in Cuba, Congress on Apr. 22 called for 200,000 volunteers and on Apr. 26 authorized the enlargement of the Regular Army from 30,000 men to 60,000. Regulars and volunteers

assembled in Florida, from where, amid much confusion, an expeditionary force of 17,000 commanded by Maj. Gen. William R. Shafter—poorly trained, organized, and equipped—sailed on June 14. It landed near Santiago June 22–26 and on July 1 captured El Caney and **San Juan Hill**, thereby commanding the heights above the city.

On July 3 Cervera's fleet left Santiago harbor only to be destroyed by Admiral Sampson's blockading force. Santiago and its garrison of 24,000 troops surrendered on July 17. On July 21 American troops landed on Puerto Rico without opposition. At the end of July, 10,000 American troops under Maj. Gen. Wesley Merritt landed in the Philippines and on Aug. 13, with Filipino insurgents under Emilio Aguinaldo, captured Manila.

The day before, a peace protocol had formally ended hostilities. The war had lasted 112 days and cost the United States 379 deaths in combat and more than 5,000 due to disease. It had been, Secretary of State John Hay wrote to Col. Theodore Roosevelt, "a splendid little war."

Peace. By the Treaty of Paris (Dec. 10, 1898), Spain surrendered all claims to Cuba and ceded to the United States the Philippines (for $20 million), Puerto Rico, and Guam.

SPANISH CIVIL WAR (1936–39). On July 17, 1936, Spanish troops under Gen. Francisco Franco rebelled against the newly elected republican government. Civil war quickly followed.

The Republican or Loyalist side was headed by a coalition government containing liberals and socialists. Franco's forces included such conservative elements as the army, monarchists, landowners and industrialists, fascists, and the Catholic Church. Nazi Germany and Fascist Italy quickly came to Franco's aid, the Soviet Union (to a lesser degree) to the aid of the republic. England and France refused to intervene. In time, the Soviet Union controlled the Republican side. Its "international brigades" included Abraham Lincoln and George Washington battalions in which nearly 3,000 Americans—many of them communists—served.

Except for the Catholic Church, which saw the civil war as a struggle between communism and the church, American public opinion strongly favored the Spanish republic. *Isolationists, however, insisted on American neutrality, and at the request of Pres. Franklin Roosevelt Congress imposed an embargo on arms shipments to either side in the conflict (see *Neutrality Acts). Franco's victory in March 1939 was generally seen as a major step in the fascist conquest of Europe.

SPECIAL PROSECUTOR. See *Independent Counsel or Special Prosecutor.

SPECIE CIRCULAR (1836). See *Bank War.

SPECIE RESUMPTION ACT (1875), legislation of the *Grant administration. Instinctively hostile to inflation, Pres. Ulysses S. Grant resisted the expansion of *greenbacks and in 1875 was happy to sign the Specie Resumption Act, which both reduced the amount of greenbacks in circulation and directed the secretary of the Treasury to accumulate a gold reserve sufficient to redeem greenbacks in gold beginning Jan. 1, 1879. The offer of redemption placed the United States firmly on the *gold standard.

SPOILS SYSTEM. Newly elected Pres. Andrew Jackson believed that the preceding John Quincy *Adams administration had been elitist and corrupt and that his first order of business was to "cleanse the Augean stables." His party managers, moreover, were eager to reward loyal Jacksonians with public offices.

For the first time, an incoming administration purged the federal bureaucracy, replacing (over Jackson's two terms) as many as 20 percent of the civil servants appointed by previous presidents with Jackson supporters. (Pres. Thomas Jefferson had replaced some Federalists with Republicans, but generally was content to appoint Republicans as offices became vacant until some "equilibrium" between the parties was reached.) The administration's action was defended by Sen. William Marcy of New York with the declaration: "to the victor belongs the spoil of the enemy."

Jackson sincerely believed that rotation in office was a democratic imperative and that any "plain and simple" man could administer any office. The spoils system lowered the quality of the federal bureaucracy, introduced incompetence and corruption on a scale not known before, but strengthened party discipline by providing tangible rewards for loyal service.

SPOTSYLVANIA COURT HOUSE. See *Wilderness Campaign.

SPUTNIK ALARM (1957), episode in the *Eisenhower administration. On Oct. 4, 1957, the Soviets launched the world's first orbiting satellite, *Sputnik*, a metal ball weighing 184 pounds that circled the earth every 92 minutes emitting a mysterious "beep beep." A month later, *Sputnik* 2, weighing 1,120 pounds, carried

scientific instruments and a live dog into space. On Dec. 6, a U.S. Vanguard missile, launched on national television, crashed on takeoff. The United States did not launch its first satellite until Jan. 31, 1958.

Misinterpreted as evidence of Soviet superiority in missile development, *Sputnik* caused widespread alarm in the United States not only about the state of the nation's defenses but of its educational system as well. Pres. Dwight D. Eisenhower knew from secret air reconnaissance photos (see *U-2 Affair) that the United States was well ahead of the Soviet Union in missile development and that the Soviets' emphasis on rocket thrust was dictated by their cruder and heavier warheads. His reassurances quieted the panic, but the episode led to the appointment of a President's Science Advisory Committee, the establishment of the National Aeronautics and Space Agency (NASA) to take rocket development out of the hands of competing armed services, and passage of a *National Defense Education Act.

SQUARE DEAL, slogan of the Theodore *Roosevelt administration. Journalist Lincoln Steffens recounts its origin:

" 'You don't stand for anything fundamental,' I said, and [Roosevelt] laughed. . . . I said with all the scorn I could put into it, 'All you represent is the square deal.'

" 'That's it,' he shouted, and rising to his feet, he banged the desk with his hands. 'That's my slogan: the square deal. . . . '

" . . . [H]e felt in his political sense how all kinds of people would take it as an ideal, as a sufficient ideal . . . and he was right. 'A square deal,' a phrase shot at him in reproach and criticism, he seized upon and published as his war cry. . . . ' "

SQUATTER SOVEREIGNTY. See *Popular Sovereignty or Squatter Sovereignty.

STAGGERS RAIL ACT (1980). See *Railroad Regulation.

STALWARTS AND HALF-BREEDS (1877–85), factions of the *Republican Party that appeared during the *Hayes administration. The Stalwarts opposed Hayes's efforts to conciliate the South. Such Stalwarts as senators Roscoe Conkling of New York, J. Donald Cameron of Pennsylvania, and John A. Logan of Illinois were also spoilsmen associated with powerful state and city machines and supporters of a third term for former president Ulysses S. Grant. Half-Breeds like senators James G.

Blaine of Maine, George F. Hoar of Massachusetts, and James A. Garfield of Ohio were more interested in *tariffs than in Southern policy. Neither faction cared for *civil service reform. Made distasteful by the assassination of Pres. James A. Garfield in 1881, the distinction had disappeared by the end of the *Garfield-Arthur administration.

STAMP ACT (1765), revenue measure of the British Parliament extending to the North American colonies the requirement—already in force in Britain—that all publications (newspapers, almanacs, pamphlets, broadsides), business and legal documents (licenses, contracts, invoices, receipts), and even dice and playing cards bear stamps of varying cost. The first direct tax levied by Parliament on the 13 colonies, it affected all Americans to some degree, regardless of section, class, or occupation.

Resistance was immediate and widespread, beginning with Patrick Henry's "treason" speech in the Virginia House of Burgesses. Riotous *Sons of Liberty attacked stamp agents and other supporters of British authority, burning stamps or otherwise preventing their sale. Merchants boycotted British goods.

The Massachusetts legislature issued a call for a **Stamp Act Congress**, which met in New York City in October 1765. Delegates from nine colonies adopted a Declaration of Rights and Grievances and insisted that the colonists could not be taxed without their consent.

A new ministry repealed the act in March 1766 but accompanied repeal with a **Declaratory Act**, which asserted that Parliament had "full power and authority to make laws and statutes of sufficient force and validity to bind the colonies and people of America, subjects of the crown of Great Britain, in all cases whatsoever."

STAMP ACT CONGRESS (1765). See *Stamp Act.

STANDARD OIL CO. OF NEW JERSEY v. UNITED STATES (1911), unanimous decision of the *White Court dissolving the Standard Oil Co. as a violator of the *Sherman Antitrust Act. In doing so, it adopted the common-law doctrine of the **rule of reason**, arguing that only those acts or agreements of a monopolistic nature that "unreasonably" affected interstate commerce—like those of Standard Oil—were to be construed as being in restraint of trade. Here the Court seemed to echo former president Theodore Roosevelt's distinction between good and bad trusts and disregarded the Sherman Act's prohibition of "every contract, combination . . . , or conspiracy in restraint of trade."

The rule of reason thus invoked meant that judges, not Congress, would determine when a particular re-

straint of trade was reasonable (permitted) or unreasonable (forbidden). Justice John Marshall Harlan concurred, but pointed out that the Court had, "by mere interpretation, modified the act of Congress, and deprived it of practical value as a defensive measure against the evils to be remedied." The Court's decision was, he declared, an act of "judicial legislation."

STANTON AND ANTHONY. Two uncommon and superior women, united in an intimate friendship that survived severe tests over half a century, founded and led the 19th-century woman suffrage movement (see *Women's Rights).

They met in 1851. Elizabeth Cady Stanton was then 35, married, the mother of four children (she would have three more). Born to wealth, she was vivacious, highly intelligent, self-confident, and stubbornly independent. She was also increasingly restive under the constraints of domesticity. The initiator in 1848 of the *Seneca Falls Convention and the principal author of its Declaration of Sentiments and Resolves, she had gained since then, through her articles and correspondence, a widening reputation as the philosopher of feminism. At the core of her philosophy was the belief that women as well as men were endowed with inalienable natural rights that made them men's equals. Only with the ballot, however, could women secure those rights and solve all the other ills arising from male despotism.

Susan Brownell Anthony was introduced to Stanton on a street in Seneca Falls, N.Y., in March 1851. "There she stood," Stanton later recalled, "with her good earnest face and genial smile, dressed in gray silk, hat and all the same color, relieved with pale blue ribbons, the perfection of neatness and sobriety. I liked her thoroughly."

Anthony was then 31. The daughter of a failed mill owner, she had been forced to support herself as a teacher for ten years. The experience taught her to prize her independence. In an age when married women had no legal existence—like single women they could not vote, hold public office, or serve on juries, but as married women they could not contract, sue, control their own property or earnings, divorce for any cause except adultery, and then lose custody of their children—Anthony never married. "The woman who will *not be ruled*," she said, "must live without marriage."

At the time of her meeting with Stanton, Anthony was looking for a cause among all the flourishing reform movements of the period to which she could wholeheartedly commit her conscience and energy. Reform work was then the only avenue to public life for a woman. Anthony was already active in the temperance movement and would soon become New York agent for the American Anti-Slavery Society. Stanton converted her to the cause of women's rights. Anthony, like Stanton, had suffered exclusion and trivialization at the hands of domineering male reformers. She readily combined women's rights with temperance and antislavery, since all shared a common theme—the despotism of white males (drunk or sober).

During the 1850s, Anthony crossed and recrossed New York State, often under arduous conditions, lecturing, organizing, petitioning, and conventioneering for abolition and women's rights. On the rare occasions when Stanton was able to leave her growing family, she proved herself a powerful speaker. Short, stout, maternal, her head crowned with a mass of curls, she swayed audiences by her ebullient charm as well as her rhetorical brilliance. Anthony lacked Stanton's rhetorical flair, but when at last she found her own voice she too proved highly effective. Her speeches were earnest, plain-spoken, enlivened by passionate conviction and sharp wit. Contrary to press reports, she impressed audiences as a woman of grace and charm. Taller than Stanton, she was lean and angular, austere in an unornamented black dress and gold-rimmed spectacles, her hair parted in the middle and pulled back into a coil on her neck.

Although they addressed each other as "Mrs. Stanton" and "Susan" all their lives, the two women forged a friendship of passionate intensity that was not uncommon among women in the 19th century. "How I do long to be with you this very minute," Anthony wrote to Stanton in 1857, "—to have one look into your very soul & one sound of your soul-stirring voice. . . ." "I long to put my arms about you once more," Stanton wrote in 1865, "and hear you scold me for all my sins and shortcomings. . . . Oh, Susan, you are very dear to me." There was always a room in the Stanton home reserved for Anthony.

Their working partnership was ideal. "In thought and sympathy we were one," Stanton recalled, "and in the division of labor we exactly complemented each other. In writing we did better work together than either could alone. While she is slow and analytical in composition, I am rapid and synthetic. I am the better writer, she the better critic. She supplied the facts and statistics, I the philosophy and rhetoric. . . ."

For their effrontery in speaking in public (no respectable woman would do that) and challenging the sacred doctrine of woman's "separate sphere" (kitchen, nursery, and church), Stanton, Anthony, and other feminists were subjected to the opprobrium and ridicule of legislators, clergy, and press. They were called unsexed, mannish, man-hating, shrewish, impudent, impious, disgusting, repulsive. "Susan is lean, cadaverous and intellectual, with the proportions of a file and the voice of a hurdy-gurdy," reported the New York World in 1866 in one of the less unkind caricatures. Stanton and Anthony took the abuse philosophically. "Cautious, careful people," Anthony reflected in 1860, "always casting about to preserve their reputation and social standing, never can bring about a reform. Those who are really in earnest must be willing to be anything or nothing in the world's estimation. . . ."

It was the opposition of other women that most depressed Stanton and Anthony. In 1870, a group of Ohio women typically declared: "Our fathers and brothers love us. Our husbands are our choice and are one with us. Our sons are what we make them. We are content that they represent us in the corn field, the battle-field, at the ballot-box, and the jury box, and we them in the church, in the school-room, at the fireside, and at the cradle." "The fact is," Anthony commented, "women are in chains, and their servitude is all the more debasing because they do not realize it."

What positively angered Anthony was the defection from the cause of fellow workers who married and began families. "Those of you who have the talent to do honor to poor . . . womanhood," Anthony complained to Stanton in 1856, "have all given yourselves over to baby-making; and left poor brainless me to do battle alone." To one defector who had just had her second child, Anthony wrote sternly, "Now, Nette, *not another baby*, is *my peremptory command*." Anthony fretted, "I am not fit to deal with anybody who is not terribly in earnest."

Of course, the worst offender was Stanton herself, who between 1842 and 1859 had seven children, which effectively tied her to her home except for rare forays to conventions or to testify before the legislature in Albany. Anthony constantly badgered her to attend important meetings or at least to write for the cause at home. "And, Mrs. Stanton," Anthony wrote in 1856, "not a *word written* on that Address for the Teachers' Convention. . . . For the love of me and for the saving of the reputation of womanhood, I beg you, with one baby on your knee and another at your feet, and four boys whistling, buzzing, hallooing *Ma, Ma*, set yourself about the work." To which Stanton replied, "Come here and I will do what I can . . . if you will hold the baby and make the puddings." The next year Anthony wrote, "Oh Mrs. Stanton how my soul longs to see you in the great Battlefield. When will the time come?" Stanton replied, "Courage, Susan, this is my last baby." It was not.

In the 1860s Stanton at last felt free to leave her

family responsibilities and take an active part in the abolition and women's rights campaigns. She was recognized as the most prominent feminist leader, and Anthony was her faithful lieutenant. Typically, Stanton served as organization president, chairperson, spokesperson, author, and editor, while Anthony worked behind the scenes as organizer, secretary, strategist, critic, and goad. Stanton was the theoretician of the movement, Anthony its manager.

During the Civil War, feminists believed that their antislavery work would be rewarded with the ballot. Instead, the 14th Amendment introduced the word *male* into the Constitution as a qualification for voting, and the 15th Amendment enfranchised the freedmen but not women, black or white. The feminists' outrage was compounded by the betrayal of their former male allies in the antislavery movement. Fearful that black rights would be jeopardized if they were coupled with women's rights, the male abolitionists argued that this was "the Negro's hour" and that women must wait their turn. The feminists had long compared their subjugation with that of the slave. Now Stanton and Anthony severed that connection and argued that educated women deserved the vote more than the former slaves. They also determined that women must have their own independent movement, without male leadership or male allies. In 1869 they founded the National Woman Suffrage Association (NWSA) with Stanton as president.

To the NWSA Stanton brought a broad and radical women's rights agenda. Not only did the NWSA seek the ballot for women, it embraced the whole range of women's issues: divorce, child custody, property rights, working conditions and wages, birth control, sexual abuse, prostitution, dress reform, child rearing, and co-education among others. To these Stanton added her personal hostility to clerical and biblical authority. Her ultimate object, in fact, was a political, social, and religious revolution. The NWSA's weekly organ between 1868 and 1870, of which Stanton was the editor and Anthony the publisher, was called *The Revolution.*

Stanton's radicalism and militancy drove conservative feminists into the rival American Woman Suffrage Association (AWSA). Whereas the New York–based NWSA was an organization of individuals that anyone could join, attend meetings, and vote, the Boston-based AWSA was an association of local societies that sent delegates to AWSA meetings. Men could join either organization, but they could not hold office in the NWSA. The NWSA distrusted both major political parties; the AWSA was virtually an auxiliary of the Republican Party. The NWSA lobbied in Washington for a 16th Amendment—"The right of citizens of the United States to vote . . . shall not be denied or abridged on account of sex"—while the AWSA lobbied state legislatures for state action.

Year after year, Anthony traveled tirelessly from coast to coast, lecturing on woman suffrage, campaigning for a woman suffrage amendment, and returning to Washington for annual NWSA conventions and to testify before congressional committees. During the 1870s, Stanton lectured eight months a year on the lyceum circuit, giving minimal attention to the NWSA, of which she was nominally president. Between 1881 and 1886, the two women collaborated on a massive three-volume *History of Woman Suffrage.*

Meanwhile, Anthony solidified her control of the NWSA with the support of younger suffragists who were devoted to "Aunt Susan." She also distanced the NWSA from Stanton's radicalism. "Beware, Susan," Stanton cautioned in 1880, "lest you become respectable." Anthony's object was to unite all reform-minded women, whatever their opinions on other subjects, on the single issue of woman suffrage. In this she succeeded, engineering in 1890 a merger of the NWSA and the AWSA into the National American Woman Suffrage Association. She dictated the election of Stanton as the first president of the new organization, then succeeded her in 1892 and served until 1900. In 1895 she loyally but fruitlessly defended her friend from a vote of censure for Stanton's *The Woman's Bible*, a feminist commentary on Scripture that scandalized even the younger suffragists. "Much as I desire the suffrage," Stanton commented, "I would rather never vote, than see the policy of our government at the mercy of the religious bigotry of such women."

By the end of the century, the woman suffrage movement had become respectable. Women had the ballot in four states and voted in municipal and school elections in many others. A woman suffrage amendment, first submitted to Congress in 1878, was 20 years away. Stanton and Anthony, "foremothers" of the movement, had become celebrities. Influential magazines published Stanton's articles and reporters hounded Anthony for interviews. Their significant birthdays were celebrated at large gatherings. Stanton died in 1902. At a celebration of her 86th birthday in Washington, D.C., in 1907, Anthony, frail and ill, responded to the suffragists' ovation with the declaration: "Failure is impossible." She died a month later.

STAR ROUTE FRAUDS (1881–83), incident in the *Garfield-Arthur administration. Starred or asterisked postal routes were those, usually in the sparsely populated South or West, where service was provided by horse, stagecoach, or wagon agencies under contract to the Post Office Department. Lax supervision permitted postal officials to collude with route operators to defraud the government by overcharging for services and improvements. When the frauds came fully to light, Pres. Chester Arthur ordered dismissals and prosecutions. In 1882–83 nine men were tried and acquitted, perhaps due to jury tampering. The affair discredited the administration.

STAR WARS. See *Missile Defense.

STATES' RIGHTS PARTY or **DIXIECRATS** (1948), political party formed by defectors from the *Democratic Party over the issue of civil rights.

Long before the Democratic national convention in July 1948, Pres. Harry S. Truman had alienated many Southern politicians by his forthright advocacy of civil rights legislation (see *Truman Administration). To mollify the Southerners, the White House drafted a moderate civil rights plank for the party's 1948 platform, but on the convention floor Hubert H. Humphrey, mayor of Minneapolis, carried a more radical plank that reflected Truman's views and proved influential in the party's victory that year.

Adoption of Humphrey's plank caused 35 Southern delegates to leave the convention and form the segregationist States' Rights or Dixiecrat Party, which nominated South Carolina governor J. Strom Thurmond for president. In November, Thurmond carried four Southern states—Alabama, Louisiana, Mississippi, and South Carolina. The Dixiecrat movement presaged the conversion of the South from Democratic to Republican as the Democratic Party embraced the *civil rights movement.

STEAMBOATS. Robert Fulton is credited with designing the first successful steamboat, the *Clermont*, a vessel with two side paddles that he took from New York City to Albany and back in 1807 in five days.

The first steamboat on western waters was the *New Orleans*, a 300-ton side-wheeler built on Fulton's design in 1811. Daniel Shreve's *Enterprise* began to ply between Louisville and New Orleans in 1815. It featured a high-pressure engine and a second deck, which thereafter became standard on river steamers. Steamboats navigated the Missouri River in 1819, the Tennessee in 1821, the upper Mississippi in 1823, and the Illinois in 1828. The number of boats operating on western rivers grew from 69 in 1820 to 494 in 1840 and 817 in 1860. The boats

brought business and population to river towns like Cincinnati, Louisville, St. Louis, and New Orleans.

Captain ownership was succeeded by corporate ownership as the boats grew larger and more elaborate. The largest boats before the Civil War were 250 feet long with 30-foot beams and 8-foot holds. The main deck carried machinery and cargo, the second deck passengers, and the third—"Texas"—deck quarters for the crew and the pilothouse. The superstructure became highly ornate and passenger quarters lavish. Boats averaged 6 miles per hour upstream, 10 to 12 down. In 1825 the *Enterprise* traveled between New Orleans and Louisville in 25 days; in 1853 another boat made the journey in less than 5.

The classic account of steamboating in its heyday is Mark Twain's *Life on the Mississippi* (1883), in which he describes his experiences as an apprentice pilot in the 1850s. By then the railroads were already taking passengers from the steamboats. Freight traffic on the rivers peaked in the 1880s but remains significant.

STEEL NAVY. Neglected after the Civil War, by 1874 the U.S. Navy had become little more than a "heterogeneous collection of naval trash," according to the *Army and Navy Journal*. Of its 37 principal ships in 1880, 33 were made entirely of wood and fully sail-powered. It ranked 12th in the world, behind the navies of the major European and some Latin American powers.

Responding in part to the propaganda of Capt. Alfred Thayer Mahan and his following of junior officers, Congress in 1883 embarked upon the construction of a modern steel navy, authorizing the construction of three cruisers, the largest of 4,500 tons. The next year it ordered five more small cruisers and two large ones, plus two second-class battleships—the *Maine* and the *Texas*—of 6,600 tons. The Naval War College in Newport, R.I., was opened in 1884.

William C. Whitney, secretary of the Navy in the first Cleveland administration, reorganized the Navy Department and pushed the construction of new vessels, insisting on naval armor and guns of domestic manufacture. His work was continued by Benjamin Franklin Tracy, secretary of the Navy in the Benjamin Harrison administration. In 1890 Congress authorized construction of three first-class battleships—the *Indiana*, the *Massachusetts*, and the *Oregon*—of 10,000 tons and the cruiser *Columbia* of 7,300 tons. By 1900 the U.S. navy ranked third in the world.

STEEL STRIKES (1892–1952). The bloody *Homestead strike of 1892 and failed attempts to organize steelworkers in 1901 and 1910 lay behind the massive union effort to organize the industry in 1919. Steelworkers comprised diverse immigrant groups unable to protest conditions in the plants. Half the workforce still worked 12 hours a day, six days a week.

When the union organizing committee demanded collective bargaining, the closed shop, the eight-hour day, and wage increases, Judge Elbert H. Gary, chairman of U.S. Steel, replied, "Our corporation and subsidiaries, although they do not combat labor unions as such, decline to discuss business with them." On Sept. 23, 1919, 350,000 steelworkers in nine states struck. The industry replied with strikebreakers, spies, local police, and federal troops while successfully portraying the strike as communist-inspired. In January 1920 the strike was called off, having achieved nothing.

In 1937, after the success of the Congress of Industrial Organizations in organizing the auto industry, U.S. Steel and more than a hundred independent companies recognized the steelworkers' union, granted the eight-hour day and 44-hour week, and raised pay 10 percent. However, **Little Steel**—Republic, Youngstown Sheet and Tube, Inland Steel, and Bethlehem—held firm. In May 1937 the union struck Little Steel, which responded with propaganda, intimidation, and force in the steel towns it controlled. The peak of violence was reached in the **Memorial Day massacre**, May 30, 1937, when Chicago police opened fire on steelworkers and their families picnicking near the South Chicago works of Republic Steel. Ten workers died, more than a hundred were injured, as were 22 of the police. The strike collapsed soon after.

Major steel strikes occurred in 1945 at the end of World War 2 and again in 1952 during the Korean War. Rather than use the injunction provisions of the *Taft-Hartley Act, Pres. Harry S. Truman seized the steel mills. The U.S. Supreme Court ruled his act unconstitutional and the strike resumed, eventually being settled without further government intervention.

STEEL WORKERS UNION. See *United Steelworkers of America (USWA).

STEWARD MACHINE CO. v. DAVIS (1937), 5–4 decision of the *Hughes Court upholding the constitutionality of the unemployment insurance provisions of the Social Security Act (see *Social Security). A companion case, *Helvering v. Davis*, decided 7–2 the same day, upheld the act's old age benefits provisions.

STIMSON DOCTRINE (1932), diplomatic pronouncement of the *Hoover administration. On Jan. 7, 1932, in response to Japan's occupation of Manchuria, Stimson announced that the United States would not recognize any change of international status contrary to the *Kellogg-Briand Peace Pact, the *Open Door Policy, or American treaty rights in China.

ST. LAWRENCE SEAWAY, international waterway connecting the St. Lawrence River with the Great Lakes. Authorized by Canada in 1951 and by the United States during the *Eisenhower administration in 1954, it opened in 1959, enabling oceangoing vessels to reach such lake ports as Toronto, Buffalo, Cleveland, Detroit, Chicago, Milwaukee, and Duluth between mid-April and mid-December.

ST.-MIHIEL. See *World War 1.

STOCK MARKET CRASH (1929). See *Panic of 1929.

STOCK-RAISING HOMESTEAD ACT (1916). See *Public Lands.

STONES RIVER. See *Murfreesboro or Stones River.

STRATEGIC DEFENSE INITIATIVE (SDI). See *Missile Defense.

STUART'S RIDE. See *Peninsula Campaign.

STUDENT NONVIOLENT COORDINATING COMMITTEE (SNCC), civil rights organization formed in 1960 by student veterans of *sit-ins. Its commitment to nonviolence eroded due to its members' experiences with the *freedom rides (1961), *Freedom Summer (1964), and the voting rights campaign in Selma, Ala. (see *Selma-to-Montgomery March, 1965). Its more militant members increasingly advocated *black power, racial separation, and radical social change. SNCC disappeared in the 1970s.

STUDENTS FOR A DEMOCRATIC SOCIETY (SDS). See *New Left.

SUBMERGED LANDS ACT (1953), legislation of the *Eisenhower administration giving to the coastal states the oil-rich tidelands extending to a distance of three miles. The federal government retained control of the continental shelf beyond the three-mile limit. Just before leaving office, Pres. Harry S. Truman, by executive order, had set aside the submerged lands as a naval petroleum reserve.

SUBSTANTIVE DUE PROCESS. See *Fuller Court.

SUBTREASURY SYSTEM. See *Independent Treasury System or Subtreasury System.

SUEZ WAR (1956), incident in the *Eisenhower administration. Pres. Dwight D. Eisenhower's great fear was that Soviet influence in the Arab world would give it control of Middle East oil, which was indispensable to U.S. allies in Western Europe. He suspected that Egypt's president Gamal Abdel Nasser might be a communist—Nasser had been armed by the Soviet bloc and had recognized Red China. When the United States withdrew its promise of financial aid for construction of Egypt's Aswan Dam, Nasser retaliated by nationalizing the Suez Canal with the intention of applying its revenues to construction of the dam.

Since the canal was managed by a company owned by British and French stockholders, Britain and France resolved to reclaim it by force, and enlisted in their scheme Israel, which had been illegally denied use of the canal and of the Gulf of Aqaba by Egypt. On Oct. 29, 1956, Israel attacked Egyptian forces in the Sinai Peninsula and drove them back toward the canal. On Nov. 5, a British and French amphibious force that had assembled at Cyprus, preceded by paratroopers, landed at Port Said at the Mediterranean entrance to the canal and quickly took control of it.

Furious at this heavy-handed reversion to 19th-century colonialism in this explosive region, Eisenhower appealed to the United Nations for a cease-fire and withdrawal, meanwhile cutting off oil and financial assistance to Britain. When the Soviets threatened to intervene, Eisenhower promised to resist them with force. Britain, France, and Israel were compelled to accept UN intervention. By the end of November, they had withdrawn from Egypt and were replaced by UN peacekeepers. The United States reaped great popularity in the third world for having defended a small country against its own allies.

SUGAR ACT (1764), first parliamentary act to raise revenue in the American colonies. An extension of the Molasses Act (1733), the Sugar Act raised old duties and established new ones on foreign products imported into the colonies; this was done for the customary purpose of regulating trade in Britain's interest. But the act also halved the duty on molasses from the French West Indies in the expectation that the colonists would pay rather than evade it; this was done for the avowed purpose of raising revenue. The act also tightened the collection of customs duties. The act's combination of trade regula-tion (long accepted by the colonists) and revenue raising (considered unconstitutional by the colonists) muted complaints.

SUMNER ASSAULT (May 22, 1856), incident in the *Pierce administration. On May 19–20, 1856, Sen. Charles Sumner of Massachusetts, a fervent abolitionist, delivered a carefully prepared but highly intemperate speech in the Senate entitled **The Crime Against Kansas**, a reference to the *Kansas-Nebraska Act and its consequences. "[T]his enormity, vast beyond comparison, swells to dimensions of wickedness which the imagination toils in vain to grasp," he declared. "It is the rape of a virgin Territory, compelling it to the hateful embrace of Slavery; and it may be clearly traced to a depraved longing for a new slave State, the hideous offspring of such a crime, in the hope of adding to the power of Slavery in the National Government." He singled out for violent personal abuse Sen. Stephen A. Douglas of Illinois, author of the act, and two Southern senators. Describing Sen. Andrew Pickens Butler of South Carolina, who was not present, as a self-imagined "chivalrous knight," Sumner said: "[H]e has chosen a mistress to whom he has made his vows, and who, though ugly to others, is always lovely to him,—though polluted in the sight of the world, is chaste in his sight: I mean the harlot Slavery."

Two days later, Rep. Preston S. Brooks of South Carolina, Butler's nephew, assaulted the seated Sumner in the Senate chamber with a light gutta-percha walking stick, beating him unconscious. Brooks was feted throughout the South for his deed. Resigning from the House, he was promptly reelected. Sumner was unable to resume his Senate seat for three years.

SUPERFUND. See *Environmentalism.

SUPPLEMENTAL SECURITY INCOME (SSI). See *Welfare.

SUPPLY-SIDE ECONOMICS. See *Reagan Administration.

SUPREME COURT, U.S. See *Marshall Court; *Taney Court; *Chase Court; *Waite Court; *Fuller Court; *White Court; *Taft Court; *Hughes Court; *Warren Court; *Burger Court; *Rehnquist Court.

SURVIVALISTS. See *Radical Right.

SUTTER'S GOLD. In 1834, 31-year-old John August Sutter—proprietor of a dry-goods shop in the Swiss town of Burgdorf—abandoned his wife and children, escaped a crowd of creditors, and fled to America. Arriving in New York in July 1834, he made his way to frontier Missouri, where he invented a fanciful past as an officer in the French army. After a failed trading venture on the *Santa Fe Trail, Captain Sutter, again leaving creditors behind, pushed west with a party of fur traders and missionaries. From Oregon, he sailed to Hawaii and then—via Alaska—to Mexican California, where he arrived in July 1839 with borrowed money and a handful of retainers hired in Hawaii. He envisioned himself becoming an *empresario,* a colonizer in California's remote Central Valley.

Three years later Sutter—hardworking, charming, and persuasive—presided like a feudal baron over a 48,000-acre Mexican grant on the American River near its junction with the Sacramento. There he erected a fort with 18-foot-high walls of adobe brick within which he built a house and all the workshops necessary for self-sufficiency. Beyond the walls were fields of wheat, corn, and beans, orchards and vineyards, herds of cattle, horses, and sheep as well as the huts of hundreds of workers—Indians, Mexican-Californians, "beached" sailors, deserted soldiers, trappers, prospectors, Mormons, and miscellaneous adventurers. Although never solvent, Sutter became famous for his expansive hospitality. Visitors were royally entertained, and when emigrants began arriving over the *California Trail, their first stop was Sutter's Fort, where they were rested, fed, reequipped, and sent on their way grateful to their host. In 1847 Sutter's men rescued the survivors of the *Donner party.

On Jan. 24, 1848, James Marshall, who was building a sawmill in partnership with Sutter 30 miles from the fort on the South Fork of the American River, discovered gold in the millrace. Sutter received the news with foreboding and attempted to keep it secret. But the news quickly spread. Sutter's workers began to desert him to scratch for gold. By summer, men all over California were abandoning farms, homes, and ships and swarming into the Sacramento valley. From an idyllic pastoral landscape, the valley became a scene of turbulent and lawless brawling. The gold seekers ignored Sutter's fences, trampled his fields, slaughtered his cattle, plundered his buildings. When they were done, business associates defrauded him of his last land claims. By the time U.S. president James K. Polk confirmed the gold discovery in his annual message to Congress on Dec. 5, 1848, unleashing the California *gold rush, Sutter was already a ruined man. James Marshall too was left destitute.

Sutter lived on in modest circumstances on a farm in the Sacramento valley, to which he brought his Swiss family. The federal government appointed him an Indian agent, and the California legislature named him commander of the state militia. But when his farm too was destroyed by an arsonist in 1865, Sutter left California for Pennsylvania. He died there in 1880.

SWANN v. CHARLOTTE-MECKLENBURG BOARD OF EDUCATION (1971), 9–0 decision of the *Burger Court upholding the power of a federal judge to order busing to achieve *school desegregation. The Charlotte school district covered 550 square miles; of its 84,000 students, 29 percent were black and concentrated in a single area. When zoning and free transfers failed to create integrated schools, the district court ordered busing to achieve a white-black ratio of 71:29 in all the district schools. Chief Justice Warren Burger upheld the power of the federal district judge to impose a desegregation plan commensurate with the problem, with the proviso that court supervision would end when the schools were sufficiently integrated.

SWING AROUND THE CIRCLE (1866), incident in the Andrew *Johnson administration. Having broken with the *Radical Republicans in Congress over *reconstruction, President Johnson determined to carry his case to the Northern people and urge the election in November of a Congress that would support him.

Late in August, Johnson embarked on a long railroad journey through Philadelphia, New York, Buffalo, Cleveland, Chicago, St. Louis, Cincinnati, and Pittsburgh—the "swing around the circle"—accompanied by Gen. Ulysses S. Grant, Adm. David Farragut, and several cabinet members. In many places he addressed audiences and dealt with hecklers in the coarse and belligerent style of a Tennessee stump speaker.

The Northern press and even his supporters were mortified by the unprecedented spectacle of a president of the United States electioneering in vulgar fashion. His intemperate speeches drove conservative and moderate Republicans into the Radical camp. In the November elections, anti-Johnson Republicans carried every Northern state legislature, won every Northern gubernatorial contest, and returned large majorities to both houses of Congress.

SYNDICALISM. See *Socialism.

T

TACNA-ARICA CONTROVERSY (1928), century-old territorial dispute between Chile and Peru over two provinces held by Chile. In 1925, Chile and Peru presented the dispute to the United States for arbitration, which was unsuccessful. In 1928, the two countries accepted a proposal of Pres. Calvin Coolidge that Chile return Tacna to Peru and retain Arica, paying a $6 million indemnity.

TAFT ADMINISTRATION (1909–13). Republican William Howard Taft, 27th president of the United States, intended to follow in the footsteps of the man who made him president, Theodore Roosevelt. "He means well, and he'll do his best," Roosevelt prophesied. "But he's weak. They'll get him."

And indeed, indolent and averse to controversy, Taft had none of Roosevelt's political skills. His first move was to summon Congress into a special session to reform the *tariff (an issue Roosevelt had prudently avoided), but he provided no leadership and was presented with the *Payne-Aldrich Tariff; his acceptance of this protective measure endeared him to the Old Guard. When Republican progressives in the House of Representatives (whom Taft disliked) sought his support against the reactionary and dictatorial Joseph G. Cannon, Taft found it easier to embrace the Speaker (see *Cannonism). A sincere conservationist, Taft earned a reputation as an enemy of *conservation by his inept handling of the *Ballinger-Pinchot controversy. The Taft administration initiated more antitrust cases than Roosevelt's had (see *Trust-Busting; *Standard Oil Co. of New Jersey v. United States), but Taft unwisely sued U.S. Steel for an acquisition that Roosevelt had personally approved in the *Panic of 1907 (see *Morgan's Career).

In foreign affairs, Taft encouraged American businessmen and bankers to invest abroad, demonstrating by his intervention in Nicaragua that he would use U.S. armed forces to protect their interests (see *Dollar Diplomacy). Perhaps to atone for the Payne-Aldrich Tariff, Taft pursued a trade reciprocity agreement with Canada, which the Canadians rejected (see *Canadian Reciprocity).

Taft's capture by the Old Guard caused a rift between him and Roosevelt (see *Roosevelt-Taft Split), who eventually placed himself at the head of Republican progressives (a position that arguably belonged to Sen. Robert M. La Follette of Wisconsin) and challenged Taft for the 1912 Republican presidential nomination. When the party chose Taft as its nominee, Roosevelt and his followers formed the *Progressive or Bull Moose Party, dividing the Republican vote and permitting the election of Democrat Woodrow Wilson.

During the Taft administration, New Mexico and Arizona became (1912) the 47th and 48th states.

TAFT COURT (1921–30), the U.S. Supreme Court under Chief Justice William Howard Taft. The Taft Court was notably more conservative than the *White Court, despite the presence of liberal justices Oliver Wendell Holmes, Louis D. Brandeis, and, after 1925, Harlan Fiske Stone. It set its face adamantly against government regulation of business, labor unions, and First Amendment freedoms.

In *Duplex Printing Co. v. Deering (1921), it upheld an injunction against a union engaged in a secondary boycott despite the *Clayton Antitrust Act's express exemption of unions from antitrust legislation. In *Bailey v. Drexel Furniture Co. (1922), it overturned a second attempt by Congress to eliminate *child labor. In *Adkins v. Children's Hospital (1927), it overturned a federal minimum-wage law for women in the District of Columbia. And in *Wolff Packing Co. v. Court of Industrial Relations (1923), it not only overturned a state law providing for compulsory arbitration of labor disputes in certain industries but specified so narrowly those businesses "affected with a public interest" that were susceptible to government regulation as to reverse judicial developments in this area since *Munn v. Illinois* (1877). Thereafter the Court used these guidelines to overturn many other government measures regulating business behavior.

In *Gitlow v. New York* (1925), the Court upheld the conviction of the author of a pamphlet advocating "class action" to establish socialism on the grounds that the pamphlet "endanger[ed] the foundations of organized government."

TAFT-HARTLEY ACT (1947), legislation of the *Truman administration, intended by its Republican sponsors, Sen. Robert A. Taft of Ohio and Rep. Fred A. Hartley Jr. of New Jersey, to correct the prolabor tilt of the National Labor Relations Act (Wagner Act) of 1937 (see *New Deal).

The growth of union membership from 3 million to 15 million since 1935 and an epidemic of postwar strikes had aroused popular sentiment for a crackdown on unions, which were often viewed as arrogant, corrupt, and communist-dominated. The act outlawed secondary boycotts and jurisdictional strikes. When a strike threatened the national interest, the president was authorized to appoint a fact-finding board and to impose an 80-day cooling-off period. The closed shop (the requirement that only union members could be hired) was outlawed, and the union shop (the requirement that all employees belong to the union) made subject to a vote by the employees. Six unfair union practices were added to the unfair management practices listed in the Wagner Act. Unions were made liable for contract violations, their political contributions were restricted, and they were required to provide annual financial reports to their members and the Labor Department. Union leaders were required to certify annually that they were not communists.

Hugely unpopular with organized labor and liberals, the Taft-Hartley Act was passed over Pres. Harry S. Truman's veto. Its repeal was regularly called for in subsequent elections. Truman, however, found the act useful in maintaining labor peace, and the labor movement was not injured by it.

TAFT-KATSURA MEMORANDUM (July 29, 1905), diplomatic accord of the Theodore *Roosevelt administration. In this secret agreement between Secretary of War William Howard Taft and Japanese prime minister Taro Katsura, the United States recognized Japan's control of Korea in exchange for Japan's disclaiming any aggressive designs toward the Philippines. Japan proclaimed a protectorate over Korea in December 1905.

TAFT-ROOSEVELT SPLIT. See *Roosevelt-Taft Split.

TAMMANY HALL, political organization that dominated the politics of New York City for more than a century. Founded in 1788 as a patriotic and fraternal society of artisans and craftsmen with an elaborate Indian ritual, it soon became identified with Thomas Jefferson's Democratic-Republican Party and became a major player in New York City's Democratic politics.

Conflict between progressive and conservative elements produced the revolt of the *Locofocos in 1835. But increasingly the organization's purpose was to profit from political patronage and the graft that came with it. Late in the century, an army of precinct captains, district leaders, and higher officers mobilized poor Irish immigrants to vote for Tammany candidates by providing them with jobs and social services. Its leaders profited not only from patronage but from bribes, kickbacks, legal fees, brokerage commissions, and what became known as "honest graft"—speculation based on insider knowledge of city affairs. Under the *Tweed Ring, the corruption extended to large-scale theft. Periodic "reform" administrations only briefly interrupted Tammany's depredations. Nevertheless, besides elevating numberless hacks to legislative, judicial, and executive positions in the city, state, and national governments, the organization in the 20th century produced two progressive politicians of national reputation—Alfred E. Smith and Robert F. Wagner Sr.

Tammany's decline began in 1898 when four outlying boroughs were consolidated with Manhattan to form the modern city of New York, introducing an enlarged cast of political players. The cutting-off of mass immigration in the 1920s altered the city's ethnic character, while the spread of civil service reduced the number of jobs in the gift of politicians. In 1932 Tammany committed a strategic error in opposing the presidential nomination of Gov. Franklin D. Roosevelt. During the *Roosevelt administration, federal patronage flowed through reform mayor Fiorello H. La Guardia, a Republican. New Deal social legislation, moreover, ended the dependence of New York's poor on Tammany's handouts. By the end of World War 2, the old Tammany Hall had disappeared.

TANEY COURT (1836–64), the U.S. Supreme Court under Chief Justice Roger B. Taney. Opponents of Pres. Andrew Jackson feared that the appointment in 1836 of

Roger B. Taney, a zealous Democrat, as chief justice signaled the dismantling of the constitutional nationalism so carefully emplaced by Chief Justice John Marshall. In fact, the Taney Court exhibited more continuity than change.

Like Marshall, Taney insisted on the Court's unique role as the interpreter of the Constitution, and he continued Marshall's work of constitutional development. There was, however, a change of emphasis—from private rights to community rights, from federal primacy to states' rights. Historians regard these as constructive shifts and—except for the Court's egregious mishandling of the slavery question—rate Taney and his Court high for intellectual power and constitutional achievement.

The Taney Court quickly demonstrated its concern for community over property rights in *Charles River Bridge v. Warren Bridge* (1837), where it disallowed an implied vested right in a monopoly to permit the free development of economic activity for a community's benefit. In *Bank of Augusta v. Earle* (1839), it recognized the right of a corporation chartered in one state to do business in others unless expressly excluded, thereby speeding the expansion of the modern corporation.

By establishing federal supremacy in the areas of constitutionally enumerated powers such as commerce, the *Marshall Court had created an imbalance in the federal system—the distribution of authority between national and state governments. Did federal supremacy mean that federal power was plenary and exclusive? To redress the balance, the Taney Court clarified the "police" or "concurrent" powers of the states to deal with local circumstances either in the absence of federal legislation or insofar as state laws did not conflict with federal laws. *Cooley v. Board of Wardens* (1851) established the necessary distinction between national subjects for which uniform national regulations were required and local subjects where diversity required local regulation.

The Taney Court's significant accomplishments in the foregoing areas were long overshadowed by its disastrous handling of the slavery issue. In *Prigg v. Pennsylvania* (1842), Justice Joseph Story for the Court ruled that state *personal liberty laws were unconstitutional and inadvertently revealed the need for a more effective *fugitive slave law, which was enacted in 1850. Under the mistaken notion that the Supreme Court could settle the slavery controversy, Taney, for a Court whose majority was Southern and proslavery, overreached himself in *Scott v. Sandford* (1857). Instead of resolving the contentious issue, the decision made political compromise impossible.

TARIFF OF ABOMINATIONS (1828), tariff passed in the John Quincy *Adams administration. The bill was introduced in Congress by supporters of presidential candidate Andrew Jackson with the intention of demonstrating his sympathy with the protectionist desires of the Middle Atlantic states and the West. They assured the antiprotectionist South that the bill would not pass because of the high duties—the "abominations"—it placed on imports necessary to New England, such as iron, hemp, and molasses. But an added duty on woolens made the bill acceptable to New England, where woolen manufacturing was new and growing, and the bill passed.

The South felt betrayed, but the Jacksonians reasoned that President Adams would lose New England if he vetoed the bill and lose the South if he signed it, thereby assuring his defeat in the 1828 presidential election. Adams signed the bill out of deference to Congress. John Randolph of Virginia observed famously that the bill pertained "to manufactures of no sort, but the manufacture of a President of the United States."

TARIFFS. Until the 20th century, the federal government had three sources of revenue: tariffs, excise taxes, and the sale of *public lands. Of these, tariffs were by far the most important. After the adoption of the *16th Amendment in 1913, the income tax became the principal source of federal revenue.

The rapid establishment of domestic manufactures during the Napoleonic Wars in Europe gave rise to a demand in the New England and Middle Atlantic states for the protection of these "infant industries." The manufacturing interest was opposed by the agrarian interest in the South and West and also by the shipping interest in the East. The contest between tariff for revenue only and a protective tariff was resolved after 1816 largely in favor of protection. The issue exacerbated growing sectional tensions (see *Tariff of Abominations; *Nullification; *Compromise of 1833). The Democratic Party, most identified with the South and West, championed low tariffs, the Whig and, later, Republican parties championed protective tariffs.

After the Civil War, tariffs soared, rationalized as protecting not only industry but industrial workers as well—although they burdened farmers and consumers (see *Morrill Tariffs; *McKinley Tariff; *Wilson-Gorman Tariff; *Dingley Tariff; *Payne-Aldrich Tariff). The attempt by the *Wilson administration to lower tariffs was cut short by World War I (see *Underwood Tariff). High tariffs remained Republican orthodoxy in the 1920s and even in the Great Depression (see *Fordney-McCumber Tariff; *Hawley-Smoot Tariff). These were mitigated in the Franklin *Roosevelt administration by the Reciprocal Trade Agreement Act (1934), which led to numerous bilateral agreements lowering barriers between the United States and its trading partners.

After World War 2, the General Agreement on Tariffs and Trade and then the World Trade Organization undertook to lower trade barriers on a multinational scale. In the United States, free trade became increasingly favored by policy makers as the best strategy in a rapidly changing global marketplace. The *North American Free Trade Agreement (1993)—aiming at the eventual elimination of trade barriers among the United States, Canada, and Mexico—was hailed by advocates of the long-term benefits of free trade but condemned by those adversely affected in the short term. Protection continued to be an issue when the United States decided that certain foreign products were being unfairly subsidized and "dumped" on the American market.

TAYLOR-FILLMORE ADMINISTRATION (1849–53).

The election of Whig Zachary Taylor, the hero of *Buena Vista, as 12th president of the United States caused joy in the South. The first president from the Deep South, Taylor was a Louisiana planter and slave owner and father-in-law of Sen. Jefferson Davis of Mississippi. It was expected that he would be solicitous of the slave owners' interests. Instead, he proved to be a nationalist of the Andrew Jackson stamp whose closest adviser was antislavery senator William H. Seward of New York.

Taylor's great concern was to avoid contentious congressional debate over the extension of slavery into the *Mexican Cession. His solution was to encourage California and New Mexico to move directly to statehood, with or without slavery as they chose (although it was universally expected that both would reject slavery), thereby bypassing the territorial stage during which Congress would again have to confront the explosive *Wilmot Proviso. He resented Sen. Henry Clay's proposing instead the broad sectional adjustment reflected in the *Compromise of 1850, which he disliked both as a challenge to his leadership and for provoking the very debate he wanted to avoid.

In his haste to see New Mexico admitted as a state, Taylor injudiciously took the New Mexico side in the *Texas boundary dispute, raising the prospect of civil war in the midst of the debate over the Compromise. War may have been averted only by Taylor's unexpected death on July 9, 1850. His successor, Millard Fillmore, 13th president, tactfully defused the Texas issue. He favored the Compromise of 1850, and although his support had little to do with its passage, it cost him the renomination of the fragmented *Whig Party in 1852.

In foreign affairs, the Taylor-Fillmore administration achieved the Clayton-Bulwer Treaty (1850; see *Panama Canal) with Great Britain and the opening of Japan (1854; see *Japan Opening). Secretary of State Daniel Webster's *Hülsemann letter (1850) expressed the bumptious nationalism of the period (see *Young America).

Fillmore was succeeded by Democrat Franklin Pierce. During the Taylor-Fillmore administration, California became (1850) the 31st state.

TEAMSTERS UNION.
See *International Brotherhood of Teamsters (IBT).

TEAPOT DOME SCANDAL (1923),
incident in the *Harding administration. In 1922 Secretary of the Interior Albert B. Fall, without competitive bidding, leased the Teapot Dome, Wyo., naval oil reserve to Harry F. Sinclair, president of Mammoth Oil Co., and the Elk Hills, Calif., reserve to Edward L. Doheny, a friend. In 1923, Senate investigators discovered that Sinclair and Doheny had loaned Fall $25,000 and $100,000, respectively, without interest. Fall was convicted of accepting bribes and sentenced to a year in prison, although Sinclair and Doheny were acquitted of bribery. In 1927 the U.S. Supreme Court declared the two leases invalid and the oil fields were returned to the government.

TECUMSEH CONFEDERACY,
league of Indian tribes in the American Northwest and Southwest formed by the Shawnee chief Tecumseh to reform the Indian character and to resist American encroachment on Indian lands.

Traveling among the tribes, Tecumseh argued that Indian lands were owned in common and could be ceded only with the consent of all the tribes. "Let the white race perish!" he exhorted the Creeks in Alabama in 1811. "They seize your land; they corrupt your women; they trample on the bones of your dead! Back whence they came, upon a trail of blood, they must be driven back!" He also preached temperance and encouraged the Indians to take up agriculture. With British support, he hoped to be able to drive the Americans south of the Ohio River, but he was careful to avoid a premature conflict.

Tecumseh's great enemy was William Henry Harrison, governor of Indiana Territory, who recognized the potential of the confederacy. In response to settler anxiety, Harrison in the fall of 1811 advanced on the Indian capital on Tippecanoe Creek while Tecumseh was absent in the south. On Nov. 11, 1811, the Indians, led by Tecumseh's brother Tenskwatawa, called the Prophet, attacked the American encampment. They were driven off, and Harrison destroyed their village and Tecumseh's stored provisions. The battle of **Tippecanoe** marked the end of the confederacy.

At the start of the *War of 1812, Tecumseh and a few followers joined the British army. He was killed at the battle of the Thames (1813).

TEHRAN CONFERENCE (1943). See *World War 2 Conferences.

TELEGRAPH. Invented by Samuel F.B. Morse in the 1830s, the telegraph was successfully demonstrated on May 24, 1844, when Morse sent the message "What hath God wrought!" from the Supreme Court room in the Capitol in Washington to his associate, Alfred Vail, in Baltimore. The Washington–Baltimore line had been paid for by Congress, but the government left further exploitation of the invention in private hands.

Numerous telegraph companies were formed, miles of telegraph lines multiplied—from 40 miles in 1846 to 200 in 1848, 12,000 in 1850, 50,000 in 1860. Rate wars bankrupted some companies and forced others to merge until the Western Union Telegraph Co. emerged as the dominant factor. Western Union's dominance was assured when the company persuaded the railroads that the telegraph would be useful to their operations. Thereafter the company was able to make use of the railroads' personnel and rights-of-way.

In 1860 Congress authorized $40,000 a year for ten years to any company that built a telegraph line between the western boundary of Missouri and San Francisco. Like the *transcontinental railroad, the transcontinental telegraph was built by two companies starting from opposite ends. The Overland Telegraph Co. built a line from Carson City, Nev., Western Union a line from Omaha, Nebr. The wires were joined at Salt Lake City on Oct. 24, 1861, when Stephen J. Field, then chief justice of California, wired Pres. Abraham Lincoln assurance of California's loyalty in the Civil War.

TELEVISION. See *Radio and Television.

TELLER AMENDMENT (1898), legislation of the *McKinley administration, the fourth of the resolutions passed by Congress on Apr. 20, 1898, authorizing forcible intervention in Cuba. Proposed by Sen. Henry M. Teller of Colorado, it disclaimed any intention by the United States "to exercise sovereignty, jurisdiction, or control" over the island.

TEMPERANCE MOVEMENT. Many observers commented on the hard drinking of Americans in the early 19th century, when (in the 1830s) the annual per capita consumption of alcohol was 7.1 gallons. The first temperance societies were founded by physicians, who saw clearly the connection between heavy drinking and disease, insanity, and early death. For Protestant and Catholic clergy, the liquor traffic became a moral issue, since drinking often led to poverty, crime, prostitution, and domestic violence.

Founded in 1826, the **American Temperance Society** published numberless pamphlets and tracts and dispatched agents across the country whose emotional appeals persuaded thousands to sign pledges of total abstinence—causing some dissent among temperance advocates who saw no harm in wine and beer. Thus temperance became one of many reform causes—abolition, prison reform, child welfare, world peace—in the "age of improvement."

Just as the temperance movement came to preach abstinence instead of moderation, it moved from moral suasion to coercion. In 1851 Maine prohibited the manufacture and sale of intoxicating liquors. By 1855, 12 more states had become "dry." The *Prohibition Party was founded in 1869 and nominated its first candidate for the presidency in 1872. Its efforts were supported by the **Women's Christian Temperance Union**, founded in 1874, which combined moral suasion—singing hymns and praying outside saloons—with political action in support of "pure homes." The nonpartisan **Anti-Saloon League**, founded in 1894, lobbied state legislatures for antiliquor laws and identified "wet" candidates of either major party.

As a result of the combined efforts of the temperance forces, by 1902 every state required temperance instruction in its public schools. By 1916 most states were dry (that is, had prohibited the sale of liquor altogether) and 21 had banned saloons. In the Congress elected that year, dries outnumbered wets two to one. This Congress passed the *18th Amendment to the U.S. Constitution, ratified in 1919, which prohibited "the manufacture, sale or transportation of intoxicating liquors within, the importation thereof into, or the exportation thereof from the United States" (see *Prohibition).

TENNESSEE VALLEY AUTHORITY (TVA). See *New Deal.

TENTH AMENDMENT. See *Bill of Rights.

TENURE OF OFFICE ACT (1867). See *Reconstruction.

TERM LIMITS, political issue that became prominent in the 1980s, when Americans' perennial dissatisfaction with their government expressed itself in a movement to limit the terms of elected officials in the belief that frequent rotation in office was both democratic and beneficial (a throwback to *Jacksonian Democracy).

The U.S. Constitution did not limit the number of terms an elected federal official could serve until the *22nd Amendment in 1951 limited presidents to two terms. An amendment introduced in 1978 to set term limits for senators and representatives failed to pass Congress. Nineteen states established term limits for elected state officials. In *U.S. v. Thornton* (1995), the U.S. Supreme Court struck down state efforts to limit the terms of congressmen.

At the start of the 21st century, a number of state and federal legislators who had been elected on voluntary term-limit platforms began to renege on promises to retire, and some term-limit states were reconsidering their earlier decisions.

TERRORISM, politically motivated criminal acts, which may have many motives: to publicize a grievance, to avenge a wrong, to intimidate authorities, to extort concessions. Those engaged in terrorism see themselves as revolutionaries or freedom fighters, not criminals.

The United States has not been a stranger to terrorism. Mobs, whether aroused by Revolutionary patriots, abolitionists or their opponents, religious or racial bigots, were terrorist weapons, as were the bombs thrown by anarchists, Wobblies, and abortion foes. Four presidential assassinations were acts of terrorism. The *Unabomber waged a one-man, 17-year terror campaign to protest modern technology. The *Oklahoma City bombing (1995) was another act of domestic terrorism, revealing the growing hostility of the native *Radical Right to the federal government.

An international terrorist movement arose out of the Iranian revolution in 1979 and the war in Afghanistan during the 1980s. Fundamentalist Muslim terrorists— some state-supported, some forming a far-flung, loose-knit network—aimed to impose medieval theocratic regimes throughout the Muslim world. The presence of "infidels" in that world—Russians in Afghanistan, Americans in Saudi Arabia, Jews in Israel—was intolerable. They opposed every manifestation of modernity, par-

ticularly as exemplified by the United States. America's power, wealth, secularism, pluralism, and cultural imperialism were hateful to third-world fundamentalist Muslims. For its support of moderate Muslim states and Israel, the United States became the "Great Satan" and the target of jihad, or holy war.

Muslim terrorists plotted numerous attacks on American interests abroad and in the United States itself. Some were discovered and forestalled, others were successful. Among the latter were: the destruction of a marine barracks in Beirut in 1983 (see *Lebanon Interventions); the downing of *Pan Am Flight 103 over Lockerbie, Scotland, in 1988; the bombing of New York City's World Trade Center in 1993 (see *World Trade Center Attack 1); the truck bombing of the Khobar Towers, which housed several thousand U.S. troops in Dhahran, Saudi Arabia, in 1996; the bombing of U.S. embassies in Nairobi, Kenya, and Dar es Salaam, Tanzania, in 1998 (see *Embassy Bombings); the attack on the U.S. missile destroyer *Cole* in Aden harbor, Yemen, in 1999. The destruction of the World Trade Center towers in New York and a simultaneous attack on the Pentagon near Washington in 2001 (see *World Trade Center Attack 2) led to the *Terrorism War.

TERRORISM WAR (2001–), war against international *terrorism, launched by Pres. George W. Bush after terrorist attacks on the World Trade Center in New York and the Pentagon near Washington (see *World Trade Center Attack 2).

"On Sept. 11," President Bush told a joint session of Congress on Sept. 20, "enemies of freedom committed an act of war against our country. . . .

"Our enemy is a radical network of terrorists and every government that supports them. . . .

"We will direct every resource at our command— every means of diplomacy, every tool of intelligence, every instrument of law enforcement, every financial influence and every necessary weapon of war—to the disruption and to the defeat of the global terror network. . . .

"Every nation in every region now has a decision to make. Either you are with us or you are with the terrorists. . . .

"Our nation, this generation, will lift the dark threat of violence from our people and our future. We will rally the world to this cause by our efforts, by our courage. We will not tire. We will not falter and we will not fail. . . .

"The course of this conflict is not known, yet its outcome is certain. Freedom and fear, justice and cruelty, have always been at war. And we know that God is not neutral between them."

Congress quickly voted war powers for the president. The Justice Department rounded up 1,200 "terror" suspects—most of them on immigration charges—and detained them in secrecy. Bush created an Office of Homeland Security, called up reserves, and stationed National Guard troops at the nation's airports. He also began to assemble a coalition of antiterrorist nations and to freeze the assets of institutions and organizations implicated in terrorism. In October Congress passed an antiterrorism act that greatly enlarged law-enforcement capabilities (see *U.S.A. Patriot Act). The next month it passed an Aviation Security Act that federalized airport baggage inspectors and provided for armed marshals to ride commercial flights.

Meanwhile, law-enforcement and intelligence agencies had quickly identified the perpetrators of the World Trade Center attack as members of Al Qaeda, an Islamic terrorist network headed by Saudi militant Osama bin Laden and based in Afghanistan, where it was protected by the Taliban, an extreme fundamentalist group that had won control of Afghanistan in the civil war that followed the Soviet evacuation in 1989.

When the Taliban refused to deliver bin Laden, the United States attacked them with military force. From aircraft carriers in the Arabian Sea and from the island of Diego Garcia in the Indian Ocean, U.S. planes began in October a systematic bombardment of Taliban command and communication facilities. U.S. special operations units were inserted into the country to identify targets for the air attack and to assist the Afghan opposition. Marines established a base in southern Afghanistan near Kandahar. In November the air attacks shifted to Taliban troop positions facing Afghan opposition forces in the northern part of the country. These forces, the Northern Alliance, then attacked, taking the Taliban strongholds of Mazar-i-Sharif, Kabul, and Kunduz in the north and Kandahar in the south. Surviving Taliban fighters were captured or dispersed. Some joined Arab Al Qaeda fighters in the caves of eastern Afghanistan, where they were pounded by U.S. bombers. U.S. special forces searched the caves for intelligence information and possible survivors, including bin Laden, whose whereabouts were unknown. In December 2001, a new Afghan government was installed in Kabul under international protection.

In 2002, President Bush announced his determination to depose Saddam Hussein, the brutal dictator of Iraq, who was suspected of aiding terrorists as well as developing biological, chemical, and nuclear weapons. In Sep-

tember, Bush issued the *Bush Doctrine, and in October received congressional authorization to launch a preemptive attack on Iraq. In November, the UN Security Council voted unanimously to require Iraq to dispose of its weapons of mass destruction or face "serious consequences."

TEST OATH CASES (1867), 5–4 decisions of the *Chase Court rejecting oaths of past loyalty—so-called **ironclad oaths** that the oath takers had not only not participated in the rebellion but had not supported it—imposed during the Civil War and Reconstruction on certain classes of Southerners. In both *Cummings v. Missouri* and *Ex parte Garland*, Justice Stephen J. Field declared that the laws imposing the oaths violated the Constitution's ban on bills of attainder (laws subjecting certain people to punishment without trial) and ex post facto laws (laws imposing punishment for acts that were not criminal when committed). Congress ignored the decisions, just months later requiring oaths of past loyalty for all voters and officeholders in the South.

TET OFFENSIVE. See *Vietnam War.

TEXAS ANNEXATION (1845). U.S. presidents John Quincy Adams and Andrew Jackson had tried to buy part or all of Texas from Mexico. When independent Texas proposed (1836) annexation, Jackson, despite pro-Southern and annexationist inclinations, decided that Texas was not worth war with Mexico (which still claimed Texas) and exacerbation of sectional conflicts in the United States. On the last full day of his administration, he only recognized Texas independence.

Jackson's successor, Martin Van Buren, was even more opposed to annexation. The mere prospect excited intense feelings in North and South. Southerners felt that annexation was essential for the preservation of slavery in the United States. Northerners felt that the addition of slaveholding Texas to the Union would enable the "slave power" to dominate the government.

Pres. John Tyler was more receptive than Van Buren to annexation. A Whig president rejected by his party, he saw the possibility of reelection as the leader of a Southern party made up of annexationist Whigs and Democrats. Secretary of State John C. Calhoun negotiated a treaty of annexation with the Texas minister in Washington, but in June 1844 the Senate rejected it due to reservations by Henry Clay, the Whig leader, and Van Buren, the Democrat leader. (Van Buren's reservations cost him the Democratic presidential nomination that year; Clay's cost him the presidential election.)

That fall, Democrat James K. Polk was elected president on an expansionist platform that embraced Oregon as well as Texas and set its sights as far afield as California. *Manifest destiny combined with Southern proslavery sentiment to overcome resistance to Texas annexation. Lame-duck President Tyler would not allow Polk to complete the project that he had carried thus far. He persuaded Congress that Texas could be annexed by a simple majority joint resolution of both houses, the way new states were admitted, subject only to Texas approval. On Feb. 27–28, 1845, Congress passed a joint annexation resolution that included an amendment permitting Texas to be divided into five slaveholding states. "[T]he heaviest calamity that ever befell myself and my country was this day consummated," John Quincy Adams wrote in his diary.

On his last day in office, Tyler dispatched a courier to Texas with the resolution. Newly inaugurated President Polk briefly halted the courier, consulted his cabinet, then let the courier proceed. Texas accepted the terms of the annexation resolution and was admitted to the Union on Dec. 29.

TEXAS BOUNDARY DISPUTE (1848–50), incident of the *Taylor-Fillmore administration. The state of Texas, like the Republic of Texas, claimed the upper Rio Grande as its western boundary. But territory east of the river was also claimed by New Mexico. In his haste to bring New Mexico directly into the Union as a state without first passing through territorial status, Pres. Zachary Taylor encouraged the drafting of a state constitution that incorporated the disputed area.

Texas was outraged and threatened to resist. Taylor vowed to use force rather than retreat. His death on July 9, 1850, brought the more tactful Millard Fillmore to the presidency. Fillmore asserted that the federal government would indeed use force against any unilateral act of Texas, but he also assured Texas that he would take no unilateral action himself but allow Congress to resolve the dispute to the satisfaction of Texas. In the end, as part of the *Compromise of 1850, Congress awarded most of the disputed area to New Mexico Territory (Fillmore had quietly buried New Mexico's statehood application) but authorized the federal government to assume Texas's preannexation public debt.

TEXAS REPUBLIC (1836–46). In December 1821, Stephen F. Austin led some 300 American families (and their slaves) across the Sabine River and occupied land between the Brazos and Colorado rivers granted to his father by Spanish authorities and later confirmed by inde-

pendent Mexico. The American settlements, which enjoyed local self-government and provincial autonomy under the liberal Mexican constitution of 1824, prospered, and Mexico offered similar grants to other *empresarios*. By 1835, some 30,000 American settlers (including 3,000 slaves) outnumbered Mexicans nearly ten to one in sparsely populated eastern and central Texas.

The Americans were disinclined to assimilate into Mexican society, from which they were separated by race, language, religion, and political tradition. Becoming distrustful of the settlers, Mexican authorities in 1830 halted further American immigration, canceled existing *empresario* contracts, stationed army garrisons in the area, and prohibited the importation of slaves (having outlawed slavery the previous year). American immigration continued illegally, and American settlers managed to evade the antislavery edicts. In 1835, Mexican president Antonio López de Santa Anna established a centralized dictatorship, ended provincial autonomy and local self-government, and prepared to occupy Texas and disarm its inhabitants.

In the **Texas Revolution** that followed, the Texans expelled Mexican garrisons from San Antonio and other places, formed (November 1835) a provisional government, and declared (March 1836) an independent Republic of Texas. In February 1836 Santa Anna crossed the Rio Grande with 6,000 troops, retook San Antonio (including on Mar. 6 the *Alamo, whose 187 defenders were killed), and massacred (Mar. 27) 371 Texas prisoners near *Goliad. In what became known as the "Runaway Scrape," thousands of panicking Texans fled before Santa Anna's army, which destroyed their farms and ranches as it advanced. But at *San Jacinto, a small Texas army under Gen. Sam Houston defeated (Apr. 21) and captured Santa Anna and forced him to sign a treaty recognizing Texas independence (which the Mexican congress repudiated). The Texans adopted a constitution modeled on that of the United States but explicitly recognizing slavery, elected Houston president, and dispatched commissioners to Washington to seek recognition or annexation. Pres. Andrew Jackson recognized Texas independence, but he and his successor, Martin Van Buren, rejected annexation.

The new republic was recognized by Great Britain, France, and other countries. Under presidents Houston (1836–38, 1841–44), Mirabeau Lamar (1838–41), and Anson Jones (1844–46), Texas struggled with insuperable problems. A vast area (its western boundary followed the Rio Grande to its source and then continued north to the 42nd parallel, almost the latitude of Boston), Texas, with a population of only 60,000 whites and 15,000 slaves in 1840, suffered from a shortage of labor, low tax revenues, a large national debt, Indian depredations, and constant border raids from Mexico. Safety for both Texans and their property in slaves lay in annexation to the United States.

Frustrated by the failure of Jackson and Van Buren to act, Houston considered the possibility of permanent independence for Texas. Great Britain preferred an independent Texas to one annexed to the United States (as did Mexico), and held out to Texans the prospect of a loan and a peace treaty with Mexico mediated by Britain. British interest in Texas alarmed U.S. Southerners, who were quick to believe that the price of British assistance to Texas would be the emancipation of Texas's slaves. A free Texas would be intolerable to Southerners, since it would act as a magnet for slaves escaping from the Deep South.

For political reasons, Pres. John Tyler put himself at the head of the Southern cause (see *Tyler Administration). When the Senate rejected a treaty of annexation with Texas, Tyler accomplished annexation by a joint resolution of the two houses of Congress, avoiding the need for the two-thirds majority required for treaty ratification.

Annexation now required only Texas approval. In June 1845 Texas president Anson Jones presented the Texas congress with a choice between annexation by the United States and a peace treaty with Mexico (which had been arranged by Great Britain). The Texas congress voted unanimously for annexation. In July, a constitutional convention drew up a state constitution; in October the people of Texas ratified annexation and the new constitution in a plebiscite; the U.S. Congress accepted the Texas constitution; and on Dec. 29, 1845, President Polk signed an act making Texas the 28th state.

TEXAS REVOLUTION (1835–36). See *Texas Republic.

TEXAS v. WHITE (1869), 5–3 decision of the *Chase Court upholding the *Radical Republicans' theory of *reconstruction. Texas, a former Confederate state not yet restored to the Union by Congress, sued in the Supreme Court to recover state-owned U.S. bonds that had been sold by the Confederate state government. Defendants argued that Texas was not a state and so not qualified to sue in federal court.

For the majority, Chief Justice Salmon P. Chase ruled in favor of Texas. "When . . . Texas became one of the United States, she entered into an indissoluble relation. All the obligations of perpetual union, and all the guaranties

of republican government in the Union, attached at once to the state. The act which consummated her admission into the Union was something more than a compact; it was the incorporation of a new member into the political body. And it was final. . . . Considered therefore as transactions under the Constitution, the ordinance of secession, adopted by the convention and ratified by a majority of the citizens of Texas, and all the acts of her legislature intended to give effect to that ordinance, were absolutely void. They were utterly without operation in law."

Although Texas was undeniably a state of the Union, at the close of the Civil War it had no government in constitutional relations with the Union. "[I]t became the duty of the United States to provide for the restoration of such a government." The power to reestablish a republican government in Texas "is primarily a legislative power, and resides in Congress." Chase reviewed the steps by which the president provisionally and then Congress definitively had restored the former Confederate states to their constitutional relations with the Union. "Nothing, in the case before us," he added significantly, "requires the court to pronounce judgment upon the constitutionality of any particular provision of these acts." The Texas authorities who instituted this case, though still provisional, were nevertheless competent to do so.

THIRD AMENDMENT. See *Bill of Rights.

THIRD PARTIES. The American political system early organized itself around two principal national parties as the most effective means for the varied groups within each to pursue their interests. Until the 19th century, these represented the business/national and the agrarian/states' rights interests; in the 20th century, they took on the coloration of conservative and liberal.

From early in the 19th century, the two principal parties have been challenged by numbers of minor or "third" parties. Some of these were organized around single issues (abolition, temperance, prohibition, greenbacks, segregation), some around ideologies (populism, socialism, communism), still others around individuals (Theodore Roosevelt, Henry A. Wallace, George Wallace, Ross Perot).

On several occasions, a third party affected the outcome of a national election. In 1844, the *Liberty Party assured the election of Democrat James K. Polk by denying New York State to Whig Henry Clay. In 1912, the *Progressive Party divided the Republican vote, assuring the election of Democrat Woodrow Wilson over Republican incumbent William Howard Taft. In 1992, Ross

Perot, self-appointed candidate of the *Reform Party, won an impressive 19 percent of the popular vote but no electoral votes. In 2000, Green Party candidate Ralph Nader may have cost Democrat Al Gore the state of Florida and thus the election.

It should be pointed out that in 1856 the new *Republican Party was not a third party but a second, having replaced the *Whig Party as one of the two principal national parties.

The chief significance of third parties has been their eventual influence on the programs of the principal parties.

THIRTEENTH AMENDMENT (1865), constitutional amendment abolishing slavery in the United States. Its first section reads: "Neither slavery nor involuntary servitude, except as a punishment for crime whereof the party shall have been duly convicted, shall exist within the United States, or any place subject to their jurisdiction."

A resolution ending slavery passed the Senate on Apr. 8, 1864, but, due to Democratic opposition, failed to get the necessary two-thirds vote in the House on June 15. Pres. Abraham Lincoln insisted that an antislavery amendment be part of the Republican Party's platform that year. The Democratic platform said nothing about slavery. The November 1864 election gave the Republicans a majority in the House sufficient to pass the amendment, but it was the old Congress, which had rejected it, that met in December 1864 for a final three-month session. Desiring a bipartisan majority for the amendment, Lincoln lobbied Democrats in the lame-duck Congress.

On Jan. 31, 1865, 16 of 80 House Democrats (14 of them lame ducks) joined 103 Republicans to pass the amendment 119–56. Ratified by 27 states (three-fourths of all the states, counting the former Confederate states, which had never legally left the Union), the 13th Amendment was declared in effect on Dec. 18, 1865.

THOMAS NOMINATION (1991), incident of the George H. W. *Bush administration. On July 1, 1991, with the failed *Bork nomination very much in mind, President Bush nominated a black conservative, Clarence Thomas, to succeed the liberal black jurist Thurgood Marshall on the U.S. Supreme Court. Thomas had been a controversial chairman of the Equal Employment Opportunity Commission (EEOC; 1982–89) and Bork's successor on the U.S. Circuit Court of Appeals for the District of Columbia (1989–91).

Interpreted by one observer as an act of "transcendent cynicism" ("Race has nothing to do with it," Bush said), Thomas's nomination confronted liberal Democrats with a painful dilemma. At hearings by the Senate Judiciary Committee in September, Thomas was opposed by black as well as white liberal organizations. On Sept. 27, the committee divided 7–7, then voted 13–1 to send the nomination to the full Senate without a recommendation.

At this point, an affidavit by Anita Hill, a black law professor at the University of Oklahoma, was leaked to the press. Hill claimed that she had been sexually harassed by Thomas when she worked for him at the EEOC. The Judiciary Committee felt compelled to reopen its hearings. On Oct. 11, on national television, Hill recounted the details of the alleged harassment. Republican senators subjected her to a hostile interrogation, and Thomas categorically denied the charges. The issue was now enlarged from Thomas's qualifications to include the male senators' sensitivity to women's issues. On Oct. 15 the Senate voted 52–48 to confirm Thomas.

THREE-FIFTHS CLAUSE, constitutional provision (Art. 1, sec. 2) that a slave would count as three-fifths of a person for the purpose of apportioning among the states direct taxes and representation in the U.S. House of Representatives. It was abrogated by the *14th Amendment, whose second section based representation on the "whole number of persons in each State, excluding Indians not taxed" but reduced a state's representation proportionally to the number of male inhabitants denied the right to vote.

THREE MILE ISLAND NUCLEAR ACCIDENT (Mar. 28, 1979), breakdown of the cooling system in a nuclear power plant near Harrisburg, Pa., that raised the danger of the overheating and "meltdown" of the plant's nuclear fuel and the spread of radioactive gases. Cleanup and other costs incurred by the owner were greater than the original construction cost. The incident brought about a reorganization of the Nuclear Regulatory Commission and increased emphasis on nuclear plant safety.

TIENTSIN TREATY (1858), diplomatic accord of the *Buchanan administration. Negotiated by the American minister in China, it gave the United States most-favored-nation status, thus permitting it to maintain diplomatic representation at Beijing and to enjoy the trading privileges recently won by Britain and France.

TIMBER CULTURE ACT (1873). See *Public Lands.

TIMBER CUTTING ACT (1878). See *Public Lands.

TIPPECANOE. See *Tecumseh Confederacy.

TITANIC SINKING (Apr. 15, 1912). On Apr. 10, 1912, the "unsinkable" British White Star liner *Titanic*, the largest, fastest, and most luxurious ship ever built, left Southampton on its maiden voyage to New York carrying 2,223 passengers and crew. At 11:40 p.m. on Apr. 14 it struck an iceberg and 2 hours and 40 minutes later sank with the loss of 832 passengers—many of them Americans—and 685 crewmen. The *Carpathia* reached the scene in time to pick up some 700 survivors, whom it brought to New York.

TORIES. See *Loyalists or Tories.

TOWNSEND PLAN (1933), old-age-pension scheme put forward in 1933 by Francis E. Townsend, a retired California physician. Under the plan, all people would retire at 60 and thereafter receive a federal pension of $200 a month on condition that they spend it within the month. To be financed by a federal sales tax, the plan was offered as a measure to both fight the *Great Depression and preserve the dignity of the elderly.

By 1935, some 4,500 Townsend clubs claimed as many as 3.5 million dues-paying members. Their pressure contributed to the passage of the Social Security Act (see *Social Security), which many elderly considered inferior to the Townsend Plan. Although an attractive figure, Townsend proved an inadequate expounder of his plan, and his reputation was sullied by his association with demagogues Charles E. Coughlin and Gerald L.K. Smith in the anti-Roosevelt *Union Party in 1936. Townsend continued to advocate his plan until his death in 1960.

TOWNSHEND ACTS (1767), acts of the British Parliament, carried by a ministry dominated by Chancellor of the Exchequer Charles Townshend. One act placed duties on American imports of glass, lead, paints, paper, and tea. These were external taxes of the kind the colonists had accepted in the past, although their avowed purpose was to raise revenue, not regulate trade. A second act established a Board of Customs Commissioners at Boston to ensure collection of the new duties.

Opposition was at first uncertain, but the rationale—that any British tax on the colonies for revenue was unconstitutional—was soon provided by John Dickinson's *Letters of a Farmer in Pennsylvania* (November 1767), a circular letter to the other colonies written by Samuel Adams and approved by the Massachusetts House of Representatives (February 1768), and a set of resolutions framed by George Mason and adopted by the Virginia House of Burgesses (May 1768). Colonial merchants everywhere except in New Hampshire acceded to nonimportation agreements enforced by patriot activists. In Boston, threats and eventual violence to the customs commissioners resulted in the stationing of British troops in the city.

In April 1770 a new British ministry headed by Lord Frederick North repealed all the Townshend duties except that on tea. Nonimportation was quickly abandoned in the colonies.

TRAIL OF TEARS (1838–39), forced migration of some 15,000 Cherokee Indians from Georgia through Kentucky, Illinois, and Missouri to *Indian Territory in present-day Oklahoma. Repudiating a treaty signed in 1835 by a minority of Cherokee leaders (see *Indian Removal), a majority of the tribe led by John Ross resisted removal until 1838. Beginning in October 1838, U.S. troops collected the Cherokees—now despoiled of their considerable property and destitute—in camps and forcibly escorted them on a disastrous winter march west. A quarter of the Indians died en route from cold, starvation, and disease.

TRANSCONTINENTAL RAILROAD. Promotion of a railroad between the Mississippi Valley and the Pacific Ocean began in 1848, but sectional rivalry prevented a decision on a route (see *Sectionalism). The absence of Southern representatives during the Civil War permitted Congress to decide on a central route from Omaha, Nebr., to Sacramento, Calif.

The Pacific Railroad Act, signed by Pres. Abraham Lincoln on July 1, 1862, assigned construction to two companies: the Union Pacific, which was to build westward from Omaha, and the Central Pacific, which was to build eastward from Sacramento. Construction did not begin until 1865. Twenty thousand men laid as much as eight miles of track a day over plains, deserts, and mountains. Costs were borne by the federal government, which loaned money to the railroads and granted them land from the public domain that they could sell or develop (see *Railroad Land Grants). On May 10, 1869, the two lines were joined by a golden spike at Promontory, Utah.

By the end of the century four other lines connected the Mississippi Valley with the West Coast—the Great Northern, the Northern Pacific, the Atchison, Topeka & Santa Fe, and the Southern Pacific.

TRENT AFFAIR (November–December 1861), incident in the *Lincoln administration. On Nov. 8, 1861,

Capt. Charles D. Wilkes, commanding the USS *San Jacinto*, stopped the British mail packet *Trent* en route from Havana and removed two passengers, James M. Mason and John Slidell, Confederate envoys bound respectively for England and France.

The seizure, which violated international law, outraged British public opinion but delighted the North, since the British had already demonstrated sympathy for the Confederate cause by "unofficially" receiving Confederate envoys and then declaring their neutrality in the war, thereby recognizing the Confederacy as a belligerent power. A British ultimatum demanding that Mason and Slidell be released was received in Washington on Dec. 18. Although fearful of the effect on American public opinion of the government's appearing to back down in the face of a British threat, Lincoln decided "One war at a time." On Dec. 26 Secretary of State William H. Seward responded to the ultimatum that Wilkes had acted without instructions and that the envoys would be released.

TRENTON (Dec. 26, 1776), *Revolutionary War battle. Driven from New York and pursued through New Jersey by British general Charles Cornwallis, Patriot general George Washington got the remnants of his army across the Delaware River into Pennsylvania by Dec. 7, first seizing or destroying all the boats in the vicinity to prevent further pursuit. The complacent British, however, gave up the campaign for the winter. To secure their position in New Jersey, they set up a number of forward posts garrisoned by German mercenaries in towns along the Delaware, including Trenton. Realizing that these isolated posts were vulnerable to attack, Washington saw an opportunity for a quick reversal of American fortunes.

On Dec. 25, Washington led 2,400 men with 18 cannon to McKonkey's Ferry, where they could be rowed across the Delaware to the Trenton side. Two other American forces were to cross the river at other points, but both turned back. The ferrying began at nightfall and was not completed until 3 a.m. because of floating ice and pelting snow, sleet, and freezing rain. A nine-mile march brought the Americans to Trenton at 7:45, in broad daylight. Nevertheless, surprise was complete. A fierce 40-minute battle resulted in 100 Germans killed and 1,000 captured with all their equipment. American casualties were four wounded.

The victory at Trenton lifted American morale and restored Washington's reputation. From Baltimore, Congress voted him dictatorial powers for six months.

TRIANGLE FIRE (Mar. 25, 1911). The Triangle Shirtwaist Co. employed 500 garment workers in the top three floors of a ten-story loft building at the corner of Washington Place and Greene Street, one block east of Washington Square in New York City. Most of the workers were the daughters of Jewish and Italian immigrant families who a year before had struck unsuccessfully against working conditions in the city's shirtwaist factories. On Saturday, May 25, 1911, shortly before 5 p.m.—the end of the six-day workweek—fire broke out on the building's eighth floor and quickly engulfed the ninth and tenth. Although the building was only ten years old and legally fireproof, narrow stairways, small elevators, and locked doors prevented many girls from escaping. Numbers leaped from the windows to their deaths. The fire was quickly extinguished, but 146 people had died.

Three months later the New York State legislature appointed a nine-member Factory Investigating Commission headed by Robert F. Wagner Sr. and Alfred E. Smith. The commission's four-year investigation led to extensive legislation improving safety and working conditions in the state's factories.

TRIANGULAR TRADE. See *Slave Trade.

TRINITY, desert site in southern New Mexico, 55 miles northwest of Alamogordo, where on July 16, 1945, the first *atomic bomb was exploded. The bomb had been developed over the preceding three years at Los Alamos, N.Mex., by a large team of scientists headed by physicist J. Robert Oppenheimer (see *Manhattan Project). A five-ton spheroid, it consisted essentially of a core of plutonium ingots surrounded by blocks of high explosives. When these were detonated, the compressed plutonium would produce an uncontrolled nuclear chain reaction releasing stupendous amounts of energy. The science of nuclear energy was well established; what was in doubt was whether the intricately constructed "gadget" would actually work. (At the time of the Trinity test, the nation's only uranium bomb, untested—uranium was extremely scarce—was aboard the cruiser *Indianapolis* destined for Hiroshima.)

In the days before July 16, the bomb was transported in sections from Los Alamos to the desert test site. There it was assembled and hoisted to the top of a 100-foot steel tower. In the early hours of July 16, Oppenheimer and a group of scientists stationed themselves in a bunkered control center 10,000 yards south of the tower. Other observers took positions 10 miles away, and a large group of Los Alamos scientists and others gathered 20 miles away. A B-29 bomber circled the site at a distance of 15 miles. All the ground observers were instructed to lie down and face away from the blast.

The bomb was detonated at 5:30 a.m. A brilliant flash of white light illuminated the desert as far as the mountain ranges on the distant horizons. A huge fireball, four times hotter than the sun's center, having vaporized the steel tower, spread out on the earth's surface, then rose upward, expanding and changing colors—yellow, orange, red, pink. At 40,000 feet it flattened out on top of a column of radioactive debris into the soon-to-be-familiar mushroom shape. Shock waves raced across the desert. The explosion had exceeded all expectations.

Reactions among the scientists to the epochal event varied. Twenty-seven-year-old physicist Richard Feynman related: "We jumped up and down, we screamed, we ran around slapping each other on the backs, shaking hands, congratulating each other." Later, Oppenheimer recalled: "We knew the world would not be the same. A few people laughed, a few people cried. Most people were silent. I remembered the line from the Hindu scripture, the *Bhagavad Gita.* . . . 'I am become Death, the destroyer of worlds.' "

TRIPOLITAN WAR (1801–5). See *Barbary Wars.

TRUMAN ADMINISTRATION (1945–53). When Pres. Franklin Roosevelt died on Apr. 12, 1945, Democratic vice president Harry S. Truman became the 33rd president of the United States. His first concern was the ending of *World War 2. Nazi Germany surrendered on May 8. From July 17 to Aug. 2, Truman met with other Allied leaders—Soviet premier Joseph Stalin and British prime minister Winston Churchill (replaced during the meeting by the new prime minister, Clement Attlee)—at Potsdam, Germany (see *World War 2 Conferences), in a final summit on the end of the war and postwar arrangements, including Soviet entry into the war against Japan, the occupation of Germany (see *German Occupation), and the trial of war criminals (see *War Crimes Trials). On Aug. 6 and 9, the United States dropped atomic bombs on two Japanese cities, compelling the Japanese to surrender (see *Atomic Bomb). U.S. troops thereupon occupied Japan (see *Japanese Occupation).

Truman then presided over a rapid demobilization of U.S. military power and the reconversion of industry from war to civilian production. This process was accompanied by an epidemic of strikes, including major strikes in the steel, coal, automobile, and railroad indus-

tries, which led Congress to pass the *Taft-Hartley Act of 1947 over Truman's veto. Truman had earlier presented Congress with a lengthy catalog of liberal legislation he wanted. Congress, controlled by Republicans for the first time since 1931, gave him little beyond the *Employment Act of 1946, an act revising *presidential succession, and another creating the *Hoover Commission on reorganization of the executive branch. By executive order, however, Truman ended segregation in the armed forces (see *Armed Forces Desegregation). A stunning victory in the 1948 presidential election gave Truman a Democratic Congress, which he hoped would enact his *Fair Deal, but Republicans and conservative Democrats continued to block his liberal program. His second term saw expansion of the *Social Security program and a National Security Act that unified the armed services (see *Armed Forces Unification). The *22nd Amendment was proposed and ratified during the Truman administration.

Abroad and at home, the *cold war increasingly occupied the administration. To the Soviet Union's perceived belligerency, Truman's response was the strategy of *containment, illustrated by the *Truman Doctrine, the *Marshall Plan, the *Berlin Airlift, creation of the *North Atlantic Treaty Organization, the decision—made with the support of the United Nations—to resist communist aggression in Korea (see *Korean War), and the development of the *hydrogen bomb. In Korea, the administration's prudent decision to fight a limited war rather than expand the war to China and the Soviet Union led to the removal of the UN commander, Gen. Douglas MacArthur (see *MacArthur Firing), and to a furious national debate over containment versus victory from which the administration emerged justified. In all these episodes, Truman was assisted by two outstanding secretaries of state, Gen. George C. Marshall (with whom he differed over the recognition of Israel; see *Israel Recognition) and Dean G. Acheson (see *Truman and Acheson).

At home, the cold war brought a climate of anxiety, intolerance, and reckless superpatriotism. When the communists won the civil war in China, Republicans accused the administration not only of incompetence but of treason (see *China "Loss"). Sensational cases of communist espionage (see *Hiss Case; *Rosenberg Case) led to passage, over Truman's veto, of the Internal Security Act of 1951 (see *Anticommunism). To disarm criticism of being "soft on communism," the administration instituted a loyalty program for federal employees and initiated prosecution of the leaders of the American *Communist Party (see *Dennis v. United States). But these moves failed to protect it from ever more irresponsible charges (see *McCarthyism).

The administration closed amid charges of corruption and in a mood of failure despite its enormous constructive achievement in establishing the defense of the West against the menace of Soviet communism. Truman was succeeded by Republican Dwight D. Eisenhower.

TRUMAN AND ACHESON. When Pres. Harry S. Truman returned to Washington from Independence, Mo., the day after the 1946 congressional elections—in which the Democrats lost control of both houses of Congress for the first time since 1928, a loss universally interpreted as humiliating to the president—he found waiting for him on the platform at Union Station not the customary group of cabinet officials but the solitary figure of the undersecretary of state, Dean Acheson. It was a gesture Truman deeply appreciated and never forgot. He invited Acheson back to the White House for drinks, and a bond was established that lasted until Acheson's death in 1971.

In the remainder of Truman's first term Acheson played a leading role in formulating the *Truman Doctrine and the *Marshall Plan. For the entirety of Truman's second term, Acheson was his secretary of state, architect of the *North Atlantic Treaty Organization, an independent Federal Republic of Germany economically and militarily integrated with the West (see *German Occupation), and a peace treaty and security alliance with a reconstructed Japan (see *Japanese Occupation).

The friendship of these two men, and their constructive partnership in creating the framework for the defense of the West in the *cold war, seemed improbable. Acheson's whole persona was an affront to the administration's enemies in Congress—the "primitives," he called them—and indeed their wrath was usually directed at him. Son of a British-born Episcopal bishop of Connecticut, product of Groton, Yale, and Harvard, always elegantly dressed in English suits and affecting a guardsman's mustache, tall, imperious Acheson drove his enemies to distraction. "I look at that fellow," cried Republican senator Hugh Butler of Nebraska, "I watch his smart-aleck manner and his British clothes and that New Dealism in everything he says and does, and I want to shout, 'Get out, get out. You stand for everything that has been wrong in the United States for years!'"

Truman seemed Acheson's total opposite. Dirt farmer, failed haberdasher, protégé of a corrupt political machine, the last president who did not go to college, Truman was simple and unpretentious and spoke in a flat Missouri twang. But each saw beneath the other's surface. Of his first meeting with then Vice President Tru-

man, Acheson wrote: "It so happened that two days before the President's [Roosevelt's] death, I had a long meeting with Mr. Truman and for the first time got a definite impression. It was a very good impression. He is straight-forward, decisive, simple, entirely honest. He, of course, has the limitation upon his judgment and wisdom that the limitations of his experience produce, but I think that he will learn fast and will inspire confidence. It seems to me a blessing that he is the President and not Henry Wallace."

The affection between Truman and Acheson was genuine. Truman, Acheson wrote, possessed "an inexhaustible supply of vitality and good spirits. He could, and did, outwork us all, with no need for papers predigested into one-page pellets of pablum. When things went wrong, he took the blame; when things went right, . . . [he gave] one of his lieutenants the credit. . . . These are qualities of a leader who builds esprit de corps. He expected, and received, the loyalty he gave. As only those close to him know, Harry S. Truman was two men. One was the public figure—peppery, sometimes belligerent, often didactic, the 'give-'em-hell' Harry. The other was the patient, modest, considerate, and appreciative boss, helpful and understanding in all official matters, affectionate and sympathetic in any private worry or sorrow. This was the 'Mr. President' we knew and loved."

Both men were realists and pragmatists. Although the son of a clergyman with firm notions of good and evil, Acheson did not believe in absolutes. Good and evil, he knew, had always coexisted. In a world of atomic and hydrogen bombs, one could not expect to destroy the enemy. Truman and Acheson's concepts of containment, limited war, and patient negotiation reflected this pragmatism and were alien to the absolutists in Congress who howled for "victory." To Republican senator William E. Jenner of Indiana, Acheson was the "communist-appeasing, communist-protecting betrayer of America."

For both men, loyalty was a great virtue. When Tom Pendergast, the Kansas City boss who had put Truman into politics without asking anything in return, was indicted for tax evasion in 1939, Senator Truman declared, "Tom Pendergast has always been my friend and I don't desert a sinking ship." When Pendergast, an ex-convict and fallen boss, died in January 1945, Vice President Truman flew to Kansas City for the funeral. The criticism he received prepared him for the assault on his secretary of state after Acheson had said that he would not "turn my back" on convicted perjurer Alger Hiss. In the resultant furor, Acheson offered to resign. Truman, he wrote, "was wonderful about it . . . said that one who had gone to the funeral of a friendless old man just out of the penitentiary had no trouble knowing what I meant and proving it."

In his farewell letter to Acheson upon leaving office, Truman wrote: "You have been my good right hand. Certainly no man is more responsible than you for pulling together the people of the free world, and strengthening their will and their determination to be strong and free. I would place you among the very greatest Secretaries of State this country has had."

TRUMAN COMMITTEE (1941–44), the Senate Special Committee to Investigate the National Defense Program, chaired by Sen. Harry S. Truman of Missouri. Alarmed by his personal discovery of waste and inefficiency in the building of army camps, Truman in February 1941 proposed to the Senate a committee to look into the awarding and execution of defense contracts. Such a committee, with himself as chairman, was appointed in March. Hardworking and scrupulously fair, Truman and his committee uncovered many examples of wrongdoing by military contractors and saved the nation hundreds of millions of dollars. The prominence Truman gained led to his selection as the Democratic nominee for vice president in 1944.

TRUMAN DOCTRINE (1947), policy statement of the *Truman administration anticipating the *cold war policy of *containment. In early 1947 Great Britain could no longer support the Greek monarchists in their civil war with Yugoslav-supported communists. At the same time, Turkey was being subjected to Soviet military pressure. On Mar. 12, 1947, Pres. Harry S. Truman described the situation to a joint session of Congress. "I believe," he declared, "that it must be the policy of the United States to support free peoples who are resisting attempted subjugation by armed minorities or by outside pressure." He requested an appropriation of $400 million for military aid to Greece and Turkey. Torn between their desires to cut the budget and to resist communism, the Republican-dominated Congress overwhelmingly passed the Greek-Turkish Aid Bill, which Truman signed on May 12.

TRUST, a form of business organization in which stockholders in a number of corporations in the same industry transfer the management of their stock to a board of trustees, which then coordinates the activities of the member corporations in such a way as to minimize competition and maximize prices and profits. A similar type of organization, the holding company, emerged in the 1890s when states began to authorize corporations chartered by them to own the stock of other corporations,

something that had not previously been permitted. To avoid legal constraints on trusts and holding companies, interlocking directorates and mergers became other methods of combination (see *Trust-Busting).

TRUST-BUSTING, energetic prosecution of large business combinations (see *Trust) in the belief that competition is the best regulator of business as well as socially beneficial. It was particularly characteristic of the Progressive Era (see *Progressivism)—the administrations of Theodore *Roosevelt, William Howard *Taft, and Woodrow *Wilson.

Many Americans first felt the power of big business in the second half of the 19th century in dealing with the railroads, which were, of course, monopolies in the areas they served (see *Railroad Regulation). The existence of industrial combinations seeking monopolistic control of their markets was not always apparent to consumers until *muckrakers and legislative investigative committees (see, e.g., *Pujo Committee) exposed the secret machinations of oil, steel, beef, and many other trusts formed around the turn of the century.

Trust regulation began with the *Sherman Antitrust Act (1890), whose imprecise language largely defeated its purpose. Pres. Theodore Roosevelt made trust-busting a principal component of his progressive program, inaugurating it with prosecution of the Northern Securities Co. (see *Northern Securities Co. v. United States). Roosevelt initiated 44 antitrust prosecutions, his successor, Taft, 90.

The *New Freedom heralded by Pres. Woodrow Wilson promised freer competition among smaller business units. The *Clayton Antitrust Act (1914) and the *Federal Trade Commission Act (1914) gave the administration more effective weapons against business concentration. But its attack on the trusts was abandoned with U.S. entry into World War 1, when it was recognized that large business organizations were highly compatible with national economic planning. Trust-busting was largely forgotten during the 1920s, suspended early in the Franklin *Roosevelt administration (see *New Deal), then revived only to be abandoned again during World War 2.

After the war, there was no great enthusiasm for trust-busting. In the latter part of the century, corporate mergers and acquisitions became ever more numerous, leading to business aggregations of unprecedented size. These encountered little opposition from the Justice Department, which regarded business practices rather than size as cause for intervention. The prosecutions of IBM in the 1960s, AT&T in the 1980s, and Microsoft in the

1990s were prompted by the companies' monopolistic practices. Regulators then believed that the requirements of global competition often justified large business aggregations. "My position on mergers," Pres. William J. Clinton said in 1998, "has always been that if they increase the competitiveness of the company and bring lower prices and higher quality services to the consumers of our country, then they are good, and if they don't, they aren't."

TRUTH-IN-LENDING ACT (1968). See *Consumer Protection.

TUBERCULOSIS, an infectious disease caused by a bacterial agent that attacks humans and animals worldwide and may involve many organs although, in humans, chiefly the lungs. Its onset is symptomless, but eventually the victim experiences fatigue, lassitude, fever, chills, sweats, and coughing of blood. The advanced stage, formerly recognized as "consumption," is marked by rapid physical wasting, fever, and death.

Tuberculosis was epidemic in Europe from the 17th century. A major epidemic extended from 1750 to 1850, when tuberculosis was the leading cause of death in North America as well as Europe. Between 1829 and 1845, Eastern U.S. cities had an average tuberculosis mortality rate of 400 per 100,000 population. This rate declined to 200 per 100,000 population in 1900. The epidemic period coincided with the vogue of Romanticism, which connected tuberculosis with artistic genius, even believing that the disease enhanced artistic creativity.

The bacterium responsible for tuberculosis was identified in 1882, and the discovery of X rays in 1895 greatly aided diagnosis. The search for a vaccine produced instead a chemical test for the presence of the bacterium at an early stage. An effective vaccine was developed in France in the 1920s. In the 19th century, the treatment of choice for tuberculosis was a regimen of rest and mild exercise in a sanitarium. In the 20th century, surgical therapy was tried and abandoned. A combination of an antibiotic (streptomycin) and two other antibiotic agents proved effective in the 1950s for treating pulmonary tuberculosis. In recent years, however, the number of cases resistant to chemotherapy has grown, raising fear of a return of epidemic tuberculosis.

TURNPIKES, surfaced toll roads built in most cases by private corporations. Between 1790 and 1820, 11,000 miles of turnpikes were built, chiefly connecting towns in New England and the Middle Atlantic states. The *National Road was a turnpike built by the federal government to facilitate westward migration.

TWEED RING (1866–71), group of corrupt politicians who looted New York City of as much as $200 million. Its leader was "Boss" William M. Tweed, who in this period combined the leadership of *Tammany Hall with the offices of state senator, Democratic county chairman, and New York City school commissioner, assistant street commissioner, and president of the Board of Supervisors. Three henchmen held the offices of mayor, city chamberlain, and comptroller. Tweed also was involved in firms that did business with the city and maintained a law office (although he was no lawyer) to which large companies paid generous retainers.

While providing progressive social programs for their constituents, mainly Catholic immigrants, Tweed and his henchmen undertook many building projects from which they siphoned large sums. His monument may be the architecturally distinguished but scandalously overpriced Tweed Courthouse, completed in 1878 and now a landmark building. Rising city debt and taxes brought investigations of the Tweed Ring by reformer Samuel J. Tilden, the *New York Times*, and cartoonist Thomas Nast in *Harper's Weekly*. Exposed, the ring was swept from office in 1871. Tweed died in prison in 1878.

TWELFTH AMENDMENT (1804), constitutional amendment passed in response to the crisis occasioned when Thomas Jefferson and Aaron Burr received the same number of *electoral college votes in the presidential election of 1800. It requires that electors vote separately for president and vice president.

TWENTIETH AMENDMENT (1933), the "lame duck" amendment, constitutional amendment that moved the start of presidential and vice presidential terms from Mar. 4 to Jan. 20 and of the terms of senators and representatives from Mar. 4 to Jan. 3, and required Congress to convene annually on Jan. 3.

The Constitution (Art. 5, sec. 4) had provided that Congress should meet at least once a year on the first Monday in December. Since representatives were elected for two-year terms, this meant that each Congress would have two sessions. To give representatives time to reach the nation's capital, Congress decided in the 18th century that members elected in November of even-numbered years would not take their seats until December of the next odd-numbered year—that is, the first session of a new Congress would begin 13 months after its election.

The result was that the second session of a Congress convened in even-numbered years after some of its members—the "lame ducks"—had been rejected by the voters the month before. Another result was a long hiatus (from March to December) between the inauguration of a new president and the convening of the Congress that had been elected at the same time.

After passage of the 20th amendment, a Congress elected in November in an even-numbered year met the following January, and a new president always found a new Congress in session. Franklin Roosevelt in 1937 was the first president to be inaugurated on Jan. 20.

The amendment also prescribed that a vice president-elect should become president if the president-elect died before inauguration.

TWENTY-FIFTH AMENDMENT (1967), constitutional amendment clarifying the issue of *presidential succession left undeveloped in Art. 2 of the Constitution. It makes clear that the vice president becomes president upon the death, removal, or resignation of the president, and it specifies how the vice president may become acting president upon the disability of the president and how the disabled president may subsequently reclaim his authority.

TWENTY-FIRST AMENDMENT (1933), constitutional amendment repealing the *18th Amendment, thereby ending *Prohibition in the United States. The only amendment to repeal a previous one, it was also the only amendment ratified by state conventions especially elected for the purpose, an alternative to ratification by state legislatures provided in Art. 5 of the Constitution.

TWENTY-FOURTH AMENDMENT (1964), constitutional amendment prohibiting the *poll tax in federal elections.

TWENTY-SECOND AMENDMENT (1951), constitutional amendment limiting U.S. presidents to two elected terms (one if the president had served more than half the term of his or her predecessor). Pres. Harry S. Truman was exempted from this limitation. The amendment is generally understood as a Republican Congress's posthumous censure of Democratic president Franklin Roosevelt, who was elected four times.

TWENTY-SEVENTH AMENDMENT (1992), constitutional amendment delaying the effect of a law changing the pay of senators and representatives until after the next election of representatives.

TWENTY-SIXTH AMENDMENT (1971), constitutional amendment setting the voting age for federal and state elections at 18.

TWENTY-THIRD AMENDMENT (1961), constitutional amendment granting the District of Columbia presidential electors not exceeding in number those of the least populous state (in effect, three).

TWO-OCEAN NAVY (1938), naval buildup authorized by the Naval Expansion Act of 1938. Previously, contemplating the prospect of one enemy at a time, Congress had been content with a one-ocean navy that could be shuttled between the Atlantic and Pacific oceans through the Panama Canal. The prospect in 1938 of enemies in both Europe and Asia moved Congress to authorize an unprecedented $1 billion for new ships. Many of those constructed as a result played a prominent part in the Pacific campaigns of World War 2.

TYLER ADMINISTRATION (1841–45). When Pres. William Henry Harrison died (Apr. 4, 1841) one month after his inauguration, John Tyler, tenth president of the United States, became the first vice president to succeed to that office upon the death of the incumbent. His succession was challenged; John Quincy Adams grumbled, "Mr. Tyler . . . styles himself President of the United States, and not Vice-President acting as President. . . . [I]t is a construction in direct violation both of the grammar and context of the Constitution, which confers upon the Vice-President, on the decease of the President, not the office, but the powers and duties of the said office." But Tyler insisted he was in fact the president, and the precedent he established has stood.

A states' rights and proslavery Whig opposed to the nationalist policies of the Whig majority (see *Whig Party), Tyler did not allow Sen. Henry Clay, the Whig leader, to dominate his administration as Clay had expected (Clay referred to Tyler contemptuously as "His Accidency"). When Clay twice carried measures chartering a Third *Bank of the United States, Tyler vetoed them. All the members of his cabinet except Daniel Webster thereupon resigned (Webster resigned in 1843), and the Whigs read Tyler out of the party.

Tyler refilled his cabinet with Southern states' rights Whigs in hopes of building Southern political support, both Whig and Democratic, for his reelection. When

Secretary of State Abel P. Upshur was killed in the *Princeton* explosion, Tyler appointed John C. Calhoun to that post and with him pursued *Texas annexation—and Southern favor.

In foreign affairs the administration accomplished the *Webster-Ashburton Treaty (1842) and the Treaty of *Wanghia (1844).

Denied renomination by the Whigs in 1844, Tyler had Democratic support in many states, but the Democrats nominated James K. Polk, who was elected on a proslavery expansionist platform. During the Tyler administration, Florida (1845) became the 28th state.

TYPHOID FEVER, disease caused by an intestinal bacillus transmitted by polluted water. Symptoms include fever, lassitude, headaches, distended abdomen, rash, and diarrhea. Severe cases result in death. The disease is associated with poor sanitary conditions. In the 19th century, it was common in U.S. cities, where death rates rose as high as 150 per 100,000 population. During the Spanish-American War, typhoid was epidemic in army training camps, killing 1,500 troops. In Cuba, the troops suffered more from *malaria and *yellow fever. Outbreaks of typhoid fever in New York during 1904–7 and in New Jersey in 1914 were traced to a cook, Mary Mallon, a carrier of the disease. She won notoriety as "Typhoid Mary."

TYPHUS, deadly epidemic disease caused by a microorganism (rickettsia) that lives in the blood of various animals—rats, mice, humans—and is transferred by various insect vectors—lice, ticks, fleas. Epidemic typhus is associated with the overcrowding, famine, and filth that accompany social disorders and war. Its toll in the armies and civilian populations of Europe from the Thirty Years' War to World Wars 1 and 2 was staggering. In the 20th century, typhus vaccine and chemical insecticides proved effective in controlling epidemic typhus.

Typhus came to America in the 18th century as "shipboard fever" at Philadelphia, New York, Baltimore, Boston, and Portsmouth. German immigrants brought it to Philadelphia in 1754. In these instances, typhus was combated by vigorous cleaning and delousing. During the Revolutionary War, typhus appeared in the Continental Army, where sanitary engineering was in its infancy. But the American experience was never comparable to the disease's ravages in Europe.

U

UNABOMBER, Federal Bureau of Investigation code name for a domestic terrorist who for 17 years protested against modern technology by mailing letter bombs to people associated with universities, airlines, computers, and other industries, killing three and injuring 23. Captured in a remote Montana cabin in 1996, the Unabomber proved to be Theodore Kaczynski, a Harvard graduate and former assistant professor of mathematics at the University of California–Berkeley. At his trial in California in January 1998, Kaczynski pleaded guilty to all charges and was sentenced to life imprisonment (see *Terrorism).

UNCLE TOM'S CABIN, antislavery novel written by Harriet Beecher Stowe and serialized (1851) in the *National Era*, an abolitionist newspaper, before being published in book form in March 1852. Stowe attempted to portray slave life—which she knew only at secondhand—with documentary accuracy while manifesting sympathy for white Southerners (all her evil characters are Northerners). Sentimental and melodramatic, the novel was immensely successful; its influence on public opinion has been compared to that of Tom Paine's *Common Sense*. Pres. Abraham Lincoln, introduced to Stowe during the Civil War, is said to have called her "the little lady who made this big war."

UNCONDITIONAL SURRENDER, in *World War 2, policy toward the Axis powers adopted by U.S. president Franklin Roosevelt and British prime minister Winston Churchill in January 1943 at Casablanca (see *World War 2 Conferences). It was intended to assure the Soviet Union that the Western Allies would not make a separate peace and to strengthen the resolve of the conquered nations and the American and British home fronts. The policy was criticized for prolonging the war by foreclosing the possibility of a negotiated peace, but Roosevelt and Churchill believed that a negotiated peace was already precluded by the behavior of the enemy, and they were resolved not to repeat the error of World War 1 when Germany was granted an armistice rather than compelled to surrender.

The policy of unconditional surrender was tacitly modified in the July 1945 Potsdam Declaration, addressed to Japan, which permitted the Japanese to retain their emperor. The emperor's authority proved indispensable in securing the surrender of widely dispersed Japanese armed forces.

UNDERGROUND RAILROAD, informal network of persons who, at considerable expense and in violation of the *fugitive slave laws, helped escaped slaves reach freedom in Northern states or in Canada. Few slaves escaped from the Deep South; most fugitives were from *Border states and reached free states—most often Ohio or Pennsylvania—without assistance. Once there, they would be fortunate to encounter a "conductor," who would shelter and clothe them and escort them by night to another conductor farther north. The most numerous conductors were *free blacks; among white conductors, Quakers, Methodists, and Congregationalists were prominent.

Harriet Tubman, an escaped slave, is reputed to have made 19 trips back to the South and to have led 300 slaves to freedom. Levi Coffin made his home at Newport, Ind., an important "station," and was called by some "president" of the underground railroad.

The number of fugitives aided by the railroad cannot be known, but it is estimated that about 1,000 slaves (a very small percentage of the slave population) made their way to freedom every year, almost all of them necessarily with some help from sympathetic Northerners.

UNDERWOOD TARIFF (1913), legislation of the *Wilson administration. Written by Rep. Oscar W. Underwood of Alabama, the act greatly expanded the free list and lowered tariff rates to an average 26 percent from the *Payne-Aldrich average of 38 percent. The coming of World War 1 less than a year later ended the brief experiment with tariff reform.

More important than the tariff schedule was the act's provision for an income tax to replace revenue lost by downward tariff revision (the tariff remained the chief source of federal revenue). The tax rose from 1 percent on personal and corporate incomes over $4,000 to 4 percent on incomes over $100,000.

UNION LEAGUE, during the Civil War and Reconstruction, patriotic clubs that originated in the North in 1862 and spread into the South after the war. In the South they were instruments by which the Republican Party mobilized black voters. They also served as centers of information and self-help for the freedmen. The clubs died out soon after the war in the North and somewhat later in the South. In New York, Philadelphia, and Chicago, Union League clubs survived into the 20th century as bastions of wealth and political conservatism.

UNION PARTY (1936), short-lived *third party created by Father Charles E. Coughlin—Detroit's "radio priest" who had founded the *National Union for Social Justice (NUSJ)—to challenge the reelection of Pres. Franklin Roosevelt in 1936. For its presidential candidate, Coughlin chose Rep. William Lemke of North Dakota, who resented administration opposition to his agricultural proposals. He also brought under the Union Party banner Dr. Francis E. Townsend, author of the *Townsend Plan, and Gerald L. K. Smith, a survivor of Huey Long's *Share Our Wealth Society. By then, however, Roosevelt's *Second New Deal had disarmed authentic progressive critics of the administration.

Coughlin, Townsend, and Smith, who offered three contradictory panaceas for the depression, were soon fighting each other. Despite Lemke's vigorous campaigning, the party garnered only 892,000 votes, less than 2 percent of the total. Chagrined at this poor showing, Coughlin, who had promised to deliver 9 million votes for Lemke, dissolved his NUSJ and retired (temporarily) from his radio ministry.

UNITED AUTOMOBILE WORKERS (UAW), labor union formed in 1935. It grew rapidly with the encouragement of *New Deal labor legislation, and in 1937 won recognition from General Motors and Chrysler through its tactic of the *sit-down strike. Recognition from Ford was won in 1941. From 1946 to 1970 the UAW was led by Walter Reuther. In 2000 it claimed 1.4 million members.

UNITED FARM WORKERS (UFW), labor union organized in 1962 by Cesar Chavez among California farm workers, originally chiefly Mexicans and Filipinos. Its first great success was a nationwide boycott of California table grapes, from which it won the right of collective bargaining and improved working and safety conditions. In the 1970s the union faced often violent competition from the *International Brotherhood of Teamsters. In 2000, the UFW claimed 50,000 members.

UNITED MINE WORKERS (UMW), labor union formed in 1890. A successful strike of bituminous miners in 1897 led to the organization, under the leadership (1898–1908) of John Mitchell, of anthracite miners and the successful *anthracite strike of 1902. After World War 1, overproduction and falling prices reduced union membership. Under the leadership (1920–60) of John L. Lewis, the UMW regained its former power. During World War 2 and shortly thereafter, Lewis led the union in four unpopular but successful strikes.

While the miners' benefits increased, their numbers declined due to modernization of the mines and a switch to low-sulfur coal, mined mostly in the nonunionized West. From 700,000 members in 1940, the UMW had declined by 2000 to 240,000 members, of whom only 30,000 were working as miners.

UNITED NATIONS CONFERENCE (Apr. 25–June 26, 1945), meeting in San Francisco of the 46 signatories of the *United Nations Declaration to complete the formation of the international organization conceived at the *Dumbarton Oaks Conference in 1944. After disputes between the Soviet Union and Western powers were resolved, the United Nations Charter was approved unanimously.

UNITED NATIONS DECLARATION (Jan. 1, 1942), World War 2 military alliance signed in Washington, D.C., by the United States, the United Kingdom, and 24 other "United Nations" against "Hitlerism." Twenty more countries subsequently adhered to the pact. The signatories accepted the goals of the *Atlantic Charter as their war aims.

UNITED STATES v. BUTLER (1936), 6–3 decision of the *Hughes Court finding the Agricultural Adjustment Act of 1933 (see *Farm Problem) unconstitutional. The act authorized payment of subsidies to farmers who voluntarily reduced the acreage devoted to certain enumerated crops, the subsidies to be paid for by a tax on the first processor of each commodity. Butler, a processor, challenged the constitutionality of the tax. The Court not only found the tax unconstitutional but overturned the entire act as invading the reserved powers of the states in attempting to regulate agricultural production.

The decision is remembered for Justice Owen Roberts's simplistic description of how the Court decided constitutional questions: "It is sometimes said that the court assumes a power to overrule or control the action of the people's representatives. This is a misconception. The Constitution is the supreme law of the land ordained and established by the people. All legislation must conform to the principles it lays down. When an act of Congress is appropriately challenged in the courts as not conforming to the constitutional mandate the judicial branch of the Government has only one duty,—to lay the article of the Constitution which is invoked beside the statute which is challenged and to decide whether the latter squares with the former."

It is also remembered for a dissent by Justice Harlan F. Stone, who not only rejected Roberts's ruling but warned the Court of its arrogance in consistently overturning *New Deal legislation: "The power of courts to declare a statute unconstitutional is subject to two guiding principles of decision which ought never to be absent from judicial consciousness. One is that courts are concerned only with the power to enact statutes, not with their wisdom. The other is that while unconstitutional exercise of power by the executive and legislative branches of the government is subject to judicial restraint, the only check upon our own exercise of power is our own sense of self-restraint. For the removal of unwise laws from the statute books appeal lies not to the courts but to the ballot and to the processes of democratic government."

UNITED STATES v. E. C. KNIGHT CO. (1895), 8–1 decision of the *Fuller Court interpreting the *Sherman Antitrust Act for the first time. In 1892, the American Sugar Refining Co. acquired the stock of its leading competitors, thereby establishing a virtual monopoly in the refining of sugar. The federal government filed suit under the Sherman Act, which prohibited combinations "in restraint of trade."

In his ruling, Chief Justice Melville Fuller distinguished between manufacturing and commerce, finding that Congress was empowered to regulate only interstate

commerce. The existence of a manufacturing monopoly was the concern of the state in which the monopoly was situated. In sole dissent, Justice John Marshall Harlan argued that a monopoly's ability to set the price of its manufactured product directly affected interstate commerce. The decision greatly reduced the effectiveness of the Sherman Act. Fuller's distinction between manufacturing and commerce prevailed until the 1930s.

UNITED STATES v. NIXON (1974), 8–0 decision of the *Burger Court denying Pres. Richard M. Nixon's claim of executive privilege in retaining possession of subpoenaed *Watergate tapes. While the Court conceded that the greatest deference must be paid to such claims where diplomatic, political, or military issues were involved, this consideration was overruled by the narrow and specific needs of a criminal investigation. The surrendered tapes did in fact establish Nixon's complicity in the Watergate cover-up.

UNITED STEELWORKERS OF AMERICA (USWA), labor union founded in 1936 as the Steel Workers Organizing Committee (SWOC) and recognized by U.S. Steel in 1937. A violent strike against "Little Steel" in 1937 failed (see *Steel Strikes), but in 1942 the courts directed the Little Steel companies to recognize the union—now the USWA—under the National Labor Relations Act. In 2000 the union claimed 750,000 members.

UNIVERSAL PEACE UNION. See *Peace Movement.

URBANIZATION. As long as water was the most economical means for transporting heavy freight, American cities were built on major bodies of water or on major navigable streams. The first important cities (Boston, Newport, New York, Philadelphia, Charleston) were seaports. As the line of settlement advanced westward, new cities were built on the inland rivers (Pittsburgh, Cincinnati, Louisville, St. Louis) and on the Great Lakes (Cleveland, Detroit, Chicago). All these cities provided markets where farmers of the hinterland exchanged their products for imported manufactures. Merchants and bankers were the leading citizens.

Concentration. The harnessing of steam power brought about an industrial revolution in America that profoundly affected urban life (see *Industrialization). The steam engine made factories independent of millstreams; now they concentrated in cities where transportation facilities and labor were available. Railroads made possible the growth of cities remote from major waterways but close to natural resources—coal, iron, oil—required by industry.

During the 19th century American cities expanded in number and size. Of the 50 largest cities in the United States at the end of the 20th century, only seven had been incorporated before 1816; 39 had been incorporated between 1816 and 1876. Most of these were in the Northeastern and North Central regions; until after the Civil War, the South preserved its predominantly agricultural economy. In the Northern cities, industrial and residential rings grew up around old commercial centers. Because workers had to live within walking distance of their jobs, developers erected three- and four-story tenements or tightly packed rows of houses close to the factories. Only the wealthy could afford to live in outlying towns and commute to their offices or factories by railroad.

The invention of the passenger elevator in the 1850s and the construction of tall, metal-framed buildings in the 1880s encouraged even denser concentrations of people by permitting the vertical stacking of offices, factories, and apartments. In 1860, only nine cities—all of them seaports—had populations of 100,000 or more; by the end of the century there were 50 cities of that size.

The transformation of the United States from a rural to an urban country was accompanied by massive migrations of population from rural areas to the cities. On each new rural generation the cities acted as magnets, offering economic opportunities and cultural amenities far more appealing than the hardship and isolation of farm life or the narrow constraints of life in small towns. Another source of urban growth was successive waves of foreign immigrants—English, Irish, Germans, Italians, Poles, Greeks, Russians (see *Immigration). Often poor and unskilled, the immigrants settled mostly in the large cities of the Northeast and Midwest, where, like native migrants, they occupied the least desirable housing and filled the least desirable jobs.

In 1920 the U.S. Census found for the first time that more than half of the nation's population was urban—that is, lived in places with populations of 2,500 or more. Since the first Census in 1790, when only 5 percent of the total population of 4 million was urban, the urban proportion of the population has steadily increased, reaching 75.2 percent in 1990.

The 1920s were the golden age of large American cities. Their physical plants were relatively new, having been built for the most part during a building boom that lasted from 1880 to 1920. Dense populations made efficient use of city facilities. These populations contained a fair balance of lower- and upper-income citizens, and the cities' economic health was assured by the presence within city limits of virtually all the area's residential, commercial, and industrial developments.

Dispersal. The concentration of dense urban masses induced by steam power began to be reversed with the coming of electricity and then the internal-combustion engine. The electric trolley, which first appeared in the 1880s, provided relatively fast transportation at prices working people could afford. As electric street railways radiated from crowded downtowns, new housing developments sprang up along them. Those city dwellers who could afford to do so abandoned densely packed old neighborhoods for one- and two-family houses in the new suburbs, which were quickly annexed to the city.

What the electric trolley began, the automobile completed. Auto registrations grew from 2.5 million in 1915 to 26 million in 1930. Mass-produced automobiles, priced within reach of the middle class and of many blue-collar workers, speeded the exodus from old neighborhoods to the city's periphery and even to suburbs altogether outside the city's jurisdiction.

Beginning in the 1920s, while the movement of population into the cities continued and even accelerated, the distribution of population within cities began to change. Increasingly, people moved out of the aging inner cities to the urban fringes and beyond. This double population movement—into urban areas but away from urban cores—reached flood proportions after World War 2. Low-cost mortgages guaranteed by the federal government, income-tax benefits for home buyers, the phenomenal multiplication of automobiles, and the construction in the 1950s and 1960s of the interstate highway system—all encouraged vast expansion of suburbs.

Industry soon followed population. Manufacturers left crowded quarters in the old industrial sections of the cities for the cheaper land and lower taxes of suburban industrial parks. Service industries followed their customers and workforce into the burgeoning suburbs. The number of jobs in the suburbs grew faster than the number in the cities; indeed, many large cities experienced net losses of jobs to their suburbs. Once merely residential communities dependent on a nearby city, suburbs developed into economically diversified towns that competed with the dominant metropolis.

Increasingly, the Census Bureau's definition of an urban place as one with a population of 2,500 or more came to have little relevance to the reality of U.S. urban civilization. Since 1950 the unit of analysis used by urbanologists has been the metropolitan area, which originally comprised a central city of at least 50,000 inhabitants, the county in which it was located, and neighboring counties that were closely associated with it by daily commuting ties. The portion of a metropolitan area outside the central city was designated suburban; it might contain residential or "bedroom" communities, industrial and commercial towns, and even large "satellite" cities. In 2000, 278 metropolitan areas embraced 19.8 percent of the nation's land and 80.3 percent of its population.

During the second half of the 20th century, the metropolitan population expanded rapidly. The metropolitan areas of the South and West mushroomed. In the slower-growing metropolitan areas of the Northeast and North Central regions, population growth was concentrated almost entirely in the suburbs. Everywhere, urban areas sprawled over the landscape until they encountered the advancing edges of other urban areas. They spilled over metropolitan borders, creating "citified country" of housing developments, shopping malls, factories, and office parks along highways and rural roads. When urban developments within one metropolitan area reached those of a neighboring metropolitan area, they formed huge new urban conglomerations extending for hundreds of miles. One such "megalopolis" stretched along the East Coast from Boston to Washington; another, in the Midwest, connected Chicago with Cleveland and Pittsburgh; on the West Coast, the area from San Francisco to San Diego was a single megalopolis.

Plight of the Central City. The exodus of their more affluent citizens left the aging central cities populated disproportionately by the poor, the elderly, and the handicapped. Many of these were new arrivals, the most recent of the successive waves of migrants who hoped to improve their lot in the large cities. After the 1920s, when the stream of foreign immigration was cut off, a swelling stream of black migrants flowed from the rural South to Northern industrial cities. Later, the blacks were joined by Hispanic migrants from Puerto Rico, Mexico, and Central America. Like previous immigrants, the blacks and Hispanics were often poor and unskilled. They arrived at a time when the industries that hired unskilled labor were already leaving Northern cities in search of cheaper labor and lower costs in the South and West or overseas. Unlike previous immigrants, blacks and Hispanics encountered racial prejudice that limited their access to jobs and housing. Their arrival exacerbated the whole range of city problems at the very time the cities' resources were diminishing.

In recent decades, there has been evidence of renewal in old central cities with diversified economies and important regional, cultural, or governmental functions. New office buildings, convention centers, hotels, and apartment houses reflected the evolution of these central cities from centers of manufacturing to centers of banking, law, accounting, and other service industries. At the same time, old sections of the central cities, historically and architecturally interesting and convenient to central business districts, were being rehabilitated—"gentrified"—by young middle-class singles and childless couples who were committed—at least temporarily—to city life.

The 2000 Census revealed that many cities continued to lose population to their suburbs—that is, central cities shrank while metropolitan areas grew. Eight of the 10 largest cities, however—Philadelphia and Detroit were the exceptions—gained population, due in part to immigration.

U.S.A. PATRIOT ACT or **ANTITERRORISM ACT** (2001), legislation of the George W. *Bush administration in response to terrorist attacks on New York and Washington (see *World Trade Center Attack 2). It enlarged the government's powers to conduct searches and electronic surveillance, to wiretap, and to track Internet communications. It banned the undeclared movement of amounts over $10,000 across U.S. borders, gave the government new tools to investigate foreign financial institutions, accounts, and transactions, and required informal money-transfer services to register with the government. It authorized the U.S. attorney general to detain indefinitely noncitizens believed to be national security risks.

UTOPIAN COMMUNITIES. Throughout American history, small groups of people have attempted to escape the vulgar culture, cruel competition, and lonely individualism of the larger society and seek a transforming communal experience informed by religious or social ideals. The Massachusetts Puritans hoped to establish an exemplary Christian commonwealth. In succeeding centuries, Mennonites, Shakers, Rappites, Perfectionists, Mormons, and numerous other sects founded religion-based communities of widely varying longevity.

In the 19th century, socialism—Christian or utopian—inspired other communal experiments. The British social reformers Frances Wright, at Nashoba, Tenn. (1825–28), and Robert Owen, at New Harmony, Ind. (1825–28), conducted communities founded on the redeeming power of education. Brook Farm (1841–47), a transcendentalist community at West Roxbury, Mass., was briefly famous for its intellectual life. Hopedale (1841–56), at Milford, Mass., hoped vainly to realize the kingdom of God on earth. Followers of the French utopian socialists Charles Fourier and Etienne Cabet founded short-lived "phalanxes" or "Icarian" communities in a number of states.

The 20th century saw a flowering of utopian communities. During the *counterculture of the 1960s and 1970s, men, women, and children sought "alternative lifestyles" that took them into "communes" of varied sizes and structures. Since then, cultists—both religious and political—have formed communities, physically or emotionally isolated, to pursue their particular ends.

The persistent hunger for affiliation that these utopian communities reveal is a poignant theme in American history, so dominated by the ethos of individualism. Experience suggests that modern society simply dissolves community, leaving the individual, for better or worse, on his own.

U-2 AFFAIR (1960), incident in the *Eisenhower administration. In 1954 the Lockheed Corp. developed a reconnaissance aircraft with a single jet engine, large wingspan, and the ability to fly long distances at altitudes above 70,000 feet that it designated the U-2. By 1956, pilots employed by the Central Intelligence Agency (CIA) were flying these planes from bases in Japan, Turkey, and elsewhere over the world's trouble spots, including the Middle East, China, and the Soviet Union. They produced valuable information, including the fact that the "missile gap" alleged by critics of the administration did not exist. This could not be revealed, however, since the flights were top secret—to the American people. They were known, of course, to the governments whose territories were used for the flights and those whose territories were overflown. The Soviets tracked the overflights by radar but, unable to bring the planes down, confined themselves to private protests.

On May 1, 1960, on the eve of a crucial Paris summit meeting on a nuclear test-ban treaty for which Pres. Dwight D. Eisenhower had great hopes, a CIA pilot named Francis Gary Powers took off in a U-2 from a base in Turkey and headed across the Soviet Union for a destination in Norway. A day later, Soviet premier Nikita Khrushchev announced that the Soviets had shot down a spy plane, and on May 5 he revealed that the Soviets had the plane, its pilot, and his film. Eisenhower, who had lied about the plane's mission when the first news broke, was humiliated, and Khrushchev went on to destroy the Paris summit in feigned outrage.

A few years later both the United States and the Soviet Union were routinely flying reconnaissance satellites over each other's territory. In 1962 Powers was exchanged for a Soviet spy held in the United States.

V

VALLEY FORGE (December 1777–June 19, 1778), *Continental Army encampment during the *Revolutionary War. Following his defeat at *Germantown, Patriot general George Washington took his army into winter quarters at Valley Forge, Pa. The site was 20 miles from Philadelphia, now occupied by the British, and some 50 miles from Lancaster and York, Pa., where the state government and the *Continental Congress, respectively, had taken refuge.

Although the winter was not notably severe, Washington's 9,000 men suffered from poor housing, inadequate food and clothing, unsanitary conditions, and disease. In large part the fault was the Quartermaster Department's, whose incompetent director, Gen. Thomas Mifflin, had resigned in November. Investigation by a congressional committee confirmed Washington's complaints and strengthened his hand. With the appointment of Gen. Nathanael Greene as quartermaster general in March, the flow of supplies—and the condition of the troops—improved rapidly.

Of no less significance was the transformation of the Patriot army from an armed rabble to disciplined professionals. This was the achievement of Baron Friedrich von Steuben, who arrived at Valley Forge as inspector general on Feb. 23. Although he spoke no English, Steuben instructed the army in a simplified version of Prussian drill—how to move and fire in compact bodies as the professional European armies did.

The revived army left Valley Forge on June 19, 1778, to follow the British army that was evacuating Philadelphia back to New York. At *Monmouth on June 28, American troops convincingly demonstrated their new professional prowess.

VAN BUREN ADMINISTRATION (1837–41). Personally unlike Andrew Jackson in every way, Martin Van Buren, eighth president of the United States, was a loyal Jacksonian Democrat. His nomination was imposed upon the unhappy Democratic Party by his chief, and he was elected over three candidates put forward by the fledgling *Whig Party.

Unfortunately for Van Buren, he inherited the consequences of Jackson's *Bank War, which contributed significantly to the *Panic of 1837 and the subsequent deep depression. He had no remedy for the distress caused by the depression but, blaming the banks for the debacle, in 1837 he proposed the *Independent Treasury System, which proved popular with radical Democrats but was opposed by conservatives. Van Buren did not obtain passage of the act until 1840, and the next year it was promptly repealed by the new Whig administration. In foreign affairs, he acted with restraint when relations with Great Britain became strained over the *Caroline affair and the *Aroostook War. Like Jackson, he opposed *Texas annexation.

Defeated in the election of 1840, Van Buren was succeeded by William Henry Harrison, a Whig.

VENEZUELAN BOUNDARY DISPUTE (1895–96), diplomatic incident in the second *Cleveland administration. A dispute between Great Britain and Venezuela over the boundary of British Guiana dating back to 1814 came to a head in 1887 when Venezuela asked the United States to arbitrate. Twice (1887, 1894) Britain rejected U.S. offers to arbitrate.

In July 1895 Secretary of State Richard Olney informed the British government that the United States would consider British pressure on Venezuela as a violation of the *Monroe Doctrine and insisted on arbitration. "Today," Olney wrote, "the United States is practically sovereign on this continent, and its fiat is law upon the subjects to which it confines its interposition.

Why? . . . It is because, in addition to all other grounds, its infinite resources combined with its isolated position render it master of the situation and practically invulnerable as against any or all other powers."

When Britain denied that the Monroe Doctrine applied and again rejected arbitration, Pres. Grover Cleveland asked Congress to create an independent boundary commission, whose decision would be backed by the United States. "[I]t will . . . be the duty of the United States to resist by every means in its power," Cleveland declared, "as a wilful aggression upon its rights and interests, the appropriation by Great Britain of any lands or the exercise of governmental jurisdiction over any territory which after investigation we have determined of right belongs to Venezuela."

This bellicose declaration forced the startled British to recognize that American friendship was indispensable in the light of growing dangers in Europe. They cooperated with the American boundary commission and then accepted international arbitration. In 1899 the arbitration board supported the British position on the disputed boundary.

VERSAILLES TREATY (1919). See *Paris Peace Conference.

VICKSBURG CAMPAIGN (November 1862–July 1863), *Civil War campaign in which Union general Ulysses S. Grant completed Union control of the Mississippi River by capturing Vicksburg, Miss.

By November 1862 all the Mississippi River was in Union hands except a 200-mile stretch from Port Hudson, La., to Vicksburg, the "Gibraltar of the West," built on bluffs on the east bank of the river. Frustrated in attempts to reach Vicksburg from the north and east, Grant took his Army of the Tennessee to the west side of the Mississippi and marched it through swamps and bayous to a point 30 miles south of Vicksburg. There Union gunboats and transports commanded by Adm. David Dixon Porter that had run the Vicksburg batteries ferried the army back across the river on Apr. 30, 1863.

Abandoning his lines of communication and determined to live off the countryside, Grant marched northeast into the state's high and dry interior, burning the state capital, Jackson, and separately defeating Confederate generals John C. Pemberton and Joseph E. Johnston in five battles (May 1–17). With Pemberton driven back into Vicksburg and Johnston helpless in his rear, Grant launched two unsuccessful attacks on the well-fortified city, then settled in for a siege. After six weeks, on July 4, 1863 (the same day that Gen. Robert E. Lee

withdrew from Gettysburg), Pemberton surrendered the starving city.

"The Father of Waters again goes unvexed to the sea," President Lincoln observed with satisfaction.

VIETNAM WAR (1957–75), America's longest and most unpopular war. It failed to achieve either of its two objectives—to defend a small, strategically unimportant country against what was seen as communist aggression and to sustain America's credibility as an ally in the *cold war.

Background. Before World War 2, the French colony of Indochina in Southeast Asia consisted of the area now comprising Vietnam, Laos, and Cambodia. Occupied by Japan during the war, it was reclaimed by France, who made its constituent countries parts of a new French Union. In Vietnam, the communist Vietminh movement, led by Ho Chi Minh, demanded complete independence. War with France began in 1946. Because France was important to U.S. policy in Europe, the United States supported France in Asia, providing 75 percent of the cost of its war in Vietnam. The fall of the French fortress at Dien Bien Phu in May 1954 ended the French effort to reconquer Vietnam.

At an international conference in Geneva, the victorious Vietminh were compelled by France, Great Britain, the Soviet Union, and China to accept a temporary division of Vietnam at the 17th parallel. North Vietnam, with its capital at Hanoi, would be governed by the Vietminh, South Vietnam, with its capital at Saigon, by the emperor Bao Dai, a French puppet. A national election would be held in 1956 to unite the country under a single government. Neither the United States nor Bao Dai subscribed to the Geneva agreement.

The next year, South Vietnamese prime minister Ngo Dinh Diem was elected president of the Republic of South Vietnam, replacing Bao Dai as head of state. Diem proved despotic and corrupt, but as a Catholic and anticommunist he enjoyed the support of the United States. With U.S. agreement, he canceled the 1956 elections, which were certain to have been won by the communists. In 1957 rebellion erupted in the South Vietnam countryside, waged by communists, nationalists, religious sectaries, and others and directed from North Vietnam. In 1960 this coalition took the name National Liberation Front (NLF). Its members became known to Americans as Vietcong—that is, Vietnamese communists.

Eisenhower and Kennedy's War. During the siege of Dien Bien Phu, in limited response to frantic French appeals for help, Pres. Dwight D. Eisenhower sent to Vietnam ten American B-26 bombers and 200 men to service them. After the French defeat and withdrawal from Vietnam, Eisenhower resolved that the remainder of noncommunist Indochina must not fall to the communists. His great fear was the "domino effect" this would have—the fall to communism of other countries in the region, beginning with Laos and Cambodia, followed by Burma, Thailand, Malaya, and Indonesia, and perhaps even by Japan, Formosa, and the Philippines. But he did not want to act unilaterally. The *Southeast Asia Treaty Organization (SEATO) was formed as an anticommunist alliance similar to NATO in Europe. With American money and arms, but not men, SEATO would ensure the independence of noncommunist Southeast Asia.

Even before Diem's rejection of national elections in 1956 precipitated an antigovernment insurgency, Eisenhower saw the need to increase American economic assistance to South Vietnam and to provide military advisers to build an army capable of resisting the expected invasion from the north. By the end of the *Eisenhower administration, the United States had 650 military advisers in South Vietnam and had suffered its first two casualties (in 1959).

Pres. John F. Kennedy saw South Vietnam as an American—indeed, a personal—challenge. His reputation for toughness and America's credibility as a cold war ally required that he continue to support South Vietnam, even after Diem was murdered (Nov. 1, 1963) in an army coup and although Diem's successors inspired little confidence in Washington. By the end of the *Kennedy administration, the United States had 16,000 military advisers in South Vietnam and had suffered 100 casualties.

Johnson's War. "I am not going to lose Vietnam," declared Pres. Lyndon B. Johnson. But in 1964 it was clear that the war was going badly, with the Vietcong controlling 40 percent of the countryside. The Military Assistance Command under Gen. William C. Westmoreland would number 23,000 by the end of the year, but a greater U.S. commitment was necessary, and for this Johnson wanted congressional approval.

On the night of Aug. 2, 1964, an American destroyer on an electronic espionage mission in the Gulf of Tonkin off the North Vietnamese coast was fired upon by North Vietnamese patrol boats. On Aug. 4, it and another destroyer erroneously reported that they had been fired upon again. Johnson seized upon this dubious event to denounce Hanoi for unprovoked attacks on U.S. ships and launched an air attack against North Vietnamese shore installations. Without revealing the provocative mission of the U.S. destroyers, Johnson requested and Congress passed almost unanimously (only two senators

voted against it) the **Gulf of Tonkin Resolution** (Aug. 7, 1964), which declared that "the Congress approves and supports the determination of the President, as Commander-in-Chief, to take all necessary measures to repel any armed attack against the forces of the United States and to prevent further aggression." The resolution was used by Johnson thereafter as authorization to conduct a U.S. war in Vietnam.

In March 1965 Johnson began a secret escalation of U.S. troops in South Vietnam. Troop levels rose from 180,000 at the end of 1965 to 550,000 in 1968. These were not military advisers but an army with orders to go onto the offensive against the NLF guerrillas. Also sent to South Vietnam were contingents from South Korea and from SEATO members Australia, New Zealand, Thailand, and the Philippines.

Meanwhile troops of the North Vietnamese army were infiltrating into the south along the **Ho Chi Minh Trail.** This system of primitive roads, passing under dense jungle cover, ran through eastern Laos half the length of Vietnam. Besides the traffic of troops going to and coming from the south, it carried the supplies and equipment provided to Hanoi by the Soviet Union and China. Another North Vietnamese supply route ran from the Cambodian port of Sihanoukville on the Gulf of Thailand into the southern part of South Vietnam.

At the same time he began the escalation of American troops in South Vietnam, Johnson ordered the strategic bombing of North Vietnam. Bombs and napalm were also rained down on suspected guerrilla concentrations in South Vietnam. By the end of the war, more bombs had been dropped on Vietnam than on all of Europe during World War 2.

Fighting the War. The Vietnam War was fought as a counterinsurgency. There was never any intention of invading North Vietnam, since that might have brought China into the war. Two main strategies were employed: pacification and "search-and-destroy." Pacification involved protecting densely populated areas from Vietcong terrorists while providing educational and social programs to win the loyalty—the "hearts and minds"—of these populations to the Saigon government.

Search-and-destroy involved massive sweeps through rural or forested areas in search of guerrilla concentrations or bases. One such sweep resulted in the **My Lai massacre** (Mar. 16, 1968), when three platoons of the Americal Division entered the hamlet of My Lai and, finding no identifiable Vietcong, vented their frustration and suspicion of the innocent-appearing villagers by massacring several hundred of them. Lt. William L. Calley, a platoon leader at My Lai, was court-martialed in 1971 on 102 counts of murder and spent three years in prison.

In this war, large-scale engagements involving regiments or divisions were infrequent; when they occurred, they were usually won by the Americans, who had the advantage of air cover and superior firepower. Typically, it was a war of small units, close and merciless, in which patrols pushed through "the bush," trying to avoid land mines and booby traps, in search of the elusive but dangerous enemy. There was no front line, and the enemy rarely wore uniforms.

In such circumstances, military progress was not measured by miles of territory gained but by numbers of enemy killed. Americans at home were regaled with weekly "body counts," numbers of enemy dead vastly greater than the number of American casualties and seemingly more than the enemy could long sustain. These were the sources of the official optimism that Washington constantly reflected.

Optimism vanished with the **Tet offensive** (January–February 1968). At the beginning of 1968, U.S. and South Vietnamese forces held the cities and were making progress against the Vietcong in the countryside. The guerrillas were believed to be too weak to conduct a major operation. But on Jan. 30, the first day of Tet (the Vietnamese lunar New Year holiday), the Vietcong struck simultaneously at cities and towns throughout South Vietnam. They seized the ancient capital of Hue, and in Saigon they penetrated to the airfield, the presidential palace, and the U.S. embassy. Taken by surprise, Americans and South Vietnamese fought back fiercely, eventually driving off the Vietcong with losses estimated at 40,000. Hue was not cleared until Feb. 24, by which time it had been reduced to rubble by American bombing. The popular uprising that the Vietcong had hoped for did not materialize, and the Vietcong themselves were permanently weakened and demoralized.

General Westmoreland claimed a great victory—then requested 200,000 more troops. But the official optimism was now exposed as fraudulent. There was, after all, no "light at the end of the tunnel." On Mar. 31 Johnson announced that he would not be a candidate for reelection in the fall. Westmoreland was recalled and replaced by Gen. Creighton Abrams (July 1). Victory in Vietnam seemed as remote as ever.

The Antiwar Movement. Opposition to the Vietnam War grew slowly due to strong anticommunist sentiment in the country and the government's deceptions. Members of religious and pacifist groups and the Old Left—socialists and other radicals—were the first

to protest. But rising draft calls and television reportage of combat began to make some Americans uneasy. In January–February 1966, Sen. William Fulbright, chairman of the Senate Foreign Relations Committee, conducted critical committee hearings on the war on national TV. Secretary of Defense Robert McNamara, the administration's leading hawk, left the cabinet in despair in February 1968. Rep. Eugene McCarthy of Minnesota declared himself an antiwar candidate for the Democratic presidential nomination, as did Sen. Robert F. Kennedy of New York.

With each new escalation, each new revelation of atrocities and official deceptions, the antiwar movement grew, spreading through the middle class, involving civil rights activists, joined too by bereaved parents and some returning veterans. Beginning with a Vietnam "teach-in" at the University of Michigan in March 1965, colleges and universities became hotbeds of antiwar agitation. Students were prominent in the growing numbers of antiwar marches, picketings, vigils, and draft-card burnings. Their chant "Hey, hey, LBJ, / How many kids did you kill today?" angered the president. The antics of radical students outside the Democratic national convention in Chicago in August 1968, and the police riot that followed, were watched by the entire nation on television. Student disturbances reached their peak after the Cambodia incursion in the spring of 1970, when students at 35 colleges and universities went on strike and the National Guard had to be called out to restore order on 21 campuses. More than 50 were forced to close for the remainder of the year.

The division between hawks and doves sometimes followed class lines. Blue-collar workers (including the police) were outraged at the unpatriotic behavior of draft-deferred college students. The police expressed their anger by the ferocity with which they dispersed campus strikers, particularly at Columbia University in the spring of 1968. Class resentment may have been at the root of the **Kent State shootings** (May 4, 1970), when members of the Ohio National Guard fired into a distant crowd of student demonstrators on the campus of Kent State University, killing four and wounding nine. A few days later, at a ceremony in New York City commemorating the Kent State victims, 200 construction workers attacked students and other middle-class participants while the police stood by.

Public opinion polls tracked declining support for the war: from 61 percent in April 1965 to 50 percent in November 1966, 44 percent in October 1967, and 35 percent in August 1968. Yet in November 1969, when in response to a large antiwar demonstration in Washington,

D.C., Pres. Richard M. Nixon reaffirmed his commitment to South Vietnam and appealed for the support of the "silent majority," he was heartened by the response.

The antiwar movement limited the government's freedom of action, depressed the morale of the troops in Vietnam, and weakened the hand of American peace negotiators. But it is not clear that it shortened the war or affected its outcome. President Nixon continued to wage war for four years, even while withdrawing American troops, and added some 20,500 U.S. battlefield deaths to the 37,500 incurred by his predecessors.

Nixon's War. "I will not be the first president of the United States to lose a war," Nixon vowed, very much like his predecessors. He was determined, however, to be tougher than his predecessors, to let the North Vietnamese know that the old rules governing the conflict no longer applied.

Nixon's basic strategy consisted of Vietnamization of the war—the enlarging, training, and equipping of the South Vietnamese army to take on an ever-larger share of the war while American troops were withdrawn. The American withdrawal began immediately, Nixon removing 60,000 troops the first year. At midyear 1970, American ground troops numbered 404,000; at midyear 1971, 225,000. At the end of 1972, only 24,000 American ground troops remained in South Vietnam.

While implementing Vietnamization and troop withdrawal, Nixon also pursued peace negotiations with the North Vietnamese in Paris, where National Security Adviser Henry Kissinger met with the chief North Vietnamese delegate, Le Duc Tho, to seek what Nixon called "peace with honor."

North Vietnamese terms for a settlement were, of course, unacceptable to the United States: the withdrawal of all U.S. troops, the remaining of North Vietnamese troops in the south, and the end of the government of Nguyen Van Thieu, president of South Vietnam since 1967. The North Vietnamese saw no need to compromise: the United States was already withdrawing, and within a few years North Vietnam would be free to deal with South Vietnam alone. Moreover, the antiwar movement in the United States was weakening American resolve, and American troops in Vietnam—reluctant to risk their lives while the war ran down—were beginning to display traces of the demoralization that became epidemic in 1971 with high frequencies of insubordination, mutiny, desertion, "fragging" (murder by hand grenade) of officers, racial conflict, and drug addiction.

Nixon determined to show that the United States was still a dangerous enemy. In March 1969 he secretly launched the bombing of North Vietnamese bases and supply depots in Cambodia. Since these bases were illegal to begin with, neither Cambodia nor North Vietnam protested. Once begun, the bombing of Cambodia continued for four years.

In May–June 1970, U.S. and South Vietnamese troops entered Cambodia (the **Cambodia incursion**, which, by expanding the war, aroused strong antiwar protests at home), destroyed large quantities of North Vietnamese supplies, and closed the supply line from Sihanoukville to the Vietcong in the southern part of South Vietnam.

In February 1971 South Vietnamese forces invaded Laos with the intention of cutting the Ho Chi Minh Trail, on which North Vietnam was now totally dependent for supplying its troops in the south. They were driven out by the North Vietnamese.

In March 1972 Hanoi, heavily resupplied by the Soviet Union, launched a major three-pronged offensive against South Vietnam, attacking south across the 17th parallel in the north, east into the central highlands, and in the south. Without the help of U.S. ground forces but with the intensive participation of U.S. tactical aircraft and B-52 bombers, the South Vietnamese contained this offensive.

Determined to meet escalation with counterescalation, Nixon renewed the bombing of North Vietnam, which had been suspended by Johnson in October 1968. These attacks included the first use of B-52s against the north. American planes also mined the port of Haiphong, through which Soviet supplies reached Hanoi. Fear of Soviet reaction had prevented this measure in the past, but now the Soviets said nothing.

Still the Paris negotiations went nowhere. In October 1972, both sides made concessions that led to a tentative peace agreement: the United States agreed to let North Vietnamese troops remain in the south after the armistice and accepted a tripartite commission composed of Saigon, the NLF, and neutrals to oversee a final settlement. This was an agreement that Nixon could have had in 1969. Indeed, South Vietnamese president Thieu rejected it, correctly seeing in it U.S. abandonment of his government and its inevitable defeat after "a decent interval" (as Kissinger cynically put it). Negotiations came to a halt.

To bring the North Vietnamese back to the negotiating table, Nixon launched the **Christmas bombing** (Dec. 18–29, 1972), when U.S. planes hit North Vietnam with unprecedented fury, leaving its economy in ruins. The bombing brought the North Vietnamese back to the Paris negotiations, and an agreement was soon signed little different from October's. This time Nixon threatened to cut off all American aid to President Thieu if he did not accept it, while promising improbably that the United States would respond "with full force" if the North Vietnamese violated the agreement. Thieu had no choice but to accept.

The armistice did not stop the fighting, although the Americans were now gone. In March 1975 Hanoi again launched a major offensive against the south, soon routing the South Vietnamese army. On Apr. 30 the North Vietnamese entered Saigon—soon to be renamed Ho Chi Minh City. In Saigon's last hours, U.S. helicopters ferried American civilians, members of the Saigon government, and other U.S. dependents from the roof of the U.S. embassy to the Seventh Fleet offshore.

Conclusion. From the start, the United States conceived the Vietnam War as a "limited war" intended only to compel North Vietnam to accept the independence of South Vietnam. But short of an invasion of North Vietnam or nuclear annihilation—both ruled out by larger considerations—the North Vietnamese could not be so compelled. When the United States finally recognized that it could not achieve its aim at any acceptable cost, it withdrew from the war.

Left to itself, although with major material aid from the United States, South Vietnam proved too weak to sustain its independence against North Vietnam. The country was at last reunited. After 30 years of devastating war, during which millions had been killed, wounded, or uprooted, when the land itself had been poisoned by massive American use of herbicides, Vietnam was condemned to another generation of extreme poverty by an American boycott and the oppressive and doctrinaire mismanagement of its communist government. Its two closest neighbors, both destabilized and then abandoned by their American allies, fell to communism in the same year—Cambodia to the genocidal Khmer Rouge, Laos to the hard-line Pathet Lao. The *Nixon Doctrine advised other Asian nations that the United States would not be back.

The Vietnam War cost the United States 58,000 killed and over 300,000 wounded. It polarized American society, radicalized or alienated youth, and sowed profound distrust of authority. The war ended the draft, which was replaced by the All Volunteer Force (see *Conscription). Until at least the *Gulf War of 1991, U.S. policy makers were burdened by the "Vietnam syndrome"—the reluctance to risk American troops anywhere without strong public support and overwhelming superiority on the ground.

VIRGINIA AND KENTUCKY RESOLUTIONS

(1798), drafted secretly by James Madison and Thomas Jefferson respectively to arouse opposition among the states to the *Alien and Sedition Acts as unconstitutional encroachments into areas where the federal government had no powers.

Jefferson's resolutions, introduced into the Kentucky legislature by John Breckinridge, argued that the U.S. Constitution was a compact among the states; that the general government had no powers beyond those specifically delegated to it; that "whensoever the general government assumes undelegated powers, its acts are unauthoritative, void, and of no force"; and that "each [state] has an equal right to judge for itself, as well of infractions as of the mode and measure of redress." The resolutions, passed by the Kentucky legislature on Nov. 16, 1798, called upon the other states to join with Kentucky "in declaring these acts void and of no force" and "in requesting their repeal at the next session of Congress." Jefferson's original language, before it was toned down by Madison and Breckinridge, was more extreme. In his draft he had written: "Where powers are assumed which have not been delegated, a nullification of the act is the rightful remedy. . . ."

Madison's resolutions, introduced into the Virginia legislature by John Taylor of Caroline and passed on Dec. 24, 1798, were couched in more moderate language. They protested the unconstitutionality of the acts and invited other states to cooperate with Virginia "in maintaining unimpaired the authorities, rights, and liberties reserved to the states respectively, or to the people."

Of the 14 states invited to join with Kentucky and Virginia in protesting the Alien and Sedition Acts, ten rejected the resolutions and took no action. Some years later, Jefferson's authorship of the Kentucky resolutions became known, and in 1832—at the height of the *nullification controversy in South Carolina—his original draft was discovered. Advocates of states' rights thereafter appealed to the "principles of '98."

VIRGINIA AND PLYMOUTH COMPANIES

(1606–24), two joint stock companies created by a royal charter of 1606 and authorized to establish colonies in North America, one in Virginia between 34 and 40 degrees North latitude, the other between 38 and 45 degrees. The colonies were to be governed by local councils subject to a council in London, which was in turn responsible to the crown.

The Virginia Company of London, which established a settlement at Jamestown in 1607, was dissolved by court order in 1624. The Virginia Company of Plymouth tried unsuccessfully to establish a colony in Maine and to exploit that region's fisheries and fur trade. It was dissolved in 1620 and replaced by the Council for New England, which succeeded in establishing a colony at Plymouth, Mass. (see *Plymouth Colony).

VIRGINIA DYNASTY (1801–25), the three successive Virginian presidents—Thomas Jefferson, James Madison, and James Monroe. George Washington was a Virginian but is not counted in the dynasty. The Federalists were particularly disturbed that four of the first five presidents should have been Virginians (and three of them Republicans). One of the resolutions adopted by the *Hartford Convention proposed a constitutional amendment to prohibit two successive presidents from the same state. Other Virginia-born presidents were William Henry Harrison, John Tyler, Zachary Taylor, and Woodrow Wilson.

VIRGINIUS AFFAIR (1873), incident in the *Grant administration. The *Virginius*, illegally flying the Ameri-can flag, was carrying arms to Cuban rebels when it was captured by Spanish authorities. Fifty-three crewmen, including some Americans, were shot. A dangerous situation was worsened by the intemperance of the U.S. minister to Spain, Daniel Sickles. Secretary of State Hamilton Fish intervened, however, and negotiated an indemnity from Spain of $80,000.

VOLSTEAD ACT (1919). See *Prohibition.

VOTING RIGHTS ACT (1965), legislation of the Lyndon *Johnson administration that dramatically remedied the disfranchisement of Southern blacks. It authorized the U.S. attorney general, in any electoral district where fewer than half of voting-age blacks were registered to vote, to suspend literacy or other discriminatory qualification tests, to send in federal registrars to register blacks if necessary, and to assign federal observers to monitor elections. Black registration in Mississippi rose from 6.7 percent in 1965 to 59.8 percent in 1968.

W

WABASH, ST. LOUIS & PACIFIC RAILWAY CO. v. ILLINOIS (1886), 6–3 decision of the *Waite Court prohibiting states from imposing "direct" regulatory burdens—such as rate regulation—on interstate commerce within their borders. ("Indirect" burdens—such as safety regulations—were permitted, but the distinction was abandoned in the 1930s.) Confirming that the regulation of interstate commerce was an exclusively federal power, the decision introduced some uncertainty into the interpretation of the Court's ruling in the *Granger Cases. The prompt result was passage of the Interstate Commerce Act (1887), the first attempt by the federal government to regulate the railroads (see *Railroad Regulation).

WACO SIEGE (Feb. 28–Apr. 19, 1993), operation of federal agents against the compound of the Branch Davidians, a disavowed sect of the Seventh-Day Adventist Church led by self-proclaimed messiah David Koresh, near Waco, Tex.

When on Feb. 28, 1993, 28 agents of the U.S. Bureau of Alcohol, Tobacco, and Firearms (ATF) attempted to serve warrants alleging that the Branch Davidians were stockpiling illegal weapons, a 45-minute gun battle ensued in which four ATF agents were killed and 16 wounded; six Branch Davidians were also killed. For the next 50 days, agents of the ATF and Federal Bureau of Investigation (FBI) sealed off the well-supplied compound while negotiations proceeded with the irrational Koresh.

Early on Apr. 19, federal agents assaulted the compound with armored vehicles and tear gas. Around noon the wooden buildings began to burn, apparently set on fire by their inhabitants. Seventy-two Branch Davidians, including 17 children and Koresh, died in the conflagration.

The incident aroused a storm of criticism of the Justice Department: Why had the final assault been necessary? Who started the fire? For members of the *Radical Right, the Waco siege was another example of a despotic government trampling on the liberties of American citizens. In their mythology, the Waco siege soon joined the 1992 siege by U.S. marshals and FBI agents of white-supremacist Randy Weaver at Ruby Ridge, Idaho, in which a marshal and Weaver's wife and teenage son were killed. In 1995, Timothy McVeigh marked the second anniversary of the Waco assault with the *Oklahoma City bombing.

From the start, U.S. attorney general Janet Reno took responsibility for the decision to attack the Branch Davidian compound and stoutly defended the acts of the ATF and FBI agents. But in 1999 it was revealed that, despite FBI denials, pyrotechnic gas grenades capable of igniting the Branch Davidian buildings had been used in the siege. In 2000, an investigation by former Republican senator John Danforth of Missouri cleared the Justice Department of any wrongdoing, and a Waco jury decided for the government in a wrongful-death lawsuit brought by surviving sect members and relatives of those who had died.

WADE-DAVIS BILL (1864). See *Reconstruction.

WAGNER ACT (1935). See *New Deal.

WAITE COURT (1877–88), the U.S. Supreme Court under Chief Justice Morrison R. Waite. Although Waite was not an outstanding jurist, his Court reclaimed some of the prestige it had lost during *Reconstruction (see *Chase Court). It became increasingly friendly toward corporations. After affirming state regulatory power in the *Granger Cases (1877), the Court lessened the force of that ruling by its decision in *Wabash, St. Louis & Pacific Railway Co. v. Illinois (1886), and in *Santa

Clara County v. Southern Pacific Railroad Co. (1886) it announced its definitive acceptance of the doctrine that the term *person* in the *14th Amendment applied to corporations as well as individuals. In the *Civil Rights Cases* (1883), the Court disclaimed federal responsibility for the protection of individuals' civil rights, although in *Ex parte* *Yarborough* (1884) it upheld (ineffectually) federal power to protect an individual's right to vote.

WALLACE'S CAREER. Between the *Great Depression and 1970, profound political, social, and cultural changes transformed the United States. Four Democratic administrations created and extended the welfare state; two moderate Republican administrations ratified it. The U.S. Supreme Court reflected the prevailing liberal climate by outlawing racial segregation, barring religion from the public schools, safeguarding the rights of criminal defendants. Blacks responded by claiming their legitimate privileges as citizens; violence flared, first in the South, then during the 1960s in cities across the country. The *Vietnam War brought new legions of demonstrators into the streets. *Welfare rolls skyrocketed as welfare became recognized as an "entitlement." A significant number of America's youth (a minority, to be sure) rejected the materialism and conformity of their parents; some "turned on" to political activism, others "dropped out" into the *counterculture.

Phenomena so unprecedented bewildered most citizens. Some, however, were frightened and outraged. To people who lived in close-knit ethnic enclaves in industrial cities, in small towns where kinship and custom ruled, in burgeoning suburbs to which new (and insecure) members of the middle class had escaped from disorderly inner cities, the familiar moral universe seemed to be under attack. Old certainties like religion, patriotism, community, family, hard work, and self-reliance were being mocked by "liberals" intent upon imposing their degenerate views on the whole society—with the backing of a "liberal" federal government, an intrusive bureaucracy, and tyrannical courts. Behind these obvious oppressors, grass-roots conservatives often saw the sinister menace of world communism. Unobserved, a backlash was preparing.

The man who gave voice—raw, angry, snarling—to that backlash was George Corley Wallace (1919–1998), four-time governor of Alabama (1963–67, 1971–79, 1983–87). Short, wiry, restless, ambitious, and totally opportunistic, Wallace needed the cheers of the crowds to still his ever-present insecurity. A son of an impoverished middle-class family, he became a protégé of James E. "Big Jim" Folsom, a populist politician who, rather than court the *Black Belt planters and Birmingham businessmen who controlled the state, campaigned directly to the rural people of Alabama. Folsom was twice elected governor (1947–51, 1955–59), only to be ruined by corruption, alcohol, and racial moderation; a populist of the old school, he believed that race was a false issue used to blind the poor to their common interests.

Wallace was shrewd enough to recognize that such moderation was unacceptable in Alabama. When in 1957 he first ran for governor, he ran as a "humane segregationist" who emphasized better roads and schools and economic development. He lost in the all-important Democratic primary to the state attorney general, who had driven the *National Association for the Advancement of Colored People out of the state. "Well, boys," Wallace promised reporters, "no other son-of-a-bitch will ever out-nigger me again."

Good as his word, Wallace ran for governor successfully in 1962 with the slogan "Vote Right—Vote White." The token integration of Southern schools was now the paramount issue. For Wallace and his hard-line supporters, even tokenism was unacceptable. Basing his defense of segregation on the long-discredited claim of states' rights, Wallace promised: "I shall refuse to abide by any such illegal federal court order even to the point of standing at the schoolhouse door"—a promise he kept on June 11, 1963, in a carefully scripted confrontation with Deputy U.S. Attorney General Nicholas Katzenbach over the registration of two black students at the University of Alabama.

"I started off talking about schools and highways and prisons and taxes," Wallace reflected to a reporter about his successful campaign, "—but I couldn't make them listen. Then I began talking about niggers—and they stomped the floor." In his inaugural address on Jan. 14, 1963, Wallace declared: "Today I have stood where once Jefferson Davis stood and took an oath to my people. It is very appropriate then that from the Cradle of the Confederacy, this very heart of the Great Anglo-Saxon Southland ... we sound the drum for freedom. ... In the name of the greatest people that have ever trod this earth, I draw the line in the dust and toss the gauntlet before the feet of tyranny. ... And I say ... segregation now ... segregation tomorrow ... segregation forever."

Few outsiders understood Wallace's complicity in the violence that racked Alabama in the civil rights campaigns of the next few years. The national press regarded him as the eccentric defender of a constitutional theory that had been put to rest in the Civil War. Invited to appear on national television interview shows and to lecture at elite universities, Wallace proved himself quick-witted and ingratiating, more than a match for the poorly prepared journalists and overconfident students.

Wallace never doubted that racism was alive and well in the North. On Mar. 6, 1964, under the slogan "Stand Up for America," he entered the Democratic presidential primary in Wisconsin, a liberal state with a small black population. He did not attack blacks, but racism was the subtext of his attack on the Civil Rights Act of 1964. With it, he uncovered a constituency, angry and vociferous, that no one had suspected was there—blue-collar workers fearful that blacks would take their jobs, white ethnics and suburbanites fearful that blacks would move into their communities, small businessmen frightened by what "big government" might do armed with new and promised civil rights legislation. These racist appeals were accompanied by derisive comments about welfare mothers "breeding children as a cash crop," federal bureaucrats who "don't know how to park their bicycles straight," and "pointy-headed" liberals, intellectuals, and long-hairs "who have been looking down their noses at us." On Apr. 7, Wallace won more than a third of the votes in the Wisconsin primary.

In May he won 30 percent of the votes in the Democratic primary in Indiana, then 47 percent of the votes in the Maryland primary. Presumably, the Democrats who voted for Wallace were not voting for him for president but "sending a message" to the leadership of both parties of their neglected discontents. When the Republicans nominated Barry Goldwater for president in July, Wallace withdrew from the Democratic race, satisfied that the message had been received.

By 1968, the Wallace issues were far more pronounced than in 1964. Wallace was then the candidate of the newly formed *American Independent Party, which collected 2.7 million signatures to put his name on the ballots of all 50 states. Wallace rallies everywhere were packed with cheering, stomping partisans. In October, polls showed Wallace's support at 20 percent. Both Hubert Humphrey and Richard Nixon, the Democratic and Republican candidates, feared that Wallace would cost them the election. In November, Wallace received 9.9 million popular votes (13 percent of the total) and carried five Southern states.

In 1972 the issue of court-ordered busing to achieve *school desegregation exercised the nation. Wallace again entered the Democratic primaries, inveighing against a tyrannical (and godless) Supreme Court for its attack on neighborhood schools and community autonomy. In Florida in March, amid a field of a dozen candidates, Wallace won with 42 percent of the votes; in

Wisconsin in April he finished second with 22 percent—behind George McGovern but ahead of Humphrey and Edmund Muskie. In May, the polls had him the front runner in the Michigan and Maryland primaries. At Laurel, Md., at 4 p.m. on May 15, a 21-year-old drifter named Arthur Bremer fired three shots at close range into the Alabama governor's shoulder, abdomen, and spine.

Paralyzed from the waist down, in constant pain, Wallace became a marginal figure in national politics. He now professed to have found religion and sought the forgiveness of those he had hurt. Surprisingly, Alabama blacks found his contrition sincere and supported him in his last campaign for governor. Meanwhile, his Northern followers had become Reagan Democrats. In the end, it was amiable Ronald Reagan—not snarling George Wallace—who reversed the course of American politics.

WANGHIA TREATY or **CUSHING'S TREATY** (1844), diplomatic achievement of the *Tyler administration. The treaty, negotiated with China by U.S. commissioner Caleb Cushing, initiated political relations between the two countries. The United States obtained the trading privileges already won by Great Britain and established the principle of extraterritoriality—American citizens in China would be governed by U.S., not Chinese, law.

WAR CRIMES TRIALS (1945–49). During World War 2, the Allies resolved to try Axis leaders for crimes against peace (planning war), crimes against humanity (genocide), war crimes (atrocities against civilians and prisoners), and conspiracy to commit these crimes. At Nuremberg, Germany, from Nov. 20, 1945, to Oct. 1, 1946, 22 Nazi leaders were tried before an international military tribunal composed of judges representing the United States, Great Britain, France, and the Soviet Union. Twelve were sentenced to death, three to life imprisonment, four to other prison terms; three were acquitted.

Other war crimes trials were held by American, British, French, and Soviet authorities in their respective occupation zones (see *German Occupation). In the American zone, Germans connected with the Dachau concentration camp, the Malmédy massacre of American prisoners, and other atrocities were tried by military tribunals. But hundreds of other German army officers, government and Nazi Party officials, doctors, and businessmen were tried in civilian courts before American judges although without juries. Meanwhile, German courts tried thousands of ordinary Nazis in the "denazification" program required by the Allies.

In Tokyo from May 3, 1946, to Nov. 4, 1948, 25 wartime Japanese leaders were tried by an international tribunal. Seven were sentenced to death, 16 to life imprisonment, and two to other prison terms.

Underlying these trials was the question whether the crimes for which the defendants were prosecuted were recognized in international law. The Allied view was that they were and that a precedent had to be firmly established for the future.

WAR DEBTS (1919–34). After World War 1, 20 countries owed the United States some $11.5 billion, loaned by the United States to its allies during the war and to other countries for relief and reconstruction shortly after the war. The Allies also owed money to each other.

The communists' repudiation of czarist debts was a major reason for Russia's postwar ostracism. But among other U.S. debtors the moral obligation to repay wartime loans was considered ambiguous. Great Britain offered to cancel debts owed her if the United States would cancel Britain's debt, but Pres. Woodrow Wilson and succeeding presidents were adamant in their insistence on repayment. (As Pres. Calvin Coolidge said famously, "They hired the money, didn't they?") In 1922, the debtor nations agreed to repay their loans over a 62-year period at an average interest rate of 2.135 percent.

The major powers expected to use German reparations to repay their debts to the United States, but Germany defaulted in 1923 and France's punitive occupation of the Ruhr led to a catastrophic German inflation that seemed to doom further reparations payments. In 1924 an international commission headed by U.S. budget director Charles G. Dawes proposed, in the **Dawes Plan**, a revised schedule of German reparations payments linked to new German taxes, currency stabilization, reorganization of the German central bank, and U.S. loans. Germany then resumed reparations payments, but by 1929 new difficulties had arisen and a new commission, headed by U.S. corporate executive Owen D. Young, worked out a "final" settlement of the reparations problem. The **Young Plan** reduced Germany's obligations (heretofore open-ended) to $8 billion payable over 58.5 years at 5.5 percent interest and established a Bank for International Settlements to facilitate payments.

Meanwhile, the worsening economic situation in Europe forced the United States to reduce both principal and interest of war debts owed it. In 1931, in the midst of the world economic crisis, Pres. Herbert Hoover proposed a one-year moratorium (the **Hoover Moratorium**) on all intergovernmental payments, war debts, and reparations. The proposal averted a panic and stabi-

lized the economic decline. Although the Allies again reduced German obligations in 1932, the United States refused to reduce its claims. Germany ceased paying reparations, and by 1934 all U.S. debtors had defaulted except Hungary, which paid interest on its debt until 1939, and Finland, which eventually paid its debt in full.

WAR HAWKS, a group of young, nationalist representatives who entered Congress in November 1811 avid for war with Great Britain. Prominent among them were Henry Clay and Richard M. Johnson of Kentucky, John C. Calhoun, William Lowndes, and Langdon Cheves of South Carolina, Felix Grundy of Tennessee, and Peter B. Porter of western New York.

WAR OF 1812 (1812–14), war between the United States and Great Britain arising out of British violations of American maritime rights.

Background. At war almost continuously from 1793, Britain and France instituted blockades of one another and seized neutral (including American) ships in violation of existing maritime law. The British, moreover, persisted in impressing alleged British deserters from American ships on the high seas (see *Impressment). The only recourse for the United States was economic sanctions against the belligerents (see *Embargo and Nonintercourse).

When French emperor Napoleon I promised to repeal his decrees prohibiting neutral trade with Britain, and Britain did not revoke its restrictions on neutral trade with French-held Europe, Pres. James Madison embargoed U.S. trade with Britain. The British finally lifted their restrictions on June 16, 1812, but Congress, ignorant of the British action, declared war on June 18. In his war message to Congress on June 1, Madison recited a long list of injuries inflicted on Americans by the British and their Indian allies to which the United States had vainly responded with "remonstrances and expostulations." "We behold, in fine," he concluded, "on the side of Great Britain a state of War against the United States; and on the side of the United States, a state of peace toward Great Britain."

Paradoxically, most of the congressmen from the maritime and commercial states of the Northeast that had suffered most from British and French depredations voted against the war. The most bellicose congressmen were nationalist politicians from the West and South, led by the *"war hawks." These representatives of farmers and frontiersmen took up the cry "Free trade and seamen's rights" because they believed war with Britain would permit an easy conquest of Canada and pacification of the

Indian tribes in the Northwest, whose hostility, they thought, was instigated by the British. The war resolution passed 79–49 in the House, 19–13 in the Senate.

The United States was ill prepared for war. The navy consisted of only 16 seagoing vessels. The army, numbering 7,000 regulars, had to be supplemented by state militias, which often did not materialize when called and proved undisciplined and ineffective when they did. Moreover, the war was widely unpopular, especially in New England, where all the state governments were in the hands of Federalists. The Federalists thought that the United States should be supporting Britain against Napoleon and considered "Mr. Madison's war" a Southern plot to ruin New England. States' rights sentiments in New England, aroused during Pres. Thomas Jefferson's embargo, now led to talk of secession, culminating in the *Hartford Convention (1814).

The War in the North. "On to Canada!" cried the war hawks. The war on the Canadian border was fought at three invasion points: Detroit; the Niagara River, between Lakes Erie and Ontario; and Lake Champlain. The first year saw a series of humiliating reverses for the Americans. Thereafter, their military competence improved, and although they never succeeded in invading Canada, they managed to check British invasions of the United States.

After a brief incursion into sparsely populated Upper Canada (July 1812), Gen. William Hull surrendered Detroit to the British (Aug. 16). On the Niagara River in October and at Plattsburg on Lake Champlain in November, undisciplined militias refused to advance into Canada.

During the winter of 1812–13, navy captain Oliver Hazard Perry built a fleet of small boats on Lake Erie and on Sept. 10, 1813, defeated a similar British fleet (see *Lake Erie). U.S. control of the lake made the British position at Detroit untenable. Withdrawing, the British were pursued by Gen. William Henry Harrison and defeated at the battle of the Thames (Oct. 5). The death in that battle of the Shawnee chief and British ally Tecumseh led to the Treaty of Greenville (July 22, 1814), by which the Northwest Indians made peace with the United States (see *Tecumseh Confederacy).

Control of Lake Ontario by an American fleet under Capt. Isaac Chauncy permitted an American force under Gen. Henry Dearborn to raid York (later Toronto), capital of Upper Canada, where the Americans burned a number of public buildings (April 1813). On the Lake Champlain front, a two-pronged attack toward Montreal led by Gens. James Wilkinson and Wade Hampton was turned back at the Châteauguay River (Oct. 25,

1813) and Chrysler's Farm (Nov. 11). In December, the British crossed the Niagara River, seized Fort Niagara, burned Buffalo, and allowed their Indian allies to ravage the countryside.

The War at Sea. While the U.S. Army was suffering humiliating setbacks on the Canadian border, the U.S. Navy was winning a series of spectacular single-ship engagements that chagrined the arrogant British and cheered the depressed American public. Among those victories: the U.S. frigate *Constitution*, Capt. Isaac Hull, over the British frigate *Guerrière* (Aug. 19, 1812); the U.S. frigate *United States*, Capt. Stephen Decatur, over the British frigate *Macedonian* (Oct. 25); the *Constitution* again, Capt. William Bainbridge, over the British frigate *Java* (Dec. 29).

Thereafter, most of the American fleet was confined to harbor by a British blockade. When the U.S. frigate *Chesapeake*, Capt. James Lawrence, ventured out of Boston harbor to accept a British challenge, it was defeated and captured by the *Shannon* (June 1, 1813). Mortally wounded, Lawrence ordered, "Don't give up the ship." American cruisers and privateers continued to harass British shipping worldwide with considerable success.

British Offensives. In 1814 the British launched invasions of the United States on the Niagara and Lake Champlain fronts. Americans under Gens. Jacob Brown and Winfield Scott stopped the first at Chippewa (July 5) and Lundy's Lane (July 25). The second invasion force turned back after Commodore Thomas Macdonough's naval victory at Plattsburg Bay (Sept. 1) denied the British control of Lake Champlain.

To create a diversion in support of the invasion thrusts in the north, a British fleet entered Chesapeake Bay in August and landed (Aug. 19) 4,500 troops at Benedict, Md. At **Bladensburg**, the British routed (Aug. 24) a hastily assembled American force and that night entered Washington, where they set fire to a number of public buildings (see *Washington Burning). They withdrew the next day and turned toward Baltimore, which was now heavily defended. On the night of Sept. 13–14 the British fleet unsuccessfully bombarded Fort McHenry in Baltimore harbor, then abandoned the campaign and in October sailed for Jamaica.

In November a British fleet carrying 7,500 troops sailed from Jamaica for New Orleans with the intention of seizing control of that city and with it the Mississippi River. At the battle of *New Orleans (Jan. 8, 1815), a well-entrenched American force under Gen. Andrew Jackson inflicted disastrous casualties on the British, who withdrew and reembarked for Jamaica.

Peace and After. In November 1813 the British

government proposed peace negotiations. Five American commissioners met with their British counterparts at Ghent in August 1814. The maritime issues that had caused the war had now been removed by the end of the war in Europe. The Treaty of *Ghent (signed Dec. 24, 1814, and ratified by the U.S. Senate Feb. 15, 1815) restored the prewar territorial status quo and provided for mixed commissions to settle U.S.-Canadian boundary disputes. Other issues involving the Great Lakes and the Atlantic fisheries were left for future negotiations.

With American successes on the Niagara front, Lake Champlain, and Baltimore—and especially the victory at New Orleans—the war ended in a burst of glory for the United States. Patriotism bloomed, political and sectional rifts healed, optimism reigned. Americans considered with satisfaction that they had successfully defended their independence a second time, that the seas were now open for their expanding commerce, that the Indians had been pacified and the West made safe for new tides of migration. President Madison's popularity, nonexistent a few months before, soared to unimagined heights. At the same time, the war instilled new respect for each other in the combatants and demonstrated their economic and political interdependence.

WAR ON POVERTY. See *Johnson (Lyndon) Administration; *Poverty.

WAR POWERS ACT (1973), legislation of the *Nixon administration, passed over the president's veto. A reaction to the unpopular *Vietnam War, which Congress had never formally declared, the act required presidents to consult with Congress before sending U.S. troops into hostilities, to report to Congress within 48 hours the deployment of U.S. troops, and to withdraw such troops within 60 days unless Congress declared war or otherwise authorized their commitment. Presidents since Nixon have consistently ignored the act as unconstitutional.

WAR REFUGEE BOARD. See *Holocaust Response.

WARREN COMMISSION. See *Kennedy Assassinations.

WARREN COURT (1953–69), the U.S. Supreme Court under Chief Justice Earl Warren. The Warren Court is often ranked second only to the *Marshall Court for the significance of its achievement—namely, reinterpreting much constitutional law in the interest of individuals rather than property, seeking social justice at the expense of long-established precedents.

In the area of civil rights, the Court's most important work was the *school-desegregation cases. In *Brown v. Board of Education of Topeka (1954), Chief Justice Warren tactfully brought together judicial activists and advocates of judicial restraint in the unanimous rejection of the 60-year-old "separate but equal" doctrine of *Plessy v. Ferguson (1896). In *Cooper v. Aaron (1958), a unanimous Court asserted its constitutional supremacy on the issue. In *Green v. County School Board of New Kent County (1968), still unanimous, the Court rejected a plausible "freedom of choice" plan intended to circumvent the desegregation order in Brown. Also unanimously, in *Heart of Atlanta Motel v. United States (1964) the Court upheld the public-accommodations sections of the *Civil Rights Act of 1964 and in *South Carolina v. Katzenbach (1966) the *Voting Rights Act of 1965.

Also in the civil rights area, the Court upheld the concept of one person, one vote in a number of reapportionment cases. In *Baker v. Carr (1962) the Court, reversing a long-standing view that the apportionment of state legislatures was a political question and thus nonjusticiable, ruled that the 14th Amendment's Equal Protection Clause required "substantial equality" among state electoral districts. Reapportionment cases from 15 states soon reached the Court, which it resolved in *Reynolds v. Sims (1964), finding that one or both houses of most state legislatures required reapportionment.

In the area of civil liberties, the Court's rulings in a series of criminal justice cases significantly enlarged the rights of the accused. In *Mapp v. Ohio (1961), the Court extended the federal exclusionary rule—that illegally seized evidence could not be used in a criminal trial—to the state courts. Similarly, in *Gideon v. Wainwright (1963) it extended to state courts the federally recognized right to counsel for indigent defendants. In *Miranda v. Arizona (1966) the Court rejected a criminal defendant's confession made during "custodial interrogation" when he had not been fully advised of his rights against self-incrimination. In In re *Gault (1967) the Court mandated procedural safeguards for defendants in juvenile courts.

Further in the area of civil liberties, in *Engel v. Vitale (1962) the Court prohibited the use in public schools of a prayer written by state officials, and in *Abington School District v. Schempp (1963) the Court prohibited Bible reading in the public schools (see *Church-State Relations). In *Yates v. United States (1957) it overturned the convictions of the second group of Communist Party leaders to be tried under the 1940 Smith Act.

In *New York Times Co. v. Sullivan (1964) it protected criticism of public officials, even when inaccurate, when no "actual malice" could be shown, and in *Griswold v. Connecticut (1965) it defined for the first time a constitutional right to privacy.

The record of the Warren Court was as controversial as it was revolutionary. In the 1960s, former president Dwight Eisenhower opined that the appointment of Earl Warren as chief justice had been his "biggest mistake."

WASHINGTON ADMINISTRATION (1789–97). Elected first president of the United States by the unanimous vote of the *electoral college, George Washington was inaugurated on Apr. 30, 1789, taking the presidential oath on the balcony of Federal Hall (previously the New York City Hall) at the corner of Wall and Broad streets in New York. In the Senate chamber within Federal Hall he delivered his inaugural address.

Washington vested the office of president with his own enormous prestige. Aware that his every act would serve as a precedent for his successors, he consciously established enduring precedents in the etiquette surrounding his office, the institutionalization of the cabinet, his direction of the federal bureaucracy, his relationship with Congress, and his limiting his tenure to two terms.

During his first term, Washington supported the efforts of Secretary of the Treasury Alexander Hamilton to strengthen the national government by establishing a sound public credit and encouraging economic development (see *Hamilton System). In 1794, he and Hamilton together led an army that suppressed resistance to Hamilton's system in the *Whiskey Rebellion.

Hamilton's program was opposed in the cabinet by Secretary of State Thomas Jefferson and in the House of Representatives by James Madison, only recently Hamilton's colleague in composing The *Federalist. Jefferson and Madison believed that the Hamilton system benefited financiers and speculators while disadvantaging farmers and workingmen. They viewed Hamilton's "loose construction" of the Constitution—his finding "implied powers" where the Constitution was silent—as aggrandizing the federal government in ways unintended by the Framers. The effect of Hamilton's policies, they believed, would be the corruption of the federal government and the ultimate establishment of a monarchy, which they were convinced that Hamilton, Vice Pres. John Adams, and perhaps even Washington himself conspired at. The conflict between *Hamilton and Jefferson led to the formation of the nation's first two political parties, the *Jeffersonian Republican Party and the *Federalist Party.

Washington was reelected unanimously in 1792. In his second term, the hostility between Federalists and Republicans was exacerbated to fever pitch by the *French Revolution and the outbreak of war between Great Britain and France. Intensely Anglophobic, Jefferson and his followers uncritically championed the French cause, even (at first) in the *Genêt affair. Washington's proclamation of neutrality (April 1793) and especially his acceptance of *Jay's Treaty (1794), which resolved a number of dangerous differences with Great Britain, they regarded as evidence of the president's pro-British bias. Criticism of Washington, which had been indirect during his first term, became direct and scurrilous. "If ever a nation was debauched by a man," editorialized Benjamin Franklin Bache in the Philadelphia Aurora, a Jeffersonian newspaper, "the American Nation has been debauched by Washington. . . . [T]he masque of patriots may be worn to conceal the foulest designs against the liberties of a people."

Party strife and personal abuse grieved and confounded Washington. Together with weariness and advancing age, they confirmed his resolution to retire at the end of his second term. With the help of Hamilton, he prepared a "farewell address" to the American people—an earnest appeal for national unity in the face of sectional and factional divisions—that was published in newspapers across the country in September 1796 (see *Washington's Farewell Address).

Washington was succeeded by his vice president, John Adams. During Washington's administration, Vermont (1791), Kentucky (1792), and Tennessee (1796) became the 14th, 15th, and 16th states.

WASHINGTON BURNING (Aug. 24–25, 1814), incident in the *War of 1812. In the summer of 1814, British general Robert Ross was ordered to create a diversion on the U.S. coast to support British operations on the Canadian border. A British fleet brought Ross and 4,500 veteran troops up Chesapeake Bay and the Patuxent River and disembarked them (Aug. 19–20) at Benedict, Md. Learning that Washington was virtually undefended, Ross approached the city from the northeast through Bladensburg, Md., on the Anacostia River.

Pres. James Madison realized only belatedly that the capital was in danger. His secretary of war, Gen. John Armstrong, assured him that it had no strategic value. Its defense was entrusted to the inexperienced Gen. William Winder, who, as the British approached, ineptly placed 7,000 raw militia across their line of march at **Bladensburg**. On Aug. 24 the British crossed the river and routed the Americans at "the Bladensburg races."

Capt. Joshua Barney with 500 sailors and marines covered the Americans' flight with naval guns, inflicting heavy casualties until he himself was wounded and captured. The panicked militia streamed through Washington, from which the government and most residents fled.

The British entered Washington at 8 p.m. A group of officers found dinner waiting at the White House, ate, and then set fire to the building. The Capitol, the Treasury, the building housing the War and State departments, the Navy Yard, and a few private buildings were also set ablaze in retaliation for similar American conduct in Canada. The fires burned all night, leaving blackened ruins.

The British left Washington the next morning, Aug. 25, and reembarked at Benedict on Aug. 30. Madison and his cabinet returned on Aug. 27 to be greeted by a surly citizenry. General Armstrong soon resigned.

WASHINGTON CONFERENCES (1941, 1943). See *World War 2 Conferences.

WASHINGTON NAVAL CONFERENCE (1921–22), diplomatic achievement of the *Harding administration. At the initiative of Secretary of State Charles Evans Hughes, representatives of nine powers—the United States, Great Britain, Japan, France, Italy, Portugal, China, Belgium, and the Netherlands—met in Washington and produced a total of nine treaties.

In the most important, the United States, Great Britain, Japan, France, and Italy agreed to suspend capital-ship construction for ten years and then to adhere to a construction ratio of 5:5:3:1.67:1.67. This treaty gave Japan naval superiority in the Western Pacific. In return, Japan signed a Nine Power Treaty pledging to maintain the *open door in China.

In a Four Power Pact, the United States, Great Britain, Japan, and France pledged to respect each other's possessions in the Pacific and to consult in case of aggression in the area by other powers. This treaty replaced the Anglo-Japanese alliance of 1902.

At a conference in London in 1935, Japan withdrew from the Washington treaties when it was denied naval parity with the United States and Great Britain.

WASHINGTON'S FAREWELL ADDRESS (1796). Determined to retire after his second term, Pres. George Washington revealed his intention in a farewell address to the American people. Drafted by Washington and amplified by Alexander Hamilton, the address was not delivered in person to an audience but given to the press and published nationwide in September 1796.

Like a father advising well-intentioned but wayward children, Washington reminded Americans that their union was the "main pillar" of their independence, peace, prosperity, and liberty. This unity was supported by sentiment: "Citizens by birth or choice of a common country, that country has a right to concentrate your affections. The name of American, which belongs to you in your national capacity, must always exalt the just pride of patriotism more than any appellation derived from local discriminations. With slight shades of difference, you have the same religion, manners, habits, and political principles. You have in a common cause fought and triumphed together. The independence and liberty you possess are the work of joint councils and joint efforts, of common dangers, sufferings, and successes."

Unity was also necessitated by their interests: The different sections of the country—North, South, East, West—found in union "greater strength, greater resource,... greater security from external danger,... an exemption from those broils and wars between themselves which so frequently afflict neighboring countries...."

To hold together so extensive a country, "a government of as much vigor as is consistent with the perfect security of liberty is indispensable." Washington admonished Americans to revere the Constitution, "the offspring of our own choice.... Respect for its authority, compliance with its laws, acquiescence in its measures, are duties enjoined by the fundamental maxims of true liberty.... The very idea of the power and the right of the people to establish government presupposes the duty of every individual to obey the established government." To preserve the government, it was necessary to resist not only "irregular opposition" to its authority but "the spirit of innovation upon its principles, however specious the pretexts."

Having warned against the divisiveness of sectional interests, Washington also warned "in the most solemn manner" against the divisive effects of party spirit: "This spirit, unfortunately, is inseparable from our nature, having its root in the strongest passions of the human mind.... It serves always to distract the public councils and enfeeble the public administration. It agitates the community with ill-founded jealousies and false alarms; kindles the animosity of one part against another;... opens the door to foreign influence and corruption...."

His experience with party divisions over foreign policy informed Washington's concluding advice: "Observe good faith and justice toward all nations. Cultivate peace and harmony with all," but avoid "permanent, inveterate antipathies against particular nations and passionate attachments for others.... Europe has a set of primary interests which to us have none or a very remote relation. . . . Our detached and distant situation invites and enables us to . . . defy material injury from external annoyance. . . . 'Tis our true policy to steer clear of permanent alliances with any portion of the foreign world."

WASHINGTON'S RESIGNATION (Dec. 23, 1783). From his emotional leave-taking of his officers at Fraunces Tavern in New York on Dec. 4, Gen. George Washington traveled to Annapolis, Md., where the *Continental Congress was then sitting. There was a rumor abroad that he would there make himself dictator. But on the morning of Dec. 23, 1783, he appeared before the small body of congressmen and nervously expressed his desire to "surrender in their hands the trust committed to me, and to claim the indulgence of retiring from the Service of my Country." He handed his commission to the president of the Congress, Thomas Mifflin, onetime disastrous quartermaster general and schemer in the *Conway Cabal. Washington left soon thereafter and reached Mount Vernon at dusk on Christmas Eve.

The event made a profound impression in Europe, where King George III was reported to have told the painter Benjamin West that if Washington resigned he would be "the greatest man in the world."

WASHINGTON'S SLAVES. George Washington was born into a world that had accepted *slavery since time immemorial. Modestly circumstanced, he inherited his first slaves along with Mount Vernon from his half brother Lawrence. His marriage to the wealthy widow Martha Custis brought him more slaves. With Martha's money he enlarged the Mount Vernon estate and bought still more slaves to work it. He was a businesslike slave owner, extending the workday, pursuing runaways, disciplining the recalcitrant, selling off the incorrigible. Washington became one of the richest men in America, his capital consisting chiefly of more than 300 slaves.

Over the years, Washington's attitude toward slavery changed. He took seriously the sentiments expressed in the Declaration of Independence. Perhaps he was impressed by the *free blacks who fought in the Continental Army. As president, he must have scorned the hypocrisy of the slave-owning Southern "republicans" who attacked his administration as monarchical. The *Hamilton system that he championed had no place for slaves. He came to see that the emancipation of the slaves was not only a humanitarian but a political imperative. "I clearly foresee," he told one visitor, "that nothing but the rooting out of slavery can perpetuate the existence of our union by consolidating it in a common bond of principle."

Washington hoped that the Southern states would gradually abolish slavery. As for his own slaves, it was impossible—and would have been inhumane—simply to turn them loose. A few he secretly left behind in freedom in Philadelphia at the end of his presidency. But many of the Mount Vernon slaves were too young or too old to care for themselves, though Washington refused to sell any of them. Unable to tell the others of his intentions for fear of precipitating an insurrection, he tried to prepare them for freedom by having them taught a variety of vocations. In this he was unsuccessful, since the slaves had no incentive to learn new skills. Vainly, he tried to rent his estate to English farmers who would retain his slaves as hired laborers.

In the end, Washington provided in his will that his slaves should be freed after his and his wife's deaths. His heirs were enjoined to care for the old and infirm and to support and educate the young (which they did as late as 1833). His hope was that the former slaves would enter Virginia society in the perilous condition of free blacks. Two years after his death and one year before her own, Martha Washington freed their personal slaves for fear that they might not wait for emancipation until her death. She could not, however, free the slaves she had inherited from her first husband, Daniel Parke Custis, because they were partly owned by the children of that marriage.

WASHINGTON TREATY (1871), diplomatic accord of the *Grant administration. A treaty between the United States and Great Britain, negotiated in Washington by Secretary of State Hamilton Fish and the earl of Ripon, it provided for arbitration of the *Alabama Claims, the *San Juan Boundary Dispute, and a U.S.-Canadian fisheries dispute.

WATERGATE (1972–74), far-reaching scandal that brought down the Nixon presidency. It arose out of Pres. Richard M. Nixon's obsession with secrecy, his fear of "enemies," and his anxiety about his reelection in 1972.

The scandal began with a little-noted arrest on June 17, 1972, at the office of the Democratic National Committee in the Watergate apartment complex in Washington of seven burglars employed by the Committee to Reelect the President (the Nixon campaign organization) and with Nixon's decision to cover up White House involvement. His efforts failed. Through the trial of the burglars, journalists' exposés, and the investigations of a

Senate committee and special prosecutors, an elaborate pattern of illegalities was disclosed—perjury, obstruction of justice, illegal wiretapping and break-ins, harassment of administration opponents, "dirty tricks" discrediting Democratic primary candidates, corrupt campaign contributions, and the president's own evasion of federal and California income taxes.

Most sensational was the revelation that Nixon had secretly recorded all conversations in the Oval Office. The struggle for possession of these tapes (which Nixon might easily have destroyed) occupied the president and investigators for months. On July 24, 1974, the U.S. Supreme Court ruled that executive privilege did not apply in a criminal matter (see *United States v. Nixon). The tapes finally surrendered revealed Nixon's desire to get the Federal Bureau of Investigation to halt its investigation of the Watergate burglary shortly after it had occurred. This was the "smoking gun" that Nixon's most loyal supporters required to change their minds.

The House Judiciary Committee voted (July 27–30) three articles of impeachment: obstruction of justice, abuse of authority, and defiance of committee subpoenas. Assured that the Senate would vote to convict, Nixon resigned on Aug. 9.

On Sept. 8, on national radio and television, Pres. Gerald Ford granted Nixon "a full, free and absolute pardon . . . for all offenses against the United States which he . . . has committed or may have committed or taken part in during the period from January 20, 1969, through August 9, 1974." Nixon never admitted any guilt.

Meanwhile, 38 members of the Nixon administration had pleaded guilty to or been indicted for crimes revealed in the Watergate investigations.

WEATHERMEN. See *New Left.

WEBSTER-ASHBURTON TREATY (1842), diplomatic achievement of the *Tyler administration. The treaty, negotiated by Secretary of State Daniel Webster and British minister Lord Ashburton, resolved a longstanding dispute over the boundary between Maine and the Canadian province of New Brunswick; the United States obtained 7,000 of the 12,000 square miles of disputed territory. Also settled was the boundary between the United States and Canada from Vermont through the St. Lawrence River and the Great Lakes to Lake of the Woods. (The U.S. boundary from Lake of the Woods to the crest of the Rocky Mountains along the 49th parallel had been fixed by the *Convention of 1818.) Another

provision established joint naval squadrons off the African coast to suppress the *slave trade.

WEBSTER-HAYNE DEBATE (Jan. 19–27, 1830), debate in the U.S. Senate about the nature of the federal Union between Daniel Webster of Massachusetts and Robert Y. Hayne of South Carolina, both noted orators. Hayne initiated the debate (Jan. 19) by attacking the Northern states as oppressive, citing *tariff and *public lands policies that benefited them at the expense of the South and West. In his first reply to Hayne (Jan. 20), Webster portrayed an active national government as a force for positive good, benefiting all sections beyond mean calculations of profit and loss. Hayne's rejoinder (Jan. 21, 25) became a defense of states' rights, *slavery, and *nullification.

Webster's second reply to Hayne (Jan. 26–27) expounded the still-novel view of the Constitution as the nation's fundamental law rather than a compact among sovereign states and of the Union as supreme and indissoluble: "It is, Sir, the people's Constitution, the people's government, made for the people, made by the people, and answerable to the people." The speech provided the authoritative text for American nationalists; Webster's peroration was memorized by generations of patriotic schoolchildren:

"When my eyes shall be turned to behold for the last time the sun in heaven, may I not see him shining on the broken and dishonored fragments of a once glorious Union; on States dissevered, discordant, belligerent; on a land rent with civil feuds, or drenched, it may be, in fraternal blood! Let their last feeble and lingering glance rather behold the gorgeous ensign of the republic, now known and honored throughout the earth, still full high advanced, its arms and trophies streaming in their original lustre, not a stripe erased or polluted, nor a single star obscured, bearing for its motto, no such miserable interrogatory as 'What is all this worth?' nor those other words of delusion and folly, 'Liberty first and Union afterwards'; but everywhere, spread all over in characters of living light, blazing on all its ample folds, as they float over the sea and over the land, and in every wind under the whole heavens, that other sentiment, dear to every true American heart,—Liberty *and* Union, now and forever, one and inseparable!"

Considered the greatest speech of his life, and indeed the greatest speech ever heard in the U.S. Senate, Webster's second reply to Hayne, delivered from notes only, occupied six hours over two successive days, enthralling an audience that filled the Senate chamber to overflowing.

The scene is preserved in a painting by George P. A. Healy that hangs in Faneuil Hall, Boston.

Both Hayne and Webster spoke again on Jan. 27, concluding the debate.

WEBSTER'S SEVENTH OF MARCH SPEECH

(Mar. 7, 1850), speech in the U.S. Senate by Sen. Daniel Webster of Massachusetts in support of Henry Clay's *Compromise of 1850. "I wish to speak to-day," he began, "not as a Massachusetts man, nor as a Northern man, but as an American. . . . I speak to-day for the preservation of the Union."

Webster's central point was that the divisive issue of the extension of slavery into the territories acquired from Mexico was already settled: in the case of Texas, by the annexation resolution; in the cases of California and New Mexico, by the facts of geography. "[U]nder one or other of these laws [going back to the Ordinance of 1787], every foot of land in the States or in the Territories has already received a fixed and decided character." He urged North and South to accept these "settled" facts and respect each other's legitimate points of view.

In the process, he criticized *abolitionists ("There are men who . . . think what is right may be distinguished from what is wrong with the precision of an algebraic equation . . . that nothing is good but what is perfect, and that there are no compromises or modifications to be made in consideration of differences of opinion or in deference to other men's judgment") and rejected the application of the *Wilmot Proviso in the *Mexican Cession ("I would not take pains uselessly to reaffirm an ordinance of nature, nor to reenact the will of God. I would put in no Wilmot Proviso for the mere purpose of a taunt or reproach . . . to wound the pride . . . of the citizens of the Southern States").

In many parts of the country, Webster's speech was received as a work of evenhanded statesmanship. But antislavery people in New England were horrified and denounced Webster as an apostate. *How came he there?* thundered Ralph Waldo Emerson. "In the final hour, when he was forced by the peremptory necessity of the closing armies to take a side—did he take the part of great principles, the side of humanity and justice, or the side of abuse and oppression and chaos? Mr. Webster decided for Slavery. . . ."

WELFARE.

Until the 1930s, aid to the needy was the concern of private charities and of state and local welfare agencies. The onset of the *Great Depression quickly exhausted the resources of those institutions. In 1933, the Franklin *Roosevelt administration established the Federal Emergency Relief Administration (FERA) to funnel federal funds into state welfare channels. At the same time, the U.S. Department of Agriculture began to distribute surplus agricultural commodities to the needy. These emergency measures of public assistance, and others that followed, were intended as temporary expedients until a revived economy reabsorbed the great numbers of unemployed.

A Federal-State Collaboration. The **Social Security Act** of 1935 created a national income-transfer system—that is, a system by which revenues derived from the better-off portions of the population would be used to maintain the incomes of the needy portions—with both social insurance and public assistance components. Although both components originated in the same act, the social insurance component is known as the *Social Security system while the public assistance component became popularly known as welfare.

Whereas the Social Security system is entirely federal, administered from Washington with payroll taxes and benefits uniform throughout the country, welfare became a federal-state collaboration, the federal government providing funds to supplement state financing of state public assistance programs. The federal government established minimum standards for these programs while the states set eligibility requirements and benefit levels and administered them. These federal-state programs preserved the traditional character of state public assistance: they were categorical (targeted to particular groups of the needy) rather than universal (accessible to all the needy). Thus the original welfare component of the Social Security Act provided for federal funds to supplement state programs of public assistance to the aged and blind and to children. Unlike Social Security, whose benefits are based on previous contributions, welfare benefits were based only on need and membership in a covered category.

The authors of the Social Security Act considered this welfare component of their system purely transitional; as social insurance became more fully operative, they believed, the need for welfare would disappear. In this they were mistaken. The steady expansion of social insurance was accompanied by an unanticipated growth in the size of the nation's welfare system.

There were three reasons for this growth. First, new welfare programs were established to meet newly perceived needs. Some of these programs were set up with little appreciation of their potential for growth and thus of their ultimate costs. Second, demographic changes resulted in greater numbers of people eligible for welfare. These included growing numbers of the elderly and of single-parent families resulting from divorce, desertion, or illegitimacy that were not covered by Social Security. Third, the participation of eligible citizens steadily grew as a result of informational campaigns conducted by welfare rights organizations, of court decisions removing arbitrary restrictive regulations, and of outreach programs conducted by welfare departments themselves.

The Welfare System. The welfare system embraced programs that provided both cash and noncash (in-kind) benefits. The principal cash programs were Aid to Families with Dependent Children (AFDC), Supplemental Security Income (SSI), pensions for needy veterans, emergency assistance (EA), and state and local general assistance (GA). The chief in-kind programs were health insurance (Medicaid), food stamps, child nutrition, and housing assistance.

Aid to Families with Dependent Children provided cash assistance to low-income, female-headed families with dependent children or to families where the male head was incapacitated. Half the states also provided AFDC benefits to two-parent families where the father was unemployed. In 1994, 4.9 million families containing 13.9 million individuals (68 percent of them children) were enrolled in AFDC. Average monthly benefits per family ranged from $556 in California to $123 in Mississippi.

Congress in 1972 consolidated three existing federal-state public assistance programs to create a single federal program called **Supplemental Security Income**. SSI provided monthly cash payments in accordance with uniform, nationwide eligibility requirements to persons with inadequate incomes (including Social Security benefits) who were 65 or over, blind, or disabled.

Other federal cash programs provided pensions for needy disabled or aged wartime veterans, their dependents, and survivors. The federal government shared with about half the states the cost of emergency assistance programs that aided low-income families during emergencies not exceeding 30 days. All the states except Arkansas had general assistance programs that aided needy persons who were ineligible for federally subsidized assistance programs.

The principal in-kind assistance program was **Medicaid**, which was enacted in 1965 at the same time that the medical insurance program for the aged, Medicare, was added to the Social Security system. Under the Medicaid program, the charges of hospitals, laboratories, nursing homes, physicians, dentists, and pharmacists for services to participants were paid by state and local governments and then partially reimbursed by the federal government. The program was administered by the states, which could choose whether to have a Medicaid

program at all (Arizona did not) and the scope of services offered (some states provided dental and eye care while others kept services to a minimum). By federal statute, AFDC recipients were automatically eligible for Medicaid where a program existed. Beyond that, states set their own eligibility standards. These varied widely.

Under the **food stamps** program, needy households received monthly allotments of stamps or coupons that were exchangeable like money for food in most food stores. The program was established in 1964 ostensibly to raise levels of nutrition among low-income families but in reality to dispose of agricultural surpluses; since it was conceived as a farm program, its administration was assigned to the Department of Agriculture rather than to the Department of Health, Education, and Welfare. In fact, the food stamp program became the nation's most successful and popular income maintenance program. It was the only noncategorical federal welfare program—that is, the only one available on the basis of need regardless of the cause of that need.

Other in-kind assistance programs included the national school lunch program, the school breakfast program, the summer feeding program, and others for children whose families lived near or below the poverty level. The federal government also provided a limited amount of housing assistance to low-income families through public housing and programs that subsidized rent and mortgage payments.

"Ending Welfare as We Know It." The welfare system was universally unpopular. The working poor resented it. Recipients found it complex, humiliating, and inadequate. By others, it was variously perceived as excessively costly, growing out of control, riddled with fraud, antiwork and antifamily, and creating intergenerational dependency. Finally, its very success at sustaining rather than eliminating the so-called underclass was deemed a fatal fault.

In 1992 Democratic presidential candidate William J. Clinton promised "to end welfare as we know it." The welfare reform bill—the **Personal Responsibility and Work Opportunity Act**—that President Clinton signed in August 1996 as an election year necessity was in fact written by a Republican Congress. Aiming to move welfare recipients from dependency to work, it ended the federal guarantee of support to needy mothers and children. Instead, the money formerly spent on AFDC and several minor programs was to be given to the states in the form of block grants to pay for welfare programs of their own devising (but approved by the federal government). Recipients of welfare benefits were expected to engage in some kind of "work activity" after two years. A lifetime limit of five years was imposed on recipients of block-grant funds.

Defenders of the long and complex act praised it for enabling the states to experiment with varied welfare strategies. Critics chiefly regretted the transfer of welfare responsibility to the states, some of which had proved incompetent and uncaring in the past. Democratic senator Daniel Patrick Moynihan of New York called it "an obscene act of social regression."

To mitigate the harshness of the act, Clinton pushed through Congress a number of measures intended to "make work pay": expansion of tax credits for low-wage workers; extension of health insurance to 3.4 million poor children; increased funds for child care and preschool education; a requirement that welfare recipients compelled to work under the reformed welfare law be paid the minimum wage and be covered by federal workplace laws. As a result, the federal government was actually spending more on welfare than ever, but now the money was targeted to the *working* poor.

In the next five years, welfare rolls fell by half, to 6 million, due in part to a booming economy. One study of the consequences of the act found that three-fourths of the women in its sample who had left welfare for work (full- or part-time) had incomes below the poverty level and no health insurance.

WELFARE CAPITALISM, policy of many American industrial corporations in the 1920s to forestall unionization of their workers by instituting company unions, profit sharing, stock options, group insurance, and pensions as well as such amenities as cafeterias, health services, and social and recreational activities. The strategy contributed to the decline of union membership and relative labor peace during that decade. After 1929, however, labor discovered that what the corporation voluntarily gave, it was free to rescind.

WEST COAST HOTEL CO. v. PARRISH (1937), 5–4 decision of the *Hughes Court upholding a Washington State minimum-wage law for women, reversing *Adkins v. Children's Hospital* (1923) on the ground that the protection of women's health overrode the liberty of contract protected by the Due Process Clause of the Fifth Amendment.

Coming soon after the announcement of Pres. Franklin Roosevelt's *court-packing plan (although it had been made several months before the announcement), the decision was widely interpreted as a tactical retreat by the Court from its resistance to *New Deal policies of economic regulation. In particular, the shift of Justice Owen Roberts from the majority in a case the year before, which upheld *Adkins*, to the majority in this case was popularly described as "the switch in time that saved nine."

WESTERN FEDERATION OF MINERS (WFM), radical labor union committed to the idea of class struggle. William D. "Big Bill" Haywood was prominent in its leadership. It conducted violent strikes in the Coeur d'Alene district of Idaho (1892, 1899), Leadville, Colo. (1894), Cripple Creek, Colo. (1894, 1903–4), and Telluride, Colo. (1901).

The forcible suppression of the Cripple Creek strike in 1904 and failed strikes in Nevada (1907), Michigan (1913), and Montana (1913–14) caused the union to abandon its revolutionary stance and adopt conventional union objectives and tactics. After participating in 1905 in the founding of the *Industrial Workers of the World, to which Haywood transferred, the WFM rejoined the *American Federation of Labor (to which it had briefly belonged in 1896–97) and in 1916 became the Union of Mine, Mill, and Smelter Workers.

WEST FLORIDA. See *Floridas, East and West.

WEST VIRGINIA STATE BOARD OF EDUCATION v. BARNETTE (1943), 6–3 decision of the U.S. Supreme Court reversing *Minersville School District v. Gobitis* (1940) and justifying Jehovah's Witnesses' refusal to salute the flag under the Free Speech Clause of the First Amendment. The decision, by Justice Robert Jackson, is considered one of the great statements of constitutional liberty:

"Struggles to coerce uniformity of sentiment in support of some end thought essential to their time and country have been waged by many good as well as by evil men. . . . Those who begin coercive elimination of dissent soon find themselves exterminating dissenters. Compulsory unification of opinion achieves only the unanimity of the graveyard.

". . . There is no mysticism in the American concept of the State or of the nature or origin of its authority. We set up government by consent of the governed, and the Bill of Rights denies those in power any legal opportunity to coerce that consent. Authority here is to be controlled by public opinion, not public opinion by authority.

". . . [W]e apply the limitations of the Constitution with no fear that freedom to be intellectually and spiritually diverse or even contrary will disintegrate the social organization. To believe that patriotism will not flourish if patriotic ceremonies are voluntary and spontaneous instead of a compulsory routine is to make an unflattering estimate of the appeal of our institutions to free minds. We can have intellectual individualism and the rich cultural diversities that we owe to exceptional minds only at the price of occasional eccentricity and abnormal attitudes. When they are so harmless to others or to the State as those we deal with here, the price is not too great. But freedom to differ is not limited to things that do not matter much. That would be a mere shadow of freedom. The test of its substance is the right to differ as to things that touch the heart of the existing order.

"If there is any fixed star in our constitutional constellation, it is that no official, high or petty, can prescribe what shall be orthodox in politics, nationalism, religion, or other matters of opinion or force citizens to confess by word or act their faith therein. . . ." (See *Church-State Relations.)

WESTWARD MOVEMENT. The Europeans who settled on the Atlantic coast of North America were awestruck by the immense continent lying before them, only sparsely populated by Native Americans. The filling of this huge space in less than three centuries—largely through the voluntary efforts of individuals, families, and small groups—is a story without parallel in world history. The experience significantly affected the American character and institutions.

The westward movement began slowly in the 17th century as colonists pushed up river valleys into the interior of New England and Virginia in search of new farmland. By 1750 the **frontier**—the line dividing settled from unsettled territory—extended from central New England south along the eastern edge of the Appalachian Mountains. The French and Indian War briefly halted the advance, which resumed in spite of official British policy and the American Revolution. Pioneers crossed the Appalachians into the broad Mississippi Valley and were quickly borne west along its rivers. By 1820 the frontier was on the Mississippi itself.

Without pause, settlers moved into the trans-Mississippi west. In the 1840s, westering pioneers crossed the Great Plains and Rocky Mountains and established settlements on the West Coast. The Great Plains were settled last. In 1890 the director of the Census observed, "There can hardly be said to be a frontier line." (As a result of the depopulation of the Great Plains during the 20th century, in 2000 nearly 900,000 square miles met the 19th-century Census Bureau definition of frontier—land with a population of six people or fewer per square mile.)

Despite the passing of the frontier, Americans continued to move westward, followed by the advancing **cen-ter of population**, a point located every ten years by the Census Bureau. The first center of population, in 1790, lay in Maryland 23 miles east of Baltimore. Thereafter it marched steadily westward, through Maryland, Virginia, West Virginia, Ohio, Indiana, Illinois, and into Missouri, where in 2000 it was located 100 miles southwest of St. Louis.

Historians identify a succession of frontiers. Everywhere, the first frontier was the fur frontier, the frontier of hunters and trappers, since fur was the most readily exploitable resource. In the Far West, the trapper was succeeded by the miner, in the North Central states by the lumberman, on the Great Plains by the cattleman. All in time gave way to the farmer. The pioneer farmer cleared the forest or broke the prairie soil. His isolated log cabin or sod hut gave way in time to a more substantial and permanent house, usually built by a later-arriving farmer, the pioneer having drifted on. In time the farmer's isolation was relieved by the rise of the rural village and small town with schools, churches, and other civilizing amenities.

The presence of the frontier through three of the nation's four centuries could not have failed to affect the people's character and institutions. Since 1893, when Frederick Jackson Turner, a historian at the University of Wisconsin, published his paper "The Significance of the Frontier in American History," historians have tried to document that influence. It is easy to find certain widely acknowledged American character traits, both good and bad, writ large on the frontier, as well as certain institutions, both democratic and antidemocratic, flourishing there. But it is doubtful if the frontier was the necessary or sole source of these.

WHAT'S THE MATTER WITH KANSAS?, title of an editorial by William Allen White published in his Emporia, Kans., *Gazette*, Aug. 15, 1896, in which White attributed the state's stagnation to its populist politicians (see *Populism):

"We have an old mossback Jacksonian who snorts and howls because there is a bathtub in the State House; we are running that old jay for Governor. We have another shabby, wild-eyed, rattle-brained fanatic who has said openly in a dozen speeches that 'the rights of the user are paramount to the rights of the owner'; we are running him for Chief Justice, so that capital will come tumbling over itself to get into the state. We have raked the old ash heap of failure in the state and found an old human hoop skirt who has failed as a businessman, who has failed as an editor, who has failed as a preacher, and we are going to run him for Congressman-at-Large. . . .

Then we have discovered a kid without a law practice and have decided to run him for Attorney General. Then, for fear some hint that the state had become respectable might percolate through the civilized portions of the nation, we have decided to send three or four harpies out lecturing, telling the people that Kansas is raising hell and letting the corn go to weed."

WHIG PARTY (1834–54), political party formed by opponents of Pres. Andrew Jackson: National Republicans, who supported a national bank, high *tariffs, and *internal improvements (see *National Republican Party); states' rights Democrats offended by Jackson's stand on *nullification and his aggrandizement of presidential power (see *Democratic Party); reform-minded Anti-Masons (see *Anti-Masonic Party); and antislavery groups. The name Whig reflected their resistance to "King Andrew" just as 18th-century Whigs had resisted royal despotism in England and colonial America.

A highly heterogeneous assemblage, the Whig Party was generally thought to represent business interests, positive but restrained government, and humanitarian reform. Young Abraham Lincoln became a Whig because the party supported internal improvements, which were important to Westerners. Although it was a national party, it was disproportionately Northern, as the Democratic Party was disproportionately Southern.

Too loosely organized to support a single presidential candidate in 1836, the Whigs backed three *favorite sons in the hope that the election might be thrown into the House of Representatives. In 1840 they passed over the great men in their party—Henry Clay and Daniel Webster—to nominate a general, William Henry Harrison, who was elected but died a month after his inauguration. His vice president and successor, John Tyler, vetoed Whig bills to reestablish a national bank and was quickly deserted by the party.

The Whigs nominated Henry Clay in 1844, but Clay equivocated on *Texas annexation and lost to Democrat James K. Polk. In 1848 the Whigs nominated another general, Zachary Taylor (president 1849–50), who was succeeded by Vice President Millard Fillmore (president 1850–53).

By this time the Whig coalition was breaking up over the slavery issue. In the presidential election of 1852, another Whig general, Winfield Scott, carried only four of 31 states. The *Kansas-Nebraska Act (1854) marked the end of the party. Northern "conscience" Whigs refused to compromise on the extension of slavery; Southern "cotton" Whigs found the proslavery Democratic Party more congenial. A remnant of the Whig Party in 1856

nominated Millard Fillmore for president; he carried only the state of Maryland. By then, most Northern Whigs were moving to the new *Republican Party.

WHISKEY REBELLION (1794), insurrection in the western counties of Pennsylvania provoked by the 1791 excise tax on whiskey, a cornerstone of Secretary of the Treasury Alexander Hamilton's funding of the national debt (see *Hamilton System).

Typically, western farmers converted their surplus grain to whiskey, which was easier to transport than the grain itself. Whiskey was also used as barter and of course it was widely consumed. Thus the excise affected a large proportion of the western population and added to their other discontents, which included hostile Indians in neighboring Ohio, continued occupation by the British of military posts in the *Northwest Territory, and restricted navigation of the Mississippi River. Westerners felt that the federal government was unmindful of their needs and that Hamilton's policy enriched eastern speculators at their expense.

Protest meetings, riots, and attacks on federal officers reached a peak in 1794. Determined to demonstrate the power of the federal government, Pres. George Washington mobilized 13,000 militia troops from Pennsylvania, New Jersey, Maryland, and Virginia, at the same time dispatching three commissioners into the rebellious counties with power to grant amnesties in return for oaths of submission.

When the commissioners failed, Washington and Hamilton, on Oct. 14, assumed command of the troops at Carlisle, Pa. Gov. Henry Lee of Virginia actually led the troops across the Allegheny Mountains, whereupon all resistance collapsed. A number of insurgent leaders were arrested and convicted but later pardoned.

WHISKEY RING SCANDAL (1875), incident in the *Grant administration. For many years, hundreds of Western distillers, federal officials in St. Louis, and Republican Party managers conspired to evade the federal tax on whiskey. Some of the proceeds went to finance Republican election campaigns. Secretary of the Treasury Benjamin H. Bristow broke up the ring in 1875, securing 230 indictments and 110 convictions. The scandal eventually reached Pres. Ulysses S. Grant's private secretary, Gen. Orville H. Babcock. Grant testified in his behalf and Babcock was acquitted.

WHITE CITIZENS COUNCILS (1954–70), organizations founded in the South after the Supreme Court's decision in *Brown v. Board of Education of Topeka*

(1953) to resist *school desegregation and black voting. Originating in Mississippi, citizens councils spread quickly throughout the lower South, enlisting white business and civic leaders who, while no less committed to white supremacy, were too respectable to join the *Ku Klux Klan. The councils compelled white politicians to resist desegregation. Against blacks, they generally favored economic intimidation but used violence on occasion. The councils declined in the 1960s after passage of the *Civil Rights Act of 1964 and the *Voting Rights Act of 1965.

WHITE COURT (1910–21), the U.S. Supreme Court under Chief Justice Edward D. White. Five members of the White Court were appointed by Pres. William Howard Taft, who also raised White himself from associate to chief justice. All were men of Taft's own conservative stamp. The duty of the Court, Taft had written, was to "preserve the fundamental structure of our government as our fathers gave it to us." The Court, however, proved less conservative than Taft expected.

In *Standard Oil Co. of New Jersey v. United States* (1911), the Court ordered the dissolution of the company under the *Sherman Antitrust Act, but did so with the explanation that Standard Oil had been "unreasonable" in its anticompetitive practices. The **rule of reason** thus invoked meant that judges, not Congress, would determine when a particular restraint of trade was reasonable (permitted) or unreasonable (forbidden). The decision gave the government a victory, but it made prosecutions under the Sherman Act more difficult. The rule of reason was applied again in *United States v. American Tobacco Co.* (1911), the Court ordering the reorganization of the tobacco trust rather than its dissolution.

In *Wilson v. New* (1917) and *Bunting v. Oregon* (1917), the Court upheld federal and state maximum-hour laws, then in *Hammer v. Dagonhart* (1918) overturned a federal law intended to eliminate *child labor. In the *Arizona Employers' Liability Cases* (1919), the Court upheld a state workmen's compensation act that established the novel principle of employer liability without fault.

Wartime decisions of the White Court upheld the draft law and the president's authority to seize the railroads. In *Schenk v. United States* (1919) and *Abrams v. United States* (1919), the Court upheld the wartime *Espionage and Sedition Acts. Notably, Justice Oliver Wendell Holmes wrote the unanimous decision in the first case, then dissented equally memorably in the second.

WHITE HOUSE CONFERENCE ON CONSERVATION (1908). See *Conservation.

WHITE PLAINS (Sept. 28, 1776), *Revolutionary War battle. Outflanked on Manhattan Island, Patriot general George Washington moved north to White Plains and positioned his army—now numbering 14,000 men, one of the largest forces he would ever command—on hills overlooking the village. British general William Howe, with 16,000 men, approached slowly, finally confronting Washington on Sept. 28. But the expected frontal assault did not materialize. Instead, the battle developed on Chatterton Hill, a mile-long ridge dominating the American right that the Patriots occupied only belatedly. There Patriot militia fought off British attacks until they panicked in the face of mounted dragoons. The British took the hill and Washington withdrew to North Castle. Instead of pursuing Washington, Howe turned west to Dobbs Ferry, intending to seize forts Washington and Lee on the Hudson River.

WHITE PRIMARY, a *primary election from which blacks were barred by a state political party, thus effectively preventing their participation in elections in one-party states. The U.S. Supreme Court upheld a Texas Democratic Party white primary in 1935 but reversed itself in 1944 when it found that white primaries violated the *15th Amendment.

WHITE SUPREMACISTS. See *Radical Right.

WHITEWATER SCANDAL (1994–2000), episode of the *Clinton administration. During the 1992 presidential election campaign, reports circulated of improper involvement by then–state attorney general Bill Clinton and his wife, Hillary, in a 1977 development project on the Whitewater River in Arkansas in partnership with James McDougal, head of Madison Guaranty, a Little Rock savings and loan institution that later failed. From 1994 to 2000, *independent counsels Robert Fisk, Kenneth W. Starr, and Robert W. Ray investigated the allegations but failed to find any wrongdoing by the Clintons.

WHOLESOME MEAT ACT (1967). See *Consumer Protection.

WHOLESOME POULTRY PRODUCTS ACT (1968). See *Consumer Protection.

WICKERSHAM COMMISSION. See *Prohibition.

WILDERNESS ACT (1964). See *Environmentalism.

WILDERNESS CAMPAIGN (May–June 1864), *Civil War campaign in which Union general Ulysses S. Grant with the Army of the Potomac, driving south toward Richmond, fought a succession of costly battles with Confederate general Robert E. Lee's Army of Northern Virginia.

On May 3–4, 1864, the Army of the Potomac, commanded by Gen. George G. Meade and accompanied by Grant, who was now general in chief of all Union armies, crossed the Rapidan River in northern Virginia and entered the Wilderness, an area of dense forest and tangled underbrush 12 miles wide and eight deep with few and narrow roads. Grant's plan was to concentrate his force in the Wilderness, then move out into the open country beyond, outflanking Lee's army, which was entrenched on the south bank of the Rapidan west of the Wilderness, and forcing a battle in which Grant's superior numbers—120,000 men to Lee's 60,000—would prevail.

Lee, however, attacked the Union army in the Wilderness, nullifying its numerical superiority. Close, confused fighting raged May 5–6, bloodying both armies. Grant's casualties were twice Lee's, but Lee was unable to attack on May 7, thus permitting Grant to disengage. In the past, after similar initial reverses, other Union commanders had retreated. But Grant had promised "There will be no turning back," and his disheartened troops broke into cheers on the night of May 7 when he led them south. The army moved around Lee's right flank and headed for a crossroads named **Spotsylvania Court House** 15 miles in Lee's rear.

Perceiving Grant's objective, Lee sent his army racing south. When the Federal column approached Spotsylvania Court House, it found the Confederates already entrenched and building breastworks that they rapidly enlarged over the next days. Day after day, from May 8 to May 12, Grant hurled his divisions against the Confederate lines, only to be repelled with heavy losses. The fighting reached a peak of ferocity on May 12 at the **Bloody Angle**, a salient in the Confederate center where Federals and Confederates, jammed together in the Confederate trenches, fought hand to hand in heavy rain from dawn to midnight.

During this week of slaughter, Grant, in a routine communication to Washington, declared that he "proposed to fight it out on this line if it takes all summer." Northern newspapers hailed Grant's statement as evidence of his bulldog tenacity.

On May 20, Grant again disengaged, moved around Lee's right, and pushed south toward the North Anna River only 25 miles from Richmond. With the advantage of shorter interior lines, Lee got there first and entrenched on the south side of the river at Hanover Junction. Deciding not to attack Lee's well-fortified position,

Grant again moved around Lee's right, down the North Anna to Totopotomy Creek. Again, Lee was waiting. Grant considered, then again moved around Lee's right toward a crossroad village in Lee's rear named Cold Harbor.

On May 31, Union cavalry under Gen. Philip Sheridan seized **Cold Harbor** and held it the next day against attack by newly arrived Confederate infantry. It took two days for Union forces to gather at Cold Harbor, during which the Confederates entrenched themselves securely on a seven-mile front west of the village. Despite costly failures in previous assaults on Confederate fortifications, Grant believed that the Confederates were now "whipped," and he preferred to attack and destroy them at Cold Harbor rather than let them reach the protection of the fortifications at Richmond, ten miles away. At dawn on June 3, in an ill-prepared attack, Grant hurled 60,000 troops against the Confederate line. In a few minutes he suffered 7,000 casualties, more than were lost all day at Bloody Angle. "I regret this assault more than any one I have ever ordered," he told his staff that night.

The disaster at Cold Harbor convinced Grant that the costly duel with Lee had to be ended. For a month the two armies had pounded away at each other indecisively, Lee refusing to give the open battle that Grant wanted. A dramatic new stroke was needed.

On the night of June 12, the Federals left their trenches before Cold Harbor, marching east and south. Lee discovered their absence only belatedly and was uncertain of their destination. The Federals moved southeast past Richmond, crossed the Chickahominy River, and then—by means of a pontoon bridge stretching 2,100 feet across tidal currents, a miracle of military engineering—crossed the James River. On June 15 the Army of the Potomac appeared before Petersburg, Va., a rail hub 20 miles *south* of Richmond through which the Confederate capital and the Army of Northern Virginia received most of their provisions (see *Petersburg Siege).

In 40 days of almost constant combat, the armies of the Potomac and Northern Virginia had sustained unprecedented casualties—60,000 in Grant's army, 20,000 in Lee's. Although these losses were largely made up by replacements, the manpower reserves on both sides were near exhaustion—temporarily in the North, permanently in the South. Throughout the campaign Grant had succeeded in denying Lee the initiative, but Lee's uncanny ability to anticipate Grant's moves and his formidable defensive skills denied Grant the opportunity for a decisive battle. Most important, Lee had preserved his army while inflicting tremendous casualties on Grant's. In the

North, praise for Grant's tenacity gave way to criticism of poor generalship and brutal indifference to casualties.

WILDERNESS ROAD,

WILDERNESS ROAD, trail blazed (1775) by frontiersman Daniel Boone from Virginia's Shenandoah Valley across the Appalachian Mountains and through the Cumberland Gap into Kentucky, terminating at Boonesboro on the Kentucky River. A branch led to Harrodsburg. Extended (1795) to Louisville and Frankfort and widened to accommodate wagons, the road was a principal avenue of western migration from 1790 to 1840.

WILLIAMS v. MISSISSIPPI

WILLIAMS v. MISSISSIPPI (1898), unanimous decision of the *Fuller Court upholding the disfranchisement of African-Americans by Southern states. A black man, Williams had been indicted for murder by an all-white grand jury and convicted by an all-white petit jury. He appealed under the Equal Protection Clause of the *14th Amendment on the ground that blacks had been excluded from the juries. This was true because Mississippi drew its jurors from lists of qualified voters, and the state's constitution, by imposing literacy and poll tax qualifications on voters, had effectively eliminated black voters. The Court ruled that an ostensibly fair law could be voided only if its application had been shown to be discriminatory, which Williams had not shown.

WILMOT PROVISO

WILMOT PROVISO (1846), amendment to a bill appropriating $2 million to be available as a down payment for territory acquired from Mexico in the *Mexican War. Introduced by David Wilmot, a prowar Pennsylvania Democrat concerned like other Northerners that the war not benefit the slave interest, the amendment, in language borrowed from the Ordinance of 1787 (see *Northwest Territory), declared "that, as an express and fundamental condition to the acquisition of any territory from the Republic of Mexico . . . neither slavery nor involuntary servitude shall ever exist in any part of said territory, except for crime, whereof the party shall first be duly convicted."

The amended appropriations bill passed the House of Representatives but failed in the Senate. Reintroduced in 1847 and again rejected, the Wilmot Proviso opened a bitter debate over the extension of slavery into the Western territories.

WILSON ADMINISTRATION

WILSON ADMINISTRATION (1913–21). Democrat Woodrow Wilson, 28th president of the United States, was a minority president, having won election only because Theodore Roosevelt and William Howard Taft divided the Republican vote, but he enjoyed Democratic majorities in both the House and the Senate.

In his inaugural address (see *Wilson's First Inaugural), Wilson offered a vision of constructive national government shared by progressives of both parties (see *Progressivism). Republican progressives who had supported Roosevelt in 1912 were surprised to find their program embraced by Democrats, a party as historically conservative as their own. Thus in short order Wilson and a Democratic Congress (with the help of Republican progressives) enacted the *Underwood Tariff (1913), the *Federal Reserve Act (1913), the *Clayton Antitrust Act (1914), the *Federal Trade Commission Act (1914), the *Smith-Lever Act (1914), the *La Follette Seamen's Act (1915), the Keating-Owen Act (see *Child Labor), and the Adamson Act (see *Railroad Regulation). The *17th Amendment, ratified in 1913, provided for the popular election of U.S. senators, and the *19th Amendment, ratified in 1919, gave women the right to vote—two major steps in the advancement of democracy.

Wilson brought to foreign affairs—an area new to him—the same high-mindedness that infused his domestic policy. He repudiated Taft's *dollar diplomacy in China (though he imposed American military governments in both Haiti and the Dominican Republic), while Secretary of State William Jennings Bryan busily negotiated *arbitration treaties. But high-mindedness proved inadequate to the dangerous complexities of the *Mexican Revolution, and even more so to the problems presented by the outbreak in 1914 of war in Europe. Wilson at first advised Americans to be neutral in thought as well as action, but although both the Allies and Germany violated neutral rights, German submarine warfare—which took American lives—made true neutrality impossible. After the *Lusitania sinking, Wilson endorsed *preparedness, and when Germany in 1917 resumed unrestricted submarine warfare he had no alternative (as his pacifist former secretary of state, Bryan, had predicted) but to ask Congress for a declaration of war—not merely in defense of neutral rights but, characteristically, to make the world safe for democracy (see *Wilson's War Message). With victory in *World War 1, Wilson went to the *Paris Peace Conference with the hope of achieving the just peace envisioned in his speeches and his *14 Points. His major achievement there was the incorporation of the covenant of the League of Nations into the highly imperfect Treaty of Versailles. But the U.S. Senate, now in Republican hands, rejected the treaty (see *Wilson and Lodge; *Wilson's Fight for the Treaty). When Wilson asked that the presidential election of 1920 be "a great and solemn referendum" on the treaty, he was even more decisively repudiated in the Republican victory of that year.

The last year and a half of the Wilson administration, when the president lay ill and largely incapacitated in the White House, was a period of government paralysis and drift, soured by U.S. intervention in Russia (1918–20; see *Russian Intervention), a scandalous *red scare (1919–20), and ratification (1919) of the *18th (Prohibition) Amendment in a mood of moral fervor that the war and perhaps Wilson himself had done much to create.

WILSON AND LODGE. The enmity between Democratic president Woodrow Wilson and Republican senator Henry Cabot Lodge, from 1919 chairman of the Senate Foreign Relations Committee, had fateful consequences for the country.

Was there an element of jealousy in their relationship? Both Wilson and Lodge were noted scholars. Both had earned Ph.D.s (an uncommon achievement in the 19th century) and had written half a dozen books. Lodge had taught at Harvard, Wilson at Princeton before becoming president of that university.

Certainly partisanship played a large role. Lodge was a Republican nationalist, a friend and follower of former president Theodore Roosevelt, who had greatly enlarged and vigorously wielded the powers of the presidency. Wilson, author of *The New Freedom*, was also a nationalist who, like Roosevelt, saw government as an instrument for advancing human welfare. Lodge, however, probably saw him only as leader of the opposition, of the traditionally antinationalist, states' rights Democratic Party—and the Democrat who had defeated Roosevelt in 1912.

Lodge prided himself on his expertise in foreign affairs. In this area, Wilson was admittedly a neophyte. On the eve of his inauguration, he confided to a friend, "It would be the irony of fate if my administration had to deal chiefly with foreign affairs." The Wilsonian program was entirely domestic; he never mentioned foreign affairs in his inaugural address. To compound his ignorance, he appointed as secretary of state the Nebraska populist William Jennings Bryan, whose ignorance of foreign affairs was even greater than his own. Lodge mortified at the consequent demoralization of the State Department. When Wilson promptly blundered into the complexities of the *Mexican Revolution, Lodge became enraged. Early in the new administration, Henry Adams observed that Lodge's "hatred for the President is demented."

Their views of the world were antithetical. Lodge was a realist who believed that force governed the world. He admired Roosevelt's maxim "Speak softly and carry a big stick." Wilson was an idealist—indeed, a moralist—who believed in the power of ideas. In World War 1, Lodge was ardently pro-Ally. He saw Britain and France as protecting American security and values. He believed that American neutrality could be legitimately tilted in their favor. And if necessary, he would enter the war on the Allied side. To Lodge, Wilson's pacifism and neutralism—his admonition that "The United States must be neutral in fact as well as in name . . . impartial in thought as well as in action"—was simply wrongheaded. When Wilson failed to protest the invasion of Belgium, to support *preparedness, and to respond forcefully to the *Lusitania sinking, Lodge despaired. Wilsonian utterances like "too proud to fight" and "peace without victory" maddened him. In 1915 he told Roosevelt that he "never expected to hate any one in politics with the hatred I feel towards Wilson."

If Lodge was a hater, Wilson had a positive genius for provocation. Superior, high-minded, self-righteous, moralistic, he was arrogant and obtuse. Having made up his mind on a subject, he was immovable. Despite his pledge that politics was adjourned for the war, he deliberately made the crucial issues of the peace partisan ones. In October 1918—with the war nearing its end and a peace conference in the offing—he appealed to American voters to elect Democrats to Congress in November; when in fact they returned Republican majorities in both houses of Congress the Republicans naturally interpreted the election as a repudiation of Wilson's leadership. Wilson consulted no Republicans—especially no Republican senators—on his peace plans, and he included only one Republican—an elderly diplomat—on the delegation he himself led to Paris. When he returned to the United States with the peace treaty, which included the covenant of the League of Nations, he presented it to Congress and the nation as unalterable.

Lodge was a conservative internationalist, not an isolationist. He would have supported a treaty guaranteeing the security of France against a German attack. But Wilson had declared that the United States "is not interested merely in the peace of Europe, but in the peace of the world. . . . We are not obeying the mandates of parties or of politics. We are obeying the mandates of humanity." Lodge had no faith in Wilson's League of Nations, which lacked the means to enforce its collective will. He was not reassured by Wilson's declaration that the League depended "primarily and chiefly upon one great force, and that is the moral force of the public opinion of the world."

But neither was Lodge one of the *irreconcilables. The *Lodge reservations may not have been intended to prevent ratification of the treaty. Indeed, the Senate's "mild reservationists," together with its Democrats, were sufficient to pass the treaty. But Wilson stubbornly refused to accept any reservations and instructed Democrats to vote against them. The result was the Senate's rejection of the peace treaty and the League on Nov. 19, 1919.

WILSON-GORMAN TARIFF (1894), legislation of the second *Cleveland administration. Pres. Grover Cleveland was committed to tariff reform, which the House version of this act promised to effect. But a protectionist Senate added more than 600 amendments, with the result that the final act reduced only slightly the high rates of the *McKinley Tariff (1890). Calling its passage "party perfidy and party dishonor," Cleveland allowed it to become law without his signature.

WILSON'S FIGHT FOR THE TREATY (Sept. 4–25, 1919). Two days after his return from the *Paris Peace Conference after *World War 1, Pres. Woodrow Wilson presented the Treaty of Versailles (which contained the covenant of the League of Nations) to the U.S. Senate.

The Senate was then divided between 49 Republicans and 47 Democrats. Opponents of the treaty needed 33 votes to block it, supporters 64 votes to ratify. Most Democrats could be counted on to support the president. Most Republicans, following the recommendations of former president William Howard Taft and former secretary of state Elihu Root and led on the Senate floor by Massachusetts senator Henry Cabot Lodge (see *Wilson and Lodge), were inclined to accept the treaty with reservations (see *Lodge Reservations) expressing the U.S. interpretation of certain clauses affecting the United States. A group of 16 *"irreconcilables," of both parties and differing views, opposed the treaty absolutely. When Wilson set himself adamantly against reservations, the "mild reservationists" began to move into opposition. By late summer, Wilson determined to take the case for ratification to the people, who he believed supported him.

On Sept. 4 Wilson left Washington on a 10,000-mile Western trip, in the course of which he delivered 37 speeches in 29 cities. Already exhausted and ill, he became progressively worse as the trip continued, enduring sleepless nights and often speaking despite splitting headaches. Although his audiences grew steadily in size and enthusiasm, the Senate remained unmoved.

St. Louis, Sept. 5: ". . . is there any man here or any woman, let me say is there any child here, who does not know that the seed of war in the modern world is industrial and commercial rivalry? The real reason that the war we have just finished took place was that Germany was afraid that her commercial rivals were going to get the better of her, and the reason why some nations went into the war against Germany was that they thought that Germany would get the commercial advantage of them. The seed of the jealousy, the seed of the deep-seated hatred was hot, successful commercial and industrial rivalry."

Des Moines, Sept. 6: ". . . the thing is going to be done whether we are in it or not. If we are in it, then we are going to be the determining factor in the development of civilization. If we are out of it, we ourselves are going to watch every other nation with suspicion, and we will be justified, too; and we are going to be watched with suspicion. Every movement of trade, every relationship of manufacture, every question of raw materials, every matter that affects the intercourse of the world, will be impeded by the consciousness that America wants to hold off and get something which she is not willing to share with the rest of mankind."

Omaha, Sept. 8: "I brought a copy of the treaty along with me, for I fancy that, in view of the criticisms that you have heard of it, you thought it consisted of only four or five clauses. Only four or five clauses out of this volume were picked out for criticism. Only four or five phrases in it are called to your attention by some of the distinguished orators who oppose its adoption. Why, my fellow citizens, this is one of the great charters of human liberty, and the man who picks flaws in it—or, rather, picks out the flaws that are in it, for there are flaws in it—forgets the magnitude of the thing, forgets the majesty of the thing, forgets that the counsels of more than twenty nations combined and were rendered unanimous in the adoption of this great instrument."

Tacoma, Sept. 13: "I wish that some of the men who are opposing this treaty could get the vision in their hearts of all it has done. It has liberated great populations. It has set up the standards of right and of liberty for the first time, where they were never unfurled before, and then has placed back of them this splendid power of the nations combined. For without the League of Nations the whole thing is a house of cards. Just a breath of power will blow it down, whereas with the League of Nations it is as strong as Gibraltar. Let them catch this vision; let them take in this conception; let them take counsel of weeping mothers; let them take counsel of bereaved fathers . . . ; let them realize that the world is hungry, that the world is naked, that the world is suffering, and that none of these things can be remedied until the minds of men are reassured."

Pueblo, Sept. 25: "What of our pledges to the men that lie dead in France? We said that they went over there, not to prove the prowess of America or her readiness for another war, but to see to it that there never was such a war again.

"It always seems to make it difficult for me to say anything, my fellow citizens, when I think of my clients in this case. My clients are the children; my clients are the next generation. They do not know what promises and bonds I undertook when I ordered the armies of the United States to the soil of France, but I know. And I intend to redeem my pledges to the children; they shall not be sent upon a similar errand.

"Again and again, my fellow citizens, mothers who lost their sons in France have come to me and, taking my hand, have shed tears upon it, not only that, but they have added, 'God bless you, Mr. President!' . . . Why should they weep upon my hand and call down the blessings of God upon me? Because they believe that their boys died for something that vastly transcends any of the immediate and palpable objects of the war. They believe, and they rightly believe, that their sons saved the liberty of the world. They believe that, wrapped up with the liberty of the world, is the continuous protection of that liberty by the concerted powers of all civilized people. They believe that this sacrifice was made in order that other sons should not be called upon for a similar gift— the gift of life, the gift of all that died."

The Pueblo speech was the last of the tour. That night Wilson experienced a nervous collapse. He was rushed back to Washington, where on Oct. 2 he suffered a stroke that left him incapacitated for more than seven months.

WILSON'S FIRST INAUGURAL (Mar. 4, 1913). For the first time in 20 years, the Democratic Party controlled both the presidency and Congress. "The success of a party means little," newly inaugurated president Woodrow Wilson observed, "except when the Nation is using that party for a large and definite purpose." That purpose was to interpret a new vision of the national life. "We see the bad with the good, the debased and decadent with the sound and vital. With this vision we approach new affairs. Our duty is to cleanse, to reconsider, to restore, to correct the evil without impairing the good, to purify and humanize every process of our common life without weakening or sentimentalizing it."

Wilson itemized the chief "things that ought to be altered": "A tariff which cuts us off from our proper part in the commerce of the world, violates the just principles of taxation, and makes the Government a facile instrument in the hands of private interests; a banking and currency system based upon the necessity of the Government to sell its bonds fifty years ago and perfectly adapted to

concentrating cash and restricting credits; an industrial system which . . . holds capital in leading strings, restricts the liberties and limits the opportunities of labor, and exploits without renewing or conserving the natural resources of the country; a body of agricultural activities never yet given the efficiency of great business undertakings or served as it should be through the instrumentality of science . . . or afforded the facilities of credit best suited to its practical needs; water-courses undeveloped, waste places unreclaimed, forests untended, fast disappearing without plan or prospect of renewal, unregarded waste heaps at every mine. . . ."

He concluded: "This is not a day of triumph; it is a day of dedication. Here muster, not the forces of party, but the forces of humanity. Men's hearts wait upon us; men's lives hang in the balance; men's hopes call upon us to say what we will do. . . . I summon all honest men, all patriotic, all forward-looking men, to my side. God helping me, I will not fail them, if they will but counsel and sustain me!"

WILSON'S WAR MESSAGE (Apr. 2, 1917). Before a joint session of Congress, Pres. Woodrow Wilson asked for a declaration of war against Germany because of its waging unrestricted submarine warfare (see *World War I). "With a profound sense of the solemn and even tragical character of the step I am taking," he said, ". . . I advise that Congress declare the recent course of the Imperial German Government to be in fact nothing less than war against the government and people of the United States; that it formally accept the status of belligerent which has thus been thrust upon it. . . .

"Our object," he continued, ". . . is to vindicate the principles of peace and justice in the life of the world as against selfish and autocratic power. . . . The world must be made safe for democracy. Its peace must be planted upon the tested foundations of political liberty. We have no selfish ends to serve. We desire no conquest, no dominion."

"It is a fearful thing," he concluded, "to lead this great peaceful people into war, into the most terrible and disastrous of all wars, civilization itself seeming to be in the balance. But the right is more precious than peace, and we shall fight for the things which we have always carried nearest our hearts,—for democracy, for the right of those who submit to authority to have a voice in their own Governments, for the rights and liberties of small nations, for a universal dominion of right by such a concert of free peoples as shall bring peace and safety to all nations and make the world itself at last free. . . . America is privileged to spend her blood and her might for the principles that gave her birth and happiness and the peace which she has treasured. God helping her, she can do no other."

WILSON v. NEW (1917), 5–4 decision of the *White Court upholding the Adamson Act's provision of an eight-hour day for railroad workers (see *Railroad Regulation). Chief Justice Edward D. White deferred to Congress's authority over interstate commerce to temporarily regulate wages and hours to avoid a strike.

WISCONSIN IDEA, term for the method of state government instituted in Wisconsin by Robert M. La Follette (governor 1901–6) and retained by his progressive successors. Its chief characteristic was the close relationship between the government and the University of Wisconsin, especially the employment of faculty experts on commissions to study problems such as taxation, regulation of public utilities, industrial relations, and conservation and to draft reform legislation. Critics argued that commission government contradicted the progressives' emphasis on direct democracy (see *Progressivism).

WISCONSIN v. YODER (1972), 6–1 decision of the *Burger Court that the state's "compelling interest" in compulsory education to age 16 did not override the free-exercise rights of the members of the Amish Mennonite Church, who believed that education beyond the eighth grade would endanger their children's faith and the survival of their community.

"It is one thing to say," wrote Chief Justice Warren Burger, "that compulsory education for a year or two beyond the eighth grade may be necessary when its goal is the preparation of the child for life in modern society as the majority live, but it is quite another if the goal of education be viewed as the preparation of the child for life in the separated agrarian community that is the keystone of the Amish faith. . . .

"Aided by a history of three centuries as an identifiable religious sect and a long history as a successful and self-sufficient segment of American society, the Amish in this case have convincingly demonstrated the sincerity of their religious beliefs, the interrelationship of belief with their mode of life, the vital role that belief and daily conduct play in the continued survival of the Old Order Amish communities and their religious organization, and the hazards presented by the State's enforcement of a statute generally valid as to others. . . .

"Courts must move with great circumspection in performing the sensitive and delicate task of weighing a State's legitimate social concern when faced with religious claims for exemption from generally applicable educational requirements."

In his dissent, Justice William O. Douglas argued that the decision supported only the interests of the parents and ignored the child's possible desire for education and emancipation (see *Church-State Relations).

WOBBLIES. See *Industrial Workers of the World (IWW).

WOLFF PACKING CO. v. COURT OF INDUSTRIAL RELATIONS (1923), unanimous decision of the *Taft Court overturning a Kansas law establishing a powerful court charged with the compulsory arbitration of labor disputes in certain key industries—those "affected with a public interest"—such as food, clothing, and fuel. Chief Justice William Howard Taft's decision included a list of guidelines for identifying businesses so "affected" and therefore susceptible to government regulation. Such businesses included public utilities, service businesses such as inns, cabs, and mills, and monopolies immune from the operation of natural economic laws. The effect of these guidelines was to put the great majority of private businesses outside the reach of state regulation.

WOMAN SUFFRAGE. See *Women's Rights; *Stanton and Anthony.

WOMEN IN THE LABOR FORCE. At the start of the 19th century, the principal occupation available to women outside their own homes was domestic service. Early in the century New England textile mills offered employment to young women. The Civil War widened opportunities for factory employment, while women were beginning to claim as their own such occupations as schoolteacher, nurse, salesclerk, and librarian. In 1900, women constituted 17 percent of the labor force.

The 20th century expanded the number of jobs open to women—for example, secretary, telephone operator, dental assistant, data processor. During World Wars 1 and 2 women entered factories in great numbers but then surrendered those jobs to the returning soldiers. The massive movement of women into the labor force after midcentury reflected important changes in the economy and society. In the postindustrial age, employment in white-collar and service occupations has grown more rapidly than employment in traditional blue-collar occupations, enlarging employment opportunities for women. Two world wars and the Great Depression changed attitudes about women's role in society, while advances in birth control assured effective family planning.

The unprecedented affluence of the post–World War 2 years had the paradoxical effect of encouraging some women to work so their families could enjoy more of the goods of a consumer society. The same economic conditions compelled other women to work to keep their families out of poverty, two-income families becoming the norm. And some women worked to find fulfillment in nontraditional ways. Between 1960 and 2000 the labor force participation rate for all women over 16 rose from 37.7 percent to 73.5 percent; in the latter year women constituted 46.9 percent of the labor force. The labor force participation rate for married women rose from 30.5 percent in 1960 to 62.0 percent in 2000; that for married women with children under six rose from 18.6 percent to 62.8 percent.

In 2000, the median income of working women was 73 percent of men's. Their lower earnings result from complex causes. First, socialization of girls in family and school tends to train them for dependency as wives and mothers. Second, women's working lives are typically shorter than men's; employers are disinclined to train or promote women to positions of responsibility when they expect that many will interrupt their work lives for marriage and family. Third, many women are segregated into low-paying "women's work"—jobs such as secretary, dental assistant, teacher, domestic, nurse, telephone operator, receptionist, and keypunch operator. Finally, women have been victimized by discrimination even when they have the qualifications for better jobs.

The progress of women into better-paying occupations and managerial jobs is largely the result of the **Equal Pay Act** of 1963, which barred sex discrimination in pay for the same job within a company, and the *Civil Rights Act of 1964, which barred sex discrimination (as well as race discrimination) in hiring and promotion. The Equal Employment Opportunities Commission (EEOC), which enforces the Civil Rights Act, has charged hundreds of companies with sex discrimination and negotiated *affirmative action programs. It has also defined and enforced rules against *sexual harassment in the workplace.

Women's entry into the professions was speeded by federal legislation in 1972 that required schools to provide equal opportunities to women or risk losing federal funds. Largely as a consequence, the number of women in accounting, architecture, law, and medicine has grown rapidly.

An issue of continuing concern to women is the establishment of the principle of **comparable worth**. Equal pay for equal work was guaranteed by the Equal Pay Act of 1963. The principle of equal pay for work of equal value—or comparable worth—maintains that work of comparable difficulty or value to an organization should receive the same pay. Thus, for example, a female nurse might argue that her work was of comparable value to that of a male accountant employed by the same hospital.

WOMEN'S CHRISTIAN TEMPERANCE UNION (WCTU). See *Temperance Movement.

WOMEN'S RIGHTS.
Following English common law, the American legal system long assigned women a separate and inferior status. Although the Constitution did not use the words *men* and *women* but always *people*, *persons*, and *citizens*, the courts did not interpret these terms to include women. Rather, they classified women with children and imbeciles as incapable of managing their own affairs.

Women were denied educations, barred from certain occupations and professions, and excluded from juries and public offices. Married women were virtually the property of their husbands. They were limited in their ability to own property, sign contracts, obtain credit, go into business, control their earnings, write wills. The law regarded home and family as the special province of women, and it did all it could to confine them there in the belief that this was in the best interests of women themselves and of society as a whole.

The 19th Century. Early in the 19th century, educated, upper-class women began to enter public life through participation in the many reform movements of the period, especially the *abolitionist crusade, often in the face of *male* hostility. The rebuff of women at a World Antislavery Convention in London in 1840 led directly to the organization of a U.S. women's rights movement in Seneca Falls, N.Y., in 1848 (see *Seneca Falls Convention). From the start, a prime objective of the movement was to win for women the right to vote (see *Stanton and Anthony).

After the Civil War, a constitutional obstacle to women's suffrage was raised when the *14th Amendment, in extending the status of citizen to former slaves, introduced the word *male* into the Constitution as a qualification for voting. The *15th Amendment, which enfranchised the former slaves, provided that the right to vote should not be denied or abridged "on account of race, color, or previous condition of servitude" but not on account of sex.

The 14th Amendment did provide new grounds on which feminists could base their demands for full citizenship for women. But when women sought the right to vote on the basis of the amendment's Privileges and Immunities Clause ("No state shall make or enforce any law which shall abridge the privileges or immunities of citizens of the United States"), the courts upheld the states' authority to fix voter qualifications. And when women appealed for equal treatment under the law on the basis of the amendment's Equal Protection Clause ("No state shall . . . deny to any person within its jurisdiction the equal protection of the laws"), the courts took a similarly restrictive view. In time, the Equal Protection Clause was extended to embrace corporations, aliens, criminals, illegitimate children, juveniles, and communists, but not—until 1971—women.

The states, however, acted to improve the position of women. During the second half of the 19th century, all the states passed **Married Women's Property Acts**, which largely ended the subordination of women under the common law by dissolving the legal unity of husband and wife. Married women thereby acquired control over their own property and earnings. By 1900 women enjoyed many of the legal advantages of citizenship, the most significant exception being the right to vote. Chivalrous legislators still exempted them from certain responsibilities of citizenship, such as jury duty and poll and property taxes. This benign attitude underlay those decisions of the courts early in the 20th century upholding the constitutionality of a number of state and federal laws intended to protect working women (but not men) by regulating their hours, pay, and working conditions (see *Muller v. Oregon).

The 20th Century. The suffrage campaign waged by feminists—those upper-class women who had the education and leisure to devote themselves to the cause of women's rights—took on new spirit during the Progressive Era (see *Progressivism) in the first decades of the 20th century. In 1890 Wyoming had entered the Union with a state constitution providing for woman suffrage. Women were voting in 17 states by 1920 when ratification of the *19th Amendment secured the vote for women nationwide and established the principle of equal political rights for women.

The suffrage did not immediately bring about the removal of gender-based classifications, which, in the guise of protecting women, actually confined them—in the feminist view—to their traditional "separate place." It was, rather, the social changes resulting from two world wars, a major depression, and, more recently, unprecedented national affluence that revolutionized the lives of women and gave new impetus to the feminist movement. Two developments were of particular importance: the de-

velopment of new and widely accessible birth-control methods liberated women from the necessity of functioning largely as child-bearers and child-rearers; and the rising flood of women into the labor force (see *Women in the Labor Force), mostly into low-paying "women's work," made women of all classes conscious of the disadvantages of their "separate place."

Feminists now perceived all gender-based classifications as discriminatory, including the legislation intended to protect women in the workplace. Not only was that legislation based on the obnoxious "separate place" doctrine, but experience showed that it prevented women who wanted to do so from working overtime at premium pay, taking higher-paying jobs that require heavy work, and getting promoted to supervisory positions. A series of federal laws and executive orders largely nullified that protective legislation. The **Equal Pay Act of 1963** ended discrimination on the basis of sex in the payment of wages. The *Civil Rights Act of 1964 ended discrimination in private employment on the basis of sex as well as race, color, religion, and national origin. Executive orders made it illegal for the federal government and for federal contractors and subcontractors to discriminate on the basis of sex. The courts have enforced women's right to enter once-all-male job fields and even military academies and sports, and they have sought to protect women once there by enforcing new laws against *sexual harassment.

To ensure enforcement of women's newly legislated rights, the **National Organization for Women (NOW)** was formed in 1966 with Betty Friedan, author of the seminal *Feminine Mystique (1963), as its first president. NOW advocated a partnership of the sexes—that is, the equality of women in both the home and the workplace—and sought to end sexual discrimination through education and political and legal action. To the left of NOW were (unorganized) radical feminists, who identified men as enemies and marriage as subjugation. The radicals aimed at the liberation of women through consciousness-raising and the elimination of sexism from institutions, relations, and language itself.

Both NOW and the radical feminists supported the *Equal Rights Amendment (ERA). In this they were opposed by conservative and working-class women who believed that the ERA was the work of an elite of radical and professional women contemptuous of traditional values of home, family, and religion and who wanted to preserve the protected position that women—in theory, at least—still retain in law and custom.

WOODSTOCK MUSIC FAIR (1969). See *Counterculture.

WORCESTER v. GEORGIA (1832), decision of the *Marshall Court attempting to modify *Cherokee Nation v. Georgia* (1831) and extend federal protection over the tribe. Chief Justice John Marshall declared Georgia law void in the tribal territory. Georgia defied the Court, and Pres. Andrew Jackson, sympathetic to Georgia, is said to have remarked, "John Marshall has made his decision, now let him enforce it."

WORKINGMEN'S PARTIES, local political parties formed in the 1830s by newly enfranchised workingmen in Philadelphia, New York, and other cities and towns in a dozen states. Reflecting the spirit of *Jacksonian democracy, they alarmed conservatives by advocating free public education, mechanics' lien laws (to protect workers' wages in the event of the employer's bankruptcy), the ten-hour day, abolition of imprisonment for debt and of the militia system, and in some cases the communistic division of property. Sometimes holding the balance of power between the larger parties, they managed to elect some members to local offices. The movement was destroyed by factional strife.

A short-lived Workingmen's Party, composed of immigrant Marxists, tried to convert the *railroad strike of 1877 into a general strike. Another Workingmen's Party, in San Francisco, instigated anti-Chinese riots in 1877 that led to the Chinese Exclusion Act of 1882.

WORK PROJECTS ADMINISTRATION (WPA). See *New Deal.

WORLD'S FAIRS. The first world's fair to be held in the United States was the *Centennial Exposition at Philadelphia in 1876. Subsequent fairs were the Columbian Exposition at Chicago in 1892, the Panama-Pacific International Exposition at San Francisco in 1915, the Century of Progress International Exhibition at Chicago in 1933–34, the World of Tomorrow at New York in 1939–40, the Century 21 Exposition at Seattle in 1962, and the New York World's Fair in 1964–65. Officially designated world's fairs were also held at Spokane, Wash. (1974), Knoxville, Tenn. (1982), and New Orleans (1984).

WORLD TRADE CENTER ATTACK I (Feb. 26, 1993), terrorist act committed by Islamic fundamentalists who detonated a rented van packed with 1,000 pounds of nitrate explosives in the underground garage of the New York City office complex—twin towers 110 stories high in lower Manhattan. The explosion killed six, injured 1,000, and caused damage estimated at more than $500 million. In March 1994, four Arab extremists

were convicted of the bombing and sentenced to life imprisonment (see *Terrorism).

The World Trade Center bombing was linked to a larger terror campaign through the person of Sheik Abdel Rahman, a blind Islamic cleric who had been implicated in the assassination of Egyptian president Anwar Sadat, had opposed the current Egyptian president, Hosni Mubarak, and had sought refuge in the United States, where he retained his influence over Muslim extremists in the United States and the Middle East. The World Trade Center bombers were his followers, as were the extremists who, apparently with support from Sudan, plotted to blow up sensitive New York City targets—including the United Nations headquarters, a federal office building, and two tunnels connecting the city to New Jersey—and assassinate a number of political figures on or about July 4, 1993. Intended to punish the United States for its support of Israel and Egypt, the plan was uncovered by the Federal Bureau of Investigation in its investigation of the World Trade Center bombing. In October 1995, Rahman and nine other extremists were convicted of conspiracy. Rahman was sentenced to life imprisonment, his codefendants to 25 years to life.

WORLD TRADE CENTER ATTACK 2 (Sept. 11, 2001). Early Tuesday morning, Sept. 11, 2001, four commercial airliners, fueled for transcontinental flights, departed from Boston, Newark, and Washington for California. Shortly after takeoff, the planes were hijacked by Arab terrorists (see *Terrorism), who took the controls and flew the planes like missiles against targets in New York City and Washington, D.C.

At 8:46 a.m., American Airlines flight 11, from Boston, crashed into floors 94–98 of the north tower of the 110-story twin-tower World Trade Center in lower Manhattan. Twenty minutes later, at 9:03 a.m., United Airlines flight 175, also from Boston, crashed into floors 78–82 of the south tower. At 9:40 a.m., American Airlines flight 77, from Washington, crashed into the west face of the Pentagon in Arlington, Va., across the Potomac River from Washington. At 10:37 a.m., United Airlines flight 93, from Newark, crashed into a field in western Pennsylvania, apparently during a struggle between passengers and hijackers. In these four crashes, all 266 passengers and crew and 19 hijackers perished.

The World Trade Center towers withstood the impacts of the two Boeing 767 airliners, but the intense heat of burning jet fuel weakened their steel frameworks and both buildings collapsed, the south tower at 9:59 a.m. and the north tower at 10:29 a.m. Casualties exceeded 2,830, among whom were nationals of some 75 foreign countries. Several nearby buildings also collapsed in whole or in part, and other buildings were severely damaged. In the crash and fire at the Pentagon, 184 military and civilian personnel died.

The attacks stunned and aroused the American public, whose sense of invulnerability was abruptly ended. The federal government instituted security measures nationwide and began to plan an appropriate response (see *Terrorism War). Meanwhile, anxiety was pervasive as the nation awaited a possible second blow—an expectation that seemed to be confirmed by the subsequent *anthrax attack.

WORLD WAR I (1914–18). War had been raging in Europe for more than two and a half years when Pres. Woodrow Wilson, on Apr. 2, 1917, asked Congress for a declaration of war against Germany because of the attacks by German submarines on U.S. and other neutral shipping (see *Wilson's War Message). "We have no selfish ends to serve," he declared. "We desire no conquest, no dominion." The object of the war was to make the world "safe for democracy," since peace could be securely planted only "upon the tested foundations of political liberty." (Wilson clarified U.S. war aims with greater particularity on Jan. 8, 1918, when he presented to Congress his *14 Points.) Wilson signed the declaration of war against Germany on Apr. 6. The United States declared war on Austria-Hungary on Dec. 7. It joined the Allies—Britain, France, Italy, and Russia—not as an ally but as an "associated power."

Mobilizing for War. To direct the nation's mobilization, Congress enlarged the president's already extensive war powers with significant new powers over the economy and the organization of executive agencies. The president worked through the Council of National Defense, consisting of six cabinet members and chaired by Secretary of War Newton D. Baker. The council established a host of committees and boards, staffed by corporation executives, to oversee every area of war production—munitions, ships, airplanes, tanks, etc. At their head was the War Industries Board, chaired (from Mar. 4, 1918) by financier Bernard M. Baruch. Besides the committees directing war production was the Railroad Administration headed by Secretary of the Treasury William G. McAdoo, the Food Administration headed by the former head of Belgian relief, Herbert Hoover, and the Public Information Committee headed by journalist George Creel. Finally, a body of academic experts known as **The Inquiry** and headed by Sidney E. Mezes, president of the College of the City of New York,

researched the issues that would be pertinent to the eventual peacemaking.

Two-thirds of the cost of the war was met by the issuance of "Liberty Bonds" for sale to the public; four "Liberty Loans" between 1917 and 1919 were oversubscribed. Congress also raised income, inheritance, corporation, excess profits, and excise taxes.

Because the war was perceived as widely unpopular—particularly among Americans of German, Austrian, Hungarian, and Irish descent and in the more isolationist Western states—the government launched a vast propaganda effort run by Creel's Public Information Committee to inflame patriotism and demonize the enemy. What propaganda could not accomplish, the law did. The *Espionage Act (1917)—made even more oppressive when amended by the Sedition Act (1918)—was zealously enforced by constituted officials and vigilantes alike, effectively stifling dissent, real and imagined.

When the United States declared war, the Regular Army stood at 200,000 men. Under the Selective Service Act of May 18, 1917 (see *Conscription), 9.6 million men aged 21–30 registered on June 5 for possible military service. Two later registrations, of men 18–45, brought the total registered to 24.2 million. The first draftees reported to hastily built training camps on Sept. 6. A total of 2.8 million men were drafted into the "National Army," while the Regular Army, National Guard, Navy, Marines, and Coast Guard continued to accept volunteers. The armed forces eventually totaled 4.5 million men.

Fighting the War. In 1917 Allied fortunes were at a low ebb. On the Western Front, failed French and British offensives suffered enormous casualties. Widespread mutinies erupted in the French army. On the Eastern Front, the Germans smashed a great Russian offensive, and in November the Bolshevik revolution effectively took Russia out of the war. In the south, Italy suffered a disaster at Caporetto in October. Meanwhile, in the Atlantic, the destruction of British shipping by German submarines peaked in April with the loss of 150 ships, confronting the British with the imminent prospect of starvation. In Berlin, the German high command calculated that a massive offensive in the spring of 1918, before American resources could be brought to bear, would win the war.

The first Americans to go into action were members of the U.S. Navy. U.S. destroyers were quickly dispatched to Queenstown, Ireland, where they joined the British navy in submarine patrol and convoy escorting. Their presence quickly reduced the toll of ships lost to submarines below replacement level. No troop transport was lost during the war. U.S. battleships joined the main British fleet at Scapa Flow that kept the German High Seas Fleet confined to its ports.

Gen. John J. Pershing, commander of the **American Expeditionary Force (AEF)**, arrived in France on June 14 and in September established his headquarters at Chaumont. On June 26 token units of the U.S. First Division reached France, but the great movement of American troops overseas came only in 1918. By July 1918 there were 1 million American troops in France, only partially trained and equipped with British and French machine guns, artillery, tanks, and airplanes. Pershing's U.S. First Army, formed on Aug. 10, took up positions in the Toul sector at the eastern end of the Western Front.

By then, the German spring offensive had spent itself in mighty drives against the British in the west and the French in the center of the front. In the desperate defensive fighting, American units under French and British command had demonstrated their fighting capacity. On May 28, the U.S. First Division, supported by French tanks, captured the German-held village of **Cantigny** and held it against repeated counterattacks. East of Cantigny, at **Château-Thierry**, the U.S. Third Division, supported by French colonial troops, prevented (May 31–June 1) the Germans from crossing the Marne River at that point. Northwest of Château-Thierry, the U.S. Second Division checked the advancing Germans and on June 6 counterattacked through difficult **Belleau Wood**, which it captured by June 21 together with several villages.

On July 18, Marshall Ferdinand Foch, newly appointed Allied supreme commander on the Western Front, counterattacked against the exhausted Germans. His immediate objectives, in preparation for a general offensive, were German salients at Amiens, below the Marne, and at **St.-Mihiel**. The last was assigned to the U.S. First Army, which efficiently reduced the salient Sept. 12–16 against light resistance (the Germans were in the process of evacuating the salient when the Americans struck), capturing 16,000 Germans and 443 guns.

The Allied general offensive began on Sept. 26. In this vast battle, extending along the entire front, the U.S. First Army, now 1.2 million strong, was moved west from St.-Mihiel to the **Meuse-Argonne** sector. There it occupied a 25-mile-wide front, its right on the marshy west bank of the Meuse River, its left in the Argonne Forest. The area, held by the Germans for four years, was heavily fortified. Taking heavy casualties, the Americans fought doggedly northward, emerging from the forest on Oct. 31. By then the Germans were withdrawing all along the Western Front. The First Army rapidly fought

its way north, reaching Sedan on the Belgian border on Nov. 11, when the armistice put a halt to hostilities.

The AEF suffered 48,909 battle deaths, 230,074 wounded. Of total U.S. deaths during the war— 112,432—more than half were caused by disease, chiefly the worldwide *influenza epidemic that ravaged training camps and battlefields.

Peacemaking. For the other Allied and Associated Powers, the war with Germany ended with the Treaty of Versailles (which included the covenant of the League of Nations), drafted at the *Paris Peace Conference. The U.S. Senate, however, rejected that treaty both with and without the Republican reservations that President Wilson opposed (see *Lodge Reservations). Four months later, responding to public pressure, the Senate on Mar. 19, 1920, considered the treaty again, and again rejected it by a vote of 49 in favor and 35 opposed, seven short of the necessary two-thirds majority. The United States was not a party to the other treaties written at the conference.

On July 2, 1921, by a joint resolution, Congress declared hostilities ended. In August the United States signed separate treaties with Germany, Austria, and Hungary, claiming whatever benefits had accrued to the other Allies by their treaties but accepting no obligations such as membership in the League of Nations would have entailed.

WORLD WAR 2 (1941–45). Japan's "sneak attack" on *Pearl Harbor on Dec. 7, 1941, united Americans for war as nothing else could. The United States declared war on Japan on Dec. 8 (see *Roosevelt's War Message). Japan's Axis partners, Germany and Italy, declared war on the United States on Dec. 11. In the next nine months, the conquests of the Axis powers reached their greatest extent. The task confronting the Allies—principally the United States, Great Britain, and the Soviet Union— appeared formidable indeed, its cost—in resources, money, and lives—incalculable.

Strike and Counterstrike in the Pacific (1941–42). In the months following the attack on Pearl Harbor, the Japanese—already in possession of Indochina, Formosa, and large parts of China—overran the Philippines, Thailand, Malaya, the Netherlands East Indies, and Burma, and seized Guam, Wake Island, Attu and Kiska in the Aleutians, the Gilbert Islands, and Hong Kong.

An air attack on the Philippines on Dec. 8, 1941, caught the U.S. air force there on the ground and destroyed it. On Dec. 10 the Japanese invaded the island of Luzon and advanced directly on the Philippine capital, Manila. American troops and their Filipino allies, commanded by Gen. Douglas MacArthur, were soon forced back onto the **Bataan** Peninsula, across Manila Bay from the capital. On Mar. 13 MacArthur left his besieged forces by submarine for Australia, promising, "I shall return." The Americans and Filipinos on Bataan surrendered on Apr. 8, those on the island of Corregidor, off the tip of Bataan, on May 6. Some 25,000 survivors died of wounds, disease, and malnutrition during a notorious "death march" to prison camps, where 9,300 Americans and 45,000 Filipinos were incarcerated.

By June 1942 Japan had carved out a vast empire, rich in rubber, oil, tin, rice, and timber, extending from the border of India almost to the north coast of Australia. (A threat to Australia had been blocked by a carrier battle in the **Coral Sea** on May 7–8 that turned back a Japanese invasion force headed for Port Moresby on the south coast of New Guinea.) Its eastern flank was protected by a perimeter of island bases extending through the Western Pacific from the Aleutians through Wake Island and the Marshall, Caroline, Mariana, Gilbert, and Bismarck archipelagos to the north coast of New Guinea. Given time to harden these defenses, the Japanese empire might become virtually impregnable.

The **Doolittle raid** signaled that the United States would not allow Japan that time. In April 1942, the U.S. carrier *Hornet*, carrying 16 B-25 medium-range army bombers commanded by Col. James Doolittle, penetrated the Japanese defense perimeter north of Midway Island to within 650 miles of Tokyo and from there on Apr. 18 launched its bombers at the Japanese capital. Thirteen B-25s hit Tokyo and other targets, then continued westward. Four landed in China, one in the Soviet Union; the rest were abandoned in flight. Seventy-one of the 80 fliers involved survived. The raid, however, was effective only in boosting U.S. morale.

Nevertheless, because of the Doolittle raid, the Japanese decided to capture Midway, which lay just east of their defense perimeter. Their assault force, which included four large carriers, was commanded by Vice Adm. Chuichi Naguma, who had led the Pearl Harbor attack. Alerted by intercepted Japanese messages, two American task forces, including the carriers *Yorktown*, *Enterprise*, and *Hornet*, engaged the Japanese in the battle of **Midway** (June 3–6, 1942) at a distance of 175 miles. Having just sent their bombers against Midway, the Japanese ships and covering fighters decimated the slow American torpedo bombers from *Yorktown* and *Hornet* attacking at sea level. American fighter escorts ran out of fuel and fell into the sea. But finally dive bombers from *Enterprise* caught the Japanese carriers unprotected from the air with their decks crowded with refueling and rearming

planes. Within five minutes, three Japanese carriers had suffered mortal damage. The fourth was sunk a few hours later as it raced from the scene. The carrier forces of the two navies were now roughly equal, and thereafter the balance would tilt increasingly in favor of the United States.

The Battle of the Atlantic (1941–43). Although Pres. Franklin Roosevelt declared the United States neutral in the war in Europe in September 1939, he himself was not neutral. He believed that a British victory was necessary for the security of the United States and the Western Hemisphere, and he hoped that he could help bring about that victory by extending military aid to Britain—and later to the Soviet Union—without involving the United States in war. In November 1939 he persuaded Congress to repeal the arms embargo of the 1937 Neutrality Act (see *Neutrality Acts) and permit belligerents to buy war materials in the United States if they paid cash and transported them in their own vessels, a provision clearly favorable to Britain and France. In September 1940, after France had fallen and when Britain faced an imminent German invasion, he negotiated the *destroyers-for-bases deal. When Britain confessed that it was running short of money to buy war supplies, Roosevelt in March 1941 guided *Lend-Lease through Congress.

The spectacle of essential war cargoes being sunk by German submarines (U-boats) caused the United States to declare (Apr. 11, 1941) a "security zone" in the Western Atlantic extending as far as Iceland in which U.S. ships and planes would patrol for German submarines and report them to British authorities. That month U.S. troops established bases in Greenland, and in August they landed in Iceland. When German submarines began to attack U.S. destroyers, the president ordered naval forces in the U.S. security zone to "shoot on sight," and the U.S. Navy began to escort British convoys as far as Iceland. In November 1941, in the last of the Neutrality Acts, Congress approved the arming of U.S. merchant ships and permitted them to carry cargoes into belligerents' ports.

As Roosevelt feared, the United States was brought into the war in December 1941 by an enemy attack. Britain's situation was then extreme. An island nation dependent on imports for half its food, all its oil, much of its nonferrous metals (copper, aluminum, etc.) and crucial manufactures like machine tools, Britain was besieged by a German submarine force based in French Atlantic ports that grew from 22 boats in January 1942 to over 100 in October. Submarine "wolf packs" lay in wait for convoys across North Atlantic sea-lanes. Off the U.S. Atlantic and Gulf coasts, single U-boats wreaked

havoc among unconvoyed U.S. tankers and freighters sil-
houetted at night against the glow of lighted American
cities. In November 1942, the worst month of the submarine war, the Allies lost 721,700 tons of shipping to
submarine attacks.

The Allies had effective weapons against the submarine. Interception and decryption of German radio communications allowed them to reroute convoys to avoid
waiting wolf packs. Land-based radar-equipped planes
patrolled portions of the sea-lanes at night, when U-boats
cruised on the surface. The convoys were generally escorted by destroyers and corvettes equipped with radar
and direction finders that could locate surfaced U-boats
by their radio transmissions.

Gradually, the battle of the Atlantic was won. Construction of new ships accelerated, especially with the development of a standardized tanker and freighter (the
Liberty ship). By October 1942 U.S. shipyards were
launching three Liberty ships a day. In February 1943
new tonnage exceeded losses for the first time. Meanwhile, U-boat losses were exceeding replacements. In
May 1943, 43 U-boats—twice the replacement number—
were sunk by aircraft and convoy escorts. From September 1939 to May 1943, the Allies lost 2,452 merchant
ships and 175 warships in the Atlantic to submarines; the
Germans lost 696 of 800 U-boats sent on patrol.

The Air War Against Germany (1942–44).
The securing of the Atlantic sea-lanes enabled Britain not
only to survive but to become the base where millions of
men and their equipment could be assembled for the invasion of the continent. Until then, for nearly two and a
half years, the war in Western Europe was an air war,
waged by British and American heavy bombers.

Massive strategic bombing of Germany began in
March 1942 with the arrival of the new British bomber,
the four-engine Lancaster. The British used it in nighttime "area bombing," having learned that they could not
fly long distances in daylight without fighter escort and
that they could not hit specific industrial targets at night.
Area bombing deliberately targeted the civilian populations of industrial cities in the expectation that their "de-
housing" and demoralization would destroy their
capacity to operate war plants effectively. In May 1942,
the British assembled the first 1,000-plane raid against
Cologne. Other massive raids against Essen and Bremen
followed in June. In July, a four-night raid on Hamburg
created a firestorm that destroyed the heart of the city
and killed 30,000 civilians. During November 1943, the
British launched 16 major raids against Berlin.

The U.S. Eighth Air Force arrived in England in the
spring of 1942. Its four-engine B-17 Flying Fortress possessed heavy defensive armament and was equipped
with a superior bombsight, causing the Americans to believe that it could fly long-distance daylight raids and hit
industrial targets with precision without fighter escort.
Its first mission, in August 1942, was against rail yards
at Rouen, France. The test of its ability to penetrate
enemy airspace in daylight without fighter support came
on Aug. 17, 1943, in a massive raid against a ball-
bearing plant at Schweinfurt in central Germany. Out of
229 B-17s in the raid, 36 were lost, a loss rate three
times what was then considered acceptable. Pending the
arrival of long-distance fighters, daylight bombing of
German targets was largely suspended, the Eighth Air
Force thereafter concentrating on targets in France and
the Low Countries where its bombers enjoyed fighter
protection.

Long-distance fighters arrived in 1944. These were
the U.S. P-51 Mustang, which was capable of reaching
Berlin from its British bases. But as the Normandy invasion approached, the heavy bombers were recalled from
Germany and concentrated on French targets behind the
invasion area. Once the armies were ashore, tactical air
forces provided close ground support, and the bombers—
both British and American—returned to round-the-clock
bombing of German targets, now escorted by fighters
that dealt effectively with diminished German air defenses. Late in 1944, as the bombers struck especially at
German oil and synthetic-oil plants and at the German
transportation network, Germany's war economy began
to collapse. Altogether, the Allies dropped 2.7 million
tons of bombs on Germany during the war, more than
70 percent of them during the war's last year. Some
600,000 German civilians were killed.

War in North Africa, Sicily, and Italy (1942–
44). When the United States entered the war, German
armies were deep in the Soviet Union, besieging
Leningrad, approaching Moscow, and driving south toward the Caucuses. Soviet premier Joseph Stalin's chief
demand of his new allies was a second front in Western
Europe to relieve the pressure in the East. But the resources for a cross-channel invasion would not be available for two more years. British prime minister Winston
Churchill proposed Allied action in North Africa, where
Germany's Afrika Korps, consisting of German and Italian troops under Gen. Erwin Rommel, threatened the
Suez Canal and the Middle East. Roosevelt agreed.

In Egypt on Oct. 23, 1942, the British Eighth Army
routed the Afrika Korps at El Alamein, only 70 miles
from Alexandria. Rommel was driven west, the British

pursuing him for 2,000 miles along the North African coast until he took shelter in the Mareth Line, French fortifications on the border between Tunisia and Libya.

Meanwhile, on Nov. 8, Anglo-American task forces from England had landed at Oran and Algiers on the Mediterranean coast of Algeria, and a third task force, sailing directly from the United States, had landed at Casablanca on the Atlantic coast of Morocco. Under the overall command of U.S. general Dwight D. Eisenhower, the three task forces moved toward Tunisia, which the Germans—having now occupied the remainder of France—had quickly seized with troops airlifted from France. Attacking the Americans approaching from Morocco, Rommel delivered a demoralizing blow at **Kasserine Pass** (Feb. 20, 1943), but the Americans quickly recovered and retook the pass five days later. On Mar. 29, the British Eighth Army outflanked the Mareth Line, and the Allies soon encircled the Germans and Italians in northern Tunisia. On May 13—after Rommel had escaped to Europe—250,000 Axis troops surrendered to the Allies in Tunisia.

Two months later, on July 10, the U.S. First Army and the British Eighth Army landed on the south coast of Sicily. The Americans turned west and against light resistance took Palermo on July 24, precipitating the overthrow of Fascist dictator Benito Mussolini in Italy. In the east, however, the British encountered tough German resistance, and the Allies did not enter Messina until Aug. 17, by which time most of the island's defenders had escaped to the mainland.

On Sept. 3 the British Eighth Army crossed the Straits of Messina onto the toe of Italy, and on Sept. 9 the U.S. Fifth Army made an amphibious landing at Salerno, south of Naples. When the Italian government then surrendered to the Allies, German troops poured into the peninsula, put down civilian and military resistance, seized Rome, and established a defensive line north of Salerno. Under Allied pressure, the Germans fell back to successive defensive lines culminating in the Gustav Line anchored at Monte Cassino. The Americans took Naples on Sept. 28, but the winter struggle northward in rugged mountain terrain was slow and costly.

On Jan. 22, 1944, the Americans outflanked the Gustav Line by an amphibious landing at **Anzio**, 30 miles south of Rome, where they found themselves trapped for three months by Germans fighting from higher ground. Reinforced, the Americans at Anzio broke out of their beachhead on May 23, at the same time that the Fifth Army captured Monte Cassino and broke through the Gustav Line. The Fifth Army's race to seize Rome on June 4 instead of encircling the Germans to its south allowed the Germans to escape north and re-form across the peninsula in the Gothic Line north of Florence in August.

The Island War in the Pacific (1942–45). From bases in Australia in August 1942 the Allies began a long offensive aimed first at the Philippines and ultimately at Japan itself. The first move was a two-armed thrust northward converging on the major Japanese base at Rabaul on New Britain Island in the Bismarck Sea. One arm of this thrust, conducted by the U.S. Navy under Adm. William F. Halsey, would drive up the Solomon chain; the other arm, conducted by the U.S. Army and Australian and New Zealand troops under General MacArthur, would reconquer the Japanese-held north coast of New Guinea.

The Solomons Campaign (Aug. 7, 1942–November 1943) began with the landing of U.S. marines on the island of **Guadalcanal**. A small Japanese garrison was quickly overcome, but Japan would not tolerate any breach in its defense perimeter. Both sides poured reinforcements into the island, and the navies that convoyed and supplied them engaged in furious battles in the narrow waters of the archipelago. In the battle of Guadalcanal (Aug. 7, 1942–Feb. 9, 1943), the marines fought a tenacious enemy at close quarters in a steaming, disease-ridden jungle. When the island was finally secure, the marines pushed north into New Georgia (June–July 1943) and Bougainville (November 1943).

The **New Guinea Campaign** (Sept. 29, 1942–July 30, 1944) began when Australian troops checked a Japanese advance across the Owen Stanley Mountains from the north in an attempt to seize Port Moresby on the south coast, opposite Australia. Australian and American troops then made their way across the mountains over the tortuous Kokoda Trail. By January 1943 they had taken Gona and Buna on the north coast. Then began a series of amphibious hooks westward along the coast. MacArthur's troops took Lae and Salamaua in September 1943, Hollandia in April 1944, and Biak in June. The conquest of New Guinea was declared complete in July 1944. Meanwhile, U.S. troops had landed on New Britain, but conquest of the Admiralty Islands in February–March 1944 had isolated Rabaul and 100,000 Japanese troops. These and many other Japanese troops on Bougainville and in the New Guinea interior were left to "wither on the vine."

By mid-1944, the archipelagos of the Southwest Pacific on the approach to the Philippines were in Allied hands. But now a second approach to the Philippines—across the Central Pacific, leapfrogging huge distances between tiny atolls—was under way, directed by Adm. Chester A. Nimitz, commander of the Pacific Theater from Pearl Harbor. On Nov. 21, 1943, marines landed on Tarawa in the Gilbert Islands. The Japanese defenders fought to the death; those not killed in battle threw themselves in a suicidal attack against marine lines. In February 1944 marines and army troops took Kwajalein and Eniwetok in the Marshall Islands, again against suicidal defense. Bypassing the major Japanese base at Truk in the Caroline Islands, U.S. troops on June 15 landed on Saipan in the Marianas. Again the defenders fought to the death, the survivors committing suicide by charging American lines or leaping off cliffs, their officers (among them Admiral Naguma) committing ritual suicide. In the battle of the **Philippine Sea** (June 19–20), initiated by the Japanese in defense of the Marianas, the U.S. Navy sank or damaged five Japanese carriers and destroyed hundreds of planes in what American pilots celebrated as the "great Marianas turkey shoot." The Marianas provided a base not only for the invasion of the Philippines but for air attacks on the Japanese home islands.

On Oct. 20, 1944, the U.S. Sixth Army, MacArthur's main ground force in New Guinea, went ashore at Leyte Gulf on the east coast of the island of Leyte in the central Philippines. MacArthur himself waded ashore toward waiting cameras and later announced by radio to the Philippine people, "I have returned." The landing was uncontested, the Japanese having planned to attack and destroy the American fleet protecting the landing site while greatly reinforced troops on the island itself pushed the stranded invasion force into the sea.

Thus on Oct. 22 an apparently powerful Japanese fleet (its four carriers had only 108 planes) left the Japanese home islands and moved south toward the Philippines, hoping to lure Admiral Halsey's Third Fleet away from its primary mission of protecting the invasion site. At the same time, two Japanese strike forces (devoid of air cover) approached from the south, intending to converge on vulnerable **Leyte Gulf**. As they moved north, these forces were mauled by U.S. submarines and carrier planes. But then Halsey, falling into the Japanese trap, raced north to deal with the approaching carrier force. On Oct. 24 his planes inflicted heavy damage on this fleet before he was urgently ordered to return to Leyte Gulf. By the time he arrived on Oct. 25, the escort carriers, destroyers, and old battleships of the Seventh Fleet had routed both southern strike forces. The battle of Leyte Gulf, the largest naval battle in history, cost the Japanese navy three battleships, four carriers, and six cruisers, losses from which it never recovered and which put an end to Japanese carrier-based naval aviation.

The conquest of Leyte continued against tenacious Japanese resistance. Not until April 1945 was the island considered secure. By then, U.S. troops had landed on Mindoro (Dec. 15, 1944) and Luzon (Jan. 8, 1945), where the fighting was no less ferocious. In house-to-house combat, ruined Manila was finally cleared (Feb. 5–23). Japanese resistance on Luzon ended only in August. Meanwhile, the U.S. Eighth Army recovered the central and southern islands of the Philippines.

U.S. possession of the Philippines cut off Japan's sea communications with its southern empire. But island bases closer to the home islands were still needed for an invasion of Japan itself. On Feb. 19, 1945, three marine divisions assaulted **Iwo Jima** in the Bonin Islands. Honeycombed with tunnels and hidden firing positions immune to naval gunfire, the island was secured at great cost only on Mar. 17, although an American flag had been raised on Mount Suribachi on Feb. 24.

Starting on Apr.1, three marine and five army divisions went ashore on **Okinawa** in the Ryukyu Islands, just 360 miles from the southernmost of the Japanese home islands. The landing was uncontested, and the northern portion of the island was quickly cleared by marines. But the mountainous southern portion proved as difficult to subdue as had Iwo Jima. When resistance ended on June 21, the Americans had taken some 7,400 prisoners, but more than 110,000 other defenders had died fighting or as suicides.

During the fighting, the 1,300-ship Allied armada offshore sustained heavy losses from suicide kamikaze attacks in which Japanese pilots tried to dive their planes into the Allied ships. Another casualty was the 70,000-ton Japanese battleship *Yamato,* which left Japan on Apr. 6 to do battle with the invasion fleet but was sunk by U.S. carrier planes the next day before even reaching Okinawa.

From D-Day to VE-Day in Europe (1944–45). On June 6, 1944—D-Day—Allied armies under the supreme command of U.S. general Dwight D. Eisenhower opened the long-awaited second front in Europe. During the night, three airborne divisions had been dropped behind the **Normandy invasion** beaches. Starting at 6 a.m. along 60 miles of the northern (Channel) coast of the Cotentin Peninsula, between Le Havre and Cherbourg, two American, two British, and one Canadian division, plus specialized units, went ashore from an armada of 4,483 ships (4,000 of them landing craft) while 12,000 planes secured the skies. At Omaha Beach, the U.S. First Division suffered heavy casualties from German guns on bluffs above the beach and on Pointe du Hoc at its western end. Landings at the other beaches—Utah, Gold, Juno, and Sword—were less diffi-cult. By nightfall, all five landing places were in Allied hands, the bridgeheads ranging from one to six miles in depth although they were still not joined. The invaders pushed rapidly inland while more troops and equipment poured into the bridgehead from two floating harbors that had been towed to the beaches.

Initially, the invaders faced only three German divi-sions, but others gathered steadily despite the devastation wreaked on French roads and railways and the constant attack of Allied tactical aircraft. The stiffening resistance threw off the Allied timetable. While British and Cana-dian troops at the east end of the bridgehead advanced on Bayeux and Caen (D-Day objectives that they did not take until July 8), the U.S. First Army at the western end reached the southern (Atlantic) coast of the Cotentin Peninsula on June 18, isolating the port city of Cher-bourg. The city surrendered on June 26, although its wrecked port facilities were not repaired until mid-July.

By July 1, the Allied bridgehead held 27 divisions (nearly 1 million men), half a million tons of supplies, and 177,000 vehicles. Nevertheless, it was still contained by smaller German forces. At the start of July, the First Army began fighting its way south through the almost impregnable hedgerow country, sustaining heavy casual-ties especially in the capture of St. Lô on July 8. A break-out was not achieved until July 25, when, after a carpet bombing of the front west of St. Lô, six divisions opened a hole in the German lines and drove forward 30 miles to Avranches.

From Avranches, the newly constituted U.S. Third Army drove southeast behind the German forces while the British and Canadians pushed south from Caen to-ward Falaise. In the battle of the **Falaise Gap** (Aug. 3–23, 1944), the Germans fought desperately to prevent their encirclement. By the time the "gap" was closed on Aug. 21, 300,000 German troops had escaped east across the Seine River through a gauntlet of Allied air and ground attacks. But 200,000 others were taken pris-oner, 50,000 German dead were counted, and the wreck-age of vast quantities of German equipment strewed the countryside.

After Falaise, the remnants of the German army re-treated north across the Schelde, Meuse, and Rhine rivers while the Allied armies poured out of their bridgehead into northern France and Belgium. The British captured Brussels on Sept. 3, Antwerp on Sept. 4. The U.S. Third Army sped eastward, en route dispatching the French Second Armored Division to liberate Paris, which it en-tered on Sept. 25. Meanwhile, on Aug. 15, the U.S. Sev-enth Army had landed in southern France between Nice

and Toulon and raced north against little opposition to join the Third Army at Dijon on Sept. 11. By mid-September, a continuous front existed from the Schelde estuary in Belgium to the Swiss border. But the Allied armies had outrun their supplies, still dependent on truck transport from Atlantic ports 500 miles away. The fail-ure of an airborne operation—"Market-Garden" (Sept. 17–24), involving two American and one British division—that attempted to leap the Meuse and lower Rhine and establish a bridgehead in northern Germany marked the end of the Allies' summer campaign.

While the Allies prepared for a spring assault against Germany itself, German dictator Adolf Hitler gathered his remaining resources for an offensive through the lightly defended Ardennes Forest aimed to divide the British and Canadian armies from the American and to seize the vital supply port of Antwerp, only 60 miles away. The German offensive, launched on Dec. 16 with 25 divisions along a 90-mile front, caught the Allies by surprise, overwhelmed the six American divisions in its path, and caused panic in Belgium and France. (On Dec. 17, an SS panzer division murdered more than 100 American prisoners at **Malmédy** in Belgium.) But the resistance of isolated American units, especially the de-fense of encircled Bastogne by the 101st Airborne Divi-sion, wrecked the Germans' timetable. They failed to reach needed Allied fuel stores; clearing weather after Dec. 26 opened them to air attack; and assaults on their right flank by the U.S. First Army and on their left flank by the U.S. Third Army drove into their 60-mile salient. By Jan. 16 the battle of the **Bulge** had ended with the front restored. German losses of men and equipment were irreplaceable.

In March, seven Allied armies—more than 80 divisions—crossed the Rhine into central Germany. (On the Eastern Front, a Soviet offensive had brought the Red Army to the Oder River opposite Berlin in the north and to Vienna in the south.) The British and Canadian armies drove through northern Germany to Bremen and Ham-burg. The U.S. First and Ninth armies encircled the Ruhr, completing its capture—with 325,000 German troops—on Apr. 18. On Apr. 11 Ninth Army troops reached the Elbe River, the previously agreed-upon demarcation line between the Soviet and Western occupation zones. The Third Army raced through southern Germany to within 30 miles of both Prague and Vienna. Farther south, the Seventh Army took Nuremberg and Munich.

On Apr. 16, the Soviets crossed the Oder River and began their final assault on Berlin. The German capital was encircled by Apr. 25. As massed Soviet artillery sys-tematically reduced the city to rubble, Soviet troops fought house to house against diehard defenders. On Apr. 30, Hitler committed suicide in his bunker under the Reichschancellery, and the city's last defenders surrendered to the Soviets on May 2. On May 7, Gen. Alfred Jodl, the German chief of staff, signed Germany's unconditional surrender at Eisenhower's headquarters at Reims, France. The war in Europe formally ended the next day, May 8 (VE-Day).

The Assault on Japan (November 1944–August 1945). Cut off from its southern empire, its merchant marine destroyed, by 1945 Japan faced steadily declining war production and actual starvation. Many people then, and some historians since, thought that the war was won and that Japan would eventually surrender without further bloodshed.

This was not the opinion of American leaders, who were struck by the suicidal defenses of Japanese island outposts and who were also privy to the internal discussions of the Japanese government through their monitoring of its communications with its diplomats in Europe. Although some people high in the Tokyo government advocated surrender, a fanatical war party insisted on fighting to the end. American leaders believed that Japan would surrender only under the double blows of an invasion of the home islands and a Soviet attack on Manchuria. On the basis of their experiences at Iwo Jima and Okinawa, they anticipated casualties as high as half a million in an invasion of Japan. Nevertheless, an invasion of the island of Kyushu was scheduled for November 1945 and logistic preparations were well under way when the war in Europe ended in May.

In preparation for the invasion, the United States launched an air assault on Japan from the newly captured Marianas, which were within the 1,500-mile flying range of the new B-29 bombers. Starting in November 1944, small but growing numbers of B-29s flew high-altitude, daylight precision-bombing raids aimed chiefly at the Japanese aircraft industry. When the results proved disappointing, the 21st Bomber Command switched to low-level nighttime attacks with incendiary bombs. On Mar. 9, 1945, B-29s attacked Tokyo with incendiaries, burning out 16 square miles of the city and killing 80–100,000 people. Thereafter fleets of B-29s raided other major cities with horrific results. But no word of surrender came from Tokyo.

On July 15, 1945, the United States successfully tested an *atomic bomb in New Mexico. From Potsdam, Germany, where he was attending a conference with Churchill and Stalin, Pres. Harry S. Truman on July 26 issued the Potsdam Declaration demanding that Japan surrender unconditionally or face "prompt and utter destruction." When Japan did not respond, the decision to use the atomic bomb on Japanese targets—a decision concurred in by all Allied leaders—went forward.

On Aug. 6, 1945, the B-29 *Enola Gay*, flying from Tinian in the Marianas, dropped a uranium bomb on the Japanese city of Hiroshima, killing 50–80,000 people. When the Japanese government failed to respond, a second bomb—this one a more powerful plutonium bomb—was dropped on Nagasaki on Aug. 9. On the same day, the Soviet Union launched a massive offensive against Manchuria. That night at an Imperial Council, Emperor Hirohito ordered the divided Japanese government to accept Allied peace terms. Later he broadcast to the Japanese people—the first time they had ever heard his voice—that they must "bear the unbearable." Japan announced its surrender on Aug. 15 (VJ-Day).

On Aug. 21, the first American occupation troops landed and found the country obedient to the emperor's command. On Sept. 2, in the presence of representatives of the Allied powers aboard the USS *Missouri* in Tokyo Bay, General MacArthur conducted the formal ceremony of surrender.

Consequences of the War. Worldwide, some 60 million people died in World War 2—25 million in the Soviet Union, 15 million in China, 6 million in Poland, over 4 million in Germany, 2 million in Japan. In the countries that had been battlefields of the war, civilian casualties far exceeded the military. Britain lost 400,000 dead, the United States 300,000. Millions more were maimed physically and psychologically. Wherever the armies or the bomber fleets had passed, the devastation was total. Millions of people were homeless and destitute. Other millions were "displaced persons," refugees, expellees, fugitives. The human and economic costs of the war are truly incalculable.

For the United States, the most dramatic effect of the war was to end the *Great Depression. As soon as war orders began to be placed by the British, French, and American governments, unemployment began to fall—from 19.0 percent in 1938 to 1.2 percent in 1944. In 1944, 54 million workers were employed in America's factories, farms, and offices while 11.4 million others served in the armed forces. Many Americans feared that the depression would return when the war ended. Vice Pres. Henry A. Wallace's prophecy of 60 million jobs after the war was greeted with ridicule—although the 60-million-jobs mark was actually passed in 1947. For the country as a whole, World War 2 began a half century of economic growth and unprecedented affluence.

The war speeded up many social changes that had been under way before the depression. One was the entry of women into the labor force, already marked during the depression. Now women replaced drafted men in defense plants. The number of working women grew from 14.2 million in 1940, when women constituted 25.2 percent of the labor force, to 19.4 million in 1944, when they constituted 29.2 percent. (The labor-force-participation rate of women in those years grew from 27.9 percent to 36.3 percent.) Women were expected to surrender their jobs to returning veterans and resume their traditional roles, and many did so. But in 1948 their numbers in the labor force turned upward again and they have continued to grow ever since (see *Women in the Labor Force).

African-Americans also found new employment opportunities during the war, which speeded their migration from the rural South to the urban North. The percentage of African-Americans living in the South declined from 77.0 in 1940 to 68.0 in 1950. New jobs and service in the still-segregated armed forces emboldened African-Americans to demand their full civil rights. The establishment of the *Fair Employment Practices Committee in 1941 under threat of a black march on Washington marked the beginnings of a civil rights campaign that reached its full force several decades later.

The war also speeded the urbanization of America and the growth of its middle class. The percentage of Americans who were classified as urban grew from 56.5 in 1940 to 59.0 in 1950. At the same time, the percentage of farmworkers in the labor force declined from 17.0 to 12.0 while the percentage of manufacturing workers grew from 20.1 to 23.9. Employees' average annual earnings, in constant dollars, rose 40.8 percent between 1940 and 1950. The *G.I. Bill of Rights enabled many veterans who might not otherwise have done so to go to college, the proportion of American men with four or more years of college growing 31.5 percent between 1940 and 1950. The same G.I. Bill helped veterans buy houses, with the result that home ownership increased 55.0 percent between 1940 and 1950.

The postwar years saw the marriages of the parents of the *baby boom generation. These newlyweds left the old inner cities and settled in new suburbs where they evolved a broad-based consumer culture that, whatever its shortcomings, kept the economy humming.

WORLD WAR 2 CONFERENCES (1941–45), meetings between Allied leaders, together with their top military and political aides, to plan war strategy and peace settlements. The principal conferences were these:

Atlantic Conference (Aug. 9–12, 1941). U.S. president Franklin Roosevelt and British prime minister Winston Churchill met aboard naval vessels anchored in Placentia Bay, Newfoundland, Canada. The first meeting of the two leaders, it revealed a fundamental conflict: Churchill wanted an Anglo-American alliance against Germany, whereas Roosevelt knew that U.S. public opinion would not support it. Both agreed on a warning to Japan against further aggression. The conference issued the *Atlantic Charter.

1st Washington Conference (Dec. 22, 1941–Jan. 6, 1942). Two weeks after Pearl Harbor, Churchill visited the White House. He and Roosevelt affirmed their strategic decision to deal with Germany first. U.S. troops would relieve British troops in Iceland and Northern Ireland. They would also land in North Africa, meeting British troops advancing from Egypt. A staff structure for the joint planning and conduct of the war was established in Washington under the title Combined Chiefs of Staff (necessitating the formation of a U.S. staff for interservice coordination that became the Joint Chiefs of Staff).

Casablanca Conference (Jan. 14–24, 1943). Roosevelt and Churchill assigned the highest priority to the war against U-boats in the Atlantic. An invasion of Sicily, and then of Italy, would follow completion of the North African campaign. A cross-Channel invasion of France was postponed to 1944, but a planning staff was to be set up. (The British persisted in subsequent meetings to advocate operations in the Mediterranean that threatened to delay the cross-Channel invasion.) A major bombing offensive against Germany was to proceed, the Americans bombing in daylight, the British at night. Both leaders agreed on the policy of *unconditional surrender toward the Axis powers.

2nd Washington Conference (May 12–25, 1943). Churchill again agreed to an invasion of France in 1944, and Roosevelt to an invasion of Italy once Sicily was secured. The bombing offensive against Germany was to continue. Air supply of the Chinese Nationalist air force was to be increased, to the neglect of the Chinese army.

1st Quebec Conference (Aug. 17–24, 1943). Churchill was forced to agree to a cross-Channel invasion (Overlord) in May 1944, for which seven divisions would be transferred from the Mediterranean. The Italian campaign would be secondary to the invasion, and there would be no offensive operations in the Balkans. A Southeast Asia Command was established under Lord Louis Mountbatten.

1st Cairo Conference (Nov. 22–26, 1943). Roosevelt and Churchill were joined by China's generalissimo Chiang Kai-shek. Roosevelt supported Chiang's desire to open a campaign in Burma, thus enlarging China's role in the war against Japan and ensuring Chiang's place among the Big Four. Churchill consented but refused to divert any British forces from the Middle East. The conference issued a declaration promising to return to China territory taken by Japan since 1894.

Tehran Conference (Nov. 28–Dec. 1, 1943). Roosevelt, Churchill, and Soviet premier Joseph Stalin finalized the decision to invade France in May 1944 from both the north and the south in conjunction with a Soviet offensive in the east. Stalin also promised to enter the war against Japan after Germany's defeat. Stalin made clear the Soviet Union's security interests in the Baltic, Eastern Europe, and Poland and pressed for a punitive settlement with Germany.

2nd Cairo Conference (Dec. 3–7, 1943). Roosevelt and Churchill met with the president of Turkey but failed to get Turkey to enter the war. They agreed to delay the promised Burma campaign, and Roosevelt decided to appoint Gen. Dwight D. Eisenhower commander of Overlord.

2nd Quebec Conference (Sept. 11–16, 1944). Roosevelt and Churchill reviewed strategic plans for the campaigns against Germany and Japan. Occupation zones in Germany were agreed upon, and the two leaders accepted (briefly) the plan of U.S. secretary of the Treasury Henry Morgenthau to deindustrialize conquered Germany (see *Morgenthau Plan). Roosevelt promised to continue *Lend-Lease to Britain after the war.

Yalta Conference (Feb. 4–12, 1945). It was attended by Roosevelt, Churchill, and Stalin. Stalin agreed to enter the war against Japan three months after the end of the war in Europe; he was promised the Kurile Islands, the southern half of Sakhalin Island, an occupation zone in Korea, and other considerations. In Europe, the demand for Germany's unconditional surrender was reaffirmed. Conquered Germany was to be divided into four occupation zones (a French zone to be carved out of the British and American zones), and the Soviet Union was to receive half of all German reparations. The United States and Great Britain accepted Soviet possession of eastern Poland, Poland to be compensated by territory taken from eastern Germany. The Soviet-sponsored Lublin government of Poland was "democratized" and free elections were promised (but never held) for Poland and other liberated countries in Eastern Europe. In the Far East, Stalin agreed to recognize Chiang as leader of the Chinese government and to urge the Chinese communists to enter a coalition with him. A meeting to draft a United Nations charter was scheduled for Apr. 25 at San Francisco; each of the major powers would have a veto in the Security Council and the Soviet Union would have two additional votes—for Ukraine and Byelorussia—in the General Assembly. For military and political reasons, most of the decisions at Yalta were kept secret.

Potsdam Conference (July 17–Aug. 2, 1945). It was attended by Stalin, the new U.S. president, Harry S. Truman, and Churchill, who was replaced on July 26 by the new British prime minister, Clement Attlee. France was not represented. Stalin agreed to enter the war against Japan on Aug. 15; on July 26 the conference issued the Potsdam Declaration calling upon Japan to surrender or suffer destruction (the newly tested *atomic bomb was not mentioned). Most of the conference's business concerned postwar Europe. A Council of Foreign Ministers of the United States, Great Britain, the Soviet Union, France, and China was created to draft peace treaties with Germany and its satellites. The leading German war criminals were to be tried by an international tribunal. The occupation of Germany would aim at demilitarization, denazification, democratization, and economic decentralization. Occupation policy was to be set by a four-power Allied Control Council in Berlin. (When French obstruction prevented it from working, the military governors of the four occupation zones had complete liberty of action.) Stalin demanded reparations in the form of capital goods. The Western Allies accepted the Oder-Neisse line as Germany's new eastern border and the transfer of 6.5 million ethnic Germans from other countries to Germany.

WOUNDED KNEE MASSACRE (1890). See *Sioux Wars.

WRIGHTS' FLIGHTS (1903). All over America in the 1890s village inventors, strapped into homemade contraptions shaped like birds, bats, or even fish, were jumping off barns or cliffs to solve the mystery of human flight. In Dayton, Ohio, the brothers Wilbur and Orville Wright—proprietors of a shop in which they repaired, built, and sold bicycles—took a more methodical approach. "I am an enthusiast, but not a crank," Wilbur explained to the Smithsonian Institution in 1899 in his request for publications on aeronautics.

The brothers, aged 32 and 28, began with large box kites, which they controlled from the ground with strings. Very early, they realized that the great problem was not flight itself but controlling the aircraft in flight. The craft was free to rotate around three axes—a horizontal axis running from wingtip to wingtip, another horizontal axis running from the nose of the craft to its tail, and a vertical axis running through the center of the craft (the rotations called respectively pitch, roll, and yaw). The Wrights controlled for pitch and yaw with horizontal and vertical rudders. Their greatest contribution was controlling for roll, which they did by "wing warping," bending the ends of the craft's wings in anticipation of later ailerons. (Not only did they learn to control roll, but they learned also to induce it and thereby cause the craft to bank, an essential maneuver in turning.) When the Wrights moved on from kites to gliders, they perfected the cambered wing design in a homemade wind tunnel, thereby increasing the craft's lift.

In 1901 and 1902, the Wrights flew manned gliders at Kitty Hawk, North Carolina, where wide flat beaches and stiff onshore winds provided ideal conditions. In December 1903 the brothers were back at Kitty Hawk ready to try powered flight. Their biplane weighed 675 pounds. It was powered by a 12-horsepower gasoline engine built in the bicycle shop that drove two pusher propellers mounted on the trailing edges of the wings and turning in opposite directions. The machine would take off into the wind from a 60-foot rail on which it rode on bicycle-wheel hubs.

At 10:35 a.m. on Dec. 17, 1903, with Orville Wright perched on the lower wing and Wilbur running alongside holding up that wing, the craft clattered down the launching rail into a 21-mile-per-hour headwind, rose unsteadily into the air, and traveled 120 feet before striking the sand 12 seconds after takeoff. Later flights that day covered as much as 852 feet in 59 seconds. That afternoon Orville telegraphed his father in Dayton: "Success. Four flights Thursday morning. . . . Inform press. Home Christmas."

WYOMING VALLEY MASSACRE (July 3, 1778), incident in the *Revolutionary War. Dispatched from Fort Niagara to devastate the New York and Pennsylvania frontiers, a force of 1,100 Loyalists and Indians commanded by Col. John Butler destroyed a force of some 400 Patriot militia in Pennsylvania's Wyoming Valley and then rampaged through the area. The incident was described as a savage massacre by Patriot propagandists.

X

XYZ AFFAIR (1797–98), incident in the diplomatic relations between the John *Adams administration and the French Directory.

To show its displeasure with *Jay's Treaty (1794), which appeared to make the United States a British ally, France refused to receive the newly appointed American minister, Charles Cotesworth Pinckney. President Adams sent two other negotiators—John Marshall and Elbridge Gerry—to join Pinckney. The French foreign minister, Charles-Maurice de Talleyrand-Périgord, seeking to embarrass the Federalist administration to the advantage of its pro-French opposition, the Jeffersonian Republicans, delayed the mission's reception by the Directory for many weeks. Finally, three agents of Talleyrand—designated X, Y, and Z in the Americans' reports—approached the mission and demanded a loan to France and a bribe to Talleyrand as conditions for its reception. The Americans temporized and sought to negotiate, but then Talleyrand declared he would deal only with Gerry—a Republican. Gerry remained in Paris after his colleagues departed.

Publication of the commissioners' reports outraged Americans and seriously embarrassed the Republican opposition. "Millions for defense but not one cent for tribute"—a toast in honor of John Marshall offered by Rep. Robert Goodloe Harper of South Carolina—became a popular slogan. Congress abrogated the 1778 treaties with France, suspended commercial relations, and prepared for war. An undeclared *naval war with France ensued.

Y

YALTA CONFERENCE (1945). See *World War 2 Conferences.

YANKEE DOODLE, American folk song that probably originated in the 1740s. Its lyrics were frequently revised to provide satiric comment on military events and social customs of the period. The version popular during the *Revolutionary War satirizes a rustic's army experience. It began: "Father and I went down to camp, / Along with Captain Gooding, / And there we see the men and boys, / As thick as hasty pudding. / Yankee Doodle, keep it up, / Yankee Doodle, dandy, / Mind the music and the step, / And with the girls be handy."

YARBOROUGH, EX PARTE (1884), unanimous decision of the *Waite Court upholding the federal government's power to punish private obstruction of a citizen's right to vote. Yarborough, convicted of beating a black man to prevent his voting in a federal election, argued that the federal laws protecting voters were unconstitutional because they lacked express authorization in the Constitution.

Justice Samuel F. Miller found the authority certainly implied if not expressed. "[I]t is the duty of [the federal] government to see that [the voter] may exercise this right freely, and to protect him from violence while so doing, or on account of so doing." This decision proved exceptional, the Court more often doubting that the federal government could interfere with private obstruction.

YATES v. UNITED STATES (1957), 6–1 decision of the *Warren Court overturning the convictions of the second group of Communist Party leaders tried under the 1940 Smith Act (see *Anticommunism).

In *Dennis v. United States* (1951), the Court had upheld the convictions of 11 Communist Party leaders

under the Smith Act; now it found significant differences between *Dennis* and the present case, in which 14 additional Communist Party leaders had been convicted. Although the Smith Act made it a crime to organize a party advocating the overthrow of the government, the word *organize* was now defined as the act creating a new organization, something in which the present appellants had not been involved. Further, the charge to the jury in *Yates* had failed to distinguish between advocacy of violent action to be undertaken immediately (not constitutionally protected) and advocacy of violent action at some future time, as an abstract doctrine (constitutionally protected). The convictions of the 14 appellants were reversed. No further prosecutions were ever brought under the Smith Act.

YAZOO LAND FRAUD (1795–1814). In 1795, a corrupt Georgia legislature sold 35 million acres of the state's western lands along the Yazoo River in present-day Alabama and Mississippi to four land companies at 1.5 cents an acre. A new legislature in 1796 rescinded the sale. Eastern speculators who had bought much of the land claimed they had been defrauded by the rescision, and when Georgia transferred its western lands to the federal government in 1802 they made their claims for compensation a national issue. Their case was strengthened by the decision of the U.S. Supreme Court in *Fletcher v. Peck* (1810) that the original sale, however corrupt the motives of the legislators, had been valid and that the 1796 rescision had violated the Contract Clause of the U.S. Constitution. In 1814 Congress provided $4.2 million to compensate the Yazoo claimants.

YELLOW FEVER, tropical viral disease transmitted solely by the female *Aedes aegypti* mosquito. Symptoms include fever, yellow skin, and black vomiting. Where no natural immunity exists, incidence and mortality may be very high.

Yellow fever may have been brought to the Western Hemisphere by African slaves, who enjoyed relative immunity to it—unlike Europeans and native Indians. In the colonial period, the disease was most active in West Africa, the Caribbean, Central and South America, and North American coastal cities.

Clergyman and scientist Cotton Mather described an outbreak of the disease in Boston in 1693 brought by a British man-of-war. New York suffered its first outbreak in 1702, when 520 people—10 percent of the population—died. There were other outbreaks in 1741 and 1747. Philadelphia was visited by yellow fever in 1699, 1743–45, 1748, and, most disastrously, in 1793, when 4,000 people died between August and October. Contemporaries described deserted streets where only hearses moved. Refugees from Philadelphia were banned by neighboring states. Charleston experienced a series of yellow fever attacks beginning in 1699 and peaking in 1758; the fever returned in six epidemics between 1790 and 1799.

In New Orleans, a series of yellow fever epidemics in the first half of the 19th century culminated in 1853, when 10,000 people—10 percent of the population— died. Outbreaks continued in the second half of the century. The last major yellow fever epidemic in the United States occurred in New Orleans in 1906.

Frequent and costly epidemics, occurring usually between August and October, seriously disrupted the social and business lives of these communities. On the positive side, they stimulated the development of public health and sanitation measures.

The role of *A. aegypti* as the vector of yellow fever was established in 1901, soon after the *Anopheles* mosquito had been implicated in the spread of malaria. In 1903, Walter Reed and James Carroll identified the cause of the disease as an ultramicroscopic virus. There followed successful mosquito eradication programs in Cuba and Panama under the direction of William C. Gorgas. After World War I, mosquito eradication programs were carried out in Central and South America. A variety of yellow fever—jungle yellow fever—persists in Africa, but a vaccine and continued mosquito eradication have reduced its incidence.

YELLOW PERIL. See *Chinese Exclusion.

YELLOW PRESS, late-19th-century newspapers that competed for circulation by sensationalizing the news,

exposing scandals, exploiting crime, gossip, and human-interest stories, and providing a variety of specialized features, including comics. The term derived from a comic strip called "The Yellow Kid" introduced in Joseph Pulitzer's New York *World* in 1896.

The invention of the web press made possible the rapid printing of great numbers of newspapers, transforming the economics of newspaper publishing from dependence upon purchasers to dependence upon advertisers, who could be charged more as circulation increased. Thus the price of some "yellow" newspapers fell to as little as one cent as they sought huge circulations among the semiliterate masses.

The classic circulation war was that between William Randolph Hearst's New York *Journal* and Pulitzer's *World*, both of which sensationalized events in Cuba and inflamed public opinion to the point that the *Spanish-American War became inevitable. Hearst—who allegedly telegraphed artist Frederic Remington in Havana in March 1898, "You furnish the pictures and I'll furnish the war"—did in fact call it "the *Journal*'s war."

YELLOW TAVERN (May 11, 1864), *Civil War battle. During May 9–25, while the Army of the Potomac fought at Spotsylvania Court House and Cold Harbor (see *Wilderness Campaign), Union cavalry general Philip Sheridan led 10,000 horsemen on a raid in the vicinity of Richmond, destroying railroad tracks, rolling stock, and three weeks' rations for Confederate general Robert E. Lee's Army of Northern Virginia, besides freeing several hundred Union prisoners.

On May 11, Confederate cavalry general J. E. B. Stuart confronted Sheridan at Yellow Tavern, six miles north of Richmond. With the advantages of numbers and firepower (they carried repeating carbines), Sheridan's cavalrymen scattered the Confederates. Stuart, age 31, was mortally wounded—his only wound of the war— and died in Richmond the next day.

YIPPIES (1960s), members of an ephemeral Youth International Party whose antics outside the Democratic national convention in Chicago in 1968 led to the prosecution of their leaders, the *Chicago Seven.

YORKTOWN SIEGE (Sept. 28–Oct. 19, 1781), episode in the *Revolutionary War. On Apr. 25, 1781, British general Charles Cornwallis left his base at Wilmington, N.C., and with 1,500 men marched north into Virginia, which he believed was the key to the war. At Petersburg he joined other British forces sent to Virginia by Gen. Henry Clinton in New York to conduct punitive raids on the colonists and intercept the flow of supplies to the Patriot army in the Carolinas and Georgia.

Cornwallis now commanded 7,500 troops, but with no major Patriot force to confront he contented himself with further raids, ravaging the Richmond area while Col. Banastre Tarleton roamed as far as Charlottesville, forcing Gov. Thomas Jefferson and the Virginia legislature to flee (June 4). At the beginning of August, Cornwallis established himself at Yorktown on the peninsula between the York and James rivers from where he had sea communications with British headquarters in New York City. A small Patriot army under the Marquis de Lafayette took up position in his rear.

Meanwhile in the north, Patriot general George Washington and French general the Comte de Rochambeau planned a Franco-American attack on New York City. When they learned of Cornwallis's position at Yorktown and of the imminent arrival in American waters of a powerful French fleet under Adm. the Comte de Grasse, they abandoned the attack on New York City in favor of an attack on Cornwallis in Virginia.

Directing de Grasse to come to Chesapeake Bay, Washington with 2,000 Continentals and Rochambeau with 5,000 French troops crossed the Hudson River in late August and began to march south, passing through Philadelphia and reaching Baltimore and Annapolis at the beginning of September. At the same time, a French naval squadron based at Newport, R.I., sailed south to join de Grasse's fleet in Chesapeake Bay.

De Grasse reached Chesapeake Bay on Aug. 30, cutting off Cornwallis from the sea and landing 3,000 French troops. Five days later a British fleet from New York arrived to challenge the French. The two fleets withdrew (Sept. 5) to sea and there fought the inconclusive battle of the Capes (capes Charles and Henry). The outnumbered British suffered damage but no losses; nevertheless, they returned to New York.

When de Grasse reentered Chesapeake Bay he found the Newport squadron awaiting him. The French sent transports north to Baltimore and Annapolis to bring the French and American armies to Yorktown. On Sept. 28, an allied army of 16,000, half American (Washington's and Lafayette's Continentals reinforced by Virginia militia), half French, laid siege to the fortified town.

The siege proceeded in classic 18th-century style. The allies dug trenches parallel to the British trenches so they could, at the appropriate time, assault the British lines with minimum exposure. Cornwallis countered by abandoning his outer works, thereby shortening his defensive perimeter. On Oct. 14 the Americans captured two redoubts in Cornwallis's defensive system, young Col. Alexander Hamilton distinguishing himself in the assault. All the while, French guns hammered the British positions.

Greatly outnumbered, Cornwallis had no hope of escaping the tightening noose except the arrival of a British relief force by sea. He launched (Oct. 16) only one futile attack from the besieged town; an attempt that night to escape across the York River was frustrated by a storm.

On Oct. 17 Cornwallis asked for terms and on Oct. 18 signed the surrender. The next day the British filed out of their fortifications between lines of resplendent French and ragged Continentals and stacked their arms. Cornwallis absented himself from the ceremonies. His second in command offered his sword to Washington but was directed to give it instead to Washington's second in command, Gen. Benjamin Lincoln, who had surrendered his sword to Clinton at Charleston 17 months before.

Five days later Clinton arrived off Chesapeake Bay with 7,000 troops to relieve Cornwallis. Discovering that he was too late, he returned to New York. Washington, too, returned to New York and resumed his position north of the city.

YOUNG AMERICA (1845–55), movement of evangelical nationalism and expansionism, largely confined to the Democratic Party. It championed youth and opposed "old fogyism." For the 1852 Democratic presidential nomination, it supported Sen. Stephen A. Douglas of Illinois, who was not yet 40. When expansionism was perceived as serving Southern interests, Young America lost popularity in the North.

YOUNG PLAN (1929). See *War Debts.

Y2K (YEAR 2000) ANXIETY or MILLENNIUM ANXIETY. The approach of the third millennium—popularly but erroneously supposed to begin on Jan. 1, 2000—precipitated the usual millennial anxieties, but unlike those at the approach of the second millennium, these were largely high-tech. The universal fear was that the world's computers, which used only the last two digits to identify the year, might misread the year 2000 as 1900—or break down altogether. The consequences of such eventualities—for government, the military, banking, business, public utilities—were incalculable, according to the experts who worked feverishly during the last years of the 20th century to prepare computer programs for the transition, at a total estimated cost in the United States alone of $100 billion. Meanwhile, many Americans, catching the experts' alarm and heeding their advice, stockpiled canned food and bottled water, hoarded cash, avoided airline reservations for Dec. 31, and even armed themselves in preparation for the apocalypse.

As it turned out, New Year's Day 2000 moved westward uneventfully from the Central Pacific with only a few minor computer glitches.

YUPPIES (1980s–90s), young *urban* *professionals*, affluent young men and women—often lawyers, stockbrokers, or corporate executives—who exemplified the economic boom of the 1980s and 1990s.

Z

ZELMAN v. SIMMONS-HARRIS (2002), 5–4 decision of the *Rehnquist Court upholding a Cleveland, Ohio, *school voucher program.

The voucher program was instituted in 1996–97 after the Cleveland City School District—comprising 75,000 students, the majority from low-income and minority families—had been declared a failure by a federal district court and placed under state control. Under the program, parents could receive as much as $2,250 a year toward tuition in a participating out-of-district public school or in a private school of their choice. In 1999–2000, 56 private schools participated in the program, 46 of which (82 percent) were religiously affiliated. No public schools in districts adjacent to Cleveland participated. Of the 3,700 students who participated in the program, 96 percent were enrolled in religious schools. The program was challenged as violating the Establishment Clause of the First Amendment (see *Church-State Relations).

In his majority decision, Chief Justice William H. Rehnquist wrote: "There is no dispute that the program challenged here was enacted for the valid secular purpose of providing educational assistance to poor children in a demonstrably failing public school system. Thus, the question presented is whether the Ohio program nonetheless has the forbidden 'effect' of advancing or inhibiting religion.

". . . [O]ur decisions have drawn a consistent distinction between government programs that provide aid directly to religious schools, and programs of true private choice, in which government aid reaches religious schools only as a result of the genuine and independent choices of private individuals." Decisions in *Mueller v. Allen* (1983), *Witters v. Washington Department of Services for the Blind* (1986), and *Zobrest v. Catalina Foothills School District* (1993) "make clear that where

a government aid program is neutral with respect to religion, and provides assistance directly to a broad class of citizens who, in turn, direct government aid to religious schools wholly as a result of their own genuine and independent private choice, the program is not readily subject to challenge under the Establishment Clause."

In dissent, Justice Stephen G. Breyer pointed out that, in the cases cited by the chief justice, public money went to support services for parochial schools such as bus transportation and computers whereas voucher money would finance religious instruction. Justice John Paul Stevens warned, "Whenever we remove a brick from the wall that was designed to separate religion and government, we increase the risk of religious strife and weaken the foundation of our democracy."

ZENGER TRIAL (1735), trial of John Peter Zenger, publisher of the *New York Weekly Journal*, for seditious libel because of articles critical of the unpopular colonial governor, William Cosby. Zenger was defended by Andrew Hamilton of Philadelphia, who argued—against the court's ruling that publication itself constituted libel—that Zenger's articles were not libelous if they were true and urged the jury to judge both the law and the facts. The jury found Zenger not guilty, setting a precedent for press freedom in America.

ZIMMERMANN NOTE (Jan. 19, 1917), incident in the *Wilson administration. The coded message from German foreign secretary Alfred Zimmermann to the German minister in Mexico during World War 1 instructed him, in case of war between the United States and Germany, to "propose an alliance on the following basis with Mexico. That we shall make war together and together make peace. We shall give general financial support, and it is understood that Mexico is to reconquer the lost territory in New Mexico, Texas, and Arizona. . . . [W]e suggest that the president of Mexico on his own initiative should communicate with Japan suggesting adherence at once to this plan. . . ."

The message was intercepted and decoded by British intelligence and transmitted to the U.S. Department of State, which released it to the press on Mar. 1. Publication created a sensation. Zimmermann himself refuted those who claimed that the note was an Allied forgery by acknowledging authorship.

THE CONSTITUTION OF THE UNITED STATES

We the people of the United States, in order to form a more perfect Union, establish justice, ensure domestic tranquility, provide for the common defence, promote the general welfare, and secure the blessings of liberty to ourselves and our posterity, do ordain and establish this Constitution for the United States of America.

ARTICLE I

Sec. 1. All legislative powers herein granted shall be vested in a Congress of the United States, which shall consist of a Senate and House of Representatives.

Sec. 2. The House of Representatives shall be composed of members chosen every second year by the people of the several states, and the electors in each state shall have the qualifications requisite for electors of the most numerous branch of the state legislature.

No person shall be a representative who shall not have attained to the age of 25 years, and been seven years a citizen of the United States, and who shall not, when elected, be an inhabitant of that state in which he shall be chosen.

Representatives and direct taxes shall be apportioned among the several states which may be included within this union, according to their respective numbers, which shall be determined by adding to the whole number of free persons, including those bound to service for a term of years, and excluding Indians not taxed, three-fifths of all other persons. The actual enumeration shall be made within three years after the first meeting of the Congress of the United States, and within every subsequent term of ten years, in such manner as they shall by law direct. The number of representatives shall not exceed one for every 30,000, but each state shall have at least one representative; and until such enumeration shall be made, the state of New-Hampshire shall be entitled to choose three, Massachusetts eight, Rhode-Island and Providence Plantations one, Connecticut five, New-York six, New-Jersey four, Pennsylvania eight, Delaware one, Maryland six, Virginia ten, North-Carolina five, South-Carolina five, and Georgia three.

When vacancies happen in the representation from any state, the executive authority thereof shall issue writs of election to fill such vacancies.

The House of Representatives shall choose their speaker and other officers; and shall have the sole power of impeachment.

Sec. 3. The Senate of the United States shall be composed of two senators from each state, chosen by the legislature thereof, for six years; and each senator shall have one vote.

Immediately after they shall be assembled in consequence of the first election, they shall be divided as equally as may be into three classes. The seats of the senators of the first class shall be vacated at the expiration of the second year, of the second class at the expiration of the fourth year, and of the third class at the expiration of the sixth year, so that one-third may be chosen every second year; and if vacancies happen by resignation, or otherwise, during the recess of the legislature of any state, the executive thereof may make temporary appointments until the next meeting of the legislature, which shall then fill such vacancies.

No person shall be a senator who shall not have attained to the age of 30 years, and been nine years a citizen of the United States, and who shall not, when elected, be an inhabitant of that state for which he shall be chosen.

The vice-president of the United States shall be president of the Senate, but shall have no vote, unless they be equally divided.

The Senate shall choose their other officers, and also a president pro tempore, in the absence of the vice-president, or when he shall exercise the office of president of the United States.

The Senate shall have the sole power to try all impeachments. When sitting for that purpose, they shall be on oath or affirmation. When the president of the United States is tried, the chief justice shall preside: And no person shall be convicted without the concurrence of two-thirds of the members present.

Judgment in cases of impeachment shall not extend further than to removal from office, and disqualification to hold and enjoy any office of honour, trust or profit under the United States; but the party convicted shall nevertheless be liable and subject to indictment, trial, judgment and punishment, according to law.

Sec. 4. The times, places and manner of holding elections for senators and representatives, shall be prescribed in each state by the legislature thereof: But the Congress may at any time by law make or alter such regulations, except as to the places of choosing senators.

The Congress shall assemble at least once in every year, and such meeting shall be on the first Monday in December, unless they shall by law appoint a different day.

Sec. 5. Each house shall be the judge of the elections, returns and qualifications of its own members, and a majority of each shall constitute a quorum to do business; but a smaller number may adjourn from day to day, and may be authorized to compel the attendance of absent members, in such manner, and under such penalties as each house may provide.

Each house may determine the rules of its proceedings, punish its members for disorderly behaviour, and, with the concurrence of two-thirds, expel a member.

Each house shall keep a journal of its proceedings, and from time to time publish the same, excepting such parts as may, in their judgment, require secrecy; and the yeas and nays of the members of either house on any question, shall, at the desire of one-fifth of those present, be entered on the journal.

Neither house, during the session of Congress, shall, without the consent of the other, adjourn for more than three days, nor to any other place than that in which the two houses shall be sitting.

Sec. 6. The senators and representatives shall receive a compensation for their services, to be ascertained by law, and paid out of the treasury of the United States. They shall in all cases, except treason, felony and breach of the peace, be privileged from arrest during their attendance at the session of their respective houses, and in going to and returning from the same; and for any speech or debate in either house, they shall not be questioned in any other place.

No senator or representative shall, during the time for which he was elected, be appointed to any civil office under the authority of the United States, which shall have been created, or the emoluments whereof shall have been increased during such time; and no person holding any office under the United States, shall be a member of either house during his continuance in office.

Sec. 7. All bills for raising revenue shall originate in the House of Representatives; but the Senate may propose or concur with amendments as on other bills.

Every bill which shall have passed the House of Representatives and the Senate, shall, before it become a law, be presented to the president of the United States; if he approve, he shall sign it, but if not, he shall return it, with his objections, to that house in which it shall have originated, who shall enter the objections at large on their journal, and proceed to reconsider it. If after such reconsideration, two-thirds of that house shall agree to pass the bill, it shall be sent, together with the objections, to the other house, by which it shall likewise be reconsidered, and if approved by two-thirds of that house, it shall become a law. But in all such cases the votes of both houses shall be determined by yeas and nays, and the names of the persons voting for and against the bill shall be entered on the journal of each house respectively. If any bill shall not be returned by the president within ten days (Sundays excepted) after it shall have been presented to him, the same shall be a law, in like manner as if he had signed it, unless the Congress by their adjournment prevent its return, in which case it shall not be a law.

Every order, resolution, or vote to which the concurrence of the Senate and House of Representatives may be necessary (except on a question of adjournment) shall be presented to the president of the United States; and before the same shall take effect, shall be approved by him, or, being disapproved by him, shall be re-passed by two-thirds of the Senate and House of Representatives, according to the rules and limitations prescribed in the case of a bill.

Sec. 8. The Congress shall have power to lay and collect taxes, duties, imposts and excises, to pay the debts and provide for the common defence and general welfare of the United States; but all duties, imposts and excises shall be uniform throughout the United States:

To borrow money on the credit of the United States:

To regulate commerce with foreign nations, and among the several states, and with the Indian tribes:

To establish an uniform rule of naturalization, and uniform laws on the subject of bankruptcies throughout the United States:

To coin money, regulate the value thereof, and of foreign coin, and fix the standard of weights and measures:

To provide for the punishment of counterfeiting the securities and current coin of the United States:

To establish post-offices and post-roads:

To promote the progress of science and useful arts, by securing for limited times to authors and inventors the exclusive right to their respective writings and discoveries:

To constitute tribunals inferior to the supreme court:

To define and punish piracies and felonies committed on the high seas, and offences against the law of nations:

To declare war, grant letters of marque and reprisal, and make rules concerning captures on land and water:

To raise and support armies, but no appropriation of money to that use shall be for a longer term than two years:

To provide and maintain a navy:

To make rules for the government and regulation of the land and naval forces:

To provide for calling forth the militia to execute the laws of the union, suppress insurrections and repel invasions:

To provide for organizing, arming and disciplining the militia, and for governing such part of them as may be employed in the service of the United States, reserving to the states respectively, the appointment of the officers, and the authority of training the militia according to the discipline prescribed by Congress:

To exercise exclusive legislation in all cases whatsoever, over such district (not exceeding ten miles square) as may, by cession of particular states, and the acceptance of Congress, become the seat of the government of the United States, and to exercise like authority over all places purchased by the consent of the legislature of the state in which the same shall be, for the erection of forts, magazines, arsenals, dock-yards, and other needful buildings: And,

To make all laws which shall be necessary and proper for carrying into execution the foregoing powers, and all other powers vested by this constitution in the government of the United States, or in any department or officer thereof.

Sec. 9. The migration or importation of such persons as any of the states now existing shall think proper to admit, shall not be prohibited by the Congress prior to the year 1808, but a tax or duty may be imposed on such importations, not exceeding 10 dollars for each person.

The privilege of the writ of *habeas corpus* shall not be suspended, unless when in cases of rebellion or invasion the public safety may require it.

No bill of attainder or *ex post facto* law shall be passed.

No capitation, or other direct tax shall be laid unless in proportion to the *census* or enumeration herein before directed to be taken.

No tax or duty shall be laid on articles exported from any state.

No preference shall be given by any regulation of commerce or revenue to the ports of one state over those of another: nor shall vessels bound to, or from one state, be obliged to enter, clear, or pay duties in another.

No money shall be drawn from the treasury but in consequence of appropriations made by law; and a regular statement and account of the receipts and expenditures of all public money shall be published from time to time.

No title of nobility shall be granted by the United States: And no person holding any office or profit or trust under them, shall, without the consent of the Congress, accept of any present, emolument, office, or title, of any kind whatever, from any king, prince or foreign state.

Sec. 10. No state shall enter into any treaty, alliance, or confederation; grant letters of marque and reprisal; coin money; emit bills of credit; make any thing but gold and silver coin a tender in payment of debts; pass any bill of attainder, *ex post facto* law, or law impairing the obligation of contracts, or grant any title of nobility.

No state shall, without the consent of the Congress, lay any imposts or duties on imports or exports, except what may be absolutely necessary for executing its inspection laws; and the net produce of all duties and imposts, laid by any state on imports or exports, shall be for the use of the treasury of the United States; and all such laws shall be subject to the revision and control of the Congress.

No state shall, without the consent of Congress, lay any duty of tonnage, keep troops, or ships of war in time of peace, enter into any agreement or compact with another state, or with a foreign power, or engage in a war, unless actually invaded, or in such imminent danger as will not admit of delay.

ARTICLE 2

Sec. 1. The executive power shall be vested in a president of the United States of America. He shall hold his office during the term of four years, and, together with the vice-president, chosen for the same term, be elected as follows:

Each state shall appoint, in such manner as the legislature thereof may direct, a number of electors, equal to the whole number of senators and representatives to which the state may be entitled in the Congress; but no senator or representative, or person holding an office of trust or profit under the United States, shall be appointed an elector.

The electors shall meet in their respective states, and vote by ballot for two persons, of whom one at least shall not be an inhabitant of the same state with themselves. And they shall make a list of all the persons voted for, and of the number of votes for each; which list they shall sign and certify, and transmit sealed to the seat of the government of the United States, directed to the president of the Senate. The president of the Senate shall, in the presence of the Senate and House of Representatives, open all the certificates and the votes shall then be counted. The person having the greatest number of votes shall be the president, if such number be a majority of the whole number of electors appointed; and if there be more than one who have such majority, and have an equal number of votes, then the House of Representatives shall immediately choose by ballot one of them for president; and if no person have a majority, then from the five highest on the list, the said House shall, in like manner, choose the president. But in choosing the president, the votes shall be taken by states, the representation from each state having one vote; a quorum for this purpose shall consist of a member or members from two-thirds of the states, and a majority of all the states shall be necessary to a choice. In every case, after the choice of the president, the person having the greatest number of votes of the electors shall be the vice-president. But if there should remain two or more who have equal votes, the Senate shall choose from them by ballot the vice-president.

The Congress may determine the time of choosing the electors, and the day on which they shall give their votes; which day shall be the same throughout the United States.

No person except a natural born citizen, or a citizen of the United States, at the time of the adoption of this constitution, shall be eligible to the office of president; neither shall any person be eligible to that office, who shall not have attained to the age of 35 years, and been 14 years a resident within the United States.

In case of the removal of the president from office, or of his death, resignation, or inability to discharge the powers and duties of the said office, the same shall devolve on the vice-president, and the Congress may by law provide for the case of removal, death, resignation, or inability, both of the president and vice-president, declaring what officer shall then act as president, and such officer shall act accordingly, until the disability be removed, or a president shall be elected.

The president shall, at stated times, receive for his services, a compensation, which shall neither be increased nor diminished during the period for which he shall have been elected, and he shall not receive within that period any other emolument from the United States, or any of them.

Before he enter on the execution of his office, he shall take the following oath or affirmation:

"I do solemnly swear (or affirm) that I will faithfully execute the office of president of the United States, and will to the best of my ability, preserve, protect and defend the constitution of the United States."

Sec. 2. The president shall be commander in chief of the army and navy of the United States, and of the militia of the several states, when called into the actual service of the United States; he may require the opinion, in writing, of the principal officer in each of the executive departments, upon any subject relating to the duties of their respective offices, and he shall have power to grant reprieves and pardons for offences against the United States, except in cases of impeachment.

He shall have power, by and with the advice and consent of the Senate, to make treaties, provided two-thirds of the senators present concur; and he shall nominate, and by and with the advice and consent of the Senate, shall appoint ambassadors, other public ministers and consuls, judges of the supreme court, and all other officers of the United States, whose appointments are not herein otherwise provided for, and which shall be established by law. But the Congress may by law vest the appointment of such inferior officers, as they think proper in the president alone, in the courts of law, or in the heads of departments.

The president shall have power to fill up all vacancies that may happen during the recess of the Senate, by granting commissions, which shall expire at the end of their next session.

Sec. 3. He shall, from time to time, give to the Congress information of the state of the union, and recommend to their consideration, such measures as he shall judge necessary and expedient; he may, on extraordinary occasions, convene both houses, or either of them, and in case of disagreement between them, with respect to the time of adjournment, he may adjourn them to such time as he shall think proper; he shall receive ambassadors and other public ministers; he shall take care that the laws be faithfully executed, and shall commission all the officers of the United States.

Sec. 4. The president, vice-president, and all civil officers of the United States shall be removed from office on impeachment for, and conviction of, treason, bribery, or other high crimes and misdemeanors.

ARTICLE 3

Sec. 1. The judicial power of the United States, shall be vested in one supreme court, and in such inferior courts as the Congress may, from time to time, ordain and establish. The judges, both of the supreme and inferior courts, shall hold their offices during good behaviour, and shall, at stated times, receive for their services a compensation, which shall not be diminished during their continuance in office.

Sec. 2. The judicial power shall extend to all cases, in law and equity, arising under this constitution, the laws of the United States, and treaties made, or which shall be made under their authority; to all cases affecting ambassadors, other public ministers and consuls; to all cases of admiralty and maritime jurisdiction; to controversies to which the United States shall be a party: to controversies between two or more states, between a state and citizens of another state, between citizens of different states, between citizens of the same state, claiming lands under grants of different states, and between a state, or the citizens thereof, and foreign states, citizens or subjects.

In all cases affecting ambassadors, other public ministers and consuls, and those in which a state shall be a party, the supreme court shall have original jurisdiction. In all the other cases before-mentioned, the supreme court shall have appellate jurisdiction, both as to law and fact, with such exceptions, and under such regulations as the Congress shall make.

The trial of all crimes, except in cases of impeachment, shall be by jury; and such trial shall be held in the state where the said crimes shall have been committed; but when not committed within any state, the trial shall be at such place or places as the Congress may by law have directed.

Sec. 3. Treason against the United States shall consist only in levying war against them, or in adhering to their enemies, giving them aid and comfort. No person shall be convicted of treason unless on the testimony of two witnesses to the same overt act, or on confession in open court.

The Congress shall have power to declare the punishment of treason, but no attainder of treason shall work corruption of blood, or forfeiture, except during the life of the person attainted.

ARTICLE 4

Sec. 1. Full faith and credit shall be given in each state to the public acts, records and judicial proceedings of every other state. And the Congress may by general laws prescribe the manner in which such acts, records and proceedings shall be proved, and the effect thereof.

Sec. 2. The citizens of each state shall be entitled to all privileges and immunities of citizens in the several states.

A person charged in any state with treason, felony, or other crime, who shall flee from justice, and be found in another state, shall, on demand of the executive authority of the state from which he fled, be delivered up, to be removed to the state having jurisdiction of the crime.

No person held to service or labour in one state, under the laws thereof, escaping into another, shall, in consequence of any law or regulation therein, be discharged from such service or labour, but shall be delivered up on claim of the party to whom such service or labour may be due.

Sec. 3. New states may be admitted by the Congress into this union; but no new state shall be formed or erected within the jurisdiction of any other state, nor any state be formed by the junction of two or more states, or parts of states, without the consent of the legislatures of the states concerned, as well as of the Congress.

The Congress shall have power to dispose of and make all needful rules and regulations repecting the territory or other property belonging to the United States; and nothing in this constitution shall be so construed as to prejudice any claims of the United States, or of any particular state.

Sec. 4. The United States shall guarantee to every state in this union, a republican form of government, and shall protect each of them against invasion; and on application of the legislature, or of the executive (when the legislature cannot be convened), against domestic violence.

ARTICLE 5

The Congress, whenever two-thirds of both houses shall deem it necessary, shall propose amendments to this constitution, or on the application of the legislatures of two-thirds of the several states, shall call a convention for proposing amendments, which, in either case, shall be valid to all intents and purposes, as part of this constitution, when ratified by the legislatures of three-fourths of the several states, or by conventions in three-fourths thereof, as the one or the other mode of ratification may be proposed by the Congress; Provided, that no amendment which may be made prior to the year 1808, shall in any manner affect the first and fourth clauses in the ninth section of the first article; and that no state, without its consent, shall be deprived of its equal suffrage in the Senate.

ARTICLE 6

All debts contracted and engagements entered into, before the adoption of this constitution, shall be as valid against the United States under this constitution, as under the confederation.

This constitution, and the laws of the United States which shall be made in pursuance thereof; and all treaties made, or which shall be made, under the authority of the United States, shall be the supreme law of the land; and the judges in every state shall be bound thereby, any thing in the constitution or laws of any state to the contrary notwithstanding.

The senators and representatives before-mentioned, and the members of the several state legislatures, and all executive and judicial officers, both of the United States and of the several states, shall be bound by oath or affirmation, to support this constitution; but no religious test shall ever be required as a qualification to any office or public trust under the United States.

ARTICLE 7

The ratification of the conventions of nine states, shall be sufficient for the establishment of this constitution between the states so ratifying the same.

DONE in convention, by the unanimous consent of the states present, the 17th day of September, in the year of our Lord 1787, and of the independence of the United States of America the 12th. In witness whereof we have hereunto subscribed our names.

[Signed by George Washington
and 37 other delegates.]

AMENDMENTS TO THE CONSTITUTION

AMENDMENT 1

Congress shall make no law respecting an establishment of religion, or prohibiting the free exercise thereof; or abridging the freedom of speech or of the press; or the right of the people peaceably to assemble, and to petition the government for a redress of grievances.

AMENDMENT 2

A well-regulated militia being necessary to the security of a free state, the right of the people to keep and bear arms shall not be infringed.

AMENDMENT 3

No soldier shall, in time of peace, be quartered in any house without the consent of the owner, nor in time of war but in a manner to be prescribed by law.

AMENDMENT 4

The right of the people to be secure in their persons, houses, papers, and effects, against unreasonable searches and seizures, shall not be violated, and no warrants shall issue but upon probable cause, supported by oath or affirmation, and particularly describing the place to be searched, and the persons or things to be seized.

AMENDMENT 5

No person shall be held to answer for a capital or other infamous crime unless on a presentment or indictment of a grand jury, except in cases arising in the land or naval forces, or in the militia, when in actual service, in time of war or public danger; nor shall any person be subject for the same offence to be twice put in jeopardy of life or limb; nor shall be compelled in any criminal case to be a witness against himself, nor be deprived of life, liberty, or property, without due process of law; nor shall private property be taken for public use without just compensation.

AMENDMENT 6

In all criminal prosecutions, the accused shall enjoy the right to a speedy and public trial, by an impartial jury of the state and district wherein the crime shall have been committed, which district shall have been previously ascertained by law, and to be informed of the nature and cause of the accusation; to be confronted with the witnesses against him; to have compulsory process of obtaining witnesses in his favor, and to have the assistance of counsel for his defence.

AMENDMENT 7

In suits at common law, where the value in controversy shall exceed twenty dollars, the right of trial by jury shall be preserved, and no fact tried by a jury shall be otherwise reexamined in any court of the United States than according to the rules of the common law.

AMENDMENT 8

Excessive bail shall not be required, nor excessive fines imposed, nor cruel and unusual punishments inflicted.

AMENDMENT 9

The enumeration in the constitution of certain rights shall not be construed to deny or disparage others retained by the people.

AMENDMENT 10

The powers not delegated to the United States by the constitution, nor prohibited by it to the states, are reserved to the states respectively, or to the people.

AMENDMENT 11

The judicial power of the United States shall not be construed to extend to any suit in law or equity, commenced or prosecuted against one of the United States, by citizens of another state, or by citizens or subjects of any foreign state.

AMENDMENT 12

The electors shall meet in their respective states, and vote by ballot for president and vice-president, one of whom at least shall not be an inhabitant of the same state with themselves; they shall name in their ballots the person voted for as president, and in distinct ballots the person voted for as vice-president; and they shall make distinct lists of all persons voted for as president, and of all persons voted for as vice-president, and of the number of votes for each, which lists they shall sign and certify, and transmit, sealed, to the seat of the government of the United States directed to the president of the Senate; the president of the Senate shall, in the presence of the Senate and House of Representatives, open all the certificates, and the votes shall then be counted; the person having the greatest number of votes for president shall be the president, if such number be a majority of the whole number of electors appointed; and if no person have such majority, then from the persons having the highest numbers not exceeding three, on the list of those voted for as president, the House of Representatives shall choose immediately, by ballot, the president. But in choosing the president, the votes shall be taken by states, the representation from each state having one vote; a quorum for this purpose shall consist of a member or members from two-thirds of the states, and a majority of all the states shall be necessary to a choice. And if the House of Representatives shall not choose a president, whenever the right of choice shall devolve upon them, before the fourth day of March next following, then the vice-president shall act as president, as in the case of the death or other constitu-

tional disability of the president. The person having the greatest number of votes as vice-president shall be the vice-president; if such number be a majority of the whole number of electors appointed, and if no person have a majority, then from the two highest numbers on the list the Senate shall choose the vice-president; a quorum for the purpose shall consist of two-thirds of the whole number of senators, and a majority of the whole number shall be necessary to a choice. But no person constitutionally ineligible to the office of president shall be eligible to that of vice-president of the United States.

AMENDMENT 13

Sec. 1. Neither slavery nor involuntary servitude, except as a punishment for crime whereof the party shall have been duly convicted, shall exist within the United States, or any place subject to their jurisdiction.

Sec. 2. Congress shall have power to enforce this article by appropriate legislation.

AMENDMENT 14

Sec. 1. All persons born or naturalized in the United States, and subject to the jurisdiction thereof, are citizens of the United States and of the state wherein they reside. No state shall make or enforce any law which shall abridge the privileges or immunities of citizens of the United States; nor shall any state deprive any person of life, liberty, or property without the due process of law; nor deny to any person within its jurisdiction the equal protection of the law.

Sec. 2. Representatives shall be apportioned among the several States according to their respective numbers, counting the whole number of persons in each state, excluding Indians not taxed. But when the right to vote at any election for the choice of electors for president and vice-president of the United States, representatives in Congress, the executive and judicial officers of a State, or the members of the legislature thereof, is denied to any of the male members of such state being of twenty-one years of age, and citizens of the United States, or in any way abridged, except for participation in rebellion or other crime, the basis of representation therein shall be reduced in the proportion which the number of such male citizens shall bear to the whole number of male citizens twenty-one years of age in such state.

Sec. 3. No person shall be a senator or representative in Congress, or elector of president and vice-president, or hold any office, civil or military, under the United States, or under any state, who, having previously taken an oath, as a member of Congress, or as an officer of the United States, or as a member of any state legislature, or as an executive or judicial officer of any state, to support the constitution of the United States, shall have engaged in insurrection or rebellion against the same, or given aid and comfort to the enemies thereof. But Congress may, by vote of two-thirds of each House, remove such disability.

Sec. 4. The validity of the public debt of the United States, authorized by law, including debts incurred for payment of pensions and bounties for services in suppressing insurrection or rebellion, shall not be questioned. But neither the United States nor any state shall assume or pay any debt or obligation incurred in aid of insurrection or rebellion against the United States, or any claim for the loss or emancipation of any slave; but all such debts, obligations, and claims shall be held illegal and void.

Sec. 5. The Congress shall have power to enforce, by appropriate legislation, the provisions of this article.

AMENDMENT 15

Sec. 1. The right of citizens of the United States to vote shall not be denied or abridged by the United States or by any state on account of race, color, or previous condition of servitude.

Sec. 2. The Congress shall have power to enforce this article by appropriate legislation.

AMENDMENT 16

The Congress shall have power to lay and collect taxes on incomes, from whatever source derived, without apportionment among the several States, and without regard to any census or enumeration.

AMENDMENT 17

The Senate of the United States shall be composed of two senators from each state, elected by the people thereof for six years; and each senator shall have one vote. The electors in each state shall have the qualifications requisite for electors of the most numerous branch of the state legislatures.

When vacancies happen in the representation of any state in the senate, the executive authority of such state shall issue writs of election to fill such vacancies; provided, that the legislature of any state may empower the executive thereof to make temporary apointments until the people fill the vacancies by election as the legislature may direct.

This amendment shall not be so construed as to affect the election or term or any senator chosen before it becomes valid as part of the Constitution.

AMENDMENT 18

Sec. 1. After one year from the ratification of this article the manufacture, sale, or transportation of intoxicating liquors within, the importation thereof into, or exportation thereof from the United States and all territory subject to the jurisdiction thereof, for beverage purposes is hereby prohibited.

Sec. 2. The Congress and the several states shall have concurrent power to enforce this article by appropriate legislation.

Sec. 3. This article shall be inoperative unless it shall have been ratified as an amendment to the Constitution by the legislatures of the several states, as provided in the Constitution, within seven years from the date of submission hereof to the states by the congress.

AMENDMENT 19

The right of citizens of the United States to vote shall not be denied or abridged by the United States or by any state on account of sex.

Congress shall have power to enforce this article by appropriate legislation.

AMENDMENT 20

Sec. 1. The terms of the president and vice-president shall end at noon on the 20th day of January, and the terms of senators and representatives at noon on the 3rd day of January, of the years in which such terms would have ended if this article had not been ratified; and the terms of their successors shall then begin.

Sec. 2. The Congress shall assemble at least once in every year, and such meeting shall begin at noon on the 3rd day of January, unless they shall by law appoint a different day.

Sec. 3. If, at the time fixed for the beginning of the term of president, the president elect shall have died, the vice-president elect shall become president. If a president shall not have been chosen before the time fixed for the beginning of his term, or if the president elect shall have failed to qualify, then the vice-president elect shall act as president until a president shall have qualified; and the Congress may by law provide for the case wherein neither a president elect nor a vice-president elect shall have qualified, declaring who shall then act as president, or the manner in which one is to act shall be selected, and such person shall act accordingly until a president or vice-president shall have qualified.

Sec. 4. The Congress may by law provide for the case of the death of any of the persons from whom the House of Representatives may choose a president, wherever the right of choice shall have devolved upon them, and for the case of the death of any of the persons from whom the Senate may choose a vice-president, whenever the right of choice shall have devolved upon them.

Sec. 5. Section 1 and 2 shall take effect on the 15th day of October following the ratification of this article.

Sec. 6. This article shall be inoperative unless it shall have been ratified as an amendment to the Constitution by the legislatures of three-fourths of the several states within seven years from the date of its submission.

AMENDMENT 21

Sec. 1. The eighteenth article of amendment to the Constitution of the United States is hereby repealed.

Sec. 2. The transportation or importation into any state, territory, or possession of the United States, for delivery or use therein of intoxicating liquors, in violation of the laws thereof, is hereby prohibited.

Sec. 3. This article shall be inoperative unless it shall have been ratified as an amendment to the Constitution by conventions in the several states, as provided in the Constitution, within seven years from the date of the submission hereof to the states by the Congress.

AMENDMENT 22

No person shall be elected to the office of the president more than twice, and no person who has held the office of president, or acted as president, for more than two years of a term to which some other person was elected president shall be elected to the office of the president more than once. But this article shall not apply to any person holding the office of the president when this article was proposed by the Congress, and shall not prevent any person who may be holding the office of president, or acting as president, during the term within which this article becomes operative from holding the office of president or acting as president during the remainder of such term.

AMENDMENT 23

Sec. 1. The District constituting the seat of government of the United States shall appoint in such manner as the Congress may direct:

A number of electors of president and vice president equal to the whole number of senators and representatives in Congress to which the District would be entitled if it were a state, but in no event more than the least populous state; they shall be in addition to those appointed by the states, but they shall be considered for the purposes of the election of president and vice president, to be electors appointed by a state; and they shall meet in the District and perform such duties as provided by the twelfth article of amendment.

Sec. 2. The Congress shall have power to enforce this article by appropriate legislation.

AMENDMENT 24

Sec. 1. The right of citizens of the United States to vote in any primary or other election for president or vice-president, for electors for president or vice-president, or for senator or representative in Congress, shall not be denied or abridged by the United States or any state by reason of failure to pay any poll tax or other tax.

Sec. 2. The Congress shall have the power to enforce this article by appropriate legislation.

AMENDMENT 25

Sec. 1. In case of the removal of the president from office or his death or resignation, the vice president shall become president.

Sec. 2. Whenever there is a vacancy in the office of the vice president, the president shall nominate a vice president who shall take the office upon confirmation by a majority vote of both houses of Congress.

Sec. 3. Whenever the president transmits to the president pro tempore of the Senate and the speaker of the House of Representatives has written declaration that he is unable to discharge the powers and duties of his office, and until he transmits to them a written declaration to the contrary, such powers and duties shall be discharged by the vice president as acting president.

Sec. 4. Whenever the vice president and a majority of either the principal officers of the executive departments or of such other body as Congress may by law provide, transmit to the president pro tempore of the senate and the speaker of the House of Representatives their written declaration that the president is unable to discharge the powers and duties of his office, the vice president shall immediately assume the powers and duties of the office as acting president.

Thereafter, when the president transmits to the president pro tempore of the Senate and the speaker of the House of Representatives his written declaration that no inability exists, he shall resume the powers and duties of the office unless the vice president and a majority of either the principal officers of the executive department or of such other body as Congress may by law provide, transmit within four days to the president pro tempore of the Senate and the speaker of the House of Representatives their written declaration that the president is unable to discharge the powers and duties of his office. Thereupon Congress shall decide the issue, assembling within 48 hours for that purpose if not in session. If the Congress, within 21 days after receipt of the latter written declaration, or, if Congress is not in session, within 21 days after Congress is required to assemble, determine by two-thirds vote of both houses that the president is unable to discharge the powers and duties of his office, the vice president shall continue to discharge the same as acting president; otherwise, the president shall resume the powers and duties of his office.

AMENDMENT 26

Sec. 1. The right of citizens of the United States, who are eighteen years of age or older, to vote shall not be denied or abridged by the United States or by any state on account of age.

Sec. 2. The Congress shall have power to enforce this article by appropriate legislation.

AMENDMENT 27

No law varying the compensation for the services of the senators and representatives shall take effect, until an election of representatives shall have intervened.